# Brief Contents

KU-605-944

# Introduction to Comparative Politics
## Political Challenges and Changing Agendas

## SIXTH EDITION

**Mark Kesselman**
Columbia University

**Joel Krieger**
Wellesley College

**William A. Joseph**
Wellesley College

## Contributors

**Ervand Abrahamian**
Baruch College

**Christopher S. Allen**
University of Georgia

**Amrita Basu**
Amherst College

**Joan DeBardeleben**
Carleton University

**Louis De Sipio**
University of California, Irvine

**Shigeko N. Fukai**
Chiba University

**Haruhiro Fukui**
University of California, Santa Barbara

**Merilee S. Grindle**
Harvard University

**Wade Jacoby**
Brigham Young University

**Halbert Jones**
Harvard University

**Darren Kew**
University of Massachusetts, Boston

**Atul Kohli**
Princeton University

**Peter Lewis**
Johns Hopkins University

**Tom Lodge**
University of Limerick, Ireland

**Alfred P. Montero**
Carleton University

**WADSWORTH**
CENGAGE Learning™

**Introduction to Comparative Politics:
Political Challenges and Changing
Agendas, Sixth Edition, International
Edition**
Mark Kesselman, Joel Krieger,
William A. Joseph

Senior Publisher: Suzanne Jeans

Executive Editor: Carolyn Merrill

Acquisitions Editor: Anita Devine

Senior Development Editor: Julia Giannotti

Assistant Editor: Laura Ross

Editorial Assistant: Nina Wasserman

Media Editor: Laura Hildebrand

Marketing Program Manager: Caitlin Green

Content Project Manager: Sara Abbott

Art Director: Linda Helcher

Print Buyer: Fola Orekoya

Senior Rights Acquisition Specialist: Jennifer
    Meyer Dare

Production Service/Compositor: Integra

Text Designer: Rokusek Design

Cover Image: GAPS/© iStockphoto

ISBN-13: 978-1-111-83419-7

ISBN-10: 1-111-83419-9

Cengage Learning International Offices

**Asia**
www.cengageasia.com
tel: (65) 6410 1200

**Brazil**
www.cengage.com.br
tel: (55) 11 3665 9900

**Latin America**
www.cengage.com.mx
tel: (52) 55 1500 6000

**Represented in Canada by
Nelson Education, Ltd.**
www.nelson.com
tel: (416) 752 9100/(800) 668 0671

**Australia/New Zealand**
www.cengage.com.au
tel: (61) 3 9685 4111

**India**
www.cengage.co.in
tel: (91) 11 4364 1111

**UK/Europe/Middle East/Africa**
www.cengage.co.uk
tel: (44) 0 1264 332 424

Cengage Learning is a leading provider of customized learning solutions
with office locations around the globe, including Singapore, the United
Kingdom, Australia, Mexico, Brazil, and Japan. Locate your local office at:
**www.cengage.com/global**.

For product information and free companion resources:
**www.cengage.com/international**

Visit your local office: **www.cengage.com/global**

Visit our corporate website: **www.cengage.com**

Printed in the United States of America
1 2 3 4 5 6 7 15 14 13 12 11

# Contents

# Contents

## PART II  CONSOLIDATED DEMOCRACIES

# Contents

# Contents

# Contents

## Chapter 6    India     236

Atul Kohli and Amrita Basu

# Contents

## PART III    TRANSITIONAL DEMOCRACIES

### Chapter 8    The Russian Federation      330
Joan DeBardeleben

# Contents

# Contents

# Contents

# Contents

# Contents

# Contents

# Contents

# Preface

The prefaces to several previous editions of *Introduction to Comparative Politics* (ICP) observed that the times, they are a changing. We reflect on how we began previous editions:

- "Politics throughout the world seems more troubled today than even a few years ago, when celebrations around the globe ushered in the new millennium."
  —*Introduction to Comparative Politics*, 3rd edition. © 2004.
- In recent years the "world of politics was as turbulent as at any time in recent memory, with clear-cut trends more elusive than ever."
  —*Introduction to Comparative Politics*, 4th edition. © 2007.
- "[We] have witnessed as much—or more—turmoil and uncertainty as the preceding years."
  —*Introduction to Comparative Politics*, 5th edition. © 2010.

The sixth edition of ICP is far from an exception to this rule. It has been published soon after prodemocracy movements overthrew decades-old dictatorships in Tunisia and Egypt, and repressive regimes unleashed deadly force against similar movements in Algeria, Bahrain, Iran, Libya, Syria, and Yemen.

It is hard to imagine that worldwide attention, riveted on the vast wave of popular movements in North Africa and the Middle East, could be diverted. Yet so it was, when an earthquake measuring 9.0 on the Richter scale rocked Japan's main island and provoked a tsunami that flattened entire villages, killed thousands, and heavily damaged a set of nuclear facilities. Japan and countries throughout the world will grapple with the social, economic, and political implications of the disaster for decades to come. ICP6 does not try to emulate the coverage of fast-breaking daily events by CNN, Fox News, and Twitter. Its mission is to provide students with a clear and comprehensive guide to these unsettled political times through comparative analysis.

## Country-by-Country Approach and Thematic Framework

The methods of comparative analysis come alive as students examine similarities and differences among countries and within and between political systems. Our thematic approach facilitates disciplined analysis of political challenges and changing agendas within each country. Like previous editions of *Introduction to Comparative Politics*, this edition (ICP6) employs a country-by-country approach structured around four core themes:

1. **A World of States** focuses on the importance of state formation, the internal organization of the state, and the impact of the interstate system on political development. We emphasize the interaction of globalization and state power.
2. **Governing the Economy** analyzes state strategies for promoting economic development and competitiveness, emphasizes the crucial role of economic performance in determining a state's political legitimacy, and stresses the effects of economic globalization on domestic politics.
3. **The Democratic Idea** explores the challenges posed to the state by citizens' demands for greater participation and influence in both democracies and authoritarian regimes, and discusses the inevitable gap between the promise of democracy and its imperfect fulfillment.

4. **The Politics of Collective Identities** considers the political consequences of the complex interplay among class, race, ethnicity, gender, religion, and nationality.

Our approach to comparative politics emphasizes the presentation of each country's politics using these four themes within a context shaped by globalization. The framework strikes a balance between the richness of each country's distinctive pattern of political development and cross-country comparative analysis.

## Four Critical Junctures in Politics

Chapter 1 helps students navigate through the text by introducing the book's thematic framework, which is combined with a thorough analysis of the political institutions and processes of each country. It sets the stage and previews the thematic focus by noting four important critical junctures in recent political history:

1. 1989, which symbolizes the end of the cold war, and the eruption of capitalist democracies that transcend East versus West divisions in Europe and much of the world;
2. 9/11, which reframes globalization, shifting attention away from the development gap and on to terrorism, security, and the use of force;
3. 2008, a year of intense financial and economic crisis around the world;
4. 2011, when prodemocracy movements confronted repressive regimes in North Africa and the Middle East, and Japan was rocked by a severe earthquake, tsunami, and nuclear disaster.

Chapter 1 also describes the comparative method; discusses our approach to studying the comparative politics of the developing world; presents in some detail our four-theme framework; and provides an overview of the organization of the country chapters.

## Consolidated Democracies, Transitional Democracies, and Authoritarian Regimes

We classify the thirteen countries in this edition of ICP in three categories:

- *Consolidated democracies* (Britain, France, Germany, India, Japan, the United States)
- *Transitional democracies* (Brazil, Mexico, Nigeria, Russia, South Africa)
- *Authoritarian regimes* (China, Iran).

In the Introduction, we define the three regime types and explain the rationale for the typology. In particular, we warn against assuming that there is a linear movement from authoritarian regimes to transitional democracies to consolidated democracies. Democratization is often a protracted process with ambiguous results or reversals, rather than a clearly delineated path toward completion. Thus, we stress that the countries we classify as transitional democracies are not riding an historical escalator mechanically leading to their transformation into stable or consolidated democracies. We call attention to "hybrid" regimes, in which the trappings and some elements of democracy co-exist with authoritarian practices.

We also emphasize that the boundaries dividing the three groups are not airtight. For one thing, politics is a moving target. Russia is a good example of a country on the cusp between a transitional democracy and an authoritarian regime. Furthermore, scholars disagree about the appropriate criteria for classifying regime types as well as about how to classify particular cases. Indeed, instructors may find it fruitful to encourage class discussion of alternative conceptual schemes for classifying groups of countries and how to best characterize the political system of given countries.

## NEW! Sixth Edition Content

The content of this edition of ICP has been shaped by our survey of what instructors found appealing about previous editions of the book and their recommended changes. Based on this feedback, we have made the following improvements:

- **NEW!** Shortened country chapters by about 25 percent compared to the previous edition. The result is a more streamlined text that strikes a balance between introducing comparative politics to students with little or no background in political science while maintaining coverage of the complexity of institutions, issues, processes, and events.
- **NEW! Focus questions** at the beginning of each major section heading in the country chapters introduce students to the section that follows, and each section concludes with a brief summary of the main points covered.
- **NEW! Chapter on South Africa** that strengthens the balance and global coverage of the book. Topics covered included apartheid, democratization, economic growth and inequality, and HIV/AIDS. The chapter is written by Tom Lodge, one of the most distinguished specialists on South African politics.
- **NEW! The thoroughly updated introduction and country chapters** provides analysis of major recent political developments throughout the world.
  - The Japan chapter gives ample attention to the earthquake, tsunami, and nuclear disaster of 2011. It has been thoroughly revised to integrate the treatment of these disasters across our thematic framework.
  - The chapters on Brazil, Britain, India, Iran, Nigeria, and the United States extensively analyze the implications of recent elections in these countries.
  - The U.S. chapter covers how the 2010 election dramatically changed the balance of power in Washington.
  - The chapters on France and Britain highlight large-scale demonstrations in 2010 opposing, in turn, pension reform and tuition hikes.
  - The chapter on Russia provides coverage of the 2010 plane crash that killed Polish president Lech Kacynski and dozens of the Polish elite, and treats the growing threats of terrorism, including the January 2011 attack on a Moscow airport.
  - The China chapter includes a new Politics in Action feature highlighting Liu Xiaobo, the 2010 winner of the Nobel Peace Prize, imprisoned by the Chinese government for "inciting subversion of state power."
  - The Nigeria case study chronicles not only the political but also the social ties between Nigeria and the United States and provides a new profile feature box about Goodluck Jonathan, who was re-elected as president in 2011.
  - The Brazil chapter includes a new Politics in Action feature describing Brazil's hosting of the 2014 World Cup and the 2016 Summer Olympics. It also covers the 2010 election of Dilma Rousseff, Brazil's first woman president.

## Consistent Country Chapter Organization

Each country chapter consists of five sections:

1. A **Chapter Opening Vignette** illustrates an important feature of the country's political patterns and describes its geographic setting, critical junctures in the historical development of the state, the state's relationship to the international political and economic system, and the country's significance for the study of comparative politics. At the beginning of each chapter, students will find a map, data on ethnicity, religion, and language specific to that country to aid in comparing countries, and some basic information about the country's political system.
2. **Description of the country's past and current political economy**, the relationship of the state and economy, economy and society, relationship to the global political economy, and political consequences of the country's economic performance.
3. **Discussion of the major institutions of governance and policy-making**, including the chief executive, cabinet, and bureaucracy, as well as other state institutions.

4. **Analysis of political representation and participation**, including the country's legislature and party system, electoral patterns, political identities, and protest movements.
5. **Review of major current issues** that confront the country and are likely to shape its political future, and how the country's politics can be understood from the perspective of the book's four major themes.

## Special Features That Teach

Maps, tables, charts, photographs, and political cartoons enliven the text and present key information in clear and graphic ways. We have provided a more visually interesting presentation of data in a way that is intended to enhance cross-country comparative analysis. In Chapter 1, a variety of data is presented in a way that facilitates comparisons among the countries covered in this book.

Sidebar boxes in each country chapter highlight three interesting and provocative aspects of politics:

1. The **Profile** feature highlights biographies of important political leaders.
2. The **Global Connection** feature provides links between domestic and international politics.
3. **The U.S. Connection** feature compares an important feature of political institutions with its American counterpart or explores a crucial aspect of the country's relationship with the United States.

   **NEW! Key terms** are set in boldface and defined in the margin of the page where the term is first introduced and in the complete glossary at the end of the book. The glossary defines many key concepts that are used broadly in comparative politics.

   **NEW! Student Research and Exploration**. In Chapter 1, students are enabled to do further research using a sidebar box that discusses the use of the Internet in the study of comparative politics. It notes a variety of websites where students can find more information about the countries covered in the book. Each chapter concludes with a list of suggested readings and websites.

## Supplemental Teaching and Learning Aids and Database Editions

### PowerLecture DVD with JoinInTM and ExamView®
ISBN-10: 1111834997 | ISBN-13: 9781111834999

This DVD provides access to Interactive PowerPoint® Lectures, a Test Bank, and the Instructor's Manual. Interactive PowerPoint® lectures make it easy for you to assemble, edit, publish, and present custom lectures for your course. The slides provide outlines specific to every chapter of Introduction to Comparative Politics, 6th edition and include tables, statistical charts, graphs, and photos from the book as well as outside sources. In addition, the slides are completely customizable for a powerful and personalized presentation. A test bank in Microsoft® Word and ExamView® computerized testing offers a large array of well-crafted multiple-choice and essay questions, along with their answers and page references. An Instructor's Manual includes learning objectives, chapter outlines, discussion questions, suggestions for class activities and projects, tips on integrating media into your class (including step-by-step instructions on how to create your own podcasts), suggested readings and Web resources. A section specifically designed for teaching assistants and adjuncts helps instructors get started teaching right away. JoinIn™ offers book-specific "clicker" questions that test and track student comprehension of key concepts. Save the data from students' responses all semester—track their progress and show them how political science works by incorporating this exciting new tool into your classroom. It is available for college and university adopters only.

### Companion Web Site
ISBN-10: 113304459X | ISBN-13: 9781133044598

Students will find open access to learning objectives, tutorial quizzes, chapter glossaries, flashcards, and crossword puzzles, all correlated by chapter. Instructors also have access to the Instructor's Manual and PowerPoints.

### WebTutor Toolbox on Blackboard

0534274897 | 9780534274894 PAC
0534274919 | 9780534274917 IAC
WebTutor Toolbox is a Web-based teaching and learning tool that integrates with your school's learning management system. It offers access to the ExamView test bank and online study tools including learning objectives, flashcards, weblinks and practice quizzes.

### WebTutor Toolbox on WebCT

0534274889 | 9780534274887 PAC
0534274900 | 9780534274900 IAC
WebTutor Toolbox is a Web-based teaching and learning tool that integrates with your school's learning management system. It offers access to the ExamView test bank and online study tools including learning objectives, flashcards, weblinks and practice quizzes.

### CourseReader: Comparative Politics

1111477604 | 9781111477608 CourseReader 0-30: Comparative Politics Printed Access Card
1111477620 | 9781111477622 CourseReader 0-30: Comparative Politics Instant Access Code
1111477612 | 9781111477615 CourseReader 0-30: Comparative Politics SSO
1111680507 | 9781111680503 CourseReader 0-60: Comparative Politics Printed Access Card
1111680493 | 9781111680497 CourseReader 0-60: Comparative Politics Instant Access Code
1111680485 | 9781111680480 CourseReader 0-60: Comparative Politics SSO
1111680531 | 9781111680534 CourseReader Unlimited: Comparative Politics Printed Access Card
1111680523 | 9781111680527 CourseReader Unlimited: Comparative Politics Instant Access Code
1111680515 | 9781111680510 CourseReader Unlimited: Comparative Politics SSO
CourseReader for Comparative Politics is a fully customizable online reader which provides access to hundreds of readings, audio, and video selections from multiple disciplines. This easy to use solution allows you to select exactly the content you need for your courses, and is loaded with convenient pedagogical features like highlighting, printing, note taking, and audio downloads. YOU have the freedom to assign individualized content at an affordable price. CourseReader: Comparative Politics is the perfect complement to any class.

As our discussion of the critical junctures of 1989, 9/11, 2008, and 2011 suggests, history and politics have not ended, and as this text will amply demonstrate, interpretive debates have not ended either. Not much is certain about what the future will hold—except that the political world will be endlessly fascinating and analysis will be quite a challenge. Welcome aboard!

## Dedication

For the first five editions of ICP, the Germany chapter was solely authored by Christopher Allen. For this edition, the chapter is co-authored with Wade Jacoby. We are delighted to welcome Dr. Jacoby, a prolific and acclaimed specialist on German and European politics. But we are immeasurably saddened by the reason that he has joined the ICP author team. In February 2011, Chris Allen passed away after years of courageously battling cancer. Chris was active to the end, and he provided valuable suggestions for revising his chapter at the planning stage for ICP6. We have been enriched and inspired by Chris' intelligence, scholarship, integrity, and, in the last decade, his great courage. As a token of our immense esteem for him, we dedicate ICP6 to Chris' memory.

## Acknowledgments

We are grateful to colleagues who have reviewed and critiqued past and current editions of ICP:

Oya Dursun-Ozkanca, *Elizabethtown College*
Debra Holzhauer, *Southeast Missouri State University*
Lisa Elizabeth Huffstetler, *University of Memphis*
Thomas Kolasa, *Troy University*
Donn Kurtz, *University of Louisiana*
Daniel Madar, *Brock University*
Julie M. Mazzei, *Kent State University*
Derwin S. Munroe, *University of Michigan at Flint*
Nicholas Toloudis, *Bowdoin College*
Dag Mossige, *Ohio State University*

In addition, we thank the talented and professional staff who helped edit and publish ICP6: Jay Boggis, Freelance Editor; Anita Devine, Acquiring Sponsoring Editor; Jeff Greene, Development Manager; Julia Giannotti, Development Editor; Laura Ross, Assistant Editor, and Nina Wasserman, Editorial Assistant.

M. K.
J. K.
W. A. J

# Introduction to
# **Comparative Politics**

# 1

# Introducing
# Comparative Politics

Mark Kesselman, Joel Krieger, and William A. Joseph

# THE GLOBAL CHALLENGE OF COMPARATIVE POLITICS

## Focus Questions

What does it mean to compare things?

What are two examples of how a comparison can bring to light features that might otherwise have been overlooked?

What are two more examples of how comparison can distort how we look at political systems?

The world of politics seems more unsettled today and the challenges even more daunting than usual. When an international financial crisis erupted in fall 2008, the global economy teetered on the edge of collapse. Economic conditions have stabilized in the intervening years, but in the United States and most other countries throughout the world, people have less to spend. Consider the situation in the United States. For years after 2008, unemployment hovered at post–World War II record levels, and job creation was sluggish. Pensions and unemployment benefits have been cut back. College graduates have a difficult time breaking into the workforce and finding meaningful, well-paying jobs. Those without college degrees have even bleaker prospects. At the same time, improved medical care and inadequate retirement accounts keep the baby boomers, those born in the two decades after World War II, working longer than ever before. Since the Great Recession of 2008, the battle has intensified over how the economic pie should be cut and the pieces distributed among different groups in society.

The result is a combustible and increasingly violent mix that seems to herald a new moment in contemporary history and a new and dramatic set of political challenges that threaten to divide societies. In the United States and elsewhere, one finds

- Young people desperate for jobs and educational opportunity sometimes sinking together with—and sometimes pitted against— the middle-aged and pensioners as the United States enters what looks and feels like the beginning of an era of perpetual austerity.
- Ordinary citizens in every corner of the globe from Tea Party activists in the United States to the heroic voices of people in many dictatorships throughout the world demanding democratic governments and the chance to enjoy the fruits of liberty.
- Ethnic, racial, and national tensions enflamed by hard times, straining national unity—a precious and increasingly rare commodity.

Like the Internet technology that speeds up and transforms our lives, creates vast far-flung social networks, and makes possible the cell phone images that flash instantly around the globe, the political world is changing rapidly, too, and the political cycles of innovation are also accelerating.

In scarcely more than twenty years, we have witnessed the collapse of the Berlin Wall in 1989, which ushered in the end of the **Cold War** era; the attack on the World Trade Center towers in 2001, ushering in a new era of global insecurity in the face of mounting terrorism; and the Great Recession of 2008, which threw the global economy into a tailspin, heightened political conflict, and heightened anxiety about the future for most people.

Just when things became too grim, we were reminded that the political wheel keeps turning, and something both unexpected and heartening may transform the political universe. And yet even the best of news doesn't last forever. As a case in point about these contradictory developments, we add 2011 to the key dates that help us chronicle the contemporary political era. This is a date of hope, turmoil,

**Cold War**

The hostile relations that prevailed between the United States and the Soviet Union from the late 1940s until the demise of the USSR in 1991.

and disaster, a date whose full implications we cannot yet interpret with certainty, but a date that we use as a marker for four remarkable developments. The year began with an inspiring democratic surge led by members of the same generation as most readers of this text. When young people took to the streets in Tunisia and Egypt, they risked everything for democratic reform. As the world watched in amazement, their widespread protests toppled decades-old dictatorships. Moreover, their courage inspired pro-democratic movements in many other countries of the Middle East and North Africa, including Algeria, Bahrain, Libya, Syria, and Yemen. However, protests elsewhere often produced a very different outcome. Rulers in most of these countries, determined not to relinquish power, unleashed massive violence against mostly peaceful and unarmed protestors. The resulting massacres abruptly shattered the optimism animating the recent wave of democratization. A United Nations–authorized military intervention in Libya, led by a coalition in which the United States played a critical role but refused to assert leadership, highlighted the complexity of this second remarkable development of 2011.

Third, even while pitched battles between repressive regimes and protestors were raging in several countries, an even more momentous tragedy was unfolding in Japan. In March 2011, Japan was devastated by a triple shock: first, an earthquake that ranked at the top of the 9-point Richter Scale measuring the intensity of earthquakes. The second shock was a gigantic tsunami unleashed by the earthquake. The 46-foot-high wall of water swept through the northeast region of Japan's largest island, flattening entire towns, tossing homes, automobiles, and boats like toys, and slaughtered tens of thousands of Japanese. Third, the tsunami heavily damaged the six nuclear reactors at the Fukushima Daiichi power station. The explosions, fires, and release of radioactive material from the crippled reactors rank with the worst nuclear disasters ever. Moreover, the catastrophe occurred in Japan, the only country that has ever suffered nuclear attack. (At the end of World War II, the United States dropped nuclear bombs on Hiroshima and Nagasaki.) As the chapter on Japan describes, the triple disaster subjected Japan's economy, social fabric, and political institutions to incredible stress, and the consequences of the nightmare rippled throughout the world.

Fourth, in a carefully planned and brilliantly executed assault by American special forces on a compound near a military academy in Pakistan, Osama bin Laden was killed in the spring of 2011. The death of the Al Qaeda leader who masterminded the devastating attacks of 9/11 produced sober reflection, national pride, and another outpouring of grief for the relatives lost and lives destroyed ten years before. Would bin Laden's demise help wind down the threat of global terrorism? It is much too early to answer that question, but most knowledgeable observers thought it likely that bin Laden's brand of terrorism might have less traction, particularly as the regional focus shifted to demands for greater democracy and economic opportunities.

The fall of the Berlin Wall in November 1989 marked the beginning of the end of the Cold War.

© AP Photo/Lionel Cironneau

*Introduction to Comparative Politics* studies how different countries both shape and are shaped by the world order created by watershed events such as those that occurred in 1989, 2001, 2008, and 2011. Each of these dates describes a particularly important moment—what we call a **critical juncture**—that helps define key transitional moments.

**critical juncture**

An important historical moment when political actors make critical choices, which shape institutions and future outcomes.

# Making Sense of Turbulent Times

The flash of newspaper headlines, television sound bites, and endless tweets can make politics look overwhelming and chaotic beyond comprehension. Through the study of comparative politics, we can better understand a rapidly changing world. Political analysis involves much more than blogging, talking head debates, or Monday-morning quarterbacking. It requires both a longer historical context and a framework for understanding unfolding developments.

This book describes and analyzes government institutions, policy-making processes, and other key aspects of politics in a wide range of countries. By analyzing and comparing similarities and differences in this representative sample of countries with reference to four key themes, we can understand longer-term causes of political changes and continuities within nations. Each country chapter that follows explores the country's political development by reference to four themes that are central for understanding politics in today's world:

- *The World of States:* the historical formation, internal organization, and interaction of states within the international order
- *Governing the Economy:* the role of the state in economic management
- *The Democratic Idea:* the spread of democracy and the challenges of democratization
- *The Politics of Collective Identities:* the sources and political impact of diverse **collective identities**, including class, gender, ethnicity, nationality, and religion

**collective identities**

The groups with which people identify, including gender, class, race, region, and religion, and which are the "building blocks" for social and political action.

These themes are valuable tools that help us make political sense of the most stable and most tumultuous times. The themes are discussed in greater detail below.

The contemporary period presents an extraordinary challenge to those who study comparative politics, but the study of comparative politics also provides a unique opportunity for understanding this uncertain era. In order to appreciate the complexity of politics in countries around the world, we must look beyond any single national perspective. Today, business and trade, information technology, mass communications and culture, immigration and travel, as well as politics, forge deep connections—as well as deep divisions—among people worldwide. It is particularly urgent that we develop a global and comparative perspective as we explore the politics of different countries and their interaction with and interdependence on one another.

There is an added benefit of studying comparative politics: by comparing political institutions, values, and processes in countries around the world, the student of comparative politics acquires analytical skills that can also be used at home. After you study comparative politics, you begin to think comparatively. As comparison becomes second nature, we hope that you will look at the politics of your own country differently, with a wider and deeper, more analytical, focus that will inspire new reflections, interpretations, and insights. The contemporary world provides a fascinating laboratory for the study of comparative politics. We hope that you share our sense of excitement in the challenging effort to understand the complex and ever-shifting terrain of contemporary politics throughout the world.

# WHAT—AND HOW—COMPARATIVE POLITICS COMPARES

To "compare and contrast" is one of the most common human mental exercises, whether in the classroom study of literature, politics, or animal behavior—or in selecting dorm rooms or arguing with friends about your favorite movie. In the observation of politics, the use of comparisons is very old, dating in the Western world from the ancient Greek philosopher, Aristotle, who analyzed and compared the city-states of Greece in the fourth century BCE according to whether they were ruled by a single individual, a few people, or all citizens. The modern study of comparative politics refines and systematizes this age-old practice of evaluating some features of country X's politics by comparing it to the same features of country Y's politics.

**Comparative politics** is a subfield within the academic discipline of political science as well as a method or approach to the study of politics.[1] The subject matter of comparative politics is the domestic politics of countries. Within the discipline of political science, comparative politics is one of four areas of specialization. In addition to comparative politics, most political science (or government) departments in U.S. colleges and universities include courses in political theory, international relations, and American politics.

Because it is widely believed that students living in the United States should study the politics of their own country in depth, American politics is usually treated as a separate subfield of political science. The pattern of separating the study of politics at home and abroad is also common elsewhere, so students in Canada study Canadian politics as a distinct specialty, and Japanese students master Japanese politics.

However, there is no logical reason why study of the United States should not be included within the field of comparative politics—and good reason to do so. Comparative study can make it easier to recognize what is distinctive about the United States and what features it shares with some other countries. This is why we have included a chapter on the United States in this book.

Special mention should be made of the distinction between comparative politics and international relations. Comparative Politics involves comparing domestic political institutions, processes, policies, conflicts, and attitudes in different countries; international relations involves studying the foreign policies of and interactions among countries, the role of international organizations such as the United Nations, and the growing influence of global actors, from multinational corporations to international human rights advocates to terrorist networks. In a globalized world, however, domestic and international politics routinely spill over into one another, so the distinction between the two fields is somewhat blurry. Courses in international relations nowadays often integrate a concern with how internal political processes affect states' behavior toward other states, while courses in comparative politics highlight the importance of transnational forces for understanding what goes on within a country's borders. One of the four themes that we use to analyze comparative politics, the "world of states," emphasizes the interaction of domestic and international forces in the politics of all nations.

That said, it makes sense to maintain the distinction between comparative politics and international relations. Much of the world's political activity continues to occur within national borders, and comparisons of domestic politics, institutions,

## Focus Questions

What do we mean by globalization?

How does increased cross-border contact among countries and peoples affect political, social, and cultural life?

**comparative politics**

The field within political science that focuses on domestic politics and analyzes patterns of similarity and difference among countries.

## THE INTERNET AND THE STUDY OF COMPARATIVE POLITICS

The Internet can be a rich source of information about the politics of countries around the world. Following are some of the types of information you can find on the Web. We haven't included URLs since they change so often. But you should be able to find the websites easily through a key word search on Google or another search engine.

- **Current events.** Most of the world's major news organizations have excellent websites. Among those we recommend for students of comparative politics are the British Broadcasting Corporation (BBC), Cable News Network (CNN), the *New York Times*, and the *Washington Post*.
- **Elections.** Results of recent (and often past) elections, data on voter turnout, and descriptions of different types of electoral systems can be found at the International Election Guide (IFES), Elections by country/Wikipedia, and the International Institute for Democracy and Electoral Assistance.
- **Statistics.** You can find data helpful both for understanding the political, economic, and social situations in individual countries and for comparing countries. Excellent sources of statistics are the Central Intelligence Agency (CIA), United Nations Development Program (UNDP), and **World Bank**.

There are many websites that bring together data from other sources. These enable you not only to access the statistics, but also to chart or map them in a variety of ways. See, for example, nationmaster.com and gapminder.com.

- **Rankings and ratings.** Many organizations provide rankings or ratings of countries along some dimension based on comparative statistical analysis. We provide the following examples of these in the data that appear at the end of this chapter: the UNDP **Human Development Index (HDI)**; the **Global Gender Gap**; the **Environmental Performance Index**; the **Corruption Perceptions Index**; and the **Freedom in the World rating**. Others you might

consult are the UNDP's Gender-Related Development Index (GDI) and Gender Empowerment Measure (GEM); the World Bank's Worldwide Governance Indicators Project; the Index of Economic Freedom; and the Press Freedom Index. *A note of caution: Some of these sites may have a political perspective that influences the way they collect and analyze data. As with any Web source, be sure to check out who sponsors the site and what type of organization it is.*

- **Official information and documents.** Most governments maintain websites in English. The first place to look the website of the country's embassy in Washington, D.C., Ottawa, or London. The United Nations delegations of many countries also have websites. Governments often have English-language versions of their official home pages, including governments with which the United States does not have official relations, such as Cuba and North Korea.
- **The United States Department of State.** The State Department's website has background notes on most countries. American embassies around the world provide information on selected topics about the country in which they are based.
- **Maps.** The Perry-Castañeda Library Map Collection at the University of Texas is probably the best currently available online source of worldwide maps at an educational institution.
- **General comparative politics.** Several American and British universities host excellent websites that provide links to a multitude of Internet resources on comparative politics (often coupled with international relations), such as Columbia University, Emory University, Keele University (UK), Princeton University, and Vanderbilt University. Do a search for "comparative politics resources" with the university name to get to these websites.

---

**globalization**

The intensification of worldwide interconnectedness associated with the increased speed and magnitude of cross-border flows of trade, investment and finance, and processes of migration, cultural diffusion, and communication.

and processes enable us to understand critical features that distinguish one country's politics from another's. Furthermore, we believe that, despite increased international economic competition and integration (a key aspect of **globalization**), countries are still the fundamental building blocks in structuring most political activity. Therefore *Introduction to Comparative Politics* is built on in-depth case studies of a sample of important countries around the world.

The comparative approach principally analyzes similarities and differences among countries by focusing on selected political institutions and processes. As students of comparative politics (we call ourselves **comparativists**), we believe that we cannot make reliable statements about most political situations by looking at only one case. We often hear statements such as: "The United States has the best health care system in the world." Comparativists immediately wonder what kinds of health care systems exist in other countries, what they cost and how they are financed, how it is decided who can receive medical care, and so on. Besides, what does "best" mean when it comes to health care systems? Is it the one that provides the widest access? The one that is the most technologically advanced? The one that is the most cost-effective? The one that produces the healthiest population? None of us would declare the winner for best picture at the Academy Awards, without seeing more than one—and even better, all—of the nominated movies!

Some comparativists focus on comparing government institutions, such as the legislature, executive, political parties, or court systems, in different countries.[2] Others compare specific political processes, such as voting or policies on a particular issue, for example, education or the environment.[3] Some comparative political studies take a thematic approach and analyze broad topics, such as the causes and consequences of nationalist movements or revolutions in different countries.[4] Comparative studies may also involve comparisons of an institution, policy, or process through time, in one or several countries. For example, some studies have analyzed a shift in the orientation of economic policy that occurred in many advanced capitalist countries in the 1980s from **Keynesianism**, an approach that gives priority to government regulation of the economy, to **neoliberalism**, which emphasizes the importance of market-friendly policies.[5] And many comparativists write in-depth analyses of politics within a single country, often within a framework that draws on similarities and differences with other countries.[6]

# Level of Analysis

Comparisons can be useful for political analysis at several different levels of a country, such as cities, regions, provinces, or states. A good way to begin the study of comparative politics is with **countries**. Countries are distinct, politically defined territories that encompass governments, composed of political institutions, as well as cultures, economies, and collective identities. Although countries are often highly divided by internal conflicts, people within their borders may have close ties to those in other countries, and business firms based in one country may have operations in many others, countries have historically been among the most important sources of a people's collective political identity. They are the major arena for organized political action in the modern world.

Within a given country, the **state** is almost always the most powerful cluster of institutions. But just what is the state? The way the term is used in comparative politics is probably unfamiliar to many students. In the United States, it usually refers to the states in the federal system—California, Illinois, New York, Texas, and so on. But in comparative politics, the state refers to the key political institutions responsible for making, implementing, and adjudicating important policies in a country.[7] Thus, we refer to the "German state" and the "Mexican state." The state is synonymous with what is often called the "government," although it also implies a more durable entity. Governments may come and go, but the state generally endures (unless overthrown from within or conquered by other states in war).

The most important state institutions are the **executive**—usually, the president and/or prime minister and the **cabinet**. Other key state institutions include the military, police, and **bureaucracy**. In some cases, the executive includes the communist party leadership (such as in China), the head of a military government (as in Nigeria until 1999), or the supreme religious leader (as in the Islamic Republic of Iran). Alongside the executive, the **legislature** and the **judiciary** comprise the institutional apex of state power, although the inter-relationships and functions of these institutions vary from country to country.

**comparativist**

A political scientist who studies the similarities and differences in the domestic politics of various countries.

**Keynesianism**

Named after the British economist John Maynard Keynes, an approach to economic policy in which state economic policies are used to regulate the economy in an attempt to achieve stable economic growth. During recession, state budget deficits are used to expand demand in an effort to boost both consumption and investment, and to create employment. During periods of high growth when inflation threatens, cuts in government spending and a tightening of credit are used to reduce demand.

**neoliberalism**

A term used to describe government policies aiming to reduce state regulation and promote competition among business firms within the market.

**country**

A territorial unit controlled by a single state.

**state**

The most powerful political institutions in a country, including the executive, legislative, and judicial branches of government, the police, and armed forces.

**executive**

The agencies of government that make and implement (execute) policy.

**cabinet**

The body of officials (e.g., ministers, secretaries) who direct executive departments presided over by the chief executive (e.g., prime minister, president).

**bureaucracy**

An organization structured hierarchically, in which lower-level officials are charged with administering regulations codified in rules that specify impersonal, objective guidelines for making decisions.

**legislature**

One of the primary political institutions in a country, in which elected members are charged with responsibility for making laws and usually providing for the financial resources for the state to carry out its functions.

**judiciary**

One of the primary political institutions in a country; responsible for the administration of justice and in some countries for determining the constitutionality of state decisions.

**legitimacy**

A belief by powerful groups and the broad citizenry that a state exercises rightful authority.

**state formation**

The historical development of a state, often marked by major stages, key events, or turning points (critical junctures) that influence the contemporary character of the state.

**nation-state**

Distinct, politically defined territory in which the state and national identity coincide.

States claim, usually, but not always, with considerable success, the right to make rules—notably, laws, administrative regulations, and court decisions—that are binding for people within the country. Even democratic states—in which top officials are chosen by procedures that authorize all citizens to participate—can survive only if they can preserve dominance internally and protect their independence with regard to other states and external groups that may threaten them. A number of countries have highly repressive states whose political survival depends largely on military and police powers. Even in such states, however, long-term stability requires that the ruling regime have some measure of political **legitimacy**; that is, the support of a significant segment of the citizenry (in particular, more influential citizens and groups) who believe that the state is entitled to demand compliance. Political legitimacy is greatly affected by the state's ability to "deliver the goods" to its people through satisfactory economic performance and at least a minimum distribution of economic resources. Moreover, as the upheavals in the Arab world in 2011 dramatized, legitimacy is much more secure when there is some measure of democracy.

Thus, *Introduction to Comparative Politics* looks closely at both the state's role in governing the economy and the pressures exerted on states to develop and extend democratic participation.

You will see from the country chapters in this book that the organization of state institutions varies widely, and that these differences have a powerful impact on political, economic, and social life. Therefore, we devote considerable attention to institutional variations, along with their political implications. Each country study begins with an analysis of how the state has evolved historically; that is, **state formation**. One critical difference among states involves the extent to which citizens in a country share a common sense of nationhood; that is, a belief that the state's geographic boundaries coincide with the political identity of the people who live within those boundaries, what can be described as a sense of solidarity and shared values based on being citizens of the same country. When state boundaries and national identity coincide, the resulting formation is called a **nation-state**.

© George Riemann

Young people were at the forefront of the democracy movements that shook the Middle East and North Africa in 2011.

A major source of political instability can occur when state boundaries and national identity do not coincide. In many countries around the world, nationalist movements within a state's borders challenge existing boundaries and seek to secede to form their own state, sometimes in alliance with movements from neighboring countries with whom they claim to share a common heritage. Such is the case with the Kurds, an ethnic group whose members live in Turkey, Syria, and Iraq. Many groups of Kurds have fought to establish an independent nation-state of Kurdistan. When a nationalist movement has distinctive ethnic, religious, and/or linguistic ties opposed to those of other groups in the country, conflicts are likely to be especially intense. India and Nigeria, for example, have experienced particularly violent episodes of what has been termed ethnonationalist conflict. Tibet is an example of ethnic conflict within a country, China, whose population otherwise has a strong sense of national identity.

# Causal Theories

Because countries are the basic building blocks in politics and because states are the most significant political organizations within countries, these are two critical units for comparative analysis. The comparativist seeks to measure and explain similarities and differences among countries or states. One widely-used approach in doing such comparative analysis involves developing **causal theories**—hypotheses that can be expressed formally in a causal mode: "If X happens, then Y will be the result." Such theories include factors (the **independent variables**, symbolized by X) that are believed to influence some outcome (the **dependent variable**, symbolized by Y) that the analyst wants to explain.

For example, it is commonly argued that if a country's economic pie shrinks, conflict among groups will intensify. This hypothesis claims what is called an inverse correlation between variables: as X varies in one direction (the economic pie shrinks), Y varies in the opposite direction (political and economic conflict over the economic pie increases). This relationship might be tested by statistical analysis of a large number of cases (Large N Analysis) or by analyzing one or several country cases in depth to determine how relevant relationships have varied historically (Small N Analysis). Even when explanation does not involve the explicit testing of hypotheses (and often it does not), comparativists try to identify significant patterns that help explain political similarities and differences among countries.

It is important to recognize the limits on just how "scientific" political science—and thus comparative politics—can be. Two important differences exist between the "hard" (or natural) sciences like physics and chemistry and the social sciences. First, social scientists study people who exercise their political will and can always act in an unpredictable way as the events of 2011 in the Middle East and North Africa powerfully demonstrate. This does not mean that people choose in a totally arbitrary fashion. We choose within the context of material constraint, institutional dictates, and cultural preferences. But there will probably always be a wide gulf between the natural and social sciences because of their different objects of study.

A second difference between the natural and social sciences is that in the natural sciences, experimental techniques can be applied to isolate the contribution of distinct factors to a particular outcome. It is possible to change the value or magnitude of a factor—for example, the force applied to an object—and measure how the outcome has consequently changed. However, political scientists and comparativists cannot apply such experimental techniques. Although some political scientists

**causal theories**

An influential approach in comparative politics that involves trying to explain why "if X happens, then Y is the result."

**independent variable**

The variable symbolized by X in the statement that "If X happens, then Y will be the result"; in other words, the independent variable is a cause of Y (the dependent variable).

**dependent variable**

The variable symbolized by Y in the statement that "If X happens, then Y will be the result"; in other words, the dependent variable is the outcome of X (the independent variable).

have constructed small groups of volunteers to conduct experiments, critics claim that there is a wide gulf between these artificial situations and what occurs in everyday life.

There is a lively debate about whether the social sciences should seek scientific explanations comparable to what prevails in the natural sciences, such as physics. An approach largely borrowed from economics, called **rational choice theory**, has become influential—and highly controversial—in political science, including comparative politics, in recent years.[8] Rational choice theory focuses on how individuals act strategically (that is, rationally) in an attempt to achieve goals that maximize their interests. Such actions involve varied activities like voting for a particular candidate or rebelling against the government. Proponents of rational choice generally use deductive and quantitative methods to construct models and general theories of political behavior that they believe can be applied across all types of political systems and cultures. This approach has been criticized for claiming to explain large-scale and complex social phenomena by reference to individual choices. It has also been criticized for dismissing the importance of variations in historical experience, political culture, identities, institutions, and other key aspects of the political world.

The study of comparative politics offers many challenges, including the complexity of the subject matter, the fast pace of change in the contemporary world, and the impossibility of manipulating variables or replicating conditions. As a result, most comparativists probably agree on a middle course that avoids either focusing exclusively on one country or blending all countries indiscriminately. If we study only individual countries without any comparative framework, comparative politics would become merely the study of a series of isolated cases. It would be impossible to recognize what is most significant in the collage of political characteristics that we find in the world's many countries. As a result, the understanding of patterns of similarity and difference among countries would be lost, along with an important tool for evaluating what is and what is not unique about a country's political life.

If we go to the other extreme and try to make universal claims, we would tend to ignore significant national differences and patterns of variation. The political world is incredibly complex, shaped by an extraordinary array of factors and an almost endless interplay of variables. Indeed, after a brief period in the 1950s and 1960s when many comparativists tried—and failed—to develop a grand theory that would apply to all countries, most comparativists now agree on the value of **middle-level theory**, that is, theories focusing on specific features of the political world, such as institutions, policies, or classes of similar events, such as revolutions or elections.

Consider an example of middle-level theory that would help us understand the developments of 2011—theories of transitions from authoritarian to more democratic forms of government. Comparativists have long analyzed the processes through which many countries with authoritarian forms of government, such as military **dictatorships** and one-party regimes, have developed more participatory and democratic regimes. In studying this process, termed **democratic transitions**, comparativists do not either treat each national case as unique or try to construct a universal pattern that ignores all differences.[9] Applying middle-level theory, we identify the influence on the new regime's political stability of specific variables such as institutional legacies, political culture, levels of economic development, the nature of the regime before the transition, and the degree of ethnic conflict or homogeneity.

**rational choice theory**

An approach to analyzing political decision-making and behavior that assumes that individual actors rationally pursue their aims in an effort to achieve the most positive net result. The theory presupposes equilibrium and unitary actors. Rational choice is often associated with the pursuit of selfish goals, but the theory permits a wide range of motivations, including altruism.

**middle-level theory**

Seeks to explain phenomena in a limited range of cases, in particular, a specific set of countries with particular characteristics, such as parliamentary regimes, or a particular type of political institution (such as political parties) or activity (such as protest).

**dictatorships**

A form of government in which power and political control are concentrated in one or a few rulers who have concentrated and nearly absolute power.

**democratic transition**

The process of a state moving from an authoritarian to a democratic political system.

Comparativists have identified common patterns and differences in the emergence and consolidation of democratic regimes in southern Europe in the 1970s (Portugal, Spain, and Greece), in Latin America, Asia, and Africa beginning in the 1980s, in Eastern and Central Europe since the revolutions of 1989, and in the Arab world and the wider Middle East in the twenty-first century.

What can we expect when the whole political world is our laboratory? When we put the method of comparative politics to the test and develop a set of themes derived from middle-level theory, we discover that it is possible to discern patterns that make sense of a vast range of political events and link the experiences of states and citizens throughout the world. Although doubtless we will not achieve definitive explanations, we remain confident that we can better understand the daily headlines, blogs, and tweets by analyzing developments with middle-range theoretical propositions.

Issues involving the appropriate choice of theory, methodology, research approaches, and strategies are a vital aspect of comparative politics. However, students may be relieved to learn that we do not deal with such issues in depth in *Introduction to Comparative Politics*. We believe that students will be in a better position to consider these questions—and provide the most powerful answers—after gaining a solid grasp of political continuities and contrasts in diverse countries around the world. It is this goal that we put front and center in *Introduction to Comparative Politics*.

# THEMES FOR COMPARATIVE ANALYSIS

SECTION **3**

We began this Introduction by emphasizing the extraordinary set of challenges that frame contemporary politics, and the fast pace of political change, from the end of the Cold War in 1989 to the popular uprisings against dictatorial regimes in North Africa and the Middle East, along with the Japanese tragedy, and the death of Bin Laden in 2011. Next, we explained the subject matter of comparative politics and described some of the tools of comparative analysis. This section discusses the four themes we use in *Introduction to Comparative Politics* to organize the description of political institutions, processes, and issues in the country chapters. These themes help explain continuities and contrasts among countries. We also suggest a way that each theme highlights a particular puzzle in comparative politics.

Our framework in *Introduction to Comparative Politics*, comprised by these core themes, provides a guide to understanding many features of contemporary comparative politics. But we urge students (and rely on instructors!) to challenge and amplify our interpretations. Further, we want to note that a textbook builds from existing theory but does not construct or test new hypotheses. That task is the goal of original scholarly studies.

## Focus Questions

Of the themes presented for comparative analysis, which one seems the most important? Why?

The least important? Why?

Give an example of how, in one particular country, features of one theme can affect the features of another theme.

## Theme 1: A World of States

Our first theme, *a world of states,* reflects the fact that for about 500 years, states have been the major actors in global politics. There are nearly 200 independent states in the world today. International organizations, such as the United

Nations, private actors like transnational corporations, such as Microsoft, and Non-Governmental Organizations (NGOs), such as Amnesty International, may play a crucial role in politics. But states still send armies to conquer other states and territories. It is the legal codes of states that make it possible for businesses to operate within their borders and beyond. States provide and enforce laws, and to varying degrees provide citizens with at least minimum social welfare, such as aid to dependent children, assistance to the unemployed, and old age pensions. States regulate the movement of people across borders through immigration law and border controls. And states seek to protect their citizens from aggressive actions by other states.

Our world-of-states theme highlights that states are still the basic building blocks in world politics. The theme also analyzes the importance of variations among the way that states are organized, in other words, the mix of political institutions that distinguishes, for example, democratic from authoritarian regimes, or, within democratic states, the contrast of presidential versus parliamentary systems. Country chapters emphasize the importance of understanding similarities and contrasts in state formation and **institutional design** across countries. We identify critical junctures in patterns of state formation: That is, key events like colonial conquest, defeat in war, economic crises, or revolutions that had a durable impact on the character of particular states. We also study variations in states' economic management strategies and capacities, diverse patterns of political institutions, such as the contrast between presidential and parliamentary forms in democratic states, the relationship of the state with social groups, and unresolved challenges that the state faces from within and outside its borders.

States may collapse when powerful rivals from inside or outside the state challenge rulers, especially when these rivals are backed by a restive and mobilized citizenry. States may also collapse when leaders violate the rule of law and become predators, preying on the population and setting off a downward spiral of state repression and social disorganization. The term **failed states** is often used to describe this extreme situation.[10] *Foreign Policy* magazine and the Fund for Global Peace, a nonprofit research organization, produce an annual "Failed States Index" that ranks the world's countries according to how vulnerable they are to political collapse according to a variety of indicators, including loss of control over territory, internal refugees, human rights abuses, and factionalized elites. Somalia, Sudan, Zimbabwe, Afghanistan, Pakistan, and Haiti were among the most vulnerable states in the 2010 rankings.[11]

The political situation in such countries approaches the nightmare of **anarchy** described by the seventeenth-century English philosopher Thomas Hobbes in his book *Leviathan*. Before the creation of the state, he suggested, human beings lived in a constant war "where every man is enemy to every man," all suffered from "continual fear, and danger of violent death," and life was "solitary, poor, nasty, brutish, and short."

Although few states decline to the point of complete failure, all states are experiencing intense pressures from an increasingly complex mix of external and internal influences. An indication of this development is that, within political science, there is increasing overlap between the study of international relations and the study of comparative politics. The world of states theme in *Introduction to Comparative Politics* emphasizes the interaction between the national and the international levels in shaping the politics of all countries. The theme points in two directions: One focuses on a state's influence in affecting other states and the international economic and political

**institutional design**

The institutional arrangements that define the relationships between executive, legislative, and judicial branches of government and between the national government and sub-national units such as states in the United States.

**failed states**

States in which the government no longer functions effectively.

**anarchy**

The absence of any form of political authority or effective rule.

arena; the other focuses on the impact of international forces on the state's activities within the country's borders.

Regarding the first direction, states still dwarf other political institutions in the exercise of power that matters, whether with regard to war, peace, and national security, or when it comes to providing educational opportunities, heath care, and pensions (social security). That said, no state, even the most powerful, such as the United States, can shape the world to fully suit its own designs or achieve its aims by acting solely on its own.

The second dimension of the world-of-states theme underlines the multiple global forces that have significant, if varying, impacts on the domestic politics of virtually all countries.[12] A wide array of international organizations and treaties, including the United Nations, the European Union, the **World Trade Organization (WTO)**, the World Bank, the **International Monetary Fund (IMF)**, and the **North American Free Trade Agreement (NAFTA)**, challenge the sovereign control of national governments within their own territories. Transnational corporations, international banks, and currency traders in New York, London, Frankfurt, Hong Kong, and Tokyo affect countries and people throughout the world. A country's political borders do not protect its citizens from global warming, environmental pollution, or infectious diseases that come from abroad.

Thanks to the global diffusion of radio, television, and the Internet, people nearly everywhere can become remarkably well informed about international developments. This knowledge may fuel popular demands that governments intervene to stop atrocities in, for example, faraway Kosovo, Rwanda, or Libya, or provide aid to the victims of natural disasters as happened after a devastating earthquake killed many thousands in China in 2008 and a multiple disaster killed many thousands in Japan in 2011. And heightened global awareness may encourage citizens to hold their own government to internationally recognized standards of human rights and democracy. Such awareness played a significant role in motivating people to join the prodemocracy movements in North Africa and the Middle East in 2011.

But international political and economic influences do not have the same impact in all countries. A handful of powerful states have the capacity to influence the institutional structure and policy of international organizations in which they participate. The more advantages a state possesses, as measured by its level of economic development, military power, and resource base, the more global influence it will likely have and the more it will benefit from globalization. Conversely, countries with fewer advantages are more dependent on other states and international organizations, and less likely to derive benefits from globalization.

*A puzzle:* To what extent can even the most powerful states (especially the United States) preserve their autonomy and impose their will on others in a globalized world? And in what ways are the poorer and less powerful countries particularly vulnerable to the pressures of globalization and disgruntled citizens?

Increasingly, the politics and policies of states are shaped by diverse international factors often lumped together under the category of globalization. At the same time, many states face increasingly restive constituencies within their country who challenge the power and legitimacy of central governments. In reading the country case studies in this book, try to assess how pressures from both above and below—outside and inside—influence a state's policies and its ability to retain citizen support.

## WTO

A global international organization that oversees the "rules of trade" among its member states. The main functions of the WTO are to serve as a forum for its members to negotiate new agreements and resolve trade disputes. Its fundamental purpose is to lower or remove barriers to free trade.

## IMF

The "sister organization" of the World Bank and also has more than 180 member states. It describes its mandate as "working to foster global monetary cooperation, secure financial stability, facilitate international trade, promote high employment and sustainable economic growth, and reduce poverty." It has been particularly active in helping countries that are experiencing serious financial problems. In exchange for IMF financial or technical assistance, a country must agree to a certain set of conditions that promote economic liberalization.

## NAFTA

A treaty among the United States, Mexico, and Canada implemented on January 1, 1994, that largely eliminates trade barriers among the three nations and establishes procedures to resolve trade disputes. NAFTA serves as a model for an eventual Free Trade Area of the Americas zone that could include most nations in the Western Hemisphere.

The cartoon claims that globalization is flattening the nation-state.

# Theme 2: Governing the Economy

The success of states in maintaining sovereign authority and control over their people is greatly affected by their ability to ensure that enough goods are produced and services delivered to satisfy the needs and demands of their populations. Citizen discontent with communist states' inadequate economic performance was an important reason for the rejection of communism and the disintegration of the Soviet Union and its allies in Eastern Europe in 1989. In contrast, China's stunning success in promoting economic development has generated powerful support for the communist regime in that country.

Effective economic performance is near the top of every state's political agenda, and "governing the economy"[13]—how a state organizes production and the extent and nature of its intervention in the economy—is a key element in its overall pattern of governance. The core of governing the economy involves the strategies that states choose in an attempt to improve economic performance, deal with economic crises, and compete in international markets. A key contrast between various strategies is the relative importance of private market forces versus government direction of the economy.

The term **political economy** refers to the interaction between politics and economics, that is, to how government actions affect economic performance and how economic performance in turn affects a country's political processes. We place great importance on political economy in *Introduction to Comparative Politics* because we

**political economy**

The study of the interaction between the state and the economy, that is, how the state and political processes affect the economy and how the organization of the economy and strategic choices made by the government and state actors affect political processes.

believe that politics in all countries is deeply influenced by the interaction between a country's government and the economy in both its domestic and international dimensions.

Is there a particular formula for state economic governance that produces maximum success in promoting national prosperity? In particular, is there an optimum balance between state direction of the economy and free markets, that is, the ability of private business firms to operate without government supervision and regulation? On the one hand, both economic winners and losers among the world's countries display a pattern of extensive state intervention in the economy. And, similarly, both winners and losers include cases of relatively little state intervention. Thus, it is not the *degree* of state intervention that distinguishes the economic success stories from those that have fared less well. It appears, from comparing the economic performance of many countries, that the winners do not share a single formula that enabled them to excel. For example, a study of the world's affluent capitalist economies identifies two quite different patterns of political economy, both of which have been associated with strong economic performance.[14] Studies seeking to explain the Asian "economic miracles"—Japan, Taiwan, South Korea, and more recently China—as well as the variable economic performance of other countries, highlight the diversity of approaches that have been pursued.[15]

Making a comparative analysis of how well different states govern their economies becomes even more complex when one considers the appropriate yardstick to measure economic success. Should economic performance be measured solely by how rapidly a country's economy grows? By how equitably it distributes the fruits of economic growth? By the quality of life of its citizenry, as measured by such criteria as life expectancy, level of education, and unemployment rate? What about the environmental impact of economic growth? These are very different measures. Although many of the dimensions are positively correlated, there is far from a complete correspondence. Recently, there has been much greater attention to the issue of **sustainable development**, which promotes ecologically sound ways to modernize the economy and raise the standard of living. (See "How is Development Measured?") We invite you to consider these questions as you study the political economies of the countries analyzed in this book.

A puzzle: What is the relationship between democracy and successful national economic performance? This is a question that students of political economy have long pondered—and to which there are no fully satisfactory answers. Although all economies, even the most powerful, experience ups and downs, all durable democracies have been notable economic success stories. On the other hand, several East Asian countries with nondemocratic regimes—notably South Korea, Taiwan, and Singapore in the 1960s and 1970s, and Malaysia and Thailand in the 1980s and 1990s—achieved remarkable records of development. China, an authoritarian **communist party-state** that has enjoyed the highest growth rate among major economies in the world since the early 1990s, provides a vivid case of development without democracy. An influential study by political scientist Adam Przeworski and colleagues concludes, after an exhaustive comparison of the economic performance of democratic and authoritarian states, that there is no clear-cut answer to the question of which regime is better able to achieve superior economic performance.[16] Similarly, Nobel Prize-winning economist Amartya Sen has argued, "There is no clear relation between economic growth and democracy in *either* direction."[17] As you read the country studies, try to identify why some states have been more successful than others in "governing the economy," that is, fostering successful economic performance.

**sustainable development**

An approach to promoting economic growth that seeks to minimize environmental degradation and depletion of natural resources.

**communist party-state**

A type of nation-state in which the communist party attempts to exercise a complete monopoly on political power and controls all important state institutions.

**democracy**

From the Greek *demos* (the people) and *kratos* (rule). A political system featuring: selection to public offices through free and fair elections; the right of all adults to vote; political parties that are free to compete in elections; government that operates by fair and relatively open procedures; political rights and civil liberties; an independent judiciary (court system); civilian control of the military.

**GDP**

The total of all goods and services produced within a country that is used as a broad measure of the size of its economy.

**GNP**

GDP plus income earned by the country's residents; another broad measure of the size of an economy.

## GLOBAL CONNECTION

### How Is Development Measured?

As we have noted, we put particular importance on understanding the relationship between the political system and the economy in the study of the politics of any country and in our overall approach to comparative politics. Each of the country case studies describes and analyzes the role of the government in making economic policy. They also take special note of the impact of the global economy on national politics.

This book makes frequent reference to two commonly used measures of the overall size or power of a country's economy:

1. **Gross domestic product** (GDP): The value of the total goods and services produced by the country during a given year.
2. **Gross national product** (GNP): GDP plus income earned abroad by the country's residents.

A country's GDP and GNP are different, but not hugely so. In this book, we usually use GDP, calculated according to an increasingly popular method called **purchasing power parity (PPP)**. PPP takes into account the real cost of living in a particular country by calculating how much it would cost in the local currency to buy the same "basket of goods" in different countries. For example, how many dollars in the United States, pesos in Mexico, or rubles in Russia does it take to buy a certain amount of food or to pay for housing? Many scholars think that PPP provides a relatively reliable (and revealing) tool for comparing the size of an economy among countries. In terms of annual total output according to PPP, the world's ten largest economies, in descending order, are the United States, China, Japan, India, Germany, Russia, Britain, France, Brazil, and Italy.

Total gross domestic product is a useful measure. It helps to understand a country's overall weight in the world economy. But because this measure does not take the size of the population into account, it does not reveal anything about the prosperity of the country's citizens. After all, although China and India are powerhouses according to their GDP, their citizens' average income ranks far below that of the majority of countries in the world. A better way to measure and compare the level of economic development and citizens' standard of living in different countries is to look at annual GDP *per capita* (per person), in other words, to divide a country's total economic output by its population. Although China has the world's second-largest economy as measured by total output, it falls to 127th out of 227 economies in terms of its annual GDP *per capita* ($7,400); India ($3,400) ranks 163rd. The United States—by far the world's biggest economy—has the tenth highest GDP per capita ($47,400). Qatar and Liechtenstein (both over $140,000), with their tiny populations rank first and second in GDP per capita. Thus, using GDP *per capita* provides a much better idea of which countries in the world are rich (developed) or poor (developing).

The comparative data charts at the end of this chapter provide total GDP and GDP *per capita* as well as other economic, geographic, demographic, and social information for our country case studies. The Comparative Rankings table also provides several ways of evaluating countries' economic, political, or public policy performance.

One of the most important measures is the **Human Development Index (HDI)**, compiled by the United Nations, which evaluates the overall well-being of people. The HDI formula considers other factors in addition to income, including, *longevity* (life expectancy at birth) and *knowledge* (adult literacy and average years of schooling). Based on this formula, countries are annually ranked and divided into four broad categories by the United Nations Development Program (UNDP): "Very High," "High," "Medium," and "Low" human development. Out of 169 countries ranked according to HDI in 2010, the top three were Norway, Australia, and New Zealand; the bottom three were Niger, the Democratic Republic of the Congo, and Zimbabwe. As you read the country case studies in this book, try to see what connections there may be between a country's politics—especially how it governs the economy—and its human development ranking.

---

**purchasing power parity (PPP)**

A method of calculating the value of a country's money based on the actual cost of buying goods and services in that country rather than how many U.S. dollars they are worth.

# Theme 3: The Democratic Idea

One of the most important and astonishing political developments in recent years has been the rapid spread of **democracy** throughout much of the world. There is powerful evidence of the strong appeal of democracy, that is, a regime in which citizens exercise substantial control over choice of political leaders and the decisions made by their governments.

According to statistical analysis of numerous measures of political freedom and civil liberties, the think tank Freedom House has calculated that in 1973, there

| Table 1.1 | The Spread of Democracy[a] | | |
|---|---|---|---|
| **Year** | **Free Countries** | **Partly Free Countries** | **Not Free Countries** |
| 1973 | 43 (35%) | 38 (18%) | 69 (47%) |
| 1983 | 54 (36%) | 47 (20%) | 64 (44%) |
| 1993[b] | 75 (25%) | 73 (44%) | 38 (31%) |
| 2010 | 87 (43%) | 60 (22%) | 47 (35%)[c] |

[a] The number of countries in each category is followed by the percentage of the world population.

[b] In 1993, the large increase in the number of free and partly free countries was mostly due to the collapse of communist regimes in the Soviet Union and elsewhere. The main reason that there was a significant drop in the percentage of world population living in free countries in 1993 was that India was classified as partly free from 1991 through 1997. It has been ranked as free since 1998.

[c] The increase in the number of countries and percentage of people rated as not free countries in 2010 compared to 1993 reflects the fact that several countries, most notably Russia, were shifted from partly free to not free. Half of the world's "not free" population lives in China.

*Source: Freedom House (www.freedomhouse.org)*

were 43 countries that could be considered "free" (or democratic), 38 that were "partly free," and 69 that should be classified as "not free."[18] In 2010, the count was 87 free, 60 partly free, and 47 not free. In terms of population, 35 percent of the world's people lived in free countries in 1973, 18 percent in partly free, and 47 percent were citizens of countries ranked as not free. In 2010, the percentages were 43 percent free, 22 percent partly free, and 35 percent not free. (See Table 1.1.) Economist Amartya Sen has observed, "While democracy is not yet uniformly practiced, nor indeed uniformly accepted, in the general climate of world opinion, democratic governance has now achieved the status of being taken to be generally right."[19] As authoritarian rulers in countries from Albania to Zaire (now called the Democratic Republic of the Congo) have learned in recent decades, once persistent and widespread pressures for democratic participation develop, they are hard to resist. However, as brutal suppression of protesters in China (in 1989) and Libya and Bahrain (in 2011) demonstrated, dictators do not easily give up their power.

What determines the growth, stagnation, or decline of democracy in a country? Comparativists have devoted enormous energy to studying this question. One scholar notes, "For the past two decades, the main topic of research in comparative politics has been democratization."[20] Yet, for all the attention it has received, there is no scholarly consensus on how and why democratization develops and becomes consolidated, remains incomplete, or is reversed. Just as there is no single route to economic prosperity, we have also learned that there is no one path to democracy, and that democratic transitions can be slow, uncertain, and reversible. Many of the country studies in *Introduction to Comparative Politics* analyze the diverse causes and sources of support for democracy; and some expose the fragility of democratic transitions.

In certain historical settings, democracy may result from a standoff or compromise among political contenders for power in which no one group can gain sufficient strength to control outcomes by itself. The result is that they "settle" for a democratic compromise in which power is shared. In some (but not all) cases,

**Human Development Index**

A composite number used by the United Nations to measure and compare levels of achievement in health, knowledge, and standard of living. HDI is based on the following indicators: life expectancy, adult literacy rate and school enrollment statistics, and gross domestic product per capita at purchasing power parity.

rival groups may conclude that democracy is preferable to civil war. Or, it may take a bloody civil war that produces stalemate to persuade competing groups to accept democracy as a second-best solution. Democracy may appeal to citizens in authoritarian nations because democratic regimes often rank among the world's most stable, affluent, free, and cohesive countries. In some cases, a regional demonstration effect occurs, in which a democratic transition in one country provokes democratic change in neighboring countries. This occurred in southern Europe in the 1970s, Latin America and parts of East Asia in the 1980s, Eastern and Central Europe in the 1990s, and in North Africa and the Middle East in 2011. Another important pressure for democracy is born of the human desire for dignity and equality. Even when dictatorial regimes appear to benefit their countries—for example, by promoting economic development or nationalist goals—citizens may demand democracy.

Let the reader beware: The authors of *Introduction to Comparative Politics* have a strong normative preference for democracy. We believe, in the oft-quoted words of Britain's World War II Prime Minister Winston Churchill, "Democracy is the worst form of government except for all those others that have been tried." Despite the many flaws of actually existing democracies, democracy seems to us to be the regime most consistent with human aspirations for freedom, prosperity, and security. However, as good social scientists, we have tried to separate our normative preferences from our analysis of politics in the countries covered in this book. With that said, we believe that political science should give high priority to rigorously analyzing normatively charged issues like repression, inequality, and injustice—as well as freedom, justice, and democracy.

It should be noted that some observers of politics have warned of dangers that may be associated with democracy. For example, political analyst Fareed Zakaria, while supportive of the democratic idea, claims that democratic policy-making tends to be dominated by what he terms "short-term political and electoral considerations," whereas wise policy requires a long-range perspective. He suggests insulating some key political institutions from partisan swings and praises agencies within the U.S. government, including the Supreme Court and the Federal Reserve Board, whose members are nominated by the president and who possess ample independent authority. He provocatively claims, "What we need in politics today is not more democracy but less."[21] Consider Zakaria's argument when you read the country studies in this book and consider to what extent and why democratic processes may promote undesirable consequences.

Is it possible to identify conditions that are necessary or sufficient for the democratic idea to take root and flourish? Comparativists have proposed, among such factors, secure national boundaries, a stable state, at least a minimum level of economic development, the widespread acceptance of democratic values, and agreement on the rules of democratic politics among those contending for power. Institutional design also matters when it comes to producing stable democracies. Do certain kinds of political institutions facilitate compromise as opposed to polarization and hence greater stability? The balance of scholarly opinion suggests, for example, that parliamentary systems that tie the fates of the legislators to that of the prime minister tend to produce more consensual outcomes than do presidential systems, where the legislature and executive are independent from each other and often compete in setting national political agendas.[22] As you read the country studies, note the patterns of similarity and difference you observe in the degree of conflict or polarization in presidential systems (such as the United States and Mexico) and compare those cases to parliamentary systems (such as Britain).

Although certain economic, cultural, and institutional features enhance the prospects of democratic transitions and consolidations, democracy has flourished in unlikely settings. India, for example, is a long-established democracy that ranks in the bottom quarter of the world's countries in terms of per capita income. Hundreds of millions of Indians live in dire poverty. Yet, despite some important instances of undemocratic practices, India has had a vibrantly functioning democratic system since it became independent in 1947.

Democracy has also failed where it might be expected to flourish, most notably and with tragic consequences in highly educated and relatively wealthy Germany in the 1930s. Democracies vary widely in terms of how they have come into existence and in their concrete historical, institutional, economic, and cultural dimensions.

Displacing authoritarian regimes and holding elections does not guarantee the survival or durability of a fledgling democracy. A wide gulf exists between what comparativists have termed a *transition* to democracy and the *consolidation* of democracy. A transition involves toppling an authoritarian regime and adopting the basic institutions and procedures of democracy; consolidation requires fuller adherence to democratic principles and making democratic government more sturdy and durable. Below we further explore the important question of how to distinguish what we term *transitional democracies* from *consolidated democracies*. We consider the distinction of such great importance that it forms one basis for our scheme for classifying countries throughout the world.

We want to emphasize that the study of comparative politics does not support a philosophy of history or theory of political development that identifies a single (democratic) end point toward which all countries will eventually converge. One landmark work, published at the beginning of a democratic wave in the mid-1970s in Portugal and Spain and then spread to Latin America, captured the tenuous process of democratization in its title: *Transitions from Authoritarian Rule: Tentative Conclusions about Uncertain Democracies*.[23] A country may adopt some democratic features, for example, elections, while retaining highly undemocratic elements as well. Scholars have suggested that it is far easier for a country to hold its first democratic election than its second or third. Historically, powerful groups have often opposed democratization because they fear that democracy will threaten their privileges. Disadvantaged groups may also oppose the democratic process because they see it as unresponsive to their deeply felt grievances. As a result, "stalled transitions" may leave a country with a mix of democratic and authoritarian features of governance. Further, reversals of democratic regimes and restorations of authoritarian rule have occurred in the past and will doubtless occur in the future.[24] Another phenomenon is "elected dictators," such as Hugo Chavez in Venezuela, who are voted into office and then use their power to dismantle important elements of the democratic system. In brief, the fact that the democratic idea is so powerful does not mean that all countries will adopt or preserve democratic institutions.

The theme of the democratic idea requires us to examine the incompleteness of democratic agendas, even in countries with the longest experiences of representative democracy. Citizens may invoke the democratic idea to demand that their government be more responsive and accountable, as in the Civil Rights Movement in the United States. **Social movements** in some democratic countries have targeted the state because of its actions or inactions in such varied spheres as environmental regulation, reproductive rights, and race or ethnic relations. Comparative studies confirm that the democratic idea fuels political conflicts in even the most durable

**social movements**

Large-scale grass-roots action that demands reforms of existing social practices and government policies.

democracies because a large gap usually separates democratic ideals and the actual functioning of democratic political institutions. Moreover, social movements often organize because citizens perceive political parties—presumably, an important vehicle for representing citizen demands in democracies—as rigid and out of touch with the people.

A puzzle: Is there a relationship between democracy and political stability? Comparativists have debated whether democratic institutions contribute to political stability or, on the contrary, to political disorder.[25] On the one hand, democracy by its very nature permits political opposition. One of its defining characteristics is competition among those who aspire to gain political office. Political life in democracies is turbulent and unpredictable. On the other hand, and perhaps paradoxically, the very fact that political opposition and competition are legitimate in democracies can deepen support for the state, even among opponents of a particular government. The democratic rules of the game may promote political stability by encouraging today's losers to reject the use of violence to press their claim to power. They may do so because they calculate that they have a good chance to win peacefully in future competition. Although deep flaws often mar democratic governance in countries that have toppled authoritarian regimes, a careful study finds that, once a country adopts a democratic regime, the odds are that it will endure.[26] As you learn about different countries, look for the stabilizing and destabilizing consequences of democratic transitions, the pressures (or lack of pressure) for democratization in authoritarian states, and the persistence of undemocratic elements even in established democracies.

# Theme 4: The Politics of Collective Identities

How do individuals understand who they are in relation to the state and other citizens? How and why do they join in groups to advance shared political or other goals within a country? In other words, what are the sources of collective political identities? At one time, social scientists thought they knew. Scholars once argued that age-old loyalties of ethnicity, religious affiliation, race, and locality were being dissolved and displaced as a result of economic, political, and cultural modernization. Comparativists thought that **social class**—solidarities based on the shared experience of work or, more broadly, economic position in society—had become the most important—indeed, nearly only—source of collective identity. They believed that in the typical political situation, groups formed on the basis of economic interest would pragmatically and peacefully pursue their interests. We now know that the formation of group attachments and the interplay of politically relevant collective identities are far more complex and uncertain.

In many long-established democracies, the political importance of identities based on class membership has declined. Economically-based sources of collective identity do remain significant in influencing citizens' party affiliation and preferences about economic policy and how the economic pie is divided and distributed. Especially in this era of austerity, the struggle over who gets what—and who decides who gets what—can be fierce. Indeed, these days class politics is making a comeback. But contrary to earlier predictions, in many countries nonclass identities have assumed growing, not diminishing, significance. Such identities are based on a sense of belonging to particular groups sharing a common language, region, religion, ethnicity, race, nationality, or gender.

**social class**

A group whose members share common world views and aspirations determined largely by occupation, income, and wealth.

The politics of collective political identity involves efforts to mobilize identity groups to influence political outcomes, ranging from the state's distribution of benefits, to economic and educational policy or the basis for political representation, and even territorial claims. Identity-based conflicts appear in most societies. Politics in democratic regimes (and, often in a more concealed way, in authoritarian regimes as well) involves a tug of war among groups over relative power and influence, both symbolic and substantive. Issues of inclusion, political recognition, representation, resource allocation, and the capacity to shape public policies, such as immigration, education, and the status of minority languages, remain pivotal in many countries.

Questions of representation are especially hard to resolve: Which groups should be considered legitimate participants in the political game? Who is included in a racial or ethnic community? Who speaks for the community or negotiates with a governmental authority on its behalf? Conflict about these issues can be intense because political leaders often seek to mobilize support by exploiting ethnic, religious, racial, or regional rivalries and by manipulating issues of identity and representation. And conflict can be all the greater because considerable material and nonmaterial stakes often derive from the outcome of these struggles. Race relations in the United States powerfully illustrates that issues about collective identities are never fully settled, although they may rage with greater or lesser intensity in particular countries and at particular times.

An especially important source of identity-based conflict involves ethnicity. And given the pace of migration and the tangled web of postcolonial histories that link colonizer to colonized, what country is not multiethnic? As political scientist Alfred Stepan points out, "...there are very few states in the entire world that are relatively homogeneous nation-states...."[27] In Britain, France, Germany, and the United States, issues of nationality, citizenship, and immigration—often linked to ethnic or racial factors—have often been hot-button issues in electoral politics. Ethnic conflicts have been particularly frequent and intense in postcolonial countries, for example, Nigeria, where colonial powers forced ethnic groups together when defining the country's boundaries and where borders were drawn with little regard to preexisting collective identities. The process of state formation has often sowed seeds for future conflict in many postcolonial nations.

Religion is another source of collective identity, as well as of severe political conflict, both within and among religious communities. Violent conflict among religious groups has recently occurred in India, Sri Lanka, Nigeria, and the United Kingdom (in Northern Ireland). Such conflicts may spill over national boundaries and involve an especially ugly form of globalization. For example, leaders of Al Qaeda targeted non-Muslim Western military forces stationed in what they regarded as the sacred soil of Saudi Arabia as a principal reason for the 9/11 attacks. At the same time, the political orientation of a particular religious community is not predetermined. The political posture associated with what it means to be Christian, Jewish, Muslim, or Hindu cannot simply be determined from holy texts. Witness the intense conflict *within* most religious communities today that pits liberal, secular elements against those who defend what they claim is a more orthodox, traditional interpretation.

**A puzzle:** How do collective identities affect a country's **distributional politics**, that is, the process of deciding how resources are distributed, concretely, who gets what? Once identity demands are placed on the national agenda, can a government resolve them by distributing political, economic, and other resources in ways that redress the grievances of the minority or politically weaker identity groups?

**distributional politics**

The use of power, particularly by the state, to allocate some kind of valued resource among competing groups.

Collective identities operate at the level of symbols, attitudes, values, and beliefs as well as at the level of material resources. The contrast between material- and non-material-based identities and demands should not be exaggerated. In practice, most groups are animated both by feelings of attachment and solidarity and by the desire to obtain material benefits and political influence for their members. Nonetheless, the analytical distinction between material and nonmaterial demands remains useful. Further, nonmaterial aspects of collective identities may make political disputes over ethnicity or religion or language or nationality especially divisive and difficult to resolve because it is harder to purchase peace through distributing material benefits.

In a situation of extreme economic scarcity, it may prove nearly impossible to reach any compromise among groups with conflicting material demands. If an adequate level of material resources is available, such conflicts may be easier to resolve through distributional politics because groups can negotiate at least a minimally satisfying share of resources.

However, as we noted above, the nonmaterial demands of ethnic, religious, and nationalist movements may be harder to satisfy by a distributional style of politics. The distributional style may be quite ineffective when, for example, a dominant linguistic group insists that a single language be used in education and government throughout the country. In such cases, political conflict tends to move from the distributive realm to the cultural realm, where compromises cannot be achieved by simply dividing the pie of material resources. The country studies in this book examine a wide range of conflicts involving collective identities. It is worth pondering whether, and under what conditions, they can be resolved by political bargaining—and when, instead, they lead to the fury and blood of political violence.

These four themes provide our analytic scaffold. With an understanding of the method of comparative politics and the four themes in mind, we can now discuss how we have grouped the country studies in *Introduction to Comparative Politics* and how the text is organized to help students master the basics of comparative analysis.

# CLASSIFYING POLITICAL SYSTEMS

## Focus Questions

What are some difficult problems involved in establishing a useful way of classifying political systems?

Can you think of another way from the one suggested in this chapter?

There are more than 200 states in the world today. Although each state is unique, to avoid being overwhelmed by the sheer number it makes sense to highlight categories of states that share some important features. That is, it is useful to identify what distinguishes one category of relatively similar states from other categories, and to study how a state moves from one category to another. When comparativists classify a large number of cases into a smaller number of categories, or types, they call the result a **typology**. A typology is an analytic construct that helps us engage in comparisons that yield useful knowledge. One of the most common typologies used to categorize states distinguishes between democratic and authoritarian political systems. As we discuss below, this is one of the bases we use to classify the countries in this book.

Typologies are also useful for making comparisons within the same political category. For example, Britain and the United States are long-established democracies. But Britain has a parliamentary form of government and the United States has a presidential one. How these very different mixes of democratic institutions work in practice is the kind of important and intriguing question that lies at the heart of comparative politics.

From the end of World War II until the 1980s, political scientists agreed that the most useful typology for classifying states involved identifying Western industrial democracies, which were called the "First World"; communist states, that were said to form the "Second World"; and economically less developed countries in Asia, Africa, and Latin America, many of which had recently gained independence and made up the "**Third World**."

The term "Third World" was coined by French authors in the 1950s to draw attention to the plight of the world's poorer nations, which they believed to be as important as the then headline-grabbing Cold War and its superpower adversaries. They drew an analogy from the history of the French Revolution of the 1780s when the impoverished common people (called the Third Estate) rose up against the privileged and powerful classes, the clergy (the First Estate) and the nobility (the Second Estate). These writers adapted this terminology of French social classes of the eighteenth century to dramatize how, in the mid-twentieth century, a long-oppressed Third World of countries in Africa, Asia, and Latin America was struggling against both the First World (the industrial democracies of the West) and the Second World (the Soviet Union and other communist countries).

From the 1960s through the late 1980s, many political scientists classified different types of states according to a typology that was based on this "Three Worlds" framework. First World capitalist industrialized countries were not only wealthy, but also stable and democratic. The communist systems of the Second World were authoritarian. Most Third World states had personal dictatorships, one-party rule, military regimes, or—at best—democracies marred by high levels of social conflict and political violence.

The term "First World" is rarely used anymore, as more countries have become both economically developed and democratic. The collapse of the Soviet Union and most other communist regimes made the "Second World" a rather meaningless concept.

Furthermore, big differences in growth rates among developing countries in recent decades make it harder to generalize about the Third World. Some countries that were considered part of the Third World, such as South Korea, are now considered high-income countries. Brazil, China, India—still relatively poor countries compared to the OECD nations—are among the world's most dynamic economies and have made substantial progress in poverty alleviation. But many developing countries have experienced little or no economic growth, and most of their people—the so-called Bottom Billion of the world's population—live in dire circumstances. The Third World has changed a lot politically, too. In 1975, most Third World countries had some kind of authoritarian government; by the early twenty-first century, scores of developing nations, from Argentina to Zambia, have become democratic, or moved in that direction. This remarkable transition toward democracy is discussed in more detail below.

The view that what Third World countries have in common is extreme poverty and brutal dictatorship is certainly not valid today, if it ever was. So should the term "Third World" be jettisoned altogether as a category for scholarly analysis? Recent trends have profoundly challenged and complicated the way that comparativists classify the world's countries. But we believe that despite major political and economic differences, the countries included in this book continue to share many distinct

**typology**

A method of classifying by using criteria that divide a group of cases into smaller cases with common characteristics.

**Third World**

refers to countries with a low or relatively low level of economic development, particularly as measured by gross national income or gross domestic product per capita.

**consolidated democracies**

Democratic political systems that have been solidly and stably established for an ample period of time and in which there is relatively consistent adherence to the core democratic principles.

**transitional democracies**

Countries that have moved from an authoritarian government to a democratic one.

**authoritarian regimes**

A system of rule in which power depends not on popular legitimacy but on the coercive force of the political authorities.

characteristics that allow us to group and study them together as part of the developing world and, indeed, that a good case can be made for the validity of "Third World" as a category for comparative analysis—even if the terms "First World" and "Second World" are outdated as typologies for classifying political systems.

If the "three worlds" method of classifying states does not help us understand how countries compare, what alternative is preferable? At present, there is a lively debate among comparativists on this question. In this book, we use a typology based on one of the most important dimensions for understanding political similarities and differences among countries in the contemporary world: The extent to which their governments are democratic.

Our typology classifies states into three groups: **consolidated democracies**, **transitional democracies**, and **authoritarian regimes**. The typology highlights the fundamental distinction between democratic and authoritarian governments. Of course, it is essential to clearly and precisely define the key terms.

# The Meaning—or Meanings—of Democracy

As with many other important concepts, the meaning of democracy is a contentious subject among political scientists—and even among politicians. Should democracy be defined solely on the basis of the procedures used to select top governmental officeholders? That is, for a political system to qualify as democratic is it sufficient that occupants of the highest offices of the state be selected on the basis of free and fair elections in which opposing parties present candidates and all citizens are entitled to cast a vote for a contending party? Or must there also be respect for civil liberties (including rights of free expression, dissent, and privacy)? And must there be an independent judiciary to protect civil liberties? Are due process and the rule of law essential components of democracy? What is the relationship between religious practice and the exercise of political power? Must a democratic regime guarantee citizens the right to worship freely—as well as the right to not worship at all? To what extent should all citizens be guaranteed economic and social rights, such as income support and access to health care, pensions, and state funded schools for all children (girls and boys) as distinct from political and civil rights (such as the right to vote and criticize the government)? These are thorny and unresolved issues.

Despite intense debate about the meaning(s) of democracy, scholars generally agree that the following conditions must be present. Disagreement involves whether additional elements just identified should also be considered necessary features of democratic regimes.

1. Selection to the highest public offices is on the basis of free and fair elections. For an election to qualify as fair, there must be procedures in place guaranteeing candidates the right to compete, all citizens must be entitled to vote, and votes must be counted accurately, with the winning candidate(s) selected according to preexisting rules that determine the kind of plurality or majority required to gain electoral victory.

2. Political parties are free to organize, present candidates for public office, and compete in elections. The opposition party or parties enjoy the right to organize and to criticize the incumbent government.

3. The elected government makes policy according to procedures that provide for transparency in decision-making and the accountability of elected officials through electoral procedures, a free media, and established judicial procedures.

4. All citizens possess political rights—the right to participate and vote in periodic elections to select key state officeholders; as well as civil liberties—the right of free assembly, conscience, privacy, and expression, including the right to criticize the government without fear of official reprisals.

5. The legal system is based on "the rule of law," according to which no person or organization is above the law, and the principle of legal equality, meaning that all citizens are treated equally by the law. The political system contains a judiciary with powers independent of the executive and legislature, charged with protecting citizens' political rights and civil liberties.

6. The elected government exercises effective authority, including control over the military and over private power-holders (including large landowners, and corporations); thus, no hidden, private groups exercise a veto power over the government, that is, effectively exercise control.

7. There is a commitment that conflicts—political, social, economic, and identity-based—will be resolved peacefully, without recourse to violence, and according to legally prescribed procedures.

We believe that these seven criteria establish the base line of any democratic political system. We invite you to use these items as a checklist while you read the case studies, noting how each of the consolidated democracies attempts to satisfy each of the seven benchmark criteria; how the transitional democracies display a mixture of success and failures; and how authoritarian political systems often fail on most, if not all of the criteria.

We stress that no country fully satisfies all these criteria for democracy. Even in long established democratic states, there remains a gap—often a substantial one—between the aspirations and ideals of democracy and the practice and results of any actually existing democracy. When you read the country studies, use this seven-point checklist to assess where the country ranks with respect to each one.

Our typology of political systems involves a further distinction between long-established, or consolidated democracies, and newly established, or transitional democracies. We claim that there is a difference in kind, and not just of degree, between the two groups. We use two criteria to distinguish these categories. The first criterion divides democratic regimes according to whether their democratic institutions and practices have been solidly established for an ample period of time. Precisely how long is open to question: more than a few years to be sure, possibly at least a decade or two? In part, the answer depends on the degree to which the next requirement is met.

The second criterion for distinguishing between consolidated and transitional democracies is the *extent* of their democratic practice. Consolidated democracies are regimes in which there is relatively consistent adherence to the seven democratic principles that we specified above. Examples of consolidated democracies are Britain, France, Germany, India, Japan, and the United States. All have been democracies for more than fifty years and generally perform fairly satisfactorily on the seven-point democratic checklist.

We do not mean to claim that consolidated democracies fully adhere to democratic norms—they don't, and they sometimes violate them in shocking ways. For example, police abuse and unequal legal treatment of citizens who are poor or from a racial or ethnic minority are all too common in countries generally considered high in the democratic rankings, like Britain and the United States. Following 9/11, intelligence agencies in many democracies—including in the United States under the terms of the Patriot Act—greatly expanded their surveillance of citizens in an effort to combat terrorism, for example, by monitoring telephone calls and e-mails and allowing government access to financial, medical, library, and other records. Such measures stirred considerable controversy (which is still stirring) about the trade-off between liberty and security in a democratic society.

The reason why we highlight the importance of adhering to democratic procedures becomes apparent when we turn to the second category of democracy that we use in this book. In many transitional democracies, a façade of democratic institutions conceals numerous practices that violate our checklist of core features of democracy. As a general matter, although there is usually greater legal protection of citizen rights and liberties in transitional democracies than in authoritarian regimes—there is considerably less than in consolidated democracies. Transitional democracies are to be found on every continent and include Russia, Brazil, Mexico, Nigeria, and South Africa.

Some transitional democracies have moved a long way toward consolidation. But many are "hybrid regimes" in which democratic forms of governance coexist with a disturbing persistence of authoritarian elements.[28] In such systems, government officials are more likely to engage in corruption, control of the media, and intimidation and violence against opponents. They use illegal means to undermine opposition parties and ensure that the ruling party is re-elected. Despite what the constitution may specify, the judiciary is often packed with ruling party faithful, and top military officers often exercise extraordinary political power behind the scenes.

How do we define authoritarian regimes—the third kind of political system in our typology? The simplest way is to change the positive sign to negative in the checklist of democratic characteristics. Thus, authoritarian regimes lack effective procedures for selecting political leaders through competitive elections based on universal suffrage; they include few institutionalized procedures for holding those with political power accountable to the citizens of the country; oppositional politics and dissent are severely restricted; people of different genders, racial groups, religions, and ethnicities do not enjoy equal rights; the legal system is highly politicized and the judiciary is not an independent branch of government capable of checking the power of the state or protecting the rights of citizens; and coercion and violence are part of the political process.

Clearly, then, authoritarian states are nondemocracies. But it isn't good social science to define something only by what it is not. The term *authoritarianism* refers to political systems in which power (or authority) is highly concentrated in a single individual, a small group of people, a single political party, ethnic group, region, or institution. Furthermore, those with power claim an exclusive right to govern and use various means, including force, to impose their will and policies on all who live under their authority.

As with states classified as democracies, there are an enormous variety of authoritarian regime types: communist party-states (e.g., China and Cuba); theocracies in which sovereign power is held by religious leaders and law is defined in religious terms (e.g., present-day Iran); military governments (e.g., Myanmar, the country formerly called Burma); absolute monarchies (e.g., Saudi Arabia); and personalistic dictatorships (e.g., Iraq under Saddam Hussein). Authoritarian regimes frequently claim that they embody a form of democracy, particularly in the contemporary era when the democratic idea seems so persuasive and powerful. For example, according to the Chinese Communist Party, the political system of the People's Republic of China is based on "socialist democracy," which it claims is superior to the "bourgeois democracy" of capitalist countries that favors the interests of wealthier citizens. But most political scientists would conclude that there is little substance to these claims and that in such states dictatorship far outweighs democracy. As the chapter on China will describe, the Communist Party monopolizes most decision-making, and its leaders are chosen by self-selection rather than popular election.

Nevertheless, even countries classified as authoritarian may include democratic values and practices. In Iran, a theocratic authoritarian regime, there are vigorously contested multiparty elections, although the extent of contestation is limited by Islamic clergy who ultimately exercise sovereign power. In China, a form of grass-roots democracy has been implemented in the more than 700,000 rural villages where a majority of the population lives. Even though the Communist Party still oversees the process, China's rural dwellers now have a real choice when they elect their local leaders. Such democratic elements in Iran and China are certainly significant in under-standing politics in those countries; however, they do not fundamentally alter the authoritarian character of the state.

Our categories of consolidated democracies, transitional democracies, and authoritarian regimes are not airtight, and some countries may straddle two cate-gories. Consider Brazil, which we designate as a transitional democracy. Ever since democracy was restored in 1974, following a period of harsh military rule, Brazil has compiled a solid record of democratic practice. For example, since the return of civilian rule there have been several peaceful electoral alternations between dramati-cally different political coalitions. One might claim that Brazil should be classified as a consolidated democracy. We believe, however, that because of repeated violations of democratic procedures, political corruption, lack of entrenched democratic values, and extensive inequality (which is heavily coded in racial terms), Brazil remains a transitional democracy.

Another example of the difficulty of classifying states: We consider India a con-solidated democracy because it has generally respected most of the democratic proce-dures on our checklist since it gained independence in 1947. There is intense political competition in India, elections are usually free and fair, and the Indian judiciary is quite independent. However, some might question our decision. For example, India has repeatedly experienced scenes of horrific communal violence, in which large num-bers of Muslim, Sikh, and Christian minorities have been brutally massacred, some-times with the active complicity of state officials.

A further point about our typology is that the boundaries among categories are fluid. Some of the countries classified as transitional democracies are experiencing such political turmoil that they could very well fall out of any category of democracy. Take Russia, for example, which we classify as a transitional democracy but whose trajectory in the last few years is in the authoritarian direction. Since Vladimir Putin's reelec-tion as president in 2004 and continuing under his handpicked successor, Dmitry Medvedev (elected in 2008), the Russian government has engaged in numerous undemocratic practices, including arbitrary detention and rigged trials of opponents, repeated violations of the constitution, and extensive political corruption. There are competitive but not fair elections, multiple parties but one dominant establishment party, press diversity in the print media but with significant restrictions, and tightly controlled television news. Therefore a good case could be made that Russia should be classified as authoritarian, even though Putin (now in the position of prime min-ister) and Medvedev enjoy extensive popular support. In fact, Freedom House now classifies Russia as "not free." However, we place Russia in the transitional democratic category because we recognize that a society like Russia may take several decades to transit to democracy, and setbacks are to be expected. But we are fully aware of the ominous tendencies that may move Russia into the authoritarian slot in our typology in the next edition of this book.

These observations about Russia underscore an important point about our typology. We do not mean to imply that there is an automatic escalator of political development that transports a country from one category to the next "higher" one. History has demonstrated that one should be wary of subscribing to a theory of inevitable progress—whether political, economic, or social. Transitional democracies may become more democratic—or may backslide toward authoritarianism.

**SECTION 5**

# ORGANIZATION OF THE TEXT

### Focus Questions

If you could choose one other country to study in a comparative politics course besides the 13 included in this book, what would it be? Why?

What would you like to know about politics in that country?

We selected the countries for the case studies in this book for their significance in terms of our comparative themes and because they provide an extensive sample of types of political regimes, levels of economic development, and geographic regions. Although each of the country studies makes important comparative references, the studies primarily provide in-depth descriptions and analyses of the politics of individual countries. At the same time, the country studies have identical formats, with common section and subsection headings to help you make comparisons and explore similar themes across the various cases. And each chapter emphasizes the four themes that anchor analyses in ICP and enables you to engage in cross-country comparisons.

The following are brief summaries of the main issues and questions covered in the country studies.

## 1: The Making of the Modern State

Section 1 in each chapter provides an overview of the forces that have shaped the state. We believe that understanding the contemporary politics of any country requires familiarity with the historical process of state formation. "Politics in Action" uses a specific event to illustrate an important political moment in the country's recent history and to highlight some of the critical political challenges it faces. "Geographic Setting" locates the country in its regional context and discusses the political implications of this setting. "Critical Junctures" looks at some of the major stages and decisive turning points in the state's development. This discussion should give you an idea of how the country assumed its current political shape and provide a sense of how relations between state and society have developed over time.

"Themes and Implications" shows how past patterns of state development continue to influence the country's current political agenda. "Historical Junctures and Political Themes" applies the text's key themes to the making of the modern state. How has the country's political development been affected by its place in position in the international order—its relative ability to control external events and its regional and global status? What are the political implications of the state's approach to economic management? What has been the country's experience with the democratic idea? What are the important bases of collective identity in the country, and how do they influence the country's politics? Section 1 ends by exploring "Implications for Comparative Politics" that is, the broader significance of the country for the study of comparative politics.

# 2: Political Economy and Development

Section 2 analyzes the pattern of governing each country's economy, and it explores how economic development has affected political change. We locate this section toward the beginning of the country study because we believe that a country's economic profile has an important impact on its politics. Within this section, there are several subsections. "State and Economy" discusses the basic organization of the country's economic system, and focuses on the role of the state and the role of markets in economic life. It also examines the relationship between the government and other economic actors. How do the dynamics and historical timing of the country's insertion into the world economy affect domestic political arrangements and shape contemporary challenges? "Society and Economy" examines the social and political implications of the country's economic situation. It describes the state's social welfare policies, such as health care, housing, and pension programs. It asks who benefits from economic change and looks at how economic development creates or reinforces class, ethnic, gender, regional, or ideological cleavages in society. The section closes by examining the country's relationship to "The Global Economy." How have international economic issues affected the domestic political agenda? How have patterns of trade and foreign investment changed over time? What is the country's relationship to regional and international economic organizations? To what degree has the country been able to influence multilateral policies?

# 3: Governance and Policy-Making

In Section 3, we describe the state's major policy-making institutions and procedures. "Organization of the State" lays out the fundamental principles on which the political system and the distribution of political power are based, the country's constitution, key state institutions, and historical experience. The chapter also outlines the basic structure of the state, including the relationship among different levels and branches of government. "The Executive" encompasses the key offices (for example, presidents, prime ministers, communist party leaders) at the top of the political system, focusing on how they are selected and how they use their power to make policy. This section also analyzes the cabinet and the national bureaucracy, their relationship to the chief executive, and their role in policy-making. "Other State Institutions" examines the military, the judiciary and the legal system, semipublic agencies, and subnational government. "The Policy-Making Process" summarizes how public policy gets made and implemented. It describes the roles of formal institutions and procedures, as well as informal aspects of policy-making, such as the influence of lobbyists and interest groups.

# 4: Representation and Participation

Section 4 focuses on the relationship between a country's state and society. How do different groups in society organize to further their political interests, how do they participate and get represented in the political system, and to what extent and how do they influence policy-making? Given the importance of the U.S. Congress in policy-making, American readers might expect to find the principal discussion of "The

Legislature" in Section 3 ("Governance and Policy-Making") rather than Section 4. But the U.S. Congress is an exceptionally powerful legislature. In most other political systems, the executive dominates the policy process, even when it is ultimately responsible to the legislature (as is the case in parliamentary systems). In most countries other than the United States, the legislature functions primarily to represent and provide a forum for the political expression of various interests; it is only secondarily (and in some cases, such as China, only marginally) a policy-making body. Therefore, although this section does describe and assess the legislature's role in policy-making, its primary focus is on how the legislature represents or fails to represent different interests in society.

"Political Parties and the Party System" describes the overall organization of the party system and reviews the major parties. "Elections" discusses the election process and recent trends in electoral behavior. It also considers the significance of elections (or lack thereof) as a vehicle for citizen participation in politics and in bringing about changes in the government. "Political Culture, Citizenship, and Identity" examines how people perceive themselves as members of the political community: the nature and source of political values and attitudes, who is considered a citizen, and how different groups in society understand their relationship to the state. The topics covered may include political aspects of the educational system, the media, religion, and ethnicity. We also ask how globalization affects collective identities and collective action. "Interests, Social Movements, and Protests" discusses how groups in civil society pursue their political interests outside the party system. What is the relationship between the state and such organizations and movements? When and how do citizens engage in acts of protest? And how does the state respond when they do?

## 5: Politics in Transition

In Section 5, we identify and analyze the major challenges confronting each country and revisit the book's four themes. "Political Challenges and Changing Agendas" lays out the major unresolved issues facing the country and how they may play out in the near future. Many of these challenges involve issues that have generated intense conflicts around the world in the recent period—globalization, economic distribution, collective identities, human rights and civil liberties, the wars in Iraq and Afghanistan, and the consequences of America's exercise of global **hegemony**. "Politics in Comparative Perspective" returns to the book's four core themes and highlights the implications of the country case for the study of comparative politics. How does the history—and how will the fate—of the country influence developments in a regional and global context? What does this case study tell us about politics in other countries that have similar political systems or that face similar kinds of political challenges?

**hegemony**

The capacity to dominate the world of states and control the terms of trade and the alliance patterns in the global order.

## Key Terms and Suggested Readings

In the margin of the text, we briefly define key terms, highlighted in bold in the text, that we consider especially important for students of comparative politics to know. The key words in each chapter are also listed at the end of the chapter and all key terms, with definitions, are included in the Glosssary at the end of the book. Each chapter also has a list of books that reflect important current scholarship in the field and/or that we think would be interesting and accessible to undergraduates. This Introduction ends with suggested readings that survey the scope and methods of comparative politics and illuminate important issues in the field. We also include a set of websites, which will help you track developments and acquire timely information in the ever-changing world of comparative politics.

We realize that it is quite a challenge to begin a journey seeking to understand contemporary politics in countries around the globe. We hope that the timely information and thematic focus of *Introduction to Comparative Politics* will prepare and inspire you to explore further the often troubling, sometimes inspiring, and endlessly fascinating world of comparative politics.

## WHAT'S IN THE COMPARATIVE DATA CHARTS?

The following charts and tables present important factual and statistical information about each of the countries included in this book. We hope most of this information is self-explanatory, but a few points of clarification may be helpful.

The social and economic data mostly come from the CIA *World Factbook*, the World Bank *World Development Indicators*, and the United Nations *Human Development Report*, all of which are issued annually. These statistics are available at the following websites:

- https://www.cia.gov/library/publications/ the-world-factbook/

- http://data.worldbank.org/
- http://hdr.undp.org/en/

The data presented are as up-to-date as possible. Unless otherwise indicated, the data are from 2008–2010. Several important terms used in the data, including gross domestic product (GDP), gross national product (GNP), purchasing power parity (PPP), and Gini Index, are explained in the Glossary and/or the feature called "How Is Development Measured?" on page 18.

## Total Geographic Area

### Land & People

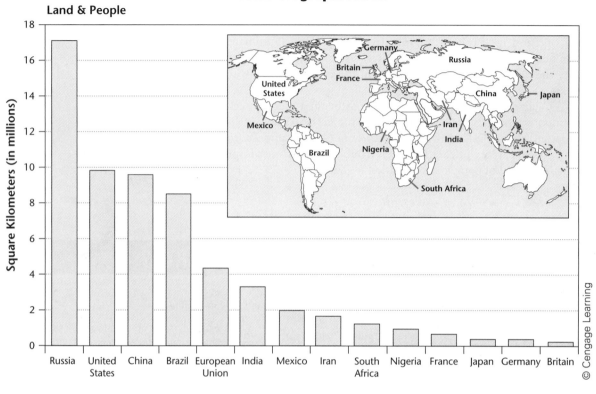

© Cengage Learning

|  | *Brazil* | *Britain* | *China* | *France* | *Germany* | *India* |
|---|---|---|---|---|---|---|
| Official name | Federative Republic of Brazil | United Kingdom of Great Britain and Northern Ireland | People's Republic of China | French Republic | Federal Republic of Germany | Republic of India |
| Capital | Brasilia | London | Beijing | Paris | Berlin | New Delhi |
| Comparative Size | Slightly smaller than the US | Slightly smaller than Oregon | Slightly smaller than the US | Slightly less than the size of Texas | Slightly smaller than Montana | Slightly more than one-third size of the US |
| Population growth per year | 1.1% | 0.6% | 0.5% | 0.5% | −0.2% | 1.3% |
| Major ethnic groups | White 53.7%, Mulatto (mixed white and black) 38.5%, Black 6.2%, Other (includes Japanese, Arab, Amerindian) 0.9%, unspecified 0.7% | White 92.1% (of which English 83.6%, Scottish 8.6%, Welsh 4.9%, Northern Irish 2.9%) Black 2%, Indian 1.8%, Pakistani 1.3%, mixed 1.2%, other 1.6% | Han Chinese 91.5%, Zhuang, Manchu, Hui, Miao, Uyghur, Mongol, Tibetan, Korean, and other nationalities 8.5% | French 76.9% other European 9%, North African 5%, other 9.1% | German 91.5%, Turkish 4.6%, other 3.9% | *The government of India does not collect statistics on ethnicity.* |
| Major religions | Roman Catholic 75.4%, Protestant 15.4%, Spiritualist 1.3%, Bantu/voodoo 0.3%, other and unspecified 0.2%, none 7.4% | Christian 71.6%, Muslim 2.7%, Hindu 1% other 1.6%, unspecified, or none 23.1% | Officially atheist, Over 16 population: Buddhist, Taoists, folk religions, 21%, Christian, 4%, Muslim, 2%. | Catholic 64.0%, No Religion 27.0%, Other 3.3%, Muslim 3.0%, Protestant 2.1%, Jewish 0.6% | Catholic 30.7%, Protestant 29.8%, Muslim 4.8%, unaffiliated 34.1%, other 0.6% | Hindu 80.5%, Muslim 13.4%, Christian 2.3%, Sikh 1.95, Buddhist 0.85%, Jain 0.4%, other 0.6%, not stated 0.1% |
| Major languages | Portuguese | English, Welsh (about 26% of the population of Wales), Scottish form of Gaelic (about 60,000 in Scotland) | Standard Chinese or Mandarin (based on the Beijing dialect), many other dialects, e.g. Cantonese and Shanghainese, and minority languages, e.g. Tibetan and Mongolian | French | German | 22 official national languages, of which Hindi is the primary tongue of about 30% of the people. English is the most important language for government and business. |

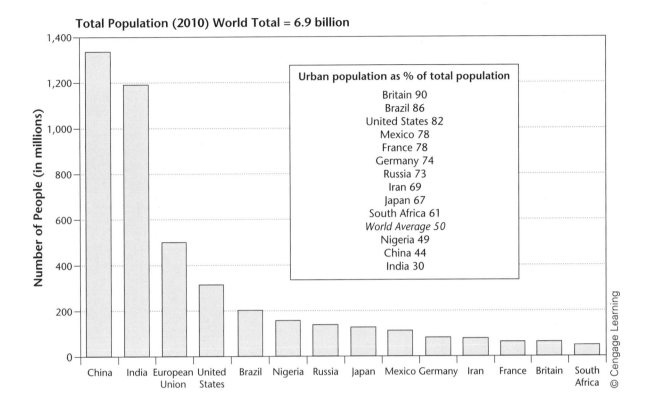

**Total Population (2010) World Total = 6.9 billion**

Number of People (in millions)

**Urban population as % of total population**

Britain 90
Brazil 86
United States 82
Mexico 78
France 78
Germany 74
Russia 73
Iran 69
Japan 67
South Africa 61
*World Average 50*
Nigeria 49
China 44
India 30

China · India · European Union · United States · Brazil · Nigeria · Russia · Japan · Mexico · Germany · Iran · France · Britain · South Africa

© Cengage Learning

| *Iran* | *Japan* | *Mexico* | *Nigeria* | *Russia* | *South Africa* | *United States* |
|---|---|---|---|---|---|---|
| Islamic Republic of Iran | Japan | United Mexican States | Federal Republic of Nigeria | Russian Federation | Republic of South Africa | United States of America |
| Tehran | Tokyo | Mexico City | Abuja | Moscow | Pretoria | Washington, D.C. |
| Slightly larger than Alaska | Slightly smaller than California | Slightly less than three times the size of Texas | Slightly more than twice the size of California | Approximately 1.8 times the size of the US | Slightly less than twice the size of Texas | About half the size of Russia |
| 1.2% | −0.3% | 1.1% | 1.9% | −0.5% | −0.4% | 1.0% |
| Persian 51%, Azeri 24%, Gilaki and Mazandarani 8%, Kurd 7%, Arab 3%, Lur 2%, Baloch 2%, Turkmen 2%, other 1% | Japanese 98.4%, Chinese 0.5%, Korean 0.4%, other 0.6% | Mestizo (Amerindian-Spanish) 60%, Amerindian or predominantly Amerindian 30%, White 9%, other 1% | More than 250 ethnic groups, the most populous and politically influential are: Hausa and Fulani 29%, Yoruba 21%, Igbo (Ibo) 18%, Ijaw 10% | Russian 79.8%, Tatar 3.8%, Ukrainian 2%, Bashkir 1.2%, Chuvash 1.1%, other or unspecified 12.1% | Black African 79%, White 9.6%, Colored 8.9%, Indian/Asian 2.5% | White, not Hispanic 63.7%, Latino, 16.3%, Black, not Hispanic 12.2%, Asian/Pacific Islander 4.8%, Native American/Alaskan Native 0.7%, two or more races/ other 2.3% |
| Muslim 98% (Shia 89%, Sunni 9%), other (includes Zoroastrian, Jewish, Christian, and Baha'i) 2% | Shintoism 83.9%, Buddhism 71.4%, Christianity 2%, other 7.8% Note: Many people practice both Shintoism and Buddhism | Roman Catholic 76.5%, Protestant 6.3% (Pentecostal 1.4%, Jehovah's Witnesses 1.1%, other 3.8%), other 0.3%, unspecified 13.8%, none 3.1% | Muslim 50.5%, Christian 48.2% (of which Catholic 13.7%, Protestant 15.0%, other Christian 19.6%), other 1.4% | Russian Orthodox 49.7%, Protestant 6.2%, Muslim 7.6%, Non-Religious 27.4%, Atheist 5.2%, other 3.9% | Zion Christian 11.1%, Pentecostal/Charismatic 8.2%, Catholic 7.1%, Methodist 6.8%, Dutch Reformed 6.7%, Anglican 3.8%, Muslim 1.5%, other Christian 36%, other 2.3%, unspecified 1.4%, none 15.1% | Protestant 51.3%, Roman Catholic 23.9%, Mormon 1.7%, other Christian 1.6%, Jewish 1.7%, Buddhist 0.7%, Muslim 0.6%, other or unspecified 2.5%, unaffiliated 12.1%, none 4% |
| Persian 51%, Turkic 26%, Kurdish 7%, Arabic 3%, other 5% | Japanese | Spanish only 92.7%, Spanish and indigenous languages 5.7%, indigenous only 0.8%, unspecified 0.8% | English (official), Hausa, Yoruba, Igbo (Ibo), Fulani, over 500 additional indigenous languages | Russian, many minority languages | IsiZulu 23.8%, IsiXhosa 17.6%, Afrikaans 13.3%, Sepedi 9.4%, English 8.2%, Setswana 8.2%, Sesotho 7.9%, Xitsonga 4.4%, other 7.2% | English, 86.1%, Spanish 13.2%, other 0.7% |

# Total Gross Domestic Product (GDP)

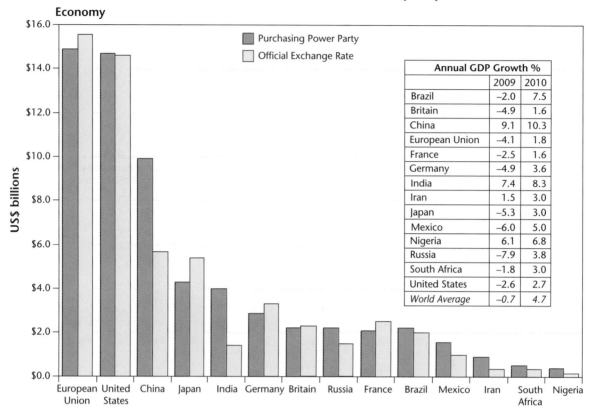

**Economy**

Legend:
- Purchasing Power Party
- Official Exchange Rate

| Annual GDP Growth % | | |
|---|---|---|
| | 2009 | 2010 |
| Brazil | −2.0 | 7.5 |
| Britain | −4.9 | 1.6 |
| China | 9.1 | 10.3 |
| European Union | −4.1 | 1.8 |
| France | −2.5 | 1.6 |
| Germany | −4.9 | 3.6 |
| India | 7.4 | 8.3 |
| Iran | 1.5 | 3.0 |
| Japan | −5.3 | 3.0 |
| Mexico | −6.0 | 5.0 |
| Nigeria | 6.1 | 6.8 |
| Russia | −7.9 | 3.8 |
| South Africa | −1.8 | 3.0 |
| United States | −2.6 | 2.7 |
| *World Average* | *−0.7* | *4.7* |

| | Brazil | Britain | China | France | Germany | India |
|---|---|---|---|---|---|---|
| GDP average annual growth: 2000–10 | 3.7% | 1.7% | 10.3% | 1.5% | 1.1% | 7.2% |
| **GDP *per capita* average annual growth:** | | | | | | |
| 2000–10 | 2.5% | 1.2% | 9.6% | 0.8% | 1.1% | 5.7% |
| 1990–99 | 0.1% | 2.0% | 8.8% | 1.4% | 1.9% | 3.7% |
| 1980–89 | 0.8% | 2.3% | 8.2% | 1.8% | *Before German* | 3.4% |
| 1970–79 | 5.9% | 2.3% | 5.3% | 3.5% | *reunification* | 0.6% |
| **GDP composition by economic sector** | | | | | | |
| Agriculture | 6.1% | 0.9% | 9.6% | 1.8% | 0.8% | 16.1% |
| Industry | 26.4% | 22.1% | 46.8% | 19.2% | 27.9% | 28.6% |
| Services | 67.5% | 77.1% | 43.6% | 79.0% | 71.3% | 55.3% |
| **Labor force by occupation** | | | | | | |
| Agriculture | 20.0% | 1.4% | 38.1% | 3.8% | 2.4% | 52.0% |
| Industry | 14.0% | 18.2% | 27.8% | 24.3% | 29.7% | 14.0% |
| Services | 66.0% | 80.4% | 34.1% | 71.8% | 67.8% | 34.0% |
| **Foreign trade as % of GDP** | | | | | | |
| Exports | 12.8% | 28.1% | 26.2% | 26.5% | 47.2% | 25.4% |
| Imports | 13.3% | 31.8% | 20.9% | 28.9% | 41.0% | 30.1% |
| **Inequality & poverty** **Household income or consumption by % share** | | | | | | |
| Poorest 10% | 1.1% | 2.1% | 3.5% | 3.0% | 3.6% | 3.6% |
| Richest 10% | 43.0% | 28.5% | 15.0% | 24.8% | 24.0% | 31.1% |
| Gini Index *(0–100; higher = more unequal)* | 55 | 36 | 42 | 33 | 28 | 37 |
| **% population in poverty** | | | | | | |
| National poverty line | 26.0% | | 2.8% | | | 25.0% |
| International poverty line (below $1.25/day) | 5.2% | 14.0% | 15.9% | 6.2% | 11.0% | 42.6% |
| International poverty line (below $2/day) | 12.7% | – | 36.3% | – | – | 75.6% |
| **Annual estimated earned income (PPP US$)** | | | | | | |
| Female | $ 7190 | $28,421 | $4323 | $25,677 | $25,691 | $1304 |
| Male | $12,006 | $42,113 | $6375 | $42,091 | $43,515 | $4102 |

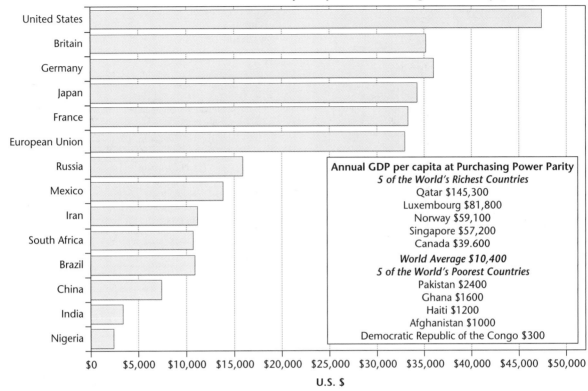

**Annual Gross Domestic Product per capita at Purchasing Power Parity (2010)**

| Iran | Japan | Mexico | Nigeria | Russia | South Africa | United States |
|---|---|---|---|---|---|---|
| 4.9% | 0.9% | 2.2% | 6.1% | 5.3% | 3.6% | 1.9% |
| | | | | | | |
| 3.4% | 0.9% | 1.1% | 3.7% | 5.7% | 2.3% | 0.9% |
| 2.9% | 1.2% | 1.6% | 0.5% | −4.8% | −0.8% | 1.9% |
| −3.7% | 3.1% | 0.1% | −1.8% | *Before collapse* | −0.3% | 2.1% |
| 2.9% | 4.1% | 3.3% | 4.2% | *of Soviet Union* | 1.0% | 2.3% |
| | | | | | | |
| 11.0% | 1.1% | 4.2% | 31.9% | 4.2% | 3.0% | 1.2% |
| 45.9% | 23.0% | 33.3% | 32.9% | 33.8% | 31.2% | 22.1% |
| 43.1% | 62.5% | 62.5% | 35.2% | 62.0% | 65.8% | 76.7% |
| | | | | | | |
| 25.0% | 3.9% | 13.7% | 70.0% | 10.0% | 9.0% | 0.7% |
| 31.0% | 26.2% | 23.4% | 10.0% | 31.9% | 26.0% | 20.3% |
| 45.0% | 69.8% | 62.9% | 20.0% | 58.1% | 65.0% | 79.0% |
| | | | | | | |
| 32.2% | 17.6% | 26.6% | 31.4% | 30.3% | 27.1% | 11.9% |
| 21.5% | 15.9% | 28.8% | 27.6% | 19.6% | 28.0% | 16.9% |
| | | | | | | |
| 2.6% | 4.8% | 1.7% | 2.0% | 1.9% | 1.3% | 2.0% |
| 29.6% | 21.7% | 36.3% | 32.4% | 30.4% | 44.7% | 30.0% |
| 38 | 25 | 52 | 43 | 44 | 58 | 42 |
| | | | | | | |
| 18.0% | 15.7% | 47.0% | 70.0% | 19.6% | 50.0% | 14.3% |
| 2.0% | – | 4.0% | 71.0% | – | 26.2% | – |
| 8.0% | – | 8.2% | 92.0% | 2.0% | – | – |
| | | | | | | |
| $5304 | $21,143 | $8375 | $1163 | $11,675 | $7328 | $34,996 |
| $16,449 | $46,706 | $21,107 | $2277 | $18,171 | $12,272 | $56,536 |

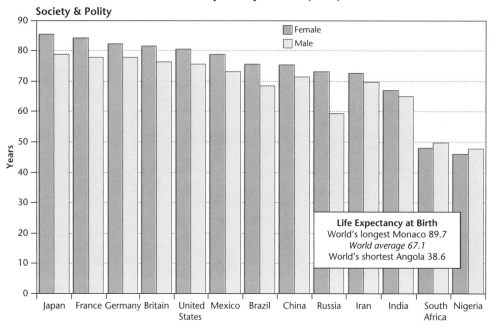

**Society & Polity**

**Life Expectancy at Birth (2010)**

Life Expectancy at Birth
World's longest Monaco 89.7
*World average 67.1*
World's shortest Angola 38.6

| | Brazil | Britain | China | France | Germany | India |
|---|---|---|---|---|---|---|
| **EDUCATION** | | | | | | |
| Adult literacy (% of population above age 15) | | | | | | |
|   Female | 90.2 | 99.0* | 90.5 | 99.0* | 99.0* | 50.8 |
|   Male | 89.8 | 99.0* | 96.7 | 99.0* | 99.0* | 75.2 |
| % age-eligible population in school | | | | | | |
|   **Primary | 127.5 | 106.4 | 113.2 | 113.2 | 104.8 | 113.1 |
|   Secondary | 100.8 | 99.0 | 76.1 | 113.2 | 101.7 | 57.0 |
|   Tertiary | 34.4 | 57.4 | 22.7 | 54.6 | 43.3 | 13.5 |
| **HEALTH** | | | | | | |
| Physicians per 1000 population | 1.7 | 2.2 | 1.5 | 3.7 | 3.5 | 0.6 |
| Maternal mortality per 100,000 live births | 58 | 12 | 38 | 8 | 7 | 230 |
| Under 5 mortality rate/1000 live births | 21.8 | 5.6 | 20.5 | 4.1 | 4.4 | 68.2 |
| Health spending as % of GDP | | | | | | |
|   Government | 3.5 | 6.9 | 1.9 | 8.7 | 8.0 | 3.0 |
|   Private | 4.9 | 1.5 | 2.4 | 2.3 | 2.4 | 1.1 |
| Adolescent fertility (births per 1000 women age 15–19) | 75.1 | 23.6 | 9.7 | 6.8 | 7.6 | 67.1 |
| **MEDIAN AGE (years)** | 29.3 | 40.0 | 35.5 | 39.9 | 44.9 | 26.2 |
| **OTHER** | | | | | | |
| Communications, Technology, & Transportation | | | | | | |
|   Telephone lines (per 100 people) | 21.4 | 54.1 | 25.7 | 47.0 | 62.6 | 3.3 |
|   Mobile cellular subscriptions (per 100 people) | 78.5 | 126.0 | 48.4 | 106.1 | 128.5 | 30.4 |
|   Internet users (per 100 people) | 37.5 | 76.0 | 22.5 | 69.1 | 75.5 | 4.5 |
|   Personal computers (per 00 people) | 16.1 | 80.2 | 5.7 | 67.8 | 65.6 | 3.3 |
|   Households with a television set (%) | 97.0 | 99.0 | 89.0 | 97.0 | 95.0 | 46.0 |
|   Motor vehicles (per 1000 people) | 198 | 527 | 32 | 600 | 623 | 12 |
| Women % members of national legislature | | | | | | |
|   Lower house or single house | 8.8 | 22.0 | 21.3 | 18.9 | 32.8 | 10.8 |
|   Upper house (if any) | 12.3 | 20.1 | | 21.9 | 21.7 | 9.0 |
| Freedom House rating (1 = most free; 7= least free) | Free (2.0) | Free (1.0) | Not Free (6.5) | Free (1.0) | Free (1.0) | Free (2.5) |
| Economist Intelligence Unit Democracy Index (10 = most democratic; 1 = least democratic) | Flawed Democracy (7.12) | Full Democracy (8.16) | Authoritarian Regime (3.14) | Flawed Democracy (7.77) | Full Democracy (8.18) | Flawed Democracy (7.28) |
| Homicides per 100K population | 22.0 | 1.5 | 1.2 | 1.4 | 0.8 | 2.8 |
| Prison inmates per 100,000 total population | 253 | 144.7 | 120 | 96 | 88 | 33 |

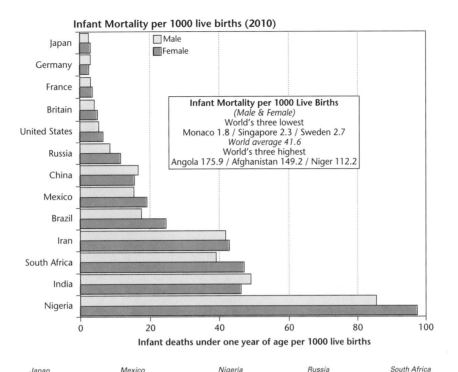

**Infant Mortality per 1000 live births (2010)**

□ Male
▨ Female

Infant deaths under one year of age per 1000 live births

Infant Mortality per 1000 Live Births
*(Male & Female)*
World's three lowest
Monaco 1.8 / Singapore 2.3 / Sweden 2.7
*World average 41.6*
World's three highest
Angola 175.9 / Afghanistan 149.2 / Niger 112.2

| Iran | Japan | Mexico | Nigeria | Russia | South Africa | United States |
|---|---|---|---|---|---|---|
| 77.2 | 99.0* | 91.5 | 48.8 | 94.7 | 85.7 | 99.0* |
| 87.3 | 99.0* | 94.6 | 71.5 | 99.7 | 87.0 | 99.0* |
| 128.4 | 101.9 | 114.3 | 93.1 | 96.8 | 104.5 | 98.8 |
| 79.7 | 100.9 | 89.9 | 30.5 | 84.8 | 95.1 | 94.1 |
| 36.1 | 58.0 | 27.2 | 10.1 | 77.2 | 14.5 | 82.9 |
| 0.9 | 2.1 | 2.9 | 0.4 | 4.3 | 0.8 | 2.7 |
| 30 | 6 | 85 | 840 | 39 | 410 | 24 |
| 32.4 | 3.4 | 17.5 | 142.9 | 13.4 | 65.3 | 7.9 |
| 3.4 | 1.5 | 2.7 | 1.7 | 1.9 | 5.0 | 8.5 |
| 3.0 | 6.5 | 3.2 | 4.9 | 3.5' | 3.6 | 7.1 |
| 18.0 | 4.8 | 64.3 | 124.1 | 24.8 | 58.4 | 35.0 |
| 26.8 | 44.8 | 27.1 | 19.2 | 38.7 | 25.0 | 36.9 |
| 34.5 | 37.7 | 19.4 | 0.9 | 31.6 | 9.1 | 50.9 |
| 59.8 | 86.4 | 70.8 | 41.7 | 140.6 | 92.4 | 89.0 |
| 32.1 | 75.2 | 22.2 | 15.9 | 31.9 | 8.6 | 75.9 |
| 10.6 | 40.7 | 14.4 | 0.9 | 13.3 | 8.5 | 80.6 |
| 76.6 | 99.0 | 93.0 | 25.0 | 98.0 | 59.0 | 98.0 |
| 16 | 595 | 244 | 31 | 245 | 159 | 820 |
| | 11.3 | 26.2 | 7.0 | 14.0 | 44.5 | 16.8 |
| 2.8 | 18.2 | 18.5 | 8.3 | 4.7 | 29.6 | 15.3 |
| Not Free (6.0) | Free (1.5) | Free (2.5) | Partly Free (4.5) | Not Free (5.5) | Not Free (2.0) | Free (1.0) |
| Authoritarian Regime (1.94) | Full Democracy (8.08) | Flawed Democracy (6.93) | Authoritarian Regime (3.47) | Hybrid Regime (4.26) | Flawed Democracy (7.79) | Full Democracy (8.18) |
| 2.9 | 0.5 | 11.6 | 1.3 | 14.2 | 36.5 | 5.2 |
| 223 | 62 | 204 | 29 | 592 | 324 | 748 |

* Developed countries have near universal adult basic literacy rates, but functional literacy is generally lower, for example, in the United States and Britain it is around 80%, and in Germany, 85%.

** Primary school enrollment may be more than 100% because of children who start school early or late or stay back.

# Comparative Rankings

International organizations and research institutions have developed statistical methods to rate and rank different countries according to various categories of economic, social, political, and environmental performance. Such rankings can be controversial, but we think they provide an interesting approach to comparative analysis. Five examples of this approach are listed below. In addition to the countries included in this book, the top and bottom 5 countries in each of the rankings are also listed.

## Human Development Index (HDI)

is a measure used by the United Nations to compare the overall level of well-being in countries around the world. It takes into account life expectancy, education, and income.

2010 HDI Rankings:

*Very High Human Development*

1. Norway
2. Australia
3. New Zealand
4. **United States**
5. Ireland
10. Germany
11. Japan
14. **France**
26. **Britain**

*High Human Development*

56. **Mexico**
65. **Russia**
70. **Iran**
73. Brazil

*Medium Human Development*

89. **China**
110. **South Africa**
119. **India**

*Low Human Development*

142. Nigeria
165. Mozambique
166. Burundi
167. Niger
168. DR Congo
169. Zimbabwe

http://hdr.undp.org/en/statistics/hdi/

## Global Gender Gap

measures the extent to which women have achieved equality with men in five critical areas: economic participation, economic opportunity, political empowerment, educational attainment, and health and well-being.

2010 Gender Gap Rankings:

1. Iceland
2. Norway
3. Finland
4. Sweden
5. New Zealand
12. **South Africa**
13. Germany
15. **Britain**
19. **United States**
45. **Russia**
46. **France**
61. **China**
85. Brazil
91. **Mexico**
94. Japan
112. **India**
118. Nigeria
123. **Iran**
129. Saudi Arabia
130. Ivory Coast
131. Mali
132. Pakistan
133. Chad
134. Yemen

http://www.weforum.org/en/initiatives/gcp/Gender Gap

## Environmental Performance Index (EPI)

measures how close countries come to meeting specific benchmarks for national pollution control and natural resource management.

2010 EPI Rankings:

1. Iceland
2. Switzerland
3. Costa Rica
4. Sweden
5. Norway
7. **France**
14. **Britain**
17. Germany
20. Japan
43. **Mexico**
61. **United States**
62. Brazil
69. **Russia**
78. **Iran**
115. **South Africa**
121. **China**
123. **India**
153. Nigeria
145. Mali
146. Mauritania
147. Sierra Leone
148. Angola
149. Niger

http://epi.yale.edu

## International Corruption Perceptions Index (CPI)

defines corruption as the abuse of public office for private gain and measures the degree to which corruption is perceived to exist among a country's public officials and politicians.

2010 CPI Rankings:

1. Denmark
1. New Zealand
1. Singapore
4. Finland
4. Sweden
15. Germany
17. Japan
20. **Britain**
22. **United States**
25. **France**
54. **South Africa**
69. Brazil
78. **China**
87. **India**
98. **Mexico**
134. Nigeria
146. **Iran**
154. **Russia**
168. Equatorial Guinea
169. Burundi
170. Chad
171. Sudan
172. Somalia

*http://www.transparency.org/ Identical numbers indicate a tie in the rankings.*

## Economist Intelligence Unit Democracy Index categorizes

four types of political systems based on five categories: electoral process and pluralism; civil liberties; the functioning of government; political participation; and political culture.

2010 Democracy Index:

*Full Democracies*

1. Norway
2. Iceland
3. Denmark
4. Sweden
5. New Zealand
14. Germany
17. **United States**
19. **Britain**
22. Japan

*Flawed Democracies*

30. **South Africa**
31. **France**
40. **India**
47. Brazil
50. **Mexico**

*Hybrid Regimes*

107. **Russia**

*Authoritarian Regimes*

136. **China**
158. **Iran**
163. Myanmar (Burma)
164. Uzbekistan
165. Turkmenistan
166. Chad
167. North Korea

http://www.eiu.com/public/

## Key Terms

Cold War
critical juncture
collective identities
comparative politics
globalization
comparativist
World Bank
Human Development Index
Global Gender Gap
Environmental Performance Index
Corruption Perceptions Index
Freedom in the World Rating
Keynesianism
neoliberalism
country
state
executive
cabinet
bureaucracy
legislature

judiciary
legitimacy
state formation
nation-state
causal theories
independent variable
dependent variable
rational choice theory
middle-level theory
dictatorships
democratic transition
institutional design
failed states
anarchy
World Trade Organization
(WTO)
International Monetary Fund
(IMF)
North American Free Trade
Agreement (NAFTA)

political economy
sustainable development
communist party-state
democracy
gross domestic product (GDP)
gross national product (GNP)
purchasing power parity (PPI)
Human Development Index
(HDI)
social movements
social class
distributional politics
typology
Third World
consolidated democracies
transitional democracies
authoritarian regime
hegemony
critical juncture

## Suggested Readings

Bates, Robert H. *The Logic of State Failure: Learning from Late-Century Africa. Dealing with Failed States*, New York: Routledge, 2009.

Bates, Robert H. *Prosperity & Violence: The Political Economy of Development*, 2nd edition. New York: W. W. Norton, 2009.

Brady, Henry E., and Collier, David, eds. *Rethinking Social Inquiry: Diverse Tools, Shared Standards*. Lanham, MD: Rowman and Littlefield, 2004.

Boix, Carles, and Susan C. Stokes, eds. *The Oxford Handbook of Comparative Politics*. New York, Oxford University Press, 2009.

Cordell, Karl, and Stefan Wolff. *Ethnic Conflict: Causes, Consequences, and Responses*. New York: Polity, 2010.

Diamond, Larry. *The Spirit of Democracy: The Struggle to Build Free Societies throughout the World*. New York: Times Books, 2008.

Diamond, Larry, and Leonardo Morlino, eds. *Assessing the Quality of Democracy*. Baltimore: Johns Hopkins University Press, 2005.

Friedman, Thomas L. *The World Is Flat: A Brief History of the Twenty-First Century*. New York: Farrar, Straus and Giroux, 2005.

Ghani, Ashraf, and Clare Lockhart. *Fixing Failed States: A Framework for Rebuilding a Fractured World*. New York: Oxford University Press, 2008.

Hall, Peter A., and David Soskice, eds. *Varieties of Capitalism: The Institutional Foundations of Comparative Advantage*. New York: Oxford University Press, 2001.

Johnston, Michael. *Syndromes of Corruption: Wealth, Power, and Democracy*. New York: Cambridge University Press, 2006.

Katznelson, Ira, and Helen V. Milner, eds. *Political Science: The State of the Discipline*. New York: Norton, 2002.

Kesselman, Mark, ed. *Readings in Comparative Politics: Political Challenges and Changing Agendas*, 2nd ed. Boston: Wadsworth, 2010.

Kesselman, Mark, ed. *The Politics of Globalization: A Reader*. Boston: Wadsworth, 2006.

Kohli, Atul. *State-Directed Development: Political Power and Industrialization in the Global Periphery*. Cambridge: Cambridge University Press, 2005.

Krieger, Joel. *Globalization and State Power: Who Wins When America Rules?* New York: Longman, 2004.

Kymlicka, Will. *Multicultural Odysseys: Navigating the New International Politics of Diversity*. New York: Oxford University Press, 2007.

Laitin, David D. *Nations, States, and Violence*. New York: Oxford University Press, 2007.

Lichbach, Mark Irving, and Alan S. Zuckerman, eds. *Comparative Politics: Rationality, Culture, and Structure*, 2nd ed. Cambridge: Cambridge University Press, 2009.

Maugeri, Leonardo. *The Age of Oil: The Mythology, History, and Future of the World's Most Controversial Resource*. New York: Praeger, 2007.

Prezworski, Adam, et al., *Democracy and Development: Political Institutions and Well-Being in the World, 1950–1990*. Cambridge: Cambridge University Press, 2000.

Roeder, Philip G. *Where Nation-States Come From: Institutional Change in the Age of Nationalism.* Princeton: Princeton University Press, 2007.

Rhodes, R. A. W., Sarah A. Binder, and Bert A. Rockman, eds. *The Oxford Handbook of Political Institutions.* New York: Oxford University Press, 2008.

Sen, Amartya. *Development as Freedom.* New York: Knopf, 1999.

Siracusa, Joseph M. *Democracy: A Very Short Introduction.* New York: Oxford University Press, 2010.

Smith, Jackie. *Social Movements for Global Democracy.* Baltimore: Johns Hopkins University Press, 2007.

Snyder, Jack L. *From Voting to Violence: Democratization and Nationalist Conflict.* W. W. Norton, 2000.

Stiglitz, Joseph E. *Globalization and Its Discontents.* New York: Norton, 2002.

Tarrow, Sidney. *Power in Movement: Social Movements and Contentious Politics,* 2nd ed. Cambridge: Cambridge University Press, 1998.

Tilly, Charles. *Democracy.* New York: Cambridge University Press, 2007.

Wolf, Martin. *Why Globalization Works.* New Haven, CT: Yale University Press, 2004.

Zakaria, Fareed. *The Future of Freedom: Illiberal Democracy at Home and Abroad.* New York: W. W. Norton, 2003.

## Suggested Websites

CIA World Factbook
**https://www.cia.gov/library/publications/the-world-factbook/index.html/**

Department of State Background Notes
**http://www.state.gov/r/pa/ei/bgn/**

Election Guide (Consortium for Elections and Political Process Strengthening)
**http://www.electionguide.org/**

Freedom House
**http://www.freedomhouse.org/**

NationMaster
**http://www.nationmaster.com/**

Politics and Government Around the World
**http://www.politicsresources.net/**

# 2 Britain

Joel Krieger

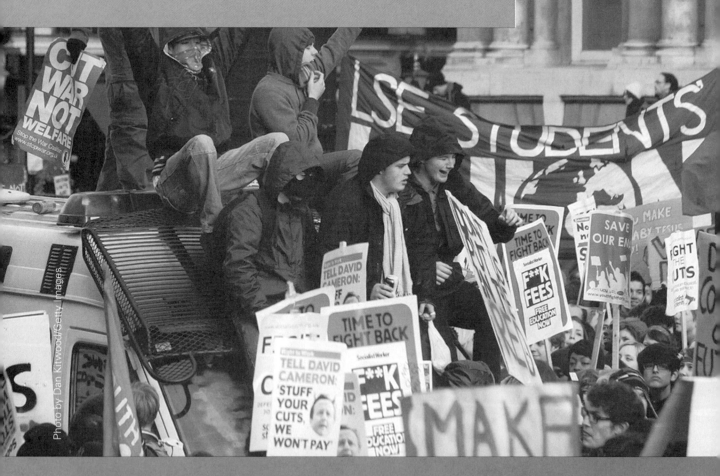

Photo by Dan Kitwood/Getty Images

**Official Name:** United Kingdom of Great Britain and Northern Ireland

**Location:** Western Europe

**Capital City:** London

**Population (2010):** 60.8 million

**Size:** 244,820 sq. km.; slightly smaller than Oregon

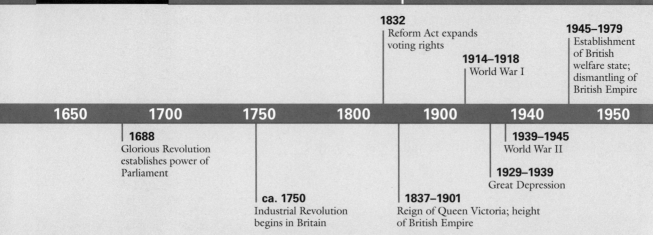

**1832**
Reform Act expands voting rights

**1914–1918**
World War I

**1945–1979**
Establishment of British welfare state; dismantling of British Empire

1650   1700   1750   1800   1900   1940   1950

**1688**
Glorious Revolution establishes power of Parliament

**1939–1945**
World War II

**1929–1939**
Great Depression

**ca. 1750**
Industrial Revolution begins in Britain

**1837–1901**
Reign of Queen Victoria; height of British Empire

# SECTION 1

# THE MAKING OF THE MODERN BRITISH STATE

## Focus Questions

Is Britain's geography still its destiny?

How does its history of empire still shape British politics today?

Why did an electoral system designed to produce a stable single-party majority result in a Conservative–Liberal coalition government in 2010?

What are the greatest challenges facing Britain today?

## Politics in Action

When the financial bubble in the U.S. housing market burst in fall 2008, the global economy teetered on the brink of collapse. Since then, financial markets have stabilized, and the global economy has begun gradually to recover lost ground. But the scars of the great recession are far from healed. In October 2010, there were sustained and massive demonstrations in France involving millions of people of all ages who turned out weekly for over a month to protest a government plan to increase the age at which people could begin to collect pensions. Public sector workers and many French from every sector of the economy and every age cohort joined the effort to preserve the rights of pensioners.

Meanwhile, in the UK, pundits ridiculed the French for taking to the streets in protest over minor adjustments in pensions, while the British were faced with far more significant austerity measures—a 20 percent reduction in public spending, half a million public sector jobs cut, a three-strikes-and-you're out plan for pressuring the unemployed to accept job offers or face a cut off of benefits, the elimination of child benefits for middle-class families, which had been a mainstay of the British welfare state for generations, and sharp increases in college tuition (traditionally low by American standards and subsidized by the government).

The British had lampooned the French for their willingness to rampage at the drop of a hat and took pride in the British "stiff upper lip"—their ability to recognize that the 2008 recession had far-reaching repercussions, the government could no longer buy its way out of the slump, and they might just as well take adversity and austerity in stride. They would go about their business and give the benefit of the doubt to the Conservative–Liberal coalition government, which had taken office just six months earlier in May 2010, promising the tough medicine that the country was now being forced to swallow.

| 1970 | 1990 | 1995 | 2000 | 2005 | 2010 |
|------|------|------|------|------|------|

**1979–1990**
Prime Minister Margaret Thatcher promotes "enterprise culture"

**1997–2007**
Prime Minister Tony Blair and Chancellor Gordon Brown lead New Labour in government

**2007**
Gordon Brown becomes prime minister and promises to renew the party and the nation, but quickly loses support and credibility as the financial crisis deepens

**2010**
New Conservative–Liberal coalition government formed

**1973**
Britain joins the European Community

**2001**
Under Blair's leadership, Britain "stands shoulder to shoulder" with America in war against terror

Photo of riots outside parliament, while inside the vote to triple tuition fees takes place.

Photo by Dan Kitwood/Getty Images

By November, however, the tables had turned: The French government had pressed ahead with its plan to cut pensions, despite protests, and France was no longer in turmoil. In Britain however, the cuts were beginning to bite hard; and increasingly restive and angry citizens, led by students who were angry at tuition hikes, were acting positively French.

In December, while Parliament debated a tuition fees bill, thousands protested in the streets and when the worst came to pass—Parliament tripled the tuition fees—resentment boiled over into mayhem. Protesters battled police, red paint was thrown at a statue of Winston Churchill, Conservative Party headquarters was attacked, and angry protesters assaulted a car in which Prince Charles was riding, shouting insults at the prince. And in comparison to Nick Clegg, leader of the Liberal Democrats, deputy prime minister, and junior coalition partner with David Cameron, Prince Charles got off lightly. The worst vitriol was reserved for Clegg, the more progressive coalition partner who was expected to counter-balance the Conservatives on social protections and civil liberties and who had promised during the election campaign not to increase fees. This high-profile flip-flop on tuition fees severely damaged Clegg's reputation and credibility and may also have farther-reaching consequences, since it represents an important fissure in the coalition government and may fuel doubts about the strength and stability of the government in an electorate which is not used to—and uneasy about—coalition government.

# Geographic Setting

Britain is the largest of the British Isles, a group of islands off the northwest coast of Europe that encompasses England, Scotland, and Wales. The second-largest island includes Northern Ireland and the independent Republic of Ireland. The term *Great Britain* includes England, Wales, and Scotland, but not Northern Ireland. We use the term *Britain* as shorthand for the United Kingdom of Great Britain and Northern Ireland.

Covering an area of approximately 94,000 square miles, Britain is roughly two-thirds the area of Japan, or approximately half the area of France. In 2007, the British population was 60.8 million (see Table 2.1).

As an island off the shore of Europe, Britain was for centuries less subject to invasion and conquest than its continental counterparts. This gave the country a sense of security. This separation has also made many Britons feel they are both apart from and a part of Europe. This feeling complicates relations with Britain's EU partners even today.

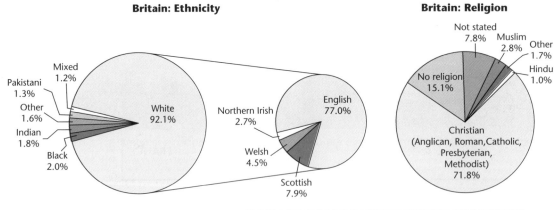

**British Currency**
Pound (£)
International Designation: GBP
Exchange Rate (2010): US$1 = .6388 GBP
50 GBP Note Design: Queen Elizabeth II (1926–)

© Ben Molyneux/Alamy

**FIGURE 2.1 The British Nation at a Glance**

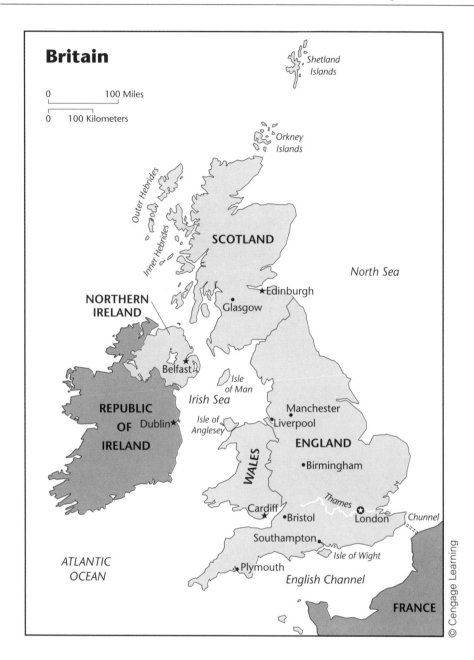

# Critical Junctures

History greatly influences contemporary politics in very important ways. Once in place, institutions leave powerful legacies. Issues left unresolved in one period may create problems for the future.

The consolidation of the British state unified several kingdoms. After Duke William of Normandy defeated the English in the Battle of Hastings in 1066, the Norman monarchy eventually extended its authority throughout the British Isles, except for Scotland. In the sixteenth century, legislation unified England and Wales legally, politically, and administratively. In 1603, James VI of Scotland ascended the English throne as James I. Although they had the same kings, Scotland and England remained separate

| Table 2.1 | Political Organization |
|---|---|
| **Political System** | Parliamentary democracy, constitutional monarchy. |
| **Regime History** | Long constitutional history, origins subject to interpretation, usually dated from the seventeenth century or earlier. |
| **Administrative Structure** | Unitary state with fusion of powers. UK parliament has supreme legislative, executive, and judicial authority. Limited powers have been transferred to representative bodies in Scotland, Wales, and Northern Ireland. |
| **Executive** | Prime minister (PM), answerable to House of Commons, subject to collective responsibility of the cabinet; member of Parliament who is leader of party or coalition that can control a majority in Commons (normally a single party but since 2010 as a two-party coalition (Conservative–Liberal Democrat)). |
| **Legislature** | Bicameral. House of Commons elected by single-member plurality system. Main legislative powers: to pass laws, provide for finance, scrutinize public administration and government policy. House of Lords, unelected upper house: limited powers to delay enactment of legislation and to recommend revisions; Since 2009, the judicial functions of parliament were transferred to the UK Supreme Court. Recent reforms eliminated voting rights for most hereditary peers. |
| **Judiciary** | Independent but with no power to judge the constitutionality of legislation or governmental conduct. UK Supreme Court, established in 2009, is final court of appeal for all UK civil cases and criminal cases in England, Wales, and Northern Ireland. |
| **Party System** | Two-party dominant, with regional variation. Principal parties: Labour and Conservative; a center party (Liberal Democrat); and national parties in Scotland, Wales, and Northern Ireland. |

kingdoms, until the Act of Union of 1707. After that, a common Parliament of Great Britain replaced the two separate parliaments of Scotland and of England and Wales.

Royal control increased after 1066, but the conduct of King John (1199–1216) fuelled opposition from feudal barons. In 1215, they forced him to consent to a series of concessions that protected feudal landowners from abuses of royal power. These restrictions were embodied in the Magna Carta, a historic statement of the rights of a political community against the monarchical state. It has served as the inspiration for constitutions around the world that contain protections for citizens and groups from the arbitrary exercise of state power. In 1236, the term *Parliament* was first used officially for the gathering of feudal barons summoned by the king whenever he required their consent to special taxes. By the fifteenth century, Parliament had gained the right to make laws.

### The Seventeenth-Century Settlement

By the sixteenth and seventeenth centuries Britain was embroiled in a complex interplay of religious conflicts, national rivalries, and struggles between rulers and Parliament. These conflicts erupted in the civil wars of the 1640s and later forced the removal of James II in 1688. This was the last successful revolution in British history.

The UK later came to be seen as a model of domestic peace and stability, but this was hardly predictable during the violent internal conflicts of the seventeenth century.

This "Glorious Revolution" of 1688 also resolved long-standing religious conflict. The replacement of the Roman Catholic James II by the Protestant William and Mary ensured the dominance of the Church of England (or Anglican Church). To this day, the Church of England remains the established (official) church. By about 1700, a basic form of parliamentary democracy had emerged.

### The Industrial Revolution and the British Empire

The Industrial Revolution from the mid-eighteenth century onward involved rapid expansion of manufacturing production and technological innovation. It also led to vast social and economic changes and created pressures to make the country more democratic. Britain's competitive edge also dominated the international order. The **Industrial Revolution** transformed the British state and changed forever the British way of life.

Despite a gradually improving standard of living throughout the English population in general, industrialization often disrupted lives and shattered old ways of life. Many field laborers lost their jobs, and many small landholders were squeezed off the land. Industrial machinery undermined the status of skilled craft workers, made them poor, and placed them on the margins of society.

**The British Empire**   Britain relied on imported raw materials, and by 1800, it sold the vast majority of finished goods overseas. Growth depended on foreign markets—not domestic consumption. This export orientation made economic growth much faster than an exclusively domestic orientation would have allowed.

Because Britain needed overseas trade, its leaders worked aggressively to secure markets and expand the empire. Backed by the British navy, international trade made England the dominant military and economic world power. Britain led the alliance that toppled Napoleon in the early nineteenth century, thus enabling the country to maintain its dominant position in the world of states.

By 1870, British trade represented nearly one-quarter of the world total (see Table 2.2). By 1900 Queen Victoria (1837–1901) ruled an empire that included 25 percent of the world's population. Britain exercised direct colonial rule over 50 countries, including India and Nigeria. Britain also dominated an extensive economic empire—a worldwide network of independent states, including China, Iran, and Brazil. Britain ruled as a **hegemonic power**, controlling alliances and the international economic order and shaping domestic political developments in countries throughout the world.

Britain's global power spurred industrial growth at home, and because domestic industry depended on world markets, the government projected British interests overseas as forcefully as possible.

**Industrial Change and the Struggle for Voting Rights**   The Industrial Revolution shifted economic power from landowners to

**Industrial Revolution**

A period of rapid and destabilizing social, economic, and political changes caused by the introduction of large-scale factory production, originating in England in the middle of the eighteenth century.

**hegemonic power**

A state that can control the pattern of alliances and terms of the international order and often shapes domestic political developments in countries throughout the world.

| Table 2.2 | World Trade and Relative Labor Productivity | |
|---|---|---|
| | **Proportion of World Trade (%)** | **Relative Labor Productivity* (%)** |
| 1870 | 24.0 | 1.63 |
| 1890 | 18.5 | 1.45 |
| 1913 | 14.1 | 1.15 |
| 1938 | 14.0 | 0.92 |

*As compared with the average rate of productivity in other members of the world economy.
*Source:* KEOHANE, ROBERT O.; AFTER HEGEMONY. © 1984 Princeton University Press. Reprinted by permission of Princeton University Press.

businessmen and industrialists. The first important step toward democratization began in the late 1820s, when the propertied classes and increasing popular agitation pressed Parliament to expand the right to vote. With Parliament under considerable pressure, the Reform Act of 1832 extended the vote to a section of the (male) middle class.

The reform was narrow. Before 1832, less than 5 percent of the adult population could vote—afterward, only about 7 percent. The reform showed the strict property basis for political participation. It inflamed class-based tensions.

The Representation of the People Act of 1867 increased the electorate to 16 percent but left cities significantly underrepresented. The Franchise Act of 1884 nearly doubled the electorate. The Representation of the People Act of 1918 finally included nearly all adult men and women over age thirty. How slow a process was it? The struggle to extend the vote took place mostly without violence, but it lasted for centuries.

## World Wars, Industrial Strife, and the Depression (1914–1945)

The development of the state was just beginning as it expanded its direct responsibility for the economy and social welfare.

State involvement in the economy increased significantly during World War I (1914–1918). The state took control of numerous industries, including railways, mining, and shipping. It set prices, restricted the flow of capital abroad, and channelled resources into war production. After World War I, the state remained active in managing industry, but in a different way. Amid tremendous industrial disputes, the state fragmented the trade union movement and resisted demands for workers' control over production. This government manipulation of the economy openly contradicted the policy of laissez-faire (minimal government interference in the operation of economic markets).

**welfare state**

A set of public policies designed to provide for citizens' needs through direct or indirect provision of pensions, health care, unemployment insurance, and assistance to the poor.

Tensions between free-market principles and interventionist practices deepened with the Great Depression—1929 through much of the 1930s—and with World War II (1939–1945). Fear of depression and yearnings for a better life after the war, transformed the role of the state and led to a period of unusual political harmony.

## Collectivist Consensus (1945–1979)

The term *collectivism* describes the consensus in politics after World War II, when most Britons and all major political parties agreed that governments should work to narrow the gap between rich and poor, and provide for basic necessities through public education, national health care, and other policies of the **welfare state** (the set of policies designed to provide health care, pensions, unemployment benefits, and assistance to the poor). They also accepted state responsibility for economic growth and full employment. Most people in Britain came to expect that the state should be responsible for economic growth and full employment (understood as a rate of unemployment at 4 percent or below). In time, however, economic downturn and political stagnation unravelled the consensus.

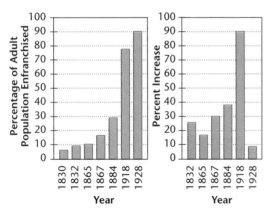

**FIGURE 2.2 Expansion of Voting Rights.**
Expansion of the franchise in Britain was a gradual process. Despite reforms dating from the early nineteenth century, nearly universal adult suffrage was not achieved until 1928.

*Source:* From RASMUSSEN. THE BRITISH POLITICAL PROCESS, 1E. © 1993 Wadsworth, a part of Cengage Learning, Inc. Reproduced by permission. www.cengage.com/permissions.

### Margaret Thatcher and the Enterprise Culture (1979–1990)

The 1970s saw the beginning of economic stagnation and declining competitiveness of key British industries in international markets. This fueled industrial strife. Class-based tensions remained near the surface of politics. No government or party could manage the economy. Edward Heath's Conservative government (1970–1974) could not resolve the economic problems or the political tensions of increased inflation and reduced growth (stagflation). The Labour government of Harold Wilson and James Callaghan (1974–1979) fared no better. Unions became increasingly disgruntled, and the country underwent a rash of strikes throughout the winter of 1978–1979, the "winter of discontent." Labour could not discipline its trade union allies to accept wage policies of the Labour government, which hurt the party in the election in May 1979. The traditional centrist Conservative and Labour alternatives seemed exhausted, at least within the collectivist mould. Many Britons were ready for a new policy agenda.

Margaret Thatcher met the challenge. Winning the leadership of the Conservative Party in 1975, she launched a set of bold policy initiatives after the Conservatives returned to power in 1979. Re-elected in 1983 and 1987, she never lost a general election.

Thatcher believed collectivism had weakened British industry and permitted powerful, self-serving unions to hold the country for ransom. To reverse Britain's relative economic slide, Thatcher sought to jump-start the economy by cutting taxes, reducing social services where possible, and using government policy to stimulate competitiveness and efficiency in the private sector.

Thatcher's leadership as prime minister (1979–1990) marks a critical dividing line in postwar British politics. Like few others, she set the tone and redefined the goals of British politics. The Thatcher government inaugurated a decisively right-wing regime, set out to divide and conquer trade unions, and to commit the country to a firm neoliberal path. A conviction politician, Thatcher led her party and the country with a style that was characterized by some as "authoritarian populism." In November 1990, a leadership challenge within Thatcher's own Conservative Party caused her sudden resignation. Her anti-EU stance and high-handed leadership style brought her down. John Major replaced her, serving from 1990 to 1997 and leading the Conservative Party to a victory in 1992 before succumbing to Tony Blair's New Labour in 1997.

### New Labour's Third Way

Under the leadership of Blair and Brown, the Labour Party was determined to modernize itself. Although its official name did not change, the party was reinvented as New Labour—a party committed to modernization that promised to fundamentally recast British politics. It offered a "third-way" alternative to Thatcherism and the collectivism of traditional Labour. New Labour rejected interest-based politics, in which unions and working people voted Labour and businesspeople and the more prosperous were Conservatives. Labour won in 1997 with support from across the socioeconomic spectrum. It rejected the historic ties between Labour governments and the trade unions and emphasized partnership with business. Early in their careers, Tony Blair and Gordon Brown had formed an alliance as rising stars in the Labour Party. Blair pushed the party to modernize and expand its political base well beyond its heritage as a labor party. Brown became shadow chancellor (the opposition party's spokesman on the economy).

But after Labour took office, Blair and Brown eventually became rivals rather than partners. Increasingly, the British government began to look and feel like a dual executive, with Brown in charge of domestic policies and Blair responsible for foreign affairs. Blair's decision to support the U.S.-led war in Iraq was very unpopular. Although he enjoyed his third electoral victory in May 2005, his parliamentary majority was slashed by nearly 100 seats. In June 2007 Blair tendered his resignation to the Queen who immediately summoned Gordon Brown to become prime minister.

A highly regarded finance minister, Brown never mastered the political skills required for a successful prime minister. Nor, despite his quick action in the face of the global financial meltdown that began in 2008, was Brown able to get out from under the shadow cast by New Labour's role in the war in Iraq, when Labour prime minister Tony Blair almost single-handedly pulled the UK into a war that was extremely unpopular in the UK, especially among Labour party stalwarts.

In the "what have you done for me lately" world of high-stakes politics, Brown's effectiveness as chancellor (finance minister) for ten years and the fact that no national leader could prevent a severe downturn in the economy once the housing bubble burst was soon forgotten. He is likely to be remembered and caricatured for his ineptitude in the 2010 election campaign, which very likely no leader of the Labour Party could have won in the dreary economic climate that prevailed and with the bitter aftertaste of the war in Iraq still defining New Labour for many. Nor could he avoid responsibility as the incumbent for the global economic downturn nor shake off the weariness voters inevitably feel for a party that seems to have been in power too long (in this case thirteen years). Nor could Brown—or any prime minister—reduce the fear of sudden terrorist attacks that ordinary people in Britain have felt ever since bombs were set off in the London transport system on July 7, 2005 (in the UK referred to as 7/7).

### The Conservative–Liberal Coalition

There is a familiar maxim: In politics, a week is a long time. If that is true, thirteen years is an eternity. Ever since the Conservatives held power in 1990, many of the core principles of New Labour's approach have become widely shared across much of the political spectrum. When the Conservatives elected David Cameron as their party leader in 2005, he took the party in a familiar mainstream direction, appealing directly to youth for political support and championing modernization and pragmatism. Young (he was born in 1966), smart and telegenic, Cameron seemed to consciously adopt, in both style and substance, much of Blair's early appeal, stealing the thunder of New Labour, and expanding the appeal of the Conservative Party by reaching out to youth and promoting agendas, such as climate change, citizen activism, and promises to reduce both the global development gap and the gap between rich and poor in the UK—issues that would have broad non-ideological appeal. As a result, when the May 2010 election produced what the British call a "hung parliament"—an outcome after a general election when no party can by itself control a majority of the seats in parliament—it was a stretch for the Conservatives and the Liberal Democrats to form a government, but it was not an unbridgeable chasm.

The Conservative–Liberal Coalition characterized their core principles this way in the jointly signed coalition agreement:

> This is an historic document in British Politics: The first time in over half a century two parties have come together to put forward a programme for partnership government.
>
> As our parties have worked together it has become increasingly clear to us that, although there are differences, there is also common ground. We share a conviction

that the days of big government are over; that centralisation and top-down control have proved a failure. We believe that the time has come to disperse power more widely in Britain today; to recognize that we will only make progress if we help people to come together to make life better.[1]

The coalition government, like New Labour before it, has tried to capture the mood in Britain, by rejecting ideological positions in favor of broad appeals to what Cameron and Clegg characterize as a radical, reforming government that attempts to blend the Conservative commitment to the dynamism of free markets with the Liberal Democrat commitment to decentralization. The result is captured in a new framework for governance, which the coalition partners call the "Big Society." The Big Society argues for wide-ranging initiatives to empower ordinary citizens to take control over their lives and shift the balance of power downward from the state to communities and individual citizens. Parents should be given the opportunity to start their own schools; citizens should be encouraged to take over the administration of post offices; to elect police commissioners; to recall MPs who violate the public trust. An innovative approach to governance in the UK, the Big Society is the "Big Idea"—the catchphrase and rebranding of politics demanded of all new governments in the UK.

Critics mocked the Big Society, and supporters have not yet been able to clearly define what it means or implement Big Society policies effectively. At a time when severe cuts in public spending demanded a roll-back of government, it remains unclear whether the Big Society is a defining vision that will drive the agenda of a strong, stable, and effective coalition government, or that it will be remembered as a catch-phrase that could not paper over the difficulties that a government would face once it was committed to making the broad, deep, and increasingly unpopular cuts demanded by the "great recession" that began in 2008.

# Themes and Implications

Our four core themes in this book, introduced in Part I, highlight the most important features of British politics.

## Historical Junctures and Political Themes

A country's position in the world of states influences its ability to manage domestic and international challenges. A weaker international standing makes it difficult for a country to control international events or insulate itself from external pressures. Britain's ability to control the terms of trade and master political alliances during the nineteenth century confirms this maxim, but times have changed.

Through gradual decolonization Britain fell to second-tier status. Its formal empire shrank between the two world wars (1919–1939) as the "white dominions" of Canada, Australia, and New Zealand gained independence. In Britain's Asian, Middle Eastern, and African colonies, pressure for political reforms that would lead to independence deepened during World War II and afterward. Beginning with the formal independence of India and Pakistan in 1947, an enormous empire dissolved in less than twenty years. Finally, in 1997, Britain returned the commercially vibrant crown colony of Hong Kong to China. The process of decolonization ended Britain's position as a dominant player in world politics.

Is Britain a world power or just a middle-of-the-pack country in Europe? Maybe both. On the one hand, resulting from its role in World War II, Britain sits as

## PROFILE

### David Cameron

Photo by Christopher Furlong - WPA Pool/ Getty Images

*The King's Speech* is a charming award-winning movie on both sides of the Atlantic, based on a true story about how an Australian speech therapist secretly aided King George VI, a stutterer, enabling him to speak unhaltingly over the radio to rally the British people to stand together against Hitler's fascism as World War II erupted. As *The Economist,* an influential weekly noted, it is a movie with deep political-cultural resonance:

"There are some lessons here for Britain's present rulers. This is a prickly, conservative and proud nation, in which grandeur must be offset with displays of humanity: David Cameron, a privileged chap who has suffered tragedies in his private life, knows this already."*

Born in 1966, in London, Cameron was brought up in Berkshire, an historic county near Oxford and the royal residence, Windsor Castle. He is the son of a stockbroker and followed generations of Cameron males who attended Eton, the historic boarding school for the privileged elite, and then Oxford, where he studied Politics, Philosophy, and Economics (PPE). Cameron graduated in 1988 with a first class honors degree. A journalist once asked Cameron, just before he became leader of the Conservative Party in 2005, if he thought his pedigree and elite schooling would hurt him politically. Cameron sighed mightily and then offered a very revealing reply. "I don't know. You can try to be logical about it and say the upside is a terrific education, the downside is the label that gets attached and mentioned in every article," replied Cameron. "Or you can just think to yourself: I am what I am. That is what I had, I am very grateful for it."**

Unlike a great many people, including many party and national leaders, Cameron seems uncommonly at home in his own skin, wears his considerable confidence gracefully, and breaks the mould of many British politicians and, in particular, Gordon Brown, his predecessor as prime minister, who was ill at ease in public, fidgety, and downcast. Cameron's jovial disposition is a considerable political asset, almost a trademark, as is his willingness to reveal publicly what many would keep behind doors, within the family. David and Samantha Cameron's first child was born with both cerebral palsy and a rare form of epilepsy. As the country came gradually to learn, David Cameron and his wife, Samantha, spent many successive nights sleeping on the floor of St. Mary's hospital by their child, Ivan, until he succumbed.

Cameron's elite education and step-by-step rise to political leadership from MP (member of parliament) to member of the Conservative Party research department, to opposition spokesman (member of the shadow cabinet with increasingly significant portfolios), to leader of the Conservative Party is very traditional, if unusually rapid. Nevertheless Cameron represents a new brand of Conservative, a "third-way" conservative who has tried to steal much of the thunder from Tony Blair, whom admirers liken to John Kennedy, and who characterizes himself as a compassionate conservative. If Cameron can lead Britain successfully through the tough economic and political times he inherited from New Labour in 2010, he will have achieved a lasting place in modern British politics—and he will have earned it the hard way.

*Bagehot, *The Economist*. January 15, 2011, p. 62 (Economist.com/blogs/Bagehot)

**Francis Elliott and James Hanning, *Cameron: The Rise of the New Conservative*, London: Harper Perennial, 2009, p. 25.

a permanent member of the United Nations Security Council and a leading member of the world's select club of nuclear powers. On the other hand, Britain almost always plays second fiddle in its special relationship to the United States, which has exposed British foreign policy to extraordinary pressures, especially since September 11. British governments also face persistent challenges in their dealings with the EU. Many countries in Europe, but not Britain, have adopted a common currency, the euro. Can Britain afford to remain aloof from such fast-paced changes of economic integration?

A second theme examines the strategies employed in governing the economy. Since the dawn of Britain's Industrial Revolution, prosperity at home has relied on superior competitiveness abroad. This is even truer today with intensified international competition and global production. Will Britain's "less-is-more" **laissez-faire** approach to economic governance, invigorated by partnerships between the state and key competitive businesses, sustain economic growth and competitiveness in a global context? Can Britain achieve a durable economic model without fuller integration into Europe?

A third theme is the potent political influence of the democratic idea, the universal appeal of core values associated with parliamentary democracy as practiced first in the United Kingdom. Even in Britain, issues about democratic governance, citizen participation, and constitutional reform have been renewed with considerable force. What are the implications of the election of May 2010 for democracy in Britain? In a sense no party won the election, but Labour was soundly defeated. The Liberal Democrats won five seats fewer than they had won in 2005 (down from 62 to 57), but won the opportunity to be the junior partner in the Conservative–Liberal Democrat coalition government; and the Conservatives, with 36.1 percent of the vote, a mere 3.7 percent increase over 2005, were unable to form a government on their own, but won the right to be responsible for shepherding the country through political uncertainty and a moment of severe economic challenges. The highly unusual outcome—the first peacetime coalition in 70 years—guarantees that 2010 will be remembered as a remarkable election, but the consequences for the democratic idea in Britain will take longer to tally.

The traditionally respected royal family, which has been rocked by improprieties, including tax scandals and infidelity over the past two decades, has seized on the marriage of Prince William as a moment of redemption. Few reject the monarchy outright, but questions about the finances and decorum of the monarchy have placed on the agenda broader issues about citizen control over government and constitutional reform. That William of Wales is now the knight in shining armor coming to the rescue of the royal family provides a graphic reminder that long-settled issues about the constitutional form and unity of the state have not been put to rest. Can the interests of England, Wales, Scotland, and Northern Ireland be balanced within a single nation-state?

The fourth theme, collective identity, considers how individuals define themselves politically through group attachments, come together to pursue political goals, and face their status as political insiders or outsiders. Through the immigration of former colonial subjects to the United Kingdom, decolonization created a multiracial and multiethnic society. Issues of race, ethnicity, and cultural identity have challenged the long-standing British values of tolerance and consensus. The concept of "Britishness"—what the country stands for and who makes up the political community—has come into question, especially since 9/11 and the bombings of the London transport system by British Muslims in July 2005.

**laissez-faire**

A term taken from the French, which means "to let be," in other words, to allow markets to act freely, with a minimum of state regulation.

## Implications for Comparative Politics

Britain was the first nation to industrialize. For much of the nineteenth century, the British Empire was the world's dominant power, with a vast network of colonies. Britain was also the first nation to develop an effective parliamentary democracy.

British politics is often studied as a model of representative government. Named after the building that houses the British legislature in London, the **Westminster model** emphasizes that democracy rests on the supreme authority of a legislature—in Britain's case, the Parliament. Finally, Britain has served as a model of gradual and peaceful evolution of democratic government in a world where transitions to democracy are often turbulent, interrupted, and uncertain.

**Westminster model**

A form of democracy based on the supreme authority of Parliament and the accountability of its elected representatives; named after the Parliament building in London.

### Summary

Despite presiding over an enviable period of economic growth and exerting high-profile leadership on the world stage, Blair lost the support of his party and was forced to hand over the reins of government to Gordon Brown for one big reason: support for the war in Iraq. The formation of an untested coalition government in 2010 is a potent reminder that democracy is an aspiration, always subject to change, and never a finished process. Britain faces many other challenges—regaining economic stability and unifying Britain as a multicultural, multiethnic, and multinational country. And it must come to terms with its role as a European country that enjoys a particularly close alliance with the United States, but has its own distinctive national and regional perspectives and interests.

SECTION

# POLITICAL ECONOMY AND DEVELOPMENT

## Focus Questions

What are the similarities and what are the differences in New Labour's approach to governing the economy compared to that of Margaret Thatcher and John Major?

On balance how successful was New Labour's approach to economic management?

What are the lessons the Conservative–Liberal coalition government should learn from New Labour?

What are the key elements of the coalition government's approach to economic management in the post-2008 context?

## neoliberalism

A term used to describe government policies aiming to promote free competition among business firms within the market, including reduced governmental regulation and social spending.

The pressures of global competitiveness and the perceived advantages of a minimalist government have encouraged the adoption in many countries of neoliberal approaches to economic management. A legacy from Thatcher's Britain, **neoliberalism** was a key feature of Tony Blair's and Gordon Brown's New Labour government. Its policies aimed to promote free competition, interfere with entrepreneurs and managers as little as possible, and create a business-friendly environment to attract foreign investment and spur innovation. Given that New Labour had long accepted the core principles of neoliberalism, the differences in economic policy between New Labour and the Conservative–Liberal coalition reflected changed circumstances—the economic crisis driven by the recession of 2008—more than ideological shifts.

## The State and the Economy

Thirty years ago, economic growth in Britain was low and unemployment high. Britain was routinely called the "sick man of Europe." But from the mid-1990s to the great recession of 2008, Britain avoided the high unemployment and recession of many EU nations. The UK economy has run on a "two-track" pattern of growth. A strong service sector (especially in financial services) offset a much weaker industrial sector. Until the global downturn of fall 2008, the British economy exhibited overall strength. With low unemployment, low interest rates, low inflation, and sustained growth, the UK performance was one of the best among the leading industrial economies.

With the transition in 2010 from a New Labour to a Conservative–Liberal government, the policy orientation did not change at a stroke. Neoliberalism drove the economic policy of New Labour and, as a result, the economic performance of the UK economy today. Two central dimensions, economic management and social policy, capture the new role of the state and show how limited this new state role really is, partly by design and partly by the sheer force of changes demanded by the recession.

## Economic Management

Like all other states, the British state intervenes in economic life, sometimes with considerable force. However, the British state has generally limited its role to broad policy instruments that influence the economy generally (**macroeconomic policy**). How has the orientation of economic policy evolved during the postwar period?

**The Consensus Era**  After World War II, the unity inspired by shared suffering during the war and the need to rebuild the country crystallized the collectivist consensus. The state broadened and deepened its responsibilities for the economy.

The state assumed direct ownership of key industries. It also accepted the responsibility to secure low levels of unemployment (a policy of full employment), expand social services, maintain a steady rate of growth (increase economic output or GDP), keep prices stable, and achieve desirable balance-of-payments and exchange rates. The approach is called Keynesian demand management, or **Keynesianism** (after the British economist John Maynard Keynes, 1883–1946).

Before Thatcher became leader of the Conservative Party in 1975, Conservative leaders generally accepted the collectivist consensus. By the 1970s, however, Britain was suffering economically without growth and with growing political discontent. Investments declined, and trade union agitation increased. Industrial unrest in the winter of 1978–1979 dramatized Labour's inability to manage the trade unions. It seemed as if everyone was on strike. Strikes by truckers disrupted fuel supplies. Strikes by train-drivers disrupted inter-city commerce and visits to granny. Some ambulance drivers refused to respond to emergency calls. Grave diggers refused to bury the dead. Thatcher came to power a few months later in May 1979. What was dubbed "the winter of discontent" destroyed Britain's collectivist consensus and discredited the Keynesian welfare state.

**Thatcherite Policy Orientation**  The economic orientations of Thatcher and John Major, her hand-picked successor, rejected Keynesianism. **Monetarism** emerged as the new economic doctrine. It assumed that there is a "natural rate of unemployment" determined by the labor market itself. State intervention to steer the economy should be limited to a few steps to foster appropriate rates of growth in the money supply and keep inflation low. Monetarism reflected a radical change from the postwar consensus regarding economic management. Not only was active government intervention considered unnecessary; it was seen as undesirable and destabilizing.

**New Labour's Economic Policy Approach**  Gordon Brown as chancellor—and later as prime minister—insisted on establishing a sound economy. He was determined to reassure international markets that the British economy was built on a platform of stability (low debt, low deficit, low inflation) and that the Labour government could be counted on to run a tight financial ship. Only after he turned the public debt into a surplus did the "iron chancellor" reinvent himself as a more conventional Labour chancellor. Even then, Brown used economic growth to increase spending (rather than cut taxes).

Brown claimed that since capital is international, mobile, and not subject to control, industrial policy and planning are futile if they focus on the domestic economy alone. Instead, government should improve the quality of labor through education and training, maintain labor market flexibility, and attract investment to Britain. Strict control of inflation and tough limits on public expenditure would promote both

---

**macroeconomic policy**

Policy intended to shape the overall economic system by concentrating on policy targets such as inflation and growth.

**Keynesianism**

Named after British economist John Maynard Keynes, an approach to economic policy in which state economic policies are used to regulate the economy to achieve stable economic growth.

**monetarism**

An approach to economic policy that assumes a natural rate of unemployment, determined by the labor market, and rejects the instruments of government spending to run budgetary deficits for stimulating the economy and creating jobs.

Kipper Williams

Chilly Economic Climate for UK as Britain is still reeling from a slew of bad economic news.

employment and investment opportunities. Economic policy should increase competitive strength through government-business partnerships and efforts to improve the skill of the work force and therefore the competitiveness of British industry.

## The Coalition Government's Economic Policy Approach

The centerpiece of the coalition government's approach to economic policy is its overarching commitment to deficit reduction as the necessary precondition for stabilizing the economy. Very soon after taking office, the coalition government engaged in a comprehensive spending review and a predictably harsh retrospective critique of the state of the economy they inherited from New Labour. To say the least, Britain's chancellor of the exchequer (finance minister) George Osborne cast significant doubt on the way New Labour handled public finances. Cameron's speech to the Tory party conference in October 2010 lambasted Labour, characterizing the result of Labour's economic policy and the urgent need for debt reduction this way:

> Back in May, we inherited public finances that can only be described as catastrophic.... This year, we're going to spend 43 billion pounds (68 billion dollars) on interest payments alone ... not to pay off the debt—just to stand still.... That's why we have acted decisively—to stop pouring so much of your hard-earned money down the drain.[2]

Key cuts announced by the chancellor, which were scheduled to be in effect for four years, included cuts in government subsidies for public housing, increases in the age for pensions, reduction in child benefits for middle-class families, a general reduction of about 10 percent in a range of social protection and welfare benefits and a cut of roughly 20 percent in public spending across the board. Of course, the new economic course set by the coalition government spurred considerable controversy. Osborne insisted that the budget was "guided fairness, reform," while his counterpart on Labour's front benches, that is, the "shadow chancellor," the likely person to be named chancellor if Labour won the next election, Alan Johnson labelled the review a "reckless gamble with people's livelihoods," and a threat to any economic recovery. On balance, the cuts were viewed as both necessary and regressive, hitting those in the lower end of the income distribution harder than those who are better off.

## Social Policy

Historically, in the UK welfare state provisions have interfered relatively little in the workings of the market, and policy-makers do not see the reduction of group inequalities as the proper goal of the welfare state. In fact, through changes in government there has been considerable continuity across the period of postwar consensus, despite differences in perspectives on the welfare state. The collectivist era enshrined the welfare state. Thatcher assailed the principles of the welfare state but accepted many of the policies as increased need triggered expanding welfare state budgets. New Labour attempted to link social expenditures to improving skills, making everyone a stakeholder in society, and tried hard—with only limited success—to turn social policy into an instrument for improving education, skills, and competitiveness.

In comparative European terms, the UK welfare state has offered few comprehensive services, and the policies are not very generous. At the same time—and the one exception—the National Health Service (NHS) provides comprehensive and universal medical care and has long been championed as the jewel in the crown of the welfare state in Britain, an exception to the rule in ordinary times because it provides fine, low cost medical care to all British citizens as a matter of right.

Will the NHS remain so when push comes to shove in these deeply troubled times when austerity rules the day? In the 2010 campaign, the Conservatives promised there would be no major changes in health care provision and that the NHS would be exempted from the across-the-board cuts faced by other government agencies. But in January 2011, the government suddenly announced a large-scale shakeup in the NHS, handing most of the responsibility for administering health care and managing health care budgets to the nation's general practitioners. Senior Liberal Democrats in the governing coalition seemed caught out by this hasty policy U-turn, warning that there was a risk of a "car crash"—an organizational and budgetary crisis that will be blamed on the coalition.

The chipping away at the NHS is a strong signal that times have changed. It is a sure bet that the budgetary entrenchment will become more severe for the first years of the coalition government and a good wager that disagreements over public spending and, in particular health policy, will produce some cracks in the coalition.

# Society and Economy

New Labour rejected both the cutbacks in social provisions of Conservative governments that seemed mean-spirited as well as the egalitarian traditions of Britain's collectivist era that emphasized entitlements or what in the United States is called "tax and spend liberalism." Instead, New Labour focused its social policy on training and broader social investment as a more positive third-way alternative.

New Labour emphasized efficiencies and attempted to break welfare dependency. Its effort to identify comprehensive solutions to society's ills and reduce the tendency for government to let marginalized individuals fall by the wayside captures the third-way orientation of the New Labour project.

The economic upturn that began in 1992, combined with Major's moderating effects on the Thatcherite social policy agenda, served to narrow inequality by the mid-1990s. Attention to social exclusion in its many forms, and strong rates of growth were good omens for narrowing the gap between rich and poor. But even before the "Great Recession" of 2008 and despite New Labour's commitment to producing a more egalitarian society and reducing poverty, it was extremely difficult to achieve success.

A 2007 report by UNICEF compared twenty-one wealthy countries (members of the OECD) on their success in securing the well-being of children along six dimensions. Both the United States and the United Kingdom are in the bottom third for five of the six dimensions under review. In the summary table that presents the overall rankings, the UK comes in dead last, just behind the United States (see Figure 2.3). Despite repeated high visibility commitments by New Labour to eliminate childhood poverty, they were unable to make any sustained headway toward that laudable goal. In a market-driven economy, it is extremely difficult for governments to effectively pursue targeted goals such as eliminating childhood poverty. The government may have the will, but it doesn't have the way (the policy instruments or the strategic capacity) to meet such goals.

## Inequality and Ethnic Minorities

Ethnic minorities disproportionately suffer diminished opportunity in the United Kingdom. More than one-third of the ethnic minority population is younger than sixteen; nearly half is under twenty-five; and more than four-fifths is under forty-five. Despite the common and often disparaging reference to ethnic minority individuals as "immigrants," members of ethnic minority groups are increasingly native-born.

Ethnic minority individuals, particularly young men, are subject to unequal treatment by the police and considerable physical harassment by citizens. They have experienced cultural isolation as well as marginalization in the educational system, job training, housing, and labor markets. There is considerable concern about the apparent rise in racially motivated crime in major metropolitan areas with significant ethnic diversity.

Poor rates of economic success reinforce the sense of isolation and distinct collective identities. Variations among ethnic minority communities are quite considerable,

Countries are listed here in order of their average rank for the six dimensions of child well-being that have been assessed. *
A light blue background indicates a place in the top third of the table; mid-blue denotes the middle third; and dark blue the bottom third.

| Dimensions of Child Well-being | Average Ranking Position (for all 6 dimensions) | Dimension 1 Material Well-being | Dimension 2 Health and Safety | Dimension 3 Educational Well-being | Dimension 4 Family and Peer Relationships | Dimension 5 Behaviors and Risks | Dimension 6 Subjective Well-being |
|---|---|---|---|---|---|---|---|
| Netherlands | 4.2 | 10 | 2 | 6 | 3 | 3 | 1 |
| Sweden | 5.0 | 1 | 1 | 5 | 15 | 1 | 7 |
| Denmark | 7.2 | 4 | 4 | 8 | 9 | 6 | 12 |
| Finland | 7.5 | 3 | 3 | 4 | 17 | 7 | 11 |
| Spain | 8.0 | 12 | 6 | 15 | 8 | 5 | 2 |
| Switzerland | 8.3 | 5 | 9 | 14 | 4 | 12 | 6 |
| Norway | 8.7 | 2 | 8 | 11 | 10 | 13 | 8 |
| Italy | 10.0 | 14 | 5 | 20 | 1 | 10 | 10 |
| Ireland | 10.2 | 19 | 19 | 7 | 7 | 4 | 5 |
| Belgium | 10.7 | 7 | 16 | 1 | 5 | 19 | 16 |
| Germany | 11.2 | 13 | 11 | 10 | 13 | 11 | 9 |
| Canada | 11.8 | 6 | 13 | 2 | 18 | 17 | 15 |
| Greece | 11.8 | 15 | 18 | 16 | 11 | 8 | 3 |
| Poland | 12.3 | 21 | 15 | 3 | 14 | 2 | 19 |
| Czech Republic | 12.5 | 11 | 10 | 9 | 19 | 9 | 17 |
| France | 13.0 | 9 | 7 | 18 | 12 | 14 | 18 |
| Portugal | 13.7 | 16 | 14 | 21 | 2 | 15 | 14 |
| Austria | 13.8 | 8 | 20 | 19 | 16 | 16 | 4 |
| Hungary | 14.5 | 20 | 17 | 13 | 6 | 18 | 13 |
| United States | 18.0 | 17 | 21 | 12 | 20 | 20 | – |
| United Kingdom | 18.2 | 18 | 12 | 17 | 21 | 21 | 20 |

* OECD countries with insufficient data to be included in the overview: Australia, Iceland, Japan, Luxembourg, Mexico, New Zealand, the Slovak Republic, South Korea, and Turkey.

**FIGURE 2.3 Child Well-Being in Rich Countries.**
Despite a strong commitment by New Labour to end child poverty, Britain comes in last in a comparison of child well-being among twenty-one wealthy countries.

*Source:* UNICEF, Child poverty in perspective. An overview of child well-being in rich countries. *Innocenti Report Card No. 7,* 2007. UNICEF Innocenti Research Centre, Florence. © The United Nations Children's Fund, 2007.

however, and there are some noteworthy success stories. For example, among men of African, Asian, Chinese, and Indian descent, the proportional representation in the managerial and professional ranks is actually higher than that for white men (although they are much less likely to be senior managers in large firms). Also, Britons of South Asian, especially Indian, descent enjoy a high rate of entrepreneurship. Nevertheless, despite some variations, employment opportunities for women from all minority ethnic groups have been limited.[3]

## Inequality and Women

Women's participation in the labor market when compared to men's also indicates inequality, although the gap is narrowing. According to 2011 government data, the pay gap for full-time employees, measured by median average pay, narrowed by two percentage points between 2009 and 2010. For full-time employees the pay gap is 10.2 percent, down from 12.2 percent in 2009. For part-time employees the gap has widened in favor of women, extending to minus 4.0 percent, compared with minus 2.5 percent in 2009. Additional good news: For all employees, the gender pay gap narrowed to 19.8 percent, from 22.0 percent in 2009.

In addition, full-time earnings for women increased more across the bottom 10 percent than men's earnings, with growth of 1.8 percent compared with 0.8 percent for their male counterparts. The hourly earnings of the top 10 percent grew by 0.8 percent for men and 2.1 percent for women.[4]

In 2008, a higher portion of men (79 percent) than women (70 percent) of working age were employed in the UK. Over the past thirty years there has been a significant increase in female employment to the point that there is virtual parity in the number of jobs performed by men and women, but almost half the jobs performed by

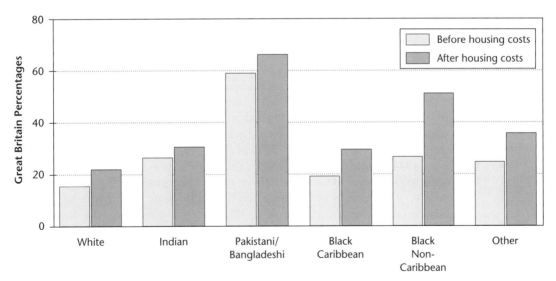

Households on low income: by ethnic group of head of household, 2001–02

**FIGURE 2.4  Distribution of Low-Income Households by Ethnicity.**
People from Britain's ethnic minority communities are far more likely than white Britons to be in lower-income households although there are important differences among ethnic minority groups. Nearly 60 percent of Pakistani or Bangladeshi households are low-income households, while about one-third of black Caribbean households live on low incomes.

*Source:* National Statistics Online: www.statistics.gov.uk/CCI/nugget.asp?ID=269&Pos=1&ColRank=2&Rank=384.

women were part-time, compared to about one-sixth performed by men.[5] In addition to broad cultural patterns, the patterns of women's employment in the UK are shaped by the chronic undersupply of affordable child care.

# Britain in the Global Economy

**foreign direct investment**

Ownership of or investment in cross-border enterprises in which the investor plays a direct managerial role.

**Foreign direct investment** (FDI) favors national systems, like those of Britain (and the United States), that rely mostly on private contractual and market-driven arrangements. Because of low costs, a business-friendly political climate, government-sponsored financial incentives, reduced trade union power, and a large pool of potential nonunionized recruits, the United Kingdom is the most highly regarded location in Europe for FDI.

The UK scores well in international comparisons of microeconomic competitiveness and growth competitiveness. It has also achieved significant competitive success in particular pockets of science-based high technology industries. Even before the Great Recession, the picture of UK global competitiveness was clouded by weak industrial performance.

Gordon Brown's Britain preached a globalization-friendly model of flexible labor markets throughout EU Europe, and its success in boosting Britain's economic performance in comparison with the rest of Europe won some reluctant admirers.

## Summary

Until the very end New Labour remained a mystery to many. Blair and Brown chalked up many successes, but people still wondered: How new was New Labour? In governing the economy New Labour tried to go back to the future. That is, the future of global competitiveness rested on traditional economics of tight finance, laissez-faire, and free trade. That approach, which was anchored in business partnerships and arms-length relationships to trade unions, was certainly new for a Labour government. On balance, New Labour was moderately successful in its approach to governing the economy. In addition, the government achieved some success in reducing child poverty and narrowing the **gender gap** in pay—but did less to reduce the unequal chances faced by ethnic minorities.

**gender gap**

Politically significant differences in social attitudes and voting behavior between men and women.

Under New Labour, Britain achieved an enviable record of growth, low inflation, and low unemployment in part because of its sustained commitment to attract foreign investment and to assume an outward-looking competitive profile. Of course that international market-driven orientation of the British economy, combined with a hands off antiregulatory approach exposed Britain to enormous risk and a very severe downturn, with reverberating political consequences, when the global recession engulfed Britain in 2008. Under the woeful conditions that the coalition government faced from their first days in office, their options for governing the economy are very limited. Rejecting the temptation to stimulate the economy through government spending, budgetary cuts are the first, second, and third priority, and effective economic management will be a daunting challenge. Government leaders are resolute and plain-spoken about the challenges they face and in the early going have impressed many by their willingness to insist on radical cuts and tight budgetary control across the board. This is bitter medicine, but if they can maintain popular support and keep their coalition afloat, they may yet have an opportunity to benefit from the recovery they anticipate around the middle of the decade.

# GOVERNANCE AND POLICY-MAKING

Britain's constitution is notable for two features: its form and its age. Britain lacks a formal written constitution in the usual sense. There is no single unified and authoritative text (like the U.S. Constitution) that has special status above ordinary law and can be amended only by special procedures. Rather, the British constitution is a combination of statutory law (mainly acts of Parliament), common law, convention, and authoritative interpretations. Although it is often said that Britain has an unwritten constitution, this is not accurate. Authoritative legal treatises are written, of course, as are the much more significant acts of Parliament that define crucial elements of the political system. These acts define the powers of Parliament and its relationship with the monarchy, the rights governing the relationship between state and citizen, the relationship of constituent nations to the United Kingdom, the relationship of the United Kingdom to the EU, and many other rights and legal arrangements. In fact, "What distinguishes the British constitution from others is not that it is unwritten, but rather that it is part written and uncodified."[6]

The conventions and acts of Parliament with constitutional implications began at least as early as the seventeenth century, notably with the Bill of Rights of 1689, which helped define the relationship between the monarchy and Parliament. "Britain's constitution presents a paradox," a British scholar of constitutional history has observed. "We live in a modern world but inhabit a pre-modern, indeed, ancient, constitution."[7]

Constitutional authorities have accepted the structure and principles of many areas of government for so long that the very appeal to convention itself has enormous cultural force. Thus, widely agreed-on rules of conduct, rather than law or U.S.-style checks and balances, set the limits of governmental power. Absolute principles of government are few, but those that exist are fundamental to the organization of the state and central to governance, policy-making, and patterns of representation. It will become clear, however, that even the most time-encrusted principles of Britain's ancient constitutional traditions are subject to quick and potentially radical changes.

## Focus Questions

What are the strengths and weaknesses of parliamentary democracy?

How significant are the changes promised in the Coalition agreement?

Is it fair to say that compared to other democracies Britain may be considered an elective dictatorship?

What is the role of the UK Supreme Court? How is it different from the U.S. Supreme Court?

How has the devolution of powers from the UK parliament to Wales, Scotland, and Northern Ireland changed both the organizing principles of the state and politics in the UK?

## Organization of the State

The core of the British system is **parliamentary sovereignty**: Parliament can make or overturn any law; the executive, the judiciary, and the throne do not have any authority to restrict, veto, or otherwise overturn parliamentary action. In a classic **parliamentary democracy**, the prime minister is answerable to the House of Commons (the elected element of Parliament) and may be dismissed by it. That said, by joining the European Economic Community in 1973 (now known as the European Union), Parliament accepted significant limitations on its power to act. It acknowledged that European law has force in the United Kingdom without requiring parliamentary assent and that European law overrides British law. Parliament has accepted the authority of the European Court of Justice (ECJ) to resolve jurisdictional disputes. To complete the circle, the ECJ has confirmed its right to suspend acts of Parliament.

**parliamentary sovereignty**

The doctrine that grants the legislature the power to make or overturn any law and permits no veto or judicial review.

**parliamentary democracy**

System of government in which the chief executive is answerable to the legislature and may be dismissed by it.

**unitary state**

In contrast to a federal system, a system of government in which no powers are reserved for subnational units of government.

**fusion of powers**

A constitutional principle that merges the authority of branches of government, in contrast to the principle of separation of powers.

**cabinet government**

A system of government in which most executive power is held by the cabinet, headed by a prime minister.

**constitutional monarchy**

System of government in which the head of state ascends by heredity but is limited in powers and constrained by the provisions of a constitution.

Second, Britain has long been a **unitary state**. By contrast to the United States, where powers not delegated to the national government are reserved for the states, no powers are reserved constitutionally for subcentral units of government in the United Kingdom. However, the Labour government of Tony Blair introduced a far-reaching program of constitutional reform that created a quasi-federal system. Specified powers have been delegated (the British prefer to say *devolved*) to legislative bodies in Scotland and Wales, and to Northern Ireland as well, now that the longstanding conflict there seems settled. In addition, powers have been redistributed from the Westminster Parliament to an authority governing London with a directly elected mayor. As part of New Labour's constitutional reform agenda, regional development agencies (RDAs), which are appointed bodies, were set up in 1999 to enhance development plans for regions throughout the UK.

Third, Britain has a system of **fusion of powers** at the national level: Parliament is the supreme legislative, executive, and judicial authority and includes the monarch as well as the House of Commons and the House of Lords. The fusion of legislature and executive is also expressed in the function and personnel of the cabinet. U.S. presidents can direct or ignore their cabinets, which have no constitutionally mandated function, but the British cabinet bears enormous constitutional responsibility. Through collective decision making, the cabinet—and not an independent prime minister—shapes, directs, and takes responsibility for government. This core principle, **cabinet government**, however, may at critical junctures be observed more in principle than in practice. Particularly with strong prime ministers, such as Thatcher and Blair, who can rally—or bully—the cabinet, power gravitates to the prime minister.

Britain is a **constitutional monarchy**. The Crown passes by hereditary succession, but the government or state officials must exercise nearly all powers of the Crown. Parliamentary sovereignty, parliamentary democracy, and cabinet government form the core of the British or Westminster model of government.

# The Executive

The term *cabinet government* emphasizes the key functions that the cabinet exercises: responsibility for policy-making, supreme control of government, and coordination of all government departments. However, the term does not capture the full range of executive institutions nor the scale and complexity of operations. Nor does it capture the realities of a system in which power invariably flows upward to the prime minister. In addition, the executive reaches well beyond the cabinet. It extends from ministries (departments) and ministers to the civil service in one direction, and to Parliament (as we shall see in Section 4) in the other direction.

## Cabinet Government

After a general election, the Crown invites the leader of the party that emerges from the election with control of a majority of seats in the House of Commons to form a government and serve as prime minister. The prime minister selects approximately two dozen ministers for the cabinet. Senior cabinet posts include the Foreign Office (equivalent to the U.S. secretary of state), the Home Office (ministry of justice or attorney general), and the chancellor of the exchequer (finance minister). Unlike the French Constitution, which prohibits a cabinet minister from serving in the legislature, British constitutional tradition *requires* overlapping membership between Parliament and cabinet. A member of the cabinet must be either a member of parliament (MP) or less commonly, a member of the House of Lords.

The cabinet room at 10 Downing Street (the prime minister's official residence) is a place of intrigue as well as deliberation. From the prime minister's viewpoint, the cabinet may appear as loyal followers or as ideological combatants, potential challengers for party leadership, and parochial advocates for pet programs that run counter to the overall objectives of the government. By contrast, the convention of collective responsibility normally unifies the cabinet. In principle, the prime minister must gain the support of a majority of the cabinet for a range of significant decisions, notably the budget and the legislative program.

The only other constitutionally mandated mechanism for checking the prime minister is the government's defeat on a vote of no confidence in the House of Commons (discussed further in Section 4). Since the defeat of a government by parliament is rare and politically dangerous, the cabinet remains the only routine check on the prime minister.

Margaret Thatcher often attempted to galvanize loyalists in the cabinet and either marginalize or expel detractors. In the end, her treatment of the cabinet, which stretched British constitutional conventions, helped inspire the movement to unseat her as party leader. John Major returned to a more consultative approach.

Tony Blair, like Thatcher, narrowed the scope of collective responsibility. The prime minister, a few key cabinet members, and a handful of advisers made many important policy decisions in smaller unofficial gatherings. Under Blair, cabinet meetings were usually less than an hour and could not seriously take up (much less resolve) policy differences.

The decision to go to war in Iraq underscored the cabinet's weakened capacity to exercise constitutional checks and balances. Blair and his close aides seemed sceptical about the effectiveness and centrality of the cabinet as well as cabinet committees. Blair preferred to coordinate strategically important policy areas through highly politicized special units in the Cabinet Office.

How Does David Cameron run his Cabinet? Carefully, no doubt, since he presides over a potentially unstable coalition in which one wrong move could bring down the government. On balance, cabinet government represents a durable and effective formula for governance, although the UK has very little experience with coalition governments. The cabinet operates within a broader cabinet system, or core executive (see Figure 2.5), and the prime minister holds or controls many of the levers of power in the core executive. Because the prime minister is the head of the cabinet, his or her office helps develop policy, coordinates operations, and functions as a liaison with the media, the party, interest groups, and Parliament.

The Cabinet is supported by a set of institutions that help formulate policy, coordinate operations, and facilitate the support for government policy. Acting within a context set by the fusion of legislature and executive, the prime minister enjoys a great opportunity for decisive leadership that is lacking in a system of checks and balances and separation of powers among the branches of government.

Cabinet committees (comprising ministers) and official committees (made up of civil servants) supplement the work of the cabinet. In addition, the treasury plays an important coordinating role through its budgetary control. The cabinet office supports day-to-day operations. Leaders in both the Commons and the Lords, the *whips*, smooth the passage of legislation sponsored by the government. Given that the government always has a working majority (except when the government declares a

**FIGURE 2.5 The Cabinet System**
The cabinet is supported by a set of institutions that help formulate policy, coordinate operations, and facilitate the support for government policy. Acting within a context set by the fusion of legislature and executive, the prime minister enjoys a great opportunity for decisive leadership that is lacking in a system of checks and balances and separation of powers among the branches of government.

*Source:* From *BRITISH POLITICS: CONTINUITIES AND CHANGE, Fourth Edition*, by Dennis Kavanagh, p. 241. © 2000. Data originally from HM Treasury Budget Bulletin. Reprinted with permission from Oxford University Press.

"free vote" which signals that a matter is either too controversial or too inconsequential to be introduced on behalf of the government), the outcome of a vote is seldom in doubt.

Because the cabinet system and the core executive concentrate power at the top, London does not suffer from Washington-style gridlock. The risk in the United Kingdom is the opposite danger of excessive concentration of power by a prime minister who is prepared to manipulate cabinet and flout the conventions of collective responsibility.

## Bureaucracy and Civil Service

Policy-making may appear to be increasingly concentrated in the prime minister's hands. When viewed from Whitehall (the London street where key UK units of government and administration are located), however, the executive may appear

## THE U.S. CONNECTION

### Comparing the U.S. Presidential System to the British Parliamentary System

Political scientists—especially those engaged in comparative politics—often discuss how the design of political institutions affects political outcomes.

Among the institutional differences that matter most is the distinction between presidential systems such as the United States and parliamentary systems such as the United Kingdom.

In a presidential system, the legislature and executive are *independent*. Both the legislature and the chief executive have their own fixed schedule for election and their own political mandate. Legislators and presidents have been elected independently of each other. They have different constituencies and often have different political agendas. Each may even gain credibility and support by opposing the other. In presidential systems the agenda and the authority of the president are often compromised when the president and the majority of legislators are from different parties—in fact this is the rule, rather than the exception in the United States and in many other presidential systems. Stalemates on key items of legislation are common. Between presidential elections, it is very difficult to remove a president, even one who has very little popular support or is suspected of acting unconstitutionally. It requires impeachment, which, in turn, requires a finding of extraordinary misconduct and a strong majority vote in the legislature.

Prime ministers, in contrast, must enjoy the support of the majority of the legislature to achieve office—and they must preserve that support to stay in office, since prime ministers and their governments can fall if they lose a vote of no confidence in the legislature. Furthermore, in a parliamentary system the timing of elections is typically not fixed (although the Cameron government has modified this rule). When riding high, the prime minister can call for a new election in an effort to win a new mandate and a deeper majority in parliament. When in trouble, a prime minister can be sent packing in an instant through a vote of no confidence.

In a parliamentary system like Britain's, because the legislators and prime minister sink or swim together, they tend to cooperate and work through differences. In a presidential system like America's, because the legislature and executive are mutually independent—one can swim, while the other sinks—the tendency for finger pointing and stalemate is much greater.

But the distinctions should not be exaggerated. Powerful prime ministers such as Thatcher and Blair were routinely criticized for being too presidential. And in Britain, the threat a prime minister faces of losing office through a vote of no confidence has all but disappeared—it has happened only once in more than 80 years. In fact, if recent history is a good predictor, an American president is more likely to face a bill of impeachment than a British prime minister is to face a serious vote of no confidence.

The analysis draws heavily from Alfred Stepan, with Cindy Skatch, "Constitutional Frameworks and Democratic Consolidation: Parliamentarism versus Presidentialism," in Mark Kesselman and Joel Krieger, eds., *Readings in Comparative Politics: Political Challenges and Changing Agendas* (Boston: Houghton Mifflin, 2006), pp. 284–293.

---

to be dominated by its vast administrative agencies. The range and complexity of state policy-making mean that the cabinet's authority must be shared with a vast set of unelected officials. Government departments are directed by members of the cabinet. Ministers are assisted by a very senior career civil servant, called a permanent secretary, who has chief administrative responsibility for running a department. Other senior civil servants, including deputy secretaries and under-secretaries, assist the permanent secretaries. In addition, the minister reaches into his or her department to appoint a principal private secretary, an up-and-coming civil servant who assists the minister as gatekeeper and liaison with senior civil servants.

Since nearly all legislation is introduced on behalf of the government and presented as the policy directive of a ministry, civil servants in Britain do much of the work of conceptualizing and refining legislation. (In the United States committee staffers in the Congress often do this work.) Civil servants, more than ministers, assume operational duties.

As a result of the ongoing modernization of Whitehall, the civil service has been downsized and given a new corporate structure. Few at the top of these agencies (agency chief executives) are traditional career civil servants. There is growing concern that the increasing importance of special advisers (who are both political policy advisers and civil servants) is eroding the impartiality of civil servants. Key special advisers played critical roles in making the case in the famous "dodgy dossier" of September 2002 alleging that the threat of weapons of mass destruction justified regime change in Iraq.

## Public and Semipublic Institutions

Like other countries, Britain has institutionalized "semipublic" agencies, which are sanctioned by the state but without direct democratic oversight. Examples include nationalized industries and Nondepartmental Public Bodies.

**Nationalized Industries** The nationalization of basic industries—such as coal, iron and steel, gas and electricity supply—was a central objective of the Labour government's program during the postwar collectivist era. By the end of the Thatcher era the idea of public ownership had clearly run out of steam and most of these giant state enterprises were privatized, that is sold to private large-scale investors or sold in small units to ordinary citizens, as was the case with British Telecom, the communications giant. More than 50 percent of the BT shares were sold to the public. When thinking of expanding state functions, we can look to a set of semipublic administrative organizations.

**Nondepartmental Public Bodies** Since the 1970s, an increasing number of administrative functions have been transferred to bodies that are typically part of the state in terms of funding, function, and appointment of staff, but operate at arms length from ministers.

These nondepartmental public bodies (NDPBs) are better known as quasi-nongovernmental organizations or **quangos**. They take responsibility for specific functions and can combine governmental and private sector expertise. At the same time, they enable ministers to distance themselves from controversial areas of policy.

Alongside quangos, in recent years the government has looked for ways to expand the investment of the private sector in capital projects such as hospitals and schools. Thus New Labour continued the private finance initiative (PFI) it inherited from the Conservatives as a key part of its signature modernization program and as a way to revitalize public services. The results are controversial: Critics and supporters disagree about the quality of services provided and about whether taxpayers win or lose by the financial arrangements. In addition, the tendency of PFI initiatives to blur the line between public and private raise important and controversial issues.[8]

**quangos**

Acronym for **quasi-nongovernmental organizations**, the term used in Britain for nonelected bodies that are outside traditional governmental departments or local authorities.

# Other State Institutions

## The Military and the Police

Those involved in security and law enforcement have enjoyed a rare measure of popular support in Britain. Constitutional tradition and professionalism distance the British police and military officers from politics.

In the case of the military, British policy since the Cold War remains focused on a gradually redefined set of North Atlantic Treaty Organization (NATO) commitments. Still ranked among the top five military powers in the world, Britain retains a global presence. In 1999, the United Kingdom strongly backed NATO's Kosovo campaign and pressed for ground troops. According to Blair, global interdependence rendered isolationism obsolete and inspired a commitment to a new ethical dimension in foreign policy. Throughout the war in Iraq and its bloody aftermath, Blair persistently sought to characterize Iraq as an extension of Kosovo, an effort to liberate Muslims from brutal dictatorships, whether Serbia's Milosevic or Iraq's Saddam Hussein. Until Blair's decision to support the American plan to shift the main venue of the war on terror from Afghanistan to Iraq, the use of the military in international conflicts generated little opposition. It may be that the Iraq war is the exception that proves the rule that the UK can play an important role in the world of states, including the use of force, when justified, without losing public support. In 2011, the Cameron government played a leading role in the international effort, endorsed by the U.N. Security Council, to protect civilians and enhance the cause of rebels fighting the regime of Libyan dictator Muammar Gaddafi. In the early stages, Cameron enjoyed strong support for his decision to participate in the international coalition.

The police have traditionally operated as independent local forces throughout the country. Since the 1980s, the police have witnessed growth in government control, centralization, and level of political use. During the coal miners' strike of 1984–1985, the police operated to an unprecedented, perhaps unlawful, degree as a national force coordinated through Scotland Yard (London police headquarters). Police menaced strikers and hindered miners from participating in strike support activities. This partisan use of the police in an industrial dispute flew in the face of constitutional traditions and offended some police officers and officials. During the 1990s, concerns about police conduct focused on police-community relations. These included race relations, corruption, and the interrogation and treatment of people held in custody.

## The Judiciary

In Britain, the principle of parliamentary sovereignty has limited the role of the judiciary. Courts have no power to judge the constitutionality of legislative acts (**judicial review**). They can only determine whether policy directives or administrative acts violate common law or an act of Parliament. Hence, the British judiciary is generally less politicized and influential than its U.S. counterpart.

**judicial review**

The prerogative of a high court to nullify actions by the executive and legislative branches of government that in its judgment violate the constitution.

Jurists, however, have participated in the wider political debate outside court. They have headed royal commissions on the conduct of industrial relations, the struggle in Northern Ireland, and riots in Britain's inner cities. In fact, inquiries led by judges with a streak of independence—or lack thereof—can prove highly embarrassing to the government and raise important issues for public debate. Take, for example, the inquiry by Lord Hutton, a senior jurist, into the death of David Kelly, a former UN weapons inspector and whistleblower who challenged the key tenet of Blair's case for the war in Iraq—that Iraq could launch weapons of mass destruction on forty-five minutes' notice. The question of Hutton's independence became very controversial, however, in light of a "finding" that exonerated the prime minister.

In recent years Britain has witnessed dramatic institutional changes in law and the administration of justice, most notably with the 2009 creation of the UK

Supreme Court, which serves as the highest court of appeal, removing that authority from the House of Lords. Although the UK Supreme Court, unlike the U.S. Supreme Court, cannot rule on the constitutionality of Acts of Parliaments and is therefore less politically influential and controversial, some British observers are concerned that without the traditional connection between parliament and the judiciary, senior judges may become more isolated and subject to political attacks from government ministers.

As a member of the EU, Britain is bound to abide by the European Court of Justice (ECJ), as it applies and develops law as an independent institution within the EU. For example, with the passage of the Human Rights Act in 1998, Britain is required to comply with the European Convention on Human Rights (ECHR). Also, the adoption of the ECHR forced Britain to curtail discrimination against gays in the military. (The Ministry of Defence confirmed in 2007 that none of its initial fears about gays in the military have been justified.)

## Subnational Government

The United Kingdom is a state comprising distinct nations (England, Scotland, Wales, and Northern Ireland). Because the British political framework has traditionally been unitary, not federal, for centuries no formal powers devolved to either the nations within the United Kingdom or to subnational (really subcentral or sub-UK) units as in the United States, Germany, or India. Historically, the UK Parliament asserted authority over all political units in the UK. No powers were reserved for any other units of government: There are no states, and no powers were reserved for nations within the UK, or for local government. Even so, nations were an aspect of collective identities in the UK, often exerting a powerful hold on their members. For many, to be Scottish or Welsh or English or Northern Irish was a core source of identity that created a sense of commonality and shared fates among members. Nations were not political units. But that is no longer true.

Recent constitutional reforms have introduced important modifications in the organizing principles of the UK. After referendums in Wales and Scotland in 1997, and in Northern Ireland, which is part of the UK, and in the Republic of Ireland (an independent country) in 1998, Tony Blair's Labour government introduced a set of power-sharing arrangements (what the British call "devolution") to govern the arrangements among the UK Westminster parliament, the Welsh Assembly, the Northern Ireland Assembly, and the Scottish Parliament.

In general, the UK government retains responsibility for all policy areas that have not been devolved, and which are the traditional domain of nation-states. Westminster controls security and foreign policy, economic policy, trade, defense, and social security for the UK as a whole, except where it doesn't, that is where specific powers have been ceded to Scotland, Northern Ireland, or Wales.

Of all the devolved nations and regions within the UK, Scotland and the Scottish government enjoy the most robust powers. Whereas Wales and Northern Ireland have relatively limited independent authority and have legislative arenas called assemblies, Scotland has a parliament, and the Scottish government is responsible for crucial areas of policy, including education, health, and the administration of justice. Clearly, devolution involves both an element of federalism and a carefully crafted compromise. The UK parliament is still the mother of all parliaments, but it has some potentially restive offspring!

It is important to note that every power devolved from the UK Parliament to the Scottish Parliament or the Welsh or Northern Ireland assembly chips away at the very core of parliamentary sovereignty that lies at the heart of the Westminster model. Devolution has also sparked a controversy that has become known as "the West Lothian Question."

What right should a Scottish MP have to vote on laws that might relate to England or Wales, while English and Welsh MPs cannot vote on some matters related to Scotland, in areas where policy had been devolved from the Westminster Parliament to the Scottish Parliament? This became a hot-button issue—when Gordon Brown, a Scotsman, was the UK prime minister and Scottish MPs were influential in winning a key vote for the government on tuition fees in England (and we know how politically combustible the issue of university fees has become).

Devolution within England is also part of the reform process. Regional Development Agencies (RDAs) were introduced throughout England in 1999 to facilitate economic development at the regional level. Even though they are unelected bodies with no statutory authority, they have opened the door to popular mobilization in the long term for elected regional assemblies. In addition, the Blair government placed changes in the governance of London on the fast track. The introduction of a directly elected mayor of London in May 2000 marked an important reform, leading to the direct election of mayors in other major cities, such as Birmingham and putting into practice a process of decentralizing power.

# The Policy-Making Process

Parliamentary sovereignty is the core constitutional principle of the British political system. But for policy-making and policy implementation, the focus is not on Westminster but rather on Whitehall.

In the UK Parliament has little direct participation in policy-making. Policy-making emerges primarily from within the executive. There, decision-making is strongly influenced by policy communities—informal networks with extensive knowledge, access, and personal connections to those responsible for policy. In this private hothouse environment, civil servants, ministers, and members of the policy communities work through informal ties. A cooperative style develops as the ministry becomes an advocate for key players and as civil servants come perhaps to over-identify the public good with the advancement of policy within their area of responsibility.

This cozy insider-only policy process has been challenged by the delegation of more and more authority to the EU. Both ministers and senior civil servants spend a great deal of time in EU policy deliberations and are constrained both directly and indirectly by the EU agenda and directives. More than 80 percent of the rules governing economic life in Britain are determined by the EU. Decisions by the EU Council of Finance Ministers and the European Central Bank shape British macroeconomic, monetary, and fiscal policies in significant ways. Even foreign and security policy are not immune from EU influences. The increasing Europeanization of policy-making has been and promises to further become one of the most interesting and potentially transformative developments in British politics.

## Summary

In almost every institutional dimension of governance and policy-making, recent years have witnessed a significant chipping away at the key organizing principles of government. The first principle of parliamentary sovereignty remains, but in practice it is weakened by the growing power of the core executive, the subordination of the UK parliament to the ultimate authority of the EU, and the reluctance of parliament to exercise its ultimate power to remove a prime minister by a vote of no confidence (to be discussed in Section 4). The second principle of Britain as a unitary state is strained by transfer of some powers to legislative and administrative bodies in Scotland, Wales, and Northern Ireland. The third principle of fusion of powers at the national level requires the effective exercise of collective responsibility of the cabinet as a check on prime ministerial power. This principle has been compromised when powerful prime ministers—such as Thatcher and Blair—find ways to work around the cabinet. As the policy-making process remained focused on Whitehall, we see a consistent picture of growing concentration of power in the executive.

SECTION 4

# REPRESENTATION AND PARTICIPATION

## Focus Question

Is Parliament still as sovereign in practice as it remains in constitutional tradition?

What are the political—and what are the constitutional—implications of the Conservative–Liberal coalition government?

Will the center hold?

As discussed in Section 3, parliamentary sovereignty is the core constitutional principle defining the role of the legislature and, in a sense, the whole system of British government. The executive or judiciary can set no act of Parliament aside, nor is any Parliament bound by the actions of any previous Parliament. Nevertheless, in practice, the control exerted by the House of Commons (or Commons)—the lower of the two houses of Parliament and by far the more powerful—is not unlimited. This section investigates the powers and role of Parliament, both Commons and Lords. It also looks at the party system, elections, and contemporary currents in British political culture, citizenship, and identity. We close by offering an analysis of surprising new directions in political participation and social protest.

## The Legislature

Today, the Commons does not really legislate in a meaningful way. Its real function is to assent to government legislation, since (with rare exceptions such as the present coalition government) a single governing party has a majority of the seats and can control the legislative agenda and pass legislation at will. In addition, the balance of effective oversight of policy has shifted from the legislature to executive agencies.

### The House of Commons

The House of Commons, the lower house of Parliament, with 650 seats at the time of the 2010 election, exercises the main legislative power in Britain. Along with the two unelected elements of Parliament, the Crown and the House of Lords, the Commons has three main functions: (1) to pass laws, (2) to provide finances for the state by authorizing taxation, and (3) to review and scrutinize public administration and government policy.

In practical terms, the Commons has a limited legislative function. Nevertheless, it serves a very important democratic role. It provides a highly visible arena for policy debate and the partisan collision of political worldviews. The flash of rhetorical skills brings drama to Westminster. One crucial element of drama, however, is nearly always missing. The outcome is seldom in doubt. MPs from the governing party (or as now, members of the Conservative–Liberal coalition) who consider rebelling against the leader of their respective parties or challenge the terms of the coalition agreement are understandably reluctant in a close and critical vote to force a general election. This would place their jobs in jeopardy. Only once since the defeat of Ramsay MacDonald's government in 1924 has a government been brought down by a defeat in the Commons (in 1979). Today, the balance of institutional power has shifted from Parliament to the governing party (or at present parties backing the coalition) and the executive.

## The Legislative Process

Bills must be introduced in the Commons and the Lords, although approval by the Lords is not required. Ideas for legislation come from political parties, pressure groups, think tanks, the prime minister's policy unit, or government departments. Proposed legislation, on behalf of the government, is then drafted by civil servants, circulated within Whitehall, approved by the cabinet, and then refined by the office of Parliamentary Counsel.

In the Commons the bill usually comes to the floor three times. The bill is formally *read* upon introduction, printed, distributed, debated in general terms, and after an interval, given a *second reading*, followed by a vote. The bill then undergoes detailed review by a standing committee reflecting the overall party balance. It then goes through a report stage during which new amendments may be introduced. In the *third reading*, the bill is considered in final form (and voted on) without debate.

A bill passed in the Commons follows a parallel path in the Lords. There the bill is either accepted without change, amended, or rejected. The Lords passes bills concerning taxation or budgetary matters without alteration, but can add technical and editorial amendments to other bills (if approved by the Commons) to add clarity and precision. Finally, it receives royal assent (which is only a formality) and becomes an Act of Parliament.

## The House of Lords

Traditionally the House of Lords (or Lords) was a wholly unelected body that was comprised of hereditary peers (nobility of the rank of duke, marquis, earl, viscount, or baron), and life peers (appointed on the recommendation of the prime minister or the recently institutionalized House of Lords Appointment Commission). The Lords also includes the archbishops of Canterbury and York and some two-dozen other bishops and archbishops of the Church of England. As part of a gradual reform agenda, in 1999, the right of all hereditary peers to sit and vote in the Lords was curtailed, and that right limited to 92 elected members. In 2011 the Lords had about 740 members.

Most significantly, the Lords serves mainly as a chamber of revision, providing expertise in redrafting legislation, with the power to suggest amendments to legislation under consideration in the Commons. The Lords can debate, refine, and delay—but not block—legislation. For example, in 2006, to protect the civil liberties of British Muslims the Lords persuaded the Commons to water down a bill that prohibited incitement to violence, on the grounds that the bill might unfairly be used to target Muslim clerics.

### Reforms in Behavior and Structure

There have been a number of contemporary changes in the House. How significant are they? How far will they go to stem the tide in Parliament's much-heralded decline?

**Behavioral Changes: Backbench Dissent**   Since the 1970s, backbenchers (MPs of the governing party who have no governmental office and rank-and-file opposition members) have been markedly less deferential. A backbench rebellion against the Major government's EU policy in 1993, which was viewed by Thatcherites as dangerously pro-European weakened the prime minister considerably and divided the party. One-third of Labour MPs defected on key votes authorizing the use of force in Iraq in 2003—an historic rebellion.

**Structural Changes: Parliamentary Committees**   In addition to the standing committees that routinely review bills, in 1979 the Commons extended the number and responsibilities of select committees, which help Parliament exert control over the executive by examining specific policies or aspects of administration.

The most controversial select committees monitor the major departments and ministries. Select committees hold hearings, take written and oral testimony, and question senior civil servants and ministers. Their reports have included strong policy recommendations at odds with government policy. These reforms have complicated the role of the civil service. Civil servants have been required to testify in a manner that may damage their ministers, revealing official culpability or flawed judgments.

## Political Parties and the Party System

Britain is often referred to as a two-party system, but as the 2010 election makes clear, that is a misnomer. It is true that from 1945 until the 2010 election, only leaders of the Labour or Conservative parties had served as prime ministers. And Conservative and Labour have been very closely matched. From 1945 through 2005, the Conservative and Labour parties each won eight general elections. In addition, throughout the postwar period, these two parties have routinely divided at least 85 percent of the seats in the Commons. But since the 1980s the Liberal Democrats (Lib Dems) have become an important alternative. Britain also has several national parties: the Scottish National Party (SNP) in Scotland and the Plaid Cymru in Wales as well as a roster of parties competing in Northern Ireland. (These parties are described below under "Trends in Electoral Behavior.")

### The Labour Party

Fifty years ago, those not engaged in manual labor voted Conservative three times more commonly than they did Labour. More than two out of three manual workers, by contrast, voted Labour. Britain then conformed to one classic pattern of a Western European party system: a two-class/two-party system.

Since the mid-1970s significant changes have developed in the party system, for example, the decline in class-based voting. It has also seen growing disaffection with even the moderate social democracy associated with the Keynesian welfare state and Labourism. The Labour party suffered from divisions between its trade unionist and parliamentary elements, constitutional wrangling over the power of trade unions to determine party policy at annual conferences, and disputes over how the leader would be selected. Divisions spilled over into foreign policy issues.

The 1980s and 1990s witnessed relative harmony within the party. Moderate trade union and parliamentary leadership agreed on major policy issues. Labour became a moderate center-left party. Under the leadership of Tony Blair, Labour was rebranded as "New Labour," although its formal name remained the Labour Party. After the party's defeat in the 2010 election, two close-knit brothers who had served in the cabinet, David Miliband with close ties to Blair as foreign minister, and Ed Miliband with close ties to Brown and former Secretary of State for Climate Change, were the top contenders to succeed Gordon Brown. In a dramatic contest for leadership of the Labour party in September 2010, Ed Miliband, the younger brother, prevailed in a very close election, signalling a turn away from New Labour and an effort to turn the party in a more progressive direction, without returning to "Old Labour." Miliband has successfully rallied the base, particularly among trade unionists and public sector employees who are feeling the pinch the hardest under the austerity policies of the Coalition government.

## The Conservative Party

The Conservative Party dates back to the eighteenth century. Its pragmatism, flexibility, and organizational capabilities have made it one of the most successful and, at times, innovative center-right parties in Europe.

In 2003, the combative and experienced Michael Howard took over as party leader. For a time, the Conservatives seemed revitalized. But it was not easy for Howard to translate his assured performances from the front bench in Parliament into popular support, as effective opposition to New Labour proved elusive. In fact, Conservatives made far less trouble for Labour Prime Minister Tony Blair on Iraq than did members of the Labour Party. Despite an energetic campaign in 2005, one likely to be remembered for the Conservatives' playing of the race and ethnicity card, electoral defeat led to his quick resignation. In December 2005, the Conservatives elected David Cameron as party leader in a landslide.

Cameron wasted little time in reorienting the party, modernizing its appeal, and reaching out beyond its traditional core values. He acknowledged that New Labour had been right in understanding the mood of Britain and right, also, to insist on achieving both social justice and economic success. Cameron promised to reduce poverty both in Britain and globally, take on climate change as a priority, and ensure security from terrorism. A testament to Blair's success, Cameron worked hard to reposition the Conservatives as a reforming more centrist party that could compete effectively with post-Blair New Labour across the economic and social spectrum.

## Liberal Democrats

Through the 1970s, the Liberal Party was the only centrist challenger to the Labour and Conservative parties. Since the 1980s, a changing roster of centrist parties posed an increasingly significant threat to the two-party dominance of Conservative and Labour. In 1981, the Social Democratic Party (SDP) formed out of a split within the Labour Party. After the Conservative victory in 1987, the Liberal Party and most of the SDP merged to form the Social and Liberal Democratic Party (now called the Liberal Democrats or Lib Dems), which quickly emerged as a major political player.

In the 2001 general election the party increased its vote tally by nearly one-fifth and won fifty-two seats, the most since 1929. This success positioned the party as a potentially powerful center-left critic of New Labour. That said, at least until Blair's fortunes declined, Labour did not make it easy for them. As the Blair government began to spend massively to improve education and health care—an approach that would come to haunt them later—it narrowed the range of policy issues on which the Liberal Democrats could challenge New Labour. Party leader Charles Kennedy won the political gamble in spring 2003 by opposing the war in Iraq. But it was not easy to take electoral advantage of Blair's political weakness. For a time, the fortunes of the Liberal Dems declined. In December 2007, after two leadership turnovers, Nick Clegg, a 40-year old ex-journalist and former member of the European Parliament took over leadership of the Liberal Democrats. Clegg and his party faced an uphill battle to make the Lib Dems a serious contender in time for the 2010 election. But the country's fatigue with New Labour, post-9/11 and post-7/7 concerns about the erosion of civil liberties that played to the party's strength, and Clegg's energetic and confident leadership—in fall 2008 Clegg launched a campaign to knock on one million doors to connect with ordinary citizens—quickly catapulted the Liberal Democrats into serious contention.

# Elections

British general elections are exclusively for seats in the House of Commons. The prime minister is not directly elected as prime minister but as a member of Parliament (MP) from a single constituency (electoral district). The Queen invites the leader of the party that can control a majority in the Commons to become prime minister. Constituencies vary widely in size, but the average number of voters remain roughly comparable. (In the 2010 election, the average number of voters in each constituency was roughly 68,000.)

Traditionally, Parliament had a maximum life of five years, with no fixed term. The 2010 coalition agreement proposed a fixed term of five years subject to dissolution by a 55 percent vote of members of parliament (MPs).

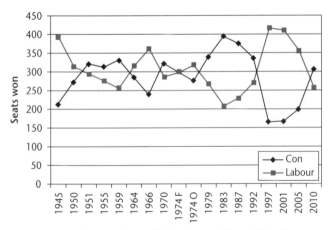

**FIGURE 2.6 Comparison of Number of Seats Won by Conservative versus Labour in UK General Elections from 1945 to 2010**

*Source:* House of Commons Research papers 08/12, 10/36. http://www.ukpolitical./ConvLab.htm.

## The Electoral System and the 2010 Election

Election for representatives in the Commons (members of Parliament, or MPs) is by a "first-past-the-post" principle in each constituency. In this single-member plurality system, the candidate who receives the most votes is elected. There is no requirement of a majority and no element of proportional representation (a system in which each party is given a percentage of seats in a representative assembly roughly comparable to its percentage of the popular vote).

This winner-take-all electoral system tends to exaggerate the size of the victory of the largest party and to reduce the influence of regionally dispersed lesser parties. This system is praised for increasing the chances that a party or coalition of parties will gain a majority of parliamentary seats and therefore form a stable government.

Critics of the electoral system charge that it does not give adequate representation to minority opinion.

Contrary to the typical tendency of the winner-take-all electoral system, the 2010 election resulted in a **hung parliament** (a situation after an election when no single party comprises a majority in the Commons). Only after a quick set of negotiations, could an arrangement be found to form a coalition government. Thus 2010 is one for the record books. On the one hand, it was the exception that proves the rule. Ordinarily Britain exhibits a stable two-party-dominant system (Conservative and Labour), with support for a third party (Liberal Democrat) spread widely across the country, but spread too thinly for the party to win a substantial number of seats. The Liberal Democrats needed an exceptional stroke of luck to buck the trend—and they got it in 2010. The campaign by the Tories peaked early, failed to inspire, and could not convince the electorate that they had the experience or were equipped to handle the enormous challenges of the economic downturn. With Blair fatigue, an unpopular successor in Gordon Brown, and a failing economy, New Labour never really stood a chance to win the election outright. The first televised debates ever in UK politics certainly enlivened the campaign. They also initially fueled a surge in popularity for the telegenic and media savvy Lib-Dem leader, Nick Clegg, who stole the show in the first debate. In fact, for a time, "Cleggmania" produced polls showing the Lib Dems with an unprecedented one-third of the electorate behind them. For a brief moment, Britain enjoyed the unlikely spectacle of a three-party contest, but one in which Labour never really had a chance.

With a two-party dominant party system, the UK electoral system tends to produce a stable single-party government. That observation seems less certain now than it did before 2010, but it will take more than one hung parliament to make observers think that the UK party system has been fundamentally transformed.

It is not clear whether the 2010 election returns signal the beginning of a critical realignment in the electoral system, but most observers recognize some grounds for improvement. For a start, the electoral system raises questions about representation and fairness. Like other winner-take-all systems, a close second place in a constituency (as in a U.S. electoral district) is simply a loss. The system reduces the competitiveness of smaller parties, like the Lib Dems, with diffuse pockets of support across the country.

In 2010 the Liberal Democrats with 23 percent of the vote won 57 seats. Labour with 29 percent of the vote won 258 seats. The Conservatives with 36.1 percent of the vote won 306 seats. Thus the Liberal Democrats achieved a share of the vote that was roughly two-thirds that of the Conservatives, but won roughly one-fifth of the seats won by the Tories. Such are the benefits of an electoral system to the victor (as well as the second major party).

Is there any wonder why more than anything else the Liberal Democrats want what neither major party would give them: A change in the electoral system to proportional representation (PR), where the number of seats allocated to parties in parliament would closely approximate the proportion of votes cast for a given party? PR would be a game changer, catapulting the Lib Dems into major party status and making them a potential kingmaker, tipping the balance in many close general elections to either the Conservatives or Labour. For that very reason, it is unlikely that such a fundamental change in the electoral system will be introduced any time soon. But parliamentary sovereignty means that any time there is a political will to change the electoral system, the electoral system can be changed by parliament.

PR seems very unlikely, but serious consideration is being given to a system called "The Alternative Vote" (AV), in which voters rank preferences among candidates. If no candidate receives a majority of first-preference votes, then second-preference

**hung parliament**

A situation after an election when no single party comprises a majority in the Commons.

votes of the candidate who finished last are redistributed, and the process is continued until a candidate achieves a majority. In fact, The Coalition Agreement calls for a Referendum Bill on electoral reform, which would introduce the Alternative Vote. It should come as no surprise, however, that the coalition partners are deeply divided on the system for electing MPs.

### Gender, Ethnicity, and Representation

The party and electoral systems contribute to the creation of a Parliament that has been and remains a bastion of white men, but it is becoming more diverse. The 2010 election produced a record number of ethnic minority MPs, with 27 elected, nearly double the number in 2005. Moreover there were a set of firsts: Labour's first Muslim female MP and first African MP; and for the Conservatives, their first Asian woman MP. Also a record percentage of women were elected in 2010 (21.5 percent, up from 19.8 percent in 2005). But this increase is hardly a surge, and in comparative terms the UK has a long way to go when it comes to women's representation: It ranks 73rd in the world in female representation. Despite the general trend of increased representation of women and minorities, they remain substantially underrepresented in Parliament.

### Trends in Electoral Behavior

Recent general elections have deepened geographic and regional fragmentation. British political scientist Ivor Crewe has referred to the emergence of two two-party systems: (1) Competition between the Conservative and Labour parties dominates contests in English urban and northern seats, and (2) Conservative-center party competition dominates England's rural and southern seats. A third two-party competition has emerged in Scotland, where Labour competes with the Scottish National Party.[9]

The national (that is regional) parties have challenged two-party dominance since the 1970s, but with only limited results. The Scottish National Party (SNP) was founded in 1934 and its Welsh counterpart, the Plaid Cymru, in 1925. The 2010 election showed the strength of Labour in Scotland, where it won 41 seats and 42 percent of the Scottish popular vote, an improvement over 2005. The Lib Dems came in a distant second with 11 seats, the Scottish National Party (SNP) won six seats. The election demonstrated once more that the Conservatives have very little traction in Scotland. They walked away with a single seat. In Wales, the Conservatives fared better, gaining five more seats than they had won in 2005 for a total of eight seats at Westminster. The Plaid Cymru won three seats, one more than in 2005. Although Labour lost four seats compared to 2005, they walked away with a very strong showing, winning 26 out of 40 seats. The results for Scotland and Wales likely indicate that devolution has weakened nationalist fervour.

## Political Culture, Citizenship, and Identity

In their study of the ideals and values that shape political behavior, political scientists Gabriel Almond and Sidney Verba wrote that the civic (or political) culture in Britain was characterized by trust, deference to authority, and pragmatism.[10] But the 1970s became a crucial turning point in British political culture and group identities that challenged this view.

During the 1970s, the long years of economic decline culminated in economic reversals in the standard of living for many Britons. Also for many, the historic bonds of occupational and social class grew weaker. Both union membership and popularity declined. At the same time, a growing number of conservative think tanks and mass-circulation newspapers worked hard to erode support for the welfare state. New social movements such as feminism, antinuclear activism, and environmentalism, challenged basic tenets of British political culture. Identities based on race and ethnicity, gender, and sexual orientation gained significance. These trends fragmented the political map and inspired a shift to the right.

Thatcher's ascent reflected these changes in political culture, identities, and values. Thatcherism rejected collectivism, the redistribution of resources from rich to poor, and state responsibility for full employment. It considered individual property rights more important than the social rights claimed by all citizens in the welfare state. Thatcherism set the stage in cultural terms for the new Labour consolidation of neoliberalism and the core political-cultural orientation in Britain.

## Social Class

A key change in political culture in the last quarter-century has been the weakening of bonds grounded in the experience of labor. During the Thatcher era, the traditional values of "an honest day's work for an honest day's pay" and solidarity among co-workers in industrial disputes were labelled "rigidities" that reduced productivity and competitiveness. New Labour continued to characterize social class as an impediment to competitiveness.

Being "tough on the unions" was a core premise of New Labour and a view that the Conservative-led coalition government has powerfully reinforced. Particularly in the context of the government's aggressive cuts in public spending, it looks like very tough days ahead for unions, particularly public sector unions, which have become a lightening rod, not only in the UK, but in the United States as well, for governments looking to cut budgets—and blame somebody for the need to make cuts. This process has contributed to a fundamental erosion of the ability of working people to improve their lot through collective bargaining or to exert influence over public policy through the political muscle of the trade union movement. Class still matters, but not in the dominating way that it shaped the nineteenth century or the collectivist era. Fewer workers belong to unions, and unions focus narrowly on enforcing individual legal rights in the workplace. Collective bargaining has been largely relegated to declining private sector industries and the public sector.[11] Strike rates in the UK have generally been below the average of both the OECD and the EU in recent decades, but intense opposition to the cuts introduced by the coalition government seems likely to reverse that trend with a vengeance.

## National Identity

Decolonization has created a multiethnic Britain. National identity has become especially complicated. Questions about fragmented sovereignty within the context of the EU, the commingled histories of four nations (England, Scotland, Wales, and Ireland/Northern Ireland), and the interplay of race and nationality have created doubts about British identity that run deep. Ethnicity, intra-UK territorial attachments, Europeanization, and globalization are complicating national identity. Can Britain foster a more inclusive sense of British identity?

Nearly 8 percent of the people who live in Britain are of African, African-Caribbean, or Asian descent. The authors of a landmark study of multiethnic Britain explained: "Many communities overlap; all affect and are affected by others. More and more people have multiple identities—they are Welsh Europeans, Pakistani Yorkshirewomen, Glaswegian Muslims, English Jews, and black British. Many enjoy this complexity but also experience conflicting loyalties."[12]

Despite many success stories, ethnic minority communities have experienced police insensitivity, problems in access to the best public housing, hate crimes, and accusations that they are not truly British if they do not root for the English cricket team. In addition, harsh criticism is directed at immigrants and asylum seekers. Since this criticism comes in the wake of intense scrutiny of the Muslim community after 9/11 and 7/7, it contributes to the alienation of the ethnic minority community, particularly among some groups of Muslim citizens. Ordinary law-abiding Muslims have experienced intensified mistrust and intimidation. But it is also true that Muslim university graduates are assuming leading roles in the professions and that dozens of Muslim city councillors have been elected across the country.

## Interests, Social Movements, and Protests

In recent years, partly in response to globalization, political protest has been on the rise. Protesters demand more accountability and transparency in the operations of powerful international trade and development agencies. For example, in 1999 London became the site of protests timed to correspond with the Seattle meeting of the World Trade Organization (WTO). The London demonstration generated some 100,000 protesters.

The intensity of environmental activism has taken off with the growing attention to genetically modified (GM) crops in the late 1990s. In November 1999, the government announced a ban on commercially grown GM crops in Britain.

A quite different kind of activism spread to the countryside among a population not usually known for political protest. Farmers had been badly hurt by the "mad cow disease" crisis in 1996 and saw an urban bias at play in New Labour and the growing threat to fox hunting. They launched massive protests, and, even after a law banning the hunt went into effect in 2005, they kept up the heat with legal challenges.

A series of antiwar rallies were held in London before the UK and the United States launched the Iraq war. In September 2002, a huge protest rally was organized in London, led by the Stop the War Coalition and the Muslim Association of Britain. Both within the United Kingdom and among observers of British politics and society, many still endorse the view that British culture is characterized by pragmatism, trust, and deference to authority. This may be true, but the persistence of a wide range of protest movements, including reverberating protests in 2011 against the very significant cuts introduced by the Conservative–Liberal Democrat coalition government qualifies this story. As the opening vignette for this chapter reveals on any given day the British are even capable of out-protesting the French!

### Summary

When we look at representation and participation in Britain we see very clearly that there is much flux, uncertainty, and room for improvement. In institutional terms the declining sovereignty of parliament leaves open the prospect of excessive power in the cabinet and the office of the prime minister.

It is not easy for Britons across national, ethnic, gender, and class distinctions to preserve a sense of shared fates and common heritage. The divisions are reflected in the upsurge of protests across the political spectrum. Things are more unsettled in Britain than people have come to expect. People in the UK are experiencing a rare level of uncertainty which has been acutely focused by a severe erosion in its economic fortunes and which coincides with what for Britain must be considered unusual political and constitutional volatility.

# BRITISH POLITICS IN TRANSITION

On July 7, 2005, four British suicide bombers, all Muslims, detonated a set of coordinated attacks on the London transport system during morning rush hour. Three bombs went off in quick succession on the London underground (subway) and one, an hour later, on a double-decker bus nearby. Fifty-six people were killed including the al-Qaeda–linked suicide bombers, and some 700 people were injured. The mayor and most inhabitants of the city, often invoking imagery of stoic Londoners withstanding the German blitz during World War II, remained calm and determined in the face of these devastating attacks. They insisted that London would remain an open and cosmopolitan city as it had been for centuries. And then the other shoe dropped.

Two weeks after 7/7, an entirely innocent Brazilian electrician, unconnected to the bombings, was shot dead by police who were under enormous pressure to prevent further attacks and mistakenly considered him responsible for the suicide attacks. The victim was travelling from his apartment to a job in Northwest London when he was killed. He was chased into a London subway station by roughly twenty police officers, where he was cornered, tripped, and shot seven times in the head and once in the shoulder. He was wearing a thick coat that, in the jittery aftermath of 7/7, raised suspicions that he might be hiding a suicide belt. He ran from the police when ordered to stop. A Brazilian could be mistaken for a person of Pakistani or Jamaican or Middle Eastern descent, as were the 7/7 bombers. Coming on the heals of 7/7, this tragic accident underscores how tense everyone is about security from terror attack and how race and ethnicity probably blinded even well-trained police officers into making an awful mistake.

## Focus Questions

Can Britain resolve the tension over national identity?

Will the center hold?

How well is Britain's ancient political system adjusting to contemporary challenges?

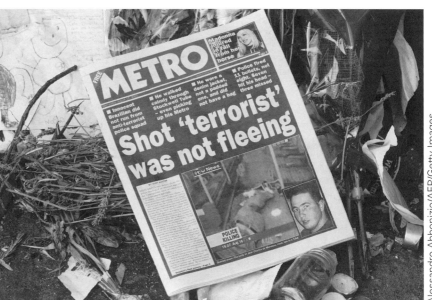

The murder of an innocent Brazilian electrician by police officers shortly after 7/7 raised new and troubling questions about security and about ethnic and racial tension in Britain.

Alessandro Abbonizio/AFP/Getty Images

# Political Challenges and Changing Agendas

As our democratic idea theme suggests, no democracy, however secure it may be, is a finished project. Even in Britain, with its centuries-old constitutional settlement and secure institutional framework, issues about democratic governance and citizens' participation remain unresolved.

## Constitutional Reform

Questions about the role of the monarchy and the House of Lords have long been simmering on Britain's political agenda. Why should the House of Commons share sovereignty with the House of Lords? What is the role of the monarchy—a very expensive institution and one subject to periodic scandals—in a modern political system? In addition, the balance of power among constitutionally critical institutions raises important questions about a democratic deficit at the heart of the Westminster model. Britain's executive easily overpowers parliament. Its strength in relation to the legislature may be greater than in any other democracy. Add to these concerns the prime minister's tendency to bypass the cabinet on crucial decisions and the bias in the electoral system that privileges the two dominant parties. Consider how tumultuous and volatile the contemporary political moment in Britain has become. The British have very little experience with coalition governments, and yet they presently have one. Moreover, not only is the capacity of the party system to produce the familiar one-party leadership in doubt, but the electoral system is under scrutiny and subject to potential change. The May 2011 referendum on the voting system—a key element in the coalition agreement—produced a decisive vote to preserve the UK's current system for electing MP's, but managed to upset the apple cart anyway. The Labour leader, Ed Miliband, who supported the "Alternative Vote" system was chastened by its resounding defeat by the electorate, and by losses in Scotland in local government elections. But the outcome was even worse for Liberal Democrat leader, Nick Clegg, for whom electoral reform was a calling card issue and a key part of the Liberal Democrat rationale for joining the coalition government. As the dust settled on the referendum on the UK voting system, held on the same day as local elections throughout the UK, the fate of Clegg and the ultimate future of the coalition remained uncertain.

## Identities in Flux

The relatively small scale of the ethnic minority community limits the political impact of the most divisive issues concerning collective identities. It is probably in this area that rigidities in the British political system most severely challenge principles of democracy and tolerance. Given Britain's single-member, simple-plurality electoral system, and no proportional representation, minority representation in Parliament remains very low. There are deep-seated social attitudes that no government can easily transform.

   The issues of immigration, refugees, and asylum still inspire a fear of multiculturalism among white Britons. Since the London bombings by British Muslims on 7/7 that killed 56 people, intense scrutiny has been focused on the Muslim community, which faces endless finger pointing and harassment. According to police, the number of hate crimes primarily affecting Muslims soared 600 percent in the weeks after the bombings. Then, in 2007, Salman Rushdie, whose book, *The Satanic Verses,* had offended many Muslims around the world and forced him into hiding in the face of a formal death threat from Iranian religious leaders, was knighted by the Queen. The honor accorded Rushdie was widely held to be an affront to the Muslim community in Britain. There is increasing concern across the political spectrum that Britain needs to find a way to deepen the ties of shared political culture and values that hold society together as well as to ensure security.

But finger pointing at the Muslim community has intensified since 9/11 and 7/7, and positions are hardening against multiculturalism. In February 2011, Prime Minister Cameron explicitly challenged the longstanding cross-party support for multiculturalism at a high-visibility security conference in Munich. Cameron condemned a culture of "hands-off" tolerance in the UK and in Europe. He criticized immigrants, and particularly Muslims (whom he seemed to define as immigrants whatever their immigration status) for leading lives apart from mainstream society. In strong terms, he warned of the dangers of multicultural policy, which made it possible for Islamic militants to radicalize Muslim youth, some of whom were likely to become terrorists. And he concluded that Europe had to defeat terrorism at home, not exclusively by the use of force elsewhere, for example, in Afghanistan.

# British Politics, Terrorism, and Britain's Relationship with the United States and the Rest of the World

In the immediate aftermath of the terror attacks on the United States, Blair's decisive support for President Bush struck a resonant chord in both countries and boosted Britain's influence in Europe. But by the spring and summer of 2002, Blair's stalwart alliance with Bush was looking more and more like a liability.

As Britons' instinctive support for America after September 11 faded, many wondered whether Tony Blair had boxed himself into a corner by aligning himself too closely with George W. Bush, without knowing where the president's foreign policy initiatives might lead in the Middle East and Asia. Yet Blair persevered in his staunch support for Bush's decision to go to war—despite Blair's strong preference for explicit Security Council authorization for the use of force and his strong preference that significant progress in resolving the Israeli-Palestinian dispute be made before any military intervention to topple the Saddam Hussein regime.

Blair refused all advice to make support of the war conditional on achievement of these ends. Blair was convinced that the threats of weapons of mass destruction (WMDs), Al Qaeda terrorism, and rogue states justified the invasion of Iraq and that Britain should and must support the United States in its leadership of a global war against terrorism. Despite initial denials by the prime minister, most Britons instinctively drew a connection between the war in Iraq and the bombs that exploded in London on 7/7.

Tony Blair came to office as a modernizer offering a "third way" alternative to the tired Tory and Old Labour recipes for governing the economy. But he left office likely to be remembered most (especially in America) for his foreign policy. Gordon Brown tried to distinguish his premiership from Blair's in this regard, by providing an accelerated schedule for withdrawing British troops from Iraq and through his key foreign policy appointments. Brown appointed Mark Malloch Brown, a vociferous critic of the UK's role in the war in Iraq as a high-profile minister with broad international affairs responsibilities. More importantly, Brown appointed David Miliband as foreign minister, a young rising star in the party known to have reservations about aspects of Blair's policy in the Middle East. Brown quickly made clear that useful lessons could be learned from the experience of the war in Iraq, leaving few in doubt that he would

# GLOBAL CONNECTION

## Britain and the Legacies of Empire

At its height during the reign of Queen Victoria (1837–1901), the British Empire encompassed fully one-quarter of the world's population and exerted direct colonial rule over some four-dozen countries scattered across the globe. In a stunning reversal of Britain's global status and fortunes, the empire fell apart in the half-century of decolonization between the independence of India in 1947 and the return of Hong Kong to China in 1997. Apart from a few scattered dependencies, the sun finally set on the British Empire, but the legacies of empire lived on to shape its relationship to the world of states in important ways.

The end of Empire did not bring the end of great power aspirations for Britain, but it shifted the emphasis as the British role in the world of states has been shaped by its determination to view its **"special relationship"** with the United States even at the expense of a full commitment to economic integration with and leadership in the European Union.

With the end of Empire it was inevitable that the special relationship between the UK and the United States would become a relationship between unequal partners. As a result, U.S. interests have tended to exert a tremendous magnetic pull on British foreign policy, to the relative neglect of European partnerships and broader international influences.

Before 9/11 New Labour stood for a coherent and progressive foreign policy framework, one that linked globalization to a growing UK commitment to narrow the development gap and in the words of Robin Cook, Blair's first foreign secretary, "to be a force for good" in the world. The Kosovo War created the context for Blair's explicit linkage of globalization with foreign and security policy.

Blair's "doctrine of international community" gave new weight to the notion of global interdependence by asserting a responsibility to use military force when necessary to achieve humanitarian objectives and contain catastrophic human rights abuses. This doctrine, as well as Blair's Atlanticist leanings, conditioned his response to 9/11 and subsequently his determination to bring the UK into the war in Iraq.

Instinctively, Tony Blair recognized the need (as he himself put it) to "stand shoulder to shoulder" with the United States, thus cementing his privileged relationship with George W. Bush and raising his international profile. In the days immediately after the terror attacks of September 2001, Blair played an important role in tamping down fears that 9/11 was demonstrating the validity of Samuel Huntington's "clash of civilizations" thesis.[13] Blair made clear that Al-Qaeda did not represent Islam and expressed his belief in a liberal and multicultural Britain in which the government had no concerns about the allegiance of Muslims.

But in the days following 9/11, the powerful attraction of the Atlantic Alliance, with Blair's distinctive inflections, took an irresistible hold over British foreign policy. At this critical juncture, several elements came together to forge the decision to support the US administration, even when the venue of the war on terror changed from Afghanistan to Iraq:

1. A fear that if the United States were left to fight the war on terror by itself, then unilateralist forces in Washington would be strengthened, and the world would be worse off.[14]
2. Blair's conviction that Iraq should be understood, like Kosovo, as an exercise in humanitarian intervention to save Muslims from catastrophic human rights abuses.[15]
3. A particular reading of the special relationship that made it imperative that the UK support the U.S. war in Iraq, viewing it as a necessary part of the global war on terror.

In Blair's doctrine of international community, the reverberations of empire were unmistakable. The civilizing mission of empire and the right of the metropolitan power to use force against the weaker dependent or failed states were both understood as an exercise of humanitarian intervention. And the use of force, however it was justified, represented an exercise in great power politics. How will the Conservative–Liberal government under the leadership of David Cameron recast the UK's role in the world of states? It seems likely that the Liberal Democrats will be more inclined to align British interests with Europe, while the Tories will remain in the Eurosceptic camp, aloof from further integration with Europe, especially so long as many of the European economies remain troubled. Perhaps to allay European concerns as well as that of his coalition partners, Cameron's first trip abroad as prime minister was to Paris and Berlin. Equally revealing, to emphasize his concerns about security, Afghani president Hamid Karzai was the first foreign leader to meet Cameron as prime minister, and at a joint press conference with Karzai at the White House, President Obama was quick to confirm "the extraordinary special relationship between the United States and Great Britain." As a sign of the times and the shifting power among British allies, Cameron has also made clear that he regards a "new special relationship with India" as a critical element in UK foreign relations and trade policy. With a proliferation of "special relationships" it may be time to wonder if the U.S. is still the UK's BFF (Best Friends Forever) or just one of several special relationships.

be reluctant to repeat such an exercise anytime soon. And in the early going, Cameron tried hard to recalibrate the special relationship by broadening its meaning to extend beyond its historic U.S.-UK definition to include other key allies and critical trading partners with special historic ties to the UK, for example India.

**special relationship**

Refers to relations between the United States and Britain and is meant to convey not only the largely positive, mutually beneficial nature of the relationship but also the common heritage and shared values of the two countries.

# British Politics in Comparative Perspective

Until the Asian financial crisis that began in 1997, it was an axiom of comparative politics that economic success required a style of economic governance that Britain lacks. Many argued that innovation and competitiveness in the new global economy required the strategic coordination of the economy by an interventionist state. But the United Kingdom escaped the recession that plagued the rest of Europe for much of the 1990s. Britain also outperformed most major world economies until the "Great Recession" of 2008 signalled a decisive downturn in Britain's economic fortunes.

In many countries throughout the world, politicians have been looking for an economic model that can sustain competitiveness while improving the plight of the socially excluded. For this reason, New Labour's third way—a political orientation designed to transcend left and right in favor of practical and effective policies—was carefully watched for more than ten years. Observers saw in New Labour a historic intellectual and political realignment, not only in Britain, but in Clinton's America and Cardoso's (and later Lula's) Brazil. Ten years is a very long time in politics, and for ten years it looked as if New Labour had found a way to mould a new political orientation that combined a sophisticated approach to competitiveness in the global economy with a pragmatic anti-ideological approach to governance. But in time, the bloom most decidedly came off the rose of New Labour, which could never recover from the war in Iraq. The electorate grew tired of Blair and never warmed up to Brown. When the financial and economic crisis struck in 2008, Britain was among the hardest hit of the core European economies. With the decline of its economic model, its refusal to participate in the Eurozone, unresolved legacies of empire, and its surprising constitutional uncertainty, it is fair to say that in comparative perspective the UK has joined the pack of middle-level European powers and, like its counterparts, faces daunting challenges across all of the four themes that frame our analysis of comparative politics.

## Summary

Since 2008, Britain has been facing daunting challenges. Almost inevitably, economic downturn produces political challenges, but it also creates opportunities for change and renewal. A new generation of untested leadership in all the major political parties and, most importantly, at the helm of the coalition government will produce new political challenges, innovative policy directions, new approaches to solving old problems, and occasional policy U-turns. Will the coalition hold or will the strains and challenges of governing shatter the coalition of convenience between the Conservatives and Liberal Democrats? Across the globe, many electorates are asking for effective pragmatic leadership in hard times. If the UK's coalition government, which came to office almost by accident and in very difficult times, stays intact and effectively manages from the center, it may last long enough to benefit both from the resourcefulness of an electorate and a country that is not easily daunted and from a rising economic tide. If that happens, it may build on the New Labour legacy of government judged on effectiveness, not ideology, and enjoy a long run in office. If not, the British distaste for coalition government will be confirmed.

## Key Terms

| | | |
|---|---|---|
| Industrial Revolution | Keynsianism | fusion of powers |
| hegemonic power | monetarism | cabinet government |
| welfare state | foreign direct investment | constitutional monarchy |
| laissez-faire | gender gap | quangos |
| Westminster model | parliamentary sovereignty | judicial review |
| neoliberalism | parliamentary democracy | hung parliament |
| macroeconomic policy | unitary state | special relationship |

## Suggested Readings

Beer, Samuel H. *Britain Against Itself: The Political Contradictions of Collectivism*. New York: Norton, 1982.

Brown, Gordon. *Beyond the Crash: Overcoming the First Crisis of Globalization* New York: Free Press, 2010.

Coates, David. *Prolonged Labour*. London: Palgrave/Macmillan, 2005.

Coates, David, and Joel Krieger. *Blair's War*. Cambridge, UK, and Malden Mass.: Polity Press, 2004.

Coates, David, and Peter Lawler, eds. *New Labour in Power*. Manchester: Manchester University Press, 2000.

Cook, Robin. *The Point of Departure*. London: Simon & Schuster, 2003.

Cronin, James E. *New Labour's Pasts*. Harrow, UK: Pearson Longman, 2004.

Driver, Stephen, and Luke Martell. *New Labour*, 3rd ed. Cambridge: Polity, 2006.

Dunleavy, Patrick, et al. *Developments in British Politics 7*. New York: Palgrave/Macmillan, 2003.

Elliott, Francis, and James Hanning. *Cameron: The Rise of the New Conservative*. Harper: 2009.

Gamble, Andrew. *Between Europe and America: The Future of British Politics*. London: Palgrave/Macmillan, 2003.

George, Bruce. *The British Labour Party and Defense*. New York: Praeger, 1991.

Giddens, Anthony. *The Third Way: The Renewal of Social Democracy*. Cambridge: Polity Press, 1998.

Gilroy, Paul. *"There Ain't No Black in the Union Jack": The Cultural Politics of Race and Nation*. Chicago: University of Chicago Press, 1991.

Hall, Stuart, and Martin, Jacques, eds. *The Politics of Thatcherism*. London: Lawrence and Wishart, 1983.

Hobsbawm, E. J. *Industry and Empire*. Harmondsworth, UK: Penguin/Pelican, 1983.

Howell, Chris. *Trade Unions and the State: The Construction of Industrial Relations Institutions in Britain, 1890–2000*. Princeton: Princeton University Press, 2005.

Jones, Bill, and Philip Norton. *Politics UK*, 7th ed., Essex, UK: Pearson, 2010.

Kampfner, John. *Blair's Wars*. London: Free Press, 2003.

Kavenagh, Dennis, and Anthony Seldon. *The Powers Behind the Prime Minister: The Hidden Influence of Number Ten*. London: Harper-Collins, 1999.

Keegan, William. *The Prudence of Mr Gordon Brown*. Chichester: John Wiley & Sons, 2004.

Krieger, Joel. *British Politics in the Global Age. Can Social Democracy Survive?* New York: Oxford University Press, 1999.

Krieger, Joel. *Globalization and State Power*. New York: Pearson Longman, 2005.

Landes, David S. *The Unbound Prometheus: Technological Change and Industrial Development in Western Europe from 1750 to the Present*. Cambridge: Cambridge University Press, 1969.

Lewis, Jane, and Rebecca Surrender, eds. *Welfare State Change: Towards a Third Way?* Oxford: Oxford University Press, 2004.

Lewis, Philip. *Islamic Britain: Religion, Politics and Identity among British Muslims*. London and New York: I. B. Taurus, 2002.

Marsh, David, et al. *Postwar British Politics in Perspective*. Cambridge: Polity Press, 1999.

Marshall, Geoffrey. *Ministerial Responsibility*. Oxford: Oxford University Press, 1989.

Middlemas, Keith. *Politics in Industrial Society: The Experience of the British System Since 1911*. London: André Deutsch, 1979.

Modood, Tariq. *Multicultural Politics: Racism, Ethnicity, and Muslims in Britain*. Minneapolis: University of Minnesota Press, 2005.

Norton, Philip. *The British Polity*, 5th ed. New York: Longman, 2011.

Parekh, Bhiku, et al., *The Future of Multi-Ethnic Britain: The Parekh Report*. London: Profile Books, 2000.

Riddell, Peter. *The Thatcher Decade*. Oxford: Basil Blackwell, 1989.

Särlvik, Bo, and Ivor Crewe. *Decade of Dealignment: The Conservative Victory of 1979 and Electoral Trends in the 1970s*. Cambridge: Cambridge University Press, 1983.

Seldon, Anthony, and Dennis Kavanagh, eds. *The Blair Effect 2001–5*. Cambridge: Cambridge University Press, 2005.

Shaw, Eric. *The Labour Party since 1945*. Oxford: Blackwell Publishers, 1996.

Thompson, E. P. *The Making of the English Working Class*. New York: Vintage, 1966.

Thompson, Noel. *Political Economy and the Labour Party*, 2nd ed. London and New York: Routledge, 2006.

## Suggested Websites

**The official UK Government website**
**www.direct.gov.uk**

The UK Parliament
**www.parliament.uk**

BBC
**www.bbc.co.uk**

The UK cabinet office
**www.cabinet-office.gov.uk**

Ipsos-Market & Opinion Research International (Mori)
Britain's leading polling organization
**http://www.ipsos-mori.com/**

The Scottish Parliament
**www.scottish.parliament.uk**

The Welsh Assembly Government
**http://wales.gov.uk/**

# 3 France

Mark Kesselman

**Official Name:** French Republic (*République Française*)

**Location:** Western Europe

**Capital City:** Paris

**Population (2007):** 63.7 million

**Size:** 634,427 sq. km.; slightly smaller than Texas

**Until 1789**
Ancien régime (Bourbon monarchy)

**1800–1814**
Consulate and First Empire (Napoleon Bonaparte)

**1814–1830**
Restoration

**1852–1870**
Second Empire
(Louis Napoleon)

**1871**
Paris Commune

| 1700 | 1780 | 1800 | 1820 | 1840 | 1860 | 1880 |
|------|------|------|------|------|------|------|

**1789–1799**
Revolutionary regimes
Constituent Assembly, 1789–1791
(Declaration of Rights of Man, Aug. 26, 1789)
Legislative, 1791; Convention, 1792–1795:
Monarchy abolished and First Republic
established, 1792; Directory, 1795–1799

**1830–1848**
July Monarchy

**1871–1940**
Third Republic

**1848–1851**
Second Republic

# SECTION 1

# THE MAKING OF THE MODERN FRENCH STATE

## Politics in Action

**Focus Question**

What are two distinctive features of French history that have led social scientists to speak of French exceptionalism?

**fundamentalism**

A term recently popularized to describe extremist religious movements throughout the world.

In the last decade, two laws passed by the French parliament involving a dress code for Muslim women have highlighted important issues in current French politics and culture. In 2004, parliament banned the display of "conspicuous signs of religious affiliation" in public schools. The prohibition applied to wearing the Jewish *yarmulke* (skullcap) and large Catholic crosses. But the main purpose of the law was to ban the *hidjab* (headscarf— or *foulard*, in French). According to official estimates, only about 1,250 of nearly 1 million Muslim schoolgirls wore the headscarf to school.[1] Just the same, the government announced that the law was necessary to preserve religious neutrality in public schools and to combat Muslim **fundamentalism**. Historian Joan Scott comments that the policy reflected "the impotence and/or unwillingness of the government to…adjust national institutions and ideologies…to the heterogeneity of [France's] current population…."[2]

In 2010, parliament went even further. Women were prohibited from wearing garments that concealed the face when they appeared in streets, parks, businesses, government buildings, and on public transportation. An overwhelming majority of legislators voted for the law, and a public opinion poll found that over 80 percent of the French supported the measure.

The principal targets of the law were the *burqa*, the head-to-toe garment worn by some Muslim women, and the *niqab*, that covers most of the face. According to a police report, only about 2,000 of France's over one million Muslim women are veiled. However, supporters claimed that the ban was needed to preserve women's independence and protect republican secular values. President Sarkozy declared, "The *burqa* is not welcome in France because it is contrary to our values and contrary to the ideals we have of a woman's dignity."

The fact that the French government imposed a national dress code reveals insecurity about French national identity and the relation of Islam to traditional

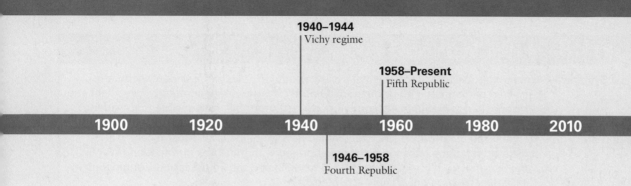

French culture and values. Further, the government's action illustrates the state's wide scope for regulating personal relations. In the United States, Congress could not legislate in this fashion because it would be considered a violation of citizens' personal rights.

## Geographic Setting

France is among the world's favored countries, thanks to its temperate climate, large and fertile land area, rich culture, and prosperous economy. Its natural beauty, superb architecture, culture, and cuisine make France the most popular tourist destination in the world.

France occupies a key strategic position in Europe. It borders the Mediterranean Sea in the south and shares borders with Belgium, Switzerland, and Germany on the north and east. Spain lies to the southwest, Italy to the southeast. With a population over 63 million, France is among the most populous countries in Western Europe. But its large area—211,000 square miles—means that population density is low (about half that of Britain, Germany, and Italy).

France has a modern and productive economy. Most people work in the industrial and service sectors. No other French city rivals Paris, the capital, in size and influence. In fact, Lille, Lyon, and Marseille are the only other large cities. In 2009, the country's gross domestic product (GDP) was just over $2 trillion and per capita income was $32,600. Most apartments and homes are equipped with modern kitchen appliances, one or more television receivers, and a line telephone. Nearly everyone has a cell phone, and most people have access to personal computers and the Internet. France ranked fourteenth among 169 countries of the world in the 2010 United Nations Development Programme's Human Development Index.

France enjoys great regional and cultural diversity, which makes the country vibrant and interesting but also prone to conflict. The French have a proverbial reputation for being argumentative. Charles de Gaulle, an influential twentieth-century leader who will be described below, remarked on the impossibility of governing a country that produces over 300 varieties of cheese! The French have a well-earned reputation for being critical—both of others and themselves. For example, a survey examining citizen happiness around the world reported that France ranks 64th out of 178 countries, compared to the United States (23rd), Germany (35th), and Britain (42nd).[3]

| Table 3.1 | Political Organization |
|---|---|
| **Political System** | Unitary republic. Semipresidential system; popularly elected president, popularly elected parliament, and prime minister and government appointed by president and responsible to National Assembly (as well as informally responsible to president). |
| **Regime History** | Frequent regime changes since the French Revolution of 1789. Most recently, a dictatorial regime based in Vichy collaborated with the Nazis during World War II; the Fourth Republic existed from 1946 to 1958; and the Fifth Republic, originating in 1958, has become universally accepted. |
| **Administrative Structure** | Unitary, with 22 mainland and five overseas regions; and 96 mainland and 5 overseas departments (as of 2011). |
| **Executive** | Dual executive: president (five-year term); PM appointed by president, generally leader of majority coalition in National Assembly, and responsible to National Assembly (as well as informally responsible to president). |
| **Legislature** | Bicameral. Senate (upper house) has power to delay legislation passed by lower house and to veto proposed constitutional amendments. National Assembly (lower house) can pass legislation and force government to resign by passing a censure motion. |
| **Judiciary** | A system of administrative, criminal, and civil courts. At the top, a nine-member independent Constitutional Council named for nonrenewable nine-year terms; president of republic names three members, president of each house of parliament names three. The Constitutional Council exercises right of judicial review. |
| **Party System** | Multiparty. Principal parties: Union for a Popular Movement (UMP); Socialist Party (PS); minor parties: National Front (FN); Communist Party (PCF); Green Party; many others throughout the political spectrum. |

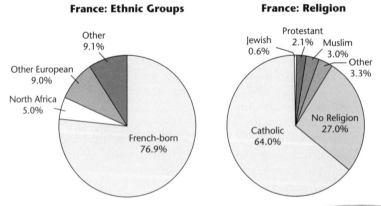

**France: Ethnic Groups**

Other 9.1%
Other European 9.0%
North Africa 5.0%
French-born 76.9%

**France: Religion**

Jewish 0.6%
Protestant 2.1%
Muslim 3.0%
Other 3.3%
No Religion 27.0%
Catholic 64.0%

**French Currency**
Euro (€)
International Designation: EUR
Exchange Rate (2010): US$1 = .755 EUR
100 Euro Note Design:
Baroque/Rococo style (the 17th and 18th century) arch

© Iurii Konoval/Shutterstock.com

FIGURE 3.1 **The French Nation at a Glance**

# Critical Junctures

## Creating Modern France

A convenient place to begin a survey of French history is with Charlemagne, who became Holy Roman emperor in 800 CE and dominated much of Western Europe, including present-day France. Following his death in 814, the empire disintegrated. Norsemen from Scandinavia established a duchy in Normandy, in northwest France. One of their rulers, William the Conqueror, invaded England in 1066 and defeated English troops at the Battle of Hastings. During the following centuries, French monarchs struggled to subdue powerful provincial leaders and regions within present-day France. Challenges came from outside and inside France's present boundaries. For example, the English invaded and nearly conquered the country during the Hundred Years' War (1337–1453). Joan of Arc, a peasant who believed she had a divine mission, led French forces to victory against the English army. Joan, however, was captured and burned at the stake. She remains a symbol of intense national pride.

During the sixteenth century, France was violently divided by a civil war called the Wars of Religion, which pitted Catholics against Protestants. Henry IV helped end religious strife, in part, by issuing the Edict of Nantes in 1598 that granted Protestants religious liberty. However, the bitter memory of religious conflict may help explain why the French became far more committed to **secularism** than was the case for neighboring countries.

The seventeenth, eighteenth, and early nineteenth centuries were the high point of France's economic, military, and cultural influence. France was the richest and most powerful country in continental Europe as well as Europe's artistic and scientific capital. In the eighteenth century, it was the center of the Enlightenment, the philosophical movement that emphasized the importance of scientific reason rather than religious belief or folk wisdom.

## The Ancien Régime

A turning point in the struggle between French monarchs and provincial rulers came when Louis XIV (r. 1643–1715) sponsored the creation of a relatively efficient state bureaucracy. Historian James Collins suggests that Louis XIV created the "mature monarchical state."[4] France began to be centrally administered by state agents, some of whom directed administrative departments in Paris, while others were posted to the provinces. The same legal code began to be applied throughout France.

Political stability involved an informal agreement between the monarchy and powerful landholding nobility. In return for the support that nobles provided to the monarchy, they were lightly taxed. The Catholic Church—a large landowner and tax collector in its own right—also enjoyed privileged status. On the other hand, Collins notes that the king "had to raise ever more money to feed his military...." The steep costs of foreign wars and the lavish lifestyle of the royal court stretched the monarchy's "financial capacity beyond its limits."[5] In response, Louis XIV and his successors levied high taxes on the rising middle classes—the most productive sectors of the economy—and on peasants and urban workers, who could least bear the burden. This complex patchwork of institutions was later described as the *ancien régime*, or old regime.

From the mid-seventeenth to the mid-eighteenth century, France was usually at war with its neighbors. Unfortunately for France, one of its main rivals—Britain—began to reap the benefits of the Agricultural and Industrial Revolutions while France's economy stagnated. In 1789, Louis XVI was forced to convene representative assemblies (the Estates General) that had not met for centuries in an attempt to raise taxes. By then, notes Collins, "The Old Regime had become so thoroughly antiquated, from local to regional to national government, that a revolution in all levels of government had to take place."[6] Louis XVI's decision to convene the Estates General backfired, for it only encouraged resistance to royal demands. On July 14, 1789, a Parisian crowd stormed the Bastille, a hated prison in the middle of Paris, and freed the prisoners. The event symbolized the crumbling of royal authority. Not long after, the monarchy and entire regime toppled.

## The Two Faces of the French Revolution, 1789–1815

The Revolution of 1789 was a *political* and a *national* **revolution**. It installed a **republic** to replace the French monarchy. This meant that political offices were supposed to be filled on the basis of individual talent rather than inheritance. It was an *international* revolution. It inspired national uprisings elsewhere in Europe, although they were often supported by French armed intervention. It was *liberal*. It championed individual liberty in the political and economic spheres, as well as secularism and

---

**secularism**

A doctrine that mandates maintaining a separation between church and state.

**ancien régime**

The monarchical regime that ruled France until the Revolution of 1789, when it was toppled by a popular uprising.

**revolution**

The process by which an established political regime is replaced (usually by force and with broad popular participation) and a new regime established that introduces radical changes throughout society.

**republic**

In contemporary usage, a political regime in which leaders are not chosen on the basis of their inherited background (as in a monarchy).

religious freedom. It was *democratic*. It proclaimed that all citizens have an equal right to participate in key political decisions.

The revolutionary regime proclaimed liberty, equality, and fraternity. But it treated opponents brutally, beheading many at the guillotine. The revolution's refusal to compromise and its hostility toward the Catholic Church, divided French society.

While the revolution toppled the *ancien régime*, it strengthened state institutions. Under the Emperor Napoleon Bonaparte, the brilliant revolutionary general who seized control of the state and ruled from 1799 to 1814, state institutions were created that survive to this day. For example, Napoleon created the system of administering the 101 *départements* that comprise present-day France. Each *département* is administered by a **prefect** appointed by the central government. Ever since the revolution, France has struggled to forge a satisfactory balance between state autonomy—the state's independence from groups within society—and democratic participation and decision making.

**prefect**

French administrators appointed by the minister of the interior to coordinate state agencies and programs within the 101 French departments or localities.

## Many Regimes, Slow Industrialization: 1815–1940

Following Napoleon's defeat in 1815, France embarked on a slow decline lasting through World War II. One problem was political instability. After 1815, France was ruled by a series of short-lived, ineffective regimes. The most durable was the Third Republic. Created after France's defeat in the Franco-Prussian War and a civil war that followed in 1871, it survived until France's defeat by Germany in World War II. The Third Republic involved an all-powerful parliament and weak executive—a sure-fire recipe to prevent decisive state action.

During the nineteenth century regimes came and went at a dizzying pace, but economic change in France was gradual. Unlike Germany, France somewhat defensively preferred the comfort of economic stability to the risk of modernization. In 1800 France was the world's second economic power behind Britain; by 1900 France trailed the United States, Great Britain, and Germany. The entrepreneurial spirit was relatively underdeveloped. French manufacturers excelled in custom-made luxury goods, like silk and porcelain. But these did not lend themselves to mechanized production. There were no mass markets for them. In addition, the French population grew quite slowly, which resulted in smaller demand and less incentive for businesses to invest.

State policies contribute to economic stability. Perhaps in order to counter political instability, the state shielded farmers, manufacturers, and artisans from foreign competition. France maintained some of the highest tariff barriers in Western Europe in the nineteenth and early twentieth centuries.

The state did promote economic modernization in some respects, however. In the 1860s, it organized an efficient rail network. The government also encouraged the formation of an investment bank to finance railroad development.

France's slow economic growth, internal divisions, and poor planning during the 1930s, when Hitler's Germany was rearming, help explain France's humiliating defeat by Germany in 1940—the second time in less than a century. (The first time was in 1870, when France lost the Franco-Prussian War.) Further, although France was on the winning side in World War I, it suffered immense losses of people and property.

## Vichy France (1940–1944) and the Fourth Republic (1946–1958)

When Germany overran France in 1940, Philippe Pétain, an aged World War I military hero was prime minister. He sealed the Third Republic's destruction and accepted France's defeat by signing an armistice with Hitler. France was divided into two. Germany occupied and directly administered the North. For several years, until Germany imposed direct rule throughout France, Pétain led a puppet state in central and southern France (often called the Vichy regime, since its capital was Vichy, a city in central France). The Vichy regime collaborated with the Nazis by repressing French opposition to Germany and sending French citizens to work in German factories. Most French passively accepted German domination. However, a handful of Communists, Socialists, and Catholic activists organized a resistance movement, at enormous personal risk to themselves.

Vichy was the only government not directly under German occupation that actively targeted Jews. It collaborated with the Nazi occupation forces to send 76,000 French and foreign Jews, including 12,000 children, to Nazi death camps.

In 1945, following the Nazi defeat, the first order of business was to create a political regime for newly independent France. Charles de Gaulle, a general who had opposed the Vichy regime and led the French Resistance movement, took the lead. He considered that France's moral decline and military defeat was due to the lack of effective political leadership. With the memory of the **authoritarian** Vichy regime still fresh, French citizens voted to reject de Gaulle's proposal to create a republic based on a strong executive. He abruptly retired from politics.

The Fourth Republic (1946–1958), created after de Gaulle's departure, embodied an extreme form of parliamentary rule and weak executive. As in the Third Republic, the constitution of the Fourth Republic delegated a near monopoly of power to parliaments. However, parliaments were often deadlocked because a large number of parties held seats. One reason was that elections to parliament were held on the basis of **proportional representation**, in which parties are awarded seats in proportion to the votes that they receive. This system compares with the single-member district, first-past-the-post system used in the United States and Britain, where the party with the most votes in a given district wins the seat in that district.

The single-member district system tends to favor larger parties and usually reduces the total number of parties represented in parliament. In the Fourth Republic, the large number of parties represented in parliament made it easier to assemble a majority to vote against the current government than to vote in support of the current government. As a result, governments were voted out of office about once every six months! The Fourth Republic did, however, help reverse a century of economic stagnation by promoting economic expansion and modernization.

Despite the waltz of governments, the Fourth Republic might have survived. However, it was toppled because of problems relating to its colonial empire. In the 1950s, the Fourth Republic was weakened by its decision to withdraw French forces from Vietnam when insurgent forces fought the army to a standstill. Even more damaging was the army's inability to crush a rebellion in Algeria, a large territory in North Africa that the French government considered part of mainland France. As the Algerian war dragged on, some French army officers feared that the government would negotiate a settlement with rebel forces. The officers threatened to direct their troops in Algeria to invade mainland France and topple the republic. The crisis ended when Charles de Gaulle came out of retirement and persuaded parliament to vote his return to power. Parliament also authorized him to scrap the Fourth Republic and replace it with a new regime based on strong executive leadership.

De Gaulle and his associates drafted a new constitution, and French voters overwhelmingly approved it in a **referendum** in 1958. The Fifth Republic has lasted ever since. Although occasionally shaken by crises, it is relatively stable and will probably prove to be the most durable regime in modern French history.

**authoritarian**

A system of rule in which power depends not on popular legitimacy but on the coercive force of the political authorities.

**proportional representation (PR)**

A system of political representation in which seats are allocated to parties within multimember constituencies, roughly in proportion to the votes each party receives.

**referendum**

An election in which citizens are asked to approve (or reject) a policy proposal.

## The Fifth Republic (1958 to the Present)

The Fourth Republic was all talk and no action. The Fifth Republic can be considered the reverse. Political leaders can act decisively—perhaps too decisively, many scholars believe—because the regime lacks strong mechanisms to hold leaders accountable.

After several years as president of the Fifth Republic, de Gaulle's high-handed governing style demonstrated what can happen when the opposition is not adequately represented within existing institutions. In May 1968, students and workers engaged in the largest general strike in Western European history. Although de Gaulle regained control of the situation, he was discredited and resigned the following year. No French president since then has rivaled de Gaulle's national and international standing.

The **conservative** forces that supported de Gaulle when he gained power in 1958 swept every election until 1981. However, economic stagnation and divisions among the ruling coalition during the 1970s enabled François Mitterrand, the opposition **Socialist** Party candidate, to win the 1981 presidential election. The peaceful transition that followed demonstrated that the political institutions of the Fifth Republic were sturdy enough to accommodate political alternation.

The Socialist government sponsored an ambitious array of reforms, including **decentralization**, expanded social benefits, and increased state control of the economy. The centerpiece was a state takeover of many industrial firms, banks, and insurance companies. Although the reforms produced important benefits, discussed in Section 2, they proved quite costly and generated intense opposition. When economic

**conservative**

The belief that existing political, social, and economic arrangements should be preserved.

**socialist**

The doctrine stating that the state should organize and direct the economy in order to promote equality and help low-income groups.

**decentralization**

Policies that aim to transfer some decision-making power from higher to lower levels of government.

Students and workers unite in a mass demonstration on the Left Bank of Paris, May 27, 1968.

*Source:* AP Images.

crisis loomed in 1983–1984, Mitterrand ordered a reversal. Since then, Socialist governments, along with the conservative governments that have alternated in power with the Socialists, have pursued market-friendly policies. The Socialist Party's right turn has contributed to reducing ideological passions between left and right that have divided France ever since the Revolution. But the 2002 presidential elections dramatically demonstrated that one cannot speak of an end to ideology in France.

### 2002: The Le Pen Bombshell

Beginning in 1981, there was frequent alternation in office between centrist governments of the center-left and the center-right. The 2002 presidential elections promised to again confirm the new centrism of French politics. Instead, the results revealed a deep and disturbing ideological fissure within French society that was not reflected in mainstream party competition.

French presidential elections are held according to a two-ballot system. Many candidates compete at the first ballot. If no candidate gains an absolute majority (over 50 percent)—the typical case—a runoff ballot between the two front-runners decides who will become president. When the 2002 election campaign opened, everyone expected that Lionel Jospin, the Socialist prime minister on the center-left, and Jacques Chirac, the conservative president on the center-right, would face off in the decisive runoff ballot. Chirac did come in first, as expected. However, to everyone's amazement far-right candidate Jean-Marie Le Pen, leader of the ultra-nationalist National Front party, nudged Jospin out for second place. This meant that Le Pen, not Jospin, would face Chirac in the runoff. Le Pen was a demagogue who targeted Muslim immigrants, Jews, and mainstream politicians.

Chirac trounced Le Pen in the second ballot. What swelled Chirac's victory was that he received the votes not only of citizens who had supported him in the first round but also those of Jospin supporters who reluctantly switched to Chirac in the runoff as the lesser evil. But the troubling results of the first round of voting in 2002 continue to be a troubling memory in French politics.

In 2007, another presidential election occurred. With the memory of Le Pen's success in 2002 still fresh, many more voters turned out than had voted in 2002.

*Le Monde's* cartoonist compares Le Pen's attack on Chirac and Jospin to the bombing of the twin towers of the World Trade Center.

*Source:* Courtesy Plantu, Cartoonists and Writers Syndicate, Cartoon Arts International, Inc., from *Le Monde*, April 23, 2002.

This time, Le Pen received only 10.5 percent of the first ballot vote and came in fourth. One reason for his poor showing was that Nicolas Sarkozy, the candidate from the mainstream center-right party, took a page out of Le Pen's play book by championing traditional conservative values and a crackdown on crime and undocumented immigrants. As a result, many former Le Pen supporters shifted to Sarkozy. It is doubtful whether repeating the themes that brought Sarkozy success in 2007 will enable him to gain re-election in 2012. Moreover, there was a good chance that Marine Le Pen, who had succeeded her father Jean-Marie Le Pen as head of National Front, would gain enough votes to participate in the runoff ballot.

## France after September 11

Since the terrorist attacks of September 11, 2001, France has been deeply involved in global conflicts. France has energetically targeted terrorism and supported the U.S. military action against Al Qaeda and the Taliban regime in Afghanistan in 2001, although it strongly opposed the U.S. invasion of Iraq in 2003. In 2011, it took the lead—ahead of the U.S.—in advocating military intervention in Libya to prevent Muammar el-Qaddafi's regime from slaughtering civilians.

France's relations with the United States have often been prickly. Indeed, anti-Americanism is an important element in French political culture shared by groups throughout the political spectrum.[7] For example, both as Resistance leader and first president of the Fifth Republic, Charles de Gaulle was notorious for opposing U.S. policies. However, President Sarkozy broke the mold. He was described in a secret U.S. diplomatic cable (leaked to the press by WikiLeaks in 2010) as "the most pro-American French president since World War II." When he lavishly praised the United States in a speech to a joint session of Congress, he was given a standing ovation. Although policy differences between France and the United States persist, a new era of cooperation began under Sarkozy's presidency.

## The French "Non"—Now or Forever?

France has traditionally been a leader seeking closer cooperation among European Union (EU) countries, the association seeking economic integration and political cooperation among the countries of Europe. Member states have greatly benefited from EU policies, including eliminating tariffs and investment restrictions among member countries, as well as EU-wide production standards that make it possible for European producers to benefit from economies of scale.

In 2005, France again took the lead—but this time in an opposite fashion. After two years of difficult negotiations, a commission had produced an EU constitution. It streamlined decision making, increased the influence of the European parliament, and created the offices of EU president and foreign minister. EU regulations require that all member states approve important changes in the EU structure. In a referendum on the EU constitution in May 2005, French voters soundly rejected it, stalling further EU integration. Many French, especially those out of work or in low-paying jobs, voted against the constitutional change because they blamed the EU for their difficult situation.

Soon after President Sarkozy was elected in 2007, he helped revive the process of European integration. Along with Chancellor Angela Merkel of Germany, he persuaded other EU member states to adopt a scaled-down version of the constitution. The Lisbon Treaty, as it is known, simplified EU decision making and created the office of EU president. However, France's membership in the EU proved a mixed blessing during the global economic crisis beginning in 2008. One example occurred in 2010 when Greece, a member of the EU and the Eurozone (the group of EU countries that share the currency known as the euro), threatened to default on its foreign debt. France took the lead in obtaining a bailout for Greece from the EU and the International Monetary Fund (IMF), an international financial institution. Although the move enabled Greece to avoid bankruptcy, it increased long-smoldering fears in France that membership in the EU was costly.

# Themes and Implications

## Historical Junctures and Political Themes

Analyzing the four themes that frame *Introduction to Comparative Politics* reveals dramatic changes and troubling questions about recent French politics.

**France in a World of States**  Although a middle-rank power, France is an important player on the world stage. It is one of the five permanent members of the UN Security Council. It has also developed nuclear weapons and sophisticated military technology. It is among the world's richest and most powerful countries.

The French state has helped the country adapt to global economic competition. In recent decades, the state promoted internationally acclaimed high-tech industrial projects. It is a world leader in telecommunications, aeronautics, and high-speed rail transport. It has led the European consortium that developed the Airbus wide-bodied airplane. France is at the forefront in developing relatively safe and cheap nuclear power. (Three quarters of all French electricity is generated by nuclear power.) The pattern of state economic guidance that prevailed in France since the end of World War II has been called **statism**. However, international economic competition, EU and other international commitments, ideological shifts, and citizens' demands for more autonomy have produced a decline of the state's role in economic management in recent decades.

**statism**

The doctrine that advocates firm state direction of the economy and society.

**Governing the Economy**  During World II, the French economy, which was already stagnant, was further devastated by the war. After the war, however, it was fundamentally transformed. Thanks to state leadership described in Section 2, the French economy was quickly rebuilt and modernized. Since the 1980s the state has taken on a more modest role.

**The Democratic Idea**  France has passionately embraced two democratic currents. The first claims that citizens should participate directly in political decisions rather than merely vote to choose leaders. This idea nourishes protest movements like that of May 1968 and more recent ones discussed below. A quite different democratic current, also powerful in France, fears direct democracy and defends the value of representative or parliamentary government.

**Politics of Collective Identity**  French national identity has always been closely linked to the central position of the state and citizenship. In principle, everyone is entitled to become a citizen. But in return citizens are expected to accept dominant republican and secular values. This tradition dictates that collective identities based on religion, ethnicity, or gender should be confined to the private sphere, and should play no role in the public arena. It is widely believed that multiculturalism threatens republican unity.

And yet, at the same time, the French are deeply divided by social, economic, and cultural cleavages. Recently, ethnic conflict and globalization have destabilized national identity. Recall the claim by Jean Marie and Marine Le Pen that Muslim immigrants and their children are responsible for unemployment, crime, and urban decay.

### Implications for Comparative Politics

French politics offers rich lessons for comparative politics. Scholars have coined the term *French exceptionalism* to highlight that French politics is distinctive. They emphasize the existence of severe ideological conflicts, which in turn have fueled political instability, including frequent regime change.

Because France has continually tried to reshape its destiny by conscious political direction, it provides a natural laboratory to test the importance of variations in institutional design. To illustrate, a 1999 constitutional amendment and a law passed in 2000 requires political parties to nominate an equal number of men and women for many political offices. As a result, the number of female representatives has soared.

Further, the French have often looked to the state to guide economic development. In countries without a strong statist tradition (for example, the United States and Britain), private groups have to rely on their own efforts.

### Summary

France is celebrated for its natural beauty, rich culture, and quality of life. But the country also has a turbulent past and deep socioeconomic and cultural divisions. For centuries, the state structured French political and social life. However, in recent decades the state has lost its preeminent role. Is the state's more modest role a blessing or a handicap? Does it mean the end of French exceptionalism? Stay tuned!

# POLITICAL ECONOMY AND DEVELOPMENT

## SECTION 2

France has the world's eighth-largest economy. It has accomplished this feat by a combination of skill, clever state management, and favorable historical and geographic circumstances. After World War II, the French state played a key role in shaping and steering the economy. However, since the 1980s, the state has assumed a more modest role. Private business firms now operate in less regulated markets. Accompanying the change has been a shift in balance from an inward-looking economic posture to an export orientation. France has become a major global economic actor. However, when it comes to economic performance, the proverbial glass is at best only half full. On the negative side, economic growth has recently been sluggish, economic inequalities are extensive, and unemployment has been at distressingly high levels for decades. Although France fared somewhat better than other West European countries and the United States during the global economic crisis of 2008–2009, it continues to confront a host of acute economic challenges.

### Focus Questions

What have been the major changes in the state's role in economic management from the Third Republic to the present?

What are the strengths and weakness of the most recent approach, adopted since the 1980s?

# The New French Revolution

During the nineteenth century, when Britain and Germany engaged in a headlong rush to industrialize, France was less ambitious. The state's main goal was not to modernize the economy but to preserve traditional society.

When the Fourth Republic was created after World War II, the groups who had opposed the Vichy regime and now governed France agreed on the need for economic and social modernization. In a few short years, an array of state agencies was created to transform the French economy and society. With only some exaggeration, one study described the postwar period as "a new French Revolution. Although peaceful, this has been just as profound as that of 1789 because it has totally overhauled the moral foundations and social equilibrium of French society."[8]

# State and Economy

France traditionally had a statist tradition of economic management. When the state shifted from guardian of the established order to energetic agent of change, it was able to steer France toward economic modernization. This approach is called ***dirigisme***, or state direction.

## French-Style Economic Management

After World War II, the state helped transform France's rural, stagnant economy into a modern, urban, industrial economy. A principal tool developed to promote economic and social modernization was **indicative planning**. A national Planning Commission of civil servants established national economic and social priorities for the next several years. They included feasible rates of economic growth and educational targets. They also identified industries, sectors, and regions that were targeted to receive special assistance.

In the new scheme, the state was the chief economic player. It financed key industrial sectors (sometimes called **industrial policy**). This approach is usually viewed as socialist. However, many conservative leaders in France at the time, such as Charles de Gaulle, supported *dirigisme*, because of the need to modernize the French economy. The state's specific tools included:

- *Subsidies, loans, tax write-offs, and price and capital controls.* State development agencies provided the bulk of capital for new investment, limited the outflow of French capital, controlled prices, and created semipublic banks for specific industries.
- *Restructuring key sectors.* The state ordered the merger of small and medium firms in important industries, including steel, machine tools, and paper products, and created new state-run firms in high-tech sectors. The goal was to sponsor what were called "national champions" able to compete in French and world markets.
- *Creating and managing entire industries.* Some national champions were world-class. For example, France became a leader in designing, building, operating, and exporting nuclear power installations.

## France's Economic Miracle

From 1945 to 1975, France's rate of economic growth was among the world's highest (see Table 3.2). Average yearly income nearly tripled between 1946 and 1962. France leapfrogged into the twentieth century.

## May 1968 and Beyond: Economic Crisis and Political Conflict

Despite the dramatic economic growth of the 1950s and 1960s, economic change caused political conflict. One reason was the state's highhanded style of governing. This served as a model for a centralized style of leadership in other sectors of French society, such as universities and workplaces. Although the regime seemed stable, massive strikes and demonstrations in May 1968 revealed its weakness.

---

***dirigisme***

A French term denoting that the state plays a leading role in supervising the economy.

**indicative planning**

A term that describes a national plan identifying desirable priorities for economic and social development.

**industrial policy**

A policy that uses state resources to promote the development of particular economic sectors.

**nationalization**

The policy by which the state assumes ownership and operation of private companies.

## Economic Instability

New problems developed in the 1970s, when the state-centered approach failed to meet the challenges of technological change and global competition. These developments required economic flexibility and decentralized economic decision making—just the opposite of the centralized style that characterized *dirigisme*. This structural problem, along with economic difficulties that increased during the 1970s, proved too much for the conservative coalition that had governed France since the creation of the Fifth Republic in 1958. After twenty-three years of conservative governments in the Fifth Republic, Socialist candidate François Mitterrand was elected president in 1981 on a platform that proposed extending the traditional *dirigiste* approach to revive economic growth, increase social benefits, and expand personal liberty. Mitterrand's Socialist Party and its allies also gained a majority in elections to the National Assembly (the more powerful legislative chamber). When a Socialist-led coalition that included Communist ministers took control of government, a new era began.

| Table 3.2 | Average Growth Rates in Gross National Product, 1958–1973 |
|---|---|
| Japan | 10.4% |
| France | 5.5 |
| Italy | 5.3 |
| West Germany | 5.0 |
| Belgium | 4.9 |
| Netherlands | 4.2 |
| Norway | 4.2 |
| Sweden | 4.1 |
| United States | 4.1 |
| United Kingdom | 3.2 |

*Source:* Reprinted by permission of the State University of New York Press, from *The Fifth Republic at Twenty* by William G. Andrews and Stanley Hoffmann (Eds). © 1981 State University of New York. All rights reserved.

## French Socialism in Practice—and Conservative Aftermath

The Socialist government sponsored a dizzying number of measures to revive the economy, create jobs, and recapture domestic markets. It substantially boosted the minimum wage, family allowances, old-age pensions, rent subsidies, and state-mandated paid vacations. It created new jobs in the public sector. The state channeled funds to develop cutting-edge technologies in biotech, telecommunications, and aerospace. A centerpiece of the program was **nationalization**, involving the state takeover of privately owned industrial firms and banks. (It might be noted that in foreign policy Mitterrand was fiercely anti-Soviet and anticommunist.)

The Socialist reforms promoted social justice and helped modernize the French economy, society, and state in the long run. But in the short run, their high cost and the opposition they provoked from French and international investors drove France to the brink of bankruptcy. Deficits soared. France's international currency reserves ran low.

The crisis cruelly demonstrated the limited margin of maneuver for a medium-rank power. In 1983, Mitterrand reluctantly ordered an about-face in economic policy. Political

"What!?? The president's a Socialist and the Eiffel Tower is still standing!??" "Incredible!"

*Source:* Courtesy Plantu, Cartoonists and Writers Syndicate/Cartoon Arts International, Inc., from *Le Monde,* May 1981.

scientist Jonah Levy observes, "A leftist administration that had been elected just two years earlier on a campaign to intensify *dirigisme* began instead to dismantle *dirigisme*."[9] Since 1983, the core elements of *dirigisme* have been abandoned and successive governments have consistently promoted a more modest and conservative orientation.

The French Socialist government's failure in the early 1980s suggests that far-reaching reforms in one medium-size country are futile. In any case, France was the victim of bad timing. At the very moment that President Mitterrand was sponsoring audacious reforms, British prime minister Margaret Thatcher and American president Ronald Reagan were pursuing an opposite strategy of deregulation and cutbacks in social benefits. France may have been too small a country to buck the international tide. In any case, the governing parties in France, whether of the center-left or center-right orientation have apparently accepted this claim. The failure of the Socialist experiment dealt a body blow to France's traditional *dirigiste* pattern.

## France's Neoliberal Modernization Strategy

**neoliberal**

A term used to describe government policies that aim to promote private enterprise by reducing government economic regulation, tax rates, and social spending. The term *liberal* is understood differently in Europe than in the United States. *Liberal* in Europe refers to protecting individual liberty; in the United States, it refers to government policies to redistribute resources from more affluent citizens to low income groups.

**privatization**

The sale of state-owned enterprises or services to private companies or investors.

**deregulation**

The process of dismantling state regulations that govern business activities.

Since 1983, the state has pursued a market-friendly "**neoliberal** modernization strategy," including **privatization**, **deregulation**, and liberalization.[10] Privatization has involved the sale to private investors of major firms and industries formerly in the public sector, notably, banks, utilities, steel producers, the Renault automobile company, and telecommunications companies. Deregulation has reduced the state's role in setting prices, wage levels, allocating credit, and hiring and firing employees. State agencies that formerly administered these important activities were weakened or eliminated. Liberalization has opened the French economy to inward and outward movements of capital and goods. The result is that France's approach to governing the economy has become quite similar to that of other rich capitalist countries. But similar does not mean identical. Political scientist Vivien Schmidt observes that France has not "abandoned its statist model.... Governments have not stopped seeking to guide business...even as they engineer the retreat of the state."[11] As a result, statism remains alive (if not altogether well). It even enjoyed a modest comeback during the severe global recession of 2007–2009. President Sarkozy had been elected in 2007 on a platform promising to reduce statism even further. But when the economic crisis erupted, he did an about-face. He now praised France's statist tradition as superior to the unregulated version of free-market capitalism practiced by the United States and Britain!

France did weather the recession somewhat better than its neighbors. In 2009, Britain and Germany's GDP fell by 4.9 percent, whereas French GDP fell by 2.5 percent. One reason may be that France retained relatively extensive state economic regulation. Another reason is France's strong safety net, discussed below. By channeling resources to less advantaged groups, social payments boosted economic demand. Even so, the French economy continues to face daunting challenges.

## Assessing French Economic Performance

French economic performance is quite mixed. For example, France devotes fewer resources than other leading countries to technological innovation. Successive governments have failed to cope with large budget deficits, heavy public debt, and high taxes. France's public debt—the amount that the government has borrowed to finance expenditures—represents 83 percent of French GDP, far above the 60 percent ceiling established by EU regulations. Moreover, rising health costs and demographic changes, especially an aging population, promise to further increase pressure for social spending. Fiscal problems will probably worsen in coming years.

Among France's most persistent and acute economic problems is unemployment. The official rate—at least 9 percent for decades—is a national disgrace. The proportion of the working age population who are employed, what economists call labor force participation, is the lowest in Western Europe. And full-time employed French workers have a shorter work week than workers elsewhere—39.1 hours, compared to 42.4 hours for British workers and 40.3 hours for German workers. At the same time, French workers are highly productive. Hourly output per worker is the highest in the world.[12]

Nicolas Sarkozy campaigned on a promise to scale back the size and scope of the state and put the French back to work. For example, he sponsored an increase in the work week and pension reforms that boosted the retirement age. However, his reforms provoked stiff resistance from groups that were asked to sacrifice long-standing benefits. And despite some success in enacting reforms, France's overall economic outlook remains bleak.

## Society and Economy

France has among the world's most ample welfare states. The network of social services has been dubbed the French social model. It reflects a deeply rooted belief that the state should help all citizens lead healthy, secure lives. An extensive array of programs channel benefits to most citizens. Cradle-to-grave social services begin with free prenatal care for pregnant women. The state provides extensive preschool facilities. (Children enter the public educational system at age 3!) Students who pass a stiff high school graduation exam are entitled to attend public universities whose tuition is virtually free. There are extensive public housing and rent subsidies, and near-universal provision for medical care. Prescription drugs as well as excellent outpatient, specialized, and hospital care are available to all, in return for a modest co-payment.

The results speak for themselves. The infant mortality rate in France is about half that in the United States. Life expectancy is 81 years old, several years more than in the United States. In 2000, the World Health Organization ranked the French health care system first in the world. No wonder that Michael Moore's documentary film *Sicko* (2007) praised the French public health care system so highly!

Workers who are laid off are eligible for extended unemployment insurance and job retraining. If they lose their jobs because of industrial restructuring, they are entitled to early retirement and good pensions. After a bitterly contested reform (described in Section 5) was enacted, the retirement age was raised in 2010. Even so, the terms are comparable to those in other West European countries. Employees can choose to retire and receive partial pension benefits at age 62 or work until age 67 and receive full pensions.

Yet inequalities in access to social programs deepen what the French call *the social fracture*. The fortunate include stably employed workers and retirees. (Seventy percent of social spending goes for pensions and other benefits for the elderly.)[13] Those who are truly needy receive free medical care and a minimum income for those over 25 years old without other income. Yet youth, women, and those from immigrant backgrounds have especially high levels of unemployment but receive relatively few social benefits.

France's social programs come with a hefty price tag: one-third of the French GDP. And costs are sure to rise in the future. An aging population means that medical and other costs will increase while revenue to finance social benefits will shrink. Currently, three adults work for every retired worker. By 2050, the ratio will drop to 1.5 employed workers for every retired worker.

## Labor Relations

Stormy relations between management and labor have traditionally damaged French economic performance. Employers have viewed unions as opponents. Workers respond by organizing strikes and pressuring the state for benefits. Even though the labor movement has historically been quite weak, unions enjoy wide public support beyond their membership. When they organize demonstrations to protest proposed government cutbacks in social benefits, a frequent occurrence in recent decades, citizens turn out by the millions.

## Inequality and Ethnic Minorities

France has long prided itself on its ability to integrate ethnic minorities. Public opinion polls repeatedly find the French less fearful of immigrants arriving from outside the EU compared to citizens in most European countries. Yet, as discussed in Section 4, this openness is flawed. For example, immigrants and their offspring are twice as likely to be unemployed as are other French. The results of a research project provide a dramatic example of why. Researchers sent 2,000 inquiries for job openings using identical CVs for two groups of fictitious applicants. The members of one group, named "Thomas Lecomte" and "Guillaume Dupont" ("traditional" French names) were invited to one job interview for every 19 applications sent. With identical qualifications, the members of the second group, "Youssuf Belkacem" and "Karim Brahimi" (obviously, Muslim names), were invited to one job interview for every 54 applications.[14]

## Inequality and Women

France provides extensive social services enabling women to work outside the home (See Figure 3.2). Government spending for family payments, child care, and maternity benefits is about double the average in other EU countries. Mothers are entitled to four to six months of paid maternity leave. Fathers receive two weeks of paid paternity leave. Daycare facilities, whose cost to parents is low thanks to public subsidies, are staffed by highly qualified and well-paid teachers. Laws mandate gender equality in the workplace and outlaw sexual harassment.

Nevertheless, gender inequalities in employment persist. The proportion of female managers and administrators is among the lowest of all industrialized countries.

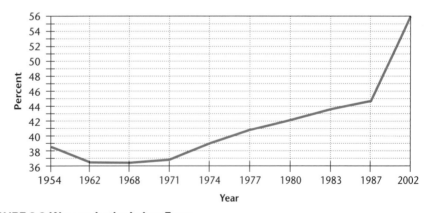

**FIGURE 3.2 Women in the Labor Force**

*Source:* INSEE, in Louis Dirn, *La Société francedillaaise en tendances* (Paris, PUF, 1990), p. 108; 2002 data from INSEE, *Tableaux de l Économie Francedillaaise, 2003–2004* (Paris: INSEE, 2003), p. 77.

Women earn about 20 percent less than men for comparable work. Time will tell whether a law passed in 2010 that fines companies not providing equal pay for men and women doing equal work will make a difference. The present situation explains why a newspaper headline recently observed, "For Women in France, Dim Outlook on Equality."[15]

## The Generation Gap

There is an informal two-tier system of employment and social welfare in France. Older workers are more likely to be employed and to receive good wages and social benefits. Young adults face special hardships. Because it is hard to dismiss workers once hired, employers are less likely to take on new workers. This lessens the chance that young workers will get a job. They are more than twice as likely to be out of work. They enjoy fewer social benefits. Recent government measures to deregulate labor markets, for example, easing restrictions on scheduling work and dismissing workers, may encourage new hiring. But two-thirds of new jobs are temporary or part-time and provide lower wages and fringe benefits.

## THE GLOBAL CONNECTION

### France and the European Union

France has been a charter member and one of the most powerful states in the European Union since its creation in 1958. (The EU was originally known as the European Economic Community.) Before World War II, France had preferred isolation to international cooperation. But three devastating wars in less than a century between France and Germany taught both countries that there was no alternative but to cooperate. The Franco-German tandem has largely shaped the pace and character of European integration. The EU has helped modernize French and other European economies. It has been highly successful in fostering closer ties between the member states of the organization. (The number of members has steadily increased to twenty-nine.) The EU has helped make Europe one of the most prosperous regions of the world.

The French economy and society have been profoundly reshaped. For example, the bulk of French international trade and investment used to be with the country's former colonies in Asia and Africa. Nowadays, over 60 percent of French imports and exports are with other member states of the EU. French farmers, in fact, receive the largest share of the EU's generous agricultural subsidies.

The EU was highly popular in France during good economic times. However, when the economy turned sour in the 1980s, many citizens began to regard the EU as a liability, not a blessing. When the EU slashed agricultural subsidies, French farmers protested. Citizens resented the EU requiring France and other member states to limit budget deficits. There was a groundswell of criticism of EU technocrats in Brussels, Belgium, the seat of the EU, who were regarded as limiting France's independence. The proportion of French expressing approval of the EU declined from 70 percent in 1987 to 43 percent in 2004.[16]

Voters expressed their discontent when they were asked to vote on a revised draft of the EU constitution in 2005. President Chirac sponsored the referendum to bolster his personal popularity and provide the EU with added legitimacy. However, his decision proved a major blunder. It came at a time when unemployment in France was at a double-digit level and when the addition of new members to the EU was quite unpopular.

The French vote to reject the constitution produced a stalemate within the EU. It also revealed a wide chasm between rank-and-file French voters and the governing parties, who lobbied for a yes vote. It took several years for the process of European integration to be revived. President Sarkozy took the lead among European leaders to do so in 2007. The result was the Lisbon Treaty, a scaled-down version of the draft EU constitution.

The economic crisis beginning in 2008 created additional strains within the EU. Most important was when several EU member states in southern Europe, especially Greece, encountered a severe fiscal crisis in 2010. Those countries in the EU who shared a common currency, the euro, were obliged to provide assistance. If they had refused, there would have been disastrous consequences for the euro, Eurozone countries, and the entire EU. In 2010, President Sarkozy persuaded a reluctant Angela Merkel, chancellor of Germany, to support a rescue package for Greece. The EU survived—but not by much. Its near implosion illustrated how closely the EU's fate is linked to the economic well-being of its member states.

# France in the Global Economy

For much of the nineteenth and twentieth centuries, France was relatively isolated from the international economy. High tariff walls limited foreign competition, protected French industry, and limited technological innovation. This cozy pattern began to change in the 1960s. France has now become tightly integrated in the wider international economy and a major global economic player. A major reason is participation in the European Union (EU).

French participation in the global economy is an important aspect of the "new French revolution" described above. Imports and exports account for over half of French GDP. Foreign investors, notably American pension funds, own nearly half of all shares traded on the Paris stock exchange. About one-third of all French workers work for firms that are at least partly foreign-owned. France ranks among the world's largest importers and exporters of capital. Yet France's participation in the global economy has caused intense strains in domestic politics because the costs and benefits of economic integration are unequally distributed. Citizens with less education and job skills are more likely to be unemployed or to have low-paying and part-time jobs. For these groups, the EU and globalization represent a threat rather than an opportunity. When citizens in Europe are polled about their attitudes toward globalization, France is the country with the highest proportion of citizens who express doubts about its benefits. One reason, no doubt, is that the EU and globalization have been associated in recent years with economic difficulties. Another may be rooted in a tendency in French political culture to cherish what is regarded as distinctively French and to view with suspicion what is considered foreign. At the same time, one should beware of generalizing: For example, the French are avid consumers of American films and popular culture!

## Summary

Following a century of relative economic stagnation, France reinvented itself after World War II. For several decades, the economy soared, and most French benefited. Central to the French economic miracle was a vigorous and effective state. The state proved the ideal agency for sponsoring large-scale industrial projects. State-sponsored development (*dirigisme*) made France a prosperous and highly industrialized country.

Eventually, however, the state proved less effective at steering an economy that demands decentralized and flexible decision making. The French increasingly resented the state's highhanded manner. The last attempt at state-sponsored development occurred at the beginning of the Mitterrand presidency. The failure of the statist features of his reform agenda shifted the balance toward a more market-based economy. Even so, statism continues to play a larger role in France than in most other industrialized capitalist countries.

The French social model is a source of great pride, great benefits—and great costs. Additional economic burdens involve high unemployment, especially concentrated among youth and ethnic minorities, an aging population that places stress on the public health and pension systems, and resulting state budget deficits. This situation forces policy-makers to choose one of two unpopular alternatives: raising taxes or cutting social services.

France's close ties to other members of EU and to the international economy more generally have produced great benefits. But these benefits have also involved economic hardships and insecurity which fall especially heavily on youth, immigrants, and the less educated.

# GOVERNANCE AND POLICY-MAKING

Charles de Gaulle, founding father of the Fifth Republic did his work well—too well, many believe. He designed the Fifth Republic to enable a strong executive to govern without much parliamentary control and other checks and balances. The result has been a relatively unchecked executive and weak parliament. The imbalance between the executive and legislature involves a fundamental design flaw in the institutional architecture of the Fifth Republic. There have, however, been reforms periodically seeking to create greater balance.

At the same time, three changes have reduced the executive's power. The first change involves decentralization of the state. The constitution specifies that the French Republic is "indivisible." It was generally assumed that an indivisible state meant a centralized state. However, in the 1980s, the Socialist government transferred substantial governmental powers to local, departmental, and regional authorities. In 2003, a conservative government transferred additional powers to subnational governments, and a constitutional amendment was passed that affirmed the principle of decentralization. These changes have produced an important reinterpretation of "indivisible." There is now a broad consensus that local and regional governments should share governmental responsibilities.

Second, as described in Section 2, the state's relation to the economy has shifted. Although the state continues to have an important role, it now consults and persuades more, and commands less.

The third change involves limits on the executive as well as legislature. Until recently, French democratic theory held that the government should have a free hand to govern because it is chosen by democratic elections. It was widely believed that the constitution should not limit the state's power, because doing so would restrict democracy. This assumption has changed. The constitution of the Fifth Republic has come to be regarded as the authoritative source for distributing power among political institutions. And the Constitutional Council, a kind of Supreme Court, has gained the vital power of **judicial review**, that is, the power to nullify legislation and executive actions that in its view violate the constitution.

## Organization of the State

The Fifth Republic is a semipresidential system. As described in the box feature on the U.S. connection, this pattern combines elements of presidential and parliamentary systems.

The semipresidential system was a product of de Gaulle's desire in 1958 to gain power that executives lacked in the Fourth Republic. He constructed a semipresidential system because he judged that a purely presidential system would be too drastic a break with France's parliamentary tradition.

Since the early 1980s, the constitutional framework has overcome two daunting political challenges. The first, in 1981, was a shift in political control (alternation) between opposing partisan coalitions, when Socialist François Mitterrand defeated conservative incumbent president Valéry Giscard d'Estaing, who was seeking re-election. Despite dire warnings of political instability, the system continued to function without disruption.

**judicial review**

The ability of a high court to nullify actions by the executive and legislative branches of government that in its judgment violate the constitution.

## THE U.S. CONNECTION

### The American Presidential System and French Semipresidential System Compared

In a presidential system, such as in the United States, the executive and the legislature are elected separately. The two branches have independent powers. Neither branch selects the other, is directly accountable to the other, or controls the other's agenda. Both institutions have fixed terms in office. This means that neither branch can force the other to resign and face new elections. The legislature can, however, impeach and force the president to resign for treason or other grave misdeeds. The French Fifth Republic has a similar impeachment procedure, by which parliament can force a president from office. However, it has never been used.

In a parliamentary system, by contrast, the executive and legislature do not have powers independent of each other. The two branches are fused. The government is accountable to parliament and must resign if parliament votes no confidence. At the same time, the government has substantial control over the parliamentary agenda. It can also dissolve parliament, which triggers new elections.

The Fifth Republic differs from both presidential and parliamentary systems. It resembles a presidential system in that both the president and parliament are directly elected. Unlike both presidential and parliamentary systems, however, the French system is directed by a dual executive, the president and a prime minister appointed by the president. The system is called *semipresidential*, not *semiparliamentary*, because every deviation from a purely parliamentary or presidential model strengthens the executive. The fusion of executive and legislative powers (as in parliamentary regimes) enables the executive to control the parliamentary agenda and dissolve parliament. In particular, the French parliament can vote to censure the prime minister. When it does so, the prime minister must resign. However, parliament cannot vote to censure the president—the more powerful member of the dual executive.

The most important difference between the American presidential system and French semipresidential system involves executive-legislative relations. American presidents confront a legislature that is usually powerful and fiercely independent. Even when Congress is controlled by the same party as the president, members of Congress have their own base of power. Further, elections to Congress occur at fixed intervals. The president cannot alter this election calendar. This vastly weakens the president's ability to influence Congress. In brief, because both branches of government are independent, agreement occurs not because one branch (that is, the president) commands—but because the two negotiate a compromise. By contrast, the French constitution renders the president powerful and parliament relatively humble and weak.

---

**cohabitation**

The term used by the French to describe the situation in the Fifth Republic when a president and prime minister belong to opposing political coalitions.

The second challenge occurred with the development of divided institutional control, that is, when the president was leader of one political coalition and a rival coalition gained a majority in parliament. The French call this ***cohabitation***, or power sharing. Many feared this would produce stalemate or crisis. It did not arise in the first decades of the Fifth Republic because conservative parties continually won both presidential and parliamentary elections. However, five years into President Mitterrand's presidential term, parliamentary elections in 1986 produced a conservative majority in the National Assembly. Mitterrand immediately bowed to political realities by appointing Jacques Chirac, leader of the conservative coalition, to be prime minister. The two seasoned politicians quickly devised workable solutions for governing. As with alternation, cohabitation has occurred several times since then. However, recent changes discussed below make it much less likely in the future.

## The Executive

France was the first major country to adopt a semipresidential system. After the fall of communism, however, Russia was inspired by the French example. Many other countries since then have adopted a semipresidential system, including Austria, Finland, Iceland, Pakistan, Portugal, Sri Lanka, and (most recently) Iraq.

## The President

Most of the time, the French president possesses more power than the U.S. president. He (there has never yet been a female president) directs the executive branch and is independent of the legislature. Yet he controls parliament's agenda and can dissolve parliament. When the same party coalition wins presidential and parliamentary elections, and there is thus united control of the two branches, the president is more powerful than the chief executive in virtually any other democratic nation.

The presidential office is so powerful because of (1) the towering personalities of Charles de Gaulle, founder and first president of the Fifth Republic, and François Mitterrand, Socialist president from 1981 to 1995; (2) the ample powers conferred on the office by the constitution; and (3) political practices of the Fifth Republic.

| Table 3.3 | Presidents of the Fifth Republic |
|---|---|
| **President** | **Term** |
| Charles de Gaulle | 1958–1969 |
| Georges Pompidou | 1969–1974 |
| Valéry Giscard d'Estaing | 1974–1981 |
| François Mitterrand | 1981–1995 |
| Jacques Chirac | 1995–2007 |
| Nicolas Sarkozy | 2007–present |

Presidential Personalities  Charles de Gaulle (1890–1970) was the most influential politician in modern France. As first president in the Fifth Republic, he set the standard for his successors. (Table 3.3 lists the Fifth Republic's presidents and their terms of office.) Thanks to his role as leader of the Resistance in World War II, he enjoyed immense popular support. He put his stamp on the presidential office by firm control of the government, executive, and entire political system.

François Mitterrand was the only one of de Gaulle's successors to further expand presidential powers. First elected in 1981, Mitterrand was largely responsible for the Socialist government's initial radical reform agenda. He then led its right turn in 1983. He worked closely with German chancellor Helmut Kohl to promote European economic integration and monetary union. Mitterrand was president from 1981 to 1995, the longest term of any president in the Fifth Republic.

Mitterrand's successor, conservative Jacques Chirac, is generally regarded as an undistinguished and weak president. Early in his presidency, he proposed a social reform that provoked massive opposition. Hoping to gain new legitimacy, he dissolved parliament in 1997 and called new elections. When his conservative coalition was defeated, he was forced to share power with Socialist opponents for the remainder of his first term in office. This period of cohabitation proved so unpopular that a constitutional reform was adopted in 2000 that was designed to reduce the chances of cohabitation in the future.

Cohabitation ended in 2002. Chirac was re-elected that year, and his conservative allies won parliamentary elections, ushering in a new period of united control. However, Chirac failed to use the opportunity to exercise bold leadership or achieve noteworthy reforms. He committed a major blunder in 2005 when he called the referendum, which the French decisively rejected, to ratify the EU's new constitution. Several major protests and opposition movements in 2005 and 2006, described in Section 5, further stymied Chirac's reform efforts. He was embroiled in a corruption scandal that led to his indictment on criminal charges. Chirac's failures explain why scholars have described his presidency as "a 'lost decade' at best and an era of inertia and decline at worst."[17]

Chirac was succeeded in 2007 by Nicolas Sarkozy, who broke the mold of dignified, distant presidents. Sarkozy is gutsy, headstrong, and impetuous. He proposed a host of reforms and succeeded in pushing through several important ones. But his proposals

## PROFILE

### President Nicolas Sarkozy

*Source:* Horacio Villalobos/epa/Corbis.

Nicolas Sarkozy, elected president in 2007, is audacious and controversial. Born in Paris in 1955, he is the first president from an immigrant background. Further, unlike most members of the political elite, Sarkozy did not attend an elite university. Instead, at a young age he was elected mayor and a member of parliament.

Sarkozy swiftly rose within the ranks of the governing conservative party, the Union for a Popular Movement (UMP: see below), and was soon appointed a junior minister and official spokesperson for the government. He quickly established a political reputation as a maverick by speaking bluntly on issues like crime and immigration in ways that his conservative supporters loved—and liberal opponents hated.

As the 1995 presidential campaign approached, Sarkozy's future seemed bright. However, he came close to destroying his political career when he supported a rival of Jacques Chirac for the UMP presidential nomination. When Chirac gained the nomination and was elected president, he refused to name Sarkozy to the government. From that time, although both men belonged to the same conservative coalition, they became political enemies.

That Sarkozy recovered from this setback is a tribute to his ambition, boundless energy, oratorical skill, knack for championing issues popular with conservative voters—and sheer luck. In 2002, when Chirac ran for re-election, Sarkozy learned the lesson of the 1995 presidential campaign and

vigorously supported Chirac. However, when Chirac was re-elected, he did not fully forgive Sarkozy for his earlier betrayal. Although this time Chirac appointed Sarkozy to the cabinet, Chirac tried to limit Sarkozy's influence. Sarkozy's luck turned when the politicians that Chirac groomed to succeed him when he retired performed poorly. Sarkozy capitalized on the opportunity, captured the UMP's nomination for the presidency in 2007, and was elected president.

President Sarkozy was soon dubbed the hyper-president because of his domineering manner and whirlwind performance in office. Rather than confining presidential interventions to rare occasions and major policy initiatives, Sarkozy was a constant but unpredictable presence. He treated François Fillon, the popular prime minister, as his lackey. His temper tantrums were notorious. Sarkozy alienated his conservative supporters by appointing Socialists to high position; he alienated moderates by profiling French from immigrant backgrounds as especially likely to be criminals. In confidential documents leaked by WikiLeaks in 2010, U.S. diplomats described Sarkozy as operating in "a zone of monarch-like impunity."[18] Another leaked document described him as "mercurial."[19]

Sarkozy's popularity plunged in 2010 after he proposed an unpopular pension reform and was implicated in a financial scandal (described in Section 5). His approval rating in public opinion polls of 30 percent was among the lowest of any president in the Fifth Republic. Scholars questioned "whether he is the man for the [president's] job—whether Sarkozy possesses the vision, discipline and commitment to provide meaningful solutions to the serious challenges still facing France."[20]

also encountered massive opposition. Further, his presidency has been marked by scandals, as will be discussed, involving cabinet ministers and Sarkozy personally.

**The Constitutional Presidency** The constitution of the Fifth Republic endows the president with the ceremonial powers of head of state. He resides in the resplendent Élysée Palace and represents France at international diplomatic gatherings. The president benefits immensely from being the only official elected by the entire French electorate.

A candidate for president must be a French citizen at least twenty-three years old. Presidents serve a five-year term. There are no limits to how many terms a president can serve. There is no vice president in France. If a president dies in office, the president of the Senate (the upper house of parliament) acts as interim president. A new presidential election is held within a short time.

A two-ballot system of election governs presidential elections. To win on the first ballot, a candidate must obtain an absolute majority (over 50 percent) of those voting. If no candidate receives a first-ballot majority—the case in every presidential election to date—a runoff election is held two weeks later to choose between the two front-runners.

The constitution grants the president the following political powers:

- The president names the prime minister, approves the prime minister's choice of other cabinet officials, and names high-ranking civil, military, and judicial officials.
- The president presides over meetings of the Council of Ministers (the government). Note that the constitution entrusts the president, not the prime minister, with this responsibility.
- The president conducts foreign affairs, through the power to negotiate and ratify treaties. He also names French ambassadors and accredits foreign ambassadors to France.
- The president directs the armed forces. A 1964 decree also granted the president exclusive control over France's nuclear forces.
- The president may dissolve the National Assembly and call new elections.
- The president appoints three of the nine members of the Constitutional Council, including its president. He can also refer bills passed by parliament to the Council to determine if they violate the constitution.
- Article 16 authorizes the president to assume emergency powers in a grave crisis. The only time this power has been used was when de Gaulle faced a military uprising. A 2008 constitutional amendment authorizes the Constitutional Council to limit the use of this clause.
- Article 89 authorizes the president, with the approval of the prime minister, to propose constitutional amendments. To pass, an amendment must be approved by both chambers of parliament and then ratified either by a national referendum or by a three-fifths vote of both houses of parliament meeting together as a congress.
- Article 11, amended in 1995, authorizes the president to organize a referendum to approve important policy initiatives or reorganize political institutions. (This procedure is distinct from the process of amending the constitution—which, as we have just seen, may also involve calling a referendum.)
- Article 5 directs the president to be an arbiter to ensure "the regular functioning of the governmental authorities, as well as the continuance of the State." The precise meaning of this clause is unclear. But the president is the sole official delegated this power.

**The Political President**  The constitution creates a powerful office on paper. But a president must translate formal powers into actual influence. Presidential preeminence is potentially further limited by the fact that the constitution also grants the prime minister and government important powers.

A key factor affecting the extent of presidential leadership is whether his coalition controls the government and parliament. When it does, he is supreme; when it does not (during cohabitation), the president is forced to share power with the prime minister, government, and parliament.

## The Prime Minister and Government

The constitution authorizes the president to appoint the prime minister. Presidents generally choose a senior politician from the party leading the majority coalition in the National Assembly. This ensures parliamentary support for the prime minister and government. The prime minister in turn nominates, and the president appoints, members of the cabinet or government, a collective body under the prime minister's direction.

The reason it matters whether the president can command a parliamentary majority is that the constitution entrusts the government not president with the power to "determine and direct the policy of the nation. It shall have at its disposal the administration and the armed forces" (Article 20). Article 21 authorizes the prime minister to "direct the action of the government. He [the prime minister] is responsible for national defense. He assures the execution of the laws." Thus, a prime minister that accepts the president's leadership does so because he or she is the junior partner of the president, that is, a political subordinate. Thus, the president's preeminence results from *political dynamics* rather than *constitutional directive*. This becomes crystal clear when a hostile majority controls parliament. At these times, the president must accept political realities and appoint a prime minister and government who are political opponents.

This description makes clear why the relationship between the president and prime minister is crucial in French politics. The relationship changes dramatically between periods of unified control, when the president and prime minister are political allies, compared to periods of cohabitation, when they are political rivals. When the president enjoys the support of a parliamentary majority, and can name a political ally as prime minister, the result is undisputed presidential supremacy. Loyal and effective prime ministers can provide the president with parliamentary support for the government's policies, sympathetic media treatment, and firm assistance in directing the state bureaucracy.

During cohabitation, the balance shifts from cooperation to competition. The constitution authorizes the prime minister to direct policy-making and policy-implementation. Thus, the president is forced to assume the mantle of dignified and ceremonial head of state, while the prime minister moves front and center to assume responsibility for leadership.

The most recent experience of cohabitation, in 1997–2002, provoked an important institutional reform. When the Socialist-led coalition won the 1997 parliamentary elections, Jacques Chirac, who had been elected president only two years earlier, was forced to name Socialist leader Lionel Jospin as prime minister. Cohabitation lasted five long years, and proved highly unpopular. There was general agreement on the need to prevent a repeat performance of this situation. The solution was to reduce the president's term from seven to five years, the same length as that of the National Assembly. By electing both at the same time, the chances are improved that the same political coalition will win both elections. This was the outcome in 2007, when Nicolas Sarkozy won the presidency and his political allies won a majority in the National Assembly. Appointing François Fillon, a loyal ally, as prime minister, enabled Sarkozy to govern freely.

To summarize the complex relationship between president and prime minister: during periods of unified control, presidents use their formal and informal powers to the hilt, and prime ministers play second fiddle. At these times, presidents can shape policy in virtually any domain they choose. The prime minister is responsible for translating general policies into specific programs and supervising the implementation of policy. The prime minister shepherds government proposals through parliament, drums up popular support for the president, takes the heat on controversial issues, and supervises the bureaucracy. During cohabitation, the president retains major responsibility for defense and foreign policy, but the prime minister assumes control over other policy areas.

Most cabinet members, also known as ministers, are senior politicians from the dominant parliamentary coalition. Cabinet ministers direct the government ministries. Positions in the cabinet are allotted to political parties in rough proportion to their strength in the majority parliamentary coalition. An attempt is also made to ensure regional balance.

The French cabinet is not an important forum for developing or debating policy. Cabinet meetings are occasions where constitutional requirements are met. For example, the cabinet must formally authorize appointment of key administrative officials. However, important government policies are shaped at the Élysée or Matignon (official residence of the prime minister) or by interministerial committees. These are informal working groups of ministers and top administrators directed by the president, prime minister, or their staff.

## Bureaucracy and Civil Service

The bureaucracy is large and sprawling. Some powerful administrators are appointed to the personal staffs of the president and prime minister. Other top administrators have large offices in ornate government ministries scattered throughout Paris. An army of civil servants—approximately 2.3 million—performs the day-to-day work of the state. Another 2.7 million staff public hospitals and subnational governmental bureaucracies. About one in five French jobholders is a civil servant!

The bureaucracy helps shape the country's social and economic life. The Fifth Republic bolstered the executive's influence by limiting parliament's legislative power and granting the government authority to issue binding regulations with the force of law. A position in the bureaucracy provides lifetime employment, considerable prestige, a good salary, and excellent fringe benefits. However, the increased power of the private sector, the smaller role for the state, ideological changes, and the power of the EU have all reduced the morale and prestige of the civil service.

The top slots in the bureaucracy rank among the most prestigious and powerful positions in France. In order to be appointed to a high-level position, one must graduate from an elite educational establishment called a ***grande école***. Over 1 million students are enrolled in French higher education at any given time (most study at public universities). A small minority—3,000 students—are admitted to highly competitive *grandes écoles.*[21] The most prestigious are the École Polytechnique, which provides scientific and engineering training, and the École Nationale d'Administration (ENA), which trains top administrators. Children from culturally and economically favored backgrounds have an immense advantage in the fierce competition for places in the *grandes écoles.*

Students who graduate at the top of their class at a *grande école* join an even more select fraternity, a ***grand corps***. These small, cohesive networks help direct government departments. Membership in a *grand corps* is for life and provides a fine salary, high status, and considerable power. Members may get plum jobs in the private sector after several years in the bureaucracy. Some run for public office and pursue political careers. Membership in a *grand corps* is a stepping stone to parliament or a cabinet appointment. Over half the prime ministers in the Fifth Republic and two former presidents have been members of *grands corps.*

## Public and Semipublic Agencies

In the past two decades, there has been a steep decline in the number of public sector enterprises in industry, banking, transportation, energy, and telecommunications. Some giant, powerful semipublic agencies remain. For example, Electricity of France monopolizes the distribution of electricity. It has been described as a state within the state. The French national railroad is another enormous public enterprise. However, like the civil service, semipublic agencies no longer enjoy the prestige and power of yesteryear. Many formerly state-owned bastions like France Télécom, Air France, and the Renault automobile company have been fully or partially privatized.

---

**grandes écoles**

Prestigious and highly selective schools of higher education in France that train top civil servants, engineers, and business executives.

---

**grands corps**

Elite networks of graduates of selective training schools in France.

# Other State Institutions

## The Judiciary

The French judicial system of Roman law differs substantially from the common law pattern prevailing in Britain and the United States. French courts pay little attention to judicial precedents. What counts are legislative texts and legal codes that regulate specialized fields like industrial relations and local government. When it comes to criminal law, a judicial authority, the *juge d'instruction*, is delegated responsibility for preparing the prosecution's case. Criminal defendants enjoy fewer rights than in the U.S. or British system of criminal justice. In the French trial system, judges actively question witnesses and recommend verdicts to juries. The Cours de cassation is the top appeals court for civil and criminal cases; its role is quite technical and apolitical.

Through much of modern French history, the judiciary was considered an arm of the executive. In the past few decades, however, this pattern has dramatically changed. The Constitutional Council, created in the Fifth Republic and described below, has grown more powerful. Independent administrative regulatory authorities have also gained extensive power in areas like broadcasting, stock market trading, and commercial competition.

**The Constitutional Council** The Constitutional Council is the Cinderella of the Fifth Republic. One study observes, "Originally an obscure institution conceived to play a marginal role in the Fifth Republic, the Constitutional Council has gradually moved toward the center stage of French politics and acquired the status of a major actor in the policy-making system."[22] The Constitutional Council has acted on some important occasions as a check on the legislature and, especially, on the executive. It became more powerful and independent after successfully claiming the right of judicial review; that is, the right to strike down legislation that it judges is in violation of the constitution or treaties. However, unlike the U.S. Supreme Court, the council must review a bill that has passed only before it is officially registered and it must rule within one month.

The nine members of the council serve staggered nine-year nonrenewable terms. The presidents of the National Assembly and Senate each appoint three members. The president of the republic names the remaining three members and also designates the council's president. The first woman was appointed to the council in 1992. Since then, four other women were appointed to the council; thus, in all, there have been five women and 61 men who have served on the council in the Fifth Republic.

Unlike members of most constitutional courts, lower court judges are rarely appointed to the French Constitutional Council. Instead, most members are prominent politicians. Since conservative parties have controlled the presidency and parliament much of the time in the Fifth Republic, most judges have been appointed by conservative politicians. At the same time, the Constitutional Council is considered a relatively nonpartisan body.

**State Council** France has a system of about thirty administrative courts that hear cases of administrative wrongdoing. They play a key role because the bureaucracy is so powerful. The most important is the *Conseil d'État* (State Council), a watchdog on the executive. This is an especially important role in the French political system, where the executive has such great autonomy.

The council decides cases brought by individuals alleging that administrative actions have violated their rights. The State Council also advises the government about the constitutionality, legality, and coherence of proposed laws that the government is drafting.

## Subnational Government

France has three layers of subnational elected governments: municipal, departmental, and regional. At the local level, there are over 36,000 municipalities, more than in all other Western European countries combined! The system seems unusually cumbersome. But polls repeatedly find that citizens hold local officials in much higher regard than national officeholders.

Until the 1980s, local governments were quite weak. Responsibility for regulating local affairs was in the hands of nationally appointed field officers. For example, prefects, supervisors of civil engineering, and financial officers all represented government ministries.

The Socialist government sponsored a fundamental overhaul of local government in the 1980s, which loosened the supervision of local governments by the national government. Regional governments were also created. Municipal, departmental, and regional governments were authorized to levy taxes and administer many aspects of education, transportation, social welfare, and cultural policy.

The reforms have brought government closer to citizens. However, decentralization has produced new problems, for example, local officials have been convicted of taking kickbacks for awarding municipal contracts to private contractors. The reforms have also increased economic inequalities among localities and regions.

## The Military and the Police

France is a middling-rank power nowadays. But it is proud of its membership in the nuclear arms club. France has many nuclear weapons and sophisticated delivery systems. The French military intervened in domestic politics on some important occasions in the past. However, for the past half century, it has remained firmly under civilian control.

Within France, the police operate with considerable freedom—too much, according to critics. Alongside police forces under the control of local governments, there is a national police force, directed by the ministry of defense and garrisoned throughout France. Judges and executive officials have rarely reined in the police. The "forces of order," as they are called in France, have a reputation for engaging in brutal tactics, illegal surveillance, arbitrary actions, and racism.

# The Policy-Making Process

As discussed above, the policy-making process differs substantially between periods of unified control and cohabitation. Under united control, the president formulates major policy initiatives in consultation with the prime minister and powerful cabinet ministers. Government ministers, assisted by top civil servants, develop legislative proposals and administrative regulations to translate broad policy into concrete action. Under divided control (cohabitation), the prime minister has the dominant voice in most areas of policy-making.

Compared with most democratic countries, France provides fewer opportunities for public and private actors outside government to influence policy-making. Executive dominance comes at the expense of legislative and popular participation. In addition, the bureaucracy is large, expert, and often domineering.

France's participation in the global economy has deeply affected the executive and the French state more generally. EU commitments have limited France's freedom of action. Yet EU membership has also enabled France to leverage its power because of its leading role in this influential organization.

France has become more integrated within the EU and the wider global arena. But the gulf has widened between policy makers and ordinary citizens, resulting in additional stress on the system of political representation, as we describe in Section 4.

### Summary

France's semipresidential system has largely achieved the goals that President de Gaulle chose when designing the Fifth Republic. However, the system has important flaws. On the one hand, during periods of unified control there are few checks on executive power. On the other hand, during periods of cohabitation the president and prime minister can engage in frequent conflict. In both cases, as described in Section 4, the result is a wide gap between the state and civil society.

# SECTION 4

# REPRESENTATION AND PARTICIPATION

### Focus Questions

Why do scholars claim that the French legislature does not adequately represent citizens and hold the executive accountable?

What are two reforms that might improve the legislature's ability to perform the functions of representation and accountability?

Charles de Gaulle believed that political parties and parliament were too powerful in the Third and Fourth Republics and had prevented vigorous executive leadership. To correct what he regarded as a dangerous imbalance, the constitution of the Fifth Republic grants the executive relatively unchecked powers. At the same time, however, it sharply limits popular participation, representation, and legislative autonomy.

De Gaulle succeeded in muzzling parliament. But he completely failed to curb political parties. Ironically, however, the development of strong, centralized parties has provided powerful support for decisive executive leadership and political stability. A major reason is the direct election of the president. To win the all-important presidential contest, formerly decentralized parties reorganized to become centralized, unified organizations.

## The Legislature

The French parliament consists of the Senate and the more powerful National Assembly. Parliament lacks the independence that legislatures enjoy in full presidential systems. It cannot hold the executive fully accountable, as parliaments can in parliamentary systems, since it can only censure the prime minister, not the president. In the Fifth Republic, parliament has lost power to the president, government, bureaucracy, judiciary, EU, television, and subnational governments!

The Constitution created a revolution in French constitutional law. Rather than providing parliament with an open-ended grant of authority, Article 34 enumerates the areas in which parliament *may* legislate and prohibits legislation on other matters. The constitution creates a large domain outside parliament's competence, within which the executive is authorized to issue legally binding regulations and decrees without need for parliamentary approval. Even within the area of parliamentary competence, Article 38 authorizes the government to request that parliament delegate authority to the government to issue ordinances (regulations) with the force of law. Governments have relied on this procedure when they wished to save time, avoid extensive parliamentary debate, or limit unwelcome amendments.

Within the limited area of lawmaking, the government has extensive power to control legislative activity. The government initiates about 90 percent of bills passed into law. Parliament has limited control over the budget.

The executive can dissolve the National Assembly before its normal five-year term ends. The executive cannot dissolve the Senate, but this matters little since the Senate cannot pass legislation without the National Assembly's assent and it cannot force the government to resign by voting censure.

The government's control over parliament is bolstered by Article 44, the package or blocked vote, by which the government can direct parliament to vote on an entire bill or a portion of a bill. The government can select which amendments to include with the text. Governments have used (or abused) the package vote to restrict debate on many key legislative bills.

The government can further curb parliament by requesting a confidence vote in the National Assembly on either its overall policies or on a specific bill (Article 49). When the government calls for a confidence vote, the measure is considered approved unless the National Assembly passes a censure motion by an absolute majority of all deputies within twenty-four hours. Deputies who abstain or are absent are, in effect, counted as voting with the government. A 2008 constitutional reform, however, has limited the government's ability to employ this procedure. It can now be used only once each parliamentary session and only for financial matters.

Deputies can also submit motions to censure the government on their own initiative, but the constitution limits the number of parliament-initiated censure motions.

Governments typically do not need to fear a censure vote because they command a majority in the National Assembly. Only one successful censure motion has ever passed in the more than fifty-year history of the Fifth Republic.

Parliament is widely perceived as a rubber stamp. Its debates are not widely reported and opposition parties cannot adequately air grievances. As a result, discontented groups often express opposition in the streets rather than by channeling demands through parliament.

Parliamentary committees (called commissions) are not very powerful. Although they are authorized to review and propose amendments to draft legislation, the government can drop amendments it dislikes before putting the text to a vote.

The National Assembly is the more powerful chamber of parliament. It alone can censure the government. It can pass laws despite the Senate's opposition. The Senate can only delay approval of legislation. However, its approval is required to pass constitutional amendments.

In response to widespread criticism of parliament's limited powers, modest reforms have been enacted to increase its powers. For example, the constitution was amended in 2008 authorizing parliament to approve nominations to some key executive positions. Opposition parties are given control of the parliamentary agenda one day a month. Yet parliament continues to have quite limited power within the French political system.

## How a Bill Becomes a Law

Following a bill's introduction in one of the two chambers (usually the National Assembly) a commission reviews the bill. It then goes to the full house for debate, possible amendment, and vote. If approved, the same procedure is followed in the second chamber.

A bill passed in identical form by the two houses becomes law (unless subsequently struck down by the Constitutional Council). If the two houses twice vote different versions of a bill (or one time each, if the government declares the bill a priority matter), a joint commission of members from both houses seeks to negotiate a compromise text. If the commission reaches agreement, the revised text is voted upon by the two houses. If they do not pass the text at this reading, the government can request the National Assembly to vote once more. If the National Assembly approves the measure, it becomes law despite the lack of senatorial approval.

Once a bill passes, the constitution authorizes the president of the republic, president of either legislative chamber, or sixty deputies or senators to submit the bill to the Constitutional Council. The council can strike down the entire text or those portions that it judges violate the constitution. The council must be asked to rule before the bill is officially registered. After this period, the law stands and can never be reviewed by the council save for the case where a citizen successfully alleges that a law violates constitutionally protected rights.

Why would the two chambers hold different positions? One reason is that they are elected by different procedures and represent different interests.

### Electing the Legislature

Elections to the 577 single-member districts of the National Assembly follow a two-ballot procedure that is similar to the one used to elect the president. Deputies, as members of the National Assembly are called, are elected for a five-year term. To be elected at the first ballot, a candidate must receive an absolute majority of the votes cast in a district. Some popular incumbent deputies (that is, members of the National Assembly) are reelected at the first ballot. Usually, though, no candidate obtains a majority at this stage. A runoff election takes place the following week.

In presidential elections, only the two front-runners are eligible to compete at the runoff ballot. But in elections to the National Assembly, all candidates in a district who receive at least 12.5 percent of the votes at the first round can compete in the runoff. However, most second-ballot elections pit a candidate on the left against one on the right. So-called triangular races among three candidates are rare, because minority candidates usually throw their support to the best-placed major party candidate on their side of the political divide. As a result, the system used to elect the National Assembly contributes to polarization. It also makes it likely that a cohesive coalition will gain a majority in parliament.

There are 348 members of the Senate. Senators have six-year terms and are not popularly elected but are chosen by electoral colleges consisting of local elected officials from France's 101 *départements* (the administrative districts into which mainland and overseas France is divided). Several overseas territories also choose senators. Mayors and town councilors from small towns, villages, and rural areas make up the largest group in the electoral college that elects senators. This over-weighting of predominantly rural areas explains why the Senate has consistently been a conservative force in the Fifth Republic.

## Political Parties and the Party System

Despite de Gaulle's fears that political parties would prevent stable leadership, they have contributed to making strong leadership and political alternation possible. Recently, however, the decline in ideological distance between the major parties has meant that many French citizens feel unrepresented. For example, the two largest parties—the center-left Socialist Party and the center-right Union pour un mouvement populaire (UMP)—are normally rivals. However, a majority of citizens voted no in the 2005 referendum on the European constitution despite the fact that both parties campaigned for a yes vote.

## The Major Parties

The UMP and PS have dominated French political life for decades. Each leads a rival coalition that has typically alternated control of key political institutions throughout the Fifth Republic. At the same time, both are constantly challenged by smaller parties on their ideological flanks.

### Union pour un mouvement populaire (Union for a Popular Movement—UMP)

Until de Gaulle reached power in 1958, right-wing parties were numerous and fragmented. De Gaulle's allies formed a new party to support his leadership, and the party was able to unify many forces on the moderate right of the political spectrum. The social base of the party reflects its conservative orientation. It is mainly composed of business executives, shopkeepers, professionals, the elderly, the wealthy, and the highly educated.

The Gaullist party—whose name was changed to the UMP in 2002—was the keystone of the early Fifth Republic. Although its fortunes flagged in the 1970s and 1980s, it regained dominance when Jacques Chirac was elected president in 1995. Nicolas Sarkozy, the dynamic UMP maverick, succeeded Chirac as president in 2007, and the party gained control of the presidency, government, and parliament.

### Parti socialiste (PS)

A perpetual and ineffective opposition party in the early Fifth Republic, the Socialist Party (PS) became a vanguard of newly modernized France in 1981. Under François Mitterrand's leadership, it swept the presidential and parliamentary elections that year. Since then, the PS and the UMP have vied for control of French political institutions. The PS reached power in 1981 by advocating substantial changes. However, it lost its ideological bearings after the right turn of 1983, as described in Section 2.

The young and unconventional Ségolène Royal was the party's nominee for president in 2007. The first female presidential candidate of a major party, Royal was a striking contrast to older, male—and stale—Socialist politicians. She came with a new ideological look, containing few references to socialism. However, when Royal lost to Nicolas Sarkozy in 2007, it was yet another in a string of electoral Socialist losses in the 21st century. To remain a major contender, the party must devise an attractive program and unite behind an effective leader.

The PS draws support from civil servants, low-income groups, and educated professionals. Its support to some extent is the mirror image of the UMP's. But both parties represent different groups within the more secure sectors of French society. Vulnerable and excluded groups, including unskilled workers, the unemployed, and school dropouts, often support fringe parties.

## Small Parties

The largest French splinter parties nowadays are the Front national (FN), Les Verts (Greens), centrist parties, and the Parti communiste français (PCF). Given space limitations, we focus on only one small party here. This requires neglecting other significant parties. For example, consider the PCF. It was among the largest parties in postwar France and is one of the few remaining self-proclaimed communist parties in the world. But its electoral support has been declining for decades, and PCF

## THE U.S. CONNECTION

### French and American Political Parties Compared

The French and American party systems are structured quite differently. The vast majority of Americans vote for either the Democratic or Republican party candidate. The combined vote for "third party" candidates, that is, candidates from other parties, rarely reaches 10 percent.

France has a multiparty system. Although in recent years two parties (the UMP and PS) have been front-runners, many smaller parties also compete and usually receive over 40 percent of the vote.

Scholars have debated the reasons for this contrast. One important factor is electoral procedures. American elections are generally governed by first-past-the-post procedures, also known as the plurality system. In elections of this kind, the candidate receiving the most votes wins. French legislative and presidential elections are governed by a two-ballot system described above. Why does this encourage the emergence of many parties? Because many French citizens calculate that voting for a small party at the first ballot will not be a wasted vote. The two-ballot procedure gives them the opportunity to express a stronger preference at the first ballot and vote "usefully" at the second ballot. Thus, having a two-ballot system gives smaller parties a boost.

At the same time, scholars have noted that the French party system is becoming "Americanized." This involves two trends: First, in part because of the importance of presidential elections, smaller parties are at a particular disadvantage, and there has thus been a tendency toward a two-party system. The UMP now dominates the center-right; the PS, the center-left. Parties that were significant players in the past are now junior partners of the two major parties.

France's party system remains quite different from the U.S. model. For example, in the 2007 president election, 57 percent of those voting supported Sarkozy and Royal at the first ballot. Nearly half of the electorate—the remaining 43 percent of voters—chose one of the other ten candidates. Thus, the French party system exhibits opposite tendencies: toward polarization, in which competition pits the two major parties against each other, and fragmentation, involving competition among a large number of parties.

A second way in which French parties and politics are coming to resemble what occurs in the United States is by a greater emphasis on personalities of political leaders and the whoopla of campaigning and governing. The United States was the first country in which television, focus groups, and polling played a central role in elections and governance. French commentators point to these elements as evidence of what they consider the Americanization of French politics.

presidential candidates nowadays receive well under 5 percent of the vote. At the same time, the PCF remains popular in some working class towns, and communist mayors continue to control a significant number of town halls. Thanks to an alliance with the PS, the PCF elected 15 deputies to parliament in 2007.

**Front national (FN)** The FN was among the first parties in Western Europe since World War II to promote racist themes. Its principal targets in the 1980s, when it first scored significant victories in local elections, were Muslim immigrants from North Africa, especially Arabs from Algeria. The FN proposed depriving immigrants of social benefits and even deporting them—a bigoted reponse to unemployment, crime, and ethnic diversity.

Jean-Marie Le Pen was the party's demagogic leader for years. His crude humor and combative style were a sharp contrast to the polished manner of most French politicians. Beginning in the 1990s, Le Pen broadened the party's focus by blaming mainstream politicians for rising crime rates, unemployment, and the loss of French sovereignty to the EU. He also adopted far-right themes by cracking anti-Semitic jokes, characterizing the Holocaust as an insignificant "historical detail," and declaring that the Nazi occupation of France during World War II was not especially inhumane.

In presidential elections in the 1990s, Le Pen received about 15 percent of the vote and came in fourth. He scored a dramatic breakthrough by gaining 17 percent of the vote in the 2002 presidential election and coming in second. This enabled him to compete with Chirac in the runoff ballot. In the 2007 presidential elections, the Le Pen vote fell back to 10 percent, and he again came in fourth. One reason was his advanced age: he was seventy-eight at the time. Further, Sarkozy stole Le Pen's thunder by adopting several of his hard-right themes, including tough talk on crime and illegal immigrants.

When Le Pen retired from active leadership of the FN, his daughter Marine, a member of the European Parliament, became head of the party. She exuberantly updated her father's approach. For example, in 2010 she compared Muslims praying in Paris streets to the Nazi occupation of France in World War II. Thanks to her youthful dynamism and the unimpressive performance of mainstream politicians, 2011 polls ranked her among the most popular politicians in France. There was a good prospect that she would repeat her father's performance in 2002 by reaching the runoff ballot in the 2012 presidential election.

The FN has profoundly influenced French politics. By fanning the flames of racism, bigotry, and xenophobia, it moved issues like immigration, crime, the place of Islam in France, and opposition to the EU and globalization to the top of the political agenda.

# Elections

France's most important elections are the legislative and presidential elections (see Tables 3.4 and 3.5). Troubling developments listed below have led some scholars to speak of a crisis of political representation and the party system.

- Support has grown for fringe parties not part of the select "cartel" of governmental parties.
- Voting patterns have been increasingly unstable. In every one of the six legislative elections between 1981 and 2002, the governing majority swung between the center-left and center-right parties. When the UMP won the 2007 parliamentary elections, it was the first time in thirty years that alternation between competing coalitions did not occur.
- Voter turnout has generally been declining in both presidential and parliamentary elections.
- Countless prominent politicians have been implicated in criminal misconduct. Starting at the top, President Chirac was convicted in 2010 of using public funds to assist the UMP while he served as mayor of Paris in the 1970s. As we describe below, in 2010 President Sarkozy was embroiled in a financial scandal. Perhaps the low point occurred in 2011. Dominique Strauss-Kahn, managing director of the International Monetary Fund (IMF), a former finance minister, the probable Socialist party candidate in the 2012 presidential election, and the most popular politician in France, was criminally charged with sexually assaulting a housekeeper in a posh New York hotel. These sordid incidents help explain why, according to one public opinion poll, 64 percent of the French regard most politicians as corrupt.[23]

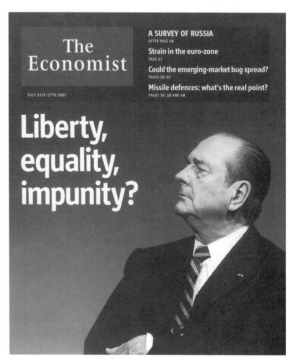

Allegations of corruption by President Chirac.

*Source:* © Philippe Wojazer/Reuters/Corbis.

## Table 3.4 — Presidential Elections in the Fifth Republic (percentage of those voting)

| Candidate | December 1965 Candidate | Ballot % | June 1969 Candidate | Ballot % | May 1974 Candidate | Ballot % | April–May 1981 Candidate | Ballot % | April–May 1988 Candidate | Ballot % | April–May 1995 Candidate | Ballot % | April–May 2002 Candidate | Ballot % | April–May 2007 Candidate | Ballot % |
|---|---|---|---|---|---|---|---|---|---|---|---|---|---|---|---|---|
| **Extreme Right** | | | | | | | | | Le Pen (FN) | 14.4 | Le Pen (FN) | 15.0 | Le Pen (FN) | 17.0 (17.9) | Le Pen (FN) | 10 |
|  | | | | | | | | | | | | | | | De Villiers | 2 |
| **Center Right** de Gaulle (Center-Right) | Pompidou (UNR) *(de Gaulle)* 43.7 (54.5) | | Pompidou (UNR) | 44.0 (57.6) | | | Chirac (RPR) | 18.0 | Chirac (RPR) | 19.9 (46.0) | Chirac (RPR) | 20.8 (52.6) | Chirac (RPR) | 19.9 (82.1) | Sarkozy (UMP) | 31 (53) |
| **Center** Lecanuet (Opposition-Center) | Lecanuet | 15.8 | Poher (Center) | 23.4 (42.4) | Giscard | 32.9 (50.7) | Giscard | 28.3 (48.2) | Barre | 16.5 | Balladur (UDF) | 18.9 | Bayrou (UDF) | 6.8 | Bayrou (UDF) | 19 |
|  | | | | | | | | | | | | | Saint-Josse (CNPT) | 4.3 | Nihous (CNPT) | 1 |
|  | | | | | | | | | | | | | Madelin (PR) | 3.9 | | |
| **Center Left** Mitterrand (Socialist-Communist) | Mitterrand (PS) | 32.2 (45.5) | Defferre (PS) | 5.1 | Mitterrand (PS) | 43.4 (49.3) | Mitterrand (PS) | 25.8 (51.8) | Mitterrand (PS) | 34.1 (54.0) | Jospin (PS) | 23.3 (47.4) | Jospin (PS) | 16.1 | Royal (PS) | 26 (47) |
|  | | | | | | | | | | | | | Chevènement | 5.3 | Voynet (Greens) | 2 |
|  | | | | | | | | | | | | | Mamère (Greens) | 5.3 | | |
| **Left** | | | Duclos (PCF) | 21.5 | | | Marchais (PCF) | 15.3 | Lajoinie (PCF) | 6.8 | Hue (PCF) | 8.6 | Hue (PCF) | 3.4 | Buffet (PCF) | 2 |
|  | | | | | | | | | | | | | 3 candidates (Extreme Left) | 10.6 | 4 candidates (Extreme Left) | 7 |
| **Abstentions** | 15.0 (15.5) | | 21.8 (30.9) | | 15.1 (12.1) | | 18.9 (14.1) | | | | 20.6 | | 27.9 (19.9) | | 16 (16) | |

*Note:* Numbers in parentheses indicate percentage of vote received in second ballot. Percentages of votes for candidates do not add to 100 because of minor party candidates and rounding errors.

*Sources:* John R. Frears and Jean-Luc Parodi, *War Will Not Take Place: The French Parliamentary Elections of March 1978* (London: Hurst, 1976), p. 6; *Le Monde, L'Élection présidentielle: 26 avril–10 mai 1981* (Paris: *Le Monde*, 1981), pp. 98, 138; *Le Monde*, April 28 and May 12, 1998; *Journal officiel*, May 14, 1995; *Le Monde*, May 5–6, 2002; *Le Monde*, May 7, 2002; www.electionresources.org/fr/president.php?election=2007&region=fr (accessed on June 18, 2007).

| Table 3.5 | Electoral Results, Elections to National Assembly, 1958–2007 (percentage of those voting) | | | | | | | | | | | | |
|---|---|---|---|---|---|---|---|---|---|---|---|---|---|
| | **1958** | **1962** | **1967** | **1968** | **1973** | **1978** | **1981** | **1986** | **1988** | **1993** | **1997** | **2002** | **2007** |
| Far Left | 2% | 2% | 2% | 4% | 3% | 3% | 1% | 2% | 0% | 2% | 2% | 3% | 2% |
| PCF | 19 | 22 | 23 | 20 | 21 | 21 | 16 | 10 | 11 | 9 | 10 | 5 | 4 |
| Socialist Party/Left Radicals | 23 | 21 | 19 | 17 | 22 | 25 | 38 | 32 | 38 | 21 | 26 | 25 | 26 |
| Ecology | — | — | — | — | — | 2 | 1 | 1 | 1 | 12 | 8 | 4 | 3 |
| Center | 15 | 15 | 18 | 10 | 16 | 21* | 19* | | 19* | 19* | 15* | | 8 |
| Center-Right | 14 | 14 | 0 | 4 | 7 | | | 42* | | | | 5* | 4 |
| UNR-RPR-UMP | 18 | 32 | 38 | 44 | 24 | 23 | 21 | — | 19 | 20 | 17 | 34 | 40 |
| Far Right | 3 | 1 | 1 | 0 | 3 | 0 | 3 | 10 | 10 | 13 | 15 | 12 | 7 |
| Abstentions | 23 | 31 | 19 | 20 | 19 | 17 | 30 | 22 | 34 | 31 | 32 | 36 | 40 |

*Number represents the percentage of combined votes for Center and Center-Right parties.
*Sources:* Françoise Dreyfus and François D'Arcy, *Les Institutions politiques et administratives de la France* (Paris: Economica, 1985), 54; *Le Monde*, March 18, 1986; *Le Monde, Les élections législatives* (Paris: *Le Monde*, 1988). Ministry of the Interior, 1993, 1997. *Le Monde*, June 11, 2002; *www.electionresources.org/fr/deputies.php?election=2007&region=fr (accessed 6/18/2007).*

More generally, French political leaders and institutions are held in pitifully low esteem. In a 2011 poll, 87 percent of the French judged all politicians to be dishonest. Nearly as many expressed little or no confidence in the government's ability to improve their personal situation.[24] France's ailing party system has contributed to the widespread belief that political institutions are in serious need of overhaul. However, it is not clear what or who can deliver effective reform.

# Political Culture, Citizenship, and Identity

Until the 1980s, two traditional subcultures powerfully shaped French political and cultural life. One subculture had a working-class flavor. It was structured by the French Communist Party (PCF) and the PCF's trade union ally, which dominated the labor movement. The other was a conservative subculture linked to the Catholic Church and its social organizations. The subcultures provided members with distinctive (and opposed) political orientations and social identities. Most French citizens, even those not fully integrated in either subculture, identified with one or the other. In recent decades, the subcultures have disintegrated. The proportion of self-identified Communists and observant Catholics has plummeted. No new, broad-based networks have replaced them.

## Social Class

For centuries, class cleavages produced intense political conflict in France. Class iden-tification, however, rapidly declined in the 1970s, as a result of changes in the econ-omy and ideological orientations. The most extensive demographic shift was a massive reduction in the number of manual workers, as basic industries, including steel, ship-building, automobiles, and textiles, drastically downsized the industrial work force. This was matched by the rise of service sector employment. This scrambling of class boundaries has eroded traditional social identities while no new social anchors have developed to replace them. When combined with a rise in unemployment beginning in the 1970s, and with no prospect of a return to full employment, the result has been a widespread sense of insecurity.

## Ethnicity and Immigration

France has traditionally attracted large numbers of immigrants. Indeed, in 1930, France had a higher proportion of immigrants than the United States.[25] A new wave of immigrants poured into France after World War II, partly thanks to a vigorous recruitment effort by the French government seeking workers to help rebuild the French economy. At the high point of postwar immigration, one ninth of the French population was foreign-born. When the French economy slowed in the 1970s, the government abruptly shifted to restricting the flow of new immigrants. New immi-grants after that have consisted of family members of immigrants already established in France, those occupying skilled positions, and undocumented immigrants. France retains a strong connection to the outside world. One French person in four these days has at least one foreign-born grandparent.

Economic stagnation and high unemployment have created insecurity that politi-cal leaders, such as the Le Pens (father and daughter), have manipulated to fan anti-immigrant flames. Their strategy has helped reshape the entire political landscape. The FN has helped move the relationship of citizens of color from immigrant backgrounds to the majority French community toward the top of the political agenda. According to one historian, "the view that immigrants represented a threat to 'national identity,' originally launched by the far right, [is now] held by large sectors of the public."[26]

President Sarkozy's rise was partly a result of his adopting the FN's anti-immigrant orientation. For example, while visiting a run-down suburb in 2005, he made inflam-matory remarks about immigrant youth that helped spark suburban riots several weeks later (they are described below). When he was elected president in 2007, he created a Ministry of Immigration and National Identity, and later launched a national debate about the meaning of France's national identity that indirectly questioned the patrio-tism of those from immigrant backgrounds. In 2010, he proposed stripping natural-ized French citizens of their citizenship if they committed serious crimes. The same year, he ordered police to destroy Roma camps (the Roma are also known as Gypsies) and forcibly deport Romas to their native Romania and Bulgaria. The European Union's minister of justice announced that she was "appalled" by the government's campaign of ethnic profiling.

## Citizenship and National Identity

France's dominant approach to immigration, citizenship, and national identity is often described as the republican model. On the one hand, the model is inclusive. There are no ethnic, racial, or religious restrictions on becoming a French citizen. No matter what their background, all newcomers are expected to adopt the values that are widely regarded as both distinctively French and universally valid. They can be summed up in the slogan dating from the French Revolution of liberty, equality, and fraternity.

The republican model, however, has an exclusionary aspect. It insists that distinctive cultural identities and values should remain private and should play no role in the public sphere. Most French regard the American conception of multiculturalism as dangerous. In the French view, multiculturalism encourages "identity politics" and creates conflicts among groups based on ethnic or religious affiliation.

France's color-blind and ethnic-blind model champions the value of individual merit. However, in practice, by studiously ignoring racial and ethnic differences, it may marginalize minorities. The government has tried to deal with the disadvantages experienced by racial and ethnic minorities indirectly, for example, by channeling benefits to what it designates as "sensitive areas," that is, urban neighborhoods which (not coincidentally) are often home to minorities. However, the failure to squarely confront racial and ethnic inequality leaves minorities economically and politically under-represented. For example, only a handful of Muslims or people of color occupy positions of political leadership.

Nicolas Sarkozy broke with this pattern in 2007 by appointing three women of North African and black African backgrounds to his cabinet. However noteworthy the decision, it did not improve the position of France's minorities.

The French are proud of their country's cultural heritage. But in an era of globalization and French membership in the EU, it is unclear what is distinctive about French identity and culture.

President Sarkozy and the UMP have highlighted the issue of national identity in ways that compound the problem. In the fall of 2009, government launched a series of meetings to discuss the contemporary meaning of French national identity. Critics charged that the debate had a partisan motive: to highlight the UMP and Sarkozy's patriotic attachments. Critics warned that ethnic minorities risked being made the scapegoat for economic and social insecurity in France. The debate soon degenerated into a national shouting match and was shelved after several months.

## Gender

French philosopher and novelist Simone de Beauvoir published *The Second Sex* after World War II. The book is a feminist landmark highlighting the social processes by which women are assigned to a secondary role in society. In the 1960s and 1970s, French feminist theorists played a major role in reshaping literary studies around the world. However, these noteworthy literary achievements have not produced gender equality in France.

Women have traditionally been highly under-represented in the French political system. Although they make up over half the electorate, there has never been a female president and only one prime minister. Thanks to long efforts by the women's movement, France took a giant step by adopting a constitutional amendment in 1999 that mandates gender parity for many elected offices. France was the first country in the world to require political parties to nominate an equal number of men and women for elected positions. Since then, over 100 other countries have followed France's lead.

The **parity law** requires parties to nominate an equal number of male and female candidates for elected political positions filled by proportional representation. Parties failing to do so can be disqualified. Where elections are held in single-member districts, public campaign subsidies are reduced if parties fail to nominate an equal number of men and women.

Following passage of the parity law, the number of women elected to town councils skyrocketed from 7,000 to 39,000. Women now make up fully half of

**parity law**

A French law passed in 2000 that directs political parties to nominate an equal number of men and women for many elections.

all members of these councils. The number of women in the Senate and regional councils has also doubled. However, the parity law has not much increased the representation of women in the National Assembly, whose members are elected from single-member districts. Parties often fulfill the parity obligation by nominating women in districts where the party is weak and they have little chance of being elected. This explains why female representation in the National Assembly has only increased slightly: from 12 percent in 2002 to 19 percent after the 2007 elections.

The parity law does not apply to presidential elections, the most important election of all. Nonetheless, it may have had an indirect influence in 2007 when, for the first time, a major political party, the PS, nominated a female presidential candidate—Ségolène Royal, president of a regional council. Royal came in second behind Nicolas Sarkozy.

Following Sarkozy's election as president, he appointed a large number of women to cabinet positions. For the first time, women were named ministers of the most powerful departments, including Interior and Finance.

While women have achieved greater political representation, thanks to the parity law and changing values, they continue to have unequal political, social, and economic representation.

# Interests, Social Movements, and Protest

## Organized Interests

Compared to the executive in countries like Britain and the United States, the French executive has typically acted on its own, without consulting much with private interest groups. Some favored interest groups, however, participate in consultative commissions and have easy access to policy-makers. Examples include the farm lobby (the FNSEA) and Medef, the umbrella business association. But as a general rule, the French state has kept interest groups at a distance.

## French Trade Unions

The French labor movement is quite weak. First, far fewer workers belong to unions than is the case in other industrial democracies. The number of union members is less than 10 percent of the labor force, the lowest figure among comparable countries. Further, the trend has been downward since the period after World War II, when over 30 percent of workers belonged to unions.

The labor movement is further weakened by internal divisions. In many industrialized democracies, including Britain, Germany, and Japan, most unions belong to a single trade union confederation. As a result, organized labor is relatively unified. France has four trade union confederations and several independent unions. Each confederation pursues its own economic and political agenda. The confederations compete with each other for members and rarely cooperate to sponsor joint activities. When they do, as occurred for jointly planned demonstrations in 2010 opposing pension reform, the whole is greater than the sum of the parts.

Yet it is only partially accurate to regard unions as weak. They have two significant resources enabling them to play an important role. First, they are represented on the governing boards of powerful public agencies, including the social security, health, pension, and unemployment insurance funds. Second, unions have the capacity to mobilize members and nonmembers alike. Unions often take the lead in organizing demonstrations to oppose plant closings or proposed cutbacks in social benefits. At these crisis points, large numbers of French turn out to support the unions. When this occurs, employers and the state appeals to union leaders to restore calm. Feverish meetings are held between government administrators, business leaders, and union officials. Unions are often able to obtain significant benefits at these times. When calm returns, unions again assume a marginal role—until the next explosion.

## Social Movements and Protest

Fifth Republic institutions were designed to discourage citizens from acting autonomously. There are fewer organized interest groups and voluntary associations in France than in comparable countries. Those that exist, such as the trade union movement, are quite weak. Perhaps partly as a result of this situation, France's centuries-old tradition of direct protest persists. France is among the European countries where the highest proportion of citizens participates in demonstrations. These protests are a substitute for adequate institutional channels of representation. A partial list of groups that have engaged in strikes and demonstrations in recent years include farmers, postal workers, teachers and professors, high school and university students, truckers, railway workers, industrial workers, sanitation workers, health care workers, retired workers, the unemployed, homeless, immigrants, actors, and research workers!

To illustrate, in late 2010 between two to three million French turned out weekly to oppose the government's plan to increase the retirement age. Demonstrations were held in Paris, Lyon, and Marseille, as well as in towns throughout the country. France ground to a halt when workers in key industries like petroleum refining and trucking went on strike. Despite the inconvenience this caused, polls report that over 70 percent of the French supported the demonstrations.[27] Nonetheless, the Sarkozy government refused to budge, and the pension reform has been implemented. The government won this skirmish, but at the price of increasing the gulf between the state and French citizens.

AP Photo/Claude Paris

Crowds gather at a demonstration protesting the French pension reform on October 5, 2010.

## Summary

French society is composed of groups from many religious, ethnic, and racial backgrounds. For generations, immigrants flocked to France from southern and eastern Europe, northern and sub-Saharan Africa, and Southeast Asia. Immigrants contributed intelligence, hard work, and vitality to making France a world cultural and economic leader. In return, France granted immigrants, or their children, the right to citizenship and social benefits.

However, immigrants are often second-class citizens. They are given the least desirable jobs, or not offered jobs at all. They live in huge and poorly maintained public housing projects and shabby neighborhoods.

The Fifth Republic has created a strong executive but lacks adequate mechanisms for representing citizens' interests. The political system has not achieved an adequate balance between executive leadership and popular participation and representation. As a result of design flaws in public institutions and the rigidity of political culture, what often appears as a calm political situation turns out to be the calm before the storm. The pattern of disruptive popular protests described in the next section is closely linked to the design of French political institutions described in Section 3 and cultural attitudes described in this section. This situation suggests a troubling question: Does the French political system have the capacity to address current challenges?

# SECTION 5

# FRENCH POLITICS IN TRANSITION

## Focus Questions

What are two major challenges facing the French political system?

Name one feature of French political institutions or culture that can help meet these challenges. Name one feature that makes it difficult to meet the challenges.

What are two features of French politics that have surprised you after reading this chapter, and why?

A juicy scandal in 2010 that appeared made to order for TV confirmed widespread French cynicism about their political leaders and highlighted disturbing features of French politics. What began as a family feud captured newspaper headlines following allegations that President Sarkozy and one of his cabinet ministers had received illegal payments by billionaire Liliane Bettencourt, heiress to the Oréal cosmetics company. The scandal quickly became known as France's Watergate after Bettencourt's accountant alleged that her former employer had for years made illegal political contributions to politicians. Most notable was the allegation that Bettencourt had made a $200,000 cash contribution to Sarkozy's 2007 presidential campaign.

As the scandal unfolded, it highlighted many unsavory connections between money and politics. When Sarkozy was elected president, he appointed Eric Woerth to be minister of budget and public finance. Woerth was responsible for policing tax fraud, and he quickly launched a well-publicized campaign against tax cheats. However, Ms. Bettencourt was never seriously investigated despite evidence that she maintained illegal bank accounts in Switzerland and failed to pay taxes on a tropical island she had purchased in the Indian Ocean.

Nor was this all. The head of a wealth management firm revealed that budget minister Woerth had contacted him to request that he hire Woerth's wife. Florence Woerth's responsibilities at the firm included helping Bettencourt minimize the tax bill that Eric Woerth's budget ministry was responsible for collecting and auditing! Adding further insult to injury was the fact that, while Mr. Woerth was serving as budget minister, he was also the UMP's treasurer. His responsibilities as budget minister included auditing the UMP's accounts and enforcing campaign finance laws!

After these details were made public, the Sarkozy government refused calls for an independent judicial investigation. Instead, the government delegated investigation of the case to a prosecutor who was under the authority of Sarkozy's minister of justice and who had close ties to Sarkozy. It was hard to avoid the impression that this was a clumsy attempt at damage control. A Socialist politician echoed a widely held view when he charged that the affair appeared to involve "corruption at the highest level of the state."[28]

The scandal highlighted close, and often unsavory, links between wealthy citizens and leading politicians, official abuses of power, and possible criminal activity by those in high places, including the president. Among many challenges confronting the French political system is how to re-establish public trust in politicians and political institutions following revelations of this kind.

# Political Challenges and Changing Agendas

### Integrating the Excluded

In November 2005, France erupted in flames following a fatal incident at a slum neighborhood outside Paris. Two adolescent boys of Algerian background were accidentally electrocuted at an electrical power substation while fleeing from the police. News of their deaths ignited riots in *cités* (impoverished neighborhoods) throughout France. For weeks, bands of young men roamed nightly through slum districts torching cars, schools, and public buildings. (Ten thousand cars were burned during the uprising.) The rebellion ended only after heavy police reinforcements occupied the turbulent neighborhoods.

Why did the young men's death provoke such widespread anger and destruction? An underlying cause is extensive unemployment among young men, especially Muslims. (Many of the rioters, although not all, were Muslim.) Another cause is the tense relations between the police and youth of immigrant background who live in what the French call "sensitive neighborhoods." A third cause is that, shortly before the uprising, then-interior minister Nicolas Sarkozy visited a suburban slum, publicly described juvenile delinquents as "scum," and proposed thoroughly disinfecting the slums. (For years after the intemperate remark, Sarkozy was unable to visit poor neighborhoods because his presence attracted angry crowds.)

Not long after the suburban riots, a government proposal triggered another massive wave of opposition. In 2006, Prime Minister Dominique de Villepin sponsored a youth employment scheme designed to create jobs for young people, especially the less-educated. The plan was called the First Employment Contract; its French initials are CPE. Villepin pointed to the 2005 urban riots as a reason to launch the CPE. The plan was designed to create jobs for young workers, especially those without advanced training. However, labor unions and student organizations charged that the reform allowed employers to hire workers at low wages and arbitrarily dismiss them.

When parliament voted to approve the plan, it produced an explosion. In no time, half of all French universities were shut down by strikes and occupations. The conflict widened when unions joined the student movement. After two million citizens throughout France participated in demonstrations, the government admitted defeat and cancelled the CPE.

President Sarkozy was determined not to back down in 2010 when he sponsored the pension reform increasing the retirement age. Although millions of people marched in September 2010 to protest the government's plan, Sarkozy did not budge. Weeks later a second nationwide demonstration was held. It was followed by a third and then a fourth. Yet Sarkozy stood firm, and the reform has been implemented. Time will tell whether Sarkozy garnered more credit or more blame for his tough stand. At the least, the incident served to highlight the wide gulf between the state and society in France and to further sour the already gloomy social climate.

## Reshaping the French Social Model?

An underlying cause of the intense confrontations described above is high unemployment and cutbacks in social spending. Protests over cutbacks have occurred in such varied sectors as health care, cultural institutions, pension benefits, and the electrical power and petrochemical industries. However, the way that cutbacks have been sponsored has contributed to conflict. Britain, Germany, and other affluent countries have sponsored social cutbacks in response to globalization, changing demography, and economic stagnation. In these countries, however, organized consultation has smoothed the process of adjustment. In France, the process has often involved a naked conflict of wills. There appears to be a pattern inscribed in France's national DNA according to which the government seeks to impose reforms in an arbitrary way and citizens respond by launching widespread protests.

## *Oui* to Roquefort Cheese, *Non* to Genetically Engineered Products

France is home to a flourishing antiglobalization movement comprised of far-leftists, intellectuals, farmers, and environmentalists. The movement's best-known leader is José Bové, a sheep farmer from southwestern France, where Roquefort cheese is produced. Small farmers like Bové oppose the standardized methods of farming that agribusiness corporations seek to impose. These methods often involve using genetically modified seed, which the movement opposes as potentially risky and designed to boost corporate profits. Farmers also oppose the way that large corporations try to centralize food processing and distribution. Bové became a popular hero after he ransacked a McDonald's construction site and served a six-week prison sentence. However, he failed to translate his popularity into political support. When he ran for president in 2007, he garnered a negligible 1.3 percent of the vote.

One of the organizations spearheading opposition to globalization is called ATTAC (which stands for Association in Support of the Tobin Tax). Yale economist and Nobel Prize winner James Tobin first proposed a tax on short-term capital movements to reduce international financial speculation and to finance development projects in poor countries. The idea of such a tax was later championed by ATTAC. The idea was given a boost during the financial crisis of 2008–2009. When President Sarkozy assumed the rotating leadership of the G-8 and G-20, organizations grouping major and developing countries, he proposed a version of the Tobin tax to prevent future financial instability.

Opposition to globalization is a major theme in French political discourse. One reason is that many French regard globalization as threatening cultural diversity. In particular, they fear that the "invasion" of American companies, products, and values will threaten France's cherished way of life. Globalization is also held responsible for exporting French jobs to low-wage countries within

Globalization. This cartoon appeared when José Bové traveled to the Seattle meeting of the World Trade Organization in 1999.

*Source:* Plantu, Cartoonists and Writers Syndicate, from Cassettes, Mensonges, et Vidéo (Paris: Le Seuil, 2000).

the EU and elsewhere. However, it should be noted that an enormous number of jobs in France are devoted to producing goods and services for export.

## The Challenge of Le Pen and the FN

The antiglobalization movement is one response to France's position in a changing world. The growth of the Le Pen phenomenon and ethnic conflicts are others. The Front national (FN) has reaped a political harvest from the presence of Muslims in French society. The five million Muslims in France is the largest number of any country in Western Europe. Political sociologist Pierre Birnbaum observes, "What the National Front proposes to the French people ... is a magical solution to their distress, to their loss of confidence in grand political visions of the nation."[29]

The FN attracts most of its support from native-born white citizens on the margins of French society. In the 2002 presidential elections, the unemployed made up one-third of its electorate. More workers voted for Le Pen than for any other candidate.[30] While Sarkozy lured many former supporters of the FN to his cause in 2007, the FN gained a new lease on life under the leadership of Marine Le Pen.

Given the FN's popularity, it is surprising that French attitudes toward immigrants of Muslim backgrounds are more positive than is the case for citizens of neighboring countries. When French, Germans, and British citizens were asked whether "it is a good thing people from the Middle East and North Africa [are] coming to your country," the French were most likely to answer yes. The same poll found that French Muslims report feeling much less alienated from the dominant culture than is the case for Muslims in Britain and Germany.[31]

## France Falling?

France has been wracked by self-doubt in recent years, as illustrated by best-selling books with titles like *France Falling*, *France's Disarray*, and *French Melancholy*. One poll found that 63 percent of the French believe their country is in decline. Indeed, one political analyst chides the French for being unduly self-critical![32]

France's political system is often described as rigid and unable to adapt. Yet, political scientist Peter A. Hall observes that "the economy, society and politics of France have changed ... profoundly during the past 25 years...."[33] Within the past decade, important reforms have involved the parity law, decentralization, and the health care, retirement, and industrial relations systems.

Another example is the civil solidarity pact (*pacte civil de solidarité*, or PACS) created in 1999. The PACS involves civil union between unmarried couples. It provides many of the legal rights and benefits enjoyed by married couples. The arrangement has proved highly popular. Nowadays, there are nearly as many PACS registered each year as marriages. The PACS law was designed to enable gay couples to obtain benefits formerly available only to married couples. However, most couples who register under the provisions of the PACS law these days are straight.

Have recent economic and social changes produced a welcome pluralism or a destructive fragmentation of French society? Many French regret that the country's formerly distinctive way of life has been destabilized. Can the positive features of the past be preserved while reforms are introduced to address pressing problems? Both

## France's Relation to Terrorism

France's relationship to terrorism is quite different from that of the United States. The United States has experienced two terrorist attacks organized from abroad. Both were directed at the World Trade Center in New York—in 1993 and September 11, 2001, when the Pentagon was also attacked. By contrast, for decades before 9/11 France was the target of domestic and international terrorist violence, often linked to its brutal colonial war in Algeria. For example, in 1996 a subway station in the Latin Quarter of Paris was bombed, killing four and wounding 170 people.

Only a handful of France's approximately 5 million Muslims support the radical variants of Islam that inspire terrorist activity. But violent opposition has been fueled in recent years, partly caused by the dispatch of French troops to serve alongside U.S. forces in Afghanistan and by French business operations throughout the world.

There have been numerous incidents in recent years of violence linked to Al Qaeda and affiliated groups. In 2003, Richard Reid, a British citizen on a plane flight between Paris and Miami, was overpowered by other passengers when he tried to ignite explosives to bring down the plane. Also in 2003, French antiterrorist police arrested eighteen Algerians and Pakistanis in the Paris area and charged them with ties to Al Qaeda. In 2006, Zacarias Moussaoui, a French citizen, was sentenced to life imprisonment in the United States on charges that he helped plan the September 11 attack. In 2007, French antiterrorism police charged eleven people with participating in a network linked to Al Qaeda.

An additional wave of incidents occurred in 2010, when police ordered the evacuation of the Eiffel Tower and arrested a dozen people linked to Al Qaeda in Marseille, Bordeaux, and elsewhere, charging them with planning bomb attacks. Five French employees of a mining company in Niger were taken hostage by an offshoot of Al Qaeda. Fears of additional hostage-taking led to the evacuation of 43,000 French citizens working in North Africa. Nonetheless, two French citizens taken hostage in 2011 were executed when Niger's armed forces tried to rescue them.

There are extensive intelligence and counterterrorist services housed in the Defense and Interior Ministries whose mission is to prevent terrorism. They have been highly effective, foiling on average two terrorist plots a year. However, these agencies operate in secret with little accountability. They have been accused of corruption, abuses of human rights, and religious and ethnic discrimination.

## French Politics in Comparative Perspective

Is French politics becoming less exceptional? For one thing, *dirigisme* and ideological conflict, two of the central features of the exceptionalist model, have declined in recent years. Yet, as discussed in Section 2, although *dirigisme* has been transformed, it has not been abandoned. Further, although left-right divisions have declined, new cleavages have developed. There is much to be learned, therefore, from including France in cross-national comparisons.

France lends itself to comparisons along the four core dimensions that have framed this book. It can usefully be compared with countries where the state plays a less central role. France's statist style of economic management offers an interesting contrast to countries in which market forces are less regulated. The French theory and practice of democracy lend themselves to comparison with democracy elsewhere. And the ways that France deals with issues involving collective identity can be usefully compared with regimes adopting a different approach.

A second kind of comparison involves historical comparisons within France. For example, the impact of institutions on political outcomes can be studied by comparing the Fourth and Fifth Republics. By studying the impact of the parity law, France provides a fine opportunity to analyze whether political institutions can be effective in reducing gender inequality.

## Summary

France occupies an enviable position in the world. The majority of French citizens enjoy a fine quality of life. In 2008, the Fifth Republic celebrated its fiftieth anniversary, a near-record for modern French regimes. Yet despite having reasons to celebrate, the French are divided and troubled about the future. Flaws in Fifth Republic political institutions make it harder to develop adequate responses to daunting challenges. Yet France's political system and society possess ample resources to meet these challenges. Nearly five decades after youthful protesters chanted in May 1968, "The struggle continues," the words have lost none of their relevance.

## Key Terms

fundamentalism
secularism
*ancien régime*
revolution
republic
prefect
authoritarian
proportional representation
referendum

conservative
socialist
decentralization
statism
*dirigisme*
indicative planning
industrial policy
nationalization
neoliberal

privatization
deregulation
judicial review
*cohabitation*
*grande école*
*grand corps*
parity law

## Suggested Readings

Berezin, Mabel. *Illiberal Politics in Neoliberal Times: Culture, Security and Populism in the New Europe.* Cambridge: Cambridge University Press, 2009.

Bleich, Erik. *Race Politics in Britain and France: Ideas and Policymaking since the 1960s.* Cambridge: Cambridge University Press, 2003.

Bowen, John R. *Why the French Don't Like Headscarves: Islam, the State, and Public Space.* Princeton: Princeton University Press, 2007.

Brouard, Sylvain, Andrew M. Appleton, and Amy G. Mazur, eds. *The French Fifth Republic at Fifty: Beyond Stereotypes.* New York: Palgrave Macmillan, 2009.

Brubaker, Rogers. *Citizenship and Nationhood in France and Germany.* Cambridge: Harvard University Press, 1992.

Cole, Alistair, Patrick Le Galès, and Jonah D. Levy, eds. *Developments in French Politics 4.* New York: Palgrave MacMillan, 2008.

Cole, A., and G. Raymond, eds. *Redefining the French Republic.* Manchester: Manchester University Press, 2006.

Culpepper, Pepper D., Peter A. Hall, and Bruno Palier, eds. *Changing France: The Politics That Markets Make.* New York: Palgrave Macmillan, 2006.

Elgie, Robert. *Political Institutions in Contemporary France.* New York: Oxford University Press, 2003.

Gordon, Philip H., and Sophie Meunier. *The French Challenge: Adapting to Globalization.* Washington, D.C.: Brookings Institution, 2001.

Knapp, Andrew. *Parties and the Party System in France: A Disconnected Democracy?* Hampshire, Eng.: Macmillan, 2004.

Laurence, Jonathan, and Justin Vaisse. *Integrating Islam: Political and Religious Challenges in Contemporary France.* Washington, D.C.: Brookings Institution, 2006.

Levy, Jonah, ed. *The State after Statism: New State Activities in the Age of Liberalization.* Cambridge: Harvard University Press, 2006.

Lewis-Beck, Michael S., ed. *The French Voter: Before and After the 2002 Elections.* London: Palgrave and Macmillan, 2004.

Murray, Rainbow. *Parties, Gender Quotas and Candidate Selection in France.* New York: Palgrave Macmillan, 2010.

Nord, Philip. *France's New Deal: From the Thirties to the Postwar Era.* Princeton: Princeton University Press, 2010.

Robb, Graham. *The Discovery of France: A Historical Geography from the Revolution to the First World War.* New York: W. W. Norton, 2007.

Schain, Martin A. *The Politics of Immigration in France, Britain, and the United States: A Comparative Study.* New York: Palgrave Macmillan, 2008.

Schmidt, Vivien A. *From State to Market? The Transformation of French Business and Government.* Cambridge: Cambridge University Press, 1996.

Scott, Joan Wallach. *The Politics of the Veil.* Princeton: Princeton University Press, 2007.

Shields, James G. *The Extreme Right in France: From Pétain to Le Pen.* London: Routledge, 2007.

Vail, Mark I. *Recasting Welfare Capitalism: Economic Adjustment in Contemporary France and Germany* (Philadelphia: Temple University Press, 2010).

Weil, Patrick. *How to Be French: Nationality in the Making since 1789.* Durham, NC: Duke University Press, 2008.

# 4 Germany

Christopher S. Allen and Wade Jacoby

**Official Name:** Federal Republic of Germany (*Bundesrepublik Deutschland*)

**Location:** Central Europe

**Capital City:** Berlin

**Population (2011):** 81.5 million

**Size:** 357,021 sq. km.; slightly smaller than Montana

**1806–1871**
Nationalism and German Unification

| 1805 | 1860 | 1870 | 1890 | 1900 | 1910 | 1915 |

**1871–1918**
Second Reich

**1919–1933**
Weimar Republic

SECTION 1

# THE MAKING OF THE MODERN GERMAN STATE

## Focus Questions

Why did German politics take such a disastrous turn in the first half of the twentieth century?

How successfully have German leaders since World War Two provided for their citizens without destabilizing the rest of Europe?

## Politics in Action

When the global financial crisis struck the United States in 2008, many Germans first thought that this was strictly an American problem. The German press was filled with stories about how the German economy was unlikely to be deeply affected. In part, this sense of security flowed from the insight that the German economy was much less driven by soaring profits in the financial sector compared to the United States and the United Kingdom. This interpretation was only strengthened by the evident problems in Europe's financial center, London, and by worrisome losses in the few German banks that had bet heavily on exotic investment instruments that originated in the United States and the United Kingdom.

When the German economy also entered into recession, it soon undermined the idea that the financial crisis was strictly a "made in America" problem or that its effects would be limited to countries with risky new financing practices and lax regulation. For one thing, when global access to capital dried up, much of the financing for trade dried up with it. Since Germany is extraordinarily active as an exporter of high quality machinery, chemicals, cars, and electronics, the decline in trade hurt Germany immediately. For another thing, it turned out that German banks were also neck-deep in lots of very messy investments abroad. Suddenly, the mood shifted and the fear in Germany was palpable.

As the crisis swept through Europe, falling exports soon threw the German economy into decline. GDP fell by about 5 percent in 2009. A number of important features of German politics immediately came into clear view. First, Germans had little faith in the power of government spending to counteract the deep recession. They worried far more (and far earlier) about government deficits than did other European governments. Second, German firms generally held onto their workers rather than laying them off as orders fell. Here, they were helped by the possibility of "short-time work," in which government paid part of the wages of workers who moved

| 1939–1945 | 1990–2000 |
|-----------|-----------|
| World War Two | The Challenge of German Unification |

| 1920 | 1930 | 1940 | 1950 | 1990 | 2001 |

| 1933–1945 | 1945–1990 | 2001– |
|-----------|-----------|-------|
| Third Reich | A Divided Germany | Germany after September 11 |

| Table 4.1 | Political Organization |
|-----------|------------------------|
| **Political System** | Parliamentary democracy. |
| **Regime History** | After the Third Reich's defeat, Germany was partitioned and occupied by the Allies in 1945. In 1949 the Federal Republic of Germany (FRG) was established in the west, and the German Democratic Republic (GDR) was established in the east. The two German states unified in 1990. |
| **Administrative Structure** | Federal, with sixteen states. Germany does not have sharp separation between levels of government. |
| **Executive** | Ceremonial president is the head of state, elected for a five-year term (with a two-term limit) by the Federal Convention. Chancellor is head of government and is a member of the *Bundestag* and a leader of the majority party or coalition. |
| **Legislature** | Bicameral. *Bundestag* (622 members after 2009 federal election) elected via dual-ballot system combining single-member districts and proportional representation. Upper house (*Bundesrat*) comprised 69 members who are elected and appointed officials from the 16 states. |
| **Judiciary** | Autonomous and independent. The legal system has three levels: Federal High Court, which is the criminal-civil system; Special Constitutional Court, dealing with matters affecting Basic Law; and Administrative Court, consisting of Labor, Social Security, and Finance courts. |
| **Party System** | Multiparty. Major parties are Christian Democratic Union (CDU), Christian Social Union (CSU), Social Democratic Party (SPD), the Greens, Free Democratic Party (FDP), and Left Party (*die Linke*). |

temporarily to part-time. This helped firms hold onto skilled workers in hopes of getting a fast start once the economy rebounded. Third, German firms were willing to accept lower profits than were many of their American counterparts. As a result, German households essentially enjoyed the same standard of living even as the economy shrank by 5 percent.

During 2010 and 2011, the German economy recovered rapidly. Yet paradoxically, this was the moment when the political side blew up. German governments

**Germany: Ethnic Groups**

**Germany: Religion**

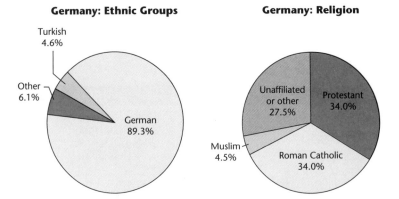

Turkish 4.6%

Other 6.1%

German 89.3%

Unaffiliated or other 27.5%

Protestant 34.0%

Muslim 4.5%

Roman Catholic 34.0%

**German Currency**
Euro (€)
International Designation: EUR
Exchange Rate (2010): US$1 = .755 EUR
100 Euro Note Design: European
historical Baroque / Rococo style
(the 17th and 18th century) arch

© Iurii Konoval/Shutterstock.com

**FIGURE 4.1 The German Nation at a Glance**

had often spent generously to promote the European Union (EU).[1] But now the German government's advice to other European countries in economic trouble can be summed up as "less risk and less debt." To an extent, this advice makes good sense. Yet if other European states consume less, to whom will Germany send its exports? Europeans are, by far, Germany's biggest trade partners. Once Greece and then Ireland and Portugal needed emergency financing from the EU, Germany's role became especially difficult. To bail them out might encourage more spending and would enrage German voters. Yet to let them go bankrupt might threaten the euro, the European currency that benefits Germany. There is no simple way out of this dilemma.

# Geographic Setting

*Gastarbeiter* (guest workers)

Workers who were recruited to join the German labor force in the 1960s and early 1970s, generally from Italy, Yugoslavia, and especially Turkey.

Located in central Europe, Germany has often been at the heart of the best and the worst of European history. It has an area of 137,803 square miles (slightly smaller than Montana). Its population is 81.5 million, the vast majority of which are ethnic German but also including about 4.6 percent Turkish and a further 6.1 percent a mixture of Kurds, Italians, Poles, Russians, and many others. The country has roughly even proportions of Roman Catholics and Protestants. For hundreds of years before unification, large German communities settled across much of central and eastern Europe. Germany has the largest population in western Europe, second only to Russia in all of Europe. Since the 1960s, ethnic diversity has been increased by several million Turks, who came to the Federal Republic as *Gastarbeiter* (guest workers)—foreign workers without citizenship. Recent immigration by about 2.4 million EU citizens has further decreased cultural homogeneity.

For a densely populated country, Germany has a high proportion of land in agriculture (54 percent). It consists of large plains in the north, smaller mountain ranges in the center, and the towering Alps at the Austrian and Swiss borders. The absence of natural borders in the west and east has been an important geographic fact, enhancing the possibilities for both commerce and conflict. Indeed, conflicts and wars with its neighbors were a frequent feature of German life until the end of World War Two. Inadequate natural resources—aside from iron ore and coal deposits in the Ruhr and Saarland regions—also shaped German history. Many of Germany's external relationships, both commercial and military, have involved gaining access to resources.

# Critical Junctures

## Nationalism and German Unification (1806–1871)

The first German "state" was the Holy Roman Empire (not the original Roman Empire). This was not a nation-state. Rather, the long-lasting empire (*Reich*) was a loose and fragmented collection of more than 300 sovereign entities, including the territories of much of present-day Germany, Austria, Italy, the Low Countries, Switzerland, Poland, the Czech Republic and even a bit of France. Many of today's sixteen **federal states** (*Bundesländer*) in Germany correspond to historic German-speaking kingdoms and principalities (Bavaria, Saxony, and Hesse) or medieval trading cities (Hamburg and Bremen), while others are fragments from larger historical units (Mecklenburg–West Pommerania is a chunk of old Prussia).

Moving from loose empire to modern federal state was difficult. Napoleon's victories against Prussia and Austria ended the Holy Roman Empire in 1806. Defeat and the resulting occupation by France aroused German nationalism, yet uncertain geographic boundaries and Protestant vs. Catholic religious division made it hard for many German-speaking lands to cooperate.[2] Still, Prussia—a powerful German-speaking state—led an alliance against Napoleon's France, leading to a new German confederation in 1815. In 1819, Prussian leaders created a tariff union that by 1834 included almost all of the German Confederation except Austria. Prussian power was based upon a strong state, dominated by a reactionary group of noble landlords in eastern Prussia (***Junkers***), a patriotic military, and a political culture of honor, duty, and service to the state. This setting was quite hostile to free-market capitalism or democracy.

The year 1848 saw many prodemocracy uprisings in Europe, including in Berlin, Frankfurt, and Vienna. But these revolutionary movements were violently and quickly suppressed. Instead, Germany was united several years later by a "revolution from above" led by Count Otto von Bismarck, who became minister-president of Prussia in 1862. Although a *Junker* himself, Bismarck realized that Prussia needed to industrialize and modernize its economy to compete with Britain, France, and the United States. Bismarck despised democracy, and he created an unlikely (and thoroughly nondemocratic) coalition of northeastern rural *Junker* lords and northwestern Ruhr Valley iron industrialists (known as the "marriage of iron and rye").

These German "revolutionaries" were elites, with an appetite for a bigger state and bigger markets. Stressing Prussia's reliance on "blood and iron," Bismarck launched three short, successful wars—against Denmark (1864), Austria (1866), and France (1870). These conquests, together with Prussia's annexation, intimidation, or inducements towards other German principalities led to the unification of Germany in 1871, when the so-called Second Reich was proclaimed. Prussia's king was made *Kaiser* (emperor).

## The Second Reich (1871–1918)

Industrial and landed elites controlled the Second Reich. It had some formal democratic features, like universal male suffrage for the lower house (*Reichstag*) of the legislature. However, this mattered little since the upper house (*Landtag*), which Bismarck controlled, had the main decision-making authority.

Bismarck's primary goal was to achieve rapid industrialization, supported by state power and a powerful banking system geared to foster large-scale industrial investment.[3] By 1900 Germany had become a leading industrial power. The state pushed **heavy industries**, often at the expense of those producing consumer goods. Lacking a strong

---

**federal state**

A state whose constitution divides power between a national (federal) government and lower units such as states, provinces, regions, *Länder*, or cantons.

**Junkers**

The land-owning nobility of Prussia, who were the grain (rye) component of Bismarck's "marriage of iron and rye."

**heavy industries**

The coal, iron, and steel sectors and the machinery and armaments production associated with them.

domestic consumer-goods economy, Germany had to export a substantial portion of what it produced.

Rapid transformation created widespread social dislocation and growing opposition to the conservative regime. A small middle class of professionals and small-business owners pressured the government—mostly unsuccessfully—to democratize and provide basic **liberal** rights. Industrialization also created a skilled manual working class and a militant Social Democratic Party (*Sozialdemokratische Partei Deutschlands*, SPD). The SPD's primary goals were economic rights in the workplace and mass participation in politics—democratization. The party was greatly influenced by revolutionary thinkers and activists Karl Marx and Friedrich Engels, whose socialist philosophy argued that workers, who produce society's goods and services, should also possess substantial economic and political power.

As German **chancellor** (head of government), Bismarck banned the SPD, yet also created the first welfare state to blunt protests at the disruption from rapid economic growth. This "Bismarckian" welfare state included some basic health benefits and the world's first state-sponsored old age pensions. Bismarck also created a powerful and centralized German state. The ***Kulturkampf*** (cultural struggle) he initiated against the Catholic Church sought to remove educational and cultural institutions from the church and place them under the state.

By 1900, Germany's primary economic challenge was obtaining raw materials and accessing world markets in which to sell its finished goods. Germany joined the general imperial adventure, sometimes called "the scramble for Africa." But as a latecomer, Germany could colonize only resource-poor southwestern and eastern Africa. This disadvantage pushed German leaders to rapidly develop the shipbuilding industry and a navy to protect and expand German economic and geopolitical interests.

Rivalries with its European neighbors eventually led to World War One, which German bears much responsibility for starting. After Bismarck was dismissed, subsequent German leaders had been far less skilled. The political system remained undemocratic and the colonies unprofitable. Meanwhile, Germany engaged Britain in a fierce naval rivalry and faced an aggressive and aggrieved France to the west. To the south, Germany's alliance with Austria-Hungary exposed it to the tinder keg of the Balkans with a host of minority nations struggling to get free of Austrian rule. To the east, Germany perceived a threat from a growing Russia with its large army. When a Serb separatist assassinated the Austrian Emperor's son, nationalists of all stripes were inflamed, including those in Germany. Germany's leaders listened to aggressive voices in the army and elsewhere and declared war in August 1914.

German leaders hoped to gain economic and political benefits from a quick victory in World War One. Instead, the long conflict cost Germany its few colonial possessions and its imperial social order. The Second Reich collapsed in November 1918 as Germany suffered a humiliating defeat in the war, leaving a weak foundation for the country's first parliamentary democracy.

## The Weimar Republic (1918–1933)

Kaiser Wilhelm II abdicated after Germany's defeat, and the **Weimar Republic** replaced the Second Reich. The SPD, the major party not discredited by the war, led Germany's first democracy. Its first task was to surrender to the Allies. The surrender was later used to discredit the party on the grounds that it had betrayed Germany by accepting defeat, even though, in fact, the war was already lost and it was the German generals who had forced the Kaiser to abdicate.

**liberal**

Economic philosophy that stresses the importance of minimizing state interference in the economy.

**chancellor**

An old German title now used by the German head of government and essentially the same as "prime minister."

***Kulturkampf***

Bismarck's fight with the Catholic Church over his desire to subordinate church to state.

**Weimar Republic**

The constitutional system of Germany between the end of World War One in 1918 and the Nazi seizure of power in 1933. So-named because the assembly to write the constitution occurred in a German city called Weimar.

**procedural democracy**

A system with formal procedures for popular choice of government leaders (especially free party competition) but which may lack other democratic elements.

**Nazi**

A German abbreviation for the National Socialist German Workers' Party, the movement led by Hitler.

The new government was a **procedural democracy** (a system with formal procedures for popular choice of government leaders, notably free party competition). However, the Weimar Republic had a fatal flaw: It lacked broad public support because both right-wing political forces and the Communists on the left rejected democratic government. The right also accused the Weimar government of "stabbing Germany in the back" by surrendering before the war was truly lost.

The Weimar Republic got off to a shaky start when SPD leaders foolishly asked the undemocratic military to guarantee order and stability. Communists had attempted to take control of some cities, and the right, including a little-known Adolf Hitler, attempted a coup. SPD leaders signed the Treaty of Versailles, which required Germany to pay heavy reparations to the victorious allies, and the government subsequently failed to stem the ruinous inflation of 1923. Although later governments eventually controlled inflation and Germany returned to some prosperity for a few years, the Depression of the 1930s struck Germany especially hard.

Into this turmoil stepped Adolf Hitler, the leader of the **Nazi** Party. Exploiting the deepening economic crisis, the Nazis mobilized large segments of the population by preaching hatred of the left and of "inferior, non-Aryan races"—especially Jews. Yet the Weimar Republic persisted, strengthening its economy (often with loans from the U.S.) and improving its foreign relations. Hitler was jailed for a time, and the Nazis might have disappeared if not for a constitutional system that allowed tiny splinter parties to remain in parliament.

The Great Depression had made Germany even more unstable. No major parties could win a majority or form lasting governments. Meanwhile, many conservative Germans underestimated Hitler's real intentions and considered his hate-filled speeches merely as political rhetoric. In early 1933 the Nazis and their conservative allies pressured President Paul von Hindenburg to appoint Hitler chancellor in a Nazi-Nationalist coalition. The Nazis immediately banned other political parties and repressed the opposition. Hitler also got Hindenburg to grant—by emergency executive order—broad, sweeping powers to the Nazi-dominated cabinet. The Nazi regime quickly consolidated its hold on power.

### The Third Reich (1933–1945)

After the Nazis obtained the chancellorship, they tried to establish complete political and social control. The Nazis used intimidation and heavy-handed use of the military, paramilitary, and police to brutally suppress the opposition and used propaganda to mobilize large parts of the population.

The Nazis centralized power and rebuilt an economy devastated by the Depression of the early 1930s. They concentrated all political authority in Berlin, removing any regional autonomy in order to repress political opposition, Jews, and other minorities. Because free trade unions had been banned, both private and state-run industries forced workers into longer hours, often for less pay. Although some segments of big business had initially feared Hitler, most of German industry eventually endorsed Nazi economic policies. The Nazis also emphasized massive public works projects and, with the onset of war, gave industrialists access to slave labor from conquered territories.[4]

Extolling a mythically glorious and racially pure German past, Hitler made scapegoats out of political opponents, homosexuals, ethnic and religious minorities, and, especially, Jews. Hitler blamed all political problems on Jews, this "external" international minority. Jews were quickly excluded from many professions, including teaching, law, medicine, and the civil service, and were prohibited from marrying non-Jews. Of course, far worse measures were adopted within a few years.

Hitler strides triumphantly through a phalanx of Nazi storm troopers (SA) in 1934.

*Source:* Ullstein Bilderdienst.

Openly defying the Treaty of Versailles (some Weimar governments had cheated quietly), Germany began to produce armaments in large quantities, and remilitarized the Rhineland, Germany's key coal and steel region. Hitler further claimed that a growing Germany needed increased space to live (*Lebensraum*) in eastern Europe. He engineered in 1938 a union (*Anschluss*) with his native Austria, most of whose leaders and citizens supported the pact with enthusiasm. His troops then occupied the German-speaking Sudetenland section of Czechoslovakia. The Nazi attack on Poland on September 1, 1939, began World War Two. Britain, France, and eventually, the Soviet Union and the United States, formed an alliance to oppose Germany, which was allied with Italy and Japan.

Despite the early Allied efforts, Hitler conquered much of Europe during 1939 and 1940. In 1941, despite having earlier signed a treaty with the USSR, Hitler attacked the Soviet Union, mistakenly calculating that it would fall as easily as his other conquests. The attack was a costly failure, and foreshadowed the Third Reich's defeat, though not until after an estimated 40 million Europeans lost their lives over the course of the war.

The most heinous aspect of the Nazi regime was the systematic extermination of 6 million Jews and the imprisonment in concentration camps of millions of Jews and other civilians. The Nazis set up the first concentration camps in 1933. Prisoners were the target of extreme brutality, and large numbers were shot or died from starvation, disease, or overwork. During the war, the Nazis created extermination camps in occupied countries like Poland, equipped with gas chambers specifically for the purpose of murdering Jews and other inmates. They also ran "scientific" experiments on camp inmates and the mentally ill and disabled.

Early on, the looting of conquered territory meant little wartime hardship for the German "homefront." As the military tide turned, however, more civilian production turned to weapons, rationing was introduced, and a fierce Allied bombing campaign killed about 300,000 civilians and razed major cities to the ground. All-told, about 2 million German civilians died in the war, in addition to about 4.5 million German soldiers.

## A Divided Germany (1945–1990)

Following Germany's total defeat in 1945, Cold War tensions led to the formal division of Germany: The Federal Republic of Germany (FRG) emerged in the west out of zones assigned to the western Allies (Britain, France, and the United States). Meanwhile, the communist German Democratic Republic (GDR) was formed out of a zone directed by the Soviet Union in the east. Postwar Germany was soon reshaped by the respective ideological visions of the two victorious sides. Democratic political institutions and a market economy were installed in the west, a communist political system and command economy in the east was controlled by the Socialist Unity Party (SED).

The two Germanys became formal nation-states in 1949, and the formal Occupation ended. Yet large military bases remained, and neither half of divided Germany was fully sovereign. The FRG deferred to the United States in international relations, as did the GDR to the Soviet Union. Neither of the two Germanys joined the Cold War's international alliances—NATO (North Atlantic Treaty Organization) and the Warsaw Pact, respectively—until 1955.

The Federal Republic (West Germany) became a democracy with constitutional provisions for free elections, civil liberties and individual rights, and an independent judiciary. The FRG's democratic system produced rapid economic growth and remarkable political stability. Under center-right Christian Democratic chancellors Konrad Adenauer (1949–1963) and Ludwig Erhard (1963–1966), the FRG established a new parliamentary regime, extensive social welfare benefits, a politically regulated market economy, and re-established strong state governments.

Under center-left Social Democratic chancellors Willy Brandt (1969–1974) and Helmut Schmidt (1974–1982), West Germany initially had robust full employment, a large increase in social services, and a diplomatic opening to the Warsaw Pact. But later in the 1970s, two economic recessions increased unemployment and forced Chancellor Schmidt to introduce moderate cutbacks in social services. Under Helmut Kohl, the Christian Democrats returned to power in 1982 as part of a center-right coalition with the Free Democratic Party (FDP) (*Time* Magazine's headline was "Germany Changes Helmuts").

As noted, the GDR was established in Soviet-occupied East Germany in 1949, a one-party state controlled by the SED. Although the state provided full employment, housing, and various social benefits, it was a rigid, Stalinist regime. The infamous *Stasi*, or secret police, was present everywhere (at the regime's end, there was a full-time Stasi official for every 180 GDR citizens. By comparison, the Soviet KGB had one for every 595 people, and the Nazi Gestapo had one for every 8,500). The Stasi kept close tabs on all East Germans and dealt ruthlessly with those suspected of opposing the regime.

Unsurprisingly, many East Germans emigrated west, and in 1961, the GDR built a wall entirely around the city of West Berlin to prevent further emigration. Over the next forty years, about 5,000 escaped through Berlin (early on, two young boys snuck out several weeks in a row to watch cowboy movies in West Berlin). But at least 136 people would lose their lives trying to flee the GDR through Berlin.

West Germany focused on rebuilding the economy and pursuing European economic integration. Although it became the strongest communist economy, East Germany lagged behind the far more developed economies of Western Europe. West Germany's allegiance to NATO was strong, and East Germany loyally toed the Soviet line in international affairs.

## The Challenge of German Unification (1990–2001)

When Soviet rule over communist regimes loosened throughout East Central Europe in 1989, the two German states at first envisioned a slow process of increased contacts and cooperation while maintaining separate sovereign states for the medium term. But contrary to expectation, German unification came rapidly, primarily because only reunification seemed able to convince East Germans not to migrate west. In 1990, the former East Germany was absorbed into the FRG as five new West German states (*Länder*).

Formal unification took place in 1990 to great fanfare. But unification euphoria did not last. The communist-planned economy was much weaker than had been recognized. East German technology was decades behind, and the unified German government spent huge sums just to rebuild communication networks and major roads that, for the first time in many years, allowed unrestricted traffic between East and West.

Aligning East Germany with the FRG was a daunting job and necessitated large tax increases. Unemployment soared, especially in eastern Germany—to approximately 20 percent—and fueled ultra-right-wing political movements who blamed foreigners for taking away jobs. Skinheads and other extremist groups often targeted Turkish immigrants.

To win the support of eastern Germans, Chancellor Kohl sugarcoated the enormity of unification. To win the support of western Germans, he had to convince them that the newly created 7.5 percent "unification tax" of the early 1990s would be enough to achieve economic integration. But the longer the unification process remained incomplete, the less patient the German electorate became.

After 16 years of Kohl's leadership, a political tidal wave occurred in the 1998 elections. SPD leader Gerhard Schröder convinced Germans that a change was necessary. Nearly 54 percent of the electorate voted for parties of the left, Schröder became chancellor, and the SPD formed a coalition government with the environmentalist Green Party.

An important aspect of unification involved extending the West German currency to East Germany. This mostly-popular move emboldened those who thought that it also might be possible to extend the Deutsche Mark (DM) to the rest of Europe. Meanwhile, as European capital flowed into East Germany, raising the value of the DM, German manufacturers nervously observed the price of German exports rising with the DM. This trend also increased their support for a European solution to national currency fluctuations.

Kohl, who had been uncertain about a European currency union, committed Germany to the idea, which France had long supported. Germany's leaders generally have been strong supporters of European integration. When the euro eventually replaced eleven European currencies in 2002, however, many Germans wondered whether the EU and the euro would provide the same stability as the formidable DM and the inflation-fighting *Deutsche Bundesbank* (Germany's central bank). Many also worried about Germany's loss of domestic control of monetary and, to a lesser extent, fiscal policies.

### Germany after September 11 (2001–)

There are no restrictions of movement on EU citizens between most member states, so as more and more countries joined the EU this highlighted the challenge that immigration poses for Germany. During the *Gastarbeiter* period of the 1960s, immigration to Germany was comparatively straightforward. Workers came from southern Europe and Turkey, supposedly for limited periods, and would then return home. What was not anticipated was that several generations of Turkish-Germans would remain in the Federal Republic. After 2000 a new wave of migrants seeking political asylum arrived from unstable and repressive countries in Africa and eastern Europe. Germany's sensitivity to the crimes of the Nazi regime had led to liberal asylum laws that not only allowed the majority of these migrants to stay but also to enjoy the benefits of Germany's generous social welfare system.

A small number of newcomers were (or became) Islamic radicals. The fact that several 9/11 terrorists had belonged to an Al Qaeda cell in Hamburg raised thorny questions about the balance between freedom and security. After 9/11 the government increased domestic surveillance and made a series of arrests and detentions. While these aggressive actions did identify threats, many Germans oppose government surveillance of residents, and Germany has strict laws regulating privacy. This combination created tension between Germany and the United States, which was widely seen to be pushing the German government to act more forcefully.

Tension with the United States ratcheted up when, during Gerhard Schröder's 2002 reelection campaign, he strongly opposed the Bush administration's preparations for war against Iraq. The Schröder government continued to oppose the war once it began in 2003. Although relations between the two countries never degenerated to the level of American–French bitterness, the strong relationship between Germany and the United States was significantly weakened.

While Schröder's foreign policy stance was popular, his government (in coalition with the Greens) lost support in a number of other areas. It was replaced in 2005 by a "Grand Coalition" of CDU-CSU and SPD. Schröder gave way as chancellor to Angela Merkel, who later won re-election in 2009 with her preferred coalition partners, the Free Democrats (FDP). Together, the coalition partners have been consumed with the economic and financial crisis, often choosing policies that left other European leaders (and, on some occasions, U.S. President Barack Obama) visibly frustrated. Germany's foreign policy has become less predictable. It has broken with its quasi-pacifist stance to send many troops abroad in recent years. And yet it resisted efforts to impose a "no-fly zone" in Libya, abstaining from the vote on UN Resolution 1973.

## Themes and Implications

### Historical Junctures and Political Themes

Germany's development can be understood in light of this book's four major themes. Consider the first theme: a world of states. Because of its earlier militarism and its history of authoritarian political culture, Germany's role in the world of states is controversial. In the nineteenth century, Germany's war-propelled unification generated anxiety among its neighbors. In the twentieth century, World War One and the crimes of the Third Reich during World War Two intensified this fear. Today, although Germany's foreign policy is constrained by the EU, many Europeans remain wary of Germany's international role. For example, many think German energy policy cooperates too much with Russia and too little with the rest of Europe. Even among Germans, a debate still rages over whether Germany can be considered a "normal" state.

As for the second theme, governing the economy, delayed unification and industrialization prevented Germany from beginning a race for empire and raw materials until the late nineteenth century. The pursuit of fast economic growth and an awakened sense of German nationalism produced an aggressive, acquisitive state. During the Third Reich, Hitler sought to fuse state and economic power. In reaction, policymakers after World War Two desired to remove the state from directly governing the economy.

The postwar period saw the development of *Modell Deutschland* (the German model), a term often used to describe the Federal Republic's distinctive socioeconomic practices. While successful for decades, it remains an open question whether these economic institutions will continue to function well in a unified Europe.[5] The EU sometimes promotes free market practices faster than Germany can absorb them. Meanwhile, Germany often produces export surpluses faster than the rest of Europe can absorb them. Both imbalances often spark frustration.

The democratic idea, our third theme, developed late in Germany. Not until 1918 and the shaky Weimar Republic did Germany attain democracy. And despite a formally democratic constitution, Weimar was a prisoner of forces bent on its destruction. Lacking a stable multiparty political system, Weimar was plagued by a sharp polarization of political parties. Germany's descent into the most brutal form of authoritarianism in the 1930s then destroyed every vestige of democracy.

The constitution of the Federal Republic in 1949 was designed to overcome both Weimar shortcomings and Nazi crimes. This was a delicate task since the first system made the state too weak while the second made it far too strong. But postwar constitution-making proved a resounding success, even if uncertainties and problems remain.

As for the fourth theme, the politics of collective identity, more than in other democratic countries, German political institutions, social forces, and patterns of life emphasize collective action more than individualism.[6] This does not imply that German citizens have less personal freedom compared to those in other developed democracies or that there are no political conflicts in Germany. It means that political expression, in both the state and civil society, generally revolves around group representation and cooperative spirit.

Certainly, Germany's history from Prussian militarism through Nazism has led many to worry about the dangers of collectivist impulses. However, Germany is unlikely to embrace an individualistic democracy like that of the United States, given the deep roots of collectivism in German political culture and because of the many positive features of collectivism. Germany's collective identity since 1945 also has been broadened by linking the country's fate to that of Europe. Germany is the economic motor of the EU, and its participation in the EU also produced a more flexible understanding of what it means to be German. For example, Germany's traditionally restrictive immigration law was changed in 1999 to enable those who had lived in Germany for decades to obtain citizenship. A big question going forward is how German voters' identification with Europe will affect their willingness to assist those countries—like Greece and Ireland—that have been hardest hit by the economic crisis.

### Implications for Comparative Politics

Germany differs from many other developed countries. Like Japan, Germany was late to industrialize and late to democratize. But the most significant difference between Germany and other western European states is, of course, the Nazi period and the destruction that the Third Reich wrought. Although concerns about this period persist, they have been substantially allayed by Germany's stable democratic experience since 1949.

Germany's significance for the study of comparative politics lies in several areas: The contrast between its nationalistic history and democratization in an integrating Europe; its distinctive form of organized capitalism that is neither state-led nor laissez-faire; its successful representative democracy that combines participation and representation of the entire electorate in a stable parliamentary regime; and a politics of identity that builds on existing groups but leaves some room for newcomers.

### Summary

Germany's turbulent history presented postwar policymakers with two daunting challenges. On the one hand, they needed to avoid re-creating a system in which the state could destroy the freedom and indeed the very lives of those whom the regime saw as its opponents. On the other hand, they needed to avoid re-creating a system where the state was so fragmented and weak that it could not tackle the very real problems Germany faced. There is no doubt that they handsomely succeeded in both these tasks. In the meantime, however, plenty of new challenges have arisen. Whether the German system is up to those challenges is something we explore in the next sections, beginning with the economy.

## SECTION 2 — POLITICAL ECONOMY AND DEVELOPMENT

## State and Economy

Germany's capitalist economy tries to capture the benefits of intense competition between firms *and* of close cooperation among firms. This is no easy trick, but Germans' standard of living is among the highest in Europe, and Germany is the world's second-largest exporter (behind far larger China). Moreover, the interplay between cooperation and conflict extends beyond companies to include Germany's two main social classes, managers and employers.

### The Role of the State Before 1945

Before unification in 1871, many of Germany's regional governments played a strong role promoting economic growth, thus blurring the distinction between the state and the market. The customs union (***Zollverein***), signed in 1834 by the leaders of several German states, propelled industrial modernization by facilitating inter-state trade.

Bismarck was also heavy-handed in developing the economy. He realized that although railroads were a primary consumer of coal and steel, they could also transport the *Junkers'* grain to market. Thus was born the famous "marriage of iron and rye." Although this rapid, Prussian-led, state-enhanced industrial growth was important, small-scale agricultural production remained in many parts of the southern states, and small-scale craft production continued in many other regions.

Business and political elites soon realized that if Germany wanted to enter a market with other industrialized countries, an economy based on small firms would face ruinous competition. To make Germany competitive, the state became a powerful force in the economy. In practice, this meant explicit coordination among government, big business, and a powerful "universal" banking system that combined savings and commercial activities.[7]

After World War One, a severe economic crisis in 1923 destabilized the Weimar economy, with inflation eventually making the currency worthless. The 1929 stock market crash and subsequent depression hit Germany's export economy especially hard. Hitler reached power in part by insisting that only his leadership could solve Germany's gigantic economic problems. During the Third Reich, between 1933 and 1945, the state encouraged German industry to repress workers, employ slave labor, and focus production on weapons (the candy company Haribo switched from gummi bears to tanks between 1939 and 1945). After the Allied victory, a number of leading industrialists, notably those who directed the Krupp steel works and the IG Farben chemical complex, were tried and convicted of war crimes.

## The Social Market Economy

After World War Two, German economic policies took a different course from either Anglo-American laissez-faire policies (generally based on "freeing" the market from the state) or state-led economic policies in countries like France and Japan. State policy was important, but indirect. It complemented the critical decisions taken by private groups like employers, trade unions, chambers of commerce, churches, and others. Broadly, this remains true today. Although the government sets guidelines, it encourages voluntary associations to play a key role. Subsequent negotiations among employers, banks, unions, and regional governments fill in key details that still respect the government's policy objectives.

The German state allows market forces to work relatively unimpeded within the general framework of government supervision. This system of **framework regulations** has enabled German economic policy to avoid the abrupt lurches between laissez-faire and state-led economic policy that have characterized post–World War Two Britain.[8] In short, this system regulates not the details, but the general rules of the game under which all actors must play. To be sure, some have criticized this system as rigid and cumbersome, charges to which we return in a moment.[9] To its advocates, however, German economic policy is flexible and encourages private actors to cooperate to devise their own solutions. As a result, the German system is often able to produce agreement on major policy directions without much social upheaval and protest.

Since the time of Adenauer, the Germans have referred to this broad approach as the **social market economy** (*Soziale Marktwirtschaft*). The social component includes conventional provisions for health insurance, unemployment, and pensions, as well as several distinctive programs, such as savings subsidies and vocational education. The system of vocational training—part tech school, part junior college, and part on-the-job training—has helped create a deep pool of human capital that has enabled Germany to produce high-quality goods for decades.

*Zollverein*

Customs union signed in the mid-1830s between Prussia, Bavaria, Hessia, Saxony, and many other German states to overcome the fragmentation of the German market.

**framework regulations**

Laws that set broad parameters for economic behavior but that require subsequent elaboration, often through formal agreements between employers and employees.

**social market economy**

A system that aims to combine the efficiency of market economies with a concern for fairness for a broad range of citizens.

The market component of the social market economy is equally critical. Germany is an intensely competitive market economy. German firms are often world leaders in anything from cars and machine tools to kitchen appliances and chocolate bars. The pattern of high-wage and high-benefits has enabled Germany to maintain its international market position far better than most of its competitors.

## Semipublic Institutions

In the late 1940s, the idea of a strong central state in Germany was discredited for two reasons: the excesses of Nazism and the American occupation authorities' preference for the private sector. West German authorities faced a dilemma. How could they rebuild society if a strong public sector role were prohibited? The answer was to create modern, democratic versions of those nineteenth-century institutions that blurred the boundaries between the public and private sectors (hence "semipublic").[10]

Semipublic institutions are responsible for much of Germany's economic policy-making. The most influential include the boards of the health insurance funds, pensions, and unemployment insurance systems, plus the employment agencies, the central bank, and the vocational education and training system. Cooperation between firms and the government requires compromise and thus helps sustain political moderation. For example, Germany's Chambers of Industry and Commerce as well as its Council of Economic Advisors are both far less partisan (and arguably far more useful) than their openly partisan American counterparts. Similarly, unions and employers sit on the boards of the pension and unemployment insurance systems. Another semipublic institution, the **health insurance funds** (*Krankenkassen*), brings all major health interests together to allocate costs and benefits through consultation and group participation. There is still disagreement, but the politics of health care is far less contentious than in the United States.

The social market economy is part of the broader system of **democratic corporatism**, in which national (and state) governments delegate certain policy-making authority to private and semipublic institutions. In countries that had a guild system in the Middle Ages, democratic corporatist representation is common. For example, we see similar systems in the Netherlands, Belgium, the Scandinavian countries, Switzerland, and Austria. In return for access to power and administration, groups representing a particular economic sector are expected to aggregate the interests of their own members and act responsibly. Semipublic institutions differ greatly from pluralist representation in countries such as the United States, where interest groups seek benefits from government agencies while keeping the implementation process at arm's length.

For the social market economy and the semipublic institutions within it to function, effective organizations representing both labor and business are a necessity. Trade unions are a powerful force in Germany, representing 6.2 million workers. They are grouped into eight countrywide, multisectoral organizations. For example, the metalworkers union organizes all union members in sectors as diverse as autos (whether or not the worker actually works with metal!), machinery, and computer chips. Similarly, the main service sector union has members from over 1,000 different trades and professions.

Because unions encompass a broad range of interests, they can negotiate with associations of employers in those same broad sectors. This means also less *state* regulation of wages, working conditions, and employment. For example, unlike almost everywhere else in Europe, Germany has traditionally had no minimum wage (though it may get one soon). At the same time, collective bargaining agreements result in German workers enjoying high wages and fringe benefits.

**health insurance funds**

Semipublic institutions that administer insurance contributions from employees and employers and thus pay for health care for covered participants.

**democratic corporatism**

A bargaining system in which important policies are established and often carried out with the participation of trade unions and business associations.

German companies are also organized into associations. Most of these associations were designed to deal with labor unions. Often, this relationship is an easy one. German firms often benefit from the fact that wages are negotiated outside the company and not between them and "their" workers. On the other hand, German firms have traditionally understood that they must pay all workers (union or not) at least the wages that their association has negotiated with the union. Firms thus cannot easily undercut one another by paying lower wages, and though firms can pay more than the union wage (and some do), it still is not easy to poach good workers from another firm. Firms also have business associations that lobby the government on policy matters.

The interplay of cooperation and conflict is not limited to the broader economy but also takes place inside each German firm through a system known as **co-determination** (*Mitbestimmung*). In the Anglo-Saxon countries, business decisions are mainly "determined" by one party: management. By contrast, co-determination is a government-sanctioned relationship that gives employees the right to participate in major decisions that affect their firms and industries. Although common in northern Europe, including the Netherlands and Scandinavia, co-determination is best known in the Federal Republic of Germany.

Co-determination allows representatives of workers and trade unions in Germany to obtain voting seats on the supervisory boards of directors of firms with 2,000 or more employees. Separate provisions are made for smaller firms. Firm managers both resent having to share management decisions with workers and appreciate that co-determination helps them reach accommodation with workers. Ultimately, German managers have seen that rather than making their firms uncompetitive, this system often has had the opposite effect. Co-determination also has allowed German workers a broader and deeper knowledge of the goals and strategies of the firms for which they work.

Another German institution providing workers a voice is the **works councils** (*Betriebsräte*). While the first form of co-determination gives trade unions a voice outside the plant (that is, on the board), the works councils represent workers inside the workplace. Their job is to address shop-floor and firm-level affairs. Whereas unions address collective bargaining issues, including the setting of wages, hours, and working conditions, works councils concentrate on social and personnel matters (although they can negotiate firm-level bonuses). About two-thirds of works councilors are also union members, a fact that minimizes but does not always prevent tension between unions and works councils.

Another useful semipublic institution is the elaborate vocational education system built on apprenticeship training. About 40 percent of German young adults go on to university. Most of the rest complete a three-year apprenticeship that combines school-based classes with at least four days a week working and learning in a company. By combining school and workplace-based learning, these apprenticeships resemble a rigorous college internship, except that they more often benefit working class people and last years rather than months. Many youth are then "taken on" as permanent employees by the firm with which they trained. The apprenticeship system long enabled Germany to avoid overreliance on the postindustrial service sector common in the United States and Britain.[11] Long after the manufacturing sector in these countries languished, nearly a third of the German economy remains engaged in manufacturing.

With its highly skilled work force, Germany long resisted the claim that it must lower wages to compete. Its competitive advantage lies in raising product quality rather than slashing wages. This has enabled Germany's highly-skilled blue-collar workers to drive expensive cars, obtain high-quality medical care, and enjoy six weeks of paid vacation each year (wages in parts of the service sector are, by contrast, much lower, and unemployment rates for the least skilled are over 20 percent in West Germany and up to 40 percent in the East).

**co-determination**

The legal right of representatives of employees to help determine the direction of the company in which they work. Co-determination often takes place through works councils.

**works councils**

Firm employees elected by their co-workers to represent the workforce in negotiations with management at that specific shop or company.

Germany's research and development strategy has complemented these economic policies. Rather than seek breakthroughs in exotic technologies that take years to commercialize, the strategy adapts existing technologies to refine already competitive sectors. During the postwar years, this policy enabled Germany to maintain competitiveness and a big trade surplus (the opposite of the United States). In recent decades, the challenges have been, first, to integrate former GDR workers raised in an East German industrial culture that told workers to follow orders rather than apply initiative and, second, to invest in formerly communist countries where high skills and lower wages can be combined.

The relentless search for technical improvements also figures into Germany's leading role in debates over global warming. German politicians from across the political spectrum have pushed for regional (EU) and global action (at Kyoto/Copenhagen) to limit and possibly reverse climate change. This position reflects a broad consensus among German voters about the reality and dangers of man-made global warming. Most Germans are shocked to hear that many Americans think global warming is a matter of "belief." German firms, including those in the all-important auto sector, generally accept regulations requiring cleaner technology. Therefore, they have a keen interest in requiring their competitors in other countries to face the same regulatory conditions. German firms and politicians also display confidence that they can meet bold targets for reductions in $CO_2$ emissions (partly because they got credit for shutting down dirty East German industries that were slated to close anyway). Angela Merkel made climate change a centerpiece of her leadership in the 2007 German presidency of the G8 and the European Council.

## Current Strains on the Social Market Economy

Over time, the social market economy has faced a growing list of strains, including the rise of new competitors, the challenge of free market ideas (especially at the EU level and among employers), the difficulties of German unification, and the burden of the financial crisis.

Germany is a trading state, and globalization involves plenty of new competitors jostling German firms long used to being world leaders. German firms face relatively high costs in wages, taxes, social contributions, and investments in apprenticeships and technology development, so they need high revenues to make a profit. Making workers more productive is one way they have done this. But this has not been enough for manufacturing firms facing ferocious competition from Asian auto and machine tool producers. Another solution for German firms is to go to lower-cost eastern and southern European countries to find the best deals rather than maintain the kind of long-standing relationships with other domestic firms that were the lynchpin of the German model. Thus, even though Germany continues to run a trade surplus in Europe and globally, its formula for export success faces a number of strains.

More fundamentally, Germany's social market economy has been increasingly attacked at the level of ideas. For years, free-market proponents from abroad criticized the German model for the "clubby" relationships among the German social partners (business associations, labor unions, and federal and state governments). Critics charged that this pattern added costs and reduced flexibility for employers. Yet as we have seen, working with unions has allowed German firms to largely maintain their competitive positions. For example, by keeping skilled workers on the payroll (with some help from the government and taxpayers), business was able to get a jump on the economic recovery after the 2008 crisis.

Free market supporters also accuse the social market economy of a failure to create sufficient jobs. However, through much of the postwar period, this too was false: For nearly 25 years, German unemployment hovered around a remarkable 1–2 percent. Since the 1970s, however, unemployment has varied from 6 to over 10 percent. Since wages are high, employers have tried to avoid creating part-time jobs, preferring to wait to hire until the need for employees becomes acute. During recession, however, employers tend to hold onto skilled workers. In fact, unemployment fell from almost 11 percent in 2005 to 6.6 percent in 2011, the lowest in two decades.

A particular problem of the social market system was caused by unification in 1990. In the early 1990s, the Kohl government badly misjudged the costs of unification, which, by the early 1990s, was consuming about 20 percent of Germany's national budget. Moreover, employers and trade unions found their long history of cooperation in the west very difficult to transfer to eastern Germany.[12] After the government privatized thousands of East German firms, the firms' new owners fired workers in droves. The problems in eastern Germany soon threatened to overwhelm the system's capacity.

In addition, the EU had already begun to disturb the intricate, mutually reinforcing pattern of German government and business self-regulation. EU rules disallowed some traditional state subsidies to promote economic development. In addition, some deregulation in European finance threatened Germany's distinctive finance-manufacturing links, which depend on long-term relationships between the two parties rather than short-term deals.[13] These challenges, along with the high wages and taxes, stoked a long-simmering debate: "Is Germany a good place to do business?" Many Germans worried that the combination of domestic and international factors made Germany a less attractive place for investment.

Substantial policy changes eventually followed from these worries. Ironically, it was the SPD-Green (left-oriented) government that sponsored far-reaching changes that made labor law, pension policy, and unemployment insurance less generous to workers. In terms of banking regulation, this reform weakened the policy of encouraging banks to maintain equity holdings in other firms. This brought the German model somewhat closer to the Anglo-American world of highly mobile capital investment, although German firms are still far less reliant than American firms on issuing stock in order to attract capital.

Finally, anxieties were compounded by the financial crisis of 2008. On the one hand, German voters and politicians were reassured that the German financial system seemed less prone to excesses than were, for example, those of the United States and the UK. On the other hand, some German financial institutions were badly burned by risky investments abroad (one bailout cost German taxpayers about $140 billion, and German banks have many bad loans still hidden in their books).

# Society and Economy

Booming economic growth after World War Two provided a sound foundation for social programs. Until the 1990s, Germany provided generous social benefits to almost everyone, including support for public transit, subsidies for the arts, virtually free higher and vocational education, and a comprehensive welfare state.

Unlike in the United States, public services receive substantial cross-party support. As such, public services in Germany dwarf those in the United States. From housing subsidies to savings subsidies, health care, and the rebuilding of the run-down cities and public infrastructure of the former GDR, public spending is remarkably generous in Germany. But the costs of unification, adjustment to the EU, and globalization have begun to challenge Germany's high standard of living and well-paid work force.

The primary workplace fault line lies between the core of mostly male, high-skilled blue-collar workers in the largest competitive industries and less-skilled workers, often employed in smaller firms with lower wages and part-time work. Immigrants and women are both over-represented in these latter sectors, whose workers benefit less from German institutions than do those in the core industries.

## Ethnicity and Economy

Germany's only large ethnic minority originated in the *Gastarbeiter* program of the 1960s, when temporary workers were recruited from southern Europe (especially Turkey) on the understanding that they would return to their native countries if unemployment increased. However, the economic boom lasted so long that when the economy did turn down in the mid-1970s, many guest workers had lived in Germany for a decade. Many stayed, but because German citizenship was not granted to these workers or their children, they were in legal limbo. The clash between German and *Gastarbeiter* cultures increased in intensity in the 1980s, particularly in areas where Turkish workers were highly concentrated. However, the SPD-Green government in 1999 allowed some second- and third-generation *Gastarbeiter* to obtain German citizenship or maintain dual citizenship.[14]

Currently, about 3.75 million people of Turkish background live in Germany, though in recent years more have left Germany than have arrived. While early Turkish migrants supplemented industrial work with niche occupations in Turkish groceries and restaurants, these niches are declining. One partial replacement is caring for the elderly, especially Turkish elderly. Increasingly, some higher-paid service jobs are held by ethnic Turks (many now German citizens). Even so, about 40 percent of Turkish families are near or below the poverty line, and Turkish unemployment levels have risen well above those for Germans during the economic crisis.

Racist attacks against Turkish immigrants and other ethnic minorities have forced Germans to confront the possibility that over fifty years of democracy have not eliminated German xenophobia. The issue was exacerbated in the 1990s and 2000s by unification and European integration. East Germans were raised in a closed society that did not celebrate, or even value, toleration. Meanwhile, in addition to the *Gastarbeiter*, the Federal Republic for many years provided generous provisions for those seeking political asylum.

Former GDR citizens, raised on a promise of guaranteed lifetime employment, suddenly faced a labor market that did not supply enough jobs. Yet they were expected to embrace immediately a much more ethnically diverse society than they had ever known. Thus, Germans who were falling through the cracks of the welfare state and were without jobs became susceptible to racist arguments blaming minorities for Germany's economic problems.

Some immigrant labor does involve high skills. For example, Germany's changing economy produced a "tech shortage" in the early 2000s that led the Schröder government to recruit software specialists from India. However, this new wave of *Gastarbeiter* was arriving precisely when some Germans were increasingly agitated about the immigration boom, and a backlash quickly occurred.

## Gender and Economy

Until the late 1970s, men monopolized positions of authority in both management and labor (though unions subsequently made greater strides than management in expanding leadership opportunities for women). Although half of all German women were in the workforce by the late 1970s, their participation only reached 66 percent by 2009, while the male participation rate remained fairly steady at 80 percent until a drop in 2009 (see Table 4.2). In East Germany, women often made greater social and economic progress than in the West. For example, both women and men received generous government support for childcare and family leave.[15] At reunification, the pay gap between men and women was nearly twice as high in West Germany as in East Germany.

| Table 4.2 | Labor Force Participation Rates (Ages 15–65) | | | | | |
|-----------|------|------|------|------|------|------|
|           | **1997** | **1999** | **2001** | **2003** | **2005** | **2009** |
| **Male**   | 80% | 81% | 80% | 79% | 80% | 76% |
| **Female** | 63% | 64% | 65% | 65% | 67% | 66% |

*Source:* Federal Statistical Office, Germany, 2007. Arbeitsagentur 2009.

Historically, women's benefits in German society have been closely tied to their roles as mothers and wives. German women often face labor market discrimination, and though they are about as likely to work outside the home as American women, they are far more likely to work part-time. It is far harder for German women to achieve positions of power and responsibility than it is for their American counterparts.

## The Generation Gap

A final social cleavage is the generation gap, which has two dimensions. First, many young people hold so-called postmaterialist values and focus more on lifestyle concerns—including ecology and personal freedom—than on bread-and-butter economic issues. Such people, however, have not been able to challenge skilled working class and middle class dominance in German politics. Youth unemployment is around 10 percent, higher than adult unemployment but far below the European average. But many young Germans suspect they will not get all the benefits their parents' generation enjoyed.

The second aspect of the generation gap comprises pensioners and older workers. The German birthrate fell markedly in the last decade of the twentieth century, particularly in the former GDR but also in the West. This placed great demographic pressure on the German welfare state because the low birthrate and the increasing age of the baby boom generation meant that fewer younger workers now contribute to the welfare and retirement benefits of an increasing elderly population. (See cartoon on page 165.) As noted, this means many young Germans find jobs, but managers worry about worker shortages, and some have called for more immigration to fill the gap.

To encourage more children, former CDU Family Minister Ursula von der Leyen (herself a physician and mother of seven) instituted policy changes that made it easier for both mothers and fathers to take paid time off for the birth of a child. Her ministry also increased daycare funding. Although there have been some modest increases in childbirths, the effectiveness of the policy remains to be seen.

# Germany in the Global Economy

Germany's relationship to the regional and international political economy is shaped by two factors: the EU and globalization.

## The European Union

As Europe's leading economic power, Germany has benefited greatly from European integration. Many actions and policies that might once have been viewed by its neighbors as German bids for domination have become more acceptable when seen as Germany's participation in the EU. German exporters depend on markets in other parts of Europe, and German banks have made large profits in the rest of Europe. But Germany also had to adapt to an unfamiliar free-market economic model quite different from the organized capitalism that emerged after World War Two.

Several difficult issues challenge Germany's international position today. One is whether German-specific institutional arrangements, such as worker (and union) participation in management, tightly organized capitalism, and the elaborate system of apprenticeship training, will flourish in wider European and global contexts.

Before the economic crisis in late 2008, most thought Germany's institutional, political, or cultural patterns could not successfully transfer beyond the Federal Republic. Since then, however, admirers have pointed to its impressive employment performance during the crisis as evidence of the value of Germany's policies and practices. At the same time, some German investments in the rest of Europe have gone spectacularly sour, and Germany has felt obliged to bail out less prosperous states. A 2009 Constitutional Court decision sent shockwaves through the EU because it limited any deeper German integration with the EU and restricted German money for bailouts for other European countries.

## Germany in a Regional Context

After World War Two, Germany faced two different criticisms. Many feared a too-powerful Germany since the country had run roughshod over its neighbors for the previous eighty years. Yet by the 1990s, Germany contended with an opposite problem: an economic giant–political dwarf syndrome in which Germany was accused of benefiting from a strong world economy while taking on too few political and military responsibilities.

Successive German chancellors Kohl, Schröder, and Merkel hoped that an integrated Europe might solve both problems. Germany's postwar political leaders have embraced European unity because they realized the opportunity that a more united continent would present. Germany remains the economic anchor of the EU, while Germany's membership in the EU has enabled it to take on political responsibilities that it would be unable to assume on its own, such as UN peacekeeping operations in the Balkans (which had borne the brunt of many of Germany's wartime crimes).

Germany's biggest test of leadership came with the euro. For decades, Germany's powerful economy both benefited from and caused a strong currency, the famous Deutsche Mark (DM). Although the DM was the very foundation of postwar German economic performance and contributed mightily to German self-confidence, a strong DM made German exports expensive. The DM's strength also sometimes frustrated other Europeans by enticing investment that might otherwise have flowed to other European countries.

Successive German chancellors judged that economic success for both Germany and Europe would require a stronger common foundation. This is where the euro came in. It promised to prevent European neighbors from weakening their currency at Germany's expense (in return, neighbors would receive less inflation and more investment capital). Kohl insisted that countries that used the euro would promise to control public spending and inflation (a promise many countries—including Germany—would subsequently break on several occasions).

Now used by over 300 million Europeans, the euro was introduced in most countries of the EU in 2002. Gone was the redoubtable DM. For most of the time since its emergence, the euro's value has traded above the U.S. dollar. This is great for European tourists wanting to visit the United States, but the higher-valued euro still makes it difficult for the export-oriented German economy to sell its goods in the Americas or Asia.

Even worse, in 2010 and 2011, Germany came under pressure to help bail out Greece, Ireland, and Portugal, members of the **Eurozone** who got in huge trouble, partly because the euro allowed them to borrow much more easily. Much-larger Spain and Italy also have worrisome levels of debt. German voters are angry, but German politicians fear that without the common currency, many of the old problems of export and capital imbalances would return. The euro may have to be reconfigured, although blowing it up entirely and going back to national currencies would be hugely expensive too. This dilemma has no easy solution, so watch it carefully. Issues such as trade, economic competition with East Asia and North America, the euro, European economic integration, climate change, and patterns of financial regulation pose daunting challenges. More than most countries, Germany's economic fortunes are tied to globalization. Management and unions realize that exports represent both profits and jobs and that protectionism would be self-defeating. The growth in world trade allowed German firms to export and prosper. Yet there are large costs, as well. When trade collapsed during 2009, Germany suffered badly. The recovery of trade then boosted German exports into record territory in 2010.

**Eurozone**

The 17 members of the EU (out of 27 total members) who share a common currency, the euro.

## Summary

From the ruins of World War Two, Germany has built one of the world's strongest economies. With only 80 million people, Germany often exports more goods than the 300 million Americans or 1.2 billion Chinese. Yet when trade declines, so do German standards of living. Globalization can be a rollercoaster for a medium-sized economy.

The German social market economy differs from more free market economies like the U.S. and statist economies like France. Government regulation establishes general framework regulations rather than detailed standards. The government sets broad licensing and performance standards for most professions and industries. Once core state requirements are announced, the government trusts that private actors will respect those broad parameters (and checks to be sure they do). In contrast, the U.S. government often produces many layers of detailed—and sometimes contradictory—regulations in the wake of economic crises, banking failures, and financial abuses.

Germany's indirect approach to regulation is bolstered by the active engagement of unions and employers, in cooperation with state and municipal policymakers. Semipublic institutions provide a forum in which these social partners help shape the German economy. At the same time, Germany is challenged to provide regional and global leadership on a wide range of issues, from the rescue of financially stressed European governments to global warming.

The German economy faces a bevy of challenges including the rise of new competitors, the challenge of free market ideas, the continuing difficulties of German unification, and the burden of the financial crisis. But Germany has some important assets to meet these challenges, notably its great economic strength and (according to some scholars) its organized and cooperative form of capitalism.[16]

# GOVERNANCE AND POLICY-MAKING

**Focus Questions**

What institutional changes aimed to fix problems of Weimar fragmentation or Nazi autocracy?

How does German federalism differ from federalism in other countries?

**Basic Law**

The 1949 proto-constitution of the Federal Republic, which continues to function today.

Most Americans expect a constitution to be a single written document. In Germany, there is a single document, but it is not called a constitution (*Verfassung*). When West Germany was founded in 1949, the Cold War kept East Germany in the communist bloc. Thus, West Germany chose to adopt a more temporary-sounding "**Basic Law**" (*Grundgesetz*), hoping reunification would come soon and permit the writing of a true constitution. When reunification finally did come—forty years later—the Basic Law had been so successful that both the term and the document itself were kept, while the old GDR was added to the FRG in the form of five new *Länder*.

In what sense did the Basic Law succeed? The primary goals of the young Federal Republic were to avoid repeating the mistakes of the Weimar Republic and to lay to rest the legacy of the Nazi regime. The Basic Law aimed to deal with both failures, and it did.

Two fundamental institutional weaknesses undermined the Weimar government: (1) The political party system's fragmentation prevented stable majorities from forming in the *Reichstag*, and (2) the president's right to exercise emergency powers made it possible to arbitrarily centralize authority and suspend democratic rights. The first weakness, (instability) encouraged the second: (the use of emergency powers to break legislative deadlocks).

Since Weimar's weakness made possible the Nazi takeover, the core reform after World War Two was to minimize the risk of extremism and the abuse of executive power. These problems were dealt with by introducing federalism and a weak presidency and by reforming electoral procedures to curb instability.

## Organization of the State

After surviving for over 60 years, the Federal Republic has clearly attained its most important goals. It has permitted successful alternations in power, although the Basic Law's provisions for federalism and divided powers tend to keep policy change slow and incremental. Undemocratic parties have received miniscule voter support despite occasional neo-Nazi threats and some incidents of racial violence.

### Government Institutions

The German state features a fairly weak president and a much stronger chancellor (prime minister), who is elected by the bicameral parliament's lower house (the *Bundestag*). The lower house is shaped, in turn, by two peculiar rules, namely the constructive vote of no confidence and the **5 percent clause** (see Section 4).

**5 percent clause**

This rule obliges a party to get at least 5 percent of the "second votes" in order to enter the Bundestag (or the state parliaments) as a party. It tends to depress votes for "splinter" parties.

Germany's parliamentary democracy resembles the parliamentary systems of Britain and Japan in that there is a fusion of powers where the chancellor, the executive or head of government, is also the leader of the leading party in the *Bundestag*. This contrasts with the separation of powers in the United States. Generally, the German executive dominates the legislature. Most members of the governing parties support the chancellor at all times, since their own positions depend on a successful government. Party voting rates in Germany are among the highest in Europe. An upper

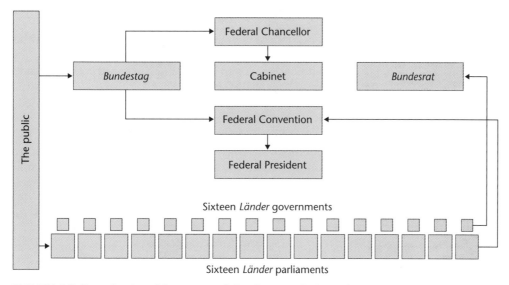

FIGURE 4.2 **Constitutional Structure of the German Federal Government**

house (the *Bundesrat*) embodies Germany's unique form of federalism where the sixteen states have considerable powers (see Figure 4.2).

# The Executive

The division between the head of government (the chancellor) and the head of state (the president) is firmly established, with responsibilities and obligations clearly distinguished between the two offices.

## The President

The German president is the head of state, but the president's role is largely ceremonial. The president is elected by the Federal Convention (*Bundesversammlung*), an electoral college of all *Bundestag* members and an equal number of delegates elected by the state legislatures. The presidential term is five years with most presidents serving only one term. No women have been elected president.

German presidents are usually senior politicians who are moderates within their parties and broadly acceptable to the electorate. However, if a political crisis were to prevent the chancellor from governing, the president could act as caretaker. For example, should a parliamentary crisis arise and no candidate could command the support of an absolute majority of *Bundestag* members, the president could authorize a chancellor to be elected by a plurality of deputies or could call new parliamentary elections.

In 2005, Chancellor Schröder's government was weakened, and the chancellor sought to engineer an early election. He gambled that voters would strengthen his hand against the opposition CDU and FDP. Both the president at the time, Horst Köhler, and the Constitutional Court feared the maneuver might set a dangerous precedent in Germany (though it is common in other parliamentary systems). In the end, the president and the court both allowed the election (which resulted in Schröder's defeat).

### The Chancellor

The chancellor is elected by a majority of the members of the Bundestag (Germany has coalition governments because no one party has typically commanded an absolute majority in the *Bundestag*). The chancellor's ability to be a strong party (and coalition) leader is thus essential to the government's success. However, even weak chancellors can usually count on their majority coalition to support their remaining in office. Only once (1998) has a government been tossed out by German voters and replaced with an entirely new one (recall how controversial it was for Schröder to call for an early election).

The chancellor determines the overall direction of government, names his or her cabinet ministers (usually in coordination with the coalition partner), and can, within limits, reorganize the number and type of ministries. The chancellor has considerable authority to govern, thanks to the Federal Chancellery (*Bundeskanzleramt*), a kind of superministry with wide-ranging powers. It enables the chancellor to oversee the entire government as well as mediate conflicts among other ministries.

Chancellors and their governments have a fair opportunity to implement their programs and take responsibility for success or failure because the interval between parliamentary elections is four years, and it is difficult to call snap elections (as in the UK). It is also hard to topple a government. Under the Weimar constitution, disparate forces could band together to unseat the chancellor but were then unable to agree on a replacement. Therefore, the Federal Republic's founders added a twist to the no-confidence vote familiar from most parliamentary systems. A German chancellor cannot be removed unless the *Bundestag* simultaneously elects a new chancellor (usually from an opposition party).

**constructive vote of no confidence**

This measure requires the Bundestag to have a new chancellor in place before ousting the current one.

This **constructive vote of no confidence** provision strengthens the chancellor in two ways. First, chancellors can more easily reconcile disputes among cabinet officials because the dispute does not threaten the chancellor's position. Second, the opposition must agree on concrete and specific alternatives to the existing government. It cannot foster opposition for its own sake.

At the same time, chancellors face significant limits on their power. As will be discussed in Section 4, the *Bundesrat* (upper house) must ratify most important legislation passed in the *Bundestag* (lower house) unless overridden by a two-thirds vote of the *Bundestag*. In addition, since the *Bundesrat* implements much legislation, chancellors have to consider the position of the upper house on most issues.

## PROFILE

### Angela Merkel

Source: © Jens Buettner/ epa/Corbis.

Angela Merkel was fifty-one years old in 2005 when she became the first female chancellor. A minister's daughter, a physicist by profession, a latecomer to political life, an eastern German, a Protestant in a party dominated by Catholics, and a woman who does not champion feminist positions, Merkel was an unlikely choice to become Germany's head of government.[17]

Like many East Germans, her political awakening came in 1989 when she took part in pro-democracy protests as the Berlin wall came down. When free political parties emerged in eastern Germany, Merkel was drawn to a small group allied with and later absorbed by the West German Christian Democrats. A quick learner, Merkel rose swiftly through the party ranks. Western parties wanted a presence in eastern Germany, and they sought skilled and astute easterners. Merkel soon caught the eye of

*(Continued)*

Helmut Kohl, won a seat in the Bundestag, and rose rapidly to Environment Minister by 1994. After her party, the CDU, was defeated in 1998, Merkel moved into the political vacuum created by Helmut Kohl's resignation as party leader after a campaign spending scandal.

In the 2005 election, the CDU lost a big lead in the polls because Merkel worried some voters with her suggestion that economic reforms should go in a more free market direction. Although her party won a plurality and Merkel became chancellor, she had to settle for a coalition with the SPD. As chancellor, however, she gradually solidified her reputation with voters. She began to speak of the "new social market economy," a vague formulation that combined appeal to tradition with a promise of renewal.

Her open opposition to Turkish membership in the EU appealed to many voters, as did her suggestion that "multiculturalism" was a poor model for German society. Merkel also raised her profile in international politics by leading an effort to put climate change on the international agenda and to reform and rescue the EU's Constitutional Treaty after its rejection by French and Dutch voters. Her government responded to the 2008 economic crisis with two medium-sized stimulus bills and the original cash-for-clunkers program (2500 euro rebates for purchases of fuel-efficient new cars).

In the 2009 election, German voters punished the SPD with its worst result ever. Thus, despite the fact that the CDU/CSU also did very badly (their worst performance since 1949), the CDU was able to form the coalition it desired with the Free Democrats. Merkel remained chancellor. By far, the defining issue of her second term was her approach to the economic crisis. She angered many other leaders—U.S. officials were skeptical at the modest size of the German stimulus package while Greek and Irish leaders chafed at her lectures about fiscal responsibility—but she understood the anger of German voters. Like Kohl before her, Merkel has also been remarkably successful in sidelining key opponents within the party. Thus, even when her popularity flags, it's not clear who might succeed her as CDU leader.

„ ... WENN DU GROß BIST, MUSST DU DAS BOOT DAHINTEN ZIEHEN ! "

Waldemar Mandzel, www.w-mandzel.de

A working-class figure tows a small boat of retirees upstream while noting to the child, "When you grow up, you get to pull the second boat." See discussion on page 159.

### The Cabinet

A government is formed after a majority of the *Bundestag* has nominated a chancellor, which usually follows a parliamentary election. The newly-nominated chancellor consults with other party (and coalition party) officials to form the cabinet. Negotiations on the policies that a coalition will pursue often become heated. The choice of cabinet ministers is made on policy as well as personal grounds. The most significant ministries are those of finance, economics, justice, interior, and foreign policy. In many cases, chancellors rely on strong ministers; some chancellors have taken ministerial responsibility themselves in key areas such as economics and foreign policy. The economics and finance ministries always work closely with the European Central Bank (ECB), which since the euro adoption has taken over the main functions of the old German Central Bank (the *Bundesbank*).

Ministers are important government actors. They have broad autonomy to set policy in their ministry, subject to the chancellor's overall right to guide the government and to the coalition agreement between the parties. Ministers are also collectively responsible for cabinet policy such that they are expected to support the government's position and not publically express any disagreements or reservations about policy.

### The Bureaucracy

**civil servants**

Employees of federal, state, and municipal governments.

An essential component of the executive is the national bureaucracy. In Germany, it is very powerful, and its members are protected by civil service provisions that give them influence and prestige (not to mention guaranteed employment for life). **Civil servants** strongly believe that their work is a profession, not just a "job."

Surprisingly, the federal government employs only about 25 percent of civil servants; the rest are employed by state and local governments. Today, most civil servants either are university graduates or come from positions within the parties. Top-level federal bureaucrats are primarily policy-makers who work closely with their ministers and the legislature. Bureaucrats at state and local levels are the main agents of policy implementation. Under Germany's distinctive form of federalism, the states administer most policies, even those determined at the national level. The links among the various levels of the bureaucracy often produce more consistent public policies than in countries where federal and state governments are at odds with one another. Indeed, overlapping responsibilities on policy issues make it difficult to state the exclusive responsibility of the three levels.

The modern German bureaucracy enjoys high, if grudging, respect from the population. German bureaucrats have a well-deserved reputation for competence. Most civil servants are politically neutral. However, a few top federal officials are partisan, consistent with the idea that parties play a critical role in German democracy and so should be represented in society's main institutions. The majority of civil servants are chosen on the basis of merit, with elaborate licensing and testing for the highest positions. Civil servants can and do run for office. About one-third of the Bundestag is typically made up of civil servants, including many teachers. This contrasts with the United States, where few legislators have any experience with administration.

## Other State Institutions

In addition to the institutions discussed so far, the military, the judiciary, and subnational governments are essential institutions for governance and policy-making.

## The Military and Police

From the eighteenth century through World War Two, the German military was powerful and aggressive. After 1945 it was disbanded because of its role in the war. It was reconstituted in the 1950s, placed under strict civilian control, and tightly limited by law and treaty. The allied occupation and German Basic law both prohibited the armed forces from operating outside Germany.

The military originally was to be used only for defensive purposes within Europe, and then in coordination with NATO authorities. Constitutional changes later ended this general prohibition, and Germany's *Bundeswehr* participated in the UN peace-keeping mission in Bosnia in 1995 (under a CDU-FDP government), the bombing of Serbia in 1999, and sent troops to Afghanistan after 9/11/2001 (both the latter decisions by SPD-Green governments). As decades pass, the post–World War Two opposition to foreign deployment of the German army is eroding somewhat.

Germany's recent abolition of the draft will make its army an all-volunteer professional force that is easier to deploy abroad. However, the military's role remains limited. Germany spends approximately 1.3 percent of its GDP on the military, less than most other large, industrialized countries. Germany also has renounced any intention to acquire nuclear weapons (in contrast to Britain and France).

German police powers are organized on a *Land* basis and, because of the excesses of the Third Reich, strong provisions are in place to protect human and civil rights. To be sure, there have been exceptions. By far the worst police abuses came not from West Germany, however, but from East Germany's notorious secret police, the *Stasi*. The Ministry for State Security (the *Stasi*'s formal name) included some 91,000 official employees; moreover, in 1989, more than 180,000 East Germans and perhaps 4,000 West Germans worked as informants for the *Stasi*.[18] The Stasi spied on virtually the entire society and arbitrarily arrested and persecuted thousands of citizens. With unification, *Stasi* archives were opened because the government believed that full disclosure of *Stasi* excesses was essential. Making public the names of informants has often created bitter confrontations.

There have been heightened challenges for German police in the wake of 9/11. Police gained some new powers, including surveillance, but the courts then cut back some of these powers. Numerous members of al Qaeda, including several of the 9/11 bombers, lived in Hamburg and other German cities. Germany has seen a number of subsequent "near misses," including a 2006 plot by two Lebanese men to explode suitcase bombs on a crowded commuter train in Cologne (other suitcase bombs on trains in Dortmund and Koblenz also failed to explode). In 2007, German police uncovered a plan by two German converts to Islam and a Turkish national to drive explosives-laden trucks into U.S. military facilities. All three young men had trained in Pakistan. In 2011, a Kosovar worker at the Frankfurt Airport opened fire on U.S. airmen, killing two and wounding two others.

## The Judiciary

The judiciary has always played a major role in German government. During the Nazi regime, it issued numerous repressive decisions, banning non-Nazi parties, allowing the seizure of Jewish property, and sanctioning the deaths of millions. The Federal Republic's founders were determined to prevent judicial abuses in the future. The Basic Law charges the judiciary with safeguarding the democratic rights of individuals, groups, and political parties. In fact, the Basic Law enumerates twenty individual rights—more than exist in the U.S. Constitution or in British common law.

Germany's legal system differs from the common law tradition of Britain and the United States. In the common law precedent-based system, characterized by adversarial relationships between contending parties, the judge merely presides over a clash between opposing lawyers. In continental Europe, including France and Germany, civil law has roots in Roman law and the Napoleonic code. The judiciary is an active administrator of the law rather than just an arbiter. In defining the meaning of laws and implementing their administration, German courts go considerably beyond those in the United States and Britain.

The German judiciary is an independent institution and remains outside the political fray on most issues. However, there are exceptions such as a controversial ruling in 1993 that limited access to abortion and overruled a more permissive law in East Germany. The judiciary was also criticized in the 1990s for showing too much leniency toward defendants who were prosecuted for allegations of racist violence.

The court system in the Federal Republic is three-pronged. One branch consists of the criminal-civil system, which has as its apex the Federal High Court. It is a unified system that tries to apply consistent criteria to cases in the sixteen states. The Federal High Court reviews cases that have been appealed from the lower courts, including criminal and civil cases, disputes among the states, and matters viewed as political in some countries, such as the abortion ruling.

The Special Constitutional Court deals with matters directly affecting the Basic Law. A postwar creation, it was founded to safeguard the new democratic order. Because of the Nazis' abuses of the judiciary, the FRG founders added a judicial layer to ensure that the democratic order was maintained. The Constitutional Court is widely respected and has issued many landmark decisions, including one in 2009 that halts any further transfer of German power to the EU unless expressly ratified by the German parliament (not just the government).

The Administrative Court system is the third branch of the judiciary. It acts as a check on the arbitrary power of the bureaucracy, an important function since public policy in Germany is so often determined by the bureaucracy. Citizens can use administrative courts to challenge bureaucratic decisions, for example, with respect to labor, welfare, or tax policies.

The courts have sometimes come under fire. Critics charged that courts did not restrain clandestine searches for leftist terrorists in the late 1970s that arguably violated the rights of citizens. The courts have recently been criticized for giving undue protection to neo-Nazis, not to mention potential al Qaeda terrorists. The judicial system as a whole must walk a fine line between maintaining civil rights in a democratic society and providing security from extremist violence.

## Subnational Government

Like the United States, Canada, and Austria, Germany is a *federal* republic. There are sixteen *Länder* (states); eleven constituted the old West Germany and five the former East Germany. German state governments enjoy considerable autonomy and independent powers. Each state has a regional assembly (*Landtag*), which functions much as the *Bundestag* does at the federal level. The governor (*Minister-Präsident*) of each *Land* is the leader of the largest party (or coalition of parties) in the *Landtag* and forms a government in the *Landtag*, just as does the chancellor in the *Bundestag*. State elections are held on independent, staggered four-year cycles, which generally do not coincide with federal elections. Subnational governments in Germany are powerful, important, and responsible for much national policy implementation, including most laws passed by the federal government. German states must also share a portion of their tax revenues, so states with stronger economies (grudgingly) support those with weaker economies and lower revenues.

The negative side of German federalism is its lack of flexibility. Since the Basic Law did not specify which powers were reserved for the federal level and which for the states, the policymaking process has grown cumbersome and contested. Since different levels have shared responsibility, this can be a recipe for conflict. At times, opposition parties have used the upper house to "blockade" the lower house for long periods. A 2006 reform attempted to clarify the policy domains of the federal and state levels and reduce the possibilities for blockades. However, it has not been very effective.[19]

State politics is organized on the same political party basis as the national parties. However, the common party names and platforms at all levels let voters see the connection among local, regional, and national issues. Because parties adopt platforms for state and city elections, voters can see the ideological differences among parties and not be swayed solely by personalities. The German party system encourages politicians to begin their careers at the local and state levels. Regional and local party members' careers are tied closely to the national, regional, and local levels of the party. Thus, ideological and policy continuity across levels is rewarded.[20]

German local governments employ about 1.5 million people and assume a wide range of tasks, providing social services (often working with semipublic institutions), implementing environmental standards, and managing the transport network. Local governments can raise revenues by owning enterprises, a reflection of historical patterns of public sector involvement in the economy. Many Germans believe that publicly-owned museums, theater companies, television and radio networks, recreational facilities, and housing complexes improve their quality of life.

# The Policy-Making Process

The chancellor and cabinet are responsible for policy-making, but the process is largely consensus-based, with contentious issues extensively debated within various public, semipublic, and private institutions. Although the legislature has a general role in policy-making, the primary driving forces are the respective cabinet departments and the experts on whom they call. The Basic Law makes the *Bundesrat* (upper house) co-equal in all areas where state interests and/or administration play a central role. In practice, this came to mean almost any important piece of domestic legislation. The 2006 federalism reforms tried to streamline these responsibilities, for example, attempting to remove the federal government entirely from higher education policy.

Policy implementation is also a shared task, in which the *Bundesrat* plays a significant role, along with corporatist interest groups and semipublic organizations. EU policy is shaped by both national and regional governments (the 2006 federalism reform guaranteed the states a role in shaping EU policies that affect them), as well as by private sector interests that use corporatist institutions to participate in the process.

Both unification and the increasing importance of the EU (for example, the adoption of the euro and the rules associated with it) have challenged this informal style of policy-making. Moreover, for all its system-maintaining advantages, the German consensual system is somewhat intolerant of dissent. This tendency helps explain why protest politics occasionally erupts in Germany, seemingly out of nowhere.

## Summary

Postwar German institutions were designed to solve two different problems: to avoid the fragmentation and weakness of Weimar and to prevent the excessive concentration of power and brutality of the Nazi period. While German institutions have succeeded admirably in both cases, the political system still struggles to generate effective policy. For one thing, its version of federalism has led to ferocious battles between the center and the states. For another, the EU has complicated policy-making at both national and subnational levels, and the Constitutional Court has made it difficult to delegate more power to the EU level. A third problem is discussed in the next section: The fragmentation of the party system has made coalition formation more complicated and governance more difficult.

SECTION 4

# REPRESENTATION AND PARTICIPATION

### Focus Questions

How has the move to a five-party system disrupted parties' traditional ways of doing business?

Why do protest politics work so differently in Germany and the United States?

German parties represent many established interests well, yet its parties and interest groups still struggle to give a voice to some major collective identities and interests. Partly, this is understandable. Incorporating disparate political cultures (like east and west Germany, for example) is a dilemma for any society. Yet the German party system is not particularly responsive to new interests and values bubbling up from society.

## Legislature

Like most parliamentary regimes, Germany "fuses" power, in that the executive branch derives directly from the legislative branch. Unlike many parliamentary systems that are tightly controlled by the government, however, both the lower house (*Bundestag*) and the upper house (*Bundesrat*) possess important partially independent powers. Both branches of the legislature are broadly representative of the major interests in German society, although some interests such as business and labor are somewhat overrepresented, whereas ecological and noneconomic interests are underrepresented.

### The *Bundestag*

**mixed member system**

An electoral system in which about half of deputies are elected from direct constituencies and the other half are drawn from closed party lists. The *Bundestag* uses the Mixed Member System, which is basically a form of proportional representation.

The lower house, the *Bundestag*, consists of 614 seats. German elections are by a two-ballot system, known as the **mixed member system**. This system blends the British and U.S. traditions of a single legislator representing one district and the European tradition of proportional representation, in which parties are allotted seats in the legislature in proportion to the percentage of popular votes they receive. To do this, the hybrid system asks voters to cast two votes on their ballot: the first for an individual candidate in a voter's local district and the second for a list of national/regional candidates grouped by party affiliation (see Figure 4.3).

Seats in the *Bundestag* are then allocated among parties by proportional representation—but with a twist produced by the single-member district feature. If a party's candidate wins a seat as an individual member, his or her party is allotted one less seat from the party's slate elected via list voting. In practice, the two large parties, the Social Democrats and the Christian Democrats, win virtually all of the district seats. In this way, the *Bundestag*'s composition is "mixed" between those deputies who are directly elected and those who enter from party lists. This mix gives the system both a constituency logic but also a mechanism for parties to influence legislators to toe the party line. Once elected, the two groups have identical powers.

Most members of the *Bundestag* are male, middle-class professionals. Fewer than 10 percent were women through the 1983 election. Since 1987, the number of women has increased substantially, reaching 32.8 percent with the 2009 election (see Table 4.3). The addition of newer parties such as the ex-communist Left Party and the continued presence of the Greens with their counterculture lifestyles has increased the variety of backgrounds among *Bundestag* members.

The proportional representation list system produces multiple parties, but it also helps strengthen parties. If legislators consistently defy their party, the leadership can give them a low list position in the next election. This is a powerful lever to promote party discipline. Party unity contributes to consistency in the parties' positions over a four-year legislative period and enables the electorate to identify each party's stance on a range of issues.

Parties must obtain at least 5 percent of the nationwide vote to benefit from proportional representation (5 percent of the vote is also required in state or municipal elections for representation in those governments). Smaller parties have tended to fade away. Thus, Germany has avoided the wild proliferation of parties that plagues some democracies, such as Italy and Israel, where coalitions are extremely difficult to form and sustain.

The tradition of strong, unified parties in the *Bundestag* has some drawbacks. New members must serve long stints as backbenchers. Individual legislators have few

**FIGURE 4.3 Bundestag Election Ballot**

With their "first vote," voters from the Bonn electoral district choose a candidate by name from the left-hand column. The winner enters the *Bundestag*. The voters next cast a "second vote" in the right-hand column for a party list. These totals give each party additional seats roughly equal to their percentage of second votes.

opportunities to make an impact. Some of the most prominent national politicians have preferred to serve their political apprenticeship in state or local government, where they have more visibility. This system, in turn, does improve the skills of young politicians.

The executive branch introduces most legislation and must initiate all federal budget and tax legislation. However, there is no sharp division between the executive and legislative branches. There is often a consensus within parties and within coalitions about what legislation should be introduced. When the executive proposes a bill, it has a quick first reading—primarily to identify any contentious issues in the bill. It then goes to a relevant *Bundestag* committee, while the Upper House is also notified. Most committee deliberations take place privately, and individual committee members have considerable latitude to shape the legislation. Committees generally consult with a wide range of groups, both pro and con. This makes it more likely that a consensus-oriented outcome will be achieved.

After the committee reports, the bill has two more readings in the *Bundestag*, with debate between governing parties and opposition generally most intense around

| Table 4.3 | Percentage of Women Members of the *Bundestag* | | |
|---|---|---|---|
| Year | Percentage | Year | Percentage |
| 1949 | 6.8 | 1980 | 8.5 |
| 1953 | 8.8 | 1983 | 9.8 |
| 1957 | 9.2 | 1987 | 15.4 |
| 1961 | 8.3 | 1990 | 20.5 |
| 1965 | 6.9 | 1994 | 26.3 |
| 1969 | 6.6 | 1998 | 30.2 |
| 1972 | 5.8 | 2002 | 32.2 |
| 1976 | 7.3 | 2005 | 31.8 |
| | | 2009 | 32.8 |

*Source:* Bundeszentrale für Politische Bildung, 2010.

**absolute veto**

In areas that directly affect the states, the *Bundesrat* can veto any bill passed by the *Bundestag.*

**suspensive veto**

In policy areas with no direct effect on the states, the *Bundesrat* has the prerogative to make the *Bundestag* pass a bill a second time.

the second reading. The primary purpose of the debate is to educate the public about the major issues of the bill. Following passage in the *Bundestag*, the *Bundesrat* must approve most bills.

### The *Bundesrat*

The *Bundesrat* is the mechanism that helps make the federal system work. Made up of sixty-nine members from the sixteen state governments, it is the point where the national and the state governments interact. When the government initiates a bill, it sends it first to the *Bundesrat*, which is also empowered to initiate bills in its own right.

The *Bundesrat* can exercise an **absolute veto** on amendments to the constitution as well as all laws that affect the fundamental interests of the states, such as taxes, territorial integrity, and basic administrative functions. Historically, laws that affect fundamental interests of states and thus require *Bundesrat* approval have amounted to slightly over half (53 percent) of bills, though a 2006 constitutional reform resulted in a subsequent decline to around 40 percent. The *Bundesrat* also can exercise a **suspensive veto**, which slows the passage of legislation. However, if the *Bundesrat* votes against a bill, the *Bundestag* can override the *Bundesrat* by passing the measure again by a simple majority. If a two-thirds majority of the *Bundesrat* votes against a bill (a rare occurrence), the *Bundestag* must pass it again by a two-thirds margin.

The political composition of the *Bundesrat* depends upon which parties are in power in the states. Each state delegation casts its votes on legislation in a bloc, reflecting the views of the state's majority party or coalition. Consequently, the party controlling the majority of state governments can have a significant effect on what legislation is passed. Because state elections usually take place between *Bundestag* electoral periods, the *Bundesrat* majority often shifts during the *Bundestag's* four-year legislative period. In fact, 2011 alone (a so-called *Superwahljahr*) ended up seeing elections in about one-third of the states.

The *Bundesrat* introduces comparatively little legislation, but its administrative responsibilities are considerable. Most members of the *Bundesrat* are also state government officials, experienced in implementing laws. The *Bundesrat* is close to the concerns and needs of the entire country and provides a forum for understanding how national legislation affects each state. Their expertise is frequently called on in the committee hearings of the *Bundestag*, which are open to all *Bundesrat* members. The *Bundesrat* also administers the world's largest public television network (ARD) and helps coordinate regional and national economic policies.

Finally, the *Bundesrat* plays a significant role in dealing with the EU. It has long advocated representation for the *Länder* in EU institutions. In 2006, it gained powers to represent the German government in Brussels in some negotiations that centrally affect the states. By the same token, the states must now pay part of the fine if Germany exceeds EU debt limits.

# Political Parties and the Party System

Germany has often been called a **party democracy** because its parties are so important in shaping state policy. Until the early 1980s, Germany had a "two-and-a-half" party system, composed of a moderate-left Social Democratic Party (SPD), a moderate-right Christian Democratic grouping (CDU in all of West Germany except Bavaria, where it is called the CSU), and a small centrist Free Democratic Party (FDP).

During the 1980s and 1990s, two new parties emerged to challenge the "two-and-a-half" major parties.[21] These were the Greens, generally on the left and favoring ecological, environmental, and peace issues; and the Party of Democratic Socialism (PDS), the former Communist Party of East Germany. In 2005, the latter formed *die Linke* (Left Party) with a group of former left-wing Social Democrats who believed Schröder's reforms undermined social democracy. Two small right-wing parties, the National Democratic Party (*Nationaldemokratische Partei Deutschlands*, NPD) and the German People's Union (*Deutsche Volksunion*, DVU), also emerged at this time. Much more conservative than the CDU/CSU, they emphasized nationalism and intolerance toward immigrants and ethnic minorities. Thus far, they have failed to clear the 5 percent threshold in national elections to gain representation in the *Bundestag*.

**party democracy**

The constitutional guarantee that political parties have a privileged place in German politics, including generous subsidies for building party organizations.

### The Christian Democrats

The CDU/CSU have dominated postwar German politics, governing, usually in coalitions, from 1949–1969, 1982–1998, and since 2005. The CDU and CSU unite Catholics and Protestants in one confessional, catchall party of the center-right. Christian Democracy champions the social market economy. Its social policies in the decades after World War Two were paternalistic and moderately conservative, but it sponsored the considerable expansion of the German welfare state. The party has been a consistent advocate of European integration since Konrad Adenauer's leadership in the early postwar period. The most significant and historic accomplishments of the long Kohl regime (1982–1998) are German unification and Germany's much deeper integration into the EU.

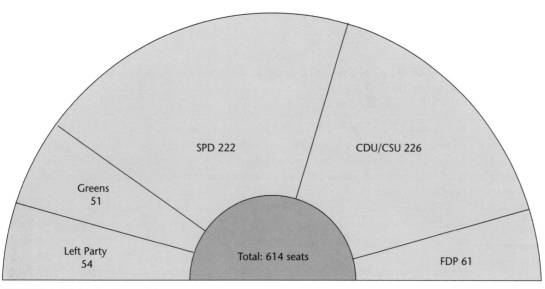

FIGURE 4.4 **Distribution of Seats**

CDU leader Angela Merkel became Germany's first female chancellor after the 2005 election. Instead of the preferred coalition with the FDP, the party's traditional coalition partner, the electoral results forced the CDU/CSU into a "Grand Coalition" with its arch-rival, the SPD. After intense negotiations among the parties over a coalition agreement, Merkel emerged as chancellor three weeks after the election. The 2009 election enabled Merkel to form her preferred coalition, although the government subsequently has been marked by substantial infighting between coalition partners (for more on Merkel, see the box in Section 3). That said, Merkel faces few challenges from within the party.

## The Social Democratic Party

The traditional leading party of the left, the SPD, was founded in 1875 in response to rapid industrialization and Bismarck's authoritarian role. Following World War One, it became the leading party—but without a majority—of the Weimar Republic during its early years.

Despite being the second-largest party in postwar Germany, the SPD obtained only about 30 percent of the vote until the early 1960s and never succeeded in even joining a government. In an attempt to broaden its constituency, it altered its party program in 1959. Deemphasizing its reliance on Marxism and its working-class base, its new goal was to recruit voters from throughout the social structure, including the middle class and among Christians.

*Ostpolitik*

The policy developed by the SPD's Willy Brandt to promote contact and commerce with the Soviet Union and its communist allies during the Cold War.

In 1969, the SPD was finally elected to office as the leading member of a majority coalition (with the FDP). It remained in power for thirteen years under chancellors Willy Brandt and Helmut Schmidt. The SPD brought to the coalition a concern for increased welfare and social spending, as well as an effort to ease strained relations with the USSR and other communist countries (***Ostpolitik***).

Out of power from 1982 to 1998, the SPD largely failed to formulate attractive alternative policies, though it governed many states. In 1998, the exhausted Kohl regime was voted out, and the SPD was able to form a coalition with the Greens. The seven years of the second SPD-led regime were initially successful, but divisions within the party about the nature of structural reform—and the direction of Social Democracy in Germany—brought the second term of the SPD-Green government to an early end. After limping through a Grand Coalition for four years, the SPD vote plunged to 23 percent in the 2009 elections, its lowest total ever. (It lost 76 seats in the *Bundestag*.)

## The Greens

citizens action groups

Non-party and often single-issue initiatives, often focused on concrete problems such as the environment, traffic, housing, or other social and economic issues.

The Greens entered the political scene in 1979 and have won seats at national and regional levels ever since. This heterogeneous party drew support from several constituencies in the early 1980s: urban-based **citizens action groups**, environmental activists, farmers, antinuclear activists, the peace movement, and small bands of Marxist-Leninists. After first overcoming the 5 percent hurdle in 1983 *Bundestag* elections, the Greens went on to win seats in most subsequent state and national elections by stressing non-economic quality-of-life issues.

Electoral success generated division within this "antiparty party." The *realos* (realists) believed it was important to moderate the party's positions in order to win power; the *fundis* (fundamentalists) opposed any collaboration with existing parties, even if this meant damaging their chances of electoral success in the short term. The squabbling between *fundis* and *realos* undercut the party's credibility, even though ecological problems in Eastern Germany presented the Greens with a tremendous opportunity.

In 1998 the Greens got their first chance to govern in a national coalition. The *fundi-realo* split emerged immediately when the divided party was unable to convince its SPD coalition partners to support ecological taxes. Green Foreign Minister, Joschka Fischer, a *realo*, further split the party by supporting Germany's participation in the NATO-led bombing campaign of Serbia. Fischer explained that his generation was raised both to say "never again war" *and* "never again Auschwitz." When forced to choose, he argued that Germany must choose the latter in order to prevent Serbian tyrant Slobodan Milosevic from sponsoring genocide against the Kosovar Albanians.

Following the 2005 election, the Greens returned to the opposition benches in the *Bundestag*. An indication of the complexity and volatility of German politics is that following the 2008 *Land* election in Hamburg, the Greens agreed to join the CDU in the regional government. At the same time, the CDU also sees the Greens as a serious competitor. Accentuating difference with the Greens was one reason for Merkel's shift toward nuclear energy, a move that backfired disastrously after the Japanese nuclear crisis. In 2011, for the first time, a Green became governor of a state. Here is yet another sign of possible increased party volatility in Germany.

## The Free Democratic Party

The FDP has specialized in turning modest numbers of votes into lots of power. Its major influence is as a swing party, in that it has allied with each of the two major parties (SPD and CDU/CSU) at different periods since 1949. The party has regularly held both the foreign and economics ministries in coalitions with the CDU/CSU and the SPD. After the 2009 elections, FDP leader Guido Westerwelle was appointed foreign minister and vice-chancellor, though he later stepped down as party leader.

The FDP's perspective encompasses two ideologies: economic liberalism (liberal in the European sense of *laissez-faire* individualism) and social liberalism (namely individual personal freedoms). During the postwar period, the FDP alternately relied on one of these two philosophies to align itself with the CDU/CSU or the SPD.

During the 1998–2005 period of SPD-Green governments, the FDP became much more explicitly a free-market party, emphasizing deregulation and privatization. The growth of the Green and Left Parties has diminished the "kingmaker" status of the FDP, but Angela Merkel made it clear in both 2005 and 2009 that she preferred governing with the FDP. In 2009, after polling an astonishingly high 15 percent, the FDP replaced the SPD in Merkel's CDU-led government coalition. However, the FDP's standing subsequently plummeted, and the party's vote dipped below 5 percent in some state elections.

## The Left Party (*die Linke*)

In 2005, the former East German Communist Party (PDS) merged with a breakaway faction of the SPD to form the Left Party. While officially a new party concentrated in the former East Germany, the PDS had a long and volatile history. Beginning in the late 1940s, the Communist Party (SED) dominated all aspects of life in East Germany. The GDR led by the SED was probably the most Stalinist and repressive regime in Eastern Europe.

After unification in 1990, the SED demonstrated tactical agility by changing its name to the PDS and modifying its program. It often polled over 20 percent in the five *Länder* of the former East Germany and won a spot in the Bundestag in each election. The Left Party was formed when it merged with left-wing dissidents from the SPD who were based primarily in western Germany. The new arrivals provided electoral support for the PDS precisely where it was weakest.

The Left Party's strong showing is largely due to its opposition to cuts in social spending. With a growing base in the west (around 5 percent) and traditional eastern support (nearly 25 percent) it has become solidly entrenched as a fifth party. All other parties oppose allying with the Left—including the SPD and Greens. Nevertheless, the Left Party's presence further makes "coalition math" far more complicated than in the simple old days of either CDU/CSU-FDP or SPD-FDP alliances. The Left Party has been part of several state coalitions, including, recently, Berlin and Brandenburg with the SPD.

The FRG is one of the few countries in western Europe that has not had a far-right and/or neo-fascist party gain seats in its national legislature. Because the Left Party's primary support in the east comes from marginalized and/or unemployed people in German society, it has provided a left-wing alternative for many voters who, in other west European countries, have turned to the far right. As noted earlier, there are two far-right political parties that have won seats in state parliaments since 2000: the DVU and NPD.[22] A Munich court struck down a planned merger between the two parties in 2011.

# Elections

Until recently, German voter turnout rates of 80 to 90 percent exceeded those in most other western European countries. There have been five major periods of party dominance (plus two shorter-lived Grand Coalitions) from 1949 leading to the CDU/CSU-FDP coalition in 2009:

1. CDU/CSU-FDP coalitions (1949–1966; CDU/CSU majority, 1957–1961)
2. Grand Coalition (CDU/CSU-SPD) (1966–1969)
3. SPD-FDP coalitions (1969–1982)
4. CDU/CSU-FDP coalitions (1982–1998)
5. SPD-Green coalitions (1998–2005)
6. Grand Coalition (CDU/CSU-SPD) (2005–2009)
7. CDU/CSU-FDP coalition (2009–)

As Figure 4.5 suggests, Germany has enjoyed relatively stable electoral allegiance, despite unification and European integration. That said, the introduction of two new parties in the *Bundestag* in recent decades may now reflect high volatility among voters and, hence, among parties. The danger is that a five-party system may often result in inconclusive elections. After the vote, it may fall to the parties to haggle amongst themselves to choose among possible coalitions. Will voters then react with even greater frustration? And will parties turn to more and more adventurous coalitions in order to form majorities?

# Political Culture, Citizenship, and Identity

**grass-roots democracy**

The idea that real democracy requires participation from rank-and-file members and not merely from organizational leaders.

With political parties representing such a broad ideological spectrum, there is wide-ranging political debate in Germany. Historically, the political right has succeeded in integrating a broad swath of right wing voters into democratic and even centrist politics. Among the democratic left, there is a strong participatory ethic, fostered by extensive participation at the workplace through the works councils. Moreover, the Greens have placed great emphasis on **grass-roots democracy**—that is, rank-and-file participation. The Greens, and now the Left Party, have forced the traditional parties to engage in grassroots efforts to mobilize support.

Germany's educational system is steeped in tradition, though it has changed considerably in recent decades. Traditionally, only a small cohort went on to university—children still begin the university prep track in the sixth grade!—while the rest went on to technical or vocational tracks. In recent years, German schools have been disappointingly middle-of-the-pack in comparative analyses.

The postwar universities long remained elitist and restrictive and often provided little critical analysis of Germany's bloody twentieth-century history. The student mobilizations of the 1960s opened up the educational system to a much wider class spectrum and also caused many of the '68 Generation (1968 was the year of the most significant student demonstrations) to challenge their parents about attitudes shaped by the Nazi period and before. Far more Germans now attend universities, but few German universities are in the very top rank globally.

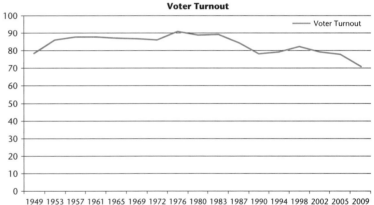

**FIGURE 4.5  FRG Election Results, 1949–2009**

*Sources:* German Information Center, 2009.

## Refugees, Immigration and Migrant Labor

The nationalism unleashed after the creation of Germany in 1871, and the following economic and political upheaval, caused catastrophe for nonethnic Germans. Because of the late-nineteenth- and early-to-mid-twentieth-century oppression of racial and ethnic minorities, postwar Germany accepted a special responsibility to Jews and other ethnic minorities. The new FRG government made large compensation payments to survivors of the Holocaust, their families, and the state of Israel. It also passed generous asylum laws to enable large numbers of those facing political persecution to obtain residency, if not citizenship in Germany. With the end of the Cold War and the opening up of east European borders, the trickle of asylum seekers turned into a flood. In response, the Kohl government drastically curtailed the right of political asylum.

At the same time, immigrants to Germany have had little chance to obtain citizenship. The 1913 Immigration Law stipulated that citizenship was based on blood (*jus sanguinis*) and not naturalization (*jus solis*). This meant that German citizenship was easy to obtain for ethnic Germans who had lived in Russia or eastern Europe for generations and did not speak German, but difficult for the *Gastarbeiter* who had lived in Germany since the 1960s. Germany's restrictive definition of identity looked remarkably insular in a Europe that was becoming more international and global until the SPD-Green government liberalized citizenship requirements in 1999.

Every European state faces a version of this dilemma. While some Germans are fearful that immigration will weaken the traditional conception of "German," globalization has opened the country to increasing migration. Adding to the economic pressures to increase immigration is a demographic time-bomb that, likewise, affects almost all European countries: a decline of the native-born population. The aging native population relies on a welfare and pension system financed by currently employed (that is, younger) workers. One partial solution to the fiscal demands of an aging population is young immigrant workers who will both revitalize economic growth and help fund the pension and welfare obligations. To do so, however, requires that Germany—and many of its neighbors—reconsider who can be a citizen.

Until the 1960s, women had been politically marginalized in the FRG. Taking to heart the slogan *Kinder, Kirche, Küche* (children, church, and kitchen), few women held positions in society outside the home. Even with the social explosions of the 1960s and the spread of feminism since the 1970s, German women have generally lagged behind women in many west European countries in obtaining adequate representation in business and civil society. However, as the data in Table 4.3 show, German women have quadrupled their representation in the Bundestag from approximately 8 percent in 1980 to almost 33 percent in 2009.

Following unification, important differences between East and West Germany on social policy affecting women provoked great controversy. Women in the former East Germany had more presence and influence in public life and in the workplace than did their counterparts in West Germany. To be sure, female employment was nearly obligatory in the GDR. Still, East German women enjoyed greater government provision for childcare and family leave. In fact, one of the hottest items of contention in Germany during the early 1990s was whether to reduce East German–style benefits to women in favor of the more conservative and restrictive ones of the Federal Republic. The West German practices and patterns prevailed after unification, to the frustration of many.

Germany's press is free, diverse, and vibrant. Newspapers appeal to a broad range of political opinion. There are a wide variety of private TV cable and satellite channels, but the three main public channels (two national, one regionally-based) provide a balance of major party positions. Until the late 1990s, most public channels prohibited paid TV campaign commercials during the two-month electoral campaigns. A rough-and-tumble tabloid press has a populist tone and is quick to punish any signs of elitism on the part of politicians. The tabloids played a key role in mobilizing opposition to German financing of the Eurozone crisis after 2008.

## Organized Interests, Social Movements, and Protest

As discussed in Section 2, Germany remains a country of organized groups: major economic producer groups such as the BDI (Federal Association of German Industry), BDA (Federal Association of German Employers), and DGB (German Trade Union Confederation); political parties (in which authentic participatory membership remains higher than in most other countries); and social groups.

Interest groups in Germany operate differently than in the United States and Britain. In Germany, interest groups have a societal responsibility beyond representing the immediate interests of their members. Laws allow private interests to perform public functions, albeit within a specified general framework. Thus, interest groups are part of the fabric of society and are virtually permanent institutions. This makes it critical that they can adapt to new issues.

Despite the emphasis on negotiation and consensus, strikes and demonstrations do occur on a wide range of economic and noneconomic issues. In some cases, strikes and other conflicts act as mechanisms pressuring institutions to be responsive.[23] Rather than being detrimental to democratic participation, such bottom-up protests contribute to a vibrant civil society.

In the best case, because they aggregate the interests of all their members, groups take a broader view of problems and policy solutions, and the state neither remains distant, as in Britain and the United States, nor intervenes in the intensive fashion typical of France and Japan. Political scientist Peter Katzenstein observes that in Germany, "the state is not an actor but a series of relationships," and these relationships are mediated and solidified in semipublic institutions.[24] Katzenstein further notes that semipublic institutions have been assigned the role of "independent governance by the representatives of social sectors at the behest of or under the general supervision of the state."[25] In other words, organizations that would elsewhere be regarded as "mere interest groups" work with semipublic agencies to fill a critical role between state and society.

Interest groups and semipublic agencies limit social conflict by regular meetings and close coordination. However, there may be a tendency for the system to leave some issues and groups unrepresented. The rise of the Green Party in the 1970s is an example of a movement that responded to the inability of existing institutions to address, mediate, and solve important issues, including environmental problems and the subordinate position of women. Another example is the Left Party, which represents those who did not feel represented by the established western-based parties. More recently, many German voters have felt enraged enough for mass demonstrations against everything from bailouts for other European states to unpopular or wasteful transport projects.

Many smaller groups fall outside this organized system, including political parties that fail to meet the 5 percent electoral threshold, such as the far-right NPD and the DVU. The substantial Turkish population, comprising 4.6 percent of Germany's inhabitants, should be included here. Many Turks have resided in Germany for decades, but unlike workers from EU countries like Italy and Spain, have few rights.

Since the student mobilizations of the late 1960s, Germany has witnessed considerable protest and mobilization of social forces outside established channels. Among the most significant have been feminists, the peace movement, the antinuclear movement, and the church-linked protests in East Germany in 1989 that catalyzed the breakdown of the communist regime. When right-wing violence in West German cities claimed the lives of three Turks (including two children) in a house bombing in 1992 and five more in an arson fire in 1993, hundreds of thousands of Germans marched to show their sympathy for the victims.

The issue of the Iraq war produced an increase in social protest beginning in 2003, largely among forces to the left of the governing SPD-Green coalition. There have also been smaller right-wing protests against continued immigration, such as a May Day Hamburg riot in 2008, but these have not approached the violent episodes of the 1990s. Among the political parties, only the Left Party actively opposed German troop deployments to Afghanistan (over 40 German soldiers have been killed since being deployed there since 2002). Most protests on this issue have been limited to hundreds rather than thousands of demonstrators.

# THE U.S. CONNECTION

## Comparing Anti-Nuclear Movements in the United States and Germany

Ever since the Japanese tsunami destroyed the Fukushima nuclear plant in 2011, concerns about nuclear power safety have increased in the United States and Germany. Both nuclear industries share some important features. Their relative size is about equal. The US gets about 20 percent of its electricity from nuclear power, generated by about 100 plants. Germany's 17 plants account for almost 25 percent of electricity. (By comparison, France's 58 plants produce 75 percent of its electricity.) In both states, the main debate involves whether to extend the life of existing plants (especially those built before the 1970s) and less about building new plants. In both countries, the government plays a critical role in licensing and inspecting plants, subsidizing R&D, and insuring against risks. In both, private companies produce nuclear power, and the government is responsible for dealing with waste.

Both states also have selected a waste dump site, which has never been used because of political opposition. In the United States, it involves tunnels bored into Yucca Mountain in the Nevada desert. In Germany, the potential dump is 1000 meters below the surface of a north German salt dome called Gorleben. Finally, in both countries an iconic nuclear accident (Three Mile Island in Pennsylvania in 1979 and Chernobyl in Ukraine in 1986) helped end construction of new nuclear plants. Yet alongside these similarities, there are striking differences in how the antinuclear movements work in both countries. The German antinuclear movement, which began in the early 1970s, has often been radical, even violent at times. It built on a cultural foundation of ecological

activism, and it eventually "broke through" an electoral system that requires coalition government and has more space for small parties than in the United States.

In the United States, however, the anti-nuclear movement split, with neither faction resembling its German counterpart. One wing of the U.S. movement has focused on legal tactics, essentially challenging the nuclear industry (and often the government) in court. The other wing has been confrontational, but non-violent.[26] Moreover, because Germans take global warming seriously, the antinuclear movement strongly supports policies involving alternative energies. In the United States, this is less true.

In Germany, the movement has been highly confrontational. Nuclear waste trains have been disrupted by protestors shooting fireworks and dropping by ropes from bridges above the train tracks. Given this context, the Japanese nuclear disaster only deepened skepticism. Merkel ordered a moratorium on a plan to extend the life of older plants, but her opponents accused her of pandering, and voters seemed to agree. In the March 2011 state elections, Merkel's party lost the state of Baden-Württemberg for the first time in 58 years. While the CDU dropped to 39 percent (from 44 percent), the Green party rocketed to 24 percent of the vote and, with the SPD, gained control of the state government. One of the government's first moves was to call on the national government to rethink its nuclear policies. Merkel's government subsequently announced the phase-out of German nuclear plants by 2022.

This gag campaign poster attacking the CDU appeared shortly after the Japanese earthquake roiled the politics of nuclear energy in Germany. Chancellor Merkel says, "We're imposing a moratorium" on re-licensing nuclear plants. *The Simpsons'* Montgomery Burns conspiratorially replies, "And then we'll start up again."

## Summary

The 2006 European Social Survey asked respondents in 19 European countries to rate their trust of national political parties. German parties scored fourteenth-lowest, tied with France and ahead only of Russia, Hungary, Portugal, Poland, and Bulgaria. At the same time, the fragmenting party landscape has now generated five seemingly durable parties. When more than one coalition may be mathematically and politically possible, parties will be more inclined to horse trade, a fact that is sure to turn off voters and cause their further alienation from parties (see figure 4.5).

Meanwhile, problems are not getting any simpler to solve. Like all European states, the German state and society must address immigration—in all its positive and negative complexity. It must do so, however, with relatively little experience in treating foreigners as potential citizens. The economic crisis, environmental and energy issues, and increasingly fierce tussles over the role of the EU all crowd the agenda in ways that parties seem increasingly unable to manage. The major advantage Germans have may lie in the remarkable capacity of German society to contribute to joint problem-solving. This legacy of the earlier historical periods will be a critical asset as Germany faces the challenges ahead.

# GERMAN POLITICS IN TRANSITION

SECTION **5**

On June 30, 2009, EU officials breathed an enormous sigh of relief as the German Constitutional Court gave its blessing to the Treaty of Lisbon, which reformed the EU's major institutions to attempt to improve the quality of decision-making. Five years earlier, the EU member states had attempted another, more thorough-going treaty reform. Both French and Dutch voters had decisively rejected this so-called Constitutional Treaty. In the aftermath, Angela Merkel placed high priority on devising a new treaty that could succeed politically where the Constitutional Treaty had failed. Eventually, the Lisbon Treaty was negotiated and signed by all 27 member states.

But the day that it was ratified by the German Bundestag, a CSU Bundestag member, acting in cooperation with the Left Party, challenged the Treaty in the Constitutional Court. If the Court had overturned German ratification, the treaty would be dead. Instead, the Court's decision was mixed. On the one hand, it found that Lisbon was acceptable because the EU's member states would remain in control of the EU. In other words, the Court did not see a federal "United States of Europe" emerging from the treaty—and the Court warned such a federal state would violate the German Basic Law.

But the Court also declared that the Treaty necessitated passage of a new German law clarifying that any future delegation of power to the EU level would require the express approval of the *Bundestag* (not just the government of the day). Moreover, the Court stated that no further power could be delegated in some policy areas. It also underscored the right of the German states to protect their prerogatives from EU interference in the areas of environmental labor and EU budget law.

**Discussion Questions**

Does the European Union require Germany to be especially generous in order for the EU to function properly?

How durable is the German economic model in the face of new regional and global competitors?

# Is European Integration Stalled?

Behind this flurry of activity lies an important truth: While European integration in the post–World War Two period could usually rely on German support and even generosity, it no longer can take these things for granted. Germany has become far more ambivalent about European integration at the same time that the EU clearly needs further reform. German elites also were long free to make deals at the European level with almost no scrutiny from voters. This also is no longer true. In fact, only about half of Germans nowadays see the EU as good for their country (10 percent fewer than in 2009).[27]

Euro-skepticism extends to political parties. Even the CDU, the party intimately identified with Europe, has ceased to see further integration as positive. In the CDU, most also do not want less integration, but not all Germans feel this way. East Germans are far more skeptical about the EU than West Germans, and perceive little benefit from membership. There are also troubles in the German-French alliance that always formed the core of major integration projects. A principle reason is the sheer impossibility for two countries out of the enlarged 27-member EU to shape integration.

Since the 1950s, Germany has depended on European integration to solve many of its problems, from its inability to run an independent foreign policy to its need for foreign consumers to purchase its enormous export surpluses. To lubricate these deals, the Germans always made side payments to other states. But its capacity and its will to do this have both waned. Changes in mass and elite opinion have been mentioned, but Germany is also in debt, having gone from 20 percent of GDP to about 80 percent today (the EU limit is 60 percent, but several states are now in violation).

# Germany and the Economic Crisis: Virtuous or Short-Sighted?

This all adds up to a Europe that clearly needs change but that cannot count on Germany to lead that change. Part of the problem is a deep chasm between two very different views of Germany's role in Europe. One view, popular with German voters, sees Germany as an economically virtuous island in a sea of European overspending and fiscal indulgence. The other view is essentially the opposite: That Germany is short-sighted and harsh, forcing indebted countries such as Ireland to pay above-market interest rates for bailouts that go primarily to repay foreign banks, many of them, you guessed it, German. Traditionally pro-German Ireland saw anti-German sentiment rise sharply after 2010.

To unravel this confusing picture, we need to understand both facts and feelings. First, the facts. As noted, Germany's economic performance during the crisis has been impressive. Exports boomed after since 2010, while unemployment soon dropped to its lowest point in years. But by holding down wages and working hard at innovation, Germans have long exported more than they import, and German voters often fail to see the crucial fact that it is the rest of Europe that absorbs this surplus (many Americans express a similar frustration with China).

The paradox is that as Germany does well, its citizens have ever less patience for countries doing poorly. Here, feelings come into play. At one level, it is understandable why German voters are frustrated. Many weren't thrilled with giving up their DM in the first place. Most feel that European governments (including their own) manipulated economic data to appear to comply with the euro rules. Meanwhile,

German competitiveness has come on the basis of flat wages and some painful cuts in social programs. Many Germans thus feel they have already sacrificed while other countries borrowed their way into trouble. This means there is little sympathy for the Greeks and the Portuguese, for example.

Angry voters handed the SPD a terrible beating in 2009, and voters' subsequent furious reaction to talk of European bailouts then hammered the Christian Democrats. Chancellor Merkel took a very cautious approach during the euro crisis of 2010 and played her cards close to her vest. When Germany passed a balanced budget law for 2011, other Europeans were startled, for Germany did not consult other states in the monetary union. Voter anger thus limits the "stimulus" that can come from Europe's largest economy.

Given voter frustration, German politicians often wait until the size and scope of financial problems in Europe is so large that German voters can finally see it. When Germany waits, the size of the problem grows, as does the pain of the adjustment. When this pain is borne mainly by other Europeans, Germany is resented. And so it will be until Germany's behavior changes. Germany may need to allow wages to rise and to expand its imports from other European states. Meanwhile, its banks must accept that they made some bad bets and that not all of those bets can or should be covered by governments. What will not do is for Germans to complain that Germany is "being punished for making good products at a good price," as many Germans like to say. Rather, it is being resented for failing to see that its trade partners cannot sustain these levels of consumption without burying themselves with debt. A July 2011 EU rescue plan for Greece—backed with lots of German money—seemed to recognize this dilemma. Time will tell if the rescue survives the challenges of the Constitutional Court and the bond markets.

## Party Fragmentation and Scandal

Political scientists have long noted the declining responsiveness of European political parties. One provocative argument is that parties have essentially learned to get along without much input from voters. As participation has declined, "cartel parties" have figured out how to safely manage competition with one another, placate (if not please) voters, and draw upon the resources of the state to benefit their party organizations (and themselves).[28]

Certainly, the two main German parties do not offer strikingly different platforms. Meanwhile, newer parties like the Greens and the Left Party have used their connection to the state to vastly increase their organizational resources. And German voters are plainly alienated from their parties. Both major parties have been hemorrhaging members for years, and voter turnout has declined by nearly 10 percent over the past decade.

Several political scandals in recent years have deepened the impression that parties respect few limits when it comes to deploying their power to build their organizations. In particular, the CDU faced a devastating financing scandal in the late 1990s that engulfed several top party officials, including former chancellor Helmut Kohl. Meanwhile, the SPD distanced itself from a core constituency—labor unions—with the so-called Hartz reforms (named after Schröder confidant and Volkswagen CEO Peter Hartz). These SPD-led reforms cut unemployment payments, obliged unemployed workers to take jobs beneath their qualifications, and reduced other social insurance benefits. This was a bitter pill for many SPD supporters. The SPD's loss of voters to the Left Party in the 2009 election is one outcome of the Hartz reforms, although the reforms also arguably helped to reduce unemployment.

The smaller parties also have had their share of scandals. A visa scandal in 2005 badly damaged the reputation of Joschka Fischer, the Green foreign minister who had been Germany's most popular politician for several years (the ministry had loosened precautions that ensured visa travel from eastern European countries did not contribute to illegal immigration or human trafficking). FDP leader and foreign minister, Guido Westewelle, has been hammered in the German press for bringing businessmen in his own family on official foreign trips. In the CSU, the aristocratic and wildly popular defense minister, Karl-Theodor zu Guttenberg, resigned from the Merkel government after evidence emerged that he had plagiarized much of his doctoral dissertation (he will likely be back). Even the Left Party, perhaps the German party least inclined to cooperate with other parties, has been enormously focused on using federal subsidies to build the party organization.

## Political Challenges and Changing Agendas

The future of German politics depends on how the country addresses the four themes identified at the outset: the world of states, governing the economy, the democratic idea, and the politics of collective identity. Germany long enjoyed a spiral of success that enabled it to confront these issues with confidence and resolve during the post–World War Two period. For example, problems of collective identities were handled in a much less exclusionary way as women, nonnative ethnic groups, and newer political parties and movements began to contribute to a healthy diversity in German politics. Democratic institutions balanced participation and dissent, offsetting the country's turbulent and often racist past by almost fifty years of a stable multiparty democracy. Germany's economic success has been significant and unique. Germany has confidently, and with the support of its neighbors and allies, taken a leading role in European integration.

Beginning with the world of states, Germany is now firmly anchored in western Europe but also has been uniquely positioned to shape the transition of the former communist central and eastern European states toward economic and political modernization and EU membership. After the collapse of communism, there were fears that German investors would "reconquer" eastern Europe. For a time, these states resisted German investment. But Germany emerged as a forceful and effective advocate of both EU and NATO enlargement, and the postcommunist states also recognized that they desired both German investments and consumer goods. Today, Germany has generally positive relations with the countries of the region. At the same time, most German politicians stress that their state is a "normal" state. By this, they mean that they intend to shape German policy to pursue German interests—to assert that they are a state and not a charitable organization.

Germany's approach to governing the economy also faces challenges in the early twenty-first century. For many years, the German economy was characterized as "high everything," in that it combined high-quality manufacturing with high wages, high fringe benefits, high worker participation, and high levels of vacation time.[29] Critics insisted that such a system could not last in a competitive world economy. Nevertheless, the German economy has remained among the world's leaders. But the huge costs of unification, globalization, and the fiscal crisis in Europe all challenge the German model anew.[30]

Democracy appears well established after over sixty years of the Federal Republic. It features high (if declining) voter turnout and a healthy civic culture.[31] Many observers believe that broad-based participation is part of the fabric of German political life. Yet the changes to party politics and the much more complex business of forming effective coalitions noted above are big challenges, as is the assimilation of the five eastern states. Can eastern Germans who have lost jobs in the transition to capitalism accept that ethnic minorities are not the main cause of their plight? Can tolerance and understanding offset a right-wing fringe that preaches hatred and blames scapegoats for the costs of unification? There is reason for optimism. On balance, eastern Germans have shown that they understand and practice democracy amazingly well.

In the area of collective identities, Germany faces many unresolved challenges. Turkish and other non-German guest workers remain essential to Germany's economy. Their long-term acceptance by the CDU/CSU, not to mention the smaller ultra-right parties, will likely be the key to a fundamental change in the concept of who is a German. More than two generations after the end of World War Two, young Germans are asking what being German actually means. Changes in citizenship laws will complicate this issue, for although this search for identity can be healthy, and immigrants can help enrich and renew the meaning of German identity, these changes can enable extremist groups to preach exaggerated nationalism and hatred of foreigners and minorities. At the same time, religious divides seem manageable: 34 percent of Germans are Catholic and 34 percent Protestant, with about 28 percent unaffiliated or other. Only about 4 percent of the population is Muslim. More difficult was the early-1990s influx of refugees and asylum seekers, which placed great strains on German taxpayers and increased ethnic tensions.

# German Politics in Comparative Perspective

Germany offers important insights for comparative politics. First, it shows that a fascist past can be put to rest. Germany's impressive democratic experience during the first sixty years of the Federal Republic has clearly exorcised the ghosts of the Third Reich. Countries such as Japan, Italy, and Spain, among developed states, also bear watching on this point. Yet some critical questions remain open for now. To what extent do the educational system, civil service, and the media bear some responsibility for the rise of right-wing violence? Have the reforms in the educational system since the 1960s provided a spirit of critical discourse in the broad mainstream of society that can withstand far right rhetoric if it increases further? Can judges effectively sentence those who abuse the civil rights of ethnic minorities? Will the news media continue to express a wide range of opinion and contribute to a healthy civic discourse? Or will strident, tabloid-style journalism stifle the more reasoned debate that any democracy must have to survive and flourish?

Second, Germany's historical development illustrates how being late to achieve political unity and late to industrialize can have negative consequences. These two factors, combined with an unfavorable institutional mix, eventually helped produce a catastrophic first half of the twentieth century for Germany and much of the world. Yet the country's subsequent transition to a successful economy with a solid democracy can provide more positive lessons for other countries. Industrializing nations may benefit, especially if they also benefit from a supportive regional context as they attempt to achieve economic growth and develop stable democracies.

Third, Germany offers a distinctive model for combining state and market. Germany's social market economy blurs the distinction between the public and private sectors. The German state pursues development plans based on its cooperative interaction with a dense network of key social and economic participants, particularly in such areas as climate change or energy policy. This approach is neither as free market as in the United States nor as statist as in France or Japan. But it requires both a state with a light touch and also an organized and self-confident society.

Fourth, while immigration politics are emotional and deeply-rooted, Germany reminds us that countries can make fundamental changes here as well. For decades, German policy essentially said, in the words of a popular CDU slogan, "Germany is not an immigration country." But the Schröder government modified Germany's immigration policies to provide a path for long-time foreign workers to gain citizenship. Again, open questions persist. Can residual ethnic tensions be resolved in a way that enhances democracy?

Finally, Germany shows us that middle-ranked powers can wield lots of clout, especially if they can emerge as regional leaders with attractive policies. For example, Germany has played a more important role in debates over such issues as climate change, where its approach has broad support in the EU, than in areas like energy policy, where Germany tends to make its own deals with countries like Russia. Germany is facing intense pressures from within its borders, notably conflict among ethnic groups, and from a complex mix of external influences. Its role as both a major western and an eastern European power puts it in a unique position. What an ironic but inspiring twist if Germany, the country whose virulent nationalism caused the most widespread destruction and destabilization in the twentieth century, took the lead at the head of the supranational EU in promoting democracy, creativity, and stability in the twenty-first century.

## Key Terms

| | | |
|---|---|---|
| *Gastarbeiter* | *Zollverein* | constructive vote of no |
| federal state | framework regulations | confidence |
| *Junkers* | social market economy | civil servants |
| heavy industries | health insurance funds | mixed member system |
| liberal | democratic corporatism | absolute veto |
| chancellor | co-determination | suspensive veto |
| *Kulturkampf* | works councils | party democracy |
| Weimar Republic | Eurozone | *Ostpolitik* |
| procedural democracy | Basic Law | citizens action groups |
| Nazi | 5 percent clause | grass-roots democracy |

## Suggested Readings

Allen, Christopher, ed. *Transformation of the German Political Party System: Institutional Crisis or Democratic Renewal?* New York: Berghahn, 2001.

Deeg, Richard. *Finance Capital Unveiled: Banks and Economic Adjustment in Germany.* Ann Arbor: University of Michigan Press, 1998.

Eley, Geoff. *Reshaping the German Right: Radical Nationalism and Political Change after Bismarck.* New Haven: Yale University Press, 1980.

Esping-Anderson, Gøsta. *Three Worlds of Welfare Capitalism.* Princeton: Princeton University Press, 1990.

Herrigel, Gary. *Manufacturing Possibilities: Creative Action and Industrial Recomposition in the U.S., Germany, and Japan.* Oxford: Oxford University Press, 2010.

Hirschman, Albert. *Exit, Loyalty, and Voice: Responses to Decline in Firms, Organizations, and States.* Cambridge: Harvard University Press, 1970.

Jacoby, Wade. *Imitation and Politics: Redesigning Modern Germany.* Ithaca, NY: Cornell University Press, 2001.

Katzenstein, Peter, *Tamed Power: Germany in Europe.* Ithaca, NY: Cornell University Press, 1997.

___. *Policy and Politics in West Germany: The Growth of a Semi-Sovereign State*. Philadelphia: Temple University Press, 1987.

Markovits, Andrei, and Simon Reich. *The German Predicament: Memory and Power in the New Europe*. Ithaca: Cornell University Press, 1997.

Piore, Michael, and Charles Sabel. *The Second Industrial Divide*. New York: Basic Books, 1984.

Rein, Taagepera, and Matthew Shugart. *Seats and Votes: The Effects and Determinants of Electoral Systems*. New Haven: Yale University Press, 1989.

Röpke, Wilhelm. "The Guiding Principle of the Liberal Programme." In H. F. Wünche, ed., *Standard Texts on the Social Market Economy*. New York: Gustav Fischer Verlag, 1982.

Schmitter, Philippe, and Gerhard Lembruch, eds. *Trends Toward Corporatist Intermediation*. Beverly Hills: Sage, 1979.

Shirer, William. *The Rise and Fall of the Third Reich*. New York: Simon & Schuster, 1960.

Steinmo, Sven, Kathleen Thelen, and Frank Longstreth, eds. *Structuring Politics: Historical Institutionalism in Historical Perspective*. New York: Cambridge University Press, 1992.

Streeck, Wolfgang. *Re-Forming Capitalism: Institutional Change in the German Political Economy*. Oxford: Oxford University Press, 2009.

## Suggested Websites

American Institute for Contemporary German Studies
**www.aicgs.org/**

*Der Spiegel* (in English)
**http://www.spiegel.de/international/**

*Deutsche Welle* (in English)
**http://www.germnews.de/dn/**

German Embassy, German Information Center
**http://www.germany.info/gic/**

German Politics
**http://www.tandf.co.uk/journals/fgrp**

German Politics and Society
**http://www.berghahnbooks.com/journals/gps/**

German Studies Web
**http://wess.lib.byu.edu/index.php/German_Studies_Web**

German World Magazine
**http://www.germanworldonline.com/**

Max Planck Institute for the Study of Societies, Cologne
**http://www.mpi-fg-koeln.mpg.de/index_en.asp**

WZB, Social Science Research Center, Berlin
**www.wz-berlin.de/default.en.asp**

# 5  Japan

Shigeko N. Fukai and Haruhiro Fukui

**Official Name:** Japan

**Location:** Eastern Asia

**Capital City:** Tokyo

**Population (2008):** 126.8 million

**Size:** 377,930 sq.km.; slightly smaller than California

**1867**
Meiji Restoration inaugurates rapid Japanese industrialization and modernization.

**1912–1926**
Taisho Democracy period.

**1925**
Universal Manhood Suffrage Law promulgated. Japan Trade Union Council formed.

**1932**
Military officers attempt but fail to take over government.

**1945**
Atomic bombs dropped on Hiroshima and Nagasaki. Soviet Union declares war on Japan. Japan surrenders. Allied occupation and reform of Japan begin.

**1947**
New Constitution of Japan, promulgated in 1946, comes into effect featuring a democratic government and a peace clause (Article 9) renouncing the right to make war.

**1976**
Lockheed scandal and arrest of former Prime Minister Tanaka Kakuei.

| 1860 | 1900 | 1920 | 1940 | 1950 | 1960 | 1980 |

**1889**
Constitution of the Great Empire of Japan establishes a bicameral legislature, the Imperial Diet.

**1900–1901**
Constitutional Party of Political Friends (Seiyukai) formed.

**1937**
Japan invades China.

**1941**
Japan attacks U.S. naval base in Pearl Harbor. United States declares war on Japan.

**1951**
Japanese Peace Treaty and United States–Japan Mutual Security Treaty signed in San Francisco.

**1955**
Socialist parties unite to form Japan Socialist Party (JSP); conservative parties merge into Liberal Democratic Party (LDP).

**1931–1932**
Japanese army takes control of Chinese Manchuria without orders from the government in Tokyo.

# SECTION 1

# THE MAKING OF THE MODERN JAPANESE STATE

## Focus Questions

How have Japan's physical, especially resource, endowments influenced its economic development and foreign policy strategies since the mid-nineteenth century?

Which watershed events in Japanese history are particularly relevant to understanding government and politics in contemporary Japan?

In what respects is the Japanese modernization and development experience similar to or different from a Western nation's, such as Germany, Britain, or the United States?

## Politics in Action

Fifteen minutes before noon on March 9, 2011, Japan's northeastern coastal region, known as Sanriku, 250–450 kilometers northeast of Tokyo, was shaken by a magnitude 7.3 offshore earthquake and washed, at several locations, by about one-meter high tsunamis. This was a major earthquake, but caused neither significant physical damage nor serious alarm in the affected coastal communities. The following day, a local seismologist was quoted in the press as saying that this quake might be followed by some magnitude 6-level aftershocks, but not by one bigger than 7.3. But around 2:45 P.M. just two days later, on March 11, an earthquake of catastrophic magnitude 9.0 struck the same region.

The biggest ever to hit Japan in its recorded history and among the biggest half dozen in world history, the temblor, with its epicenter some twenty-five kilometers deep under the seabed about 130 kilometers east of the city of Sendai, violently shook the ground in the coastal region for as long as three minutes and for more than two minutes even as far away as Tokyo. The earthquake was followed by a two-meter high tsunami wave barely ten minutes later, at virtually the same time as the first tsunami warning was sounded in most coastal communities in the region. This was followed by other, and much bigger, waves, which surged westward toward the Sanriku coast, traveling initially at more than 200 kilometers per hour, then losing the speed but gaining in height as they approached the shoreline. Rising to a

## Timeline

**1985**
Telecommunications and tobacco industries privatized. Equal Employment Law enacted.

**1993**
LDP loses in House of Representatives general election; first non-LDP government since 1955 formed by coalition centered on the JNP.

**1994**
New House of Representatives election law passed. LDP returns to power in coalition with the JSP.

**1998**
LDP cabinets implement a series of measures to resuscitate stagnant economy, but to no significant effect. Japan's economy remains depressed into the first decade of the twenty-first century.

**2001**
National government ministries and agencies reorganized. Self-Defense Force ships dispatched to Indian Ocean to assist U.S. Navy in its antiterrorism operations.

**2009**
DPJ wins in House of Representatives election and forms government.

**2011**
A magnitude 9.0 earthquake strikes northeastern Japan, triggering huge tsunamis, laying waste to a wide swath of residential and farm land on the coast, crippling a nuclear plant.

**1985  1990  1995  2000  2005  2011**

**1992**
Japan New Party (JNP) founded by LDP dissidents.

**1990**
Prince Akihito ascends throne as Heisei emperor.

**1989**
Showa emperor, Hirohito, dies. LDP loses in House of Councilors election.

**1997**
Asian financial crisis shakes Japanese stock market and economy.

**1996**
LDP forms first single-party cabinet since 1993.

**2007**
LDP led by Abe Shinzo loses to opposition Democratic Party of Japan (DPJ) in House of Councilors election.

**2005**
LDP led by Koizumi Junichiro wins landslide victory in House of Representatives election.

**2004**
SDF troops sent to Iraq to assist U.S. postwar mission.

---

maximum height of twenty-four meters as they hit the rugged saw-tooth shoreline, the waves either smashed through or went over all breakwaters and seawalls, some ten-meter tall and twenty-meter thick reinforced concrete structures, to inundate 450 square kilometers of residential and farm land, as far as five kilometers inland in some areas.

As the walls of water roared through the coastal towns and villages, they uprooted, tossed around, and splintered everything in their paths—ships, docks, homes, stores, schools, hospitals, cars, roads, bridges, and people. They left the region's hub airport under a thick cover of sandy sludge littered with upended, broken, and partially buried small aircraft. The waves also washed away or destroyed most of the tsunami detection and relay stations along the coast, making it impossible either to count the number and timing of the waves that reached the coast or to make precise measurements of their velocity, strengths, and heights. This caused great confusion in the initial estimates of the scale of the disaster until the scenario was reconstructed several days later by simulations and aerial photographs.

REUTERS/Ho New

Prime Minister Kan Naoto at the port of Rikuzentakata City, Iwate Prefecture, three weeks after it was devastated by the March 11, 2011, disaster.

### Japan: Ethnic Groups

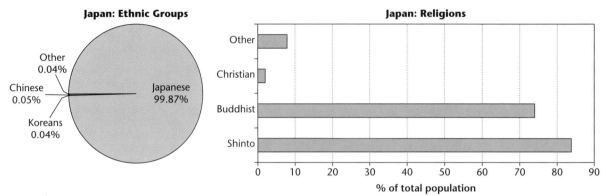

Other
0.04%

Chinese
0.05%

Koreans
0.04%

Japanese
99.87%

### Japan: Religions

Other

Christian

Buddhist

Shinto

0  10  20  30  40  50  60  70  80  90

**% of total population**

*Note*: Many people practice both Shintoism and Buddhism.

**Japanese Currency**
Yen (¥)
International Designation: JPY
Exchange Rate (2010): US$1 = 87.78 JPY
10,000 Yen Note Design: FukuzawaYukichi
(1834–1901), political theorist and founder
of Keio University.

© jpskenn/Shutterstock.com

FIGURE 5.1 **The Japanese Nation at a Glance**

The combination of the monster earthquake and tsunamis destroyed about 20,000 homes, claimed an estimated 21,000 lives, and left nearly 300,000 people homeless. This spelled the worst catastrophe Japan had suffered since World War II, and it was vastly aggravated and complicated by the damage done to a nuclear plant built just above the shoreline, which was owned and operated by Japan's largest electricity utility, Tokyo Electric Power Company (TEPCO). When the earthquake struck, three of its six reactors at the plant, known as Fukushima Daiichi (Fukushima Number One) were in operation, while the other three had been shut down, but housed spent fuel rods in their cooling pools. The earthquake and tsunami knocked out the plant's power-operated cooling system, triggering fires and gas explosions at all three reactors in operation and at one of the three that had been shut down, followed by radiation leaks at one or more of them. The subsequent efforts to repair the cooling system and stop the radiation leaks were hampered and delayed by the potential recurrence of explosions and the extremely high levels of radioactivity inside and around the plant.

Some 200,000 residents of the area within a twenty kilometer radius of the crippled plant and a ten kilometer radius of the only slightly damaged Fukushima Daini (Number Two) plant about ten kilometers away were ordered to evacuate. The radioactive materials leaked by the damaged reactors contaminated not only their immediate environs, including nearby farms and their produce and seawater in the area adjacent to the plant, but even tap water at locations as far away as Tokyo. The region's fishing industry, which accounted for about one-third of Japan's fisheries output, was wiped out. The total economic cost of the triple disaster was estimated to amount to more than $200 billion, while the human, social, and political costs were,

**Japan**

© Cengage Learning

| Table 5.1 | Political Organization |
|---|---|
| **Political System** | Parliamentary democracy and constitutional monarchy, in which the emperor is merely a symbol of national unity. |
| **Regime History** | Current constitution promulgated in 1946 and in effect since 1947. |
| **Administrative Structure** | Unitary state, 47 units of intermediate-level subnational government "prefectures," and 1,790 lower-level units designated as city, town, or village. |
| **Executive** | Prime minister selected by legislature; a cabinet of about twenty ministers appointed by prime minister. |
| **Legislature** | Bicameral. The upper house (House of Councilors) has 242 members elected for six-year terms. Half of the members are elected every three years. One hundred forty-six are elected from multiple-seat prefecture-wide districts; 96 are elected nationally by a party list proportional representation method. The lower house (House of Representatives) has 480 members elected for four-year terms, which may be shortened by the dissolution of the house. Three hundred lower house members are elected from single-seat constituencies; 180 are elected by party list proportional representation from eleven regional electoral districts. |
| **Judiciary** | Supreme Court has fifteen judges appointed by the cabinet, except the chief judge who is nominated by the cabinet and appointed by the emperor; all are eligible to serve until seventy years of age, subject to popular review. |
| **Party System** | One-party dominant (Liberal Democratic Party) from mid-1950s to mid-1990s, evolving into a quasi-two-party system since. Major parties: Liberal Democratic Party, Democratic Party of Japan, Clean Government Party, Social Democratic Party, Japan Communist Party. |

and likely would forever remain, incalculable. The physical and spiritual reconstruction of the devastated communities, and the nation as a whole, was bound to take many years or even decades.

## Geographic Setting

The nation of Japan consists of some 6,850 islands lying off the northeastern coast of Asia. With a territory of about 377,915 square kilometers (146,000 square miles), Japan is slightly smaller than California, slightly larger than Germany, and one twenty-fifth the size of China. All but four of its islands—Honshu, Hokkaido, Kyushu, and Shikoku—are less than 500 square kilometers in size.

Japan is the tenth most populous country in today's world, with about 127 million people. With about 336 people per square kilometer, it has about ten times the population density of the United States. Over 85 percent of the total population lives in about 450 cities with 50,000 or more people per square kilometer.

Japan is poorly endowed with natural resources, except for normally plentiful rainfall that feeds the paddy fields and ensures an adequate supply of the nation's dietary staple, rice. Moreover, only about 13 percent of land in Japan is arable, compared to about 20 percent in the United States, 25 percent in Britain, and well over

30 percent in Germany and France. Because it needs to import natural resources and foodstuffs, modern Japan has been a natural trading state.

Japan's closest neighbors are Korea and China. Ancient and medieval Japan imported not only large amounts of material goods from these neighbors, but also wide-ranging forms of culture, such as religion, literature, law, architecture, and fine arts. The name of the country comes from Chinese characters that mean, "sun's origin," which is why Japan is often referred to as the "Land of the Rising Sun."

Medieval Japan also developed trading and diplomatic relationships with peoples who lived in Southeast Asia. Starting in the mid-nineteenth century, Japan developed extensive contacts—and sometimes violent conflicts—with Russia and the United States.

# Critical Junctures

## Ancient and Medieval Japan

Archeological evidence shows that hunters and gatherers inhabited the Japanese archipelago as early as 30,000 BCE. By about 7,000 BCE, some inhabitants began to build and live in small settlements and raise livestock. By the middle of the third century CE, several tribal states had emerged in the southwestern regions of the country. A century or so later, they came under the control of a legendary "heavenly sovereign" or "emperor," who was said to be descended from a prehistoric deity, the Sun Goddess.

These early rulers frequently sent representatives to Korea and China who returned with products of more advanced civilizations. These included the teachings of the Chinese philosopher, Confucius (551–479 BCE), with emphasis on reverence for one's ancestors and deference to authority, ideas that have had an enduring effect on Japanese society. Buddhism from India reached Japan via China and Korea in the middle of the sixth century CE. Combined with the native religion, Shinto, Confucianism and Buddhism continue to shape everyday life.

The offspring of the first emperor founded the world's longest reigning—and still surviving—monarchy. They or their regents ruled the young Japanese state until the late twelfth century, when power began to shift to a rising class of warlords, a few of whom assumed the title of **shogun** (general) as if they were the emperor's military guardian.[1] In the early seventeenth century, one of these warlords named Tokugawa Ieyasu* established a military government, or shogunate, in the new capital city of Edo, today's Tokyo, which lasted for the next 265 years. A figurehead emperor resided in the old imperial capital city, Kyoto.

During its iron-fisted rule, the Tokugawa shogunate closed Japan nearly completely from the outside world. The state was divided into a vast complex of estates under the shogun's authority, which included all major cities and mining towns, and 270 or so mostly rural domains governed by local subordinate lords. The latter were required to visit Edo every few years to pay homage to the shogun and to contribute funds and labor to a variety of public works undertaken by the central government. These requirements kept the local lords poor and weak enough to prevent them from being a threat to the Tokugawa rulers.

The Tokugawa shogunate divided the Japanese people into six classes—warriors, farmers, artisans, merchants, "filthy hordes," and "nonhumans." Warriors, called **bushi** or samurai in Japanese, about 8 percent of the population, were the ruling class. The last two classes were "outcastes." Members of the several classes were strictly segregated both

**shogun**

The title, meaning general, assumed by a succession of hereditary leaders of the three military dynasties—the Minamotos, the Ashikagas, and the Tokugawas—that ruled Japan one after another from the late twelfth century to the mid-nineteenth century. Their government was called the shogunate.

**bushi (samurai)**

The warrior class in medieval Japan, also known as samurai. The class emerged around the tenth century CE, and a dominant band established Japan's first warrior government in the twelfth century. The last warrior government was overthrown in the Meiji Restoration of the mid-nineteenth century.

---

* In Japanese, *family* names come before the *given* (or personal) name.

occupationally and residentially. Women were treated as inherently inferior and subordinate to men and could not participate in public affairs. Most children from samurai families—and increasingly those of well-to-do farmers and merchants—received elementary school education. In addition to reading, writing, and simple arithmetic, these children learned Confucian teaching about the correct social order and proper personal behavior.[2]

## Japan in the Meiji-Taisho Era (1868–1925)

In 1868 a revolution toppled the Tokugawa regime. This revolution was a reaction to the forcible entry in 1853 and 1854 of a small flotilla of American warships under the command of Commodore Matthew C. Perry into a bay some 160 kilometers (100 miles) southwest of Edo. These ships had defied the centuries-old official policy that banned unauthorized foreigners from entering Japanese territory. The shogun capitulated to Commodore Perry's demand that Japan open its ports to American naval and merchant ships. This gave anti-Tokugawa local lords and their followers an excuse to revolt against the shogunate.

The revolution established a new government in 1868. They installed a young heir to the imperial throne as the nation's new sovereign. The young emperor's reign title was Meiji ("enlightened rule"), and the revolution came to be known as the Meiji Restoration. Over the next fifty years, Japan's government was led by a small group of leaders of the anti-Tokugawa revolution, who quickly transformed a feudal state into a major industrial and military power.

The Meiji government replaced the six-class system with a three-class system. The samurai class was retained, but farmers, artisans, and merchants were lumped into a single "commoner" class, and those in the two outcaste categories became a "new commoner" class. A national public education system, composed of primary, secondary, and post-secondary institutions, was introduced. Education opened new avenues for members of all classes to change and improve their life opportunities.

The introduction of the democratic idea to Japan in the late nineteenth century gave rise to a "freedom and people's rights" movement, led by the Liberal and the Reform parties. The Meiji oligarchy responded in 1889 by issuing a constitution modeled after that of Prussia (which later became part of Germany), and setting up a two-house legislature, the Imperial Diet. The upper house, the House of Peers, consisted exclusively of hereditary and appointed members, such as male adult members of the imperial family, former feudal lords, who had been given the title of a peer (noble) after the Meiji Restoration, and men credited with distinguished service to the state. The lower house, the House of Representatives, was elected by an all-male electorate of top-bracket taxpayers, who at first accounted for a little over 1 percent of Japan's total population, rising to about 5.5 percent by the early 1920s.

The 1889 "Constitution of the Great Empire of Japan" guaranteed civil rights and freedoms to the people "subject to the limitations imposed by law" and required every law to be enacted with the consent of the Imperial Diet. But, in theory and to a large extent in practice as well, the emperor retained the right to approve and issue all laws; open, close, and adjourn the Diet; and declare war, make peace, and conclude international treaties. In fact, the oligarchy of the emperor's senior advisors continued to rule the state by controlling powerful non-elective institutions of government, such as the Privy Council, the House of Peers, and the civil and military services.

During the reign of the Meiji emperor's successor, the Taisho ("great righteousness") Emperor, Japan made significant progress toward political liberalization, in a period known as **Taisho Democracy** (roughly 1912–1926). The two main political parties were renamed Seiyukai (Constitutional Party of Political Friends) and Kenseito (Constitutional Government Party) and alternately formed a government through

**Taisho democracy**

A reference to Japanese politics in the period roughly coinciding with Emperor Taisho's reign, 1912–1926. The period was characterized by the rise of a popular movement for democratization of government by the introduction of universal manhood suffrage and the reduction of the power and influence of authoritarian institutions of the state.

electoral competition. This led to a series of government turnovers that reflected progress towards democratization.[3]

In 1925 the House of Representatives enacted the Universal Manhood Suffrage Law. This law removed the tax payment requirement for the vote, quadrupling overnight the size of the electorate to about 20 percent of the total population, although women still could not vote.

Despite important political changes, Taisho Democracy was fundamentally superficial and fragile. Class inequalities still divided and destabilized Japanese society. Rural Japan was dominated by a small class of wealthy landlords and urban Japan by a few giant industrial and financial conglomerates, known as **zaibatsu**. The government bureaucracy was controlled by graduates of a single government-run university. As the Japanese economy became mired in a long recession after World War I and was then devastated by the Great Depression in the early 1930s, advocates of democracy at home and peace abroad increasingly faced savage attacks by the military and ultra-nationalist civilian groups.

Buoyed by Japanese victories in the Sino-Japanese War (1894–1895) and the Russo-Japanese War (1904–1905), the military's political power and influence grew steadily throughout the Meiji-Taisho eras. Under the new Showa ("enlightened peace") Emperor's reign, which began in 1926, the military became increasingly free from civilian control and started to pursue its own defense and foreign policy goals. This eventually led to the Japanese invasion and occupation of northern Chinese provinces and the creation of a puppet state called Manchukuo in 1932.[4]

In that same year, a band of young naval officers attacked several government offices in Tokyo and shot to death the prime minister in an abortive coup d'état. In a similar attempt in February 1936, army troops led by radical officers invaded a number of government offices, murdered the finance minister and several others, and occupied a whole block in central Tokyo for four days.[5] These events intimidated and silenced opponents of the military inside and outside the government. All political parties were also effectively muzzled, then disbanded by government order in 1941.

When the League of Nations condemned the Japanese invasion of China in 1933, Japan walked out of the organization. Faced with growing international criticism and ostracism, Japan entered a supposedly defensive military alliance with Nazi Germany in 1936. Fascist Italy joined the following year. In the summer of 1937, the Japanese army began a full-scale invasion of China. During the following winter, Japanese troops unleashed a murderous rampage against civilians in the capital city of China, an incident now known as the "Rape of Nanking." In an effort to contain Japanese military aggression, the United States nullified its trade agreement with Japan in 1939. This cut off Japan from a major source of raw materials. The government in Tokyo decided to seek an alternative source of supplies in Southeast Asia. In July 1941, Japan moved troops into French Indochina (now Vietnam, Laos, and Cambodia). In response, Washington froze Japanese-owned assets in the United States and banned the sale of oil to Japan.

Faced with the prospect of exhausting its limited fuel supplies, the Japanese government, now led by General Tojo Hideki, decided to start a war against the United States. On December 7, 1941, Japanese naval air units executed a carefully planned surprise attack on the U.S. naval base at Pearl Harbor in Hawaii. The United States immediately declared war on Japan.

Japan had some notable military successes early in the war, but it soon began to lose one major battle after another. By late 1944, its effort was reduced to a desperate defense of its homeland from increasingly frequent and devastating air raids by American bombers. In early August 1945, Japan's resistance ended when the first atomic bombs used in war annihilated two major cities, Hiroshima and Nagasaki. On August 15, Japan surrendered unconditionally to the Allied Powers.

**zaibatsu**

Giant holding companies in pre–World War II Japan, each owned by and under the control of members of a particular family. The largest were divided into a number of independent firms under the democratization program during the postwar occupation but were later revived as *keiretsu*, although no longer under the control of any of the original founding families.

AP Photo/Stanley Troutman

Hiroshima in the wake of the atomic bombing in August 1945.

*Source*: The Big Picture—Boston.com, " #28 (AP photo), at http://www.boston.com/
bigpicture/2009/08/hiroshima_64_years_ago.html.

## The Allied Occupation (1945–1952)

The Allied Occupation of Japan transformed an authoritarian militarist state into a
pacifist democracy.[6] The occupation, which lasted from 1945 to 1952, was formally
a joint operation by the major Allies: the United States, the British Commonwealth,
the Soviet Union, and China. In practice, the United States, represented by General
Douglas MacArthur, who held the position of **Supreme Commander for the Allied
Powers (SCAP)**, played the dominant role.

    During the first year and a half of the occupation, SCAP pursued two major goals:
the complete demilitarization and democratization of Japan. The Japanese armed forces
were swiftly dismantled, troops were demobilized, military production was halted, and
wartime leaders were either arrested or purged from their positions in the government.
Seven of them, including General Tojo, were executed for war crimes. Militaristic and
antidemocratic institutions and practices were banned. At the same time, workers'
right to organize was recognized, women were given the vote, and major *zaibatsu*
were dissolved. Only the government bureaucracy was left largely intact.

    The most important step taken toward the democratization and demilitarization of
Japan during the Occupation was the replacement of the Meiji Constitution by a democratic constitution. Based on a draft prepared by a handful of American lawyers, the new
constitution gave the emperor a purely symbolic role, while naming the people as the sovereign of the state. It also made the bicameral Diet the state's sole law-making body. All
its members, including those in the reorganized and renamed upper house, the House
of Councilors, were directly elected by the people. Article 9, known as a "peace clause,"
declared the reborn Japan a permanently disarmed pacifist nation. The article reads:

> Aspiring sincerely to an international peace based on justice and order, the Japanese
> people forever renounce war as a sovereign right of the nation and the threat or use
> of force as means of settling international disputes.

**Supreme Commander
for the Allied Powers
(SCAP)**

The official title of
General Douglas
MacArthur between 1945
and 1951 when he led
the Allied Occupation of
Japan.

In order to accomplish the aim of the preceding paragraph, land, sea, and air forces, as well as other war potential, will never be maintained. The right of belligerency of the state will not be recognized.

Despite this unique constitutional ban, the **Self-Defense Forces (SDF)** were created in the early 1950s, which have since grown into one of the largest and best-equipped military forces in the world. But their status and operations are rigidly defined and limited under the pacifist constitution.

## Contemporary Japan (1952 to the Present)

Competitive party politics revived after the war. The prewar Seiyukai party reemerged as the Japan Liberal Party, which dominated Japanese politics for much of the occupation period. The Liberals' major rival, the Japan Socialist Party (JSP), won a slim plurality in the Diet elections in 1947 and formed a coalition government with the Japan Progressive Party (later renamed the Democratic Party), which was descended from the prewar Kenseito party. But the Liberals returned to power a year and a half later in the second government turnover in postwar Japan, and thereafter steadily consolidated their hold on the Diet. The Liberal and the Democratic parties merged into the Liberal Democratic Party (LDP) in 1955, which would effectively monopolize control of government until the early 1990s.

A major political crisis occurred in 1960 over the revision of the U.S.-Japan Mutual Security Treaty that had been signed at the end of the occupation in 1951 and that allowed the United States to station troops in Japan. The LDP government's decision to revise, but maintain, the treaty provoked fierce opposition both in the Diet and in the streets of Tokyo and other major cities. Hundreds of thousands of protesters, led by JSP and Japan Communist Party (JCP) Diet members, marched against the treaty and Prime Minister Kishi Nobusuke's government. The protesters warned that the treaty would make Japan a semipermanent military dependency of the United States and an enemy of Japan's closer neighbors, China and the Soviet Union. Even so, the government pushed the revised treaty through the Diet, where the LDP had a strong majority.

The government's action provoked such a violent public reaction with an anti-American tinge that President Eisenhower's scheduled state visit to Japan was canceled and Prime Minister Kishi and his cabinet resigned.

The 1960 political crisis led Kishi's successors to avoid addressing controversial constitutional and security policy issues and concentrate on economic problems. This change in the LDP's strategy ushered in a period of political stability and phenomenal economic growth. The country was jolted, however, by the oil shocks of 1973 and 1979. Afterward, the Japanese economy never regained the vigor of the preceding two decades.

The LDP maintained its majority in the Diet through the end of the 1980s. The socialist parties, in contrast, suffered a steady decline in electoral performance, due mostly to the diminishing influence of left-wing labor unions in an increasingly middle-class society.

**Self-Defense Forces (SDF)**

Inaugurated in Japan as a police reserve force with 75,000 recruits in August 1950, following the outbreak of the Korean War. Known as SDF since 1954, it today consists of approximately 250,000 troops equipped with sophisticated modern weapons and weapons systems.

Demonstrators against renewal of U.S.-Japan Mutual Security Treaty in front of Diet Building in Tokyo, May 1960.

*Source:* AP Images.

## Asian Development Bank (ADB)

A regional bank established in 1966 to promote economic development in and cooperation among nations in Asia. The bank mediates public and private investments in, and loans for, selected developmental projects. The current members include forty-eight nations and areas within the Asian and Pacific region and nineteen outside the region, including the United States.

## Asia-Pacific Economic Cooperation (APEC)

A regional organization of Asian and Pacific Rim nations established in 1989 to promote cooperation among member states, especially in foreign investment and the standardization and compilation of statistical data. Currently composed of twenty-one members (including the United States and Canada), it advocates "open regionalism," cooperation among nations within the region that neither precludes nor impedes cooperation between them and nations outside the region.

## Association of Southeast Asian Nations (ASEAN)

An organization formed in 1967 to promote regional economic and political cooperation. As of 2010, ASEAN consisted of ten member states: Brunei, Cambodia, Indonesia, Laos, Malaysia, Myanmar, the Philippines, Singapore, Thailand, and Vietnam.

A number of scandals hurt the LDP in election, but never threatened its control of government until Japan fell into a long economic downturn in the 1990s. As noted earlier, the LDP's stable one-party rule has now ended, and Japanese politics has come to be characterized by extremely high electoral volatility, frequent government turnovers, and a widespread sense of political, as well as economic, instability and uncertainty.

# Themes and Implications

## Historical Junctures and Political Themes

Japan joined the modern world of states in the late nineteenth century after two and a half centuries of self-imposed isolation. To its leaders and people, the world then appeared divided between powerful, self-aggrandizing states and powerless and often conquered states. To survive in such a world, a state must make itself powerful both economically and militarily, as Meiji Japan quickly did. World War II, particularly the horror of the atomic bombings, however, led most Japanese to abandon faith in military force. The only choice left for postwar Japan was cooperation with other nations. Japan has thus become an internationalist state committed to an active role in global and regional organizations.

Japan did not join the UN until 1956, mainly because the Soviet Union at first opposed admitting a major U.S. ally, but it is now the second-largest contributor to the UN budget. It is the second-largest financial contributor, after the United States, to the International Monetary Fund (IMF) and the World Bank, and has a de facto permanent seat on the boards of the IMF and the World Bank. Japan has been very active and visible in Asian and Pacific economic organizations. It is not only the largest contributor to the **Asian Development Bank (ADB)**, but has also provided all its past governors. It is a founding member and a major promoter of the **Asia-Pacific Economic Cooperation (APEC)** forum and actively supports the **Association of Southeast Asian Nations (ASEAN)**.

In the wake of the September 11, 2001, terrorist attacks on the United States, Japanese public opinion overwhelmingly favored participating in the war on terrorism. When the war turned out to be a military campaign against the Taliban in Afghanistan, however, the Japanese public reaction turned more cautious and when the war came to include the invasion of Iraq in the spring of 2003, Japanese public opinion became overwhelmingly negative. Nonetheless, the Japanese government has supported American-led military actions in Afghanistan and Iraq with the dispatch of Self-Defense Force troops, arms, and equipment to noncombat duties in conflict areas.

Japan's entry into the modern world also exposed its citizens to the democratic idea. By the 1890s, Meiji Japan had formally become a constitutional monarchy with a partially elected parliament and vocal political parties. Pre–World War II Japan was far more committed to rapid industrialization and military buildup than to democratization, but its experiment with democratic politics prepared the nation for the far more complete democratization that was introduced after the war. The democratic idea has become an integral element of Japanese political culture today.

Meiji Japan developed an industrial economy in a country that had neither the natural resources nor the technologies believed to be essential to successful modernization. Meiji-era development therefore involved extensive and systematic intervention by the state in governing the economy, an approach later known as **industrial policy.** This model of economic growth was spectacularly successful in both prewar and postwar Japan and was copied by many other nations, especially those in East Asia. Industrial policy, however, ceased to work in the late twentieth century. Since the early 1990s, the Japanese economy has been mired in a recession that seems to defy any remedy based on industrial policy.

The Japanese developed a strong sense of national identity early in their history. Following the failed attempt by Mongolian forces to invade the country in the late thirteenth century, a nationalist ideology was deliberately constructed and propagated with the aid of a divine-land myth. The nationalist ideology was subsequently systematically cultivated by leaders of Meiji and early Showa Japan and successfully harnessed to their aggressive foreign and military policies, which eventually led to the Pacific War (1941–1945).

## Implications for Comparative Politics

Japan's geography, history, and culture make it particularly interesting to compare its politics with those of other Asian nations, especially those in the Confucian cultural zone of Northeast Asia: China, including Taiwan, and North and South Korea. Japan also shares the rice paddy culture with these countries as well as those in Southeast Asia, with which it also has close historical ties. Rice paddy culture encouraged, on the one hand, early development of sophisticated water management, irrigation, and hydraulic engineering technologies necessary for the successful cultivation of rice and, on the other hand, a certain humility and deference to the forces and whims of nature. Many elements of this culture still influence religion, festivals, art, and a variety of government practices and politics throughout the region.

The evident ethnic and cultural similarities and affinities between Japan and other East Asian nations raise questions about the many important differences between them. Why, for example, did Japan begin to modernize its political system and social institutions and industrialize its economy so much earlier than its Asian neighbors? Why has postwar Japan had a stable democratic system, while most Asian nations have experienced authoritarian government, unstable multiparty politics, or extensive political violence?

Japan's geography, history, and culture are certainly markedly different from those of Western nations. Yet there are many fruitful comparisons to be made between Japan and the West. Why, for example, did Japan develop national identity and unite the nation earlier than most Western nations? How has Japan adopted institutions, ideas, and values from the West in the modernization of its economy and the democratization of its politics, while still maintaining many core aspects of its unique culture and national identity?

Comparisons between modern Japan and modern Germany are particularly interesting. These nations entered the modern world at about the same time in the nineteenth century, pursued rapid economic development, became major military powers by the early twentieth century, started and lost World War II, were occupied and transformed by their wartime enemies, and reemerged in the postwar world as two of the world's most economically powerful and politically stable democracies.[7] What explains such remarkable similarities between these two very different countries? What are the political lessons of the Japanese and German transition from autocracy to democracy?

## Summary

Over the nearly two millennia of its recorded history, the Japanese state has experienced several dramatic changes, both internally and in its relationship with the outside world. It originated in the third century CE as a primitive state under powerful political, economic, and cultural influence of its closest neighbors, China and Korea. By the eighth century, however, it had developed into a unified and distinctive state with its own ruling dynasty of emperors and, after the twelfth century, those of a

**industrial policy**

A generic term to refer to a variety of policies designed to shape leading sectors of the economy and enhance competitiveness, especially for industries that are considered strategic to national interests. Countries differ substantially regarding the degree to which their states consciously pursue industrial policies.

succession of warlord families, until one of whom, the Tokugawas, turned it into a tightly centralized and internationally closed feudal state at the beginning of the seventeenth century. This regime was toppled, and Japan was opened again to the world by the United States navy in the mid-nineteenth century. The new Japan under the "restored" rule of the imperial family grew rapidly into a major economic and military power in the late nineteenth century and early twentieth century, fought and won wars with China and Russia, then fought and lost the Pacific theater of World War II, was occupied and reformed by the United States and its allies, then re-emerged as a miraculously successful nonmilitary economic power in the postwar world. The Japanese miracle ended in the last decade of the twentieth century and it has since been mired in an endless recession and growing political instability.

# SECTION 2    POLITICAL ECONOMY AND DEVELOPMENT

## Focus Questions

In what ways is the historical pattern of the evolution of the modern Japanese political economy unique?

Why and in what ways has it served as a model for other developing nations, particularly for those in East Asia?

Why did the Japanese "economic miracle" plunge into an ongoing deep recession?

What structural and/ or behavioral features of the private sector of the Japanese economy have set it apart from its counterparts in most Western nations, and how have those features changed due to Japan's integration into the global political economy?

## State and Economy

The growth of the Japanese economy in the late 1950s through the early 1970s was an economic miracle. This performance, however, did not begin after World War II. Japan's economy had been growing steadily by an average of about 3 percent per year from the Meiji Restoration in 1868 through the early twentieth century. In the 1930s the pace had accelerated to more than 5 percent per year.[8]

The worldwide depression of the early 1930s devastated the Japanese economy, especially its agrarian sector, causing widespread suffering. Unlike most other industrial nations, however, Japan recovered remarkably quickly, thanks initially to vastly increased public spending, especially military expenditures, and subsequently to rapidly growing exports of industrial goods. Between 1932 and 1937, the total value of Japanese exports tripled. The production of industrial goods also increased very rapidly. By 1941, Japan was one of the world's fastest-growing and most competitive economies.

This performance resulted from a combination of factors, including the entrepreneurial talent and initiative of business leaders and a motivated, literate, and increasingly skilled work force. The Sino-Japanese War (1894–1895) and the Russo-Japanese War (1904–1905) also spurred Japanese heavy industries. World War I was also a windfall for Japanese businesses. The wartime boom left Japan's international trade balance with a surplus for the first time in history.[9]

Even Japan's defeat in World War II turned out to be an economic blessing. The prewar Japanese economy had been hobbled with a structural problem that impeded growth and development: the grossly uneven distribution of income and wealth. The resulting widespread poverty not only generated considerable social tension, but also prevented the formation of a sufficiently large domestic market for Japanese manufacturers. After World War II, Occupation-sponsored reforms—ranging from the dissolution of *zaibatsu* conglomerates to the unionization of well over half of Japan's urban workers, and extensive agricultural land reforms—significantly reduced the concentration of wealth and economic power and prepared the country for vast expansion of its middle class and its domestic consumer markets.

The Occupation's demilitarization program also freed Japan from military spending, which had swallowed one-third of the annual government budget in the early 1930s and three-quarters at the beginning of World War II. Japan could now devote its capital, labor, and technology to producing goods and services for civilian consumption. Japan soon emerged as one of the most productive, competitive, and wealthiest nations in the postwar world.

During the Korean War of the 1950s and the Vietnam War of the 1960s, Japanese factories were the main suppliers of the goods and services for the U.S. military. Both wars triggered long economic booms for Japan. By the time these booms ended in the early 1970s, Japan had become the second-largest market economy in the world in terms of total Gross Domestic Product.

The Cold War also contributed to the Japanese economic miracle. American policy toward both Japan and Germany dramatically shifted. By 1948, Washington's primary objectives were no longer the total demilitarization and democratization of the two occupied nations, but their swift economic recovery and incorporation into the U.S.-led anticommunist bloc. After China came under communist rule in 1949 and the Korean War broke out in 1950, Japan's new role as a key ally of the United States in Asia became even more prominent.

From 1947 to 1951, the United States helped Japan rebuild its economy by providing aid, including food, worth about $1.8 billion. The Occupation authorities also helped the Japanese government overcome postwar economic chaos, especially rampant inflation, by balancing the government budget, raising taxes, imposing price and wage freezes, and resuming limited foreign trade. After the Occupation ended in 1952, the United States continued to help Japan's economic recovery by opening its markets to Japanese exports and granting Japanese firms access to advanced industrial technology developed by U.S. firms. The United States supported Japan's admission to the United Nations, the International Monetary Fund (IMF), the World Bank, and the General Agreement on Tariffs and Trade (GATT). Membership in such international organizations enabled Japanese manufacturers to gain access to raw materials, merchandise, and capital markets, advanced industrial technology, and scientific information.

The role of government, however, has been of central importance in Japan's economic development. In the mid-nineteenth century, the Meiji state founded and operated munitions factories, mines, railroads, telegraph and telephone companies, and textile mills, and sold them at token prices to private entrepreneurs, some of whom became heads of *zaibatsu* conglomerates.[10] These corporate empires spearheaded the rapid expansion of the economy, helped by subsidies, tax breaks, tariff protection, as well as roads, railroads, port facilities, and communications networks, all provided by the state.

The state's role as the patron and protector of domestic industry continued after the post–World War II Allied Occupation. No sooner had the Occupation ended in 1952 than the Japanese government began to devise and implement policies and programs to jump-start the economy. Under its refined and expanded industrial policy, the government provided investment funds, tax breaks, foreign exchange, and foreign technologies to targeted strategic industries.

By the 1980s, surging Japanese exports had made Japan the world's largest creditor nation, and the United States began to view Japanese trade as a serious threat to its own industries. This led to a series of bilateral and multilateral trade and financial negotiations. Of particular importance was the 1985 Plaza Accord—a joint decision by representatives of the U.S., Japanese, and European financial authorities to force the dollar to decrease in value against other major currencies, Japan's currency, the *yen*, in particular. This would make Japanese exports more expensive and less competitive. Alarmed by the impending negative impact on Japan's export-driven economy, the Bank of Japan (BOJ)—equivalent to the Federal Reserve in the

United States—abruptly and drastically cut interest rates, inadvertently triggering a hyperinflation (a "bubble") of stock and real estate prices. Toward the end of 1989, the Japanese government belatedly and again abruptly tightened lending regulations in a panic, and the BOJ raised interest rates. This sudden policy reversal burst the bubble and touched off a protracted recession that continues to this day in Japan.

Protection of domestic agriculture is another example of failed policy in governing Japan's economy. Until the early 1990s, Japan maintained a nearly total ban on the import of foreign rice. Despite, or rather because of, such an exclusive focus on its rice farming instead of crop diversification, Japan's self-sufficiency in food supply plummeted from about 80 percent in 1960 to about 40 percent in 2007.

This obsession with the protection of domestic rice farming dates back to the period of extreme food shortages immediately following the end of World War II. Early postwar policies gave birth to a gigantic national network of farmers organized in agricultural cooperatives, Diet members from rural districts, and Ministry of Agriculture bureaucrats. These vested interests have continued to block effective reform of the country's outdated food-supply system.

Japan's financial sector also has been under strong state control and protection. An informal system of government influence known as **administrative guidance** has led the nation's major banks and securities firms to form tight networks of mutual cooperation and assistance, backed by an implicit government commitment to bail out their members in trouble. This so-called convoy system helped weak and internationally uncompetitive financial institutions survive. In the 1990s and early 2000s, many of these financial institutions—saddled with defaulted loans accumulated in the earlier bubble economy—went bankrupt. Those that survived stopped lending, especially to small businesses, effectively starving them of investment funds and aggravating the recession. The Japanese government set up a Financial Services Agency in 2001 to help banks and securities firms rid themselves of bad loans and begin to lend again. The agency has since mediated a series of bank mergers to create some of the largest financial institutions in the world. This move, however, has so far failed to lift Japan out of the recession.

The record of the Japanese state's "interventionism" has been very mixed, generally more positive early on, but more negative in later years.

## Society and Economy

The private industrial sector of the Japanese economy is characterized by interdependence and networking among a small number of giant firms, on the one hand, and a vast number of small firms, on the other. Most big businesses are affiliated with one or another of several huge business alliances, known as **keiretsu**. Each *keiretsu* is composed of a major bank and several large manufacturing, trading, shipping, construction, and insurance companies that are of comparable size and horizontally linked with one another. There are also more than a dozen similar but vertically linked *keiretsu*, including those built around the major automobile manufacturers, that provide a company with most of what is needed to produce its final products.

The Mitsubishi Group is a good example of a horizontally organized *keiretsu*. It is composed of about thirty formally independent, coequal corporations. Each member corporation is a leading firm in its own line of business, including Mitsubishi Motors, Nikon Corporation, and Kirin Brewery, as well as the Bank of Tokyo–Mitsubishi UFJ financial group.

By contrast, the Toyota Group represents a vertically organized *keiretsu*. Its top layer consists of 15 or so large corporations that maintain stable subcontracting relationships

**administrative guidance**

Informal guidance, usually not based on statute or formal regulation, that is given by a government agency, such as a ministry and its subdivisions, to a private organization, such as a firm or a lower-level government. The lack of transparency of the practice makes it subject to criticisms as a disguised form of collusion between a government agency and a firm.

**keiretsu**

A group of closely allied Japanese firms that have preferential trading relationships and often interlocking directorates and stock-sharing arrangements. The relationships among *keiretsu* member firms have been regarded as collusive and harmful to free trade by some of Japan's principal trading partners.

with about 340 smaller firms. In turn, many of these subcontractors hand down some of their work to even smaller firms. The Toyota Group is a huge pyramid made up of several hundred legally independent but operationally interdependent firms.

Since the late 1990s, both types of *keiretsu* have met challenges posed by the accelerating process of globalization and rapidly increasing cross-border mergers and acquisitions (M&A) and business alliances. While some *keiretsu* links have been tightened, many have been weakened.

The percentage of women in Japan's labor force has grown in recent decades and is now at about 50 percent. Sixty-three percent of women over the age of sixteen (the female labor participation rate) were working in 2009. According to the International Labor Organization, however, women made up only 9 percent of Japanese legislators, senior government officials, and company managers in 2008, compared with 43 percent in the United States, 39 percent in France, 38 percent in Germany, 34 percent in Britain, and 17 percent in China. The gender gap in wages has narrowed, but female workers are still paid on average less than 70 percent as much as male workers. A little over half of Japanese female workers hold "non-regular" jobs, which are part-time or temporary and come with few, if any, benefits. Between 1945 and 1955, intense, often violent, labor disputes rocked an impoverished Japan. During the three and a half decades of vigorous economic growth that followed, radical and militant labor unionism steadily declined, until it virtually disappeared. The proportion of labor union members in the nation's industrial work force declined from about 35 percent in 1970 to about 20 percent by 2010. Until recently, thanks to a relatively egalitarian pattern of income distribution (see Figure 5.2), most Japanese regarded themselves as members of the "middle class," that is, economically as well off as most other Japanese.

This situation began to change in the late 1990s as the Japanese economy began to shrink. Japan's rate of relative poverty—defined as the percentage of households with incomes less than 60 percent of the median household income in the given country—had risen to one of the highest levels among OECD member states by the mid-2000s, due importantly to an increase in the number of nonregular workers (34 percent of the total labor force by 2008).

The typical Japanese worker's wage or salary consists of relatively low basic monthly pay, substantial semiannual bonuses, and several allowances; for example, for dependent support, housing, and commuting costs. Retirement benefits for most regular employees consist of lump-sum severance pay and a contribution-based pension.

Japan's social welfare system is relatively undeveloped compared to its counterparts in most Western nations. Not until after World War II did the Japanese government begin to make a systematic effort to provide tax-supported pension, medical insurance, unemployment insurance, and workers' compensation programs for all citizens. The development of a comprehensive national social welfare system was mandated by the 1947 Constitution. During the four decades following the Allied Occupation, a number of state-sponsored and wholly or partially state-financed social welfare programs were established.

Today, virtually all Japanese citizens are provided with some social welfare benefits. However, the amounts of these benefits are not enough to meet the needs of most citizens, which creates a vicious circle: swelling ranks of citizens unable or reluctant to spend their diminished or

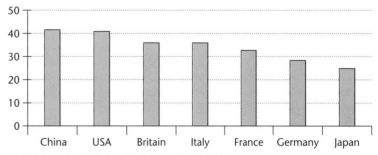

**FIGURE 5.2  GINI Coefficients, 1992–2007**

*Source:* UNDP 2009; http://hdrstats.undp.org/en/indicators/161.html.

**Japan's New National Symbol**

*Source*: Roger Dahl, "Dahl's Japan," *Japan Times*, March 14, 2010, http://www.japantimes.co.jp/life/cartoons/ca20100314ed.html.

diminishing incomes on anything but essential necessities of life, aggravating the persistent deflation and prolonging the recession.

A key to cut this vicious circle would be expansion of the social security programs. Social security spending, however, is already the largest government expenditure item. The rapidly aging population automatically ratchets it up each year, while tax revenue remains stagnant or even declines.

The recession-induced decline in the amount of private money available for investment has been made up mostly by public funds generated not by tax revenue, which has also declined, but by issue of new government bonds. As a result, the accumulated value of long-term public bonds amounted to about 904 trillion yen (about US$10.7 trillion) in June 2010, or 190 percent of Japan's GDP, by far the highest ratio among OECD countries. How to restore fiscal health, while stimulating the economy to create jobs and improving the social welfare system is one of the biggest challenges faced by the Japanese government and people.

# Japan in the Global Economy

## The Trading State

**newly industrialized countries (NICs)**

A term used to describe a group of countries that achieved rapid economic development beginning in the 1960s, largely stimulated by robust international trade (particularly exports) and guided by government policies. The core NICs are usually considered to be Taiwan, South Korea, Hong Kong, and Singapore, but other countries, including Argentina, Brazil, Malaysia, Mexico, and Thailand, are often included in this category.

Following the 1868 Meiji Restoration Japan pursued rapid industrialization, initially by exporting relatively cheap products of labor-intensive industries, such as textiles, and then increasingly higher-value-added products of more capital-intensive industries, including iron and steel, shipbuilding, and machinery. After World War II, especially since the 1960s, this export-led development strategy has been followed by the **newly industrialized countries (NICs)** in East Asia: South Korea, Taiwan, and Singapore early on, and then Thailand, Malaysia, Indonesia, and China.

About 90 percent of Japan's $781.4 billion exports in 2008 consisted of industrial goods, especially machinery and automobiles, and 50 percent of its $762.5 billion imports in the same year consisted of fuels, industrial raw materials, and foodstuffs. While Japan continues to import raw materials, turn them into industrial products, and sell them back to the rest of the world, often at large profits, its imports of industrial goods have vastly increased in recent years.

Japan continues to have chronic deficits (imports exceeding exports) in its trade balances with nations that export fuels, raw materials, and foodstuffs. These deficits are more than made up for by larger surpluses (exports exceeding imports) in Japan's trade with the United States, some European nations such as Britain and the Netherlands, and, above all, most nations in Asia, with the exception of China, Indonesia, and Malaysia (see Figure 5.3).

Washington used to charge Tokyo with unfair trade practices, and the two governments used to carry on endless trade disputes and negotiations. The United States' complaint shifted from Japan's high tariffs to protect domestic industries in the 1950s to **nontariff barriers (NTBs)**, such as import quotas, discriminatory application of safety and technical standards against imports, and a government procurement policy favoring domestic products in the 1960s.[11] In the 1980s, Japan was accused of creating and maintaining structural impediments to foreign imports and investments, including a complex domestic distribution system, collusive business practices among *keiretsu* companies, and predatory trade practices, such as dumping (selling goods abroad at prices lower than those charged at home).

In response, Japan has removed or significantly reduced the tariff and nontariff import barriers and abandoned most of the alleged predatory trade practices. Meanwhile, China has replaced Japan as the trading partner of the United States with the largest bilateral trade surplus and with the largest foreign exchange reserves in the world.

Increasing international competition has led many Japanese manufacturers to relocate their plants to China and other developing countries, especially in Southeast and South Asia. Some Japanese firms have begun to invest in development of oil, natural gas, and other energy-related resources abroad, while others are increasingly involved in the mergers and acquisitions of foreign firms. Japan's income from foreign direct investment (FDI) has been larger than its trade account surplus since 2004. As a result, Japan has become more dependent on returns from overseas investment than on earnings from trade for its income from international transactions, a major shift in the pattern of Japan's engagement with the world economy.

**nontariff barriers (NTBs)**

Policies—such as quotas, health and safety standards, packaging and labeling rules, and unique or unusual business practices—designed to prevent foreign imports in order to protect domestic industries. A form of protectionism that does not use formal tariffs.

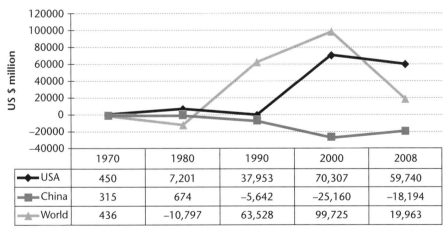

| | 1970 | 1980 | 1990 | 2000 | 2008 |
|---|---|---|---|---|---|
| USA | 450 | 7,201 | 37,953 | 70,307 | 59,740 |
| China | 315 | 674 | –5,642 | –25,160 | –18,194 |
| World | 436 | –10,797 | 63,528 | 99,725 | 19,963 |

**FIGURE 5.3** **Japan's Trade Balances with the United States, China, and the World**

*Note:* Dollar values converted from yen values at each year's average exchange rate.

*Sources:* Yano Tsuneta kinenkai, ed., *Suji de miru nihon no 100-nen*, 3rd ed. [Japan's 100 years in numbers] (Tokyo: Kokuseisha, 1991), pp. 325–326; Keizai kikakucho chosakyoku [Research Bureau, Economic Planning Agency], ed., *Keizai yoran* (*Heisei 6-nen ban*) [Economic handbook, 1994 edition] (Tokyo: Ministry of Finance Printing Office, 1994), pp. 188–189, 192–193; Somucho tokeikyoku [Bureau of Statistics, Management and Coordination Agency], ed., *Sekai no tokei* [Statistics of the World] (Tokyo: Ministry of Finance Printing Office, 1998), pp. 202, 220–221; Somusho tokei kenshujo [Statistical Research and Training Institute, Ministry of Internal Affairs and Communications], eds., *Sekai no tokei 2010* [Statistics of the World 2010] (Tokyo: Ministry of Finance Printing Office, 2010), pp. 231–232, Table 9-6.

The expansion of Japan's investments abroad has contributed to domestic unemployment. At the same time, foreign investment *in* Japan remains the lowest among the OECD countries. This is also the case with imports as a percentage of GDP, as well as the proportion of foreign workers in its labor force. Since around 2000, inward FDI has come to be accepted as a positive factor in the revival of the long-stagnant Japanese economy. It increased 2.8 times from 2003 to 2008, although it was a mere 3.6 percent of GDP in the latter year as compared to the OECD average of 27.2 percent. The Japanese economy is still relatively closed.

The Asia-Pacific region has been of special economic and strategic interest to Japan since long before World War II. But, in contrast to its earlier efforts to dominate the region through military power, Japan now tries to play the role of a leading partner in the development of regional cooperation. The rising tide of regionalism around the world in recent years, highlighted by the expansion of the European Union (EU), the conclusion of the North American Free Trade Agreement (NAFTA), and, above all, China's increasingly active involvement in the East Asian regional political economy, has spurred Japan's interest in improving regional cooperation in its own backyard.

The currency crisis that swept the region in 1997 gave birth to a sense of shared "Asian identity" and triggered a move to expand economic cooperation among nations in the region with a view to preventing a similar crisis. Japan has concluded economic partnership agreements (EPAs) so far with seven ASEAN member states, Mexico, Chile, and Switzerland, and is now trying to integrate and expand most of them into a comprehensive regional EPA.

In the meantime, steadily intensifying trading and investment activities by private firms in the region, notably Japanese firms, have led to the development of multiple networks of intraregional economic cooperation characterized by, above all, cross-border exchanges in intermediate, or producer, goods such as steel and plywood. Intraregional trade now accounts for nearly 60 percent of the combined total of foreign trade by the thirteen "ASEAN Plus Three" nations, namely, the ten ASEAN members plus China, Japan, and South Korea. This percentage of intraregional trade is higher than NAFTA's and approaches the EU's. A broad consensus has emerged among leaders in the region that they should make concerted efforts to build a more focused intraregional demand-based economic structure by raising living standards, so that more industrial goods produced in Asia are consumed in Asia.

## Summary

Following the Meiji Restoration of the mid-nineteenth century, the Japanese economy grew rapidly, largely according to government plans and under government direction, based on an approach broadly known as industrial policy. After World War II, the Occupation-sponsored demilitarization and democratization reforms within Japan, in the context of the free trade environment throughout the world, led to spectacular growth of the Japanese economy in the late 1950s through the early 1970s. Japan became one of the world's most competitive exporters and began even to threaten domestic industries in the United States and Western Europe. In 1985 the world's major industrial nations took concerted action, known as the Plaza Accord, in order to blunt Japan's export drive by raising the value of the yen relative to the dollar. The Japanese government's inopportune response to the anticipated detrimental effects of the accord on the Japanese economy, especially export-dependent small businesses, gave birth to a huge economic bubble, which burst in the early 1990s and plunged Japan into a prolonged recession. Two decades later, Japan has not yet dug itself out of the recession, which has been aggravated by a rapidly aging population and intensifying competition posed by the fast-growing emerging economies in the region.

# GOVERNANCE AND POLICY-MAKING

## Organization of the State

Japan is divided into forty-seven prefectures (provinces), which are, in turn, subdivided into about 1,727 municipalities (as of March 2010), ranging from large cities like metropolitan Tokyo with about 8.5 million residents and Yokohama with about 3.7 million residents, to half a dozen villages with no more than a few hundred inhabitants. Japan is a unitary state in which the prefectures and municipalities are subordinate, both economically and politically, to the national government and enjoy much more limited decision-making power than their counterparts in federal states, such as the United States, Canada, and Germany.

Japan is a constitutional monarchy and a parliamentary democracy, much like Britain and Sweden. The monarch (the emperor) is the symbolic head of state, but the people exercise sovereign power through their elected representatives in the national parliament, the Diet. The constitution gives the Diet the power to nominate the prime minister, enact laws, approve the government budget, ratify international treaties, and audit the financial transactions of the state. Nevertheless, the cabinet rather than the Diet initiates most legislation and in effect makes laws.

## The Executive

### The Prime Minister and the Cabinet

The prime minister is elected by the Diet and is usually the leader of the party that has a majority or plurality of seats in the House of Representatives. The House of Representatives and the House of Councilors separately elect a candidate for prime minister by a simple majority. If different candidates are elected by the two houses, the one elected by the lower house becomes prime minister. The prime minister must be a current Diet member and retains his or her seat in the Diet while serving as head of the executive branch.

Between 1955, when the Liberal Democratic Party was founded and formed its first government, and 2009, when the Democratic Party of Japan took over in the wake of its landslide victory in the lower house election of that year, all but three of Japan's 25 prime ministers were LDP leaders. They were first chosen as the party's president by consensus, often forged through backdoor negotiations among intraparty faction leaders. This process usually produced "everybody's second choice" as party president, someone who had held important cabinet and/or party positions in previous governments, usually in accordance with a seniority-based promotion system built on intraparty factional balance. (Factions are discussed in Section 4.) All but two of the nine LDP presidents and prime ministers who served during the last two decades (1991–2010) were so-called hereditary Diet members, who used their family connections and political influence inherited from their relatives, typically their own fathers, who had served in the Diet, to establish their political careers. Most have turned out to be ineffectual as party and government leaders and have served very short terms.

### Focus Questions

What is the influence of "iron triangles" in policy-making processes in Japanese government for the quality and strength of democracy in the country?

What factors or circumstances have constrained most significantly the exercise of political leadership by Japanese prime ministers and their cabinets in the last two decades?

In what ways is Japan's military force unique?

## PROFILES

### The Japanese Monarchy

Photo by KURITA KAKU/Gamma-Rapho via Getty Images

Japan has the oldest surviving monarchy in the world with the reign of the first legendary emperor dating back to the mid-7th century CE and that of the first documented emperor to the late 7th century CE. According to tradition, Akihito, the present occupant of Japan's Chrysanthemum Throne—so-called after the flower chosen as the crest of the imperial family in 1868—is the 125th in an unbroken line of emperors and empresses. His ancestors were Japan's actual rulers from the late seventh through the early tenth centuries and thereafter remained the nation's titular rulers until shortly after the end of World War II. Under the Meiji Constitution (1889–1947), the emperor was not only Japan's sovereign ruler but also a demigod whose person was considered sacred and inviolable. The 1947 Constitution, written during the Allied Occupation, relegated the emperor to the status of a symbol of the Japanese state in which the people were sovereign. The Japanese monarchy has both survived and been transformed by the country's devastating defeat in World War II and the far-reaching postwar reforms, and continues to thrive as an important national symbol.

The contemporary Japanese imperial family is a small group. As of January 2011, it consisted of 23 individuals, most prominently Emperor Akihito and Empress Michiko; the emperor's oldest son and heir apparent, Crown Prince Naruhito, his wife, Masako, and their daughter.

Succession to the Chrysanthemum Throne is governed by strict traditional rules of patrilineage, and only males are allowed to succeed to the throne, as stipulated in the 1947 Imperial Household Law. Under these rules, Prince Akishino, the crown prince's younger brother, is second and his young son, Prince Hisahito, third in the line of succession. Until Prince Hisahito was born in September 2006, no male had been born to any branch of the imperial family since Akishino's birth in 1965. This situation had given rise to intense and emotional debates both inside and outside the government over the need to amend the 1947 law to allow a female heir to succeed to the throne—a common practice among contemporary European monarchies—and the historical and doctrinal implications of the proposed change. Once the potential male heir was born, however, the highly charged debates ended almost overnight.

Compared to his aloof and enigmatic father, Hirohito, who at least figuratively led Japan into and out of the disastrous world war and whose role in that war remains controversial,[12] Emperor Akihito is a far more modern and cosmopolitan monarch. An eleven-year-old boy at war's end, he lived through the austere early postwar years as an impressionable young man, mingled freely with classmates from commoner families, learned English from an American Quaker woman, and married a businessman's daughter. Nonetheless, with the rigidly male-centered succession rule in place, the Japanese monarchy remains an extraordinarily tradition-bound institution.

The only notable exception was Koizumi Junichiro, who served as prime minister from April 2001 to September 2006. Although he "inherited" his Diet seat from his father, his own rise to the top was due more to his own public and media popularity for his aggressive antiestablishment, populist posture than to his being a favorite among the LDP elite.

The prime minister has the constitutional right to submit bills to the Diet in the name of the cabinet; to exercise control and supervision of the national civil service; and, in rare cases, to suspend a cabinet member's constitutionally guaranteed immunity from an adverse legal action during his or her tenure in office. The prime minister is also the commander-in-chief of Japan's military and may order, subject to the Diet's consent, the Self-Defense Forces to take appropriate actions in a national emergency.

If the House of Representatives passes a vote of no confidence against a cabinet, the prime minister must either resign, in which case the ruling party will choose a new party leader and prime minister, or dissolve the house and call a new election. Japanese prime ministers may also resign for other reasons, such as poor health, loss of support from important elements of his party, corruption scandals, and, increasingly, loss of support among the general public, as measured by frequent public opinion polls. As a result, the average tenure in office of prime ministers in postwar Japan has been just a little over two years, with several serving for less than a year. The frequent turnover of cabinets seriously impairs their ability to implement their policy agendas and also damages public trust in the government.

The executive powers and responsibilities of the Japanese cabinet include the following:

- Advising and taking responsibility for any of the emperor's ceremonial actions that are of concern to the state, such as the promulgation of laws and international treaties, convocation of the Diet, dissolution of the House of Representatives, and receiving foreign ambassadors and ministers;
- Designating the chief justice of the Supreme Court, who is formally appointed by the emperor;
- Appointing all other judges of the Supreme Court and those of the lower courts;
- Calling the Diet into extraordinary session and the upper house into emergency session;
- Approving expenditure of the state's reserve funds.

## The National Bureaucracy

At the core of the Japanese state are eleven national government ministries, each with virtually exclusive jurisdiction over a specific area or areas of public policy. Each ministry is headed by a minister, one to three parliamentary vice-ministers, and one or two administrative vice-ministers. The core organization of a ministry consists of a minister's secretariat; several staff bureaus, which are concerned mainly with broad policy issues; and several line bureaus, responsible for the implementation of specific policies and programs. The bureaus are each subdivided into divisions and departments. These core components are supplemented, as a rule, by several auxiliary agencies, commissions, committees, and institutes.

In the 1970s and 1980s, Japan's government bureaucracy was greatly admired, both within the nation and abroad, as the exceptionally intelligent, energetic, and dedicated architect of the nation's post–World War II economic success. By the end of the 1990s, however, its enviable reputation had largely dissipated. First, the depressed state of the Japanese economy was blamed on the bureaucrats. Second, a series of headline-grabbing scandals involving officials in some of the traditionally most powerful and prestigious ministries and agencies tainted the reputation of Japanese bureaucrats as unselfish, public-minded, and incorruptible mandarins. Third, politicians began to claim a greater share of policy-making power at the expense of bureaucrats. Fourth, diminishing tax revenue and tighter spending discipline spelled a shrinking war chest for bureaucrats to tap into for greasing their relationships with politicians and special interest groups, thus seriously eroding their influence. Finally, largely as a result of these developments, the bureaucrats themselves began to lose their self-confidence and sense of mission.

An entrenched tradition of ministerial autonomy has often seriously interfered with cooperation among ministries. For example, in the aftermath of the devastating earthquake that hit Kobe City in January 1995, ministerial egoism and parochialism were widely blamed for long delays, often with tragic consequences, in the national government's response to the disaster.

Japanese national civil service entrance examinations are highly competitive, especially in the fast-track category, officially called Class I. In 2010, roughly one out of 20 initial applicants and one out of ten of those who actually took the exam passed it.

| Table 5.2 | Cabinet Positions (June 2010) |
|---|---|
| Prime Minister | |
| Minister of Internal Affairs and Communications cum Minister of State for Promotion of Local Sovereignty | |
| Minister of Justice | |
| Minister of Foreign Affairs | |
| Minister of Finance | |
| Minister of Education, Culture, Sports, Science, and Technology cum Minister of State for Science and Technology Policy | |
| Minister of Health, Labor, and Welfare cum Minister of State for Pension Reform | |
| Minister of Agriculture, Forestry, and Fisheries | |
| Minister of Economy, Trade, and Industry | |
| Minister of Land, Infrastructure, Transport and Tourism cum Minister of State for Okinawa and Northern Territories Affairs | |
| Minister of Environment | |
| Minister of Defense | |
| Chief Cabinet Secretary | |
| Minister of State for Financial Services cum Minister of State for Postal Reform | |
| Minister of State for National Policy cum Minister of State for Economic and Fiscal Policy cum Minister of State for Consumer Affairs and Food Safety | |
| Minister of State for Civil Service Reform cum Minister of State for the New Public Commons cum Minister of State for Social Affairs and Gender Equality | |
| Chairman of the National Commission on Public Safety cum Minister of State for Disaster Management cum Minister of State for the Abduction Issue | |

**amakudari**

A Japanese practice, known as "descent from heaven," in which government officials retiring from their administrative positions take jobs in public corporations or private firms with which their own ministry has or recently had close ties.

The current mandatory retirement age for most national civil servants is 60. This relatively early retirement age, combined with relatively modest retirement benefits, leads most civil service retirees to seek new jobs upon retirement. Many find high-paying positions in public or semipublic corporations or in major private firms through their ministry's good offices. This manner of gaining post-retirement employment is known as **amakudari**, or "descent from heaven."

The "descent" is usually arranged in advance between the ministry ("heaven") from which the official is retiring and a public, semipublic, or private enterprise with which the ministry has a close relationship. The Japanese civil service law forbids employment of a retired civil servant within two years of his or her retirement by a private enterprise that has had a close relationship with the government office where the retired official was employed in the last five years. This restriction, however, may be lifted at the National Personnel Authority's discretion, which is routinely done for several dozen retiring senior bureaucrats each year. Moreover, there are no legal restrictions on the "descent" of a retired official to a public or semipublic organization.

In 2009, Japan's national government, including its auxiliary organizations and Self-Defense Force staff and troops, had on its payroll about 600,000 people, or less than 1 percent of the approximately 64 million gainfully employed people in the country. Civil servants cost about 7.2 percent of the national government's annual expenditures and 0.8 percent of Japan's GDP. Japan's national civil service is thus relatively lean and thrifty.

In addition to the national government ministries and agencies, there were, as of 2010, about 7,000 public and semipublic enterprises funded wholly or substantially by the central government. Their activities ranged from energy resource development to promotion of international cooperation to oversight of publicly managed gambling. Many had outlived their usefulness and served primarily as destinations of retiring bureaucrats' lucrative descent from heaven. They have been the main targets of the DPJ government's civil service reform drive.

# Other State Institutions

## The Military

Japan's military establishment was totally dismantled by the Allied Occupation authorities after World War II, and the nation was forbidden to rearm by the peace clause of the 1947 Constitution. Nonetheless, the outbreak of the Korean War in 1950 led the

---

## THE U.S. CONNECTION

### U.S.-Japan Alliance and the Japanese Self-Defense Forces

As Figures 5.4 and 5.5 show, Japan spends far less for defense as a percentage of GDP than its military ally, the United States. Not surprisingly, U.S. leaders have persistently demanded a larger defense effort by Tokyo. Japan has responded not by large increases in defense spending, which would be financially difficult and politically unpopular, but mainly by expanding its participation in UN-sponsored peacekeeping operations and, more recently, to limited support of U.S. actions in Iraq and Afghanistan.[13]

Beginning with the dispatch of three civilian election watchers to Angola in 1992, Japanese, including SDF troops in an increasing number of cases, have participated during the past decade in peacekeeping activities in Cambodia, Mozambique, El Salvador, Rwanda, Syria/Golan Heights, Bosnia/Herzegovina, and East Timor.

Following the September 11, 2001, terrorist attacks on the United States, the Japanese government dispatched, with little overt public or media opposition, half a dozen warships to the Indian Ocean to assist the U.S. forces in their military operations in and around Afghanistan. This was soon followed by Diet passage of a Special Anti-Terrorism Measures Bill and the adoption by the cabinet of a Basic Plan of Special Anti-Terrorism Measures, which authorized the SDF to assist American and British forces in Afghanistan and later in Iraq. The SDF operation in the Indian Ocean continued until January 2010.

Nevertheless, Japan continues to rely heavily on the United States for its military security. This arrangement is based on the 1960 Treaty of Mutual Cooperation and Security between Japan and the United States. By virtue of the treaty and the Agreement on the Status of U.S. Armed Forces, the United States maintains an extended network of military bases and facilities and about 45,000 troops in Japan.

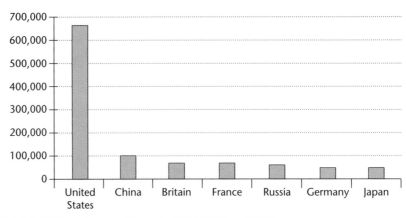

**FIGURE 5.4 Military Expenditures in US$ Million, 2008**

*Source:* Information from the Stockholm International Peace Research Institute (SIPRI): http://www.sipri.org/research/armaments/milex; SIPRI, Signalistgatan 9, SE-169 70 Solna, Sweden.

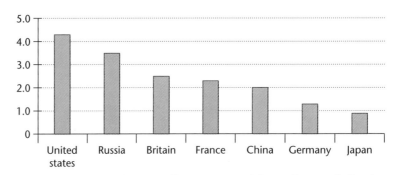

**FIGURE 5.5 Military Expenditures as Percentages of Gross Domestic Product, 2008**

*Source:* Information from the Stockholm International Peace Research Institute (SIPRI): http://www.sipri.org/research/armaments/milex; SIPRI, Signalistgatan 9, SE-169 70 Solna, Sweden.

Japanese government, with strong American prompting, to launch a rearmament program. Initially, a so-called police reserve force was created, to avoid provoking controversy over its constitutionality. By 1954, this force had evolved into the Self-Defense Forces (SDF). In 1959, the Supreme Court ruled that Article 9 of the constitution allowed Japan to take necessary measures to defend itself as an independent nation.

The SDF is today roughly equal—in operational capability if not in physical size—to the armed forces of a major Western European nation. In 2009, Japan's defense budget of $46.9 billion was ranked seventh in the world, after the United States, China, Britain, France, Russia, and Germany.

## The Judiciary

The judicial branch of the Japanese government operates according to the rules set by the Supreme Court, which consists of the chief judge and fourteen other judges. All judges are appointed by the cabinet, except for the chief judge of the Supreme Court, who is nominated by the cabinet and formally appointed by the emperor. Supreme Court judges are subject to popular review and potential recall in the first House of

Representatives election following their appointment and every ten years thereafter. None, however, has ever been recalled as a result of the popular review.

The Supreme Court, eight higher (regional) courts, and fifty district (prefectural) courts possess, and occasionally use, the constitutional power of judicial review. But the Supreme Court has been extremely reluctant to declare an existing law unconstitutional. In the little over sixty years since its institution in 1947, the Supreme Court has declared only 20 existing laws unconstitutional. This apparent timidity may be attributed mainly to the influential legal opinion that holds that the judiciary should not intervene in decisions of the legislative or executive branches of government, which represent the people's will more directly than the judiciary.

Until May 2009, professional judges alone decided the outcome of cases brought to court. A quasi-jury system has now been introduced, however, under which even a major criminal case is heard and verdicts are determined by a panel composed of three professional judges and six randomly chosen citizens. Many consider the introduction of this **"Lay Judge System"** (*saiban-in-seido*) one of the most radical government reforms in post–Occupation Japan and a major step toward democratizing its legal system.

## The Police

From early 1948 to mid-1954, local municipalities held direct control over about three-quarters of the Japanese police force, with the national government controlling the rest. Since then, the Japanese police have operated under the direct control of prefectural governors and prefectural public safety commissions. Forty-seven prefectural police headquarters and safety commissions are directly responsible for the maintenance and activities of all Japanese police forces, although the National Police Agency exercises supervisory authority and has coordinating power over the prefectural organizations and their personnel. This relatively decentralized structure reflects, in part, a reaction against the much dreaded coercive power wielded by the prewar and wartime Japanese police.

Until the 1980s, the Japanese police enjoyed a reputation, both at home and abroad, as a highly disciplined, efficient, and effective guardian of peace and order in the country. Since then, however, that enviable reputation has been damaged by a growing incidence of mediocre performance, low motivation, and even widespread corruption. According to the National Police Agency's annual report, the incidence of criminal offenses reported in the country increased by about 23 percent between 1980 and 2008, from about 1,160 to about 1,424 per 100,000 citizens; but the percentage of criminals apprehended fell by nearly 50 percent. The change is attributable partly to the increasing cultural and behavioral heterogeneity of Japanese society, resulting from growing generational gaps and a slow but steady increase in the number of resident and visiting foreigners. It is also due partly to a decline in the number of applicants for police jobs and the resulting decline in the police/crime ratio.

Nonetheless, Japan remains a relatively crime-free society, with less than half as many victims of criminal offenses per capita reported in 2005 as Britain, a little over half as many as the United States, and substantially fewer than either France or Germany. When it comes to the percentage of offenders apprehended, Japan's record of a little under 32 percent in 2007 was considerably higher than the United States' 20 percent and Britain's 28 percent, but significantly lower than France's 36 percent and, especially, Germany's 55 percent. Once a case comes to trial, Japan boasts a conviction rate of 99.9 percent.

The criminal justice system in Japan has been criticized for abuse of prisoners and suspects, and the arbitrary and often inhumane way the prison system is run. The astoundingly high conviction rate is achieved largely by prosecutors' heavy reliance on confessions.

**"Lay Judge System"** (*saiban-in-seido*)

The quasi-jury system for major criminal cases that was introduced into Japan's judicial system in May 2009. Guilt or innocence of the accused—and, if convicted, the sentence—are determined by a judicial panel composed of three professional judges and six laypersons.

Confessions are often coerced by abusive interrogations in the "substitute prisons" where suspects can be detained for up to 22 days by police and prosecutors, and are given very restricted access to their lawyers—in violation of the constitutional guarantee (Article 34) of the right to counsel and *habeas corpus*, which directs that a person either be charged before a judge or released. The quasi-jury system introduced in May 2009 is expected to open the judicial system to greater public scrutiny and help reduce human rights abuses.

Japan is, along with the United States, one of the very few developed countries that still practice capital punishment. Executions in Japan are carried out by hanging and conducted in great secrecy. In 2008, Japan executed 15 people, while the U.S. executed 37. In a 2010 Cabinet Office public opinion poll, 85.6 percent of respondents supported the death penalty on the grounds that it prevents personal vendettas and deters future crimes. There was a nonpartisan group of 80 Diet members opposed to capital punishment, including the former chief of the National Police Agency, at the end of 2009. This number, however, represented a sharp drop from 120 of such lawmakers counted two years earlier, a drop probably due to the weight of public opinion in favor of the death penalty.

### Subnational Government

Japanese prefectures and their subdivisions have long been under the administrative and financial control of the national government and enjoy only limited decision-making authority. In this respect, Japan differs from most other industrial democracies, where subnational levels of government have greater autonomy.

The lopsided distribution of decision-making power in the Japanese political system has been sustained by an equally lopsided division of taxation power. The national government collects nearly two-thirds of the taxes levied by all levels of governments and provides the funds for nearly one-third of local government expenditures.

The 1947 Constitution of Japan devotes its last substantive chapter to local self-government and refers to "the principle of local autonomy." There has always been a broad, although more implicit than explicit, consensus among Japanese scholars and a large segment of the general public that robust local autonomy is an essential element of modern democracy. This academic and public opinion, which has been increasingly embraced and articulated by the powerful national associations of prefectural and local politicians, began to move the LDP government to act in the mid-1990s, when a Local Decentralization Promotion Law was enacted by the Diet and a prime minister's advisory commission on the implementation of the law was set up. This has since been followed by a series of similar legislative and executive actions both under the LDP and DPJ cabinets. In late 2009, the government appointed a blue-ribbon group with a grandiose title "Local Sovereignty Strategy Conference," which was composed of half-dozen cabinet ministers, several leading local politicians, and a few scholars.

The decentralization campaign, however, has so far been more rhetoric than action, importantly due to strong opposition among LDP Diet members and senior bureaucrats, as well as the very short tenure of most prime ministers and cabinets. The weak and dependent status of local government vis-à-vis national government is still widely perceived to be detrimental to the deepening of Japanese democracy.

# The Policy-Making Process

Until recently, policy-making in postwar Japan was dominated by informal coalitions called "iron triangles" that were made up of Liberal Democratic Party politicians, national civil servants (bureaucrats), and major interest group leaders. Draft bills were reviewed and approved by the LDP's Policy Research Council, which operated through a dozen standing committees, each corresponding to a government ministry and an abundance of ad hoc committees. The recommendations of these committees were presented to the Council's executive committee and then to the party's Executive Council. If approved at both levels, the recommendations usually became government policies to be implemented through legislative actions of the Diet or administrative actions of the bureaucracy.

Most LDP policy committees were led by veteran Diet members with experience and knowledge in specific areas. Over the years, they formed close personal relationships with senior civil servants and leaders of special interest groups. These LDP legislative leaders, who formed among themselves what were popularly known as **zoku** (tribes), worked through iron triangles with their bureaucratic and business allies. Such tribes and iron triangles dominated policy-making in all major policy areas, but especially agriculture, construction, education, telecommunications, and transportation.

The iron triangles promoted special interests favored by politicians and bureaucrats. Bureaucrats had their turfs protected and often expanded by sympathetic politicians, and politicians had their campaign war chests filled with contributions from the interest groups that they supported. The LDP tribes were the principal actors in Japan's widespread **pork-barrel politics** and the major sources of political corruption. Big businesses, small shop owners, farmers, builders, insurers, and doctors were all represented by their own tribes that protected them against those who threatened their interests, whether they were Japanese consumers, insurance policy holders, patients, or foreign producers and exporters.

The resistance and obstruction by powerful entrenched interests, determined to hang on to and perpetuate the status quo, stymied reformist efforts in virtually all major policy areas, making Japanese politics look like a downtown intersection in a perennial gridlock. This political paralysis made it extremely difficult to change old policies, practices, and procedures in any significant or timely way and aggravated already bad situations, such as the protracted economic slump and the mounting public debt.

Since the DPJ took over the reins of government in 2009, its leadership has made sporadic attempts to reduce the influence of tribes and iron triangles in the policy-making process, but with no tangible results. The moribund system, which has significantly alienated the Japanese public from the government, and politics generally, under the LDP rule, appears to have survived the recent change of governments, at least in the short run.

Bureaucrats have also suffered a significant decline in their political influence, but still play a central role in policy-making. Often with the help of advisory groups of academic and professional experts, they develop the majority of new policies and draft the majority of new bills debated and voted into law by members of the Diet. The policies approved and laws enacted by legislators are then implemented by the same civil servants and elicit diverse reactions from citizens and especially from organized special interests. These reactions in turn lead bureaucrats and politicians to develop new policies, revise existing laws, and enact new laws.

**zoku**

Members of the Japanese Diet (parliament) with recognized experience and expertise in particular policy areas such as agriculture, construction, and transportation, and close personal connections with special interests in those areas.

**pork-barrel politics**

A term originally used by students of American politics to refer to legislation that benefits particular legislators by funding public works and projects in their districts. More broadly, the term refers to preferential allocation of public benefits or resources to particular districts or regions so as to give electoral advantage to particular politicians or political parties.

## Summary

A unitary state, Japan grants an overwhelming policy-making role to its national government, formed and controlled by the elected national legislature, the Diet, at the expense of its prefectural and local governments. Under its 1947 constitution, the Japanese monarchy, while the oldest in the world, plays a merely symbolic role, and the military is under strict civilian control. During much of the Liberal Democratic

Party's four-decade long control of government, the ruling party's policy-savvy veteran Diet members formed iron triangle coalitions with ministry bureaucrats and major interest group leaders to dominate policy-making in all major policy areas. Most legislative bills were drafted by bureaucrats and ratified by the LDP-controlled Diet. The judiciary, while constitutionally independent from both the legislative and executive branches of government, tended to be deferential to them, especially in exercising its constitutional right of judicial review. As the Japanese economy fell into a long recession in the last decade of the twentieth century, both the LDP and the bureaucracy began to lose the confidence of the public and the support of the electorate, leading to rival parties' rise to power. The DPJ, which took over the reins of government in 2009, has embarked on major political and administrative reform, but neither the influence of iron triangles nor the role of the bureaucracy in Japan's policy-making process is likely to significantly diminish in the foreseeable future.

# REPRESENTATION AND PARTICIPATION

## Focus Questions

What have been some of the major changes in the Japanese party and electoral systems in recent years?

Japanese government is often portrayed as misogynistic. Is this an accurate and fair description of the reality?

Is Japan a homogeneous and egalitarian nation?

What is the status of minority and marginalized groups in Japanese society?

How do citizen interests get represented in Japan?

What forms have citizen protests taken, and why have they declined in recent years?

The most important institutions through which Japanese citizens express their interests are the parliament (the Diet) and local legislatures. The principal actors who represent them are therefore Diet members, most of whom are affiliated with political parties, and members of prefectural and municipal assemblies, the majority of whom are independents. There are, however, other organizations and activities that represent citizens' concerns and opinions outside the legislatures, such as interest groups and social movements.

## The Legislature

According to the postwar Japanese constitution, the Diet is the highest and sole law-making organ of the state. The constitution gives it the power to nominate the prime minister, enact laws, approve the government budget, ratify international treaties, and audit the financial transactions of the state. The Diet is bicameral, with an upper chamber, the House of Councilors, and a lower chamber, the House of Representatives. Both houses consist of popularly elected members. The lower house is the larger and more powerful of the two, with the power to override the opposition of the upper house in votes on the budget, ratification of international treaties, and the nomination of a new prime minister. The speaker and vice-speaker of the House of Representatives and the president and vice-president of the House of Councilors nominally give up their party affiliations and become independent members.

The Diet also has the power to investigate any matter of national interest, whereas the prime minister and the cabinet must report to the Diet on the state of the nation and its foreign relations. In fulfilling this constitutional requirement, cabinet ministers regularly attend meetings of Diet committees and answer members' questions.

Nevertheless, as discussed in the previous section, the cabinet rather than the Diet initiates most legislation and in effect makes laws. This is mostly because members of the Diet have virtually no legislative staff of their own, whereas cabinet ministers enjoy easy access to the substantial staff and resources of the civil service. During the

LDP's long one-party rule, civil servants drafted the majority of bills, most of which were then passed by the LDP-dominated Diet. This style of legislative politics ended with the defeat of the LDP-CGP ruling coalition in the 2007 upper house election, making the legislative process and procedure far more complicated and unpredictable.

The House of Representatives, the lower and more powerful house of the Diet, currently has 480 members. The full term of office for its members is four years, but the lower house is frequently dissolved and new elections held at the discretion of the prime minister and the cabinet. The House of Councilors, the upper house of the Diet, currently has 242 members. Their term of office is six years. Their terms are staggered, as with U.S. senators, so that 121 members are elected every three years.

An ordinary session of the Diet sits for 150 days each year, beginning in mid-January. It may be extended once. An extraordinary session may be called at any time by the cabinet or by one-quarter or more of the members of either house. As in the U.S. Congress, a good deal of business is conducted in the standing and ad hoc committees of each house. In mid-2010, there were seventeen standing and seven ad hoc committees in the lower house and seventeen standing and six ad hoc committees in the upper house. A bill may be first introduced in either house of the Diet, but must be considered and approved by both houses in order to become a law. A bill may be introduced by the cabinet, the house as a whole, a committee of the house, or a group of members of the house. A member's bill that does not require a budget appropriation must be cosigned by twenty or more lower house members or ten or more upper house members; one that requires a budget appropriation must be cosigned by fifty or more lower house or twenty or more upper house members.

A bill approved by a committee of either house is referred to and debated by the whole house and, if approved, transmitted to the other house, where the same process is repeated. A simple majority is required for the passage of a bill or a resolution by either house or a committee, unless it is a proposal to revise the constitution, which requires the consent of two-thirds or more of all members in each house and then is put to the vote in a national referendum for final approval. A bill that has been approved by both houses is signed by the speaker of the lower house or the president of the upper house, whichever has approved it last, and presented to the emperor for *pro forma* promulgation.

An ordinary bill already passed by the lower house, then rejected by the upper house, may be voted on again and into law by a two-thirds majority of lower house members present and voting. Following the advent of the "twisted" Diet in 2007 (discussed below), the ruling LDP-led coalition resorted several times to this method of passing its key bills. Following the advent of the second "twisted" Diet in 2010, the DPJ government may use the same method.

The annual government budget must be introduced first to the lower house and may be passed by that house alone, regardless of the upper house's action or opinion. The same applies to international treaties. Unlike members of the U.S. Congress, but like legislators in other parliamentary democracies, Japanese Diet members normally vote strictly along party lines.

The overwhelming majority of Japanese legislators are men. In the 2009 lower house and 2010 upper house elections, 54 and 44 women, respectively, were elected. They accounted for about 11 percent and 18 percent of the total membership of each house. On a list compiled in June 2010 by the Inter-Parliamentary Union, Japan ranked 92nd among 186 nations in the percentage of women in the lower or single house of parliament. As one woman candidate's experience described in the profile box suggests, however, the Japanese attitude toward women in politics is slowly but steadily changing and likely to gradually change the gender ratios of members of the Diet and local legislatures in the decades to come.

## PROFILES

### Renho

**Triumphant DPJ candidate Renho with her campaign staff, July 11, 2010**

*Source*: Yomiuri Online, http://www.yomiuri.co.jp/politics/photograph/garticle.htm?ge=761&gr=2462&id=77798.

Photo by Sankei via Getty Images

One candidate in the 2010 upper house election attracted special public and media attention verging on the sensational. The candidate, Renho, ran for a second term in the house from the Tokyo prefectural district, the largest of such districts, where 24 candidates vied for five seats. She not only won a seat in the very crowded field, but did so spectacularly, winning 1.7 million votes, or over 28 percent of the total vote cast in the district. No other candidate in the whole nation received as many as one million votes in this election. This record was of great historic interest and significance for several reasons.

First, this candidate was a woman. Second, she was a Chinese-Japanese, born in Japan of a Chinese father from Taiwan and a Japanese mother. Third, she was a media celebrity well known for her previous careers as a savvy newscaster and a successful host of popular television shows. And last, but not least, she had made a name most recently as a particularly active and vocal member of the Administrative Reform Council set up within the Office of the Cabinet in late 2009 and, especially, as an undaunted and sharp-tongued critic of wasteful bureaucratic programs and practices. She had been appointed Minister of State for Civil Service Reform in the DPJ cabinet just a month before the election.

Incidentally, "Renho" is the Japanese pronunciation of the Chinese characters for her given name, Lien-fang. Her family name is Murata. As a rule, Japanese use their full name, that is, family name followed by given name, in their public lives. Renho, however, has been officially authorized by the cabinet to publicly and regularly use her given name only, an unprecedented exception never before granted to a Diet or cabinet member.

Renho's triumph in the 2010 upper house election points up several important aspects of contemporary Japanese politics and society, including the growing tolerance and acceptance of ethnic differences among its citizens, the enormous power of the media, especially television, and the intense public dissatisfaction with the political and social status quo. It suggests, above all, that performance, whether political or nonpolitical, trumps ethnicity, gender, and tradition in today's politics. It is worth noting that the second-ranked winner in the Tokyo prefectural district in the 2010 upper house election was another woman and that the three male winners all trailed the two women.

When an incumbent LDP or DPJ Diet member retires or dies, he or she is often succeeded by a relative, typically a son. Thanks to the campaign organization and personal networks bequeathed by the predecessor, such a successor has significant advantage over rivals. In the 2009 House of Representatives general election, such "hereditary" candidates accounted for 17 percent of all winners and 42 percent of the LDP-affiliated winners. All but two LDP prime ministers who served between 1991 and 2009 were "hereditary" lower house members.

## Political Parties and the Party System

There are now five major political parties in Japan: the Democratic Party of Japan (DPJ), the Liberal Democratic Party (LDP), the Japanese Communist Party (JCP), the Social Democratic Party (SDP), and the Clean Government Party (CGP), which was founded in the 1960s as the political arm of a lay Buddhist association, *Sokagakkai* (Value Creation Academy) (see Table 5.3). The current ruling party, the DPJ, was established in 1998, from a merger of several smaller parties that were opposed to the LDP and included defectors from the LDP itself.

Ideologically, the LDP is a conservative party and stands at the right end of the political party spectrum; the JCP and SDP are at the left end; and the DPJ and CGP are centrist, but both lean toward the conservative end. There were a few minor, and likely ephemeral, parties running candidates in Diet elections and winning a few seats in each house. The party system as a whole, however, has become a virtual two-party-dominant pattern, with the DPJ and LDP competing for power virtually between themselves.

The LDP has been divided into several entrenched rival factions. Until the late 1980s, the boss of each faction and his followers used to be bound by close **clientelist** ties of mutual help and dependence. The boss, as a rule a well-heeled veteran lower house member and an aspiring party and government leader, helped his followers with campaign funds at election time and sponsored their appointment to Diet, cabinet, and party offices. His followers reciprocated by pledging support for the boss's bid for the office of the LDP president, which was, given the LDP's control of the Diet, virtually synonymous with the office of prime minister. In recent years, however, the ties between a leader and his followers in an LDP faction and among faction members in general have substantially loosened.

The DPJ and the SDP have also been host to entrenched intraparty factions. In fact, their factions have been more intractable and disruptive of intraparty harmony and unity than their LDP counterparts. While LDP factions have been concerned primarily with fundraising and the distribution of government and party offices among its Diet members, the factions in the DPJ and the SDP have been divided primarily along ideological and policy lines. Both parties have been seriously handicapped by the factional divisions among their leaders and members in competing with the LDP and other parties both in the legislature and at the ballot box.

Japanese political parties are all formed primarily by and for Diet members with very modest grassroots memberships. In a nation with an electorate of well over 100 million, the LDP has about one million grass-roots members, or less than 1 percent of the electorate, the CGP and the JCP a little over 400,000 each, the DPJ about 340,000, and the SDP less than 40,000. They are all elite, as opposed to mass, parties.

**clientelism (or patron-client networks)**

An informal aspect of policy-making in which a powerful patron (for example, a traditional local boss, government agency, or dominant party) offers resources such as land, contracts, protection, or jobs in return for the support and services (such as labor or votes) of lower-status and less powerful clients; corruption, preferential treatment, and inequality are characteristic of clientelist politics.

| Table 5.3 | Japan's Political Parties | | Diet Seats | |
|---|---|---|---|---|
| | Party Name | Year Founded | Lower House 2009 Elections | Upper House 2010 Elections |
| Right | Liberal Democratic Party (LDP) | 1955 | 119 | 84 |
| Center | Democratic Party of Japan (DPJ) | 1998 | 308 | 106 |
| | Clean Government Party (CGP) | 1964 | 21x | 19 |
| Left | Social Democratic Party (SDP) | 1955 | 7 | 4 |
| | Japan Communist Party (JCP) | 1945 | 9 | 6 |
| | Others and Independents | | 16 | 23 |
| Total Seats | | | 480 | 242 |

Source: *Asahi Shimbun*, August 31, 2009; July 12, 2010.

**Single Non-Transferable Vote (SNTV)**

A method of voting used in a multimember election district system. Each voter casts only one ballot for a particular candidate and that vote may not be transferred to another candidate even of the same party. As many candidates with the most votes are elected as the number of posts available in each district.

*koenkai*

A Japanese campaign organization for a particular candidate, consisting mainly of the candidate's relatives, friends, fellow alumni, coworkers, and their acquaintances. For most conservative politicians, especially LDP and DPJ members of the Diet and local legislatures, networks of *koenkai* organizations are far more important and effective than political parties in assisting politicians' election campaigns. Since it costs politicians a great deal of money to maintain these networks, *koenkai*-centered elections encourage corruption.

**Mixed Member Proportional (MMP)**

An electoral system that combines (mixes) the proportional features of a party list proportional representation system with the local representation features of a single-member plurality system. Under this mixed system, each voter casts one vote for a party list and another for an individual candidate in a single-member electoral district.

Under a political reform law passed in 1994, major Japanese political parties are subsidized by the state, which means the taxpayers. Each party receives an amount that equals 250 yen multiplied by Japan's current population, in proportion to the sum of the number of seats it currently holds in the two houses and the average share of the vote it has won in the most recent lower house and the two most recent upper house elections. According to this formula, DPJ received in 2010 about 17.3 billion yen, or $162 million, and the LDP 10.4 billion yen, or $120 million. The law was intended to reduce the parties' susceptibility to corruption due to fund-raising pressures.

Japanese local government and politics are generally nonpartisan. All of the current 47 prefectural governors and nearly all of the 1,790 mayors are independents, and so are nearly 80 percent of municipal assembly members. The only exception is prefectural assembly members, three-quarters of whom are affiliated with one or another major national party, about half with the LDP.

# Elections

Elections to the House of Representatives must be held at least once every four years. A new election is called if the House is dissolved. Diet election campaign costs are partially borne by the government. Candidates receive free posters, stamped postcards, space in the official gazette, radio and television advertisements, use of public halls for campaign speeches, and passes for public means of transportation during the legally defined campaign periods.

Under the system in effect from the mid-1920s to 1994, all lower house members, as well as some of the House of Councilors, were elected in multimember districts by the **Single Non-Transferrable Vote (SNTV)** method in which several candidates are elected, but every voter has only one vote. This system tended to pit candidates of the same party against each other within a district and led each to highlight his or her constituency services, rather than policy positions and commitments. Constituency service activities were carried out primarily by the candidate's personal campaign organization, generically known as ***koenkai*** (support association).

During election campaigns, the *koenkai* mobilized local community groups, such as agricultural cooperatives and shopkeepers' associations, to get out the vote for their candidates. It took large amounts of money and hard work to set up and maintain a viable *koenkai* organization. The LDP's long rule depended on the extensive and sturdy networks of clientelist relationships between LDP politicians, their *koenkai* organizations, and loyal constituents. This highly personalized, *koenkai*-centered style of campaigning and fundraising was blamed for widespread political corruption.

In the 1994 reform, the SNTV system for House of Representatives elections was replaced by a **Mixed Member Proportional (MMP)** system that combines a **single-member district (SMD)** and **proportional representation (PR)** system similar to that used in Germany. There are now 300 single-member districts in which the winners are decided on a "first-past-the-post" basis; in other words, whichever candidate gets the most votes wins the seat. The other 180 members are elected according to what is called a *party list* system of proportional representation (PR) from eleven regional electoral districts that have between six and thirty seats to fill. To run a candidate or candidates in a PR district, a party must hold at least five current Diet seats, have won at least 2 percent of the vote in the most recent Diet election, or have at least ten candidates running in the current election. Each qualified party submits a ranked list of its candidates in that regional district to the election management committee in advance of the voting. Voters mark ballots for their preferred political party. The 180 multimember district seats in the House of Representatives are then allocated to the parties in numbers proportionate to their shares of the total vote, and those seats are, in turn, allocated to the candidates according to their rank on the party's list. In sum, each voter casts two ballots in a lower house election, one for a particular candidate in the single member district and one for a party in the multimember regional district.

The 242 members of the House of Councilors are elected to six-year terms. Councilors' terms are staggered, so half of the members (121) are elected every three years. Unlike the House of Representatives, the House of Councilors cannot be dissolved, and elections occur regularly every three years. Ninety-six members (forty-eight in each triennial election) are elected by a party list proportional representation (PR) method, on a *nationwide* basis rather than by regional districts. The remaining 146 (or 73 every three years) members are elected from prefectures, between two and ten per prefecture, by the SNTV method.

The LDP dominated the Diet under the pre-1994 House of Representatives election system and continued to do so for a decade under the new system. As Table 5.4 suggests, however, its grip on Diet elections has begun to slip. The LDP beat the DPJ in the 2005 lower house election, but, in the 2007 upper house election, the DPJ-led opposition beat the LDP-led ruling coalition 127 to 103, while the LDP held a two-thirds majority in the lower house. This created a "twisted" Diet, a situation in which the party of the prime minister—the government party—controlled one house but the opposition controlled the other. Because, as a rule, all bills must be passed by both houses to become law, this situation led to a constant legislative gridlock. Then, in 2009, the DPJ won a landslide victory in the lower house election and formed the first non-LDP government since 1994. In the July 2010 upper house election, however, the LDP won more seats than the DPJ. Only half of the house's 242 seats are open to contest in each triennial election, and when the newly won seats and those unaffected by this election were combined, the DPJ still had 106 seats to the LDP's 84. When all the seats in the House of Councilors were counted, however, the DPJ and

**single-member district (SMD)**

An electoral district in which only one representative is elected, most commonly by the first-past-the-post method. In a system that uses this method, the candidate who wins the most votes in each district is elected, whether or not he or she wins an absolute majority of the votes.

**proportional representation (PR)**

A system of political representation in which seats are allocated to parties within multimember constituencies, roughly in proportion to the votes each party receives. PR usually encourages the election to parliament of more political parties than single-member-district winner-take-all systems.

| Table 5.4 | Percentage Shares of Seats and Proportional Representation Votes by Party | | | | | | |
|---|---|---|---|---|---|---|---|
| | Lower House | | | | Upper House | | |
| | Seats % | | Votes % | | Seats % | | Votes % | |
| | 2005 | 2009 | 2005 | 2009 | 2007 | 2010 | 2007 | 2010 |
| Liberal Democratic Party | 61.6 | 24.8 | 38.2 | 26.7 | 30.6 | 42.1 | 28.1 | 24.1 |
| Democratic Party of Japan | 23.5 | 64.2 | 31.0 | 42.4 | 49.6 | 36.4 | 39.5 | 31.6 |
| Clean Government Party | 6.4 | 4.4 | 13.3 | 11.5 | 7.4 | 7.4 | 13.2 | 13.1 |
| Japan Communist Party | 1.9 | 1.9 | 7.3 | 7.0 | 2.5 | 2.5 | 7.5 | 6.1 |
| Social Democratic Party | 1.5 | 1.5 | 5.5 | 4.3 | 1.7 | 1.7 | 4.5 | 3.8 |
| Other parties & independents | 3.5 | ? | 4.7 | 8.1 | 8.3 | ? | 6.3 | 21.3 |

*Sources:* Government of Japan, Ministry of Internal Affairs and Communications, website: http://www.soumu.go.jp/senkyo/senkyo_s/data/index.html.

its coalition partner, the People's New Party, were outnumbered by the opposition 133 to 109. This created a twisted Diet for the second time. This situation was thus the exact reverse of its predecessor of three years before. Both were dramatic signs of the growing volatility in Japanese electoral and party politics.

The experiences of the electoral upsets in 1993 and especially in 2007 and 2010 suggest that Japanese politics has metamorphosed from an uncommonly stable **predominant-party regime** to an unstable and unpredictable two-party-dominant system. The change may have turned Japan into a more "normal" democratic state, but it has also seriously burdened the country with problems and challenges of an increasingly independent, active, impatient electorate and an ever-present and very outspoken mass media.

Until the late 1980s, voter turnout fluctuated between 68 and 77 percent in lower house elections and 57 and 75 percent in upper house elections. Turnout rates hit low points in the mid-1990s, a period characterized by a series of political corruption scandals, at about 60 percent for the House of Representatives and 45 percent for the House of Councilors. The rates subsequently recovered to 69 percent in the 2009 lower house election and 58 percent in the 2010 upper house election.

**predominant-party regime**

A multiparty political system in which one party maintains a predominant position in parliament and control of government for a long period of time.

## Political Culture, Citizenship, and Identity

Compared to most other countries in today's world, Japan is an ethnically and culturally homogeneous country, and its citizens have a very well-developed sense of national identity. This identity was molded into a strong and aggressive nationalist ideology before World War II, when Japan attempted to build a colonial empire in East Asia. Japan's defeat in World War II put an end to the country's aggressive nationalism and dreams of empire building. The strong sense of national identity, however, remains an important feature of Japanese political culture.

Most Japanese are nominally Shintoist or Buddhist, but many are counted as both. As a result, there are about 107 million self-proclaimed Shintoists and nearly 98 million Buddhists, for a total of 205 million, in the nation of 127 million or so total population, without even counting about 3 million Christians and 10 million affiliated with other religious groups.

Shinto has been historically identified with the imperial family and, in prewar Japan, it was the orthodox state religion and used by the government to nurture the idea of a unique family-nation ruled and protected by descendants of its original divine creator. The postwar Japanese constitution, like its U.S. model, provides for the separation of state and religion. The only explicitly political organization affiliated with a particular religion in postwar Japan is the Buddhist-affiliated Clean Government Party, which was the LDP's coalition government partner from 2000 to 2009, but has won on its own less than one-eighth of the total vote in any recent Diet election.

The Japanese are among the best-schooled people in the world. Six-year elementary and three-year lower secondary school education is compulsory, and virtually all children finish. Moreover, over 95 percent of lower secondary school graduates go to three-year upper secondary schools, and over half of upper secondary school graduates attend and graduate from four-year universities. Schools are predominantly public, and private schools differ little from public schools in either organization or curriculum. All schools use similar textbooks in all subject areas, thanks to a national textbook certification system. All drafts of textbooks must be submitted to the Ministry of Education, Science, Sports, and Culture for inspection, often resulting in extensive revisions, before they can be adopted for use in schools.

Japan boasts publication of 2.5 newspapers per person, 78,000 new books per year, and over 4,000 monthly magazines. Japan's mainstream mass media tend to be politically and socially passive and noncommittal by American standards, due mainly to the importance of advertising as a revenue source and to the influence of "press clubs." A press club consists of one or more reporters from each accredited member newspaper, television station, radio station, or news service agency. Each club is provided with office space by the organization it covers, and its members gather information mainly from the organization's official spokespersons. A reporter who seeks unofficial information risks losing good standing with the host organization and even club membership. The system works to suppress publication of news critical of the organizations concerned, such as a government ministry or a major firm.[14] Moreover, all major Japanese newspapers and privately owned television and radio stations depend heavily on advertisements and tend to avoid publishing information that might alienate their advertisers.

The major Japanese political parties publish their own newspapers. The JCP's *Akahata* (Red Flag) is the largest in circulation, with some 300,000 subscribers for its daily edition and about 1,400,000 subscribers for its Sunday edition as of 2010, followed by the CGP's *Komei* (Clean Government) with 800,000 subscribers, the LDP's *Jiyuminshu* (Liberal Democracy) with about 680,000 subscribers, the SDP's *Shakai Shimpo* (social news) with 150,000 subscribers, and the DPJ's *Press Minshu* (Democracy Press) with about 70,000 subscribers. Unlike the mainstream commercial newspapers, these partisan papers are far more politically articulate and assertive, but are read only by very small numbers of partisan readers.

The ethnic and cultural homogeneity of Japanese society has been gradually eroded by its increasing contact with the outside world, especially since the late twentieth century when the process of globalization significantly intensified. Compared with the developed nations of North America and Western Europe, however, Japan remains far less physically exposed to and penetrated by foreign influences. The number of resident foreigners in Japan in 2010, for example, was slightly over 2 million, or about 1.6 percent of Japan's total population. Moreover, nearly a third of these foreigners were Chinese, a little over a quarter Koreans, and about 15 percent Japanese Brazilians and Peruvians. In other words, about 70 percent of resident foreigners have ethnic and cultural backgrounds shared with or very similar to the Japanese.

# Interests, Social Movements, and Protests

### Environmental and Energy Issues

The environmental protection movement in postwar Japan emerged in the 1950s and 1960s as a series of sporadic local protests against the extreme, often lethal, pollution of water, soil, and air, which resulted mainly from rapidly expanding industrial and mining operations and caused serious illnesses and fatalities among the affected local populations. Three particularly serious water pollution cases and one air pollution case from that period led to widely publicized litigation, collectively known as the **Four Great Pollution Trials**, which all ended in the plaintiffs' victory in the early 1970s. These trials and the public outrage over these and other similar cases moved the Diet to enact a set of stiff anti-pollution laws.[15]

The nation had since been spared an environmental disaster as serious as any of these cases until March 2011, although the overall level of the pollution of air, water, and soil in the nation had not substantially declined. As public attention shifted increasingly to other pressing or looming economic and social issues in the

**Four Great Pollution Trials**

Include a mercury poisoning case in Minamata City, thus known as the Minamata Disease, a very similar case in another city, thus known as the Second Minamata Disease, a cadmium poisoning case known as the *itai-itai* (ouch-ouch) disease, and a case of severe asthma caused by inhalation of sulfur dioxide that occurred in Yokkaichi City, hence known as the Yokkaichi Asthma.

post-bubble "lost decades," environmental issues had been pushed onto back burners, and the environmental protection movement had run out of steam.

Japan was the host for the December 1997 Conference of the Parties to the United Nations Framework Convention on Climate Change (UNFCCC), which adopted the Kyoto Protocol that aimed to get governments to commit to reducing greenhouse gases. Since then, however, Japan had been the worst laggard among advanced industrial nations in the global effort to reduce greenhouse gasses and halt climate change.

Japan is one of the world's major users of nuclear energy, with fifty-four reactors supplying about 30 percent of the electric power used in the country in early 2011. Still, a number of local communities and governments have objected to the construction of reactors in their own backyards. The opposition was particularly intense in the wake of accidents, in 1997 and 1999, at one of Japan's major nuclear power plant sites, **Tokai Village**. In more recent years, however, the concern about hazards associated with nuclear reactors had substantially diminished, until an accident far more catastrophic than the Tokai Village disaster occurred in March 2011, at one of the two nuclear plants owned and operated by Tokyo Electric Power Company (TEPCO) on the Pacific coast of Fukushima Prefecture.

While the 2011 accident was a result of an earthquake and tsunamis it triggered, both clearly natural disasters, TEPCO had been explicitly warned by several independent scientists that an earthquake and tsunamis of a comparable scale had hit the same region in the year 869, and possibly also a millennium or so earlier, and that there was a distinct possibility that another would strike in the future. The warning had been apparently ignored by TEPCO, which had kept insisting that its plants could withstand the biggest conceivable earthquake of magnitude 8.6 and whatever tsunamis any earthquake could trigger in the region. Moreover, TEPCO's position had been endorsed by the government, which had approved in February 2011 the renewal of the company's permit to operate those plants for the next ten years.

What happened on March 11, 2011, shocked the entire nation so profoundly that it was bound to lead to a wholesale review and revision of Japan's energy and environmental policies in general and nuclear power development policy in particular. In light of its real and acute need for new and accessible sources of energy, the nation will face an excruciating dilemma in such a review. However, the immensity of the disaster and tragedy the nation experienced in the spring of 2011 will not allow its government and people to avoid confronting and resolving the dilemma one way or another.

**Tokai Village**

A seaside community lying about 145 kilometers northeast of Tokyo that is Japan's major nuclear research center that hosts reprocessing and enrichment plants. It is also known as the site of the two serious nuclear accidents the nation has experienced.

## Former Outcaste Class

The discrimination against and physical segregation of Japan's outcaste class dates back to the pre–Tokugawa era and survived until after World War II. For centuries, members of the class were condemned to pariah status and lived in ghettos, called *Buraku* (hamlets) and known in recent times as "discriminated hamlets" or "unliberated hamlets." The discrimination and segregation were legally abolished more than a century ago, in the wake of the Meiji Restoration, but the prejudice persisted.[16]

In the 1970s, a series of laws was passed to help eliminate the approximately 4,600 discriminated hamlets that still existed and integrate the more than 1 million residents into the broader national community. Since then, considerable improvement has been made in the economic conditions of former outcaste communities, but complete equality and full integration into the national community remain goals yet to be fulfilled.

## Women's Movement

The movement to improve the social and political status of women dates back to the early part of the Meiji period. Japan's first major women's organization was the Tokyo Women's Temperance Union, founded in 1886, which campaigned mainly for the abolition of prostitution. The Bluestocking Society, formed in 1911 by a group of younger women writers, attacked the traditional patriarchal family system and called for the expansion of educational and professional opportunities for women.

The Taisho Democracy era after World War I saw the birth of women's organizations more explicitly committed to achieving gender equality in politics. The Society of New Women founded in 1920 successfully lobbied the Imperial Diet to amend the Peace and Police Law, a 1900 law, which prohibited women's participation in political parties and other political organizations. This was followed by the formation of Japan's first suffragist organization in 1924 and its first openly socialist women's organization in 1929. In the militarist climate of the 1930s, however, all of these liberal women's organizations were disbanded and replaced by organizations promoting the traditional status and role of women as good homemakers, wives, and mothers.

The emancipation of women was one of the most important goals of the postwar reforms undertaken during the Allied Occupation. Japanese women were enfranchised for the first time and began to participate actively in politics as voters. Numerous women's organizations were founded. Informal, and often covert, discrimination against women, however, still remains a conspicuous characteristic of contemporary Japanese society and politics.

According to the 2009 edition of the United Nations *Human Development Report* (HDR), Japan ranked 10th in the Human Development Index (HDI), which measures overall quality of economic and physical life, among 182 nations. But, according to the 2009 edition of the World Economic Forum's *Global Gender Gap Report*, which measures degrees of gender equality, Japan ranked 101st among 134 nations. Japan has a very long way to go to achieve gender equality.

"Japan Lagging in Gender Equality" (An old Japanese saying instructed women to walk three steps behind men).

*Source:* Roger Dahl, "Dahl's Japan" *Japan Times*, October 24, 2010: http://www.japantimes.co.jp/life/cartoons/ca20101024ed.html.

## Ethnic Minorities: Ainu, Okinawans, Koreans, and New Immigrants

Japan is a homogeneous society in comparison with most other nations, but identity issues have been of considerable concern to the ethnic minority known as the Ainu, those from Japan's southernmost island prefecture, Okinawa, and Koreans and other resident foreigners.

The Ainu are descendants of the ancient hunter-gatherers believed to have once inhabited the greater part of the northern regions of Japan. With their distinct language and culture, they were treated as a quasi-foreign community before the Meiji Restoration. They traditionally had no concept or institution of private property, and during the Meiji period, when they began to be treated as integral members of the Japanese nation, they lost their communally owned land to immigrants from other regions of the country. They were also forced to abandon hunting by government decree. Most Ainu fell into extreme poverty. As the number of non-Ainu immigrants in their home territories grew, intermarriage increased. Today, as few as about 25,000 and as many as 200,000 Japanese are believed to have some Ainu blood, but no accurate and reliable statistics exist.

Until the late 1990s, the Ainu were, in theory, protected by an archaic 1899 law. In 1994, an Ainu scholar and author filled a vacancy in the upper house of the Diet left by a deceased JSP member and was instrumental in the enactment of the 1997 Law to Promote Ainu Culture, which replaced the Meiji law.

The pre-Meiji status of the people in Japan's southernmost island chain, the prefecture of Okinawa, was somewhat similar to the Ainus'. They were subjects of the Kingdom of the Ryukyus, a state under Chinese suzerainty until the early seventeenth century, when it was invaded and occupied by a military force sent by the lord of a Japanese feudal domain in southern Kyushu and came under ambiguous dual suzerainty of Qing China and Tokugawa Japan. The Meiji government unilaterally incorporated the island kingdom into the newly created system of local administration in 1879.

Like the Ainu, Okinawans, with their own distinctive language and culture, have faced prejudice and discrimination. Throughout its history, Okinawa has remained the poorest prefecture in the country in terms of per capita income. In the three-month-long Battle of Okinawa, by far the bloodiest fought between Japanese and U.S. forces within Japanese territory at the end of World War II, about two-thirds of the approximately 190,000 Japanese killed or missing were Okinawans and nearly 80 percent of them were civilians.

After the war ended in August 1945, Okinawa was administratively separated from the rest of the country, placed under U.S. military rule, and turned into a key outpost of U.S. forces during the cold war. The island prefecture was returned to Japanese administration in 1972, but it remains host to three-quarters of the U.S. military bases in Japan. These bases take up 10 percent of its land area, which accounts for only 0.6 percent of Japan's territory. Moreover, it still ranks at the bottom of the nation's forty-seven prefectures in per capita income. The Okinawan identity as an ethnic minority has considerably weakened over the years, but neither their collective historical memories nor their grievances about their present economic conditions, political status, and especially the United States military bases, have declined.

After the Meiji Restoration and especially after Japan annexed Korea in 1910, many Koreans migrated to Japan. Initially, most came voluntarily. By the 1930s, however, they were increasingly brought by force to work in some of the nation's most poorly equipped and accident-prone factories and mines. At the end of World War II,

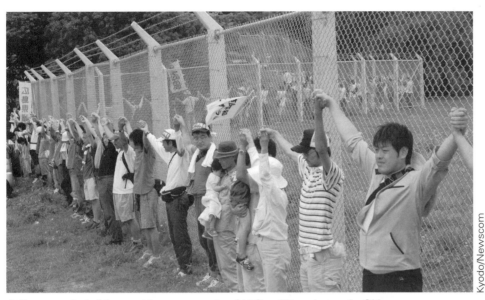

A "human chain" formed by opponents of U.S. military bases in Okinawa.

*Source: Yomiuri Online,* at http://www.yomiuri.co.jp/politics/photograph/garticle. htm?ge=761&gr=2459&id=70906.

more than 2 million Koreans were living in Japan. A majority returned to South or North Korea, but approximately 650,000 stayed in Japan.[17]

Unlike some other states, such as the United States, that grant citizenship, as a rule, to any person born within their territories regardless of their parents' citizenship status based on the *jus soli* ("right of the soil") principle, Japan grants citizenship to anyone born of a parent who is a Japanese citizen regardless of where he or she is born, but to nobody else except through naturalization based on the *jus sanguinis* ("right of blood") principle. Moreover, Japan does not permit dual citizenship. Most of the million or so ethnic Koreans who currently live in Japan were born of Korean parents and therefore were denied Japanese citizenship at birth. A minority of them have applied for and acquired Japanese citizenship after they reached the legally required age of 20. The majority, estimated to be about 590,000, remain resident aliens. About 410,000, or 70 percent, of them are recognized as having been colonial Japanese citizens before 1945 or their descendants and are entitled to permanent residence in Japan. Like other alien residents, however, these Koreans cannot vote in Japanese elections, nor receive publicly funded social security or pension benefits.

The most important and difficult problems related to ethnic minorities are no longer physical hardships or material deprivations inflicted on them by deliberate government policy. In fact, many former minority enclaves have received generous financial assistance from both the national and local governments during the last three decades. The core issue facing the minorities is the social and cultural discrimination they continue to experience, especially in employment and marriage.

Like many other advanced industrial societies, contemporary Japan attracts foreign workers, most of whom enter the country legally, but who often overstay their visas. As of 2008, about 925,000 foreign workers, mainly from Asia, were employed in Japan, nearly 20 percent of them illegally. These immigrant workers are increasingly indispensable to many Japanese businesses suffering from chronic shortages of young and cheap labor. Unlike the situation in some European countries with much higher percentages of foreign workers and much higher unemployment rates, no organized violence against foreign workers by Japanese citizens has yet been reported.

Introduced as an integral component of the Occupation-sponsored democratization program, the postwar Japanese labor movement was initially led by left-leaning public service unions allied with the Socialist and Communist parties. At the peak of its strength in 1949, the movement boasted 35,000 unions with 6.6 million members, representing about 55 percent of the nation's total urban labor force, engaging in frequent, and often violent, actions against management, and winning major concessions over wages and working conditions for the members. As the nation's postwar economic reconstruction progressed and its living conditions steadily improved in the next few decades, until most Japanese families came to identify themselves as middle class, the labor movement lost not only its militancy but its effective grip on rank and file workers. The rate of unionization had fallen to one-third of the total urban labor force by the mid-1970s, to one-quarter by the mid-1990s, and to less than one-fifth by 2010. The number of labor disputes involving organized strikes or walkouts lasting for more than a half day, or four hours, peaked in the mid-1970s at about 5,200 per year and plummeted thereafter, until it fell below 100 by the first year of the twenty-first century. Acrimonious, not to mention violent, labor disputes have been virtually absent from the Japan of the "Lost Decades," when over a third of the nation's urban labor force consists of nonunion temporary and part-time employees.

# SECTION 5 JAPANESE POLITICS IN TRANSITION

## Focus Questions

How has the March 2011 earthquake disaster affected Japanese politics and political economy?

Why is the graying population one of Japan's most serious problems?

How has mounting public debt become a major challenge facing the Japanese government?

What are the main costs and benefits of frequent government turnovers?

# Political Challenges and Changing Agendas

At the time of this writing just a month after the mega earthquake struck, Japan is desperately struggling to bring the radiation-spewing crippled nuclear reactors under control, while searching for bodies in the rubble in the stricken region, caring for the well over 170,000 survivors still living at shelters across the nation, and beginning to plan to rebuild the severely damaged regional and national economy and society. Many of Japan's best known manufacturing companies, such as Toyota and Sony, have suspended operations at their plants in the region, due mainly to power blackouts and shipment difficulties, causing cancellations and delays in the delivery of their name-brand products to both domestic and overseas markets. They are trying, with considerable difficulty, to get their production and delivery schedules back on track and minimize their sales losses. The entire nation is in a trauma amidst an unfolding disaster, the long-term economic and political consequences of which are still unknown.

There are, however, a few consequences of transitional, if not transformative, significance that have already become fairly discernible. First, the disaster has cost the nation far more than any other natural disaster has ever cost it, to the tune of $200 billion or more, and the bulk of the cost will have to be paid by the Japanese government; that is, taxpayers, who are already deep in debt and mired in a two-decade long recession. This additional financial burden is bound to further sap Japan's economic strength and worsen its citizens' condition of life.

Second, the nuclear disaster has revealed serious inadequacies in the regulatory system in operation in the Japanese nuclear power industry. TEPCO, the owner and operator of the damaged nuclear plant, had apparently been left to run its plants and nuclear reactors pretty much as it deemed fit, with little effective oversight by the government watchdog, the Nuclear and Industrial Safety Agency (NISA). As implicitly admitted by Prime Minister Kan Naoto and his cabinet in the wake of the disaster, the problem was, at least partly, that the NISA was a regulatory arm of the Agency for Natural Resources and Energy (ANRE), which was essentially the public custodian of the entire energy industry with a more collusive than regulatory relationship with the industry and its member firms. The iron triangle alliance of ANRE bureaucrats, industry leaders, and the mostly LDP Atomic Power Tribe politicians in the Diet had effectively neutralized and corrupted NISA as a public watchdog agency and ensured that TEPCO and other nuclear power companies were largely left alone to run their potentially unsafe nuclear plants. The March 2011 disaster is bound to lead the Japanese public and the DPJ government to question, and possibly reform, this ineffectual and dangerous regulatory regime.

Finally, the disaster was nearly as shocking to peoples and governments in other nations as to Japanese, thanks importantly to the news, photographs, and videos of the frightening scenes of the triple disaster transmitted virtually instantly from the Japanese coastal towns and villages to far corners of the world. The shock quickly turned into sympathy and solidarity and offers of support and help to Japanese people in general and victims in particular. Within a few days of the disaster, nearly 100 governments and international organizations offered various forms of assistance, represented most dramatically by a huge group of warships, military aircraft, and soldiers dispatched almost overnight by the United States, and search and rescue teams dispatched by a dozen nations, including the United States, Australia, New Zealand, Germany, Turkey, South Korea, and Singapore. Others, including China and Russia, readily offered technical and monetary assistance. The American Red Cross collected and passed to its Japanese counterpart $120 million in less than three weeks. This spectacle of a worldwide campaign to help them in their time of crisis was something Japanese had never experienced before. The unprecedented experience has left such a profound and lasting impact on so many Japanese that their images of themselves and the world they live in will likely become far less parochial and susceptible to chauvinist propaganda and far more trusting of other peoples' basic goodwill and humanity than previously. This may well prove to be one positive long-term consequence of the national crisis and tragedy of spring 2011.

Even before the earthquakes and tsunamis shook Japan, the country faced several serious social, economic, and political challenges. The rapid aging of the nation's population is one of those challenges. Japan has the world's second-longest average life expectancy: 79.0 years for men and 86.1 for women in 2010. At the same time, Japan's birthrate of 7.87 per 1,000 population (2008) is the lowest in the world. As a result of these two trends, Japan now has a higher percentage of citizens 65 years old and over than any other country. This has led to a sharp rise in the cost of health care for elderly people and a significant shortfall in the number of younger, productive workers.

The May 2010 monthly demographic report of the Japanese Ministry of Internal Affairs and Communications showed that the number of minors under 15 years old in Japan was about 1,694,000, or 13.3 percent of Japan's total population. The percentage share of this age group had been steadily declining over the last three decades, at accelerating rates in recent years. Back in 1950, under-15-year-olds had accounted for more than one-third of the nation's total population. The ranks of that age group fell below those of 65 years old and over for the first time in 1997. The elderly now account for 23 percent of the total population, or nearly 10 percent more than minors. This makes Japan one of the fastest graying nations in the world, roughly equal to Germany or Italy, but much faster aging than the United States or China. The question many Japanese ask is: Who will be providing for the rapidly growing ranks of the elderly and how?

Prompted by a widespread public shock over the fall of the total fertility rate to a historical low of 1.57 in 1990—thus known as the "1.57 shock"—the Japanese government set up a special four-minister task force in 1994 to devise and implement a series of legislative, budgetary, and administrative steps to reverse, or at least halt, the alarming trend. These initially emphasized financial support for the construction and maintenance of local day care centers and nursery schools, but have subsequently been expanded to include a variety of assistance to mothers and would-be mothers, delivered, as a rule, through local governments, such as providing free or subsidized prenatal and postnatal care and services.

In 1999, the cabinet-level task force was expanded to a six-minister group. Since the turn of the millennium, prefectural and municipal governments have begun to initiate a number of similar programs and projects on their own, such as funding special discounts for pregnant women at designated retail stores. In the 2006–2007 fiscal year, the combined spending by the national and local governments on the problem of "birthrate decline" rose to about $1 billion. However, all these government efforts have not resulted in higher birth or total fertility rates.

In the meantime, the growing, but so far ineffectual, public spending for birthrate-boosting efforts substantially adds to the national and local governments' overall annual spending for social security–related programs and to the chronic and mounting government debt, which is another very serious challenge the nation faces. The situation is particularly alarming in light of the failure of the succession of governments to regain control of the national economy, which was lost more than two decades ago when the financial bubble formed, ballooned, then popped to plunge Japan into deep and seemingly endless recession. Over the last two decades, Japan's GDP has grown by 19 percent and its annual national government's budget by 28 percent, while the annual government spending for social security-related programs has grown by 95 percent, or nearly doubled. As a result, the Japanese government budget has been chronically in deficit, which has been routinely covered by newly issued government bonds, the accumulated amount of the public debts has steadily increased, and debt service has inevitably claimed an increasing share of the annual government budget.

In fact, the prospects for Japan's economy look grimmer, even without counting the costs of recovery from the March 2011 disaster. According to the Japanese Cabinet Office's statistics, the nation's GDP did not grow but declined in 2008 and 2009, by –3.7 and –2.0 percent respectively. As mentioned in Section 2, the amount of the outstanding national government debt was nearly double Japan's GDP, or about $84,000 per citizen, in mid-2010.

The outstanding public debt seriously constrains government activities and compromises the overall quality of life. Recent cabinets have therefore tried seriously to increase revenue and cut spending. In 1989, the effort to increase revenue had led to the introduction of a 3 percent national value-added tax, officially called consumption tax. The rate was raised to 5 percent in 1997 and another rise to 10 percent has recently been proposed both by the LDP and, informally, by the DPJ. A serious effort to cut spending has also been under way since the 1980s and significantly accelerated under the DPJ government. In the fall of 2009, a series of systematic and rigorous evaluations and "culling" of all government agencies and their affiliated organizations and their programs was launched, with a view to eliminating or scaling down as many nonessential entities and programs as possible. Both these efforts, however, have so far made no tangible dent in the enormous government debt problem, much less in the stagnant state of the general economy.

The sorry state of the Japanese economy and government finance inevitably affects its international economic role and status. Once touted as the world's most dynamic industrial economy, Japan ranked only twenty-seventh on the 2010 relative economic competitiveness list of fifty-eight-nations, compiled by the International Institute for Management Development of Lausanne, Switzerland, below all Asian countries except India and the Philippines, not to mention all other state-members of the Group of Eight (G8) large economies other than Russia. Japan was the largest donor of official development assistance (ODA) funds throughout the 1990s, but, according to the Japanese Ministry of Foreign Affairs statistics, fell by 2009 to the fifth rank below the United States, France, Germany, and Britain.

Another serious challenge today's Japan faces concerns the quality and operation of its democratic institutions, particularly its parliamentary and electoral systems. Under the LDP's seemingly unassailable and permanent one-party rule from the mid-1950s to the mid-1990s, Japan was an "uncommon democracy," sometimes cited, albeit incorrectly, as a prime example of a young and immature democracy. It had not experienced two changes of ruling parties, which was seen by many political scientists as a key test of the consolidation of a country's democracy.[18] Even after it was driven out of power in 1993, the LDP quickly managed to return to power and stay in power for another decade and a half, although only in coalition with one or more other parties.

But, with the turnover of ruling parties since the mid-1990s, Japanese democracy has now clearly passed the **"two turnover" test of consolidation**. On the other hand, the extremely short lifespan of nearly all cabinets in recent years raises serious questions about their ability to perform their executive functions and the party or parties in power to perform their legislative functions.

The quick cabinet turnovers have resulted mainly from the extreme, unpredictable swings in the electoral fortunes of the major political parties, which in turn reflect fast shifting voter preferences and behavior. The temporary, and often fleeting, support for a particular party's candidates by an increasingly independent electorate may lead the party to an unforeseen victory, but it may, and often does, swing to a rival party in the next election.

Independent voters tend to be more demanding and critical of a current government and its performance. Elections subject to the decisive influence of such voters tend inevitably to favor turnovers in winning parties, changes in cabinets, and short life spans for cabinets. Frequent turnovers often produce a divided government with different parties controlling important parts of the government. As the recent experiences of Japan and the United States show, this can enormously complicate the business of government.

**two-turnover test of democratic consolidation**

A test proposed by Samuel P. Huntington in *The Third Wave: Democratization in the Late Twentieth Century* (1991), which requires a new democratic regime born of a recent transition from authoritarianism to experience two peaceful changes in the party or parties in power before it is considered a consolidated, or viable, democracy.

# Japanese Politics in Comparative Perspective

Japan thus faces a number of extremely complex and seemingly intractable political, economic, and social challenges. In broader comparative perspective, however, few of them are unique to Japan. Its graying population problem may be acute, but it is nearly as serious in most advanced industrial nations, especially in Western Europe, and increasingly even elsewhere in East Asia, as in South Korea and China. Japan's economic and fiscal problems, such as low and falling growth rates and growing budget deficits, are also widely shared by most high-income countries, including the United States. They all find it as excruciatingly difficult and have by and large so far failed, as Japan has, to either deeply cut public spending, or substantially increase revenue, especially by tax increases. Natural disasters such as earthquakes and tsunamis, and even those caused by humans, such as accidents at nuclear power plants, pose as real and great threats to many other nations as to Japan.

Most, if not all, of the serious challenges the country faces today are thus not unique to Japan. What separates Japan from other established democracies, however, is the roots of its contemporary democracy itself and its unique constitutional pacifism. These were both planned and planted by the post–World War II Allied Occupation authorities in the wake of history's biggest and bloodiest conflict, which ended with the total annihilation of two major cities by the only nuclear weapons ever used in war. The roots of democracy and pacifism planted in soil of a nation fresh with memories of the horrors of war have grown for more than six decades. Contemporary Japan is unique among nations in its official and public commitment to antimilitarism, and the democratic idea is deeply embedded in its political culture.

## Key Terms

shogun
*bushi* (samurai)
Taisho Democracy
*zaibatsu*
Supreme Commander for the Allied Powers (SCAP)
Self-Defense Forces (SDF)
Asian Development Bank (ADB)
Asia-Pacific Economic Cooperation (APEC)
Association of Southeast Asian Nations (ASEAN)

industrial policy
administrative guidance
*keiretsu*
newly industrialized countries (NICs)
nontariff barriers (NTBs)
*amakudari*
"Lay Judge System" (*saibanin-seido*)
*zoku*
pork-barrel politics
clientelism (or patron-client networks)

Single Non-Transferable Vote (SNTV)
*koenkai*
Mixed Member Proportional (MMP)
single-member district (SMD)
proportional representation (PR)
predominant-party regime
Four Great Pollution Trials
Tokai Village
two-turnover test of democratic consolidation

## Suggested Readings

Amyx, Jennifer A. *Japan's Financial Crisis: Institutional Rigidity and Reluctant Change*. Princeton, N.J.: Princeton University Press, 2004.

Barnhard, Michael A. *Japan Prepares for Total War: The Search for Economic Security, 1919–1941*. Ithaca, N.Y.: Cornell University Press, 1987.

Calder, Kent E. *Crisis and Compensation: Public Policy and Political Stability in Japan, 1949–1986*. Princeton, N.J.: Princeton University Press, 1988.

Cargill, Thomas F., and Takayuki Sakamoto. *Japan since 1980*. New York: Cambridge University Press, 2008.

Cargill, Thomas F., and Naoyuki Yoshino. *Postal Savings and Fiscal Investment in Japan: The PSS and the FILP*. Oxford: Oxford University Press, 2003.

Colignon, Richard A., and Chikako Usui. *Amakudari: The Hidden Fabric of Japan's Economy*. Ithaca, N.Y., and London: Cornell University Press, 2003.

Curtis, Gerald L. *The Logic of Japanese Politics: Leaders, Institutions, and the Limits of Change*. New York: Columbia University Press, 1999.

Dower, John. *Embracing Defeat: Japan in the Aftermath of World War II*. London: Penguin Books, 1999.

Gluck, Carol. *Japan's Modern Myths: Ideology in the Late Meiji Period*. Princeton, N.J.: Princeton University Press, 1985.

Hall, John Whitney, et al., eds., *The Cambridge History of Japan*, 6 vols. Cambridge: Cambridge University Press, 1988–1993.

Hook, Glenn D., et al. *Japan's International Relations: Politics, Economics and Security*. London: Routledge, 2001.

Kohno, Masaru. *Japan's Postwar Party Politics*. Princeton, N.J.: Princeton University Press, 1997.

Leonardsen, Dag. *Japan as a Low-Crime Nation*. Houndmills, UK: Palgrave Macmillan, 2004.

Lockwood, William W. *The Economic Development of Japan: Growth and Structural Change, 1868–1938.* Princeton, N.J.: Princeton University Press, 1954.

McVeigh, Brian J. *Nationalisms of Japan: Managing and Mystifying Identity.* Lanham, MD.: Rowman and Littlefield, 2004.

Pempel, T. J. *Regime Shift: Comparative Dynamics of the Japanese Political Economy.* Ithaca, N.Y.: Cornell University Press, 1998.

Samuels, Richard J. *Securing Japan: Tokyo's Grand Strategy and the Future of East Asia.* Ithaca, N.Y.: Cornell University Press, 2007.

Stockwin, J. A. A. *Governing Japan: Divided Politics in a Resurgent Economy,* 4th ed. Oxford: Blackwell, 2008.

Upham, Frank K. *Law and Social Change in Postwar Japan.* Cambridge: Harvard University Press, 1987.

Vogel, Steven K. *Japan Remodeled: How Government and Industry are Reforming Japanese Capitalism.* Ithaca, N.Y.: Cornell University Press, 2006.

## Suggested Websites

*Asahi Shimbun,* a newspaper
**www.asahi.com/english**

Cabinet Office, Government of Japan
**www.cao.go.jp/index-e.html**

*Daily Yomiuri Online,* a newspaper
**www.yomiuri.co.jp/dy**

Japan Guide
**jguide.stanford.edu**

Japan Politics Central
**jpcentral.virginia.edu**

Nikkei Net International, economic news
**www.nni.Nikkei.co.jp**

Portal Site of Official Statistics of Japan
**http://www.e-stat.go.jp/SG1/estat/eStatTopPortalE.do**

Prime Minister of Japan and His Cabinet
**http://kantei.go.jp/foreign/index-e.html**

*The Mainichi Daily News,* a newspaper
**http://mdn.mainichi.jp**

# 6 India

Atul Kohli and Amrita Basu

AP Photo/Kevin Frayer

**Official Name:** Republic of India (Bharat)

**Location:** South Asia

**Capital City:** New Delhi

**Population (2011):** 1.2 billion

**Size:** 3,287,590 sq. km.; slightly more than one-third the size of the United States

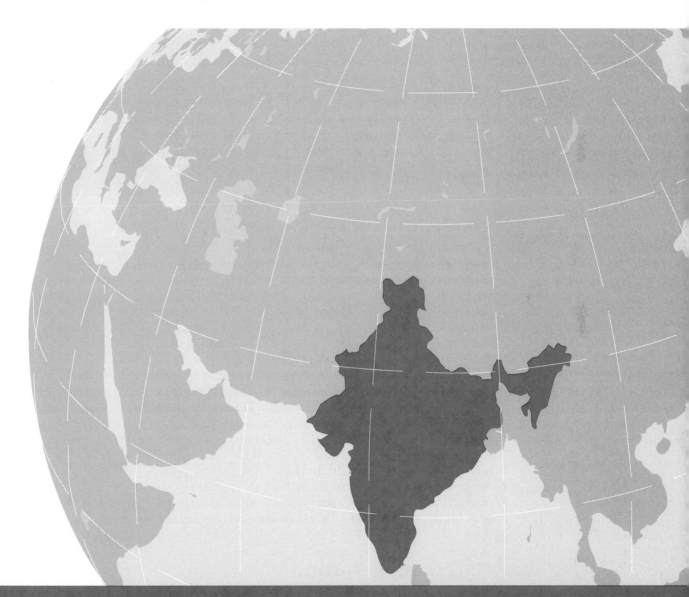

| | | | | | | | |
|---|---|---|---|---|---|---|---|
| **1526** Mughal dynasty founded. | | | | | | **1757** Britain establishes informal colonial rule. | |
| 1500 | 1550 | 1600 | 1650 | 1700 | 1750 | 1800 | |

**1612–1690**
British East India Company establishes trading stations at Surat, Bombay, and Calcutta.

# SECTION 1

# THE MAKING OF THE MODERN INDIAN STATE

## Focus Questions

What accounts for India's ability to maintain democratic institutions for most of its post-independence history?

What lessons does India hold for the prospects of establishing democracy in multiethnic societies?

## Politics in Action

Political and economic developments in India continue to be a study in contrasts. Over the last three decades India has had among the world's fastest-growing economies. But it also has the largest number of malnourished and illiterate children in the world. As the Commonwealth Games in 2010 revealed, Indian democracy is characterized by government incompetence, inefficiency, and corruption. While the games in the end went off smoothly, a number of other corruption scandals, including vote-buying in parliament exposed by Wikileaks, further tarnished India's image, leading India's eminent industrialist, Ratan Tata, to characterize India—somewhat unfairly—as a "banana republic." But a nationwide anticorruption movement soon followed. "India Against Corruption" galvanized public attention through four million Twitter messages and protests by high-profile Bollywood actors and actresses. Political activist Ana Hazare embarked on a "fast unto death" on April 4, 2011, demanding that the government enact a law that would effectively address corruption in public office. Four days later, the government conceded to his demand and agreed to create a joint committee of state and civil society representatives to draft an effective bill. India's long tradition of democracy has survived and succeeded amidst, despite and through its turbulence.

## Geographic Setting

In area, India is the seventh-largest country in the world and the third-largest country in Asia. It is called a subcontinent because of its large and distinct land mass. India's rich geography includes three diverse topographic zones (the mountainous northern zone, the basin formed by the Ganges River, and the peninsula of southern India) and a variety of climates (mountain climate in the northern mountain range; dry, hot

**1857**
Britain establishes formal colonial rule
in response to Sepoy Rebellion.

**1947**
India achieves independence from Britain; India and
Pakistan are partitioned; modern Indian state is founded.

**1966–1984**
Indira Gandhi is prime minister (except
for a brief period from 1977 to 1980).

1850    1885    1920    1955    1990    2025

**1885**
Indian National Congress is
created.

**1947–1964**
Jawaharlal Nehru is prime
minister.

**2004-present**
Congress Party-dominated
coalition government, the United
Progressive Alliance.

**1999–2004**
Bharatiya Janata Party-dominated
coalition government.

Construction Site for the 2010 Commonwealth Games

AP Photo/Kevin Frayer

weather in the arid, northern plateau; and subtropical climate in the south). Along with Pakistan and Bangladesh, the region is isolated from the rest of Asia by the Himalayas to the north and the Indian Ocean to the east, south, and west. Only the northwest frontier is easily passable and has been used for thousands of years.

With 1.2 billion people, India has the second-largest population in the world, after its neighbor China. Although the Indian economy is growing rapidly, so are the numbers of its inhabitants. Population growth strains physical infrastructure and increases the need for social services, especially when many children are born into poverty. The Indian government's family planning policies have been meager and ineffective.

India is the world's largest democracy and the oldest democracy in Asia, Africa, and Latin America. It has had democratic institutions since it became an independent country in 1947 after nearly two centuries of British colonial rule. The durability of

## Sikhs

Sikhs, a religious minority, constitute less than 2% of the Indian population and 76% of the state of Punjab. Sikhism is a monotheistic religion that was founded in the fifteenth century.

## caste system

India's Hindu society is divided into castes. According to the Hindu religion, membership in a caste is determined at birth. Castes form a rough social and economic hierarchy.

## Brahmin

The highest caste in the Hindu caste system of India.

Indian democracy is especially intriguing considering the country's huge population and enormous social and regional diversity. India has twenty-two official national languages. Hindi, the largest, is spoken by about 30 percent of the population. There are also numerous regional dialects. India contains many different ethnic groups, a host of regionally concentrated tribal groups, and followers of every major religion in the world. In addition to Hindus, who represent 81 percent of the population, India includes Muslims, **Sikhs**, Christians, Jains, Buddhists, and several tiny Jewish communities. India's 160,000,000 Muslims are the third-largest Muslim population in the world, after Indonesia and Pakistan.

Indian society, especially Hindu society, is divided into many caste groupings. Mainly based on occupation, castes tend to be closed social groups into which people are born, marry, and die. Historically, the **caste system** compartmentalized and ranked the Hindu population through rules governing daily life, such as eating, marriage, and prayer. Sanctioned by religion, caste hierarchy is based on a conception of the world as divided into realms of purity and impurity. Each hereditary and endogamous group (that is, a group into which one is born and within which one marries) constitutes a *jati*, which is itself organized by *varna*, or shades of color. The four main *varnas* are the **Brahmin**, or priestly caste; the *Kshatriya*, or warrior and royal caste; the *Vaishyas*, or trading caste; and the *Shudra*, or artisan caste. Each *varna* is divided into many *jatis* that correspond to occupational groups (such as potters, barbers, and carpenters).

Seventy percent of the Indian population lives in far-flung villages in the countryside. However, the major cities, Bombay (renamed Mumbai), Calcutta (renamed Kolkata), and New Delhi, the national capital, are among the largest and most densely populated cities in the world. See Figure 6.1 for more details.

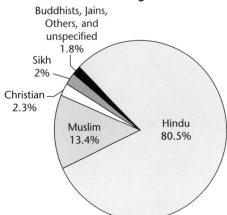

**Religions**

Buddhists, Jains, Others, and unspecified 1.8%
Sikh 2%
Christian 2.3%
Muslim 13.4%
Hindu 80.5%

**Languages**

The Constitution of India recognizes twenty-two national languages, of which Hindi, the primary tongue of about 30% of the population, is the official language of the country. The Constitution also allows for the use of English for official purposes. There are 844 different dialects spoken in various parts of the country.

**Indian Currency**
Rupee (₹)
International Designation: INR
Exchange Rate (2010): US$1 = 46.163 INR
500 Rupee Note Design: Mahatma Gandhi (1869–1948)

**FIGURE 6.1 The Indian Nation at a Glance**

# Critical Junctures

Indian civilization dates back to the Indus Valley Civilization of the third millennium B.C.E. The subcontinent, comprising present-day Pakistan, India, and Bangladesh, has witnessed the rise and fall of many civilizations and empires. Alexander the Great's invasion of northwestern India in 326 B.C.E. introduced trade and communication with western Asia. The Maurya dynasty (322–185 B.C.E.) under Emperor Ashoka then united separate kingdoms in northern India into a single empire. The Mughal kingdom (early sixteenth century to mid-nineteenth century) further expanded to include most of the Indian subcontinent and parts of what is now Afghanistan.

As the Mughal Empire declined, several new states emerged, and independent states that had previously existed expanded. The most important among them formed the Maratha Empire which, at its height, controlled most of central and northern India. Other important regimes in the post-Mughal period include the Sikh Empire in the north, and the Mysore kingdom and state of Hyderabad in the south.

| Table 6.1 | Political Organization |
|-----------|------------------------|
| **Political System** | Parliamentary democracy and a federal republic. |
| **Regime History** | In 2009 the government was formed by the United Progressive Alliance; the Congress Party is the single largest party in the government, and Manmohan Singh is prime minister. |
| **Administrative Structure** | Federal, with twenty-eight state governments. |
| **Executive** | Prime minister, leader of the party or coalition with the most seats in the parliament. |
| **Legislature** | Bicameral, upper house elected indirectly and without much substantial power; lower house, the main house, with members elected from single-member districts, winner-take-all. |
| **Judiciary** | Independent constitutional court with appointed judges. |
| **Party System** | Multiparty system. The Congress Party is the dominant party; the Bharatiya Janata Party (BJP) is the major opposition party. |

Individual princely states were the most authoritative sources of power in precolonial India. However the power of these princely rulers was limited by a powerful social order that they were unable to change.

### The Colonial Legacy (1757–1947)

The British started gaining control of the subcontinent in the late seventeenth and early eighteenth centuries. British influence began when the East India Company, a large English trading organization, developed commercial interests in India. With strong backing from the British Crown, it played off one Indian prince against another. After the **Sepoy Rebellion**, also known as the Mutiny of 1857, a large-scale revolt by Indian soldiers, Britain assumed direct control from the East India Company.

**Sepoy Rebellion**

An armed uprising by Indian soldiers against expansion of British colonialism in India in 1857.

The British described India, its most valuable colonial possession, as the "jewel in the [British] crown." India provided Britain raw materials, most notably cotton, and a profitable market for Britain's growing industry, especially textiles. (Britain dismantled India's own textile industry to create demand for British products.) Colonial rule ended shortly after World War II in 1947, when the Indian nationalist movement succeeded in expelling the British and making India an independent country. India was among the first colonies in the developing world to gain independence.

The British created a relatively efficient administrative structure to control the vast subcontinent. Important instruments included an all-India civil service, police force, and army. At first, only British nationals were permitted to serve in these institutions. Eventually, some educated Indians were permitted to join. The civil administration, police, and armed services in India continue to be organized along the principles the British colonialists established in the nineteenth and twentieth centuries. Britain started constructing a railway system in east India in the 1840s; by 1880, it had created over 9,000 miles of rail lines throughout the country. The rail system continued to grow throughout the twentieth century and is currently the largest in Asia. It continues to be an important and efficient means for transporting people and freight.

### The Nationalist Movement and Partition (1885–1947)

British rulers and traditional rural Indian elites became allies of sorts, squeezing resources from the peasantry to maintain the bureaucratic state and support the conspicuous lifestyles of a parasitic landlord class. However, this exploitative pattern generated growing intellectual and cultural opposition. The growth of commerce, education, and urbanization gave rise to urban, educated upper-caste privileged Indians who resented being treated as second-class citizens. They formed the Indian National Congress (INC) in 1885.

In its early years, the INC periodically met and petitioned British rulers for a greater voice in administering India's affairs. They sought political equality and access to higher administrative offices. Eventually, requests turned into demands. Some nationalists resorted to violence; others adopted a strategy of nonviolent mass mobilization. Thanks to the brilliant and inspiring leadership of Mohandas Gandhi, the INC was able to preserve a fragile unity. Gandhi led India's nationalist movement for decades, and his strategy of militant but nonviolent protest has set a high standard for political activists. Civil rights leader Martin Luther King, Jr., for example, was deeply inspired by Gandhi's example.

As support for the INC grew, the British either had to repress it or make concessions. They tried both. The turning point occurred when Britain's struggle against Nazi Germany increased the political, economic, and symbolic costs of maintaining

**scheduled castes**

The lowest caste in India; also known as the untouchables.

---

## PROFILE

### Mohandas Karamchand Gandhi

Born into a prominent, although poor Bania (merchant caste) family with a tradition of government service, Mohandas Karamchand Gandhi was raised in Porbander, a small town in the Indian state of Gujarat. He married at the age of thirteen, and after completing his secondary schooling, traveled to Great Britain to pursue a university education. Gandhi studied law in London for two years and then moved to Durban, South Africa, where he worked as a lawyer and activist for twenty-one years. While in South Africa, he developed the political strategy of nonviolence or *satyagraha* (grasp of truth) as a means of defending the rights of South Africa's Indian population. On his return to India in 1915, he transformed the Indian National Congress into a mass party by recruiting the urban and rural poor, non-Hindu religious groups, and members of **scheduled castes**, whom he called *Harijans*, or Children of God. When the British massacred civilians in a peaceful demonstration at Jallianwala Bagh in the Punjab in April 1919, Gandhi and his close associate, Jawaharlal Nehru,

organized a noncooperation movement. This involved a boycott of British legal and educational institutions as well as British merchandise in favor of *swadeshi*, or indigenous goods. Under Gandhi's leadership, the Indian National Congress mobilized millions of Indians to demand independence from Britain. Although they were extraordinarily successful, independence was accompanied by the tragedy of partition. Just as Britain was preparing to grant India independence in 1947, it divided the Indian subcontinent into two countries. The larger area, the majority of whose population was Hindu, became independent India; the North, most of whose population was Muslim, became a separate country, Pakistan.

Gandhi considered the partition of India along religious lines in 1947 a disaster that should be avoided at all costs. However, he was unable to avert it.

Five months after India achieved self-rule, Gandhi was murdered by a Hindu extremist who considered him overly sympathetic to Muslim interests.

control over India. To gain Indians' support for the war effort, Britain promised to grant India independence. In August, 1947, soon after the war ended, India became a sovereign nation.

The euphoria of Indian independence was tempered by the human tragedy that accompanied the partition of the subcontinent. Influential members of India's minority Muslim elite regarded the Hindu-dominated INC with suspicion, in part because of the legacies of colonial divide-and-rule policies. When the INC refused to concede to their demands for separate political rights, they pressed for the creation of an independent Muslim state in northern India, where there was a large Muslim population. Britain divided the subcontinent into two sovereign states in 1947—the Muslim state of Pakistan and the secular state of India, the majority of whose citizens were Hindu. Partition, as it was called, was turbulent and destructive. Millions of Muslims fled from India to Pakistan, and millions of Hindus fled the other way. More than 10 million people migrated and nearly a million died in inter-ethnic violence. The Muslim population of India declined from 24 percent before independence to 10 percent thereafter.

Three features of the nationalist movement greatly influenced Indian state building and democracy. First, the INC proclaimed the value of preserving a broad tent within which political, ethnic, and religious conflicts could play themselves out. This helped India to create and maintain a relatively stable political system. However, second, Hindu-Muslim tensions which gave rise to Partition, resulted in enduring hostilities between the neighboring states of India and Pakistan. The two countries have fought three wars since Partition. Although some recent initiatives have defused tensions, there is an ever-present possibility of war between these two nuclear powers.

Third, the nationalist movement laid the foundations for democracy in India. Many of the INC's prominent leaders, like Gandhi and Jawaharlal Nehru, were educated in England and were committed democrats. Moreover, the INC chose its leaders through internal elections, participated in provincial elections, and ran democratic governments with limited powers in British-controlled Indian provinces. These pre-independence democratic tendencies were valuable future resources.

### The Nehru Era (1947–1964)

After independence, India adopted a Westminster model of British-style parliamentary democracy. The INC transformed itself from an opposition movement into a political party, the Congress Party. It was highly successful in the first years of independence, both because of its popularity in having led India to independence and because the Congress government created a nationwide **patronage system** that rewarded supporters with posts and resources.

Jawaharlal Nehru wanted India to play a global role. Together with other leaders of newly independent countries in Asia and Africa, he initiated what became known as the **nonaligned bloc**, a group of countries wishing to maintain a distance from the two superpowers. He attempted to set India on a rapid road to industrialization by promoting heavy industry. He was also committed to redistributing wealth through land reform. However much of India's land remained concentrated in the hands of traditional rural elites. While Nehru and the Congress Party proclaimed pro-poor, socialist commitments, they generally failed to deliver on their promises. To this day, India remains divided between a small affluent elite and hundreds of millions of poor peasants and urban workers. In recent years, India's economic growth has created a sizeable middle class between these two extremes. Nonetheless, the majority of

**patronage system**

A political system in which government officials appoint loyal followers to positions rather than choosing people based on their qualifications.

**nonaligned bloc**

Countries that refused to ally with either the United States or the USSR during the Cold War years.

Indians in both cities and countryside remain poor. Despite India's amazingly fast economic growth in the past two decades, the per capita income of her citizens places India among the poorest countries in the world.

An important change in the decade following independence was the creation of states based on the principal language in the region. Many non-Hindi groups feared domination by Hindi speakers and demanded that the Indian union be reorganized into linguistically defined states. Nehru reluctantly agreed to the creation of fourteen such states in 1957. In later years, additional states were carved out of existing ones, and there are now twenty-eight major states within India.

### The Indira Gandhi Era (1966–1984)

When Nehru died in 1964, the Congress Party was divided over the choice of a successor and hastily selected a compromise candidate, mild-mannered Lal Bahadur Shastri as prime minister. When Shastri died in 1966, rivalry among potential successors broke out. Party elites chose another compromise candidate, Nehru's daughter, Indira Gandhi (no relation to Mohandas Gandhi). They calculated that, as Nehru's daughter, she would help the Congress Party garner sufficient electoral support to remain in power. They also thought that she would be a weak woman who they could manipulate. Their first calculation was correct, their second was wholly inaccurate.

Indira Gandhi was India's second longest-serving prime minister. Her father was the longest-serving. She held office from 1966 to 1984, except for the years between 1977 and 1980. Her rule had several long-term legacies for contemporary Indian democracy. First, she quickly consolidated control over the Congress Party, replacing existing leaders with loyal allies. Gandhi also adopted a populist rhetoric that was popular with India's poor, but she failed to translate it into real gains. Like her father, she was unable to redistribute agricultural land from large landowners to small farmers and agricultural laborers or to generate employment, provide welfare, and broaden access to education and medical services.

Indian politics became increasingly turbulent under Indira Gandhi. As her power grew, so did opposition to her. In 1974, the political situation in India became quite unstable. When the opposition organized strikes and demonstrations, Gandhi declared a State of Emergency in 1975. She suspended many democratic rights, arrested most opposition leaders and ruled by decree. The **Emergency** lasted nearly two years, the only period since independence in 1947 that India did not function as a democracy (see Table 6.2 for a list of Indian prime ministers).

**Emergency (1975–1977)**

The period when Indian Prime Minister Indira Gandhi suspended many formal democratic rights and ruled in an authoritarian manner.

Gandhi ended the Emergency in 1977 and called for national elections, confident that she would be re-elected. However, opposition groups hastily formed an umbrella organization, the Janata Party. Gandhi and the Congress Party were soundly defeated. For the first time since independence, a non-Congress government briefly came to power. Soon after the elections, Janata leaders became factionalized, and the government collapsed. Indira Gandhi regained power in the 1980 parliamentary elections.

Indira Gandhi's tenure in power between 1980 and 1984 was marked, as it had been when she governed earlier, by a personal and populist political style, an increasingly centralized political system, failure to implement antipoverty policies, and political turbulence. However, Gandhi departed from her previous approach in two ways. First, she abandoned a socialist commitment and started changing the rules that governed India's economy. The new orientation embraced India's private sector as a means to improve India's poor economic performance. Second, she abandoned

| Table 6.2 | Prime Ministers of India, 1947–Present | |
|---|---|---|
| | **Years in Office** | **Party** |
| Jawaharlal Nehru | 1947–1964 | Congress |
| Lal Bahadur Shastri | 1964–1966 | Congress |
| Indira Gandhi | 1966–1977 | Congress |
| Morarji Desai | 1977–1979 | Janata |
| Charan Singh | 1979–1980 | Janata |
| Indira Gandhi | 1980–1984 | Congress |
| Rajiv Gandhi | 1984–1989 | Congress |
| V. P. Singh | 1989–1990 | Janata |
| Chandra Shekhar | 1990–1991 | Janata (Socialist) |
| Narasimha Rao | 1991–1996 | Congress |
| Atal Bihari Vajpayee | 1996 (13 days) | BJP & Allies |
| H. D. Deve Gowda | 1996–1997 | United Front |
| I. K. Gujral | 1997–1998 | United Front |
| Atal Bihari | 1998–1999 | BJP & Allies |
| Atal Bihari Vajpayee | 1999–2004 | |
| Manmohan Singh | 2004–present | Congress & Allies |

secularism and began to use religious appeals to mobilize India's Hindu majority. Gandhi contributed to polarization and conflict by depicting Punjabi Sikhs' grievances as religious rather than territorial. She also covertly encouraged the rise of an extremist faction among Sikhs. The movement turned violent and took over the holiest of the holy Sikh temples in Amritsar as a sanctuary. In 1984, Gandhi made the fatal mistake of dispatching troops to root out the militants. Sikhs were outraged when the operation badly damaged the temple and left many dead and injured. Months later, Gandhi was assassinated by her Sikh bodyguards. Immediately after her death, Hindu mobs, led by members of the Congress Party, murdered 3,700 Sikhs in New Delhi and other north Indian cities. Decades later, some of the leaders responsible for the carnage were finally convicted.

Under Indira Gandhi's leadership, Indian politics became more personalized, populist, and nationalist. While her foreign policies strengthened India's international position, her domestic policies weakened democratic institutions. For example, whereas during the Nehru era, local elites had helped select the Congress Party's higher political officeholders, Gandhi changed the procedure and directly appointed national and regional-level party officials. Although the strategy enabled her to gain a firm grip over the party, it isolated her from broader political forces and eroded the legitimacy of regional leaders.

Gandhi's death ushered in a new generation of the Nehru–Gandhi dynasty, when her son Rajiv Gandhi, became prime minister and served until 1989. Rajiv Gandhi won a landslide victory in the elections that followed his mother's death as a result of the sympathy that his mother's assassination generated. He came to office promising clean government, a high-tech economy that would carry India into the next century, and reduced ethnic conflict. He was somewhat successful in easing tensions in the Punjab. But he inflamed relations between Hindus and Muslims by sponsoring a law that sharply limited the rights of Muslim women. His leadership was also marred by allegations of corruption.

## Coalition Governments (1989 to the Present)

For the first three decades after independence, many parties competed for office. However, none came close to rivaling Congress, particularly in national politics. The Congress Party led all governments from independence to 1989, except for one brief interlude (1977–1980). The decline of the Congress party ushered in an era of instability with no clearly dominant party. In each national election since 1989, coalition governments have depended on the support of federal parties. The BJP-dominated National Democratic Alliance (1999–2004) depended heavily on regional allies.

However, in 2004 the Congress coalition government enjoyed a stronger mandate than it had in many years. The leader of Congress was Sonia Gandhi, widow of slain Prime Minister Rajiv Gandhi. Although she had demonstrated her ability to lead Congress, party elites feared that her Italian background made her a risky choice as prime minister. Instead they named Manmohan Singh, a respected former cabinet minister and influential member of the Congress Party, but not its leader, prime minister.

For the first time, a politician who was neither a leader of his own party nor that of the ruling alliance became prime minister. Although not a charismatic figure, Manmohan Singh proved a highly capable and popular prime minister. His Congress-led coalition government was re-elected to power in 2009 by a larger margin than in 2004. However as described below his reputation has been recently tarnished by not acting swiftly enough to address widespread corruption by Congress government officials.

## September 11th and its Aftermath

India was deeply affected by the September 11, 2001, attacks on the World Trade Center in New York and on the Pentagon in Washington. Although none of the Al Qaeda terrorists who hijacked the planes on September 11th was from India or neighboring Pakistan, the global network of violence that flourished after 9/11 cast a shadow over Indo-Pakistan relations. On the Pakistani side, high-level units of Pakistan's powerful and shadowy intelligence services, the Inter-Services Intelligence (ISI), provided support for groups linked to Al Qaeda. For years before 9/11, these

One hundred sixty four people were killed and 308 people were injured in the November 29, 2008, bombing of the Taj Hotel in Mumbai. The Lashkar-e-Taiba claimed responsibility for this attack.

AP Photo/Lefteris Pitarakis

groups carried out attacks on Indian armed forces and civil officials in Kashmir, a territory controlled by India but claimed by Pakistan.

After 9/11, militants based in Pakistan, and supported by the ISI, began to launch attacks on the Indian heartland. Two incidents were especially dramatic. First, militants bombed and damaged the Indian Parliament in Delhi on December 13, 2001, killing fifteen people. In another major attack in November 2008, ten Pakistani gunmen—all of whom were members of the terrorist organization Lashkar-e-Taiba—stormed some of Mumbai's most iconic and busiest sites, including the Taj Intercontinental Hotel and the Chhatrapati Shivaji Terminus. With guns blazing, they barricaded themselves in the hotel and executed scores of guests (selecting Westerners as their prime target). For three horrifying days, television stations around the world portrayed the standoff at the hotel. The crisis ended when Indian elite forces stormed the hotel and killed all but one militant; 164 people were killed and 308 people were injured during the several-day crisis. The lone surviving gunman was tried and sentenced to death in May 2010.

Tensions between India and Pakistan dramatically escalated when the surviving militant provided details of the ISI's involvement in the massacre. Although war was avoided thanks to Prime Minister Singh, the Mumbai attack highlighted the fragile relations between India and Pakistan.

# Themes and Implications

## Historical Junctures and Political Themes

India in a World of States India is well positioned, by its large size, growing wealth, democratic legitimacy, and geographic location, to play a powerful role in world affairs. Yet for this to occur, Indian leaders must prevent domestic pressures from escalating into international conflicts and must nurture peaceful relations with India's powerful neighbors, Pakistan and China.

India's first nuclear test in 1974 signaled the dawn of a new era. India shares borders with two nuclear powers, China and Pakistan, and has engaged in wars and frequent border skirmishes with both. Indo-Pakistani relations are especially tense. Kashmir has been a perpetual source of conflict. More recently, Pakistani leaders fear that India, the far larger and more powerful country, is attempting to encircle Pakistan by its growing influence in Afghanistan, Pakistan's neighbor on the North.

Fire officers stand near a train coach destroyed by a bomb blast at Matunga railway station in Mumbai, India, in this July 11, 2006 photo. More than 200 people were killed in the bombings.

**Governing the Economy**   Indian policymakers first sought to achieve economic self-sufficiency through state-led industrialization focused on satisfying the needs of India's large internal market. This economic strategy required protectionist measures (such as high tariffs) to shield India from foreign economic competition. It succeeded in creating some important basic industries but also generated extensive inefficiencies and failed to reduce severe poverty. Like many developing nations, India has recently adjusted its economic strategy to meet the demands of competitive and interdependent global markets. During the 1980s, these reforms consisted mainly of government incentives to India's established private sector to increase production. Since 1991, reforms have opened the Indian economy to the outside world. The results include both a growing economy but also growing inequalities. Among the daunting challenges facing Indian leaders is how to ensure sustained growth while sponsoring measures to reduce economic inequalities.

## The Democratic Idea

India has recently become more democratic in some ways but less democratic in others. A larger number of people, with more diverse identities, are participating in politics than ever before. The Indian political class is no longer recruited from a single region, caste, and class. However, business leaders wield much more political influence than do the far more numerous poor. Further, a key ingredient of democracy is the protection of minority rights. On this count India is less democratic than in the past because of recent assaults on Muslims, Christians, and lower caste groups.

**The Politics of Collective Identity**   Democracy is supposed to provide a level playing field in which diverse interests and identities seek to resolve their differences. India has demonstrated how an incredibly large and diverse country can process conflicts peacefully and democratically. However, political parties and leading politicians have sometimes mobilized the electorate along ethnic lines and targeted minority groups.

### Implications for Comparative Politics

India offers a fascinating profile that can deepen our understanding of comparative politics. First, it is a poor yet vibrant democracy. Despite widespread poverty and illiteracy, most Indians value their citizenship rights and exercise them vigorously. Against great odds, India became and remains a thriving democracy, an especially striking achievement given the authoritarian fate of most newly independent countries in Asia and Africa.

Second, the Indian state has managed to remain fairly cohesive and stable—although this must be qualified by political violence in a variety of states and regions. Third, with well over a billion people of diverse cultural, religious, and linguistic identities, Indian democracy is an excellent arena for analyzing various theories and dilemmas of comparative politics. At its best, India offers instructive lessons in multi-ethnic democracy. At its worst, it can provide lessons in how democracy can be used and misused.

Fourth, theorists of democratic change in Latin America and Eastern Europe have puzzled over what constitutes a consolidated democracy and how to achieve it. Here, a comparison between India and Pakistan is instructive. Whereas the two countries were formed at the same moment, India has functioned as a democracy for all but two years since 1947 whereas Pakistan has been an authoritarian state for most of the same period.

Fifth, comparativists have explored whether democracy and social equity can be achieved simultaneously in poor countries. The case of Kerala, a state in southern India, suggests that the answer can be a cautious yes. Although one of the poorest states in India, Kerala has achieved near-total literacy, long life expectancy, low infant mortality, and widespread access to medical care. Kerala's development indicators compare favorably with those in the rest of India, other low-income countries, and even wealthy countries like the United States.

Finally, comparativists have long engaged in a lively debate about the impact of democracy on economic growth. While cross-national evidence remains inconclusive, India's record of steady per capita growth of 4–5 percent annually in the past thirty years powerfully demonstrates how successful economic management can occur within a democratic framework. At the same time, India's failure to adequately redistribute its economic resources provides a more sobering lesson.

### Summary

India is a vast and complex amalgam of diverse religious, cultural, and societal influences. Because its' linguistic, regional, class, religious, and caste divisions have traditionally cross-cut one another, this has often prevented any one cleavage from becoming polarized and any one identity from becoming dominant. Conversely, when a political leader or party has mobilized on the basis of one identity to the exclusion of others, the result has been a dangerous tendency toward polarization and violence.

This discussion of critical junctures in Indian history highlights the central challenge of contemporary Indian politics: how to establish a coherent, legitimate government that will facilitate both economic growth and equitable distribution. The remainder of this chapter deals with India's successes and failures in dealing with these challenges.

# POLITICAL ECONOMY AND DEVELOPMENT

At independence, India had a poor, largely agricultural economy. Although a majority of Indians, especially the poor, still work and live in the countryside, India has developed a substantial industrial base, a booming service sector, and a vibrant middle class. Since the Congress government introduced economic liberalization policies in 1991, all governments have supported economic reforms to reduce heavy-handed state economic direction that discouraged private initiative. Liberalization has helped spur rapid economic growth. For example, although per capita income in India grew less than 1 percent a year during the decade 1970–1979, it grew 5.5 percent annually during 2000–2009. At the same time, hundreds of millions of people have been deprived of the fruits of economic growth.

## State and Economy

### The Economy after Independence

One of the central tasks that Indian leaders faced after 1947 was to modernize the sluggish economy. During Nehru's rule, India adopted a model of development based on the creation of public enterprises and state guidance of private economic activity. Nehru created a powerful planning commission that established government investment priorities. Unlike the planning process in communist states, Indian plans included a large role for private entrepreneurs. Some large, private family-owned firms in industries like steel were a powerful force in the Indian economy. But the government also limited the start-up and expansion of private industries. It imposed high tariffs on imports, arguing that newly created Indian industries required protection from foreign competitors.

This government-planned mixed economy enabled India to create an impressive industrial base but did little to help the poor. The protected industries were quite inefficient by global standards, and they were hindered from acting boldly by mountains of red tape administered by government bureaucrats.

Given the predominantly rural character of India, the highly unequal distribution of agricultural land presented a particularly significant challenge. Although the government passed legislation in the early 1950s reducing the size of some of the largest landholdings, it reallocated little of the reclaimed land to poor tenants and agricultural laborers. Most land remained in the hands of medium-to large-sized landowners, who became part of the Congress political machine. This weakened the Congress Party's ability to assist the rural poor and undermined its socialist commitments.

Rather than fulfilling its promise to enact substantial land reforms, the government adopted an alternative strategy in the late 1960s. Known as the **green revolution**, the strategy aimed to increase agricultural production by providing farmers with improved seeds, subsidized fertilizer, and irrigation. The Green Revolution made India self-sufficient in food and even a food exporter. This represented a sharp contrast with the past, when famines resulted in mass starvation.

However, the benefits of the Green Revolution were highly uneven. While production increased sharply in the Punjab, for example, other regions (and especially

**SECTION**
**2**

## Focus Questions

What have been two major achievements and two major failures of Indian economic development strategy?

How successfully has India managed to balance the goals of promoting economic efficiency and social equity? Suggest one or more ways that the tradeoff could be improved.

**green revolution**

A strategy for increasing agricultural (especially food) production, involving improved seeds, irrigation, and abundant use of fertilizers.

poor farmers in less favored regions) were left behind. The very success of the Green Revolution created other long-term problems. In particular, intensive use of fertilizers depleted the soil. Purchasing costly agricultural machinery forced farmers to borrow large sums—often from money-lenders at high interest rates. In recent years, the states that were the standard bearers of the Green Revolution have experienced a severe agricultural crisis. One tragic result has been a wave of suicides by farmers who are unable to repay massive debts.

**state-led economic development**

The process of promoting economic development using governmental machinery.

To summarize, the period between 1950 and 1980 consisted of **state-led economic development** that expanded the public sector, protected the domestic sector from foreign competition, and closely supervised private sector activity. Political leaders hoped to strengthen India's international position by promoting self-sufficient industrialization. This policy was somewhat successful. State-led development insulated the Indian economy from global influences. The strategy resulted in modest economic growth, whose main beneficiaries were the business classes, medium and large landowning farmers, and political and bureaucratic elites. A substantial urban middle class also developed. By 1980, India was a significant industrial power that produced its own steel, airplanes, automobiles, chemicals, military hardware, and many consumer goods. Although land reform failed, the Green Revolution greatly increased food production.

However, state-led development also had substantial flaws. Shielded from competition, industry was often inefficient, and the entire economy stagnated. The elaborate rules and regulations controlling private economic activity encouraged corruption, as entrepreneurs bribed bureaucrats to evade the rules. And the focus on heavy industry meant that most investment involved purchasing machinery rather than creating jobs: 40 percent of India's population, primarily poor tenant farmers and landless laborers, were unable to escape poverty; indeed, the number of desperately poor people increased substantially.

## Economic Liberalization

**economic liberalization**

The removal of government control and regulation over private enterprise.

Political and economic elites became increasingly dissatisfied with India's inadequate economic performance compared with that of other Asian countries. For example, during the 1970s, whereas India's economy grew at the rate of 3.4 percent per year, South Korea's grew at 9.6 percent. India's business and industrial classes began to regard government regulation of the economy as a hindrance rather than a help. They became aware that poverty limited the possibility for expanding domestic markets. A turning point occurred in the 1980s and accelerated after 1991, when India moved toward **economic liberalization**. Under the leadership of Finance Minister (and later prime minister) Manmohan Singh, the Indian government loosened its tight grip on the economy by eliminating price controls, reducing state intervention in day-to-day economic affairs, easing import regulations, reforming the tax system, and doing away with many state-run monopolies. As a result, the private sector began to grow rapidly, foreign investment poured into the country, and the economy soared.

India's economic performance has been highly impressive since then, with growth rates maintaining a pace of 5–7 percent annually. This record is especially noteworthy compared to the dismal performance of many debt-ridden African economies. An important reason for this success is that Indian entrepreneurs have been able to operate with fewer government restrictions. Since 1991, the reduction of tariffs and other restrictions has further integrated India into the global economy.

However, this pattern of economic growth required borrowing capital from abroad to expand productive equipment. The need to repay foreign loans exerted enormous pressure on the government. In the 1990s, India was forced to borrow from the International Monetary Fund (IMF) and the World Bank to repay past loans. In return, these international organizations required the Indian government to reduce subsidies to the poor and sell government shares in public enterprises. Government policies reduced the workforce in public enterprises and reduced public spending and deficits. The government has also enacted legal restrictions limiting employers' ability to lay off workers.

## Reforms in Agriculture

Since the 1990s, governments have reduced subsidized food supplies in order to limit public spending. In order to comply with the dictates of the World Trade Organization (WTO), the government removed restrictions on imports. This has harmed millions of impoverished families. Although industrialized countries have maintained trade barriers on agricultural products and continue to subsidize their domestic farmers, India's safety net has shrunk as its agricultural economy has opened up to global forces.

India's intensive agricultural development, substantial industrial growth, and ineffective government regulation, have created serious environmental problems. India suffers from severe air pollution in large cities and contaminated lakes and rivers. There is a shortage of drinking water partly due to industrial overuse. Urbanization, commercial logging, and the use of wood for fuel have caused deforestation, provoking droughts, floods, and cyclones. The emission of carbon dioxide has contributed to the worldwide greenhouse effect, leading to an increase in temperature, a rise in the sea level, and the destruction of coastal croplands and fisheries.

Over the past several years, India has established policies that seek to increase the efficiency of coal, oil, and natural gas consumption. But it has made clear that it will not adopt policies that jeopardize the country's economic growth rate. It has refused to enforce measures that will drastically reduce the country's carbon emissions output or forestall India's growing demand for energy. At the 2009 United Nations Climate Change Conference in Copenhagen, for example, India opposed drastic carbon cutting steps unless developed countries did so and provided monetary assistance to help developing countries do the same.

There are substantial successes on the positive side of the economic ledger. Some industries, such as information technology, have taken off. The service sector is expanding and contributes significantly to economic growth. Liberalization policies have accelerated industrial expansion. The stock of modern technology continues to grow, and the closer relationship between government and business has encouraged substantial domestic and foreign investment. At the same time, India has yet to devise an adequate balance between economic development, environmental protection, and social equity. The booming economy consumes enormous amounts of scarce resources and further burdens the Indian and global ecosystem.

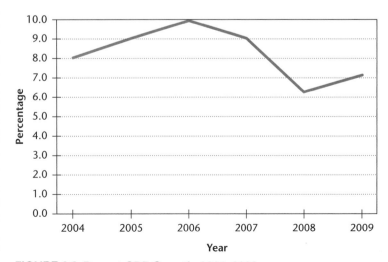

**FIGURE 6.2  Recent GDP Growth, 2004–2009**

*Source:* World Bank National Accounts data, devdata.world-bank.org/data-query/SMChartExp.asp.

# Society and Economy

## Inequality and Social Welfare Policy

India is deeply stratified by class and income. At the top of the income pyramid, a small group of Indians have made incredible fortunes in business and industry. The wealth of the Ambanis, Tatas, and Birlas rivals that of the richest corporate tycoons in the world. About 100 million Indians are relatively well off and enjoy a standard of living comparable to that of middle or upper-middle-class people anywhere in the world. Moreover, thanks to a large pool of low-wage labor, middle-class Indians generally employ one or more full-time domestic workers.

India's lower-middle classes, about half the population, are mainly self-employed business owners, small farmers, and urban workers. India has the largest number of poor people in the world, though measures of poverty differ. According to the Indian government's definition of poverty, 25 percent of India's population is living in poverty. According to the World Bank, the official international measure of poverty is $2 per day and of absolute poverty, $1.25 per day. By these measures, 76 percent of Indians are below the poverty line, and 43 percent of Indians are living in absolute poverty. If one employs the measures used by the Indian government, the proportion of those who are defined as poor has halved since independence. However, India's rapid population growth has increased the absolute number of the poor: from about 200 million in the 1950s to about 300 million currently.

About three-quarters of the poor live in rural areas. Most are landless laborers and live in India's thousands of villages. The urban poor are concentrated in giant slums with few public services, such as electricity and indoor plumbing. Although the economic boom has improved conditions for hundreds of millions, many more Indians are mired in poverty, and their children have little prospect of leading a better life.

The sizable number of poor people encourages many Indian politicians to adopt populist or socialist electoral platforms—although often in name only. In some cases, the poor influence electoral outcomes. For example, the states of West Bengal and Kerala have a long history of radical politics; the poor in these states are well organized and elect left-leaning state governments. These governments have redistributed land to the poor and implemented antipoverty programs. The poor have also fueled many social movements. The **Naxalite** revolutionary movement is an important example. Influenced by Maoist ideals, it has organized the landless poor to engage in land seizures and attacks on the state and dominant classes.

Over the years, Indian governments have pursued various poverty alleviation programs. The present national government has undertaken a reform of the employment guarantee scheme to provide the poor with jobs constructing roads and bridges and cleaning agricultural waterways. Because the rural poor are unemployed for nearly half the year when agricultural jobs are not available, these schemes have become an important source of off-season jobs and income.

However overall, India has a poor record when it comes to reducing poverty. Antipoverty programs and land reforms have generally failed to reduce economic inequality and help the poor. India has few Western-style welfare programs, such as unemployment insurance and comprehensive public health programs. Especially noteworthy is that India does not provide universal primary education. Thus, only 75 percent of boys and men are literate. The situation is far worse for girls and women, of whom only 51 percent are literate. This increases the likelihood that poverty will be perpetuated in future generations.

A variety of inequalities in India have increased over the last two decades. The most serious are the growing inequalities across Indian regions as well as across Indian

**Naxalite**

The Naxalite movement emerged as a breakaway faction of the CPM in West Bengal in 1967. It is a radical, often violent, extra-parliamentary movement.

cities and the countryside. For example, the average per capita income of someone living in one of India's richer states, such as Gujarat, is four times higher than the per capita income of an individual living in the poor state of Bihar. An average citizen living in India's villages is also likely to be much poorer than someone living in a city. Class inequalities within cities have also become more skewed. These growing inequalities can become politicized and add to the problems of India's democracy.

India's population continues to grow at a rapid pace—double the rate of China. Before long it will be the world's largest country. India's democratic government has generally resisted coercive population control policies, such as those practiced by China. But it has also failed to practice more progressive ways to reduce population growth. For example, although literate women are more likely to marry later in life and engage in family planning, the Indian government has failed to make education a priority, and as noted above girls and women are especially likely to be illiterate. Since India has more people than it can use productively, a growing population hinders economic growth.

India is one of the few countries in the world with a lower percentage of females than males. Evidence that Indian society favors boys over girls can be inferred from such social indicators as lower female literacy, nutrition rates, and survival of female versus male infants. Prejudice against girls is reinforced through traditions like the dowry system (the Hindu custom of giving the groom and his family substantial money and goods at the time of a daughter's wedding). Although giving and receiving a dowry is illegal, it continues to be practiced, and the sums involved have grown alongside increased materialism and aspirations for upward social mobility, particularly among the urban middle and lower-middle classes.

India also has the world's largest population of child labor, though this has been declining in recent years. Children are employed in agricultural labor and in match production, rug weaving, and selling refreshments at train stations. Children often work long hours at low wages. Because they cannot attend school, they have limited prospects for upward mobility. The issue of child labor is closely related to India's failure to provide universal primary education (see Figure 6.3).

Many Indian elites claim that compulsory primary education is an unaffordable luxury in a poor country like India. However, this argument is not persuasive; many poor African countries have higher rates of primary school enrollment than India. The more likely obstacle to universal primary education is poverty and caste inequality. Many poor families see large families as a form of insurance, for they depend on their children's labor for support. And many upper-caste elites do not consider educating lower-caste children a priority. Over the last decade or two, the government has increased public spending on primary education, and enrollments have increased sharply. Unfortunately, the quality of education in most public schools remains very poor.

Those who suffer most are at the bottom of the caste hierarchy: the **untouchables**. The Indian census classifies nearly 10 percent of India's population as belonging to the untouchables or scheduled castes, as they are officially known. Untouchables engage in occupations such as cleaning and leather work, which is considered "unclean," and they are not considered members of organized Hindu society. The members of this group are stigmatized and excluded from meaningful participation in social and economic life.

The caste system has had a destructive impact on Indian social and economic life. By assigning people to specific occupations at birth, it limits individual choice and impedes social and economic mobility. Although the link between caste and

**untouchables**

The lowest caste in India's caste system, whose members are among the poorest and most disadvantaged Indians.

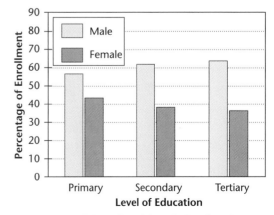

**FIGURE 6.3  Educational Levels by Gender**

*Source:* UNESCO Institute for Statistics, www.uis. unesco.org/en/stats/stats.

occupation has weakened, especially in urban areas, it remains an important organizing principle for employment. Caste groups sometimes re-designate their caste identities to achieve group mobility without undermining the principles governing caste hierarchies. In the political arena, voting blocs are often organized on a caste basis. Because caste divides the lower classes in rural India, it makes it difficult for the poor to organize to defend their interests.

# India in the Global Economy

Although for decades starting in the 1950s India pursued an active foreign policy as a leader of the nonaligned bloc, its leaders sought to minimize global economic exchange. During the period when India's economy was relatively closed to outside influences, powerful groups emerged with vested interests in preventing change. Many bureaucrats accepted bribes from business executives to issue licenses or evade regulations. Moreover, labor unions, especially in government-controlled factories, supported inefficient operations because this kept employment at high levels. These well-entrenched groups resisted liberalization and threatened to support opposition parties if the government sponsored a decisive policy shift.

By the 1980s, the negative effects of this pattern finally forced a change. When the government opened the economy, foreign investment soared from $100 million a year to nearly $4 billion annually between 1992 and 1998, and then to nearly $8 billion annually in 2006–2007. However, foreign investment in India remains several times lower than in China and Brazil. Furthermore, it is concentrated in industries producing for the domestic market; it has not facilitated export promotion, potentially a major source of hard currency.

One high-tech sector in which India excels is computer software. Indian firms and multinational corporations employ large numbers of highly skilled, low-cost, English-speaking scientific and engineering talent to make India a world leader in the production of software. India boasts the equivalent of California's Silicon Valley in Bangalore in southern India, home to a large number of software firms. Furthermore, within the past few years, transnational corporations have hired graduates of India's superb higher institutions of engineering and technology.

For the same reason, India has become a prime destination for corporate call centers, tech support, and back office operations of banks, insurance companies, and financial firms. Scores of high-rise office buildings, shopping malls, and housing complexes have sprung up outside major cities like Delhi and Mumbai. They provide graphic evidence of the new India. However, because they are so cut off from traditional Indian society, they further intensify the country's extreme social fragmentation.

India's integration within the global economy has increased as a result of a WTO agreement on trade in services, which has required the government to ease restrictions on banking, insurance, and other services. More than forty foreign banks have opened in India, and the government has also opened up the insurance sector to private and foreign investment. This has been a mixed blessing. For example, foreign banks focus on retail banking in profitable urban areas and ignore less lucrative areas of lending. This reduces the possibilities for farmers and small-scale industrialists in rural and poorer regions to obtain loans.

India has compiled an enviable growth record in the last decade, and the prospects for future growth are favorable, in part due to the need to improve the country's poor infrastructure. As a result, India has become an attractive destination for foreign investment, and capital from all over the world has poured into the country. India has catapulted into the first ranks of large developing countries. It is a charter member of

## GLOBAL CONNECTIONS

### India in the Global Economy

Since 1991 India's economy has globalized. Tariffs on trade have come down. India's exports have as a result grown rapidly, but so have imports. Laws on foreign investment have also become more liberal. While direct foreign investment is significantly lower in India than in China, foreign investment into India has continued to grow over the last two decades. Foreign monies in the form of portfolio invest-ments have also flown into India, buoying the stock markets but also adding volatility. In terms of financial markets, India is not as well integrated into the global economy as many Latin American and some East Asian economies. While crit-icisms of this selective integration abound, India suffered a lot less during a variety of global financial crises than other developing markets.

the so-called BRIC countries: Brazil, Russia, India, and China—a bloc of developing countries that wields significant clout in the international arena.

### Summary

India has come a long way since the heavy-handed state and entrenched Indian-owned firms cooperated to stifle economic progress. Thanks to clever economic pol-icy, a large, well-trained, and low-cost skilled labor force, and a growing number of world-class corporations, India is poised to become an economic giant. Globalization has promoted the rapid expansion of a middle class that enthusiastically participates in global consumer culture. At the same time, however, globalization has increased eco-nomic inequality by generating more benefits for those in the middle and upper ranks than for the rural and urban poor. As a result, Indian society increasingly consists of socially and economically segregated worlds. The challenge for the government is to devise ways to make globalization work for all.

# GOVERNANCE AND POLICY-MAKING

SECTION 3

## Organization of the State

The 1950 constitution, adopted soon after India gained independence, created a democratic republic with a parliamentary system of national government and a weak, mostly ceremonial, president. India's political system is federal, and the states have substantial autonomy, power, and responsibilities. For much of the period since 1947, India has been a stable, democratic country with universal suffrage and periodic local, state, and national elections. This record of democratic stability is remarkable among developing countries. Indian democracy has proved so durable because its political institutions have been able to accommodate many challenges. (See Table 6.1 for an outline of Indian political organization.)

Unlike the British constitution, which it resembles in many respects, the Indian constitution is a written document that has been periodically amended. Because the Indian constitution is highly detailed, it leaves less room for interpretation than many

### Focus Questions

How well do Indian political institutions enable decisive govern-ment action while creat-ing checks and balances that limit governmental abuses of power?

Suggest two ways to improve the system of governance and policy-making, and explain why they are desirable and how feasible it would be to adopt them.

## PROFILE

### The Nehru–Gandhi Dynasty

Jawaharlal Nehru was a staunch believer in liberal democratic principles. When India became independent in 1947, Nehru became prime minister and retained that position until his death in 1964. Nehru was a committed nationalist and social democrat. He sought to strengthen India's autonomy and national economy and improve the lives of the Indian poor. He tried to establish a socialist, democratic, and secular state, although India often failed to live up to these lofty ideals. Nehru attempted to set India on a rapid road to industrialization by promoting heavy industry. He advocated redistributing wealth through land reform, although much of India's land remained concentrated in the hands of traditional rural elites. Finally, Nehru championed democratic and individual rights, including the right to private property.

Upon his death, India inherited a stable polity, a functioning democracy, and an economy characterized by a large public sector and a complex pattern of state control over the private sector.

Indira Gandhi became prime minister shortly after the death of her father, Jawaharlal Nehru, and dominated the Indian political scene until her assassination in 1984. While her foreign policies strengthened India's international position, her domestic policies weakened democratic institutions. Her tendency to centralize and personalize authority within the Congress contributed to the erosion of the party. She engaged in repressive measures to curtail growing political opposition. She was ultimately assassinated by her Sikh bodyguards.

other national constitutions. Three special features are worth noting. First, unlike many constitutions, the Indian constitution directs the government to promote social and economic equality and justice. The constitution thus outlines policy goals, rather than simply enumerating formal procedures of decision-making and allocating powers among political institutions. Although the impact of these constitutional provisions on welfare and social justice is limited, political parties and movements have appealed to them when seeking reforms.

Second, the Indian constitution, like the U.S. constitution, provides for freedom of religion and defines India as a secular state. And third, the constitution allows for the temporary suspension of many democratic rights under emergency conditions. These provisions were used, for understandable reasons, during wars with Pakistan and China. But they have also been invoked, more disturbingly, to deal with internal political threats, most dramatically during the national Emergency from 1975 to 1977.

Further, the constitution specifies that, in the event that state governments are unable to function in a stable manner, the national government is authorized to declare President's Rule, which involves suspending the elected state government and administering the state's affairs from Delhi. President's Rule was designed to be used as a last resort to temporarily curb unrest in federal states. However, by 1989 the central government had declared President's Rule sixty-seven times. Prime Minister Jawaharlal Nehru only invoked President's Rule eight times from 1951 to 1964. By contrast it was invoked thirty-nine times from 1975 to 1989, mainly while Indira Gandhi was prime minister. The Congress government used it to remove governments formed by opposition parties from office and to strengthen its own control. Under pressure from the opposition, Indira Gandhi created the Sarkaria Commission in 1983 to review center-state relations. It issued a report in 1987, which claimed that President's Rule had been necessary only twenty-six of the sixty-seven times it had been used and urged the central government to exercise restraint in imposing it. A landmark 1994 Supreme Court ruling, (*S. R. Bommai* v. *Union Government of India*) affirmed the Sarkaria Commission findings, called for judicial review of central government decisions to impose President's Rule, and affirmed the possibility of the courts striking it down. The coalition governments that have held office since 1989 have been reluctant to invoke President's Rule. An important reason is that parties that are members of national governing coalitions oppose the national government suspending state governments that they lead.

In India's federal system, the central government controls most essential government functions, such as defense, foreign policy, taxation, public expenditures, and economic planning. State governments formally control agriculture, education, and law and order. However, because states are heavily dependent on the central government for funds to finance programs in these policy areas, their actual power is limited.

The ***Lok Sabha***, or House of the People, is the lower chamber of parliament and the ***Rajya Sabha***, the upper house. (India's parliament will be described in Section 4.) Following elections to the Lok Sabha, the leader of the political party with the most seats becomes the prime minister. Effective power is concentrated in the prime minister's office. The prime minister in turn nominates members of the cabinet, mostly members of parliament belonging to the ruling coalition. The prime minister and cabinet members also head various ministries.

## The Executive

### The Prime Minister and the Cabinet

The prime minister governs with the help of the cabinet, which periodically meets to discuss important issues, including new legislative proposals. Because they lead the majority party coalition in parliament, passing a bill is not as complicated as it can be in a presidential system. The permanent bureaucracy, especially senior- and middle-level bureaucrats, is responsible for policy implementation. Nevertheless, as in most other parliamentary systems, such as those in Britain, Germany, and Japan, there is considerable overlap in India between the executive and the legislative branches of the government.

---

**Lok Sabha**

The lower house of parliament in India, where all major legislation must pass before becoming law.

**Rajya Sabha**

India's upper house of parliament; considerably less politically powerful than the *Lok Sabha*.

---

# THE U.S. CONNECTION

## Comparing Chief Executives in India and the United States

In the U.S. presidential system, the positions of head of state and chief executive are combined in one office: the president. The president thus both symbolizes the unity of the entire country and is a political party leader and head of government.

This pattern is quite unusual. In most countries, there are two offices. The head of state is mostly a ceremonial office, occupied by a monarch or a president indirectly elected by the legislature or an electoral college. In India, the president is elected for a five-year term by an electoral college composed of elected representatives from the national and state governments, and can be subsequently re-elected. The president symbolizes the unity of India and is expected to rise above partisan conflicts. However, presidential approval is necessary for most parliamentary bills to become laws. Presidents can veto bills by refusing assent or delaying their enactment. Presidents can also name the prime minister when parliamentary elections do not produce a clear verdict as to which party should lead the new government.

By combining the functions of head of state and head of government, the United States concentrates enormous power in one person. The Indian system assigns the two functions to different officials, thus leaving the president generally above the political fray and making the prime minister a more partisan figure. What are the strength and weaknesses of each system?

### The Prime Minister

The prime minister is the head of India's Council of Ministers, and is therefore in charge of all government ministries. As such, the prime minister is ultimately responsible for all of the daily activities of the central government. Among other things, the prime minister has the power to appoint individuals to various government offices, establish policy on issues such as defense and foreign affairs, and administer the civil service. Between 1947 and 1984, except for several brief interludes, India had only two prime ministers: Nehru and Indira Gandhi (see Table 6.2). This is nearly unique among democracies; it underlines the powerful hold that the Nehru–Gandhi family had on India's political destinies.

### The Cabinet

The prime minister chooses the cabinet, mostly from among the governing party's senior members of parliament. Being named to the cabinet is among the most sought-after prizes in Indian politics. The main criteria guiding a prime minister's choice are seniority, competence, and personal loyalty. Regional and caste representation are also considered. In recent years, because governments are coalitions of many parties, representatives from each one must be named to the cabinet. The result is that cabinets nowadays are often large, unwieldy, and divided.

Cabinet ministers have three roles. First, they are members of the government and participate in shaping its general policy orientation. Second, they are leaders of their own parties and must try to maintain party cohesion and support for the government. This may be difficult, especially if the government pursues a policy that is unpopular with the party's members. Third, cabinet ministers direct a ministry responsible for a particular policy area. They must thus supervise the ministry's civil servants and try to ensure that the department performs competently. Complicating a minister's situation is that what brings success in one area may detract from success in another.

### The Bureaucracy

The prime minister and cabinet ministers supervise the bureaucracy in close collaboration with senior civil servants. Each senior minister oversees a sprawling department staffed by some highly competent, overworked, senior civil servants and many not-so-competent, underworked, lowly bureaucrats.

**Indian Administrative Service (IAS)**

India's civil service, a highly professional and talented group of administrators who run the Indian government on a day-to-day basis.

The **Indian Administrative Service (IAS)**, an elite corps of top bureaucrats, constitutes a critically important but relatively thin layer at the top of India's bureaucracy. Recruitment occurs through a highly competitive examination. Many more candidates compete than are chosen, since IAS appointments provide lifetime tenure, excellent pay, and great prestige. In 2009, for example, out of the nearly 600,000 applicants for IAS civil service posts, just 7,000 were selected for an interview, and only 2,500 of those interviewed were appointed. Whereas political leaders come and go, senior civil servants stay—and accumulate a storehouse of knowledge and expertise that makes them powerful and competent.

Many of India's most talented young men and women were attracted to the IAS in the decades after independence, an indication of the prestige that came with service in national government. The attraction of the IAS has declined, however, and many of India's most talented young people now go into engineering and business administration, or leave the country for better opportunities abroad. Government service has become tarnished by corruption, and the level of professionalism within the IAS has declined as politicians increasingly prefer loyalty over merit and seniority when making promotions. Nevertheless, the IAS continues to recruit highly talented young people, many of whom become dedicated senior civil servants who constitute the backbone of the Indian government.

Below the IAS, the level of talent and professionalism drops sharply. The national and state-level Indian bureaucracy is infamous for corruption and inefficiency. Civil servants are powerfully organized and, thanks to lifetime tenure, free to resist orders coming from their superiors. There has been a marked decline in the competence and integrity of the Indian bureaucracy through the years. Its lack of responsiveness and accountability pose a major problem for Indian democracy. These problems contribute to the gap between good policies and their poor implementation at the local level.

# Other State Institutions

### The Military and the Police

With more than 1 million well-trained and well-equipped members, the Indian military is a highly powerful and professional organization. It has never intervened directly in politics. Over the years, the continuity of constitutional, electoral politics and a relatively apolitical effective military have come to reinforce and strengthen each other. Civilian politicians provide ample resources to the armed forces and, for the most part, encourage them to function as a professional organization. The armed forces, in turn, accept direction from democratically elected civilian leaders.

The Indian police forces have never been as professionalized as the armed forces. The police come under the jurisdiction of state governments, not the central government. Because state governments are generally less effective and honest than the national government, the Indian police are not apolitical civil servants. State-level politicians regularly interfere in police personnel issues, and police officers in turn regularly oblige politicians. The police are easily bribed and often allied with criminals or politicians. The police generally favor dominant social groups such as landowners, upper castes, and the majority Hindu religious community. A large, sprawling, and relatively ineffective police service remains a problematic presence in Indian society.

In addition to the regular armed forces and state-level police forces, the national government controls paramilitary forces that number nearly half a million men. As Indian politics became more turbulent in the 1980s, paramilitary forces steadily expanded. Because the national government calls on the regular armed forces only as a last resort to manage internal conflicts, and because state-level police forces are generally unreliable, paramilitary forces are often used to maintain order.

### The Judiciary

An independent judiciary is another component of India's state system. The major judicial authority is the Supreme Court, comprising a chief justice and seventeen other judges. The president appoints judges on the advice of the prime minister. Once appointed, judges cannot be removed from the bench until retirement at age sixty-five.

The main political role of the Supreme Court is to ensure that legislation conforms to the constitution. The Supreme Court has acted as a bulwark against state abuses of power in some landmark civil rights judgments. It introduced a system of public interest litigation that enabled bonded laborers, disenfranchised tribal people, the homeless, and indigent women to redress their claims. In recent years, the Supreme Court has defended environmental causes. In 1996–1997, the Court ordered that clean water and air laws in New Delhi be enforced, which involved removing polluting cars and buses from the streets and shutting down polluting enterprises.

A principal source of conflict is that the constitution simultaneously protects private property yet also directs the government to pursue social justice. Indian leaders have often promulgated socialist legislation, for example, requiring the redistribution of agricultural land. The Supreme Court considers legislation of this nature because it potentially violates the right to private property. For instance, during the early years of independence, the courts overturned state government laws to redistribute land from (***zamindars***), traditional landowners, on the grounds that the laws violated *zamindars'* fundamental rights. Parliament retaliated by amending the constitution to protect the executive's authority to promote land redistribution. But matters did not end there. The Supreme Court responded that parliament lacked the power to abrogate fundamental rights. During the Emergency period, Indira Gandhi directed parliament to pass an amendment limiting the Supreme Court's right of judicial review to procedural issues. After the Emergency ended, the newly elected government reversed the change.

Over the years, the Supreme Court has clashed head to head with the parliament as a result of the contradiction between principles of parliamentary sovereignty and judicial review that is embedded in India's constitution. For example, it has required central and state governments to prevent starvation by releasing food stocks and to promote education by providing school lunches and daycare facilities.

Like other Indian political institutions, the judiciary suffers from what has been described as institutional decay. The caseload on the Supreme Court, as with much of the Indian legal system, is extremely heavy, and there is a significant backlog of cases. When cases drag on for years, public confidence in the judiciary crumbles. Still the Supreme Court remains a powerful and valuable institution.

Compared to other large, multiethnic democracies, India has generally protected fundamental civil rights, including an independent judiciary, universal suffrage, and a free and lively press. India's media, especially its newspapers and magazines, are as free as any in the world. The combination of a vocal intellectual stratum and a free press is a cherished element in India's democracy.

Nevertheless, the tradition of a strong, interventionist state has enabled the government to violate civil liberties. After September 11, the Indian parliament passed the Prevention of Terrorism Act (POTA) whose definition of terrorism was extremely vague. A citizen could be charged under POTA without having committed a specific act. Grounds included conspiring, attempting to commit, advocating, abetting, advising, or inciting terrorism. Penalties ranged from stiff prison sentences to death. Confessions made to police officers were admissible as evidence in courts, contrary to ordinary law, and the police used torture to extract confessions.

The government used POTA in a highly arbitrary manner. The largest number of arrests took place in India's newest state, Jharkhand, where members and supporters of radical groups were incarcerated under POTA. The government also portrayed pro-independence groups in Kashmir and Muslim groups throughout India as terrorists.

**zamindars**

Landlords who served as tax collectors in India under the British colonial government. The *zamindari* system was abolished after independence.

Shortly after Manmohan Singh became prime minister in 2004, the cabinet repealed POTA on grounds that it had been misused. Instead, it amended existing laws to tackle terrorism. However, Singh's government did not dismiss charges against those who had previously been arrested under POTA.

### Subnational Government

The structure of India's twenty-eight state governments parallels that of the national government. Each state has a government, headed by a chief minister, who is the leader of the party with most seats in the lower house of the state legislature. The chief minister appoints cabinet ministers, who head various ministries staffed by a state-level, permanent bureaucracy. The quality of government below the national level is often poor.

Each state has a governor, who is appointed by the national president. Governors are supposed to serve under the direction of the chief minister. However, in practice they often become independently powerful, especially in states where the national government is at odds with the state government or where state governments are unstable. Governors can dismiss elected state governments and proclaim temporary Presidential Rule if they determine that the state government is ineffective.

There is an ongoing power struggle between state and central governments. States often demand a greater allocation of resources from the central government. They have also demanded the devolution of power and recognition of their distinctive cultural and linguistic identities. When conflicting political parties are in power at the national and state levels, center-state relations can be inflamed by political and ethnic conflicts.

Indian politics has become increasingly regionalized in recent years. States have become more autonomous economically and politically. State parties play an increasingly important role in national governance. Economic liberalization has provided them with the opportunity to seek out foreign investment independent of the national government. One consequence is that regional inequalities are widening.

India also has an elaborate system of local governance. The ***panchayats*** are locally elected councils at the local, district, and state levels. They were strengthened in 1992 by a constitutional amendment that stipulated that *panchayat* elections should be held every five years and required that one-third of all seats on the *panchayats* should be reserved for women and that scheduled castes and tribes should be represented in proportion to their numbers in the locality. Most states have met the 33 percent women's **reservations** at all three levels and several have exceeded it.

The resources and planning capabilities of the *panchayats* are relatively limited. State legislatures determine how much power and authority they can wield. Most *panchayats* are responsible for implementing rural development schemes but not devising them. Although *panchayats* are provided with considerable resources, they have little discretion over how to allocate funds. Corruption is common because local political elites, bureaucrats, and influential citizens often siphon off public funds. Thus, many of the funds spent on poverty alleviation programs have been wasted.

*panchayats*

Elected bodies at the village, district, and state levels that have development and administrative responsibilities.

**reservations**

Jobs or admissions to colleges reserved by the government of India for specific underprivileged groups.

# The Policy-Making Process

The government in New Delhi formulates major policies. Behind the scenes, senior civil servants in each ministry, as well as in cross-ministry offices like the prime minister's secretariat and the planning commission, play an important role identifying problems, synthesizing data, and presenting political leaders with alternative solutions. Because the prime minister usually has a clear majority in parliament, passage of most legislation is ensured, except in extremely controversial areas.

The real policy drama in India occurs when major bills are under consideration and during the process of implementation. Consider the policy shift to economic liberalization. The new course was formulated at the highest level of government by only a handful of senior ministers and bureaucrats. To reach the decision, however, a fairly complex set of political activities took place. Decision-makers consulted some of the most important interest groups, such as associations of Indian businessmen and representatives of international organizations like the World Bank and International Monetary Fund (IMF). Other groups, including those who might be harmed, made their positions known. Organized labor, for example, called a one-day general strike to oppose any attempt to privatize the public sector. Newspapers, magazines, and intellectuals weighed in. Political parties announced their positions. Members of the ruling party, the Congress in this case, did not necessarily support their own leaders at the early stage. Opposition parties emphasized the harm that the reform might inflict on their constituents. These pressures modified the policy that the government eventually adopted.

After policies have been adopted, their implementation is far from assured. Regarding liberalization, some aspects of the new policy package proved easier to implement than others. Changing the exchange rate was relatively easy because both the policy decision and its implementation require the actions of only a handful of politicians and bureaucrats. By contrast, simplifying the procedures for creating new business enterprises proved far more complicated. Implementation involves layers of bureaucrats; most benefit from the control they would need to give up. Consequently, many dragged their feet and tried to sabotage the newly simplified procedures.

## Summary

That India has functioned as a democracy for most of its sixty-year history has a great deal to do with the political institutions and processes created after 1947 and the constitution it adopted in 1950. Among the key sources of democratic stability are its largely free, fair, regular local, state and national elections, which entail relatively high levels of voter turnout. India has usually protected civil rights by creating an independent judiciary and ensuring freedom of the press. The executive has generally maintained stability and order without greatly abusing power. Federal states have substantial autonomy, power, and responsibilities, and federal parties have come to play increasingly important roles in national governance.

However democratic processes and institutions have periodically come under strain. This is partly because the highly centralized state that has existed since independence has sometimes undermined civil liberties and removed elected federal governments from office on dubious claims of ensuring stability. The autonomy and strength of key political institutions has eroded under regimes that have sought to centralize and personalize power. Well designed policies are often not implemented because they face resistance from a variety of vested interests at state and local levels. Thus while Indian democracy has endured despite the odds, maintaining strong, autonomous political institutions that prevent excessive power from being concentrated in the executive is an ongoing challenge, as is the struggle to provide competent governance.

# REPRESENTATION AND PARTICIPATION

## The Legislature

The Indian parliament is bicameral, consisting of the *Lok Sabha* and the *Rajya Sabha*. *Lok Sabha* elections are of vital importance. First, the outcome determines which party coalition will control the government. Second, although members of parliament cannot shape policies, they enjoy considerable status, access to resources, and influence over allocations of government funds.

Elections to the *Lok Sabha* are held at least every five years. However, as in other parliamentary systems, the prime minister may choose to call elections earlier. India is divided into 544 electoral districts of roughly equal population, each of which elects one representative to the national parliament by a first-past-the-post electoral procedure. Since party leaders control nominations, most legislators are beholden to them for securing a party ticket. Given the importance of the party label for nominations, members of parliament support party leaders and maintain strong voting discipline in the *Lok Sabha*.

The main tasks of the *Lok Sabha* are to elect the prime minister (that is, the leader of the winning party coalition), pass legislation, and debate government actions. Although any member of parliament can introduce bills, the government sponsors those that get serious consideration and are eventually passed. After bills are introduced, they are assigned to parliamentary committees for detailed study and discussion. The committees report the bills back to the *Lok Sabha* for debate, possible amendment, and preliminary votes. They are then sent to the *Rajya Sabha*, the upper house, which generally approves bills passed by the *Lok Sabha*. Most members of the *Rajya Sabha* are elected indirectly by state legislatures. It is much weaker than the *Lok Sabha* because its assent is not required for the passage of spending measures that the *Lok Sabha* approves, it cannot introduce no-confidence motions, and it is much smaller than the *Lok Sabha*. After the *Rajya Sabha* votes on (and possibly amends) bills, they return to the *Lok Sabha* for a third reading, after which the final text is voted on by both houses and, if passed, sent to the president for approval.

Although the *Lok Sabha* can make and unmake governments (by voting to bring them down), it does not play a significant role in policy-making. Keep in mind that (1) the government generally introduces new legislation; (2) most legislators are politically beholden to party leaders; and (3) all parties maintain tight discipline to ensure voting along party lines.

One indication of parliament's relative ineffectiveness is that changes in its social composition do not have significant policy consequences. Whether members of parliament are business executives or workers, men or women, or members of upper or lower castes is unlikely to significantly influence policy. Nevertheless, groups in society derive symbolic recognition from having one of their own in parliament.

The typical member of parliament is a male university graduate between forty and sixty years old. Over the years, there have been some changes in the social composition of legislators. For example, legislators in the 1950s were likely to be urban men and were often lawyers and members of higher castes. Today, nearly half of all members of parliament come from rural areas, and many have agricultural backgrounds. Members

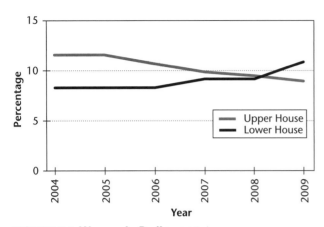

**FIGURE 6.4 Women in Parliament**

*Source:* Women in Parliaments World Classification. Http://www.ipu.org/wmn-e/arc/classif300908.htm.

of the middle castes (the so-called backward castes) are also well represented today. These changes reflect some of the broad shifts in the distribution of power in Indian society. By contrast, the proportion of women and of poor, lower-caste individuals in parliament remains low. The representation of women in parliament has gradually increased from 4.4 percent (or 22 women) in the first parliament (1952–1957) to 10.8 percent (58 women) in 2009. (See Figure 6.4.)

Following many years of deliberation and debate, the upper house of parliament supported a constitutional amendment in 2010 guaranteeing at least 33 percent seats for women in parliament and the legislative assemblies; it awaits approval by the lower house of parliament.

# Political Parties and the Party System

Political parties and elections are where much of the real drama of Indian politics occurs. Since parties that control a majority of seats in the national or state parliaments form the government and control public resources, parties devote substantial political energy to contesting elections. Since independence, the party system has evolved from being dominated by Congress to one in which Congress is merely one among the major parties but far from dominant (see Table 6.3.) What thus began as a virtually one-party system has evolved into a real multiparty system with three main political tendencies: centrist, center-left, and center-right.

| Table 6.3 | Major Party Election Results | | | | | | | | | | | |
|---|---|---|---|---|---|---|---|---|---|---|---|---|
| | **1991** | | **1996** | | **1998** | | **1999** | | **2004** | | **2009** | |
| | % | Seats | % | Seats | % | Seats | % | Seats | % | Seats | % | Seats |
| Congress | 37.3 | 225 | 29 | 143 | 25.4 | 140 | 28.4 | 112 | 26.69 | 145[a] | 28.55% | |
| BJP & Allies | 19.9 | 119 | 24 | 193 | 36.2 | 250 | 41.3 | 296 | 35.9 | 1.189 | 24.63% | |
| Janata | 10.8 | 55 | Joined with UF | | Joined with UF | | 1 | 1 | Joined with Congress | | 0% | |
| United Front | — | — | 31 | 180 | 20.9 | 98 | — | — | — | — | — | — |
| Communists[b] | — | 48 | Joined with UF | | Joined with UF | | 5.4 | 32 | 7.0 | 53 | 1.43% | |
| Others | | | | | | | 23.9 | 107 | 19.9 | 78 | 34.71% | |

[a]The more relevant figures in 2004 for Congress and allies were 35.82 and 219, respectively.
[b] Includes both the CPM and the CPI.
*Source: India Today,* July 15, 1991, March 16, 1998; *Economic Times* website, economictimes.indiatimes.com; and *The Hindu,* May 20, 2004.

India's major national parties are ideologically diverse. As a centrist party, the Congress stands for secularism, economic liberalization, and mild redistribution of wealth. The Bharatiya Janata Party (BJP), by contrast, has championed religious nationalist and antiminority positions. In addition to these two main contenders, other major competitors include the Janata, the all-India CPM, and nearly thirty-four regional parties with a presence in the parliament.

The major parties are unable to form a government on their own, so they must stitch together coalitions that include many small, usually regionally based, parties. As one would expect, there are feverish negotiations among coalition parties over the allocation of cabinet positions and the policies that the governing coalition will pursue.

## The Congress Party

Following independence, with Nehru at its helm, Congress was the unquestioned ruling party of India. Over the years, especially since the mid-1960s, this hegemony came to be challenged. By the time Indira Gandhi assumed power in 1966, the old Congress Party had begun to lose its political sway, and anticolonial nationalism was fading. In a short time, many poor, lower-caste citizens became independent from the political guidance of village big men. As a result, numerous regional parties started challenging the Congress party's monopoly on power.

Indira Gandhi sought to reverse the decline in Congress's electoral popularity by mobilizing the poor, who were India's vast majority. Her promise to end poverty struck a popular chord and propelled Gandhi to the top of India's political pyramid. Her personal success, however, split the party. Indira Gandhi replaced the party's decentralized bottom-up structure with a centralized organization. The top-down structure enabled leaders to control the party, but it was a major liability in achieving grassroots support.

Whereas during the 1970s Congress had a left-of-center, pro-poor political platform, beginning in 1984 it became centrist under Rajiv Gandhi (see Section 2). For much of the 1980s and 1990s, the Congress Party tilted right of center, championing economic efficiency, business interests, and limited government spending on health, education, and welfare. However, the 2004 and 2009 national elections, that returned Congress to power, have been interpreted as a victory for the forces of secularism and limited redistribution over the more conservative politics of the religious nationalists.

## The Janata Party

The Janata Party, India's other centrist party, with support from other parties, formed short-lived national governments in 1977, 1989, 1996, and 1997. The Janata Party is not a cohesive political party but a changing coalition of small parties and factions. It was created in 1977 when several small parties formed an alliance to oppose Indira Gandhi's Emergency. Much to everyone's surprise, Janata won the national elections. This loose coalition lasted only a little over two years, when conflicting leadership ambitions tore it apart.

Under the leadership of breakaway Congress leader V. P. Singh, the Janata Party again briefly controlled national government during the late 1980s. Singh undertook one major policy initiative that identified the Janata Party with a progressive cause. He supported a proposal by the **Mandal Commission**, an official government agency that recommended quotas in government jobs and admissions to universities to what are described as other backward classes, generally, the middle, rural castes. The policy is known as reservation, similar to the policy of reserving seats for women in the *panchayats* described above, and to affirmative action programs in the United States. The "**other backward classes**," who became beneficiaries of reservations constitute between 32 to 52

**Mandal Commission**

A government-appointed commission headed by J. P. Mandal to consider seat reservations and quotas to redress caste discrimination.

**other backward classes**

The middle or intermediary castes in India that have been accorded reserved seats in public education and employment since the early 1990s.

percent of the population. Prime Minister Singh's attempt to garner electoral support backfired when threatened upper castes organized demonstrations, riots, and political violence. Not only did this disruption contribute to the downfall of Singh's government, but it also transformed local and regional caste conflicts into national conflicts.

In recent years, the Janata Party has been able to survive only as part of the United Front, a broad coalition of small parties. It has ceased to command sufficient independent strength to be designated a national party. The Janata Party continues to have a weak organizational structure, and it lacks a distinctive, coherent political platform. To distinguish itself from Congress, it claims that it is more faithful to Mahatma Gandhi's vision of modern India as decentralized and village-oriented. The Janata Party is viewed as a party of small, rural agriculturalists who generally fall somewhere in the middle of the rigid caste hierarchy between Brahmins and untouchables. It is unclear whether the backward castes will continue to identify with the Janata Party.

### The Bharatiya Janata Party (BJP)

The BJP is a descendant of the Jana Sangh Party, which entered the Indian political scene in 1951. The Jana Sangh joined the Janata Party government in 1977, but its members left and formed the BJP in 1980. The BJP is a right-leaning, Hindu-nationalist party, the first major Indian party to seek support on the basis of religious identity, and the first party to adopt an openly anti-Muslim stance. Unlike Congress and Janata, the BJP is highly centralized and well organized. It has disciplined party members who become party cadres only after long apprenticeship.

The BJP differs from Congress and the Janata Party in another respect. It has close ties to a large nonparliamentary organization, the Rashtriya Swayam Sevak Sangh (RSS). The RSS recruits young people (especially educated youth in urban areas) by emphasizing cultural activities. It champions a chauvinistic reinterpretation of India's "great Hindu past." The BJP also has close ties with another RSS affiliated group, a religious organization, the Visva Hindu Parishad (VHP).

Until the late 1980s, the Jana Sangh and the BJP were mainly supported by the urban, lower-middle-classes, especially small traders and commercial groups. Since their numbers were relatively small, the BJP was a minor actor on the Indian political scene. The party widened its base of support in the late 1980s by appealing to Hindu nationalism, especially in north-central and western India, as well as in the southern state of Karnataka. The BJP found in Indian Muslims a convenient scapegoat for the frustrations of various social groups.

In the 1989 elections, the BJP emerged as the third-largest party after the Congress and Janata parties. In 1991, it gained the second-largest number of seats in parliament. The BJP sought to attract Hindu support by allying with the RSS and VHP in a campaign challenging the legitimacy of a Muslim mosque (the babri masjid) located at Ayodhya, in northern India. BJP and VHP leaders claimed that centuries ago, a Muslim ruler had destroyed a Hindu temple at the birth place of the Hindu god Ram to construct the mosque. The BJP, RSS, and VHP organized a nationwide campaign, which culminated in the destruction of the mosque on December 6, 1992. Seventeen hundred people, mostly Muslim, were killed in subsequent riots.

When the BJP was twice defeated in parliamentary elections following the destruction of the mosque at Ayodhya, it formed the National Democratic Alliance, a coalition with regional political parties. In an attempt to gain legitimacy, it shelved contentious issues that promoted the interests of Hindus over those of religious minorities.

The BJP renounced some of its chauvinist positions after attaining power in the National Democratic Alliance in 1999. However, it retained close ties to the antiminority, far right RSS and VHP. Moreover, all of the BJP's top-ranking leaders are RSS members. The BJP, in alliance with the VHP, continued to engage in antiminority violence in several federal states. The most important instance was in Gujarat in February–March 2002 when the BJP state government orchestrated a campaign of terror against the Muslim population, which resulted in approximately 2,000 deaths. The BJP capitalized on Hindu electoral support to return to office in Gujarat in 2002 and 2007.

However, the BJP's leading role in the anti-Muslim riots in Gujarat may have contributed to its defeat in the 2004 and 2009 national parliamentary elections. Testimony to the broad appeal of secularism is that the Congress government's rejection of sectarian religious appeals and at least verbal support for improving the situation of minorities has contributed to its repeated electoral victories. This may be a reason why the BJP has downplayed its Hindu-nationalist platform in recent years.

## The Communist Party of India (CPM)

India remains one of the only democratic countries in the world with a self-proclaimed communist party. The CPM is an offshoot of the Communist Party of India, which was formed during the colonial period. Although the CPM is communist in name, it has evolved into a social democratic (or center-left) party that accepts democracy and the limits of a market economy. At the same time, it seeks to obtain greater benefits for the poor. The CPM's political base today is concentrated in two Indian states, West Bengal and Kerala. CPM candidates are often elected to the *Lok Sabha* from these states, and the CPM has frequently run governments in the two states.

The CPM is a disciplined party, with party cadres and a hierarchical authority structure. Within the national parliament, CPM members often strongly criticize government policies that are likely to hurt the poor. CPM-run state governments in West Bengal and Kerala have provided relatively honest and stable administration. They have sponsored moderate reforms that seek to ensure the rights of agricultural tenants (for example, by preventing landlords from evicting them), provide services to those living in shantytowns, and channel public investments to rural areas.

However, in 2007 the CPM government in West Bengal sponsored an economic project that proved highly unpopular. The West Bengal government sought to promote industrial development by acquiring farmland to create special economic zones (SEZs). It tried to attract foreign and domestic companies to invest in these zones by offering tax and other subsidies. Villagers in Nandigram, a town in one zone, organized demonstrations to protest the government's acquiring a large tract of land. When the state government ordered the police to fire on the protesters, it provoked nationwide opposition. The CPM's relatively poor showing in the 2009 elections can partly be explained by the crackdown and, more generally, to the CPM's sponsorship of SEZs.

The Indian party system has changed dramatically since 1989. A multiparty system has emerged amidst the growth of federal parties, and the power of federal states has grown. Federal parties have largely determined the outcome of the last three elections and participated in every coalition government since 1989. Even in the 2009 elections, which are commonly seen as a victory for the national Congress party, federal parties won 29.2 percent of the vote. As a result, national parties have become dependent on federal parties to form and sustain governing coalitions. Neither of the two major electoral contenders, the Congress or the BJP is at present able to muster anything close to a majority of parliamentary seats to form a government.

Taken together, the thirty-four officially recognized state parties have significant weight in Indian politics. Some are regional powerhouses and control state governments. While the fragmentation of the party system enables the representation

Rally for the 2009 Parliamentary Elections.

AP Photo/Rajesh Kumar Singh

of multiple interests, it also deters the government from acting decisively. Cabinets are large, unwieldy, and cautious. If the government acted boldly, it could lose the support of one or more coalition partners, lose its parliamentary majority and be forced to resign.

## Elections

Elections in India are a colossal event. Nearly 500 million people are eligible to vote, and close to 300 million cast ballots. The turnout rate is far higher than in the United States. Although television plays an increasingly important role, much campaigning still involves personal contacts between politicians and the electorate. Senior politicians fly around the country making speeches at election rallies amid blaring music. Lesser politicians and party supporters travel the dusty streets in tiny villages and district towns. Political messages boom from loudspeakers.

Given India's low literacy rates, pictures of party symbols are critical: a hand for Congress; lotus flower for the BJP; and hammer and sickle for the CPM. Illiterate voters vote by putting a thumb mark on the preferred symbol. During the campaign, therefore, party officials work hard to associate the party's candidate and election platform with the appropriate symbol.

Members of parliament are elected by a single-member district first-past-the-post system. Many candidates compete in each electoral district; the candidate with a plurality wins the seat. This system privileges the major political parties.

A pillar of Indian democracy is the fact that its elections are open, competitive, and honest. Much of the credit for this goes to the Election Commission, which functions independently of the executive. Particularly since 1991, with the appointment of a respected chief, the Election Commission has been highly successful in protecting the integrity of the electoral process.

## Political Culture, Citizenship, and Identity

Several aspects of Indian political culture are noteworthy. First, the political/public and private spheres are not sharply differentiated. One undesirable result is corruption, since politicians frequently seek personal and family enrichment through public office. A more attractive result is a high level of citizens' political involvement. Second, the Indian elite is extremely factionalized. Personal ambition prevents leaders from pursuing collective goals, such as forming cohesive parties, running stable governments, or giving priority to national development. Unlike many East Asian countries, for example, where consensus is powerful and political negotiations take place behind closed doors, politics in India involves open conflicts.

Third, regions are highly differentiated by language and culture, villages are poorly connected with each other, and communities are stratified by caste. Some observers regard group fragmentation as playing a positive role in promoting political stability. Others stress that it obstructs implementing national reforms to improve the lot of the poor.

India's highly open style of democratic politics often fuels political conflicts involving identity politics. Region, language, religion, and caste help Indians define themselves. Ethnic conflicts were minimal during the period of Nehru's secular nationalism and when Indira Gandhi's poor-versus-rich cleavage defined the core political issues. In the 1980s and 1990s, however, the decline of the Congress Party and developments in telecommunications and transportation accentuated group differences. As a result, identity-based political conflicts have mushroomed. Two especially significant conflicts deserve mention. First, caste conflicts, that were formerly local and regional, have become national in character. V. P. Singh initiated this process when he introduced reservations for other backward classes. This gave rise to political parties that sought to advance the interests of lower caste groups and to increasing caste-based contestation.

The second destructive identity-based conflict pits Hindus against Muslims. For most of the post-independence period, when Hindu-Muslim conflicts occurred they were triggered by tensions on the local level. However, in the mid-1980s and 1990s, the BJP whipped up anti-Muslim emotions in an effort to attract Hindu support. The resulting violence against Muslims illustrates the dangers of stirring up identity-based political passions.

# Interests, Social Movements, and Protest

India has a vibrant tradition of political activism that has both enriched and complicated the workings of democracy. Social movements, nongovernmental organizations (NGOs), and trade unions have pressured the state to address the interests and needs of underprivileged groups and check authoritarian tendencies. Labor has played a significant role. Unions frequently engage in strikes, demonstrations, and an Indian protest technique called *gherao*, when workers hold executives of a firm hostage to press their demands.

Labor unions are politically fragmented, particularly at the national level. Instead of the familiar model of one factory/one union, unions allied to different political parties often organize within a single factory. Rival labor organizations compete for workers' support at higher levels as well. The government generally stays out of labor-management conflicts. India's industrial relations are thus closer to the pluralist model found in Anglo-American countries than to the corporatist model of Mexico.

Social movements date back to the mid-1970s. Prime Minister Indira Gandhi distrusted voluntary organizations and movements, and sought to restrict their activities. During the national Emergency (1975–1977), the government imprisoned members of the opposition. However, activists reacted by forming political parties and social movements, often with close ties to one another. Socialist leader Jai Prakash Narain organized the most influential movement opposing Emergency rule. It helped bring about the downfall of Congress and the election of the Janata Party. A decade later, V. P. Singh resigned from Congress and formed the *Jan Morcha* (Peoples' Front), a movement that brought new groups into politics and helped elect the National Front in 1989.

There was also a significant growth in the number of NGOs from the 1980s on. When Rajiv Gandhi came to power in 1984, he cultivated a closer relationship with

NGOs. Over the years, the government's financial support for NGOs has steadily increased.

The large number and extensive activities of social movements make India quite distinctive among developing countries. The most significant social movements include the women's movement, the environment movement, the farmers' movement, and the *dalit* movement. The term *dalit* is derived from the Indo-Aryan root, "dal," which means suppressed or crushed. *Dalit* is widely used today in preference to the terms "scheduled castes" or "untouchables."

The roots of the *dalit* movement lie in a reform movement among Hindus that began in 1875, whose members first used the term. The modern *dalit* movement was inspired by Dr. Balasaheb Ambedkar, the *dalit* author of the Indian constitution, who formed the Republican Party in the late 1960s. When the party disintegrated, it was succeeded by the Dalit Panthers, a movement that demanded that *dalits* be treated with dignity and provided with better educational opportunities. Today, the *dalit* movement seeks a greater share of electoral power and public office. Among its most notable successes is the Bahujan Samaj Party (BSP), created in 1989 with the goal of increasing dalits' political representation and acquisition of political power. The BSP grew rapidly in the 1990s by championing *dalit* empowerment while appealing to a broad cross-caste base of support. The BSP succeeded in forming coalition governments with other political parties in Uttar Pradesh (UP), India's most populous state. In 2007, it was elected to state office independently, and its powerful female leader, Mayavati (known by one name only), became UP's chief minister.

The environmental movement has been spurred by the magnitude of the country's environmental crisis, described in Section 2. Some groups have opposed state policies that have permitted deforestation. The Chipko movement, which emerged in the early 1970s in the Himalayas is one of the best-known and oldest movements against deforestation. It has influenced similar forms of activism in other regions of the country. Other groups have challenged industries that operate with little regard for the health and safety of their workers and the local community. The 1984 Union Carbide disaster in Bhopal, when a gas leak caused an explosion that resulted in thousands of deaths and injuries, generated movements demanding greater compensation for victims of the gas leak, as well as the adoption of environmental regulations to prevent similar disasters in the future.

One of India's largest environmental movements has opposed the construction of a dam that it claimed would benefit already prosperous regions to the detriment of poor regions, as well as displace millions of people who would not be provided with adequate resettlement. A large proportion of those displaced are tribals who do not possess land titles. The Narmada Bachao Andolan (NBA) began protesting the construction of the giant Sardar Sarvodaya Dam in western India in 1986. The Narmada movement galvanized tens of thousands of people to engage in nonviolent protest. It caused the World Bank to rescind promised loans, but the Indian government continued to pursue the project.

Women and questions of gender inequality have been at the forefront of environmental struggles like the Chipko and Narmada movements. The 1980s also witnessed the formation of a number of autonomous urban women's organizations. They campaigned against rape in police custody, dowry murders, *sati* (the immolation of widows on their husbands' funeral pyres;), female feticide (facilitated by the use of amniocentesis), media misrepresentation of women, harmful contraception dissemination, coercive population policies, and the adverse impact of economic reforms.

Four important developments have influenced the character and trajectory of social movements in recent years. First, many social movements have developed close relationships to the state and to electoral politics. In the past, social movements tended to be community-based and issue-specific. Once a movement achieved some success, by

---

**dalit**

The dalit movement is organized by untouchables or scheduled caste against caste discrimination and oppression.

---

**sati**

*Sati*, or widow immolation, was outlawed by the British in the nineteenth century. *Satis* have occurred, although they are uncommon, in post-Independence India.

limiting the felling of forest trees, stopping the construction of a dam, or obtaining higher prices for agricultural subsidies, it would dissolve. Although many social movements remain limited in focus, duration, and geographic reach, some have sought to overcome these difficulties by engaging in electoral politics. The *dalit* movement and Hindu nationalism are two important examples. Other movements have sought to work with particular branches of the state. The women's movement, for example, has worked closely with the bureaucracy and the courts.

Second, the growth of the religious right has confronted left-wing social movements with a serious challenge. Although the religious right and the secular left disagree on most issues, they have adopted the same stance on some questions, like opposing economic liberalization and globalization. The dilemma this poses is whether groups that are fundamentally opposed on some issues should form tactical alliances on the issues where they agree.

Third, as the state has abandoned its socialist commitments, social movements and political parties have also ceased to focus on poverty and class inequality. The most important exception is the Naxalites. Although the Naxalites have strong support among some of India's poorest and most marginal communities, its use of violence has limited its appeal among social activists.

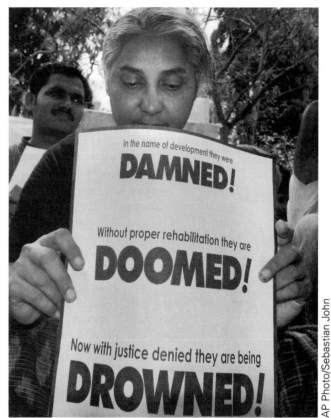

Crowds gathered to protest the construction of the Sardar Sarovar Dam.

Fourth, many NGOs and social movements have developed extensive transnational connections. The consequences for social movements have been double-edged. On the positive side, funding from foreign sources has been vital to the survival of NGOs and social movements since they have received limited funding from Indian corporate groups. However, NGOs that receive foreign funding are often viewed with suspicion. Moreover, foreign funding has created a division between activists with and without access to foreign donors.

## Summary

Political participation over the years has broadened in scope and deepened in intensity. A single-party system dominated by the Congress Party has slowly been replaced by a multiparty system of parties across the left-right spectrum. Similarly, caste hierarchies have eroded in Indian society, and upper castes cannot readily control the political behavior of those below them. The result is that many groups feel empowered and seek to translate this new consciousness and sense of efficacy into material gains by influencing government policies. The developments described in this section, including the development of a genuine multiparty system, the rise of state-based parties, and the growth of social movements, all point toward an explosion of participation along with a fragmentation of Indian society. These trends raise questions about the relationship between the expansion of democracy and the challenges of democratic governance.

# INDIAN POLITICS IN TRANSITION

## Focus Questions

Identify two or three major challenges confronting India. How well equipped are Indian political institutions to meet these challenges?

In what ways does India provide a useful model of economic and political development for other countries?

What are two features of India's political system that make the Indian model less attractive?

## Political Challenges and Changing Agendas

India has come a long way in the more than six decades since independence. On the positive side of the ledger, Indians can justly be proud of the fact that this large, poor, and incredibly diverse country has survived intact. Beyond this, the fact that India has been fairly well governed during this period represents another achievement. The disturbing record of failed states in the world, in far smaller countries, suggests grounds to celebrate the fact that the Indian state is reasonably effective. A further achievement is that India has been a well-functioning democracy for virtually its entire existence and by and large has upheld the rule of law and protected equal rights, notably those of minorities. Finally, Indians can be proud of the fact after decades of economic stagnation, their country is leapfrogging into the twenty-first century. By scoring sustained and rapid economic growth for the last three decades, India has become a leader of the world's emerging economies.

However, these are the impressive features of the proverbially half-filled glass. We conclude the chapter by highlighting several of the many pressing challenges that India must surmount to fulfill its rich and promising potential.

### The Challenge of Ethnic Diversity

The future of Indian democracy is closely bound up with how the country confronts the growing politicization of ethnic identities; that is, the attempt by organized ethnic groups to obtain state power and state-controlled economic resources. Caste, language, and religion are the basis for political mobilization. Democracy can encourage political parties and leaders to manipulate group identities for electoral purposes.

Political struggles in India are simultaneously struggles for identity, power, and wealth. Identity politics is characterized by two distinct trends: the tendency for a variety of diverse non–class-based regional and ethnic groups to make demands on parties and governments; and pressure on political parties to broaden their electoral appeals to the poor; that is, the middle and lower strata of Indian society. If India's growth dividend is sufficiently large, it may be possible to satisfy both sets of demands. However, this requires an unusually favorable set of circumstances, including continued economic growth, skillful political leadership, and a commitment to distribute economic gains broadly enough to satisfy all significant groups.

### Political Violence

In recent years, India has experienced the growth of two forms of violence in addition to Hindu nationalist violence described earlier. The first is on the part of the poor and dispossessed who have participated in the Naxalite-led insurgency in thirteen out of India's twenty-eight states. Prime Minister Singh has characterized the

"Maoist rebels" as India's major "law and order problem." In 2009 alone, more than 900 people, most of them civilians, were killed in attacks related to the Naxalite-led insurgency.

Second, India has become a prime site of terrorist violence in recent years. In the 1990s, most attacks were linked to regional conflicts in the Punjab, Kashmir, and the Northeast. While violent attacks continue in Kashmir, they have extended to other parts of the country. The sources of terrorist attacks have also become more varied. Organizations with links to the RSS have planned several of them, although they have made them appear to be the work of Muslim militants. Pakistan's ISI and other transnational Islamic networks have been responsible for many others.

## India-Pakistan Tensions

From the moment that India and Pakistan became separate states, relations between them have varied from tense to violent. Their troubled relations include a history of three wars, simmering tensions over Kashmir, and periodic violence between their armed forces. Indo-Pakistani tensions are a major reason for the two countries' high military expenditures.

The attack on the Indian parliament in 2001 sent tensions between the two countries to the boiling point. India charged that the attacks were orchestrated by the Pakistani government and assembled over 1 million troops at the Pakistani border. The threat of nuclear war was a distinct possibility. Intense intervention by the United States helped defuse the situation, and the two countries withdrew most of their troops from the border.

Relations since then have ebbed and flowed. They improved in 2005, when the Indian and Pakistani governments initiated bus service across the cease-fire line for the first time in fifty years. However, the attack in Mumbai in 2008, once again escalated tensions. A high point in their relations occurred during the Asian semifinals of the Cricket World Cup tournament in 2011, which pitted India against Pakistan and was played in India. Prime Minister Singh took the unprecedented step of inviting the Pakistani prime minister Asaf Ali Zardari to India as his guest and Zardari accepted his invitation.

A key issue is how India can prevent conflict with Pakistan from spiraling into nuclear war. The fact that both countries possess nuclear weapons aimed at the other makes the stakes incredibly high. Moreover, India has tense relations with not one but two nuclear-armed neighbors. Conflict with China, its powerful neighbor to the North and East, is never far from the surface.

## Nuclear Weapons

Soon after the BJP was first elected to power in May 1998, it fulfilled an electoral promise by gate-crashing the nuclear club. Although it cited threats from China and Pakistan as the key reason to develop nuclear weapons, the BJP's decision can also be traced to electoral considerations. The Hindu bomb, as the BJP described it, was an excellent way to mobilize Indians' national pride and thereby deflect attention from domestic, economic, and political problems.

After India detonated a nuclear bomb, Pakistan responded in kind, triggering fears of a nuclear arms race in South Asia. Worldwide condemnation and sanctions on both India and Pakistan swiftly followed. The Manmohan Singh government took a dramatic step toward defusing tensions over the nuclear issue in 2004 when it proclaimed India's commitment to preventing the proliferation of weapons of mass destruction. As a result of this commitment, the United States and India signed an agreement in 2005 that authorized India to secure international help for its civilian nuclear reactors while retaining its nuclear arms. The agreement was followed by the removal of a U.S. ban on selling nuclear technology to India. The Indo-U.S. nuclear treaty, which both countries ratified in 2008, provides for cooperation on nuclear issues despite India's continuing violation of nonproliferation norms. (For example, India has refused to sign the Comprehensive Test Ban Treaty and the Nuclear Nonproliferation Treaty.)

## Kashmir in a World of States

The roots of the conflict over Kashmir go back to the origins of India and Pakistan. The status of Kashmir—whether it should be part of India, part of Pakistan, or an independent state—was unresolved in 1947 and remains unresolved today. Tensions have often been attributed to the ethnic and religious diversity of the state's population, which is roughly 65 percent Muslim and 35 percent Hindus and other minorities. The non-Muslim minorities—Hindus, Sikhs, and Buddhists, concentrated in the areas of the state called Jammu and Ladakh—largely prefer living under Indian sovereignty. However, separatist sentiments cannot be explained primarily by religious and ethnic differences. Rather, one must explain why so many Kashmiri Muslims became violently opposed to India.

The Kashmir problem reveals the limits of Indian democracy. Despite the Indian government's pledge to grant Kashmiris the right to determine their future, the Indian government has used repression, direct control, and manipulation for decades to install unrepresentative and unpopular governments in Kashmir favorable to India. The government has repeatedly engaged in fraud and violence to shape election outcomes in Kashmir. Although recent elections were somewhat more open and inclusive, the Kashmir problem remains a major source of tension with Pakistan.

## India's Regional Relations

India's relations with regional powers have been inconsistent historically but have improved in recent years as a result of globalization. Relations with China have been especially tumultuous. Although the two countries fought only one war, in 1962, recurrent border disputes reflect their competition for regional and international influence. Over the past few years, however, India and China have come to emphasize their shared economic interests. In 2005, for example, New Delhi and Beijing signed a series of political and economic agreements, signaling a move towards greater cooperation. Today China is India's major trading partner.

Although India and Nepal established strong economic and political ties through the 1950 Indo-Nepal Treaty of Peace and Friendship, relations between the two countries have sometimes been fraught. Tensions between the two countries escalated after Nepal became an absolutist monarchy in 2005. Relations have improved since the king was deposed and democracy re-established in Nepal in 2008.

India's relations with Sri Lanka and Bangladesh have been deeply influenced by their shared ethnic compositions. India is home to fifty-five million Tamils who live in the southern state of Tamil Nadu. The Liberation Tigers of Tamil Eeelam (LTTE), which waged a secessionist movement resulting in a prolonged civil war, acquired significant support of Indian Tamils. India sent troops to Sri Lanka to disarm the

LTTE in 1987 but actually enflamed the conflict. India withdrew its troops in 1990 and maintained a distance from the conflict after that. Since the end of the civil war in Sri Lanka, India and Sri Lanka have strengthened their diplomatic and trade relations.

The creation of Bangladesh as a predominantly Bengali nation that seceded from Pakistan in 1971 was in good measure a result of India's intervention. India's Bengali population strongly identified with Bangladesh's claims to nationhood, and India's military helped engineer Bangladesh's breakaway from Pakistan. However Bangladesh has expressed resentment at trade imbalances, India's control over water resources, and Indian army incursions into its territory. In 2010, the Bangladeshi prime minister's visit to India signaled increased economic and political cooperation between the two countries.

## Economic Performance

India's economic experience is neither a clear success nor a clear failure. India has maintained strong and steady economic growth rate for decades. As a result, from being held up as an example of economic failure, India has recently emerged as a leader of developing countries. Several factors may explain this outcome. The first is the relationship between political governance and economic growth. In this, India has been fortunate to have enjoyed relatively good government: Its democratic system is mostly open and stable, its most powerful political leaders are public spirited, and its upper bureaucracy is well trained and competent.

The second factor concerns India's strategy for economic development. In the 1950s, India chose to insulate its economy from global forces, limiting the role of trade and foreign investment and emphasizing the government's role in promoting self-sufficiency in heavy industry and agriculture. The positive result was that India grew enough food to feed its large and growing population and produced a vast range of industrial goods. This strategy, however, was not without costs. India sacrificed the additional economic growth that might have come from competing effectively in global markets. Moreover, during this period it made little effort to alleviate its staggering poverty: Land redistribution failed, job creation by heavy industries was minimal, and investment in the education and health of the poor was relatively limited. In addition to the terrible human and social costs of this neglect, the poor became a drag on economic growth because they were unable to buy goods and stimulate demand for increased production; an uneducated and unhealthy labor force is not a productive labor force.

Yet the sluggish phase is now long past, and the Indian economy has grown briskly over the last three decades. However, India's numerous poor are not benefiting sufficiently from growth. Cuts in public spending on education and health services have been especially hard on the poor. The government has not succeeded in distributing the gains of growth to reduce poverty and inequality.

## International Power and Domestic Prosperity

India's attempts to become a strong regional and international power are shaped and constrained by the international environment. The increasing interdependence of global economies was illustrated by the global effects of the 2008 economic crisis. India's growth rate declined as did the demand for its exports and foreign investments, and the fiscal deficit rose to nearly 7 percent of GDP. However, the Indian economy quickly regained strength, and soon began to surge ahead again.

## Institutional Decay

Institutional decay is at the root of many of India's other challenges. Competent, honest, and responsive institutions are required to deal with the far-ranging problems identified above of Indian-Pakistan relations, ethnic diversity, and economic performance. Yet such institutions are in short supply. Disturbing evidence periodically surfaces of corruption that tarnishes key sectors of the state, such as the police, civil service, and political parties. Official corruption is not limited to accepting bribes in exchange for favors. For example, in 2010, it became evident that cabinet ministers and their associates had received kickbacks from India's purchase of weaponry and the sale of telecommunication rights. India's telecom minister, Andimuthu Raja, was accused of selling licenses to use Indian airwaves to cell phone operators at extremely low prices, costing the Indian government $40 billion in lost revenues. The incident led to further investigations, which revealed corruption at the highest levels of the central government. Although there was no evidence that Prime Minister Singh was directly involved, his refusal for months to launch an official investigation undermined his authority. Without a thorough housecleaning to eliminate institutional decay, India will make little progress in dealing with its many other pressing challenges.

In brief, India has an enviable array of resources and a daunting host of challenges. How well it will use its resources to confront these challenges is an open question. Will it be able to capitalize on its positive achievements, such as the longstanding democratic ethos framed by functioning institutions, a vibrant media and civil society, and a growing and ambitious middle class? Or will it be crippled by ethnic hostility resulting in inaction at best and disintegration of the country at worst?

The alleviation of poverty and class inequality remains a pressing challenge. So too does the Naxalite insurgency. The state's repressive response to Naxalism has only contributed to its growth. Tensions with Pakistan and instability in Kashmir continue to simmer. Understanding how India meets—or fails to meet—these challenges will be of enormous interest to students of comparative politics in the years to come. How India reconciles its national ambitions, domestic demands for greater economic redistribution, and global pressures for an efficient economy will affect its influence on regional and global trends.

# Indian Politics in Comparative Perspective

India provides an incredibly interesting and important laboratory for studying issues in comparative politics. Consider the issue of democratic consolidation. Although democracy was introduced to India by its elites, it has established firm roots within society. A clear example is when Indira Gandhi declared Emergency rule (1975–1977) and curtailed democratic freedoms. In the next election, in 1977, Indian citizens decisively voted Gandhi out of power, registering their preference for democratic rule. Most Indians value democracy and advance their claims within democratic institutions, even when those institutions are flawed.

Comparativists debate whether democracy or authoritarianism is better for economic growth. In the past, democratic India's economic performance did not compare well with the success stories of authoritarian regimes in East Asia and China. However, India's impressive economic growth in recent years suggests that the returns are not yet in. India provides a fine laboratory for studying the relationship of democratic institutions and economic performance.

Another issue within Indian politics with important comparative implications involves the relationship between democratic institutions and multiethnic societies. By studying India's history, particularly the post-1947 period, comparativists can explore how cleavages of caste, religion, and language have been contained and their destructive consequences minimized. Yet the repeated instances of ethnic violence in India suggest the need for caution. Comparativists have also puzzled over the conditions under which multiple and contradictory interests within a democratic framework can generate positive economic and distributional outcomes. Here, the variable performance of different regions in India can serve as a laboratory. For instance, what can be learned from studying two communist-ruled states, Kerala and West Bengal, which sponsored land redistribution policies and extensive social welfare programs? Many scholars have praised the Kerala model because it abolished tenancy and landlord exploitation, provided effective public food distribution of subsidized rice to low-income households, enacted protective laws for agricultural workers and pensions for retired agricultural laborers, and provided extensive government employment for low-caste communities.

Another question engaging comparativists is whether success in providing education and welfare inevitably leads to success in the economic sphere. Again, the case of Kerala provides pointers for further research. Kerala scores high on human development indicators such as literacy and health, and its economy has also grown in recent years. At the same time, Kerala remains one of the poorest states in India.

It is not yet clear whether India will be able to build upon and extend its achievements or will fail to cope with many severe challenges in coming years. Political scientists will doubtless find much to learn from studying India's future development. The results will be of vital importance to over one billion Indian citizens. And, given India's immense size and strategic importance, developments in Indian politics will affect the fate of people throughout the world.

## Key Terms

| | | |
|---|---|---|
| Sikh | green revolution | *zamindars* |
| caste system | state-led economic development | *panchayats* |
| Brahmin | economic liberalization | reservations |
| Sepoy Rebellion | Naxalite | Mandal Commission |
| scheduled castes | untouchables | other backward classes |
| patronage system | *Lok Sabha* | *dalits* |
| nonaligned bloc | *Rajya Sabha* | *sati* |
| Emergency (1975–1977) | Indian Administrative Service (IAS) | |

## Suggested Readings

Bardhan, Pranab. *The Political Economy of Development in India*. New Delhi: Oxford University Press, 1984.

Basu, Amrita. *Two Faces of Protest: Contrasting Modes of Women's Activism in India*. Berkeley: University of California Press, 1992.

Basu, Amrita., and Atul Kohli, eds. *Community Conflicts and the State in India*. New Delhi: Oxford University Press, 1998.

Basu, Amrita, and Srirupa Roy, eds. *Violence and Democracy in India*. Calcutta: Seagull Books, 2006.

Brass, Paul. *The Production of Hindu-Muslim Violence in Contemporary India* (University of Washington Press, 2003).

Chatterjee, Partha, ed. *State Politics in India*. New Delhi: Oxford University Press, 1997.

Corbridge, Stuart, and John Harriss. *Reinventing India*. Cambridge, U.K.: Polity Press, 2000.

Dreze, Jean, and Amartya Sen, eds. *Economic Development and Social Opportunity*. New Delhi: Oxford University Press, 1995.

Frankel, Francine. *India's Political Economy, 1947–2004: The Gradual Revolution*. New Delhi: Oxford University Press, 2005.

Gangly, Sumit, Larry Diamond, and Marc Plattner, eds. *The State of India's Democracy*. Baltimore: Johns Hopkins University Press, 2007.

Guha, Ramachandran, *India after Gandhi: The World's Largest Democracy*. New York: Harper Perennial, 2008.

Hasan, Zoya, *Politics of Inclusion: Caste, Minority and Representation in India*. Delhi: Oxford University Press, 2009.

Jaffrelot, Christophe. *The Hindu Nationalist Movement and Indian Politics, 1925 to the 1990s: Strategies on Identity Building, Implantation and Mobilization*. New York: Columbia University Press, 1996.

Jalal, Ayesha. *Democracy and Authoritarianism in South Asia*. Cambridge: Cambridge University Press, 1995.

Jayal, Niraja Gopal, and Pratap Mehta, eds. *The Oxford Companion to Politics in India*. New Delhi: Oxford University Press, 2010.

Jenkins, Rob. *Regional Reflections: Contemporary Politics across India's States*. New Delhi: Oxford University Press, 2004.

Kohli, Atul. *Democracy and Discontent: India's Growing Crisis of Governability*. Cambridge: Cambridge University Press, 1991.

___. *State Directed Development: Political Power and Industrialization in the Global Periphery*. Cambridge: Cambridge University Press, 2004.

___. *The State and Poverty in India: The Politics of Reform*. Cambridge: Cambridge University Press, 1987.

___, ed. *The Success of India's Democracy*. Cambridge: Cambridge University Press, 2001.

Panagariya, Arvind. *India: The Emerging Giant*. New York: Oxford University Press, 2008.

Ray, Raka, and Mary Katzenstein, eds. *Social Movements in India: Poverty, Power and Politics*. Lanham, MD: Rowman and Littlefield, 2005.

Rudolph, Lloyd, and Susanne Rudolph, *In Pursuit of Lakshmi: The Political Economy of the Indian State*. Chicago: University of Chicago Press, 1987.

Sarkar, Sumit. *Modern India: 1885 to 1947*. Madras: Macmillan, 1983.

Varshney, Ashutosh. *Ethnic Conflict and Civic Life: Hindus and Muslims in India*. New Haven: Yale University Press, 2002.

___, ed. *India and the Political Economy of Developing Countries: Essays in Honor of Myron Weiner*. New Delhi: Sage Publishers, 2004.

Wilkinson, Steven. *Votes and Violence: Electoral Competition and Ethnic Riots in India*. Cambridge: Cambridge University Press, 2004.

## Suggested Websites

Indian National Congress
http://www.congress.org.in/new/

Bharatiya Janata Party (BJP)
www.bjp.org

Times of India
http://timesofindia.indiatimes.com/

*Economic and Political Weekly*, a good source of information on Indian politics
www.epw.org.in

*Frontline*, a magazine with coverage of Indian politics
www.flonnet.com

*The Hindu*, an English daily paper in India
www.hinduonnet.com

*Hindustan Times*
www.hindustantimes.com

Directory of Indian government websites
goidirectory.nic.in

*Sabrang Communications*, providing coverage of human rights issues in India
www.sabrang.com

# 7 The United States

Louis DeSipio

AP Images/Moshe Bursuker

**Official Name:** United States of America

**Location:** North America, between Canada and Mexico

**Capital City:** Washington, D.C.

**Population (2010):** 308.7 million

**Size:** 9,826,630 sq. km.; about half the size of South America; slightly larger than China

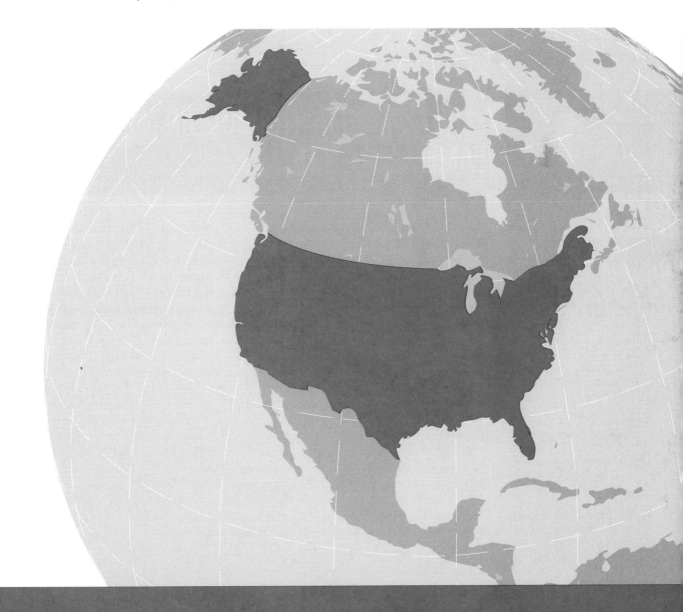

**1788**
U.S. Constitution replaced Articles of Confederation.

**1803**
Supreme Court establishes judicial review in *Marbury* v. *Madison*.

**1861–1865**
U.S. Civil War.

| 1700 | 1780 | 1800 | 1820 | 1840 | 1860 | 1880 |

**1803**
Louisiana Purchase.

**1776**
Independence from Great Britain declared.

**1830s**
Mass political parties emerge, and electorate expands to include a majority of white men.

**1865–1876**
Reconstruction era: The United States establishes but fails to guarantee voting rights for freed slaves.

SECTION 1

# THE MAKING OF THE MODERN AMERICAN STATE

## Focus Questions

The outcomes of several of the previous critical junctures have seen an expansion in the powers and responsibilities of the federal government relative to the states. The political mood in the United States as evidenced by the outcome of the 2010 elections, however, would appear to suggest that many in the electorate desire a diminished role for the federal government. Based on your reading of the issues that led to the previous critical outcomes and their resolutions, what do you think will be the trigger of the next critical juncture and its outcome?

How does geographic setting shape the governing structures that have emerged in the United States over the past 225 years?

Barack Obama's election in 2008 saw the largest presidential victory margin in recent elections. His victory was accompanied by increases in the size of the Democratic majorities in the U.S. House and Senate. Having one party in control of both houses of Congress and the presidency was unusual in contemporary politics. The sizes of Democratic majorities in the House and Senate were also substantial. Obama used these majorities to pass a series of major bills including a large economic stimulus bill, national health insurance (discussed later), civil rights legislation focusing on workplace discrimination, and reform of the financial services industry. The Senate also confirmed two members of the U.S. Supreme Court nominated by President Obama.

The 2010 election dramatically changed the balance of political power in Washington and reduced the likelihood that the Obama administration would be able to continue to promote its agenda. The Democrats lost 63 seats in the House of Representatives (out of 435), 6 Senate seats, 6 governorships, 134 state Senate seats (out of 1,971), and 547 state House seats (out of 5,411). The losses in the U.S. House gave control of that body to the Republicans. Although Democrats maintained a slight majority in the U.S. Senate, it seems unlikely that they will be able to hold onto that majority in the 2012 elections (in which they have many more party members up for reelection than do the Republicans).

## Politics in Action

In the words of President Obama, the 2010 election was a "shellacking" for his administration and the Democrats. As important as the number of offices that changed from Democrat to Republican was the fact that many of the defeated candidates were moderates in both parties. After the election, Republican officeholders

## Timeline

**1933–1940**
The New Deal responds to the economic distress of the Great Depression.

**1974**
Richard Nixon resigns the presidency in the face of certain impeachment.

**1978**
California passes Proposition 13.

**2001**
The World Trade Center and the Pentagon are targets of terrorist attacks using hijacked civilian airliners.

| 1900 | 1930 | 1960 | 1980 | 1990 | 2010 |
|------|------|------|------|------|------|

**1896**
Voter turnout in elections begins century-long decline.

**1941–1945**
U.S. participates in World War II.

**1964**
Tonkin Gulf Resolution authorizes military actions in Vietnam.

**2008**
Barack Obama elected President of the United States.

**1996**
Federal government ends the guarantee of social welfare programs to the poor established during the New Deal.

---

were more conservative than their predecessors and Democrats more liberal, adding to the polarization between the parties in Congress and in many state legislatures. The meanings of *liberal* and *conservative* are far from consistent in U.S. politics; in the context of the 2010 elections, conservatives called for lower taxes and a diminished role of the federal (national) government relative to state governments. They opposed many initiatives of the Obama administration, and some argued that Obama was far outside of the American mainstream. Of particular concern for conservatives in 2010 was the national health insurance plan passed by Congress and signed into law by President Obama earlier in 2010.

The Democrat's success in terms of passing so much and such far-reaching legislation spurred widespread mobilization to change course. The electorate in 2010 was sufficiently different than the 2008 electorate to ensure the dramatic change in officeholders; there is less evidence that voters who supported Obama and the Democrats in 2008 shifted their support in large numbers to the Republicans in 2010.

The consequences of these electoral changes will be felt well beyond the next election. The Republican majority in the U.S. House of Representatives returns the country to what has been the norm since 1968: divided government with different parties controlling different branches of the government. Divided government increases the need for compromise. Compromise, however, is more difficult in the absence of moderate Republicans and Democrats. States have become increasingly resistant to some federal programs, a power they have as a result of the constitutional division between federal and state governments: **federalism**. This assertion of a heightened state role in governance will expand with new Republican majorities in state houses and governorships. State legislatures assume a constitutional role each decade in the year ending in 1; to account for population changes, they redistrict U.S. House and state legislative seats, changes that will be in place for the next decade.

Looking to the future, the voters who gave the Democrats House and Senate majorities and the presidency after 2008 and the Republicans House and state legislative majorities after 2010 will be further frustrated by what they perceive as gridlock and a failure of elected leaders to live up to their 2008 or 2010 promises. The 2012 presidential race will shift the electorate, in part, to that of 2008, likely undercutting some of the 2010 Republican gains. These major shifts obscure the larger phenomenon of American politics, since at least 2000, of an evenly divided electorate with increasing numbers dissatisfied with both parties and frustrated that government institutions fail to speak to their needs.

---

**federalism**

A system of governance in which political authority is shared between the national government and regional or state governments. The powers of each level of government are usually specified in a federal constitution.

# Geographic Setting

**North American Free Trade Agreement (NAFTA)**

A treaty among the United States, Mexico, and Canada implemented on January 1, 1994, that largely eliminates trade barriers among the three nations and establishes procedures to resolve trade disputes. NAFTA serves as a model for an eventual Free Trade Area of the Americas zone that could include most nations in the Western Hemisphere.

The United States occupy nearly half of North America. Its only two neighbors, Mexico and Canada, do not present a military threat and are linked in a comprehensive trade agreement: the **North American Free Trade Agreement (NAFTA)**. U.S. territory is rich in natural resources, arable land, navigable rivers, and protected ports. This abundance has led Americans to assume they will always have enough resources to meet national needs. Finally, the United States has always had low population densities and has served as a magnet for international migration.

European colonization led to the eventual unification of the territory that became the United States under one government and the expansion of that territory from the Atlantic to the Pacific Oceans. This process began in the early 1500s and reached its peak in the nineteenth century, when rapid population expansion was reinforced by an imperialist national ideology **(manifest destiny)** to expand all the way to the Pacific. Native Americans were pushed aside. The United States experimented with colonialism around 1900, annexing Hawaii, Guam, the Northern Marianas Islands, and Puerto Rico.

**manifest destiny**

The public philosophy in the nineteenth century that the United States was not only entitled but also destined to occupy territory from the Atlantic to the Pacific.

Puerto Rico is a colony of the United States with autonomy in local governance, but only limited autonomy in trade and foreign policy. Puerto Ricans are U.S. citizens by birth and can travel freely to the United States. Although some in Puerto Rico seek independence, most want either a continuation of Commonwealth status or statehood. Guam is an "unincorporated territory" (a U.S. territory that is not on the road to statehood and does not have all of the protections of the U.S. Constitution).

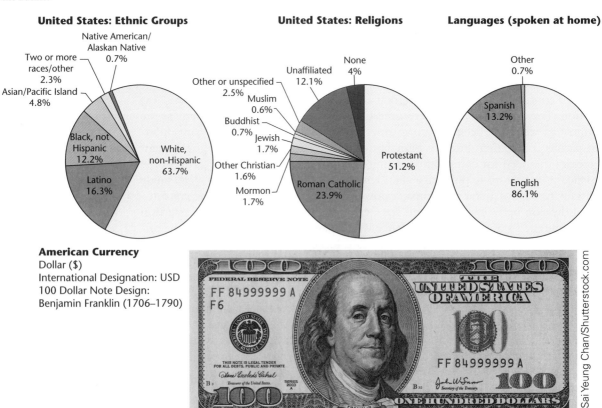

**American Currency**
Dollar ($)
International Designation: USD
100 Dollar Note Design:
Benjamin Franklin (1706–1790)

FIGURE 7.1 **The American Nation at a Glance**

*Source:* Pew Forum on Religion and Public Life, U.S. Religious Landscape Survey, 2007.

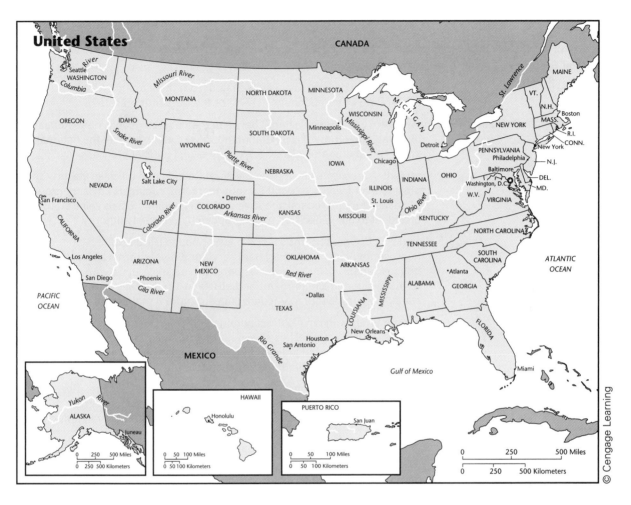

# Critical Junctures

The first four critical junctures in U.S. political history appeared at points when mass discontent organized itself enough to change governing institutions or relationships. Each juncture challenged dominant ideas about who should have a voice in democratic government and what the relationship between government and citizen should be. Four periods of focused popular demand are explored here:

1. From the beginning of the American Revolution through the ratification of the Constitution and Bill of Rights
2. The Civil War and Reconstruction
3. The New Deal
4. The contemporary period of routinely divided national government and frequent shifts in which party controlled the presidency, the Senate, and the House of Representatives that began with the 1968 national elections

It was into this ongoing period of divided national government that the United States experienced the attacks of September 11, 2001.

## The Revolutionary Era (1773–1789)

Mass and elite discontent with British colonial rule sparked the American Revolution and the signing of the **Declaration of Independence**. Mass interests wanted to keep

**Declaration of Independence**

The document asserting that the British colonies in what is now the United States had declared themselves independent from Great Britain. The Declaration of Independence was signed in Philadelphia on July 4, 1776.

| Table 7.1 | Political Organization |
|---|---|
| Political System | Presidential system. |
| Regime History | Representative democracy, usually dated from the signing of the Declaration of Independence (1776) or the Constitution (1787). |
| Administrative Structure | Federalism, with powers shared between the national government and the fifty state governments; separation of powers at the level of the national government among legislative, executive, and judicial branches. |
| Executive | President, "directly" elected (with Electoral College that officially elects president and vice president) for four-year term; cabinet is advisory group of heads of major federal agencies and other senior officials selected by president to aid in decision-making but with no formal authority. |
| Legislature | Bicameral. Congress composed of a lower house (House of Representatives) of 435 members serving two-year terms and an upper house (Senate) of 100 members (two from each state) serving six-year terms; elected in single-member districts (or, in the case of the Senate, states) by simple plurality (some states require a majority of voters). |
| Judiciary | Supreme Court with nine justices nominated by president and confirmed by Senate, with life tenure; has specified original and appellate jurisdiction and exercises the power of judicial review (can declare acts of the legislature and executive unconstitutional and therefore null and void). |
| Party System | Essentially two-party system (Republican and Democrat), with relatively weak and fractionalized parties; more than in most representative democracies, the personal following of candidates remains very important. |

**Articles of Confederation**

The first governing document of the United States, agreed to in 1777 and ratified in 1781. The Articles concentrated most powers in the states and made the national government largely dependent on voluntary contributions of the states.

government close to home, in each colony, and wanted each colony to have substantial independence from the others. Elite interests advocated a national government with control over foreign policy, national assumption of state Revolutionary War debts, and the ability to establish national rules for commerce.

Mass interests won the first round of this battle. From 1777 to 1788, the **Articles of Confederation** governed the nation. Because the national government could not implement foreign or domestic policy, raise taxes, or regulate trade between the states without the cooperation of the individual states, elite interests gained support for replacing the Articles with the Constitution. The limited powers of the national government under the Articles rested in a legislature, but the states had to ratify most key decisions. States also established their own foreign policies, often different from each other. They also established their own fiscal policies and financed state budgets through extensive borrowing.

The Constitution maintained most power with the states but granted the federal (or national) government authority over commerce and foreign and military policy. It also gave the federal government a source of financing independent of the states. And, most important, it created a president, who had powers independent of the legislature. The Constitution delegated specific, but limited, powers to the national government. These included establishing post offices and roads, coining money, promoting the progress of science, raising and supporting an army and a navy, and establishing a uniform rule of naturalization. These powers (Article I, Section 8 of the Constitution) tended to give the federal government the power to create a national economy. Finally, the Constitution limited citizens' voice in government. Presidents were elected indirectly, through the Electoral

College, a body of political insiders from each state who are elected on election day and meet the following month to formally elect the president. As became clear after the 2000 election, the Electoral College ensures that candidates who win the majority of the popular vote do not necessarily win the presidency. Members of the Senate were originally elected by state legislatures. Only the members of the House of Representatives were elected by the people, but the states determined who could vote for members of the House. At first, only property-holding men held the vote in most states. By the 1840s, most white adult men could vote. Women did not receive voting rights nationally until 1920.

As popular support for ratifying the Constitution grew, many who had supported the Articles of Confederation made a new demand: The newly drafted U.S. Constitution should include enumerated protections for individuals from governmental power. Meeting this demand for a **Bill of Rights** was necessary to ensure the ratification of the Constitution. Although the specific rights guaranteed in the Bill of Rights did not mean much for Americans in the 1790s, they later came to offer protections against the excesses of national and state government. Because federal judges had to interpret these rights, the federal courts later played a growing role in the national government, particularly in the twentieth century.

## The Civil War and Reconstruction (1861–1876)

The morality of slavery convulsed the nation before the war, but the war itself began over the question of whether the states or the national government should be dominant. Many states believed they could reject specific federal laws. Any time Congress threatened to pass legislation to restrict slavery in the South, one or more southern state legislatures would threaten to nullify it. Many believed that if any state could nullify federal laws, the union would be put at risk. The Civil War resolved this issue in favor of the indivisibility of the union. The war also established an enforceable national citizenship to supplement state citizenship, which had existed even before the Constitution.[1] Establishing national citizenship began a slow process that culminated in the New Deal, as citizens looked to the federal government to meet their basic needs in times of national crisis.

To establish full citizenship for the freed slaves, Congress revisited the question of individual liberties and citizenship. These post–Civil War debates on the relationship of citizens to the national government established several important principles in the Fourteenth Amendment to the Constitution (1868). First, it extended the protections of the Bill of Rights to cover actions by states as well as by the federal government. Second, it extended citizenship to all persons born in the United States. This made U.S. citizens of freed slaves and also guaranteed that U.S.-born children of immigrants who migrated would become U.S. citizens at birth. Third, Congress sought to establish some federal regulation of voting and to grant the vote to African Americans. When the federal government failed to continue enforcing black voting rights, African Americans, particularly in the South, could not routinely exercise the vote until the Voting Rights Act in 1965. These fundamental guarantees that ensure electoral opportunities today limit prerogatives recognized as the states' responsibilities in the Constitution.

## The New Deal Era (1933–1940)

The third critical juncture in U.S. political development was the New Deal, the Roosevelt administration's response to the economic crisis of the Great Depression. The federal government tapped its constitutional powers to regulate interstate commerce in order to vastly expand federal regulation of business. It also established a

**Bill of Rights**

The first ten amendments to the U.S. Constitution (ratified in 1791), which established limits on the actions of government. Initially, the Bill of Rights limited only the federal government. The Fourteenth Amendment and subsequent judicial rulings extended the provisions of the Bill of Rights to the states.

## Social Security

National systems of contributory and non-contributory benefits to provide assistance for the elderly, sick, disabled, unemployed, and others similarly in need of assistance. The specific coverage of social security, a key component of the welfare state, varies by country.

nationally guaranteed safety net, which included such programs as **Social Security** to provide monthly payments to the elderly who had worked, housing programs to provide housing for the working poor, and food subsidies for children in poor households. Finally, the federal government subsidized agriculture and offered farmers protections against the cyclical nature of demand. The legislative and judicial battles to establish such policies represent a fundamental expansion of the role of the federal government.

The federal government now asserted dominance over the states in delivering services to the people. Equally important, during the New Deal the presidency asserted dominance over the Congress in policy-making. The New Deal president, Franklin D. Roosevelt, found powers that no previous president had exercised. All post–New Deal presidents remain much more powerful than any of their predecessors, except perhaps for Abraham Lincoln, who served during the Civil War. Beginning in the 1960s, however, Congress began to challenge growth in executive power.

The expanded role of the federal government in the 1930s appeared amidst demands for even more dramatic changes. Unemployment rates as high as 40 percent, a worldwide decline in demand for U.S. manufactures, and ecological changes that made much agricultural land unproductive spurred widespread demand for wealth redistribution and centralization of power in the federal government. Although the New Deal programs represented a significant change from the policies that preceded the Great Depression, they also reflected underlying American political values (see Section 4). Even in the New Deal era, class-based politics was kept to a minimum.

As the Depression came to a close, the United States geared up for its involvement in World War II. Although the United States had previously been involved in international conflicts beyond its borders, the experience of World War II was different at the beginning of U.S. involvement and at the end. The United States entered the war after U.S. territory was attacked. After the war, the United States was at the center of a multilateral strategy to contain the Soviet Union.

### Divided Government, Frequently Shifting Partisan Dominance, and Political Contestation of the Scope of Government (1968 to the Present)

The fourth critical juncture, which began with the 1968 presidential election, is ongoing today. This critical juncture has two dimensions. First, the national government has been routinely divided between the two political parties with dominance of each branch of government shifting regularly. This division exacerbates the inefficiency that was designed into the American constitutional order and increases popular distrust of government (see Section 3).

In 1968 Richard Nixon (a California Republican) became president. Through Nixon's term and that of his Republican successor, Gerald Ford, the Democrats maintained control of both houses of Congress. In the period since 1968, one of the parties has controlled the presidency, the U.S. Senate, *and* the U.S. House of Representatives only five times. The Democrats controlled all three from 1977 to 1980, from 1993 to 1994, and from 2009 to 2010. The Republicans controlled all three from late January to June 2001 and again from 2003 to 2007. One party has replaced the other in the presidency five times since 1968. This division of the federal government between the parties and the routine shift in party control of the Congress or the presidency slow government response to controversial policy issues.

The second ongoing dimension of the contemporary critical juncture emerges from the apparent inefficiency caused by divided government. Many in the United States began to question the steady increase in the scope of governmental services. The electoral roots of this popular discontent can be found in the passage of Proposition 13 by California voters in 1978, which limited California's ability to increase **property taxes**. The passage of Proposition 13 began an era that continues today, in which many citizens reject the expansion of government.

Popular discontent in the contemporary era is not limited to taxes; it also focuses on the scope of government. This period saw popular mobilization to reshape government's involvement in "values" issues, such as abortion, gay marriage, and the role of religion. Advocates on all sides of these issues want government to protect their interests, while condemning government for allegedly promoting the interests of groups with opposing positions. Ultimately, the courts become the venue to shape government policies on social issues.

While divided government had become the norm in 1968, the division became even more razor thin in the late 1990s. Each election raises the possibility of a switch in partisan control of the Senate or the House and the intense focus of both parties and **interest groups** on winning the handful of seats that could switch from one party to the other.

## September 11, 2001, and Its Aftermath

It is in this environment, that the United States responded to the terrorist attacks of September 11. Initially, Congress and the populace rallied behind the president to increase the scope of federal law enforcement powers and to provide financial assistance for New York City, the families of the victims of the attack, and the airlines. With Congress closely divided and neither side actively seeking compromise, the United States soon saw the consequences of the structure and scope of government during the fourth critical juncture.

In the weeks after September 11, 2001, the United States experienced a rare period of national consensus and international support. Domestically, President Bush's popularity surged to 90 percent. Largely without debate, Congress passed a dramatic expansion of government's ability to conduct surveillance, to enforce laws, to limit civil liberties, and to fight terrorism, especially through the **USA PATRIOT Act** of 2001.

Popular support for President Bush and his administration's initial efforts to respond to the challenges of September 11 continued as the administration prepared for an invasion of Afghanistan. The United States also experienced a period of international support immediately following the September 11, 2001, attacks. In addition to immediate offers of humanitarian assistance, initial U.S. military responses to the attacks won widespread backing around the world.

The initial domestic cohesion and international support for the United States dissipated quickly. U.S. efforts to extend the war on terrorism to Iraq became the focus of many of the objections to growing U.S. power and unilateralism in international affairs.

Domestically, Bush saw steadily declining popular support. It dropped below 50 percent in 2005 and below 30 percent in 2008. A sizeable minority of the U.S. population opposed the U.S. invasion of Iraq without the support of the United Nations or other international bodies. This opposition grew in the period after the military phase of the war ended when it became evident that the peace would be harder fought than the war. Bush's support also declined when he advocated strongly partisan positions on contentious domestic issues such as tax cuts that benefited high-income earners, the partial privatization of Social Security, and support for the social conservative

---

**property taxes**

Taxes levied by local governments on the assessed value of property. Property taxes are the primary way in which local jurisdictions in the United States pay for the costs of primary and secondary education. Because the value of property varies dramatically from neighborhood to neighborhood, the funding available for schools—and the quality of education—also varies from place to place.

**interest groups**

Organizations that seek to represent the interests—usually economic—of their members in dealings with the government. Important examples are associations representing people with specific occupations, business interests, racial and ethnic groups, or age groups in society.

**USA PATRIOT Act**

Legislation passed by the United States Congress in the wake of the September 11, 2001 attacks on New York and Washington. The legislation dramatically expanded the federal government's ability to conduct surveillance, to enforce laws, to limit civil liberties, and to fight terrorism.

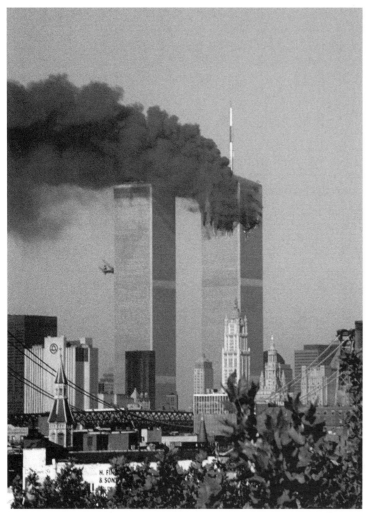

A jet crashes into the World Trade Center on September 11, 2001.
*Source:* AP Images/Moshe Bursuker.

agenda. Many had expected that Bush would govern more consensually during a period of national crisis. The Bush administration also paid a political price for the multiple failures in the federal government's response to Hurricane Katrina's destruction of New Orleans and the Gulf Coast. Bush's policies and overall stridency in domestic and foreign policy returned the country to the near-even partisan division that had characterized the country in the 1990s.

The United States also faced significant opposition from its allies. Germany and France, in particular, opposed U.S. intervention in Iraq and prevented both United Nations and NATO support for U.S. military activities. The growing opposition to U.S. unilateralism in international affairs resulted in a dramatic decline in positive feelings for the United States among residents of other countries.

In the years immediately after September 11, 2001, the United States won and squandered international support, and the Bush administration lost some of its domestic support. In retrospect, neither of these outcomes is surprising. Allies of the United States have increasingly sought multilateral solutions to international affairs and are suspicious of U.S. unilateralism.

# Themes and Implications

### Historical Junctures and Political Themes

**separation of powers**

An organization of political institutions within the state in which the executive, legislature, and judiciary have autonomous powers and no one branch dominates the others. This is the common pattern in presidential systems, as opposed to parliamentary systems, in which there is a fusion of powers.

The conflict between the president and Congress, the centralization of federal power in the twentieth century, and the growing concern about the cost and scope of government represent ongoing themes in U.S. politics. These are not quickly or easily resolved because the Constitution slows resolution by creating a system of federalism and **separation of powers** (see Section 3). The framers of the Constitution were wary of allowing the federal government to intervene too readily in matters of individual liberties or states' prerogatives, so they created a governing system with multiple powers. These limits remain today even as the United States has achieved sole superpower status, and other countries, as well as U.S. citizens, expect the United States to lead.

With such a system of government, the United States may now be at a disadvantage relative to other governing systems that can react more quickly and decisively to societal needs and shifts in public opinion. In parliamentary systems, even when they are burdened by the compromises necessary to maintain coalition governments, prime ministers can exercise power in a way that a U.S. president or Congress can never expect to do. In the United States, elections are held on a regular cycle, regardless of the popularity of the president. The presidency and Congress are routinely controlled by the two opposing parties. Federalism further slows government action.

Until the New Deal and World War II, the United States pursued a contradictory policy toward the rest of the world of states: It sought isolation from international politics but unfettered access to international markets. World War II changed the first of these stances, at least at elite levels (see Section 2): The United States sought to shape international relations through multilateral organizations and military force. It designed the multilateral organizations so that it could have a disproportionate voice (for example, in the United Nations Security Council). The United States used military force to contain communism around the world. With the end of the Cold War, some now call for a reduced role of the U.S. government in the world of states or, at a minimum, a greater willingness to use a unilateral response to international military crises. This decline in interest in the U.S. role in the world among some U.S. citizens reflects the fact that foreign policy has never been central to the evolution of U.S. politics and governance.

The federal government and the states have sought to manage the economy by building domestic manufacturing, exploiting the nation's natural resources, and regulating the banking sector, while interfering little in the conduct of business (see Section 2). This hands-off attitude toward economic regulation can come at a price.

To build industry and exploit resources, the government built roads and other infrastructure, educated citizens, and opened its borders to guarantee a workforce. It also sought access to international markets. Only in exceptional circumstances has it limited the operations of business through antitrust or environmental regulation.

The democratic idea in the U.S. context was one of an indirect, representative democracy with checks on democratically elected leaders. The emergence of a strong national government after the New Deal era meant that national coalitions could often focus their demands on a single, federal government, rather than always having to target a host of state governments as well. The decline in mediating institutions that can channel these demands reduces the ability of individual citizens to influence the national government (see Section 4).

As a nation of immigrants, the United States must unite immigrants and descendants of immigrants from Europe, Africa, Latin America, and Asia with the established U.S. population. Previous waves of immigrants experienced only one to two generations of political and societal exclusion. Whether today's immigrants (particularly those who enter the United States without legal immigrant status) experience the same relatively rapid acculturation remains an open question. Preliminary evidence indicates that the process may be even quicker for immigrants who possess skills and education but slower for those who do not.[2] National economic decline or the rise of a virulent anti-immigrant sentiment could slow or even stop the acculturation process. The United States has never fully remedied its longest-lasting difference in collective identities with full economic and political incorporation of African Americans.

## Implications for Comparative Politics

Scholars of U.S. politics have always had to come to terms with the idea of American exceptionalism—the idea that the United States is unique and cannot easily be compared to other countries. In several respects, the United States *could* be considered exceptional: Its geography and natural resources offer it advantages that few other nations can match; its experience with mass representative democracy is longer than that of other nations; it has been able to expand the citizenry beyond the descendants of the original citizens; and U.S. society has been much less divided by class than have the societies of other states.[3]

The U.S. Constitution, for all of its limitations, has served as the model for the constitutions of many newly independent nations. Some form of separation of powers (see Section 3) has become the norm in democratic states. Similarly, district-based and **single-member-plurality (SMP) electoral systems** (see Section 4) have been widely adapted to reduce conflict in multiethnic states, of which the United States was the first large-scale example. Through its active role in multilateral institutions such as the United Nations (UN) and international financial institutions such as the International Monetary Fund (IMF), the United States also attempts to impose its will on other nations.

### Summary

In the post–New Deal and post–World War II era, the United States faces increasing demands from its own people as well as from other nations and multinational organizations with a system of governance that was designed to impede government and check the powers of each branch of government. The 2010 elections reflected ongoing popular concerns among some that the United States was moving too quickly away from core American values. Yet the American people expect rapid response from government in times of crisis. The ongoing critical juncture raises the question of how the United States will evolve its systems of governance and political culture to meet its citizens' needs and to play its ongoing central role in the system of states while maintaining government's traditionally limited role.

**single-member-plurality (SMP) electoral system**

An electoral system in which candidates run for a single seat from a specific geographic district. The winner is the person who receives the most votes, whether or not they amount to a majority. SMP systems, unlike systems of proportional representation, increase the likelihood that two national coalition parties will form.

# SECTION 2 POLITICAL ECONOMY AND DEVELOPMENT

## Focus Questions

What principles guide U.S. governmental decisions about economic regulation?

How does federalism shape U.S. decision-making on protections for workers and social welfare programs for citizens?

What challenges does the euro pose for the dollar and for the U.S. role in the international political economy?

## State and Economy

When national leaders present the accomplishments of the United States, they often claim that by governing the economy less, the United States allows the private economy to thrive. In this simplified version of this story, the private sector is the engine of national growth, and this private sector is most successful when left alone by government. Economic success, then, is tied to the **free market**—*the absence of government regulation* and the opportunity for entrepreneurs to build the nation's economy.

Relative to other advanced democracies, the U.S. economy is much less regulated. The U.S. government has traditionally taken a **laissez-faire** attitude toward economic actors. This absence of regulation allowed for the creation and expansion of many new types of production that subsequently spread throughout the world, but it also can come at a cost. U.S. policymakers cede power to private actors who are not concerned with the impact of their activities on the broader economy, such as the mortgage lenders who built the subprime lending industry or the investment banks that bought the subprime loans.

The Constitution reserves for the federal government authority to regulate *inter*-state commerce and commerce with foreign nations. As a result, state and local governments are limited in their ability to shape the economy. Over time, however, states have established the ability to regulate workplace conditions as part of their **police powers** or of jurisdiction over public health and safety.

Except for agriculture, higher education, and some defense-related industries, the size of various sectors of the economy is almost entirely the result of the free market. The federal government does try to incubate some new industries, but it primarily uses grants to private agencies—often universities—to accomplish this end. This stimulation of new economic activity makes up a very small share of the nation's gross national product. The United States also occasionally supports ailing industries.

Since the New Deal, the federal government has guaranteed minimum prices for most agricultural commodities and has sought to protect agriculture by paying farmers to leave some land fallow. It has also considerably reduced the costs of production and risks associated with agriculture by providing subsidized crop insurance, canals and aqueducts to transport water, and flood control projects. It has subsidized the sale of U.S. agricultural products abroad and purchased some surplus agricultural production for storage and distribution in the United States. Although a less explicit form of subsidy, weak regulation of U.S. immigration laws has ensured a reliable, inexpensive labor supply.

The federal government has also limited its own ability to regulate the economy. With the formation of the **Federal Reserve Board** in 1913, it removed control of the money supply from elected officeholders. Today, unelected leaders on the Federal Reserve Board, many with ties to the banking industry, control the volume of money in the economy and the key interest rates that determine the rates at which banks lend money to businesses and individuals. As the United States slid toward recession in 2008, the Federal Reserve was the central U.S. policy-making agency seeking to avert recession. The Federal Reserve also assumed new responsibilities that may signal an expansion of its role in U.S. society (while making it more subject to Congressional oversight). It provided direct subsidies and low-cost loans to banks, allowing them to survive, but also allowing them to pay their executives high salaries and bonuses. As the recession continued, the Federal Reserve purchased government bonds owned by banks to keep interest rates low, but also in the expectation that the banks would use their newly available cash to lend to private borrowers. Many in U.S. society expressed concerns that the resources used to make these bond purchases were simply money created out of whole cloth by the Federal Reserve that will eventually lead to inflation. The Federal Reserve will likely face levels of scrutiny in the 112th Congress (2011–2013) that it has not since the 1960s. These congressional challenges to the Federal Reserve's autonomy will likely raise concerns among other nations that the United States will be less able to act as a global banker and lender of last resort in the future.

The U.S. government does not regulate the flow of capital. As a result, many large U.S.-based firms have evolved into multinational corporations, removing themselves from a great deal of U.S. government regulation and taxation.

It is important to recognize that from the nation's earliest days, the federal government promoted agriculture and industry, spurred exports, and (more recently) sought to stabilize the domestic and international economy. These promotional efforts included tariffs, which sought to disadvantage products that competed with U.S. manufactures; roads and canals, so that U.S.-produced goods could be brought to market cheaply and quickly; the distribution of federally owned lands in the West

## free market

A system in which government regulation of the economy is absent or limited. Relative to other advanced democracies, the United States has traditionally had a freer market economically.

## laissez-faire

A term taken from the French, which means, "to let do," in other words, to allow to act freely. In political economy, it refers to the pattern in which state management is limited to such matters as enforcing contracts and protecting property rights, while private market forces are free to operate with only minimal state regulation.

## police powers

Powers that are traditionally held by the states to regulate public safety and welfare. Police powers are the form of interaction with government that citizens most often experience. Even with the growth in federal government powers in the twentieth century, police powers remain the primary responsibility of the states and localities.

## Federal Reserve Board

The U.S. central bank established by Congress in 1913 to regulate the banking industry and the money supply. Although the president appoints the chair of the board of governors (with Senate approval), the board operates largely independently.

to individuals and to railroads, so that the land could contribute to national economic activity; and large-scale immigration, so that capital would have people to produce and consume goods (see Section 3).

Efforts to promote U.S. industry often came at the expense of individual citizens, who are less able to organize and make demands of government. Tariffs, for example, kept prices high for domestic consumers.

Through much of the nation's history, the United States used its diplomatic and military resources to establish and maintain markets for U.S.-produced commodities and manufactures abroad. The United States, for example, uses its position in the world economy and on multilateral lending institutions to open markets, provide loans for nations facing economic distress, and protect some U.S.-produced goods from foreign competition. Despite national rhetoric to the contrary, the United States has consistently promoted economic development, though not by regulating production or spurring specific industries.

The U.S. economy has increasingly come to rely on two unintentional forms of international subsidy. First, it has built up a steadily increasing international trade deficit. In other words, the United States has bought much more abroad than it has sold. Although some aspects of these trade deficits could well reflect a strength in the U.S. economy (for example, being able to purchase goods produced inexpensively abroad), continuing deficits of this level act as a downward pressure on the U.S. dollar (see Figure 7.2). Slowing this downward pressure for the time being is the second form of international subsidy: The U.S. dollar is the international reserve currency. This means that many nations and individual investors keep their reserves (their savings) in dollars. By doing this, they keep demand for the dollar up, reducing the downward pressure that comes from trade deficits. By buying U.S. government bonds, they are lending the United States money. The euro, the European common currency, however, is increasingly serving as a reserve currency. The long-term stability of the U.S. economy and the value of the dollar as a reserve currency are being challenged by an increasing national debt (discussed later in this chapter) and market concerns about unfunded liabilities in federal and state pension, health care, and insurance programs.

Beginning in 1890, the United States enacted antitrust legislation that gave it the ability to break up large businesses that could, by their very size, control an entire

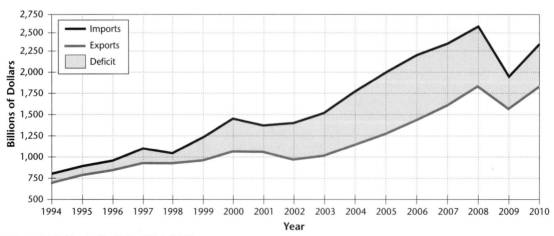

**FIGURE 7.2 U.S. Trade Deficit, 1994–2010**

*Source:* U.S. Bureau of the Census. 2011. "U.S. Trade in Goods and Services—Balance of Payments (BOP) Basis," http://www.census.gov/foreign-trade/statistics/historical/gands.pdf (accessed February 15, 2011).

market. These antitrust powers have been used sparingly. Antitrust legislation gives the government a power that is very much at odds with a laissez-faire ideology, but its unwillingness to use this authority except in the most egregious cases reflects the underlying hands-off ideology.

In the twentieth century, the U.S. government took on new responsibilities to protect citizens and to tax businesses, in part, to provide government-mandated services for workers. The government also expanded regulation of workplace safety, pension systems, and other worker-management relations issues (see Section 3). Despite this expansion of the government role in providing protections to workers, the United States offers fewer guarantees to its workers than do other advanced democracies.

The public sector has traditionally been smaller in the United States than in other advanced democracies. Nevertheless, the U.S. government and the states conduct activities that many believe could be better conducted by the private sector. The federal government operates hospitals for veterans, provides water and electrical power to Appalachian states, manages lands in the West and Alaska, runs the civilian air traffic control system, and, after September 11, manages passenger and luggage screening at commercial airports. Roads have traditionally been built and maintained by the state and federal governments, and waterways have been kept navigable (and open to recreational use) by the federal government.

The U.S. government has privatized some activities in recent years. The postal service, for example, became a semi-independent corporation in 1970. The federal government is trying to end subsidies for Amtrak that it inherited when the company's private sector owners went bankrupt in 1971.

Often left out of the story of the development of the U.S. economy is the role of its natural resources and the environment. The nation's territory is diverse in terms of natural resources and environments, stretching from tropical to arctic. The territory includes arable land that can produce more than enough year round for the domestic market as well as for extensive exports. Land has become increasingly concentrated in a few hands, but in the past, it was held in small plots tilled at least in part by the owners. This tradition of equitable land distribution (encouraged by government policies in the nineteenth century that distributed small plots to resident landholders) dampened the class tensions that appeared in societies with entrenched landholding elites. Not all Americans were eligible for this land giveaway, however. Recently freed slaves could not obtain free lands in the West, and some share of the gap in wealth between whites and blacks today can be attributed to the access that whites had to western lands in the last century.[4]

The United States has protected ports and navigable rivers, and few enemies can challenge U.S. control over these transportation resources. For more than a century, it was able to expand trade while not investing in a large standing military to defend its trade routes.

One area in which the United States has taken a limited role in regulating the activities of private actors in the American economy is environmental regulation. When the environment first became an issue in international politics, the United States took aggressive action to clean the air and the nation's oceans and navigable waterways. In each of these regulatory areas, federal legislation had dramatic impacts. Emissions standards have made the air much healthier, even in the nation's most car-focused cities. Waterways that were dangerous to the touch are now open to swimming. New lands were added to the national park system.[5] The visible successes of the early environmental **regulations** reduced the salience of environmental issues. These 1970s-era environmental regulations have not been followed by a continuing national commitment to environmentalism.

**regulations**

The rules that explain the implementation of laws. When the legislature passes a law, it sets broad principles for implementation, but how the law is actually implemented is determined by regulations written by executive branch agencies. The regulation-writing process allows interested parties to influence the eventual shape of the law in practice.

The United States has fewer environmental regulations than other advanced democracies and has been less willing to engage in multilateral agreements on environmental issues than on issues such as international security and economic cooperation. The United States, for example, is a signatory to the Kyoto Protocols to limit climate change (primarily through the reduction of greenhouse gases), but the treaty was never ratified by the U.S. Senate and is nonbinding on the United States. Nine U.S. states and 740 U.S. cities have passed emissions caps that broadly follow Kyoto guidelines (though often less rapidly than Kyoto would mandate). Unlike an international treaty, however, these state and city efforts can be amended with a majority vote in a legislature and are more difficult to enforce.

Early in his term, President Obama proposed "cap and trade" energy regulation that would have set limits on carbon emissions while allowing factories and other carbon emitters to sell unused carbon emissions to create incentives for conversion to renewable energy sources. Despite some early bipartisan support, this legislation ultimately failed, losing support from all Senate Republicans and some Democrats. Again, however, states are acting in the absence of federal action. California, New Mexico, and several states in the Northeast have proposed state-level carbon emissions limits that would create a national market to trade the bounty of energy conservation.

## Society and Economy

The United States adheres more strictly to its laissez-faire ideology in terms of the outcomes of the economic system. The distribution of income and wealth is much more unequal in the United States than in other advanced democracies, and that gap has been steadily widening over the past 30 years. In 2009, the top 5 percent alone earned more than 21.7 percent of the total amount earned. Wide differences exist between women and men and between racial groups. Women, on average, earned $11,227 annually less than men. Non-Hispanic whites earned an average of $41,000 in 2005 compared to $36,000 for Asian Americans, $29,000 for blacks, and $27,000 for Hispanics.

The United States has always tolerated these conditions and sees them as an incentive for people at the lower end of the economic spectrum. Wealth and income have become more skewed since 1980, a phenomenon that has not been an issue of national political concern. In fact, the mere mention in an election of the class implications of a policy, particularly tax policy, will usually lead to the charge of fomenting class warfare. This became particularly apparent in the month after the 2010 election. Tax cuts enacted in the early 2000s (early in the Bush administration) were set to expire, and President Obama proposed extending them only for taxpayers earning less than $250,000 annually. Republicans in Congress sought to extend them for all taxpayers. The economic consequences of these proposals were of little concern in the debate; instead each side alleged the other was promoting class division. In the end, Obama and the Democrats backed down, and the Bush tax cuts were extended for all tax payers for two years. Consequently, they will again be subject to debate in the middle of the 2012 presidential race.

Federal income taxation of individuals is progressive, with higher-income people paying a higher share of their income in taxes. Rates range from 0 percent for individuals with incomes less than $9,350 to 35 percent for individuals with incomes exceeding approximately $373,650. The progressive nature of federal taxes is reduced considerably by two factors. Upper-income taxpayers receive a much higher share of

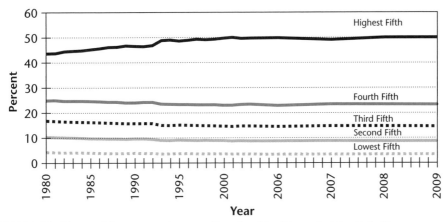

**FIGURE 7.3  Share of Aggregate Income Received by Households, Quintiles, 1980–2009**

*Source:* U.S. Bureau of the Census. 2011. "Historical Income Table—Households" Table H-2. Share of Aggregate Income Received by Each Fifth and Top 5 Percent of Households. http://www.census.gov/hhes/www/income/data/historical/household/index.html (accessed February 15, 2011).

their income from investments, which are taxed at lower rates. Second, all taxpayers with salary income are subject to a regressive tax for Social Security and disability benefits. The tax for Social Security and Medicare is currently 7.65 percent paid by the worker (lowered to 5.65 percent in 2011) and 7.65 percent paid by the employer. The Social Security share of this tax is imposed only on the first $106,800 of income and not at all on higher incomes.

State and local taxes tend to be much less progressive. Most states levy a sales tax. This is a flat tax, ranging between 2.9 and 8.25 percent depending on the state. For lower-income people, sales taxes act as a flat tax on most or all of their income. Upper-income people pay a smaller share of their income because they do not have to spend all of their income on consumption. Not all states have income taxes. No state has an income tax that is as progressive as the federal income tax. The final major form of individual taxation is property taxes. Property owners pay them directly and can deduct the tax payment from their federal and, in some cases, state income taxes. Renters pay them as part of their rent payment but do not directly get any tax benefits. Governments in the United States have increasingly supplemented taxes with user fees charged for the provision of specific services.

Thus, the gap between rich and poor in the United States is not remedied by progressive taxation. This gap might well have led to the emergence of class-based political movements, but immigration policy, which also promoted economic development, focused workers' attention away from class and toward cultural differences that reduced the salience of class divisions in U.S. society. Unions, which could also have promoted class-based politics and focused workers' attentions on income inequalities, have traditionally been weak in the United States. This weakness reflects individual-level antipathy toward unions, but also state and federal laws that limit the abilities of unions to organize and collectively bargain.

Agriculture and industry could not have grown in the United States without the importation of immigrant labor. The United States has generally sought to remedy labor shortages with policies that encouraged migration. Today, the United States is one of just four countries that allow large-scale migration of those who do not already have a cultural tie to the receiving nation. Contemporary immigration to the United States numbers approximately 1,100,000 people annually, who immigrate under the provisions of the law to a permanent status that allows for eventual eligibility for U.S. citizenship (see Figure 7.4).[6] Until the economy soured in 2008, these legal immigrants were joined by as many as 500,000 additional unauthorized migrants each year.[7] Despite new enforcement policies, it is likely that the size of the unauthorized immigrant population will likely again begin to grow when the U.S. economy recovers from recession.

Although the United States tolerates the unequal distribution of income and wealth, in the twentieth century, it intervened directly in the free market to establish protections for workers and, to a lesser degree, to guarantee the welfare of the most disadvantaged in the society. The programs for workers, which are primarily **distributive policies**, receive much more public support than do programs to assist the poor, which are primarily **redistributive policies**. Distributive policies allocate resources into an area that policymakers perceive needs to be promoted without a significant impact on income or wealth distribution. Redistributive policies take resources from one person or group in society and allocate them to a more disadvantaged group in the society. Most worker benefits, such as health insurance, childcare, and pensions, are provided by private employers, if they are provided at all, but are regulated by the government.

Best known among the federal programs aimed toward workers is Social Security, which taxes workers and their employers to pay for benefits for retired and disabled workers (and nonworker spouses). In the past, retirees almost always received more than they had paid into the system (a form of intergenerational redistribution), but it will take significant reforms to guarantee that this outcome continues when today's workers reach retirement age. Actuarial estimates indicate that the Social Security Trust Fund will be exhausted in 2036 if there are no changes to the tax used to pay for Social Security or the benefit rates or age of eligibility. Medicare—the government health plan for the elderly—will run out of funds in 2024 (an estimate contingent on the full implementation of

**distributive policies**

Policies that allocate state resources into an area that lawmakers perceive needs to be promoted. For example, leaders today believe that students should have access to the Internet. In order to accomplish this goal, telephone users are being taxed to provide money for schools to establish connections to the Internet (which, in large part, uses telephone lines to transfer data).

**redistributive policies**

Policies that take resources from one person or group in society and allocate them to a different, usually more disadvantaged, group. The United States has traditionally opposed redistributive policies to the disadvantaged.

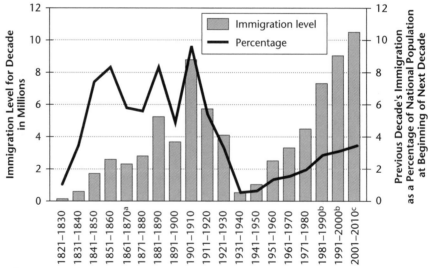

a Until 1867, the federal government recorded as immigrants only people who arrived at seaports.

b These figures include recipients of legalization under the Immigration Reform and Control Act of 1986 who immigrated to the United States prior to 1982 but were recorded as having entered in the year in which they received permanent residence.

c Author's estimate based on 2001–2009 data.

**FIGURE 7.4 Immigration to the United States, 1821–2010**

*Source:* Adopted from DeSipio, Louis, and Rodolfo O. de la Garza, *Making Americans/Remaking America: Immigration* and Immigrant Policy (Boulder, Colo: Westview Press, 1998), Table 2.1.

the national health insurance plan; if it is not implemented the estimates are that the Medicare trust fund will run out of funds at least a decade earlier). The U.S. government faces the dilemma of having to lower benefits for each of these programs, raising taxes, or paying benefits out of general revenues. Changing the tax basis of Social Security and Medicare now (or lowering benefits now) would delay this point of reckoning.

In 2010, in response to growing numbers of uninsured Americans and spiraling health care costs, Congress created a new national health care program for U.S. citizens and permanent residents. The new program is largely distributive in nature with some additional subsidies (redistribution) for low-income individuals. It builds on the private health insurance that many Americans receive through their employers or unions. This national health care plan, which will not be fully implemented until 2014, is controversial for several reasons. Some fear that it will undermine the incentive for employers, particularly small employers, to provide insurance. Governments would then have to provide a higher share of insurance and assume costs currently paid by employers. Others resent that government is not more central to the provision of insurance and that private insurance, with its overhead costs and quest for profits, will absorb health care expenditures that could go to providing better treatments. When the national health care bill was debated, some in Congress called for government to replace the role of private insurers (the so-called single-payer option). States are concerned that they will have to provide insurance to residents who are not otherwise able to get private insurance and that they will have to assume at least 10 percent of the costs of providing this insurance (the federal government will pay the rest). Finally, some feel that the new mandate that all Americans have health insurance after 2014 or be fined violates the Constitution.

The government also established a minimum wage and a bureaucratic mechanism to enforce this wage. Some states and localities have established higher minimum wages than the federal minimum wage. Citizen groups in several cities nationwide over the past decade have promoted a further expansion of the idea of a minimum wage to a "living wage," a wage sufficient to live in high-cost cities and often double the federal minimum wage.

The states regulate worker-employer relations through unemployment insurance and insurance against workplace injuries. Benefits and eligibility requirements vary dramatically by state, although the federal governmental mandates that all workers be eligible for twenty-six weeks of unemployment benefits (assuming the worker has been employed for more than six months).

Beginning in the 1930s, the United States also established social welfare programs to assist the economically disadvantaged. As one would expect in a system organized around the free market, these programs have never been as broad-based or as socially accepted as in other economies. The states administered these programs—which provide food, health care, housing assistance, some job training, and some cash assistance to the poor—with a combination of federal and state funds. Eligibility and benefit levels varied dramatically from state to state. Prior to 1996, there was a federal guarantee of some food and cash assistance for everyone who met eligibility thresholds. This guarantee disappeared in 1996 when recipients were limited in the duration of their eligibility and states were entrusted with developing programs to train recipients for work and to find jobs for them. Although enacted separately from the 1996 welfare reform, the federal government also reduced the availability of federally managed housing for the poor and expanded subsidies for the poor to secure housing in the private market.

In today's economy, public benefits and public employment are increasingly limited to U.S. citizens. Over time, these policies could enhance differences between the non-Hispanic white and black populations, on the one hand, and ethnic groups with large shares of immigrants, such as Latinos and Asian Americans, on the other.

Both the federal and state governments are facing gaps between income and expenditures. The federal government can continue to run a large annual deficit. The sum of these deficits—the national debt—totals nearly $14.3 trillion. Most states do not have this option and must either raise revenues or cut services annually.

Deficits can have a salutary effect on the national economy during weak economic times because the federal government can more easily borrow and then spend this money to stimulate the economy and support individuals who are out of work. In the long run, however, this federal debt absorbs money that could be invested in private-sector activities and will slow national economic growth. In 2011, the federal government will pay approximately $250 billion in interest on its debt, an amount that will increase considerably when the economy recovers and interest rates rise.

# The United States in the Global Economy

Since colonial times, the United States has been linked to world trade. By the late twentieth century, the United States had vastly expanded its role in international finance and was an importer of goods produced abroad (often in low-wage countries that could produce goods less expensively than U.S. factories) as well as an exporter of agricultural products.

After World War II, the United States reversed its traditional isolationism to take a leading role in regulating the international economy. The increasing interdependence of global economies was the result, in part, of conscious efforts by world leaders at the end of World War II, through the Bretton Woods Agreement, to establish and fund multinational lending institutions. Chief among these institutions were the World Bank and the International Monetary Fund. Since their establishment in the 1940s, they have been supplemented by a network of international lending and regulatory agencies and regional trading agreements.

The United States is also part of regional trading networks, such as NAFTA with Canada and Mexico. After its passage, the United States also entered into an agreement with neighboring countries in the Caribbean to reduce tariffs on many goods.

The U.S. government plays a central role in the international political economy. It achieves this through its domination of international lending agencies and regional defense and trade organizations. But these efforts are ultimately limited by domestic politics. Thus, while presidents may promote an international agenda, Congress often limits the funding for international organizations. The United States then appears to many outside the country as a hesitant and sometimes resentful economic leader.

In recent years, another multilateral institution has emerged that can potentially challenge U.S. economic dominance. The European Union (EU) is much more than a trading alliance. It is an organization of twenty-seven European nations with growing international influence. Seventeen EU members share a common currency, the euro. As the euro came into widespread use, the dollar faced its first challenge in many years as the world's dominant trading currency. The debit levels of some Eurozone countries, such as Greece and Ireland, as the post-2008 recession deepened, reduced the international appeal of the euro and of European debt. At least temporarily, this worked to the advantage of the dollar.

The United States also funds binational international lending through such agencies as the Export-Import Bank and the Overseas Private Investment Corporation. These agencies make loans to countries and private businesses to purchase goods and services from U.S.-owned businesses. The United States also provides grants and loans to allies to further U.S. strategic and foreign policy objectives or for humanitarian reasons.

The United States has slowly, and grudgingly, adapted to a world where it can no longer simply assert its central role. Thus, the U.S. government and, more slowly, the American people have seen their problems and needs from a global perspective. The separation of powers between the executive and legislative branches, and the local constituencies of members of Congress, ensures continuing resistance to this new international role (see The Global Connection: Arizona SB 1070 and U.S. relations with Mexico).

## Summary

The role of the United States in regulating the domestic economy and shaping the international economy may be tested in coming years in a manner that has not been seen since the formation of the multilateral organizations after World War II. The strength of the U.S. economy is increasingly determined by decisions of multinational corporations that are able to transfer capital and production across national boundaries with little control by governments and international actors. As the domestic U.S. economy is increasingly shaped by these international forces, U.S. citizens will demand economic stability from their government. The U.S. government was designed to be weak, so it will not be able to respond easily. The seeming lack of response will strengthen calls by some to isolate the United States from the regulation of the international economy. If these voices become dominant, the United States may find itself at odds with the international organizations that it helped create and that promote U.S. trade internationally.

"The decision to build a fence along parts of the U.S. border with Mexico appeared to many as a metaphor for the barriers that the United States was establishing with other nations in other policy arenas."

*Source:* TOLE © 2006 *The Washington Post.* Reprinted with permission of UNIVERSAL PRESS SYNDICATE. All rights reserved.

## THE GLOBAL CONNECTION

### Arizona SB 1070 and U.S. Relations with Mexico

Many issues divide the United States and Mexico: trade disputes, migration, drug smuggling and violence, and gun smuggling among others. In 2010, Arizona added to this list. Reflecting popular concerns over Congress's failure to reform immigration, it passed a law requiring police to verify the legal immigration status of people arrested or detained by the police. The law, SB 1070, also criminalized giving assistance to an unauthorized alien, such as allowing a unauthorized immigrant family member to live in your home.

Many in the United States were concerned by these requirements. Under the Constitution, regulation of immigration is an enumerated power of the federal government. Aside from this constitutional concern, many raised concerns of racial profiling. Would police in Arizona verify the legal status of all people detained or just of those who were Latino or Asian American? Mexico also objected to SB 1070. Mexico officially protested that its nationals will be subject to harassment in Arizona.

Arizona's enactment of the law made it more difficult for the U.S. government to negotiate with Mexico on issues of joint importance. SB 1070 demonstrates the inherent difficulty in a federalist system for the making of foreign policy. The U.S. government opposes SB 1070 as strongly as does Mexico (it has sued in federal court to have it ruled unconstitutional), but it cannot control the actions of Arizona or any other state to pass legislation that can muddy bi-national relations.

SECTION **3**

# GOVERNANCE AND POLICY-MAKING

## Organization of the State

**Focus Questions**

What powers does the Constitution give to U.S. presidents and how have twentieth-century presidents been able to expand these powers?

What are the constitutional and structural strengths and weaknesses of the federal judiciary in the United States?

How can citizens influence the policy-making process in the United States?

The U.S. Constitution was drafted in 1787 and ratified the following year. The Constitution established a central government that was independent of the states but left the states most of their pre-existing powers (particularly police powers and public safety). Although it had limited powers, the new U.S. government exercised powers over commerce and foreign policy that were denied to the states.

The Constitution has been amended twenty-seven times since 1787. The first ten of these amendments (ratified in 1791) make up the Bill of Rights, the set of protections of individual rights that were a necessary compromise to ensure that the Constitution was ratified. The remaining seventeen amendments have extended democratic election practices and changed procedural deficiencies in the original Constitution that came to be perceived as inconsistent with democratic practice. Examples of amendments to extend democratic election practices are the extension of the vote to women and to citizens between the ages of eighteen and twenty (the Nineteenth and Twenty-Sixth Amendments, respectively) or the prohibition of poll taxes, a tax that had to be paid before an individual could vote (the Twenty-Fourth Amendment). Changes to procedural deficiencies included linking presidential and vice-presidential candidates on a single ticket, replacing a system where the candidate with the most votes in the Electoral College won the presidency and the second-place candidate won the vice-presidency (the Twelfth Amendment), and establishing procedures to replace a president who becomes incapacitated (the Twenty-Fifth Amendment).

Each amendment requires three-quarters of the states to agree to the change. Although the Constitution allows states to initiate amendments, all twenty-seven have resulted from amendments initially ratified by Congress. When Congress initiates an amendment to the Constitution, two-thirds of the members of the House and the Senate must vote in favor of the amendment before it is sent to the states. States set their own procedures for ratifying constitutional amendments.

Understanding two principles is necessary to understand American constitutional government: federalism and separation of powers.[8] Federalism is the division of authority between multiple levels of government: in the United States, between the federal and state governments. Separation of powers is an effort to set government against itself by vesting separate branches with independent powers so that any one branch cannot permanently dominate the others.

These two characteristics of American government—federalism and separation of powers—were necessary compromises to guarantee the ratification of the Constitution. They are more than compromises, however. They reflect a conscious desire by the constitutional framers to limit the federal government's ability to control citizens' lives. To limit what they perceived as an inevitable tyranny of majorities over numerical minorities, the framers designed a system that set each part of government against all the other parts. Each branch of the federal government could limit the independent action of the other two branches, and the federal government and the states could limit each other.

Federalism and separation of powers have a consequence that could not be fully anticipated by the framers of the Constitution: U.S. government is designed to be inefficient. Because each part of government is set against all others, policy-making is difficult. No single leader or branch of government can unequivocally dominate policy-making as the prime minister can in a parliamentary system. Although a consensus across branches of government can sometimes appear in times of national challenge, such as in the period immediately after the September 11 attacks, this commonality of purpose quickly dissolves as each branch of government seeks to protect its prerogatives and position in the policy-making process.

Federalism establishes multiple sovereigns. A citizen of the United States is simultaneously a national citizen and a citizen of one of the states. Each citizen has responsibilities to each of these sovereigns and can be held accountable to the laws of each. Over the nation's history, the balance of power has shifted, with the federal government gaining power relative to the states, but to this day, states remain responsible for many parts of citizens' lives and act in these areas independently of the federal government.

Many powers traditionally reserved to the states have shifted to the federal government. The most rapid of these shifts occurred during the New Deal, when the federal government tapped its commerce regulation powers to create a wide range of programs to address the economic and social needs of the people. In part, the current court challenges to national health insurance focus on the questions of federalism: whether Congress has the authority to mandate individual health coverage and to require the states to establish insurance pools for their residents who cannot buy insurance from private insurers under Congress's authority to regulate interstate commerce.

The second organizing principle of American government is separation of powers. Each of the three branches of the federal government—the executive, the legislative (see Section 4), and the judiciary—shares in the responsibilities of governing and has some oversight over the other branches. In order to enact a law, for example, Congress must pass the law, and the president must sign it. The president can block the action of Congress by vetoing the law. Congress can override the president's veto through a two-thirds vote in both houses of Congress. The courts can review the constitutionality of laws passed by Congress and signed by the president. Congress and the states acting in unison can reverse a Supreme Court ruling on the constitutionality of a law by passing a constitutional amendment by two-thirds votes in each house that is subsequently ratified by three-quarters of the states. The Senate must ratify senior appointments to the executive branch, including members of the cabinet, as well as federal judges. The president nominates these judges, and Congress sets their salaries and much of their jurisdiction (except in constitutional matters). In sum, separation of powers allows each branch to limit the others and prevents any one branch from carrying out its responsibilities without the others' cooperation. It also allows for the phenomenon of divided government in which different political parties control the executive and legislative branches of government. This complexity encourages an ongoing competition for political power.

# The Executive

## The Presidency

The American presidency has grown dramatically in power since the nation's first days. The president, who is indirectly elected, serves a fixed four-year term and is limited to two terms by a constitutional amendment ratified in 1951. The president is both head of state and head of government.

Through much of U.S. political history, the president was not at the center of the federal government. Quite the contrary: The Constitution established Congress as the central branch of government and relegated the president to a much more poorly defined role whose primary responsibilities are administering programs designed and funded by Congress. Even now, the structural weaknesses of the presidency remain. The president must receive ongoing support from Congress to implement his agenda. But the president cannot control Congress except to the degree that public opinion (and, to a much lesser degree, party loyalty) encourages members of Congress to support the president. U.S. presidents are far weaker than prime ministers in parliamentary systems; they can, however, stay in office long after they have lost popular support.

The president is the commander-in-chief of the military and may grant pardons, make treaties (with the approval of two-thirds of the Senate), and make senior appointments to the executive branch and to judicial posts (again with the Senate's concurrence). The president is required to provide an annual state of the union report to Congress and may call Congress into session. Finally, the president manages the bureaucracy, which at the time of the Constitution's ratification was small but has subsequently grown in size and responsibility. In terms of formal powers, the president is far weaker than Congress.

With one exception, presidents until the turn of the twentieth century did not add considerably to the delegated powers. The exception was Abraham Lincoln, who dominated Congress during the Civil War. His example was one that twentieth-century presidents followed. He became a national leader and was able to establish his own power base directly in the citizenry. Lincoln realized that each member of Congress depended on a local constituency (a district or state), and he labeled their activities as being local or sectional. Lincoln created a national power base for the presidency by presenting himself as the only national political leader, an important position during the Civil War. He had an advantage in being commander-in-chief during wartime; however, the foundation of his power was not the military but his connection to the people.

In the twentieth century, presidents discovered that they had a previously untapped resource. Beginning with Theodore Roosevelt, twentieth-century presidents used the office of the president as a bully pulpit to speak to the nation and propose public policies that met national needs. No member of Congress or the Senate could claim a similar national constituency.

Later in the twentieth century, presidents found a new power. As the role of the federal government expanded, they managed a much larger federal bureaucracy that provided goods and services used by nearly all citizens. Thus, a program like Social Security connects almost all citizens to the executive branch. Beginning with the New Deal, presidents proposed programs that expanded the federal bureaucracy and, consequently, the connection between the people and the president. Some of the Congressional opposition to the 2010 national health insurance bill focused on the creation of another program that linked the individual welfare of all Americans to a program administered by the Executive Branch.

Finally, twentieth-century presidents learned another important lesson from the experience of Abraham Lincoln. The president has an authority over the military that places the office at the center of policy-making in military and international affairs. Thus, in the period from World War II to the collapse of the Soviet Union, the presidency gained strength from the widely perceived need for a single decision-maker.

## PROFILE

### Barack Obama

Barack Obama's 2008 election to the presidency surprised many observers of U.S. society and politics. Obama self-identifies as, and is understood to be, African American in a society that has persistently discriminated against blacks. Many observers felt that this would prevent many white Americans from supporting his candidacy. In the end, the majority of white voters did oppose Obama, but his victory was sealed by strong support from African Americans, Latinos, and Asian Americans. Obama's African roots come from his father, who migrated to the United States as a student in the early 1960s, which makes him unique on another dimension. No previous President is the child of an immigrant to the United States.

Obama's preparation for his candidacy and for the presidency included service as a community organizer and later as a civil rights attorney. On many other dimensions, Obama shared characteristics with people recently elected to the presidency. He is trained as a lawyer, is married, and held elective office at the time of his candidacy.

President Obama began his administration facing greater challenges than most of his predecessors. The United States was engaged in two ground wars abroad as well as the war on terrorism. Obama's resources to address these international challenges were limited by a collapse in the global economy that worsened in the months before his election. A collapse in the financial services sector spurred a recession that more than doubled unemployment rates and the federal deficit. Personal bankruptcies and home foreclosures grew to new record levels.

During his first two years in office, President Obama had a resource that few of his predecessors did—sizeable Democratic majorities in the Senate and House of Representatives. The result was an ambitious agenda that saw the passage of more major pieces of legislation than any president since Lyndon Johnson had been able to pass, including: the national health care bill, two economic stimulus bills to help the nation recover from the recession, a bill to regulate the financial services industry, ratification of an arms control treaty with Russia, the end of the military's restrictions on gay and lesbian service members, civil rights legislation focusing on the workplace, and the confirmation of two Supreme Court justices, one of whom was the first Latino on the high court.

*Source:* Official White House Photo by Pete Souza.

Although the presidency gained powers in the twentieth century, the office remains structurally weak relative to Congress. Presidential power is particularly undercut by the norm of divided government: Presidents have little power over Congresses controlled by the other party. Since Congress retains the power to appropriate funds, the president must ultimately yield to its will on the design and implementation of policy.

Until the election of Barack Obama in November 2008, all presidents had been white men. All but one (John F. Kennedy) have been Protestant. While being a former general was once a stepping-stone to the presidency, in today's politics having served as a governor works to a candidate's advantage. Despite a common assumption, only four vice presidents have been elected to the presidency immediately at the end of their terms. It is more common for vice presidents to move to the presidency on the death (or, in one case, the resignation) of the president.

## The Cabinet and the Bureaucracy

To manage the U.S. government, the president appoints (and the Senate confirms) senior administrators to key executive branch departments. The chief officers at each of the core departments make up the president's cabinet. These senior officers include heads of prominent departments such as the secretary of state, the attorney general, and the secretary of defense, as well as lesser-known officials such as the secretary of veterans affairs. The U.S. cabinet has no legal standing, and presidents frequently use it only at a symbolic level. The president is also free to extend membership to other senior appointed officials (such as the U.S. ambassador to the United Nations), so the number of cabinet members fluctuates from administration to administration.

The senior officers of the executive branch agencies manage a workforce of approximately 2.1 million civilian civil servants (the bureaucracy). Although formally part of the executive branch, the bureaucracy must also be responsive to Congress. Under certain circumstances, it operates independently of both elective branches and, rarely, under the direction of the courts. The presidential appointees who lead the federal agencies establish broad policy objectives and propose budgets that can expand or contract the responsibilities of executive-branch offices. Congress must approve these budgets, and it uses this financial oversight to encourage bureaucrats to behave as their congressional monitors wish. Although the size of the federal bureaucracy had been in steady decline since the early 1980s, the new federal military and security responsibilities established after the September 11 attacks reversed this trend.

Arguably, the inability of either Congress or the president to control the bureaucracy fully should give it some independence. But the bureaucracy as a rule does not have the resources to collect information and shape the laws that guide its operations. Interest groups have steadily filled this informational role, but the information comes at a cost. Bureaucracies often develop symbiotic relations with the interests that they should be regulating. The interest groups have more access to Congress and can shape the operations of the regulatory agencies. These **iron triangle relationships** (among a private interest group, a congressional committee or subcommittee overseeing the policy in question, and a federal agency implementing the policy) often exclude new players who represent alternative views on how policies should be implemented. Without an independent source of authority, the bureaucracy must depend on both the elected branches and also on interest groups.

**iron triangle relationships**

A term coined by students of American politics to refer to the relationships of mutual support formed by particular government agencies, members of congressional committees or subcommittees, and interest groups in various policy areas.

# Other State Institutions

Besides the presidency and the Congress (see Section 4), several other institutions are central to the operation of U.S. government: the military, national security agencies, the judiciary, and state and local governments.

### The Military

The U.S. Army, Navy, Marine Corps, Coast Guard, and Air Force include approximately 1.4 million active-duty personnel plus an additional 1.3 million reserve and national guard troops. The president is commander-in-chief of the U.S. military, but on a day-to-day basis, U.S. forces serve under the command of a nonpolitical officer corps.

Because of the unique geographic resources of the United States, the military has had to dedicate few of its resources to defending U.S. territory. Beginning with the new U.S. geopolitical role after World War II, the military was given new responsibilities to support U.S. multilateral and regional defense agreements.

The United States increasingly looks to its allies to support U.S. military objectives abroad. In preparation for war with Iraq, U.S. military leaders designed an invasion force of 130,000, with 100,000 ground troops and the remainder in support positions abroad. These 100,000 U.S. military ground troops were supported by at least 15,000 British ground troops. They were supplemented by approximately

160,000 contractors.[9] International forces in Afghanistan in 2010 numbered 140,000 with 90,000 from the U.S. and the remainder from 36 other countries.

Many of the traditional responsibilities of the military, such as support of troops and specialized technical activities, have been transferred to reserve units and to private firms who work under contract to the Defense Department. Reserve troops are now called to active duty more frequently. They have been required to serve multiple long-term commitments in Iraq and Afghanistan and have been prohibited from leaving the reserves at the end of their commitments.

The repeated deployment of troops since the beginning of the U.S. military presence in Afghanistan has led to concerns that the U.S. military is stretched too thin and could not respond if the U.S. faced a new military challenge.

With the increased expectations for the military came increased reliance on defense technologies. U.S. nuclear weapons, intelligence technologies, and space-based defense technologies, as well as the maintenance of conventional weaponry and troop support, have significantly raised the cost of maintaining the military. This has led to ongoing national debates about the cost of the military and whether defense resources should go to technology or for troops. Industries have emerged to provide goods and services to the military. Proposals to cut defense spending often face opposition from these industries.

## National Security Agencies

The September 11, 2001, attacks focused the attention of policy-makers on domestic security. Agencies with responsibility in this area had been dispersed throughout the federal government. They were now concentrated in the Department of Homeland Security under a single cabinet secretary. Although it took somewhat longer, intelligence-gathering agencies were placed under the administrative control of a director of national intelligence. Funding for domestic security and international intelligence gathering increased by approximately one-third.

Legislation passed in the months after September 11, 2001, also subjected U.S. citizens and permanent residents to greater levels of government scrutiny and to potential violations of civil rights. The Bush administration asserted (and the courts rejected) a position that suspected terrorists could be seized and held indefinitely, without charges.

## The Judiciary

Of the three branches of federal government, the courts are the most poorly defined in the Constitution. Initially, it was unclear what check the courts had on other branches of government. Equally important, the courts were quite dependent on the president, who appointed judges, and on Congress, which approved the nomination of judges and set the jurisdictional authority of the courts.

In 1803, the Supreme Court established the foundation for a more substantial role in federal policy-making. It ruled in ***Marbury v. Madison*** that the courts inherently had the right to review the constitutionality of the laws. This ruling, though used rarely in the nineteenth century, gave the judiciary a central place in the system of **checks and balances**.

Even with the power of judicial review, the judicial branch remained weaker than the other branches. In addition to Congress's ability to establish court jurisdiction in nonconstitutional cases and the president's ability to fill the courts with people of his choosing, the courts have other weaknesses. They must rely on the executive branch

***Marbury v. Madison***

The 1803 U.S. Supreme Court ruling that the federal courts inherently had the authority to review the constitutionality of laws passed by Congress and signed by the president. The ruling, initially used sparingly, placed the courts centrally in the system of checks and balances.

**checks and balances**

A governmental system of divided authority in which coequal branches can restrain each other's actions. For example, the U.S. president must sign legislation passed by Congress for it to become law. If the president vetoes a bill, Congress can override that veto by a two-thirds vote of the Senate and the House of Representatives.

to enforce their decisions. Enforcement proves particularly difficult when a court's rulings are not in line with public opinion, such as when the courts ruled that busing should be used as a tool to accomplish racial integration in the schools. The courts' own rules have also limited their powers. Traditionally, the courts limit standing—the ability to bring suits—to individuals who saw their rights directly challenged by a law, policy, or action of government.

Beginning in the second half of the twentieth century, the federal courts gained power relative to the other branches of government. In part, this came from expanding the rules of standing so that groups as well as individuals could challenge laws, policies, or government actions and by maintaining longer jurisdiction over cases as a tool to establish limited enforcement abilities. The courts also gained relative power because of the expansion of federal regulatory policy. Unclear laws and regulations, often requiring technical expertise to implement, placed the courts at the center of many policy debates. The courts have also gained power because they became a venue for individuals and groups whose interests were neglected by the democratically elected institutions but who could make claims based on constitutional guarantees of civil rights or civil liberties. African Americans, for example, received favorable rulings from federal courts before Congress and the president responded to their demands. Since the September 11 attacks, the executive branch and majorities in Congress showed that they were willing to limit individual rights in a search for collective security. Courts—including the Supreme Court—have been more cautious.

The power of the courts ultimately rest with their ability to persuade the citizenry that their procedures are fair and their judgments are based on the Constitution and the law. This may become more difficult in the future as the courts and particularly the Supreme Court have moved steadily to the ideological right. Analysis in 2010, at the time of the retirement of long-time Justice John Paul Stevens, demonstrated that each of the current nine justices is more conservative that his or her predecessor on the Court and that majority opinions have become more conservative, on average, than under any of the three previous chief justices. With the courts increasingly involved in contentious national issues, the Senate has taken its role in reviewing appointments more seriously and has slowed the confirmation of appointees, leaving some judicial circuits severely short of judges.

AP Photo/J. Scott Applewhite

Supreme Court nominee Sonia Sotomayor prepares to testify before the Senate Judiciary Committee as part of her confirmation process.

The steady increase in judicial power in the twentieth century should not obscure the fundamental weaknesses of the courts relative to the elected branches. The courts are more dependent on the elected branches than the elected branches are on them.

### Subnational Government

State governments serve as an important part of government in the United States. Their responsibilities include providing services to people more directly than does the federal government. Most important among these is education, which has always been a state and local responsibility in the United States.

States and localities are able to experiment with new policies. If a policy fails in a single state, the cost is much lower than if the entire country had undertaken a new policy that eventually failed. Successes in one state, however, can be copied in others or nationally.

In addition to state governments, citizens pay taxes to, and receive services from, local governments that include counties, cities, and districts for special services such as water and fire protection, and townships. These local entities have a different relationship to the states, however, than do states to the federal government. The local entities are statutory creations of the state and can be altered or eliminated by the state (and are not a form of federalism).

Local governments provide many of the direct services that the citizenry receives from the government. Because states and localities have different resources (often based on local property taxes) and different visions of the responsibilities of government, people in the United States may receive vastly different versions of the same government service, depending simply on where they live. Education provides an example. Property tax–poor areas may spend only a few thousand dollars per year educating students, while property tax–rich areas may spend $15,000 to $20,000 per student.

# The Policy-Making Process

Because of separation of powers and constitutional limits on each branch of government, the federal policy-making process has no clear starting or ending point. Instead, citizens and organized interests have multiple points of entry and can fight outcomes through multiple points of attack. Without centralization, policies often conflict with each other. The United States, for example, subsidizes tobacco cultivation but seeks to hamper tobacco companies from selling cigarettes through high taxes, health warnings, and limits on advertising. Federalism further complicates policy-making. Each state sets policy in many areas, and states often have contradictory policies. In sum, policy advocates have many venues in which to propose new policies or to change existing policies: congressional committees, individual members of Congress, executive branch regulatory agencies, state governments, and, in some states, direct ballot initiatives.

With so many entrance points, there are equally many points at which policies can be blocked. Once Congress passes a law, executive branch agencies must issue regulations to explain specifically how the law will be implemented. Subtle changes can be inserted as part of this process. On controversial issues, senior political appointees set policy for the writing of regulations.

Furthermore, people or interest groups that feel disadvantaged by the regulations can fight regulations in the courts. They also can contest the law itself, if they can find a way to claim that the law is unconstitutional or conflicts with another law or with state government responsibilities. Once a policy is in place, it can be opposed or undermined by creating a competing policy in another agency or at the state level.

The Constitution gives no guidance about the origins and outcomes of policy initiatives. The president must present an annual report to Congress on the state of the nation. This has evolved into an organized set of policy proposals. Without presidential leadership in policy-making, Congress partially filled the void. Enumerated powers in the Constitution direct Congress to take action in specific policy areas, such as establishing a post office or building public roads. Once Congress established committees to increase its efficiency (see Section 4), these committees offered forums for discussion of narrow policy. These committees, however, are not mandated in the Constitution and are changed to reflect the policy needs of each era. Thus, while presidents can propose policies (and implement them), only Congress has the ability to deliberate about policy and pass it into law.

Beginning in the 1970s some federal courts experimented with initiating policy as a way of maintaining jurisdiction in cases brought before them. These efforts, such as court-mandated control over state prison or mental health care systems, spurred much national controversy and caused the judiciary to decline in public opinion. Today, the courts are much more likely to block or reshape policies than to initiate them.

Without any clear starting point, individual citizens have great difficulty when they seek to advocate a new policy. Into this void have come extragovernmental institutions, some with narrow interests and some promoting collective interests. Prominent or wealthy individuals or groups can get Congress's or the president's attention through campaign contributions and other types of influence.

Mediating institutions have also emerged to represent mass interests. Political parties organize citizen demands and channel them to political leaders. The parties balance the needs of various interests in society and come as close as any other group in society to presenting comprehensive policy proposals (often summarized in the parties' platforms). Group-based interests also organize to make narrow demands. Veterans are an early example of a group that made a group-specific demand on federal policy-making. In the twentieth century, as both federal and state governments began to implement more widespread distributive and redistributive policies, more organized interest groups appeared. These interest groups have become the dominant form of mediating institution in U.S. politics (see Section 4). Unlike political parties, however, interest groups represent only a single issue or group of narrowly related issues.

## Summary

The twentieth century saw a dramatic increase in the responsibilities of the presidency, the executive branch, and the courts relative to the Congress. Arguably, these changes reflect a fundamental shift in the balance of powers between the branches established in the Constitution. These increases in executive and judicial responsibilities each responded to popular demands for a more expansive government role in U.S. society and a government that protects individual rights. Late in the century, however, many in the electorate challenged this new scope of government. It is this question of the appropriate size and scope of government that animates the ongoing critical juncture in U.S. politics and that explains, in part, the dramatic shift from widespread electoral support for President Obama and the Democrats in 2008 to support for Republicans in 2010 (and likely future equally dramatic shifts in national leadership).

# REPRESENTATION AND PARTICIPATION

## The Legislature

Of the three branches in the federal government, the founders envisioned that Congress would be at the center and would be the most powerful. They concentrated the most important powers in it and were most explicit about its responsibilities. For most of the nation's history, their expectations for the powers of Congress have been met.

One of the most important compromises of the Constitutional Convention involved the structure of Congress. States with large populations wanted seats in the national legislature to be allocated based on population. Small states feared they would be at a disadvantage under this system and wanted each state to have equal representation. The compromise was a **bicameral** system with two houses, one allocated by population—the House of Representatives—and the other with equal representation for each state—the Senate. This compromise has remained largely uncontested for the past 200 years despite the growing gap in population between large and small states. The senatorial vote of each resident of Wyoming has sixty-five times the impact of each Californian.

The two legislative bodies are structured differently. The House has 435 members and is designed to be more responsive to the popular will. Terms are short (two years), and the districts are smaller than Senate seats except in the smallest states. The average House seat has approximately 716,000 constituents and will continue to grow. The Senate has 100 members and is designed to be more deliberative, with six-year, staggered terms. Although unlikely, it is possible every two years to vote out an entire House of Representatives; the Senate could see only one-third of its members unseated during any election year.

Membership in the U.S. Congress is slightly more diverse than the people who have held the presidency, although most members of Congress are white male Protestants. In the 112th Congress (2011–2013), approximately 17 percent of office-holders were women, 9 percent were African American, 6 percent were Latino, and 3 percent were Asian American. Most members of Congress, regardless of gender, race, or ethnicity, are highly educated professionals. Law is the most common profession. The Senate is less racially diverse but has a comparable share of women to the House: two Latinos, two Asian Americans, and 17 women served in the Senate in 2011. No African Americans served in the Senate.

The two central powers of Congress are legislation and oversight. For a bill to become law, it must be passed in the same form by both the House and the Senate and signed by the president. Equally important, Congress has the ability to monitor the implementation of laws that it passes. Since it continues to control the appropriation of funds for programs each year, Congress can oversee programs being administered by the executive branch and shape their implementation through allocations of money or by rewriting the law.

Congress has organized itself to increase its efficiency. Discussion and debate take place primarily in committees and subcommittees. The committee system permits each member to specialize in specific areas of public policy. Committees are organized topically, and members often seek to serve on committees that are of particular

### Focus Questions

How do Congress's constitutional powers and its organizational structure ensure that it is the most powerful branch of the U.S. government?

Who votes and who doesn't in U.S. politics? Why?

What aspects of the organization and structure of the U.S. government and the electorate diminish the likelihood of the establishment of more than two political parties?

How do U.S. political values manifest themselves in the U.S. Constitution?

**bicameral**

A legislative body with two houses, such as the U.S. Senate and the U.S. House of Representatives. Just as the U.S. Constitution divides responsibilities between the branches of the federal government and between the federal government and the states, it divides legislative responsibilities between the Senate and the House.

interest to their constituencies—for instance, a member of Congress from a rural area may seek to serve on the Agriculture Committee. All members seek to serve on committees that have broad oversight of a wide range of government activities, such as the Appropriations Committee, through which all spending bills must pass. Specialization allows each member to have some influence while not requiring that she or he know the substance of all facets of government.

For a bill to become law, it must be reviewed by the committee and subcommittee that have responsibility for the substantive area that it covers. When a member proposes a bill, it goes to a committee based on its subject matter and usually never gets any further. In each session, relatively few bills receive hearings before a subcommittee or committee. The House and Senate leadership (the Speaker of the House, the Senate Majority Leader, and committee chairs) are central to deciding which bills receive hearings. If the bill receives support from the committee, it must then be debated by the body as a whole. In the House, this may never occur because that institution has another roadblock: the Rules Committee, which determines what can be debated on the floor and under what terms. Only in the Senate can debate be unlimited (although it can be limited by cloture, a vote of sixty senators to limit debate). These hierarchical structures strengthen the powers granted to the House and the Senate in the Constitution because they allow Congress to act efficiently and to use its powers to investigate federal programs, even though it does not administer them. As a result, Congress places itself at the center of the policy-making process. Although congressional power waned somewhat in the late twentieth century, Congress remains the foremost branch of American government. This specialization and hierarchy ensure that congressional leaders are more central to the design and oversight of policy than are members of European parliaments.

This tension between the constitutional powers of Congress and the national focus on the president as the national leader became evident in the federal government's response to the September 11 attacks. Initially, President Bush shaped the public policy response, including a large emergency appropriation that included financial assistance for New York City, grants and loans to the airlines, an increase in defense and intelligence spending, and military action against Afghanistan. As Bush administration policies evolved and the response came to focus on structural changes in the federal government, however, Congress began to reassert its constitutional prerogatives. Congressional concern about the growth in executive power after September 11 was probably most evident in its reaction to the Bush administration's reorganization of more than fifty federal agencies into the cabinet-level Department of Homeland Security.

Congress also asserted itself to ensure that the National Commission on Terrorist Attacks on the United States, unofficially known as the 9/11 Commission, would be formed, funded, and given sufficient time to conduct its investigation and write its report. Initially, the Bush administration opposed forming such an investigative commission and, once it relented in the face of strong congressional opposition to its position, sought to limit the scope, funding, and longevity of the commission. The commission documented executive branch intelligence-gathering failures and provided the political pressure necessary to force the Bush administration to create a new federal official—the Director of National Intelligence—who would oversee most U.S. intelligence-gathering agencies.

Congressional oversight of presidential leadership in the U.S. response to September 11 and the wars in Afghanistan and Iraq demonstrate that Congress has not yielded as the president gained power. It passed legislation to undermine presidential power and, equally important, applied its authority to investigate federal programs to weaken the presidency. These investigations of presidents and their senior appointees weaken the connection between the presidency and the people and weaken not just the presidents as individuals, but also the presidency as an office.

# Political Parties and the Party System

The roots of two-party politics can be found both in the nation's political culture and in the legal structures that govern elections. The Democrats can trace their origins to the 1800 election, while the Republicans first appeared in 1856. Despite the fact that today's parties have consistently competed against each other, the coalitions that support them (and which they, in turn, serve) have changed continually.

Today, the Republicans depend on a coalition of upper-income voters, social conservatives, small-business owners, residents of rural areas, and evangelical Christians. They receive more support from men than from women and are strongest in the South and the Mountain West.

The Republicans have tried to make inroads in minority communities but have been largely unsuccessful, with the exception of Cuban Americans and some Asian American groups (see Figure 7.5). For Republicans to win Latino (or African American) votes on a wider scale, the party would have to be willing to alienate some core Republican constituencies.

The contemporary Democratic coalition includes urban populations, the elderly, racial and ethnic minorities, workers in export-oriented businesses, unionized labor, and, increasingly, working women. Suburban voters have increasingly joined the Democratic coalition. Today's Democrats are concentrated in the Northeast and on the West Coast. The Democrats have built a steady advantage among women voters.

Democratic partisanship grew steadily over the Bush years and declined slightly in the first two years of the Obama administration. In 2010, Democrats made up 32 percent of the electorate, Republicans 25 percent, and Independents 37 percent. Although the Independents have seen the most growth over the past two decades, they tend to lean reliably toward one party or the other. When these "leaners" are accounted for, the Democrats maintain a slight advantage, though a narrower one—roughly 44 percent to 41 percent in late 2010. Generally, Democrats, who

|  | 1992 Percent | 1996 Percent | 2000 Percent | 2004 Percent | 2008 Percent |
|---|---|---|---|---|---|
| Whites | 49.4 | 48.3 | 43.8 | 41.4 | 43.9 |
| Blacks | 89.2 | 87.5 | 91.8 | 88.9 | 96.0 |
| Hispanics | 70.9 | 77.4 | 68.4 | 56.6 | 68.9 |
| Asian Americans | 36.0 | 47.3 | 56.8 | 56.0 | 63.9 |

*Note:* These calculations exclude votes for candidates other than Democratic and Republican candidates. Each of these elections include many candidates other than the Democrat and Republican. The non-major party candidates who received the most votes in these elections were: Ross Perot in 1992 and 1996, who earned approximately 19 percent and 8 percent of the vote in 1992 and 1996, respectively; and Ralph Nader who won 3 percent and 1 percent of the vote in 2000 and 2004, respectively.
*Source:* Author's calculations based on *New York Times*. 2008. "Election Results 2008." http://elections.nytimes.com/2008/results/president/national-exit-polls.html (accessed February 15, 2010).

**FIGURE 7.5  Democratic Party Share of Two-Party Vote, Presidential Elections 1992–2008**

are more likely to be poor, less educated, and younger than Republican voters, are less likely to turn out on Election Day, particularly in "off-year" (nonpresidential) elections. After the 2010 election, the Republicans controlled governorships in 29 states, and the Democrats controlled 20. Rhode Island's Governor is Independent Lincoln Chafee. The Republicans won a majority of members of the House of Representatives in 2010 (242 to 193). Democrats hold the majority in the Senate (53 to 47).

These majorities will likely be in flux for the next several elections. The electorate is much more evenly divided than the U.S. House or the governorships suggest; both saw Democratic gains in 2006 and 2008 and gains for the Republicans in 2010. Of the two parties, the Republicans have a more fragile coalition. Beginning in the 1990s, internal conflicts grew in the Republican Party. Moral conservatives and fiscal conservatives each wanted the party to focus on their interests and jettison the others' issues as a way of expanding the party's base of support. In 2010, this division manifested itself in the emergence of the Tea Party activists who sought to move the Republican Party to the right out of concerns that the federal government was spending too much and usurping powers that should be held by the states (see U.S. Connection: The Tea Party).

These party divisions lead to speculation that new parties might emerge. But the political culture of the United States dampens the likelihood that a faction of one of the parties will break off and form a party that competes in election after election. Instead, two coalitional parties are the norm, an unusual pattern among advanced democracies.

## U.S. CONNECTION

### The Tea Party

The 2010 U.S. elections saw the emergence of a new political movement—the Tea Party. Despite its name, it is a social movement not a party, and largely organizes within the Republican Party. Tea Party activism emerged in response to anger in the electorate over federal government spending and growing federal budget deficits, to Federal Reserve actions to support the banking sector and to keep interest rates low, and to the enactment of the national health care plan and its requirement that all Americans be required to purchase insurance. Tea Party activism is highly decentralized, so there is no single Tea Party, and it rejects centralized leadership.

Various Tea Party organizations and chapters endorsed 129 candidates for the House of Representatives and 9 Senate candidates. In several cases, tea party candidates defeated the preferred candidates of Republican leaders in party primaries. Although the tea party saw some major victories in the U.S. House of Representatives, several of the Tea Party candidates who defeated establishment Republicans in primaries went on to defeat in the general election. Most notable among these were Nevadan Sharon Angle, Delaware's Christine O'Donnell, New York's Carl Palodino, and Coloradan Ken Buck. Had the mainstream Republicans

been their party's candidate, it is likely that they would have won. Had all four won, Republicans would have controlled the Senate in 2011.

Today's Tea Party reflects the latest in a long line of U.S. populist movements that appear in eras when the national government is perceived to be distant and out of touch. Over time, its energy will likely dissipate. Its rejection of formal organization and leadership structures make it difficult to sustain the high levels of citizen involvement seen in the period leading up to the 2010 elections. That said, it will undoubtedly be a force in the 2012 elections. Candidates for the 2012 Republican presidential nomination will need to win support from the activists who have been mobilized by the Tea Party movement and local Tea Party members will challenge incumbent moderate Republicans in party primaries. The outcome of the 2012 elections at the federal and state levels will determine how long the Tea Party movement as an organization will be a part of national political debates. Its organizing principles of reducing the size and scope of the federal government, on the other hand, will likely be part of U.S. political debates for the foreseeable future.

Electoral law reinforces this situation. Most U.S. elections are conducted under a single-member-plurality election system in district-based elections. Single-member district-based elections reward coalitional parties and diminish opportunities for single-issue parties or narrowly focused parties, such as the Green Party or the Tea Party, should it break off from the Republican Party. Broad coalitional parties can contest seats in election after election, while smaller parties in the United States are likely to dissolve after several defeats.

There are more than 600,000 elected offices in the United States. To compete regularly in even a small percentage of these, a party must have a national presence and a national infrastructure. Most third parties fail long before they are able to compete in more than a few hundred races.

Finally, the heterogeneity of the U.S. population and the range of regional needs and interests rewards parties that can form coalitions prior to elections, as does a system with just two political parties. The Constitution-driven inefficiency of the U.S. government would become all the more dramatic if multiple parties (rather than two that must, by their nature, be coalitions) were competing in legislatures to shape outcomes.

# Elections

As an example of its commitment to democratic norms, the United States points to the frequency of elections and the range of offices filled through elections. Unlike the case in parliamentary systems, these elections are conducted on a regular schedule: presidential elections every four years, Senate elections every six years, House of Representatives elections every two years. States and localities set the terms of state and local offices, but almost all have fixed terms.

Fundamental to understanding U.S. elections is federalism. States set the rules for conducting elections and for who can participate and how votes are counted. When the country was founded, this authority was almost complete, since the Constitution said little about elections. At the country's founding, most states limited electoral participation to white male landholders. By the 1830s, many states had eliminated the property-holding requirement, in part in response to the emergence of competitive political parties that sought to build membership.

Further expansion of the U.S. electorate required the intervention of the federal government and amendment of the Constitution to reduce state authority in determining voter eligibility. The first of the efforts to nationalize electoral rules was initially a failure. This was the effort to extend the franchise to African Americans after the Civil War through the Fourteenth and Fifteenth Amendments. More successful was the Nineteenth Amendment, ratified in 1920, which extended the vote to women.[10] The Civil War amendments finally had an impact with the passage of the Voting Rights Act (VRA) in 1965, which secured African Americans access to the ballot box. In 1975, Congress extended the VRA to other ethnic and racial groups who had previously seen their right to vote abridged because of their origin or ancestry—Hispanics, Asian Americans, Native Americans, and Alaskan Natives. In 1971, the Twenty-Sixth Amendment gave the vote to all citizens aged eighteen and older.

States continue to regulate individual participation in elections through their control of voter registration. In most advanced democracies, the national government is responsible for voter registration rather than the individual. Individual registration prescreens potential voters to ensure they meet the state's requirements for voting:

residence in the jurisdiction for a set amount of time and, in many states, the absence of felony convictions. While this may appear minimal and necessary to prevent voter fraud such as an individual's voting multiple times in the same election, the requirement to register in advance of the election prevents many from being able to vote.[11]

There is a second consequence of federalism on U.S. elections: The responsibility for holding elections, deciding which nonfederal offices are filled through elections, and determining how long nonfederal officeholders will serve before again having to be elected is the responsibility of the states and, if the states delegate the power, to localities. Thus, a local office that is elected in one state could be an appointed office in another. Terms for state and local offices, such as governors, vary. Elections are held at different points throughout the year. Finally, federalism shapes elections by delegating to the states responsibilities for determining how votes are collected and how they are counted, even in elections to national office.

What are the consequences of this federalist system of elections? At a minimum, it leads to confusion and burnout among potential voters. Many voters are unaware of elections that are not held on the same schedule as national elections. Others who are aware become overloaded with electoral responsibilities in jurisdictions that have frequent elections and so choose not to vote in local races.

One result of this decentralized system with a legacy of group-based exclusion is that increasing numbers of citizens do not vote. In the late 1800s, for example, turnout in national elections exceeded 80 percent of those eligible to vote, and the poor participated at rates comparable to the rich. By 1996, turnout in the presidential election dropped below 50 percent (returning to 64 percent in the 2008 election). In state and local races, turnouts in the range of 10 to 20 percent are the norm. Perhaps more important, turnout varies dramatically among different groups in society. The poor are less likely to vote than the rich, the young less likely than the old, and the less educated less likely than the more educated.[12] Because blacks and Hispanics are more likely to be young, poor, and have lower levels of formal education, they are less likely to vote than are whites. Hence, political institutions are less likely to hear their demands and respond to their needs.

These class- and age-driven differences in participation are not entirely the result of federalism and variation in the rules for individual participation and the conduct of elections. Declining party competitiveness at the state level also plays a role. Nevertheless, the steady elimination of formal group-based exclusion has been replaced by the marginalization of the majority of some groups, such as Asian Americans and Hispanics. The United States has yet to live up to its democratic ideals.

This declining participation should not obscure the dramatic changes in leadership and issues addressed that result from elections (see Figure 7.6). In 2006, the Democrats regained control of the Senate and House of Representatives and elected the first woman to serve as Speaker of the House (Nancy Pelosi). In 2010, the Republicans gained control of the House as well as many governorships and state house majorities. These Republican majorities in many state governments allowed them to guide redistricting that will determine Congressional and state legislative seats for the remainder of the decade.

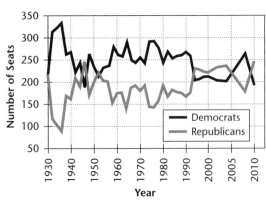

**FIGURE 7.6 Party Control of the U.S. House of Representatives, 1930–2010**

*Source:* U.S. House of Representatives, Office of the Clerk. 2011. "Party Divisions of the House of Representatives (1789 to Present)." http://clerk.house.gov/art_history/house_history/partyDiv.html (accessed February 15, 2011).

# Political Culture, Citizenship, and Identity

The United States is a large country with distinct regional cultures, ongoing immigration leading to distinct languages and cultures, class divisions, and a history of denying many Americans their civil rights. Despite these cleavages, the United States has maintained almost from its first days a set of core political values that has served to unify the majority of the citizenry. These values are liberty, equality, and democracy.

Liberty, as it is used in discussions of U.S. political culture, refers to liberty from restrictions imposed by government. A tangible form of this notion of liberty appears in the Bill of Rights, which provides for the rights of free speech, free assembly, free practice of religion, and the absence of cruel and unusual punishment. Support for liberty takes a second form: support for economic liberty and free enterprise. Property and contract rights are protected at several places in the Constitution. Furthermore, Congress is empowered to regulate commerce.

Clearly, these liberties are not mutually exclusive. But protections of the Bill of Rights often conflict with each other: Economic liberties reward some in the society at the cost of economic opportunities for others. Nevertheless, the idea that citizens should be free to pursue their beliefs and their economic objectives with only limited government interference has been a unifying element in U.S. political culture.

Equality is the second unifying American political value. In the Declaration of Independence, it is "self-evident" that "all men are created equal." Nevertheless, at various times in the nation's history, women, Native Americans, African Americans, Mexican Americans, Chinese Americans, Japanese Americans, and immigrants who had naturalized have been excluded from membership in the polity and, consequently, from access to this equality. But each of the excluded groups, such as African Americans during the civil rights movement, has used the widespread belief in equality to organize and demand that the United States live up to its ideals.

It is important to observe what this belief in equality is not. The equality that has long been sought is equality of opportunity, not equality of result, such as that sought in the communist states. There is support for the notion that people should have an equal opportunity to compete for economic rewards, not that they should end up at the same point.

The final unifying value is representative democracy. Throughout the nation's history, there has been a belief that government is legitimate only to the degree that it reflects the popular will. As with the notion of equality, the pool of citizens whose voices should be heard has changed over time, from white male property holders at the

Despite a steady liberalization of rules on who can vote, voting rates in the United States have declined for the past 100 years.

*Source:* By permission of Gary Varvel and Creators Syndicate, Inc.

time of the founding to most citizen adults today (convicted felons are excluded from the franchise in many states).

The United States has never had a national religion and, at times in the nation's history, conflicts between Protestants and Catholics have been divisive. In contemporary society, division over religion is more between those for whom religion provides routine guidance in politics and social interactions and those for whom religion is a more private matter that does not shape political activities.

In 2008, 51 percent of U.S. adults were Protestant, 24 percent were Roman Catholic, and 2 percent were Jewish or Mormon. Less than 1 percent were Muslim. Nearly 17 percent of U.S. adults reported no religious preference. Despite the fact that there is no national religion in the United States, religion plays a more central role in U.S. politics than it does in the politics of European democracies. Moral issues—such as abortion and gay rights—guide the votes of a sizeable minority of the population. Many elected leaders are overt in their religiosity to a degree that would not be acceptable in European politics (and would not have been in U.S. politics as recently as twenty-five years ago).

Values are very much at the heart of contemporary political debates. Leaders have marshaled these values throughout the nation's history to reduce potential cleavages in U.S. society. Since the United States cannot look to a common ethnicity of its people (as, for example, Germany can), to a sovereign with a historical tie to the citizenry (as in a monarchy like the United Kingdom), or to a purported common religion or ideology among its citizens (as does Iran or Cuba), the belief in these values has been used to unify the diverse peoples of the United States.[13]

## Interests, Social Movements, and Protest

In the United States, political participation has long included activities other than elections and party politics. In the nation's story about its origins, protest proves central; the Revolution was spurred by acts of civil disobedience such as the Boston Tea Party. Similarly, protest and social movements repeatedly forced the United States to live up to its democratic ideals. From the woman's suffrage movement of the nineteenth century to the civil rights movement of the 1950s and 1960s, people defined as being outside the democratic community organized to demand that they be included.

These protest movements have also been able to tap the willingness of Americans to become involved in collective action. This voluntarism and civic involvement have long been identified as stronger in the U.S. democracy than in other advanced democracies.

In recent years, however, observers of U.S. politics have noted a decline in civic involvement, a decline that has also appeared in the other advanced democracies. Although social movements remain, they have become much more driven by elites than were their predecessors. At the same time, voluntarism and civic involvement have declined, and the likelihood of participation has followed the patterns of voting, with the more educated, wealthier, and older generally more likely to volunteer and be civically engaged.[14] This decline in civic involvement in U.S. politics has serious long-term implications for society. As civic involvement declines, Americans talk about politics less with their peers and have a lessened sense that they can shape political outcomes. They are less likely to be part of networks that allow for collective political action. Political scientist Robert Putnam has identified this as the "bowling alone" phenomenon in which social capital—the networks of relationships with norms of behavior, trust, and cooperation that increase the likelihood that society will function effectively—is in decline.[15] Americans traditionally had many social venues, such as bowling leagues, where they had an outlet to talk about politics and, potentially, to organize when they were frustrated with political outcomes. There are fewer of these today (people are busier, have more job responsibilities, and spend more time watching television), and the decline in civic engagement has led to reduced political efficacy and greater frustration with the course of politics.

Protest, of course, remains an option for people who feel neglected by the political order. In 2006, for example, as many as 5 million immigrants, their families, and their supporters took to the streets to protest anti-immigrant legislation in the U.S. House of Representatives. Mass protests such as these, however, are very much the exception. Despite the fact that many in the United States oppose immigration at current levels, the social movement organizations that have formed to promote this cause—most notably the Minuteman organization—have rarely been able to generate much mass participation. National polling indicates that for the population as a whole—who neither joined the street protests nor the militias—immigration is an area of continuing concern. Each of the last three Congresses has sought to reform immigration in a comprehensive manner, but has failed, suggesting that neither the street protests, nor the anti-immigrant militias were of sufficient gravity or organization to pressure Congress into action on immigration.

The decline in social movements and other ways to organize the politically marginalized (such as labor unions), however, has shifted the focus of protest from organized collective actions to more isolated and, often, violent protests (such as the 1995 bombing of the federal building in Oklahoma City or the antiglobalization protests in Seattle in 1999) that fail to build more support for the demands of the people organizing the protest. Militia movements—organizations of individuals willing to take up arms to defend their own notion of U.S. political values and the Constitution, for example—represent the concerns of some in today's society, but few support their activities.

The twentieth century saw the rise of a new form of organized political activity: interest groups. Like political parties and candidates for office, these organizations try to influence the outcome of public policy by influencing policy-makers. They differ, however, in that they are usually organized to influence a single issue or a tightly related group of issues. Also unlike social movements, they rely on money and professional staff rather than on committed volunteers. Interest groups increased in prominence as the federal and state governments increasingly implemented distributive and redistributive policies. Beginning in the 1970s, a specialized form of interest group, the **political action committee (PAC)**, appeared to evade restrictions on corporations and organized labor to make financial contributions to political candidates and political parties.

Interest groups are so numerous in U.S. politics that it is not possible to even venture a guess as to their number. They include national organizations, such as the National Rifle Association, as well as local groups, such as associations of library patrons who seek to influence city council appropriations. They include mass organizations, such as the American Association of Retired Persons, and very narrow interests, such as oil producers seeking to defend tax protections for their industry.

Although interest groups and PACs are now much more common than social movements in U.S. politics, they do not replace one key function traditionally fulfilled by the social movements, which seek to establish accountability between citizens and government. Interest groups by definition protect the needs of a cohesive group in the society and demand that government allocate resources in a way that benefits the interests of that group. They usually include as members people who already receive

**political action committee (PAC)**

A narrow form of interest group that seeks to influence policy by making contributions to candidates and parties in U.S. politics.

rewards from government or are seeking new benefits. Their membership, then, tends to include more socially, financially, and educationally advantaged members of U.S. society. There is no place in the network of interest groups for individuals who are outside the democratic community or whose voices are ignored by the polity. The key role that social movements and protest have played in U.S. politics is being replaced by a more elite and more government-focused form of political organization.

## Summary

The Constitution places the U.S. Congress at the center of U.S. policymaking. To influence its actions, political parties and interest groups mobilize the citizenry to vote in elections and to advocate to officeholders. As the size and scope of government has increased, citizen participation and involvement has diminished. The complexity of policies and multiple points of access discourage many from believing that their voices will be heard. Over time, this frustration leads to a perception that government is "out of control" and dominated by special interests. For the United States to meet its democratic ideals, however, it must find a means to balance the growing complexity of modern governance with the need for regular citizen input into shaping government activities. These new resources to connect government and the governed will need to build on core U.S. political values.

# SECTION 5   UNITED STATES POLITICS IN TRANSITION

## Focus Questions

In what ways can effective mediating institutions overcome the roadblocks to governance built into the U.S. Constitution?

How has the U.S. role in global governance and global institutions changed in the period since World War II?

What are the likely ongoing barriers to U.S. integration into the growing network of multinational organizations and interstate relations?

The election of Barack Obama signaled a significant transition for U.S. electoral politics. Had only non-Hispanic whites voted, John McCain would have easily won the presidency. Instead, Obama won large majorities of the African American, Latino, and Asian American votes, and with the 43 percent of the White vote he carried, was elected President. The Senate and House elections in 2008 saw the highest number of minorities elected in U.S. history.

Obama's victory should not, however, obscure the fact that the U.S. electorate has a dramatically lower share of minority participants than does the population as a whole. Latinos, for example made up 15 percent of the population in 2008, but just 7 percent of the electorate; Asian Americans made up 5 percent of the population and 3 percent of the electorate. The gap was narrower for African Americans: 13 percent of the population and 12 percent of the electorate, but 2008 was uniquely significant for the black community.

Without question, some of these gaps will narrow over time. Minority populations tend to be younger, for example, than non-Hispanic whites, and voting increases with age. The minority voting gap, nevertheless, presents an ongoing challenge for the American democracy, one that will likely grow in the short term. The gap is even greater in the states with large minority populations. At the state level, the pool of regular voters is dominated by older upper-income white voters; this population is more resistant to pay for the services needed by many of the minority nonvoters, such as K–12 education, social services, and adult education. Candidates and office holders, however, often speak to the needs of voters over the societal need to ensure that all Americans have access to the resources they need to succeed.

# Political Challenges and Changing Agendas

The United States today faces some familiar and some new challenges that result from the nation's new place in the world of states. Primary among the continuing challenges is the need to live up to its own definition of the democratic idea and to balance this goal of representative government elected through mass participation with the divergent economic outcomes that result from its laissez-faire approach to governing the economy. The United States must address these challenges with a system of government that was designed to impede the actions of government and a citizenry that expects much of government but frequently does not trust it to serve popular needs.

The United States has assumed a relatively new role and set of responsibilities in the world of states, at least new as far as the past seventy years; U.S. governing institutions must now respond not just to their own people, but more broadly to an international political order that is increasingly interconnected and seeks rapid responses to international security, political, and economic crises. The institutional arrangements of U.S. government hamper quick responses and increase the likelihood of parochial responses that the rest of the world can hear as isolationism or unilateralism. These institutional arrangements are reinforced by a citizenry that for the most part cares little about foreign policy (except when war threatens), expects quick and often painless solutions to international crises, and has little respect, and sometimes open animosity, for multinational political and economic institutions such as the U.N. and the I.M.F. Despite the citizenry's continued focus on domestic concerns, U.S. jobs and national economic well-being are increasingly connected to international markets and to the willingness of governments and individuals to buy U.S. bonds. Over time, many in the United States may come to resent this economic integration.

Economics is not the only role that the United States plays in the world of states, as has been brought home in the period since the September 11 attacks. Although the citizenry has demonstrated a willingness to pay the financial cost of a global military, it has been much less willing to sacrifice lives. As a result, U.S. leaders must continually balance their military objectives and responsibilities to allies and international organizations with an inability to commit U.S. forces to conflicts that might lead to substantial casualties.

This tension between U.S. reliance on a global economic order among developed nations and a willingness to pursue a unilateral military and defense policy appeared repeatedly after the September 11 attacks. The initial approach of national leaders as well as the citizenry was to pursue military actions against Afghanistan and Iraq alone if necessary. Although alliances formed for each military engagement, this threat of unilateral action made the building of long-term multilateral alliances all the more difficult.

In addition to its economic and military roles, the United States exports its culture and language throughout the world. This process contributes to economic development in the United States; equally important, it places the United States at the center of an increasingly homogenizing international culture. But this process also creates hostility in countries that want to defend their national and local cultures.

The substantial changes in the U.S. connections to the world of states have not been matched by equally dramatic changes in the U.S. role in governing the economy. Laissez-faire governance continues. The United States tolerates income and wealth disparities greater than those of other advanced democracies. Business is less regulated and less taxed in the United States than in other democracies. Few in the polity contest this system of economic regulation.

Since the Great Depression, the United States has seen an expansion of redistributive programs to assist the poor. In the period of divided government, however, the United States has reduced its commitment to assisting the poor and has established time limits for any individual to collect benefits. It seems highly unlikely that the United States will develop targeted programs to assist citizens in need that compare to those of other advanced democracies.

Distributive programs targeted to the middle class, such as Social Security, Medicare, and college student loans, have also been implemented in the twentieth century. These have much more support among voters and are harder to undermine, even if they challenge traditional laissez-faire approaches. The costs of these programs, however, are putting an increasing long-term burden on the federal budget and, because of deficit spending, on the national economy. There is little political will to deal with these long-term costs. Divided government, with routinely shifting Democratic and Republican majorities adds to this complexity; each party must treat each election as the opportunity to reenter the majority.

The U.S. government faces a challenge to its sense of its own democratic idea that is more dramatic than that faced by other advanced democracies. The 64 percent of the electorate who turned out in 2008 was high by recent standards, but it's not clear that this pattern will continue. Turnout in non–presidential-year elections is even lower: This was approximately 42 percent of registered voters in 2010. Participation is not spread evenly across the population: older, more affluent, and more educated citizens are much more likely to vote than are the young, the less educated, and the poor. Elected representatives are receiving less guidance from a narrower subset of the people.

The breadth of nonelectoral politics is also narrowing. Previous study of the United States found rich networks of community-based organizations, voluntary organizations, and other forms of nonelectoral political activity. Community politics in the United States, however, began to decline in the 1950s (roughly when electoral turnout began to decline) and appears to be at record lows today.

The politics of collective identities has always been central to U.S. politics because the country has been a recipient of large numbers of immigrants through much of its history. Each wave of immigrants has differed from its predecessors in terms of culture and religion. These differences forced the country to redefine itself in order to live up to its democratic idea. The "old" group of each era also perceived the "new" group as a threat to the political values of the nation. Today, Asian and Hispanic immigrants are seen as a challenge by the descendants of European immigrants.

The United States has experienced a long period of sustained high levels of immigration since 1965. The current period of high immigration has seen higher levels of overall immigration than the previous period of sustained high immigration (beginning after the Civil War and extending to the 1920s). Many in Congress today are proposing legislation to further deter undocumented migration, but there have been few proposals to reduce the opportunities for legal immigration.

Without strong political parties, mediating institutions, and nonelectoral community politics, the political integration of these immigrants and their children may stall. The preliminary evidence is that naturalization rates are increasing, but that naturalized citizens vote and participate in other forms of politics at lower levels than comparably situated U.S.-born citizens. If these patterns continue, the United States faces a new risk: Contemporary immigrants and their children may not be represented in the political order, even when these immigrants become U.S. citizens.

In the past, institutional arrangements and mediating institutions could partly overcome the weaknesses of the U.S. constitutional system. Congress dominated the executive until the New Deal era, after which the president dominated Congress until Watergate. This institutional dominance reflected the framers' intent through the Great Depression and after, at least in terms of the dominance of one branch. It is unclear that the framers envisioned a system where two, and occasionally all three, branches of government would compete for dominance and where the Congress and the presidency would be routinely controlled by different political parties.

Mediating institutions once played a role that they cannot tackle today. Once the political parties formed as mass institutions in the 1830s, they served a necessary role in unifying popular opinion and forcing elite compromise. Today, parties are in decline and have been replaced by a distinct type of mediating institution that does not seek compromise across issues and instead promotes narrow interests. Interest groups connect the citizenry to political institutions, but they only advance a narrow agenda.

The United States faces the same challenges it has always faced, and it is still limited by a governing system that seeks to inhibit government activity. In the past, it has overcome these challenges when citizens participated actively, often working through mediating institutions and mobilizing new groups to active political participation. With citizen participation becoming more selective and mediating institutions less broadly based, the United States will have trouble facing challenges. Because of our central position in the world economy, if we cannot meet our challenges, the whole world will suffer with us.

## United States Politics in Comparative Perspective

From the perspective of the study of comparative politics, the United States may well remain an enigma. Its size, wealth, unique experiences with immigration, history of political isolation from the world, and reliance on separation of powers and federalism do not have clear parallels among other advanced democracies. This distinctness comes through perhaps most clearly in the way the United States engages its international political responsibilities. While the president has traditionally directed the scope of U.S. foreign policy, Congress, as it reasserts power relative to the president, will likely play an increasing role. Members of Congress, who represent narrow geographic districts and are more directly connected to mass interests, are less likely to take an internationalist perspective than the president does. When Congress speaks on international issues, it is often with multiple voices, including some that oppose U.S. involvement in multilateral organizations. This conflict over control and direction of foreign policy has increased since the end of the Cold War.

The relationship of the United States to Cuba offers an example. Since the Cuban revolution (1959), the United States has not recognized Cuba and has imposed economic sanctions in an effort to remove Fidel and, now, Raul Castro from power and to encourage economic reforms. Increasingly, however, interests in the United States across the ideological spectrum (agricultural producers, recent Cuban émigrés, the travel and tourism industry, and liberals who never supported the sanctions) have sought to expand opportunities for trade with Cuba. These efforts, however, have been effectively blocked by Cuban American leaders, who raise the prospect of Cuban American voters fleeing a candidate who supports a change in policy, and by Cuban American members of Congress who use leadership positions to slow policy change. In the 112th Congress (2011–2013), Cuban American Ileana Ros-Lehtinen will chair the U.S. House Foreign Affairs Committee. Her position on the committee and in the Republican leadership makes it unlikely that Congress will approve any change in U.S. economic sanctions on Cuba.

The impact of the constitutionally mandated structural and institutional weaknesses of U.S. government is not limited to the American people. The United States plays a dominant role in the world economy, as well as a central political role in international organizations. Thus, the inefficiencies and multiple entry points into U.S. policy-making shape the ability of the United States to respond to crises and develop coherent long-term policies in conjunction with its allies. In 1998, for example, as the world economy declined, the president, with the support of the chair of the Federal Reserve, proposed that the United States increase its contribution to the IMF by $18 billion. Congress initially balked at this request for several reasons, none of which were apparent to the U.S. allies. While the power of intransigence and horse trading makes sense to analysts of U.S. politics, analysts abroad cannot so easily understand the seeming failure of the United States to act in a time of crisis. Eventually Congress passed the added IMF appropriation.

In sum, despite its central role in the international economic system and in multilateral organizations, the United States often remains reluctant to embrace fully the international system that it helped shape. This hesitancy appears despite the active role of U.S. economic interests abroad and the importance of international trade to the U.S. economy. The United States does not hesitate to impose its will abroad when it perceives its security threatened, or when it perceives that the rules made by the international organizations undermine its economic or political interests. Thus, despite its central role in the world of states, the United States is sometimes a hesitant leader. The post–9/11 world makes this a much more difficult position to sustain. The challenge of the contemporary era is not states—as it was in the Cold War era—but instead international non–state-based networks. These cannot so easily be controlled through economic dominance and multilateral political alliances. As the United States faces the new challenges of a post–9/11 world, it must again reexamine the degree to which it is willing to act unilaterally and to pay the price for global concern about its occasional unilateralism.

### Summary

Throughout its history, the United States has faced and overcome challenges to grow into the world's largest economy and a respected and emulated model for representative democratic political institutions. This need for evolutionary change continues as its own population and the world of states continues to change. Its success in these efforts—what is needed to guarantee its continuing global leadership—depends on its ability to live up to its democratic ideal and ensure that all Americans have equal voice and a sense of efficacy, that their voices will be heard by their leaders.

## Chapter Summary

The U.S. democratic model remains a powerful force in the world of nations. It has survived for over two centuries and has adapted to the pressures of an increasingly globalized world. The United States will continue to face many challenges to live up to its own democratic ideals and to serve as an international political and economic leader. Most important among these are the constitutional limits that often impede governmental action and a citizenry that has seen a ongoing decline in civic engagement in recent years and an increasing frustration with their connections to government.

The outcome of the 2010 elections, however, show that mass organization can significantly change the focus and direction of government. Organization by the Tea Party movement and by the Republican Party in 2010 will likely lead to organization and mobilization on the left that will advocate for positions quite different from those advocated by the winners of many 2010 elections. The constitutional system may slow the influence of this organization on policy-making, but ensures that the citizenry's voice will be heard every two years and that governing institutions will change to reflect changing demands among voters and other organized interests in U.S. society.

## Key Terms

| | | |
|---|---|---|
| federalism | interest groups | regulations |
| North American Free Trade Agreement (NAFTA) | USA PATRIOT Act | distributive policies |
| manifest destiny | separation of powers | redistributive policies |
| Declaration of Independence | single-member-plurality (SMP) electoral system | iron triangle relationships |
| Articles of Confederation | free market | *Marbury* v. *Madison* |
| Bill of Rights | laissez-faire | checks and balances |
| social security | police powers | bicameral |
| property taxes | Federal Reserve Board | political action committee (PAC) |

## Suggested Readings

Amar, Akhil Reed. *The Bill of Rights: Creation and Reconstruction.* New Haven, CT: Yale University Press, 1998.

Burns, Nancy, Kay Lehman Schlozman, and Sidney Verba. *The Private Roots of Public Action: Gender, Equality, and Political Participation.* Cambridge: Harvard University Press, 2001.

Dawson, Michael C. *Black Visions: The Roots of Contemporary African-American Political Ideologies.* Chicago: University of Chicago Press, 2002.

Deering, Christopher J., and Steven S. Smith. *Committees in Congress,* 3rd ed. Washington, D.C.: Congressional Quarterly Books, 1997.

DeSipio, Louis. *Counting on the Latino Vote: Latinos as a New Electorate.* Charlottesville: University Press of Virginia, 1996.

Elkins, Stanley, and Eric McKitrick. *The Age of Federalism.* New York: Oxford University Press, 1993.

*The Federalist Papers.* Edited by Clinton Rossiter. New York, Mentor, 1961.

Fenno, Jr., Richard F. *Home Style: House Members in Their Districts.* Glenview, Ill.: Scott, Foresman, 1978.

Hartz, Louis. *The Liberal Tradition in America.* New York: Harvest/HBJ, 1955.

Judis, John B., and Ruy Teixeira. *The Emerging Democratic Majority.* New York: Scribner, 2002.

Kupchan, Charles. *The End of the American Era: U.S. Foreign Policy and the Geopolitics of the Twenty-First Century.* New York: Knopf, 2002.

Levinson, Sanford. *Constitutional Faith.* Princeton, NJ: Princeton University Press, 1988.

Lowi, Theodore J. *The End of Liberalism: The Second Republic of the United States,* 2nd ed. New York: Norton, 1979.

Nye, Joseph, Jr. *The Paradox of American Power: Why the World's Only Superpower Can't Go It Alone.* New York: Oxford University Press, 2002.

Sniderman, Paul, and Thomas Piazza. *The Scar of Race.* Cambridge: Harvard University Press, 1993.

Verba, Sidney, Kay Lehman Schlozman, and Henry Brady. *Voice and Equality: Civic Voluntarism in American Politics.* Cambridge: Harvard University Press, 1995.

Wilson, Woodrow. *Congressional Government: A Study in American Politics.* Baltimore: Johns Hopkins University Press, 1885.

Wolfinger, Raymond, and Steven Rosenstone. *Who Votes?* New Haven, CT: Yale University Press, 1980.

Zaller, John. *The Nature and Origins of Mass Opinion.* New York: Cambridge University Press, 1992.

Zolberg, Aristide. *A Nation by Design: Immigration Policy in the Fashioning of America.* Cambridge: Harvard University Press, 2006.

## Suggested Websites

The 9/11 Commission Report
**http://www.gpoaccess.gov/911/index.html**

FindLaw—Cases and Codes: U.S. Constitution
**findlaw.com/casecode/constitution/**

*New York Times*
**www.nytimes.com**

Thomas—Legislative Information from the Library of Congress
**thomas.loc.gov**

U.S. Census Bureau
**www.census.gov**

White House
**www.whitehouse.gov**

# 8

# The Russian Federation[1]

Joan DeBardeleben

ITAR-TASS /Landov

**Official Name:** Russian Federation (Rossiiskaia Federatsiia)

**Location:** Eastern Europe/Northern Asia

**Capital City:** Moscow

**Population (2009):** 141.9 million

**Size:** 17,075,200 sq. km.; approximately 1.8 times the size of the United States

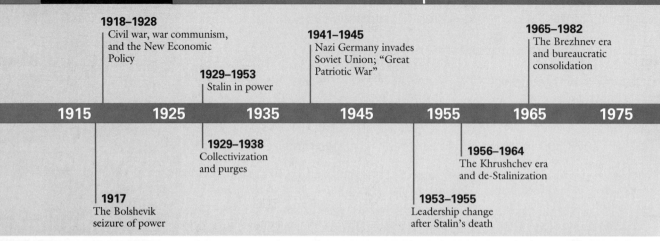

**1918–1928**
Civil war, war communism, and the New Economic Policy

**1929–1953**
Stalin in power

**1941–1945**
Nazi Germany invades Soviet Union; "Great Patriotic War"

**1965–1982**
The Brezhnev era and bureaucratic consolidation

1915     1925     1935     1945     1955     1965     1975

**1929–1938**
Collectivization and purges

**1956–1964**
The Khrushchev era and de-Stalinization

**1917**
The Bolshevik seizure of power

**1953–1955**
Leadership change after Stalin's death

# SECTION 1

# THE MAKING OF THE MODERN RUSSIAN STATE

## Focus Questions

Consider three crucial junctures in Russian history. In what ways was each juncture a reaction to a recurring problem in Russian history?

What were Russia's principal challenges in the 1990s and how have they changed since the year 2000?

## Politics in Action

The town of Pikalyova, located about 150 miles southeast of St. Petersburg, Russia, and with only around 22,000 residents, suddenly became a well-known symbol among Russia's political elites following dramatic events in the spring of 2009. This industrial town represents a Soviet legacy, the so-called monocity—a relatively small urban settlement that is dependent for its survival on a single interdependent industrial complex. When the global financial/economic crisis of 2008–2009 hit, Pikalyovo lived from the production of three intertwined factories, one of them the linchpin—BaselCement Pikalyovo, owned by a powerful businessman, Oleg Deripaska. In spring 2009, the town began to experience difficulties because Deripaska's firm could no longer supply materials to the other two factories. The rupture sparked public protests when the city's heating and hot water supply was interrupted and wages weren't being paid; civil unrest spread, as residents blocked the federal highway and descended on city hall, demanding the resignation of the governor of the region. When Russia's prime minister, Vladimir Putin, arrived on the scene to deal with the crisis in early June, the country's elite watched. After some heavy-handed talks, local economic and political figures were cajoled to rustle up alternative supply sources, production was partially restored, and back wages were paid. With the prime minister's intervention, the crisis was contained.[2]

Pikalyovo came to be a power symbol. The crisis itself reflected the vulnerable position of Russia's inherited industrial legacy. Overall in 2009 over 200 mass-protest actions were inspired in one way or another by the economic crisis. Demands were primarily economic and only rarely mentioned political grievances. Nonetheless, the political leadership was clearly worried about the potential spread of the "Pikalyovo effect,"[3] and concessions were often offered preemptively to contain unrest elsewhere.

At the same time the Pikalyovo events exemplified the continuing interdependence of politics and economics in contemporary Russia: A crisis in a small provincial town required the personal attention of the country's top leaders.

| 1982–1985 | 1991 | 1998 | 2007–2008 |
| Leadership change after Brezhnev's death | Collapse of the USSR and establishment of the Russian Federation as an independent state | Financial crisis and devaluation of the ruble | Parliamentary and presidential elections establishing dominance of United Russia and smooth transition to the presidency of Dmitry Medvedev |
| | | **2000–2008** Putin presidency, with recentralization of state power | |

**1985**    **1990**    **1995**    **2000**    **2005**    **2010**

| **1985–1991** The Gorbachev era and *perestroika* | **1993** Adoption of the new Russian constitution by referendum; first (multiparty) parliamentary elections in the Russian Federation (December) | **2004** Beslan hostage-taking, southern Russia; Putin announces new centralizing measures | **December 2011– March 2012** State Duma elections and Presidential elections |
| | **1991–1999** Yeltsin presidency, with market and democratic reforms | | |

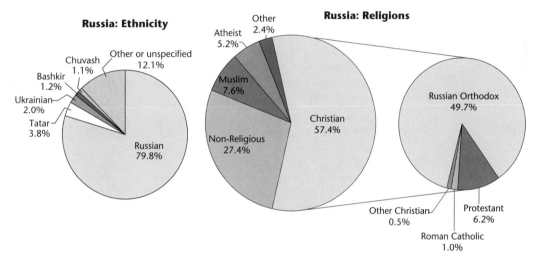

**Russia: Ethnicity**

- Chuvash 1.1%
- Bashkir 1.2%
- Ukrainian 2.0%
- Tatar 3.8%
- Other or unspecified 12.1%
- Russian 79.8%

**Russia: Religions**

- Other 2.4%
- Atheist 5.2%
- Muslim 7.6%
- Non-Religious 27.4%
- Christian 57.4%

- Russian Orthodox 49.7%
- Other Christian 0.5%
- Roman Catholic 1.0%
- Protestant 6.2%

**Russian Currency**
Ruble
International Designation: RUB
Exchange Rate (2010): US$1 = 30 RUB
100 Ruble Note Design: Sculpture on the portico of the Bolshoi Theatre in Moscow

© 4780322454/Shutterstock.com

**FIGURE 8.1 The Russian Nation at a Glance**

# Geographic Setting

After the Soviet Union broke up in 1991, fifteen newly independent states emerged on its territory. This section focuses on the Russian Federation, the largest successor state and the largest European country in population (141.9 million in November 2009)[4] and, in area, the largest country in the world, spanning eleven time zones.

| Table 8.1 | Political Organization |
|---|---|
| Political System | Constitutionally a presidential system |
| Regime History | Re-formed as an independent state with the collapse of communist rule in December 1991; current constitution since December 1993. |
| Administrative Structure | Constitutionally a federal system, with eighty-three subnational governments; politically centralized. |
| Executive | Dual executive (president and prime minister). Direct election of president; prime minister appointed by the president with the approval of the lower house of the parliament (State Duma). |
| Legislature | Bicameral. Upper house (Federation Council) appointed by heads of regional executive and representative organs. Lower house (State Duma) chosen by direct election, national proportional representation system with 450 deputies. Powers include proposal and approval of legislation, approval of presidential appointees. |
| Judiciary | Independent constitutional court with nineteen justices, nominated by the president and approved by the Federation Council, holding twelve-year terms with possible renewal. |
| Party System | Dominant establishment party (United Russia) within a multi-party system |

Russia underwent rapid industrialization and urbanization under Soviet rule. Only 18 percent of Russians lived in urban areas in 1917, at the time of the Russian Revolution; 73 percent do now. Less than 8 percent of Russia's land is arable, while 45 percent is forested. Russia is rich in natural resources, concentrated in western Siberia and northern Russia. These include minerals (even gold and diamonds), timber, oil, and natural gas, which now form the basis of Russia's economic wealth.

Before the communists took power in 1917, the Russia's czarist empire extended east to the Pacific, south to the Caucasus Mountains and the Muslim areas of Central Asia, north to the Arctic Circle, and west into present-day Ukraine, eastern Poland, and the Baltic states. In the USSR the Russian Republic formed the core of a multiethnic state. Russia's ethnic diversity and geographic scope have made it a hard country to govern. Currently Russia faces pockets of instability on several of its borders, most notably in Tajikistan and Afghanistan in Central Asia, and in Georgia and Azerbaijan in the south. Russia's western neighbors include Ukraine, Belarus, and several member states of the European Union (EU), namely Finland, Estonia, Latvia, Lithuania, and Poland. Located at a critical juncture between Europe, the Islamic world, and Asia, Russia's regional sphere of influence is now disputed.

## Critical Junctures

### The Decline of the Russian Tsarist State and the Founding of the Soviet Union

**patrimonial state**

A system of governance in which the ruler treats the state as personal property (patrimony).

Until 1917, an autocratic system headed by the tsar ruled Russia. Russia had a **patrimonial state** that not only ruled the country but also owned the land.[5] The majority of the peasant population was tied to the nobles, the state, or the church (through serfdom). The serfs were emancipated in 1861 as a part of the tsar's effort to modernize Russia and to make it militarily competitive with the West.

The key impetus for industrialization came from the state and from foreign capital. Despite some reforms, workers became increasingly discontented, as did liberal intellectuals, students, and, later, peasants, in the face of Russia's defeat in the Russo-Japanese war and continued tsarist repression. Revolution broke out in 1905. The regime maintained control through repression and economic reform until March, 1917, during the height of World War I, when revolution deposed the tsar and installed a moderate provisional government. In November, the Bolsheviks, led by Vladimir Lenin, overthrew that government.

## The Bolshevik Revolution and the Establishment of Soviet Power (1917–1929)

The Bolsheviks were Marxists who believed their revolution reflected the political interests of the proletariat (working class). Most revolutionary leaders, however, were not workers, but came from a more educated and privileged stratum, the intelligentsia. Their slogan, "Land, Peace, and Bread," appealed to both the working class and the discontented peasantry—over 80 percent of Russia's population.

The Bolshevik strategy was based on two key ideas: democratic centralism and vanguardism. **Democratic centralism** mandated a hierarchical party structure in which leaders were, at least formally, elected from below, but strict discipline was required in implementing party decisions once they were made. The centralizing elements of democratic centralism took precedence over the democratic elements, as the party tried to insulate itself from informers of the tsarist forces and later from real and imagined threats to the new regime. The concept of a **vanguard party** governed the Bolsheviks' relations with broader social forces. Party leaders claimed to understand the interests of working people better than the people did themselves. Over time, this philosophy was used to justify virtually all actions of the party and the state it dominated.

In 1922 the Bolsheviks formed the Union of Soviet Socialist Republics (USSR), the first communist party to take state power. Prior to this, the Bolsheviks had faced an extended civil war (1918–1921), when they introduced war communism, which involved state control of key economic sectors and forcible requisitioning of grain from the peasants. The *Cheka*, the security arm of the regime, was strengthened, and restrictions were placed on other political groups. By 1921, the leadership had recognized the political costs of war communism. In an effort to accommodate the peasantry, the New Economic Policy (NEP) was introduced in 1921 and lasted until 1928. Under NEP, state control over the economy was loosened so that private enterprise and trade were revived. The state, however, retained control of large-scale industry.

Gradually, throughout the 1920s, the authoritarian strains of Bolshevik thinking eclipsed the democratic elements. Lacking a democratic tradition and bolstered by the vanguard ideology of the party, the Bolshevik leaders were plagued by internal struggles following Lenin's death in 1924. These conflicts culminated in the rise of Joseph Stalin and the demotion or exile of other prominent figures such as Leon Trotsky and Nikolai Bukharin. By 1929 all open opposition, even within the party itself, had been silenced.

The Bolshevik revolution also initiated a period of international isolation; to fulfill their promise of peace, the new rulers had had to cede important chunks of territory to Germany under the Brest-Litovsk Treaty (1918), which were returned to Russia only after Germany was defeated by the United States, France, and Britain. However

**democratic centralism**

A system of political organization developed by V. I. Lenin and practiced, with modifications, by all communist party-states. Its principles include a hierarchical party structure.

**vanguard party**

A political party that claims to operate in the "true" interests of the group or class that it purports to represent, even if this understanding doesn't correspond to the expressed interests of the group itself.

these countries were hardly pleased with Russia's revolution, which led to expropriation of foreign holdings and which represented the first successful challenge to the capitalist order. The former allies sent material aid and troops to oppose the new Bolshevik government during the civil war.

### The Stalin Revolution (1929–1953)

From 1929 until his death in 1953, Joseph Stalin consolidated his power as Soviet leader. He brought changes to every aspect of Soviet life. The state became the engine for rapid economic development, with state ownership of virtually all economic assets. By 1935, over 90 percent of agricultural land had been taken from the peasants and made into state or collective farms. **Collectivization** was rationalized as a means of preventing the emergence of a new capitalist class in the countryside. But it actually targeted the peasantry as a whole, leading to widespread famine and the death of millions. Rapid industrialization favored heavy industries, and consumer goods were neglected. Economic control operated through a complex but inefficient system of central economic planning, in which the state planning committee (Gosplan) set production targets for every enterprise in the country. People were uprooted from their traditional lives in the countryside and catapulted into the rhythm of urban industrial life. Media censorship and state control of the arts strangled creativity as well as political opposition. The party/state became the authoritative source of truth; anyone deviating from the authorized interpretation could be charged with treason.

Gradually, the party became subject to the personal whims of Stalin and his secret police. Overall, an estimated 5 percent of the Soviet population was arrested at one point or another under the Stalinist system, usually for no apparent cause. Forms of resistance were evasive rather than active. Peasants killed livestock to avoid giving it over to collective farms. Laborers worked inefficiently. Absenteeism was high.

Isolation from the outside world was a key tool of the Stalinist system of power. But the policy had costs. While it shielded Soviet society from the Great Depression of the 1930s, the Soviet economy, protected from foreign competition, also failed to keep up with the rapid economic and technological transformation in the West.

In 1941, Nazi Germany invaded the Soviet Union, and Stalin joined the Allied powers. Casualties in the war were staggering, about 27 million people, including 19 million civilians. War sacrifices and heroism have remained powerful symbols of pride and unity for Russians up through the present day. After the war, the other Allied powers allowed the Soviet Union to absorb new territories into the USSR itself (these became the Soviet republics of Latvia, Lithuania, Estonia, Moldavia, and portions of western Ukraine). The Allies also implicitly granted the USSR free rein to shape the postwar governments and economies in East Germany, Poland, Hungary, Czechoslovakia, Yugoslavia, Bulgaria, and Romania. Western offers to include parts of the region in the Marshall Plan were rejected under pressure from the USSR. Local Communist parties gained control in each country. Only in Yugoslavia were indigenous Communist forces sufficiently strong to hold power largely on their own and thus later to assert their independence from Moscow.

The USSR emerged as a global superpower as the Soviet sphere of influence encompassed large parts of Central and Eastern Europe. In 1947, the American president Harry Truman proclaimed a policy to contain further Soviet expansion (later known as the Truman Doctrine). In 1949, the North Atlantic Treaty Organization (NATO) was formed involving several West European countries, the United States, and Canada, to protect against potential Soviet aggression. In 1955 the Soviet

**collectivization**

A process undertaken in the Soviet Union under Stalin from 1929 into the early 1930s and in China under Mao in the 1950s, by which agricultural land was removed from private ownership and organized into large state and collective farms.

# Russian Federation, March 2010

*Yamal-Nenets (A Ok) and Khanty-Mansiisk (A Ok) are also part of Tyumen oblast.
**Nenetsia (A Ok) is also part of Arkhangel'sk oblast.

© Cengage Learning

Occupied by the Soviet Union in 1944, administered by Russia, claimed by Japan

**Legend:**

― Republic, oblast, or krai boundary
--- Autonomous okrug (A Ok) boundary, when the A Ok is also part of an oblast.
An oblast is named only when its name differs from that of its administrative center.

Republic
Oblast or Krai
Autonomous Okrug (A Ok)
Autonomous Oblast (AO)

0    800 km
0    800 Miles

| | | |
|---|---|---|
| 1 Krasnodar Krai | 7 Ingushetia | |
| 2 Stavropol' Krai | 8 Chechnya | |
| 3 Adygea | 9 Mordovia | |
| 4 Karachay-Cherkessia | 10 Chuvashia | |
| 5 Kabardino-Balkaria | 11 Mari El | |
| 6 North Ossetia | 12 Udmurtia | |

Union initiated the Warsaw Pact in response. These events marked the beginning of the Cold War, characterized by tension and military competition between the two superpowers, leading to an escalating arms race that was particularly costly to the Soviet Union.

The Soviet Union isolated its satellite countries in Central and Eastern Europe from the West and tightened their economic and political integration with the USSR. Some countries within the Soviet bloc, however, had strong historic links to Western Europe (especially Czechoslovakia, Poland, and Hungary). Over time, these countries served not only as geographic buffers to direct Western contacts but also as conduits for Western influence.

### Attempts at De-Stalinization (1953–1985)

Even the Soviet elite realized that Stalin's terror could be sustained only at great cost. The terror destroyed initiative and participation, and the unpredictability of Stalinist rule inhibited the rational formulation of policy. From Stalin's death in 1953 until the mid-1980s Soviet politics became more regularized and stable. Terror abated, but political controls remained in place, and efforts to isolate Soviet citizens from foreign influences continued.

In 1956, Nikita Khrushchev, the new party leader, embarked on a bold policy of de-Stalinization, rejecting terror as an instrument of political control. The secret police (KGB) was subordinated to the authority of the Communist Party of the Soviet Union (CPSU), and party meetings resumed on a regular basis. However, internal party structures remained highly centralized, and elections were uncontested. Khrushchev's successor, Leonid Brezhnev (party head 1964–1982) partially reversed Khrushchev's de-Stalinization efforts. Controls tightened again in the cultural sphere. Individuals who expressed dissenting views through underground publishing or publication abroad were harassed, arrested, or exiled. However, unlike in the Stalinist period, the political repression was predictable. People generally knew when they were transgressing permitted limits of criticism.

From the late 1970s onward, an aging political leadership was increasingly ineffective at addressing mounting problems. Economic growth rates declined, living standards improved only minimally, and opportunities for upward career mobility declined. To maintain the Soviet Union's superpower status, resources were diverted to the military sector, gutting the consumer and agricultural spheres. An inefficient economic structure raised the costs of exploiting new natural resources. High pollution levels and alcoholism contributed to health problems. At the same time, liberalization in some Eastern European states and the telecommunications revolution made it increasingly difficult to shield the Soviet population from exposure to Western lifestyles and ideas. Among a certain critical portion of the population, aspirations were rising just as the capacity of the system to fulfill them was declining.

### Perestroika and Glasnost (1985–1991)

**glasnost**

Gorbachev's policy of "openness," which involved an easing of controls on the media, arts, and public discussion.

Mikhail Gorbachev took office as a Communist Party leader in March 1985. He endorsed a reform program that centered around four important concepts intended to spur economic growth and bring political renewal. These were *perestroika* (economic restructuring), *glasnost* (openness), *demokratizatsiia* (a type of limited democratization), and "New Thinking" in foreign policy.[6] Gorbachev's reform program was designed to adapt the communist system to new conditions rather than to usher in its demise.

The most divisive issues were economic policy and demands for republic auton-omy. Only half of the Soviet population was ethnically Russian in 1989. Once Gorbachev opened the door to dissenting views, demands for national autonomy arose in some of the USSR's fifteen union republics. This occurred first in the three Baltic republics (Latvia, Lithuania, and Estonia), then in Ukraine, Georgia, Armenia, and Moldova, and finally in the Russian Republic itself. Gorbachev's efforts failed to bring consensus on a new federal system that could hold the country together.

Gorbachev's economic policies failed as well. Half-measures sent contradictory messages to enterprise directors, producing a drop in output and undermining estab-lished patterns that had kept the Soviet economy functioning, although inefficiently. To protect themselves, regions and union republics began to restrict exports to other regions, despite planning mandates. In "the war of laws," regional officials openly defied central directives.

Just as his domestic support was plummeting, Gorbachev was awarded the Nobel Peace Prize, in 1991. Under his New Thinking, the military buildup in the USSR was halted, important arms control agreements were ratified, and many controls on international contacts were lifted. In 1989, Gorbachev refused to prop up unpopular communist governments in the Soviet bloc in Central European countries. First in Hungary and Poland, then in the German Democratic Republic (East Germany) and Czechoslovakia, pressure from below pushed the communist parties out of power. To Gorbachev's dismay, the liberation of these countries fed the process of disintegration of the Soviet Union itself.

## Collapse of the USSR and the Emergence of the Russian Federation (1991 to the Present)

In 1985 Mikhail Gorbachev drafted Boris Yeltsin into the leadership team as a nonvoting member of the USSR's top party organ, the Politburo. Ironically, later Yeltsin played a key role in the final demise of the Soviet Union. In June 1991 a popular election confirmed Yeltsin as president of the Russian Republic of the USSR (a post he had held since May of the previous year). In August 1991 a coalition of conservative figures attempted a coup d'état to halt Gorbachev's program to reform the Soviet system. While Gorbachev was held captive at his summer house (*dacha*), Boris Yeltsin climbed atop a tank loyal to the reform leadership and rallied opposition to the attempted coup. In December 1991, Yeltsin and the leaders of Ukrainian and Belorussian Republics declared the end of the Soviet Union, proposing to replace it by a loosely structured entity, the Commonwealth of Independent States.

As leader of the newly independent Russian Federation, Yeltsin took a more radi-cal approach to reform than Gorbachev had done. He quickly proclaimed his com-mitment to Western-style democracy and market economic reform. However, that program was controversial and proved hard to implement. The executive and legis-lative branches of the government also failed to reach consensus on the nature of a new Russian constitution; the result was a bloody showdown in October 1993, after Yeltsin disbanded what he considered to be an obstructive parliament and laid siege to its premises, the Russian White House. The president mandated new parliamentary elections and a referendum on a new constitution, which passed by a narrow margin in December 1993.

Yeltsin embarked on a program of radical economic reform, which confronted Russians with an increasingly uncertain future marked by declining real wages, high inflation, and rising crime. Yeltsin's initial popularity was also marred by an extended military conflict to prevent Chechnya, a southern republic of Russia, from seceding from the country. Concern that separatism could spread to other regions was an important motivation for the military intervention. Despite these problems, with the help of an active public relations effort, Yeltsin was reelected president in 1996, winning 54 percent of the vote against the Communist Party candidate, Gennady Zyuganov, in a second round of voting. During his second term in office Yeltsin was plagued by poor health and continuing failed policies. In 1998 a major financial crisis triggered a political one.

In 1999, Yeltsin appointed Vladimir Putin prime minister. Putin, a little-known figure from St. Petersburg, was a former KGB operative in East Germany. His political advance was swift, and the rise in his popularity was equally meteoric. In December 1999, Yeltsin resigned as president of the Russian Federation. In presidential elections that followed in March 2000 Putin won a resounding victory. Putin benefited from auspicious conditions. In 1999 the economy began a period of sustained economic growth that lasted until the 2008–2009 global financial crisis. High international gas and oil prices fed tax dollars into the state's coffers.

Just as economic growth revived, worries about security increased. Instability associated with the Chechnya problem underlay a string of terrorist attacks, beginning in 1999. One particularly tragic event involved a hostage-taking on the first day of school (September 1, 2004) in the town of Beslan in southern Russia, which ended in tragedy, with more than 300 hostages killed—the majority children. Meanwhile, in March 2003, Russian authorities tried to set Chechnya on a track of normalization, holding a referendum that would confirm Chechnya's status within the Russian Federation. However, intermittent violence continued.

Despite these problems, Putin recorded consistently high levels of popular support throughout his tenure and successfully managed the transition to his handpicked successor as president, Dmitry Medvedev, who won the 2008 presidential elections handily. However, throughout this period, Putin also introduced political reforms marked by increased political centralization, restrictions on political opposition, and the growing dominance of one political party, United Russia. Since 2000 Russia has been characterized by a drift to a form of **soft authoritarianism**, in which formal and informal mechanisms secure the dominance of the ruling group. While Western experts debate whether authoritarian tendencies might yet be reversed, many Russians just hope that the enhanced powers of the central authorities may help ensure a secure and stable way of life. When the economic-financial crisis took hold in 2008 a new source of insecurity arose. With the decline in oil and gas prices, Russia's main export commodities, the economic upturn was interrupted. In 2009 Russian President Medvedev announced a modernization program to address some of the imbalances in the Russian economy, but the momentum for reform has proven to be weak. As Russia approached the 2011–2012 election cycle, foreign observers and domestic critics wondered whether Medevdev's conception of modernization might include a gradual turn away from the authoritarian tendencies of the previous decades, but most were skeptical.

In the international sphere, following the attacks on the World Trade Center and the Pentagon on September 11, 2001, Russia and the United States shared a common interest in combating terrorism. However, tensions with the United States quickly emerged as Russia opposed the American incursion into Iraq. Russian leaders were also wary of increasing U.S. influence in neighboring countries, which included support for admitting countries such as Ukraine and Georgia into NATO and for installation of an antimissile defense system in Central Europe. A further crisis point occurred in August 2008 with Russia's military intervention in Georgia to support the secessionist regions of South Ossetia and Abkazia; Western leaders

**soft authoritarianism**

A system of political control in which a combination of formal and informal mechanisms ensure the dominance of a ruling group or dominant party, despite the existence of some forms of political competition and expressions of political opposition.

Pikalyovo residents protest against job cuts and worsening living standards. Slogans on the signs read "Why do you sack my mom?," "BasEl's politics is crisis itself!," and "Authorities are political impotent!"

*Source*: http://www.mr7.ru/news/economy/story_14348.html.

objected strongly to the Russian action. Nonetheless, in March 2009, following Barack Obama's inauguration as U.S. President, the new Secretary of State Hillary Clinton made a dramatic gesture of calling for a "reset"[7] of U.S.-Russian relations, generating hope that the grand hopes of the 1990s for an end to East-West tensions could again be revived.

# Themes and Implications

### Historical Junctures and Political Themes

Following the collapse of the USSR in 1991, international support for the new reform-oriented government in Russia surged, with the proliferation of aid programs and international financial credits. In the 1990s, Russia's status as a world power waned, and the expansion of Western organizations (NATO, EU) to Russia's western border undermined its sphere of influence in Central and Eastern Europe. Russia's western neighbors, except Belarus, looked more to Europe than to Russia as a guidepost for the future. But Russia's economic recovery following 1998, the rise of energy prices, and Europe's dependence on imports of Russian natural gas and oil provided an important basis for Russia's renewed international influence. No longer simply a supplicant in its relationship to the West, Russia reasserted its role as a major European power under Putin's leadership. But with its "near abroad," Russia has had difficulties establishing itself as a respected regional leader. Russia's defense of a disputed presidential election outcome during Ukraine's Orange Revolution in November 2004 suggested the primacy of Russian national interest over democratic values. Russian intervention in Georgia in 2008, to support secessionist claims there, evoked concern in other neighboring countries. At the same time, by 2008 tensions between Russia and the West had reached a level unprecedented in the post-communist period. Will new diplomatic efforts begun in 2009 reverse this trend?

For nearly a decade after the collapse of the Soviet system, the Russian Federation seemed mired in a downward spiral of economic collapse and political paralysis. By the late 1990s, the Russian public was disillusioned and distrustful of its leaders, and resentment remained over the dismal results of the Western-inspired reform program. After 1998, however, growth rates recovered, budget surpluses became routine, and the population experienced a marked increase in economic confidence. Questions arose, however, about the depth of the economic recovery, and indeed the drop in energy prices with the 2008 financial crisis and ensuing global recession posed a significant challenge for Russia. However, in previous years the government had wisely created a Reserve Fund and Prosperity Fund (generated from high oil and gas revenues) for just such a contingency, providing a buffer against the worse effects. Since energy prices recovered relatively quickly and the government sought to protect social welfare measures from severe cutbacks, Russia withstood the financial and economic crisis relatively well. At the same time, wide disparities in wealth and income, as well as important regional inequalities, continue to plague the system. Although many important policy problems have been addressed, others remain unresolved, including inadequate levels of foreign investment, capital flight, continuing high levels of inequality, and the decline in the agricultural sector.

Concerns about the fate of Russian democracy have also become widespread in the West as well as among opposition groups inside Russia. On the positive side, the constitution adopted in 1993 has gained a surprising level of public acceptance, even as observers express intensifying concern that key reforms adopted after 2000 may be undermining real political competition. The regime justifies these changes as necessary to ensure state capacity to govern and to secure continuing economic growth, but critics see the Russian desire for order as leading the country down an authoritarian path with only the trappings of political democracy, under the tutorship of a dominant establishment political party, United Russia. High and rising levels of corruption still pervade the Russian political and economic system, despite the proclaimed commitment of the political leadership to curtail them.

Finally, Russians continue to seek new forms of collective identity. The loss of superpower status, the dominance of Western economic and political models in the 1990s, and the absence of a widely accepted ideology have all contributed to uncertainty about what it means to be Russian and where Russia fits into the world of states. Meanwhile, Russia itself suffers from internal divisions. Although overt separatism has been limited to the Republic of Chechnya, differing visions of collective identity have emerged in some of Russia's ethnic republics, particularly in Muslim areas. A revival of Russian nationalism, directed partly at the West and partly at non-Christian ethnic minority groups, is a phenomenon of increasing concern. Other aspects of identity, including social class and gender roles, are also being reconsidered.

## Implications for Comparative Politics

Many countries have attempted a transition from authoritarian rule to democratic governance. In Russia's case, one of the most important factors affecting this process is the tradition of strong state control, stretching from tsarist times through the Soviet period, and now influencing present developments. In addition, the intertwined character of politics, economics, and ideology in the Soviet Union has made democratization and economic reform difficult to realize at the same time. In effect, four transition processes were initiated simultaneously in the early 1990s: democratization, market reform, a redefinition of national identity, and integration into the world economy. Whereas other democratizing countries may have undergone one or two of these transitions, Russia initially tried to tackle all four at once. Because the former communist elites had no private wealth to fall back on, corrupt or illegal methods were sometimes used by Russia's emerging capitalist class to maintain former privileges. Citizens, confronted with economic decline and an ideological vacuum, have been susceptible to appeals for strong state control, as well as nationalist appeals. No doubt, economic uncertainty has made the Russian public willing to accept strong leadership and limits on political expression that would be resisted in many Western countries. Russia's current "backsliding" from democratic development may, in part, reflect the difficulties of pursuing so many transitions at once.

## Summary

Russian history has been characterized by a series of upheavals and changes that have often made life unpredictable and difficult for the citizen. The revolutions of 1917 replaced tsarist rule with a political system dominated by the Communist Party. In the Stalinist period Communist rule involved a process of rapid industrialization, collectivization of agriculture, and purges of the party, followed by large losses of population associated with World War II. With the death of Stalin came another important transition, as politics was transformed into a more predictable system of bureaucratic authoritarianism, characterized by relative stability but without political competition or democratic control. The most recent transition, ushered in by the collapse of Communist Party rule in 1991, resulted in the emergence of the Russian Federation as an independent state. The new Russia experienced an almost immediate period of economic decline in the midst of halting efforts to democratize the system in the 1990s. However, beginning in 1999, the economy took a turn for the better, at the same time that limits on political competition seem to be reversing some of the earlier democratic gains.

# POLITICAL ECONOMY AND DEVELOPMENT

SECTION **2**

The collapse of the Soviet system in late 1991 ushered in a sea change, radically reducing the state's traditionally strong role in economic development and opening the Russian economy to foreign influence. However, the process of market reform that the Russian government pursued after 1991 brought with it an immediate dramatic decline in economic performance as well as fundamental changes in social relationships. To respond, the Russian government struggled to create tools to regulate the new market forces and to manage impacts of global economic forces. After experiencing an unprecedented period of economic depression from 1991 to 1998, Russia experienced renewed economic growth, but this growth has been built largely on the country's wealth of energy and natural resources. With the economic/financial crisis of 2008–2009, prices of oil and natural gas declined precipitously, with serious consequences for Russia. However, the relatively quick recovery in price levels prevented severe economic impacts. The Russian economy remains, however, highly dependent on natural resource exports, and that dependence introduces long-term economic risks. In addition, extreme levels of social inequality and corruption remain. Overall the relative costs and benefits of Russia's transition from a state-run economy to a mixed market system are still contested.

## Focus Questions

Describe Russia's most difficult problems in moving from a command economy toward a market economy. What are the main advantages and disadvantages of each form of economy?

How have social policies changed in Russia since the collapse of the Soviet system?

As Russia has become more closely tied to the world economy, what economic adjustments has Russia had to make?

# State and Economy

In the Soviet period, land, factories, and all other important economic assets belonged to the state. Short- and long-term economic plans defined production goals, but these were frequently too ambitious. Except in the illegal black market and peasant market, prices were controlled by the state. Firms and individuals were not permitted to develop direct links to foreign partners; these were all channeled through the central economic bureaucracy.

The Soviet economic model registered some remarkable achievements: rapid industrialization, provision of social welfare and mass education, relatively low levels of inequality, and advances in key economic sectors such as the military and space industries. Nonetheless, over time, top-heavy Soviet planning could neither sustain rising prosperity at home nor deliver competitive products for export. Gorbachev's efforts at the end of the Soviet period to adapt Soviet economic structures to meet these challenges were largely unsuccessful.

Following the collapse of the USSR, in 1992 Boris Yeltsin endorsed a more radical policy of **market reform**. Four main pillars of his program were (1) lifting price controls, (2) encouraging small private businesses and entrepreneurs, (3) privatizing most state-owned enterprises, and (4) opening the economy to international influences. In January 1992, price controls on most goods were loosened or removed entirely. As a result, the consumer price index increased by about 2,500 percent between December 1991 and December 1992. Real wages declined by 50 percent.

Privatization was rapid compared to most other post-communist countries. By early 1994, 80 percent of medium-sized and large state enterprises in designated sectors of the economy had been transformed into **joint-stock companies**. The most widely adopted method for privatizing state enterprises, called **insider privatization**, gave managers and workers of the enterprise (jointly) the right to acquire a controlling packet (51 percent) of enterprise shares at virtually symbolic prices. Each citizen of Russia was issued a **privatization voucher** with a nominal value of 10,000 rubles (at various times between four and twenty U.S. dollars), which could be used to acquire shares in their own enterprise.

Many analysts believe that insider privatization hampered reform of business operations and reduced the expected gains of privatization. Managers, many of whom did not have the skills needed to operate in a market environment, were reluctant to lay off excess labor or resisted overtures by outside investors who might gain control of the enterprise. Some managers extracted personal profit from enterprise operations rather than investing available funds to improve production. Productivity and efficiency did not increase significantly; unprofitable firms continued to operate; investment was weak; and the benefits of ownership were not widely or fairly distributed. The government continued to subsidize ineffective operations, leaving most Russian firms uncompetitive.

In 1995, a second stage of privatization was launched. Firms could sell remaining shares for cash or investment guarantees. However, many firms were unattractive to investors because backward technology would require massive infusions of capital. Some of the more attractive enterprises fell into the hands of developing financial-industrial conglomerates that had acquired their wealth through positions of power or connections in the government. At the same time, new ventures, which were generally more efficient than former state firms, faced obstacles: confusing regulations, high taxes, lack of capital, and poor infrastructure (transport, banking, communications).

Reform of agriculture was even less satisfactory. Large joint-stock companies and associations of individual households were created on the basis of former state and collective farms. These privatized companies operated inefficiently, and agricultural

**market reform**

A strategy of economic transformation that involves reducing the role of the state in managing the economy and increasing the role of market forces.

**joint-stock companies**

Business firms whose capital is divided into shares that can be held by individuals, groups of individuals, or governmental units.

**insider privatization**

The transformation of formerly state-owned enterprises into joint-stock companies or private enterprises in which majority control is in the hands of employees and/or managers.

**privatization voucher**

A certificate worth 10,000 rubles (at various times between four and twenty U.S. dollars) issued by the government to each Russian citizen in 1992 to be used to purchase shares in state enterprises undergoing privatization.

© Yadid Levy/Alamy

Russians shop at the Apraksin Dvor market in St. Petersburg.

output declined. Foreign food imports also undercut domestic producers, contributing to a downward spiral in agricultural investment and production.

By the late 1990s, it appeared that the government's reform program had failed. Russia was in the grip of a severe depression. Industrial production was less than half the 1990 level. The depression fed on itself, as declining capacity in one sector deprived other sectors of buyers or suppliers.

A key obstacle to the success of the market reform agenda in the 1990s was the weakness of state institutions. Without an effective tax collection system, for instance, the government could not acquire revenues to pay its own bills on time, provide essential services to the population, and ensure a well-functioning economic infrastructure (such as transportation, energy, public utilities). A weak state meant inadequate regulation of the banking sector and poor enforcement of health, safety, and labor standards. As the state failed to carry out these functions, businesses took matters into their own hands, for example, by hiring private security services, turning to the **mafia** for protection, or by paying bribes. Ineffective government fed corruption and criminality.

The central state in Moscow also had difficulty exerting its authority in relation to regional authorities and in the face of increasing power of business **oligarchs**. These oligarchs, wealthy individuals who benefited from privatization, often wielded significant political influence.[8] Diverse methods of laundering money to avoid taxes became widespread. Corruption involving government officials, the police, and operators abroad fed a rising crime rate. Rich foreigners, Russian bankers, and outspoken journalists became targets of the Russian mafia.

A financial crisis in August 1998 brought the situation to a head. The government successively took on new loans at progressively higher rates of interest in order to pay off existing debts, creating a structure of **pyramid debt**. Following a sharp upturn in 1996–1997, in August 1998 the Russian stock market lost over 90 percent of its value. The government defaulted on its bonds. Many Russian banks, holders of the Russian government's short-term bonds, faced imminent bankruptcy. The

**mafia**

A term borrowed from Italy and widely used in Russia to describe networks of organized criminal activity.

**oligarchs**

A small group of powerful and wealthy individuals who gained ownership and control of important sectors of Russia's economy in the context of privatization of state assets in the 1990s.

**pyramid debt**

A situation in which a government or organization takes on debt obligations at progressively higher rates of interest in order to pay off existing debt.

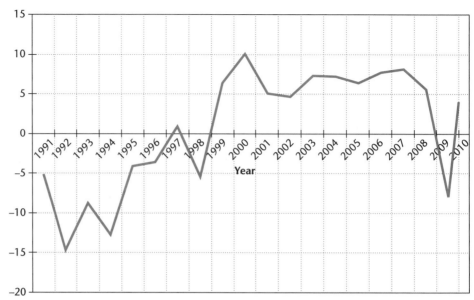

**FIGURE 8.2 Economic Decline and Recovery (gross domestic product)
Constant prices, as percent of previous year**

*Sources:* Data for 2000 to 2009, Federal State Statistics Service (Goskomstat) of the Russian Federation website; data from 1991 to 2000 are from *Introduction to Comparative Politics* (Houghton Mifflin, 2004), p. 361.

government began to print more of the increasingly valueless rubles, threatening to undermine the ruble's value further and thus intensify the underlying financial crisis.

The government finally allowed a radical devaluation of the ruble. Within a two-week period, the ruble lost two-thirds of its value against the U.S. dollar, banks closed or allowed only limited withdrawals, supplies of imported goods decreased, and business accounts were frozen—forcing some firms to lay off employees and others to close their doors. However, despite these immediately disastrous effects, the 1998 financial crisis ushered in positive changes. First, the devalued ruble made Russian products more competitive with foreign imports. Firms were able to improve their products, put underused labor back to work, and thus increase productivity. The state budget benefited from improved tax revenues. Barter declined, as did payment arrears. Economic growth revived, beginning in 1999.

When Vladimir Putin became president in the year 2000, he faced many challenges and introduced a set of legislative reforms to spur recovery. A 13 percent flat income tax, deemed easier to enforce, was one very visible aspect of the package. A budget surplus replaced a deficit. By 2007 the Russian government had lowered its debt burden to 3 percent of GDP. Foreign reserves grew from just $12 billion (U.S.) in 1998 to about $500 billion (U.S.) in March 2008.[9] Prospects for Russia's membership in the World Trade Organization also fueled optimism about Russia's trade growth.

Meanwhile, Putin made clear that economic oligarchs who used their financial positions to affect political outcomes would suffer sanctions. However, enforcement efforts were selectively directed at critics of the government. A particularly prominent case involved Mikhail Khodorkovsky, the chief executive officer and major shareholder of the giant Russian oil company Yukos. In October 2003 Khodorkovsky was placed under arrest for fraud and tax evasion, and in May 2005 he was sentenced by a Russian court to nine years in prison. And in 2010 additional charges extended his jail time

REUTERS/Alexander Natruskin.

Russian oil oligarch Mikhail Khodorkovsky, shown under arrest, displayed in a cage.

further. The attack on Yukos undermined investor confidence with fears that political pretexts might justify future government economic takeovers.

Corruption is another major obstacle to effective economic management. Transparency International produces an annual Corruption Perceptions index, based on a compilation of independent surveys. In 2010, Russia received a poor ranking, 2.1 on a 10-point scale, with 10 being the least corrupt.[10] Russia ranked 154 out of the 178 countries surveyed. One form of corruption, referred to as "**state capture**," is based on "the efforts of firms to shape the laws, policies, and regulations of the state to their own advantage by providing illicit private gains to public officials."[11] Efforts of the Russian leadership to control the power of some oligarchs could be seen as an effort to reign in this type of activity. However, corruption remains pervasive and is still a key hindrance not only to economic reform but also to political development.

**state capture**

The ability of firms to systematically turn state regulations to their advantage through payoffs or other benefits offered to state officials

## Society and Economy

The Soviet leadership established priorities with little input from society. One was military production, but the regime's social goals also produced some of the most marked achievements of the Soviet system. Benefits to the population included free health care, low-cost access to essential goods and services, maternity leave (partially paid), child benefits, disability pensions, and mass education. In a short period of time, universal access to primary and secondary schooling led to nearly universal literacy under Soviet rule. Postsecondary education was free of charge, with state stipends provided to university students. Guaranteed employment and job security were other priorities. Almost all able-bodied adults, men and women alike, worked outside the home. Citizens received many social benefits through the workplace, and modest pensions were guaranteed by the state, ensuring a stable but minimal standard of living for retirement.

The Soviet system, however, was plagued by shortages and low-quality service. For example, advanced medical equipment was in limited supply. Sometimes under-the-table payments were required to prompt better-quality service. Many goods and services were scarce. Housing shortages restricted mobility and forced young families to share small apartments with parents. Productivity was low by international standards, and work discipline weak. Drunkenness and absenteeism were not unusual. A Soviet saying illustrated the problem: "We pretend to work, they pretend to pay us."

As a matter of state policy, wage differentials between the best- and worst-paid were lower than in Western countries. This approach reduced the incentive for outstanding achievements and innovation. Due to state ownership, individuals could not accumulate wealth in real estate, stocks, or businesses. Although political elites had access to scarce goods, higher-quality health care, travel, and vacation homes, these privileges were hidden from public view.

The Soviet experience led Russians to expect the state to ensure a social welfare network, but in the 1990s, budget constraints necessitated cutbacks, just when social needs were greatest. Although universal health care remained, higher-quality care and access to medicine depended more obviously on ability to pay. Benefits provided through the workplace were cut back, as businesses faced pressures to reduce costs.

Some groups have benefited from market reforms introduced in the 1990s more than others, Those with Western language skills and those employed in the natural resources, banking, and financial sectors have better-than-average prospects. At the top of the scale are the super-wealthy, including people who took advantage of privatization to gain positions in lucrative sectors like banking, finance, oil, and gas. But losers have been more numerous. Poverty is highest among rural residents, the unemployed, children, the less educated, pensioners, and the disabled. As a result of low wage levels, the majority of those in poverty are the working poor.

Alongside more objective factors, culture affects economic change. Incentive structures of the Soviet period were internalized by older population groups, including features that encouraged risk avoidance, low productivity, poor punctuality, absenteeism, lack of personal initiative, and a preference for security over achievement.[12] However, young people in Russia are adapting to a new work environment. They

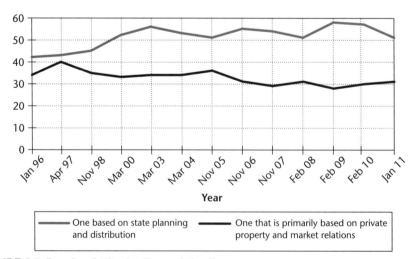

**FIGURE 8.3 Russian Attitudes Toward the Economy**
Which kind of economic system seems to you the most correct: one based on state planning and distribution, or one that is primarily based on private ownership and market relations?

*Source:* Levada Center. 2011 data is from a survey of 1600 respondents 18 years of age and older, from 45 regions, January 21–24, 2011, and data reported is also from earlier surveys, http://www.levada.ru/press/2011020803.html, accessed February 13, 2011.

are more flexible, in part due to their age, but also because of differing socialization experiences that have resulted in altered expectations. Consequently, they are inclined to support the market transition and are more oriented toward maximizing self-interest and demonstrating initiative. Nevertheless, many Russians of all age groups still question values underlying market reform, preferring an economy that is less profit driven and more oriented to equality and the collective good.

Following the economic upturn that began in 1999, large differentials in income and wealth have persisted, but the portion of the population living below the subsistence level declined after 1999. In addition average real disposable income has increased. Beginning in 2000, levels of personal consumption began to rise, but many individuals (particularly men) still hold two to three jobs just to make ends meet. Social indicators of economic stress have begun to decline only slowly, and the economic-financial crisis of 2008–2009 introduced new economic uncertainties just when many Russians were beginning to feel that life was returning to normal.

A particularly contentious issue led to massive street demonstrations in several Russian cities in early 2005 over changes to social welfare policy. Called "monetarization of social benefits," the reforms involved replacing certain services (such as public transport) that had been provided free to disadvantaged groups (pensioners, veterans, the disabled) with a modest monetary payment to the individual. Many Russians viewed the measures as involving direct reductions in social welfare benefits. After large-scale demonstrations, the government agreed to accompany the reforms by a modest increase in pensions and to restore subsidized transport. Learning from this experience, during the 2008–2009 financial-economic crisis, the government attempted to avoid cuts in social welfare measures and pensions.

Wearing shirts that read "Is something wrong? Give birth," Russian pensioners took part in a flash mob in Moscow city's underground in May 2011. According to organizers, the goal of the action was to encourage Russian women to get pregnant and increase the nation's birth rate.

*Source: Rossiiskie vesti,* August 18, 2004, p. 3.

In 2005, Putin announced a new program of National Projects intended to address inadequacies in the social sector and to reverse Russia's decline in population. The Projects focus on four priority areas: health care, education, housing, and agriculture. The National Projects were put under the stewardship of First Deputy Prime Minister Dmitry Medvedev, who was elected to the post of president in March 2008.

Russia saw a steady decline in population until 2009, mitigated to some extent by a positive inflow of immigrants, particularly from other former Soviet republics.[13] Life expectancy for Russian men in 2009 was estimated at 63 years and 75 years for women. Primary factors contributing to the high mortality rates include stress related to social and economic dislocation and unnatural causes of death (accidents, murders, suicides).[14]

To boost the birthrate, in May 2006 Putin announced a doubling of monthly child support payments and a large monetary bonus for women having a second child. Another pronatalist measure was Medvedev's announcement in 2010 instructing government officials to "design a program of free land allocation for house/dacha construction, when a third and every subsequent child is born."[15] Although declining birth rates often accompany economic modernization, in the 1990s many couples were especially reluctant to have children because of daily hardships, future uncertainty, a declining standard of living, and continuing housing shortages. Furthermore, women continue to carry the bulk of domestic responsibilities while still working outside the home to boost family income; fathers play a relatively small role in child rearing. Many women take advantage of the permitted three-year maternity leave, which is only partially paid, but difficulties in reconciling home and work duties no doubt contribute to low birthrates as well.

## Russia in the Global Economy

Right up to the end of the Soviet period, the economy remained relatively isolated from outside influences. Foreign trade was channeled through central state organs, so individual enterprises had neither the incentive nor even the possibility to seek external markets. Over time, the ruble has been allowed to respond to market conditions, and firms are allowed to conclude agreements directly with foreign partners. In response, in the 1990s Western governments (especially Germany) made fairly generous commitments of technical and humanitarian assistance. The World Bank, the International Monetary Fund (IMF), and the European Union (EU) also contributed substantial amounts of economic assistance, often in the form of repayable credits. In the past, release of IMF credit, issued to stabilize the ruble, was made contingent on Russia's pursuing a strict policy of fiscal and monetary control and lifting remaining price controls. The Russian government had difficulties in meeting these conditions, and thus the funds were released intermittently. After the August 1998 crisis, the Russian government defaulted, first on the ruble-denominated short-term debt, and then on the former Soviet debt. Since then, debt repayments have been made on time. In 2001, the government decided to forgo additional IMF credits. By 2005, it had paid off its IMF debt.

Russia has had problems attracting foreign investment. Levels still remain low compared to other East European countries, despite some improvements since 2004. An upward trajectory was interrupted by the 1998 financial crisis. Major sources of foreign direct investment since 2000 have been Germany, the United States, and Cyprus (mainly recycled Russian capital, previously exported for tax reasons), but foreign investors are, since 2006, prevented from gaining a majority share in certain sectors of the economy that are identified as of strategic importance After ironing out some specific contentious trade issues, both the EU and the United States have confirmed their support for Russian membership in the World Trade Organization (WTO), which many experts expect to occur sometime in 2011, fueling concern in some sectors of the Russian economy about their continuing competitiveness in the face of increased international exposure. Many experts, however, consider that WTO membership will offer Russia considerable economic benefits overall.

The geographic focus of Russia's foreign trade activity has shifted significantly since the Soviet period. Whereas in 1994 Ukraine was Russia's most important trading partner, in 2008 the most important trading partners were Germany (receiving more than 6.9 percent of Russian exports, and providing 12.6 percent of imports to Russia), the Netherlands (receiving 12.2 percent of Russian exports), Italy (with 9 percent of Russian exports), and China (the largest source of Russian imports, 12 percent). Overall the expanded EU accounts for more than 50 percent of Russia's trade, compared to 14 percent for the countries of the Commonwealth of Independent States (CIS).[16] A substantial portion of export commodities to Europe are energy resources.

## GLOBAL CONNECTION

### Russia and International Organizations

Russia is open to global influences. The government has achieved membership in many international and regional organizations such the World Bank, the International Monetary Fund, and the Council of Europe, and is seeking membership in others, such as the World Trade Organization. In other cases Russia has forged partnerships with organizations for which membership is currently not foreseen (e.g., the European Union or the North Atlantic Treaty Organization, NATO). Relations with three regional organizations are profiled here:

*The European Union (EU).* Russia has not expressed a desire to join the European Union, but in 1997 a ten-year Partnership and Cooperation Agreement (PCA) between the EU and Russia went into effect, setting the basis for a "strategic partnership," which in 2003 was reinforced by the creation of four "Common Spaces" of cooperation in areas relating to economic cooperation; common borders; external security; and research, education, and culture. With the lapsing of the PCA, in late 2008 negotiations commenced for a new agreement. In 2007 the EU and Russia initiated a process to facilitate the issuance of visas for Russians wishing to visit the EU, and in 2010 they announced a Modernization Partnership.

*The Council of Europe* (distinct from the European Union) is the major European vehicle for the defense of human rights, enforced through the European Court of Human Rights (ECHR) in Strasbourg, France. The Council defines its mandate as being "to develop throughout Europe common and democratic principles based on the European Convention on Human Rights and other reference texts on the protection of individuals."* Russia acceded to the organization in 1996 and ratified the European Convention on Human Rights in 1998. In joining the

Council of Europe, Russia subjected itself to periodic reviews and to the judgments of the ECHR, along with a number of other obligations. Thousands of human rights cases involving Russia have been brought to the ECHR and most judgments have gone against Russia, leading to a controversial suggestion by the Chief Justice of the Russian Constitutional Court that Russia could consider withdrawal from the Court's jurisdiction.[17] However, observers doubt that this proposal will be implemented and evidence suggests that Russia's leaders support continued Council of Europe membership.

*The North Atlantic Treaty Organization (NATO)* was originally formed after World War II to safeguard its members from the Soviet threat. Following the collapse of the communist system, NATO has had to rethink its mandate and the nature of potential threats. Among its redefined duties are crisis management, peacekeeping, opposing international terrorism, and prevention of nuclear proliferation. Since 1999 many countries of Central and Eastern Europe have been admitted as members. Russia has objected to the expansion of NATO at each step, most recently to the proposed admission of Ukraine and Georgia. Russia has, over time, nonetheless developed a stronger working relationship with the organization, including the agreement on the NATO-Russia Founding Act on Mutual Relations in 1997, formation of the NATO-Russia Council in 2002, and, most recently, an agreement at the Russia-NATO summit in Lisbon in November 2010 regarding a commitment to undertake a Joint Review of 21st Century Common Security Challenges.

---

*http://www.coe.int/aboutCoe/index.asp?page=quisommesnous&l=en.

Russia's position in the international political economy remains undetermined. With a highly skilled workforce, high levels of educational and scientific achievement, and a rich base of natural resources, Russia has many of the ingredients necessary to become a competitive and powerful force in the global economy. However, if the country's industrial capacity is not restored, reliance on natural resource exports will leave Russia vulnerable to global economic fluctuations in supply and demand. In the first nine months of 2010, about 69 percent of exports were fuels and energy resources, whereas only about 5.2 percent were machinery and equipment, with other resources such as metals and timber making up a large part of the balance.[18] Furthermore, levels of capital investment and technological innovation have not been adequate to fuel increased productivity; even in the lucrative energy sector, experts raise serious concerns about the ability of Russian firms to develop new reserves adequate to meet both domestic needs and contractual obligations to foreign (mainly European) consumers in future years. At the same time, its wealth in natural resources has given Russia advantages compared to its neighbors, since these expensive materials do not need to be imported. Ultimately, Russia's position in the global economy will depend on the ability of the country's leadership to fashion a viable approach to domestic economic challenges and to facilitate differentiation of the country's export base.

## Summary

The heavy hand of state control contributed to the inefficiency of the Soviet economy, but in contemporary Russia the state has often been ineffective in providing the legal framework and institutional structures necessary for the new market economy. In the early 1990s, the government lifted price controls, privatized state enterprises, and opened the economy to international influences. The result was rapid inflation, a fall in the standard of living, and dramatic economic decline. Ever since an economic recovery began in 1999, a wider range of goods has been available to the consumer, but many people still have difficulty making ends meet, and inequality is much higher than in the Soviet period. Under Soviet rule, Russians came to expect the government to provide a certain level of social welfare, but market economic reform undermined many of these policies. The Russian economy is highly dependent on exports of oil, gas, and other natural resources, making it susceptible to global economic influences such as the financial-economic crisis of 2008–2009.

# SECTION 3   GOVERNANCE AND POLICY-MAKING

In the 1990s the Russian leadership, under Boris Yeltsin, endorsed liberal democratic principles, and subsequent Russian presidents, both Vladimir Putin and Dmitry Medvedev, have reaffirmed their commitment to democracy. However, over time, the interpretation of how democratic governance should be applied and interpreted to make it compatible with Russia's unique political tradition and realities has become contested. Skeptics have abounded as Putin's measures to strengthen presidential power seem to have undermined many of the Russian Federation's founding democratic principles. Since 2008, when Dmitry Medvedev was elected to succeed

Vladimir Putin as president , speculation has arisen as to whether Medvedev's approach would be more sympathetic to liberal democratic principles and, if so, whether he might develop his own political base to reverse some of the authoritarian tendencies introduced by Putin.

# Organization of the State

In the Soviet period, before Gorbachev's reforms, top organs of the Communist Party of the Soviet Union (CPSU) dominated the state. The CPSU was hierarchical. Lower party bodies elected delegates to higher party organs, but elections were uncontested, and top organs determined candidates for lower party posts. The Politburo, the top party organ, was the real decision-making center. A larger body, the Central Committee, represented the broader political elite, including regional party leaders and representatives of various economic sectors. Alongside the CPSU were Soviet state structures, which formally resembled Western parliamentary systems but had little decision-making authority. The state bureaucracy had day-to-day responsibility in both the economic and political spheres but followed the party's directives in all matters. People holding high state positions were appointed through the ***nomenklatura*** system, which allowed the CPSU to fill key posts with politically reliable individuals. The Supreme Soviet, the parliament, was a rubber-stamp body.

The Soviet constitution was only symbolic, since many of its principles were ignored. The constitution provided for legislative, executive, and judicial organs, but separation of powers was considered unnecessary because the CPSU claimed to represent the interests of society as a whole. When the constitution was violated (frequently), the courts had no independent authority to enforce or protect its provisions. Likewise, the Soviet federal system was phony, since all aspects of life were overseen by a highly centralized Communist Party. Nonetheless, the various subunits that existed within the Russian Republic were carried over into the Russian Federation in an altered form.

Gorbachev introduced innovations into the Soviet system: competitive elections, increased political pluralism, reduced Communist Party dominance, a revitalized legislative branch of government, and renegotiated terms for Soviet federalism. He also tried to bring the constitution into harmony with political reality. These changes moved the political system haltingly and unevenly closer to the liberal democratic systems of the West.

Even before the collapse of the USSR, political institutions began to change in the Russian Republic, which was only one constituent unit of the Soviet Union. A new post of president was created, and on June 12, 1991, Boris Yeltsin was elected by direct popular vote as its first incumbent. Once the Russian Federation became independent, a crucial turning point was the adoption by referendum of a new Russian constitution in December 1993. This constitution provides the legal foundation for current state institutions (see Figure 8.4). Ratification of a new Russian constitution followed a violent confrontation between the president and the parliament in 1993. Nonetheless, the new constitution seems to have acquired broad-based popular legitimacy.

The document affirms many established principles of liberal democratic governance—competitive multiparty elections, separation of powers, an independent judiciary, federalism, and protection of individual civil liberties. At the same time, the president and executive branch are granted strong powers. In the face of radical institutional change, however, in the 1990s the state demonstrated only a weak

**Focus Questions**

Why has the Russian leadership viewed centralization as necessary and what centralizing measures have been taken since 2000?

How have the military, judiciary, and subnational governments evolved since the fall of the Soviet Union? Have they gained or lost importance?

What is the relationship between the prime minister and the president in Russia? How have the particular individuals who have filled these posts helped to shape this relationship?

*nomenklatura*

A system of personnel selection in the Soviet period under which the Communist Party maintained control over the appointment of important officials in all spheres of social, economic, and political life.

capacity to govern, involving dysfunctional conflict between major institutions of government. Subnational governments demanded increased autonomy, even sovereignty, generating a process of negotiation and political conflict between the center and the regions that sometimes led to contradictions between regional and federal laws. The constitution made the executive dominant but still dependent on the agreement of the legislative branch to realize its programs. Under President Yeltsin, tension between the two branches of government was a persistent obstacle to effective governance. In addition, establishing real judicial independence remained a significant political challenge.

Beginning with Vladimir Putin's presidency (2000–2008) the power of the presidency was augmented further in an effort to address the weakness of central state authority. Many observers feel, however, that Putin's centralizing measures have undermined the very checks and balances that were supposed to protect against reestablishment of authoritarian control. In fact, some observers see in Putin's reforms a partial reversion to practices and patterns reminiscent of the Soviet period, namely, centralization of power and obstacles to effective political competition. In addition, poor salaries and lack of professionalism in the civil service have made it difficult to control widespread corruption and misuse of political power.

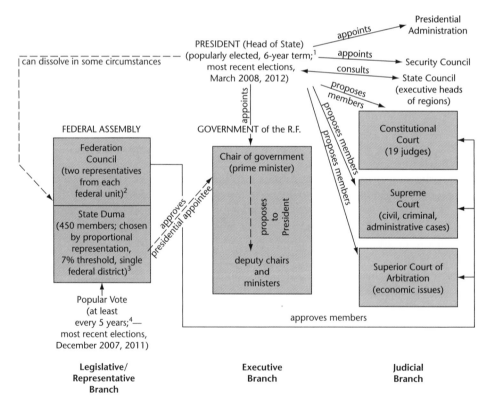

[1]As of 2012 the term is 6 years, previously 4 years.
[2]One representative appointed by the regional legislature and one by the regional excutive.
[3]Changed to nation-wide proportional representation system in 2007 with 7% threshold. Until 2007 half of seats were chosen in single-member-districts and half by proportional representation with a 5% threshold.
[4]As of 2011 the term will be maximum 5 years, previously 4 years.

**FIGURE 8.4 Political Institutions of the Russian Federation (R.F.) 2011**

# The Executive

The constitution establishes a semipresidential system, formally resembling the French system but with stronger executive power. As in France, the executive itself has two heads (the president and the prime minister), introducing a potential venue for intrastate tension. The president is also the head of state, and until 2008 this office held primary power. The prime minister, appointed by the president but approved by the lower house of the parliament (the State Duma, hereafter Duma), is the head of government. As a rule of thumb, the president has overseen foreign policy, relations with the regions, and the organs of state security, while the prime minister has focused his attention on the economy and related issues. However, with Yeltsin's continuing health problems in 1998 and 1999, operative power shifted in the direction of the prime minister. In December 1999, Yeltsin resigned from office, making the prime minister, Vladimir Putin, acting president until the March 2000 elections. Following the election of Vladimir Putin as president in March 2000 the primary locus of power returned to the presidency. Putin's 2004 electoral victory was stunning (71 percent of the vote), reinforcing his authority. Since the constitution excludes the same person from holding three consecutive terms as president, Putin proposed Dmitry Medvedev as his successor, who was elected to the post in March 2008. Since 2008 the actual balance of power between the president and prime minister has been a perennial topic of discussion within the Russian Federation and among foreign observers.

One of the president's most important powers is the authority to issue decrees, which Yeltsin used frequently for contentious issues. Although presidential decrees may not violate the constitution or specific legislation passed by the bicameral legislature, policy-making by decree allows the president to ignore an uncooperative or divided parliament. Yeltsin's decision in 1994, and again in 1999, to launch the offensive in Chechnya was not approved by either house of parliament, despite strong objections. Under Putin and Medvedev the power of decree has been used more sparingly, partly because both leaders have had strong support in the legislature.

The president can also call a state of emergency, impose martial law, grant pardons, call referendums, and temporarily suspend actions of other state organs if he deems them to contradict the constitution or federal laws. Some of these actions must be confirmed by other state organs (such as the upper house of the parliament, the Federation Council). The president is commander-in-chief of the armed forces and conducts affairs of state with other nations. Impeachment of the president involves the two houses of the legislative body (the Duma and the Federation Council), the Supreme Court, and the Constitutional Court. If the president dies in office or becomes incapacitated, the prime minister fills the post until new presidential elections can be held.

The Russian government is headed by the prime minister, flanked by varying numbers of deputy prime ministers. The president's choice of prime minister must be approved by the Duma. During Yeltsin's presidency, six prime ministers held office, the longest being Viktor Chernomyrdin, from December 1992 until March 1998, and the final one being Vladimir Putin, appointed in August 1999. After becoming acting president in December 1999, Putin had three prime ministers (and one acting prime minister). The first of these, Mikhail Kasyanov (May 2000 to February 2004), later became an outspoken opposition figure. Following his election as president in 2008, Medvedev selected Putin as his prime minister. A governing Medvedev-Putin tandem was put in place. As prime minister, Putin created a new organ, the Presidium of the Russian cabinet, a body that meets weekly and acts as a kind of executive committee of the larger cabinet.

The prime minister can be removed by the Duma through two repeat votes of no confidence passed within a three-month period. Even in the 1990s when there was

## PROFILES

## Dmitry Medvedev

Following the presidential election of March 2008, the new Russian president, Dmitry Medvedev (left), nominated the highly popular former president, Vladimir Putin (right), to serve as his prime minister.

*Source:* AP Images/ITAR-TASS, Presidential Press Service, Vladimir Rodionov.

Dmitry Medvedev was elected third president of the Russian Federation on March 2, 2008 in a landslide victory, receiving 70 percent of the popular vote. Just forty-two years old, Medvedev is the youngest leader to take power since the fall of the tsars. Medvedev was born in Leningrad (now St. Petersburg), completed his education there, and received his Ph.D. in law from Leningrad State University in 1990.

He began his academic career as an associate professor at the same university, while working as an adviser to the chairman of the Leningrad City Council and an expert consultant to the St. Petersburg city hall's Committee for External Affairs.

In 1999 Medvedev moved to Moscow, where he worked in the Presidential Executive Office under Vladimir Putin, first as deputy and first deputy chief of staff, then, in 2003, as chief of staff. He continued to rise under Putin's leadership, becoming first deputy prime minister of the Russian Federation in November 2005. At the same time, from 2000 to 2008, Medvedev was the Chairman of the Board of Directors of OAO Gazprom—the Russian natural gas monopoly.

As the nation's president, Dmitry Medvedev has proposed a strategic program of modernization under the title "Go, Russia!" The plan would make Russia into "a country whose prosperity is ensured not so much thanks to commodities but by intellectual resources: the so-called intelligent economy, creating unique knowledge, exporting new technologies and innovative products."*

In a speech in Yaroslavl (Russia) at the Global Policy Forum on September 10, 2010, Medvedev also stated his criteria for democracy: In addition to assurance of basic legal rights, he mentioned an advanced level of technological development, protection of citizens from crime and terrorism, a high level of culture and education, and the belief among citizens themselves that they live in a democratic society. Medvedev concluded that "there is democracy in Russia . . . young, immature, incomplete and inexperienced, but it's a democracy nevertheless."[19] Observers debated whether Medvedev is likely to promote real political liberalization.

The Russian president is famous for being an active Internet user. He has his own blog and is on "Twitter" and other social networks. He uses state-of-the art IT products (iPhone, iPad), and he likes photography and hard-rock music. Deep Purple is reportedly one of his favorite bands.

*Dmitry Medvedev, "Rossia Vpered" (Go, Russia), gazeta.ru 10.09.2009; http://www.kremlin.ru/news/5413, accessed January 30, 2011.

tension with President Yeltsin, the Duma was unable or unwilling to exercise this power, presumably in part because this action could lead to dissolution of the Duma itself. Until 2008, the prime minister was never the leader of the dominant party or coalition in the Duma. This changed when Putin became prime minister in 2008 because he was also elected as chairperson of the dominant party, United Russia, in that year.

One of the most intriguing questions in the current period relates to the relationship between the current president, Dmitry Medvedev, and his appointee as prime minister, Vladimir Putin. The interdependence of the two leaders has aroused much speculation about whether Medvedev is building an independent political base or whether he is primarily a vehicle of Putin's continued dominance. Observers wonder whether Medvedev will cede to Putin in the next presidential elections in 2012, when Putin would, under the constitution, be permitted to run again.

### The National Bureaucracy

The state's administrative structure includes ministries, state committees, and other agencies. Based on an administrative reform adopted in 2004, ministries are concerned with policy functions or political aspects, whereas services and agencies generally undertake monitoring functions or implementation. Most observers agree that these administrative reforms have not improved bureaucratic efficiency or government responsiveness.

Some government ministries (such as the Foreign Affairs Ministry, the Federal Security Service, and the Defense Ministry) report directly to the president. The president has created various advisory bodies that solicit input from important political and economic actors and also co-opt them into support for government policies. The most important are the Security Council and the State Council. Formed in 1992, the Security Council advises the president in areas related to foreign policy and security (broadly conceived) and includes heads of the so-called power ministries such as Defense and the Federal Security Service, the prime minister, and in recent years the heads of seven newly created federal districts. The 2009 State Security Strategy of the Russian Federation accorded the Security Council a coordinating role in this area, but the body remains only advisory. The State Council was formed in September 2000 as part of Putin's attempt to redefine the role of regional leaders in federal decision-making (see below). A smaller presidium, made up of seven of the regional heads selected by the president, meets monthly.

Ministers other than the prime minister do not require parliamentary approval. The prime minister makes recommendations to the president, who appoints these officials. Ministers and other agency heads are generally career bureaucrats who have risen through an appropriate ministry, although sometimes more clearly political appointments are made. Many agencies have been reorganized, often more than once. Sometimes restructuring signals particular leadership priorities. For example, the State Committee for Environmental Protection was abolished by a May 2000 decree; these responsibilities now lie with the Ministry of Natural Resources and Ecology. The mixing of responsibility for overseeing both use and protection of natural resources in this single agency may be an indicator of the low priority of environmental protection (as compared to resource use). In May 2008, Putin created a new Ministry of Energy, splitting off these functions from those of the Ministry of Industry and Trade. This move reflected the growing importance of this sector to Russia's economy.[20]

Top leaders also use restructuring to place their clients and allies in key positions. For example, Putin drew heavily on colleagues with whom he worked earlier in St. Petersburg or in the security establishment, referred to as ***siloviki***, in staffing a variety of posts in his administration. ***Clientelistic networks*** continue to play a key role in both the presidential administration and other state organs. These linkages are similar to old-boys' networks in the West; they underscore the importance of personal loyalty and career ties between individuals as they rise in bureaucratic or political structures. While instituting a merit-based civil service system has been a state goal, it has not yet been achieved in reality. The Russian state bureaucracy continues to suffer low levels of public respect and continuing problems with corruption.

Despite efforts to reduce the size of the state bureaucracy during Putin's term of office, its size increased substantially, in part through the creation of new federal agencies. As an apparent cost-cutting measure, in December 2010 Medvedev issued a presidential decree mandating a 5 percent cut in staff during 2011, with a decline of 20 percent by April 2013. The exact mechanism for achieving this result is unclear.

## Public and Semipublic Institutions

In limited sectors of the economy, partial or complete state ownership has remained fairly intact or even been restored after earlier privatization was carried out. Public or quasi-public ownership may take the form of direct state or municipal ownership of assets or

*siloviki*

Derived from the Russian word *sil*, meaning "force," Russian politicians and governmental officials drawn from the security and intelligence agencies, special forces, or the military, many of whom were recruited to important political posts under Vladimir Putin.

*clientelistic networks*

Informal systems of asymmetrical power in which a powerful patron (e.g., the president, prime minister, or governor) offers less powerful clients resources, benefits, or career advantages in return for support, loyalty, or services.

majority control of shares in a "privatized" firm. Economic sectors more likely to involve public or semipublic ownership include telecommunications (the nonmobile telephone industry in particular), public transport (railways, municipal transport), the electronic media (television), and the energy sector. A prime example from the energy sector is Gazprom, the natural gas monopoly, in which the federal government controls just over 50 percent of the shares. Several television channels are publicly owned. Indirect state influence is also realized through the dominant ownership share in many regional TV channels by Gazprom-Media, a subsidiary of the state-controlled natural gas company.

In other areas, such as education and health care, while some private facilities and institutions have emerged in recent years, these services are still primarily provided through tax-supported agencies. Some prestigious new private universities, often with Western economic support, have cropped up in major urban areas, but Russia's large historic universities remain public institutions. Likewise, a state-run medical care system assures basic care to all citizens, although private clinics and hospitals are increasingly servicing the more affluent parts of the population. In public transport, smaller private companies that provide shuttle and bus services have grown up alongside publicly owned transport networks. In general, public or semipublic agencies offer services at a lower price, but often also with lower quality.

Significant parts of the social infrastructure remain under public or semipublic control. In the Soviet period, many social services were administered to citizens through the workplace. These services included daycare, housing, medical care, and vacation facilities, as well as food services and some retail outlets. Between 1991 and the end of the 1990s, a process of divestiture resulted in the transfer of most of these assets and responsibilities to other institutions, either to private owners or, often, to municipalities. For example, while many state- or enterprise-owned apartments were turned over to private ownership by their occupants, an important part of the country's housing stock was placed in municipal ownership.

Political authorities, including the president, are responsible for appointing executive officials in many public and semipublic institutions. This situation indicates a continuing close relationship between major economic institutions and the state, likely to remain due to the Russian tradition of a strong state and the discrediting of privatization by its association with dismal economic results in the 1990s. Indicative of this trend, the overall share of GDP created in the nonstate sector increased from 5 percent in 1991 to 70 percent in 1997, then fell from 70 percent in 1997 down to 65 percent in 2005–2006.[21]

# Other State Institutions

## The Military and Security Organs

Because of Vladimir Putin's career background in the KGB, he drew many of his staff from this arena. Thus, while the formal rank of the Federal Security Service (the successor to the KGB) has not changed, the actual impact of the security establishment acquired increasing importance under Putin, even before 9/11. The Russian government attributes repeated bombings since 1999 to Chechen terrorists and has claimed that the terrorists have international links to Al Qaeda (see page 376). Since the September 11 attacks, cooperation between Russian and Western security agencies has increased, as Russia has shared security information. Because many Russians are alarmed by the crime rate and terrorist bombings in the country, restrictions on civil liberties have not elicited strong popular concern. At the same time, there is widespread public cynicism about the honesty of the ordinary police. Many believe that payoffs by the mafia and even by ordinary citizens can buy police cooperation in overlooking crimes or ordinary legal infractions such as traffic tickets.

The Soviet military once ranked second only to that of the United States, but the size of the armed forces has declined to a quarter of its size at the end of the Soviet period. Defense spending declined in the 1990s, then increased again after 2000, but is still far below Soviet levels.[22] The Soviet and Russian military have never usurped civilian power. The Communist Party controlled military appointments and, during the August 1991 coup attempt, troops remained loyal to Yeltsin and Gorbachev, even though the Minister of Defense was among the coup plotters. Likewise, in October 1993, despite some apparent hesitancy in military circles, military units defended the government's position, this time firing on civilian protesters and shocking the country.

The political power and prestige of the military have suffered, in part as a result of its failure to implement a successful strategy in Chechnya. Accordingly, the government increased the role of the Federal Security Service there instead of relying on the army alone.[23] Reports of deteriorating conditions in some Russian nuclear arsenals have raised international concerns about nuclear security. In addition, the situation of military personnel, from the highest officers to rank-and-file soldiers, has dramatically worsened. As of 2007, the Russian Federation still maintains universal male conscription, but noncompliance and draftees rejected for health reasons have been persistent problems. In 2008 mandatory service was reduced from two years to one year; women have never been subject to the military draft. A law to permit alternative military service for conscientious objectors took effect in 2004. Government proposals to supplement the conscript army by a smaller professional military corps are on the agenda, but there are no definite plans to abolish the military draft entirely.

High crime rates indicate a low capacity of the state to provide legal security to its citizens. Thus, in addition to state security agencies, there is a range of private security firms that provide protection to businesses and individuals. A network of intrigue and hidden relationships can make it hard to determine the boundaries of state involvement in the security sector, and the government's inability to enforce laws or to apprehend violators may create an impression of state involvement even where they may be none. A prominent example is the case of a former agent of the Russian Federal Security Service, Alexander Litvinenko, who claimed in 1998 that he was threatened after failing to fulfill an FSB order to kill Boris Berezovsky, an out-of-favor businessman in self-imposed exile in the United Kingdom (UK);[24] in 2000 Litvinenko himself took political asylum in the UK and continued his outspoken criticism of the Russian government. In November 2006, Litvinenko was fatally poisoned in London with the rare radioactive isotope Polonium-210. On his deathbed, Litvinenko accused the Kremlin of being responsible for his death, an undocumented accusation. In May 2007, the United Kingdom formally requested extradition of Andrei Lugovoi, an ex-KGB agent and Russian politician, to stand trial for the murder, but the Russian government refused, citing a constitutional prohibition. The issue sparked tension between the two countries, including expulsion of diplomats on both sides. These kinds of incidents have generated an atmosphere of insecurity and bizarre linkages reminiscent of Cold War spy novels.

## The Judiciary

Concepts such as judicial independence and the rule of law were poorly understood in both pre-revolutionary Russia and the Soviet era. These concepts have, however, been embedded in the new Russian constitution and are, in principle, accepted both by the public and political elites. However, their implementation has been difficult and not wholly successful.

In Russia, a Constitutional Court was formed in 1991. Its decisions were binding, and in several cases even the president had to bow to its authority. After several controversial decisions, Yeltsin suspended the operations of the court in late 1993. However, the Russian constitution now provides for a Constitutional Court again, with the power to adjudicate disputes on the constitutionality of federal and regional laws, as well as jurisdictional disputes between various political institutions. Judges are nominated by the president and approved by the Federation Council, a procedure that produced a stalemate after the new constitution was adopted, so that the new court became functional only in 1995. Since 1995, the court has established itself as a vehicle for resolving conflicts involving the protection of individual rights and conformity of regional laws with constitutional requirements. The court has, however, been cautious in confronting the executive branch.

Alongside the Constitutional Court is an extensive system of lower and appellate courts, with the Supreme Court at the pinnacle. These courts hear ordinary civil and criminal cases. In 1995, a system of commercial courts was also formed to hear cases dealing with issues related to privatization, taxes, and other commercial activities. The Federation Council must approve nominees for Supreme Court judgeships, and the constitution also grants the president power to appoint judges at other levels. Measures to shield judges from political pressures include criminal prosecution for attempting to influence a judge, protections from arbitrary dismissal, and improved salaries for judges. One innovation in the legal system has been the introduction of jury trials for some types of criminal offenses.

## Subnational Governments

The collapse of the Soviet Union was precipitated by the demands of some union republics for more autonomy and, then, independence. After the Russian Federation became an independent state, the problem resurfaced of constructing a viable federal structure within Russia itself. Some of the federal units were very assertive in putting forth claims for autonomy or even sovereignty. The most extreme example is Chechnya, whose demand for independence led to a protracted civil war. The ethnic dimension complicates political relations with some other republics as well, particularly Tatarstan and Bashkortostan, which occupy relatively large territories in the center of the country and are of Islamic cultural background.

**power vertical**

A term introduced by Vladimir Putin when he was president to describe a unified and hierarchical structure of executive power ranging from the national to the local level.

Putin's most controversial initiatives relating to Russia's regions were part of his attempt to strengthen what he termed the **"power vertical."** This concept refers to an integrated structure of executive power from the presidential level down through to the local level. Critics have questioned whether this idea is consistent with federal principles, and others see it as undermining Russia's fledgling democratic system. A first step in creating the power vertical was the creation of seven federal districts on top of the existing federal units. Although not designed to replace regional governments, the districts were intended to oversee the work of federal offices operating in these regions and to ensure compliance with federal laws and the constitution.

A second set of changes to create the power vertical involved a weakening of the independence of governors and republic presidents. Beginning in 1996, the governors, along with the heads of each regional legislative body, sat as members of the upper house of the Russian parliament, the Federation Council. This arrangement gave the regional executives a direct voice in national legislative discussions and a presence in Moscow. In 2001, Putin gained approval for a revision to the composition of the Federation Council, removing regional executives. Now one regional representative

## U.S. CONNECTION

### Federalism Compared

Russia is a **federal system**, according to its constitution. This means that, at least in theory, powers are divided between the central government and Russia's eighty-three constituent units. In comparison to the American federal system, the Russian structure seems complicated. Some of Russia's federal units are called republics (21), while others are *oblasts* (regions) (49), *krais* (territories) (6), one autonomous republic (1), autonomous *okrugs* (4), and cities of federal status (2, Moscow and St. Petersburg). Russia's size and multiethnic population underlie this complexity. Because many ethnic groups are regionally concentrated in Russia, unlike in the United States, these groups form the basis for some federal units, notably the republics and okrugs, which are named after the ethnic groups that reside there.

In the 1990s, Russia's federal government had difficulty controlling what happened in the regions. Regional laws sometimes deviated from federal law. Bilateral treaties with the federal government granted some regional governments special privileges, producing what some called "**asymmetrical federalism**." During his term as president, Vladimir Putin put measures in place to ensure a greater degree of legal and political uniformity throughout the country. One such measure, adopted in 2004, involved replacing

direct election of governors by a quasi-appointment procedure, making the governor dependent on the president

Russia's federal units are represented in the upper house of the national legislature, the Federation Council. Just as the U.S. Senate includes two representatives from each state, in Russia each region also has two delegates in this body; however, their method of selection has varied over time. In 1993 they were elected directly by the electorate, as in the United States. From the mid-1990s, the regional chief executive (hereafter referred to as the governor) and the head of each regional legislature themselves sat on the Federation Council. Now the members of the Federation Council are appointed, one by the region's governor and the other by the region's legislature. As the president has considerable influence over appointment of the governor, this system weakens accountability of the Federation Council to the public.

All of these measures have led some observers to question whether Russia is really a federal system at all. Although Russia does have a constitutional court to resolve disputes over the jurisdictions of the federal government and the regions, unlike in the United States the constitution does not provide a strong basis for regional power, since it places many powers in the hands of the central government while most others are considered "shared" jurisdictions.

---

is appointed by the regional executive and the other by the regional legislature. Some governors resisted this change, seeing it as an assault on their power. Putin made concessions to make the change more palatable, for example, giving governors the right to recall their representatives. The State Council was formed to try to assure the regional executives that they would retain some role in the federal policy-making arena.

Following the Beslan terrorist attack in 2004, Putin identified corruption and ineffective leadership at the regional level as culprits in allowing terrorists to carry out the devastating school hostage taking. Accordingly, Putin proposed an additional reform that created the decisive element of central control over regional politics. This change eliminated the popular election of governors. They are now nominated by the president and approved by the regional legislature. However, if the regional legislature refuses the nomination three times, the president may disband the body and call for new legislative elections. The president's nominees have been approved by the regional legislature in every case, usually with an overwhelming majority or even unanimously. In his first two years in office, Medvedev replaced eighteen incumbent governors in this way, apparently seeking individuals who would both be politically loyal and managerially competent.[25] With governors and republic presidents dependent on the goodwill of the president for appointment and reappointment, a self-perpetuating power structure has taken on a formal character.

The distribution of tax revenues among the various levels of government has been another contentious issue. The Soviet state pursued a considerable degree of regional equalization, but regional differences have increased in the Russian Federation. Putin

**federal system**

A political structure in which subnational units have significant independent powers; the powers of each level are usually specified in the federal constitution.

**asymmetrical federalism**

A form of federalism in which some subnational units in the federal system have greater or lesser powers than others.

created a more regularized system for determining the distribution of revenues, taking account of both the regional tax base and differences in the needs of various regions (for instance, northern regions have higher expenses to maintain basic services). However, in fact, an increasing proportion of tax revenues are now controlled by Moscow, and regional governments are constantly faced with shortfalls in carrying out their major responsibilities, for example, in social policy. Disparities between rich and poor regions have reached dramatic proportions, with Moscow and areas rich in natural resources being the best off.

# The Policy-Making Process

Policy-making occurs both formally and informally. The federal government, the president and his administration, regional legislatures, individual deputies, and some judicial bodies may, according to the constitution, propose legislation. In the Yeltsin era, conflict between the president and State Duma made policy-making contentious and fractious; under Putin and Medvedev, the State Duma has generally gone along with proposals made by the president and the government, and the proportion of legislation initiated by the executive branch has increased significantly.

In order for a bill to become law, it must be approved by both houses of the parliament in three readings and signed by the president. If the president vetoes the bill, it must be passed again in the same wording by a two-thirds majority of both houses of parliament in order to override the veto. Many policy proclamations have been made through presidential or governmental decrees, without formal consultation with the legislative branch. This decision-making process is much less visible and may involve closed-door bargaining rather than an open process of debate and consultation.

Informal groupings also have an important indirect impact on policy-making. During the Yeltsin period, business magnates were able to exert behind-the-scenes influence to gain benefits in the privatization of lucrative firms in sectors such as oil, media, and transport. Putin attempted to reduce the direct political influence of these powerful economic figures, but at the cost of also reducing political competition.

A continuing problem is weak policy implementation. Under communist rule, the party's control over political appointments enforced at least some degree of conformity to central mandates. Under Yeltsin, fragmented and decentralized political power gave the executive branch few resources to ensure compliance. Pervasive corruption, including bribery and selective enforcement, hindered enforcement of policy decisions. Although Putin and Medvedev both have stated their commitment to restrict these types of irregularities, they no doubt continue. However, the commitment to reestablishing order and a rule of law has been an important justification for the centralization of power.

## Summary

When the Russian Federation was formed in 1991, new political structures needed to be constructed. A constitution was adopted in 1993, which involved a directly elected president who had strong political powers. In addition, a federal system was established with the result that the central government had difficulty controlling actions of regional governments in the 1990s. Since 1999, however, the political system has seen increased centralization, including a harmonization of central and regional laws, quasi-appointment of regional governors, and a more unified executive structure in the country. Under Putin the role of the security forces increased; the military lost its previous stature; and the judiciary took on increased, although not complete, independence. Policy-making is largely under the guidance of the executive organs of the state with little real influence from society or political parties. Whereas in the 1990s the relationship between the executive and legislative branches (Federal Assembly) was characterized by conflict that often produced political deadlock, since 2000 the legislative branch has been relatively compliant, reinforcing the president's dominant role.

# REPRESENTATION AND PARTICIPATION

SECTION 4

Gorbachev's policies in the 1980s brought a dramatic change in the relationship between state and society, as *glasnost* sparked new public and private initiatives. Most restrictions on the formation of social organizations were lifted, and a large number of independent groups appeared. Hopes rose that these trends might indicate the emergence of **civil society**. Just a few years later, only a small stratum of Russian society was actually actively engaged; the demands of everyday life, cynicism about politics, and increasing controls on political opposition led many people to withdraw into private life. However, with hardships imposed by the economic crisis of 2008–2009, there is evidence of increasing political activism among a small but important sector of society.

## The Legislature

The Federal Assembly came into being after the parliamentary elections of December 12, 1993, when the referendum ratifying the new Russian constitution was also approved. The upper house, the Federation Council, represents Russia's constituent federal units. The lower house, the State Duma (hereafter the Duma), has 450 members and involves direct popular election based on a national **proportional representation** electoral system.

Within the Duma, factions unite deputies from the same party. In May 2008 there were four party factions representing the parties elected in the December 2007 vote; in January 2011, 315 (or 70 percent) of the 450 deputies in the State Duma were part of the faction of the dominant party, United Russia.[26] The Duma has a council (ten members) and thirty-two committees. The Duma elects its own speaker (or chair); since July 2003 this has been Boris Gryzlov of the United Russia party.

Compared to the communist period, deputies reflect less fully the demographic characteristics of the population at large. For example, in 1984, 33 percent of the members of the Supreme Soviet were women; in 2005 they constituted less than 10 percent, rising to a bit over 13 percent in 2010.[27] The underrepresentation of women and workers in the present Duma indicates the extent to which Russian politics is primarily the domain of male elites.

The upper house of the Federal Assembly, the Federation Council, has two members from each of Russia's federal regions and republics. Many prominent businessmen are among the appointees, and in some cases the posts may be granted in exchange for political loyalty. Party factions do not play a significant role in the Federation Council. Deputies to the Federation Council, as well as to the Duma, are granted immunity from criminal prosecution.

The constitution grants parliament powers in the legislative and budgetary areas, but if there is conflict with the president or government, these powers can be exercised effectively only if parliament operates with a high degree of unity. In practice, the president can often override the parliament through mechanisms such as the veto of legislation. Each house of parliament has the authority to confirm certain presidential appointees. The Federation Council must also approve presidential decrees relating to martial law and state emergencies, as well as to deploying troops abroad.

Following electoral rebuffs in the 1993 and 1995 parliamentary elections, Yeltsin confronted a parliament that obstructed many of his proposed policies, but the parliament did not have the power or unity to offer a constructive alternative. Since the 2003 election, however, parliament has cooperated with the president, since about two-thirds or more of the deputies have been tied to the United Russia faction, closest to the president. In general, however, the process of gaining Duma acceptance of government proposals has depended more on the authority of the president and on the particular configuration of power at the moment rather than on the existence of disciplined party accountability such as exists in some European countries.

Society's ability to affect particular policy decisions through the legislative process is minimal. Parties in the parliament are isolated from the public at large, suffer low levels of popular respect, and the internal decision-making structures of parties are generally elite-dominated.

## Political Parties and the Party System

One of the most important political changes following the collapse of communism was the shift from a single-party to a multiparty system. In the USSR, the Communist Party (CPSU) not only dominated state organs but also oversaw all social institutions, such as the mass media, trade unions, youth groups, educational institutions, and professional associations. It defined the official ideology for the country, set the parameters for state censorship, and ensured that loyal supporters occupied all important offices. Approximately 10 percent of adults in the Soviet Union were party members, but there were no effective mechanisms to ensure accountability of the party leadership to its members.

National competitive elections were held for the first time in the USSR in 1989, but new political parties were not formal participants in Russia until 1993. Since then, a confusing array of political organizations has run candidates in elections. In early 2007, thirteen registered parties met conditions required for official registration, with eleven appearing on the Duma ballot and four winning at least some seats; in January 2011 only seven parties met conditions of legal registration.[28]

In the 1990s, many parties formed around prominent individuals, making politics very personalistic. Furthermore, other than the Communist Party, Russian parties are young, so deeply rooted political identifications have not had time to develop. Finally, many citizens do not have a clear conception of their own interests or of how parties might represent them. In this context, image making is as important as programmatic positions, so parties appeal to transient voter sentiments.

While individual leaders play an important role in political life in Russia, some key issues have divided opinions in the post-1991 period. One such issue is economic policy. Nearly all political parties have mouthed support for creation of a market economy. However communist/socialist groupings have been more muted in their enthusiasm and have argued for a continued state role in providing social protection and benefits for vulnerable parts of the population. The liberal/reform groupings, on

| Party or bloc | Percent of 1999 party list vote | Percent of 2003 party list vote | Percent of Duma seats 2003 | Percent of 2007 party list vote | Percent of Duma seats 2007 | Comment | Current or last party leader |
|---|---|---|---|---|---|---|---|
| **Table 8.2** Top Parties in the Russian State Duma, 2003, 2007 | | | | | | | |
| **Centrist/establishment** | | | | | | | |
| United Russia | 23.3 (Unity Party) | 37.6 | 49.3 | 64.3 | 70.0 | Formed as Unity Party in 1999, then merged with Fatherland, All-Russia to form United Russia | Vladimir Putin (since 2007) |
| Rodina (2003)/A Just Russia (2007) | — | 9.0 | 8.2 | 7.7 | 8.4 | Rodina formed a constituent element of A Just Russia, formed Oct. 2006 | Sergei Mironov (A Just Russia) |
| Fatherland, All-Russia | 13.3 | | | | | Merged into United Russia, 2001 | Yuri Lyzhkov, Evegenii Primakov (1999) |
| **Communist/Socialist** | | | | | | | |
| Communist Party of the Russian Federation | | 12.6 | 11.6 | 11.6 | 12.7 | Most popular party in the 1990s | Gennady Zyuganov |
| **Nationalist/Patriotic** | | | | | | | |
| Liberal Democratic Party of Russia | 6.0 | 11.5 | 8.0 | 8.1 | 8.9 | Ran as Bloc Zhironovsky in 1999 | Vladimir Zhironovsky |
| **Liberal/Westernizing** | | | | | | | |
| Union of Rightist Forces/now Pravoe delo (Just Cause) | 8.5 | 4.0 | 0.7 | 1.0 | 0 | Joined with other parties in Nov. 2008 to form Pravoe delo | Georgii Bovt, Leonid Gozman |
| Yabloko | 5.9 | 4.3 | 0.9 | 1.6 | 0 | Under the leadership of Grigory Yavlinksy until 2008 | Sergey Mitrokhin |

the other hand, have advocated more rapid market reform, including privatization, free prices, and limited government spending. United Russia charts a middle ground, appealing to voters from a wide ideological spectrum.

Another dividing line relates to national identity. Nationalist/patriotic parties emphasize the defense of Russian interests over Westernization. They strongly criticize the westward expansion of NATO into regions neighboring Russia. They favor a strong military establishment and protection from foreign economic influence. Liberal/reform parties, on the other hand, advocate integration of Russia into the global market and the adoption of Western economic and political principles. Again, the United Russia party has articulated an intriguing combination of these viewpoints, identifying Europe as the primary identity point for Russia, but at the same time insisting on Russia's role as a regional power, pursuing its own unique path of political and economic development.

Ethnic and regional parties have not had a significant impact on the national scene. Similarly, religion, although an important source of personal meaning and a strong social presence, has not emerged as a significant basis of political cleavage for ethnic Russians, who are primarily Russian Orthodox Christians.

Russian political parties do not fit neatly on a left-right spectrum. Nationalist sentiments crosscut economic ideologies, producing the following party tendencies:

- The traditional left, critical of market reform and often mildly nationalistic
- Liberal/reform forces, supporting assertive Western-type market reform and political norms
- Centrist "parties of power," representing the political elite
- Nationalist/patriotic forces, primarily concerned with identity issues and national self-assertion

The most important parties in all four groupings have not challenged the structure of the political system but have chosen to work within it. Since 2000, liberal/reform parties have been marginalized and are no longer represented in political institutions. Of the four parties represented in the State Duma, two are centrist (United Russia and A Just Russia). The second-strongest party after United Russia, the Communist Party of the Russian Federation, is a traditional left party. The fourth party, the Liberal Democratic Party of Russia (led by Vladimir Zhirinovsky) is nationalist/patriotic.

### The Dominant Party: United Russia

**dominant party**

A political party that manages to maintain consistent control of a political system through formal and informal mechanisms of power, with or without strong support from the population.

Since 2003, one political party, United Russia, has taken on clear dominance. Its predecessor, the Unity Party, rose to prominence, together with Vladimir Putin, in the elections of 1999 and 2000. While the Unity Party gained 23.3 percent of the vote in Duma elections in 1999, United Russia received 37.6 percent in 2003, and 64 percent in 2007. In April 2008, at a party congress, United Russia's delegates unanimously approved creation of a custom-made post for Vladimir Putin as party chairman. United Russia has served as a major source of political support for Putin, and in January 2011 Medvedev gave the party the right to use his photo as well in United Russia campaign materials, although he does not hold a formal position in the party.[29]

What explains United Russia's success? An important factor is the association with Putin, but the party has also built a political machine that could generate persuasive incentives for regional elites. The party is truly a party of power, focused on winning to its side prominent people, including heads of Russia's regions, who then use their influence to further bolster the party's votes. Combined with increasingly centralized control within the party, the result is a political machine reinforced by the president's power over gubernatorial appointments. The party has a rather poorly defined program, which emphasizes the uniqueness of the Russian approach (as distinct from Western models), an appeal to values of order and law, and a continued commitment to moderate reform.

The question now facing the party is whether it has adequate institutional strength to impose accountability on its leaders and whether it can develop an organizational footing in society. When Dmitry Medvedev removed the long-time mayor of Moscow, Yuri Luzhkov, from office in 2010 (citing corruption), this raised questions about United Russia's future strategy. Luzhkov's removal left the Moscow branch of United Russia, which Luzhkov had dominated, in a difficult position, given its dependence on the national power structure. Luzhkov's replacement, Sergei Sobrianin, who has ties to both Putin and Medvedev, received the unanimous support of the 32 United Russia deputies in the Moscow city council (called the city Duma).

### Other Parties Represented in the State *Duma* (2007–2011)

Many consider the Communist Party of the Russian Federation (CPRF) to be the only party that could be considered a real opposition force. The CPRF was by far the strongest parliamentary party after the 1995 elections, winning over one-third of the seats in the Duma. Since then its strength has steadily declined. With the second-strongest showing, after United Russia, in the 2007 Duma elections, the party's vote was nonetheless weak, winning only 11.7 percent of the vote. The party defines its goals as being democracy, justice, equality, patriotism and internationalism, a combination of civic rights and duties, and socialist renewal. Primary among the party's concerns are the social costs of the market reform process.

Support for the party is especially strong among older Russians, the economically disadvantaged, and rural residents. The CPRF appears to represent those who have adapted less successfully to the radical and uncertain changes of recent years, as well as some individuals who remain committed to socialist ideals. Its principal failures have been an inability to adapt its public position to attract significant numbers of new adherents, particularly among the young, as well as the absence of a charismatic and attractive political leader. Although one might expect Russia to offer fertile ground for social democratic sentiments like those that have been successful in the Scandinavian countries of Western Europe, the CPRF has not capitalized on these sentiments, nor has it made room for a new social democratic party that could be more successful.

Two other parties were represented in the State Duma after the 2007 elections. The Liberal Democratic Party of Russia (LDPR) placed a close third behind the Communist Party. Neither liberal nor particularly democratic in its platform, the party can be characterized as nationalist and populist. Its leadership openly appeals to the antiwestern sentiments that grew in the wake of Russia's decline from superpower status. Concern with the breakdown of law and order seems to rank high among its priorities. The party's leader, Vladimir Zhirinovsky, has garnered especially strong support among working-class men and military personnel. However, most often this party has not challenged the political establishment on important issues.

The same is true of A Just Russia, founded in 2006, based on an amalgam of three smaller parties. Many observers consider that A Just Russia was formed, from above, to demonstrate the competitive nature of Russia's electoral system, while undermining opposition parties that might pose a real threat to United Russia. The leadership espouses support for socialist principles, placing it to the left of United Russia on the political spectrum and offering a political magnet for dissatisfied supporters of the Communist Party. In highly exceptional cases A Just Russia has been able to win mayoral elections in smaller cities;[30] however, the party does not pose a real challenge to the position of United Russia and has generally supported the president and government.

While these three parties, singly or combined, cannot challenge the power of United Russia, they have on occasion issued protests over what they consider to be unfair electoral procedures. For example, in October 2009 deputies from all three factions abandoned a session of the State Duma as a sign of protest against the results of regional elections, accusing United Russia of infringement of proper electoral procedures and demanding that the results be nullified. After consultations with the president, the demands were withdrawn.

### The Liberal Democratic Parties: Marginalized

The liberal/reform parties (those that most strongly support Western economic and political values) have become marginalized since 2003, when they won only a handful of seats in the Duma. These groups have organized under a variety of party names since 1993, including Russia's Choice, Russia's Democratic Choice, and, most recently, the Union of Rightist Forces, as well as the Yabloko party. These parties have espoused a commitment to traditional liberal values, such as a limited economic role for the state, support for free-market principles, and the protection of individual rights and liberties. Prominent figures such as Boris Nemstov and Grigory Yabloko were visible and sometimes influential in the 1990s as representatives of reform policies, but they have since found it hard to build a stable and unified electoral base. Many Russians hold policies associated with these figures, such as rapid privatization and price increases, responsible for Russia's economic decline. Often referred to as "democrats," their unpopularity also creates confusion as to what democracy really implies. An additional source of weakness has been their difficulty in running under a uniform and consistent party name. Support for liberal/reform parties generally has been stronger among the young, the more highly educated, urban dwellers, and the well-off. Thus, ironically, those with the best prospects for succeeding in the new market economy have been the least successful in fashioning an effective political party to represent themselves.

# Elections

Turnout in federal elections remains respectable, generally between 60 and 70 percent; it stood at 63 percent in the 2007 Duma election and close to 70 percent in the 2008 presidential vote. National elections receive extensive media coverage, and campaign activities begin as long as a year in advance. The political leadership has also actively encouraged voter turnout, to give elections an appearance of legitimacy. Up until 2003, national elections were generally considered to be reasonably fair and free, but international observers have expressed serious concerns about the fairness of both the 2003–2004 and 2007–2008 election cycles, related, for example, to slanted media coverage.[31]

Until 2007, the electoral system for selecting the Duma resembled the German system in some regards, combining proportional representation (with a 5 percent threshold) with winner-take-all districts. In addition, voters were given the explicit option of voting against all candidates or parties (4.7 percent chose this in 2003). Until 1999, despite the electoral rebuffs in 1993 and 1995, the public gave strongest support to the Communist Party and the Liberal Democratic Party; in contrast, in 1999 and 2003, parliamentary elections offered qualified support for the government.

The 2007 election was governed by a new electoral system involving one national proportional representation district, with a minimum threshold for representation of each party raised to 7 percent. Parties are required to include regional representatives on their lists from across the country. For those parties above the 7 percent threshold, choice of deputies from the party list must reflect strength of the vote in the various regions. In addition, according to the 2001 law on political parties, in order to participate in the election, a party must have affiliates in more than half of the regions of Russia, with a certain number of registered members in these regions. Therefore, parties with a strong political base in one or several regions would only be represented in the national parliament if they had organizations of the requisite size in half of the regions in the country and if they had gained 7 percent of the national vote. In 2006, national legislation removed the "against all" option from the ballot.

With the rapid ascent of United Russia since 1999, opposition parties have experienced a sharp decline in electoral success. One reason is genuine popular support for Putin (and later Medvedev), as well as the failure of the opposition parties to develop appealing programs or field attractive candidates. Media coverage has also strongly favored United Russia and the president. Administrative control measures and selective enforcement have delimited the scope of acceptable political opposition, sometimes providing pretexts to disqualify opposition forces. In addition, the carrot-and-stick method has wooed regional elites, producing a bandwagon effect that has been reinforced by the abolition of elections of regional executives.

Russia has yet to experience a real transfer of power from one political grouping to another, which some scholars consider a first step in consolidating democratic governance. Under the Russian constitution, presidential elections have been held every four years, but beginning with the 2012 election the term will be extended to six years; the Duma mandate will be extended from four to five years.

# Political Culture, Citizenship, and Identity

Political culture can be a source of great continuity in the face of radical upheavals in the social and political spheres. Attitudes toward government that prevailed in the tsarist period seem to have endured with remarkable tenacity. These include a tradition of personalistic authority, highly centralized leadership, and a desire for an authoritative source of truth. The Soviet regime embodied these and other traditional Russian values, such as egalitarianism and collectivism. At the same time, the Soviet development model glorified science, technology, industrialization, and urbanization; these values were superimposed on the traditional way of life of the largely rural population. When communism collapsed, Soviet ideology was discredited, and in the 1990s the government embraced Western political and economic values. Many citizens and intellectuals are skeptical of this "imported" culture, partly because it conflicts with other traditional civic values such as egalitarianism, collectivism, and a broad scope for state activity. Public opinion surveys over time do, however, suggest at least general support for liberal democratic values such as an independent judiciary, a free press, basic civil liberties, and competitive elections, but at the same time a desire for strong political leadership. During Putin's presidency the leadership espoused a particular Russian concept of **sovereign democracy**, emphasizing the importance of adapting democratic principles to the Russian context.

**sovereign democracy**

A concept of democracy articulated by President Putin's political advisor, Vladimir Surkov, to communicate the idea that democracy in Russia should be adapted to Russian traditions and conditions rather than based on Western models.

| Table 8.3 | Russian Views on Political and Economic Systems |
|---|---|

**Which type of political system seems to you to be better: the Soviet, the current system, or democracy according to the model of Western countries?**

| | Feb96 | Nov97 | Dec98 | Mar00 | Mar03 | Mar04 | Nov05 | Dec06 | Nov07 | Feb08 | Feb09 | Feb10 | Feb11 |
|---|---|---|---|---|---|---|---|---|---|---|---|---|---|
| The Soviet one, which we had until the 1990s | 45 | 38 | 43 | 42 | 48 | 41 | 42 | 35 | 35 | 24 | 38 | 34 | 33 |
| The current system | 10 | 11 | 5 | 11 | 18 | 19 | 23 | 26 | 17 | 36 | 25 | 28 | 19 |
| Democracy of Western countries | 26 | 28 | 32 | 26 | 22 | 24 | 20 | 16 | 19 | 15 | 18 | 20 | 23 |
| Other | 7 | 8 | 7 | 4 | 6 | 5 | 6 | 7 | 7 | 7 | 7 | 7 | 8 |
| Hard to say | 13 | 16 | 13 | 17 | 7 | 12 | 10 | 16 | 12 | 18 | 12 | 12 | 16 |

*Source:* Levada Center. 2011 data is from a survey of 1600 respondents 18 years of age and older, from 45 regions, January 21–24, 2011, and data reported is from earlier surveys, http://www.levada.ru/press/2011020803.html (accessed February 13, 2011).

In the USSR, just over 50 percent of the population was ethnically Russian. Since most of the major ethnic minorities now reside in other Soviet successor states, Russians now make up just under 80 percent of the population of the Russian Federation. The largest minority group is the Tatars, a traditionally Muslim group residing primarily in Tatarstan, a republic of Russia. Other significant minorities are the neighboring Bashkirs, various indigenous peoples of the Russian north, the many Muslim groups in the northern Caucasus region, and ethnic groups (such as Ukrainians and Armenians) of other former Soviet republics. Some 25 million ethnic Russians reside outside the Russian Federation in other former Soviet republics.

Because Russia is a multiethnic state, one important aspect of the state's search for identity relates to what it means to be Russian. The Russian language itself has two distinct words for Russian: *russkii*, which refers to an ethnicity, and *rossiiskii*, a broader concept referring to people of various ethnic backgrounds who make up the Russian citizenry. Both anti-Semitic and anti-Muslim sentiments surface in everyday life. In recent years there have been increasing concerns about the rise of an exclusionary form of Russian nationalism among certain parts of the population. Official state policy, while explicitly opposing ethnic stereotypes, may, in some cases, have implicitly fed them. A somewhat controversial phenomenon is the youth group, Nashi (Ours), that was formed in 2005. While claiming to oppose fascism in Russia, some observers consider the group itself to nurture intolerance and extremist sentiments. Among Nashi's goals are to educate youth in Russian history and values, and to form volunteer groups to help maintain law and order. The group has been highly supportive of Putin, seeing him as a defender of Russia's national sovereignty.

Today, the Russian Orthodox Church appeals to many citizens who are looking for a replacement for the discredited values of the communist system. A controversial law, directed primarily at Western proselytizers, passed in 1997, made it harder for new religious groups to organize. Human rights advocates and foreign observers protested strongly, again raising questions about the depth of Russia's commitment to liberal democratic values.

Attitudes toward gender relations in Russia reflect traditional family values. It is generally assumed that women will carry the primary responsibility for child care and a certain standard of "femininity" is expected of women both inside and outside the workplace. Feminism is not popular in Russia, as many women consider it inconsistent with traditional notions of femininity or with accepted social roles for women. At the same time, a number of civil society organizations have sprung up to represent the interests of women; some of them advocate traditional policies to provide better social supports for mothers and families, while others challenge traditional gender roles and definitions.

Changing cultural norms affect gender relations in other ways as well. A permissive cultural environment, propagated in advertising and through the mass media, represents women more frequently as sex objects. Advertising also reinforces commercialized images of female beauty that may not correspond to cultural expectations or to healthy lifestyles. In the face of unemployment and the breakdown in traditional social linkages, increasing numbers of young women have turned to prostitution to make a living; HIV/AIDS rates are also increasing at a rapid rate, fueled by prostitution, low levels of information, and the rise of drug trafficking related to Russia's permeable eastern border.

Social class identity was a major theme in the Soviet period. The Bolshevik revolution was justified in the name of the working class, and the Communist Party of the Soviet Union claimed to be a working-class party. However, many dissidents and average citizens perceived an "us–them" relationship with the political elite in Soviet times, which some dissident intellectuals conceptualized in terms of class conflict between the party leadership and the mass of the Soviet population. Because social class was a major part of the discredited Soviet ideology, in the postcommunist period many Russians remain skeptical of claims made by politicians to represent the working class, and trade unions are weakly supported. Even the Communist Party of the Russian Federation does not explicitly identify itself as a working-class party.

## Interests, Social Movements, and Protest

Since the collapse of the USSR, numerous political and social organizations have sprung up in every region of Russia, representing the interests of groups such as children, veterans, women, environmental advocates, pensioners, and the disabled. Many observers saw such blossoming activism as the foundation for a fledgling civil society that would nurture the new democratic institutions established since 1991. Despite limited resources and small staffs, these nongovernment organizations (NGOs) provided a potential source of independent political activity. However, there have been many obstacles to realizing this potential. In the past, many groups relied on Western aid to support their activities, potentially diverting them from concerns of their constituents toward priorities of their foreign sponsors. Others depend on support from local governments or commercial activities.

In January 2006 Putin signed legislation amending laws on public associations and noncommercial organizations. These controversial changes, protested widely by Western governments, placed new grounds for denying registration to such organizations, established new reporting requirements (particularly for organizations receiving funds from foreign sources), and increased government supervisory functions. Particular requirements are placed on foreign noncommercial nongovernmental organizations operating in Russia. The new measures were justified as necessary to respond to external terrorist threats, but many commentators saw them as an effort to reduce the likelihood that civil society activists with external contacts might foment a colored revolution in Russian similar to what happened in Ukraine in 2004 or in Georgia in 2005.

The government has attempted to channel public activism through official forums. These have included the Civic Forum, organized with government support in 2001, and more recently, the Public Chamber, created in 2005 by legislation proposed by the president.[32] Based on voluntary participation by presidential appointees and representatives recommended by national and regional societal organizations, the organization is presented as a mechanism for public consultation and input, as well as a vehicle for creating public support for government policy. It likely involves an effort to co-opt public activists from more disruptive forms of self-expression, but also to mobilize the assistance of citizens' groups in delivering social services.

A variety of mass-based political organizations protest the current political direction of the government, but since 2007 the authorities have tried to restrict use of public demonstrations and protests. An alternative political grouping, The Other Russia, unites a wide range of opposition figures from both the left and right end of the political spectrum. On July 31, 2009, leaders of The Other Russia initiated a series of monthly protests, each held on the 31st of months with 31 days, to affirm the right to free assembly provided for in Article 31 of the Constitution. On December 31, 2010, dozens of protesters were arrested, including prominent liberal figure Boris Nemtsov, who was held in detention for fifteen days. Gary Kasparov, the world chess champion, is another figure active in such opposition demonstrations. In 2010 the level of public protests of one sort or another seemed to show a marked increase.[33]

Alexander Weinstein/Kommersant

Boris Nemstov, an opposition leader (second left), shown during a protest action "Waiting for Justice" in Moscow on December 27, 2010, the day of Mikhail Khodorkovsky's second sentencing.

*Source:* http://kommersant.ru/photo/photo.aspx?y=2011&m=1.

The official trade unions established under Soviet rule have survived under the title of the Federation of Independent Trade Unions (FITU). However, FITU has lost the confidence of large parts of the workforce. In some sectors, such as the coal industry, new independent trade unions have formed, mainly at the local level. Labor actions have, at various times, included spontaneous strikes, transport blockages, and even hunger strikes. Immediate concessions are often offered in response to such protests, but the underlying problems are rarely addressed. According to data from the Federal Statistical Service of the Russian government, strikes showed a radical decline after 2005–2006,[34] suggesting that working-class organizations are only weakly oriented toward or able to support sustained collective action.

The media itself has an important impact on how interests are expressed. While much of the television coverage is subject to more or less direct influence by the government, some newspapers and independent journalists, as well as Internet sources, do offer a critical perspective on political developments. An estimated fifty-two journalists have been murdered since 1992, making Russia the third-most-dangerous country for journalists in the world.[35] Many cases involve reporting in war-torn Chechnya; others are contract murders or assassinations. One reason journalists are at risk is the incapacity of the state to enforce law and order, but they also face other obstacles. Article 29 of the Russian constitution guarantees "freedom of the mass media" and prohibits censorship. However, Russia ranked 140th out of 178 countries in 2010 in terms of press freedom, according to *Reporters without Borders*.[36] The organization also noted increasing control of major media outlets by industrial groups close to Putin. While Russians have access to a wide range of independent newspapers, readership has declined radically, and the most visible source of news coverage, television, is often openly biased.

At the time of this writing, one cannot say that civil society has truly formed in Russia. Whatever forms of collective identity have emerged, social forces do not easily find avenues to exert constructive and organized influence on state activity.

## Summary

The bicameral legislature of the Russian parliament has played a relatively ineffective role in policy-making, despite its legal power to approve legislation. In the 1990s the legislature lacked the necessary unity to act decisively; more recently the legislature tends to carry out the wishes of the executive branch. Despite the introduction of competitive elections, political parties have had a hard time establishing themselves as credible vehicles of popular influence; most political parties have weak linkages to society, are strongly marked by the image of their leaders, and have not played a significant role in forming the government. High levels of political party fragmentation characterized Russian politics until 2003, when United Russia, a party of the political establishment, projected itself as the dominant political force in the country, enjoying a rapid rise in electoral success and popular support. This was in part due to its close association with Vladimir Putin and partly due to a bandwagon effect in which regional politicians and other important political figures have rushed to join the "party of power." While elections in the 1990s were considered by most international observers to be relatively fair, observers now have greater doubts about whether there is a level playing field, as opposition forces have been subject to various types of political controls that limit their ability to gain support or even compete in elections, or to exercise other forms of political power.

## SECTION 5

# RUSSIAN POLITICS IN TRANSITION

### Focus Questions

Describe three of the most important political challenges now facing the Russian state. For each one, outline how you think Russia might meet these challenges.

In what ways might terrorism affect Russia's democratization processes?

What kind of international role is Russia seeking for itself, and how have Russia's leaders tried to establish this role?

On April 10, 2010, a tragic plane crash in Russia shook Europe. When approaching its destination of Smolensk, Russia, a Polish-piloted plane carrying the Polish president (Lech Kaczynski), his wife, and dozens of other members of the Polish political elite attempted to land in thick fog, defying the repeated warnings of Russian air traffic controllers. The ensuing crash left 97 people dead. The ill-fated trip was intended to mark the beginning of an historic reconciliation between Poland and Russia; the previous week Prime Minister Putin became the first Russian leader to officially acknowledge Soviet responsibility for the 1940 massacre of thousands of Polish military officers in the Katyn Woods near Smolensk. It was at Katyn that the commemorative events were to be held. Putin's gesture was intended to begin a healing process between the two countries, whose history left many Poles resentful of Russia.

News of the plane crash evoked immediate apprehension that the reconciliation efforts would be derailed, as Poland dealt with a monumental national tragedy. However, quite the opposite occurred. Outpourings of sympathy from the Russian leadership and a statement passed by the Russian State Duma condemning Stalin's actions in relation to Katyn ushered in a period of new political dialogue between the two countries. In early December 2010 Medvedev visited the Polish capital, Warsaw, and declared: "The spirit of our relations is changing, . . ." indicating Russia's willingness "to discuss the most difficult, the darkest and most weighing pages in our mutual history."[37] This moment was one of several that seemed to offer new hope for a period of warmer relations between Russia and the West.

# Political Challenges and Changing Agendas

Russia's future path continues to remain unclear. Will the country move in a "two steps forward, one step backward" progression to a more democratic political system? Or does the free-wheeling atmosphere and political relaxation that occurred in the 1990s more likely recall the temporary liberalization that occurred in the 1920s or the short-lived thaw of the Khrushchev period? Will Russia be able to reestablish a respected role as a regional and global power, to bring corruption under control, to establish trust in political institutions, and to diversify the economy? These are some of the key challenges facing the Russian Federation.

When the first edition of this book was published in 1996, five possible scenarios for Russia's future were presented:

1. A stable progression toward marketization and democratization
2. The gradual introduction of "soft authoritarianism"
3. A return to a more extreme authoritarianism of a quasifascist or communist variety
4. The disintegration of Russia into regional fiefdoms or de facto individual states
5. Economic decline, civil war, and military expansionism

At the time of this writing, the "soft authoritarian" scenario seems most likely; however, there are still significant forces that may move Russia back to a more democratic trajectory.

## Russia in the World of States

In the international sphere, Russia's flirtation with Westernization in the early 1990s produced ambiguous results, leading to a severe transitional recession and placing Russia in the position of a supplicant state requesting international credits and assistance from the West. Russia's protests against unpalatable international developments, such as NATO enlargement, and NATO's bombing of Yugoslavia in 1999, revealed Moscow's underlying resentment against Western dominance, as well as the country's relative powerlessness in affecting global developments. The events of September 11, 2001, however, provided an impetus for cooperative efforts in the battle against international terrorism. Evidence of warmer relations included the formation of a NATO-Russia Council in May 2002, but new tensions arose around American withdrawal from the Anti-Ballistic Missile Treaty in 2002, Russian objections to the American incursion into Iraq in March 2003, American proposals to erect a missile defense system in Central Europe, and the 2008 Russian incursion into Georgia.

One of Russia's main challenges has been to reestablish itself as a respected regional leader in neighboring countries, particularly those that were formerly part of the Soviet Union. The relationship to Ukraine has been wrought with particular difficulties. Ukraine's own internal political divisions have provided Russia with an opportunity to exert political leverage, building on business interests and sympathies for closer Russian ties among a significant portion of the Ukrainian population, despite the country's declared aspiration for eventual membership in the European Union.

# TERRORISM

## The Russian Case

The threat of terrorism has become a reality for Russians, with a growing list of disturbing tragedies resulting in hundreds of casualties: a series of apartment bombings in Moscow and two other cities in 1999; a hostage-taking in a popular Moscow theatre in 2002; a school hostage-taking in the southern town of Beslan in 2004; an attack on the popular Nevskiy express train that links Moscow and St. Petersburg in 2009; bombings in and outside the Moscow subway in 2010; and an attack at an important Moscow airport (Domodedovo) in January 2011.

Attacks in Russia initially had indigenous roots in the separatist region of Chechnya. Terrorism became a tool of Chechen militants to counter Russian military efforts to defeat separatist forces. In several terrorist incidents, female suicide bombers, the so-called black widows of fallen Chechen militants, have played a visible role.

Because Russia includes several Muslim population groups, authorities have been careful not to give antiterrorist rhetoric an anti-Muslim tone. As President Putin noted in 2004, "to vent anger towards terrorists against people of different beliefs . . . in a country with such a diversity of religions and ethnicities . . . is completely destructive." He emphasized that the terrorists themselves want to undermine Russian unity not only by pushing for Chechen separatism, but also by driving a wedge of distrust and hostility between diverse ethnic and religious groups. According to Putin, the battle against terrorism is "truly a fight for the unity of the country."* Over time, linkages between Russian terrorist groups and international Islamic fundamentalist organizations have become increasingly important.

Russian authorities have found it difficult to isolate terrorist elements because of the indigenous roots of Chechen grievances. Ethnic profiling has tainted both government actions and popular sentiments. Individuals with a south Caucasian appearance have felt themselves subject to various forms of harassment, including complaints of arbitrary identity checks, planting of drugs and weapons, and obstruction of registration for residence permits. In 2003 the Russian government adopted a partial amnesty for former rebels in an attempt to undermine the terrorist appeal in Chechnya and surrounding areas. In terms of policy, recent amendments to a 1998 antiterrorism law restrict the media from disseminating information that might hinder or prevent counter-terrorist measures; some critics view these measures as potentially placing restrictions on freedom of speech. The Beslan tragedy also led to a broadened legal definition of terrorism that critics felt could be used to ban antigovernment meetings or demonstrations; in 2008 jury trials were limited in cases involving terrorism. There has been only minimal domestic opposition to most of these measures.

*Speech at a meeting of the Presidential Council for Coordination with Religious Organisations, September 29, 2004, website of the Embassy of the Russian Federation to the Republic of South Africa, http://russianembassy.org.za/statements/text/oct04/dputin290904.html.

Ukraine's role as a transit country for gas pipelines between Russia and Western Europe has led to repeated conflicts, most notably in 2009, when Russian gas supplies to Western Europe were temporarily interrupted.

The massive popular protests in Ukraine that followed the contested presidential election in 2004 (the Orange Revolution) elicited apprehension in Moscow, with Russia's leaders claiming they were nurtured by Western organizations. In February 2010 relations with Ukraine improved, as presidential elections in Ukraine saw the victory of the more pro-Russian candidate, Viktor Yanukovych, who subsequently concluded an agreement with Russia providing a twenty-five-year lease on a naval base in Ukraine's Crimea for use by Russia's Black Sea fleet in exchange for lower natural gas prices.

Relations with some other neighboring post-Soviet countries (e.g., Georgia) have been equally fraught with difficulties, as Russia has struggled to establish itself as a positive role model in the region. Efforts to form regional organizations to strengthen ties between these countries and Russia have taken a variety of forms. The largely ineffective Commonwealth of Independent States, formed in 1991 when the Soviet Union collapsed, was joined later by the Collective Security Treaty Organization (CSTO), the Eurasian Economic Forum, and the Shanghai Cooperation Organization (SCO, including China and the post-Soviet Central Asian states).[38] Each has a subset of countries from the former Soviet space as members, but neither Ukraine nor Georgia is in any of the three newer groupings. None of these efforts has brought the type of regional unity under Russia's leadership that Moscow has aspired to.

Another challenge has been Russia's efforts to establish itself as an equal partner with the United States and Europe. Following U.S. Secretary of State Clinton's effort to reset U.S.-Russian relations in March 2009, progress was made on key issues of conflict at a NATO-Russia Summit in Lisbon in November 2010. In the face of the expiration of the Strategic Arms Reduction Treaty in December 2009, a new agreement was signed in Prague between the United States and Russia in April 2010 and ratified by both the Russian State Duma and the U.S. Congress to go into effect in January 2011. All of these developments suggest the possibility of a more positive trajectory for Russia's relations with the West in the next decade.

One area where such cooperation with the West will be particularly important is in the economic arena, where Russia's longer-term prospects remain marred by an unbalanced economic structure and widespread corruption. Russia has resisted opening natural gas transit pipes to European firms, while itself seeking access to retail markets in Europe. At the same time, experts believe that without increased Western investment and technological know-how, Russia will not be able to develop untapped deposits quickly enough to meet both domestic demands and export commitments. In 2010 Medvedev reached out to foreign partners (including the European Union and Germany) to help push forward Russia's modernization effort, including support for Russia's WTO (World Trade Organization) accession and limits on protectionist measures. In November 2010, Putin used an article in a leading German newspaper to call for the creation of an economic community that would extend "from Lisbon to Vladivostok," while soon thereafter chastising the EU for energy legislation that adversely affects Russian companies.[39]

The backdrop for these overtures to the West was the impact of the 2008–2009 global financial-economic crisis on Russia; a sharp drop in gas and oil prices temporarily undercut the foundation of Russia's economic motor. The crisis had wide-ranging

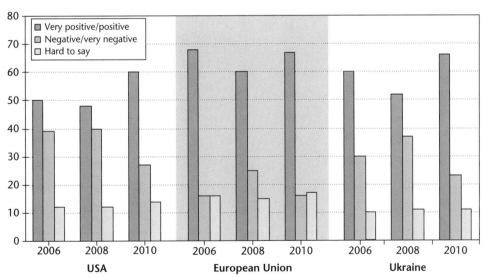

FIGURE 8.5 **Attitudes of the Russian Population toward Foreign Countries***
"Overall, how do you feel about the following at the current time?"

*The 2010 data is based on a survey carried out between May 1 and May 25, 2010, by the Levada Center, among 1800 respondents from 46 regions of Russia, 3.4% margin of error; other data is from earlier surveys. http://www.levada.ru/press/2010062301.html, accessed 28 January 2011.

effects, including devaluation of the ruble, a decline in the inflow of money from abroad, a plummeting stock market, reduced state revenues, higher unemployment, reduced work hours, and wage arrears. From positive growth rates in the previous ten years, Russia moved to a dramatic fall by the first quarter of 2009. Because energy prices recovered fairly quickly and Russian had reserve funds to fall back on, the crisis did not push Russia back to the disastrous economic situation of the 1990s, but the dramatic shift in economic performance may have reminded both the Russian public and its leaders of the potential fragility of the economic recovery.

In November 2009 President Medvedev published a much-discussed article entitled "Go Russia" in which he called for a modernization program, primarily through the development of high-technology sectors.[40] Perhaps the greatest economic challenge facing the president elected in 2012 will be to establish policies to ensure a greater diversity of Russia's economic base, while limiting the influence of powerful economic forces without undermining legitimate political pluralism.

Whether Medvedev's modernization program includes a concept of political liberalization remains unclear. Russia's move toward a more authoritarian political path remains a continued irritant in the country's relationship with both the United States and Europe, and also has the potential to trigger internal political instability. The continuing disjuncture between high personal support for Putin and Medvedev alongside a continuing lack of confidence in the ability of political institutions to address the country's problems effectively suggests that the legitimacy of the system is still on thin ice. The more positive working relationship between the executive and legislative branches that emerged under Putin's leadership and continued into the Medvedev presidency has been at the cost of permitting a real parliamentary opposition to function. Efforts to regularize relations between the center and regions provide prospects for improved institutional performance, but the reduction of vehicles for popular input and heavy-handed efforts to keep regional elites

**FIGURE 8.6 Structure of Russian Exports, Jan–Oct 2010**

*Source:* Adapted from Russian State Statistical Service website, http://www.customs.ru/ru/stats/arhiv-stats-new/trfgoods/popup.php?id286=731.
*Note:* The percentages do not add up to 100% due to rounding.

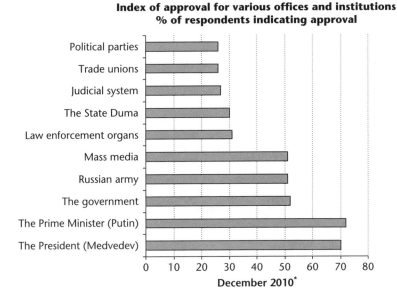

**Index of approval for various offices and institutions
% of respondents indicating approval**

December 2010*

*Figures for the President, Prime Minister, government, Council of the Federation, and State Duma are from December 25. Exact date in December for other institutions not specified.

**FIGURE 8.7 Approval Ratings of Leaders and Institutions**

*Sources:* Data from the website of the Russian Public Opinion Research Center (VTsIOM), reports on weekly and monthly surveys or approval ratings of public institution, http://wciom.ru/index.php?id=172; http://wciom.ru/index.php?id=173 (accessed Jan. 31, 2011).

in line and to control political opposition already show signs of producing poor policy choices that in 2010 elicited more widespread public protests and reinforced public cynicism about the motives of politicians and the trustworthiness of institutions. Underlying all of these problems is the key issue of widespread corruption that pervades every walk of life.

Despite changes in social consciousness, the formation of new political identities also remains unfinished business. Many people are still preoccupied by challenges of everyday life, with little time or energy to forge new forms of collective action to address underlying problems. Under such circumstances, the appeal to nationalism and other basic sentiments can be powerful. The weakness of Russian intermediary organizations (interest groups, political parties, or associations) means that politicians can more easily appeal directly to emotions because people are not members of groups that help them evaluate the political claims. These conditions reduce safeguards against authoritarian outcomes.

Nevertheless, the high level of education and increasing exposure to international media and the Internet may work in the opposite direction. Many Russians identify their country as part of Europe and its culture, an attitude echoed by the government. Exposure to alternative political systems and cultures may make people more critical of their own political system and seek opportunities to change it.

Russia remains in what seems to be an extended period of transition. In the early 1990s, Russians frequently hoped for "normal conditions," that is, an escape from the shortages, insecurity, and political controls of the past. Now, "normality" has been redefined in less glowing terms than those conceived in the late 1980s. Russians seem to have a capability to adapt to change and uncertainty that North Americans find at once alluring, puzzling, and disturbing.

# Russian Politics in Comparative Perspective

The way in which politics, economics, and ideology were intertwined in the Soviet period has profoundly affected the nature of political change in all of the former Soviet republics and generally has made the democratization process more difficult. How has Russia fared compared to some of the other post-communist systems that faced many of these same challenges, and what can we learn from these comparisons? A rule of thumb, simple as it seems, is that the further east one goes in the post-communist world, the more difficult and prolonged the transition period has been (with the exception of Belarus, which lies adjacent to the European Union and has therefore liberalized less than one might expect). This is partly because the more westerly countries of Central Europe that were outside the USSR (Poland, Hungary, Czech Republic, Slovakia), as well as the Baltic states (Estonia, Latvia, Lithuania), were able to accede to the EU, producing a strong motivation to embark on fundamental reform. This illustrates the potentially powerful impact of international forces on domestic political developments, if domestic actors are receptive. Also these countries were under communist rule for a shorter period of time. In addition most of these countries had a history of closer ties and greater cultural exposure to Western Europe; ideas of liberalism, private property, and individualism were less foreign to citizens in countries such as Czechoslovakia, East Germany, Poland, and Hungary than in regions farther east, including Russia. Historical legacies and cultural differences do matter.

Russia's experience demonstrates the importance of strong political institutions if democracy is to be secured. Their weakness in the 1990s contributed to high levels of social dislocation, corruption, and personal stress, as well as to demographic decline and poor economic adaptation to the market. However, Russia's rich deposits of natural resources have sheltered it from difficulties facing some neighboring countries like Ukraine. At the same time, Russia's natural resource wealth has made it difficult to untangle economic and political power, reducing political accountability to the public. The "resource curse" produces economic hazards as well, including the so-called Dutch disease, in which heavy reliance on export income pushes the value of the currency up, making it more difficult for domestic producers to export successfully and feeding inflationary pressures.

Progression along the various dimensions of the quadruple transition are uneven across post-communist countries, and Russia seems now to be progressing economically, while regressing politically, with nationalism on the rise and aspirations to status of a regional superpower resurfacing. In all of the post-Soviet states (except the Baltic states), the attempt to construct democratic political institutions has been characterized by repeated political crises, weak representation of popular interests, executive–legislative conflict, faltering efforts at constitutional revision, and corruption. Terrorist attacks persist, reinforcing a sense of insecurity and producing fertile ground for nationalist sentiments and a strong role for the security forces, which themselves enjoy a low level of popular legitimacy and are marred by corruption. Nonetheless, with the exception of the Chechnya conflict and its spillover into the neighboring areas in Russia's European south, Russia has escaped major domestic violence and civil war, unlike parts of the former Yugoslavia, Georgia, Moldova, and the Central Asian state of Tajikistan.

Will Russia be able to find a place for itself in the world of states that meets the expectations of its educated and sophisticated population? Even after the first decade of the new millennium, prospects are still unclear. One thing is certain: Russia will continue to be a key regional force in Europe and Asia by virtue of its size, its rich energy and resource base, its large and highly skilled population and its nuclear arsenal. However, while Russia's leaders have shown a desire and willingness to identify as a European country, Russia has had an ambivalent relationship to accepting crucial norms that would underlie an effective and enduring partnership with the West.

If the Russian leadership gradually moves Russia on a path closer to liberal democratic development, then this may provide an example to other semiauthoritarian countries in Russia's neighborhood. On the other hand, if the continuation of existing authoritarian trends is associated with sustained economic growth and stability that benefits the majority of the population, then Russia may settle into a extended period of soft authoritarianism that reinforces the East–West divide, and that could, if not resisted by the political leadership, feed destructive nationalist tendencies. Finally, if the Russian leadership's insulation generates unpopular and ineffective policy outcomes, or if world energy prices trigger an economic downslide, this may stimulate a new process of reflection on Russia's future path and offer an opportunity for democratic forces to reassert themselves and find popular resonance.

## Summary

Russia's political course since 1991 has been profoundly influenced by the fact that the country underwent simultaneous and radical transformations in four spheres: politics, economics, ideology, and geopolitical position in the world. Managing so much change in a short time has been difficult and has produced mixed results. Efforts to democratize the political system have been only partially successful, and experts disagree both about whether the political controls initiated by Putin were needed to ensure stability and whether they can be easily reversed. In the economic sphere, after recovering from a period of deep economic decline in the 1990s, Russia's renewed growth depends largely on exports of energy and natural resources, making the country vulnerable to external shocks such as the 2008–2009 global crisis. The country faces the challenge of effectively using its natural resource wealth to rebuild other sectors of the economy. In terms of ideology, nationalism threatens to reinforce intolerance and undermine social unity. Continuing high levels of corruption also undermine popular confidence in state institutions. Whereas countries that have joined the European Union seem, for the most part, to have successfully established viable democratic systems with functioning market economies, other post-Soviet states in Eastern Europe and Central Asia face similar challenges to Russia's in consolidating democracy and market reform. Russia has sought to reassert its role as a regional and global force, and a possible reduction in tensions with the West are still on shaky ground.

## Key Terms

| | | |
|---|---|---|
| patrimonial state | privatization voucher | asymmetrical federalism |
| democratic centralism | mafia | federal system |
| vanguard party | oligarchs | civil society |
| collectivization | pyramid debt | proportional representation (PR) |
| *glasnost* | state capture | dominant party |
| soft authoritarianism | *nomenklatura* | sovereign democracy |
| market reform | *siloviki* | vanguard party |
| joint-stock companies | clientelistic networks | |
| insider privatization | power vertical | |

## Suggested Readings

Åslund, Anders. *Russia's Capitalist Revolution: Why Market Reform Succeeded and Democracy Failed?* Washington, DC: Peterson Institute for International Economics, 2007.

Black, J. L. *Vladimir Putin and the New World Order: Looking East, Looking West?* Lanham, MD: Rowman and Littlefield Publishers, 2004.

Colton, Timothy J. *Yeltsin: A Life.* New York: Basic Books, 2008.

Donaldson, Robert H., and Joseph L. Nogee. *The Foreign Policy of Russia: Changing Systems, Enduring Interests.* Armonk, NY: M.E. Sharpe, 2009.

Evans, Jr., Alfred B., Laura A. Henry, and Lisa McIntosh Sundstrom, eds. *Russian Civil Society.* Armonk, NY: M.E. Sharpe, 2006.

Freeland, Chrystia. *Sale of the Century: Russia's Wild Ride from Communism to Capitalism.* New York: Doubleday, 2000.

Gel'man, Vladimir, and Cameron Ross, eds. *The Politics of Sub-National Authoritarianism in Russia.* Farnham, Surrey UK: Ashgate, 2010.

Getty, J. Arch. *Origins of the Great Purges: The Soviet Communist Party Reconsidered.* Cambridge: Cambridge University Press, 1985.

Hale, Henry E. "Regime Cycles, Democracy, Autocracy and Revolution in Post-Soviet Eurasia." *World Politics* 58 (October 2005): 133–165.

Hendley, Kathryn. "Rule of Law, Russian-Style." *Current History* (October 2009).

Herspring, Dale, and Stephen Wegren, eds. *After Putin's Russia*, 4th ed. Lanham, MD: Rowman and Littlefield Publishers, 2010.

Hopf, Ted, ed. *Russia's European Choice.* New York: Palgrave MacMillan, 2008.

Hough, Jerry, and Merle Fainsod. *How the Soviet Union Is Governed.* Cambridge: Harvard University Press, 1979.

Ledeneva, Alena V. *How Russia Really Works: The Informal Practices That Shaped Post-Soviet Politics and Business.* Ithaca, NY: Cornell University Press, 2006.

Lewin, Moshe. *The Gorbachev Phenomenon: A Historical Interpretation.* Berkeley: University of California Press, 1991.

Pipes, Richard. *Russia under the Old Regime.* New York: Scribner, 1974.

Remington, Thomas F. *Politics in Russia*, 6th ed. Boston: Longman, 2010.

Sakwa, Richard. *Putin: Russia's Choice.* London and New York: Routledge, 2008.

Shevtsova, Lilia. *Russia Lost in Transition: The Yeltsin and Putin Legacies.* Washington, D.C.: The Carnegie Endowment for International Peace, 2007.

Tolz, Vera. *Russia.* London: Arnold; New York: Oxford University Press, 2001.

Wengren, Stephen K., *Land Reform in Russia.* New Haven and London: Yale University Press, 2009.

## Suggested Websites

The Carnegie Moscow Center
www.carnegie.ru/en/

Itar-TASS News Agency
www.itar-tass.com/eng/

Johnson's Russia List
www.cdi.org/russia/johnson/default.cfm RECHECK

Radio Free Europe/Radio Liberty
http://www.rferl.org/section/Russia/161.html

*The Moscow News*
www.mnweekly.ru

*Russian Analytical Digest*
http://www.laender-analysen.de/index.php?topic=russland&url=http://www.res.ethz.ch/analysis/rad/

Russia Profile
http://russiaprofile.org/politics/

Open Democracy (Russia)
http://www.opendemocracy.net/russia

Center for Eastern Studies (Warsaw), Eastweek
http://www.osw.waw.pl/en/publikacje/tagi/Russian%20Federation

# 9 Brazil

Alfred P. Montero

**Official Name:** Federative Republic of Brazil (Republica Federativa do Brasil)

**Location:** Eastern South America

**Capital City:** Brasília

**Population (2008):** 196.3 million

**Size:** 8,511,965 sq. km.; slightly smaller than the United States

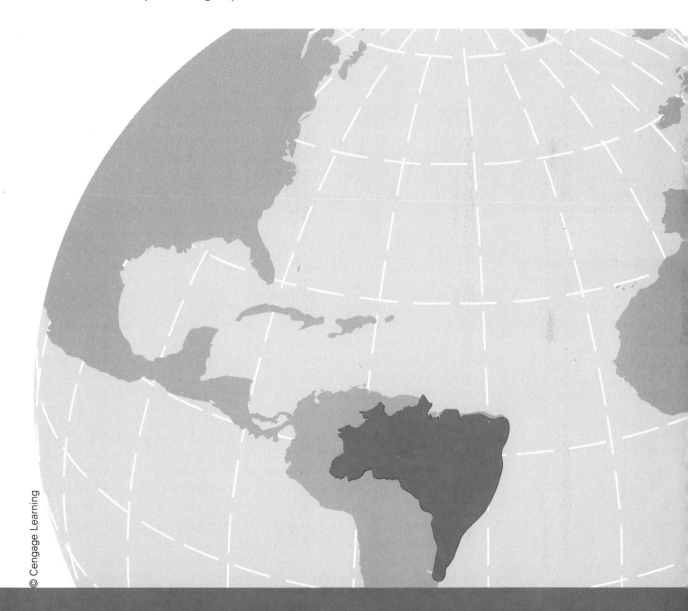

**1822** Dom Pedro I declares himself emperor of Brazil, peacefully ending three hundred years of Portuguese colonial rule.

**1888** Abolition of slavery

**1930** Getúlio Vargas gains power after a coup led by military and political leaders. His period of dictatorship (1937–1945) is known as the New State.

**1950** Vargas is elected president. Scandals precipitate his suicide in 1954.

**1960** Jânio Quadros becomes president.

| 1700 | 1800 | 1850 | 1900 | 1930 | 1950 | 1960 |

**1824** Constitution drafted

**1891** A new constitution establishes a directly elected president.

**1889** Dom Pedro II, who assumed throne in 1840, is forced into exile; landowning elites establish an oligarchical republic.

**1945** Vargas calls for general elections. General Eurico Dutra of the Social Democratic Party wins.

**1956** Juscelino Kubitschek becomes president.

# SECTION 1

# THE MAKING OF THE MODERN BRAZILIAN STATE

## Focus Questions

How has the authority of the national government varied over the history of Brazil from independence to the present?

In what major ways has Brazilian democracy been limited since independence?

## Politics in Action

On October 2, 2009, Brazilian president, Luiz Inácio Lula da Silva, celebrated the International Olympic Committee's (IOC) decision to award Rio de Janeiro the 2016 Summer Games. The recognition followed Brazil's successful bid to host the 2014 World Cup of Football (Soccer). These designations were apt for a country that by 2010 looked like a winner. Riding a boom in exports, Brazil's economy grew quickly, putting it on a faster pace to become the world's fifth-largest economy (up from ninth just ten years before). The discovery of deep wells of oil off the coast of Rio de Janeiro state in 2007 held out the hope that future growth would be financed by oil exports. Yet even without oil, rising median household incomes were already making Brazilians richer and more equal in a country known for notorious inequality. To those assembled in Copenhagen to hear the IOC's decision, Brazil was already wearing a gold medal in several political and economic events as a mature democracy, a growing and industrialized economy; a society prepared to host the biggest sports events on the planet.

## Geographic Setting

Larger than the continental United States, Brazil occupies two-thirds of South America. Its 192 million inhabitants are concentrated in the urban southern and southeastern regions; the northern Amazon region, with 5.3 million, is sparsely populated.

Brazil includes thick rain forest in the Amazon valley, large lowland swamps (the *pantanal*) in the central western states, and vast expanses of badlands (the *sertão*) in the north and northeast. Brazil is rich in natural resources and arable land. The Amazon has an abundance of minerals and tropical fruit; the central and southern regions provide iron ore and coal; offshore and onshore sources of petroleum are also significant and may become even more so. Brazil's farmlands are particularly fertile.

## Timeline

**1961** Quadros resigns. João Goulart gains presidency despite an attempted military coup.

**1964** A military coup places power in the hands of successive authoritarian regimes.

**1984** *Diretas Já!*, a mass mobilization campaign, calls for direct elections.

**1985** Vice-presidential candidate José Sarney becomes president on the sudden death of elected president Tancredo Neves.

**1988** A new constitution grants new social and political rights.

**1989** Fernando Collor is elected president.

**1992** Collor is impeached; Vice President Itamar Franco assumes presidency.

**1994** Fernando Henrique Cardoso is elected president after his Real Plan controls inflation.

**1998** Cardoso is reelected.

**1999** The Real Plan weathers a financial crisis.

**2002** Lula da Silva is elected president.

**2006** Lula is reelected after surviving a corruption scandal.

**2010** Dilma Rousseff, Lula's former chief-of-staff, is elected Brazil's first woman president.

1970 — 1985 — 1990 — 1995 — 2000 — 2010

---

The Amazon's climate is wet, the *sertão* is dry, and the agricultural areas of the central, southeastern, and southern regions are temperate. The importance of the Amazon as the "green lungs of the planet" make its fragile ecology and the exploitation of its resources a matter of international concern.

Immigration of Europeans and Africans has contributed to an ethnically mixed society. Approximately 53.7 percent of the population is white, 38.5 percent *pardo* (brown or mulatto), 6.2 percent black, and 0.5 percent Asian.[1] These numbers probably ignore people of mixed race, who are sometimes classified erroneously as being white or *pardo*. The indigenous people of the Amazon basin are estimated to number 250,000.[2] The Asian population, which numbers just over a million, is dominated by people of Japanese descent who immigrated from 1908 through the 1950s.

Brazil is a blend of different cultural influences, although Portuguese as the common language helps keep Brazilians united. Brazilians are not greatly divided over religious differences. Roman Catholicism was imposed by the Portuguese and

**Brazil: Ethnic Groups**
- Other (includes Japanese; Arab; Amerindian) .9%
- Unspecified .7%
- Black 6.2%
- Mulatto (mixed white and black) 38.5%
- White 53.7%

**Brazil: Religion**
- Other and unspecified 2.0%
- Bantu/Voodoo 0.3%
- Spiritualist 1.3%
- None 7.4%
- Protestant 15.4%
- Roman Catholic 75.4%

**Brazilian Currency**
Real/Reais (R$)
International Designation: BRL
Exchange Rate (2010): US$1 = 1.77 BRL
100 Reais Note Design: Effigy of the Brazilian Republic.

**FIGURE 9.1 The Brazilian Nation at a Glance.**

| Table 9.1 | Political Organization |
|---|---|
| **Political System** | Federal republic, presidential with separation of powers. |
| **Regime History** | Democratic since 1946 with periods of military authoritarianism, especially 1964–1985. |
| **Administrative Structure** | Federal, with twenty-six states plus the Federal District, which also functions as a state. Subnational legislatures are unicameral. State governments have multiple secretariats, the major ones commonly being economy, planning, and infrastructure. The states are divided into municipalities (more than 5,500), with mayors and councilors directly elected. |
| **Executive** | President, vice president, and cabinet. The president and vice president are directly elected by universal suffrage in a two-round runoff election for four-year terms. Since 1998, the president and vice president may run for a second term. |
| **Legislature** | Bicameral: The Senate is made up of three senators from each state and from the Federal District, elected by plurality vote for an eight-year term; the Chamber of Deputies consists of representatives from each state and from the Federal District, elected by proportional vote for a four-year term. |
| **Judiciary** | Supreme Court, High Tribunal of Justice, regional courts, labor courts, electoral courts, military courts, and state courts. Judiciary has financial and administrative autonomy. Most judges are appointed for life. |
| **Party System** | Multiparty system including several parties of the right, center-left, and left. Elections are by open-list proportional representation. There is no restriction on the creation and merging of political parties. |

reinforced by immigration from Italy, Spain, and Portugal. Evangelical Protestants have recently made inroads. Protestants now compose about 15.4 percent of the population. Afro-Brazilian and indigenous religions also operate alongside the Catholic liturgy (see Figure 9.1 and Table 9.1).

**moderating power
(poder moderador)**

A term used in Brazilian politics to refer to the situation following the 1824 constitution in which the monarchy was supposed to act as a moderating power, among the executive, legislative, and judicial branches of government, arbitrating party conflicts, and fulfilling governmental responsibilities when nonroyal agents failed.

**oligarchy**

Narrowly based, undemocratic government, often by traditional elites.

# Critical Junctures

### The Brazilian Empire (1822–1889)

Brazil was a Portuguese colony, not a Spanish one, so it escaped the violent wars of independence and the comparatively spasmodic collapse of the Spanish colonial system. Brazilian independence was declared peacefully by the Crown's own agent in the colony in 1822.

To control its sprawling territory, Brazil centralized authority in the emperor, who acted as a **moderating power** (*poder moderador*), mediating conflicts among the executive, legislative, and judicial branches of government and powerful landowning oligarchy. This centralization contrasted with other postcolonial Latin American states, which suffered numerous conflicts among territorially dispersed strongmen (*caudillos*).

Imperial Brazil enjoyed several features of representative democracy: regular elections, alternation of parties in power, and scrupulous compliance with the constitution. Liberal institutions, however, only regulated political competition among the rural, oligarchical elites, leaving out the mass of the Brazilian population who were neither enfranchised nor politically organized.

## The Old Republic (1889–1930)

In 1889 came the peaceful demise of the empire, the exile of Emperor Dom Pedro II, and the emergence of a republic ruled by the landowning oligarchy. The decline of slavery and the rise of republicanism had effectively ended the empire. Liberal political values in opposition to centralized political authority had also taken root among the coffee oligarchy. As these elites grew suspicious of attempts to centralize power, they discounted the need for a moderating power in the national state.

The Old Republic (1889–1930) consolidated the coffee oligarchy and a small urban industrial class and commercial elite linked to the coffee trade. The constitution of 1891, inspired by the U.S. model, established a directly elected president, guaranteed separation of church and state, and gave the vote to all literate males (about 3.5 percent of the population before 1930). The **legitimacy** of the republican political system was established on governing principles that were limited to a privileged few, but no longer determined by the hereditary rights of the emperor. The states gained greater authority to formulate policy, spend money, levy taxes, and maintain their own militias.

Although the constitution expressed liberal ideas, most Brazilians lived in rural areas where the landed oligarchy squashed dissent. As in the southern United States and in Mexico, landed elites manipulated local political activity. In a process known as *coronelismo,* these elites, or colonels, gathered their poor workers and used their votes to elect officials they favored.

These ties between patron (landowner) and client (peasant) became the basis of modern Brazilian politics. In return for protection and occasional favors, the client

**legitimacy**

Norms and rules that are conceived and codified in law. Also refers to leaders, groups, and organizations that exist and behave within the bounds of the law.

**clientelism**

An informal aspect of policy-making in which a powerful patron (for example, a traditional local boss, government agency, or dominant party) offers resources such as land, contracts, protection, or jobs in return for the support and services (such as labor or votes) of lower-status and less powerful clients; corruption, preferential treatment, and inequality are characteristic of clientelist politics.

**politics of the governors**

In Brazil, refers to periods of history in which state governors acquire extraordinary powers over domains of policy that were previously claimed by the federal government. The term refers most commonly to the Old Republic and the current state of Brazilian federalism.

**interventores**

In Brazil, allies of Getúlio Vargas (1930–1945, 1950–1952) picked by the dictator during his first period of rulership to replace opposition governors in all the Brazilian states except Minas Gerais. The *interventores* represented a shift of power from subnational government to the central state.

did the bidding of the patron. As cities grew and the state's administrative agencies expanded, the process of trading favors and demanding political support in return became known as **clientelism**.

The empire had centralized, but the Old Republic consecrated the power of local elites. The **politics of the governors** empowered regional elites, mainly from coffee and cattle regions.

## The 1930 Revolution

As world demand for coffee plummeted during the Depression of the 1930s, the coffee and ranch elites faced their worst crisis. Worker demonstrations and the Brazilian Communist Party challenged the legitimacy of the Old Republic. Among the discontented political elites, a figure emerged who transformed Brazilian politics forever: Getúlio Vargas (see "Profile: Getúlio Dornelles Vargas" in Section 3).

Vargas came to power as the head of a new "revolutionary government" that swiftly crushed middle-class and popular dissent. He built a political coalition around a new project of industrialization led by the central government and based on central state resources. Unlike the Old Republic, Vargas controlled regional governments by replacing all governors (except in Minas Gerais) with handpicked allies (***interventores***). The center of gravity of Brazilian politics swung back to the national state. Vargas, as "father of the people," could not be upstaged by competing political images and organizations. Brazilian society would be linked directly to the state and to Vargas as the state's primary agent.

Vargas believed he could win the support of landed elites, commercial interests, bureaucrats, and the military by answering their demands in a controlled way. They were allowed to participate in the new political order, but only as passive members of state-created and state-regulated unions and associations. This model of **state corporatism** rejects the idea of competition among social groups by having the state arbitrate all conflicts. For instance, when workers requested increases in their wages, state agencies determined to what extent such demands would be met and how business would pay for them.[3]

By 1937, Vargas had achieved a position of virtually uncontested power. During the next eight years, he consolidated his state corporatist model with labor codes, the establishment of public firms to produce strategic commodities such as steel and oil, and paternalistic social policies. These policies were collectively called the New State (*Estado Novo*).

## The Populist Republic (1945–1964)

The ever-growing mobilization of segments of the working and middle classes, and U.S. diplomatic pressure forced Vargas to call for full democratic elections to be held in 1945. Three political parties fought the election: The Social Democratic Party (PSD) and the Brazilian Labor Party (PTB) were pro-Vargas, while the National Democratic Union (UDN) stood against him. The PSD and the PTB, which operated in alliance, were both creations of the state, while the UDN brought together regional forces that wanted a return to liberal constitutionalism. The campaign was so bitter that the military forced Vargas to resign, two months before the general election.

The turn to democracy in 1946 did not break with the past. The new constitution guaranteed periodic elections, but the most important economic and social policies were still decided by the state bureaucracy, not by the national legislature.

**Populism**, but not democracy, defined the new political order. In Brazil, the terms *populist* and *populism* refer to politicians, programs, or movements that seek to expand citizenship to previously disenfranchised sectors of society in return for political support. Populist governments grant benefits to guarantee support, but discourage lower-class groups from creating their own organizations. Populists do not consider themselves accountable to the people.

Brazilian workers supported Vargas for his promises to improve the social insurance system, and elected him in 1950. However, economic limitations and opposition claims that he was preparing a new dictatorship made Vargas politically vulnerable.[4] He was soon swept up in a bizarre scandal involving the attempted assassination of a popular journalist. During the crisis, Vargas combated accusations of his own complicity that increasingly wore on him, leading him to kill himself on August 24, 1954. Under Vargas's democratic successor, Juscelino Kubitschek (1956–1960), the economy improved. Brazilian industry expanded tremendously. Kubitschek was a master of political symbolism and **nationalism**, promoting images of a new, bigger Brazil that could create "fifty years of development in five." His chief symbol was his decision to move the capital from Rio de Janeiro to a planned city called Brasília—a utopian city that rallied support for Kubitschek's developmentalist policies.

The presidents after Kubitschek proved much less competent.[5] João Goulart, for instance, began an ill-fated campaign for structural reforms, mainly in education and agriculture. But peasant league movements, students, and professional organizations organized protests, strikes, and illegal seizures of land. As right-wing organizations battled leftist groups in the streets of the capital, the military ended Brazil's experiment with democratic populism in March 1964.

## The Rise of Bureaucratic Authoritarianism (1964–1985)

The military government installed what the Argentine political sociologist Guillermo O'Donnell termed **bureaucratic authoritarianism (BA)**.[6] Such regimes respond to severe economic crises and are led by the armed forces and key civilian allies, most notably by professional economists, engineers, and administrators. BA limited civil rights and other political freedoms, sometimes going so far as wholesale censorship of the press, torture of civilians, and imprisonment without trial.

The military government first planned a quick return to civilian rule and even allowed limited democratic institutions to continue. After being purged in 1964 of the BA's opponents, the national congress continued to function, and direct elections for federal legislators and most mayors (but not the president or state governors) took place at regular intervals. In November 1965, the military replaced all existing political parties with only two: the National Renovation Alliance (ARENA) and the Brazilian Democratic Movement (MDB). ARENA was the military government's party, and MDB was the "official" party of the opposition. Former members of the three major parties joined one of the two new parties.[7]

Although these democratic institutions were more than a sham, their powers were severely limited. The military government used institutional decrees to legislate the most important matters, preventing the congress from having an important voice. Few civilian politicians could speak out directly against the military for fear of being removed from office.

---

**state corporatism**

A system of interest representation in which the constituent units are organized into a limited number of singular, compulsory, noncompetitive, hierarchically ordered, and functionally differentiated categories, recognized or licensed (if not created) by the state and granted a deliberate representational monopoly within their respective categories in exchange for observing certain controls in their selection of leaders and articulation of demands and supports.

**populism**

Gaining the support of popular sectors. When used in Latin American politics, this support is often achieved by manipulation and demagogic appeals.

**nationalism**

An ideology seeking to create a nation-state for a particular community; a group identity associated with membership is such a political community. Nationalists often proclaim that their state and nation are superior to others.

**bureaucratic authoritarianism (BA)**

A term developed by Argentine sociologist Guillermo O'Donnell to interpret the common characteristics of military-led authoritarian regimes in Brazil, Argentina, Chile, and Uruguay in the 1960s and 1970s. According to O'Donnell, bureaucratic authoritarian regimes led by the armed forces and key civilian allies emerged in these countries in response to severe economic crises.

Brazil's capital, Brasília. The planned city was designed by the world-famous Brazilian architect Oscar Niemeyer.

*Source:* George Holton/Photo Researchers, Inc.

**state-led economic development**

The process of promoting economic development using governmental machinery.

**abertura**

(Portuguese for "opening"; *apertura* in Spanish) In Brazil, refers to the period of authoritarian liberalization begun in 1974 when the military allowed civilian politicians to compete for political office in the context of a more open political society.

In economic policy, the military reinforced the previous pattern of state interventionism. The government promoted **state-led economic development** by creating hundreds of state corporations and investing enormous sums in established public firms. Brazil implemented one of the most successful economic development programs among newly industrialized countries. Often called the "Brazilian miracle," these programs demonstrated that, like France, Germany, and Japan in earlier periods, a developing country could create its own economic miracle.

## The Transition to Democracy and the First Civilian Governments (1974–2001)

After the oil crisis of 1973 set off a wave of inflation around the world, the economy began to falter. Increasing criticism from Brazilian business led the last two ruling generals, Geisel and Figueiredo, to begin a gradual process of democratization. Initially, these leaders envisioned only a liberalizing, or opening (*abertura*), of the regime to allow civilian politicians to compete for political office. As was later the case with Gorbachev's *glasnost* in the Soviet Union, however, control over the process of liberalization gradually slipped from military hands and was captured by organizations within civil society. In 1974, the opposition party, the MDB, stunned the military government by increasing its representation in the Senate from 18 to 30 percent and in the Chamber of Deputies from 22 to 44 percent. The party did not have a majority, but it did capture a majority in both chambers of the state legislatures in the most important industrialized southern and southeastern states.

In the following years, the opposition made successive electoral gains and obtained concessions from the government. The most important were the reestablishment of direct elections for governors in 1982, political amnesty for dissidents, the elimination of the government's power to oust legislators from political office, and the restoration of political rights to those who had previously lost them. In the gubernatorial elections of November 1982 the opposition candidates won landslide victories in the major states.

The military wanted to maintain as much control over the succession process as possible and preferred to have the next president selected within a restricted electoral college. But mass mobilization campaigns demanded the right to elect the next president directly. The *Diretas Já!* ("Direct Elections Now!") movement, comprising an array of social movements, opposition politicians, and labor unions, expanded in size and influence in 1984. Their rallies exerted tremendous pressure on the military at a moment when it was not clear who would succeed General Figueiredo. The military's fight to keep the 1984 elections indirect alienated civilian supporters of the generals. Many former supporters broke with the regime and backed an alliance (the Liberal Front) with Tancredo Neves, the candidate of the opposition PMDB, the Party of the MDB. Neves's victory in 1984, however, was marred by his sudden death on the eve of the inauguration. Vice President José Sarney became the first civilian president of Brazil since 1964.

The events leading to Sarney's presidency disappointed those who had hoped for a clean break with the authoritarian past. Most of the politicians who gained positions of power in the new democracy hailed from the former ARENA or its misleadingly named successor, the Democratic Social Party (PDS). Most of these soon joined Sarney's own PMDB or its alliance partner, the Party of the Liberal Front (PFL).[8] A political transition that should have produced change, led to considerable continuity.

A chance for fundamental change appeared in 1987 when the national Constituent Assembly met to draft a new constitution. Given the earlier success of the opposition governors in 1982, state political machines became important players in the game of constitution writing. The state governments petitioned for the devolution of new authority to tax and spend. Labor groups also exerted influence through their lobbying organizations. Workers demanded constitutional protection of the right to strike and called for extending this right to public employees. The constitution also granted workers the right to create their own unions without authorization from the Ministry of Labor.[9]

Soon after Sarney's rise to power, annual rates of inflation began to skyrocket. The government sponsored several stabilization plans, but without success. By 1989, the first direct presidential elections since the 1960s, Brazilian society was calling for a political leader to remedy runaway inflation and remove corrupt and authoritarian politicians.

Fernando Collor de Mello, became president after a grueling campaign against Lula da Silva, the popular left-wing labor leader and head of the Workers' Party (*Partido dos Trabalhadores,* or PT). To counteract Lula's following, Collor's rhetoric appealed to the poor, known as the *descamisados* ("shirtless ones"), with his attacks against politicians and social problems caused by bureaucratic inefficiency.

The Collor presidency began the privatization of state enterprises, deregulation of the economy, and the reversal of decades of policies that had kept Brazil's markets closed to the rest of the world. But Collor failed to solve the nagging problem of inflation. Ironically, he was soon accused of bribery and influence peddling and was impeached in September 1992.

Collor's impeachment brought Itamar Franco to the presidency. Despite uncertainty during his first year, his government played an important stabilizing role. In July 1994, Fernando Henrique Cardoso, his minister of finance implemented the Real Plan, which created a new currency, the *real*. Monthly inflation fell from 26 percent to 2.82 percent in October 1994 (see Section 2).

Cardoso rode the success of the Real Plan to the presidency, beating out Lula and the PT in 1994 and again in 1998. He proved adept at keeping inflation low and consolidating some of the structural reforms of the economy. But Brazil's budget and trade deficits increased, and financial crises in Asia and Russia in 1997 and 1998 eventually led to a crisis in the Real Plan. In January 1999, the value of the *real* collapsed. But the currency soon stabilized, and hyperinflation did not return. The Cardoso administration was also able to pass the Law of Fiscal Responsibility in 2000, which addressed many of the pernicious effects of runaway spending by state and municipal governments.

### After September 11, 2001

September 11 and the collapse of the Argentine economy that same year produced a fundamental crisis of confidence in Brazil. In particular, Argentina's crisis threatened to destabilize the recovery of the *real*. Meanwhile, Washington's war on terror threatened to displace social and economic priorities in Brazil's relations with the United States. Diplomacy with Washington became particularly bitter over the Bush administration's insistence on going to war with Iraq and its heavy-handed approach to dealing with foreigners.

The election of Lula da Silva as president in October 2002 stemmed from a popular desire to put the social agenda ahead of the American focus on security. Lula's election also reflected the maturation of democracy. Once a proponent of socialism, Lula embraced Cardoso's reform agenda. He passed major social security reforms in 2003 and 2004, but, similar to his predecessor's difficulties, his reforms became stalled in congress during the run-up to municipal elections in late 2004. Worse still, PT-led municipal governments, once a model of good governance in Latin America, were accused of procuring kickbacks to fund electoral activities. PT leaders surrounding Lula were implicated in a second scandal involving the purchase of votes in the congress for reform legislation. However, Lula won reelection in 2006 anyway, and he continued to garner high presidential approval ratings well into his second term. He expanded public expenditures on infrastructure and industry as part of his Plan for the Acceleration of Growth. Improved growth, higher median incomes, and decreased inequality set the stage for Lula to promote the election of his chief-of-staff, Dilma Rousseff, as his successor in 2010. She is Brazil's first woman president.

In the post 9/11 world, Brazil's politics are less affected by the themes of the war on terror or the wars in Iraq and Afghanistan, than other countries that emphasize security. In Brazil, development and democracy continue to dominate the agenda of domestic and international policy.

## Themes and Implications

### Historical Junctures and Political Themes

Both international and domestic factors have influenced the Brazilian state's structure, capacity, and relations with society. During the empire, international opposition to slavery forced powerful oligarchs to turn to the state for protection. The coffee and ranch economies provided the material base for the Old Republic and were intricately tied to Brazil's economic role in the world. Even the *Estado Novo*, with its drive to organize society, was democratized by the defeat of fascism in Europe. The return to democracy during the 1980s was part of a larger global experience, as authoritarian regimes gave way all over Latin America, Eastern Europe, southern Europe, and the Soviet Union.

The Brazilian state adjusted to changes in the distribution of power; the rise of new, politically active social classes; and the requirements of development. Power shifted regularly between the central and subnational governments. These swings between centralizing periods and decentralizing ones punctuated critical junctures of Brazilian politics.

The entry of the working and middle classes as political actors reshaped the Brazilian state during the twentieth century. Vargas's New State mobilized workers and professionals. Populist democracy later provided them protection from unsafe working environments, the effects of eroding wages, and the prohibitive expense of health care. Public firms employed hundreds of thousands of Brazilians and transformed the development of the country. During the 1980s and 1990s, neoliberal reforms dramatically altered the role of the Brazilian state (see Section 2). Brazil's governance of the economy highlights the strategic role of the state in the maintenance of growth. State-led growth built the foundation for governing the economy, and developmentalism moved Brazil from a predominantly agrarian economy into an industrialized one. Growth was poorly distributed, however, and the social problems that emerged from it remain at the heart of Brazil's struggles with democracy. The country's high growth trajectory in recent years has generated a positive pattern, one in which the state has promoted growth through wise economic policy-making and social spending. Regarding the democratic idea, Brazil certainly has the institutions of a democracy, but patrimonialism, populism, corporatism, and corruption undermine them. Brazilian politicians typically cultivate personal votes (**personalist politicians**) and avoid following the rule of parties or alliances. Many switch parties several times in a career, making Brazilian political parties extremely weak (see Section 4). Personalism persists because it is well rewarded.

Even with its shortcomings, Brazilians prefer this form of government. They appreciate that democracy gives them more say in policy-making. Thousands of new political groups, social movements, civic networks, and economic associations have emerged. The Brazilian state is highly decentralized into twenty-six states, a federal district, and 5,564 municipalities. Each center of power is a locus of demand-making by citizens and policy-making by elites. Centralized rule following the model of the New State or the bureaucratic authoritarian period is impossible and undesirable today.

In assessing the politics of collective identity, the first question to answer is who are the Brazilians? This has always been a vexing issue, especially because heavy flows of international commerce, finance, and ideas have made Brazil's borders obsolete. One common answer is that the symbols of the Brazilian nation still tie Brazilians together: carnival, soccer, samba, and bossa nova. Even though these symbols have become more prevalent, they have lost some of their meaning because of commercialization. Catholicism is a less unifying force today, as Pentecostalism and evangelism have eaten into the church's membership. Women have improved their social position and political awareness as gender-based organizations have become important resources of civil society. Yet even here, Brazil remains extremely patriarchal: Women are expected to balance motherhood and other traditional roles in the household, even while economic needs pressure them to produce income.

**personalist politicians**

Demagogic political leaders who use their personal charisma to mobilize their constituency.

Race remains the most difficult issue to understand. Racial identity continues to divide Brazilians, but not in the clear-cut manner it divides blacks and whites in the United States. Categories are multiple, especially since racial mixing defies the kind of stark, black-white segregation in the United States.

Class continues to separate Brazilians. Economic reforms and the erosion of populist redistribution have widened social gaps, making Brazil a highly fragmented society. Although it is one of the world's ten wealthiest economies, that wealth is poorly distributed. Like India, Brazil's social indicators consistently rank near the bottom in the world, though these indicators are improving. Income disparities mirror racial differences. The poor are mostly blacks and mulattos, while the rich are mostly white. The poverty of the north and northeast contrasts with the more industrialized and prosperous southeastern and southern states.

## Implications for Comparative Politics

As a large, politically decentralized, and socially fragmented polity, Brazil presents several extraordinary challenges to the study of comparative politics. First, the Brazilian state is an anomaly. It has been both highly centralized and decentralized during different periods of its history. In each of these periods, the state produced lasting political legacies that have both strengthened and weakened its capacity for promoting development, democracy, and social distribution. Although political centralization has been an important factor in making the French state strong, decentralized states such as the United States and German federations have also proven to be successful formulas for government. The Brazilian case is a laboratory for evaluating which approach is likely to be more successful in other large, decentralized states in the developing world, such as India.

While the complexity of the Brazilian state represents one problem area, the weakness of the country's democratic institutions suggests another, and perhaps more troubling, concern. Along with Russia, Brazil demonstrates how the lack of coherent party systems and electoral institutions can endanger democracy. Paradoxically, as Brazil developed economically and made its way back to democracy in the 1980s, it also became a more socially unequal country. Other democracies have also found that democratization does not improve the distribution of wealth. Finally, the complex divisions afflicting Brazilians' collective identities challenge all attempts to address the country's problems. In this regard, Brazil presents a puzzle for theories about collective identities: How has such a socially fragmented society remained a coherent whole for so long?

## Summary

Brazil is a country of continental size with a long history of building a national state and, in recent decades, a more democratic system of government. Both processes have been shaped at different points by presidents such as Vargas, Cardoso, and Lula. Central characteristics of Brazilian politics such as clientelism, personalism, and corporatism have endured and adapted to the modernization of the state and the economy. Despite these tendencies, Brazilian democracy has survived and prospered since 1985, and it now does so in the context of a new period of accelerated growth and development.

**export-led growth**

Economic growth generated by the export of a country's commodities. Export-led growth can occur at an early stage of economic development, in which case it involves primary products, such as the country's mineral resources, timber, and agricultural products; or at a later stage, when industrial goods and services are exported.

**interventionist**

An interventionist state acts vigorously to shape the performance of major sectors of the economy.

# POLITICAL ECONOMY AND DEVELOPMENT

Like most developing countries, Brazil's politics has always been shaped by the quest for economic and social development. Two processes have left enduring legacies: the pattern of state intervention in the domestic market and the effects of external economic change. External economic crises have compelled the state to intervene through protection, subsidies, and even the production of goods it previously imported. These policies have made Brazil one of the faster-growing newly industrialized countries of the world, alongside India and China. But globalization has made the Brazilian economy once again highly dependent upon the country's strategic position in world markets. Without the state-led development that guided Brazil during the last half century, the country faces a crossroads in its model of economic growth.

## State and Economy

Brazil's economic development prior to the New State depended on **export-led growth**, that is, on the export of agricultural products. During the Old Republic, international demand for Brazilian coffee gave Brazil a virtual global monopoly. Cotton, sugar, and cereals also continued to be important export products.

Coffee kept Brazil active in the world market with minimal state involvement in the period before the Great Depression. Export receipts provided a reservoir of capital to build railroads, power stations, and other infrastructure. These investments then spurred the growth of light industries, mostly in textiles, footwear, and clothing. With ample domestic capital, public finance was relegated to a minor role.

The state became far more **interventionist** during the 1930s when international demand for coffee declined. As exports fell, imports of manufactured goods also declined. These forces prompted **import substitution industrialization (ISI)**, a model of development that promoted domestic production of previously imported manufactured goods. At first, Brazil did not need large doses of state intervention. This so-called light, or easy, phase of ISI focused on products that did not require much capital or sophisticated technology. Most of these industries were labor intensive and created jobs.

At the end of World War II, new ideas about Third World development became popular among various international agencies. The new goal was to "deepen" the ISI model by promoting heavy industry and capital-intensive production. In Brazil, a new generation of **state technocrats** designed new policies. Inspired by the United Nations Economic Commission for Latin America (ECLA), these technocrats targeted particular industrial sectors. Then, through industrial policies including planning, subsidies, and financial support, state agencies promoted the quick growth of these sectors.

During the 1950s Brazil was a prime example of ECLA-style **developmentalism**, the ideology and practice of state-sponsored growth. More than any other Latin American state, Brazil was organizationally capable of deepening ISI. The state promoted private investment by extracting and distributing raw materials

### Focus Questions

How did the Brazilian state's role in promoting development change as the country moved from import-substitution to market-oriented reform?

Identify some of the persisting problems of Brazilian economic development and how progress has been made during the New Republic in addressing them.

**import substitution industrialization (ISI)**

Strategy for industrialization based on domestic manufacture of previously imported goods to satisfy domestic market demands.

**state technocrats**

Career-minded bureaucrats who administer public policy according to a technical rather than a political rationale. In Mexico and Brazil, these are known as the *técnicos*.

**developmentalism**

An ideology and practice in Latin America during the 1950s in which the state played a leading role in seeking to foster economic development through sponsoring vigorous industrial policy.

| Table 9.2 | Governing the Economy: GDP Growth Rates |
|-----------|-----------------------------------------|
| 1940–1949 | 5.6% |
| 1950–1959 | 6.1% |
| 1960–1969 | 5.4% |
| 1970–1979 | 12.4% |
| 1980–1989 | 1.5% |
| 1990–1996 | 2.1% |
| 1997–2000 | 0.8% |
| 2001–2003 | 1.0% |
| 2004–2007 | 3.2% |
| 2008–2010 | 5.7% |

*Source:* IBGE and Werner Baer. THE BRAZILIAN ECONOMY: GROWTH AND DEVELOPMENT, Fourth Edition. Copyright © 1995. Reproduced with permission of ABC-CLIO, LLC.

for domestic industries at prices well below the international market. Other firms, if they were linked to sectors of the economy receiving these supports, would benefit in a chain reaction.

Growth rates achieved impressive levels during the 1950s and early 1960s and even higher levels in the 1970s (see Table 9.2), but the first serious contradictions of ISI emerged during this period. Protection led to noncompetitive, inefficient production. Industries grew, but they depended too heavily on public subsidies. ISI also became import-intensive. Businesses used subsidized finance to import technology and machinery, since the government overvalued the currency to make import prices cheaper. But this overvaluation hurt exports, by making them more expensive; and the revenue from exports was needed to pay for imports. Because the export sector could not supply the state with much-needed revenues to sustain growth, the government printed money, which in turn led to inflation. Under the Goulart government (1961–1964), the economy's capacity to import and export dwindled, and stagnation set in. A crisis soon followed that contributed to the coup of 1964.

The failures of ISI during the 1960s inspired new thinking. The dependency school emerged, claiming that underdeveloped or "peripheral" countries faced tremendous obstacles to achieving sustained levels of industrialization and growth in a world dominated by "core" economies in North America and Western Europe. ISI's failures, it was argued, were due to the ill-fated attempt to adjust marginally the inherently exploitative structure of world markets. Because pursuing capitalist development only favored the core economies, the dependency school advocated de-linking Brazil from the world economy. The fall of Brazilian democracy, however, provided little opportunity to apply these ideas outside the universities.

The military governments promoted reform but eventually tried to deepen ISI through state-led development. From 1964 to 1985, the state continued to promote industrialization, especially durable consumer goods for the domestic market. Multinational firms also invested and transferred technology. Table 9.3 highlights the important contribution of industry to the Brazilian gross domestic product.

**para-statals**

State-owned, or at least state-controlled, corporations, created to undertake a broad range of activities, from control and marketing of agricultural production to provision of banking services, operating airlines, and other transportation facilities and public utilities.

**Para-statals** (public or state firms) played an important role in the military's development model. Large-scale projects were financed and managed by bureaucratic agencies and state firms, and often included foreign companies. Peter Evans characterized these complex relations among the state, foreign investors, and domestic capitalists as a "triple alliance."[10] But the state remained the dominant partner.

### The Environmental Costs of State-Led Growth

The central and southern states of São Paulo, Minas Gerais, Rio de Janeiro, and Rio Grande do Sul led the country's development, but they also became sites of environmental degradation. In the 1970s Guanabara Bay and the Paraiba do Sul River basin, both in Rio de Janeiro state, approached the brink of biological death. Urban pollution in São Paulo devastated the Tietê River, threatening the health of millions. In Cubatão, an industrial city east of metropolitan São Paulo, conditions became so bad that by 1981, one city council member reported that he had not seen a star in twenty years.

Big development projects reached the Amazon River basin in the 1970s. These industrial projects threatened the tropical forests, as did cattle ranching, timber extraction, and slash-and-burn agriculture by poor farmers. By the 1980s, it was clear that the primary result of these practices was the deforestation of the Amazon.

| Table 9.3 | Governing the Economy: Sector Composition of the GDP, 1970–2007 | | |
|---|---|---|---|
| **Year** | **Agriculture** | **Industry** | **Services** |
| 1970 | 11.6% | 35.9% | 52.6% |
| 1980 | 10.2% | 41.0% | 48.8% |
| 1990 | 9.3% | 34.2% | 56.5% |
| 2000 | 9.0% | 29.0% | 62.0% |
| 2007 | 5.1% | 30.8% | 64.0% |

Source: IBGE and Werner Baer. THE BRAZILIAN ECONOMY: GROWTH AND DEVELOPMENT, Fourth Edition. Copyright © 1995. Reproduced with permission of ABC-CLIO, LLC.

Partly because of the return to democracy in 1984, new environmental movements within and outside Brazil began to influence official and public opinion. The Amazon, one of the world's major mechanisms for absorbing excess $CO_2$, suffered deforestation at a rate of 19,500 square kilometers per year between 1996 and 2005. Though the Brazilian government backed away from making sweeping commitments to reduce $CO_2$, it has renewed efforts to reduce deforestation under pressure from domestic and international nongovernmental organizations. These efforts have paid off in that the annual rate of deforestation fell by two-thirds after 2008, partly due to new federal protection of land against farming, and improved policing of these areas by satellite. Improvements to the land registry system, which monitors land ownership and use, have enhanced enforcement. As the agricultural sector turns to more productive methods and the Brazilian government emphasizes energy efficiency, the pressure may subside to develop the Amazon further.

## The Fiscal System

As the Brazilian economy became more complex after the 1960s, new opportunities for evading taxes emerged. An **informal economy** of small firms, domestic enterprises, street vendors, and unregistered employees proliferated, outside the taxable economy. Economists estimate that the informal economy could be as large as twenty percent of Brazil's gross domestic product ($420 billion), and it may employ about 40 million to 60 million people. Figures estimate that federal coffers lose more than $70 billion a year in forgone tax revenues.

The new constitution of 1988 allowed states and municipalities to expand their collection of taxes and to receive larger transfers of funds from Brasília. Significant gaps then emerged in tax collection responsibilities and public spending. Although the central state spent less than it collected in taxes between 1960 and 1994, Brazil's 5,564 municipal governments spent several times more than they collected. Subnational governments also gained more discretion over spending, since the destination of most of these funds was not predetermined by the federal government. The governors also used public banks held by the state governments to finance expenditures, thus expanding their debt.

**informal economy**

That portion of the economy largely outside government control in which employees work without contracts or benefits. Examples include casual employees in restaurants and hotels, street vendors, and day laborers in construction or agriculture.

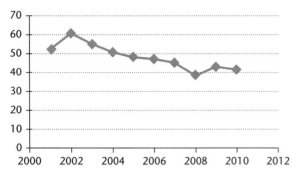

**FIGURE 9.2  Governing the Economy: Brazilian Public Sector Debt as a Percentage of GDP, 2001–2010**

*Source:* Based on numbers produced by the Central Bank of Brazil.

The Collor administration began to reverse some of the adverse effects. But the Cardoso administration's efforts to recover federal tax revenues and reduce the fiscal distortions of Brazil's federal structure made the greatest difference. The Fiscal Responsibility Law of 2000 set strict limits on federal, state, and municipal expenditures, but its enforcement is still in doubt. With large civil service payrolls, governments are hard-pressed to implement the law. Despite these problems, improved tax collection and economic growth have reduced the public debt from 60 percent of GDP in 2002 to 43 percent in 2010 (see Figure 9.2).

In 2003, Lula's government passed a simplified tax code and a tax reform permitting increases in federal taxes. But it postponed legislation to address fiscal competition among the states, the simplification and unification of the states' value-added tax, and efforts to reduce the overall tax burden on business. The government also failed to do something about the weight of sales taxes that fall more heavily on the poor. Still, the Lula government was able to reduce the public sector debt, as Figure 9.2 illustrates.

### The Problem of Inflation

In Brazil, inflation accompanied state-led development. The Brazilian state, business, and unions all distorted the value of goods and services by manipulating prices, interest rates, and wages. Successive attempts to control inflation fell apart as different interest groups attempted to retain these controls. No fewer than seven "stabilization" plans between 1985 and 1994 collapsed, sometimes generating "hyperinflation" (600 percent or more annual inflation). Figure 9.3 illustrates this terrible track record.

Only Cardoso's Real Plan proved successful. The Real Plan anchored the *real*, the new currency, to the dollar. It did not fix the real to the dollar strictly but allowed it to float within bounds, thus achieving more flexibility in the exchange rate.

But success itself can create problems. In 1995, Central Bank managers in Brasília became convinced that the *real* was overvalued, which made exports more expensive abroad, raised the costs of production, and made imports cheaper. Brazil's trade deficit rose by more than 140 percent after 1995. The *real* then fell by more than 50 percent against the dollar in January 1999. Despite the devaluation, hyperinflation did not return, and the government moderated growth in public spending. Renewed growth and good fiscal management by the Lula administration began to reduce the massive public debt.

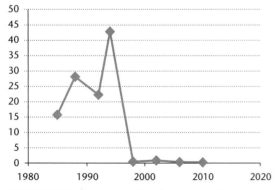

**FIGURE 9.3  Governing the Economy: Average Monthly Rates of Inflation, 1985–2010**

*Source:* Author's design based on Brazilian Central Bank figures, accessed in October 2010.

# Society and Economy

Between 1950 and 1980, employment in industry jumped from 14 percent to 24 percent, while employment in agriculture declined from 60 percent to 30 percent. Import substitution had created industrial jobs by expanding the size of both the working and the middle classes.

Nevertheless, the jobs created in industry did not begin to absorb the huge number of unemployed. Many new jobs required skilled and semiskilled specialized labor. In the late 1980s and 1990s, even skilled workers faced losing their jobs because of intense industrial restructuring. During the 1990s, manufacturing jobs fell by 48 percent, and unemployment rose above 18 percent in metropolitan areas. Service-sector employment increased, but not enough to make up for industrial job losses. These jobs also paid less and offered fewer protections from arbitrary dismissal.

Industrialization also failed to eradicate the racial inequalities inherited from slavery. Despite the impressive industrial development of Brazil, Afro-Brazilians continued to make less than their white colleagues and had fewer opportunities for upward mobility. According to one study, nonwhite men and women in Brazil have made real gains in their income because of improvements in education and occupation, but the gap separating nonwhite income from white income remains significant.[11] On average, blacks make 41 percent and mulattos make 47 percent of what whites make.

Women make up 28 percent of the economically active population and continue to enter the labor market in record numbers. Working women typically have more years of schooling than men, but they still receive lower salaries for the same job. Women make 57 percent of what men make. Afro-Brazilian women, who are doubly disadvantaged by race and gender, are more likely to have underpaid and menial work. The uneven effects of industrialization patterns and other demographic and policy factors discussed below have all worked against the equalization of income distribution historically. Income remains more maldistributed in Brazil than it is in most other developing countries (see Table 9.4). Yet recent economic growth and rising median incomes have begun to reverse decades of worsening inequality.

| Table 9.4 | Governing the Economy: Brazilian Income Distribution in Comparative Perspective | | | |
|---|---|---|---|---|
| Country | 10% Richest | 20% Richest | 20% Poorest | 10% Poorest |
| Brazil | 43.0 | 58.7 | 3.0 | 1.1 |
| Mexico | 41.3 | 56.4 | 3.8 | 1.2 |
| Chile | 41.7 | 56.8 | 4.1 | 1.6 |
| China | 31.4 | 47.8 | 5.7 | 2.4 |
| Nigeria | 32.42 | 48.6 | 5.1 | 2.0 |
| India | 31.1 | 45.3 | 8.1 | 3.6 |
| United States | 29.9 | 45.8 | 5.4 | 1.9 |
| United Kingdom | 28.5 | 44.0 | 6.1 | 2.1 |
| France | 25.1 | 40.2 | 7.2 | 2.8 |
| Russia | 34.3 | 50.2 | 5.6 | 2.2 |

*Source:* World Bank, *World Development Indicators 2010* (Washington, D.C.: World Bank, 2010).

### The Welfare System

In a country of startling social inequalities, welfare policy plays a remarkably small role. Although welfare and education expenditures constitute about 11 percent of the GDP, among the highest levels in the world, the money has not improved Brazil's mediocre welfare state.

Salaried workers receive benefits such as health care, worker's compensation, retirement pensions, paid vacations, and overtime pay, but only about 15 percent of the population qualify. Workers in the informal sector generally cannot collect welfare since technically the federal government does not consider them employed. Corruption, clientelism, and outright waste prevent benefits from going to the people who need them the most.[12]

More people need welfare than actually contribute to the welfare state. That means the government must finance the shortfall with debt. Between 1960 and 2000, the population doubled, but the number of retired people multiplied eleven-fold. Retirement benefits and pensions now exceed the salaries of working employees by 30 percent. These fiscal problems fall most heavily on the public system. More than 70 percent of all income transfers are retirement benefits that go to middle-class and upper-class individuals. The indigent receive only 1.5 percent of these funds.

The Cardoso administration laid some of the groundwork for reversing poverty and inequality. In addition to several programs to provide grants directly to poor families to improve their health and the education of their children, Cardoso also targeted the rural poor. The Family Health Program, for instance, provides community health workers for areas that have historically been underserved. Some studies have shown that this program has accelerated the decline in infant mortality and, along with other programs, has improved prenatal care and family reproductive medicine, including reductions in the rates of HIV/AIDS.[13]

The Lula administration focused even more on social reform. In the fall of 2003, the government passed a social security reform that raised the minimum retirement age, placed stricter limits on benefit ceilings, reduced survivor benefits, and taxed pensions and benefits. Issues including the taxation of social security benefits for judges and military officers and the reduction of survivor benefits for the latter group became stumbling blocks in cross-party negotiations. The government made concessions on these and other issues, but the total annual savings were less than half of the original target.

The most notable new social reform is *Bolsa Família* (the Family Grant Program), which consolidated three programs started by the Cardoso government. Lula expanded the funding of *Bolsa Família*, which grants modest monthly sums to families that keep their children in school and see the doctor for regular vaccinations and check-ups. Since 2003, 11.1 million families or 20 percent of the Brazilian population (46 million people) have benefited from *Bolsa Família*.[14] Both Cardoso's and Lula's sustained efforts in social welfare have generated some aggregate results: Poverty rates have fallen since 1994 and other improvements such as reduced illiteracy, particularly in the poorest regions, have been recorded in recent years.

### Agrarian Reform

Landownership remains in the hands of only 1 percent of the landowning class. The arable land held by this small group of owners (about 58,000 owners) is equal to the size of Venezuela and Colombia combined. Over 3 million other farmers survive on only 2 percent of the country's land.

The Cardoso administration expropriated some unproductive estates and settled 186,000 families on them. Perhaps because the Lula government seemed more sympathetic, the rate of land invasions dramatically increased in 2003–2005. Rhetoric and direct action continued to escalate tensions and test the Lula government's commitment to fiscal probity and modest social reform, but the administration failed to initiate anything close to a land reform during the president's two terms. The issue was one that enlivened the presidential campaign in 2010 of a former PT member, Marina Silva, of the small Green Party, whose 19 percent share of the first-round vote reflected how neglected social issues involving land and ecology still remain salient issues in Brazilian politics.

The landless poor have swelled the rings of poverty around Brazil's major cities. During the 1950s and 1960s, the growth of industry in the south and southeast enticed millions to migrate in the hopes of finding new economic opportunities. By 1991, 75 percent of Brazil's population was living in urban areas.

The pressures on Brazilian cities for basic services overwhelmed the budgets of municipalities and state governments. Squatters soon took government land, settling on the outskirts of the major cities. They built huge shantytowns called *favelas* around cities like Rio and São Paulo.

Regional disparities in income worsened during this period. The military governments addressed this problem by transferring revenues from the industrialized south and southeast to the poor north and northeast, where many of their supporters were based. The federal government subsidized communication and transportation in the poorer regions and created new state agencies to run regional developmental projects. The poor regions increased their share of GDP. The economic gap between regions narrowed, but social and income disparities within the underdeveloped regions increased. Industrialization in the poorer regions was capital intensive and therefore labor saving, but it did not create jobs. Only the most skilled workers in these regions benefited from these changes. Poor agricultural management, ecological destruction, the murder of native Brazilians in order to expropriate land for mining and agriculture, and corruption all weakened the distributive effect of these policies. The northern and northeastern regions remain much poorer today than those in the south and southeast.

## Brazil in the Global Economy

Because the financing needs of state-led industrialization outstripped the resources of the national development bank and domestic bankers, Brazil pursued international sources of credit to deepen ISI and became the largest debtor country in the developing world.

By the end of the 1970s, the world economy had been hit with two oil price shocks that sent inflation rates soaring in the United States and other industrialized countries. Many of these countries also held Brazilian debt. As central banks ratcheted interest rates upward to force prices back down, Brazil's interest payments soared.[15]

### favelas

A Portuguese-language term for the shantytowns that ring many of the main cities in Brazil. The shantytowns emerge where people can invade unused land and build domiciles before the authorities can remove them. Unfinished public housing projects can also become the sites of *favelas*. *Favelas* expanded after the 1970s as a response to the inadequate supply of homes in urban centers to meet the demand caused by increasing rural-urban migration.

Brazilian President Luiz Inacio Lula da Silva is shown in this photo attending a re-election campaign wearing a cap of the Landless Movement (MST).

AP Photo/Victor R. Caivano

Private investors began to shun Brazil and other Latin American debtors so that the IMF and the World Bank became important suppliers of badly needed credit. But these institutions would only help debtors who promised to take harsh measures to reduce inflation, such as reducing social expenditures, opening their domestic markets to foreign competition, promoting exports, and privatizing state industries.

Brazil rejected these conditions. The Sarney government refused to implement the free-market policies demanded by the international financial institutions. In 1987, his government took the ultimate gamble in resisting creditors by declaring a moratorium on debt repayment. It was lifted a few months later under intense pressure from the international financial community. The Brazilian business community also opposed the moratorium, fearing that such aggressive action would scare off foreign investors and ruin the country's already tattered credit rating.

Collor reversed course. He agreed to put Brazil on the path of free-market policies with reforms that included the privatization of state enterprises and the deregulation of the economy. Collor also began to normalize relations between Brazil and the multilateral agencies, especially the IMF.

Because the liberalization of markets opened Brazilian industry to increased foreign competition, the competitiveness of domestic firms emerged as a core problem. Inefficiencies caused by poor infrastructure, untrained labor, and lack of access to technology and capital continue as key obstacles.

Brazil's success in an interconnected and competitive global marketplace depends on its external political relations. Brazil's trade relations with the United States have been particularly troubled. At present, negotiations to establish the Free Trade Area of the Americas (FTAA) have slowed to a crawl. Unlike his predecessor, George W. Bush, Barack Obama said little and did less about the hemispheric integration process. For the Brazilians, Washington's refusal to discuss agricultural policies remains a sticking point to further negotiations since American subsidies to domestic producers coupled with temporary tariffs on agricultural imports have caused the Brazilians to distrust the U.S. commitment to free trade more generally. Brazil's commitment to the international free-trade system will likely expand with the growing importance of its export sector. Due to increased prices for soy, oranges, wheat, coffee, and other products that Brazil exports, the country's account enjoyed a healthy surplus of $20 billion in October 2010. Brazil is becoming one of the major manufacturing and agrindustry nodes in the globalized system of production and consumption. Ties to China, in particular, are growing stronger as Brazilian soy and iron ore exports provide the raw materials the Chinese need to develop further. As China moves to emphasize domestic consumption more, Brazilian exporters and multinational firms will benefit from their growing access to the second-largest market in the world.

Domestic and international opposition to globalization might constrain the Dilma Rousseff presidency from pursuing further integration into global markets. But the export commodity boom will likely motivate the government to stick to its commitments to expand the country's position in global markets. Lula's good fiscal management and modest social reforms have satisfied the IMF's requirements and pleased many looking for meaningful social change. Lula even found ways of making Brazil's relations with the international financial institutions work in favor of his administration's social justice goals. During his two terms in office, Lula signed several agreements with the World Bank and the Inter-American Development Bank to create and fund new social assistance programs.

# GLOBAL CONNECTION

## Governing the Economy in a World of States: MERCOSUL

In January 1995, after several years of negotiating the Treaty of Asunción, Brazil, Argentina, Paraguay, and Uruguay inaugurated MERCOSUL, a regional common market group. Under MERCOSUL (Mercosur in Spanish), Brazil and its trade partners agreed to reduce tariffs on imports from signatories gradually and impose a common external tariff (CET) ranging from 0 to 23 percent on the imports of non-members.

During the negotiations over the Treaty of Asunción between March 26, 1991, and MERCOSUL's inauguration, trade among the partners increased from 8 to 20 percent, making the case for a subhemispheric common market stronger. Efforts to remove gradually tariff protections and nontariff protections, such as regulations that slow the flow of trade, proceeded with few disruptions.

MERCOSUL is only the latest in a list of common market schemes in Latin America. In 1960, the Latin American Association of Free Trade (ALALC) initiated a process for forming a common market in twelve years. Although this goal was unfulfilled because of persistent differences among the group's members, intraregional trade increased from 7.7 percent in 1960 to 13.8 percent in 1980. Subhemispheric common market groups unconnected to ALALC also emerged as the Andean Group in 1969 (Bolivia, Colombia, Ecuador, and Venezuela) and the Central American Common Market in 1960 (Costa Rica, Guatemala, El Salvador, Honduras, and Nicaragua). ALALC was replaced in 1980 with the Latin American Integration Association (ALADI). Unlike ALALC's mission of forming a common market, ALADI's goal was to foster the formation of preferential trade agreements among subhemispheric groups. These efforts received their most important boost soon after the administration of George H. W. Bush delivered its Enterprise for the Americas Initiative (EAI) in 1990, a plan of lofty goals for hemispheric economic integration, which are being implemented now through the Free Trade Area of the Americas (FTAA). Soon after the EAI was announced, the existing regional groups and a new wave of other groups formed preferential organizations. Besides MERCOSUL, the most important of these was the North American Free Trade Agreement (NAFTA), initiated on January 1, 1994.

MERCOSUL differs from NAFTA in several ways. First, it is designed to be a common market among developing countries and not, as NAFTA is, a tripartite free-trade area organized to reduce tariffs primarily across the U.S.–Mexico border. Second, MERCOSUL can evolve in ways unimagined in NAFTA, such as the creation of a common currency. Finally, MERCOSUL can and has negotiated free-trade agreements with other global blocks such as the European Union (EU). This gives these four developing countries more leverage on the international level. Mexico's interests as a developing country are arguably not given the same priority by its trade partners in NAFTA.

MERCOSUL also differs markedly from the EU. Because the EU is a supranational organization, its members shift important sovereign areas of policy such as commercial; competition; increasingly justice and home affairs; and for the members of the euro zone, monetary policy to Brussels. The signatories of MERCOSUL do not envision more than a commercial and perhaps monetary agreement, and all this is negotiated multilaterally. MERCOSUL does not have an executive body such as the EU Commission that regulates the behavior of members. It has dispute resolution mechanisms, but nothing like the European Court of Justice whose decisions are binding on EU members.

Like its predecessors, MERCOSUL was a product and a cause of increased commercial integration among its signatories. Since its creation, MERCOSUL has contributed to a threefold increase in trade among its members, but with an upsurge in world prices for soya, grains, and minerals, trade with the rest of the world has increased more rapidly than inter-MERCOSUL trade since 2004. MERCOSUL is also at a diplomatic crossroads regarding the role it will play in the continuing FTAA process. President Lula da Silva used Brazil's leadership within MERCOSUL to extract concessions from Washington on the type and pacing of trade liberalization in the hemisphere, but the results have not substantially deepened the level of regional integration as originally envisioned in the Treaty of Asunción.

*Source:* Lia Valls Pereira, "Tratado de Assunção: Resultados e Perspectivas," in Antônio Salazar P. Brandão and Lia Valls Pereira, eds., *Mercosul: Perspectivas da Integração* (Rio de Janeiro: Fundação Getúlio Vargas, 1996), p. 11; *The Economist*, July 5, 2007.

## Summary

During the past three decades, Brazil has emerged from being an inward-oriented industrializer dependent on the state and foreign credit to becoming a market-oriented industrialized country that has achieved an enviable new competitive position in the world. Old problems of inflation and run-away government debt have been brought under control. Even persistent social inequalities and poverty are now improving and the objects of more efficiently targeted social policies. The ecological and land-ownership dimensions of development will continue to be areas for improving the quality of life for more of Brazil's people. The economy is now more interconnected with other markets than at any other time in the country's history. So navigating domestic and international priorities in foreign economic policy will become more prominent tasks for the government of Dilma Rousseff.

# SECTION 3 GOVERNANCE AND POLICY-MAKING

## Organization of the State

Brazilian state institutions have changed significantly since independence. Even so, a number of institutional legacies continue to shape Brazilian politics. The most important is the centralization of state authority in the executive. This process began with the rise of Getúlio Vargas and the New State during the 1930s (see "Profile: Getúlio Dornelles Vargas"). Vargas' legacy is paradoxical because it reflects not only the centralization of the state but also the way in which the decentralized federal structure of Brazil continues to shape the country's politics. The constitution of 1988 attempted to construct a new democratic order but left these contradictory tendencies in place.

Some general features of the Brazilian state can be identified. First, church and state are officially separated. The Catholic Church has never controlled any portion of the state apparatus or directly influenced national politics as it has in other Catholic countries. This does not mean, however, that the Catholic Church plays no role in Brazilian politics (see Section 4).

Second, the Brazilian state has traditionally placed vast power in the hands of the executive. The directly elected president is the head of state, head of government, and commander-in-chief of the armed forces. Although the executive is one of three branches of government (along with the legislature and the judiciary), Brazilian presidents have traditionally been less bound by judicial and legislative constraints than most of their European or North American counterparts. Brazilian constitutions have granted more discretion to the executive than to the other branches in enforcing laws or making policy.

Brazil's executive and the bureaucracy manage most of the policy-making and implementation functions of government. The state lacks the checks and balances of the U.S. government system. It differs also from the semipresidentialism of France. Both the Brazilian federal legislature and state governments look to the president and to the minister of the economy for leadership on policy. The heads of the key agencies of the economic bureaucracy—the ministers of the economy and of planning, the president of the Central Bank, and the head of the national development bank—have more discretion over the details of policy than the president does. Recent presidents have also had little choice but to delegate authority to the bureaucracy, given the growing complexity of economic and social policy. Ultimate authority nevertheless remains in the hands of the president, who may replace the cabinet ministers.

## PROFILE

### Getúlio Dornelles Vargas

Getúlio Vargas as president in 1952.

*Source:* Keystone/ Stringer/Hulton Archive/Getty Images.

Getúlio Dornelles Vargas (1883–1954) came from a wealthy family in the cattle-rich southernmost state of Rio Grande do Sul. Vargas's youth was marked by political divisions within his family between federalists and republicans, conflicts that separated Brazilians during the Old Republic and particularly in Rio Grande do Sul. Political violence, which was common in the state's history, also affected Vargas's upbringing. His two brothers were each accused of killing rivals, one at the military school in Minas Gerais that Getúlio attended with one of his older siblings. After a brief stint in the military, Vargas attended law school in Porto Alegre, where he excelled as an orator.

After graduating in 1907, he became a district attorney. Later, he served as majority leader in the state senate. In 1923, Vargas was elected federal deputy for Rio Grande do Sul, and in 1924 he became leader of his state's delegation in the Chamber of Deputies. In 1926, he became finance minister. He served for a year before winning the governorship of his home state. Never an ideologue, Vargas practiced a highly pragmatic style of governing that made him one of Brazil's most popular politicians.

Vargas's position as governor of Rio Grande do Sul catapulted him into national prominence in 1929. The international economic crisis forced several regional economic oligarchies to unite in opposition to the coffee and pro-export financial policies of the government and in favor of efforts to protect their local economies. The states, including the state of São Paulo, divided their support between two candidates for the presidency: Julio Prestes, who was supported by President Luis, and Vargas, head of the opposition. The two states of Minas Gerais and Rio Grande do Sul voted as a bloc for Vargas, but he lost the 1930 election. Immediately afterward, a coup by military and political leaders installed Vargas in power.

The reforms of Vargas's New State, as his program was called, established the revised terms that linked Brazilian society to the state. Even today, his political legacy continues in the form of state agencies designed to promote economic development and laws protecting workers and raising living standards for families so that they do not suffer from poverty and hunger.

*Source:* For more on Vargas's life, see Robert M. Levine, *Father of the Poor? Vargas and His Era* (New York: Cambridge University Press, 1998).

Although the Brazilian president is the dominant player among the three branches of government, the powers of the legislature and the judiciary have become stronger. The 1988 constitution gave many oversight functions to the legislature and judiciary, so that much presidential discretion in economic and social policy is now subject to approval by either the legislature or the judiciary, or both. However, this power is not often employed effectively. Centralizing traditions are still strong in Brazil, making the obstacles to the deconcentration of executive power enormous (see Table 9.1).

## The Executive

A majority of delegates to the 1987 National Constituent Assembly that drafted the new democratic constitution favored the creation of a parliamentary system but a popular referendum in 1993 reaffirmed the existing presidential system. Even so, rules designed to rein in the federal executive found their way into the 1988 constitution. Partly in reaction to the extreme centralization of executive authority during military rule, the delegates restored some congressional prerogatives from before 1964, and they granted new ones, including oversight of economic policy and the right to be consulted on executive appointments. Executive decrees, which allowed the president to legislate directly, were replaced by "provisional measures" (also known as "emergency measures"). Provisional measures preserved the president's power to legislate for sixty days, at the end of which congress can pass, reject, or allow the provisional law to expire. Presidential power also met with a restriction on the power to reissue provisional measures, which both houses of Congress passed in 2001.

Despite these new constraints, Brazilian presidents were still able to use emergency measures with considerable success when the economy is in trouble. In crisis conditions, how could Congress deny the president the right to railroad through much-needed reform legislation? Worse still, the Supreme Tribunal, the highest court in Brazil, has done little to curb obvious abuses of constitutional authority by the president. The use of presidential discretionary power has only reinforced the powers of the executive to legislate.[16] The Brazilian president is elected for a four-year term with the opportunity to stand for re-election in a consecutive term. The major presidential candidates since the Cardoso presidency have tended to be prominent government ministers or governors from states such as São Paulo and Rio de Janeiro. These elites often capture party nominations with the organizations to which they are already affiliated, making national conventions nothing less than coronations. Political allies then shift resources to those candidates they believe will most likely win and shower patronage back at supporters once in government. Though there are parallels with the U.S. presidency, Brazilian presidents are institutionally empowered differently (see "The U.S. Connection: The Presidency").

Since the beginning of the military governments, the ministry of economy has had more authority than any other executive agency of the state. These powers

---

# U. S. CONNECTION

## The Presidency

Like the American president, the Brazilian president is the only executive elected by all eligible voters throughout the country. He or she is the figure that the voters most identify as the head of government. Yet the Brazilian presidency has powers that exceed those of the American president. Brazilian presidents legislate regularly. Over 85 percent of all bills before congress first emerged from the Palácio do Planalto, home of the president's offices in Brasília. The most important legislation is the annual budget, which is crafted by the chiefs of the economic bureaucracy and the presidency and then sent to congress. The Senate and the Chamber of Deputies may amend legislation, but that is usually done with an eye to what the president will accept. Like the American president, the Brazilian president maintains a pocket veto, but unlike most American presidents, also a line-item veto. Brazilian presidents may also impound approved funds, which makes legislators mindful of enacting policies in ways not favored by the president. Like American presidents, Brazilian presidents can enact legislation using executive orders. But "provisional measures," as they are called in Brazil, are employed more regularly and with less judicial oversight. Fernando Collor, for example, severely

abused these powers. In his first year in office, Collor handed down 150 emergency measures. Technically, this meant that the country experienced an "emergency" situation every forty-eight hours. Since 2001, congress has developed greater oversight on the president's ability to issue and reissue provisional measures.

Given the Brazilian state's extensive bureaucratic apparatus, the president has extensive powers of appointment. During the New Republic, presidents have had the power to appoint upwards of 48,000 civil servants, eight times more than the 6,000 appointed by American presidents. Of these, only ambassadors, high court justices, the solicitor general, and the president of the Central Bank are subject to Senate approval.

Similar to the American president, the Brazilian president is the commander-in-chief of the armed forces. In practice, however, the military branches have retained some prerogatives over internal promotion, judicial oversight, and the development of new weapons systems. Brazilian presidents since Collor have exerted their authority over the military, restricting the autonomy of the armed forces over some of these areas.

grew in response to the economic problems of the 1980s and 1990s. As a result of their control of the federal budget and the details of economic policy, recent ministers of the economy have had levels of authority typical of a prime minister in a parliamentary system.

## The Bureaucracy: State and Semipublic Firms

Bureaucratic agencies and public firms have played a key role in Brazilian economic and political development. After 1940, the state created a large number of new agencies and public enterprises. Many of these entities were allowed to accumulate their own debt and plan development projects without undue influence from central ministries or politicians. Public firms became a key part of the triple alliance of state, foreign, and domestic capital that governed the state-led model of development. By 1981, the federal government owned ten of the top twenty-five enterprises in Brazil, and state governments owned eight others. Public expenditures as a share of GDP increased from 16 percent in 1947 to more than 32 percent in 1969, far higher than in any other Latin American country except socialist Cuba.

Much of this spending (and the huge debt that financed it) was concentrated on development projects, many of gigantic proportions. Key examples include the world's largest hydroelectric plant, Itaipú; Petrobrás's petroleum processing centers; steel mills such as the gargantuan National Steel Company in Volta Redonda, Rio de Janeiro; and Vale do Rio Doce (today known only as Vale), which maintains interests in sectors as diverse as mining, transport, paper, and textiles. On the eve of the debt crisis in 1982, the top thirty-three projects accumulated U.S. $88 billion in external debt, employed 1.5 million people, and contributed $47 billion to the GDP.

Managing the planning and finance of these projects calls for enormous skill. Recruitment into the civil service requires passage of exams, with advanced degrees required of those who aspire to management positions in the more technical economic and engineering agencies. For example, the National Bank for Economic and Social Development (BNDES) remains the most important financier of development projects in Brazil. Founded in the early 1950s, the BNDES plays a key role in channeling public funds to industrial projects such as the automobile sector and domestic suppliers of parts and labor. The experience of the BNDES demonstrated that despite Brazil's clientelist legacies, the Brazilian bureaucracy could function effectively. Meritocratic advancement and professional recruitment granted these agencies some autonomy from political manipulation. They were considered islands of efficiency in a state apparatus that was characterized by patronage and corruption.[17] BNDES's technocracy took on larger responsibilities during the Cardoso and Lula presidencies. At present, the bank manages an array of investment and development projects that make it the largest development bank in the world; even larger than the World Bank.

The 1988 constitution did not alter significantly the concentration of power in the economic bureaucracy. In fact, the new constitution reinforced certain bureaucratic monopolies. For example, the state's exclusive control over petroleum, natural gas, exploration of minerals, nuclear energy, and telecommunications was protected constitutionally.

The writers of the new constitution did, however, place restraints on the activity of state-directed industries. State firms, for instance, could incur only limited amounts of debt. The constitution also imposed the requirement that Congress approve any new state enterprises proposed by the executive branch.

After his election in 1989, Fernando Collor began a sweeping reform of Brazil's public bureaucracy, beginning with the privatization of large public firms in steel, chemicals, and mining. In 1990, his government launched the National Destatization Program (*Programa Nacional de Destatização,* PND). Under the PND, public firms, amounting to a total value of $39 billion, were sold ($8.5 billion in the steel sector alone). The Cardoso administration went even further. It convinced Congress to amend the constitution to remove the public monopoly on petroleum refining, telecommunications, and infrastructure, making these sectors available for auction to private firms. In 1998, much of the public telecommunications sector was privatized, bringing in about $24 billion.

Paradoxically, the agency at the center of the privatization process in Brazil is the BNDES. Faced with the fiscal crisis of the 1980s, BNDES managers adopted a new perspective on the state's role in the economy. Instead of targeting industries and spending large sums to promote them, its new mission became providing financing to productivity-enhancing investments such as new technology and labor retraining.

## The Military and the Police

Like many other South American militaries, the Brazilian armed forces retain substantial independence from civilian presidents and legislators. Brazil has suffered numerous coups; those in 1930 and 1964 were critical junctures, while others brought in caretaker governments that eventually yielded to civilian rule. The generals continue to maintain influence in Brazilian politics, blocking policies they do not like and lobbying on behalf of those they favor.

The military's participation in Brazilian politics became more limited, if still quite expansive, following the transition to democracy. Several laws gave the military broad prerogatives to "guarantee internal order" and to play a "tutelary role" in civilian government. During the Sarney administration, members of the armed forces retained cabinet-level rank in areas of importance to the military, such as the ministries of the armed forces and the nuclear program. Most important, the military succeeded in securing amnesty for human rights abuses committed during the preceding authoritarian regime. In an effort to professionalize the armed forces, the Collor government slashed the military budget, thereby reducing the autonomy that the military enjoyed during the authoritarian period. Collor also replaced the top generals with officers who had few or no connections to the authoritarian regime and were committed to civilian leadership.

The military police are only nominally controlled by state governors; they are, in fact, trained, equipped, and managed by the armed forces, which also maintain a separate judicial system to try officers for wrongdoing. The state police consists of two forces: the civil police force, which acts as an investigative unit, and the uniformed military police force, which maintains order. The military police do not just regulate military personnel but civilians as well. They often partake in specialized commando-type operations in urban areas, especially in the *favelas*, and they engage in riot control.

During the 1990s, economic crisis and press coverage made urban crime one of the most important political issues facing the country. Perhaps the most telling indicator of the rising level of violence is the fact that more than fifty mayors were assassinated in Brazil between 1990 and 2000.

The specter of criminal violence has shocked Brazilians into voting for politicians who promise better police security. But Brazilians have learned that police forces themselves are often part of the problem. Despite official oversight of police authorities, in practice the military and civil police forces in many cities of the northeast, in São Paulo, and in Rio de Janeiro often act abusively. Cases of arbitrary detention, torture, corruption, and systematic killings by Brazilian police have received much international attention. Human rights investigations have found that off-duty police officers are regularly hired by merchants and assorted thugs to kill street urchins whom they accuse of theft. Human Rights Watch reported during the 1990s that at least 10 percent of the homicides in Rio de Janeiro and São Paulo were committed by the police.[18] The police are also targets of violence, as organized crime syndicates, especially in São Paulo, have become more brazen in their attacks on police installations.

The federal police force is a small unit of approximately 3,000 people. It operates like a combined U.S. Federal Bureau of Investigation, Secret Service, Drug Enforcement Agency, and Immigration and Naturalization Service. Despite its limited size, the federal police force has been at the center of every national investigation of corruption. Thanks to the federal police and the Public Ministry, the official federal prosecutor with offices in each of Brazil's states and the federal district, the federal government's capacity for investigation and law enforcement has expanded considerably.

# Other State Institutions

## The Judiciary

Brazil has a network of state courts, with jurisdiction over state matters, and a federal court system, not unlike the one in the United States, which maintains jurisdiction over federal crimes. A supreme court (the Supreme Federal Tribunal), similar in jurisdiction to the U.S. Supreme Court acts as the final arbiter of court cases. The Supreme Federal Tribunal's eleven justices are nominated by the president and confirmed by an absolute majority of the Senate. The Superior Court of Justice, with thirty-three sitting justices, operates beneath the Supreme Federal Tribunal as an appeals court. The Supreme Federal Tribunal decides constitutional questions. The military maintains its own court system.

The judiciary adjudicates political conflicts as well as civil and social conflicts. The Electoral Supreme Tribunal (*Tribunal Supremo Eleitoral,* TSE) has exclusive responsibility to organize and oversee all issues related to elections. The TSE has the power to investigate charges of political bias by public employees, file criminal charges against persons violating electoral laws, and validate electoral results. In addition to these constitutional provisions, the TSE monitors the legal compliance of electoral campaigns and executive neutrality in campaigns. Political candidates with pending charges are allowed to run for office, but they are prohibited from taking their elected seats if they do not resolve the charges. Dozens of "dirty record" (*ficha suja*) candidates have been impeded from office, reinforcing the power that the TSE and its regional electoral courts have to oversee all elections.

As in the rest of Latin America, penal codes established by legislation govern the powers of judges. This makes the judiciary less flexible than in North America, which operates on case law, but it provides a more effective barrier against judicial activism— the tendency of the courts to render broad interpretations of the law. The main problem in the Brazilian system has been the lack of judicial review. Lower courts do not have to follow the precedents of the STF or STJ, though that has been changing due to judicial reforms passed since 2004. The powers of the courts in Brazil continue to expand in ways that build up judicial review functions that were never established completely by the 1988 Constitution.

In recent years, the judiciary has been severely criticized for its perceived unresponsiveness to Brazil's social problems and persistent corruption in the lower courts.

In rural areas, impoverished defendants are often denied the right to a fair trial by powerful landowners, who have undue influence over judges and procedures. Courts have also refused to hear cases prosecuting those who organize child prostitution, pornography, and murder of street urchins.

Corruption in the judiciary is an important and high-profile issue. The federal police has initiated a number of investigations since 2003 to root out corrupt judges. Typically, these cases expose criminal rings that implicate state and federal judges, police officers, and other agents of the court system.

Restructuring the judiciary continues to receive attention. In December 2004, Congress passed a comprehensive reform meant to increase the capacity of the STF and STJ to set precedent and reduce the number of appeals. The reform established a National Judicial Council to regulate the lower courts, where judges are more tolerant of nepotism and conflict of interest. Some critics view these reforms as inadequate, on the grounds that the structure of the judiciary and its approach to interpreting and implementing laws are the central obstacles to accomplishing policy goals.

## Subnational Government

Like Germany, Mexico, India, and the United States, the Brazilian state has a federal structure. The country's twenty-six states are subdivided into 5,564 municipal governments. The structure of subnational politics in Brazil consists of a governor; his or her chief advisers, who also usually lead key secretariats such as economy and planning; and a unicameral legislature often dominated by the supporters of the governor. Governors serve four-year terms and are limited to two terms in office.

By controlling patronage through their powers of appointment and spending, governors and even some mayors can wield extraordinary influence.[19] The 1982 elections were the first time since the military regime when Brazilians could elect their governors directly. This lent legitimacy to the governors' campaign to decentralize fiscal resources. In recent years, attempts to mollify this subnational constituency have watered down key pieces of reform legislation. Political decentralization, which was accelerated with the constitution of 1988, has further fragmented the Brazilian polity. Nevertheless, some subnational governments have created innovative new policies.[20] The 1988 constitution gave the states and municipalities a larger share of tax revenues. At the same time, however, the governors and mayors deflected Brasília's attempts to devolve additional spending responsibilities to subnational government, particularly in the areas of health, education, and infrastructure. The governors also were able to protect state banks from a major overhaul. This reform was greatly needed, because these financial institutions continued to accumulate huge debts.

During the Collor administration, the federal government began to regain much of the fiscal authority it had lost to the states and municipalities. The Central Bank intervened in bankrupt state banks and privatized them. The federal government also refused to roll over state debt without a promise of reform, including the privatization of money-losing utility companies. The Cardoso administration required states and municipalities to finance a larger share of social spending, including education and health care.

Despite these efforts, Brazilian presidents must continue to negotiate the terms of reform with governors and Congress. Lula's reforms achieved only limited savings, however, because he had to concede shares of new taxes and yield control of some state revenues that might otherwise have been used to contain spending and reduce the mounting federal debt.

Most subnational politics are still preoccupied with distributing political favors in return for fiscal rewards, but certain governors and mayors have devised innovative solutions to social and economic problems. One study of the state of Ceará has demonstrated that even the most underdeveloped subnational governments can promote industrial investment, employment, and social services.[21] Mayors affiliated with Lula's PT have had much electoral success based on a solid record of effective local government.

# The Policy-Making Process

Although policy-making continues to be fluid and ambiguous, certain domains of policy are clearly demarcated. Foreign policy, for example, is exclusively the responsibility of the executive branch. Political parties and the Congress still have only inconsistent power over investment policies. Bureaucratic agencies retain command over the details of social and economic policies.

Clientelism injects itself at every stage of policymaking, from formulation and decision-making to implementation. Established personal contacts often shape who benefits from policy-making. Quid pro quos, nepotism, and other kinds of favoritism, if not outright corruption, regularly obstruct or distort policy-making.[22]

Complex formal and informal networks link the political executive, key agencies of the bureaucracy, and private interests. These networks are the chief players in clientelist circles. Cardoso described these clientelistic networks as **bureaucratic rings**. He considered the Brazilian state to be highly permeable, fragmented, and therefore easily colonized by private interests that make alliances with midlevel bureaucratic officers. By shaping public policy to benefit these interests, bureaucrats gain the promise of future employment in the private sector. Because they are entrenched and well connected, few policies can be implemented without the support of the most powerful bureaucratic rings.

One example of the role of bureaucratic rings is the creation of large development projects. Governors and mayors want lucrative public projects to be placed in their jurisdictions; private contractors yearn for the state's business; and politicians position themselves for all the attendant kickbacks, political and pecuniary.[23]

Among the key sources of influence outside the state is organized business. Unlike business associations in some Asian and West European countries, Brazilian business groups have remained independent of corporatist ties to the state. Business associations have also remained aloof from political parties. Lobbying by Brazilian entrepreneurs is common, and their participation in bureaucratic rings is legendary. Few major economic policies are passed without the input of the Federation of São Paulo Industries (*Federação das Industrias do Estado de São Paulo,* or FIESP).

The country's labor confederations and unions have had less consistent access to policymaking. Although unions were once directly organized and manipulated by the corporatist state, they gained autonomy in the late 1970s and the 1980s. From then on, they sought leverage over policymaking through outside channels, such as the link between the *Central Única dos Trabalhadores* (CUT, Workers' Singular Peak Association) and Lula da Silva's Workers' Party. Attempts to bring labor formally into direct negotiations with business and the state have failed. Widening cleavages within the Brazilian union movement tended to split sectors of organized labor, causing some segments to refuse to be bound by any agreement.

Debate and lobbying do not stop in Brazil once laws are enacted. Policy implementation is a subject of perpetual bargaining. The Brazilian way (*o jeito brasileiro*)

**bureaucratic rings**

A term developed by the Brazilian sociologist and president Fernando Henrique Cardoso that refers to the highly permeable and fragmented structure of the state bureaucracy that allows private interests to make alliances with midlevel bureaucratic officers. By shaping public policy to benefit these interests, bureaucrats gain the promise of future employment in the private sector. While in positions of responsibility, bureaucratic rings are ardent defenders of their own interests.

is to scoff at the law and find a way around it. Paradoxically, this can be the source of great efficiency in Brazilian society, for it enables policy to be implemented—but it carries a heavy price in that the rule of law is not respected.

### Summary

The Brazilian state is a mixture of professionalism and clientelism, and both of these dimensions have remained even as the country has democratized and developed. While regular citizens sometimes resort to *jeito* to get around rules and elites can regularly subvert the law, it is also true that Brazilian democracy has strengthened law enforcement. The prosecutorial, oversight and investigative functions of the state have become more adept at detecting corruption. But accountability requires that the guilty be punished and that the courts adjudicate more efficiently and without excusing lawbreaking by privileged groups.

## SECTION 4

# REPRESENTATION AND PARTICIPATION

### Focus Questions

In what ways do Brazilian political institutions impede representation and elite accountability?

How does the mobilization of civil society in Brazil enhance the country's democratic governance?

The fragmentation of legislative politics, the weaknesses of political parties, and the interests of particular politicians and their clientelistic allies make enacting reform on behalf of the national interest extremely difficult. Politicians and parties that can best dispense patronage and cultivate clientele networks are the most successful. More often than not, the main beneficiaries are a small number of elite economic and political interests who develop ongoing relationships with legislators, governors, and presidents.

The transition to democracy, however, coincided with an explosion of civil society activism and mobilization. The expansion of voting rights and the involvement of gender and ethnic groups, urban social movements, and environmental and religious organizations in Brazilian politics have greatly expanded the range of political participation. Just the same, political institutions have failed to harmonize the demands of conflicting forces.

## The Legislature

The 594-member national legislature has an upper house, the Senate, with 81 members, and a lower house, the Chamber of Deputies, with 513 members. Every state and the federal district elect three senators by simple majority. Senators serve for eight-year terms and may be reelected without limit. Two-thirds of the Senate is elected at one time, and the remaining one-third is elected four years later. Senatorial elections are held at the same time as those for the Chamber of Deputies, all of whose members are elected on a four-year cycle. Federal deputies may be reelected without limits. Each state is allowed a minimum of eight and a maximum of seventy deputies, according to population. This introduces severe malapportionment in the allocation of seats. Without the ceiling and floor on seats, states with large populations, such as São Paulo, would have more than seventy deputies, and states in the underpopulated Amazon, such as Roraima, would have fewer than eight.

The two houses of the legislature share equal authority to make laws, and both must approve a bill for it to become law. Each chamber can propose or veto legislation passed by the other. When the two chambers pass bills on a given topic that contain different provisions, they go back and forth between houses without going through a joint conference committee, as in the United States. Once a bill is passed by both houses in identical form, the president may sign it into law, reject it as a whole, or accept some and reject other parts of it. The legislature can override a presidential veto by a majority vote in both houses during a joint session, but such instances are rare. Constitutional amendments must be passed twice by three-fifths of the votes in each house of congress. Amendments may also be passed by an absolute majority in a special constituent assembly proposed by the president and created by both houses of congress. The Senate is empowered to try the president and other top officials, including the vice president and key ministers and justices, for impeachable offenses. It also approves the president's nominees to high offices, including justices of the high courts, heads of diplomatic missions, and directors of the Central Bank.

Complex constitutional rules for determining representation in the legislature favor sparsely populated states. Because these states are the most numerous in the federal system, voters from small states tend to be greatly overrepresented in the legislature. A vote in some states counts 33 times more than a vote in São Paulo! The least-populated states are also the poorest and most rural. Typically, they have been political bases for conservative landowning interests and, more recently, agribusiness. These traditions have continued into the democratic period and largely explain why conservative landowners and agribusiness elites maintain positions of great influence in the Brazilian Congress.

Legislators view their service primarily as a means to enhance their own income, thanks to generous public pensions and kickbacks earned from dispensing political favors. Election to the federal legislature is often used as a stepping stone to even more lucrative, especially executive, posts. After the presidency, the most coveted positions are the governorships of industrialized states. Appointment to head the premier ministries and state firms also ranks high. Most members of Congress come from the middle or upper-middle classes; most of these have much to gain if they can step into well-paid posts in the executive and the para-statal enterprises following their congressional service. A mere 3 percent of seats in Congress are held by Afro-Brazilians. Only 9 percent of the seats in the Chamber and 14 percent of those in the Senate are held by women.

The Congress has largely failed to use the expanded powers that it was granted by the 1988 constitution. Lack of a quorum to vote is a frequent problem, and Congress's recently acquired powers have increased legislators' opportunities to practice corruption and backroom dealing. The many deficiencies of the Brazilian legislature were highlighted in recent years by several corruption scandals. Vote buying in the Congress by the Lula government is the most prominent example, but kickbacks from public contracts are even more common. With the matter of corruption very much in the news cycle in Brazil, Congress is often criticized for its lack of accountability. One response to legislative corruption has been to use parliamentary commissions of inquiry to review allegations of malfeasance by elected officials. Although these temporary committees have demonstrated some influence, they have rarely produced results. The temporary committees work alongside sixteen permanent legislative committees that treat issues as diverse as taxation and human rights. These committees, however, are not nearly as strong as the major committees in the U.S. Congress. Legislative committees, both temporary and permanent, often fail to conclude an investigation or find solutions to persistent dilemmas in policy.

# Political Parties and the Party System

Party names, affiliations, and the structure of party alliances are constantly in flux. Like many of the country's current problems, party instability stretches back to the New State of Getúlio Vargas and the centralization of politics in the Brazilian state. State corporatism and populism were hostile to the development of independent party organizations. Populist redistribution reinforced these tendencies, as workers and the middle class became accustomed to asking what they would receive from a politician in return for support.

Many of the traditional weaknesses of the party system were reinforced after the transition to democracy, making parties even more anemic. Politicians switched parties nearly at will to increase their access to patronage, sometimes during their terms in office. A Supreme Court decision in 2007 ruled against this practice but allowed switching prior to elections. Other rules of the electoral system create incentives for politicians to ignore party labels. Brazil's experience with **proportional representation (PR)**, which is used to elect federal and state deputies, is particularly important in this regard. Proportional representation may be based on either a closed-list or an open-list system. In a closed-list PR, the party selects the order of politicians, and voters cannot cross party lines. Because voters are effectively choosing the party that best represents them, this system encourages party loyalty among both the electorate and individual politicians. In an open-list PR system, the voters have more discretion and can cross party lines. Brazil's PR system is open-list. On electronic voting machines, voters cast their ballots for individuals not parties by punching in the candidate's electoral number. The geographic boundaries of electoral districts in Brazil for state and federal deputies are entire states. There are few limits on how many individuals and parties may run in the same electoral district. Crowded fields discourage party loyalty and emphasize the personal qualities of candidates, who must stand out in the minds of voters. Worse still, the open-list PR system creates incentives for politicians to ignore party labels, because voters can cross party lines with ease.

Open-list proportional representation explains why there are so many parties in Brazil. With so much emphasis on the personal qualities of politicians, ambitious individuals can ignore the established party hierarchies while achieving elected office. As a result, Brazil has the most fragmented party system in Latin America and one of the most fragmented in the world. This makes parties extremely poor vehicles for representing political alternatives. Brazil's electoral system further fragments power because state, not national, parties select legislative candidates. In most cases, Brazilian governors exert tremendous influence over nominations. This further weakens national party leaders, who remain beholden to governors who can reward them with supportive nominees or rivals.

Brazil's mix of presidentialism and multiparty democracy creates other problems. Given the political fragmentation of the legislature and the weakness of the party system, presidents cannot maintain majority alliances in Congress, a requirement for stability. In parliamentary systems, the governing party typically has an absolute majority or heads an alliance of parties that compose a majority. The ruling party or alliance can then implement its program by sponsoring legislation. By contrast, Brazilian presidents have often attempted to govern above parties, dispensing favors to key congressional politicians to get legislation approved. Alternatively, presidents have often railroaded reform through Congress by using their discretionary authorities.

**proportional representation (PR)**

A system of political representation in which seats are allocated to parties within multimember constituencies, roughly in proportion to the votes each party receives. PR usually encourages the election to parliament of more political parties than single-member-district winner-take-all systems.

Within Brazil's confusing party system, a number of political organizations have emerged over the last few years. These parties can be defined ideologically, although the categories are not as internally consistent or cut and dry as they might seem (see Table 9.5).

Political parties on the right currently defend neoliberal economic policies designed to shrink the size of the public sector. They support the reduction and partial privatization of the welfare state. On constitutional reform, right-wing parties are fairly united in favor of rolling back social spending; they also advocate electoral reform—specifically, the establishment of a majority or mixed, rather than purely proportional, district voting system.

A loose set of conservative parties currently struggles for the mantle of the right. In front of the pack is the PFL (Party of the Liberal Front), which was refounded in 2007 as the Democrats (DEM). PFL/DEM is one of the larger parties in the Senate and the Chamber and has generally opposed President Lula. Many small parties have allied with right-wing and center-right parties or advocated right-wing issues,

| Table 9.5 | The Democratic Idea: The Major Parties in Brazil |
|---|---|
| **Conservative/Right-Wing Parties** | |
| PFL/DEM | *Partido da Frente Liberal* (Party of the Liberal Front) (refounded as the *Democratas* (Democrats) in 2007) |
| PL/PR | *Partido Liberal (Liberal Party)* (refounded as the Party of the Republic in 2007) |
| PP | *Partido Progressista* (Progressive Party) |
| **Centrist Parties** | |
| PMDB | *Partido do Movimento Democrático Brasileiro* (Party of the Brazilian Democratic Movement) |
| PSDB | *Partido da Social Democracia Brasileira* (Party of Brazilian Social Democracy) |
| **Populist/Leftist Parties** | |
| PT | *Partido dos Trabalhadores* (Workers' Party) |
| PSB | *Partido Socialista Brasileiro* (Brazilian Socialist Party) |
| PCdoB | *Partido Comunista do Brasil* (Communist Party of Brazil) |
| PDT | *Partido Democrático Trabalhista* (Democratic Labor Party) |
| PPS | *Partido Popular Socialista (ex-Partido Comunista Brasileiro)* (Popular Socialist Party) |

Luiz Inácio "Lula" da Silva, founder of the Workers' Party and Brazilian president (2002–2006.)

*Source:* © *Jornal do Brasil,* August 19, 1998.

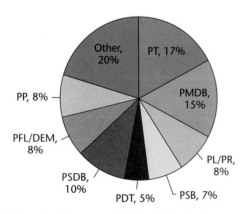

**FIGURE 9.4 Share of Seats of the Major Parties in the Chamber of Deputies, Based on October 2010 Election Results**.

*Source:* Data from final TSE numbers.

such as the Brazilian Labor Party (PTB), the Progressive Party (PP), and the evangelistic Liberal Party/Party of the Republic (PL/PR).

The two other largest parties in congress are the PMDB (Party of the Brazilian Democratic Movement, the successor to the old MDB) and the PSDB. These parties, while having disparate leftist and rightist elements, tend to dominate the center and center-left segments of the ideological spectrum. Along with the PFL/DEM, these have been the key governing parties during the democratic era. There is agreement that these parties have become more cohesive in favor of neoliberal reform, and hence they can be characterized as being on the right or center-right.[24]

Political parties on the left advocate reducing deficits and inflation but also maintaining the present size of the public sector and improving the welfare state. Left-oriented parties want to expand the state's role in promoting and protecting domestic industry. On constitutional reform, they support the social rights guaranteed by the 1988 constitution.

The Workers' Party (PT) has been the most successful of the leftist parties, having elected Luiz Inácio "Lula" da Silva twice to the presidency. The PT was founded by workers who had defied the military government and engaged in strikes in São Paulo's metalworking and automobile industries in 1978 and 1979. Although the PT began with a working-class message and leftist platform, its identity broadened and moderated during the 1980s and early 1990s. Under Lula's leadership the party increasingly sought the support of the middle class, rural and urban poor, and even segments of business and the upper classes. In the years preceding Lula's presidency, the party moderated its criticism of capitalism, ultimately accepting many of the economic reforms that Cardoso implemented. During Lula's presidency, the PT moved further to the center, leaving its left-most flank exposed in elections. Former PT member Marina Silva's third-place showing in the 2010 presidential race is probably a result of allowing leftist candidates to capture the support of voters displeased with the increasing conservatism of the mainstream PT.

Although the PT has occupied much of the left's political space, other leftist parties have gained some notable support in the New Republic. The Democratic Labor Party (PDT), a populist organization, advocates Vargas-era nationalism and state-led development. The PPS was once led by Ciro Gomes, a former finance minister (under Itamar Franco) and former governor of Ceará. In 2003, Lula appointed him minister of national integration, a position that the president hoped would keep Gomes's party on the government's side in congress. When the PPS left the government in 2004, Gomes remained in his cabinet post, and switched to the PSB.

Currently, no party has more than 25 percent of the seats in either house of Congress (see Figures 9.4 and 9.5). Cardoso's multiparty alliance of the PSDB-PFL-PTB-PPB controlled 57 percent of the vote in the lower house and 48 percent in the upper house. Lula failed to organize a similar "governing coalition"; his government depended on enticing centrist and center-right parties to vote for his legislation. His successor, Dilma Rousseff, enjoys a larger support base in Congress than Lula or even Cardoso, given the erosion of conservative parties' seat shares. Although party switching has now been limited by law, party merging and routine clientelism still make the loyalty of so-called pro-government parties remarkably soft. This situation has reinforced the executive's claim to be the only source of political order in the Brazilian democratic system.

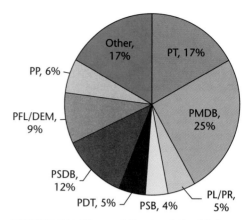

**FIGURE 9.5 Share of Seats of the Major Parties in the Senate, Based on October 2010 Election Results**

*Source:* Data from final TSE numbers.

# Elections

Because of urbanization and economic modernization, the Brazilian electorate grew impressively after 1945. Improved literacy and efforts by political parties to expand voter registration increased the number of citizens eligible to vote. A literacy requirement was eliminated in 1985, the voting age was reduced from eighteen to sixteen in 1988, and voting was made compulsory, except for illiterates and citizens over seventy.

With the return to democracy in the 1980s, newly independent labor unions and special-interest organizations emerged, making new alliances in civil society possible. Mass appeal became an important element in campaigns and political alliances. Nevertheless, the richness of political organization was restrained by the legacies of state-centered structures of social control.

Contests for public office in Brazil are dominated by the rules of proportional representation (PR), which, as was discussed above, distort democratic representation. In addition to its effects on the party system, open-list PR weakens the incentives for politicians to listen to the electorate. Given the multiplicity of parties, unbalanced apportionment of seats among the states, and the sheer size of some state-sized electoral districts, candidates often have few incentives to be accountable to their constituencies. In states with hundreds of candidates running in oversized electoral districts, the votes obtained by successful candidates are often widely scattered, limiting the accountability of those elected. In less-populated states, there are more seats and parties per voter; and the electoral and party quotients are lower. As a result, candidates often alter their legal place of residence immediately before an election in order to run from a safer seat, compounding the lack of accountability.

With the *abertura,* political parties gained the right to broadcast electoral propaganda on radio and television. All radio stations and TV channels are required to carry, at no charge, two hours of party programming each day during a campaign season. The parties are entitled to an amount of time on the air proportional to their number of votes in the previous election.

The 1989 presidential election gave Brazilians their first opportunity to elect the president directly. Collor's (PRN) election became an important precedent that further strengthened Brazilian democracy. Ironically, his impeachment two years later also promoted democracy because it reinforced the rule of law and enhanced the oversight functions of the Congress. Fernando Henrique Cardoso's election in 1994 and reelection in 1998 reinforced the 1989 precedent of direct elections for the presidency.

Although most Brazilians are suspicious of authoritarianism and oppose the return of the military or any other form of dictatorship, they seem disappointed with the results of democracy. The weakness of political parties, coupled with the persistence of clientelism and accusations of corruption against even previously squeaky clean parties such as the PT, have disillusioned average Brazilians.

## Political Culture, Citizenship, and Identity

The notion of national identity describes a sense of national community that goes beyond mere allegiance to a state, a set of economic interests, regional loyalties, or kinship affiliations. A national identity gains strength through a process of nation building during which a set of national symbols, cultural terms and images, and shared myths consolidate around historical experiences that define the loyalties of a group of people.

Several developments made Brazilian nation building possible. Unlike nation formation in culturally, linguistically, and geographically diverse Western Europe, Africa, and Asia, Brazil enjoyed a homogeneous linguistic and colonial experience. As a result, Brazilian history largely avoided the ethnic conflicts that have become obstacles to nation building in Eastern Europe, Nigeria, and India. Immigrants added their ideas and value systems at the turn of the century, but they brought no compelling identities that could substitute for an overarching national consciousness. Regional secessionist movements were uncommon in Brazilian history and were short-lived episodes when they did emerge in the twentieth century.

Despite Brazil's rich ethnic makeup, racial identities in Brazil have seldom been the basis for political action. Brazilians often agreed on the spurious idea that Brazil was a racial democracy. Even in the face of severe economic and political oppression of native peoples, Afro-Brazilians, and Asians, the myth of racial democracy has endured in the national consciousness. It is sustained by a strong sense of national identity and nationalism that opposes the idea that there are multiple experiences for Brazilians beyond the obvious ones regarding class differences.

Like the myth of racial democracy, the major collective political identities in Brazilian history have sought to hide or deny the real conflicts in society. For example, the symbols and images of political nationalism tended to boost the quasi-utopian visions of the country's future development. Developmentalists under the military governments and democratic leaders such as Kubitschek espoused optimism that "Brazil is the country of the future." (More cynical Brazilians quipped afterwards that Brazil is the country of the future, and will always be.)

And as with racial identities, socioeconomic realities belie the widely perceived view that women have equal citizenship with men. Brazilian women make only 70 percent of what men make, and black women do even worse at 40 percent. In rural areas, women are substantially disadvantaged in the granting of land titles. Female heads of families are routinely passed over by official agencies distributing land titles to favor oldest sons, even when these are minors. Thirty-four percent of illiterate women earn the minimum wage or less, versus 5 percent of illiterate males. Despite women's improved economic, social, and political importance, progress on women's issues is slow.

The persistence of optimistic myths about the country in the face of socioeconomic and political realities often leads to angry disengagement from politics. Pervasive corporatism and populism in twentieth-century Brazilian politics, and the current crisis in these forms of mobilizing popular support, have limited Brazilians' avenues for

Carnival in Brazil, the world's largest floor show, is also an insightful exhibition of allegories and popular myths about the country, its people, and their culture.
*Source:* Bettman/Corbis.

becoming more involved in politics. Also, an underfunded primary and secondary educational system and a largely uncritical media leave most Brazilians without the resources to become more politically aware. Maintaining continuous political identities is made difficult by the frenetic nature of political change that has characterized much of the New Republic period.

One of the key outcomes of the sense of powerlessness the majority of Brazilians retain is the belief that the state should organize society. The primacy of the state manifests itself in Brazilian political culture in the notion that the state has a duty to provide for its citizens' welfare. These ideas are not just imposed on Brazilians by savvy politicians; they reflect a consensus that is the product of many decades of social and political conflict.

The political sentiments of Brazilian society are actually quite static because most Brazilians feel powerless to change their fates. Brazilians have always considered liberal democratic institutions, particularly individual rights, as artificial or irrelevant. Since the end of the nineteenth century, Brazilians have made a distinction between the "legal" Brazil—that is, the formal laws of the country—and the "real" Brazil— what actually occurs. Brazilian intellectuals developed the phrase *para ingles ver* ("for the English to see") to describe the notion that liberal democracy had been implanted to impress foreign observers, hiding the fact that real politics would be conducted behind the scenes. As Brazil struggles to balance the interests of foreign investors with those of its own people, many Brazilians continue to believe that much of the politics they observe is really "for the English to see."

During the redemocratization process, new trends in Brazilian political culture emerged. Most segments of Brazilian society came to embrace "modernization with democracy," even if they would later raise doubts about its benefits. One prominent example is the role played by the Catholic Church in promoting democracy. During the transition, a number of Catholic political organizations and movements aided by the church organized popular opposition to the military governments. After the transition, archbishops of the Catholic Church helped assemble testimonials of torture victims. The publication of these depositions in the book *Nunca Mais* (*Never Again*) fueled condemnation of the authoritarian past. In this way, an establishment that previously had been associated with social conservatism and political oppression became a catalyst of popular opposition to authoritarianism. Another trend that developed during and after the transition to democracy was the growth of a profound distrust of the state. Business groups assailed the failures of state-led development, while labor unions claimed that corporatist management of industrial relations could not satisfy the interests of workers. As a result, Brazilians became increasingly receptive to fringe voices that promised to eradicate the previous economic-political order. By ceding their authority to untested figures, Brazilians sometimes fail one of the most important tests of democracy: ensuring that elected officials will be accountable to the electorate.

Soon after the transition to democracy, many journalists, economists, politicians, intellectuals, and entrepreneurs began to embrace the notion that national institutions could be adjusted incrementally to strengthen democracy and promote economic growth. Constitutional, administrative, and economic reform became priorities of politicians such as Fernando Henrique Cardoso.

Cardoso delivered in 1994 when his Real Plan reduced inflation and increased the buying power of most Brazilians. That success gave him the popular support he needed to become president and launch an array of institutional reforms. In 1998, facing another presidential contest and with his reforms stuck in Congress, Cardoso barely outcompeted Lula. When Lula's turn came to occupy the presidential office, he managed to end his presidency with much higher approval ratings than any of his predecessors. Such support came largely from popular social policies such as the Bolsa Família. Lula's success then led voters to elect his hand-picked successor, Dilma Rousseff, in 2010. One hopeful lesson from this is that more than Lula's personal charisma was at play in Dilma's election. The policies of Lula's government probably contributed to the 2010 election results. The challenge of selling a complex set of policies to a population with weak political socialization and poor general education has become central to gaining and maintaining political power in Brazil. The Brazilian media are free to criticize the government, and most broadcast businesses are privately owned. Although the government has considerable influence over the resources necessary for media production and the advertising revenue from government campaigns, there is no overt government censorship, and freedom of the press is widely and constitutionally proclaimed. The largest media organizations are owned by several conglomerates. The Globo network is Brazil's preeminent media empire and one of the five largest television networks in the world. Conglomerates like Globo play favorites, and, in return, they expect licensing concessions and other favors from their political friends.

Unlike the situation in the United States, the events of 9/11 did not fundamentally change Brazilian political culture or increase the nation's sense of vulnerability. Having suffered the military regime's torture and arbitrary killings—a kind of state terrorism—in their own country, Brazilians are well aware that democracy and decency have enemies capable of the greatest cruelty. Many Brazilians also live with everyday terrors—poverty, hunger, disease, and violence—that they regard as far more dangerous than terrorism.

# Interests, Social Movements, and Protest

Despite the growing disengagement of most Brazilians from politics and the country's legacy of state corporatism, autonomous collective interests have been able to heavily influence the political landscape. The role of business lobbies, rural protest movements, and labor unions, particularly those linked to the Workers' Party, are all examples of how Brazilian civil society has been partially able to overcome the vise of state corporatism and social control.

After the profound liberalizing changes in Catholic doctrine following the Second Vatican Council in the early 1960s, the church in Brazil became more active in advocating social and political reform. The Brazilian church, through the National Conference of Brazilian Bishops (CNBB), produced an array of projects to improve literacy, stimulate political awareness, and improve the working and living conditions of the poor.

One well-known outcome of these changes was the development of liberation theology, a doctrine that argued that religion should seek to free people not only from their sins but from social injustice. By organizing community-based movements to press for improved sanitation, clean water, basic education, and, most important, freedom from oppression, Catholic groups mobilized millions of citizens. Among the Brazilian church's most notable accomplishments was the development of an agrarian reform council in the 1970s, the Pastoral Land Commission. The commission called for extending land ownership to poor peasants. The Brazilian church also created ecclesiastical community movements to improve conditions in the *favelas*.

In the mid-1970s, Brazil witnessed an explosion of social and political organization: grass-roots popular movements; new forms of trade unionism; neighborhood movements; professional associations of doctors, lawyers, and journalists; entrepreneurial associations; and middle-class organizations. At the same time, a host of nongovernmental organizations (NGOs) became more active in Brazil; among them were Amnesty International, Greenpeace, and native Brazilian rights groups. Domestic groups active in these areas increasingly turned to the NGOs for resources and information, adding an international dimension to what was previously an issue of domestic politics.

By the 1980s, women were participating in and leading popular initiatives on a wide variety of issues related to employment and the provision of basic services. Many of these organizations enlisted the support of political parties and trade unions in battles over women's wages, birth control, rape, and violence in the home. Although nearly absent in employers' organizations, women are highly active in rural and urban unions. In recent years, Brazilian women have created more than 3,000 organizations to address issues of concern to women. A good example are special police stations (*delegacias de defesa da mulher*, DDMs) dedicated to addressing crimes against women. The DDMs have been created in major Brazilian cities, and particularly in São Paulo.

Women's groups have been given a boost as more women have joined the work force. More than 20 percent of Brazilian families are supported exclusively by women. Social policies such as Bolsa Família reinforce the importance of women in society by focusing their resources on women as the heads of households.

Women have also made strides in representative politics and key administrative appointments. Ellen Gracie Northfleet became the first woman to head the Supreme Court; Lula appointed a second woman to the court in 2006. A woman was also named to the board of directors of the Central Bank. Women in formal politics have in recent years become mayors of some major cities, such as São Paulo. Although in recent years, the number of women with seats in congress has nearly doubled, the rate remains one of the lowest in Latin America.

In contrast to the progress of women's movements, a movement to address racial discrimination has not emerged. Only during the 1940s did some public officials and academics acknowledge that prejudice existed against blacks. At that time, the problems of race were equated with the problems of class. Attacking class inequality was thus considered a way to address prejudice against blacks. This belief seemed plausible because most poor Brazilians are either *pardo* (mulatto) or black. But it might be just as logical to suggest that they are poor because they are black. In any case, the relationship between race and class in Brazil is just as ambiguous as it is in the United States and other multiethnic societies.

Some analysts believe that a gradual and peaceful evolution of race relations is possible. Others argue that as a consequence of white domination, blacks lack the collective identity and political organization necessary to put race relations on the political agenda. Both sides seem to agree, however, that although poverty and color are significantly correlated, overt confrontation among races is uncommon.

Over the past half-century, large-scale and poorly regulated economic development of the Amazon has threatened the cultures and lives of Indians. Miners, loggers, and land developers typically invade native lands, often with destructive consequences for the ecology and indigenous people. For example, members of the Ianomami, a tribe living in a reserve with rich mineral resources, are frequently murdered by miners. During the military government, the national Indian agency, FUNAI, turned a blind eye to such abuses, claiming that indigenous cultures represented "ethnic cysts to be excised from the body politic."[25] With the *abertura*, many environmental NGOs defended the human rights of indigenous people as part of their campaign to defend the Amazon and its people. The end of military rule and the economic crisis of the 1980s slowed exploitation of the Amazon.

The 1988 constitution recognized the rights of indigenous peoples for the first time and created large reserves for tribes like the Ianomami. But President Cardoso, under pressure by landowning conservative allies from the northeast, implemented a policy to allow private interests to develop over half of all indigenous lands. Allied against these interests are members of the Workers' Party, a coalition of indigenous groups known as COIAB, and church-based missionary organizations. The Kayapó tribe and their resistance to large-scale development projects in the Amazon are a key example of how environmental, labor, and indigenous issues are melding together to form a powerful grassroots campaign. Their struggle continues, but without more federal protection, Amazonian Indians will continue to be threatened. The sprouting of movements, associations, and interest groups may seem impressive, but they represent specific constituencies. Most Brazilians are not interested in participating in parties, movements, and unions, in part because government does not provide them with such basic services as security, justice, education, and health care. When confronted with immediate deprivations, many Brazilians avoid organized and peaceful political action, and often take to the streets in sporadic riots. Such events suggest that many Brazilians believe that the only responses in the face of unresponsive political and state organizations are violent protest or passivity.

## Summary

The Brazilian political system suffers from weak partisan identities among voters, low discipline within political parties, and inconsistent relations between the presidency and Congress. The open-list PR electoral system makes these tendencies worse, and further confuses voters. At the same time, civil society remains actively engaged in politics, often in sustained and organized ways. The performance of the Lula government and the election of his hand-picked successor, Dilma Rousseff, who enjoys ample support in the Congress, suggests that Brazil may gain an opportunity to reform the political system.

# BRAZILIAN POLITICS IN TRANSITION

SECTION 5

## Political Challenges and Changing Agendas

The contrast between Lula's campaign to become president in 2002 and the Brazil led by Lula that captured the right to stage the 2014 World Cup and the 2016 Olympic Summer games, could not be more stark. In 2002, investment banks and even some policy-makers around the world worried out loud that a Lula presidency would reject capitalism and lead the country to default on its external debt. The giant Wall Street firm, Goldman Sachs, even published a "Lulameter" to inform clients about the probability of a Lula victory and, therefore, impending economic disaster in South America. We now know that those fears were misplaced. Not only did Lula continue Cardoso's market-oriented reforms, he expanded the social policies of his predecessor. High annual growth rates, rising median incomes, and a fall in poverty and inequality levels are Lula's legacy after eight years in office. Far from his being what one investment firm called "Da Lula Monster" of anticapitalism, Lula led Brazil through its most prosperous period since the days of Juscelino Kubitschek and the military's "miracle" economy. With the World Cup and Olympics within view, and sustained high growth rates for years, Brazil can even claim to be a rising world power on a par with China, India, and Russia.

As his successor, Dilma Rousseff, will be the chief beneficiary of Lula's legacy. Her election as Brazil's first woman president caps off perhaps the most meteoric of political careers, though one completely dependent on Lula. A former militant against the authoritarian regime, Dilma was jailed and tortured in 1970 and 1972. After finishing her degree in economics, she ventured again into politics during the New Republic but as an appointee in municipal and state government in Rio Grande do Sul and its capital, Porto Alegre. She joined the PT late in her career, in 2000, and was plucked from obscurity by Lula in 2002 to become his Minister of Energy. Following the departure of Lula's chief of staff due to corruption allegations in 2005, Dilma became the president's closest adviser. Having no real experience in elected office, Dilma ran and won the presidency in 2010.

The central challenge of her presidency will be the core weakness in the Brazilian political and economic system: the persistence of many of the old clientelist forms of doing politics and the lack of political reform. Like their predecessors, Lula and Dilma have had to curry center-right support by embracing the very mechanisms of clientelism that create a deadlock in the country's democratic institutions. Given a weak party system and constitutional requirements that all amendments must be passed twice by 60 percent majorities in both houses of congress, clientelism has become

**Focus Questions**

What are some of the legacies of the Lula presidency that may shape Dilma Rousseff's presidency?

Is Brazil prepared to be considered a global power?

the presidency's most powerful mechanism for cultivating support in order to piece together large, fractious majorities needed to pass reform bills.

These reforms have suffered the watering down effect that comes with making compromises to secure passage. Neither Cardoso nor Lula did much to strengthen the discipline of political parties or reduce the fragmentation of the legislature. Political reform must remain the top priority for the Dilma government if any headway is going to be made. The open-list electoral system should be replaced by a closed-list system to increase the internal discipline of parties. Public financing of campaigns should replace private spending, which reinforces the clientelist networks that too often interfere with the representative function. Lula was able to make many more poor Brazilians feel included in the economy, if not in the political system, and he did so without fundamentally threatening property holders and capitalists. The *Bolsa Família* has become a model for how to target social benefits to lift millions out of misery if not poverty. But moving more of these Brazilians into self-sustaining employment in the formal sector will require the creation of jobs. As long as the economy continues to grow under favorable international conditions for Brazil, Dilma may well enjoy the political room she will need to reduce chronic inequality further.

The social and ecological costs of the maldistribution of income and the abuse of natural resources will continue to limit Brazil's potential unless more aggressive action is taken. Another challenge involves balancing economic development and environmental concerns. The fact that many of Brazil's exports are still extractive (such as iron ore and lumber), or agricultural commodities, places ever more pressure on the country's ecology. Deforestation of the Amazon and international climate change are intricately linked. A key issue is whether Brazil can help preserve the rain forest and reduce its own production of greenhouse gases at the same time that it maintains a brisk rate of economic growth. Another question is what responsibilities Brazil will have in dealing with man-made causes of climate change in the future as it transitions to become a large, net oil exporter. Despite all of the attention that the Amazon's rain forest receives in the international media, in Brazil, "Amazonian defense"—the securing of the huge, jungle borders of Brazil's north from the encroachment of drug cartels and illegal miners—gets more attention than the "defense of the Amazon." The work of Brazilian and international NGOs in the Amazon is still relatively a recent—since the democratic transition—phenomenon, while development and security concerns are much older and run deeper in the national psyche.

Brazil may be moving into a new moment in its history where it can renew the grand visions of development sponsored by Vargas, Kubitschek, and the military governments. Sustained by large capital inflows, Lula's government was able to redirect substantially more resources to the National Development Bank. The BNDES is now the largest development bank in the world, and it handles a range of loan programs to finance everything from the biggest infrastructure projects to innovations by small firms. Brazil has not had access to international capital, the presence of more open and deregulated markets, and the capacity of the public sector to provide direction and finance in this way since the 1950s. Juscelino Kubitschek's mantra of "fifty years of development in five years" may become, with perhaps a less exaggerated timeframe, the label for this historic moment in Brazilian history.

In other ways, the central state has become a far more passive agent. Brazilian workers no longer negotiate labor issues with state mediation, as they still do in Germany. Instead, labor unions, when they are capable, negotiate directly with business.

In most cases the interests of business usually prevail. Urban workers receive little or no compensation from the state when they suffer layoffs or reductions in their salaries and workplace benefits. Most rural workers, the millions of workers in the informal sector, and minorities are in an even more precarious position. The weakness of the judiciary, human rights violations by police and security forces, and the tendency to vigilantism and class conflict in poor, rural areas reinforce the anemia of civil society.

In this context, Brazilian democracy has suffered greatly. The poor feel doubly divorced from politics, both socially and politically disenfranchised from a process they view as unresponsive to their needs. Over time, this sense of disengagement has turned into open doubt about the utility of democracy itself. The weakness of political party loyalties and well-documented instances of corruption involving organizations such as the PT suggest a lack of accountability. By contrast, stronger democracies, such as Germany, the United States, France, and Britain rely on well-defined rules that force political leaders to be accountable to other branches of government and to their own constituencies.

Brazil is one of the world's key platforms for agricultural production and manufacturing. It is a crucial supplier of raw materials to other countries, as well as a large market for multinational producers. It has advantages few other developing countries enjoy. Integration in the global economy, however, also means that Brazilian firms and workers (not to mention the public sector) must be able to adapt to greater competition from abroad and the needs of foreign capital. Given the pace of technological change, the pressures to train workers, boost productivity, and enhance research and development have grown tremendously. While Brazil is benefiting from an upsurge in demand for its natural resource exports, commodity booms do not tend to last. Gains from capital inflows must be put to work in the form of investment for the future in everything from road-building and port modernization to education.

As globalization and democratization have made Brazilian politics less predictable, older questions about what it means to be Brazilian have re-emerged. Brazil highlights the point made in the Introduction that political identities are often reshaped in changed circumstances. What it means to be Brazilian has become a more complex question. Democracy has given ordinary Brazilians more of a voice, but they have become active mostly on local issues, not at the national level. Women, nongovernmental organizations, Catholics, Pentecostals, blacks, landless peasants, and residents of *favelas* have all organized in recent years around social and cultural issues. On the one hand, these movements have placed additional pressure on an already weakened state to deliver goods and services. On the other hand, these groups have supplied alternatives to the state by providing their own systems of social services and cultural support. Because the domain of the state is constrained by the need to compete in the global economy, space is created for nonstate actors to provide goods and services that were previously produced by the state. How are all these disparate groups linked? Do they have a common, national interest?

One recent development involves the way that Brazilian elites see the role of their country in forging a counterweight to the hegemonic power of the United States. In Brazil's engagement with the United States in trade policy (in the FTAA and the WTO), as well as in security and other diplomatic relations, Lula's approach was summed up by his foreign minister, Celso Amorim, as "benign restraint." Following this policy, Brazil opposed the United States on issues such as the war in Iraq and American agricultural subsidies, but it cooperated with Washington in the war against terrorism and regional integration. Lula's government was committed to fighting terrorism but it was unwilling to ignore social justice or to bend to the security policies of the United States.

# Brazilian Politics in Comparative Perspective

The most important lesson that Brazil offers for the study of comparative politics is that fragmented polities threaten democracy, social development, and nation building. The Brazilian political order is fragmented on several levels. The central state is fragmented by conflicts between the executive and the legislature, divided alliances and self-interested politicians in Congress, decentralized government, and an indecisive judiciary with a complicated structure and an uncertain mission. Political parties are fragmented by clientelism and electoral rules that create incentives for politicians and voters to ignore party labels. Finally, civil society itself is fragmented into numerous, often conflictual, organizations, interest groups, professional associations, social movements, churches, and, most important, social classes and ethnic identities.

In some socioeconomically fragmented societies, such as the United States and India, institutions have been more successful in bridging the gap between individualistic pursuits and the demand of people for good government. Political parties, parliaments, and informal associations strengthen democracy in these countries. Where these institutions are faulty, as they are in Brazil, fragmentation exacerbates the weakness of the state and the society.

A weak state deepens the citizenry's sense that all politics is corrupt. Moreover, police brutality, human rights violations, judicial incompetence, and the unresponsiveness of bureaucratic agencies further discourage citizens from political participation. These problems reinforce the importance of creating systems of accountability. Unfortunately, the English word *accountability* has no counterpart in either Portuguese or Spanish. Given Brazil's (and Latin America's) long history of oligarchical rule and social exclusion, the notion of making elites accountable to the people is so alien that the languages of the region lack the required vocabulary. Systems of accountability must be built from the ground up; they must be nurtured in local government and in community organizations, and then in the governments of states and the central state. The judiciary, political parties, the media, and organizations of civil society must be able to play enforcement and watchdog roles. These are the building blocks of accountability that are the fulcrum of democracy.

Without a system of elite accountability, representation of the citizenry is impossible. In particular, the poor depend on elected officials to find solutions to their problems. Brazilian politicians have shown that through demagoguery and personalism, they can be elected. But being elected is not the same as representing a constituency. For this to occur, institutions must make political elites accountable to the people who elected them.

Lula's success in reducing hunger, poverty, and inequality—the most important goals of his presidency—produced a laudable record that strengthened democracy. *Bolsa Família* has not only made a substantial change in the lives of millions of poor Brazilians, it may even have begun to cut the ties of dependency, especially in the countryside, that make rural workers and their families dependent on landowners and local political barons. This might lead these people to vote without concern for what the erstwhile local *coroneis* prefer, an outcome that could change 500 years of Brazilian history.

Part of the problem is that sustaining even these successful reform efforts requires great political unity, but political fragmentation can have a virulent effect on a country's sense of national purpose. Collective identities, by definition, require mechanisms that forge mutual understandings among groups of people. Fractured societies turn to age-old ethnic identities that can produce destructive, internecine conflict, as the India–Pakistan and Nigerian experiences demonstrate. In Brazil, such extreme conflict has been avoided, but the divisive effects of a fragmented polity on collective identities are serious nonetheless. Divided by class, poor Brazilians continue to feel that politics holds no solutions for them, so they fail to mobilize for their rights. Blacks, women, and indigenous peoples share many interests. Yet few national organizations have been able to unite a coalition of interest groups to change destructive business practices. Finally, all Brazilians are harmed by the clearing of rainforests, pollution of rivers and lakes, and destruction of species; yet the major political parties and Congress seem incapable of addressing these issues.

Perhaps the most serious effect of political fragmentation on Brazil has involved the struggle to defend the country's interests in an increasingly competitive, global marketplace. While globalization forces all countries, and particularly developing countries, to adapt to new technology, ideas, and economic interests, it also provides states with the opportunity to attract investment. Given the weakness of the Brazilian state, the social dislocation produced by industrial restructuring (such as unemployment), and the current instability of the international investment climate, Brazil maintains only an ambiguous vision of its role in the global capitalist order. Although Brazilian business, some unions, and key political leaders speak of the need to defend Brazil's interests in the international political economy, the country has few coherent strategies. But dealing with these issues requires a consistent policy created by a political leadership with clear ideas about the interests of the country. In Brazil's fragmented polity, developing such strategies is difficult.

In the world since September 11, 2001, issues of security are outpacing matters of equity and development. Dilma's government has followed Lula's lead in its commitment to fighting terrorism at the same time that it has sought to pursue social justice and refused to bend to the security policies of the United States. Brazil's successful bids to host the World Cup and the Olympics are evidence that it does not seek to isolate itself from the world. If Brazil becomes an increasingly fair and just nation, it will prove to be influential simply through its example to other developing countries. Finally, Brazil's experience with economic restructuring and democratization will continue to influence other countries undergoing similar transformations in Latin America and elsewhere. As a large and resource-rich country, Brazil presents a useful case for comparison with other big developing countries such as Mexico, Russia, India, and China. Among the dimensions on which useful comparisons can be made are its evolving federal structure, as well as its efforts to manage its resources while dealing with environmental costs.

As a transitional democracy, Brazil can provide insights into governance systems. As a negative example, Brazil's ongoing experiment with presidentialism, multiparty democracy, and open-list PR may well confirm the superiority of alternative parliamentary systems in India and Germany or presidentialism in France and the United States. As a positive example, Brazil's ability to keep a diverse country united through trying economic times has much to teach Russia and Nigeria, since these countries too are weighed down by the dual challenges of economic reform and nation building.

Within Latin America, Brazil continues to consolidate its position as the preeminent economy of the region. Through MERCOSUL, Brazil exercises regional leadership on commercial questions, and with its continued dominance of the Amazon basin, the country commands the world's attention on environmental issues in the developing world. Brazil's experiences with balancing the exigencies of neoliberal economic adjustment with the sociopolitical realities of poverty will keep it at center stage.

Brazil may not be "the country of the future," but it is a country with a future. None of the problems of Brazilian politics and social development are immune to improvement. If political reform is consolidated in the next few years, the groundwork will have been laid for transforming Brazil into a country that deserves the respect of the world.

## Summary

Despite the persistence of institutional impediments to reform and more efficient democratic governance, Brazil is poised to make the most of its increasing prosperity to address erstwhile social problems and emerge on the global stage as a power to be respected. Much depends on the quality of the country's new leadership, which will work with Lula's legacy of good social and economic policy performance. To the extent that voters come to identify and reward good government, the incentives of Brazilian politics, which currently favor particular interests, will come to embrace the provision of good policies. The same expectations for the performance of political organizations can provide support for efforts under the Dilma Rousseff presidency for political reform.

## Key Terms

moderating power (*poder moderador*)
oligarchy
legitimacy
clientelism
politics of the governors
*interventores*
state corporatism
populism

nationalism
bureaucratic authoritarianism (BA) state-led development
*abertura*
personalist politicians
export-led growth
interventionist
import substitution industrialization (ISI)

state technocrats
developmentalism
para-statals
informal economy
*favelas*
bureaucratic rings
proportional representation (PR)

## Suggested Readings

Alvarez, Sonia. *Engendering Democracy in Brazil*. Princeton, NJ: Princeton University Press, 1990.

Ames, Barry. *The Deadlock of Democracy in Brazil: Interests, Identities, and Institutions in Comparative Politics*. Ann Arbor: University of Michigan Press, 2001.

Evans, Peter B. *Dependent Development: The Alliance of Multinational, State, and Local Capital in Brazil*. Princeton, NJ: Princeton University Press, 1979.

Furtado, Celso. *The Economic Growth of Brazil: A Survey from Colonial to Modern Times*. Berkeley: University of California Press, 1963.

Goldstein, Donna M. *Laughter Out of Place: Race, Class, Violence, and Sexuality in a Rio Shantytown*. Berkeley: University of California Press, 2003.

Hochstetler, Kathryn, and Margaret Keck. *Greening Brazil: Environmental Activism in State and Society*. Durham, NC: Duke University Press, 2007.

Hunter, Wendy. *The Transformation of the Workers' Party in Brazil, 1989–2009*. New York: Cambridge University Press, 2010.

Kingstone, Peter R., and Timothy J. Power, eds. *Democratic Brazil Revisited*. Pittsburgh: University of Pittsburgh Press, 2008.

Mainwaring, Scott. *Rethinking Party Systems in the Third Wave of Democratization: The Case of Brazil*. Stanford: Stanford University Press, 1999.

Matta, Roberto da. *Carnivals, Rogues, and Heroes: An Interpretation of the Brazilian Dilemma*. Notre Dame, IN: University of Notre Dame Press, 1991.

Samuels, David J. *Ambition, Federalism, and Legislative Politics in Brazil*. New York: Cambridge University Press, 2003.

Scheper-Hughes, Nancy. *Death without Weeping: The Violence of Everyday Life in Brazil*. Berkeley: University of California Press, 1992.

Schneider, Ben Ross. *Politics within the State: Elite Bureaucrats and Industrial Policy in Authoritarian Brazil*. Pittsburgh: University of Pittsburgh Press, 1991.

Sheriff, Robin E. *Dreaming Equality: Color, Race, and Racism in Urban Brazil*. New Brunswick: Rutgers University Press, 2001.

Skidmore, Thomas E. *Black into White: Race and Nationality in Brazilian Thought.* Durham, NC: Duke University Press, 1993.

———. *The Politics of Military Rule in Brazil, 1964–85.* New York: Oxford University Press, 1988.

Stepan, Alfred. *Rethinking Military Politics: Brazil and the Southern Cone.* Princeton, NJ: Princeton University Press, 1988.

———, ed. *Democratizing Brazil: Problems of Transition and Consolidation.* New York: Oxford University Press, 1989.

Tendler, Judith. *Good Government in the Tropics.* Baltimore: Johns Hopkins University Press, 1997.

Weyland, Kurt. *Democracy Without Equity: Failures of Reform in Brazil.* Pittsburgh: University of Pittsburgh Press, 1996.

## Suggested Websites

LANIC database, University of Texas—Austin, Brazil Resource page
**lanic.utexas.edu/la/brazil/.=**

YouTube, President Lula da Silva's 2007 address at Davos
**http://www.youtube.com/watch?v=RqsDMU3ASgo**

Electronic Voting Simulator by the Supreme Electoral Tribunal
**http://www.tse.gov.br/internet/eleicoes/urna_ eletronica/simulador_Votacao_2010/br.htm**

The U.S. Library of Congress Country Study Page for Brazil
**lcweb2.loc.gov/frd/cs/brtoc.html**

SciELO Brazil, Searchable Database of Full-Text Articles on Brazil
**www.scielo.br**

National Development Bank of Brazil, Searchable Database of Documents on Brazilian Economy and Development (many in English)
**http://www.bndes.gov.br/SiteBNDES/bndes/bndes_ en/**

# 10 Mexico

Merilee S. Grindle and Halbert M. Jones

AP Photo/Gregory Bull

**Official Name:** United Mexican States (Estados Unidos Mexicanos)

**Location:** Southern North America

**Capital City:** Mexico City

**Population (2010):** 112.5 million

**Size:** 1,972,550 sq. km.; slightly less than three times the size of Texas

**1810–1821**
War of independence from Spain

**1876–1911**
Dictatorship of Porfirio Diaz

**1917**
Mexican Constitution

**1934–1940**
Presidency of Lázaro Cárdenas; entrenchment of corporatist state

| 1500 | 1830 | 1860 | 1890 | 1920 | 1950 | 1980 |

**1521**
Spaniards led by Hernán Cortés capture the Aztec capital, initiating three centuries of colonial rule.

**1910–1920**
Mexican Revolution

**1929**
Plutarco Elías Calles founds PRI.

**1968**
Massacre of Tlaltelolco; an unknown number of protesting students killed

# SECTION 1

# THE MAKING OF THE MODERN MEXICAN STATE

## Politics in Action

### Focus Questions

In what ways have the critical junctures of Mexican history grown out of the country's relations with other countries, especially the United States?

How did the Revolution of 1910 shape Mexico's development? A century later, is the Revolution still relevant to Mexican politics today?

What were the bases of political stability in Mexico through most of the twentieth century? What factors contributed to Mexico's democratic transition at the end of the century?

How has recent drug-related violence in Mexico affected the country's politics?

On June 28, 2010, just days before state elections were due to be held in many parts of Mexico, gunmen intercepted and opened fire on the motorcade in which the leading candidate for the governorship of Tamaulipas was traveling, killing the candidate, Rodolfo Torre Cantú of the Institutional Revolutionary Party (PRI), and six of his aides. Though the motive behind the attack was unclear, the shocking incident took place in a state strategically located on the country's Gulf coast, south of the border with Texas, an area that has been wracked by violence between competing drug trafficking organizations and between those organizations and Mexican authorities, especially since President Felipe Calderón launched an effort to crack down on organized crime shortly after taking office in December 2006. The assassination was part of a wave of violence that is reckoned to have claimed some 35,000 lives in less than five years, and it raised fears that the fight against drug cartels could have a profoundly destabilizing effect on the nation's politics.

The bloodshed in Tamaulipas and elsewhere has been an alarming development in a country that had experienced decades of stability under PRI administrations during the second half of the twentieth century. Moreover, for a nation that optimistically embraced the transition to a more pluralistic, more democratic political system after an opposition victory in the 2000 presidential election brought an end to the PRI regime, the violence, political stalemate, and economic stagnation of recent years have been deeply discouraging. More than a decade after the fall of the PRI's "perfect dictatorship"—so-called because of its ability to perpetuate itself, generally without having to resort to overt repression—Mexico and its 112 million people are facing the challenges of institutional reform, economic development, and integration into complex global networks, even as they continue to adjust to new and evolving political realities.

**1982**
Market reformers come to power in PRI.

**1988**
Carolos Salinas is elected amid charges of fraud.

**1996**
Political parties agree on electoral reform.

**1997**
Opposition parties advance nationwide; PRI loses absolute majority in congress for first time in its history.

**2009**
PRI makes major gains in congressional elections as the country faces a wave of drug-related violence.

**1985**      **1990**      **1995**      **2000**      **2005**      **2010**

**1978–1982**
State-led development reaches peak with petroleum boom and bust.

**1989**
First governorship is won by an opposition party.

**1994**
NAFTA goes into effect; uprising in Chiapas; Colosio assassinated.

**2000**
PRI loses presidency; Vicente Fox of PAN becomes president, but without majority support in congress.

**2006**
Felipe Calderón Hinojosa of PAN is elected president; no party has a majority of seats in congress.

The results of the elections that followed Torre's assassination gave an indication of some of the ways in which the Mexican political landscape continues to shift. Voters in twelve of Mexico's thirty-one states went to the polls on July 4, 2010, to elect new governors (re-election is not permitted in the Mexican political system). In Tamaulipas, Egidio Torres Cantú took the place of his murdered brother on the ballot and became one of nine PRI candidates to win election, highlighting the continuing viability and nationwide presence of a party that many had dismissed as a discredited and spent political force after it lost the presidency in 2000. In three other states, however, coalitions of parties opposed to the PRI captured the governorship. These political alliances were remarkable in that they brought together the right-of-center National Action Party (PAN) and the left-of-center Party of the Democratic Revolution (PRD), which were bitter rivals during the 2006 presidential campaign. Indeed, the PRD's candidate that year, Andres Manuel López Obrador, refused to concede defeat to Felipe Calderón of the PAN, claiming that he had been the victim of electoral fraud and proclaiming himself the "legitimate" president of Mexico. The willingness of these two parties to cooperate in state elections in 2010, despite their ideological differences, reflected their shared fear of a comeback by the PRI. In the most closely watched contest of the day, the poor southern state of Oaxaca, which had been governed for decades by a ruthlessly effective PRI political machine, opted for the opposition candidate for the governorship by a narrow margin, giving the PAN and the PRD cause for celebration.

Perhaps the most remarkable aspect of the July 4 election results, however, was the fact that so many of both the PRI and the PAN-PRD victories represented a defeat for the incumbent party in states where elections were held that day. PRI candidates unseated one PRD and two PAN administrations, and all three PAN-PRD victories came in states governed by the PRI. These outcomes can be interpreted as a reflection of Mexicans' disillusionment with many of their leaders but also as an encouraging sign that voters in what was until recently an authoritarian state have come to see alternation in power and peaceful transitions between parties as a natural and desirable part of the political process. As Mexicans turn their attention to what is expected to be a fiercely contested presidential election in 2012, these democratic values will surely influence their choice of the candidate who is, in their view, best equipped to meet the daunting challenges that the country faces: restoring a sense of security in a society that has been scarred by violence, establishing the rule of law and combating impunity in a country whose police forces and criminal justice system are undergoing a difficult process of reform, reducing inequality in a nation that is home to both the world's richest man and to millions who live in extreme poverty, and creating jobs and opportunities in an economy that has found growing integration into global markets to be both a blessing and a curse.

# Geographic Setting

Mexico includes coastal plains, high plateaus, fertile valleys, rain forests, and deserts within an area slightly less than three times the size of Texas. Two imposing mountain ranges run the length of Mexico: the Sierra Madre Occidental to the west and the Sierra Madre Oriental to the east. Mexico's geography has made communication and transportation between regions difficult and infrastructure expensive. Mountainous terrain limits large-scale commercial agriculture to irrigated fields in the north, while the center and south produce a wide variety of crops on small farms. The country is rich in oil, silver, and other natural resources, but it has long struggled to manage those resources wisely. (See Figure 10.1 for the Mexican nation at a glance.)

Mexico is the second-largest nation in Latin America after Portuguese-speaking Brazil and the largest Spanish-speaking nation in the world. Sixty percent of the population is ***mestizo***, or people of mixed **Amerindian** and Spanish descent. About 30 percent of the population claims Amerindian descent, although only 6 percent

**mestizo**

A person of mixed white, indigenous (Amerindian), and sometimes African descent.

**Amerindian**

Original peoples of North and South America; indigenous people.

**Mexican Currency**
Peso ($)
International Designation: MXN
Exchange Rate (2010): US$1 = 12.69 MXN
100 Peso Note Design: Nezahualcoyotl (1402–1472), pre-Columbian ruler and poet

© PhotoSpin, Inc/Alamy

FIGURE 10.1 **The Mexican Nation at a Glance**

| Table 10.1 | Political Organization |
|---|---|
| **Political System** | Federal republic |
| **Regime History** | Current form of government since 1917 |
| **Administrative Structure** | Federal system with thirty-one states and a federal district (Mexico City) |
| **Executive** | President, elected by direct election with a six-year term of office; reelection not permitted |
| **Legislature** | Bicameral Congress. Senate (upper house) and Chamber of Deputies (lower house); elections held every three years. There are 128 senators, 3 from each of the thirty-one states, 3 from the federal (capital) district, and 32 elected nationally by proportional representation for six-year terms. The 500 members of the Chamber of Deputies are elected for three-year terms from 300 electoral districts, 300 by simple majority vote and 200 by proportional representation. |
| **Judiciary** | Independent federal and state court system headed by a Supreme Court with eleven justices appointed by the president and approved by the Senate. |
| **Party System** | Multiparty system. One-party dominant (Institutional Revolutionary Party) system from 1929 until 2000. Major parties: National Action Party, Institutional Revolutionary Party, and the Party of the Democratic Revolution. |

speaks an indigenous language rather than Spanish. The largest **indigenous groups** are the Maya in the south and the Náhuatl in the central regions, with well over 1 million members each. Although Mexicans pride themselves on their Amerindian heritage, issues of race and class divide society.

**indigenous groups**

Population of **Amerindian** heritage in Mexico.

Mexico became a largely urban country in the second half of the twentieth century. Mexico City, in fact, is one of the world's largest metropolitan areas, with about 20 million inhabitants. Migration both within and beyond Mexico's borders has become a major issue. Greater economic opportunities in the industrial cities of the north lead many men and women to seek work there in the *maquiladoras*, or assembly industries. Many job seekers continue on to the United States. On Mexico's southern border, many thousands of Central Americans look for better prospects in Mexico and beyond.

*maquiladoras*

Factories that produce goods for export, often located along the U.S.–Mexican border.

# Critical Junctures

## Independence and Instability (1810–1876)

After a small band of Spanish forces led by Hernán Cortés toppled the Aztec Empire in 1521, Spain ruled Mexico for three centuries. Colonial policy was designed to extract wealth from the territory, ensuring that economic benefits flowed to the mother country. The rulers of New Spain, as the colony was known, sought to

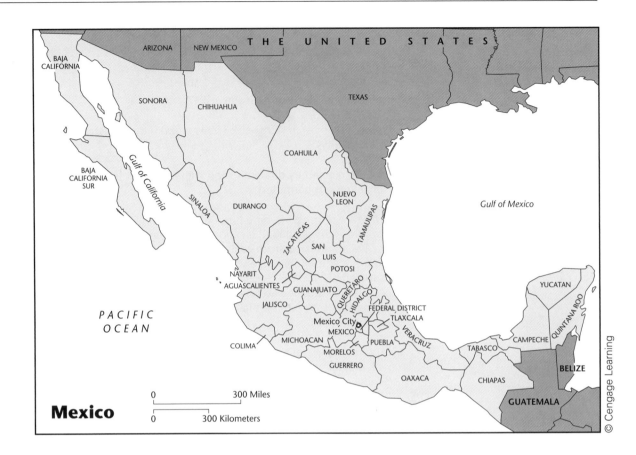

Mexico

maintain a commitment to the Roman Catholic religion and the subordination of the Amerindian population.

In 1810, a parish priest in central Mexico named Miguel Hidalgo began the first of a series of wars for independence. Although independence was gained in 1821, Mexico struggled to create a stable and legitimate government for decades afterward. Liberals and conservatives, monarchists and republicans, federalists and centralists, and those who sought to expand the power of the church and those who sought to curtail it were all engaged in the battle. Between 1833 and 1855, thirty-six presidential administrations came to power.

During the disorganized period after independence, Mexico lost half its territory. Central America (with the exception of what is today the Mexican state of Chiapas) rejected rule from Mexico City in 1823, and the northern territory of Texas won independence in a war ending in 1836. After Texas became a U.S. state in 1845, a border dispute led the United States to declare war on Mexico in 1846. U.S. forces invaded the port city of Veracruz, and with considerable loss of civilian lives, they marched toward Mexico City, where they fought the final battle of the war at Chapultepec Castle. An 1848 treaty recognized the loss of Texas and gave the United States title to what later became the states of New Mexico, Utah, Nevada, Arizona, California, and part of Colorado for about $18 million, leaving a legacy of deep resentment toward the United States.

After the war, liberals and conservatives continued their struggle over issues of political and economic order and, in particular, the power of the Catholic Church. The Constitution of 1857 incorporated many of the goals of the liberals, such as a somewhat democratic government, a bill of rights, and limitations on the power of the church. In 1861, Spain, Great Britain, and France occupied Veracruz to collect debts owed by Mexico. The French army continued on to Mexico City, where it subdued the weak government, and installed a European prince as the Emperor Maximilian (1864–1867). Conservatives welcomed this respite from liberal rule. Benito Juárez returned to the presidency in 1867 after defeating and executing Maximilian. Juárez is still hailed in Mexico today as an early proponent of more democratic government.

### The Porfiriato (1876–1911)

Over the next few years, a popular retired general named Porfirio Díaz became increasingly dissatisfied with what he thought was a "lot of politics" and "little action." After several failed attempts to win the presidency, he finally took the office in 1876. He established a dictatorship—known as the *Porfiriato*—that lasted thirty-four years and was at first welcomed by many because it brought sustained stability to the country.

Díaz imposed a highly centralized authoritarian system to create political order and economic progress. Over time, he relied increasingly on a small clique of advisers, known as *científicos* (scientists), who wanted to adopt European technologies and values to modernize the country. Díaz and the *científicos* encouraged foreign investment and amassed huge personal fortunes. During the *Porfiriato*, this small elite group monopolized political power and reserved lucrative economic investments for itself. Economic and political opportunities were closed off for new generations of middle- and upper-class Mexicans, who became increasingly resentful of the greed of the Porfirians and frustrated by their own lack of opportunities.

### The Revolution of 1910 and the Sonoran Dynasty (1910–1934)

The legacies of the distant past are still felt, but the most formative event in the country's modern history was the Revolution of 1910, which ended the *Porfiriato* and was the first great social revolution of the twentieth century. The revolution was fought

---

# GLOBAL CONNECTION

## Conquest or Encounter?

The year 1519, when the Spanish conqueror Hernán Cortés arrived on the shores of the Yucatán Peninsula, is often considered the starting point of Mexican political history. The land that was to become New Spain and then Mexico was home to extensive and complex indigenous civilizations that were advanced in agriculture, architecture, and political and economic organization. By 1519, diverse groups had fallen under the power of the militaristic Aztec Empire, which extended throughout what is today central and southern Mexico.

Cortés and the colonial masters who came after him subjected indigenous groups to forced labor; robbed them of gold, silver, and land; and introduced flora and fauna from Europe that destroyed long-existing aqueducts and irrigation systems. They also brought alien forms of property rights and authority relationships, a religion that viewed indigenous practices as the devil's work, and an economy based on mining and cattle—all of which soon overwhelmed existing structures of social and economic organization. Within a century, wars, savage exploitation at the hands of the Spaniards,

and the introduction of European diseases reduced the indigenous population from an estimated 25 million to 1 million or fewer. Even so, the Spanish never constituted more than a small percentage of the total population, and massive racial mixing among the Indians, Europeans, and to a lesser extent Africans produced a new *raza*, or *mestizo* race.

What does it mean to be Mexican? Is one the conquered or the conqueror? While celebrating Amerindian achievements in food, culture, the arts, and ancient civilization, middle-class Mexico has the contradictory sense that to be "Indian" nowadays is to be backward. But perhaps the situation is changing, with the upsurge of indigenous movements from both the grassroots and the international level striving to promote ethnic pride, defend rights, and foster the teaching of Indian languages.

The collision of two worlds still resonates. Is Mexico colonial or modern? Third or First World? Southern or Northern? Is the United States an ally or a conqueror? Many Mexicans at once welcome and fear full integration into the global economy, asking themselves: Is globalization a new form of conquest?

by a variety of forces for a variety of reasons, which made the consolidation of power that followed as significant as the revolution itself.

Díaz had promised an open election for president, and in 1910, Francisco I. Madero presented himself as a candidate. Madero and his reform-minded allies hoped that a new class of politically ambitious citizens would move into positions of power. When this opposition swelled, Díaz jailed Madero and tried to repress growing dissent. But the clamor for change forced Díaz into exile. Madero was elected in 1911, but he was soon using the military to put down revolts by reformers and reactionaries alike. When Madero was assassinated during a **coup d'état** in 1913, political order collapsed.

At the same time that middle-class reformers struggled to displace Díaz, a peasant revolt that focused on land claims erupted in the central and southern states of the country. This revolt had roots in legislation that made it easy for wealthy landowners and ranchers to claim the lands of peasant villagers. Villagers armed themselves and joined forces under a variety of local leaders. The most famous was Emiliano Zapata. His manifesto, the Plan de Ayala, became the cornerstone of the radical agrarian reform that became part of the Constitution of 1917.

In the north, Francisco (Pancho) Villa's forces combined military maneuvers with banditry, looting, and warlordism. In 1916, troops from the United States entered Mexico to punish Villa for an attack on U.S. territory. The presence of U.S. troops on Mexican soil resulted in increased public hostility toward the United States. Feelings against the United States were already running high because of the 1914 occupation of the city of Veracruz by American forces sent by President Woodrow Wilson in response to an incident involving the detention of several U.S. sailors by Mexican authorities.

**coup d'état**

A forceful, extra-constitutional action resulting in the removal of an existing government.

In 1914, Pancho Villa met with Emiliano Zapata in Mexico City to discuss the revolution and their separate goals for its outcome.

*Source:* http://www.russellmeansfreedom.com/tag/emiliano-zapata/.

© Underwood & Underwood/CORBIS

The Mexican Constitution of 1917 was forged out of the diverse and often conflicting interests of the various factions that arose during the 1910 Revolution. It established a formal set of political institutions and guaranteed citizens a range of progressive social and economic rights: agrarian reform, social security, the right to organize in unions, a minimum wage, an eight-hour workday, profit sharing for workers, universal secular education, and adult male suffrage. Despite these socially advanced provisions, the constitution did not provide suffrage for women, who had to wait until 1953 to vote in local elections and 1958 to vote in national elections. To limit the power of foreign investors, only Mexican citizens or the government could own land or rights to water and other natural resources. Numerous articles severely limited the power of the Roman Catholic Church, long a target of liberals who wanted Mexico to be a secular state. Despite such noble sentiments, violence continued as competing leaders sought to assert power and displace their rivals.

Power was gradually consolidated in the hands of a group of revolutionary leaders from the north of the country. Known as the Sonoran Dynasty, after their home state of Sonora, these leaders were committed to a capitalist model of economic development. Eventually, one of the Sonorans, Plutarco Elías Calles, emerged as the *jefe máximo,* or supreme leader. After his presidential term (1924–1928), Calles managed to select and dominate his successors from 1929 to 1934. The consolidation of power under his control was accompanied by extreme **anticlericalism**, which eventually resulted in the outbreak of a violent conflict, known as the *Cristiada,* between the government and devout followers of the Catholic Church's conservative leadership.

In 1929, Calles brought together many of the most powerful contenders for leadership to create a political party. The bargain he offered was simple: Contenders for power would accommodate each other's interests in the expectation that without political violence, the country would prosper and they would be able to reap the benefits of even greater power and economic spoils. For the next seven decades, Calles's bargain ensured nonviolent conflict resolution among elites and the uninterrupted rule of the Institutional Revolutionary Party (PRI) in national politics.

Although the revolution that began in 1910 was complex and the interests contending for power in its aftermath were numerous, there were five clear results of this protracted conflict. First, the power of traditional rural landowners was undercut. But in the years after the revolution, wealthy elites would again emerge in rural areas, even though they would never again be so powerful in national politics nor would their power be so unchecked in local areas. Second, the influence of the Catholic Church was strongly curtailed. Third, the power of foreign investors was severely limited. Henceforth, Mexican nationalism would shape economic policy-making. Fourth, a new political elite consolidated power and agreed to resolve conflicts through accommodation and bargaining rather than through violence. And fifth, the new constitution and the new party laid the basis for a strong central government that could assert its power over agricultural, industrial, and social development.

**anticlericalism**

Opposition to the power of churches or clergy in politics. In some countries, for example, France and Mexico, this opposition has focused on the role of the Catholic Church in politics.

## Lázaro Cárdenas, Agrarian Reform, and the Workers (1934–1940)

In 1934, Plutarco Elías Calles handpicked Lázaro Cárdenas as the official candidate for the presidency. He fully anticipated that Cárdenas would go along with his behind-the-scenes management of the country. To his great surprise, Cárdenas executed a virtual coup that established his own supremacy.[1] Even more unexpectedly, Cárdenas mobilized peasants and workers in pursuit of the more radical goals of the 1910 revolution. During his administration, more than 49 million acres of land were distributed, nearly twice as much as had been parceled out by all the previous

**ejido**

Land granted by Mexican government to an organized group of peasants.

**ejidatario**

Recipient of an *ejido* land grant in Mexico.

post revolutionary governments combined.[2] Most of these lands were distributed in the form of *ejidos* (collective land grants) to peasant groups. *Ejidatarios* (those who acquired *ejido* lands) became one of the most enduring bases of support for the government. Cárdenas also encouraged workers to form unions and demand higher wages and better working conditions. In 1938, he wrested the petroleum industry from foreign investors and placed it under government control.

During the Cárdenas years (1934–1940), the bulk of the Mexican population was incorporated into the political system. Organizations of peasants and workers, middle-class groups, and the military were added to the official party. In addition, the Cárdenas years witnessed a great expansion of the role of the state as the government encouraged investment in industrialization, provided credit to agriculture, and created infrastructure.

### The Politics of Rapid Development (1940–1982)

In the decades that followed, Cárdenas's successors used the institutions he created to counteract his reforms. Gradually, the PRI developed a huge patronage machine, characterized by extensive chains of personal relationships based on the exchange of favors. These exchange relationships, known as **clientelism**, became the cement that built loyalty to the PRI and the political system.

**clientelism**

An informal aspect of policy-making in which a powerful patron (for example, a traditional local boss, government agency, or dominant party) offers resources such as land, contracts, protection, or jobs in return for the support and services (such as labor or votes) of lower-status and less powerful clients; corruption, preferential treatment, and inequality are characteristic of clientelist politics.

This kind of political control reoriented the country's development away from the egalitarian social goals of the 1930s toward a development strategy in which the state actively encouraged industrialization and the accumulation of wealth. Economic growth rates were high during the 1940s, 1950s, and 1960s. By the 1970s, however, industrial development policies were no longer generating rapid growth.

The country's economy was in deep crisis by the mid-1970s. Just as policy-makers began to take actions to correct the problems, vast new amounts of oil were discovered in the Gulf of Mexico. Soon, rapid economic growth in virtually every sector of the economy was refueled by extensive public investment programs paid for with oil revenues. Unfortunately, international petroleum prices plunged in the early 1980s, and Mexico plunged into a deep economic crisis.

### Crisis and Reform (1982–2000)

**North American Free Trade Agreement (NAFTA)**

A treaty between the United States, Mexico, and Canada implemented on January 1, 1994, that largely eliminates trade barriers among the three nations and establishes procedures to resolve trade disputes.

This economic crisis led two presidents, Miguel de la Madrid (1982–1988) and Carlos Salinas (1988–1994), to introduce the first major reversal of the country's development strategy since the 1940s. New policies were put in place to limit the government's role in the economy and to reduce barriers to international trade. This period marked the beginning of a new effort to integrate Mexico more fully into the global economy. In 1993, President Salinas signed the **North American Free Trade Agreement (NAFTA)**, which committed Mexico, the United States, and Canada to the elimination of trade barriers between them. The economic reforms of the 1980s and 1990s were a turning point for Mexico and meant that the country's future development would be closely tied to international economic conditions.

Globalization brought with it new opportunities, but the increased exposure to the world economy also led to greater vulnerability to international capital flows and financial crises. After one such crisis hit at the end of 1994, for example, the Mexican economy shrank by 6.2 percent, inflation soared, taxes rose while wages were frozen, and the banking system collapsed. Mexico was likewise deeply affected by the global economic crisis of 2008, largely because of its strong links with the hard-hit U.S. economy.

The economic volatility of the early to mid-1990s was accompanied by worrying signs of political instability. On January 1, 1994, a guerrilla movement, the Zapatista

Army of National Liberation (EZLN), seized four towns in the southern state of Chiapas. The group demanded land, democracy, indigenous rights, and an immediate repeal of NAFTA. Many citizens throughout the country openly supported the aims of the rebels. The government and the military were also criticized for inaction and human rights abuses in the state.

Following close on the heels of rebellion came the assassination of the PRI's presidential candidate, Luis Donaldo Colosio, on March 23, 1994, in Tijuana. The assassination shocked all citizens and shook the political elite deeply. Although the self-confessed "lone gunman" was jailed, the ensuing investigation raised concerns about a possible conspiracy involving party and law enforcement officials as well as drug cartels. Some Mexicans were convinced that the assassination was part of a plot by party "dinosaurs," political hardliners who opposed any kind of democratic transformation. Rumors circulated about a cover-up scandal. Eventually, skepticism about the integrity of the inquiry was so great that President Salinas called for a new investigation. Even today, little is known about what exactly happened in Tijuana and why.

With the election of replacement candidate Ernesto Zedillo in August 1994, the PRI remained in power, but these shocks provoked widespread disillusionment and frustration with the political system. In 1997, for the first time in modern Mexican history, the PRI lost its absolute majority in the Chamber of Deputies, the lower house of the national congress. Since then, the congress has shown increasing dynamism as a counterbalance to the presidency. The 2000 election of Vicente Fox as the first non-PRI president in seven decades was the culmination of this electoral revolution.

## Since 2000: Mexico as a Multi-Party Democracy

After taking office in December 2000, Vicente Fox found it difficult to bring about the changes that he had promised to the Mexican people. Proposals for reform went down to defeat, and the president was subjected to catcalls and heckling when he made his annual reports to the congress. The difficulties faced by Fox as he attempted to implement his ambitious agenda arose in part because he and his administration lacked experience. However, a bigger problem for the president was that he lacked the compliant congressional majority and the close relationship with his party that his PRI predecessors had enjoyed.

With his legislative agenda stalled, Fox hoped that achievements in international policy would enhance his prestige at home. He was particularly hopeful that a close connection with the U.S. president, George W. Bush, would facilitate important breakthroughs in relations with the United States. The events of September 11, 2001, dramatically changed the outlook, however. The terrorist attacks on the United States led officials in Washington to seek to strengthen border security and to shift much of their attention away from Mexico and Latin America and toward Afghanistan and the Middle East. As a result, Mexican hopes for an agreement under which a greater number of their citizens would legally be able to migrate to and work in the United States were dashed. Thus, Fox found both his domestic and international policy priorities largely blocked.

As Fox's term in office came to a close, his National Action Party (PAN) turned to Felipe Calderón Hinojosa, the former secretary of energy, as its candidate in the 2006 presidential election. His main opponent was Andrés Manuel López Obrador of the Party of the Democratic Revolution (PRD). López Obrador accused Calderón of favoring the rich at the expense of Mexico's poor; Calderón argued that López Obrador had authoritarian tendencies that imperiled Mexico's democracy and that his economic policies would threaten Mexico's stability.

When Calderón won by a small margin, López Obrador refused to concede defeat. López Obrador's defiant response had the unintended effect of dividing the opposition and allowing Calderón to consolidate his hold on power. The new president also benefited from a general perception that his administration was more competent and more politically savvy than the previous Fox administration. His government passed a political reform bill that changed the way political campaigns were financed. He also pushed through a fiscal reform bill that raised corporate taxes.

By far the greatest challenge Mexico faced, however, was the increasing cost of fighting the war on drugs and organized crime. Calderón relied on the army and federal police to launch military offensives against drug cartels throughout the country. Within weeks of taking office, he had deployed thousands of troops and police to states plagued by the drug trade, such as Baja California, Michoacán, and Guerrero. The offensive has resulted in the apprehension or killing of many leading drug traffickers, but it has also triggered an ongoing and unexpectedly intense wave of violence that has claimed tens of thousands of lives, damaged the country's image abroad, and undermined the confidence of many Mexicans in the ability of their government to maintain order and assure their safety.

# Themes and Implications

### Historical Junctures and Political Themes

The modern Mexican state emerged from a revolution that proclaimed goals of democratic government, social justice, and national control of the country's resources. In the chaotic years after the revolution, the state created conditions for political and social peace. By incorporating peasants and workers into party and government institutions, by providing benefits to low-income groups during the 1930s, and by presiding over considerable economic growth after 1940, it became widely accepted as legitimate. These factors worked together to create a strong state capable of guiding economic and political life. Only in the 1980s did this system begin to crumble.

Mexico has always prided itself on ideological independence from the world's great powers. For many decades, Mexico considered itself a natural leader of Latin America and the developing world in general. After the early 1980s, however, the government rejected this position in favor of rapid integration into the global economy. The country aspired to the status enjoyed by the **newly industrialized countries (NICs)** of the world, such as South Korea, Malaysia, and Taiwan. However, many concerned citizens believed that in pursuing this strategy the government was accepting a position of political, cultural, and economic subordination to the United States.

Economic and political crises after 1980 highlighted the conflict between a market-oriented development strategy and the country's philosophical tradition of a strong and protective state. The larger questions of whether this development strategy can generate growth, whether Mexican products can find profitable markets overseas, whether investors can create extensive job opportunities for millions of unemployed and part-time workers, and whether the country can maintain the confidence of those investors over the longer term continue to challenge the country.

After the Revolution of 1910, the country opted not for true democracy but for representation through government-mediated organizations within a **corporatist state**, in which interest groups became an institutionalized part of state structure rather than an independent source of advocacy. This increased state power in relation to **civil society**. The state took the lead in defining goals for the country's development and, through the school system, the party, and the media, inculcated in the population a broad sense of its legitimate right to set such goals. In addition, the

---

**NICs**

A term used to describe a group of countries that achieved rapid economic development beginning in the 1960s, largely stimulated by robust international trade (particularly exports) and guided by government policies.

**corporatist state**

A state in which interest groups become an institutionalized part of the state structure.

**civil society**

Refers to the space occupied by voluntary associations outside the state, for example, professional associations (lawyers, doctors, teachers), trade unions, student and women's groups, religious bodies, and other voluntary association groups.

state had extensive resources at its disposal to control or co-opt dissent and purchase political loyalty. The PRI was an essential channel through which material goods, jobs, the distribution of land, and the allocation of development projects flowed to increase popular support for the system or to buy off opposition to it.

Although many Mexicans were actively involved in local community organizations, religious activities, unions, and public interest groups, traditionally the scope for challenging the government was very limited. At the same time, Mexico's strong state did not become openly repressive except when directly challenged.

By the 1980s, cracks began to appear in the traditional ways in which Mexican citizens interacted with the government. As the PRI began to lose its capacity to control political activities and as civic groups increasingly insisted on their right to remain independent from the PRI and the government, the terms of the state-society relationship were clearly in need of redefinition. Mexico's future stability depends on how well a more democratic government can accommodate conflicting interests while at the same time providing better economic opportunities to its very large number of poor citizens.

## Implications for Comparative Politics

In a world of developing nations wracked by political turmoil, military coups, and regime changes, the PRI established enduring institutions of governance and conditions for political stability in Mexico. Other developing countries have sought to emulate the Mexican model of stability based on an alliance between a dominant party and a strong development-oriented state, but no other government has been able to create a system that has had widespread legitimacy for so long.

Currently, Mexico is transforming itself from a corporatist state to a democratic one. At the same time, it struggles to resolve the conflicts of development through integration with its North American neighbors. The country has

In recent years, Mexican authorities have moved forcefully against the country's drug trafficking organizations, which had amassed considerable resources through their criminal activities.

made significant strides in industrialization, which accounts for about 32.9 percent of the country's gross domestic product (GDP). Agriculture contributes about 4.3 percent to GDP, and services contribute some 62.8 percent. This structure is very similar to the economic profiles of Argentina, Brazil, Poland, and Hungary. But unlike those countries, Mexico is oil rich. The government-owned petroleum industry is a ready source of revenue and foreign exchange, but this commodity also makes the economy extremely vulnerable to changes in international oil prices.

Mexico is categorized by the World Bank as an upper-middle-income developing country. The country's industrial and petroleum-based economy gives it a per capita income ($13,200) comparable to that of countries such as Brazil, Russia, and South Africa, and higher than those of most other developing nations. But the way the country has promoted economic growth and industrialization is important in explaining why widespread poverty has persisted and why political power is not more equitably distributed.

## Summary

The Mexican political system is unique among developing countries in the extent to which it managed to institutionalize and maintain civilian political authority for a very long time. The country's development has been significantly shaped by its proximity to the United States, and its contemporary economic development is linked to the expansion of globalization. Yet the critical junctures in the country's history also show the importance of domestic political and economic conflicts. Although the Revolution of 1910 happened a century ago, its legacies continue to mark development in Mexico, as does its earlier history of industrialization and urbanization. And the impact of particular leaders and their presidential administrations also marks the emergence of the country. In a world of developing nations wracked by political turmoil, military coups, and regime changes, the PRI regime established important conditions for political stability, even though it stifled democratic freedoms. Currently, Mexico is undergoing significant political change, transforming itself from a corporatist state to a democratic one. At the same time, Mexican society is experiencing high levels of violence as the state confronts drug trafficking organizations that represent a challenge to its authority and to the rule of law. Industry and oil give the country a per capita income higher than those of most other developing nations, but the country suffers from great inequalities in how wealth is distributed, and poverty continues to be a grim reality for millions. The way the country promoted economic growth and industrialization is important in explaining why widespread poverty has persisted and why political power is not more equitably distributed.

# POLITICAL ECONOMY AND DEVELOPMENT

## State and Economy

During the *Porfiriato* (1876–1911), policy-makers believed that Mexico could grow rich by exporting raw materials. Their efforts to attract domestic and international investment encouraged a major boom in the production and export of products such as henequin (for making rope), coffee, cacao (cocoa beans), cattle, oil, silver, and gold. Soon, the country had become so attractive to foreign investors that large amounts of land, the country's petroleum, its railroad network, and its mining wealth were largely controlled by foreigners. Nationalist reaction against these foreign interests played a significant role in the tensions that produced the Revolution of 1910.

After the revolution, this nationalism combined with a sense of social justice inspired by revolutionary leaders such as Zapata. The country adopted a strategy in which the government guided industrial and agricultural development. This development strategy (often called **state capitalism**) relied heavily on government actions to encourage private investment and reduce risks for private entrepreneurs. At the same time, many came to believe that Mexico should begin to manufacture the goods that it was then importing.

**state capitalism**

An economic system that is primarily capitalistic but in which there is some degree of government ownership of the means of production.

## Import Substitution and Its Consequences

Between 1940 and 1982, Mexico pursued a form of state capitalism and a model of industrialization known as import substitution, or **import substitution industrialization (ISI)**. Like Brazil and other Latin American countries during the same period, the government promoted the development of industries to supply the domestic market by encouraging domestic and international investment. Initially, the country produced mainly simple products like shoes, clothing, and processed foods. But by the 1960s and 1970s, it was also producing consumer durables, intermediate goods, and capital goods.

With the massive agrarian reform of the 1930s (see Section 1), the *ejido* had become an important structure in the rural economy. After Cárdenas left office, however, government policy-makers moved away from the economic development of the *ejidos*. They became committed instead to developing a strong, entrepreneurial private sector in agriculture. For them, "the development of private agriculture would be the 'foundation of industrial greatness.'"[3] They wanted this sector to provide foodstuffs for the growing cities, raw materials for industry, and foreign exchange from exports. To encourage these goals, the government invested in transportation networks, irrigation projects, and agricultural storage facilities. It provided extension services and invested in research. It encouraged imports of technology to improve output and mechanize production. Since policy-makers believed that modern commercial farmers would respond better to these investments and services than would peasants on small plots of land, the government provided most of its assistance to large landowners.

Between 1940 and 1950, GDP grew at an annual average of 6.7 percent, while manufacturing increased at an average of 8.1 percent. In the 1950s, manufacturing achieved an average of 7.3 percent growth annually, and in the 1960s, that figure rose to 10.1 percent. Agricultural production also grew rapidly as new areas were brought under cultivation and **green revolution** technology was extensively adopted on large farms. Even the poorest Mexicans believed that their lives were improving. Table 10.2 presents data that summarize a number of advancements during this period. So impressive was Mexico's economic performance that it was referred to internationally as the "Mexican Miracle."

It was not long before a group of domestic entrepreneurs developed a special relationship with the state. Government policies protected their products through high tariffs or special licensing requirements, limiting imports of competing goods. Business elites in Mexico received subsidized credit to invest in equipment and plants; they benefited from cheap, subsidized energy; and they rarely had to pay taxes. These protected businesses emerged as powerful players in national politics. They were able to veto efforts by the government to cut back on their benefits, and they lobbied for even more advantages.

Workers also became more important players in Mexico's national politics. As mentioned in Section 1, widespread unionization occurred under Cárdenas, and workers won many rights that had been promised in the Constitution of 1917. The policy changes initiated in the 1940s, however, made the unions more dependent on the government for benefits and protection; the government also limited the right to strike. Union membership meant job security and important benefits such as housing subsidies and health care. These factors compensated for the lack of democracy within the labor movement. Moreover, labor leaders had privileged access to the country's political leadership and benefited personally from their control over jobs, contracts, and working conditions. In return, they guaranteed labor peace.[4]

In agriculture, those who benefited from government policies and services were primarily farmers who had enough land and economic resources to irrigate

### Focus Questions

In what ways have various theories of economic development affected government policies in Mexico? Which policies have been the most successful? The least successful?

Which economic developments in Mexico have most greatly affected social progress, for better or worse? To what degree had government policy affected those developments? To what degree were they shaped by outside forces?

What accounts for the Mexican government's decision to seek greater integration into the global economy? In what ways have global linkages helped or harmed the lives of various social groups?

**import substitution industrialization (ISI)**

Strategy for industrialization based on domestic manufacture of previously imported goods to satisfy domestic market demands.

**green revolution**

A strategy for increasing agricultural (especially food) production, involving improved seeds, irrigation, and abundant use of fertilizers.

| Table 10.2 | Mexican Development, 1940–2010 | | | | | | |
|---|---|---|---|---|---|---|---|
| | **1940** | **1950** | **1960** | **1970** | **1980** | **1990** | **2010**[a] |
| Population (millions) | 19.8 | 26.3 | 38.0 | 52.8 | 70.4 | 88.5 | 112.5 |
| Life expectancy (years) | – | 51.6 | 58.6 | 62.6 | 67.4 | 68.9 | 76.5 |
| Infant mortality (per 1,000 live births) | – | – | 86.3 | 70.9 | 49.9 | 42.6 | 17.3 |
| Illiteracy (% of population age 15 and over) | – | 42.5 | 34.5 | 25.0 | 16.0 | 12.7 | 7.0 |
| Urban population (% of total) | – | – | 50.7 | 59.0 | 66.4 | 72.6 | 78.0 |
| Economically active population in agriculture (% of total) | – | 58.3 | 55.1 | 44.0 | 36.6 | 22.0 | 13.5 |
| | **1940–1949** | **1950–1959** | **1960–1969** | **1970–1979** | **1980–1989** | **1990–1999** | **2000–2009** |
| GDP growth rate (average annual percent) | 6.7 | 5.8 | 7.6 | 6.4 | 1.6 | 3.4 | 1.3 |
| Per capita GDP growth rate | – | – | 3.7 | 3.3 | –0.1 | 1.6 | 0.3 |

[a] Or most recent year available.

*Sources:* Statistical Abstract for Latin America (New York: United Nations, Economic Commission for Latin America, various years); Roger Hansen, *The Politics of Mexican Development* (Baltimore, MD: Johns Hopkins University Press, 1971); *Statistical Bulletin of the OAS*; World Bank Country Data for Mexico, World Bank, World Development Indicators; Central Intelligence Agency, *CIA World Factbook*.

**informal sector (economy)**

That portion of the economy largely outside government control in which employees work without contracts or benefits. Examples include casual employees in restaurants and hotels, street vendors, and day laborers in construction or agriculture.

and mechanize. By the 1950s, a group of large, commercially oriented farmers had emerged to dominate the agricultural economy.[5]

Government policies eventually limited the potential for further growth.[6] Industrialists who received extensive subsidies and benefits from the government had few incentives to produce efficiently. High tariffs kept out foreign competition, further reducing reasons for efficiency or quality in production. Importing technology to support industrialization eventually became a drain on the country's foreign exchange.

As the economy grew, many were left behind. The ranks of the urban poor grew steadily, particularly from the 1960s on. By 1970, a large proportion of Mexico City's population was living in inner-city tenements or squatter settlements surrounding the city.[7] Mexico developed a sizable **informal sector**—workers who produced and sold goods and services at the margin of the economic system and faced extreme insecurity.

Also left behind in the country's development after 1940 were peasant farmers. Their lands were often the least fertile, plot sizes were minuscule, and access to markets was impeded by poor transportation and exploitive middlemen who trucked products to markets for exorbitant fees. Farming in the *ejido* communities, where land was held communally, was particularly difficult.

Increasing disparities in rural and urban incomes, coupled with high population growth rates, contributed to the emergence of rural guerrilla movements and student protests in the mid- and late 1960s. The domestic market was limited by poverty; many Mexicans could not afford the sophisticated manufactured products the country would need to produce in order to keep growing under the import substitution model.

By the late 1960s, the country was no longer able to meet domestic demand for basic foodstuffs and was forced to import increasingly large quantities of food, costing the government foreign exchange that it could have used for other purposes.

## Sowing the Oil and Reaping a Crisis

In the early 1970s, Mexico faced the threat of social crisis brought on by rural poverty, chaotic urbanization, high population growth, and the questioning of political legitimacy. The government responded by increasing investment in infrastructure and public industries, regulating the flow of foreign capital, and increasing social spending. It was spending much more than it generated, causing the public internal debt to grow rapidly and requiring heavy borrowing abroad. Little progress was made in changing existing policies, however, because just as the seriousness of the economic situation was being recognized, vast new finds of oil came to the rescue.

Between 1978 and 1982, Mexico became a major oil exporter. As international oil prices rose rapidly, so too did the country's fortunes, along with those of other oil-rich countries. The administration of President José López Portillo (1976–1982) embarked on a policy to "sow the oil" in the economy and "administer the abundance" with vast investment projects in virtually all sectors and with major new initiatives to reduce poverty and deal with declining agricultural productivity.

Oil accounted for almost four-fifths of the country's exports, causing the economy to be extremely vulnerable to changes in oil prices. And change they did. Global overproduction led to a steep drop in international prices for Mexican petroleum in 1982, and prices fell even lower in the years that followed. At the same time, the United States tightened its monetary policy by raising interest rates, and access to foreign credit dried up. In August 1982, the government announced that the country could not pay the interest on its foreign debt, triggering a crisis that reverberated around the world.

The economic crisis had several important implications for structures of power and privilege in Mexico. The crisis convinced even the most diehard believers that import substitution created inefficiencies in production, failed to generate sufficient employment, cost the government far too much in subsidies, and increased dependency on industrialized countries. In addition, the power of privileged interest groups and their ability to influence government policy declined.

Similarly, the country's labor unions lost much of their bargaining power with government over issues of wages and protection. A shift in employment from the formal to the informal economy further fragmented what had once been the most powerful sector of the PRI.

A wide variety of interests began to organize outside the PRI to demand that government do something about the situation. Massive earthquakes in Mexico City in September 1985 proved to be a watershed for Mexican society. Severely disappointed by the government's failure to respond to the problems created by death, destruction, and homelessness, hundreds of communities organized rescue efforts, soup kitchens, shelters, and rehabilitation initiatives. A surging sense of political empowerment developed, as groups long accustomed to dependence on government learned that they could solve their problems better without government than with it.[8]

The elections of 1988 became a focus for protest against the economic dislocation caused by the crisis and the political powerlessness that most citizens felt. For the first time in decades, the PRI was challenged by the increased popularity of opposition political parties, one of them headed by Cuauhtémoc Cárdenas, the son of the country's most revered president, Lázaro Cárdenas. When the votes were counted, it was announced that Carlos Salinas, the PRI candidate, had received a bare majority of 50.7 percent, as opposition parties claimed widespread electoral fraud.

### New Strategies: Structural Reforms and NAFTA

Between 1988 and 1994, the mutually dependent relationship between industry and government was weakened as new free-market policies were put in place. Deregulation gave the private sector more freedom to pursue economic activities and less reason to seek special favors from government. A constitutional revision made it possible for *ejidatarios* to become owners of individual plots of land; this made them less dependent on government but more vulnerable to losing their land. In addition, Salinas and his successor, Ernesto Zedillo, pursued an overhaul of the federal system and the way government agencies worked together by delegating more authority and resources to the country's traditionally weak state and local governments.

Among the most far-reaching initiatives was the North American Free Trade Agreement (NAFTA). This agreement with Canada and the United States created the basis for gradual introduction of free trade among the three countries. However, the liberalization of the Mexican economy and opening of its markets to foreign competition increased Mexico's vulnerability to changes in international economic conditions. These factors, as well as mismanaged economic policies, led to a major economic crisis for the country at the end of 1994 and profound recession in 1995. NAFTA has meant that the fate of the Mexican economy is increasingly linked to the health of the U.S. economy.

## Society and Economy

Mexico's economic development has had a significant impact on social conditions in the country. Overall, the standard of living and quality of life rose markedly after the 1940s. Provision of health and education services expanded until government cutbacks on social expenditures in the early 1980s. Among the most important consequences of economic growth was the development of a large middle class, most of whom live in Mexico's numerous large cities.

These achievements reflect well on the ability of the economy to increase social well-being in the country. But in terms of standard indicators of social development—infant mortality, literacy, and life expectancy—Mexico fell behind a number of Latin American countries that grew less rapidly but provided more effectively for their populations. Costa Rica, Colombia, Argentina, Chile, and Uruguay had lower overall growth but greater social development in the period after 1940. These countries paid more attention to the distribution of the benefits of growth than did Mexico. Moreover, rapid industrialization and urbanization has made Mexico City one of the most polluted cities in the world, and in some rural areas oil exploitation left devastating environmental damage.[9]

Mexico's economic development resulted in a widening gap between the wealthy and the poor and also among different regions in the country. As the rich grew richer, the gap between the rich and the poor increased. In 1950, the bottom 40 percent of the country's households accounted for about 14 percent of total personal income, while the top 30 percent had 60 percent of total income.[10] In 2008, it is estimated, the bottom 40 percent accounted for about 11.9 percent of income, while the top 40 percent shared 75.6 percent.[11]

Harsh conditions in the countryside have fueled a half-century of migration to the cities. Nevertheless, some 25 million Mexicans continue to live in rural areas, many of them in deep poverty. Many work for substandard wages and migrate seasonally to search for jobs in order to sustain their families. This land is often not irrigated and depends on erratic rainfall. It is often leached of nutrients as a result of centuries of cultivation, population pressure, and erosion. When the Zapatista rebels in Chiapas called for jobs, land, education, and health facilities, they were clearly reflecting the realities of life in much of the countryside.

Poverty has a regional dimension in Mexico. The northern areas of the country are significantly better off than the southern and central areas. In the north, large commercial farms using modern technologies grow fruits, vegetables, and grains for export. Moreover, industrial cities such as Monterrey and Tijuana provide steady jobs for skilled and unskilled labor. Along the border, a band of *maquiladoras* (manufacturing and assembly plants) provides many jobs, particularly for young women who are seeking some escape from the burdens of rural life or the constraints of traditional family life.

In the southern and central regions of the country, the population is denser, the land poorer, and the number of *ejidatarios* eking out subsistence greater. Transportation is often difficult, and during parts of the year, some areas may be inaccessible because of heavy rains and flooding. Most of Mexico's remaining indigenous groups live in the southern regions, often in remote areas where they have been forgotten by government programs and exploited by regional bosses for generations.

The general economic crisis of the 1980s had an impact on social conditions in Mexico as well. Wages declined by about half, and unemployment soared as businesses collapsed and the government laid off workers in public offices and privatized industries. The informal sector expanded rapidly. Here, people manage to make a living by hawking chewing gum, umbrellas, sponges, candy, shoelaces, mirrors, and a variety of other items in the street; jumping in front of cars at stoplights to wash windshields and sell newspapers; producing and repairing cheap consumer goods such as shoes and clothing; and selling services on a daily or hourly basis.

The economic crisis of the 1980s also reduced the quality and availability of social services. Expenditures on education and health declined after 1982 as the government imposed austerity measures. Salaries of primary school teachers declined by 34 percent between 1983 and 1988. Per capita health expenditures declined from a high of about $19 in 1980 to about $11 in 1990. Although indicators of mortality did not rise during this troubled decade, the incidence of diseases associated with poverty—malnutrition, cholera, anemia, and dysentery—increased. Since the 1980s, periods of slow improvement in conditions for the poor have been punctuated by new economic shocks, including sharp downturns in the mid-1990s and late 2000s. Though economic recovery has been slow and fitful in recent decades, the Mexican government has begun to fill the void left by cuts in social spending during the depths of the crisis. Recent years have seen the launch of successful programs that provide

## THE U.S. CONNECTION

### Mexican Migration to the United States

Mexicans began moving to the United States in substantial numbers late in the nineteenth century, and their ranks grew as many fled the chaotic conditions that had been created by the Revolution of 1910. Most settled in the border states of California and Texas, where they joined preexisting Mexican communities that had been there since the days when the American southwest had been part of Mexico. Even greater numbers of migrants began to arrive during World War II, when the U.S. government allowed Mexican workers, known as *braceros*, to enter the country to help provide much-needed manpower for strategic production efforts. The *bracero* program remained in place after the war, and under it, a predominantly male Mexican workforce provided seasonal labor to U.S. employers, mostly in agriculture. After the *bracero* program came to an end in 1964, Mexicans continued to seek work in the United States, despite the fact that most then had to enter the country illegally. To a large extent, the U.S. government informally tolerated the employment of undocumented migrants until the 1980s, when policy-makers came under pressure to assert control over the border. The 1986 Immigration Reform and Control Act (IRCA) allowed migrants who had been in the United States for a long period of time to gain legal residency rights, but it called for tighter controls on immigration in the future.

IRCA and subsequent efforts to deter illegal immigration simply turned a pattern of seasonal migration into a flow of migrants that settled permanently north of the border. Before 1986, most Mexican migrant workers left their families at home and worked in the United States for only a few months at a time before returning to their country with the money they had earned. The money that these migrants send back to Mexico helps to sustain not just their own families but entire regions that have been left behind by the migrants who gained amnesty under IRCA and then sent for their families to join them, creating a more permanent immigrant community. Also, as increased vigilance and new barriers

making the crossing of the border more difficult, more of the migrants who arrived in the United States decided to remain there rather than risk apprehension by traveling back and forth between the two countries. High-profile efforts to patrol the border around urban areas such as San Diego and El Paso led migrants to use more remote crossing points, and although the number of Mexicans who died trying to reach the United States rose as many attempted to travel through the desolate deserts of Arizona, the overall rate of illegal immigration was not affected by the government's crackdown.

In the 1990s and 2000s, growing Mexican communities in the United States spread into areas such as North Carolina, Georgia, Arkansas, and Iowa, where few Mexicans had lived before. They also became increasingly mobilized politically as they organized to resist anti-immigrant voter initiatives such as Proposition 187 in California in 1994 and Proposition 200 in Arizona in 2004, both of which threatened to cut off social services for undocumented migrants. At the same time, their political importance in Mexico has reached unprecedented heights as officials at all levels of government there recognize the critical importance to the Mexican economy of the $21.3 billion that the country receives each year in remittances from migrants working in other countries. Mexican governors, mayors, and federal officials now regularly visit representatives of migrant groups in the United States, often seeking their support and funding for projects at home. Moreover, a 1996 law allowing Mexicans to hold dual citizenship makes it possible for many Mexican migrants to have a voice in the governance of both the country of their birth as well as the country where they now reside. In 2005, Mexican legislators finally approved a system under which registered Mexican voters living abroad could participate in federal elections using mail-in ballots, and it is easy to imagine that this huge group could play a decisive role in future electoral contests.

vastly expanded access to basic health care and cash grants to poor families that keep their children in school.

The contrast between the poverty of the developing world and the prosperity of industrialized nations is nowhere on more vivid display than it is along the 2,000-mile-long border between Mexico and the United States. As the number of Mexican migrants seeking opportunities abroad has grown in recent years, their presence in the United States has come to have profound ramifications for the politics of both nations (see The U.S. Connection: Mexican Migration to the United States).

# Mexico in the Global Economy

The crisis that began in 1982 altered Mexico's international economic policies. In response to that crisis, the government relaxed restrictions on the ability of foreigners to own property, reduced and eliminated tariffs, and did away with most import licenses. Foreign investment was courted in the hope of increasing the manufacture of goods for export. The government also introduced a series of incentives to encourage the private sector to produce goods for export. In 1986, Mexico joined the General Agreement on Tariffs and Trade (GATT), a multilateral agreement that sought to promote freer trade among countries and that later became the basis for the World Trade Organization (WTO). In the 1990s and early 2000s, Mexico signed trade pacts with many countries in Latin America, Europe, and elsewhere.

The government's effort to pursue a more outward-oriented development strategy culminated in the ratification of NAFTA in 1993, with gradual implementation beginning on January 1, 1994. In 2009, 80.7 percent of the country's exports were sent to the United States, and 48.1 percent of its imports came from that country, making Mexico's northern neighbor its most important trading partner by a wide margin.[12] Access to the U.S. market is essential to Mexico and to domestic and foreign investors. NAFTA signaled a new period in U.S.–Mexican relations by making closer integration of the two economies a certainty.

NAFTA also entails risks for Mexico. Domestic producers worry about competition from U.S. firms. Farmers worry that Mexican crops cannot compete effectively with those grown in the United States; for example, peasant producers of corn and beans have been hard hit by the availability of lower-priced U.S.-grown grains.[13] In addition, many believe that embracing free trade with Canada and the United States indicates a loss of sovereignty. Certainly, Mexico's economic situation is now more vulnerable to the ebb and flow of economic conditions in the U.S. economy. Indeed, after the United States plunged into a deep recession in 2008, Mexico's economy contracted by more than 7 percent, despite the fact that the crisis was not of its own making. Moreover, some in Mexico are also concerned with evidence of "cultural imperialism" as U.S. movies, music, fashions, and lifestyles increasingly influence consumers. Indeed, for Mexico, which has traditionally feared the power of the United States in its domestic affairs, internationalization of political and economic relationships poses particularly difficult problems of adjustment.

On the other hand, the United States, newly aware of the importance of the Mexican economy to its own economic growth and concerned about instability on its southern border, hammered together a $50 billion economic assistance program composed of U.S., European, and IMF commitments to support its neighbor when economic crisis struck in 1994. The Mexican government imposed a new stabilization package that contained austerity measures, higher interest rates, and limits on wages. Remarkably, by 1998, Mexico had paid off all of its obligations to the United States.

Globalization is also stripping Mexico of some of the secrecy that traditionally surrounded government decision-making, electoral processes, and efforts to deal with political dissent. International attention increasingly focuses on the country, and investors want clear and up-to-date information on what is occurring in the economy. The Internet and e-mail, along with lower international telephone rates, are increasing the flow of information across borders. The government can no longer respond to events such as the peasant rebellion in Chiapas, alleged electoral fraud, or the management of exchange rates without considering how such actions will be perceived in Tokyo, Frankfurt, Ottawa, London, or Washington.

## Summary

Mexico's development from the 1930s to the 1980s was marked by extensive government engagement in the economy. During this period, the country industrialized and became primarily urban. At the same time, the living conditions of most Mexicans improved, and standards of health, longevity, and education grew. Yet, along with these achievements, development strategies led to industrial and agricultural sectors that were often inefficient and overly protected by government, inequalities in the distribution of income and opportunities increased, and growth was threatened by a combination of domestic policies and international economic conditions. In the 1980s, the earlier model of development collapsed in crisis, and more market-oriented policies have significantly reduced the role of government in the economy and opened the country up to global economic forces. Yet growth has been slow under the new policies and inequalities have increased. Economic growth, social inequality, and the legacies of an authoritarian past continue to affect the development of the country.

SECTION **3**

# GOVERNANCE AND POLICY-MAKING

## Organization of the State

**Focus Questions**

In what ways does the actual exercise of state power differ from the model outlined in the Constitution? What are the main reasons for these discrepancies?

In what ways do Mexican officeholders exercise power in addition to the powers formally granted to them by law?

To what extent is federalism a reality in Mexico today? How is power divided between administrations at the national, state, and local levels?

Are state institutions like the military and the judiciary truly independent of the executive branch of government? In what ways have these institutions promoted or hindered the growth of democracy in recent years?

Under the Constitution of 1917, Mexico's political institutions resemble those of the United States. There are three branches of government, and a set of checks and balances limits the power of each. The congress is composed of the Senate and the Chamber of Deputies. One hundred twenty-eight senators are elected, three from each of the country's thirty-one states; three from the Federal District, which contains the capital, Mexico City; and another thirty-two elected nationally by **proportional representation (PR)**. The 500 members of the Chamber of Deputies are elected from 300 electoral districts—300 by simple majority vote and 200 by proportional representation. State and local governments are also elected. The president, governors, and senators are elected for six years, an important institutional feature of Mexican politics referred to as the *sexenio*. Congressional deputies (representatives in the lower house) and municipal officials are elected for three years.

In practice, the Mexican system is very different from that of the United States. The constitution is a long document that can be easily amended, especially when compared to that of the United States. It lays out the structure of government and guarantees a wide range of human rights, including familiar ones such as freedom of speech and protection under the law, but also economic and social rights such as the right to a job and the right to health care. Economic and social rights are acknowledged but in practice do not reach all of the population. Although there has been some decentralization, the political system is still much more centralized than that of the United States. Congress is now more active as a decision-making arena and as a check on presidential power, but the executive remains central to initiating policy and managing political conflict.

# The Executive

## The President and the Cabinet

The presidency is the central institution of governance and policy-making in Mexico. Until the 1990s, the incumbent president always selected who would run as the PRI's next presidential candidate, appointed officials to all positions of power in the government and the party, and often named the candidates who almost automatically won elections as governors, senators, deputies, and local officials.[14] Even with a non-PRI incumbent, the president continues to set the broad outlines of policy for the administration and has numerous resources to ensure that those policy preferences are adopted. Until the mid-1970s, Mexican presidents were considered above criticism in national politics and revered as symbols of national progress and well-being. While economic and political events of the 1980s and 1990s diminished presidential prestige and politicians are increasingly willing to stand up to the chief executive in today's multiparty system, the extent of presidential power remains a legacy of the long period of PRI dominance.

Mexican presidents have a set of formal powers that allows them to initiate legislation, lead in foreign policy, create government agencies, make policy by decree or through administrative regulations and procedures, and appoint a wide range of public officials. More important, informal powers allow them to exert considerable control. The president manages a vast patronage machine for filling positions in government and initiates legislation and policies that were, until recently, routinely approved by the congress.

Mexican presidents, though powerful, are not omnipotent. They must, for example, abide by a deeply held constitutional norm, fully adhered to since 1940, by stepping down at the end of their six-year term, and they must adhere to tradition by removing themselves from the political limelight to allow their successors to assume full presidential leadership. All presidents, regardless of party, must demonstrate their loyalty to the myths and symbols of Mexican nationalism, such as the indigenous roots of much of its culture and the agrarian goals of the revolution, and they must make a rhetorical commitment to social justice and sovereignty in international affairs.

In the 1990s, President Zedillo gave up a number of the traditional powers of the presidency. He announced, for example, that he would not select his PRI successor but would leave it up to the party to determine its candidate. This created considerable conflict and tension as the PRI had to take on unaccustomed roles and as politicians sought to fill the void left by the "abandonment" of presidential power. Vicente Fox and Felipe Calderón inherited a system in which the president is expected to set the policies and determine the priorities for a very wide range of government activity, yet needs a strong party in congress and experienced people in his administration to enact legislation and implement policies.

Under the PRI, presidents were always male and almost always members of the outgoing president's cabinet. With the victory of the PAN in 2000, this long tradition came to an end. Prior to running for president, Vicente Fox had been in business and had served as the governor of the state of Guanajuato. Calderón, although he had served briefly as Fox's secretary of energy, was not his chosen successor. Fox had hoped to be succeeded by his secretary of the interior, Santiago Creel. In this respect, Calderón's victory in 2006 continued a trend toward greater independence of parties from presidential preferences.

**proportional representation (PR)**

A system of political representation in which seats are allocated to parties within multimember constituencies, roughly in proportion to the votes each party receives. PR usually encourages the election to parliament of more political parties than single-member-district winner-take-all systems.

*sexenio*

The six-year term in office of Mexican presidents.

Mexican presidential candidates since the mid-1970s have had impressive educational credentials and have tended to be trained in economics and management rather than in the traditional field of law. Presidents since López Portillo have had postgraduate training at elite institutions in the United States. By the 1980s, a topic of great debate in political circles was the extent to which a divide between *políticos* (politicians) and *técnicos* (**technocrats**) had emerged within the national political elite.

Once elected, the president moves quickly to name a cabinet. Under the PRI, he usually selected those with whom he had worked over the years as he rose to political prominence. He also used cabinet posts to ensure a broad coalition of support; he might, for example, appoint people with close ties to the labor movement, business interests, or some of the regional strongholds of the party. Only in rare exceptions were cabinet officials not active members of the PRI. When the PAN assumed the presidency in 2000, the selection of cabinet members and close advisers became more difficult. Until then, the PAN had elected officials only to a few state and local governments and to a relatively small number of seats in congress. As a consequence, the range of people with executive experience to whom Fox could turn was limited. He appointed U.S.-trained economists for his economic team and business executives for many other important posts. Few of these appointees had close ties to the PAN, and few had prior experience in government. Fox's powers were curtailed to some degree by a more forceful congress and his administration's lack of experience in governing. Whereas Fox preferred technocrats with limited political experience, Calderón filled his cabinet positions with longtime members of the PAN who have a longer history of political engagement. Over the years, few women have been selected for ministry-level posts. Initially, they only presided over agencies with limited influence over decision-making, like the ministries of tourism and ecology. More recently, however, women have headed the foreign ministry, and in 2011, at a moment when the fight against organized crime was at the top of the Calderón administration's agenda, a woman was named to serve as attorney general.

The president has the authority to fill numerous other high-level positions, which allows him to provide policy direction and keep tabs on what is occurring throughout the government. The range of appointments that a chief executive can make means that the beginning of each administration is characterized by extensive turnover of positions, and as a result, progress on the president's policy agenda can be slow during his first year in office as newly appointed officials learn the ropes and assemble their staff. The president's power to make appointments allows him to build a team of like-minded officials in government and ensure their loyalty. This system traditionally served the interests of presidents and the PRI well; under the PAN, given the limited number of its partisans who have experience at the national level, the system has not guaranteed the president as much power over the workings of the executive branch.

## The Bureaucracy

Mexico's executive branch is large and powerful. Almost 1.5 million people work in the federal bureaucracy, most of them in Mexico City. An additional 1 million work in state-owned industries and semiautonomous agencies of the government. State and local governments employ over 1.5 million people.

Officials at lower levels in the bureaucracy are unionized and protected by legislation that gives them job security and a range of benefits. At middle and upper levels, most officials are called "confidence employees"; they serve as long as their bosses have confidence in them. These officials have been personally appointed by

---

**technocrats**

Career-minded bureaucrats who administer public policy according to a technical rather than a political rationale.

their superiors at the outset of an administration. Their modest salaries are compensated for by the significant power that they can have over public affairs. For aspiring young professionals, a career in government is often attractive because of the challenge of dealing with important problems on a daily basis. Some employees also benefit from opportunities to take bribes or use other means to promote their personal interests.

## The Parastatal Sector

The **parastatal** sector—composed of semiautonomous or autonomous government agencies, many of which produce goods and services—was extremely large and powerful in Mexico prior to the 1990s. As part of its post-1940 development strategy, the government engaged in numerous activities that in other countries are carried out by the private sector. Thus, until the Salinas administration, the country's largest steel mill was state-owned, as were the largest fertilizer producer, sugar mills, and airlines. In addition, the national electricity board still produces energy, which it supplies to industries at subsidized prices. The state-owned petroleum company, PEMEX, grew to enormous proportions in the 1970s and 1980s under the impact of the oil boom. NAFIN, a state investment corporation, provides a considerable amount of investment capital for the country. At one point, a state marketing board called CONASUPO was responsible for the importation and purchase of the country's basic food supplies, and in the 1970s, it played a major role in distributing food, credit, and farm implements in rural areas.

This large parastatal sector was significantly trimmed by the economic policy reforms that began in the 1980s. In 1970, there were 391 parastatal organizations in Mexico. By 1982, their number had grown to 1,155, in part because of the expansion of government activities under presidents Echeverría and López Portillo and in part because of the nationalization of private banks in 1982. Shortly afterward, concerted efforts were made to privatize many of these industries, including the telephone company, the national airlines, and the nationalized banks. By 1994, only 215 state-owned industries remained, and efforts continued to sell or liquidate many of them. However, some core components of the parastatal sector will likely remain in government hands for the foreseeable future because an influential bloc of nationalist political actors insists on the symbolic importance of public ownership of key industries.

**parastatal**

A government-owned corporation or agency. Parastatal institutions generally engage in or seek to promote and organize commercial activity in a particular sector. Because of their connection to the state, these enterprises can also serve as instruments of official policy, as sources of patronage opportunities, or as important generators of government revenue.

# Other State Institutions

## The Military

Mexico is one of only a few countries in the developing world, particularly in Latin America, to have successfully marginalized the military from centers of political power. Although former military leaders dominated Mexican politics during the decades immediately after the Revolution of 1910, Calles, Cárdenas, and subsequent presidents laid the groundwork for civilian rule by introducing the practice of rotating regional military commands so that generals could not build up geographic bases of power. In addition, post-revolutionary leaders made an implicit bargain with the military leaders by providing them with opportunities to engage in business so that they did not look to political office as a way of gaining economic power. After 1946, the military no longer had institutional representation within the PRI and became

The principle of civilian authority over the Mexican armed forces has been established for decades, but today both the army and navy are playing a large role in the fight against organized crime. Here, President Felipe Calderón appears in a parade alongside military leaders.

*Source:* http://media3.washingtonpost.com/wp-srv/photo/gallery/100914/GAL-10Sep14-5722/media/PHO-10Sep14-251759.jpg

clearly subordinate to civilian control. No military officer has held the presidency since that time.

This does not mean that the military has operated outside politics. It has been called in from time to time to deal with domestic unrest: in rural areas in the 1960s, in Mexico City and other cities to repress student protest movements in 1968, in Chiapas beginning in late 1994, and to manage the Mexico City police in 1997. The military was also called in to deal with the aftermath of the earthquake in Mexico City in 1985, but its inadequate response to the emergency did little to improve its reputation. When the PAN government made it possible for citizens to gain greater access to government information, it was discovered that the military had been involved in political repression, torture, and killing in the 1970s and 1980s. The scandal created by such revelations further lowered its reputation, though polls show that Mexicans continue to have more confidence in and admiration for the armed forces than for many other institutions, including the police forces, which are widely regarded as corrupt and ineffective.

In recent years, the military has been heavily involved in efforts to combat drug trafficking, and rumors have at times arisen about deals struck between military officials and drug barons. The military continues to be used to fight drug cartels and organized crime. Within weeks of taking office, Calderón had deployed thousands of military troops to Michoacán and Baja California to combat criminal organizations engaged in the drug trade. When the president dressed in military fatigues to address the troops in Michoacán in late January 2007, it was a dramatic manifestation of the increased role the military would play under his administration in the fight against crime. In some regions particularly hard-hit by drug-related violence, the military has taken over many policing functions. Though the army is seen as less corrupt than many of the local police forces they have replaced, concerns about their ongoing presence on the streets of Mexican cities have arisen, particularly as allegations of civil and human rights violations by soldiers have emerged in some areas.

Whenever the military is called in to resolve domestic conflicts, some Mexicans become concerned that the institution is becoming politicized and may come to play a larger role in political decision-making. Thus far, such fears have not been realized, and many believe that as long as civilian administrations are able to maintain the country's tradition of stability, the military will not intervene directly in politics. The fact that the country successfully observed the transfer of power from the PRI to the PAN also has increased a sense that the military will remain subordinate to civilian control.

## The Judiciary

Unlike Anglo-American legal systems, Mexico's law derives from the Roman and Napoleonic tradition and is highly formalized. Because Mexican law tends to be very explicit and because there are no punitive damages allowed in court cases, there are fewer lawsuits than in the United States. One important exception to this is the *amparo* (protection), whereby individual citizens may ask for a writ of protection, claiming that their constitutional rights have been violated by specific government actions or laws.

There are both federal and state courts in Mexico. The federal system is composed of the Supreme Court, which decides the most important cases; circuit courts, which take cases on appeal; and district courts, where cases enter the system. As in the United States, Supreme Court justices are nominated by the president and approved by the Senate. Since most of the important laws in Mexico are federal, state courts have played a subordinate role. This is changing, however. As Mexican states become more independent from the federal government, state law has been experiencing tremendous growth. In addition, there are many important specialized federal courts, such as labor courts, military courts, and electoral courts.

Like other government institutions in Mexico, the judiciary was for many decades politically, though not constitutionally, subordinate to the executive. The courts occasionally slowed the actions of government by issuing *amparos*; however, in almost every case in which the power of government or the president was at stake, the courts ruled on the side of the government. The Zedillo administration tried to change this by emphasizing the rule of law over that of powerful individuals. Increasing interest in human rights issues by citizens' groups and the media added pressure to the courts to play a stronger role in protecting basic freedoms. Zedillo's refusal to interfere with the courts' judgments also strengthened the judiciary. This trajectory continued under Fox and Calderón.

Although the judicial system remains the weakest branch of government, reforms continue to be proposed. In 2008, in response to concern for the rights of defendants who fall victim to police and prosecutorial misconduct, constitutional amendments called for the introduction of public trials with oral testimony and the presumption of innocence. When fully implemented, the reforms will represent one of the most significant changes to the judiciary in modern Mexican history. The northern state of Chihuahua has been the first to adopt the new system, but the new procedures have been controversial there, and progress elsewhere in the country has been slow.

### Subnational Government

As with many other aspects of the Mexican political system, regional and local government in Mexico is quite different from what is described in the constitution. Under Mexico's federal system, each state has its own constitution, executive, unicameral legislature, and judiciary. Municipalities (equivalent to U.S. counties) are governed by popularly elected mayors and councils. But most state and municipal governments are poor. Most of the funds they command are transferred to them from the central government, and they have little legal or administrative capacity to raise their own revenue. States and localities also suffer greatly from the lack of well-trained and well-paid public officials. As at the national level, many jobs are distributed as political patronage, but even officials who are motivated to be responsive to local needs are generally ill equipped to do so. Since the early 1990s, the government has made several serious efforts to decentralize and devolve more power to state and local governments. At times, governors and mayors have resisted such initiatives because they meant that regional and local governments would have to manage much more complex activities and be the focus of demands from public sector workers and their unions. Local governments were also worried that they would be unable to acquire the budgetary resources necessary to carry out their new responsibilities.

Until 1988, all governors were from the PRI. Finally, in 1989, a non-PRI governor assumed power in Baja California, an important first. By 2011, eleven states and the Federal District were governed by parties other than the PRI. Also, municipalities have increasingly been the focus of authentic party competition. As opposition parties came to control these levels of government, they were challenged to improve services such as police protection, garbage collection, sanitation, and education. PRI-dominated governments have also tried to improve their performance because they are now more threatened by the possibility of losing elections.

# The Policy-Making Process

The Mexican system is very dependent on the quality of its leadership and on presidential understanding of how economic and social policies can affect the development of the country. As indicated throughout this chapter, the president's single six-year term of office, the *sexenio,* is an extremely important fact of political life in Mexico. New presidents can introduce extensive change in positions within the government. They are able to bring in "their" people, who build teams of "their" people within ministries, agencies, and party networks. This generally provides the president with a group of high- and middle-level officials who share the same general orientation toward public policy and are motivated to carry out his goals. When the PRI was the dominant party, these officials believed that in following presidential leadership, they enhanced their chances for upward political mobility. In such a context, even under a single party, it was likely that changes in public policies could be introduced every six years, creating innovation or discontinuity, or both.

Together with the bureaucracy, the president is the focal point of policy formulation and political management. Until 1997, the legislature always had a PRI majority and acted as a rubber stamp for presidentially sponsored legislation. Since then, the congress has proven to be a more active policy-maker, blocking and forcing the negotiation of legislation, and even introducing its own bills. The president's skills in negotiating, managing the opposition, using the media to acquire public support, and maneuvering within the bureaucracy can be important in ensuring that his program is fully endorsed.

Significant limits on presidential power occur when policy is being implemented. At times, policies are not implemented because public officials at the lower levels disagree with them or make deals with affected interests in order to benefit personally. This is the case, for example, with taxes that remain uncollected because individuals or corporations bribe officials to overlook them. In other cases, lower-level officials may lack the capacity or skills to implement some policies, such as those directed toward improving education or rural development services. For various reasons, Mexican presidents cannot always deliver on their intentions. Traditionally, Mexican citizens have blamed lower-level officials for such slippage, but exempting the president from responsibility for what does or does not occur during his watch has become much less common since the 1970s.

## Summary

On paper, Mexico's government resembles that of the United States, with three branches of government, checks and balances among them, and federalism defining the relationship between national, state, and local governments. In practice, however, the country developed a political system that concentrated most power in the hands of the president and the executive branch and managed political conflict through a dominant party. Much of the power of the president and the PRI was based on their capacity to use patronage to respond to political conflicts. This system is undergoing rapid change, as the legislature and court systems develop more independent roles, state and local governments acquire more independence, and the PRI no longer dominates the party system. Mexico, like the United States and Canada, is a federal republic with important power-sharing arrangements between the national and subnational levels of government. However, until the 1990s, state and local governments had few resources and a limited sphere of action when compared with the national level. Under the PRI, the executive branch held almost all power, while the legislative and judiciary branches followed the executive's lead and were considered rubber-stamp bodies. During the years of PRI hegemony, the government was civilian, authoritarian, and corporatist. Currently, Mexico has multiparty competitive elections, and power is less concentrated in the executive branch and the national government. Since the mid-1980s, great efforts have been made to reinvigorate the nation's laws and institutions and to make the country more democratic.

# REPRESENTATION AND PARTICIPATION

SECTION 4

How do citizen interests get represented in Mexican politics, given the high degree of centralization, presidentialism, and, until recently, PRI domination? Is it possible for ordinary citizens to make demands on government and influence public policy? In fact, Mexico has had a relatively peaceful history since the revolution, in part because the political system offers some channels for representation and participation. Throughout this long history, the political system has emphasized compromise among contending elites, behind-the-scenes conflict resolution, and distribution of political rewards to those willing to play by the formal and informal rules of the game.

It has also responded, if only reluctantly and defensively, to demands for change. (See Table 10.1 for an outline of Mexico's political organization.)

Often, citizens are best able to interact with the government through a variety of informal means rather than through the formal processes of elections, campaigns, and interest group lobbying. Interacting with government through the personal and informal mechanisms of clientelism usually means that the government retains the upper hand in deciding which interests to respond to and which to ignore. For many interests, this has meant "incorporation without power."[15] Increasingly, however, Mexican citizens are organizing to alter this situation, and the advent of truly competitive elections has increased the possibility that citizens who organize can gain some response from government.

# The Legislature

Students in the United States are frequently asked to study complex charts explaining how a bill becomes a law because the formal process of lawmaking affects the content of legislation. Under the old reign of the PRI in Mexico, while there were formal rules that prescribed such a process, studying them would not have been useful for understanding how the legislature worked. Because of the overwhelming dominance of the ruling party, opposition to presidential initiatives by Mexico's two-chamber legislature, the Senate and the Chamber of Deputies, was rarely heard. If representatives did not agree with policies they were asked to approve, they counted on the fact that policy implementation was flexible and allowed for after-the-fact bending of the rules or disregard of measures that were harmful to important interests.

Representation in Congress has become more diverse since the end of the 1980s. A greater number of political parties are now represented; women have begun to be elected to more positions; and some representatives have also emerged from the ranks of community activists.

After 1988, the PRI's grip on the legislature steadily weakened. By 2006, the party had only 106 representatives in the Chamber of Deputies, fewer than either of its two main rivals (see Figure 10.2). The PRI subsequently made large gains

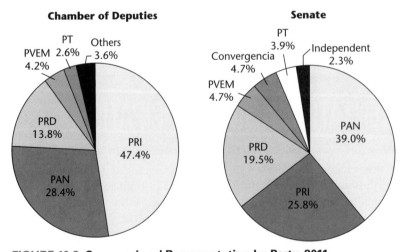

**FIGURE 10.2 Congressional Representation by Party, 2011**

*Source:* CIA World Factbook, www.cia.gov/library/publications/the-world-factbook/geos/mx.html#Govt; see also www.senado.gob.mx and www.camaradediputados.gob.mx.

in mid-term legislative elections in 2009, again becoming the largest party in the Chamber of Deputies, but the Congress remains divided between strong PRI, PAN, and PRD blocs, with no single party able to dominate proceedings. In large part because the PRI has lost its stranglehold on congressional representation, the role of the legislature in the policy process has been strengthened considerably since the late 1990s.[16] The cost of greater power sharing between the executive and the legislature, however, has been a slow-down in the policy process. The biggest change, therefore, has been that the Congress has evolved from a rubber-stamp institution to one that must be negotiated with by the executive branch.

# Political Parties and the Party System

Even under the long reign of the PRI, a number of political parties existed in Mexico. By the mid-1980s, some of them were attracting more political support, a trend that continued into the 1990s and 2000s (see Table 10.3). Electoral reforms introduced

| Table 10.3 | Voting for Major Parties in Presidential Elections, 1934–2006 | | | |
|---|---|---|---|---|
| Year | Votes for PRI Candidate | Votes for PAN Candidate | Votes for PRD Candidate | Voter Turnout (% of eligible adults) |
| 1934 | 98.2 | — | — | 53.6 |
| 1940 | 93.9 | — | — | 57.5 |
| 1946 | 77.9 | — | — | 42.6 |
| 1952 | 74.3 | 7.8 | — | 57.9 |
| 1958 | 90.4 | 9.4 | — | 49.4 |
| 1964 | 88.8 | 11.1 | — | 54.1 |
| 1970 | 83.3 | 13.9 | — | 63.9 |
| 1976 | 93.6 | — | — | 29.6 |
| 1982 | 71.0 | 15.7 | — | 66.1 |
| 1988 | 50.7 | 16.8 | 30.95 | 49.4 |
| 1994 | 50.1 | 26.7 | 16.59 | 77.16 |
| 2000 | 36.1 | 42.5 | 16.64 | 64.0 |
| 2006 | 22.26 | 35.89 | 35.31 | 58.55 |

*Source:* From *Comparative Politics Today: A World View*, 4th ed., Gabriel Almond and G. Bingham Powell, Jr. © 1988. Reprinted by permission of Addison-Wesley Educational Publishers, Inc. For 1988: *El Universal*, "*Resultados Electorales,*" graficos.eluniversal.com.mx/tablas/presidente/presidentes.htm. For 1994: Instituto Federal Electoral, *Estadística de las Elecciones Federales de 1994, Compendio de Resultados* (Mexico, D.F., 1995). For 2000 and 2006: Instituto Federal Electoral, www.ife.org.mx.

by the López Portillo, de la Madrid, Salinas, and Zedillo administrations made it easier for opposition parties to contest elections and win seats in the legislature. In 1990, an electoral commission was created to regulate campaigns and elections, and in 1996 it became fully independent of the government. Now all parties receive funding from the government and have access to the media. Furthermore, in 2008, Calderón successfully pushed through congress an electoral reform law that changed how political campaigns were financed.

## The PRI

Mexico's Institutional Revolutionary Party (PRI) was founded by a coalition of political elites who agreed that it was preferable to work out their conflicts within an overarching structure of compromise than to continue to resort to violence. In the 1930s, the forerunner of the PRI (the party operated under different names until 1946) incorporated a wide array of interests, becoming a mass-based party that drew support from all classes in the population. Over seven decades, its principal activities were to generate support for the government, organize the electorate to vote for its candidates, and distribute jobs and resources in return for loyalty to the system.

Until the 1990s, party organization was based largely on the corporatist representation of class interests. Labor was represented within party councils by the Confederation of Mexican Workers (CTM), which included industry-based unions at local, regional, and national levels. Peasants were represented by the National Peasant Confederation (CNC), an organization of *ejido* and peasant unions and regional associations. The so-called popular sector, comprising small businesses, community-based groups, and public employees, had less internal cohesion but was represented by the National Confederation of Popular Organizations (CNOP). Of the three, the CTM was consistently the best organized and most powerful. Traditionally, the PRI's strongest support came from the countryside, where *ejidatarios* and independent small farmers were dependent on rewards of land or jobs. As the country became more urbanized, the support base provided by rural communities remained important to the PRI, but produced many fewer votes than were necessary to keep the party in power.

Within its corporatist structures, the PRI functioned through extended networks that distributed public resources—particularly jobs, land, development projects, and access to public services—to lower-level activists who controlled votes at the local level. In this system, those with ambitions to hold public office or positions within the PRI put together networks of supporters from above (patrons), to whom they delivered votes, and supporters from below (clients), who traded allegiance for access to public resources. For well over half a century, this system worked extremely well. PRI candidates won by overwhelming majorities until the 1980s (see Figure 10.3). Of course, electoral fraud and the ability to distribute government largesse are central explanations for these numbers, but they also attest to an extremely well-organized party.

Within the PRI, power was centralized, and the sector organizations (the CTM, the CNC, and the CNOP) responded primarily to elites at the top of the political pyramid rather than to member interests. Over time, the corporate interest group organizations, particularly the CTM and the CNC, became widely identified with corruption, bossism, centralized control, and lack of effective participation. By the 1980s, new generations of voters were less beholden to patronage-style politics and much more willing to question the party's dominance. When the administrations of de la Madrid, Salinas, and Zedillo imposed harsh austerity measures, the PRI was held responsible for the resulting losses in incomes and benefits. Simultaneously, as the government cut back sharply on public sector jobs and services, the PRI had far fewer

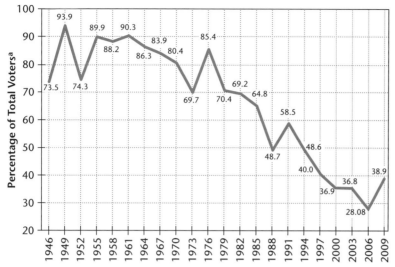

*a* Percentage base includes annulled votes and those cast for nonregistered candidates.

**FIGURE 10.3  PRI Support in Congressional Elections, 1946-2009**

*Source:* For 1946–1988: Juan Molinar Horcasitas, *El tiempo de la legtimidad: Elecciones, autoritarismo y democracia en México* (México, D.F.: Cal y Arena, 1991). For 1991: Secretaría Nacional de Estudios, Partido Acción Nacional, *Análisis del Proceso Federal Electoral 1994, 1995.* For 1994: Instituto Federal Electoral, *Estadístca de las Elecciones Federales de 1994, Compendio de Resultados* (Mexico, D.F., 1995). For 1997: www.ife.org.mx/ww-worge/tablas/mrent.htm. For 2000, 2003, and 2006: Instituto Federal Electoral, www.ife.org.mx. In 2003 and 2006, the PRI formed the senior partner in the *Alianza para Todos* (Alliance for Everyone), which brought the PRI and the much smaller PVEM together on a single ticket in some states in 2003 and at the national level in 2006. In 2006, the PRD formed the senior partner of the *Coalición por el Bien de Todos* (Coalition for the Good of All), which was formed with the Partido del Trabajo (Labor Party) and *Convergencia* (Convergence). *Source:* For 2009: Instituto Federal Electoral, http://prep2009.ife.org.mx/PREP2009/index_prep2009.html.

resources to distribute to maintain its traditional bases of support. Moreover, it began to suffer from increasing internal dissension between the old guard—the so-called dinosaurs—and the "modernizers" who wanted to reform the party.

In the late 1980s, the PRI began to be challenged by parties to the right and left, and outcomes were hotly contested by the opposition, which claimed fraudulent electoral practices. As the PRI faced greater competition from other parties and continued to suffer from declining popularity, efforts were made to restructure and reform it. Party conventions were introduced in an effort to democratize the internal workings of the party, and some states and localities began to hold primaries to select PRI candidates, a significant departure from the old system of selection by party bosses.

After the PRI lost the presidency in 2000, the party faced a difficult future. In the twenty-first century, Mexico's voters are younger, better educated, and more middle class than they were during the period of PRI dominance. They are also more likely to live in urban areas than they were in the days of the party's greatest success. The 1988 presidential elections demonstrated the relevance of changing demographic conditions when only 27.3 percent of the population of Mexico City voted for the PRI candidate and only 34.3 percent of the population in other urban areas supported him. By 2006, support for the party had fallen so far in the nation's capital that only 11.68 percent of voters in the Federal District cast their ballots for PRI congressional candidates. With the vast majority of the country's population now living in cities, the PRI will have to win the support of more urban voters. Nonetheless, the PRI continues to be one of Mexico's most important political parties, and many observers believe that the party could return to power. It did not, as some predicted, dissolve once it lost the ability to control the presidency. It is still the only party that has a presence in every region of the country, and after the violence and legislative gridlock of recent years, some Mexicans believe that the PRI could draw upon its long experience in government to offer a greater degree of order and stability.

### The PAN

The National Action Party (PAN) was founded in 1939 to represent interests opposed to the centralization and anticlericalism of the PRI. It was established by those who believed that the country needed more than one strong political party and that opposition parties should oppose the PRI through legal and constitutional actions. Historically, this party has been strongest in northern states, where the tradition of resistance to Mexico City is also strongest. It has also been primarily an urban party of the middle class and is closely identified with the private sector. The PAN has traditionally campaigned on a platform endorsing greater regional autonomy, less government intervention in the economy, reduced regulation of business, clean and fair elections, rapprochement with the Catholic Church, and support for private and religious education. When PRI governments of the 1980s and 1990s moved toward market-friendly and export-oriented policies, the policy differences between the two parties were significantly reduced. Nevertheless, a major difference of perspectives about religion continued to characterize the two parties.

For many years, the PAN was able to elect only 9 to 10 percent of all deputies to the national congress and to capture control of only a few municipal governments. Beginning in the 1980s and 1990s, it was able to take advantage both of the economic crises (and the PRI's subsequent weakened ability to control the political process) and political reforms to increase its power. By 2011, the PAN controlled the governorships of seven states, was the largest party in the Mexican Senate, and was the second-largest party in the Chamber of Deputies, after the PRI.

In 2000, the party took the unusual step of nominating Vicente Fox for the presidency, despite the fact that he was not a longstanding member of the party. Many party insiders considered him to be an opportunistic newcomer, and they worked to limit his ability to run for office, forcing him to look for other sources for financing his campaign. Starting in 1997, the "Friends of Fox" organization began to raise funds and promote his candidacy for president. Fox gained in popularity throughout the country, and in 1999, the party had little option but to nominate him as its candidate. The Friends of Fox continued to provide the most important source of campaign support, however, and when Fox won the presidential election, the PAN organization was weak and not at all united in backing him. His inability to capitalize on his electoral victory and push forward a more ambitious package of reforms allowed the party insiders to regain control of the nominating process and advance the candidacy of Felipe Calderón in 2006. Unlike Fox, he was a lifelong member of the PAN and was the son of one of the PAN's founding members.

### The PRD

Another significant challenge to the PRI has come from the Party of the Democratic Revolution (PRD), a populist, nationalist, and leftist alternative to the PRI. Its candidate in the 1988 and 1994 elections was Cuauhtémoc Cárdenas, the son of Mexico's most famous and revered president. He was a PRI insider until party leaders virtually ejected him for demanding internal reform of the party and a platform emphasizing social justice. In the 1988 elections, Cárdenas was officially credited with winning 31.1 percent of the vote, and his party captured 139 seats in the Chamber of Deputies. He benefited from massive political defection from the PRI and garnered support from workers disaffected with the boss-dominated unions, as well as from peasants who remembered his father's concern for agrarian reform and the welfare of the poor.

Even while the votes were being counted, the party began to denounce widespread electoral fraud and claim that Cárdenas would have won if the election had been honest. The party challenged a number of vote counts in the courts and walked out on the inaugural speech given by the PRI's Salinas. Considerable public opinion supported the party's challenge. After the 1988 elections, then, it seemed that the PRD was a strong contender to become Mexico's second-most-powerful party. It was expected to have a real chance in future years to challenge the PRI's "right" to the presidency.

Nevertheless, in the aftermath of these elections, the party was plagued by internal divisions over its platform, leadership, organizational structure, and election strategy. By 1994, it still lagged far behind the PRI and the PAN in establishing and maintaining the local constituency organizations needed to mobilize votes and monitor the election process. In addition, the PRD found it difficult to define an appropriate left-of-center alternative to the market-oriented policies carried out by the government. In the 1994 elections, Cárdenas won only 17 percent of the vote.

Thanks to the government's continued unpopular economic policies and the leadership of a successful grassroots mobilizer named Andrés Manuel López Obrador, who was elected to head the party in 1996, the PRD began to stage a remarkable turnaround. Factional bickering was controlled, and organizational discipline increased. In addition, the PRD proved successful in moving beyond its regional strongholds and established itself as a truly national party.

Thanks largely to its control over the capital city and the existence of PRD administrations on the municipal level in parts of the country, the party was able to boast that about a quarter of the country's population lived under a PRD government. Furthermore, under the leadership of López Obrador, the PRD's prospects for the 2006 elections looked good. Indeed, for most of 2005, polls indicated that López Obrador was the clear favorite to win the presidency. In early 2006, however, Calderón was able to shift the focus of his campaign and raise fears that a López Obrador presidency would threaten the stability of Mexico's economy. The election was hard fought and characterized by growing animosity. In the end, Calderón was able to win by a narrow margin. López Obrador refused to concede defeat and staged several protests, including a shadow inauguration where he declared himself the "legitimate" president of Mexico.

López Obrador's response to the outcome of the 2006 election split public opinion and created another debilitating divide in the PRD, this time between those who supported López Obrador's claims and more pragmatic party leaders who favored looking to the future. The pragmatists won control of the party, and in several recent state elections, the PRD has even formed alliances with the PAN, despite a lack of ideological common ground, in order to defeat a resurgent PRI. Meanwhile, López Obrador and his allies have criticized this strategy and cultivated the support of smaller parties. Though the PRD continues to govern the Federal District and several states, these deep divisions within the party make its future prospects uncertain.

## Other Parties

There are a number of smaller parties that contest elections in Mexico. In 2011, the most important small parties were: *Convergencia* (Convergence); *Partido del Trabajo* (PT, Labor Party); *Partido Verde Ecologista Mexicana* (PVEM, Green Party); and

*Partido Nueva Alianza* (New Alliance Party). Since Mexican law requires parties to receive at least 2.5 percent of the vote to be able to compete in future elections, the long-term viability of some of these organizations is doubtful. Small parties, however, usually do win a few of the seats in the Chamber of Deputies and the Senate that are filled by proportional representation. Also, these groups sometimes wield influence on national politics by forming alliances with the larger parties, either endorsing their candidates for president or governor in national and state elections or backing a single slate of candidates for congress. For example, in 2006, Convergence and the PT formed an alliance—the Coalition for the Good of All—with the PRD, while the Green Party joined with the PRI in the Alliance for Mexico. Though these parties can boost the fortunes of larger parties by forming alliances with them, they also have the potential to become a place of refuge for dissident factions that have lost out in internal struggles within the major parties, as is illustrated by the growing ties between the PT and supporters of Andrés Manuel López Obrador of the PRD.

## Elections

Each of the three main political parties draws voters from a wide and overlapping spectrum of the electorate. Nevertheless, a typical voter for the PRI is likely to be from a rural area or small town, to have less education, and to be older and poorer than voters for the other parties. A typical voter for the PAN is likely to be from a northern state, to live in an urban area, to be a middle-class professional, to have a comfortable lifestyle, and to have a high school or even a university education. A typical voter for the PRD is likely to be young, to be a political activist, to have an elementary or high school education, to live in one of the central states, and to live in a small town or an urban area. As we have seen, the support base for the PRI is the most vulnerable to economic and demographic changes in the country. Voting for opposition parties is an urban phenomenon, and a large majority of the Mexican population today lives in urban areas. This means that in order to stay competitive, the PRI will have to garner more support from cities and large towns. It must also be able to appeal to younger voters, especially the large numbers who are attracted to the PRD and the PAN.

Since 1994, elections have been more competitive and much fairer than they were during decades of PRI dominance, and subsequent congressional, state, and municipal elections reinforced the impression that electoral fraud is on the wane in many areas. The PAN's victory in 2000 substantially increased this impression. When López Obrador claimed in 2006 that Calderón's victory was fraudulent, the legitimacy of the federal electoral authorities was questioned, but no evidence of wide-scale fraud or election tampering was ever uncovered.

## Political Culture, Citizenship, and Identity

Most Mexicans have a deep familiarity with how their political system works and the ways in which they might be able to extract benefits from it. They understand the informal rules of the game in Mexican politics that have helped maintain political stability despite extensive inequalities in economic and political power. Clientelism has long been a form of participation in the sense that through their connections, many people, even the poorest, are able to interact with public officials and get something out of the political system. This kind of participation emphasizes how limited resources, such as access to health care, can be distributed in a way that provides maximum political payoff. This informal system is a fundamental reason that many Mexicans continued to vote for the PRI for so long.

However, new ways of interacting with government are emerging, and they coexist along with the clientelistic style of the past. An increasing number of citizens are seeking to negotiate with the government on the basis of citizenship rights, not personal patron-client relationships. The movements that emerged in the 1980s sought to form broad but loose coalitions with other organizations and attempted to identify and work with reform-oriented public officials. Their suspicion of traditional political organizations such as the PRI and its affiliates also led them to avoid close alliances with other parties, such as the PAN and the PRD.

As politics and elections became more open and competitive, the roles of public opinion and the mass media have become more important. Today, the media play an important role in forming public opinion in Mexico. As with other aspects of Mexican politics, the media began to become more independent in the 1980s, enjoying a "spring" of greater independence and diversity of opinion.[17] There are currently several major television networks in the country, and many citizens have access to CNN and other global networks. The number of newspapers is expanding, as is their circulation, and several news magazines play the same role in Mexico that *Time* and *Newsweek* do in the United States. To be sure, there is some concern that many of the most important and influential media outlets in the country are controlled by a small number of individuals and corporations. Also, violence against and intimidation of Mexican journalists by drug trafficking organizations has limited the ability of the press to report on the important issues raised in the context of the fight against organized crime in recent years. Nonetheless, citizens in Mexico today hear a much wider range of opinion and much greater reporting of debates about public policy and criticism of government than at any time previously.

# Interests, Social Movements, and Protest

The Mexican political system has long responded to groups of citizens through pragmatic **accommodation** to their interests. This is one important reason that political tensions among major interests have rarely escalated into the kind of serious conflict that can threaten stability. Where open conflict has occurred, it has generally been met with efforts to find some kind of compromise solution. Accommodation has been particularly apparent in response to the interests of business. Mexico's development strategy encouraged the growth of wealthy elites in commerce, finance, industry, and agriculture (see Section 2).

Labor has been similarly accommodated within the system. Wage levels for unionized workers grew fairly consistently between 1940 and 1982, when the economic crisis caused a significant drop in wages. At the same time, labor interests were attended to through concrete benefits and limitations on the rights of employers to discipline or dismiss workers. Union leaders controlled their rank and file in the interest of their own power to negotiate with government, but at the same time, they sought benefits for workers who continued to provide support for the PRI. The power of the union bosses has declined, in part because the unions are weaker than in the past, in part because union members are demanding greater democratization, and in part because the PRI no longer monopolizes political power. Likewise, in the countryside, rural organizations have gained greater independence from the government. Indigenous groups have also emerged to demand that government be responsive to their needs

**accommodation**

An informal agreement or settlement between the government and important interest groups in response to the interest groups' concerns for policy or program benefits.

Mexicans are accustomed to making demands on their leaders, and protest is an established feature of Mexican political culture. Here, protesters march into Mexico City's central square, the Zócalo.

and respectful of their traditions. Since 1994, the Zapatista rebels in Chiapas, who are still engaged in largely nonviolent opposition to the Mexican state, have become a focal point for broad alliances of those concerned about the rights of indigenous groups (ethnic minorities) and rural poverty.

Despite the strong and controlling role of the PRI in Mexico's political history, the country also has a tradition of civic organizations that operate at community and local levels with considerable independence from politics. Urban popular movements, formed by low- and modest-income (popular) groups, gained renewed vitality in the 1980s.[18] When the economic crisis resulted in drastic reductions of social welfare spending and city services, working- and middle-class neighborhoods forged new coalitions and greatly expanded the national discussion of urban problems. The Mexico City earthquake of 1985 encouraged the formation of unprecedented numbers of grassroots movements in response to the slow and poorly managed relief efforts of the government. The elections of 1988 and 1994 provided these groups with significant opportunities to press parties and candidates to respond to their needs. As the opposition parties expanded rapidly, some leaders of urban movements enrolled as candidates for public office.

Urban popular movements bring citizens together around needs and ideals that cut across class boundaries. Neighborhood improvement, the environment, local self-government, economic development, feminism, and professional identity have been among the factors that have forged links among these groups. Women have begun to mobilize in many cities to demand community services, equal pay, legal equality, and opportunities in business that have traditionally been denied to them.

Previously, parties of the left focused most of their attention on questions of economic redistribution, but this has recently begun to change. Political issues that are commonly discussed in the United States, such as abortion and gay rights, have recently begun to be debated publicly in Mexico. In April 2007, the PRD-controlled legislature of Mexico City voted to decriminalize abortions in the first trimester (in the rest of Mexico abortion continues to be illegal except in cases of rape or severe birth defects, although in fact gaining access to a legal abortion even under these circumstances is exceedingly difficult). And in November 2006, the PRD voted to legalize gay civil unions in the Federal District. The PAN remains vehemently opposed to these measures. For example, in 2000 the PAN-dominated legislature of Guanajuato voted to ban abortion even in the case of rape, and established penalties of up to three years in prison for women who violated the law.

Although President Vicente Fox was opposed to abortion, he did attempt to distance himself from the Guanajuato law and for the most part avoided discussing contentious social and cultural subjects. But under his administration condom use was encouraged and a campaign against homophobia was launched. In 2004, he caused a furor within his own party when his administration approved the distribution of the morning-after pill in public clinics. These policies were denounced by Calderón, who vowed in his 2006 campaign to ban the use of this pill and openly expressed his opposition to abortion and gay rights.

## Summary

Democratic politics is growing stronger in Mexico. The elections of 2000 and 2006 demonstrated that a transition of power from a civilian authoritarian regime to a more democratic one could take place relatively peacefully. The causes of this important change emerged gradually, as Mexican citizens developed the capacity to question the dominance of the PRI regime and as the government introduced important changes that opened up opportunities for opposition parties to develop and for people to vote more easily for these parties. Parties such as the PAN and the PRD are developing greater capacity to campaign effectively for office, and civil society groups are becoming better organized and more capable of having an impact on government policies. Citizens are also enjoying greater access to a variety of sources of information about government. Challenges remain in terms of how citizens in Mexico relate to the political system and the government, but trends toward the consolidation of an effective democratic political system are positive.

# MEXICAN POLITICS IN TRANSITION

SECTION **5**

The Mexican political landscape has been transformed over the past twenty years, as a long period of dominance by a single party has given way to a competitive multiparty system. The country's institutions, leaders, and citizens are still adjusting to this ongoing process of change. While most Mexicans are proud that their political system has become more democratic, many also lament that the division of power between political parties and branches of government at times seems to make the state less efficient and possibly less able to address effectively the challenges of development and governance faced by Mexico.

One particularly dramatic illustration of how much Mexican politics has changed in recent decades can be seen on September 1 of each year, when, in accordance with

**Focus Questions**

In what ways is economic integration with the rest of the world affecting political and social changes in Mexico? Which groups of people is it hurting most? Helping most?

What challenges does the process of globalization pose to Mexicans' strong sense of national identity?

How successful has Mexico been in confronting the legacy of authoritarian rule? To what extent have recent administrations been able to make the government more accountable and transparent?

Does Mexico offer lessons for other countries moving from authoritarian forms of governance to more democratic ones? What features of the Mexican experience might other countries usefully follow? What features are so peculiar to Mexico that they offer little guidance to the rest of the world?

Article 69 of the Constitution of 1917, the executive branch delivers a report on the state of the nation and the actions of the administration to the Mexican congress at the opening of its annual session. For decades, this date was known informally as the "Day of the President," as the ritual surrounding the address highlighted the prestige and authority of the chief executive. The president would don his ceremonial red, white, and green sash before traveling to the legislative chambers from the National Palace, the symbolic seat of power in Mexico since the days of the Spanish viceroys. While delivering his *informe* (report), the president could count on a respectful hearing from an attentive audience of deputies and senators who were overwhelmingly drawn from the ranks of his own party. Though the spectacle of the *informe* during the heyday of PRI dominance excluded dissenting voices, it projected an image of a strong, stable political system. Even in 1982, when President José López Portillo broke into tears while reporting on his failure to avert a debt crisis that sent the country into an economic tailspin, legislators dutifully applauded.

That deference to the president began to break down in 1988, however. After a contentious presidential election marred by allegations of fraud, a legislator who had broken away from the PRI to support opposition candidate Cuauhtémoc Cárdenas dared to interrupt President Miguel de la Madrid's September 1 speech. More recently, after members of the PRD charged that Felipe Calderón's election in 2006 was illegitimate, outgoing President Vicente Fox was prevented from even reaching the rostrum when he arrived to give his address on September 1 of that year. He complied with his constitutional mandate by submitting a printed copy of his report and then left the building without delivering his speech. In 2007, President Felipe Calderón likewise appeared before a deeply divided Congress only long enough to hand over a printed version of his *informe*, and new rules introduced in 2008 eliminated the requirement that the president deliver his report in person. Since then, the annual report of the executive branch has been transmitted by a government minister to the legislature, where representatives of all the parties represented in Congress then deliver a response. Thus, the number of voices heard on important national issues has increased, though to many the fact that the president is no longer able to appear before Congress suggests that the capacity of the state has been diminished.

# Political Challenges and Changing Agendas

As Mexicans adjust and adapt to the dramatic political transition of recent years, they are conscious that their nation faces many challenges, and they are struggling to build a political system that will be both democratic and effective. They are calling upon the state to be open about abuses of authority in the past and to protect citizens from such abuses in the future. They seek to address long-standing inequalities in Mexican society, in part by ensuring that women and ethnic minorities have access to economic opportunities and social services. They also hope to preserve Mexican identity while, at the same time, realizing the economic benefits of integration into global networks.

Mexico today provides a testing ground for the democratic idea in a state with a long history of authoritarian institutions. The democratic ideas of citizen rights to free speech and assembly, free and fair elections, and responsive government are major reasons that the power of the PRI came under so much attack beginning in the 1980s. As part of its commitment to delivering a sharp change from the practices of the past, the administration of Vicente Fox (2000–2006) pledged to make government more transparent and to improve the state of human rights in Mexico. In the past, the government had been able to limit knowledge of its repressive actions, use the court system to maintain the political peace, and intimidate those who objected to its actions. Fox appointed human rights activists to his cabinet and ordered that secret police and military files be opened to public scrutiny. He instructed government ministries to supply more information about their activities and about the rights that citizens have to various kinds of services. Fox also invited the United Nations to open a human rights office in Mexico. He encouraged the ratification of the Inter-American Convention on Enforced Disappearance of Persons. The government also sought to protect the rights of Mexicans abroad, and the United States and Mexico established a working group to improve human rights conditions for migrants.

The results of these actions have been dramatic. For the first time, Mexicans learned of cases of hundreds of people who had "disappeared" as a result of police and military actions. In addition, citizens have come forward to announce other disappearances, ones they were unwilling to report earlier because they feared reprisals. In 2002, former president Luis Echeverría was brought before prosecutors and questioned about government actions against political dissent in 1968 and 1971, a kind of accountability unheard of in the past. The National Human Rights Commission has been active in efforts to hold government officials accountable and to protect citizens nationally and abroad from repetitions of the abuses of the past.

Yet challenges to human rights accountability remain. Opening up files and setting up systems for prosecuting abusers needs to be followed by actions to impose penalties on abusers. The Mexican judicial system is weak and has little experience in human rights cases. In addition, action on reports of disappearances, torture, and imprisonment has been slowed by disagreement about civil and military jurisdictions. In a revelation that was embarrassing to the government, Amnesty International reported several cases of disappearances that occurred after Fox assumed leadership of the country. There were also reports of arbitrary detentions and extrajudicial executions. In October 2001, Digna Ochoa, a prominent human rights lawyer, was shot. In the aftermath of this assassination, the government was accused of not doing enough to protect her, even when it was widely known that she had been targeted by those opposed to her work. Human rights activists claimed that police and military personnel, in particular, still had impunity from the laws, and human rights concerns have grown as the military has taken a more direct role in law enforcement in the context of the Calderón administration's effort to dismantle drug trafficking organizations. Human rights advocates point to recent alleged abuses by members of the armed forces and call for greater accountability from an institution that is still shielded from much civilian scrutiny. Although human rights are much more likely to be protected than in the past, the government still has a long way to go in safeguarding the rights of indigenous people, political dissidents, migrants, gays and lesbians, and poor people whose ability to use the judicial system is limited by poverty and lack of information.

Currently, Mexico is struggling with opening up its political institutions to become more democratic. However, efforts to bring about greater transparency in the Mexican political system often run up against obstacles. These setbacks have left some Mexicans skeptical of claims that a truly open, democratic political culture is being forged.

Mexico is also confronting major challenges in adapting newly democratic institutions to reflect ethnic and religious diversity and to provide equity for women in economic and political affairs. The past two decades have witnessed the emergence of more organized and politically independent ethnic groups demanding justice and equality from government. These groups claim that they have suffered for nearly 500 years and that they are no longer willing to accept poverty and marginality as their lot. The Roman Catholic Church, still the largest organized religion in the country, is losing members to Protestant sects that appeal particularly to the everyday concerns of poor Mexicans. Women, who make up 37 percent of the formal labor force and 42 percent of professional and technical workers, are becoming more organized, but they still have a long way to go before their wages equal those of men or they have equal voice in political and economic decisions.

Another significant challenge for Mexico today is reconciling its strong sense of national identity with the strains placed on a country's sovereignty by the process of global economic integration. Mexicans define themselves in part through a set of historical events, symbols, and myths that focus on the country's troubled relationship with the United States. The myths of the Revolution of 1910 emphasize the uniqueness of the country in terms of its opposition to the capitalists and militarists of the northern country. In the 1970s, Mexicans were encouraged to see themselves as leading Third World countries in arguing for enhanced bargaining positions in relation to the industrialized countries of the north. This view stands in strong contrast to more recent perspectives touting the benefits of an internationally oriented economy and the undeniable post-NAFTA reality of information, culture, money, and people flowing back and forth across borders.

The country's sense of national identity is also affected by international migration. Every year, large numbers of Mexicans enter the United States as workers. Many return to their towns and villages with new values and new views of the world. Many stay in the United States, where Hispanics have become the largest ethnic minority population in the country. Although they believe that Mexico is a better place to nurture strong family life and values, they are nevertheless strongly influenced by U.S. mass culture, including popular music, movies, television programs, fast food, and consumer goods.

The inability of the Mexican economy to create enough jobs pushes additional Mexicans to seek work in the United States, and the cash remittances that migrants abroad send home to their families and communities are now almost as important a source of income for Mexico as PEMEX's oil sales. However, the issues surrounding migration have become even more complex since the attacks of September 11, 2001. Hopes for a bilateral accord that would permit more Mexicans to enter and work in the United States legally evaporated after U.S. officials suddenly found themselves under greatly increased pressure to control the country's borders. Whether or not the U.S. government approves, the difference in wages between the United States and Mexico will persist for a long time, which implies that migration will also persist.

There is disagreement about how to respond to the economic challenges that Mexico faces. Much of the debate surrounds the question of what integration into a competitive international economy really means. For some, it represents the final abandonment of Mexico's sovereignty. For others, it is the basis on which future prosperity must be built. Those who are critical of the market-based, outward-oriented development strategy are concerned about its impact on workers, peasants, and national identities. They argue that the state has abandoned its responsibilities to protect the poor from shortcomings of the market and to provide for their basic needs. They believe that U.S. and Canadian investors have come to Mexico only to find low-wage labor for industrial empires located elsewhere, and they point out that many of those investors did not hesitate to abandon Mexico when the opportunity arose to move to even lower-wage countries such as China. They see little benefit in further industrial development based on importation of foreign-made parts, their assembly in Mexico, and their export to other markets. This kind of development, they argue, has been prevalent in the *maquiladoras,* or assembly industries, many of which are located along the U.S.–Mexico border. Those who favor closer integration with Canada and the United States acknowledge that some foreign investment does not promote technological advances or move the work force into higher-paying and more skilled jobs. They emphasize, however, that most investment will occur because Mexico has a relatively well-educated population, the capacity to absorb modern technology, and a large internal market for industrial goods.

Inequality represents another daunting challenge for Mexican society. While elites enjoy the benefits of sumptuous lifestyles, education at the best U.S. universities for their children, and luxury travel throughout the world, large numbers of Mexicans remain ill-educated, poorly served with health care, and distant from the security of knowing that their basic needs for food, shelter, and employment will be met. As in the United States, some argue that the best solutions to these problems are economic growth and expanded employment. They believe that the achievement of prosperity through integration into the global economy will benefit everyone in the long run. For this to occur, however, they insist that education will have to be improved and made more appropriate for developing a well-prepared work force. They also believe that improved education will come about when local communities have more control over schools and curricula and when parents have more choice between public and private education for their children. From their perspective, the solution to poverty and injustice is fairly clear: more and better jobs and improved education.

For those critical of the development path on which Mexico embarked in the 1980s and 1990s, the problems of poverty and inequity are more complex. Solutions involve understanding the diverse causes of poverty, including not only lack of jobs and poor education but also exploitation, geographic isolation, and discriminatory laws and practices, as well as the disruptive impact of migration, urbanization, and the tensions of modern life. In the past, Mexicans looked to government for social welfare benefits, but their provision was deeply flawed by inefficiency and political manipulation. The government consistently used access to social services as a means to increase its political control and limit the capacity of citizens to demand equitable treatment. Thus, although many continue to believe that it is the responsibility of government to ensure that citizens are well educated, healthy, and able to make the most of their potential, the populace is deeply suspicious of the government's capacity to provide such conditions fairly and efficiently.

# Mexican Politics in Comparative Perspective

Mexico faces many of the same challenges that beset other countries: creating equitable and effective democratic government, becoming integrated into a global economy, responding to complex social problems, and supporting increasing diversity without losing national identity. Indeed, these are precisely the challenges faced by the United States, as well as by India, Nigeria, Brazil, Germany, and others. The legacies of its past, the tensions of the present, and the innovations of the future will no doubt evolve in ways that continue to be uniquely Mexican.

Mexico represents a pivotal case of political and economic transition for the developing world. If it can successfully bridge the gap between its past and its future and move from centralization to effective local governance, from regional vulnerability to global interdependence, and from the control of the few to the participation of the many, it will set a model for other countries that face the same kind of challenges.

## Summary

What will the future bring? How much will the pressures for change and the potential loss of national identity affect the nature of the political system? In 1980, few people could have foreseen the extensive economic policy reforms and pressures for democracy that Mexico would experience in the next three decades. Few would have predicted the defeat of the PRI in the elections of 2000 or the electoral outcome of 2006. In considering the future of the country, it is important to remember that Mexico has a long tradition of relatively strong institutions. It is not a country that will easily slip into sustained political instability. Despite real challenges faced as Mexico confronts criminal organizations and seeks to reform its police forces and judicial system, the country is not in danger of becoming a "failed state," as some outside observers have been tempted to suggest. A tradition of constitutional government, a strong presidency, a political system that has incorporated a wide range of interests, little military involvement in politics, and a deep sense of national identity—these are among the factors that need to be considered in understanding the political consequences of democratization, economic integration, and greater social equality in Mexico.

## Key Terms

| | | |
|---|---|---|
| *mestizo* | North American Free Trade | green revolution |
| Amerindian | Agreement (NAFTA) | informal sector |
| indigenous groups | newly industrializing | proportional representation |
| *maquiladoras* | countries (NICs) | (PR) |
| coup d'état | corporatist state | *sexenio* |
| anticlericalism | civil society | technocrats |
| *ejidos* | state capitalism | parastatal |
| *ejidatarios* | import substitution | accommodation |
| clientelism | industrialization (ISI) | |

## Suggested Readings

Babb, Sarah L. *Managing Mexico: Economists from Nationalism to Neoliberalism.* Princeton, NJ: Princeton University Press, 2001.

Call, Wendy. *No Word for Welcome: The Mexican Village Faces the Global Economy.* Lincoln: University of Nebraska Press, 2011.

Camp, Roderic Ai. *The Metamorphosis of Leadership in a Democratic Mexico.* Oxford University Press, 2010.

Ibid. *Politics in Mexico: The Democratic Consolidation,* 5th ed. New York: Oxford University Press, 2007.

Chand, Vickram K. *Mexico's Political Awakening.* Notre Dame, IN: University of Notre Dame Press, 2001.

Davidow, Jeffrey. *The U.S. and Mexico: The Bear and the Porcupine.* Princeton, NJ: Markus Wiener Publishers, 2004.

Delano, Alexandra. *Mexico and its Diaspora in the United States: Policies of Emigration since 1848.* New York: Cambridge University Press, 2011.

Dominguez, Jorge I., and Chappell H. Lawson (eds.). *Mexico's Pivotal Democratic Election: Candidates, Voters, and the Presidential Campaign of 2000.* Stanford, CA: Stanford University Press, 2004.

Eisenstadt, Todd A. *Politics, Identity, and Mexico's Indigenous Rights Movements* (Cambridge Studies in Contentious Politics). New York: Cambridge University Press, 2011.

Fitzgerald, David. *A Nation of Emigrants: How Mexico Manages Its Migration.* Berkeley: University of California Press, 2008.

Gauss, Susan M. *Made in Mexico: Regions, Nation, and the State in the Rise of Mexican Industrialism, 1920s–1940s.* University Park: Pennsylvania State University Press, 2011.

Grayson, George. *Mexico: Narco-Violence and a Failed State?* Piscataway, NJ: Transaction Publishers, 2009.

Grindle, Merilee S. *Challenging the State: Crisis and Innovation in Latin America and Africa.* Cambridge: Cambridge University Press, 1995.

Hamilton, Nora. *Mexico: Political, Social and Economic Evolution*. New York: Oxford University Press, 2010.

Harvey, Neil. *The Chiapas Rebellion: The Struggle for Land and Democracy*. Durham, NC: Duke University Press, 1998.

Henderson, Timothy J. *Beyond Borders: A History of Mexican Migration to the United States*. New York: Wiley-Blackwell, 2011.

Joseph, Gilbert M., Timothy J. Henderson, Robin Kirk, and Orin Starn. *The Mexico Reader: History, Culture, Politics*. Durham, NC: Duke University Press, 2002.

Katz, Friedrich. *The Life and Times of Pancho Villa*. Stanford, CA: Stanford University Press, 1998.

Lawson, Chappell H. *Building the Fourth Estate: Democratization and the Rise of a Free Press in Mexico*. Berkeley: University of California, 2002.

Levy, Daniel C., and Kathleen Bruhn. *Mexico: The Struggle for Democratic Development*. Berkeley: University of California Press, 2001.

Meyer, Michael C., William L. Sherman, and Susan M. Deeds. *The Course of Mexican History*, 9th ed. New York: Oxford University Press, 2010.

Paz, Octavio *The Labyrinth of Solitude: The Other Mexico, Return to the Labyrinth of Solitude, Mexico and the United States, the Philanthropic Ogre*. Revised edition. New York: Grove Press, 1994.

Preston, Julia, and Samuel Dillon. *Opening Mexico: The Making of a Democracy*. New York: Farrar, Straus and Giroux, 2004.

Salinas de Gortari, Carlos. *México: The Policy and Politics of Modernization*. Trans. by Peter Hearn and Patricia Rosas. Barcelona: Plaza & Janés Editores, 2002.

Selee, Andrew, and Jacqueline Peschard. *Mexico's Democratic Challenges: Politics, Government, and Society*. Stanford, CA: Stanford University Press, 2010.

Speed, Shannon. *Rights in Rebellion: Indigenous Struggle and Human Rights in Chiapas*. Stanford, CA: Stanford University Press, 2007.

Trevizo, Dolores. *Rural Protest and the Making of Democracy in Mexico, 1968–2000*. University Park: Pennsylvania State University Press, 2011.

Ugalde, Luis Carlos. *The Mexican Congress: Old Player, New Power*. Washington, DC: Center for Strategic and International Studies, 2000.

Womack, John, Jr. *Zapata and the Mexican Revolution*. New York: Vintage Books, 1968.

Wuhs, Steven T. *Savage Democracy: Institutional Change and Party Development in Mexico*. University Park: Pennsylvania State University Press, 2011.

## Suggested Websites

Office of the President (in Spanish and English)
**www.presidencia.gob.mx**

Secretariat of Foreign Relations (in Spanish and English)
**www.sre.gob.mx**

Mexican Embassy to the United States
**http://embamex.sre.gob.mx/usa/**

Office of Mexican Affairs, U.S. Department of State
**http://www.state.gov/p/wha/ci/mx/**

The Mexico Project, National Security Archive
**www2.gwu.edu/~nsarchiv/mexico**

# 11 South Africa

Tom Lodge

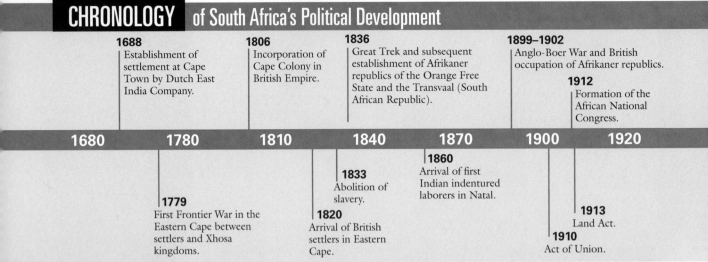

**1688**
Establishment of settlement at Cape Town by Dutch East India Company.

**1806**
Incorporation of Cape Colony in British Empire.

**1836**
Great Trek and subsequent establishment of Afrikaner republics of the Orange Free State and the Transvaal (South African Republic).

**1899–1902**
Anglo-Boer War and British occupation of Afrikaner republics.

**1912**
Formation of the African National Congress.

1680    1780    1810    1840    1870    1900    1920

**1833**
Abolition of slavery.

**1860**
Arrival of first Indian indentured laborers in Natal.

**1779**
First Frontier War in the Eastern Cape between settlers and Xhosa kingdoms.

**1820**
Arrival of British settlers in Eastern Cape.

**1913**
Land Act.

**1910**
Act of Union.

# THE MAKING OF THE MODERN SOUTH AFRICAN STATE

## Focus Questions

Why did institutionalized racism become such a central characteristic of South African social life in the twentieth century?

How was apartheid ended in South Africa?

In which ways does racial segregation persist in South Africa?

Why has South Africa attracted so much international attention?

## Politics in Action

In 2009 South Africa's president, Jacob Zuma, seemed to have achieved what was once unthinkable. To many observers over the preceding decade he had appeared such an unlikely claimant to his party's and his country's highest office, despite his appointment as deputy president in 1999. His accession to the state presidency followed a fierce conflict within in his own party in which a majority of delegates at a conference of the ruling African National Congress (ANC) at the end of 2007 voted against the re-election of the incumbent president, Thabo Mbeki, a set-back that led to Mbeki's resignation from public office in August the following year.

At the conference Zuma's supporters came from two groupings within the ANC, its youth activists, mobilised by the Congress's Youth League, many of them young unemployed men, and from the ANC's left wing allies within the trade union movement and the Communist Party. Their combined influence was sufficient to challenge the authority of the party notables assembled in support of Mbeki. To these groups, Jacob Zuma appeared a champion: a people's person, open and sympathetic. Leftwingers within the ANC disliked the pro-business orientation of Mbeki's policies, especially with respect to the ways in which public enterprises were being managed. Youth Leaguers liked Zuma's heroic track record as an anti-apartheid guerrilla organiser and political prisoner, and in certain quarters, Zuma's "traditionalist" lifestyle—his polygamous marriages and easy familiarity with rural etiquette—represented powerful qualifications for the highest position.

To his opponents within the ANC Zuma's lack of formal education, his bucolic habits, his inability to master the arcane phraseology in the language ANC leaders liked to use in public, and his tangles with the law all made him a most unsuitable candidate for office. In truth, though, even Zuma's legal difficulties helped to generate public approval. In 2007 he was still facing charges for accepting bribes offered during the negotiation of a government defence contract in 1999. The previous year

**1923**
Native Urban Areas Act codifies urban racial segregation.

**1960**
Sharpeville massacre and prohibition of the two main African nationalist organizations, the ANC and the PAC.

**1976**
Soweto uprising.

**1992**
Opening of constitutional negotiations.

**1996**
Adoption of final constitution.

**1999**
Thabo Mbeki succeeds Nelson Mandela as president.

**2008**
Thabo Mbeki resigns from the presidency after criticism for putting pressure on the Directorate for Public Prosecutions.

| **1925** | **1950** | **1980** | **1990** | **2000** | **2010** |
|---|---|---|---|---|---|

**1922**
Rand Rebellion by white mineworkers.

**1926**
Institution of job reservation for white workers in the Mines and Works Amendment Act.

**1948**
Election into power of National Party and the inception of Apartheid program.

**1986**
Repeal of the pass laws.

**1994**
First universal suffrage election under a transitional constitution.

**1990**
Unbanning of the ANC and the PAC and release of political prisoners.

**2010**
South Africa hosts the World Cup Soccer tournament, a recognition of the country's transition from apartheid to democracy.

**2009**
ANC wins fourth victory in national elections. Jacob Zuma becomes president.

he was acquitted in a rape case in which his defence had been that his accuser, a houseguest, had signalled her availability, by wearing a short skirt and failing to cross her legs, wanton behavior from the standpoint of decorous Zulu convention. If he was mistaken, Zuma told the court, he would "have had his cows ready if his accuser had agreed to marry him." The judge found him not guilty for other reasons, but Zuma's explanation of his actions resonated morally with the honor code of so many of his supporters, socially marginalised young men, still emotionally rooted in a rural patriarchal culture.

By 2011, the coincidences of interests that had assembled behind Zuma's claims for leadership between 2007 and 2009 had weakened. This became obvious in an unusually open quarrel amongst ANC notables, prompted by Zuma's friendship with the three Gupta brothers, entrepreneurs who had arrived in South Africa from India in 1993 to seek out new business opportunities, hoping to exploit social networks created by earlier migrations from India to South Africa. The Guptas established a computer company, Sahara, not to be confused with the Indian conglomerate with the same name. For the next decade or so, they prospered modestly, making useful political friendships. Rajesh Gupta became friendly with Essop Pahad, a minister in the president's office, and in 2001 Sahara Computers hired Jacob Zuma's son, Duduzane, as an intern. In 2006 the Guptas joined forces with one of the key "black empowerment" companies. Mvelephanda, owned by Tokyo Sexwale, an important ANC personality who himself would line up beside Zuma in his efforts to depose Mbeki. After Zuma's accession to the presidency in 2009, connections between the Zuma and Gupta families proliferated. Two additional young Zumas, a daughter and a nephew, joined Gupta-owned companies. More worryingly, a new enterprise, Mabengele, directed by Duduzane Zuma and the Gupta brothers secured a succession of partnerships with foreign investments in significant strategic sectors, deals that were "facilitated" by the government, or which depended upon official concessions. Meanwhile the Guptas began to boast about their political influence, informing deputy ministers about their impending promotions before a cabinet reshuffle at the end of 2010. Senior ANC officials complained to journalists that the Guptas were able to subvert the party's control over public appointments, ensuring their associates were put into key posts in parastatal corporations.

By February 2011, anxieties over the "Gupta rampage" were placed emphatically in the public domain, when the ANC's trade union partner, COSATU, issued a statement in which it announced it would set up an investigation to assess allegations that the Guptas were "plundering the economy." That month, Julius Malewa, the volatile president of the Youth League, and in the past a fervent Zuma supporter, chose a key occasion, the ANC's launch of its local government program, to attack the Guptas: "This is not a democracy of families" he said.

Malewa's intervention represented a step too far, however, for such a public criticism of the leadership still represents a violation of ANC norms, and his breach of protocol gave his enemies a key opportunity. Within the ANC, the Youth League president is not a universally admired figure, and not withstanding their joint support of Zuma's candidacy, left-wingers view him as a dangerous demagogue and a racial nationalist, a self-professed admirer of Zimbabwe's Robert Mugabe, widely regarded as one of the world's worst despots. Accordingly, the South African Communist Party's secretary general Blade Nzimande warned that whilst communists should be concerned about people using political connections to become wealthy, complaints about the Guptas might be prompted simply by jealousies among people who had lost out in the spoils system. The ANC's secretary general, Gwede Mantashe, himself a communist, seemed to agree with this view: Criticism of the Guptas' influence was prompted by racial prejudice, he told journalists.

In reality, no top ANC leaders can really be very anxious about the use of political connections to build private fortunes; such behavior has become institutionalized through the party's own procedures. Differences over the Guptas' friendship with President Zuma signal rather a deeper struggle for power within the ANC. Rivalries between the left wing and the Youth League are set to intensify before the elections for top party positions in 2012. Each group hopes to settle unresolved issues about the ANC's long-term trajectory. Is the ANC to be a movement still largely driven by its traditional ideological mooring with the socialist left, or is it rather, as Malewa and his comrades would prefer, to be more prompted by African **irredentism** and ideas about racial dignity? Today, whether Jacob Zuma himself can survive such a conflict and secure a second term in office looks very questionable.

**irredentism**

In this setting, irredentism is the belief that South Africa should be governed mainly or even exclusively by "indigenous' Africans."

| Table 11.1 | Political Organization |
|---|---|
| **Political System** | Parliamentary democracy and federal republic. |
| **Regime History** | Governed by an African National Congress–led coalition from 1994. Between 1910 and 1994 governments were formed by parties representing a white minority and were elected through racially restricted franchises. A British dominion until 1961 and then a republic. |
| **Administrative Structure** | Nine regional governments sharing authority with a national administration. Regional governments have few exclusive legislative powers and can be overridden on most significant issues by national legislatures. |
| **Executive** | President elected by parliament. President selects cabinet. |
| **Legislature** | National assembly and regional legislatures elected on the basis of party list proportional representation. National Council of Provinces made up by delegations from each regional government serves as a second chamber of parliament. |
| **Judiciary** | Independent constitutional court with appointed judges. |
| **Party System** | Multiparty system. African National Congress predominates. Other important parties: Democratic Alliance, Congress of the People, Inkatha Freedom Party, United Democratic Movement, Freedom Front. |

# Geographic Setting

South Africa is about twice the size of Texas. In 2011 the population was around 50 million. Sixty-one percent of this population lives in towns and cities. Government statistics divide the population into four main race groups: nearly 40 million Bantu-language-speaking ***Africans***, who are descended from successive waves of migrants from Central Africa. The first European settlers arrived in the seventeenth century. Their descendants make up 4.5 million *Whites*. The 4.4 million *Coloureds* (the term used universally in South Africa) represent a group whose ancestry includes the earliest indigenous hunter-gatherers, as well as slaves from Indonesia and the offspring from unions between white settlers and these groups. 1.2 million Indians are mostly descendants of indentured laborers who were recruited from India during the nineteenth century. Under the apartheid regime (1948–1993), each group had a different legal status. Today, racial segregation is no longer the law, but the communal identities created by official racial classification still influence social life. Most blacks still live in historically segregated ghetto-like neighborhoods, and most whites live in the more comfortable suburbs. (See Figure 11.1 for the South African nation at a glance.)

### African

South African usage refers to Bantu language speakers, the demographic majority of South African citizens.

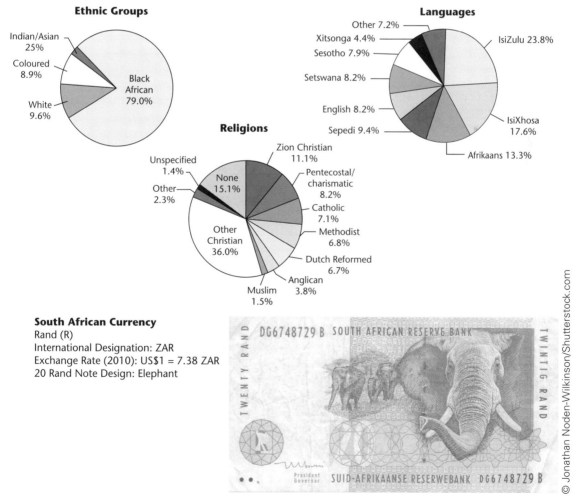

**South African Currency**
Rand (R)
International Designation: ZAR
Exchange Rate (2010): US$1 = 7.38 ZAR
20 Rand Note Design: Elephant

© Jonathan Noden-Wilkinson/Shutterstock.com

**FIGURE 11.1 The South African Nation at a Glance**

*Source*: From Tom Lodge, South African Politics Since 1994, pp. vi–vii. Reprinted with permission.

# Critical Junctures

### Settlement, 1688–1911

In 1652 the Dutch East India Company established a reprovisioning station for its merchant ships at the southern tip of Africa. The Dutch settlers did not arrive first. Bantu-language-speaking Africans had settled in the region at least 2,000 years previously. Bantu speakers drove away or merged with earlier San and the Khoi-Khoi hunter-gatherer and pastoral communities.

By the eighteenth century Dutch settlers in South Africa were identifying themselves as **Afrikaners**. They spoke a distinctive variant of Dutch called Afrikaans. In 1806, Britain took control of the territory as part of its imperial expansion. Because they resented British policies (including the abolition of slavery in 1833), about one-tenth of the Afrikaner population—the *voortrekkers*—migrated northwards between 1836 and 1840. The voortrekkers established the Orange Free State in 1852 and the Transvaal in 1854.

### Dynamics of the Frontier, 1779–1906

White settlement quickly overwhelmed the pastoral economies of the Khoi-San in the northern areas. The settlers encountered more formidable adversaries among Xhosa-speaking Africans along the eastern coast. The frontier wars between 1779 and 1878 fixed the boundaries between white farmers and the Xhosa kingdoms.

The strongest African resistance arose in the Zulu Kingdom, an impressive militarized state. The wars that created the Zulu state in the early nineteenth century

## Afrikaner

Descendants of Dutch, French, German, and Scots settlers speaking a language (Afrikaans) derived heavily from Dutch and politically mobilized as an ethnic group through the twentieth century.

## voortrekkers

Pastoralist descendants of Dutch-speaking settlers in South Africa who moved north from the British-controlled Cape in 1836 to establish independent republics; later regarded as the founders of the Afrikaner nation.

had forced other peoples to migrate. These peoples formed their own powerful states derived from the Zulu model. But huge areas had been depopulated, which were available for white settlers. The white settlers usually preserved some pre-colonial African institutions, but these played a subordinate role in colonial administrations.

In 1843, Britain annexed Natal, which had been part of the Zulu kingdom. From 1860, British immigrants established sugar plantations and began recruiting Indian labor. Today about 80 percent of South Africa's Indian population lives in the province of KwaZulu-Natal.

## Imperialists against Republicans, 1867–1910

After gold was discovered in the Witwatersrand region of the Transvaal in 1886, a massive mining industry grew up. By 1898 the mine owners, mainly British, increasingly objected to the Afrikaner government in Pretoria, the Transvaal capital, mostly because the government tended to favor landholders over mine owners in official programs to enlist African labor. By the late 1890s, however, the British government had become more receptive to the mine owners, or "Randlords," since global competition from Germany and the United States had increased the strategic value of the Transvaal gold reserves. Before Britain could invade, the Afrikaner republics declared war on October 11, 1899. The savage Anglo-Boer War (1899–1902) was prolonged by the guerrilla campaign launched against the British by Afrikaner farmers called **Boers**.

**Boer**

Literally "farmer"; modern usage is a derogatory reference to Afrikaners.

But Britain prevailed. Casualties included 28,000 Afrikaner civilians who died in concentration camps. One hundred thousand Africans served in the armies on both sides, and 14,000 Africans died in internment camps. Voting was already color-blind in the British Cape Colony region, and Africans hoped that after the war they would be able to vote throughout the country. But during the 1902 peace negotiations, the British prioritized good relations between the Afrikaners and the English. In the Cape, a small African elite retained the vote, but in the other provinces the agreement denied Africans any enfranchisement.

Britain's ascendency in South Africa was confirmed by its victory in the Anglo-Boer War. Under the new British administration, officials constructed an efficient bureaucracy. A customs union between the four South African territories eliminated tariffs. A new Native Affairs Department reorganized labor recruitment. In 1910, under the Act of Union the four territories of Cape, Natal, Transvaal, and the Orange Free State became provinces of the Union of South Africa, which became a dominion of the British empire. Africans outside the Cape would be excluded from voting.

## The Origins of Modern Institutionalized Racism, 1910–1945

These arrangements confirmed the essential features of South Africa's racist order. The need to coerce African labor guided policy. In gold mining, profits depended on very cheap labor. The gold mines used a closed compound system, which was originally developed to stop smuggling in the diamond fields, but on the Witwatersrand it became a totalitarian system of control. Recruiting workers demanded repressive political order.[1] Beginning with the 1913 Land Act, laws were passed to enforce racial discrimination. These laws were supposed to meet the needs of a mining economy, which needed cheap labor that could not rebel.[2] The Land Act allowed Africans to own land only inside a patchwork of native reserves.

In the 1880s Afrikaner nationalists constructed an "imagined community" based on language standardization and literary culture. This community attracted white people who had been forced off the land during the Anglo-Boer War.[3] During a white miners' armed insurrection in 1922, Afrikaner workers resurrected a Boer commando system.

The miners protested because their employers were giving certain semiskilled work to Africans, previously jobs reserved for whites. In putting down the rebellion, 153 people were killed. Two years later, a coalition government of the Labour Party and the (Afrikaner) National Party set up a "civilized labor" policy. It meant that all whites, even ones without any skills, should earn enough to maintain a "civilized" standard of living. Semiskilled and certain unskilled jobs were reserved for whites. The new government also invested in public industries. The pace of industrialization accelerated after 1933. After the currency was devalued, fresh waves of investment flowed in from overseas.

### Apartheid and African Resistance, 1945–1960

In 1934, a new United Party was created by a fusion between the National Party and the pro-British South African Party led by Jan Smuts, who became prime minister in 1939. Social tensions prompted two different sets of political challenges to Smuts' United Party administration.

After moderate Afrikaner nationalists joined Jan Smuts in the United Party, breakaway factions formed a Purified National Party. Meanwhile, Afrikaner nationalism became a mass movement under the direction of a secret *Broederbond* (Brotherhood) that sponsored savings banks, trade unions, and voluntary organizations. During the early 1940s, the National Party developed a program around the idea of **apartheid** (apartness). This emphasized even more rigid racial separation than already existed in South Africa. Apartheid policies would restrict Indians and Coloureds, and halt African migration into the urban areas. This appealed to white workers who feared African competition for their jobs. The National Party also drew support from farmers, who found it difficult to recruit labor during rapid industrialization. The National Party won a narrow electoral victory in 1948, marking the formal beginning of the apartheid era in South African history. More racist legislation followed. **Pass laws** required all Africans to carry internal passports at all times and interracial sex was banned. Blacks needed special permits to travel to or live in towns.

African politics also became a mass movement in the 1940s. The African National Congress party had been founded in 1912 in response to the racialist policies of the government of the Union of South Africa. It was not very active until the 1940s. In 1945 the Natal Indian Congress, an organization first formed in 1894 by Mohandas Gandhi (who lived in South Africa from 1893 to 1914) to protest discrimination against Indians, led a nonviolent resistance movement that inspired ANC leaders.

### The Sharpeville Massacre and Grand Apartheid, 1960–1976

In the 1950s, African politicians had reacted to fresh restrictions and new segregation laws with civil disobedience campaigns, general strikes, and consumer boycotts. After the government banned the South African Communist Party in 1950, the ANC and allied Indian and Coloured organizations became more radical, as communists began to play a more assertive role in their leadership. White communists remained secretly active in black trade unions.

On March 21, 1960, South Africa police killed approximately eighty people who had assembled outside a police station to protest the pass laws. After the Sharpeville massacre, the authorities banned the ANC and a more militant offshoot, the Pan-Africanist Congress, which had organized the antipass protests.

**apartheid**

In Afrikaans, "separateness." First used in 1929 to describe Afrikaner nationalist proposals for strict racial separation and "to ensure the safety of the white race."

**pass laws**

Laws in apartheid South Africa that required Africans to carry identity books in which were stamped the permits required for them to travel between the countryside and the cities.

While the African liberation movements reorganized in exile and prepared for guerrilla warfare, National Party governments under Hendrik Verwoerd and John Vorster ratcheted up their program of racial separation in what became known as "Grand Apartheid."[4] Under the 1970 Black Homeland Citizenship Act all Africans would become citizens of ten supposedly sovereign states within the territory of South Africa. Blacks would no longer be citizens of South Africa. The ten **homelands** became increasingly overcrowded as 1.4 million farm workers were forcibly resettled within them. In addition, several hundred thousand city dwellers were deported to the homelands. African urban workers would become permanent **migrant laborers**, renewing their contracts every year and leaving their families in the homelands.

To prepare for this change, the central government took control of the administration of the African **townships** in the cities where the migrant workers lived. Construction of family housing for Africans in the major cities was halted, the authorities building instead huge dormitory-like hostels for "bachelor" workers. A program of Bantu education, stressing menial vocational training introduced into primary schools in 1954 was extended to African secondary schooling. Restrictions were placed on African, Indian, and Coloured enrolment in the major universities. Special segregated colleges were established. New laws allowed detention without trial and made it easier to torture prisoners. Through a far-reaching network of informers, the police located most of the networks responsible for brief campaigns of sabotage and insurgency that had been mounted by the ANC and the Pan-Africanist Congress. By 1965, most significant African leaders who had not left the country were beginning life sentences on Robben Island, a former leper colony offshore from Cape Town. These leaders included Nelson Mandela, ANC deputy president and commander-in-chief of its armed wing, ***Umkhonto-we-Sizwe*** (Spear of the Nation).

**homelands**

Areas reserved for exclusive African occupation, established through the provisions of the 1913 and 1936 land legislation and later developed as semi-autonomous ethnic states during the apartheid era.

**migrant laborers**

Laborers who move to another location to take a job, often a low-paying, temporary one.

**township**

South African usage refers to a segregated residential area reserved for Africans, during apartheid tightly controlled and constituted mainly by public housing.

***Umkhonto-we-Sizwe***

Zulu and Xhosa for "Spear of the Nation," the armed wing of the African National Congress, established in 1961 and integrated into the South African National Defence Force in 1994.

Central Press/Getty Images

A policeman stands over a corpse after the Sharpeville massacre. Survivors today claim that some of the wounded were killed as they lay on the ground by black police constables brought in from Johannesburg.

**sanctions**

International embargos on economic and cultural contracts with a particular country; applied selectively to South Africa by various governments and the United Nations from 1948 until 1994.

During this era of Grand Apartheid, foreign capital and public investment built up strategic industries such as armaments and synthetic fuels, in anticipation of international **sanctions** that were beginning to be imposed on South Africa because of its racist policies. The country experienced substantial economic growth and modernization.

As Africans moved into semiskilled manufacturing jobs created by the expanding economy, black workers obtained new leverage against employers. Wildcat strikes broke out in 1973 as a combative trade union movement gained strength. Daily tabloid newspapers aimed at township readers had appeared in the mid-1960s. These papers took advantage of mass literacy and helped form a new generation of political organizations that were inspired by the U.S. black power movement and were led by the expanding numbers of graduates from the segregated universities.

### Generational Revolt and Political Reform, 1976–1990

In the mid-1970s, the collapse of Portuguese colonial power in Angola and Mozambique and the rise of radical black governments in those countries inspired South African anti-apartheid activists. The ideas of the racially assertive black consciousness movement percolated down to secondary schools, quickly finding followers in an educational system that discriminated terribly against Africans.

The Education Ministry rashly decided to enforce a decades-old requirement that half the curriculum in Black schools should be taught in Afrikaans. This provoked demonstrations on June 16, 1976, in the townships around Johannesburg. The police fired into a crowd of 15,000 children, killing two. In the following days, the revolt spread to fifty Transvaal centers. The next year saw street battles, strikes, and classroom boycotts. At least 575 protesters died. Several thousand more crossed South Africa's borders to join the liberation organizations.

By the mid-1970s, Afrikaner nationalism had changed. Two-thirds of Afrikaners were now white-collar workers. Afrikaner firms were now among the most advanced manufacturers. Their directors were increasingly bothered by apartheid regulations that restricted the mobility of black labor.[5] Reflecting this change, African workers gained collective bargaining rights. Black trade unions won legal recognition. Another series of reforms followed, which attempted to solicit support from the most urbanized Africans. By 1986 these reforms included the repeal of the pass laws and other means of **influx control** that had been used to regulate Black migration to the cities.

**influx control**

A system of controls that regulated African movement between cities and between towns and the countryside, enforcing residence in the homelands and restricting African choice of employment.

In 1983, the United Democratic Front (UDF) was formed by anti-apartheid organizations drawn from the student movement, trade unions, and township-based civic associations. They proclaimed their loyalty to the "non-racial" ideology of the ANC. UDF affiliates were conspicuous in the insurrectionary climate that developed in the townships in late 1984 in response to rent hikes. Township rioting, military repression, guerrilla warfare, and conflict between supporters of liberation movements and the adherents of homeland regimes each contributed to a new bloody phase of South Africa's political history. Between 1984 and 1994, politically motivated killings claimed 25,000 lives.

### The South African Miracle, 1990–1999

On February 12, 1990, a new president, F. W. De Klerk created a bombshell when he announced the repeal of prohibitions on the ANC and other proscribed organizations. He also announced that Nelson Mandela would be released unconditionally from prison. His government was ready to begin negotiating. De Klerk was a conservative, but he was disturbed by the prospect of tightening economic sanctions and was encouraged by the collapse of the communist governments, such as the

Soviet Union, that had previously been important supporters of the ANC. He hoped that through abandoning apartheid and beginning negotiations for power-sharing, the National Party could build black support. The existence of a powerful political movement organized around the KwaZulu homeland authority, the Inkatha Freedom Party, led by a Zulu prince, Chief Mangosuthu Buthelezi, represented another reason he believed that an anti-ANC coalition could prevail. ANC leaders, in turn, were willing to make concessions, acknowledging that they could not seize power through revolution. Opinion polls assured them of their growing public support.

At the time, it seemed miraculous that such bitter adversaries could be ready to collaborate so closely in designing a new political system. Their success was even more remarkable, because political hostilities continued between their supporters. Between 1990 and 1994, 14,000 people died in warfare between the ANC, Inkatha, and various state-sponsored vigilante groups. In 1993 two years of bargaining produced a transitional constitution in which the main parties would hold cabinet positions in accordance with their shares of the vote in **proportional representation** elections. All participants in politically motivated violence, including torture of prisoners and terrorist attacks, could obtain immunity from prosecution. Even senior public servants (mostly white) would keep their jobs. Power would be divided between a national assembly and nine provincial legislatures. These legislatures would absorb the homeland bureaucracies. Parliament would sit as a constitutional assembly to draw up a final constitution, which would have to follow the fundamental principles agreed to in the 1993 document.

On April 27, 1994, with just over 62 percent of the ballot, the ANC achieved an overwhelming majority among black voters except in KwaZulu-Natal, where Inkatha obtained a narrow victory. With 20 percent of the national vote, De Klerk's New National Party drew substantial support among Coloureds and Indians, along with most white votes. Eight more parties achieved parliamentary representation. On May 10, the Government of National Unity (GNU) took office, led by Nelson Mandela and including representatives of the ANC, the National Party, and the Inkatha Freedom Party (see Profile: Nelson Mandela). For many observers South Africans had achieved an astonishing historical turnaround.

In office, the GNU began the Reconstruction and Development Programme (RDP), a plan drawn up originally by the ANC's labor ally, the Congress of South African Trade Unions (COSATU). The RDP emphasized "people-driven development" including fairer allocation of public goods. ANC leaders in power still used the Marxist-Leninist terms for what they called a national democratic revolution. But their policies were surprisingly moderate. Under both Mandela and his successor, Thabo Mbeki, ANC-led administrations attempted

**proportional representation (PR)**

A system of political representation in which seats are allocated to parties within multimember constituencies, roughly in proportion to the votes each party receives. In South Africa the entire country serves as a single 400-seat parliamentary constituency.

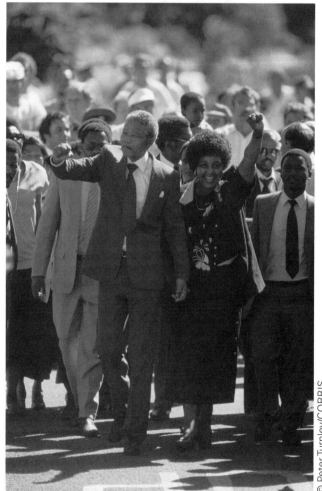

Nelson Mandela walks through the gates of Pollsmoor Prison on the day of his release, hand in hand with his wife, Winnie.

© Peter Turnley/CORBIS

## PROFILE

# Nelson Mandela

Born in a tiny Transkei village in 1918, Nelson Mandela could claim Thembu royal lineage. After he rebelled against an arranged marriage and was suspended from Fort Hare University for his role in a student strike, he travelled to Johannesburg to begin work as a legal clerk. He joined the ANC in 1942 and helped to establish the Youth League. This group wanted to radicalize the ANC's moderate philosophy in favor of a militant, racially exclusive nationalism. By 1951, however, Mandela had become friends with Indian activists and white Communists. This led him to revise his belief that African nationalists should not cooperate across race lines. That year, Mandela helped plan a "defiance campaign" against "unjust laws." Thereafter, as the ANC's deputy president, Mandela, played a major role as an ANC strategist. In 1952, he founded a law firm with his comrade Oliver Tambo.

Following the Sharpeville massacre in March 1960, Mandela was detained for five months, and the ANC was outlawed. In May 1961, he led a nationwide general strike. In October, he helped form a sabotage organization, *Umkhonto-we-Sizwe* (Spear of the Nation). Mandela left South Africa in January 1962 to seek financial and military support. He returned in July and was arrested. He was ultimately convicted of sabotage and other crimes against the state and sentenced to life in prison.

During nearly thirty years of imprisonment, Mandela maintained his authority over successive generations of convicted activists. Beginning in 1985, he began a secret series of meetings with government leaders to persuade the authorities to initiate constitutional negotiations with the ANC.

On February 11, 1990, Mandela was unconditionally released. As ANC president from 1991, his leadership was crucial in curbing the expectations of his organization's often unruly following. He shared the Nobel Peace Prize in 1993 with President F. W. De Klerk. After the ANC's electoral victory in 1994, he served as South African president until 1999. His personal achievements during this period included symbolic acts of reconciliation with the Afrikaner minority and vigorous defense of constitutional undertakings. Remaining active after his retirement from public office, he became chair of the Burundi peace talks in 2000.

Nelson Mandela contributed significantly to the ANC's ideological formation in the 1950s. He was a powerful proponent of the multiracial Congress Alliance. Although influenced by Marxism, he maintained an admiration for British parliamentary democracy. Although he advocated working-class mobilization, Mandela took advantage of his social connections with the rural aristocracy, and he skilfully balanced his pronouncements to the various constituencies within the ANC's popular following. After 1960, his personal courage and theatrical style were vital in keeping the rank-and-file militants loyal to the ANC. He pioneered the ANC's transformation to a clandestine insurgent body and led its second transformation into an electorally oriented political party. His speech at his trial in 1964 increased his stature making him, in the words of the *London Times*, "a colossus of African nationalism." Four decades later, he remains Africa's most internationally influential statesman.

to address the basic needs of poor people. Social expenditure was limited, however, by tight budgetary discipline. After adopting the Growth, Employment, and Redistribution policy (GEAR) in 1996, the ANC leadership embraced free-market reforms, including **privatization** and tariff reduction, despite objections from their trade union allies. In 2007, Mbeki's opponents succeeded in electing his deputy Jacob Zuma to replace him as the ANC's party leader and shortly thereafter Mbeki resigned from the state presidency. Mbeki's resignation followed the dismissal of corruption charges against Zuma, charges that the judge suggested were instigated from the president's office.

**privatization**

The sale of state-owned enterprises to private companies or investors.

### South Africa after 9/11

International terrorist networks have only a very limited presence in South Africa. By 2001, police had immobilized the main domestic terrorist agency, a clandestine Islamist network that had operated within the Cape Town–based vigilante group, People Against Drugs and Gangsterism (PAGAD). This group undertook a series of attacks targeting tourist facilities, a gay bar, and a synagogue. The government drafted additional antiterrorism legislation. This gave the police new powers of search and allowed detention without charge for up to fourteen days. By the end of 2001 officials were defending the draft bill against criticism from human rights groups. Officials claimed it was a necessary measure in the global fight against terrorism. Such reasoning is disputed by most specialists given the absence of a significant local constituency that might support terrorist activity. South African Muslims are relatively affluent and are increasingly middle class, and they are more likely to live outside traditional Muslim neighborhoods. Local Islamist political parties perform poorly in elections.

Several suspected Al Qaeda operatives were deported in May 2004, and police subsequently supplied information leading to further arrests in Jordan, Syria, and Britain. Five months later, however, the U.S. Central Intelligence Agency (CIA) suggested that South Africa might still be accommodating "second tier" Al Qaeda leaders.

South Africa's relatively restrained response to the security issues posed by the Anglo-American war on terror supplies a final set of comparative insights. As we have noted, a fairly secularized and relatively affluent Muslim minority provides quite limited local hospitality and rhetorical support for the more radical strands of Islamic activism. The ANC's historical experience of seeking and balancing its support from governments across international geostrategic divisions has led the South African government to withhold formal public support for America's offensive against fundamentalist Islamic movements while offering discreet cooperation with both American and British intelligence. More generally, however, South Africans do not view their political world as significantly altered by Al Qaeda's attack of 9/11. Distance from the main theaters of the global war on terror and still recent memories of a brutal civil war help to explain why South African politicians identify their chief strategic priorities differently from their counterparts in Washington and London.

Diplomatically, South Africa has taken a relatively independent tack. The government withheld any endorsement of the American-led invasion of Iraq in 2003. The ANC itself maintained quite friendly relations with Saddam Hussein's administration, and the party benefited from illicit donations that accompanied South African purchases of Iraqi oil. One month after the fall of Baghdad, however, Thabo Mbeki hosted a visit by President Bush during which the two leaders discussed a program of American assistance to strengthen South African border security.

# Themes and Implications

## Historical Junctures and Political Themes

### South Africa in a World of States
Ever since the Anglo-Boer War, South Africa has attracted an unusual degree of international political attention. Its political economy has been shaped decisively by inflows of capital and population. Throughout the twentieth century the economy depended on imported technology, which made it vulnerable to international pressure. Although the major powers set up sanctions only reluctantly, the country's institutionalized racial segregation attracted unanimous censure within the post–World War II world of states.

These external influences have complicated South Africa's relationship with the rest of Africa. As a **settler state**, South Africa was perceived by pan-African politicians as a leftover element of the colonial world, a perception that was reinforced by apartheid South Africa's alignment with Western powers during the Cold War. Even after democracy came and an African government took power, South Africa's economic dominance as the most developed country in Africa excited resentment as much as admiration. Its status as Africa's leading economy has brought it new kinds of international influence. In 1999, South Africa became the only African member of the G20 grouping, an annual convention of finance ministers and heads of reserve banks from the world's biggest economies. In December 2010, the BRIC (Brazil, India and China) economic grouping became BRICS when South Africa joined the informal

**settler state**

Colonial or former colonial administrations controlled by the descendants of immigrants who settled in the territory.

bloc of rapidly growing emerging economies that seeks to transform global financial and trading relations in favor of developing countries.

**Governing the Economy** State-directed industrialization in South Africa was encouraged with the establishment in 1928 of the public Iron and Steel Corporation. Such expansion of public enterprise accelerated during the apartheid era. The threat of foreign trade embargoes led the regime to increase protective trade tariffs to encourage import substitution industrialization during the 1960s.

Between 1993 and 2001 South Africa removed about two-thirds of these tariffs largely in response to the conditions of membership in the World Trade Organization. Tariff reform affected some industries harshly but was gentler on others in which South Africa might expect to become competitive internationally. South African policy-makers could decide the details of trade reform independently of foreign institutions because the government owed a relatively low foreign debt, an effect of financial sanctions during the 1980s when it was not eligible for international loans.

**The Democratic Idea** South African democracy is the product of many traditions. Immigrants reinforced key features of South African political culture. In the twentieth century, this included a tradition of militant socialism that accompanied the influxes of workers from English tin mines and Australian gold fields before World War I. Baltic Jewish refugees included in their numbers veterans of Russian revolutionary movements. Communists, working with African nationalists, helped to ensure that black opposition to apartheid was led by advocates of a racially inclusive South African nation. Non-racial themes in South African politics were also shaped by the heritage of liberal institutions that had accompanied earlier arrivals from Europe, for example, the influential network of Methodist-sponsored secondary schools and colleges attended by ANC leaders. Modern South African democratic thought reflects each of these different legacies, as well as the social ethics derived from indigenous African statecraft, with its traditions of consensual decision making and the etiquette of kinship.[6]

Modern democracy in South Africa is also influenced by the ideas of an African trade union movement that was built in the late 1970s and that emphasized accountable leadership. South Africa's adoption of a constitutionally entrenched bill of rights was colored by important new sources of inspiration from other countries. The negotiators across the political spectrum who found a way from apartheid to democracy were inspired by the succession of transitions from authoritarian regimes that unfolded in many parts of the world in the 1980s and 1990s.

**Collective Identity** In seven sets of elections since 1994, parliamentary and municipal, post-apartheid South African voters for the most part still appear to be influenced by their feelings of racial identity. Africans overwhelmingly support African nationalist parties. Despite the conspicuous presence of whites in its leadership, only tiny numbers of white South Africans support the ANC. Among all groups, material interests may reinforce notions of racial community. Virtually all very poor people are African; for them it can be very difficult to feel any sense of shared social identity with generally affluent white South Africans. The prospects for democratic progress are limited when racial solidarities are so decisive.

## Implications for Comparative Politics

**democratization**

Transition from authoritarian rule to a democratic political order.

The most recent comparative analysis of South African politics emphasizes its significance as a relatively successful example of **democratization**. Post-apartheid politics in South Africa offers to comparativists useful insights into the factors that build and consolidate democratic life: These factors certainly include a pattern of economic growth in which the construction of a modern economy came before universal enfranchisement; the role played in making democracy work by a vigorous civil society; as well as the effects of a carefully assembled set of state institutions designed to promote social inclusion and reward consensus. South Africa may yet offer an encouraging model of a racially segmented society that has succeeded in nurturing stable and democratic political institutions.

## Summary

A unified South Africa was established in the aftermath of the Anglo-Boer War of 1899–1902, a conflict that made the British Empire the dominant force in the subcontinent. A modern administration was geared to providing cheap labor to the gold mining industry and restricted African access to land. In the decades following Union, white workers succeeded in gaining rights and privileges as citizens, but the legal status of black South Africans deteriorated. Afrikaner nationalists held office from 1948 and established a strict regime of racial apartheid. Popular African resistance was suppressed in 1960. In exile, the main African movements embraced guerrilla warfare. From 1976 onwards, urbanization, industrialization, and mass literacy prompted powerful challenges to white minority rule. In 1990, in response to insurgency and international pressure, the South African political leadership lifted the ban on the main African political organizations and began to negotiate a political settlement. In 1994 a democratically elected government began attempting to reduce poverty and inequality while also encouraging economic regeneration.

# POLITICAL ECONOMY AND DEVELOPMENT

SECTION 2

# State and Economy

### Apartheid Economics

Extensive economic intervention by the South African state reinforced apartheid policies. From 1952, laws prohibited Africans from living in any town unless they had been born there or had worked for the same employer for ten years. Migrant workers without urban residential rights had to live in tightly controlled hostels in segregated townships. By the mid-1960s, political repression had virtually eliminated most of the more militant African trade unions. In 1968 the Armaments Development and Manufacturing Corporation (Armscor) was created. This greatly expanded the scope of public industrial enterprise. By 1981, Armscor was at the center of a defense industry employing 100,000 people.

Apartheid economics was buttressed by a welfare state, even though it functioned in a racially discriminatory fashion. Public construction of African housing began on a significant scale outside Johannesburg during the 1930s. This was the first of a series of projects of a vast township—later named Soweto (the administrative acronym from

## Focus Questions

In what ways has the state's role in the economy changed since 1970 and especially since the end of apartheid?

In what ways and why is South Africa so socially unequal today?

How did international sanctions affect the South African apartheid economy and what role did they play in hastening the end of apartheid?

southwestern townships). Wartime industrialization led the government to suspend pass laws. During the 1940s, as Africans rapidly moved to the cities, illegal shanty settlements mushroomed on the fringes of most major cities. Although they restricted further African urbanization, governments after 1948 funded a rapid expansion of public housing to accommodate Africans who were permitted to live in towns. In 1971, African public housing totalled more than 500,000 family dwellings. During the 1960s, official policy increasingly favored single workers' hostel construction instead of family housing. Most townships included bleak barrack-like hostels in which African migrant workers slept in bunks and used communal bathrooms and kitchens.

In the 1960s, the state spread its control over African educational institutions. But it also increased school enrolment massively. By the end of the decade, most children of school-going age were attending public schools, although there were huge inequalities in the amount of public money spent per capita on white and black children. Pension payments between the races were equalized only in 1993 as apartheid was ending. South Africa's universal public pension, together with disability grants and other kinds of welfare payments, remain unusual in sub-Saharan African states today.

## Liberalization and Deregulation

**economic deregulation**

The lifting or relaxation of government controls over the economy, including the reduction of import taxes (tariffs) and the phasing out of subsidized prices for producers and consumers.

The dismantling of apartheid was accompanied by wider kinds of **economic deregulation**. Effectively by 1984, most official employment discrimination had been removed except in gold mining. In the mid-1980s, the government began to dismantle the protections and subsidies that had supported white agriculture. Parallel to these developments, the Iron and Steel Corporation and the public road freight company were privatized. In the late 1980s rising defense spending and expanding public debt brought fresh reasons to deregulate and privatize. When the government abolished influx control in 1986, this should have opened up the labor market, at least in theory, but by this time the main labor shortages were in skilled sectors. These shortages resulted because generations of Africans had not been able to receive industrial training and technical education. Once Africans were allowed to move to the cities, urban growth quickly picked up. In the last two decades of the twentieth century, most South African towns have at least doubled in population.

Since 1994, ANC governments have maintained and expanded the liberal economic policies of the late apartheid era. Redistributive policies have attempted to expand the scope of private ownership rather than broaden the public sector. For instance, between 1994 and 2010 the government helped to finance the construction of more than 2.3 million low-cost houses, but this is through one-time grants to impoverished families. The grants enable them to buy their own houses, built by private contractors on cheap former public land. For many residents in the townships, home ownership was more expensive than public rented housing or the site payments they had made to "shacklords" in squatter camps: The housing subsidies usually did not cover construction costs, and poor families who moved into the houses often ended up paying more on bond repayments at commercial interest rates than they had paid on rents. Moreover, rural urban migration and demographic pressure combined to push up the figures for the "housing backlog": Today to meet the needs of shanty dwellers another 2.1 million houses need to be built.

In 1994, the government agreed to reduce industrial tariffs by two-thirds by 2001 and agricultural tariffs by 36 percent within a decade as a condition for joining the World Trade Organization. In 1997, industries stopped receiving export incentive subsidies. Currency exchange controls were substantially relaxed as well to promote foreign investment.

Since 1994, privatization policies have had their most profound effect on munici-pal administration. Heavily indebted local authorities now contract out basic services such as water supply and garbage collection. Despite trade union opposition Telkom, the telephone utility, was largely privatized by 2003, with the government retaining a 40 percent stake. To put the railroad network on a commercial footing, most smaller rural stations were closed. Effectively, the state abandoned a major share of its former duty to provide cheap, subsidized public transport. Even so, the transport corporation remains wholly state-owned after successive failures to engage foreign investors and local black empowerment groups. To offset the social effects of withdrawing from many of its traditional areas of activity, the state has made a considerable effort to address basic needs and reduce poverty. The government is also beginning to expand its authority over environmental issues.

By the beginning of the 1990s, trade union opposition to unsafe working condi-tions was expanding into a broader concern with the effects of industrial pollution. The environmental movement acquired a popular base, and its causes broadened to embrace "brown" issues of the urban landscape, such as poor access to clean water and unsafe waste disposal, as well as the more traditional interests of "green" conser-vationism like vehicle emissions and energy efficiency.

In 1993, ANC negotiators insisted that clauses on environmental health and ecological sustainability should go into the post-apartheid constitution. Since 1994, government policies have attempted to integrate ecological concerns with the require-ments of social justice. A series of land restitution court cases have produced settle-ments in which historically dispossessed communities have signed "co-management" agreements with the National Parks Board. The 1998 Marine Living Resources Act has opened up fishing grounds to impoverished village communities. In return, villag-ers are expected to keep the size of their catches within sustainable limits. New mining laws have introduced tighter regulations against pollution.

Meanwhile, environmental protests have become increasingly likely to draw mass participation. Activists are not always successful, however. When nongovern-mental organizations (NGOs) oppose industrial development, they sometimes stir up strong hostility from local people suffering from unemployment. This happened in Saldanha Bay in 1998 when environmentalists opposed building a new steel fac-tory and were accused of elevating the welfare of penguins over the livelihoods of people. Environmental groups are likely to oppose the government's plans to build an additional reactor at the existing nuclear facility at Koeberg, just 30 kilometers from Cape Town, which is the only nuclear power station on the entire continent of Africa. To date, efforts to halt the building of a second reactor have been confined to relatively decorous public meetings. Greenpeace activists did scale the walls of the Koeburg compound to post a placard in 2002, but since then there has been no mili-tant protest. However, there remains evident public anxiety, particularly as residential settlement has extended closer to the power station. The Nuclear Regulator issued a defensively phrased statement in the wake of the Fukushima disaster, pointing out that designs for both the existing and projected reactors at Koeberg were intended to withstand level 7 earthquakes and eight meter tidal waves.

# Society and Economy

South Africa remains one of the most unequal societies in the world despite the gov-ernment's efforts to alleviate poverty. Measured through the Gini coefficient statisti-cal measure of income inequality in which 0 is "perfectly equal" and 1 is "perfectly unequal," South Africa inequality in 2009 was measured at 0.58, a disturbingly high degree, and only slightly below the 1991 estimate. To be sure, large numbers of Africans have been joining the richer population: Those living in the top fifth of income earners rose from 0.4 million in 1994 to 1.9 million in 2008, though this has meant that among Africans, income inequality has increased dramatically. Unemployment, chiefly affecting Africans remains very high at 24 percent at the end of 2010, according to Statistics South Africa (SSA), though slightly lower than the 2001 figure of 28 percent, itself an increase from 23.4 percent in 1996.

South African social inequality is, to a large extent, the historic product of government policies. Whites moved ahead economically at the expense of Africans. For example racial inequities in government expenditure were especially obvious in education. In the 1950s, more whites than Africans were trained as teachers, even though five times as many African children were of school-going age. The 1960s saw a swift expansion of African enrolment, but as late as 1984, the number of Africans completing the final grade of high school was only 60 percent of the total of white pupils in grade 12. In 1985, the government was still spending half its educational budget on white schools.

After 1994, government policies attempted to equalize entitlements and allocations as well as broaden access to public goods, but without dramatic expansion in public spending. Today, public expenditure on education is roughly uniform. Africans now outnumber other racial groups attending universities. As noted above more people receive welfare grants, 12 million today, up from 3 million in 1994. Measures to alleviate poverty have also included housing subsidies and setting up running water for about a third of the rural population. In 1999, municipalities began to implement free water and electricity allowances. During the 1990s, the electricity supply commission substantially expanded the electricity network to embrace poorer rural communities. In addition, 1,300 new clinics have given free public health care to millions of pregnant women and small children. However, hospitals in the main urban centers have deteriorated because health funding has gone to the countryside.

Have such efforts resulted in less poverty? Certainly since 1994, poor people have benefited more from government services and public support, but their absolute numbers have not changed much. Between 2000 and 2010 poverty may have declined slightly, though in 2010, Statistics South Africa calculations show that 47 percent of the population was still living below the poverty line. Sharp increases in the provision of welfare grants, costing nearly 2 percent of GDP in 2001 and 3.3 percent in 2007 may have helped to alleviate poverty slightly.[7] Dramatic rises in economic growth are needed to alleviate poverty significantly, though.

Unemployment and the HIV/AIDS pandemic have offset the government's efforts to address poverty. The manufacturing work force shrank by 400,000 in ten years after 1988, a 25 percent fall. At the same time 500,000 workers left farms. More recently, however, the number of manufacturing jobs has stabilized, and the numbers employed on commercial farms have increased. Public sector employment shrank only slightly, a reflection of the leverage exercised by public sector trade unions. In the late 1990s they were the major players in the still powerful union movement. Despite unemployment, union membership grew rapidly. In 2003 overall union membership was 2.7 million. Unemployment is concentrated among school dropouts and rural people. Africans are still much more likely to be unemployed than other groups.

Between 1996 and 2010, as a consequence of wider access to public health facilities, infant mortality fell slightly from 51 per 1,000 to 49 per 1,000. However life expectancy also fell from 64 in 1996 to 51 in 2007 (UNDP statistics). Falling life expectancy reflects the devastating impact of HIV/AIDS, which, according to South Africa's Medical Research Council, was responsible for 25 percent of deaths in 2000. Between 1990 and 2010 six million South Africans were estimated to have died of AIDS.[8] South Africa's rate of HIV/AIDS infection remains among the highest in the world. In the late 1980s and early 1990s, accelerating urbanization combined with structural unemployment, political violence, and labor migration to loosen social cohesion in poor communities, creating an especially severe version of the high-risk situation identified by HIV/AIDS epidemiologists.[9]

Significantly higher percentages of women live in poverty than men, and the growing number of households headed by women are especially likely to be very poor. Women are at higher risk of HIV/AIDS infection.

## Black Empowerment

Enlarging the share of black ownership in the economy was a major policy priority for Thabo Mbeki's administration. In Mbeki's words, "the struggle against racism in our country must include the objective of creating a black bourgeoisie." Drawing its inspiration from both U.S. and, more importantly, Malaysian experience, the government has enacted a series of laws since 1999 to promote black business. The Preferential Procurement Act established a set of criteria in awarding government contracts that require companies that win them to allocate shares to "previously disadvantaged" people. The Promotion of Equality Act set up a monitoring system to record how well companies were "deracializing" their managements. The National Empowerment Fund Act reserves 2 percent of the proceeds from the sale of public corporations to finance black shareholding in these concerns. Mining and energy have traditionally benefited from government protection and subsidies. Here the government has used its leverage to extract commitments to black empowerment. The government has been providing black entrepreneurs about 2.5 billion rand ($375 million) a year of start-up capital.

How successful has this program been in "deracializing" South African capitalism? Measured by the proportion of black-owned companies on the Johannesburg stock exchange, the share of the economy owned by a "black bourgeoisie" remains modest: between 2 and 5 percent. In certain sectors, black companies are more significant, in oil for example (14 percent).

However, black participation in the economy is not limited to predominantly black-owned companies. Political pressure has prompted all major companies to appoint black people to their boards: In 2002 for example, more than 11 percent of company directors were black, a proportion that has probably increased since then. Shareholding has spread swiftly among black South Africans. For example, nearly a million black people registered for the sale of shares in 2002 in the previously state-owned telecommunications company. Black participation in the real estate business, almost non-existent in 1990, now matches the numbers of white realtors, a telling instance of the proliferation of property ownership in black communities.

Whether black empowerment has made South Africa more socially stable is another question. With the rising black share of economic ownership the government certainly has an incentive to maintain business-friendly policies. The people who have benefited most from these empowerment measures have often been politically well-connected, many of them former activists. And black empowerment has not reduced black poverty. Indeed it may have promoted economic inefficiencies that have curbed growth and job creation. To most poor black South Africans, wealth still appears predominantly white.

# South Africa and the International Political Economy

From the mid-1940s, protectionist policies promoted manufacturing for the domestic market. These policies, together with the restrictions on the use of black labor, caused growing inefficiencies, which economists believe constrained growth by the early 1970s.[10]

Protectionist policies favored the manufacture of consumption rather than capital goods. This helps explain why, in contrast to other middle-income developing countries, South Africa lagged behind in producing machines and equipment. In comparison to most primary commodity producers, high gold prices and well-diversified markets for exports helped to keep terms of trade in South Africa's favor throughout most of the apartheid era, despite the rising cost of oil imports.

One important consequence of the international sanctions campaign that began in the 1970s in order to put pressure on South Africa to end apartheid was that the government began to invest in local branches of production, fearing a time when sanctions might become more effective. For example, threats of an oil embargo imposed extra costs on the South African economy, but it also stimulated a petrochemical industry that remains one of South Africa's more competitive export sectors.

More significant in its political effect than trade sanctions on South African policy-makers was the impact of divestment and credit denial by companies and banks, principally American, in reaction to the state of emergency that was imposed in 1985. Divestment was a direct response to threats by colleges as well as state and local governments to withdraw their holdings in companies with South African interests. The divestment campaign culminated in the passage in the U.S. Congress of the Comprehensive Anti-Apartheid Act in October 1986. Divestment did not directly hurt South African economic activity since South African domestic capital formation was the major source of investment in the economy. However, the prospect of future limitations in the country's ability to secure foreign loans was extremely alarming to the government. By 1987, South African industrialists were dismayed about the troubles they expected to have in obtaining access to advanced technology.[11]

Traditionally, South Africa dominated its regional economy through such arrangements as the South African Customs Union (which linked South Africa, Namibia, Lesotho, Swaziland, and Botswana in a free-trade and revenue-sharing zone). During the 1980s, however, the region's economic significance as a trading partner with South Africa substantially increased at the same time that labor migration from the region into South Africa slackened. In the early 1980s, at a time of balance-of-payments difficulties, regional annual trade surpluses in South Africa's favor reached $1.8 billion. South Africa's regional trading partners bought 40 percent of its manufacturing exports. By the end of the decade, however, regional trade was contracting because of the warfare that stepped up when South Africa sponsored insurgencies against the Marxist governments in Angola and Mozambique. Such destabilization created growing unease within industrial circles, as well as disagreements within government itself.

The effects of South Africa's post-1994 reintegration into international market were initially disheartening. Through the rest of the decade, growth levels remained modest—2.3 percent increases in GDP while foreign investors remained wary. The ending of sanctions helped to increase South African trade with other African countries, but it also prompted an outflow of South African investment into countries with lower labor costs. WTO-mandated tariff reductions exposed hitherto protected industries to foreign competition with heavy job losses resulting in textiles and clothing factories.

After 2000, though, growth began to accelerate, reaching levels above 5 percent from 2005 onwards. Major public investments, much of it dependent on foreign lending, into the upgrading of harbors and railways, the construction of a petroleum pipeline between Johannesburg and Maputo, and the re-equipping of electrical power stations stimulated other sectors of the economy and created nearly half a million new jobs. Export-oriented manufacturing has expanded though not as much as government hoped: The most buoyant export sector is in energy; electricity to African neighbours and coal to the rest of the world. Local industries continue to encounter fierce foreign competition in the domestic market, though, particularly from the growing volume of Chinese imports. This has ensured that macroeconomic policy issues remain profoundly contested in South Africa's political life, even within the ruling party.

## Summary

Racial segregation required considerable state intervention in the economy. In particular until 1986 the state restricted Africans' mobility, in order to ensure adequate supplies of cheap black labor for mining and agriculture. State-owned enterprises, however, helped to develop a substantial manufacturing sector from the late 1920s onward. During the 1960s and 1970s public investments in strategic synthetic fuel and armaments diversified the industrial base further. Increasingly comprehensive social welfare programs accompanied these developments. From the 1970s, external anti-apartheid pressures as well as shortages of crucial skills began to prompt liberalization. Even before the advent of universal suffrage in 1994, most apartheid restrictions had been dismantled. Since then, democratic governments have continued to expand economic liberalization, reducing tariffs and selling public enterprises. Rising unemployment, partly a consequence of market reform, as well as the effects of the HIV/AIDS pandemic, have frustrated the government's efforts to reduce poverty and inequality.

# GOVERNANCE AND POLICY-MAKING

SECTION 3

# Organization of the State

Modern state organization in South Africa emerged from four years of bargaining between 1992 and 1996. A transitional constitution settled the details of how South African would be governed after the first democratic elections, which were held in 1994. Parliament, acting as a constitutional assembly, then debated a final document that had to incorporate key principles adopted at the earlier multiparty talks. This was a way of ensuring that racial and other minority concerns would receive enduring protection. A bill of rights supplies safeguards that range from traditional civil liberties to environmental protections and sexual choice. Most clauses of the constitution can be changed through a two-thirds vote in the National Assembly. However, an opening section of the Constitution lists a set of key values for which a 75 percent majority is needed for amendment.

## Focus Questions

How is the South African political system similar to and different from the British and the American?

Why is the executive branch of government so powerful in South Africa?

Why is public confidence in the legal system so limited?

Since 1994, the South African state has been a quasi-federal system. The national government has the power to override laws passed by nine provincial regional legislatures. The provincial administrations depend on funds allocated by the central government.

Between 1994 and 1999, the transitional constitution compelled the executive of the Government of National Unity be composed of a coalition of party representatives, with posts being distributed roughly proportionately to parties that achieved more than 5 percent of the vote. The National Party withdrew from the GNU in 1996, partly because of its failure to impose its will on the drafting of the 1996 constitution. The requirement for **power sharing** did not feature in the 1996 constitution.

**power sharing**

Constitutional arrangements to ensure that the major political parties share executive authority. These can include mandatory coalitions and allocation of senior official positions between parties.

## The Executive

Although the South African system of government has inherited many features of the Westminster model, the South African president is considerably more powerful than the British prime minister. South African governments are formed by the president, who must be a member of the National Assembly. When elected by the Assembly, the president vacates his or her parliamentary seat and appoints and subsequently chairs a cabinet of ministers as well. The president, who can only serve two five-year terms, also chooses a deputy president, a post with no constitutionally designated special powers.

South Africa's first president after universal suffrage elections in 1994 was Nelson Mandela, who served one term, declining to serve another on grounds of age. His single term was decisive in establishing the prestige of the new government both abroad, and more importantly, at home. His successor, Thabo Mbeki, followed Mandela's example in taking care to cultivate strong personal relationships with members of the Afrikaner elite. Prior to becoming president of the Republic, both

Dressed in his warrior kilt (Ishebu), Jacob Zuma demonstrates his mastery of traditional dance steps while his supporters sing his anthem from the Umkhonto camps, Umshini Wami, My Machine Gun.

Mandela and Mbeki had been elected (though secret ballots) as the head of the ANC at delegate conferences. The president can be impeached or removed from office by a two-thirds vote of the National Assembly, but only on grounds of disability or serious misconduct.

As Mandela's deputy president, Mbeki was largely responsible for the day-to-day management of the administration as well as managing the cabinet. After he became president in 1999, the office accumulated functions and resources. Although he was elected to a second term in 2004, Mbeki lost his party's support in ANC leadership elections at the end of 2007 and resigned the following year, to be replaced by his deputy, Kgalema Motlanthe. After the 2009 election the new National Assembly elected Jacob Zuma as president and Motlanthe reassumed his former role as deputy.

Unlike the president, cabinet ministers remain members of parliament and are accountable to it through question-time sessions. These are regularly scheduled occasions, in which ministers have to reply to queries from backbenchers. Ministers are also accountable to various parliamentary standing committees. Parliamentarians lose office if they are expelled from membership by their parties. This gives the executive great power. Elected by a parliamentary majority, the president will normally

## PROFILE

### Jacob Zuma

Jacob Zuma used to be regarded as a stalwart party loyalist. After he was elected deputy president of the ANC in 1997 and then appointed deputy head of state in 1999, the ANC thought that it could delay deciding who would eventually replace Thabo Mbeki. Zuma himself had no higher ambitions, party insiders believed. Polygamous marriages and very limited formal education also seemed to make it unlikely that Zuma would ever become president.

Among ANC leaders, however, Jacob Zuma was unusual in his command of personal support within the organization and its political allies. Zuma's enthusiastic maintenance of his Communist Party affiliations encouraged trade unionists to think he was a champion of their concerns. He also stands out among the ANC's present leadership for the depth of his political experience. His "struggle history" includes ten years in prison for his role in an early anti-apartheid sabotage campaign. Also, his reputation as a "traditionalist" man of the people makes him especially popular in the countryside. With his warm manner and down-to-earth style, he is also well liked among ordinary ANC members. His efforts in the early 1990s to broker peace in KwaZulu Natal earned him respect and trust outside the ANC. Because there were no other obvious replacements for Thabo Mbeki after the president had completed his constitutionally limited two terms, Jacob Zuma's political stock began to rise.

In 2005, on the day of his arraignment on rape charges, several thousand Zuma supporters surrounded the Supreme Court building, singing his personal anthem, "Bring Me My Machine Gun," and wearing T-shirts printed with the slogan, "Zuma: 100 percent Zulu Boy." The reference to Zuma's ethnicity reflected a popular belief that Xhosa politicians (who supposedly predominate within the ANC's senior ranks) were blocking his rise to the presidency. Ethnic sensitivities are not unusual within the ANC's internal politics but it is very common for such feelings to be voiced so publicly.

Zuma also faced formidable corruption charges. In the 2005 trial of Shabir Shaik, Zuma's former financial adviser, prosecutors were able to demonstrate that Shaik had negotiated a bribe from a French arms contractor on Zuma's behalf. In the evidence accepted by the court in Shaik's trial, Jacob Zuma was an active and knowing accomplice in corrupt business practices. However, under pressure from the president's office, the Directorate of Public Prosecutions in their efforts to press charges against Zuma made various procedural errors, which in 2008 supplied the justification for a high court to dismiss the case on technical grounds that Zuma's rights had been violated.

Jacob Zuma's substantial support within the ANC was overwhelmingly evident at the party's congress held in December 2007. He easily defeated Mbeki in the contest for the party presidency. With the collapse of state's efforts to prosecute him in August 2008, his election to the state presidency in 2009 became inevitable. In office, Zuma's political support base, which depends on an uneasy alliance between different disaffected groups within the ANC, has begun to fragment and various scandals have weakened his personal authority.

be a political party leader, enjoying a controlling influence over the makeup of parliamentary representation. Given the president-as-party-leader's de facto power over parliamentary office holding, a revolt by ruling party backbenchers is extremely unlikely. In 1999, Thabo Mbeki could appoint his cabinet without any restrictions. He chose, however, to include members of the Inkatha Freedom Party, which had been a fierce rival of the ANC. Inkatha turned down an invitation to participate in Mbeki's second cabinet in 2004, but made room in his cabinet for Marthinus van Schalwyk, then the leader of the National Party, who became Minister for the Environment and Tourism. In 2009, Jacob Zuma appointed to his cabinet Pieter Mulder, the leader of the Freedom Front, which is the main representative of Afrikaner irredentist politics. Although there is no formal requirement for socially representative cabinets, ANC governments embody a racial cross-section. Twenty-six ministers and deputy ministers are women, a reflection of the ANC's commitment to gender equity, which has also ensured that at least one-third of ANC parliamentarians are female.

There are very few checks other than constitutional restraints on the leadership of the ruling party. Certainly, Thabo Mbeki attempted to impose his personal authority more frequently than his predecessor. For example, he dictated the choice of premiers to the ANC regional organization. In 1998 an ANC "deployment committee" was set up. This was intended to decide on key appointments in parastatal organizations, as well as having the final decision in the makeup of the party's electoral lists. Since Zuma's accession to the presidency, though, the management of political patronage has become increasingly personalized, and as the outcry over the Gupta family's influence suggests, the party's deployment committee has been sidelined by the president's office. Zuma has blamed the party's policy of "cadre deployment" for appointments of unqualified or corrupt people to high positions and has promised to correct such practices.

Unlike Mandela's charismatic authority within the ANC, the accession of both Mbeki and Zuma to the party leadership have been contested. Accordingly leaders now are expected to reward their political allies. Both Mbeki and Zuma have used their powers of appointment to favor trusted associates, displacing rivals and opponents in the process. Such political patronage has resulted in a proliferation of factionalism within both the ANC, impeding the development of competent public administration and feeding corruption. Estimates of the annual cost of public corruption suggest that as much as four billion rand ($600 million) a year is lost through corruption and waste, much of it through procurements in which suppliers cooperate with officials in charging inflated prices. In 2010, investigators discovered that 6,000 civil servants failed to disclose their business interests, interests that often involved companies with government contracts

After 1994, ANC-led administrations attracted praise for their restraints on public expenditure, their efforts to reduce public employment, and their success in reducing the deficit. But government spending for public welfare investment have been subverted by a weak bureaucracy, especially in several of the nine provinces that together employ the vast majority of the country's public servants (750,000 of 1.1 million) as well as spending two-thirds of the budget. This bureaucracy is partly controlled by the central government and partly by the provinces. Certain departments—defense, security, justice, finance, trade and industry, and home affairs—are administered in a centralized fashion by national government ministries. For other departments—education, social services, and health—provincial administrations headed by elected governments enjoy considerable discretion. Certain central ministries are extremely efficient—finance, for example, especially with respect to tax collection; but others have reputations for corruption and incompetence.

## THE U.S. CONNECTION

### Organization of the State, South Africa Compared to the United States

In South Africa, as in the United States, the Constitution lays down the essential features of state organization. In the United States the Supreme Court has the final say on constitutional interpretation. In South Africa the Constitutional Court performs this function. In both countries the president appoint the judges, but in South Africa Constitutional Court judges hold office for fixed terms (12 years) whereas in the United States Supreme Court judges are appointed for life. In South Africa, it is easier to amend the constitution. Most changes require only a two-thirds vote in parliament. In the United States, however, three-fourths of the fifty states must approve constitutional amendments, which also need two-thirds votes in Congress and the president's approval.

South Africa follows the Westminster system of government in which the party winning parliamentary elections sets up the executive. This is different from the American separation of presidential and legislature elections. American presidents have formidable powers, but Congress can check these powers to some degree. In South Africa the parliament tends to defer to the presidency. South African executive authority has grown through the use of national list proportional representation for legislative elections, which centralizes party organization and empowers party leaders. Unlike in the United States parliamentarians do not represent particular districts.

In both countries presidents may serve only two terms, and in both presidents can be removed from office through impeachment (and, in the case of the United States, trial by the Senate). In South Africa, political parties can use any method they want to choose presidential candidates and all other candidates for elected public offices. The relative weakness of American political parties is partly a result of the primary elections that give ordinary citizens such an important role in deciding who runs for office. Cabinet ministers remain subject to the normal rules of parliamentary accountability, but because one party (the ANC) dominates the political system, the executive enjoys considerable autonomy. In both countries executive power derives partly from a spoils system in which politicians appoint senior officials in the civil service.

Both countries are federal systems, but in South Africa the nine provinces depend almost entirely upon the central government for their budgets. Provincial governments can pass legislation, but the National Assembly can override all their laws. This is very different from the considerable powers that American states, cities, and towns exercise in areas such as welfare and education. The United States possesses a relatively accessible political system with a great many places where citizens and lobbies can affect policy-making. This openness is the result of several factors: federalism, a decentralized party system, separation of powers, and the fact that office holders are personally accountable to the voters. In comparison, the South African political system is less open and more centralized.

## Other State Institutions

### The Judiciary and the Police

The senior levels of the judiciary are freer of political influence than they were during the apartheid era. All judges are appointed through a constitutional process that limits executive discretion. Court judgments demonstrate robust judicial independence, despite complaints by cabinet ministers that judges are trying to make themselves policy-makers.

Judicial independence has been especially obvious with respect to the Constitutional Court. In two key judgments, in 2001 and in 2002, the court ruled on how the government should allocate public resources, to meet its constitutional duty to supply shelter for a group of forcibly evicted squatters in Grootboom near Cape Town and to provide antiretroviral medication for HIV/AIDS patients. More recently, in 2009, the Court again showed its assertiveness in according voting rights to certain groups of foreign residents, a decision that probably benefited the ANC's opponents in upcoming elections.

Public respect for legal institutions needs to be based on more than the autonomy and integrity. For most citizens, courts are inaccessible and inefficient. Huge caseloads make legal proceedings extremely slow. Nearly half of South Africa's prisoners are awaiting trial. Several thousand cases a year do not reach trial because criminal syndicates bribe court officials to destroy dockets.

South Africa has one of the highest crime rates in the world. This is a consequence of gross social inequalities, a violent political history, and a general disrespect for the law that apartheid engendered, although rising rates of youth unemployment supply a more contemporary explanation for crime.

Overall, conviction rates in South Africa, at 8 percent in 2002, represent one of the lowest levels in the world. This is a reflection of poor police work and courtroom shortcomings. Up to the 1990s judges tolerated routine use of torture to extract confessions even in petty criminal cases. Today, judges are much more discerning, but reports suggest that the police still torture suspected criminals quite routinely. Between March 2008 and April 2009, the Independent Complaints Directorate investigated 828 cases of assaults by police officers of people held in their custody, many of these sufficiently severe to rate as torture.

Since 1994, despite efforts at reform, police competence remains patchy. The unification of the national police force with a number of separate homeland forces has resulted in an organization that is top heavy in its rank structure. Only a third of South Africa's 17,000 police officers work in the field. One reason that conviction rates are low is that semiliterate constables ignore basic rules of evidence. Pay scales for rank-and-file police officers are the lowest in the public sector, which makes the force

To date, the judiciary has generally resisted political pressure. During the efforts to prosecute Jacob Zuma for corruption, his supporters were outspokenly critical of the legal system, maintaining that it was impossible for Zuma to receive a fair trial. Many observers including the *Mail and Guardian's*, Zapiro, as in this cartoon, expressed concern that Zuma's allies were themselves attempting to exert political pressure on judicial decisions.

exceptionally prone to corruption. In 2010, Jackie Selebi, a one-time head of Interpol (International Criminal Police Organization), and the most senior South African police officer was convicted on corruption charges and sentenced to fifteen years in prison.

## National Security Organizations

The South African military is not in much better shape than the police forces. The South African National Defence Force (SANDF), an amalgamation of the old South African Defence Force, homeland militias, and the guerrilla armies, employed 75,000 soldiers, sailors, and airmen in 2005, about half the size of the full-time army during the apartheid era. One reason that has made South Africa reluctant to play a major role in continental peacekeeping operations is the poor quality of its forces, which ceased active recruitment between 1994 and 2000. The transformation of apartheid's aggressive war machine into what opposition politicians deride as "an armed welfare department" may not be permanent. In 1998, the government committed itself to an ambitious program of expenditure on military aircraft, submarines, and light destroyers for the navy, while recruitment was to be stepped up to an annual rate of 10,000. Despite this resolution, more than a decade later the Defence Force remains too underequipped and undermanned to play even the fairly confined defensive role envisaged for it in the 2009 Defence White paper. The shortcomings are most evident in the airforce where half the combat pilot positions are unfilled as well as a similar proportion of the posts allocated to technical support. The army continues to make do with obsolete equipment, some of it over thirty years old. Budgetary increases in 2009 intended for recruitment and material were absorbed in a major pay increase awarded when soldiers joined civil servants in striking for a 10 percent pay raise. With expenditure on the SANDF equalling 1.3 percent of GDP, experts agree that South African defense is underfunded. However, since the al Qaeda 9/11 attacks, the budgets of the externally oriented Secret Service and the larger domestically focused National Intelligence Agency have both expanded. The services may have become increasingly affected by factional politics, though. Jacob Zuma enjoys close personal relationships with senior intelligence officials, a reflection of his pre-1994 role in the ANC's intelligence service, and both he and Mbeki engaged intelligence officials in their political rivalry with each other.

## Subnational Government

A more serious limitation on the power of the South African state than its military weakness is shortcomings of the subnational governments, both in provincial administrations and in municipal authorities.

The nine provincial governments are led by premiers, who are limited to two terms in office. In principle, premiers are elected by their legislatures, but in the seven provinces in which the ANC predominates, such elections are formalities. Premiers are in reality appointed and dismissed by the president.

Each premier appoints a minicabinet, called an executive council. Provincial revenues derive mainly from central government. In addition, provinces receive conditional grants for particular projects from the national ministries. Provincial administrations must allocate their expenditure between departments in accordance with national budgetary guidelines. However, within these structures they enjoy a measure of financial discretion, in contracting for services and equipment, for example.

In the beginning, most of the provinces had to amalgamate several civil services from different homelands or from the separate establishments that existed for white,

Coloured, and Indian people. The new provincial boundaries brought together rival elites who sometimes remained jealous of each other's influence. In many of the former homelands, bureaucratic systems had suffered considerable degeneration. Because governments did not have strong accountability mechanisms, provincial administrations were often short of key skills such as financial record keeping, and civil servants were as a consequence often very corrupt.

Reforming such administrations was extremely difficult, particularly because it was impossible to dismiss public servants during the Mandela era—an unfortunate consequence of the transition guarantees in the 1993 constitution. Additionally, militant public service unions affiliated to COSATU, the ANC's ally, often protect identifiably corrupt officials. Most of the new provincial governments lack basic information, even about the number of their employees or the location of public property. Finally, South Africa's current public administration inherited hierarchical and authoritarian traditions from the apartheid regime, which in practice have proved very difficult to change.

In any case as citizen entitlements have expanded in social reforms—free prenatal health care, abortions on demand, housing subsidies, a wider range of welfare grants, and so forth—the bureaucracy has acquired a whole range of new tasks, even though it was already badly managed and poorly qualified. It has also become slightly smaller and has lost many skilled personnel. Public service managers in regional departments often find it difficult to interpret and understand policy designed in national ministries.

Partly because of the failings of the provincial administrations, from 1999 onwards national policy-makers increasingly emphasized municipal government as the key agency in the delivery of development projects. Because of their taxation powers, local governments in many respects have greater discretionary power than provincial administrations, especially in the case of the metropolitan councils in South Africa's six main cities. Although the big cities draw most of their revenues from local taxes, the smaller local authorities remain heavily dependent on government grants. Today about 75 percent of South Africa's cities are governed by ANC-dominated administrations.

However, there has been very low voter turnout in local elections, and heavy criticism at public meetings of the way local councils were performing. The public was clearly disappointed with the first decade of democratic local government. The Ministry of Provincial and Local Government has invested considerable effort to train councillors as well as to set up a system of ward committees to improve accountability and public participation in planning. But reforms do not seem to have improved the quality of representation in local government. In 2009 there were 100 "service delivery" protests, four times as many as in 2008. Corruption is especially entrenched in local government. Municipal administration personnel also lack basic skills. For example in 2007, one-third of city governments employed no engineers, an effect of the exodus during the preceding decade of white apartheid-era officials. As the cabinet minister responsible for municipalities conceded in 2010, outside the big cities, local government was "not working."

## The Policy-Making Process

Before it came to power in 1994, the ANC appeared to be committed to participatory ways of making policy. This was reflected in the way the post-apartheid Reconstruction and Development Programme (RDP) was adopted and the new governments rhetoric about "stakeholder" consultation in development planning and institutional accountability.

The early Mandela administration seemed to put this approach into practice when it came to making policy. Assertive parliamentary committees and ministers who were prepared to work closely with them made the process more open to interest groups and the infant lobbying industry. Departments conscientiously circulated Green Papers and White Papers (successive drafts of policy proposals) to all conceivably interested parties, and they encouraged public feedback at policy presentations up and down the country.

The minister of finance's announcement of the essential tenets of an official Growth, Employment, and Redistribution (GEAR) policy in 1996 represented an abrupt turnaround. From then on, the minister warned, macroeconomic management would stress deficit reduction, the removal of tariff protection, government right-sizing, privatization, exchange control relaxation, and the setting of wage increases below rates of productivity growth. The ANC's trade union allies clearly could not endorse these objectives. After a currency crisis in late 1995, creating jobs in the private sector became the main engine for social progress. The government itself, the minister warned, was not in the business of creating jobs.

The minister's statement, immediately after GEAR's publication, that its content was non-negotiable, also made it different from any other official policy announcements released in the form of Green or White papers. GEAR's adoption set the tone for the new style of policy-making in South Africa. Since 1996, policy shifts have occurred in a characteristically sudden fashion, without elaborate consultative procedures. The surest way to influence policy from outside government is through direct access to the president's office and the informal networks that surround it.

Successive ANC governments, including Jacob Zuma's, have retained commitment to fiscally conservative policies. This has put economic issues at the center of political conflict. COSATU hostility to GEAR has been expressed in several national strikes. Other kinds of dissent, both by unions and the broader public, have shown hostility to official financial policies. Trade unions joined civic associations to mobilize popular protest against contracting out municipal services as well to challenge the moral right of municipalities to evict delinquent tenants and to withdraw services from payment defaulters. The austerity measures implicit in GEAR's economies have had an especially severe effect on municipalities, which have received less and less funding from the central government. At the beginning of the Mandela government, ANC leaders hoped to maintain their activist traditions in the ways in which they made decisions and exercised power. In South African democracy's second decade, the worlds of policy decision-making and popular political activism, have become increasingly insulated from each other.

## Summary

For the post-apartheid transition period, between 1994 and 1999, a power-sharing coalition helped to reassure racial minorities. Nine provincial governments give South African politics a quasi-federal character and offer smaller political parties the possibility of executive office. Despite such safeguards, the ruling party and its leaders are very powerful because of large ANC majorities in the National Assembly. Presidential authority gains strength from an electoral system that makes members of parliament very dependent on the party leadership. Continuing shortcomings in the police, the judicial system, and the provincial administrations effectively limit executive power. Meanwhile policy-making has become increasingly centralized.

# REPRESENTATION AND PARTICIPATION

# The Legislature

South Africa's legislature consists of a 400-member National Assembly located in Cape Town, as well as the National Council of Provinces. In general elections, parties compete for National Assembly seats by offering single lists of candidates rather than by running candidates in individual districts or constituencies. If a ruling party's leadership predominates within the executive branch, as is the case with the ANC, then the executive branch's power over parliament is much greater than in most other systems in which the executive branch is accountable to parliament. This is because MPs hold their seats at the will of party leadership, not through being personally elected.

Parliamentary committees review the work of different government departments. Standing Committees on Public Accounts and Public Finance monitor general public spending, and they can summon ministers and public servants to appear before them. In practice, most of the legislation since 1994 has been drafted by government ministers and their departments, not by members or committees of parliament. Draft laws must be read in the National Assembly before portfolio committees review their content. These committees usually call for public recommendations on the bill before calling for revision, acceptance, or rejection of the law. Once a bill has received its second reading in the National Assembly, it can be enacted.

In 1999, a second chamber of the parliament was set up, the National Council of the Provinces. Its ninety members are made up of nine equal delegations drawn from the provincial legislatures. To encourage consensus within provincial delegations, each province can cast only one vote within the Council. The National Council for the Provinces reviews all legislation. But for most laws its functions are only advisory.

Much of what happens in parliament depends on the ANC caucus, which represents nearly two-thirds of the votes in the National Assembly. On the whole, ANC parliamentarians have tended to defer to the executive. This can be partly because of the country's electoral system. South Africa uses a national list system of proportional representation. In national and provincial elections (held simultaneously every five years), parties nominate lists of candidates—one list for the National Assembly and one for each of the nine provinces. Voters use two ballot papers, one for the Assembly and one for their provincial legislature, on which they indicate their preferred party. In this way, voters can divide their support between two parties. Names of candidates do not appear on the ballot papers. Seats are allocated in proportion to each party's share of the votes. The list system through which MPs hold their seats at the discretion of party leaders means that MPs can defy party policy or leadership directives only if they are willing to risk heavy penalties, including losing their seat in parliament.

During the Mandela presidency ANC MPs were occasionally willing to confront the executive branch. During the Mbeki administration, parliamentary committee assertiveness became much rarer, and government ministers treated committees scornfully. In any case, ANC parliamentarians may have other priorities than ensuring executive accountability. In 2007 40 percent of the ANC caucus listed themselves as company directors.

In 2001, the ANC established a political committee to monitor the hearings of the Select Committee on Public Accounts (SCOPA), which was investigating allegations of corrupt arms contracting. SCOPA's inquiry followed allegations that a former defence minister had accepted an 11 million rand ($1.6 million) bribe. SCOPA, chaired according to convention by an opposition MP but containing a majority of ANC members, recommended in November 2000 that the Special Investigations Unit should participate in the official investigation. President Mbeki rejected this recommendation. The leader of the ANC group within SCOPA, Andrew Feinstein, was demoted and subsequently resigned, complaining of ministerial efforts to "rein me in."[12] In January 2001, the ANC chief parliamentary whip, Tony Yengeni, established a special political committee of twenty-two senior ANC MPs "to provide greater political direction to the ANC's parliamentary caucus." Yengeni announced that he would attend ANC study group meetings of SCOPA members to supply "political authority and guidance."[13] Two years later, however, Yengeni was compelled to leave parliament after being convicted for accepting a vehicle from one of the arms contractors under investigation. In February 2001, the official joint investigation committee published its report. This did not implicate senior politicians, but it did accuse top civil servants of nepotism and lying. After 2002, SCOPA ceased to play any further role in the arms contracting saga, despite later courtroom revelations about much more serious wrongdoings than those identified in the joint report. For its critics, SCOPA's inability to investigate the arms purchases was proof enough of the ANC leadership's tight control of parliament.

## Political Parties and the Party System

The main parties that emerged as the leading groups in the 1994 election were well established organizations: the African National Congress founded in 1912, the (Afrikaner) National Party in 1914, the Democratic Party in its original incarnation as the Progressive Party in 1959, Inkatha in 1975, and the Pan-Africanist Congress in

**Focus Questions**

Why has the South African National Assembly been so ineffective in checking executive power?

Why have opposition parties remained so weak in South African politics?

What factors encourage parties to take up centrist or moderate positions during elections?

Why may racial identity continue to influence political behavior?

Why do social movements and social organizations remain racially separate in South Africa?

1959. Each party drew support mainly from a different ethnic or racial group. Even after apartheid, the pattern of racial or ethnic bloc voting has changed only slightly. There have, however, been some important changes in South Africa's party system.

## The African National Congress

The ANC began in a conference of African notables that assembled in 1912 to protest the impending South African Land Act. Years later, during World War II, the ANC began to build a mass membership. By this time, several of its leaders were also members of the Communist Party. Within the ANC, both Communists and Africanists (racially assertive African nationalists) who formed the Youth League influenced the ANC to embrace more aggressive tactics. The Communist Party was banned in 1950; its members then worked within the ANC and allied organizations. Communist influence and older liberal traditions instilled by Methodist schools, which trained most African political leaders, ensured that although the ANC itself remained an exclusively African body, it defined its program on a broader basis. In 1956, the ANC's Freedom Charter proposed a democratic future in which all races would enjoy equal rights. A "Defiance Campaign" of civil disobedience against new apartheid laws swelled membership.

A breakaway movement, the Pan-Africanist Congress (PAC), formed in 1959 as a more radical alternative to the ANC. After the uproar that followed the Sharpeville massacre in March 1960, the government banned both the ANC and the PAC. Moving underground and into exile, they began planning armed insurgencies.

During its thirty years in exile, the ANC strengthened its alliance with the Communist Party. Partly because of this alliance, it opened its ranks to whites, Indians, and Coloureds. Because survival in exile required discipline and authority, the ANC patterned its internal organization on the centralized model of communist parties.

After 1976, ANC guerrillas attracted public attention with attacks on symbolic targets. A charismatic cult developed around the imprisoned leaders on Robben Island, especially Nelson Mandela. Mandela's stature helped the ANC to achieve recognition and acceptance internationally. By the late 1980s, meetings between its leaders and Western statesmen underlined its status as a government-in-waiting. The ANC established secret preliminary contacts with South African officials in the mid-1980s. After the party was unbanned and Mandela was released from prison in 1990, the international recognition the ANC had obtained in exile brought the financial resources needed to build a sophisticated mass organization in South Africa.

In its first two terms in office, authoritarian tendencies within the ANC strengthened. Its 1997 amendments to the party constitution endorsed centralism and prohibited factionalism. This was supposed to make it difficult for caucuses to emerge around a policy position that disagreed with the leadership. Party officials also tried to promote authoritarian patterns of party discipline by reinforcing a new Africanist advocacy of deference and respect for elders in society. However, the rank and file rebellion against Thabo Mbeki's effort to secure a third term in the party presidency at its national conference in 2007 may have helped to strengthen the ANC's commitment to internally democratic procedures.

Today the ANC's overwhelming predominance in South African political life is partly a result of its legitimacy as a national liberation movement in the struggle against apartheid. Its political authority also results from an extensive political organization, represented through local branches throughout the country. The 2009 elections were contested by the new Congress of the People Party (Cope), constituted mainly by Thabo Mbeki's supporters in the Eastern Cape, the first really significant defection from the ANC. It obtained a small, but encouraging 7 percent share of the national ballot.

## Smaller Parties

After Sharpeville, the largely Afrikaner-based National Party maintained its commitment to racial segregation and white privilege, but it defined its vision and programs in more universal language to win supporters among conservative groups in western countries. Portraying Southern Africa as a strategic area in the conflict between the West and the Soviet Union in the Cold War was a key ingredient in this project. A narrow majority of English-speaking South Africans supported the National Party during the 1980s. Meanwhile, the Progressive Party, represented in parliament by the lone voice of Helen Suzman between 1961 and 1974, won twenty-six seats and 20 percent of the white vote in 1981. Traditionally, their support derived from affluent urban English-speaking neighborhoods. During the 1960s, Suzman ensured that the party's appeal rested on advocating civil liberties.

Progressive Party constitutional proposals emphasized decentralization and minority protection. Such proposals appealed to the leadership of Inkatha, the ruling party in the Zulu homeland, which had its own reasons for favoring federal constitutional arrangements. Control of state machinery as well as its association with the Zulu royal house enabled Inkatha to build a formidable organization. This became increasingly militarized throughout the 1980s during the ferocious struggle for territorial dominance in the shanty communities on the outskirts of the homeland's urban centers.

During the constitutional negotiations of the early 1990s, most parties attempted to broaden their support bases. The ANC built branches outside African neighborhoods. The "New" National Party (NNP)—as the National Party came to be called after apartheid—attracted a Coloured following. Although working-class Coloureds suffered racial oppression to some extent, they had also benefited from apartheid, which had protected their jobs from African competition. In 1990, the Progressives combined with a group of breakaway parliamentarians from the National Party to form the Democratic Party (DP). The Democrats recruited fresh support from Indian and Coloured politicians while positioning their organization as the party of meritocracy, business, and free enterprise. Meanwhile, the Inkatha Freedom Party (IFP) gave conspicuous positions to a number of white sympathizers.

Seven parties won seats in the National Assembly in the first universal suffrage election of 1994. As well as the historic organizations, there were two new groups. The Freedom Front hoped to secure future arrangements for Afrikaner self-determination. More realistically, they believed their presence in parliament would protect the status of existing Afrikaner institutions, especially in education. The African Christian Democratic Party was a product of an evangelical Protestant revival movement, especially influential within middle-class Coloured areas in the Western Cape.

## The Democratic Alliance and Opposition Politics

After 1994, the New National Party's fortunes plummeted. The party's ineffectual role as a junior coalition partner in the Government of National Unity between 1994 and 1996 undermined confidence among its white supporters who would have preferred combative opposition to the ANC. The NNP joined in an alliance with the Democratic Party between 1999 and 2002, but this introduced new sources of ideological tension between the parties. This partnership, called the Democratic Alliance (DA), was not politically viable. Democrats disliked the NNP's old-style patronage machine, while New National Party organizers perceived Democrats as organizationally weak and finicky amateurs, who were not prepared for the rough and tumble tactics of winning power in poor communities.

By the beginning of 2002, the Democratic Alliance had fallen apart, though the Democrats retained their new name running in subsequent elections as the Democratic Alliance. In withdrawing from the alliance, NNP leaders emphasized that their differences with the Democrats involved issues of political substance, not just personal conflicts. They were more predisposed than the DP to the ANC's vision of cooperative participatory government, and they maintained that they too, like the ruling party, had a historical affinity with poor people. The NNP favored a constructive opposition, not one that had been "reduced to an angry white voice, mudslinging and character assassination."[14] Despite their agreement about policy issues, the two parties were still influenced by quite different philosophies—the Democrats rooted in a liberal conception of individual citizenship and the Nationalist based on community-centered notions of rights and obligations. Many NNP politicians also had fewer principled objections to the ANC's performance in government than the liberal free marketers who lead the Democratic Party. Opinion polls indicate that NNP supporters tended to be more concerned by the kinds of issues that animated the ANC's social base (job creation, for example) and less inclined than Democrats to assign the first government priority to fighting crime.

In 2002, the New National Party announced that in the future it would cooperate with the ANC government, another turnaround that diminished its credibility further among many of its constituents. In the 2004 elections the support for NNP fell to a quarter of its level in 1999. However, the NNP leader, Marthinus van Schalkwyk received a cabinet position, and he and the six other NNP parliamentarians joined the ANC in 2005. The NNP announced its dissolution in 2006, ninety-two years after its foundation.

In 2009, the Democratic Alliance obtained about 3 million votes, nearly 17 percent of the total and won 67 out of the 136 opposition seats in parliament, as well as winning control of the Western Cape regional government. More generally opposition has consolidated into three main parties, the DA, Congress of the People, and the IFP with the other parties obtaining progressively smaller vote shares in successive elections. Any future IFP collapse—almost certain after the departure of its aging leader, Chief Buthelezi—would probably see an exodus of IFP supporters to the ANC. But the DA can reasonably hope to be the main beneficiary of other parties' declines. Though the DA has invested effort in trying to recruit black members and establish African township branches, the 2009 election results confirmed it had yet to win serious numbers of African votes even in the Western Cape where it emerged as the most popular party among Coloured voters. DA officials themselves acknowledge that they have yet to take votes from the ANC and that so far their gains have been at the expense of smaller parties. In the Western Cape, its fortunes among Africans may change, though, with the benefits of incumbency.

Between 1994 and 2009, electoral support for the ANC has remained fairly stable, 62.65 percent in 1994, 66.35 percent in 1999, 69.69 percent in 2004 and 65.90 percent in 2009 (see Table 11.2). Most of the ANC's support in these elections was African, although it also succeeded in winning substantial minorities of the votes in Indian and Coloured communities. Over the four elections, the most significant changes have been in the configuration of opposition parties, with successive advances enjoyed by the Democrats, the collapse of National Party vote, and the decline of Inkatha. The use of a proportional representation system encourages the inclusion of small parties in parliament, which the South African constitutional architects had planned. Voters no longer identify quite so emotionally with parties. People are less likely to believe that they "belong" to a party or that it is "theirs."[15] Party membership remains extensive, however.

Neither white-led democrats nor ethnic regionalists appear very likely to create a popularly credible opposition to the ANC. The ruling party's monopoly on black electoral support will probably be challenged only when tensions between right and left wings within the ANC reach the breaking point. To date, the ANC's alliance with

| Party | 1994 | 1999 | 2004 | 2009 |
|---|---|---|---|---|
| African Christian Democratic Party | 88,104 (0.45%) | 228,976 (1.43%) | 250,272 (1.60%) | 142,658 (0.81%) |
| ANC | 12,237,655 (62.55%) | 10,601,330 (66.35%) | 10,880,915 (69.69%) | 11,650,748 (65.90%) |
| Congress of the People | - | - | - | 1,311,027 (7.42%) |
| Democratic Party/Alliance | 338,426 (1.73%) | 1,527,337 (9.56%) | 1,931,201 (12.37%) | 2,945,829 (16.66%) |
| Freedom Front | 424,555 (2.17%) | 127,217 (0.80%) | 139,465 (0.89%) | 146,796 (0.83%) |
| Inkatha | 2,058,294 (10.94%) | 1,371,477 (8.58%) | 1,088,664 (6.97%) | 804,260 (4.55%) |
| New National Party | 3,983,690 (20.39%) | 1,098,215 (6.87%) | 257,824 (1.65%) | - |
| Pan-Africanist Congress | 243,478 (1.25%) | 113,125 (0.71%) | 113,512 (0.35%) | 48,530 (0.27%) |
| United Democratic Movement | - | 546,790 (3.42%) | 355,717 (2.28%) | 149,680 (0.85%) |
| Others | 149,296 (0.81%) | 362,676 (2.19%) | 595,101 (3.80%) | 480,416 (2.73%) |
| **Total Votes** | **19,533,498** | **15,977,142** | **15,612,671** | **17,680,729** |
| Turnout of registered voters | - | 89.3% | 76.7% | 77.3% |
| Turnout of voting age population | 86% | 71.8% | 57.8% | 59.8% |

**Table 11.2  South African General Elections, 1994–2009**

organized labor and the Communist Party has held up, despite deep and frequently voiced disagreements about the government's commitment to privatization, liberalization, and deficit reduction. Generally, workers have been among the beneficiaries of ANC rule: Wages have risen faster than inflation, and the government has been reluctant to cut public sector jobs. Legal reforms have enhanced the collective bargaining capacity of trade unions as well as instituting new rights and entitlements for workers. Nevertheless, relations between trade unions and the government are often fractious. In 2010, a massive strike by nearly a million civil servants secured a 10 percent wage increase.

# Elections

South African elections are generally judged to be free and fair, and arguably in certain respects have become more so rather than less. Most importantly, it has become progressively easier for candidates of all parties to canvass voters outside the areas where their core supporters live. In 1994 there were "no go" areas in which canvassers from certain parties were forcibly excluded by their competitors' activists and supporters. The Inkatha-dominated Northern Natal represented a no-go area for the ANC in 1994, as did Soweto for the Democrats in 1994. Such areas were much less extensive in 1999. By 2004 each of the main parties were routinely deploying door-to-door canvassers in the same neighbourhoods sometimes at the same time. Over the four national elections, electoral management by the Independent Electoral Commission has become increasingly effective, and in 2009 more than two million new voters were added to the electorate in an especially successful registration drive, especially among people aged 20–29. All the available evidence suggests that voters are confident about ballot secrecy as well as the integrity of the count.

Access to public broadcasting actually improved for opposition parties in 2009 with new rules for election broadcasting, and if anything coverage of the 2009 campaign by the state-owned South African Broadcasting Corporation (SABC) was less biased in favor of the ruling party than in 1999 and 2004. This was possibly a consequence of the internal tensions within the ANC accompanying Jacob Zuma's accession, which also affected the SABC's Board. During the 2009 election ANC leaders complained that the Board was biased in favor of Zuma's disaffected opponents, now campaigning in the new Congress of the People Party (Cope).

Running against these positive trends, though, was an increased propensity for ruling party speakers at mass meetings to suggest that electoral support would be rewarded with grants or other benefits. Moreover in the run-up to formal campaigning, observers noted an increased incidence of "robust" electioneering including attacks on rival activists. In general, though, the weight of the evidence suggests that the ANC continues to win its victories through persuasive campaigning rather than as a consequence of coercion, threats, or untoward inducements.

Arguably, South Africa's electoral system promotes the formation of socially inclusive political parties and civil electioneering. In South Africa, the nationwide double-ballot, list-proportional representation electoral system contains strong incentives for moderation because the electorate is so spread out. All parties are encouraged to seek votes outside their core support or base areas, a consideration that helps to encourage them to adopt programs with broad social appeal. Party leaders put people on their lists who might not win popular support in electoral contests that were focused around individual candidates: members of racial minorities or women, for example. The drawback is that parliamentarians hold their seats at the will of party leaders, and this has produced a parliament that tends to be deferential toward the executive.

# Political Culture, Citizenship, and Identity

Relatively high turnout rates in national elections are encouraging signs of a strong citizenship identity among South Africans. So were rising levels of approval and satisfaction with democracy during the Mandela administration, although opinion polls suggest such sentiments are less widely shared today. All pollsters agree that people are more likely to trust the national government than provincial or local authorities.

Opinion polls indicate that South Africans tend to believe that race relations have improved since 1994. But racial divisions continue to affect patterns of political support. Although public schools and middle-class neighborhoods have become desegregated, most black people still live in ghetto-like townships or in the historical homeland areas; racial distinctions still remain very conspicuous in South African social geography. However, since 1994, new patterns of public behavior seem to have created more conciliatory attitudes among South Africans. A national survey in May 2004 found that 60 percent of South Africans believed that race relations were improving, and 30 percent thought they had remained the same. Blacks were more likely than other groups to think that race relations were better. In general among all groups perceptions about the future are becoming more optimistic.[16]

Even so, there remain sources of racial tension. The government is critical of what it takes to be the slow progress of black business, and ANC leaders routinely blame the absence of quicker social change on "white economic selfishness" (Thabo Mbeki's phrase). Class-based politics was generally quite comfortably accommodated within the ANC's fold during the anti-apartheid struggle since most of its active followers were workers and their families, and the war against apartheid could just as easily be considered an offensive against capitalism. Even today, union leaders hold back from organizing a workers' party separately from the ANC, recognizing that many workers are likely to retain the loyalties fostered by decades of nationalist politics. Therefore populist racial invective directed against white privilege and wealth remains politically compelling, especially for leaders of the ANC's Youth League, with their constituency among unemployed school dropouts.

In the 1950s, a powerful women's movement developed within the ANC to resist extending the pass laws to African women. More and more women were heading single-parent households, and many women were moving into industrial occupations and higher education, which led to feminist movements. One of the first major social reforms enacted by Mandela's government was legalizing abortion on demand. In general, its female members have forced the ANC to pay at least some attention to women's rights and entitlements.

# Interests, Social Movements, and Protests

Social movements continue to be unusually well organized for a developing country. Although participation at union meetings may have dwindled, the unions have extensive financial resources, since dues are automatically deducted from workers' wages, and unions often organize entire economic sectors. The ranks of organized labor include 2.8 million members.

In townships, residents' associations have created an impressive associational network. Surveys suggest that people are more likely to participate in civic associations than in political parties. From 2002, a new generation of local single-issue movements began to address the problems of landlessness, electricity cut-offs, and evictions of bond or municipal tax defaulters. Around these concerns a strong vein of assertive protest has gathered momentum in which the activist repertoire often includes forceful behavior that borders on the violent: damage to public buildings, tire-burning, and skirmishing with police. The frequency of "major service delivery protests" as monitored by the authorities has risen through the decade: 10 in 2004, more than 50 in 2009. Participants tend to be young, often unemployed school dropouts. The focus of their anger is often the venality of local politicians, but the aggression can also direct itself at more vulnerable targets. In 2008 sixty immigrants, mainly from Mozambique and Zimbabwe, were killed by xenophobic rioters in a series of incidents around Johannesburg, these killings spurred ostensibly by widely shared convictions that foreigners were depriving local people of their jobs.

Such behavior contrasts with more benign predispositions that seem to prevail in South African associational life. For example surveys confirm that about half the population does voluntary work for charitable organizations. The proportion increases among younger people.[17] With the exception of COSATU, which invites white participation, associational life remains racially segregated, though. Business organizations, for example, continue to represent white and black firms separately. The larger corporations are still perceived to represent white privilege. Churches may have racially integrated hierarchies (Anglicans, Methodists, and Catholics have black leaders), but most South Africans worship in racially exclusive congregations. Only black South Africans attend soccer games in significant numbers to watch the multiracial teams in the Premier Soccer League. Rugby and cricket fans remain predominantly white despite efforts within the sporting administrations to make the teams more diverse. South African democracy is still weakened by divisions between ethnic groups that prevent people from recognizing common interests and shared enthusiasms.

### Summary

On the whole, members of the post-apartheid parliament within the ruling party have failed to exercise formal oversight. Party caucuses within parliament are generally tightly disciplined, a reflection of a strong party system. The African National Congress inherited from an eighty-year liberation struggle a tightly centralized organization structure and a mass following that was grouped into an extensive network of local branches. It remains the predominant organization among black South Africans. Any effective challenge to its authority will require smaller parties, mainly based among racial or ethnic minorities, to draw away significant numbers of the ANC's core support. The more likely scenario may be a future split among ANC voters as a consequence of union opposition to free-market policies. South Africa may represent a racially divided dominant-party democracy, but elections are fair, and strong social movements increase the prospects for democratic consolidation.

# SOUTH AFRICAN POLITICS IN TRANSITION

## Focus Questions

What are likely to be the long-term effects of HIV/AIDS in South Africa?

In certain respects it has been easier to institute and consolidate democracy in South Africa than in many other developing countries that underwent democratic transitions in the 1980s and 1990s. Why?

## Political Challenges and Changing Agendas

The impact of AIDS on South African society is hard to overestimate. More that 10 percent of the population is currently HIV-positive, 5.7 million people, according to UN figures for 2009. A million South Africans have already died of HIV/AIDS. AIDS is likely to kill between 5 and 7 million South Africans in the next ten years. Its victims tend to be young, between the ages of fifteen and fifty—the most economically active members of the population. Because of these deaths, the dependency ratio between income earners and those they support may double. Poor households that support AIDS patients can spend up to two-thirds of their income on the cost of care.[18] This public health holocaust is destroying a whole generation of parents.

In contrast to other African governments that have attempted to cope with the epidemic, South Africa's initial efforts to combat its spread and deal with its effects were tentative and confused. Belatedly, a public education program, including the free distribution of condoms began, toward the end of the Mandela presidency, to promote awareness of the disease. At the beginning of the program, however, education was presented as an alternative to medical treatment. Surveys suggest that AIDS awareness is not enough. It does not seem to reduce the sexual behavior that spreads the disease.

In October 1998, the minister of health announced that the government would cease supplying antiretroviral drugs to hospitals that up to then had prescribed them to pregnant women to prevent mother-to-child transmission of AIDS. The 80 million rand ($12 million) saving would be used instead for distributing 140 million contraceptives and training 10,000 teachers in life skills. One month later, Thabo Mbeki, who then was chairman of a ministerial committee on AIDS, defended the minister's decision by claiming that the drug concerned, azidothymidine (AZT), was "dangerously toxic."

Hostility to the public prescription of drugs stemmed from more complicated considerations, however. President Mbeki began publicly expressing doubts about the scientific status of the disease in late 1999 and in particular questioned the generally accepted link between HIV and AIDS. He believed that conventional scientific explanations about the disease's causes stem from racial prejudice. In 2001, Mbeki referred to the "insulting" theory that AIDS originated in Africa. In reality, Mbeki contended, South Africans who were dying of the illnesses that immune deficiency exposed them to (tuberculosis for example) were not victims of a virus; they were instead the casualties of poverty. Mbeki was aligning himself with a small minority of dissident scientists and doctors who have either denied AIDS' existence altogether or have disputed the causal link between HIV and AIDS. In 2000, the president established a panel to investigate the scientific evidence about the causes of AIDS and appointed several dissidents to join this body.

Mbeki's scepticism about AIDS certainly undermined attempts to combat the pandemic. Between 1998 and 2001, public hospitals were prevented from using antiretroviral drugs, including nevirapine, a much cheaper alternative to AZT—even for treating rape victims. But several provinces, including two ANC administrations in the Eastern Cape and Gauteng, resumed using nevirapine quite widely during 2001, but elsewhere provincial health ministers loyally maintained the ban for several years more, firing doctors who questioned such policy. Taking their cue from the president, cabinet ministers began questioning AIDS statistics and projections, suggesting these were derived from faulty sampling procedures. After the Treatment Action Campaign successfully obtained a Constitutional Court judgment compelling the government to use nevirapine in hospitals, ANC nominees on the Medical Control Council began warning that the drug might need to be deregistered on grounds of toxicity.

In addition to aggravating the death rates attributable to HIV/AIDS, the most serious consequences of government support for "dissident" positions is the absence of any serious planning to cope with the consequences of the pandemic. At the very least, increased numbers of child-care facilities, the introduction of public hospices, and a comprehensive overhaul of social security and medical insurance would be reasonable things to expect from government; no such measures have yet been adopted. Although in August 2002, after a Constitutional Court judgment, and in response to internal pressures within the ANC, the cabinet appeared to commit itself to provision of antiretroviral treatment, the health ministry resisted. The Treatment Action Campaign organized a civil disobedience protest during 2003 against the delay.

Really full-hearted compliance with the Court's decision only began after the ANC's leadership change in 2008 that led to Mbeki's fall from power. By 2009, with a new health minister in charge, 850,000 patients were receiving medication, still well short of what was needed, but a substantial advance all the same. In October that year, the government committed increased funding to drug purchases. Today the major difficulties are administrative: The health system simply cannot manage the scale of the treatment required. But with Zuma himself publically undergoing an AIDs test, the leadership's support for an effective program to counter the pandemic is no longer in doubt. With a 32 percent infection rate among women in their late 20s, according to a survey undertaken by the Human Sciences Research Council in 2009, this fresh commitment may just be too late.

## Economic Challenges

Despite increasing death rates among the economically active population, high-level unemployment is likely to persist. HIV/AIDS will cut already low saving rates and deepen the shortages of skilled workers. Every year half a million students leave high school without graduating. When they enter the labor market without skills, they ensure that unemployment will remain at high levels for a long time.

Modern governments are not in the business of creating jobs, Mbeki's ministers used to insist, and they argued that the removal of subsidies and tariffs encouraged more competitive industries. In their view, South Africa had adopted the "correct macro financial policy fundamentals." Critics of Mbeki's government argued that one factor that deterred investors, high crime rates, was partly the result of the government's failure to undertake thorough police reform. Fairly modest levels of public debt compared to that of most other developing countries prompted left-wing economists to suggest that heavier foreign borrowing might finance higher levels of public investment in services and fighting poverty and stimulate the kinds of growth rates needed to reduce unemployment significantly. This advice may have had some impact. During Mbeki's second term after 2004, foreign loan–funded investment in infrastructure did help to expand employment, mainly though in short-term jobs in construction, much of it linked to the building of new facilities for South Africa's hosting of the Soccer World Cup in 2010.

Government social expenditure has helped to soften the effects of poverty, but social inequality remains as strong as ever before. Absolute poverty has probably receded a little given the construction of more than two million houses now inhabited by poor people and the much wider distribution of welfare grants. Since 1994, the rise of Africans into leadership positions in the public sector, social organizations, and certain sectors of business may have helped to soften popular perceptions of social injustice.

Agricultural landownership is one domain, however, in which white privileges remain especially visible, and so far the government has made only very gradual progress to change racial patterns of landholding. Since 2000, a succession of illegal land occupations, both urban and rural, by homeless people outside towns, has underlined how volatile landlessness can be as a political issue, especially when many Africans bitterly remember being forced off the land. South African land reform is based on a principle of paying market-level prices to landowners. Even when historically dispossessed communities win back their original land rights, the process of restitution is subject to protracted negotiations over compensation.

The prospects for South Africa's transitional democracy will be fragile if its institutions are too frequently invoked to protect property rights. On the other hand, it is also possible that constitutional arguments help the poor and helpless by raising awareness of their circumstances. Defending and extending democracy may become much more challenging, however, if resources available for public services become scarcer and it becomes more difficult to decide who should receive them. Polls confirm that the South African public's ideas of democracy emphasize improvements in living conditions. In other words, people associate democracy with the provision of livelihoods and basic necessities. They attach less importance to its institutional and political dimensions. In this sense, the challenges of governing the economy and deepening the democratic idea come together in ways that define politics in South Africa today.

Public trust in authority is unlikely to be strengthened by new draft legislation for the Protection of Information, though. This threatens to extend the scope of official secrecy in such a way that newspapers might risk heavy penalties if they investigate venal politicians. At the time of writing the Bill is being redrafted, though, after extensive protest including opposition from key trade unionists and key ANC notables. Most recently the ANC's Pallo Jordan has criticised the Bill as the expression of a "fool's errand", asking the question, "How did the ANC paint itself in a corner where it can be portrayed as being opposed to press freedom"? Concern to shield top politicians from corruption allegations may have received fresh impetus with Jacob Zuma's accession given his own notoriety as a rent-seeker.

# South African Politics in Comparative Perspective

Unlike many of the countries that moved from authoritarian regimes to democratic governments in the late 1980s and early 1990s, South Africa's political economy was developed through a settler minority that became a permanent part of its population. This made the transition to democracy both easier and more challenging.

Between two world wars, a politically independent settler state could invest the revenues from the local production of primary commodities to develop a relatively diversified industrial economy. It expropriated land from its African subjects and recruited a modern working class from them. Later, unlike many former colonial countries in Africa, powerful and well-organized social forces could mobilize to support democratization in South Africa, in particular the African trade unions, which had evolved around industrial assembly lines even under apartheid. Democratic politics within the white settler minority prompted wider kinds of political organization across the population almost from the beginning of South Africa's Act of Union in 1910. Today the organizations that are represented in the South African parliament are among the oldest political parties in the developing world. Ironically, despite its often brutal efforts during the apartheid era to promote ethnic division, the effective authority of the South African state through most of the twentieth century was probably a more decisive influence in stimulating a national identity than many more benign governments elsewhere in the colonial and postcolonial world.

Nevertheless, South African society was deeply divided in the 1990s at the beginning of democratization. Except for the churches, most institutions and organizations were segmented, separated, or stratified by race. In addition, economic inequalities between rich and poor were among the most polarized in the world, and their injustice was reinforced because they ran along racial lines.

In certain respects, South African democratization represents a success story. The national government has created trust among citizens. Its political procedures are recognized to be fair, and political leaders have generally observed its rules. A constitution that was designed to be socially inclusive has fostered widely representative institutions. Popular support of the government is partly a result of its efforts to extend services to poor people, distribute resources fairly, and expand and improve infrastructure and education. Disciplined public finance has encouraged a revival of GDP growth to the point that South Africa is now recognized as one of the most important emerging economies.

One reason that democratization since 1994 has brought about more effective governance is that it was preceded by a much longer process of political and economic reform. The dismantling of the tariffs and subsidies that nurtured and protected industry and commercial agriculture began more than a decade before the universal right to vote. Unlike in the countries of the post-communist world, the coming of democracy did not bring a sudden exposure to the harsh shocks of international competition. Economic liberalization has continued at a relatively measured pace compared to the experience of many Third World countries, which have been compelled to undergo very rapid structural adjustment of their economies. The welfare state created under apartheid has maintained many of its provisions and extended certain of them, in sharp contrast to the shrinking scope of social services offered by most governments in the developing world.

Similarly, political liberalization preceded universal enfranchisement over a relatively long period. Industrial relations reform enabled black trade unions to participate in institutionalized collective bargaining through the 1980s. This encouraged the growth of well-structured associational life, both inside and outside the workplace, which reinvigorated older political organizations. Elsewhere, new democracies have been fragile because they have not had strong representative movements and parties. In South Africa, constitutional negotiations did not take place in a political vacuum or in a situation of near state collapse. Until the 1994 elections, the apartheid state retained effective authority, and because the negotiations that moved the country towards democracy unfolded over several years, the settlement reached a high degree of consensus.

Will South Africa manage to deal with its economic challenges under democratic conditions? To redress poverty and reduce inequality significantly, the state will have to make much more serious inroads into minority privileges. Although the constitution makes meeting basic needs of citizens a government obligation, it was also designed to reassure economically minority dominant groups that their interests would be safeguarded under democracy. It is likely that the constitution's meaning will become increasingly challenged if the government attempts to address inequality through expanding the scope of administrative regulation, for example, through compulsory purchases to accelerate land reform, for example.

Today, South Africa's political leaders sometimes blame the constitutional compromises of the transition from apartheid for their slow progress in creating a fairer society, even though these compromises were necessary at the time. But as we have seen, shortcomings in government performance may be more attributable to administrative incapacity (as in policing and justice) or deference to presidential eccentricity (as with AIDS policy). Even so, South Africa provides grounds for hope that democracy and economic growth can be combined in the developing world.

## Summary

The four main challenges to South Africa's political leadership are HIV/AIDS, unemployment, social inequality, and deepening democracy. Extreme social inequality may reduce public support for democracy and open up opportunities for populist authoritarian politics. Compared to other new democracies, however, the South African political future appears hopeful. South Africans began their democracy with a relatively diversified economy and strong political institutions. The government has tried to reduce economic hardship, and support for the political system is widespread.

## Key Terms

| | | |
|---|---|---|
| apartheid | homelands | privatization |
| irredentism | migrant laborers | settler state |
| *African* | township | democratization |
| Afrikaner | *Umkhonto-we-Sizwe* | economic deregulation |
| *voortrekkers* | sanctions | power sharing |
| Boer | influx control | |
| pass laws | proportional representation (PR) | |

## Suggested Readings

Davenport, Rodney, and Christopher Saunders. *South Africa: A Modern History*, 5th ed. New York: St. Martin's Press, 2000.

Feinstein, Andrew, *After the Party: Corruption, the ANC and South Africa's Uncertain Future*. London: Verso, 2009.

Gevisser, Mark. *Thabo Mbeki: The Dream Deferred*. Johannesburg: Jonathan Ball, 2007.

Gibson, James L. *Overcoming Apartheid: Can Truth Reconcile a Divided Nation?* New York: Russell Sage Foundation, 2004.

Glaser, Darryl. *Politics and Society in South Africa*. Thousand Oaks, CA: Sage, 2001.

Gumede, William Mervin. *Thabo Mbeki and the Battle for the Soul of the ANC*. Cape Town: Zebra Press, 2005.

Lipton, Merle. *Capitalism and Apartheid: South Africa, 1910–1986*. Aldershot, England: Wildwood House, 1986.

Lodge, Tom. *Sharpeville: An Apartheid Massacre and its Consequences*. Oxford: Oxford University Press, 2011.

Mandela, Nelson. *Long Walk to Freedom*. New York: Little, Brown, 1994.

Marais, Hein. *South Africa: Limits to Change: The Political Economy of Transition*. New York: Zed Books, 2001.

Marx, Anthony. *Making Race and Nation: A Comparison of the United States, South Africa and Brazil*. Cambridge: Cambridge University Press, 1998.

Nattrass, Nicoli. *The Moral Economy of AIDS in South Africa*. Cambridge: Cambridge University Press, 2004.

Picard, Louis. *The State of the State: Institutional Transformation, Capacity and Political Change in South Africa*. Johannesburg: Witwatersrand University Press, 2005.

Robins, Steven L. *Limits to Liberation after Apartheid: Citizenship, Governance and Culture*. Athens: Ohio University Press, 2005.

Seekings, Jeremy. *The UDF: A History of the United Democratic Front in South Africa, 1983–1991*. Athens: Ohio University Press, 2000.

Sparks, Allister. *Tomorrow Is Another Country: The Inside Story of South Africa's Negotiated Revolution*. Sandton: Struik Book Distributors, 1994.

Spitz, Richard, and Matthew Chaskelson. *The Politics of Transition: A Hidden History of South Africa's Negotiated Settlement*. Oxford: Hart Publishing and Johannesburg: Witwatersrand University Press, 2000.

Welsh, David, *The Rise and Fall of Apartheid*, Johannesburg: Jonathan Ball, 2009.

Wilson, Richard. *The Politics of Truth and Reconciliation in South Africa: Legitimizing the Post-Apartheid State*. Cambridge: Cambridge University Press, 2001.

## Suggested Websites

Electoral Institute for Sustainability of Democracy in Africa
http://www.eisa.org.za

Institute for Democracy in Africa
http://www.idasa.org

South African Institute of Race Relations
http://www.sairr.org.za

Statistics South Africa
http://www.stats.gov.za

# 12 Nigeria

Darren Kew and Peter Lewis

© Pius Utomi Ekpei/Afp/Getty Images

**Official Name:** Federal Republic of Nigeria

**Location:** Western Africa

**Capital City:** Abuja

**Population (2009):** 154.7 million

**Size:** 923,768 sq. km.; slightly more than twice the size of California

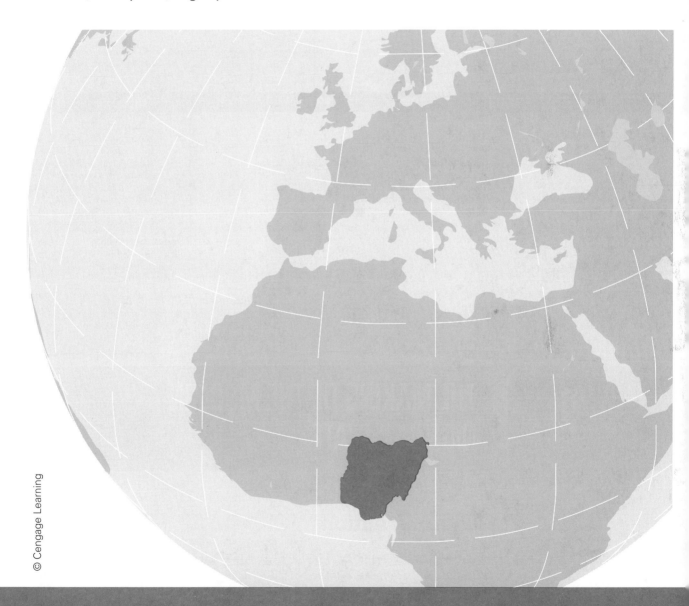

© Cengage Learning

**1960**
Independence. Nigeria consists of three regions under a Westminster parliamentary model. Abubakar Tafawa Balewa, a northerner, is the first prime minister.

**January 1966**
Civilian government deposed in coup. General Aguiyi Ironsi, an Igbo, becomes head of state.

**1967–1970**
Biafran civil war

**July 1975**
Military coup deposes Gowan; led by General Murtala Muhammed, a northerner.

**February 1976**
Murtala Muhammed assassinated in failed coup led by Middle Belt minorities. Muhammed's second-in-command, General Olusegun Obasanjo, a Yoruba, assumes power.

**October 1979**
Elections held. A majority in both houses is won by NPN, led by northern/Hausa-Fulani groups. Alhaji Shehu Shagari is elected Nigeria's first executive president.

| 1960 | 1965 | 1970 | 1975 | 1980 | 1985 | 1990 |
|------|------|------|------|------|------|------|

**July 1966**
Countercoup is led by General Yakubu Gowan (an Anga, from the Middle Belt) with aid from northern groups.

**August 1985**
Buhari is overthrown by General Ibrahim B. Babangida, a Middle Belt Muslim, in a palace coup. Babangida promises a return to democracy by 1990, a date he delays five times before being forced from office.

**December 1983**
Military coup led by General Muhammadu Buhari, a northerner.

**September 1978**
New constitution completed, marking the adoption of the U.S. presidential model in a federation with 19 states.

**SECTION 1**

# THE MAKING OF THE MODERN NIGERIAN STATE

## Politics in Action

In late November 2009, President Umaru Musa Yar'Adua collapsed for at least the third time since coming to office in 2007 from an ailment that he had never fully explained to the nation. He was rushed unconscious to a hospital in Saudi Arabia, and only his wife and a handful of his closest advisors saw him directly. For over three months, Nigerians had no direct evidence that their president was conscious or alive, and even his own ministers and a delegation of Senators were refused access. Government activity at the federal level ground to a halt.

Shockingly, for the first two months, neither the National Assembly nor the cabinet raised any public concern that the nation in effect had no president. The

## June 12, 1993
Moshood Abiola wins presidential elections, but Babangida annuls the election eleven days later.

## July–September 1994
Pro-democracy strike by the major oil union, NUPENG, cuts Nigeria's oil production by an estimated 25 percent. Sympathy strikes ensue, followed by arrests of political and civic leaders.

## June 1998
General Abacha dies; succeeded by General Abdulsalami Abubakar, a Middle Belt Muslim from Babangida's hometown. Abubakar releases nearly all political prisoners and installs a new transition program. Parties are allowed to form unhindered.

## 2000
Communal conflicts erupt in Lagos, Benue, Kaduna, and Kana states at different times over localized issues.

## Spring 2002
The Supreme Court passes several landmark judgments, overturning a PDP-biased 2001 electoral law, and ruling on the control of offshore oil and gas resources. In November the Court opens the legal door for more parties to be registered.

## May 2006
President Obasanjo tries to amend the constitution to allow himself a third term in office, but is defeated by the National Assembly.

## April 2011
Jonathan wins the presidential election despite opposition from Northern factions for violating an informal ethnic rotation principle. The PDP again takes the majority of contests, but improved elections under a reformist chairman allow opposition parties to make some inroads.

**1995   1999   2000   2005   2007   2011**

## November 1993
Defense Minister General Sani Abacha seizes power in a coup. Two years later he announces a three-year transition to civilian rule, which he manipulates to have himself nominated for president in 1998.

## August 1993
Babangida installs Ernest Shonekan as "interim civilian president" until new presidential elections could be held later that autumn.

## November 1999
Zamfara state in the north is the first of twelve to institute the *shari'a* criminal code. That same month, President Obasanjo sends the army to the Niger Delta town of Odi to root out local militias, leveling the town in the process.

## 1999
Former head of state Olusegun Obansanjo and his party, the PDP, sweep the presidential and National Assembly elections, adding to their majority control of state and local government seats. The federation now contains thirty-six states.

## August 2002
The National Assembly begins impeachment proceedings against President Obasanjo over budgetary issues. The matter ends by November, with the president apologizing.

## April–May 2007
The ruling PDP again takes a vast majority of election victories across the nation amid a deeply compromised process. Umaru Musa Yar'Adua becomes president. Yar'Adua promises reform, but spends his first year trying to solidify his tenuous hold on power.

## December 2008
The Supreme Court upholds President Yar'Adua's election in a narrow 4–3 decision.

## May 2010
President Yar'Adua dies in office, after several months incapacitated in a Saudi hospital. Vice President Goodluck Jonathan assumes the presidency.

First Lady and the president's inner circle released occasional statements that the president was recovering well, but prevented any direct contact with him and blocked all attempts to have Vice President Jonathan step in as acting president as the constitution directs. Finally, under both international pressure and the threat of a military coup, the National Assembly declared Jonathan Acting President in February 2010. President Yar'Adua returned to the country shortly thereafter, but was clearly too ill to govern, and he passed away in May 2010. Goodluck Jonathan then was sworn in as president.

The fact that Nigeria could persist for months without a functioning president, during which time his wife and a few advisors could seek to run the country themselves—and that they would go largely unchallenged—speaks volumes about the state of the nation's politics. Democratization in Nigeria—nearly a decade after the exit of the military from power—has yet to produce good governance. Instead, authoritarian rule has given way to competitive oligarchy, in which an increasingly greedy, oil-rich political elite fight to expand their power, while more than 90 percent of Nigerians struggle to survive on less than two U.S. dollars per day. This impoverished majority is so disenfranchised by the state that their president could disappear for months, and a small cabal could hold the nation hostage, without much public outcry.

## Focus Questions

What are some of the key impacts that colonialism and military rule left on the development of the Nigerian state?

What role has ethnicity played in the development of Nigeria's political parties, and in the collapse of Nigeria's First Republic and descent into civil war?

How have clientelism and corruption continued to undermine political development in the Fourth Republic?

**authoritarianism**

A system of rule in which power depends not on popular legitimacy but on the coercive force of the political authorities. Hence, there are few personal and group freedoms. It is also characterized by near absolute power in the executive branch and few, if any, legislative and judicial controls.

**legitimacy**

A belief by powerful groups and the broad citizenry that a state exercises rightful authority. In the contemporary world, a state is said to possess legitimacy when it enjoys consent of the governed, which usually involves democratic procedures and the attempt to achieve a satisfactory level of development and equitable distribution of resources.

**accountability**

A government's responsibility to its population, usually by periodic popular elections, transparent fiscal practices, and by parliament's having the power to dismiss the government by passing a motion of no confidence. In a political system characterized by accountability, the major actions taken by government must be known and understood by the citizenry.

**unfinished state**

A state characterized by instabilities and uncertainties that may render it susceptible to collapse as a coherent entity.

Under the surface of this fiasco, however, were some important signs that a decade of democracy has had some impact. First and foremost, throughout the crisis, as opposition grew it insisted on the constitution as the framework for resolving the dispute. Ultimately, elites turned to the National Assembly, not the military, and military leaders rejected pressure from some junior officers to stage a coup. Moreover, the politicians clearly sensed that they could not neglect public opinion forever. Discontent has grown with the slow pace of change and the intrigues of the oligarchy, and the public has begun to demand a greater share of the nation's wealth and a greater say in political decisions.

Nigeria thus encapsulates many characteristics that more broadly identify Africa, as the young democracy faces the challenge of managing the country's contentious ethnic and religious diversity in conditions of scarcity and weak institutions, while facing the constant struggle between **authoritarian** and democratic governance, the push for development amidst persistent underdevelopment, the burden of public corruption, and the pressure for accountability. Nigeria, like most other African countries, has sought to create a viable nation-state out of the incoherence created by its colonial borders. More than 250 competing ethnic groups, crosscut by two major religious traditions, have repeatedly clashed over economic and political resources. The result: a Nigeria with low levels of popular **legitimacy** and **accountability**, and a persistent inability to meet the most basic needs of its citizens. Nigeria today remains an **unfinished state** characterized by instabilities and uncertainties. Will Nigeria return to the discredited path of authoritarianism and greater underdevelopment, or will the civilian leadership rise to achieve a consolidated democracy and sustainable growth?

# Geographic Setting

Nigeria, with 130 million people inhabiting 356,669 square miles, is the most populous nation in Africa. A center of West African regional trade, culture, and military strength, Nigeria borders four countries—Benin, Niger, Chad, and Cameroon. Nigeria, like nearly all African states, is not even a century old.

Nigeria was a British colony from 1914 until 1960. Nigeria's boundaries had little to do with the borders of the precolonial African societies, and merely marked the point where British influence ended and French began. Britain ruled northern and southern Nigeria as two separate colonies until 1914, when it amalgamated its Northern and Southern Protectorates. In short, Nigeria was an arbitrary creation reflecting British colonial interests. This forced union of myriad African cultures and ruling entities under one political roof remains a central feature of Nigerian political life today.

Nigeria is a hub of regional activity. Its population is nearly 60 percent of West Africa's total. Nigeria's gross domestic product (GDP) typically represents more than half of the total GDP for the entire subregion.

Nigeria includes six imprecisely defined "zones." The Hausa-Fulani, Nigeria's largest ethnic group, dominate the northwest (or "core North"). The northeast consists of minority groups, the largest of whom are the Kanuri. Both northern regions are predominantly Muslim. The Middle Belt includes minority groups, both Muslim and Christian. The southwest is dominated by the country's second-largest ethnic group, the Yoruba, who are approximately 40 percent Muslim, 50 percent Christian (primarily Protestant), and 10 percent practitioners of Yoruba traditional beliefs. The southeast is the Igbo homeland, Nigeria's third largest group, who are primarily Christian. Between the Yoruba and Igbo regions is the southern minority zone, which stretches across the Niger Delta areas and east along the coast as far as Cameroon.

**Languages:** English (official), Hausa, Yoruba, Igho (Ibo), Fulani, 100–200 additional indigenous

**Nigerian Currency**
Niara (₦)
International Designation: NGN
Exchange Rate (2010): US$1 = 150.88
500 Naira Note Design: Aliyu Mai-Bornu
(1919–1970) and Clement Isong (1920–2000),
economists and governors of the Central Bank
of Nigeria

© iStockphoto.com/Johnny Greig

**FIGURE 12.1 The Nigerian Nation at a Glance**

# Critical Junctures

Nigeria's recent history reflects influences from the precolonial period, the crucial changes caused by British colonialism, the postcolonial alternation of military and civilian rule, and the economic collapse from 1980 to 2000, caused by political corruption and overreliance on the oil industry, which has been reinforced by the post–2003 oil boom.

## The Precolonial Period (1800–1900)

In contrast to the forest belt to the south, the more open terrain in the north, with its need for irrigation, encouraged the early growth of centralized states. Such states from the eighth century included Kanem-Bornu and the Hausa states. Another attempt at state formation led to the Jukun kingdom, which by the end of the seventeenth century was a subject state of the Bornu Empire.

Trade across the Sahara Desert with northern Africa shaped developments in the savanna areas of the north. Trade brought material benefits as well as Arabic education and Islam, which gradually replaced traditional spiritual, political, and social practices. In 1808, the Fulani, from lands west of modern Nigeria, fought a holy war (***jihad***), and established the Sokoto Caliphate, which used Islam and a common language, Hausa, to unify the disparate groups in the north. The Fulani Empire held sway until British colonial authority was imposed on northern Nigeria by 1900.

**jihad**

Literally "struggle." Although often used to mean armed struggle against unbelievers, it can also mean to fight against socio-political corruption or a spiritual struggle for self-improvement.

| Table 12.1 | Political Organization |
|---|---|
| **Political System** | Federal republic |
| **Regime History** | Democratic government took office in May 1999, after sixteen years of military rule. The most recent national elections were held in 2011. |
| **Administrative Structure** | Nigeria is a federation of thirty-six states, plus the Federal Capital Territory (FCT) in Abuja. The three tiers of government are federal, state, and local. Actual power is centralized under the presidency and the governors. |
| **Executive** | U.S.-style presidential system, under Goodluck Jonathan |
| **Legislature** | A bicameral civilian legislature was elected in April 2011. The 109 senators are elected on the basis of equal representation: three from each state, and one from the FCT. The 360 members of the House of Representatives are elected from single-member districts. |
| **Judiciary** | Federal, state, and local court system, headed by the Federal Court of Appeal and the Supreme Court, which consists of fifteen appointed associate justices and the chief justice. States may establish a system of Islamic law (*shari'a*) for cases involving only Muslims in customary disputes (divorce, property, etc.). Most Nigerian states feature such courts, which share a Federal Court of Appeal in Abuja. Non-Muslim states may also set up customary courts, based on local traditional jurisprudence. Secular courts retain supreme jurisdiction if conflict arises between customary and secular courts. |
| **Party System** | Nearly fifty parties have been registered by the Nigerian electoral commission since 2002. The largest are the People's Democratic Party (PDP), the All Nigerian People's Party (ANPP), the Action Congress of Nigeria (ACN), and Congress for Progressive Change (CPC). PDP won the presidency, majorities in both houses of the National Assembly, as well as a majority of governorships, state assemblies, and local governments. |

**acephalous societies**

Literally "headless" societies. A number of traditional Nigerian societies, such as the Igbo in the precolonial period, lacked executive rulership as we have come to conceive of it. Instead, the villages and clans were governed by committee or consensus.

Toward the southern edge of the savanna, politics generally followed kinship lines. Political authority was so diffuse that later Western contacts described them as "stateless," or **acephalous societies**. Because such groups as the Tiv lacked complex political hierarchies, they escaped much of the upheaval experienced under colonialism by the centralized states, and retained much of their autonomy.

Southern Nigeria included the highly centralized Yoruba empires and the kingdoms of Oyo and Ife; the Edo kingdom of Benin in the Midwest; the acephalous societies of the Igbo to the east; and the trading city-states of the Niger Delta and its hinterland, peopled by a wide range of ethnicities.

Several precolonial societies had democratic elements that might have led to more open and participatory polities had they not been interrupted by colonialism. Governance in the Yoruba and Igbo communities involved principles of accountability and representation. Among the Islamic communities of the north, political society was highly structured, reflecting local interpretations of Qur'anic principles. Leadership structures were considerably more hierarchical than those of the south, and women were typically consigned to subordinate political status. The Islamic Fulani Empire was a confederation in which the rulers, emirs, owed allegiance to the

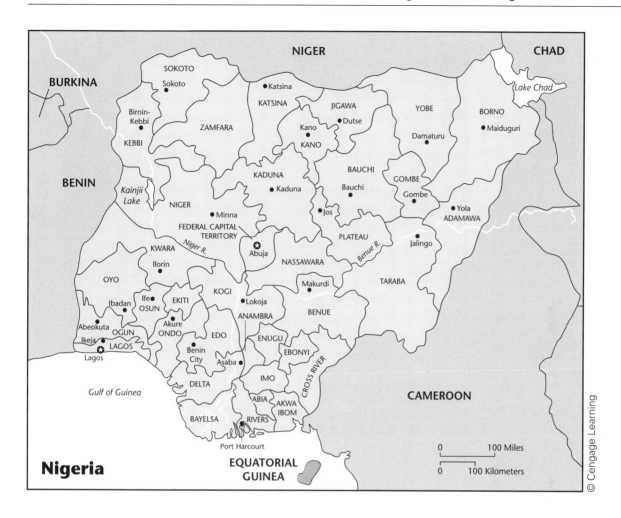

**Nigeria**

sultan, who was the temporal and spiritual head of the empire. The sultan's powers, in turn, were limited by his duty to observe Islamic principles.

## Colonial Rule and Its Impact (1860–1945)[1]

Competition for trade and empire drove the European imperial powers further into Africa. Colonial rule deepened the extraction of Nigeria's natural resources and the exploitation of Nigerian labor. Colonialism left its imprint on all aspects of Nigeria's political and economic systems.

Where centralized monarchies existed in the north, the British ruled through **indirect rule**, which allowed traditional structures to persist as subordinates to the British governor and a small administrative apparatus. With more dispersed kingships, as among the Yoruba, or in acephalous societies, particularly among the Igbo and other groups in the southeast, the colonizers either strengthened the authority of traditional chiefs and kings or appointed **warrant chiefs** (who ruled by warrant of the British Crown), weakening the previous practices of accountability and participation.

The British played off ethnic and social divisions to keep Nigerians from developing organized political resistance to colonial rule. When resistance did develop, the colonizers were not afraid to employ repressive tactics, even as late as the 1940s. Yet the British also promoted the foundations of a democratic political system. This dual

**indirect rule**

A term used to describe the British style of colonialism in Nigeria and India in which local traditional rulers and political structures were used to help support the colonial governing structure.

**warrant chiefs**

Leaders employed by the British colonial regime in Nigeria. A system in which "chiefs" were selected by the British to oversee certain legal matters and assist the colonial enterprise in governance and law enforcement in local areas.

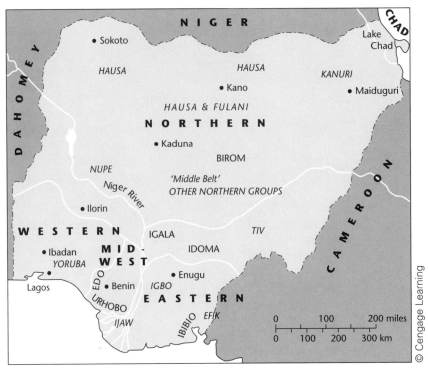

Regions are shown in
bold text, ethnic groups
are shown in italic text.

Nigeria under the First Republic, divided into four regions, with the
massive Northern Region encompassing two-thirds of the nation's
territory and more than half its population.

standard left a conflicted democratic idea: formal democratic institutions within an
authoritarian political culture. Colonialism also strengthened the collective identities
of Nigeria's multiple ethnic groups by fostering political competition among them,
primarily among the three largest: the Hausa-Fulani, Yoruba, and Igbo.

### Divisive Identities: Ethnic Politics under Colonialism (1945–1960)

Based on their experience under British rule, leaders of the anticolonial movement
came to regard the state as an exploitative instrument. Its control became an opportunity to pursue personal and group interests rather than broad national interests.
When the British began to negotiate a gradual exit from Nigeria, the semblance of
unity among the anticolonial leaders soon evaporated. Intergroup political competition became increasingly fierce.

Nigerian leaders quickly turned to ethnicity as a way to pursue competition and
mobilize public support. The three largest ethnic groups, the Hausa-Fulani, Igbo,
and Yoruba, though each a minority, together comprise approximately two-thirds
of Nigeria's population. They have long dominated the political process. By pitting
ethnic groups against each other for purposes of divide and rule, and by structuring
the administrative units of Nigeria based on ethnic groups, the British ensured that
ethnicity would be the primary element in political identification and mobilization.

Initially, ethnically based associations were concerned with nonpolitical issues:
promoting mutual aid for housing and education, and sponsoring cultural events.
With the encouragement of ambitious leaders, however, these groups took on a more

political character. Nigeria's first political party, the National Council of Nigeria and the Cameroons (later the National Convention of Nigerian Citizens, NCNC), initially drew supporters from across Nigeria. As independence approached, however, elites began to divide along ethnic lines to mobilize support for their differing political agendas.

In 1954, the British divided Nigeria into a federation of three regions with elected governments. Each region soon fell under the domination of one of the major ethnic groups and their respective parties. The Northern Region came under the control of the Northern People's Congress (NPC), dominated by Hausa-Fulani elites. In the southern half of the country, the Western Region was controlled by the Action Group (AG), which was controlled by Yoruba elites. The Igbo, the numerically dominant group in the Eastern Region, were closely associated with the NCNC, which became the ruling party there.

Chief Obafemi Awolowo, leader of the AG, captured the sentiment of the times when he wrote in 1947, "Nigeria is not a nation. It is a mere geographical expression. There are no 'Nigerians' in the same sense as there are 'English,' 'Welsh,' or 'French.' The word 'Nigerian' is merely a distinctive appellation to distinguish those who live within the boundaries of Nigeria from those who do not."[2]

### The First Republic (1960–1966)

The British granted Nigeria independence in 1960 to an elected parliamentary government. Nigerians adopted the British Westminster model at the federal and regional levels, with the prime minister chosen by the majority party or coalition. Northerners came to dominate the federal government by virtue of their greater population. The ruling coalition for the first two years quickly turned into a northern-only grouping when the NPC achieved an outright majority in the legislature. Having benefited less from the economic, educational, and infrastructural benefits of colonialism, the northerners who dominated the First Republic set out to redistribute resources to their benefit. This NPC policy of "northernization" brought them into direct conflict with their southern counterparts, particularly the Yoruba-based AG and later the Igbo-dominated NCNC.

Rivalries intensified as the NPC sat atop an absolute majority in the federal parliament with no need for its former coalition partner, the NCNC. Nnamdi Azikiwe, the NCNC leader who was also president in the First Republic (then a largely symbolic position), and Tafawa Balewa, the NPC prime minister, separately approached the military to ensure that if it came to conflict, they could count on its loyalty. Thus, "in the struggle for personal survival both men, perhaps inadvertently, made the armed forces aware that they had a political role to play."[3]

### Civil War and Military Rule (1966–1979)

With significant encouragement from contending civilian leaders, a group of largely Igbo officers seized power in January 1966. General Aguiyi Ironsi, also an Igbo, was killed in a second coup in July 1966, which brought Yakubu Gowon, a Middle Belt Christian, to power as a consensus head of state among the non-Igbo coup plotters.[4]

Because many northern officials had been killed in the initial coup, a tremendous backlash against Igbos flared in several parts of the country. Ethnic violence sent many Igbos fleeing to their home region in the east. By 1967, the predominantly Igbo population of eastern Nigeria attempted to secede and form its own independent country, named Biafra. Gowon built a military-led government of national unity in what remained of Nigeria (the north and west) and, after a bloody three-year war of attrition and starvation tactics, defeated Biafra in January 1970. The conflict claimed at least a million deaths.

Precolonial Nigeria, showing the Sokoto Caliphate at its greatest extent in the early 19th Century. The British conquest brought many nations under one roof.

After the war, Gowon presided over a policy of national reconciliation, which proceeded fairly smoothly with the aid of growing oil revenues. Senior officers reaped the benefits of the global oil boom in 1973–1974, however, and corruption was widespread. Influenced by the unwillingness of the military elite to relinquish power and the spoils of office, Gowon postponed a return to civilian rule, and was overthrown in 1975 by Murtala Muhammad, who was assassinated before he could achieve a democratic transition. General Olusegun Obasanjo, Muhammad's second-in-command and successor, peacefully ceded power to an elected civilian government in 1979, which became known as the Second Republic. Obasanjo retired but would later reemerge as a civilian president in 1999.

### The Second and Third Republics, and Predatory Military Rule (1979–1999)

The president of the 1979–1983 Second Republic, Shehu Shagari, and his ruling National Party of Nigeria (NPN, drawn largely from the First Republic's northern-dominated NPC), did little to reduce the mistrust between the various parts of the federation, or to stem rampant corruption. The NPN captured outright majorities in the 1983 state and national elections through massive fraud and violence. The last vestiges of popular tolerance dissipated, and a few months later the military, led by Major General Muhammadu Buhari, seized power.

When General Buhari refused to pledge a rapid return to democratic rule and failed to revive a plummeting economy, his popular support wavered, and in August 1985 General Ibrahim Babangida seized power. Babangida and his cohort quickly announced a transition to democratic rule, then stalled and subsequently annulled the presidential election of June 1993. In stark contrast to all prior elections, the 1993 election was relatively fair, and was evidently won by Yoruba businessman Chief Moshood Abiola. The annulment provoked angry reactions from a population weary of postponed transitions, lingering military rule, and the deception of rulers. Babangida resigned, and his handpicked successor, Ernest Shonekan, led a weak civilian caretaker government. General Sani Abacha, who had been installed by Babangida as defense minister, soon seized power. Like Babangida, Abacha announced a new program of transition to civilian rule and regularly delayed the steps in its implementation. He cracked down on political opposition, severely restricted civil liberties and political rights, and fomented corruption on a massive scale. Only Abacha's sudden death in June 1998 saved the country from certain crisis. General Abdulsalami Abubakar, Abacha's successor, quickly established a new transition program and promptly handed power to an elected civilian government led by President Olusegun Obasanjo and the People's Democratic Party (PDP) in May 1999.

Olusegun Obasanjo ruled Nigeria first as military head of state from 1976 to 1979 and then as civilian president from 1999 to 2007. As president, he instituted a number of important reforms, but also tried—and failed—to change the constitution to extend his term in office.

## The Fourth Republic (1999 to the Present)

Obasanjo was called out of retirement by the leaders of the PDP to run for president. Obasanjo, although a Yoruba, handed over power as military head of state in 1979 to the northerner Shehu Shagari at the dawn of the Second Republic. The northern political establishment had concluded that Obasanjo was a Yoruba candidate they could trust. In addition, many perceived that an ex-military leader could better manage to keep the armed forces in the barracks once they left power.

Obasanjo claimed a broad mandate to arrest the nation's decline by reforming the state and economy. Within weeks, he electrified the nation by retiring all the military officers who had held positions of political power under previous military governments, seeing them as the most likely plotters of future coups.

Obasanjo targeted the oil sector for new management and lobbied foreign governments to forgive Nigeria's massive debts. The minimum wage was raised significantly, a "truth and reconciliation" commission was set up to address past abuses, and commissions were formed to fight corruption and channel oil revenues back to the impoverished and environmentally ravaged Niger Delta region, where oil is extracted. Civil society groups thrived on renewed political freedom, and the media grew bold in exposing corrupt practices in government. Despite this ambitious reform agenda, however, Obasanjo had political debts to his party, and his political survival, notably his bid for reelection in 2003, required that the anticorruption campaign leave entrenched interests unscathed and corrupt politicians in place. He was openly disdainful of the National Assembly and eventually faced three motions to impeach him. Avoiding impeachment, however, Obasanjo secured renomination from his party (the PDP) in the 2003 elections through a series of political accommodations with key party barons. The PDP political machine engaged in widespread electoral malpractices, which saved the president's second term and secured PDP dominance, but public confidence plummeted. Faced with increasing political turmoil and social conflict, the president called a National Political Reform Conference in early 2005. The conference, designed to review the constitution and to bolster government legitimacy, led to an effort—which in the end failed—to remove the two-term limit on the president. A 2006 effort to extend his term also failed under enormous media scrutiny and public outcry, prompting its rejection by the Senate.

Stymied by the legislature, the president's supporters moved to Plan B. A massively fraudulent election was planned for April 2007, with sufficiently blatant rigging and confusion to provoke the public into the streets in order to declare a state of emergency and allow President Obasanjo to stay in office. PDP dominance in the National Assembly, state legislatures, and governorships would also be assured. Meanwhile, the president chose a little-known, reclusive governor from the north with health problems to be his successor: Umaru Musa Yar'Adua of Katsina state. Obasanjo misjudged both the Nigerian people and Yar'Adua. Despite local and international condemnation of the April 2007 polls, the public did not erupt, and Obasanjo had little choice but to hand over to Yar'Adua in May 2007. President Yar'Adua, for his part, quickly demonstrated his independence and set out to gain control of the PDP and to restrain Obasanjo, reversing a number of Obasanjo's controversial decisions.

President Yar'Adua, however, remained burdened with a legitimacy gap from the sham 2007 polls, helped only partly by a split 4–3 decision of the Supreme Court in December 2008 upholding his election. Yar'Adua's first year and a half in office saw little action on the ambitious "Seven Point Agenda" he made during the campaign; instead, he focused on solidifying his control of the PDP and on winning the court challenge to his election. A respectable Electoral Reform Committee was named, but its recommendations were largely ignored. These and other good intentions, such as an amnesty program for the insurgency-torn Niger Delta, soon ran aground on the president's declining health. His sudden collapse and evacuation to Saudi Arabia in November 2010 made clear that the rumors about his health were not far-fetched, and that the president was dying. Normal government activity all but ceased, as cabinet ministers felt paralyzed with no clear direction, and a small circle of advisors around the president usurped presidential powers and secured government contracts.

After several weeks with no word from the president, however, discontent began to grow over the cabal surrounding him and the inaction of his ministers, and international pressure, particularly from the United States and Britain, mounted for a constitutional handover to the vice president. These pressures, along with word of coup threats within the rank and file of the military, finally pushed the National Assembly to act after over 70 days of Yar'Adua's absence to name Vice President Goodluck Jonathan the acting president. Jonathan, from the oil-rich Niger Delta, moved cautiously to assure Northern powerbrokers that they could work with him. His deft political efforts, backed in part by support from former President Obasanjo, ensured a smooth transition when President Yar'Adua at last passed away in May 2010.

Like Obasanjo and Yar'Adua, President Jonathan came to office without control of his own party, the PDP, and so, like his predecessors, Jonathan moved quickly to establish his influence using the largesse of Nigeria's massive state-controlled oil wealth. Within several months, he made clear his intention to run for president in April 2011. In stark contrast to his predecessors, however, President Jonathan appointed a credible chairman to head the electoral commission, who promptly undertook efforts to reform the deeply compromised election system.

No longer able to buy the favor of the electoral commission at the federal level, the political parties—the ruling PDP in particular—shifted their rigging tactics to the state and local levels where the new chairman had yet to institute major reforms. Consequently, the 2011 elections were much improved from the disastrous 2007 contests, but the PDP still utilized its massive resource advantage to shift many outcomes by buying local election staff to inflate vote tallies, spreading largess around communities to buy votes, and using thugs to intimate voters in opposition strongholds. Opposition parties still won more victories than in the past, but the PDP likely would have lost its majority hold over the federal House and Senate, and more of the governorships and state assemblies, were it not for its rigging efforts.

Heightened public expectations of cleaner elections sparked greater outrage over these malpractices, leading to over 800 deaths in postelection riots, particularly in the north. President Jonathan thus returned to office with a stronger popular mandate than his predecessor because of the increased technical credibility of the electoral commission, but tarnished by the persistence of rigging and the widespread deaths. Many northern factions also remained antagonistic over the shift of power so quickly back to a southerner. Jonathan took the oath of office in 2011, again promising reforms.

# Themes and Implications

## Historical Junctures and Political Themes

Federalism and democracy have been important strategies in the effort to build a coherent nation-state in Nigeria out of more than 250 different ethnic groups. The legacy of colonial rule and many years of military domination, however, have yielded a unitary system in federal guise: A system with an all-powerful central government surrounded by weak and largely economically insolvent states.

When the military returned to the barracks in 1999, it left an overdeveloped executive arm at all levels of government—federal, state, and local—at the expense of weak legislative and judicial institutions. Unchecked executive power has encouraged the arbitrary exercise of authority and patronage politics, which sap the economy and undermine the rule of law. Since the return of democratic rule, however, the state governments, the National Assembly, and the judiciary have been whittling away at the powers of the national executive.

### Nigeria in the World of States
Nigeria, with its natural riches, has long been regarded as a potential political and economic giant of Africa. Nigerian leaders have long aspired to regional leadership, undertaking several peacekeeping operations and an ambitious diplomatic agenda—through the United Nations, the African Union, and on its own—to broker peace initiatives and to foster democracy in some instances. Recent efforts include Sudan's troubled Darfur region, Côte d'Ivoire, and Zimbabwe.

### Governing Nigeria's Economy
Instead of independent growth today Nigeria depends on unpredictable oil revenues, sparse external loans, and aid. Owing to neglect of agriculture, Nigeria moved from self-sufficiency in basic foodstuffs in the mid-1960s to heavy dependence on imports less than twenty years later. Manufacturing activities, after a surge of investment by government and foreign firms in the 1970s, suffered from inefficiency and disinvestment in subsequent decades.

Years of predatory military rule made Nigeria a political and economic pariah in the 1990s, and deteriorating political institutions made the country a way station for international drug trafficking and for international commercial fraud. Although the most recent accession of democratic government ended the nation's political isolation, its economy remains subject to the fluctuations of the international oil market. The government has been favored since 2003 by high oil prices and increasing U.S. consumption of Nigerian oil and gas, but there has been little effective restructuring or diversification of the petroleum monoculture so far. Nigeria is now again suffering the consequences of not addressing its oil dependence, as its projected oil revenues have dropped more than half as oil prices fell in late 2008 under global recession pressures.

**Democratic Ideas amid Colonialism and Military Rule**   The very concept of the state was introduced to restructure and subordinate the local economy to European capitalism. The Nigerian colonial state was conceived and fashioned as **interventionist**, with broad license to intrude into major sectors of the economy and society. A secondary concern was the creation of an economy hospitable to free markets and private enterprise. Nigeria's interventionist state extended its management of the economy, including broad administrative controls and significant ownership positions in many areas of the economy.

**interventionist**

An interventionist state acts vigorously to shape the performance of major sectors of the economy.

After independence in 1960, Nigeria's civilian and military rulers alike expanded the interventionist state. Successive governments began in the late 1980s to reverse this trend, but privatization and economic reform have been piecemeal. President Obasanjo's efforts to promote better macroeconomic management and to root out endemic corruption bore some results, but unemployment and poverty remain virtually unchanged—or worse.

Colonialism introduced a cultural dualism between the traditions of social accountability in precolonial society and emerging Western ideas of individualism. These pressures weakened indigenous democratic bases for the accountability of rulers and responsibility to the governed, along with age-old checks on abuses of office. Although colonial rulers left Nigeria with the machinery of parliamentary democracy, they largely socialized the population to be passive subjects rather than responsive participants. In practice, colonialism bequeathed an authoritarian legacy to independent Nigeria. Military rule continued this pattern from 1966 to 1979 and again from 1983 to 1999, as juntas promised democratization but governed with increasing severity.

This dualism promoted two public realms to which individuals belonged: the communal realm, in which people identified by ethnic or subethnic groups (Igbo, Tiv, Yoruba, and others), and the civic realm in which citizenship was universal.[5] Because the colonial state and its "civic" realm began as an alien, exploitative force, Nigerians came to view the state as the realm from which rights must be extracted, duties and taxes withheld, and resources plundered (see Section 4). Morality was reserved for the ethnic or communal realm. Military rule reinforced this pattern, and the democratic idea in Nigeria has also been filtered through deep regional divisions.

The south experienced the benefits and burdens of colonial occupation. The coastal location of Lagos, Calabar, and their surrounding regions made them important hubs for trade and shipping activity, around which the British built the necessary infrastructure—schools (promoting Christianity and Western education), roads, ports, and the like—and a large African civil service to facilitate colonialism. In northern Nigeria, where indigenous hierarchical political structures were better established, the British used local structures and left intact the emirate authorities and Islamic institutions of the region and prohibited Christian missionary activity. The north consequently received few infrastructural benefits, but its traditional administration was largely preserved.

The south thus enjoyed the basis for a modern economy and exposure to democratic institutions, but the north remained largely agricultural and monarchical, and tried to use its numerical advantage to control government and redistribute resources. Despite these setbacks and divisions, the democratic idea remained vibrant across Nigeria throughout even the darkest days of military rule, and it remains strong even as frustrations rise with the current democratic government. Nigeria's incredible diversity continually demands constant processes of negotiation and protections of interests that democracy promises.

**Nigeria's Fragile Collective Identity** This division between north and south is overlaid with hundreds of ethnic divisions across the nation, which military governments and civilians alike have been prone to manipulate for selfish ends. These many cultural divisions have been continually exacerbated by the triple threats of **clientelism**, corruption, and unstable authoritarian governing structures, which together stir up ethnic group competition and hinder economic potential.[6] Clientelism is the practice by which particular individuals or segments receive disproportionate policy benefits or political favors from a political patron, usually at the expense of the larger society. In Nigeria, patrons are often linked to clients by ethnic, religious, or other cultural ties, but these ties have generally benefited only a small elite. By fostering political competition along cultural lines, clientelism tends to undermine social trust and political stability, which are necessary conditions for economic growth.

Nevertheless, the idea of Nigeria has taken root among the country's ethnic groups almost 50 years after independence. Most Nigerians enjoy many personal connections across ethnic and religious lines, and elites in both the north and the south have significant business activities throughout the country. Even so, ethnicity remains a critical flashpoint.

## Implications for Comparative Politics

Nigeria is by far the largest country in Africa and among the ten most populous countries in the world. One out of every five black Africans is Nigerian. Unlike most other African countries, Nigeria has the human and material resources to overcome the vicious cycle of poverty and **autocracy**. Hopes for this breakthrough, however, have been regularly frustrated over five decades of independent rule.

Nigeria remains the oldest surviving federation in Africa, and it has managed through much travail to maintain its fragile unity. That cohesion has come under increasing stress, however, and a major challenge is to ensure that Nigeria does not ultimately collapse. Nigeria's past failures to sustain democracy and economic development also render it an important case for the study of resource competition and the perils of corruption, and its experience demonstrates the interrelationship between democracy and development. Democracy and development depend on leadership, political culture, institutional autonomy, and the external economic climate; Nigeria has much to teach us on all these topics.

## Summary

British colonialism forced together a host of nations under one political roof that had little experience governing as a single entity. Political mobilization through these ethnic identities led to the collapse of Nigeria's first democratic experiment and civil war. Thirty years of military rule reunited the country under a federal system, but left deep patterns of clientelism and corruption that have characterized the politics of Nigeria's Fourth Republic since the military returned to the barracks in 1999.

**clientelism**

An informal aspect of policy-making in which a powerful patron (for example, a traditional local boss, government agency, or dominant party) offers resources such as land, contracts, protection, or jobs in return for the support and services (such as labor or votes) of lower-status and less powerful clients; corruption, preferential treatment, and inequality are characteristic of clientelist politics.

**autocracy**

A government in which one or a few rulers has absolute power, thus, a dictatorship.

# POLITICAL ECONOMY AND DEVELOPMENT

**Focus Questions**

What were some of the key impacts of the oil boom on Nigeria's political economy?

What efforts has Nigeria made to try to address poverty and spur development?

Colonialism bequeathed Nigeria an interventionist state, and governments after independence continued this pattern. The state became the central fixture in the Nigerian economy, stunting the private sector and encumbering industry and commerce. As the state began to unravel in the late 1980s and 1990s, leaders grew more predatory, plundering the petroleum sector, and preventing the nation's vast economic potential from being realized.

## State and Economy

**rents**

Economic gains that do not compensate those who produced them and do not contribute to productivity, typically associated with government earnings that do not get channeled back into either investments or policies that benefit the public good. Pursuit of economic rents (or "rent-seeking") is profit seeking that takes the form of nonproductive economic activity.

Through direct ownership of industry and services or through regulation and administrative control, the Nigerian state plays the central role in economic decision-making. Most of the nation's revenues, and nearly all of its hard currency, are channeled through the government, which control these earnings, known as **rents**. Consequently, winning government contracts becomes a central economic activity, and those who control the state become the gatekeepers for many lucrative arrangements.[7] Those left out of these rent-seeking opportunities—perhaps 70 percent of Nigerians—must try to survive on petty trade and subsistence agriculture (the so-called informal sector of the economy) where taxes and regulation rarely reach. This informal sector accounts for about one-fifth of the entire Nigerian GDP, much of it earned through cross-border trade.

### Origins of Economic Decline

In the colonial and immediate postcolonial periods, Nigeria's economy was centered on agricultural production for domestic consumption as well as for export. Despite the emphasis on exports, Nigeria was self-sufficient in food production at the time of independence. Later in the 1960s emphasis shifted to the development of nonfood export crops through large-scale enterprises.

Small farmers received scant government support. Predictably, food production suffered, and food imports were stepped up to meet the needs of a burgeoning population. Three factors effectively undermined the Nigerian agricultural sector:[8] the Biafran War (1967–1970); severe drought, and the development of the petroleum industry. Agricultural export production plummeted from 80 percent of exports in 1960 to just 2 percent by 1980. With the 1970s boom in revenues from oil, Nigeria greatly increased its expenditures on education, defense, and infrastructure. Imports of capital goods and raw materials required to support this expansion rose more than seven-fold between 1971 and 1979. Similarly, imports of consumer goods rose dramatically (600 percent) in the same period as an increasingly wealthy Nigerian elite developed a taste for expensive imported goods.[9] By 1978, the government had outspent its revenues and could no longer finance many of its ambitious projects, causing external debt to skyrocket.

The acceleration in oil wealth spurred increasing corruption, as some officials set up joint ventures with foreign oil companies and others stole public funds. The economic downturn of the 1980s created even greater incentives for government corruption. Within three years of seizing power in 1993, General Abacha allowed all of Nigeria's oil refineries to collapse, forcing this giant oil-exporting country into the absurd situation of having to import refined petroleum. Abacha's family members and friends, who served as fronts, shamelessly monopolized the contracts to import this fuel in 1997, a pattern that continued into the Fourth Republic. Elsewhere, outside the oil sector, small-time scam artists proliferated such that by 2002, Internet scams had become one of Nigeria's top five industries, earning more than $100 million annually.

On the one hand, the oil boom generated tremendous income; on the other, it became a source of external dependence and badly skewed the Nigerian economy. Since the early 1970s, Nigeria has relied on oil for more than 90 percent of its export earnings and about three-quarters of government revenues, as shown in Table 12.2.[10]

## From 1985 to the Present: Deepening Economic Crisis and the Search for Solutions

**Structural Adjustment**   The year 1985 marked a turning point for the Nigerian state and economy. Within a year of wresting power from General Buhari in August 1985, the Babangida regime developed an economic **structural adjustment program (SAP)** with the active support of the World Bank and the IMF (also referred to as the **international financial institutions, or IFIs**). The decision to embark on the SAP was made against a background of increasing economic constraints arising from the continued dependence of the economy on waning oil revenues, a growing debt burden, **balance of payments** difficulties, and lack of fiscal discipline.[10]

The large revenues arising from the oil windfall enabled the state to increase its involvement in direct production. Beginning in the 1970s, the government created a number of parastatals (state-owned enterprises; see Section 3), including large shares in major banks and other financial institutions, manufacturing, construction, agriculture, public utilities, and various services. Although the government has since sold many of its parastatals, the state remains the biggest employer as well as the most important source of revenue, even for the private sector.

**Privatization**, which is central to Nigeria's adjustment program, means that state-owned businesses would be sold to private (nonstate) investors, domestic or foreign, to generate revenue and improve efficiency, but both domestic and foreign investors have been hesitant to risk significant capital in light of persistent instability, unpredictable economic policies, and endemic corruption. Only a few attractive areas such as telecommunications, utilities, and oil and gas are likely to draw significant foreign capital.

**Economic Planning**   Beginning in 1946, when the colonial administration announced the ten-year Plan for Development and Welfare, national plans have been prepared by the ministries of finance, economic development, and planning. Five-year plans were the norm from 1962 through 1985, when their scope was extended to fifteen years. The national plan, however, has not been an effective management tool. The reasons are the absence of an effective database for planning and a great lack of discipline in plan implementation.

**structural adjustment program (SAP)**

Programs established by the World Bank intended to alter and reform the economic structures of highly indebted Third World countries as a condition for receiving international loans. SAPs often involve the necessity for **privatization,** trade liberalization, and fiscal restraint, which typically requires the dismantling of social welfare systems.

**international financial institutions (IFIs)**

This term generally refers to the International Bank for Reconstruction and Development (the World Bank) and the International Monetary Fund (IMF), but can also include other international lending institutions.

**balance of payments**

An indicator of international flow of funds that shows the excess or deficit in total payments of all kinds between or among countries. Included in the calculation are exports and imports, grants, and international debt payments.

**privatization**

Selling state-owned assets to private owners and investors, intended to generate revenue, reduce wasteful state spending, and improve efficiency.

## Table 12.2    Oil Sector Statistics, 1970–2009

| Year | Oil Exports Value (Millions $)[1] | Total Exports (Millions $)[2] | Oil Exports as % of Total Exports[3] | Government Oil Revenue (Naira Millions)[4] | Government Oil Revenue (Millions $)[5] | Total Government Revenue (Naira Millions)[6] | Percent of Total Revenue |
|---|---|---|---|---|---|---|---|
| 1970 | | | | 166 | 232 | 634 | 26 |
| 1974 | | | | 3724 | 5911 | 4537 | 82 |
| 1979 | | | | 8881 | 14704 | 10912 | 81 |
| 1980 | | | | 12353 | 22583 | 15234 | 81 |
| 1981 | | | | 8564 | 13858 | 13291 | 64 |
| 1985 | | | | 10924 | 12219 | 15050 | 73 |
| 1987 | | | | 19027 | 4738 | 25381 | 75 |
| 1989 | | | | 39131 | 5313 | 53870 | 73 |
| 1993 | | | | 162012 | 7342 | 192769 | 84 |
| 1994 | | | | 160192 | 7283 | 201911 | 79 |
| 1998 | | | | 324311 | 14818 | 463609 | 70 |
| 2001 | | | | 1707563 | 15352 | 2231533 | 77 |
| 2002 | | | | 1230851 | 10208 | 1731838 | 71 |
| 2003 | | | | 2074281 | 10791 | 2575096 | 81 |
| 2004 | | | | 3354800 | 25245 | 3920500 | 86 |
| 2005 | 49722 | 52402 | 95 | 4762400 | 36279 | 5547500 | 86 |
| 2006 | 54607 | 62772 | 87 | 5287567 | 41100 | 5965102 | 89 |
| 2007 | 51170 | 59907 | 85 | 4462950 | 35474 | 5715500 | 78 |
| 2008 | 74053 | 87459 | 85 | 6530630 | 55088 | 7866590 | 83 |
| 2009 | 26471 | 33256 | 80 | 3191938 | 21445 | 4057499 | 79 |

[1]OPEC Annual Stat Bulletin 2009.
[2]OPEC.
[3]OPEC.
[4]Central Bank of Nigeria.
[5]Converted using average annual exchange rates from OPEC report 2009 and 2005, http://www.opec.org/library/annual%20statistical%20bulletin/interactive/2005/filez/sumtbl.htm.
[6]Central Bank of Nigeria.
*Source:* Recent data compiled by Evan Litwin and Mukesh Baral.

Nigerian and foreign business leaders revived dialogue with government on economic direction with the 1994 establishment of the annual Nigerian Economic Summit Group (NESG). This differed from previous planning efforts in that it was based on the coequal participation of government and private sector representatives. Two years later, General Abacha initiated the Vision 2010 process (see "Global Connection: From Vision 2010 to NEEDS"). Participants in Vision 2010 advocated reductions in government's excessive role in the economy with the goals of increasing market efficiency and reducing competition for control of the state. The Obasanjo administration accepted much of the Vision 2010 agenda at the outset of its first term, and advice from the NESG continues to influence economic policies.

President Obasanjo opened his second term in office in 2003 with a renewed focus on economic reform and development. Nigeria stabilized its macroeconomic policy, restructured the banking sector, and established a new anticorruption agency, the Economic and Financial Crimes Commission (EFCC). Unfortunately, many of these ambitious goals were followed by lackluster implementation, and President Jonathan has so far provided little economic policy. Buoyant oil revenues have helped to spur the economy higher since 2005, but poverty has not significantly diminished, and there remain basic questions about the sustainability of growth without a more diversified productive foundation.

# GLOBAL CONNECTION

## From Vision 2010 to NEEDS

In the early 1990s, concerned with the nation's economic decline, a number of the larger Nigerian businesses and key multinational corporations decided to pursue new initiatives, including the first Economic Summit, a high-profile conference that advocated numerous policies to move Nigeria toward becoming an "emerging market" that could attract foreign investment along the lines of the high performing states in Asia.

Through Vision 2010, the government pledged to adopt a package of business-promoting economic reforms, while business pledged to work toward certain growth targets consistent with governmental priorities in employment, taxation, community investment, and the like. Along with government and business leaders, key figures were invited to participate from nearly all sectors of society, including the press, nongovernmental organizations, youth groups, market women's associations, and others. Government-owned media followed Vision 2010's pronouncements with great fanfare, while the private media reviewed them with a healthy dose of skepticism regarding Abacha's intentions and the elitist nature of the exercise. Vision 2010's final report called for:

- Restoring democratic rule
- Restructuring and professionalizing the military
- Lowering the population growth rate
- Rebuilding education
- Meaningful privatization
- Diversifying the export base beyond oil
- Supporting intellectual property rights
- Central bank autonomy

Whatever its merits, Vision 2010 was imperiled because of its association with Abacha. When the new Obasanjo administration took office in 1999 lacking a comprehensive economic plan of its own, however, it quietly adopted the general economic strategy and objectives of Vision 2010. President Obasanjo repackaged and developed many of these goals into a new economic initiative for his second term, the National Economic Empowerment and Development Strategy (NEEDS). Upon taking office in 2007, President Yar'Adua announced his intention to continue the thrust of the policy goals of NEEDS and Vision 2010, announcing his own Vision 2020 and a Seven Point Agenda that included economic reforms. His declining health, however, left little of these plans enacted, and President Jonathan has yet to undertake any ambitious economic efforts.

*Source:* Vision 2010 Final Report, September 1997; Federal Government of Nigeria, the *National Economic Empowerment and Development Strategy,* March 2004.

| Table 12.3 | Selected Economic Indicators, 1980–2009 | | |
|---|---|---|---|
| **Years** | **Real GDP (in billions)** | **GDP % Growth** | **Inflation Rate % (CPI)** |
| 1980 | 64.2 | 4.2 | 9.97 |
| 1985 | 28.4 | 9.7 | 7.44 |
| 1990 | 28.5 | 8.2 | 7.36 |
| 1993 | 21.4 | 2.2 | 57.17 |
| 1995 | 28.1 | 2.5 | 72.84 |
| 1997 | 36.2 | 2.7 | 8.53 |
| 1999 | 34.8 | 1.1 | 6.62 |
| 2000 | 46 | 5.4 | 6.93 |
| 2001 | 48 | 3.1 | 18.87 |
| 2002 | 59.1 | 1.55 | 12.88 |
| 2003 | 67.7 | 10.3 | 14.03 |
| 2005 | 112.2 | 5.4 | 17.86 |
| 2007 | 165.9 | 6.45 | 5.38 |
| 2008 | 207.1 | 6 | 11.58 |
| 2009 | 173 | 5.6 | 11.54 |

*Source:* World Bank. Recent data compiled by Evan Litwin and Mukesh Baral.

Perhaps Obasanjo's greatest economic achievement was paying off most of Nigeria's heavy foreign debt (see Table 12.4). On taking office in 1999 he promptly undertook numerous visits to Europe, Asia, and the United States to urge the governments of those countries to forgive most of Nigeria's obligations. After persistent international lobbying, along with progress on economic reforms during Obasanjo's second term, Nigeria eventually secured an agreement for a substantial reduction of the country's debt. In June 2005, the Paris Club of official creditors approved a package of debt repayments, repurchases, and write-offs that reduced Nigeria's external debt by 90 percent.

President Yar'Adua vowed to continue President Obasanjo's reforms, promising to declare a "state of emergency" on the power sector in particular, in order to address this most basic infrastructural need. He also pledged to be the "rule of law" president to crack down on corruption. Yet neither of these goals was achieved, and the president also hobbled the EFCC's anticorruption efforts and relied on a number of corrupt figures to run his government, including one under investigation for money-laundering in Britain. President Jonathan removed some of these figures on taking office, but others remain in his administration as well.

Social Welfare The continued decline in Nigeria's economic performance since the early 1980s has caused great suffering. Since 1986, there has been a marked deterioration in the quantity and quality of social services, complicated by a marked decline in household incomes (see Table 12.5). The SAP program and subsequent austerity measures emphasizing the reduction of state expenditures have forced cutbacks in spending on social welfare.

Budgetary austerity and economic stagnation have hurt vulnerable groups such as the urban and rural poor, women, the young, and the elderly. Life expectancy is barely above forty years, and infant mortality is estimated at more than 80 deaths per 1,000 live births. Nigeria's provision of basic education is also inadequate. Moreover, Nigeria has failed to develop a national social security system, with much of the gap filled by family-based networks of mutual aid. Moreover, most Nigerians do not have access to formal sector jobs, and roughly 70 percent of the population must live on less than a dollar per day, while 92 percent of Nigerians live on less than two dollars per day.

| Table 12.4 | Nigeria's Total External Debt (millions of US$ at current prices and exchange rates) | |
|---|---|---|
| **Years** | **Total Debt/GDP** | **Total Debt Service/ Exports** |
| 1977 | 8.73 | 1.04 |
| 1986 | 109.9 | 38.03 |
| 1996 | 88.97 | 14.79 |
| 1997 | 78.54 | 8.71 |
| 1999 | 83.76 | 7.54 |
| 2000 | 68.18 | 8.71 |
| 2001 | 64.67 | 12.9 |
| 2002 | 51.55 | 8.13 |
| 2003 | 51.16 | 5.96 |
| 2007 | 5.2 | 1.79 |
| 2008 | 5.55 | 0.67 |
| 2009 | 4.53 | 0.81 |

*Source:* World Bank. Recent data compiled by Evan Litwin and Mukesh Baral.

| Table 12.5 | Index of Real Household Incomes of Key Groups 1980/81–1986/87, 1996, 2001 (Rural self-employed in 1980/81 = 100) | | | | | | | | |
|---|---|---|---|---|---|---|---|---|---|
| | **1980/81** | **1981/82** | **1982/83** | **1983/84** | **1984/85** | **1985/86** | **1986/87** | **1996*** | **2001*** |
| Rural self-employed | 100 | 103 | 95 | 86 | 73 | 74 | 65 | 27 | 32 |
| Rural wage earners | 178 | 160 | 147 | 135 | 92 | 95 | 84 | 48 | 57 |
| All rural households | 105 | 107 | 99 | 89 | 74 | 84 | 74 | 28 | 33 |
| Urban self-employed | 150 | 124 | 106 | 94 | 69 | 69 | 61 | 41 | 48 |
| Urban wage earners | 203 | 177 | 164 | 140 | 101 | 101 | 90 | 55 | 65 |
| All urban households | 166 | 142 | 129 | 109 | 80 | 80 | 71 | 45 | 53 |

*Estimated, based on 1980/81 figures adjusted for a 73 percent drop in per capita GDP from 1980 to 1996, and an 18 percent increase in per capita GDP from 1996 to 2001. The Federal Office of Statistics (FOS) lists annual household incomes for 1996 as $75 (N 6,349) for urban households and $57 (N 4,820) for rural households, suggesting that the gap between urban and rural households is actually 19 percent closer than our estimate.

*Sources:* National Integrated Survey of Households (NISH), Federal Office of Statistics (FOS) consumer price data, and World Bank estimates. As found in Paul Collier, *An Analysis of the Nigerian Labour Market*, Development Economics Department Discussion Paper (Washington, D.C.: World Bank, 1986). From Tom Forrest, *Politics and Economic Development in Nigeria* (Boulder: Westview Press, 1993), 214. 1996 data from FOS *Annual Abstract of Statistics: 1997 Edition*, p. 80.

Health care and other social services—water, education, food, and shelter—remain woefully inadequate. In addition to the needless loss of countless lives to preventable and curable maladies, the nation stands on the verge of an AIDS epidemic of catastrophic proportions. The government has made AIDS a secondary priority, leaving much of the initiative to a small group of courageous but underfunded nongovernmental organizations. The Obasanjo administration began providing subsidized antiretroviral medications in 2002, but the UN estimates that these are reaching only about 17 percent of Nigerians who are HIV positive.

# Society and Economy

Because the central government controls access to most resources and economic opportunities, the state has become the major focus for competition among ethnic, regional, religious, and class groups.[11]

## Ethnic and Religious Cleavages

Nigeria's ethnic relations have generated tensions that sap the country's economy of much-needed vitality.[12] The dominance of the Hausa-Fulani, Igbo, and Yoruba in the country's national life, and the conflicts among political elites from these groups, distort economic affairs.

Government ineptitude (or outright manipulation), and growing Islamic and Christian assertion, have also heightened conflicts.[13] Christians have perceived past northern-dominated governments as being pro-Muslim in their management and distribution of scarce resources, some of which jeopardized the secular nature of the state. These fears have increased since 1999, when several northern states instituted expanded versions of the Islamic legal code, the *shari'a*. For their part, Muslims feared that President Obasanjo, a born-again Christian, tilted the balance of power and thus the distribution of economic benefits against the north, and such fears are again on the rise under President Jonathan, also a Christian. Economic decline has contributed to the rise of Christian and Muslim fundamentalisms, which have spread among unemployed youths and others in a society suffering under economic collapse. Disputes have sometimes escalated into violence.

Since the return of democracy in 1999, many ethnic-based and religious movements have taken advantage of renewed political freedoms to organize to press the government to address their grievances. Some mobilization has been peaceful, but many armed groups have also formed, at times with the encouragement or complicity of the mainstream political movements. In the oil-producing regions, these militias live off the pay they receive in providing security for oil "bunkering": illegal criminal networks (often including individuals in the oil industry, political leaders, and the military) that tap into pipelines, siphon oil, and resell it on the black market.

Youths from the Niger Delta minorities, primarily the Ijaw, have occupied Shell and Chevron facilities on several occasions to protest their economic marginalization. One spectacular incident on an offshore oil platform in 2002 saw a group of local women stage a peaceful takeover using a traditional form of protest: disrobing in order to shame the oil companies and local authorities. Some of these protests have ended peacefully, but since 2003 the number and firepower of the militias have increased, making the region increasingly militarized. The government has periodically responded to these incidents and other disturbances with excessive force.

In the Niger Delta, the struggle of the minority communities with the federal government and multinational oil corporations has been complicated by clashes among the minority groups themselves over control of land and access to government rents. Ethnic-based mobilization, including the activities of militias and vigilante groups, has increased across the country since the transition to civilian rule. Political leaders have sometimes built alliances with such groups and are increasingly using them to harass and even kill political opponents. These practices have reached a dangerous threshold in the Niger Delta, where an ethnic militia attacked a state capital in late 2004 and forced the flight of the governor. Since that time, a host of new militant groups have arisen, engaging in oil bunkering and kidnapping to make money, and occasionally attacking oil installations. The largest such group, the Movement for the Emancipation of the Niger Delta (MEND), has repeatedly threatened to drive out foreign oil interests if their demands for a greater share of oil revenues are not met. The activities of MEND and other militants have forced more than a quarter of Nigeria's onshore oil operations to shut down through persistent attacks on offshore and onshore installations. President Yar'Adua initiated an amnesty program for the militias in 2009 that lowered the number of attacks, but his sickness and death limited the implementation of the program.

These divisive practices overshadow certain positive aspects of sectional identities. For example, associations based on ethnic and religious affinities often serve as vehicles for mobilizing savings, investment, and production, such as informal credit associations. Sectional groups such as the Igbo *Ohaneze* or the Yoruba *Afenifere* have also advocated more equitable federalism and continued democratic development.

## Gender Differences

Although the Land Use Act of 1978 stated that all land in Nigeria is ultimately owned by the government, land tenure in Nigeria is still governed by traditional practice, which is largely patriarchal. Despite the fact that women, especially from the south and Middle Belt areas, have traditionally dominated agricultural production and form the bulk of agricultural producers, they are generally prevented from owning land, which remains the major means of production. Trading, in which women feature prominently, is also controlled in many areas by traditional chiefs and local government councilors, who are overwhelmingly male.

Women's associations in the past tended to be elitist, urban based, and mainly concerned with issues of trade, children, household welfare, and religion.[14] The few that did have a more political orientation have been largely token appendages of the male-dominated political parties or instruments of the government. Women are grossly underrepresented at all levels of the governmental system; only 8 (of 469) national legislators are women.

Reflecting the historical economic and educational advantages of the south, women's interest organizations sprouted in southern Nigeria earlier than in the north. Although these groups initially focused generally on nonpolitical issues surrounding women's health and children's welfare, they are now also focusing on explicit political goals, such as getting more women into government and increasing funds available for education.

Northern groups also showed tremendous creativity in using Islam to support their activities, which was important considering that tenets of the religion have been regularly used by Nigerian men to justify women's subordinate status. Women's groups in general have been more dynamic in developing income-generating projects to make their organizations and constituents increasingly self-reliant, compared with male-dominated NGOs that depend heavily on foreign or government funding.

## Nigeria in the Global Economy

The Nigerian state has remained comparatively weak and dependent on Western industrial and financial interests. The country's acute debt burden was dramatically reduced in 2005, but Nigeria is still reliant on the developed industrial economies for finance capital, production and information technologies, basic consumer items, and raw materials. Mismanagement, endemic corruption, and the vagaries of international commodity markets have squandered the country's economic potential. Apart from its standing in global energy markets, Nigeria has receded to the margins of the global economy.

## Nigeria and the Regional Political Economy

**Economic Community of West African States (ECOWAS)**

The West African regional organization, including 15 member countries from Cape Verde in the west to Nigeria and Niger in the east.

Nigeria's aspirations to be a regional leader in Africa have not been dampened by its declining position in the global political economy. Nigeria was a major actor in the formation of the **Economic Community of West African States (ECOWAS)** in 1975 and has carried a disproportionately high financial and administrative burden for keeping the organization afloat. Under President Obasanjo's initiative, ECOWAS voted in 2000 to create a parliament and a single currency for the region as the next step toward a European Union–style integration. The lackluster results of past integration efforts do not bode well for success.

Nigeria was also the largest contributor of troops to the West African peacekeeping force, the ECOWAS Monitoring Group (known as ECOMOG). Under Nigerian direction, the ECOWAS countries dispatched ECOMOG troops to Liberia from 1990 to 1997 to restore order and prevent the Liberian civil war from destabilizing the subregion. Ironically, despite military dictatorship at home, Nigerian ECOMOG forces invaded Sierra Leone in May 1997 to restore its democratically elected government. Nigeria under President Obasanjo also sought to mediate crises in Guinea-Bissau, Togo, and Ivory Coast, and in Darfur (Sudan), Congo, and Zimbabwe outside the ECOWAS region.

Because it is the largest economy in the West African subregion, Nigeria has at times been a magnet for immigration. At the height of the 1970s oil boom, many West African laborers, most of them Ghanaians, migrated to Nigeria in search of employment. When the oil-based expansion ceased and jobs became scarce, Nigeria sought to protect its own workers by expelling hundreds of thousands of West Africans in 1983 and 1985. Many Nigerians now flock to the hot Ghanaian economy for work and to countries across the continent, including far-off South Africa.

## Nigeria and the Political Economy of the West

Shortly after the 1973–1974 global oil crisis, Nigeria's oil wealth was perceived by the Nigerian elite as a source of strength. In 1975, for example, Nigeria was selling about 30 percent of its oil to the United States and was able to apply pressure to the administration of President Gerald Ford in a dispute over Angola.[15] By the 1980s, however, the global oil market had become a buyers' market. Thereafter, it became clear that Nigeria's dependence on oil was a source of weakness, not strength. The depth of Nigeria's international weakness became more evident with the adoption of structural adjustment in the mid-1980s. Given the enormity of the economic crisis, Nigeria was compelled to seek IMF/World Bank support to improve its balance of payments and facilitate economic restructuring and debt rescheduling, and it has had to accept direction from foreign agencies ever since.

## THE U.S. CONNECTION

### Much in Common

Since the 1970s Nigeria has had a strong relationship with the United States. Most of Nigeria's military governments during the Cold War aligned their foreign policies with the West, although they differed over South Africa, with Nigeria taking a strong anti-apartheid stance. Beginning with the Second Republic constitution, Nigeria closely modeled its presidential and federal systems on those of the United States, and Nigerian courts will occasionally turn to American jurisprudence for legal precedents. Since President Carter's visit to Nigeria in 1978, Washington has supported Nigerian efforts to liberalize and deepen democratic development.

Overwhelmingly, however, the key issue in U.S.-Nigerian relations has been oil. The United States buys roughly 8 percent of its petroleum imports from Nigeria, and has repeatedly pushed Abuja to increase production of its "sweet crude," the especially high quality oil Nigeria offers. Nigeria also discovered massive gas reserves off its coasts that it has begun to export in recent years as well. Nigeria's military governments used America's oil addiction to force it to moderate its pressure on Abuja to democratize. The civilian governments since 1999 have also largely ignored U.S. complaints over declining election quality, and the Yar'Adua administration cultivated ties with China after the United States suspended high-level diplomatic relations over the farcical 2007 elections. Shortly thereafter, the Bush administration welcomed President Yar'Adua to Washington. President Jonathan, however, came to office in part with the help of U.S. pressure, and he has cultivated close ties with the Obama administration.

Nigeria and the United States also share strong societal ties. Since the 1960s, Christian Nigerians have been avid consumers of American Pentecostalism, sprouting thousands of new churches over the years and infusing them with a uniquely Nigerian flair, such that many of these churches are now opening satellites in the United States and around the globe. In addition, a growing number of Nigerians have migrated to the United States, such that nearly 300,000 are now U.S. citizens. Since 2000, this diaspora has begun to exercise some influence over U.S. policy, and they have also used their financial resources to support development projects and exercise political influence in Nigeria.

In addition to its dependence on oil revenues, Nigeria remains dependent on Western and Chinese technology and expertise for exploration and extraction of its oil reserves. The United States is now turning toward Nigerian oil to diversify its supply base beyond the Middle East, which should improve Nigerian government revenues but may not significantly alter the overall dependency of the economy.

Nigeria remains a highly visible and influential member of the Organization of Petroleum Exporting Countries (OPEC), selling on average more than 2 million barrels of petroleum daily (although militancy in the Niger Delta has reduced this figure) and contributing approximately 8 percent of U.S. oil imports. Nigeria's oil wealth and its great economic potential have tempered the resolve of Western nations in combating human rights and other abuses, notably during the Abacha period from 1993 to 1998.

The West has been supportive of the return of Nigerian leadership across Africa. Together with President Thabo Mbeki of South Africa, President Obasanjo was instrumental in convincing the continent's leaders to transform the OAU into the African Union (AU) in 2002, modeled on European-style processes to promote greater political integration across the continent. The AU's first item of business was to endorse the New Partnership for Africa's Development (NEPAD), through which African governments committed to good governance and economic reforms in return for access to Western markets and financial assistance. NEPAD remains a central element in Nigerian and South African foreign policy.

Despite its considerable geopolitical resources, Nigeria's economic development profile remains harsh. Nigeria is listed very close to the bottom of the UNDP's Human Development Index (HDI), 142 out of 174, behind India and Haiti. Gross national product (GNP) per capita in 2001 was $300, less than 2 percent of which was recorded as public expenditures on education and health, respectively.

## Summary

Nigeria built an interventionist state on the massive earnings from the 1970s oil boom. Instead of delivering prosperity, however, the oil revenues have been mismanaged and fostered corruption. Repeated development plans have been promised over the years but have been poorly implemented. Nevertheless, Nigeria remains an important oil producer, which gives it some voice in regional and global politics. Yet the failure to deliver broad-based economic growth at home has raised ethnic and religious divisions, particularly in the oil-producing regions of the Niger Delta.

SECTION 3

# GOVERNANCE AND POLICY-MAKING

### Focus Questions

What is the "National Question," and how have Nigerians tried to resolve it?

What is prebendalism, and how has the "Big Man" problem played out in the civilian governments since 1999?

What have been some of the challenges and/or benefits for Nigeria in having parallel *shari'a* courts alongside the secular legal system?

The rough edges of what has been called the "unfinished Nigerian state" appears in its institutions of governance and policy-making. What seemed like an endless political transition under the Babangida and Abacha regimes was rushed through in less than a year by their successor, Abdulsalami Abubakar. President Obasanjo thus inherited a government that was close to collapse, riddled with corruption, unable to perform basic tasks of governance, yet facing high public expectations to deliver rapid progress. He delivered some important economic reforms over his eight years as president, but he gradually succumbed to the "Big Man," prebendal style of corrupt clientelist networks, and tried to change the Constitution to allow himself to stay in power indefinitely. The Nigerian public, however, rejected his ambitions, providing his political opponents, civil society, and the media a strong base to mobilize and force him to leave in May 2007. President Yar'Adua, like Obasanjo, came to power without a client network of his own and immediately set out to build one. President Jonathan also took office without much of a network, and quickly turned Nigeria's massive state resources to the task of getting himself elected in 2011.

## Organization of the State

### The National Question and Constitutional Governance

After almost five decades as an independent nation, Nigerians are still debating the basic political structures of the country, who will rule and how, and in some quarters, if the country should even remain united. They call this fundamental governance issue the "national question." How is the country to be governed given its great diversity? What should be the institutional form of the government? How can all sections of the country work in harmony and none feel excluded or dominated by the others? Without clear answers to these questions, Nigeria has stumbled along since independence between democracy and constitutionalism, on the one hand, and military domination on the other. The May 2006 rejection of President Obasanjo's third-term gambit, and the fact that most elites insisted on a constitutional solution to the crisis over President Yar'Adua's incapacitation and death suggest, however, that Nigeria may have turned a corner in terms of a growing respect for constitutional rule.

Since the amalgamation of northern and southern Nigeria in 1914, the country has drafted nine constitutions—five under colonial rule and four thereafter. Nigerian constitutions have suffered under little respect from military or civilian leaders, who have often been unwilling to observe legal and constitutional constraints. Governance and policy-making in this context are conducted within fragile institutions that are swamped by personal and partisan considerations.

## Federalism and State Structure

Nigeria's First Republic experimented with the British-style parliamentary model, in which the prime minister is chosen directly from the legislative ranks. The First Republic was relatively decentralized, with more political power vested in the three federal units: the Northern, Eastern, and Western Regions. The Second Republic constitution, which went into effect in 1979, adopted a U.S.-style presidential model. The Fourth Republic continues with the presidential model: A system with a strong executive who is constrained by a system of formal checks and balances on authority, a bicameral legislature, and an independent judicial branch charged with matters of law and constitutional interpretation.[16]

Like the United States, Nigeria also features a federal structure comprising 36 states and 774 local government units empowered, within limits, to enact their own laws. The judicial system also resembles that of the United States, with a network of local and appellate courts as well as state-level courts. Unlike the United States, however, Nigeria also allows customary law courts to function alongside the secular system, including *shari'a* courts in Muslim communities.

In practice, however, military rule left an authoritarian political culture that remains despite the formal democratization of state structures. The control of oil wealth by this centralized command structure has further cemented economic and political control in the center, resulting in a skewed federalism in which states enjoy nominal powers, but in reality are highly dependent on the central government. Another aspect of federalism in Nigeria has been the effort to arrive at some form of elite accommodation to moderate some of the more divisive aspects of cultural pluralism. The domination of federal governments from 1960 to 1999 by northern Nigerians led southern Nigerians, particularly Yoruba leaders, to demand a "power shift" of the presidency to the south in 1999, leading to the election of Olusegun Obasanjo. Northerners then demanded a shift back to the north in 2007, propelling Umaru Yar'Adua, a northern governor, into office. This ethnic rotation principle is not formally found in the constitution, but all the major political parties recognize it as a necessity. Moreover, the parties practice ethnic rotation at the state and local levels as well.[17]

A central issue in both the 2009–2010 crisis over Yar'Adua's incapacitation and the 2011 election of President Jonathan, a southerner from the Niger Delta, is that Jonathan's ascension has broken the ethnic rotation principle. Northern factions argued that under this rule the presidency should have stayed with them for two terms until 2015. These factions were unable, however, to unite and block Jonathan from winning the PDP nomination and election in 2011. Consequently, northern groups are certain to demand rotation of the presidency back to their region in 2015.

This informal norm of ethnic rotation has built upon an older, formal practice, known as "federal character." Federal character calls for ethnic quotas in government hiring practices, and was introduced into the public service and formally codified by the 1979 constitution, although the armed forces have long observed such quotas. Although this principle is regarded by some as a positive Nigerian contribution to governance in a plural society, its application has also intensified some intergroup rivalries and conflicts. In recent years, there have been calls for the use of merit over federal character in awarding public sector jobs. The establishment of the ethnic rotation principle—a "power shift"—by the end of the Obasanjo years, however, was a tremendously positive development in moving toward addressing the national question. Some critics have argued that a power shift is antidemocratic, meaning that it is antimajoritarian and encourages elite bargaining at the expense of public votes. Yet it also encourages elite accommodation and introduces greater predictability in the system, reducing the perception that control of political offices is a zero-sum game. President Jonathan's breaking of this principle though his election in 2011 raised significant tensions in the PDP primaries and was partly responsible for the election riots that killed 800 people, but has yet to produce a major north-south clash, as feared. Nonetheless, northern factions are certain to demand that principle dictates that it is their turn to succeed the southerner Jonathan when his term in office ends.

## The Executive

### Evolution of the Executive Function

In the Second Republic, the earlier parliamentary system was replaced by a presidential system based on the American model. The president was chosen directly by the electorate rather than indirectly by the legislature, based on a widespread belief that a popularly elected president could serve as a symbol of national unity. The framers of the Second Republic's constitution believed that placing the election of the president in the hands of the electorate, rather than parliament, would mitigate a lack of party discipline in the selection of the executive. The Second Republic's experiment with presidentialism lasted for only four years before it was ended by the 1983 coup.

### The Executive under Military Rule

The leadership styles among Nigeria's seven military heads of state varied widely but, in general, under military administrations, the president, or head of state, made appointments to most senior government positions.[18] Since the legislature was disbanded, major executive decisions (typically passed by decrees) were subject to the approval of a ruling council of high-level military officers, although by Abacha's time this council had become largely a rubber stamp for the ruler. Although the military became increasingly repressive, nearly all the juntas spoke of making a transition to democracy in order to gain legitimacy.

Given the highly personalistic character of military politics, patron-client relationships flourished. The military pattern of organization, with one strongman at the top and echelons of subordinates below in a pyramid of top-down relationships, spread throughout Nigerian political culture and subcultures.

Having been politicized and divided by these patron-client relationships, the military was structurally weakened during its long years in power. Under Babangida and Abacha, the military was transformed from an instrument that guarantees national defense and security into a predatory apparatus, one more powerful than political parties. Over four decades after the first military coup of January 1966, most Nigerians now believe that the country's political and economic development has been profoundly hampered by military domination and misrule. While there have been reports of coup plots on a number of occasions during the Fourth Republic, the military establishment has so far remained loyal and generally within its constitutional security roles.

President Obasanjo paid close attention to keeping the military professionally oriented—and in the barracks. U.S. military advisers and technical assistance were invited to redirect the Nigerian military toward regional peacekeeping expertise—and to keep them busy outside of politics. So far, this strategy has been effective, but the military remains a threat. Junior and senior officers threatened coups over the farcical 2007 elections and the refusal of Yar'Adua's advisors to hand power to Jonathan in 2009–2010. So long as civilian leaders continue the corrupt politics of their patronage networks and fail to deliver broad-based development, the military will loom in the background as a possible alternative to civilian rule.

## The Fourth Republic: The Obasanjo, Yar'Adua, and Jonathan Administrations

President Obasanjo's first six months in office were marked by initiatives to reform the armed forces, revitalize the economy, address public welfare, and improve standards of governance. The president sought to root out misconduct and inefficiency in the public sector. Soon, however, familiar patterns of clientelism and financial kickbacks for oil licenses resurfaced. Obasanjo proposed an anticorruption commission with sweeping statutory powers to investigate and prosecute public officials. Delayed in its establishment, the commission had little impact. A second anticorruption commission, however, the Economic and Financial Crimes Commission (EFCC), has since its founding in 2003 had an impressive record of indictments.

Nonetheless, a major impediment to reform came from the ruling party itself. The PDP is run by a collection of powerful politicians from Nigeria's early governments, many of whom grew rich from their complicity with the Babangida and Abacha juntas. With a difficult reelection bid in 2003, these fixers again delivered a victory for the president and the PDP, accomplished through massive fraud in a third of Nigeria's states and questionable practices in at least another third of the country.

After the 2003 election President Obasanjo appeared convinced that he needed to build his own prebendal network if he were to govern and if he were to pursue his ambition to stay in office past two terms. He and his supporters soon moved to gain control of the PDP, offering benefits for loyalty, and removing allies of rival Big Men in the party. The president then signaled the EFCC to investigate his rivals, arresting some and forcing others to support his plans. When Obasanjo's third-term amendment was quashed by the National Assembly in May 2006, the president then had himself named "Chairman for Life" of the PDP, with the power to eject anyone from the party, even his successor as president.

Not surprisingly, President Yar'Adua spent his first year in office trying to gain control over the PDP. He halted many of the last-minute privatizations of state assets into the hands of Obasanjo loyalists and replaced the chairman of the EFCC. The Yar'Adua administration also did nothing to prevent the National Assembly from instigating a series of investigations into the Obasanjo administration that unearthed massive corruption, including the discovery that more than $10 billion had been sunk into the power sector that had produced no results. President Yar'Adua also assisted many of the PDP governors—twelve of whom had their elections overturned by the courts—to retain their seats in rerun elections. By 2009, Yar'Adua had greater control of the PDP, and Obasanjo was on the decline. Yar'Adua's incapacitation later that year and death thereafter, however, reversed Obasanjo's fortunes; and he threw his support behind Goodluck Jonathan at the key moment when Yar'Adua loyalists were preventing him from becoming acting president.

With Obasanjo's support, Jonathan moved to build other alliances to gain influence in the PDP, particularly with the powerful state governors. Their support, bought with the massive resources in the hands of the presidency, won him the PDP nomination and swept him to victory in April 2011.

These developments demonstrated the continuing deficits of legitimacy for the government as well as the democratic system. As Nigeria's political elites continue to flout the rules of the system, it is inevitable that patronage, coercion, and personal interest will drive policy more than the interests of the public. President Jonathan's first year has so far followed this pattern of "Big Man" prebendal politics—with one important exception: He appointed a credible chairman of the nation's electoral commission, Attahiru Jega. Jega had only a few months to prepare for the April 2011 election, but his reforms assured a more credible outcome than 2007, and hold the promise of significant change for 2015 as more sweeping reforms within the commission begin to take hold.

## The Bureaucracy

As government was increasingly "Africanized" before independence, the bureaucracy became a way to reward individuals in the patrimonial system (see "Current Challenges: Prebendalism"). Individuals were appointed on the basis of patronage, ethnic group, and regional origin rather than merit.

It is conservatively estimated that federal and state government personnel increased from 72,000 at independence to well over 1 million by the mid-1980s. The salaries of these bureaucrats presently consume roughly half of government expenditures. Several of President Obasanjo's progressive ministers undertook extensive reforms within their ministries, with some successes, but which the bureaucracy fought at every turn.

## Semipublic Institutions

**parastatals**

State-owned industries or businesses. Sometimes the government will own and manage the company outright, or only own a majority share of its stock but allow members of the private sector to run it.

Among the largest components of the national administration in Nigeria are numerous state-owned enterprises, usually referred to as **parastatals**. In general, parastatals are established for several reasons. First, they furnish public facilities, including water, power, telecommunications, ports, and other transportation, at lower cost than private companies. Secondly, they were introduced to accelerate economic development by controlling the commanding heights of the economy, including steel production, petroleum and natural gas production, refining, petrochemicals, fertilizer, and certain areas of agriculture. Thirdly, there is a nationalist dimension that relates to issues of sovereignty over sectors perceived sensitive for national security.

## Prebendalism

Prebendalism is the disbursing of public offices and state rents to one's ethnic clients. It is an extreme form of clientelism that refers to the practice of mobilizing cultural and other sectional identities by political aspirants and officeholders for the purpose of corruptly appropriating state resources. Prebendalism is an established pattern of political behavior that justifies the pursuit of and the use of public office for the personal benefit of the officeholder and his clients. The official public purpose of the office becomes a secondary concern. As with clientelism, the officeholder's clients comprise a specific set of elites to which he is linked, typically by ethnic or religious ties. This linkage is key to understanding the concept. There are thus two sides involved in prebendalism, the officeholder and the client, and expectations of benefits by the clients (or supporters) perpetuate the prebendal system in a pyramid fashion with a "Big Man" or "godfather" at the top and echelons of intermediate Big Men and clients below.[19]

As practiced in the Babangida and Abacha eras, when official corruption occurred on an unprecedented scale, prebendalism deepened sectional cleavages and eroded the resources of the state. It also discouraged genuinely productive activity in the economy and expanded the class of individuals who live off state patronage.

As long as prebendalism remains the norm, a stable democracy will be elusive. Because these practices are deeply embedded, they are more difficult to uproot. The corruption resulting from prebendal practices is blamed for the enormous overseas flight of capital into private accounts of each president in turn. For instance, much of the $12.2 billion oil windfall of the early 1990s is believed to have been pocketed by Babangida and senior members of his regime. General Abacha diverted at least $5 billion from the Nigerian central bank, and President Obasanjo and members of his administration were questioned for the disappearance of more than $10 billion into the power sector alone. Transparency International regularly lists Nigeria among the most corrupt countries in the world.

Privatizing the parastatals was a central plank of the reform strategy under the Obasanjo administration. The telecommunications and power industries were put up for sale, and the administration promised to sell parts of the oil industry and privatize part or all of the NNPC. Open licensing in the telecommunications sector after 1999 ushered in a cellular phone boom that has revolutionized Nigerian society and made the country one of the fastest-growing cellular markets in the world. Privatization of the national landline network and the power industries, however, became patronage boondoggles rife with corruption.

# Other State Institutions

Other institutions of governance and policy-making, including the federal judiciary and subnational governments (incorporating state and local courts), operate within the context of a strong central government dominated by a powerful chief executive.

### The Judiciary

At one time, the Nigerian judiciary enjoyed relative autonomy from the executive arm. Aggrieved individuals and organizations could take the government to court and expect a judgment based on the merits of their case. This situation changed as each successive military government demonstrated a profound disdain for judicial practices, and eventually it undermined not only the autonomy but also the very integrity of the judiciary as a third branch of government.

The Buhari, Babangida, and Abacha regimes, in particular, issued a spate of repressive decrees disallowing judicial review. Through the executive's power of appointment of judicial officers to the high bench, as well as the executive's control of judicial budgets, the government came to dominate the courts. In addition, the once highly competent judiciary was undermined severely by declining standards of legal training and bribery. The decline of court independence reached a low in 1993 when the Supreme Court placed all actions of the military executive beyond judicial review. The detention and hanging of Ken Saro-Wiwa and eight other Ogoni activists in 1995 underscored the politicization and compromised state of the judicial system.

With the return of civilian rule in 1999, however, the courts have slowly begun to restore some independence and credibility. In early 2002, for instance, the Supreme Court passed two landmark judgments. The first struck down a 2001 election law that would have prevented new parties from contesting the national elections in 2003—a decision that contravened the wishes of the president and the ruling party. The Court also decided against the governors of Nigeria's coastal states over control of the vast offshore gas reserves, declaring these to be under the jurisdiction of the federal government. Since the farcical 2007 elections, the courts have overturned twelve gubernatorial races and a host of legislative contests, and the Supreme Court reviewed the presidential election as well.

*shari'a*

Islamic law derived mostly from the Qur'an and the examples set by the Prophet Muhammad in the Sunnah.

**State and Local Judiciaries** The judiciaries at the state level are subordinate to the Federal Court of Appeal and the Supreme Court. Some of the states in the northern part of the country with large Muslim populations maintain a parallel court system based on the Islamic ***shari'a*** (religious law). Similarly, some states in the Middle Belt and southern part of the country have subsidiary courts based on customary law (see Table 12.1). Each of these maintains an appellate division. Otherwise, all courts of record in the country are based on the English common law tradition, and all courts are ultimately bound by decisions handed down by the Supreme Court.

How to apply the *shari'a* has been a source of continuing debate in Nigerian politics. For several years, some northern groups have participated in a movement to expand the application of *shari'a* law in predominantly Muslim areas of Nigeria, and some even have advocated that it be made the supreme law of the land. Prior to the establishment of the Fourth Republic, *shari'a* courts had jurisdiction only among Muslims in civil proceedings and in questions of Islamic personal law. In November 1999, however, the northern state of Zamfara instituted a version of the *shari'a* criminal code that included cutting off hands for stealing, and stoning to death for those (especially women) who committed adultery. Eleven other northern states adopted the criminal code by 2001, prompting fears among Christian minorities in these states that the code might be applied to them. Two thousand people lost their lives in Kaduna in 2000 when the state installed the *shari'a* criminal code despite a population that is half Christian.

Although the *shari'a* criminal code appears to contradict Nigeria's officially secular constitution, President Obasanjo refused to challenge it, seeing the movement as a "fad." His refusal to challenge *shari'a* saved the nation from a deeply divisive policy debate and gave northern political and legal systems time to adjust. In fact, although the *shari'a* systems in these states have created more vehicles for patronage, they have also opened up new avenues for public action to press government for accountability and reform. In addition, women's groups mobilized against several questionable local *shari'a* court decisions to challenge them at the appellate level, winning landmark decisions that helped to extend women's legal protections under the code.

## State and Local Government

Nigeria's centralization of oil revenues has fostered intense competition among local communities and states for access to national patronage. Most states would be insolvent without substantial support from the central government. About 90 percent of state incomes are received directly from the federal government, which includes a lump sum based on oil revenues, plus a percentage of oil income based on population. In all likelihood, only the states of Lagos, Rivers, and Kano could survive without federal subsidies; the rest are thoroughly dependent upon federal revenues.

Despite attempted reforms, most local governments have degenerated into prebendal patronage outposts for the governors to dole out to loyalists. For the most part, they do little to address their governance responsibilities.

| Table 12.6 | Percentage Contribution of Different Sources of Government Revenue to Allocated Revenue, 1980–2009 | | | |
|---|---|---|---|---|
| Years | Oil Revenue (Naira Millions) | Non-Oil Revenue (Naira Millions) | Oil as % of Revenue | Non-Oil as % of Revenue |
| 1980 | 12353 | 2880 | 81 | 19 |
| 1981 | 8564 | 4726 | 64 | 36 |
| 1983 | 7253 | 3256 | 69 | 31 |
| 1985 | 10924 | 4127 | 72.5 | 27.5 |
| 1987 | 19027 | 6354 | 75 | 25 |
| 1992 | 164078 | 26375 | 86 | 14 |
| 1994 | 160192 | 41718 | 79 | 21 |
| 1995 | 324548 | 135440 | 70.5 | 29.5 |
| 1996 | 408783 | 114814 | 78 | 22 |
| 2001 | 1707563 | 523970 | 76.5 | 23.5 |
| 2002 | 1230851 | 500986 | 71 | 29 |
| 2003 | 2074281 | 500815 | 80.5 | 19.5 |
| 2007 | 4462950 | 1252550 | 78 | 22 |
| 2008 | 6530630 | 1335960 | 83 | 17 |
| 2009 | 3191938 | 865561 | 78.6 | 21.4 |

*Source:* Federal Ministry of Finance and Economic Development, Lagos. From Adedotun Phillips, "Managing Fiscal Federalism: Revenue Allocation Issues," *Publius: The Journal of Federalism*, 21, no. 4 (Fall 1991), p. 109. Nigerian Federal Office of Statistics, *Annual Abstract of Statistics: 1997 Edition.* Nigerian Economic Summit Group, *Economic Indicators* (Vol. 8, no. 2, April–June 2002). Recent data compiled by Evan Litwin and Mukesh Baral.

The federal, state, and local governments have the constitutional and legal powers to raise funds through taxes. However, Nigerians share an understandable unwillingness to pay taxes and fees to a government with such a poor record of delivering basic services. The result is a vicious cycle: Government is sapped of resources and legitimacy and cannot adequately serve the people. Communities, in turn, are compelled to resort to self-help measures to protect these operations and thus withdraw further from the reach of the state. Because very few individuals and organizations pay taxes, even the most basic government functions are starved of resources, and the states become more dependent upon federal oil wealth in order to function.

The return of democratic rule has meant the return of conflict between the state and national governments. The primary vehicle for conflict since 1999 has been a series of "governors' forums" asserting greater legal control over resources in

| Table 12.7 | Share of Total Government Expenditure | |
|---|---|---|
| **Share of Total Government Expenditure** | **2008** | **2009** |
| Federal[1] | 3,240,800 | 3,456,900 |
| State[2] | 3,021,600 | 2,776,900 |
| Local[3] | 1,387,900 | 1,067,614 |
| Total Expenditure (Naira Millions) | 7,650,300 | 7,301,414 |

[1]Central Bank of Nigeria, Annual Report 2009, section 5.4.3; Annual Report 2008, section 5.3.3.
[2]Central Bank of Nigeria, Annual Report 2009, section 5.5.3; Annual Report 2008, section 5.4.3.
[3]Central Bank of Nigeria, Table B.3.1, Summary of Local Govt's Finances. Figures can also be cross-referenced with Annual Report 2009.
*Source:* Recent data compiled by Evan Litwin and Mukesh Baral.

**prebendalism**

Patterns of political behavior that rest on the justification that official state offices should be utilized for the personal benefit of officeholders as well as of their support group or clients.

their states. A number of governors have turned to armed militias and vigilante groups to provide security and to intimidate political opponents. Many of these groups were initially local responses to the corrupt and ineffective police force, or enforcers of the new *shari'a* codes in the north, but the governors have sensed the larger political usefulness of these groups. Consequently, political assassinations and violence increased as the 2003, 2007, and 2011 elections approached. Some of these militias in the Niger Delta or political thugs in other parts of the country have grown independent and turned on their former masters, raising the spectre of local warlords that have ruined other African nations.

# The Policy-Making Process

Nigeria's prolonged experience with military rule has resulted in a policy process based more on top-down directives than on consultation, political debate, and legislation. A decade of democratic government has seen important changes, as the legislatures, courts, and state governments have begun to force the presidency to negotiate its policies and work within a constitutional framework. But military rule has left indelible marks on policy-making in Nigeria. Because of their influence in recruitment and promotions, as well as through their own charisma or political connections, senior officers often developed networks of supporters, creating what is referred to as a "loyalty pyramid."[20] Once in power, the men at the top of these pyramids in Nigeria, whether military or civilian, gained access to tremendous oil wealth, passed on through the lower echelons of the pyramid to reward support. Often these pyramids reflect ethnic or religious affiliations (see the discussions of corruption in Section 2 and **prebendalism** in Section 3).[21] Many of the current civilian politicians belonged to the loyalty pyramids of different military men, and their networks resemble the politics of loyalty pyramids among the military.

Civilian policy-making in present-day Nigeria centers largely on presidential initiative in proposing policies, which are then filtered through the interests of the "Big Men." Invariably, their agendas conflict with those of the president and with each other, and policies are consequently blocked or significantly altered. Frequently, the reformist agenda is stalled or ineffectual.

## Summary

Nigeria has sought a number of institutional and informal solutions to manage the "National Question" posed by its great diversity. Federalism has helped to decentralize government somewhat and preserved a basic measure of unity, but the state- and federal-level executives still retain much of the enormous advantages bestowed upon them by military rule. Military rule also left behind corrupt, prebendal patterns that created the current "Big Man" system dominating the PDP and the nation's politics.

## President Goodluck Jonathan

President Goodluck Jonathan, casting his vote in his Bayelsa state village and wearing a traditional hat common to many Niger Delta communities. He was elected vice president in 2007, named Acting President by the National Assembly on the incapacitation of President Yar'Adua in 2010, and elected president in 2011.

© PIUS UTOMI EKPEI/AFP/ Getty Images

The story goes that President Jonathan's father, a canoe maker from Bayelsa state, had an innate sense that his son was born lucky, and so named him Goodluck. Whether the story is truth or legend, events certainly support its conclusion: Fortune has so far smiled on the president, rocketing him from humble beginnings in the Niger Delta to the center of Nigerian politics. Jonathan worked as both a lecturer and an environmental official while finishing his Ph.D. in zoology. In 1998 he joined the PDP and won the office of deputy governor of Bayelsa state. He then became governor in 2005 when his predecessor was impeached for corruption. When President Obasanjo picked the little-known Yar'Adua as the 2007 presidential candidate for the PDP, he sought to balance the ticket with someone from the Niger Delta. The other regional governors—having been in office longer—were richer and deemed more powerful, so Obasanjo turned to Jonathan for the vice presidency. As President Yar'Adua's health failed, Jonathan found himself acting president in February 2010 and then president when Yar'Adua passed away in May 2010.

Given this quick ascent, the president has little track record to suggest what direction he will take now that his April 2011 election victory is behind him. Bayelsa politics is infamous for corruption and militant activity, and militias dynamited Jonathan's house the night he was elected vice president in 2007. His wife, Patience, was accused by the EFCC of money laundering in 2006 and forced to return $13.5 million, although she was never prosecuted. While vice president, Jonathan sought to play a peacemaking role with the major Niger Delta militias without much success, and as president he has promised to revive electricity production and push electoral reform. The latter promise he delivered upon, naming a respected civil society leader to head the electoral commission.

President Jonathan is the first Nigerian head of state to have a Facebook page (http://www.facebook.com/ jonathangoodluck), and is even believed to take the time to write some of the postings himself.

# REPRESENTATION AND PARTICIPATION

SECTION 4

Representation and participation are two vital components of modern democracies. Nigerian legislatures have commonly been sidelined or reduced to subservience by the powerful executive, while fraud, elite manipulation, and military interference have marred the formal party and electoral systems. Thus, we emphasize unofficial methods of representation and participation through the institutions of **civil society**, which are often more important than the formal institutions.

## The Legislature

Nigeria's legislature has been a primary victim of the country's political instability. Legislative structures and processes historically suffered abuse, neglect, or peremptory suspension by the executive. Until the first coup in 1966, Nigeria operated its legislature along the lines of the British Westminster model, with an elected lower house and a smaller upper house composed of individuals selected by the executive.

**civil society**

Refers to the space occupied by voluntary associations outside the state, for example, professional associations (lawyers, doctors, teachers), trade unions, student and women's groups, religious bodies, and other voluntary association groups.

**Focus Questions**

What accounts for the weakness of legislatures in Nigeria since independence?

What have been the benefits and costs of the move from ethnic parties under the early republics to the multiethnic parties of the Fourth Republic?

What role has civil society played in resisting military rule and voicing the public interest under civilian government?

For the next thirteen years of military rule, a Supreme Military Council performed legislative functions by initiating and passing decrees at will. During the second period of civilian rule, 1979–1983, the bicameral legislature was introduced similar to the U.S. system, with a Senate and House of Representatives (together known as the National Assembly) consisting of elected members.

Election to the Senate is on the basis of equal state representation, with three senators from each of the thirty-six states, plus one senator from the federal capital territory, Abuja. The practice of equal representation in the Senate is identical to that of the United States, except that each Nigerian state elects three senators instead of two. Election to the Nigerian House of Representatives is also based on state representation but weighted to reflect the relative size of each state's population, again after the U.S. example. Only eight women were elected in 1999 to sit in the Fourth Republic's National Assembly; by 2007 this number rose slightly to 33, but still constituting only 7 percent of the legislature's membership. This reflects the limited political participation of Nigerian women in formal institutions, as discussed in Section 2.

Nigerian legislatures under military governments were either powerless or nonexistent. Even under civilian administrations, however, Nigerian legislatures were subjected to great pressure by the executive and have never assumed their full constitutional role. Since independence, the same party that won the executive has almost always managed to win the majority in the National Assembly and state assemblies either outright or in coalitions. Amid all the changes, one aspect of Nigerian politics has been consistent: the dominance of the executive. In fact, the president controls and disburses public revenues, despite the constitutional mandate that the National Assembly controls the public purse. The presidency typically disburses funds as it wishes, paying little attention to the budgets passed by the National Assembly.

Given this history of executive dominance, the National Assembly that took office in 1999 began its work with great uncertainty over its role in Nigerian politics. With both the House and the Senate controlled by the PDP, along with the presidency, the familiar pattern of executive dominance of the legislature through the party structures continued. Legislators spent most of their time clamoring for their personal spending funds to be disbursed by the executive and voted themselves pay raises. Other legislators, however, tested the waters for the first time with a variety of radical bills that never emerged from committee, including one that would have asked the United States to invade Nigeria if the military staged another coup. President Obasanjo, meanwhile, referred to legislators as "small boys" and rarely accorded them the respect of an equal branch of government. Legislatures at the state level face a similar imbalance of power with the governors, who control large local bureaucracies and control the funds received from the federally shared revenues.

Gradually, however, the National Assembly began to assert itself and gain some relevance. In annual budget negotiations, Assembly leaders struggled to resist presidential dominance. In August 2002, the House and the Senate, led by members of Obasanjo's own party, began impeachment proceedings against the president for refusing to disburse funds as agreed in that year's budget. The president compromised, but continued to ignore subsequent budgets, leading to two additional—and unsuccessful—attempts to impeach him.

Perhaps the greatest victory for the National Assembly was when it rejected President Obasanjo's constitutional amendments in May 2006 that would have allowed him additional terms in office. The president, however, ensured that these victories for the institution came at a heavy price for its members: Nearly 80 percent of legislators elected in 1999 were not returned in 2003, and another 80 percent did not return in 2007—not because their constituents voted them out, but because they were removed in the PDP primaries, a process that President Obasanjo and the governors largely controlled. President Yar'Adua showed greater respect for the National Assembly during his few years in office. Most importantly, during his incapacitation, political leaders after months of inaction finally turned to the National Assembly to declare Goodluck Jonathan the acting president, rather than having the cabinet or military do so as was more common in the past. This move demonstrated that, at the very least, politicians have gained a growing respect for the legislature's constitutional role.

# The Party System and Elections

An unfortunate legacy of the party and electoral systems after independence was that political parties were associated with particular ethnic groups.[22] The three-region federation created by the British, with one region for each of the three biggest ethnic groups (Hausa-Fulani, Yoruba, and Igbo), created strong incentives for three parties—one dominated by each group—to form. This in turn fostered a strong perception of politics as an ethnically zero-sum (or winner-takes-all) struggle for access to scarce state resources. This encouraged the political and social fragmentation that ultimately destroyed the First Republic and undermined the Second Republic. Unlike Ghana and Côte d'Ivoire, Nigeria did not develop an authoritarian dominant-party system after independence, which might have transcended some of these social cleavages.

In addition to the three-region structure of the federation at independence, Nigeria's use of a first-past-the-post plurality electoral system produced legislative majorities for these three parties with strong ethnic identities. During subsequent democratic experiments, many of the newer parties could trace their roots to their predecessors in the first civilian regime. Consequently, parties were more attentive to the welfare of their ethnic groups than to the development of Nigeria as a whole. In a polity as potentially volatile as Nigeria, these tendencies intensified political polarization and resentment among the losers.

In the Second Republic, the leading parties shared the same ethnic and sectional support, and often the same leadership, as the parties that were prominent in the first civilian regime. In his maneuvering steps toward creating the civilian Third Republic, General Babangida announced a landmark decision in 1989 to establish only two political parties by decree.[23] The state provided initial start-up funds, wrote the constitutions and manifestos of these parties, and designed them to be "a little to the right and a little to the left," respectively, on the political–ideological spectrum. Interestingly, the elections that took place under these rules from 1990 to 1993 indicated that the two parties cut across the cleavages of ethnicity, regionalism, and religion, demonstrating the potential to move beyond ethnicity.[24] The Social Democratic Party (SDP), which emerged victorious in the 1993 national elections, was an impressive coalition of Second Republic party structures, including elements of the former UPN, NPP, PRP, and GNPP. The opposing National Republican Convention (NRC) was seen as having its roots in northern groups that were the core of the National Party of Nigeria (NPN).

Table 12.8 shows historical trends in electoral patterns and communal affiliations. As clearly outlined, northern-based parties dominated the first and second experiments with civilian rule. Given this background, it is significant that Moshood Abiola was able to win the presidency in 1993, the first time in Nigeria's history that a southerner electorally defeated a northerner. Abiola, a Yoruba Muslim, won a number of key states in the north, including the hometown of his opponent. Southerners therefore perceived the decision by the northern-dominated Babangida regime to annul the June 12 elections as a deliberate attempt by the military and northern interests to maintain their decades-long domination of the highest levels of government.

| Table 12.8 | Federal Election Results in Nigeria, 1959–2011 |
| --- | --- |

**Presidential Election Results, 1979–2011**

| | *Victor (% of the vote)* | *Leading Contender (% of the vote)* |
| --- | --- | --- |
| 1979 | Shehu Shagari, NPN (33.8) | Obafemi Awolowo, UPN (29.2) |
| 1983 | Shehu Shagari, NPN (47.3) | Obafemi Awolowo, UPN (31.1) |
| 1993 | M.K.O. Abiola, SDP (58.0) | Bashir Tofa, NRC (42.0) |
| 1999 | Olusegun Obasanjo, PDP (62.8) | Olu Falae, AD/APP alliance (37.2) |
| 2003 | Olusegun Obasanjo, PDP (61.9) | Mohammadu Buhari, ANPP (31.2) |
| 2007 | Umaru Yar'Adua, PDP (69.8) | Mohammadu Buhari, ANPP (18.7) |
| 2011 | Goodluck Jonathan, PDP (58.9) | Mohammadu Buhari, CDC (32.0) |

**Parties Controlling the Parliament/National Assembly (Both Houses) by Ethno-Regional Zone, First to Fourth Republics**

| | | *Northwest* | *North-Central* | *Northeast* | *Southwest* | *South-South* | *Southeast* |
| --- | --- | --- | --- | --- | --- | --- | --- |
| First | 1959 | **NPC** | **NPC** (NEPU) | **NPC** | *AG* | *AG* | *NCNC*[*] |
| | 1964–65 | **NPC** | **NPC** | **NPC** | NNDP[*] (AG)[**] | NNDP[*] (AG)[**] | *NCNC* |
| Second | 1979 | **NPN** | PRP (**NPN,** UPN) | GNPP (**NPN**) | *UPN* (**NPN**) | **NPN** (*UPN*) | NPP[*] |
| | 1983 | **NPN** | **NPN** (PRP) | **NPN** | *UPN* (**NPN**) | **NPN** | NPP[**] |
| Third | 1992 | **NRC** | *SDP* (**NRC**) | *SDP* (**NRC**) | *SDP* | **NRC** (*SDP*) | **NRC** |
| Fourth | 1999 | **PDP** (*APP*) | **PDP** | **PDP** (*APP*) | AD (**PDP**) | **PDP** (*APP*) | **PDP** |
| | 2003 | *ANPP* (**PDP**) | *ANPP* (**PDP**) | **PDP** (*ANPP*) | **PDP** AD | **PDP** (*ANPP*) | **PDP** (APGA) |
| | 2007 | *ANPP* (**PDP**) | **PDP** ANPP | **PDP** ANPP | **PDP** AC | **PDP** | **PDP** PPA |
| | 2011 | **PDP** CDC | **PDP** CDC | **PDP** ANPP | *ACN* **PDP** | **PDP** ACN | **PDP** ACN |

Boldfaced: Ruling party
Italicized: Leading opposition
[*]Coalition with ruling party
[**]Coalition with opposition

*(continued)*

| **Table 12.8** | (continued) |
|---|---|

### National Assembly and State-Level Elections

| Senate | 1999 | 2003 |
|---|---|---|
| PDP | 63 | 73 |
| APP/ANPP | 26 | 28 |
| AD | 20 | 6 |

| House | 1999 | 2003 |
|---|---|---|
| PDP | 214 | 213 |
| APP/ANPP | 77 | 95 |
| AD | 69 | 31 |
| Other | | 7 |

| Governorships | 1999 | 2003 |
|---|---|---|
| PDP | 21 | 28 |
| APP/ANPP | 9 | 7 |
| AD | 6 | 1 |

| State Houses of Assembly | 1999 | 2003 |
|---|---|---|
| PDP | 23 | 28 |
| APP/ANPP | 8 | 7 |
| AD | 5 | 1 |

### 2007 Election Results

| Parties | House of Representatives | | Senate | |
|---|---|---|---|---|
| | Votes % | Seats | Votes % | Seats |
| People's Democratic Party | 54.5 | 223 | 53.7 | 76 |
| All Nigeria People's Party | 27.4 | 96 | 27.9 | 27 |
| Action Congress | 8.8 | 34 | 9.7 | 6 |
| Others | 2.8 | 7 | 2.7 | – |

| Governorships | | State Assemblies | |
|---|---|---|---|
| 26 | PDP | 28 | PDP |
| 5 | ANPP | 5 | ANPP |
| 2 | PPA | 1 | PPA |
| 2 | AC | 2 | AC |
| 1 | APGA | | |

### 2011 Elections

| Party | House Votes % | House Seats | Senate Votes % | Senate Seats | Governorships | State Assemblies |
|---|---|---|---|---|---|---|
| PDP | 54.4 | 152 | 62.4 | 53 | 23 | 26 |
| ACN | 19.0 | 53 | 21.2 | 18 | 6 | 5 |

*(continued)*

| Table 12.8 | | (continued) | | | | |
|---|---|---|---|---|---|---|
| CDC | 11.1 | 31 | 7.1 | 6 | 1 | 0 |
| Others | 15.4 | 43 | 9.4 | 8 | 6 | 5 |

**List of Acronyms Used in Table 12.8**

| | | | |
|---|---|---|---|
| AC (later ACN) | Action Congress (of Nigeria) | NPC | Northern People's Congress |
| AG | Action Group | | |
| AD | Alliance for Democracy | NPF | Northern Progressive Front |
| ANPP | All Nigerian People's Party (formerly APP) | NPN | National Party of Nigeria |
| APGA | All People's Grand Alliance | NPP | Nigerian People's Party |
| APP | All People's Party | NRC | National Republican Convention |
| CDC | Congress for Democratic Change | PPA | Progress People's Alliance |
| GNPP | Great Nigerian People's Party | | |
| NAP | Nigerian Advance Party | PRP | People's Redemption Party |
| NCNC | National Convention of Nigerian Citizens (formerly National Council of Nigeria and the Cameroons) | PDP | People's Democratic Party |
| NEPU | Northern Elements Progressive Union | SDP | Social Democratic Party |
| NNDP | Nigerian National Democratic Party | UPN | Unity Party of Nigeria |

## Old Roots and New Alignments: The PDP and the Other Parties of the Fourth Republic

Nigerians generally reacted with anger to General Abacha's 1993 coup and his subsequent banning of the SDP and NRC. With the unions crushed and Abiola in jail by the end of 1994, democracy deteriorated. In late 1996, the Abacha government registered only five parties, most of whose members had no public constituency and little political experience. During 1997, the five parties, branded by the opposition as "five fingers of a leprous hand," began to clamor for General Abacha to run for president. The presidential election scheduled for August 1998 was reduced to a mere referendum, endorsed by the chief justice of the Supreme Court as legally permissible. The "transition" process had become a travesty.[25] Once Abacha's plan to be certified as president became a certainty, domestic opposition increased. A group of former governors and political leaders from the north (many former NPN and PRP members) publicly petitioned Abacha not to run for president and human rights and pro-democracy groups protested. Even General Babangida voiced his opposition to Abacha's continuing as president. The only real obstacle to Abacha's plan for "self-succession" was whether the military would allow it.

Although there had been frequent rumors of Abacha's ill health, his death on June 8, 1998, was still a great surprise. The following day, General Abubakar, chief of Defense Staff, was sworn in as head of state. Shortly afterward, he promised a speedy transition to democracy and began releasing political prisoners, but Abiola died suspiciously a month after Abacha. New parties quickly formed, and even Yoruba political leaders agreed to participate, although they insisted that the next president should be a Yoruba to compensate their people for having been robbed of their first elected presidency.

Once again, political associations centered on well-known personalities, and intense bargaining and mergers took place. The G-34, the prominent group of civilian leaders who had condemned Abacha's plans to perpetuate his power, created the People's Democratic Party (PDP) in late August, minus most of their Yoruba members, who joined the Alliance for Democracy (AD). At least twenty more parties applied for certification to the electoral commission (INEC); many of them were truly grass-roots movements, including a human rights organization and a trade union party.

To escape the ethnic-based parties of the First and Second Republics, INEC required that parties earn at least 5 percent of the votes in twenty-four of the thirty-six states in local government elections in order to advance to the later state and federal levels. This turned out to be an ingenious way of reducing the number of parties, while obliging viable parties to broaden their appeal. The only parties to meet INEC's requirements were the PDP, AD, and the All People's Party (APP). To assuage the Yoruba over Abiola's lost 1993 mandate, the PDP turned to retired General Obasanjo, who went on to defeat an AD/APP alliance candidate in the 1999 presidential contest.

The parties of the Fourth Republic are primarily alliances of convenience among Big Men from across Nigeria. Their sole purpose is to gain power. They have no ideological differences or policy platforms that distinguish them, such that politicians who lose in one party will frequently shift to another. Yet these parties do feature one terribly important innovation that distinguishes them from those of the First and Second Republics: The PDP, APP (now ANPP), and other leading parties of the Fourth Republic are multiethnic. They rely on elite-centered structures established during previous civilian governments and transition programs, and demonstrate the cross-ethnic alliances that developed over the last quarter-century, particularly through the two mega-parties of the Third Republic. The PDP includes core members of the northern established NPN, the northern progressive PRP, and the Igbo-dominated NPP of the Second Republic, as well as prominent politicians from the Niger Delta. The APP (now ANPP) is also a multiethnic collection, drawing from the Second Republic's GNPP, a party dominated by the northeastern-based Kanuri and groups from the Middle Belt, and also features politicians who had prominent roles in the Abacha-sponsored parties. The ANPP also includes northwestern politicians of royal lineage, Igbo business moguls, and southern minority leaders. The AD, however, was as Yoruba-centered as its predecessors, the UPN in the Second Republic and the AG in the First Republic. The party would later pay at the polls for its lack of national appeal, however, and would join with breakaway factions of the PDP to form the Action Congress (AC, later ACN; see below).

This rise of multiethnic political parties is one of the most significant democratic developments of the Fourth Republic. In multiethnic parties there is a strong incentive for politicians to bargain and bridge their ethnic differences *within* the party, so that they may then compete with the other parties in the system, which would preferably be multiethnic as well.[26] In Nigeria, ethnic divisions—supported by prebendal networks—still dominate national politics, but the multiethnic parties have at least done fairly well at bridging these many divides during election periods and at fostering a climate of compromise during particularly divisive national debates. Greasing the wheels of these compromises among the elites, however, is preferential treatment in access to public offices, government contracts, and the corrupt spoils of oil wealth. In short, multiethnic parties have widened the circle of corruption, allowing the biggest politicians to build vast patronage networks across ethnic lines and diluting—but not erasing—the ethnocentric aspects of the prebendal system. Lower ethnic tensions have come at the price of greater elite corruption, which may be seen as progress, but which must transition to more accountable party politics if the 92 percent of Nigerians who live on less than $2 per day are to share in the nation's great wealth.

The main vehicle whereby other African countries like Ghana have begun to rise out of this elite corruption trap is through the rise of a unified, viable political opposition, which has not developed in Nigeria. The two main opposition parties, the ANPP and AD (later ACN), never organized a working relationship or a serious policy challenge to the PDP, except in the weeks prior to elections. ANPP leaders generally preferred to work with the PDP in order to gain access to government largesse, and most of its governors joined the PDP by 2010. The courts, however, overturned gubernatorial races in Edo, Osun, Ondo, Ekiti, Imo, and Abia, handing these seats to opposition parties. Complicating matters has been an explosion in the number of political parties.

The PDP took power again in 2011 with a massive majority across Nigeria, controlling the presidency, 23 governorships and 26 state assemblies, and more than half of the seats of the National Assembly. Yet it was also a party in disarray. Amid this infighting, President Jonathan moved to assert control of the party through liberal use of state finances and backed by former President Obasanjo. Jonathan struck a deal with the PDP governors to clinch the party nomination and win the election in 2011, facing down a divided opposition.

# Political Culture, Citizenship, and Identity

Military rule left Nigeria with strong authoritarian influences in its political culture. Most of the younger politicians of the Fourth Republic came of age during military rule and learned the business of politics from Abacha, Babangida, and their military governors. Nigeria's deep democratic traditions discussed in Section 1 remain vibrant among the larger polity, but they are in constant tension with the values imbibed during years of governance when political problems were often solved by military dictate, power, and violence rather than by negotiation and respect for law. This tension was manifest in the irony that the leading presidential contenders in 2003 were all former military men, one of whom—Buhari—was the ringleader of the 1983 coup that overthrew the Second Republic. Perhaps symbolic of a growing shift in Nigerian political culture away from its authoritarian past, however, Umaru Yar'Adua was the nation's first university graduate to become president, and Goodluck Jonathan has a Ph.D. in zoology.

### Modernity versus Traditionalism

The interaction of Western (colonial) elements with traditional (precolonial, African) practices has created the tensions of a modern sociopolitical system that rests uneasily on traditional foundations. Nigerians straddle two worlds, each undergoing constant evolution. On one hand, the strong elements in communal societies that promoted accountability have been weakened by the intrusion of Western culture oriented toward individuality, and exacerbated by urbanization. On the other hand, the modern state has been unable to free itself fully from rival ethnic claims organized around narrow, exclusivist constituencies.

As a result, exclusivist identities continue to dominate Nigerian political culture and to define the nature of citizenship.[27] Individuals tend to identify with their immediate ethnic, regional, and religious groups rather than with state institutions, especially during moments of crisis. Entirely missing from the relationship between state and citizen in Nigeria is a fundamental reciprocity—a working social contract—based on the belief that there is a common interest that binds them.

## Religion

Religion has been a persistent source of comfort and a basis for conflict throughout Nigerian history. Islam began to filter into northeast Nigeria in the eleventh and twelfth centuries, spread to Hausaland by the fifteenth century, and greatly expanded in the early nineteenth century. In the north, Islam first coexisted with, then gradually supplanted, indigenous religions. Christianity arrived in the early nineteenth century, but expanded rapidly through missionary activity in the south. The amalgamation of northern and southern Nigeria in 1914 brought together the two regions and their belief systems. The nation is now evenly divided between Muslims and Christians, and the Middle Belt states where the fault line runs have often been particularly volatile. A handful of violent Islamist groups, notably Boko Haram, have become active in recent years, attacking police stations and setting off bombs in several states and Abuja. Their political agendas are primarily local, but they share an interest in establishing an Islamist state in Nigeria and express common cause with global jihadist groups like Al Qaeda, although they do not yet coordinate activities.

These religious cultures have consistently clashed over political issues such as the secular character of the state. The application of the *shari'a* criminal code in the northern states has been a focal point for these tensions. For many Muslims, the *shari'a* represents a way of life and supreme law that transcends secular and state law; for many Christians, the expansion of *shari'a* law threatens the secular nature of the Nigerian state and their position within it. The pull of religious versus national identity becomes even stronger in times of economic hardship.

## The Press

The plural nature of Nigerian society, with the potential to engender a shared political culture, can be seen in virtually all aspects of public life. The Nigerian press has long been one of the liveliest and most irreverent in Africa. The Abacha regime moved to stifle its independence, as had Babangida. In addition, members of the media are sometimes regarded as captives of ethnic and regional constituencies, a perception that has weakened their capacity to resist attacks on their rights and privileges. Significantly, much of the Nigerian press has been based in a Lagos-Ibadan axis in the southwestern part of Nigeria and has frequently been labeled "southern." Recently, however, independent television and radio stations have proliferated around the country, and forests of satellite towers now span Nigerian cities to support the boom in Internet cafés and telecommunications. Internet-based investigative journalists such as saharareporters. com have utilized the uncensored medium of the Internet to print stories that the mainstream newspapers have been afraid to publish, exposing the corrupt activities of some of Nigeria's biggest politicians.

# Interests, Social Movements, and Protest

Because the political machinery was in the hands of the military throughout the 1980s and 1990s, Nigerians sought alternative means of representation and protest. Historically, labor has played a significant role in Nigerian politics, as have student groups, women's organizations, and various radical and populist organizations. Business groups have frequently supported and colluded with corrupt civilian and military regimes. In the last year of the Abacha regime, however, even the business class, through mechanisms like Vision 2010, began to suggest an end to such arbitrary rule. The termination of military rule has seen civil society groups flourish across Nigeria.

## Labor

**state corporatism**

A political system in which the state requires all members of a particular economic sector to join an officially designated interest group. Such interest groups thus attain public status, and they participate in national policymaking. The result is that the state has great control over the groups, and groups have great control over their members.

Organized labor has played an important role in challenging governments during both the colonial and postcolonial eras in several African countries, Nigeria among them. Continuous military pressure throughout the 1980s and 1990s forced a decline in the independence and strength of organized labor in Nigerian politics. The Babangida regime implemented strategies of **state corporatism** designed to control and co-opt various social forces such as labor. When the leadership of the Nigerian Labour Congress (NLC), the umbrella confederation, took a vigorous stand against the government, the regime sacked the leaders and appointed conservative replacements. Pro-democracy strikes in mid-1994 by the National Petroleum Employees Union (NUPENG) and other sympathetic labor groups significantly reduced oil production and nearly brought the country to a halt, whereupon the Abacha regime arrested and disbanded its leadership.

The Nigerian labor movement has been vulnerable to reprisals by the state and private employers. The government has always been the biggest single employer of labor in Nigeria, as well as the recognized arbiter of industrial relations between employers and employees. Efforts by military regimes to centralize and co-opt the unions caused their militancy and impact to wane. Moreover, ethnic, regional, and religious divisions have often hampered labor solidarity, and these differences have been periodically manipulated by the state. Nevertheless, labor still claims an estimated 2 million members across Nigeria and remains one of the most potent forces in civil society. The unions have a great stake in the consolidation of constitutional rule in the Fourth Republic and the protections that allow them to organize and act freely on behalf of their members. Given the strength of the NLC, the PDP has sought to break it into its constituent unions to dilute its impact, but has so far been unsuccessful. The NLC has called national strikes on a number of occasions since 2000, typically over wages and fuel price hikes.

## The Business Community

Nigeria has a long history of entrepreneurialism and business development. This spirit is compromised by tendencies toward rent-seeking and the appropriation of state resources. Members of the Nigerian business class have been characterized as "pirate capitalists" because of the high level of corrupt practices and collusion with state officials.[28] Many wealthy individuals have served in the military or civilian governments, while others protect their access to state resources by sponsoring politicians or entering into business arrangements with bureaucrats.

Private interests have proven surprisingly resilient, as organized groups have emerged to represent the interests of the business class and to promote general economic development. There are numerous associations throughout Nigeria representing a broad variety of business activities and sectoral interests. National business associations, such as the Nigerian Association of Chambers of Commerce, Industry, Mines, and Agriculture (NACCIMA), the largest in the country, have taken an increasingly political stance, expressing their determination to protect their interests by advocating for better governance.

## Other Social Groups

Student activism continues to be an important feature of Nigerian political life. Since the 1990s, many universities have seen the rise of what are called "cults"—gangs of young men who are typically armed and sometimes do have cultish rituals associated with their groups. Many of these cultists "graduated" to join the militias and thugs of the politicians after 2000, while the cults are also often employed by elites for their power plays. In partial response to the cult phenomenon, religious movements have proliferated across Nigerian universities, providing students with an alternative way of life to these violent groups. Yet the religious groups on campuses have also provided vehicles for encouraging and recruiting both Christian and Muslim fundamentalists.

Growing restiveness over economic hardship and military oppression led to a sharp increase in the number of human rights groups and other nongovernmental organizations (NGOs) since the 1990s.[29] Greater funding for NGOs from foreign governments and private foundations assisted the growth of this sector, most notably in the south but gradually in the north as well. They have generally focused on such issues as civil protection, gender law, health care, media access, and public housing. Most are urban based, although efforts to develop rural networks are underway.

The movement to resist President Obasanjo's third-term bid in May 2006 resurrected some of civil society's previous level of alliance building, as did some of the labor-led protests to Obasanjo's many—and often successful—efforts to raise the price of fuel. Civil society groups also condemned Obasanjo's efforts to provoke an election crisis in 2007, but faced a quandary: If they organized protests to the flawed elections, they might give Obasanjo the excuse he needed to declare a state of emergency. Consequently, few groups resisted the election outcomes, preferring to accept Yar'Adua in order to get rid of Obasanjo, and to fight the more flagrant election violations at the tribunals.

Overall, civil society groups are making substantial contributions to consolidating democracy in Nigeria. In particular, many groups have built good working relationships with the National Assembly and state legislatures, from which both sides have benefited. Their relationships with the political parties, however, remain distant. Nigeria's prospects for building a sustainable democracy during the Fourth Republic will depend, in part, on the willingness of many of these advocacy groups to increase their collaboration with the political parties, while avoiding cooptation and maintaining a high level of vigilance and activism.

## Summary

Legislatures in Nigeria have long been overshadowed by the powerful executive branch, which dominated politics in the military years. Yet in fits and starts, the National Assembly and some state legislatures have begun to reclaim some of their constitutional prerogatives. Another important shift in recent years is from the ethnic parties of the early republics to the multiethnic parties of the present, which create incentives for politicians to build bridges across ethnic lines. These multiethnic parties have, however, been built in part through corruption. Civil society groups, particularly the labor movement, resisted executive dominance under the military and, since 1999, have tried to press for reforms under civilian rule.

# NIGERIAN POLITICS IN TRANSITION

## Focus Questions

What role can political opposition and civil society play in reversing prebendalism and the politics of the "Big Men"?

What other reforms can help to settle the National Question and harness the strong democratic yearnings of the Nigerian public?

Despite the slow progress of the Fourth Republic, Nigerians overwhelmingly favor democratic government over military rule. About 70 percent of respondents in a recent survey said that they still prefer democracy to any other alternative, although popular frustration is growing with the slow pace of reform and continued corruption in politics.[30] Will democracy in Nigeria be consolidated sufficiently to meet minimal levels of public satisfaction, or will the nation again succumb to destructive authoritarian rule?

Nigerian politics must change in fundamental ways for democracy to become more stable and legitimate. First and foremost, the nation must turn from a system of politics dominated by "Big Men"—for all intents and purposes, a competitive oligarchy—to a more representative mode of politics that addresses the fundamental interests of the public. Second, Nigerians must conclusively settle the national question and commit to political arrangements that accommodate the nation's diversity. In short, Nigeria's Fourth Republic must find ways of moving beyond prebendal politics and develop a truly national political process in which mobilization and conflicts along ethnic, regional, and religious lines gradually diminish, and which can address Nigeria's true national crisis: poverty and underdevelopment.

## Political Challenges and Changing Agendas

Nigeria's fitful transition to democratic rule between 1985 and 1999 was inconclusive, largely because it was planned and directed from above. This approach contrasts sharply with the popular-based movements that unseated autocracies in Central and Eastern Europe. The military periodically made promises for democratic transition as a ploy to stabilize and legitimate their governments. General Abubakar dutifully handed power to the civilians in 1999, but only after ensuring that the military's interests would be protected under civilian rule and creating an overly powerful executive that reinforces prebendalism and its patronage system. The military's rapid transition program produced a tenuous, conflicted democratic government that faces daunting tasks of restoring key institutions, securing social stability, and reforming the economy. The continuing strength and influence of collective identities, defined on the basis of religion or ethnicity, are often more binding than national allegiances. The parasitic nature of the Nigerian economy is a further source of instability. Rent-seeking and other unproductive, often corrupt, business activities remain accepted norms of wealth accumulation.

Nonetheless, Nigerians are sowing seeds of change in all of these areas. Attitudes toward the military in government have shifted dramatically. Military attitudes themselves have changed significantly as well, as evidenced by the restraint shown by the armed forces during Yar'Adua's incapacitation and long absence. The decline in the appeal of military rule can be attributed to the abysmal performances of the Babangida and Abacha regimes in economic oversight and governance. Many now recognize that the military, apart from its contributions to national security, is incapable of promoting economic and social progress in Nigeria. With the armed forces seemingly secure in their barracks, the nature of the struggles among civilian political elites will decide the direction of political and economic change. Thus, democratic development may be advanced in the long run if stable coalitions appear over time in a manner that balances the power among contending groups, and if these key elites adapt to essential norms and rules of the political game.

Initially, members of the new political class confined their struggles within the constraints of the democratic system: using the courts, media, legislative struggles, and even legal expediencies such as impeachment. Political actors largely worked through formal institutions, contending openly and offsetting the power of a single group or faction. Since the 2003 elections, however, the political elite have also shown a growing willingness to use extra-systemic measures to forward their interests through election rigging, corruption, and militia-led violence. The Niger Delta has grown particularly violent, with increasingly well-armed militias that in some cases have shown a measure of independence from their political patrons.

The next critical step down the long road of democratic development for Nigeria is the creation of a viable, multiethnic opposition party that is also loyal, meaning that it plays by the rules of the system. Opposition parties help to reduce corruption in the system because they have an interest in exposing the misconduct of the ruling party, which in turn pressures them to restrain their own behavior. Furthermore, in order to unseat the ruling party and win elections, opposition parties need to engage the public to win their votes. In this manner, issues of interest to the public are engaged by the parties. This is the basis of the social contract: Elites gain the privilege of power so long as they use it to promote the public interest.

The introduction of so many new parties since 2002 has hurt the development of a viable, loyal opposition, further diluting it and allowing the PDP to govern largely unchecked. The PDP has also worked to absorb or co-opt opposition leaders when possible. Worse, several minor parties have managed to win only narrow ethnic constituencies, raising the specter that Nigeria may return to the ruinous ethnic party politics of the past. Yet the larger of these opposition parties could also provide the

© PIUS UTOMI EKPEI/AFP/Getty Images

Protests over federal exploitation of the oil-producing Niger Delta sparked a region-wide insurgency by 2003, with heavily armed militias engaged in both political disputes and criminal activities, cutting Nigeria's oil production by more than a quarter.

building blocks of a viable opposition party or coalition if the PDP implodes along its strong internal divisions.

The project of building a coherent nation-state out of competing nationalities remains unfinished. Ironically, because the parties of the Fourth Republic generally do not represent any particular ethnic interest—indeed, they do not represent anyone's interests except those of the leaders and their clients—ethnic associations and militias have risen to articulate ethnic-based grievances. Ethnic consciousness cannot—and should not—be eliminated from society, but ethnicity cannot be the main basis for political competition. If current ethnic mobilization can be contained within ethnic associations arguing over the agenda of the parties, then it can be managed. If, however, any of the ethnic associations captures one of the political parties or joins with the militias to foment separatism, instability will result. The Niger Delta has gone furthest down this road, with a number of militias that have voiced ethno-nationalist demands, some of which verge on separatism.

Democratic development also requires further decentralization of power structures in Nigeria. The struggle on the part of the National Assembly and the state governors to wrest power from the presidency has advanced this process, as has the growing competence and role of the judiciary. Privatization of government parastatals could also reduce the power of the presidency over time, since it will no longer control all the primary sectors of the economy. A more decentralized system allows local problems to be solved within communities rather than involving national institutions and the accompanying interethnic competition. Decentralization also lowers the stakes for holding national offices, thereby reducing the destructive pressures on political competition and political office. The devolution of power and resources to smaller units, closer to their constituents, can substantially enhance the accountability of leaders and the transparency of government operations.

Civil society groups are the final link in democratic consolidation in Nigeria. These groups are critical players in connecting the Nigerian state to the Nigerian people. They aggregate and articulate popular interests into the policy realm, and they provide advocacy on behalf of their members. If the political parties are to reflect anything more than elite interests and clientelist rule, the parties must reach out and build alliances with the institutions of civil society. For opposition parties to become a viable opposition movement capable of checking the power of the PDP, they will have to build alliances with civil society groups in order to mobilize large portions of the population, particularly labor unions. Foreign pressure also plays an important role in maintaining the quest for democracy and sustainable development. In recent years, major external forces have been more forthright in supporting civil society and democratization in Nigeria. The United States, Britain, and some member states of the European Union quite visibly exerted pressure on Babangida and Abacha to leave and applied modest sanctions in support of democracy. These same governments again pressed Nigerian leaders to name Jonathan acting president during the crisis over President Yar'Adua's incapacitation.

Nevertheless, the Western commitment to development and democracy in Africa is limited by the industrial powers' addiction to oil, which has blunted the impact of such pressure on Nigeria, and is now exacerbated by growing competition from China for energy resources. Much of the initiative for Africa's growth therefore needs to emerge from within. In Nigeria, such initiatives will depend on substantial changes in the way Nigerians do business. It will be necessary to develop a more sophisticated and far less corrupt form of capitalist enterprise and the development of entrepreneurial, particularly middle class interests within Nigeria who will see their interests tied to the principles of democratic politics and economic initiative. The middle class is beginning to grow under democratic rule, but it remains small and vulnerable to economic and political instability.

Nigerian politics has been characterized by turmoil and periodic crises ever since the British relinquished colonial power. Over fifty years later, the country is still trying to piece together a fragile democracy, while per capita incomes are scarcely higher than at independence. Despite a number of positive trends, the nation continues to wrestle with overdependence of its economy on oil, enfeebled infrastructure and institutions, heightened sociopolitical tensions, an irresponsible elite, and an expanding mass culture of despondency and rage. Only responsible government combined with sustained civil society action can reverse this decline and restore the nation to what President Obasanjo called "the path to greatness."

# Nigerian Politics in Comparative Perspective

The study of Nigeria has important implications for the study of African politics and, more broadly, of comparative politics. The Nigerian case embodies a number of key themes and issues that can be generalized. We can learn much about how democratic regimes are established and consolidated by understanding Nigeria's pitfalls and travails. Analysis of the historical dynamics of Nigeria's ethnic conflict helps to identify institutional mechanisms that may be effective in reducing ethnic conflict in other states. We can also learn much about the necessary and sufficient conditions for economic development, and the particular liabilities of oil-dependent states. Each of these issues offers comparative lessons for the major themes explored in this book: the world of states, governing the economy, the democratic idea, and the politics of collective identities.

## A World of States

Nigeria exists in two "worlds" of states: one in the global political economy and the other within Africa. We have addressed at length Nigeria's position in the world. Economically, Nigeria was thrust into the world economy in a position of weakness, first as a British colony and later as an independent nation. Despite its resources and the potential of oil to provide the investment capital needed to build a modern economy, Nigeria has grown weaker. It has lost much of its international clout, and in place of the international respect it once enjoyed as a developing giant within Africa, the country became notorious throughout the 1990s for corruption, human rights abuses, and failed governance. The return of democracy and soaring oil prices have restored some of Nigeria's former stature, but its economic vulnerability and persistent corruption keep it a secondary player in the world of states.

The future of democracy, political stability, and economic renewal in other parts of Africa, and certainly in West Africa, will be greatly influenced for good or ill by unfolding events in Nigeria, the giant of the continent. Beyond the obvious demonstration effects, the economy of the West African subregion could be buoyed by substantial growth in the Nigerian economy. In addition, President Obasanjo conducted very active public diplomacy across Africa, seeking to resolve major conflicts, promote democracy, and improve trade. President Yar'Adua was far less active in foreign policy, and cultivated stronger ties with China. President Jonathan has strong ties with the United States, but has yet to define his African policy further abroad.

Thus far, international political and business attention has shifted elsewhere on the continent, focusing on such countries as South Africa, Botswana, and Ghana. Growing insurgency in the Niger Delta has also meant that Nigeria has even fallen behind Angola as the largest oil producer on the continent. This portends a danger of greater marginalization, reflecting the expanding patchwork of Africa among areas of stability and growth, contrasted with areas of turmoil and decay.

## Governing the Economy

Nigeria provides important insights into the political economy of underdevelopment. At independence in 1960, Nigeria was stronger economically than its Southeast Asian counterparts Indonesia and Malaysia. Independent Nigeria appeared poised for growth, with a wealth of natural resources, a large population, and the presence of highly entrepreneurial groups in many regions of the country. Today, Nigeria is among the poorest countries in the world in terms of per capita income, while many of its Asian counterparts have joined the ranks of the wealthy countries. One critical lesson Nigeria teaches is that a rich endowment of resources is not enough to ensure economic development. In fact, it may encourage rent-seeking behavior that undermines more productive activities.[31] Sound political and institutional development must come first.

Other variables are critically important, notably democratic stability and a capable developmental state. A developmentalist ethic, and an institutional structure to enforce it, can set limits to corrupt behavior and constrain the pursuit of short-term personal gain at the expense of national economic growth. Institutions vital to the pursuit of these objectives include a professional civil service, an independent judiciary, and a free press. Nigeria has had each of these, but they were gradually undermined and corrupted under military rule. The public "ethic" that has come to dominate Nigerian political economy has been prebendalism. Where corruption is unchecked, economic development suffers accordingly.

Nigeria also demonstrates that sustainable economic development requires sound economic policy. Without export diversification, commodity-exporting countries are buffeted by the price fluctuations of one or two main products. This situation can be traced back to overreliance on primary commodity export-oriented policies bequeathed by the British colonial regime. Yet other former colonies, such as Malaysia and Indonesia, have managed to diversify their initial export base. Nigeria, by contrast, has substituted one form of commodity dependence for another, and it has allowed its petroleum industry to overwhelm all other sectors of the economy. Nigeria even became a net importer of products (for example, palm oil and palm nuts) for which it was once a leading world producer. Nigeria is even in the absurd position of being unable to feed itself, despite rich agricultural lands. In comparative perspective, we can see that natural resource endowments can be tremendously beneficial. The United States, for example, has parlayed its endowments of agricultural, mineral, and energy resources into one of the world's most diversified modern economies. Meanwhile Japan, which is by comparison poorly endowed with natural resources, has one of the strongest economies in the world, achieved in large part through its unique developmental strategies. Each of these examples illustrates the primacy of sound economic policies implemented through consolidated political systems.

## The Democratic Idea

Many African countries have experienced transitions from authoritarian rule.[32] With the end of superpower competition in Africa and the withdrawal of external support for Africa's despots, many African societies experienced a resurgence of popular pressures for greater participation in political life and more open forms of governance.

Decades of authoritarian, single-party, and military rule in Africa left a dismal record of political repression, human rights abuses, inequality, deteriorating governance, and failed economies. A handful of elites acquired large fortunes through wanton corruption. The exercise of postcolonial authoritarian rule in Africa has contributed to economic stagnation and decline. The difficulties of such countries as Cameroon, Togo, and Zimbabwe in achieving political transitions reflects, in large part, the ruling elites' unwillingness to cede control of the political instruments that made possible their self-enrichment.

Nigeria exemplifies the harsh reality of authoritarian and unaccountable governance. Nigerians have endured six military regimes, countless attempted coups, and a bloody civil war that claimed more than 1 million lives. They have also seen a once-prospering economy reduced to a near shambles. Today, democracy has become a greater imperative because only such a system provides the mechanisms to limit abuses of power and render governments accountable.

## Collective Identities

Nigeria presents an important case in which to study the dangers of communal competition in a society with deep cultural divisions. How can multiethnic countries manage diversity? What institutional mechanisms can be employed to avert tragedies such as the 1967–1970 civil war or the continuing conflicts that have brought great suffering to Rwanda and the former Yugoslavia? This chapter has suggested institutional reforms such as multiethnic political parties, decentralization, and a strengthened federal system that can contribute to reducing tensions and minimizing conflict.

Insights from the Nigerian experience may explain why some federations persist, while identifying factors that can undermine them. Nigeria's complex social map, and its varied attempts to create a nation out of its highly diverse population, enhances our understanding of the politics of cultural pluralism and the difficulties of accommodating sectional interests under conditions of political and economic insecurity. Federal character in Nigeria has become a form of ethnic and regional favoritism and a tool for dispensing patronage. Yet the country has benefited in some ways from the attention devoted to creating state and local governments, and from giving people in different regions a sense of being stakeholders in the entity called Nigeria.

## Summary

Despite 30 years of military rule followed by over a decade of corrupt civilian government, the democratic yearning of the Nigerian public remains strong. If viable political opposition backed by civil society and public support can rise to balance the PDP and break its near-monopoly on power, then in time prebendalism will give way to more responsible, democratic government. Public frustrations, however, are growing at the slow pace of reform and economic development.

## Chapter Summary

Colonialism forced many nations under one political roof, ensuring that ethnic divisions would dominate the nation's politics after independence in 1960, leading to collapse and civil war. Military rule for nearly 30 years after the war, greased by rents from the oil industry, reunified Nigeria under a federal system, but also fed the prebendal pattern that has corrupted the politics of the Fourth Republic.

Nigeria's challenges reflect the frustrated hopes of its people for a better life, stable government, and a democratic political order, while suggesting the potential contributions that this country could make to the African continent and the wider international arena. Such potential depends upon responsive and capable democratic governance. If Nigeria cannot reverse the corrupt, prebendal status quo, however, then the specter will remain of military entrepreneurs, or ethnic and religious extremists, plunging Nigeria into another cycle of coups, decline, and possibly collapse.

## Key Terms

authoritarianism
legitimacy
accountability
unfinished state
*jihad*
acephalous societies
indirect rule
warrant chiefs
interventionist

clientelism
autocracy
rents
structural adjustment program
    (SAP)
international financial institutions
    (IFIs)
balance of payments
privitization

Economic Community
    of West African States
    (ECOWAS)
parastatals
*shari'a*
prebendalism
civil society
state corporatism

## Suggested Readings

Aborisade, Oladimeji, and Robert J. Mundt. *Politics in Nigeria*, 2nd ed. New York: Longman, 2002.

Achike, Okay. *Public Administration: A Nigerian and Comparative Perspective*. London: Longman, 1978.

Adamolekun, L. *Politics and Administration in Nigeria*. London: Hutchinson, 1986.

Agbaje, Adigun. *The Nigerian Press: Hegemony and the Social Construction of Legitimacy, 1960–1983*. Lewiston, NY: Edwin Mellen Press, 1992.

Agbaje, Adigun. "Twilight of Democracy in Nigeria." *Africa Demos* 3, no. 3:5. Atlanta: The Carter Center of Emory University, 1994.

Beckett, Paul A., and Crawford Young, eds. *Dilemmas of Democracy in Nigeria*. Rochester, NY: University of Rochester Press, 1997.

Bienen, Henry. *Political Conflict and Economic Change in Nigeria*. London: Frank Cass, 1988.

Diamond, Larry. *Class, Ethnicity and Democracy in Nigeria: The Failure of the First Republic*. London: Macmillan, 1988.

Diamond, Larry. "Nigeria: The Uncivic Society and the Descent into Praetorianism." In Larry Diamond, J. Linz, and S. M. Lipset, eds., *Politics in Developing Countries: Comparing Experiences with Democracy*, 2nd ed. Boulder, CO: Lynne Rienner Publishers, 1995, pp. 417–491.

Decalo, Samuel. *Coups and Army Rule in Africa*, 2nd ed. New Haven: Yale University Press, 1990.

Dudley, Billy. *An Introduction to Nigerian Government and Politics*. Bloomington: Indiana University Press, 1982.

Ekeh, Peter P., and Eghosa E. Osaghae, eds. *Federal Character and Federalism in Nigeria*. Ibadan: Heinemann, 1989.

Falola, Toyin. *Violence in Nigeria: The Crisis of Religious Politics and Secular Ideologies*. Rochester, NY: University of Rochester Press, 1999.

Forrest, Tom. *Politics and Economic Development in Nigeria*. Boulder, CO: Westview Press, 1993.

Horowitz, Donald L. *Ethnic Groups in Conflict*. Berkeley: University of California Press, 1985.

Joseph, Richard A. *Democracy and Prebendal Politics in Nigeria: The Rise and Fall of the Second Republic*. Cambridge: Cambridge University Press, 1987.

Kew, Darren. "Nigerian elections and the neopatrimonial paradox: In search of the social contract," *Journal of Contemporary African Studies* 28, no. 4 (2010): 499–521.

Kirk-Greene, Anthony, and Douglas Rimmer. *Nigeria since 1970: A Political and Economic Outline*. London: Hodder and Stoughton, 1981.

Lewis, Peter M. "Endgame in Nigeria? The Politics of a Failed Democratic Transition." *African Affairs* 93 (1994): 323–340.

Lewis, Peter M., Barnett R. Rubin, and Pearl T. Robinson. *Stabilizing Nigeria: Pressures, Incentives, and Support for Civil Society*. New York: Century Foundation for the Council on Foreign Relations, 1998.

Lubeck, Paul. *Islam and Urban Labor in Northern Nigeria*. Cambridge: Cambridge University Press, 1987.

Luckham, Robin. *The Nigerian Military: A Sociological Analysis of Authority and Revolt, 1960–67*. Cambridge: Cambridge University Press, 1971.

Melson, Robert, and Howard Wolpe, eds. *Nigeria: Modernization and the Politics of Communalism*. East Lansing: Michigan State University Press, 1971.

Nyang'oro, Julius, and Tim Shaw, eds. *Corporatism in Africa: Comparative Analysis and Practice*. Boulder, CO: Westview Press, 1989.

Olukoshi, Adebayo, ed. *The Politics of Structural Adjustment in Nigeria*. London: James Currey Publishers, 1993.

Osaghae, Eghosa. *Crippled Giant: Nigeria since Independence*. Bloomington: Indiana University Press, 1998.

Oyediran, Oyeleye, ed. *Nigerian Government and Politics under Military Rule*. London: Macmillan, 1979.

Reno, William. *Warlord Politics and African States*. Boulder, CO: Lynne Rienner Publishers, 1998.

Sklar, Richard L. *Nigerian Political Parties: Power in an Emergent African Nation*. New York: NOK Publishers, 1983.

Soyinka, Wole. *Open Sore of a Continent*. Oxford: Oxford University Press, 1996.

Suberu, Rotimi. *Federalism and Ethnic Conflict in Nigeria*. Washington, DC: U.S. Institute of Peace, 2001.

Watts, Michael, ed. *State, Oil, and Agriculture in Nigeria*. Berkeley: University of California Press, 1987.

Wunsch, James S., and Dele Olowu, eds. *The Failure of the Centralized State: Institutions and Self-Governance in Africa*. Boulder, CO: Westview Press, 1990.

Young, Crawford. *The Rising Tide of Cultural Pluralism: The Nation-State at Bay?* Madison: University of Wisconsin Press, 1993.

## Suggested Websites

British Broadcasting Corporation: A 2002 interview with President Obasanjo
**news.bbc.co.uk/2/hi/talking_point/1800826.stm**

Gamji: A collection of news stories from Nigerian newspapers, as well as opinion pieces and other news links
**www.gamji.com**

*The Guardian,* Nigeria's leading daily newspaper
**www.ngrguardiannews.com**

Human Rights Watch reports
**hrw.org/doc/?t=africa&c=nigeri**

International Institute for Democracy and Electoral Assistance
**archive.idea.int/frontpage_nigeria.htm**

Stanford University's Center for African Studies
**http://africanstudies.stanford.edu/**

# 13  Iran

Ervand Abrahamian

**Official Name:** Islamic Republic of Iran (Jomhuri-ye Eslami-ye Iran)

**Location:** Middle East (West Asia)

**Capital City:** Tehran

**Population (2010):** 66.4 million

**Size:** approximately 1,648,000 sq. km.; slightly larger than Alaska

## CHRONOLOGY of Modern Iran's Political Development

**1925**
Reza Khan establishes
the Pahlavi dynasty.

**1953**
CIA-supported coup
overthrows Mossadeq.

**1941–1945**
Allied occupation
of Iran during
World War II.

**1963**
Shah launches
"White
Revolution."

| 1920 | 1940 | 1950 | 1960 | 1965 | 1970 | 1975 |
|---|---|---|---|---|---|---|

**1941**
Muhammad Reza
Pahlavi becomes
Shah of Iran.

**1975**
Shah establishes
the Resurgence
Party.

**1921**
Colonel Reza Khan's
military coup.

**1951**
Nationalization of
the oil industry by
government of Prime
Minister Mossadeq.

**1905–1911**
Constitutional Revolution.

# SECTION 1 THE MAKING OF THE MODERN IRANIAN STATE

## Focus Questions

To what extent does language, history, and religion give Iran a distinct identity?

How did Muhammad Reza Shah come to power, and what role did the United States play in supporting him?

What led to the Islamic Revolution of 1979?

Who was Ayatollah Ruhollah Khomeini, and what influence did he have on the Islamic Republic of Iran?

**ayatollah**

Literally, "sign of God." High-ranking cleric in Iran.

**civil society**

Refers to the space occupied by voluntary associations outside the state, for example, professional associations, trade unions, and student groups.

## Politics in Action

In 1997, Iran elected Muhammad Khatami president of the Islamic Republic. He was reelected in 2001 by an increased majority. Khatami a middle-ranking cleric was not a high-ranking **ayatollah**. He had promised to create a more open **civil society** and improve the country's "sick economy." He stressed the importance of protecting individual liberties, freedom of expression, women's rights, political pluralism, and the rule of law. He even promoted better relations with the United States and other Western nations.

Commentators, inside and outside the country, had considered the election a shoo-in for Khatami's conservative rival. But Khatami won 70 percent of the vote. Once in office, President Khatami liberalized the press, established new political parties, and initiated a "dialogue of civilizations" with the West.

In 2005, Iranian voters again voted for change—in the opposite direction. Mahmoud Ahmadinejad, the ultraconservative mayor of Tehran, won over 60 percent of the vote. He had promised to reduce poverty, promote social justice, and end corruption. He also promised to reverse many of the liberal changes implemented under Khatami. He denounced the West as "decadent" and took a hard line on relations with the United States and on Israel, which he said should be "wiped off the map." He particularly defended Iran's right to develop nuclear energy, which he claimed would be used only for peaceful purposes. He insisted the United States had no right to tell other nations what types of technology they could develop. Ahmadinejad was reelected in 2009 in a highly controversial election that resulted in mass protests and widespread accusations of ballot rigging.

These very different electoral outcomes illustrate the contradictory political forces at work in the Islamic Republic of Iran. Iran is a mixture of **theocracy** and democracy. Its political system is based on both clerical authority and popular sovereignty, on the divine right of the clergy and the rights of the people, on concepts

## Timeline

**1979**
Islamic Revolution; Shah forced into exile; Iran becomes an Islamic Republic; Ayatollah Khomeini becomes Leader.

**March 1980**
Elections for the First Islamic *Majles* (parliament). Subsequent Majles elections every four years.

**June 1981**
President Bani-Sadr ousted by Khomeini, replaced by Muhammad Ali Rajai.

**2005**
Ultraconservative Mahmoud Ahmadinejad elected president.

| 1979 | 1980 | 1985 | 1990 | 2000 | 2005 |
|------|------|------|------|------|------|

**1979–1981**
Hostage crisis—52 U.S. embassy employees held by radical students.

**December 1979**
Referendum on the Islamic constitution.

**October 1981**
Ayatollah Ali Khamenei elected president.

**January 1980**
Abol-Hassan Bani-Sadr elected president.

**1980–1988**
War with Iraq.

**1989**
Khomeini dies; Khamenei appointed Leader; Rafsanjani elected president (reelected in 1993).

**1997**
Muhammad Khatami elected president on reform platform (reelected in 2001).

**2009**
Ahmadinejad re-elected; large-scale protests against alleged electoral fraud take place in Tehran and other cities.

---

derived from early Islam and from modern democratic principles. Iran has regular elections for the presidency and the **Majles** (Parliament), but the clerically dominated **Guardian Council** determines who can run. The president is the formal head of the executive branch. But he can be overruled, even dismissed, by the chief cleric, the **Leader** known in the West as the **Supreme Leader**. The president appoints the minister of justice, but the whole judiciary is under the supervision of the chief judge, who is appointed directly by the Leader. The *Majles* is the legislature, but bills do not become law unless the Guardian Council deems them compatible with Islam and the Islamic constitution.

## Geographic Setting

Iran is three times the size of France, slightly larger than Alaska, and much larger than its immediate neighbors. Most of its territory is inhospitable to agriculture. Rain-fed agriculture is confined mostly to the northwest and the provinces along the Caspian Sea. Only pastoral nomads can survive in the semiarid zones and in the high mountain valleys. Thus, 67 percent of the total population of near 66 million is concentrated on 27 percent of the land—mostly in the Caspian region, in the northwest provinces, and in the cities of Tehran, Mashed, Isfahan, Tabriz, Shiraz, and Qom.

Iran is the second-largest oil producer in the Middle East and the fourth-largest in the world, and oil revenues have made Iran an urbanized and partly industrialized country. Nearly 68 percent of the population lives in urban centers; 70 percent of the labor force is employed in industry and services; 83 percent of adults are literate; life expectancy has reached over seventy years; and the majority of Iranians enjoy a standard of living well above that found in most of Asia and Africa. Iran can no longer be described as a typically poor underdeveloped Third World country. It is a middle-income country with a per capita income above that of Mexico, Brazil, and South Africa.

Iran lies on the strategic crossroads between Central Asia and Turkey, between the Indian subcontinent and the Middle East, and between the Arabian Peninsula and the Caucasus Mountains, which are often considered a boundary between Europe and Asia. This has made the region vulnerable to invaders.

The population today reflects these historic invasions. Some 51 percent speak Persian (**Farsi**), an Indo-European language, as their first language; 26 percent speak dialects of Turkic, mainly Azeri and Turkman; 8 percent speak Gilaki or Mazandarani, distinct Persian dialects; 7 percent speak Kurdish, another Indo-European language; and 3 percent speak Arabic. Use of Persian, however, has dramatically increased

---

**theocracy**

A state dominated by the clergy, who rule on the grounds that they are the only interpreters of God's will and law.

**Majles**

The Iranian parliament, from the Arabic term for "assembly."

**Guardian Council**

A committee created in the Iranian constitution to oversee the *Majles* (the parliament).

**Leader/Supreme Leader**

A cleric elected to be the head of the Islamic Republic of Iran.

**Farsi**

Persian word for the Persian language. Fars is a province in Central Iran.

| Table 13.1 | Political Organization |
|---|---|
| **Political System** | A mixture of democracy and theocracy (rule of the clergy) headed by a cleric with the title of the Leader. |
| **Regime History** | Islamic Republic since the 1979 Islamic Revolution. |
| **Administrative Structure** | Centralized administration with 30 provinces. The interior minister appoints the provincial governor-generals. |
| **Executive** | President and his cabinet. The president is chosen by the general electorate every four years. The president chooses his cabinet ministers, but they need to obtain the approval of the Majles (parliament). |
| **Legislature** | Unicameral. The Majles, formed of 290 seats, is elected every four years. It has multiple-member districts with the top runners in the elections taking the seats. Bills passed by the Majles do not become law unless they have the approval of the clerically dominated Council of Guardians. |
| **Judiciary** | A Chief Judge and a Supreme Court independent of the executive and legislature but appointed by the Leader. |
| **Party System** | The ruling clergy restricts most party and organizational activities. |

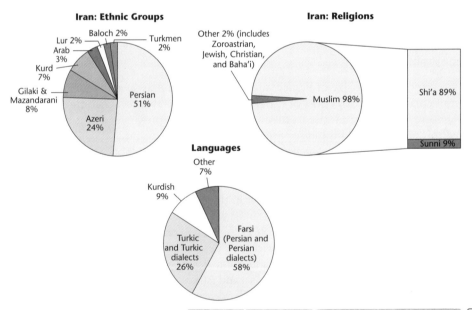

**Iran: Ethnic Groups**

Baloch 2%
Lur 2%
Turkmen 2%
Arab 3%
Kurd 7%
Gilaki & Mazandarani 8%
Persian 51%
Azeri 24%

**Iran: Religions**

Other 2% (includes Zoroastrian, Jewish, Christian, and Baha'i)
Muslim 98%
Shi'a 89%
Sunni 9%

**Languages**

Other 7%
Kurdish 9%
Turkic and Turkic dialects 26%
Farsi (Persian and Persian dialects) 58%

**Iranian Currency**
Rial (ریال)
International Designation: IRR
Exchange Rate (2010): US$1 = 10,308
1000 Rial Note Design: Ayatollah Ruhollah Khomeini (1902–1989),
Supreme Leader (1979–1989)

**FIGURE 13.1 The Iranian Nation at a Glance**

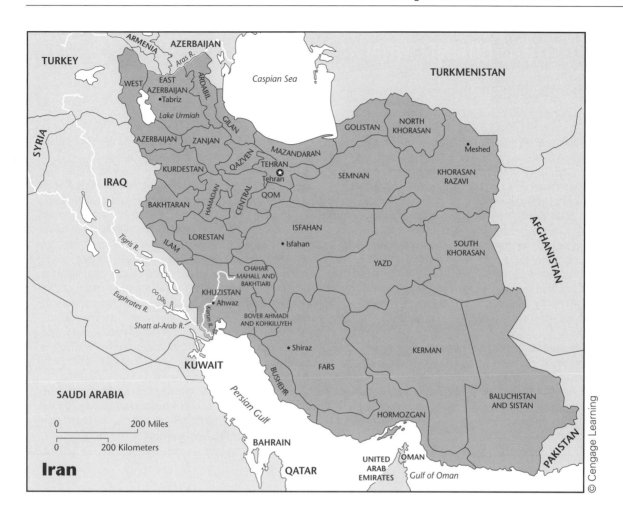

**Iran**

in recent years because of successful literacy campaigns. Over 90 percent of the population can now communicate in Persian, the national language. Although Iran shares many religious and cultural features with the rest of the Middle East, its Persian heritage gives it a national identity distinct from that of the Arab and Turkish world. Iranians by no means consider themselves part of the Arab world.

# Critical Junctures

### The Safavids (1501–1722)

The Safavid dynasty conquered the territory that is now Iran in the sixteenth century and forcibly converted their subjects to Shi'ism, even though the vast majority had been Sunnis. By the mid-seventeenth century, Sunnism survived only among the tribal groups at the periphery.

Safavid Iran also contained small communities of Jews, Zoroastrians, and Christians. The Safavids tolerated religious minorities as long as they paid special taxes and accepted royal authority. According to Islam, Christians, Jews, and Zoroastrians were to be tolerated as legitimate **People of the Book**, because they were mentioned in the Holy **Qur'an** and possessed their own sacred texts: the Bible, the Torah, and the Avesta.

**People of the Book**

The Muslim term for recognized religious minorities, such as Christians, Jews, and Zoroastrians.

**Qur'an**

The Muslim Bible.

## THE GLOBAL CONNECTION

### Islam and Shi'ism

Islam, with over 1 billion adherents, is the second-largest religion in the world after Christianity. Islam means literally "submission to God," and a Muslim is someone who has submitted to God—the same God that Jews and Christians worship. Islam has one central tenet: "There is only one God, and Muhammad is His Prophet." Muslims, in order to consider themselves faithful, need to perform the following four duties to the best of their ability: give to charity; pray every day facing Mecca, where Abraham is believed to have built the first place of worship; make a pilgrimage at least once in a lifetime to Mecca, which is located in modern Saudi Arabia; and fast during the daytime hours in the month of Ramadan to commemorate God's revelation of the Qur'an (Koran, or Holy Book) to the Prophet Muhammad. These four, together with the central tenet, are known as the Five Pillars of Islam.

From its earliest days, Islam has been divided into two major branches: Sunni, meaning literally "followers of tradition," and Shi'i, literally "partisans of Ali." Sunnis are by far in the majority worldwide. Shi'is constitute less than 10 percent of Muslims worldwide and are concentrated in Iran, southern Iraq, Bahrain, eastern Turkey, Azerbaijan, and southern Lebanon.

Although both branches accept the Five Pillars, they differ mostly over who should have succeeded the Prophet Muhammad (d. 632). The Sunnis recognized the early dynasties that ruled the Islamic empire with the exalted title of caliph ("Prophet's Deputy"). The Shi'is, however, argued that as soon as the Prophet died, his authority should have been passed on to Imam Ali, the Prophet's close companion, disciple, and son-in-law. They further argue that Imam Ali passed his authority to his direct male heirs, the third of whom, Imam Husayn, had been martyred fighting the Sunnis in 680, and the twelfth of whom had supposedly gone into hiding in 941.

The Shi'is are also known as Twelvers since they follow the Twelve Imams. They refer to the Twelfth Imam as the *Mahdi*, the Hidden Imam, and believe him to be the Messiah who will herald the end of the world. Furthermore, they argue that in his absence, the authority to interpret the **shari'a** (religious law) should be in the hands of the senior clerical scholars—the ayatollahs. Thus, from the beginning, the Shi'is harbored ambivalent attitudes toward the state, especially if the rulers were Sunnis or lacked genealogical links to the Twelve Imams. For Sunnis, the *shari'a* is based mostly on the Qur'an and the teachings of the Prophet. For Shi'is, it is based also on the teachings of the Twelve Imams.

---

**shari'a**

Islamic law derived mostly from the Qur'an and the examples set by the Prophet Muhammad.

The Safavids governed through Persian scribes and Shi'i clerics as well as through tribal chiefs, large landowners, religious notables, city merchants, guild elders, and urban ward leaders.

The Safavid army was formed mostly of tribal cavalry led by tribal chieftains. Safavid revenues came mostly from land taxes levied on the peasantry. The Safavids claimed absolute power, but they lacked a central state and had to cooperate with many semi-independent local leaders.

### The Qajars (1794–1925)

In 1722 Afghan tribesmen invaded the capital. After a half-century of civil war the Qajars—a Turkic-speaking Shi'i tribe—reconquered much of Iran. They moved the capital to Tehran and recreated the Safavid system of central manipulation and court administration. They also declared Shi'ism to be the state religion, even though they, unlike the Safavids, did not boast of genealogical links to the Twelve Imams. Since these new shahs, or kings, did not pretend to wear the Imam's mantle, Shi'i clerical leaders could claim to be the main interpreters of Islam.

Qajar rule coincided with the peak of European imperialism in the nineteenth century. The Russians seized parts of Central Asia and the Caucasus region from Iran and extracted major economic concessions. The British Imperial Bank won the monopoly to issue paper money. The Indo-European Telegraph Company got a contract to extend communication lines throughout the country. Exclusive rights to drill for oil in the southwest were sold to a British citizen. Iranians increasingly felt their whole country had been auctioned off.

These resentments led to the constitutional revolution of 1905–1909. The 1906 constitution introduced elections, separation of powers, laws made by a legislative assembly, and the concepts of popular sovereignty and the nation (*mellat*). It retained the monarchy, but centered political power in a national assembly called the *Majles*.

The constitution gave the *Majles* extensive authority over all laws, budgets, treaties, loans, concessions, and the make-up of the cabinet. The ministers were accountable to the *Majles*, not to the shah. The constitution also included a bill of rights guaranteeing equality before the law, protection of life and property, safeguards from arbitrary arrest, and freedom of expression and association.

Shi'ism was declared Iran's official religion. Clerical courts continued to implement the *shari'a*. A Guardian Council of senior clerics elected by the *Majles* had veto power over parliamentary bills it deemed un-Islamic.

The initial euphoria soon gave way to deep disillusionment. Pressures from the European powers continued, and a devastating famine after World War I took some 1 million lives, almost 10 percent of the total population. Internal conflicts polarized the *Majles* into warring liberal and conservative factions. Liberals, mostly members of the intelligentsia, championed social reforms, especially the replacement of the *shari'a* with a modern legal code. Conservatives, led by landlords, tribal chiefs, and senior clerics, vehemently opposed such reforms, particularly land reform, women's rights, and the granting of full equality to religious minorities.

The central government, without any real army, bureaucracy, or tax-collecting machinery, could not administer the provinces. During World War I, Russia and Britain formally carved up Iran into three zones. Russia occupied the north, Britain the south. Iran was left with a small middle "neutral zone."

By 1921, Iran was in complete disarray. According to a British diplomat, the propertied classes, fearful of communism, were anxiously seeking "a savior on horseback."[1]

### The Pahlavis (1925–1979)

In February 1921 Colonel Reza Khan carried out a **coup d'état**. He replaced the cabinet and consolidated power in his own hands. Four years later, he deposed the Qajars and crowned himself shah-in-shah—king of kings—and established the Pahlavi dynasty. This was the first nontribal dynasty to rule the whole of Iran.

Reza Shah ruled with an iron fist until 1941, when the British and the Soviets invaded Iran to stop Nazi Germany from establishing a foothold there. Reza Shah promptly abdicated in favor of his son, Muhammad Reza Shah, and went into exile, where he soon died. In the first twelve years of his reign, the young shah retained control over the armed forces but had to tolerate a free press, an independent judiciary, competitive elections, assertive cabinet ministers, and boisterous parliaments. He also had to confront two vigorous political movements: the communist Tudeh (Masses) Party and the National Front, led by the charismatic Dr. Muhammad Mossadeq (1882–1967).

The Tudeh drew its support mostly from working-class trade unions. The National Front drew its support mainly from the salaried middle classes and campaigned to nationalize the British company that controlled the petroleum industry. Mossadeq also wanted to sever the shah's links with the armed forces. In 1951, Mossadeq was elected prime minister and promptly nationalized the oil industry. The period of relative freedom, however, ended abruptly in 1953, when royalist army officers overthrew

**coup d'état**

A forceful, extra-constitutional action resulting in the removal of an existing government, usually carried out by the military.

Mossadeq and installed the shah with absolute power. The coup was financed by the U.S. Central Intelligence Agency (CIA) and the British. This intensified anti-British sentiment and created a deep distrust of the United States. It also made the shah appear to be a puppet of foreign powers.

The Pahlavi dynasty built Iran's first highly centralized state. The armed forces grew from fewer than 40,000 in 1925 to 124,000 in 1941, and to over 410,000 in 1979. The armed forces were supplemented by a pervasive secret police known as SAVAK.

Iran's bureaucracy expanded to twenty-one ministries employing over 300,000 civil servants in 1979. The Education Ministry grew twentyfold. The powerful Interior Ministry appointed provincial governors, town mayors, district superintendents, and village headmen; it could even rig *Majles* elections and create rubber-stamp parliaments.

The Justice Ministry supplanted the *shari'a* with a European-style civil code and the clerical courts with a modern judicial system culminating in a Supreme Court. The Transport Ministry built an impressive array of bridges, ports, highways, and railroads known as the Trans-Iranian Railway. The Ministry of Industries financed numerous factories specializing in consumer goods. The Agricultural Ministry became prominent in 1963 when the shah made land reform the centerpiece of his "White Revolution." This White Revolution was an effort to promote economic development and such social reform as extending the vote to women. It also created a Literacy Corps for the countryside. Thus, by the late 1970s, the state had set up a modern system of communications, initiated a minor industrial revolution, and extended its reach into even the most outlying villages.

The state also controlled the National and the Central Banks; the Industrial and Mining Development Bank; the Plan Organization in charge of economic policy; the national radio-television network; and most important, the National Iranian Oil Company.

The dynasty's founder, Reza Shah, had used coercion, confiscation, and diversion of irrigation water to make himself one of the largest landowners in the Middle East. This wealth transformed the shah's imperial court into a large military-landed complex, providing work for thousands in its numerous palaces, hotels, casinos, charities, companies, and beach resorts. This patronage system grew under his son, Muhammad Reza Shah, particularly after he established his tax-exempt Pahlavi Foundation, which eventually controlled 207 large companies.

The Pahlavi drive for secularization, centralization, industrialization, and social development won some favor from the urban propertied classes. But arbitrary rule; the 1953 coup that overthrew a popular prime minister; the disregard for constitutional liberties; and the stifling of independent newspapers, political parties, and professional associations produced widespread resentment. The Pahlavi state, like the Safavids and the Qajars, hovered over, rather than embedded itself into, Iranian society.

In 1975, the shah formed the Resurgence Party. He declared Iran a one-party state and threatened imprisonment and exile to those refusing to join the party. The Resurgence Party was designed to create yet another organizational link with the population, especially with the **bazaars** (traditional marketplaces), which, unlike the rest of society, had managed to retain their independent guilds and thus escape direct government control. The Resurgence Party promptly established its own bazaar guilds as well as newspapers, women's organizations, professional associations, and labor unions. It also prepared to create a Religious Corps to teach the peasants "true Islam."

**bazaar**

An urban marketplace where shops, workshops, small businesses, and export-importers are located.

### The Islamic Revolution (1979)

These grievances were best summed up by an exile newspaper in Paris on the very eve of the 1979 revolution. In an article entitled "Fifty Years of Treason," it charged the shah and his family with establishing a military dictatorship; collaborating with the CIA; trampling on the constitution; creating SAVAK, the secret police; rigging parliamentary elections; organizing a fascistic one-party state; taking over the religious establishment; and undermining national identity by disseminating Western culture. It also accused the regime of inducing millions of landless peasants to migrate into urban shantytowns; widening the gap between rich and poor; funneling money away from the middle class bourgeoisie into the pockets of the wealthy comprador bourgeoisie (entrepreneurs linked to foreign companies and multinational corporations); wasting resources on bloated military budgets; and granting new capitulations to the West.

These grievances took sharper edge when the leading opposition cleric, Ayatollah Ruhollah Khomeini—exiled in Iraq—formulated a new version of Shi'ism (see Profile: "Ayatollah Ruhollah Khomeini"). His version of Shi'ism has often been labeled Islamic **fundamentalism**. It would be better to call it **political Islam** or even more accurately as Shi'i populism. The term *fundamentalism*, derived from American Protestantism, implies religious dogmatism, intellectual inflexibility and purity, political traditionalism, social conservatism, rejection of the modern world, and the literal interpretation of scriptural texts. While Khomeinism shares some of these characteristics, Khomeini was not so much a social conservative as a political revolutionary who rallied the people of Iran against a decadent elite.

Khomeini denounced monarchies in general as part of the corrupt elite exploiting the oppressed masses. Oppressors were courtiers, large landowners, high-ranking military officers, wealthy foreign-connected capitalists, and millionaire palace dwellers. The oppressed were the masses, especially landless peasants, wage earners, bazaar shopkeepers, and shantytown dwellers.

Khomeini gave a radically new meaning to the old Shi'i term *velayat-e faqih* (**jurist's guardianship**). He argued that jurist's guardianship gave the senior clergy all-encompassing authority over the whole community, not just over widows, minors, and the mentally disabled (the previous interpretation). Only the senior clerics could understand the *shari'a;* the divine authority given to the Prophet and the Imams had been passed on to their spiritual heirs, the clergy. He further insisted the clergy were the people's true representatives, since they lived among them, listened to their problems, and shared their everyday joys and pains. He claimed that the shah secretly planned to confiscate all religious endowment funds and replace Islamic values with "cultural imperialism."

In 1977–1978, the shah tried to deal with a 20 percent rise in consumer prices and a 10 percent decline in oil revenues by cutting construction projects and declaring war against "profiteers," "hoarders," and "price gougers." Shopkeepers believed the shah was diverting attention from court corruption and planning to replace them with government-run department stores. They also thought he intended to destroy the bazaar.

The shah was also subjected to international pressure on the sensitive issue of human rights—from Amnesty International, the United Nations, and the Western press, as well as from the recently elected Carter administration in the United States. In 1977, the shah gave the International Red Cross access to Iranian prisons and permitted political prisoners to have defense attorneys. This international pressure allowed the opposition to breathe again after decades of suffocation.[2]

**fundamentalism**

A term recently popularized to describe radical religious movements throughout the world.

**political Islam**

A term for the intermingling of religion with politics and often used as a substitute for fundamentalism.

**jurist's guardianship**

Khomeini's concept that the Iranian clergy should rule on the grounds that they are the divinely appointed guardians of both the law and the people.

This slight loosening of the reins sealed the fate of the shah. Political parties, labor organizations, and professional associations—especially lawyers, writers, and university professors—regrouped after years of being banned. Bazaar guilds regained their independence. College, high school, and seminary students took to the streets—with each demonstration growing in size and vociferousness. On September 8, 1978, remembered in Iran as Black Friday, troops shot and killed a large but unknown number of unarmed civilians in central Tehran. This dramatically intensified popular hatred for the regime. By late 1978, general strikes throughout the country were bringing the whole economy to a halt. Oil workers vowed that they would not produce any petroleum for the outside world until they had exported the "shah and his forty thieves."[3]

In urban centers, local committees attached to the mosques and financed by the bazaars were distributing food to the needy, supplanting the police with militias known as ***pasdaran*** (Revolutionary Guards). They replaced the judicial system with ad hoc courts applying the *shari'a*. Anti-regime rallies were now attracting as many as 2 million protesters. Protesters demanded the abolition of the monarchy, the return of Khomeini, and the establishment of a republic that would preserve national independence and provide the downtrodden masses with decent wages, land, and a proper standard of living.

Although led by pro-Khomeini clerics, these rallies drew support from a broad variety of organizations: the National Front; the Lawyer's, Doctor's, and Women's associations; the communist Tudeh Party; the Fedayin, a Marxist guerrilla group; and the Mojahedin, a Muslim guerrilla group formed of nonclerical intellectuals. The rallies also attracted students, from high schools and colleges, as well as shopkeepers and craftsmen from the bazaars. A secret Revolutionary Committee in Tehran coordinated protests throughout the country. This was one of the first revolutions to be televised worldwide. Many would later feel that these demonstrations had inspired the revolutions that swept through Eastern Europe in the 1980s.

Confronted by this opposition and by increasing numbers of soldiers who were deserting to the opposition, the shah decided to leave Iran. A year later, when he was in exile and dying of cancer, many speculated that he might have mastered the upheavals if he had been healthier, possessed a stronger personality, and received full

**pasdaran**

Persian term for guards, used to refer to the army of Revolutionary Guards formed during Iran's Islamic Revolution.

---

## PROFILE

### Ayatollah Ruhollah Khomeini

Ruhollah Khomeini was born in 1902 into a landed clerical family in central Iran. During the 1920s, he studied in the famous Fayzieh Seminary in Qom with the leading theologians of the day, most of whom were scrupulously apolitical. He taught at the seminary from the 1930s through the 1950s, avoiding politics even during the mass campaign to nationalize the British-owned oil company. His entry into politics did not come until 1963, when he, along with most other clerical leaders, denounced Muhammad Reza Shah's White Revolution. Forced into exile, Khomeini taught at the Shi'i center of Najaf in Iraq from 1964 until 1978. During these years, Khomeini developed his own version of Shi'i populism by incorporating socioeconomic grievances into his sermons and denouncing not just the shah but also the whole ruling class. Returning home triumphant in the midst of the Iranian Revolution after the shah was forced from power in 1979, he was declared the Imam and Leader of the new Islamic Republic. In the past, Iranian Shi'is, unlike the Arab Sunnis, had reserved the special term *Imam* only for Imam Ali and his eleven direct heirs, whom they deemed infallible, and, therefore, almost semidivine. For many Iranians in 1979, Khomeini was charismatic in the true sense of the word: a man with a special gift from God. Khomeini ruled as Imam and Leader of the Islamic Republic until his death in 1989.

support from the United States. But even a man with an iron will and full foreign backing would not have been able to deal with millions of angry demonstrators, massive general strikes, and debilitating desertions from his own pampered armed forces.

On February 11, 1979, a few hours of street fighting provided the final blow to the fifty-four-year-old dynasty that claimed a 2,500-year-old heritage.

## The Islamic Republic (1979–present)

Seven weeks after the February revolution, a nationwide referendum replaced the monarchy with an Islamic Republic. Liberal and lay supporters of Khomeini, including Mehdi Bazargan, his first prime minister, had hoped to offer the electorate the choice of a *democratic* Islamic Republic. But Khomeini overruled them. He declared the term *democratic* was redundant because Islam itself was democratic. Khomeini was now hailed as the Leader of the Revolution, Founder of the Islamic Republic, Guide of the Oppressed Masses, Commander of the Armed Forces, and most potent of all, Imam of the Muslim World.

A new constitution was drawn up in late 1979 by the **Assembly of Experts** (*Majles-e Khebregan*). Although this seventy-three-man assembly—later increased to eighty-six—was elected by the general public, almost all secular organizations as well as clerics opposed to Khomeini boycotted the elections because the state media were controlled, independent papers had been banned, and voters were being intimidated by club-wielding vigilantes known as the **Hezbollahis** ("Partisans of God"). The vast majority of those elected, including forty *hojjat al-Islams* (middle-ranking clerics) and fifteen ayatollahs were pro-Khomeini clerics. They drafted a highly theocratic constitution vesting much authority in the hands of Khomeini in particular and the clergy in general—all this over the strong objections of Prime Minister Bazargan, who wanted a French-style presidential republic that would be Islamic in name but democratic in structure.

When Bazargan threatened to submit his own constitution to the public, the state television network, controlled by the clerics, showed him shaking hands with U.S. policy-makers. Meanwhile, Khomeini denounced the U.S embassy as a "den of spies" plotting a repeat performance of the 1953 coup. This led to mass demonstrations, a break-in at the embassy, the seizure of dozens of American hostages, and eventually the resignation of Bazargan. Some suspect that the hostage crisis had been engineered to undercut Bazargan.

A month after the embassy break-in, Khomeini submitted the theocratic constitution to the public and declared that all citizens had a divine duty to vote; 99 percent of those voting endorsed it.

In the first decade after the revolution, a number of factors helped the clerics consolidate power. First, few people could challenge Khomeini's overwhelming charisma and popularity. Second, the invasion of Iran in 1980 by Saddam Hussein's Iraq rallied the Iranian population behind their endangered homeland. Third, international petroleum prices shot up, sustaining Iran's oil revenues. The price of a barrel of oil, which had hovered around $30 in 1979, jumped to over $50 by 1981, which enabled the new regime, despite war and revolution, to continue to finance existing development programs.

The second decade after the revolution brought the clerics serious problems. Khomeini's death in June 1989 removed his decisive presence. His successor, Ali Khamenei, lacked not only his charisma but also his scholastic credentials and seminary disciples. The 1988 UN-brokered cease-fire in the Iran-Iraq War ended the foreign danger. A drastic fall in world oil prices, which plunged to less than $10 a barrel by

**Assembly of Experts**

Group that nominates and can remove the Supreme Leader in Iran. The assembly is elected by the general electorate, but almost all its members are clerics.

*Hezbollahis*

Literally "partisans of God." In Iran, the term is used to describe religious vigilantes. In Lebanon, it is used to describe the Shi'i militia.

*hojjat al-Islam*

Literally, "the proof of Islam." In Iran, it means a medium-ranking cleric.

The shah's statue on the ground, February 1979.

1998, placed a sharp brake on economic development. Even more serious, by the late 1990s, the regime was facing a major ideological crisis, with many of Khomeini's followers, including some of his closest disciples, now stressing the importance of public participation over clerical hegemony, of political pluralism over theological conformity, and of civil society over state authority—in other words, of democracy over theocracy.

### Iran after 9/11

The terrorist attacks of September 11, 2001, and the subsequent American invasions of Afghanistan in October 2001 and Iraq in March 2002, had profound consequences for Iran. At first, the American war on terror brought Iran and the United States closer together since Iran for years had seen both the Taliban and Saddam Hussein as its own mortal enemies. Saddam Hussein was hated for the obvious reason that he had waged an eight-year war on Iran. The Taliban was hated in part because it had been created by Pakistan—Iran's main rival to the east; in part because it had massacred large number of Shi'i Afghans; and in part because being Sunni fundamentalists financed by the Wahhabis, the main Sunni fundamentalists in Saudi Arabia, the Taliban considered Shi'ism as well as all innovations since the very beginnings of Islam to be unacceptable heresies. In fact, these Sunni fundamentalists consider Shi'is to be as bad if not worse than non-Muslim infidels. Not surprisingly, Iran helped the United States replace the Taliban in 2001. It also used its considerable influence among the Iraqi Shi'is to install a pro-American government in Baghdad in 2003. It offered the United States in 2003 a "grand bargain" to settle all major differences, including those over nuclear research, Israel, Lebanon, and the Persian Gulf. Iran also offered to give a greater hand in helping the United States stabilize Iraq.

These hopes, however, were soon dashed—first because President George W. Bush named Iran (along with Iraq and North Korea) as part of an "Axis of Evil," that supported terrorism and were developing weapons of mass destruction. He then refused to enter serious negotiations until Iran unconditionally stopped nuclear research. This cold-shouldering played a major role in both undermining the Iran's liberal President Khatemi and paving the way for the electoral victory of the bellicose and ultraconservative Ahmadinejad in 2005. Reformers did not want to be associated with an American administration that not only insisted Iran should not have a nuclear program but also aggressively advocated regime change in Tehran. For most Iranians, this again resurrected memories of the 1953 CIA coup. These issues increased tensions and brought Iran and the United States closer to a diplomatic, if not military, confrontation. The United States still insists that it will not negotiate with Iran unless it stops its nuclear enrichment program. Iran insists that its nuclear program has no military purpose and that it conforms to guidelines set by international treaties.

The United States would like to see "behavioral" change if not "regime change" in Iran. But the United States needs Iran's cooperation in Iraq to prevent the situation there from getting completely out of control. For now, the situation appears to be at a stalemate. Only time will show how the crisis will work itself out.

# Themes and Implications

## Historical Junctures and Political Themes

Khomeini argued that Islam and democracy were compatible since the vast majority of people in Iran respected the clerics as the true interpreters of the *shari'a*, and wanted them to oversee state officials. Islam and the democratic idea, however, appear less reconcilable now that much of the public has lost its enthusiasm for clerical rule. Khomeinism has divided into two divergent branches in Iran: political liberalism and clerical conservatism. These ideological currents, which will be discussed later in this chapter, are at the heart of Iranian politics today.

Democracy is based on the principles that all individuals are equal, especially before the law, and that all people have inalienable natural rights. The *shari'a* is based on inequalities—between men and women, between Muslims and non-Muslims, between legitimate minorities, known as the People of the Book, and illegitimate ones, known as unbelievers. Moderate clerics, however, advocate reforming the *shari'a* to make it compatible with individual freedoms and human rights.

By denouncing the United States as an "arrogant imperialist," canceling military agreements with the West, and condoning the taking of United States diplomats as hostages, Khomeini asserted Iranian power in the region but also inadvertently prompted Saddam Hussein to launch the Iraq-Iran War in 1980.

Khomeini's policies made it difficult for his successors to improve relations with the West. He called for revolutions throughout the Muslim world, denouncing Arab rulers in the region, particularly in Saudi Arabia, as the "corrupt puppets of American imperialism." He strengthened Iran's navy and bought nuclear submarines from Russia. He launched a research program to build medium-range missiles and nuclear power—possibly even nuclear weapons. He denounced the proposals for Arab-Israeli negotiations over Palestine. He sent money as well as arms to Muslim dissidents abroad, particularly Shi'i groups in Lebanon, Iraq, and Afghanistan. He permitted the intelligence services to assassinate some one hundred exiled opposition leaders living in Western Europe. These policies isolated Iran not only from the United States but also from the European Community, human rights organizations, and the United Nations.

## THE U.S. CONNECTION

### The Nuclear Power Issue

At the heart of U.S.-Iran tensions lies the nuclear issue. For Iran, nuclear technology—always defined as a "civilian program"—is a non-negotiable right of an independent nation, essential not only for its long-term energy needs but also to attain the hallmark of a developed country. It sees nuclear power as a matter of both sovereignty and modernity.

For the United States, any nuclear technology—even for peaceful purposes—in the hands of Iran is fraught with many risks. The United States argues that such technology could be expanded into a weapons program, and nuclear weapons could then be used on Israel or passed on to "terrorist organizations." It seems that the only way to resolve the issue is for the United States to accept Iran's civilian program, and Iran, in return, to provide verifiable

guarantees that its program would not trespass into the military realm. Under the Bush administration, negotiations broke down since the United States demanded that Iran cease forthwith all enrichment. Under the Obama administration, the United States has implicitly accepted Iran's right to enrich so long as it provides verifiable guarantees that it would not enrich to the point of producing weapons. To pressure Iran to provide such guarantees, the Obama administration has persuaded the UN to place economic sanctions on Iran—especially on the Revolutionary Guards and elite members of the regime. These sanctions, however, will probably have little impact at a time when petroleum-exporting countries such as Iran are enjoying windfall wealth from soaring oil prices.

The Islamic Republic is determined to remain dominant in the Persian Gulf and to play an important role in the world of states. It has one of the biggest armies in the region, a large land mass, considerable human resources, a respectable gross domestic product (GDP), and vast oil production. Iran also has the potential to become a nuclear power, the major source of tension in U.S.-Iranian relations.

But Iran's GDP is only about equal to that of New Jersey, and its military hardware has been exhausted by war, age, and lack of spare parts. In the last years of the shah, military purchases accounted for 17 percent of the GDP; they now account for 2 percent. In 2005, Iran spent only $4.1 billion on arms whereas Turkey spent as much as $10 billion, Saudi Arabia $21 billion, and even tiny Kuwait and United Arab Emirates together more than $6.6 billion. What is more, Iran's plans to develop nuclear power have been delayed because the United States has persuaded Europe not to transfer such technology to Iran and by a successful joint U.S.-Israeli cyber-sabotage program that injected a software "worm" into the computers used to control the production of enriched uranium. Therefore, Iran is unlikely to be able to develop nuclear weapons in the near future. Moreover, the United States, after 9/11 and the occupation of Iraq in March 2003, surrounded Iran with military bases in the Persian Gulf, Turkey, Azerbaijan, Georgia, Afghanistan, and Central Asia.

In the early years of the Islamic Republic in the 1980s, peasants continued to migrate to the cities because of the lack of both agricultural land and irrigation. Industry suffered from lack of investment capital. Inflation and unemployment were high. The population steadily increased, and real per capita income fell due to forces outside state control. To deal with these problems, some leaders favored state-interventionist strategies. Others advocated **laissez-faire** market-based strategies. Such differences over how to govern the economy are still being debated in Iran and are the source of much political contention.

The state-enforced emphasis on Shi'ism has alienated the 10 percent of Iranians who are Sunnis. In addition, the regime's insistence on a theocratic constitution

**laissez-faire**

A term taken from the French, which means "to let be," in other words, to allow to act freely.

antagonized some important clerics as well as lay secular Muslims, who lead most of the political parties. Similarly, the strong association of Shi'ism with the central, Persian-speaking regions of the country could alienate the important Turkic minority in Azerbaijan province. All of these trends put a strain on Iran's collective national identity.

## Implications for Comparative Politics

The Khomeinist movement culminating in the 1979 revolution helped expand Islam from a personal religion concerned with the individual's relations with God into an all-encompassing ideology that dealt with political, legal, social and economic matters as well as personal ones. The slogan of the revolution was "Islam is the Solution." This expanded interpretation of Islam became known as **Islamism** and political Islam. Some social scientists substitute these terms for fundamentalism and religious populism. The direct product of this form of Islam was the creation of an Islamic Republic that was theocratic—a regime in which the clergy claimed special authority on grounds that as experts on theology they had better understanding of religion and therefore greater expertise than laymen in supervising the running of the state. This authority is based not on the claim they enjoy direct communications with God—they do not claim such privilege—but that they have scholarly knowledge of the scriptures and God's laws—the *shari'a*. This made the Islamic Republic a unique political system in the modern world.

**Islamism**

A new term for the use of Islam as a political ideology. Similar to political Islam and fundamentalism.

Although this was the main contribution of the Islamic Republic to comparative politics, the reform movement of the 1990s did its best to counter it. The leading reformers, who labeled themselves the new Muslim intellectuals, argued that their intellectual fathers, the revolutionary generation, had mistakenly "bloated religion" and expanded it from personal ethics into an all-encompassing political ideology. In other words, they had turned faith into a total system of thought similar to twentieth-century European totalitarian ideologies—the other major isms. The new Muslim intellectuals set themselves the task of slimming down, narrowing, and lightening this over-bloated system of thought. In short, they turned away from Islamism back to a more conventional understanding of Islam.

It is this two contrasting interpretations of Islam that help explain the bitter conflict in contemporary Iran between reformers and conservatives, between so-called fundamentalists and liberal pragmatists, between supporters of Khatami and those of Ahmadinejad, between the generation that made the 1979 revolution and the new generation that came of age during the same revolution. They both consider themselves Islamic but have sharply different interpretations of Islam—especially when it comes to politics.

## Summary

The Iranian state—unlike many others in the Middle East—is viable and well established. It has a long history. Its official religion—Shi'ism—binds the elite with the masses, the government with the governed, the rulers with the ruled. Its ministries are embedded deep into society, providing multiple social services. It has substantial oil revenues, which, although fluctuating, provide the government the means to finance the ever-growing ministries. What is more, the recent past—especially the Islamic Revolution and the eight-year war with Iraq—has helped create a strong sense of national solidarity against the outside world—not just against the West but also much of the Sunni Muslim World.

# POLITICAL ECONOMY AND DEVELOPMENT

**Focus Questions**

What are some of the ways in which the oil industry has advanced or distorted development in Iran?

What impact did the shah's economic policies have on Iranian society?

Has life improved for most people in the Islamic Republic—especially in the 1990s?

What role do oil revenues play in integrating Iran into the global economy?

**rentier state**

A country that obtains much of its revenue from the export of oil or other natural resources.

## State and Economy

British prospectors struck oil in Iran's Khuzistan province in 1908, and the British government in 1912 decided to fuel its navy with petroleum rather than coal. It also decided to buy most of its fuel from the Anglo-Iranian Oil Company. Iran's oil revenues increased modestly in the next four decades, reaching $16 million in 1951. After the nationalization of the oil industry in 1951 and the agreement with a consortium of U.S. and British companies in 1955, oil revenues rose steadily, from $34 million in 1955 to $5 billion in 1973 and, after the quadrupling of oil prices in 1974, to over $23 billion in 1976. Between 1953 and 1978, Iran's cumulative oil income came to over $100 billion.

Oil financed over 90 percent of imports and 80 percent of the annual budget and far surpassed total tax revenues. Oil also enabled Iran not to worry about feeding its population. Instead, it could undertake ambitious development programs that other states could carry out only if they squeezed scarce resources from their populations. In fact, oil revenues made Iran into a **rentier state,** a country that obtains a lucrative income by exporting raw materials or leasing out natural resources to foreign companies. Iran as well as Iraq, Algeria, and the Gulf states received enough money from their oil wells to be able to disregard their internal tax bases. The Iranian state thus became relatively independent of society. Society, in turn, had few inputs into the state. Little taxation meant little representation.

From the 1950s through the 1970s, Muhammad Reza Shah tried to encourage other exports and attract foreign investment into non-oil ventures. Despite some increase in carpet and pistachio exports, oil continued to dominate. In 1979, on the eve of the Islamic Revolution, oil still provided 97 percent of the country's foreign exchange. Foreign firms invested no more than $1 billion in Iran—and much of this was not in industry but in banking, trade, and insurance. In Iran, as in the rest of the Middle East, foreign investors were put off by government corruption, labor costs, small internal markets, potential instability, and fear of confiscation.

Despite waste and corruption, there was significant growth in many modern sectors of the economy under the shah. (See Table 13.2.) GNP grew at an average rate of 9.6 percent per year from 1960 to 1977. This made Iran one of the fastest-growing economies in the world. Land reform created over 644,000 moderately prosperous farms. The number of modern factories tripled. The Trans-Iranian Railway was completed. Roads were built connecting most villages with the provincial cities.

| Table 13.2 | Industrial Production | |
|---|---|---|
| **Product** | **1953** | **1977** |
| Coal (tons) | 200,000 | 900,000 |
| Iron ore (tons) | 5,000 | 930,000 |
| Steel (tons) | — | 275,000 |
| Cement (tons) | 53,000 | 4,300,000 |
| Sugar (tons) | 70,000 | 527,000 |
| Tractors (no.) | — | 7,700 |
| Motor vehicles (no.) | — | 109,000 |

*Source:* E. Abrahamian, "Structural Causes of the Iranian Revolution," *Middle East Research and Information Project,* no. 87 (May 1980), 22.

# Iran's Economy under the Islamic Republic

Iran's main economic problem has been instability in the world oil market. Oil revenues, which continued to provide the state with 80 percent of its hard currency and 75 percent of its total revenues, fell from $20 billion in 1978 to less than $10 billion in 1998. Oil revenues did not improve until the early 2000s when they increased to $17 billion in 2000, $44 billion in 2005, and over $55 billion per year by the late 2000s. This increase was due not to rise in production—in fact, total production in 2005 was a third less than in 1975—but to the dramatic rise in the price of oil in the international market. The price of a barrel of oil jumped from $14 in 1998 to $30 in 2000, $56 in 2005, and topped near $100 in 2008.

Contemporary Iran is awash in oil money. But the country's economic situation has been complicated by the population explosion, the Iran-Iraqi war, and the emigration of some 3 million Iranians. The annual population growth rate, which had hit 2.5 percent in the late 1970s, jumped to nearly 4 percent by the late 1980s, the highest rate in the world. The war wrought on Iran as much as $600 billion in property damage and over 218,000 dead. The Islamic Revolution itself frightened many professionals and highly skilled technicians, as well as wealthy entrepreneurs, and industrialists into fleeing to the West.

The overall result was a twenty-year economic crisis lasting well into the late 1990s. The value of real incomes, including salaries and pensions, dropped by as much as 60 percent. Unemployment hit 20 percent; over two-thirds of entrants into the labor force could not find jobs. Peasants continued to flock to urban shantytowns. Tehran grew from 4.5 million to 12 million people. The total number of families living below the poverty level increased. By the late 1990s, over 9 million urban dwellers lived below the official poverty line.[4] Shortages in foreign exchange curtailed vital imports, even of essential manufactured goods. What is more, the regime that came to power advocating self-sufficiency now owed foreign banks and governments over $30 billion, forcing it to renegotiate foreign loans constantly. In the 2005 presidential elections, these problems help explain the strong victory of Ahmadinejad, the conservative populist candidate.

Nevertheless, the Islamic Republic has scored some notable economic successes. The Reconstruction Ministry built 30,000 miles of paved roads, 40,000 schools, and 7,000 libraries. It brought electricity and running water to more than half of the country's 50,000 villages. The number of registered vehicles on the roads increased from 27,000 in 1990 to over 3 million in 2009. More dams and irrigation canals were built, and the Agricultural Ministry distributed some 630,000 hectares of confiscated arable land to peasants and gave farmers more favorable prices.

The government has exercised control over most of Iran's economy for the entire history of the Islamic Republic. Reformist president Khatami took steps to reduce the role of the state in governing the economy by allowing privatization in some sectors of the economy (including banking) and relaunching a stock market to sell shares of government businesses to private investors. Even Ayatollah Khamenei, the chief religious leader, and current conservative president Ahmadinejad have endorsed privatization. Ahmadinejad has initiated a program to give "justice shares" of state-owned industries to low-income citizens. Nevertheless, about 70 percent of the Iranian economy continued to be under state control.

The recent rise in petroleum prices has greatly helped the situation. Foreign reserves have increased to $4.8 billion, stabilizing the currency and improving the country's creditworthiness. Iran has become one of the few developing countries to be free of foreign debt. It has been able to set aside some oil revenues as a hedge against leaner times. Both the official unemployment and inflation rates, while still high, have fallen, and the currency has stabilized. The government has floated its first international bond, and foreign investments have been contracted to flow into oil and gas ventures, petrochemicals, minerals, and car factories. UN sanctions, however, have stymied such inflows. Of course, oil revenues have also allowed the government to channel large additional funds into the infrastructure. President Ahmadinejad has promised to steer more of the oil wealth to projects and programs that directly help the poor.

Despite initial setbacks, Iran has been able to become more self-sufficient in food production. Ironically, the impressive growth in private cars and public transport strained the refineries and forced Iran to become more dependent on imported gasoline. What is more, the oil revenues enabled the government to allocate as much as $100 billion a year subsidizing essential goods such as bread, heating fuel, gasoline, sugar, rice, milk, and cooking oil. In 2011, it made the bold move of trimming these subsidies, and, instead, giving cash directly to the poor.

# Society and Economy

During the shah's reign, a huge amount of state investment went into social welfare. Enrollment in primary schools grew from fewer than 750,000 to over 4 million; in secondary schools from 121,000 to nearly 740,000; in vocational schools from 2,500 to nearly 230,000; and in universities from under 14,000 to more than 154,000. Between 1963 and 1977, the number of hospital beds increased from 24,126 to 48,000; medical clinics from 700 to 2,800; nurses from 1,969 to 4,105; and doctors from 4,500 to 12,750. These improvements, together with the elimination of epidemics and famines, lowered infant mortality and led to a population explosion.

The shah's approach to development, however, increased his unpopularity with many sectors of Iranian society. The shah believed that if economic growth benefited those who were already better off, some of the wealth would gradually trickle down to the lower levels of society. But these benefits got stuck at the top and never trickled down.

In fact, wealth trickled up: In 1972, the richest 20 percent of urban households accounted for 47.1 percent of total urban family expenditures; by 1977, it accounted for 55.5 percent. In 1972, the poorest 40 percent accounted for 16.7 percent of urban family expenditures; by 1977, this had dropped to 11.7 percent. In Iran's cities, the rich were getting richer, and the poor were getting poorer.

The new factories drew criticism that they were mere assembly plants that used cheap labor and were poor substitutes for real industrial development that would benefit the nation. The shah's public health programs still left Iran with one of the worst doctor-patient ratios and child mortality rates in the Middle East. The per capita income in the richest provinces was ten times more than in the poorest ones. The ratio of urban to rural incomes was 5 to 1. Land reform created a small layer of prosperous farmers but left the vast majority of peasants landless or nearly landless (see Table 13.3). By the mid-1970s, Iran was one of the most unequal countries in the world.[5]

These inequalities created a **dual society**—on one side the modern sector, headed by elites with close ties to the oil state, on the other side the traditional sector, the

**dual society**

A society and economy that are sharply divided into a traditional, usually poorer, and a modern, usually richer, sector.

clergy, the bazaar middle class, and the rural masses. Each sector, in turn, was sharply stratified into unequal classes (see Figure 13.2).

The upper class—the Pahlavi family, the court-connected entrepreneurs, the military officers, and the senior civil servants—made up less than 0.01 percent of the population. In the modern sector, the middle class—professionals, civil servants, salaried personnel, and college students—formed about 10 percent of the population. The bottom of the modern sector—the urban working class, factory workers, construction laborers, peddlers, and unemployed—constituted over 32 percent. In the traditional sector, the middle class—bazaar merchants, small retailers, shopkeepers, workshop owners, and well-to-do family farmers—made up 13 percent; the rural masses 45 percent.

| Table 13.3 | Land Ownership in 1977 |
|---|---|
| **Size (Hectares)** | **Number of Owners** |
| 200+ | 1,300 |
| 51–200 | 44,000 |
| 11–50 | 600,000 |
| 3–10 | 1,200,000 |
| Landless | 700,000 |

*Note:* One hectare is equal to approximately 2.47 acres.
*Source:* E. Abrahamian, "Structural Causes of the Iranian Revolution," *Middle East Research and Information Project*, no. 87 (May 1980).

These inequalities fueled resentments, which were expressed more in cultural and religious terms than in economic and class terms. Among the fiercest critics was Jalal Al-e Ahmad (1923–1969). He argued that the ruling class was destroying Iran by mindlessly imitating the West; neglecting the peasantry; showing contempt for popular religion; worshipping mechanization, regimentation, and industrialization; and flooding the country with foreign ideas, tastes, luxury items, and mass-consumption goods. He stressed that developing countries such as Iran could survive this "plague" of Western imperialism only by returning to their cultural roots and developing a self-reliant society, especially a fully independent economy. Al-e Ahmad is deemed to be not only the main intellectual critic of the old order but also the founder of the "back to roots" movement in Iran that influenced the Islamic Revolution that overthrew the shah.

Al-e Ahmad's ideas were developed further by another young intellectual, Ali Shariati (1933–1977). Studying in Paris during the 1960s, Shariati was influenced by Marxist sociology, Catholic liberation theology, the Algerian revolution, and, most important, Frantz Fanon's theory of violent Third World revolutions against colonial oppression as laid out in *The Wretched of the Earth* (1961).

Shariati argued that history was a continuous struggle between oppressors and oppressed. Each class had its own interests, its own interpretations of religion, and its own sense of right and wrong. God periodically sent down prophets, such as Abraham, Moses, Jesus, and Muhammad. Muhammad had been sent to launch a dynamic community in "permanent revolution" toward the ultimate utopia: a perfectly classless society.

Although Muhammad's goal had been betrayed by his illegitimate successors, his radical message had been preserved by the Shi'i Imams, especially by Imam Husayn, who had been martyred to show future generations that human beings had the moral duty to fight oppression in all places at all times. According to Shariati, the contemporary oppressors were the imperialists, the modern-day feudalists, the corrupt capitalists, and their hangers-on. He criticized the conservative clerics who had tried to transform revolutionary religion into an apolitical public opiate. Shariati died on the eve of the revolution, but his prolific works were so widely read and so influential

**Upper Class**

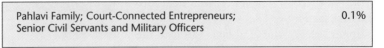

| Pahlavi Family; Court-Connected Entrepreneurs; Senior Civil Servants and Military Officers | 0.1% |

**Middle Class**

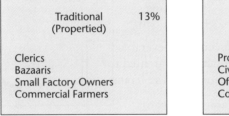

| Traditional (Propertied) 13% | Modern (Salaried) 10% |
|---|---|
| Clerics<br>Bazaaris<br>Small Factory Owners<br>Commercial Farmers | Professionals<br>Civil Servants<br>Office Employees<br>College Students |

**Lower Classes**

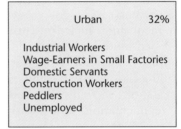

| Rural 45% | Urban 32% |
|---|---|
| Landed Peasants<br>Near Landless Peasants<br>Landless Peasants<br>Unemployed | Industrial Workers<br>Wage-Earners in Small Factories<br>Domestic Servants<br>Construction Workers<br>Peddlers<br>Unemployed |

**FIGURE 13.2 Iran's Class Structures in the Mid-1970s.**
Iranian society was divided sharply not only into horizontal classes, but also into vertical sectors—the modern and the transitional, the urban and the rural. This is known as a dual society.

that many felt that he, rather than Khomeini, was the true theorist of the Islamic Revolution.

In recent decades, life has improved for most Iranians. On the whole, the poor in Iran are better off now than their parents had been before the founding of the Islamic Republic. By the late 1990s, most independent farmers owned radios, televisions, refrigerators, and pickup trucks. The extension of social services narrowed the gap between town and country and between the urban poor and the middle classes. The adult literacy rate grew from 50 percent to 83 percent, and by 2000 the literacy rate among those in the six to twenty-nine age range hit 97 percent. The infant mortality rate fell from 104 per 1,000 in the mid-1970s to 30 per 1,000 in 2009. Life expectancy climbed from fifty-five years in 1979 to sixty-eight in 1993 and further to over seventy in 2009—one of the best in the Middle East. The UN estimates that by 2000, 94 percent of the population had access to health services and 95 percent to safe water.

The Islamic Republic also made major strides toward population control. At first, it closed down birth control clinics. But it reversed direction once the ministries responsible for social services felt the full impact of this growth. In 1989, the government declared that Islam favored healthy rather than large families and that one literate citizen was better than ten illiterate ones. It reopened birth control clinics, cut subsidies to large families, and announced that the ideal family should consist of no more than two children. It even took away social benefits from those having more than two children. By 2003, population growth had fallen to 1.2 percent a year; and by 2005 to 0.66 percent.

# Iran in the Global Economy

The integration of Iran into the world system began in the latter half of the nineteenth century. Several factors account for this integration: concessions granted to the European powers; the Suez Canal and the Trans-Caspian and the Batum-Baku railways; telegraph lines across Iran linking India with Britain; the outflow of capital from Europe after 1870; and, most important, the Industrial Revolution in Europe and the subsequent export of European manufactured goods to the rest of the world. In the nineteenth century, Iran's foreign trade increased tenfold.

Economic dependency resulted, a situation common in much of the Third World. Less-developed countries become too reliant on developed countries; poorer nations are vulnerable to sudden fluctuations in richer economies and dependent on the export of raw materials, whose prices often stagnate or decline, while prices for the manufactured products they import invariably increase.

Cash crops, especially cotton, tobacco, and opium, reduced the acreage for wheat and other edible grains in Iran. Many landowners stopped growing food and turned to commercial export crops. This led to disastrous famines in 1860, 1869–1872, 1880, and 1918–1920.

The clerical regime relies on two crutches of power: the bayonet and the oil well.

*Source:* Courtesy Mojahed (in exile).

Furthermore, many local merchants, shopkeepers, and workshop owners in the bazaars now formed a national propertied middle class aware of their common interests against both the central government and the foreign powers. This new class awareness played an important role in Iran's constitutional revolution of 1905.

Under the shah, Iran became the second-most-important member (after Saudi Arabia) of the **Organization of Petroleum Exporting Countries (OPEC)**; Iran could cast decisive votes for raising or moderating oil prices. At times, the shah curried Western favor by moderating prices. At other times, he pushed for higher prices to finance his ambitious projects and military purchases. These purchases rapidly escalated once President Richard Nixon began to encourage U.S. allies to take a greater role in policing their regions. Moreover, Nixon's secretary of state, Henry Kissinger, argued that the United States should finance its ever-increasing oil imports, by exporting more military hardware to the Persian Gulf. Arms dealers joked that the shah read their technical manuals the same way that some men read *Playboy*. The shah's arms buying from the United States jumped from $135 million in 1970 to a peak of $5.7 billion in 1977.

This military might gave the shah a reach well beyond his immediate boundaries. Iran occupied three small but strategically located Arab islands in the Strait of

**OPEC (Organization of Petroleum Exporting Countries)**

An organization dedicated to achieving stability in the price of oil, avoiding price fluctuations, and generally furthering the interests of the member states.

Hormuz, thus controlling the oil lifeline through the Persian Gulf but also creating distrust among his Arab neighbors. The shah talked of establishing a presence well beyond the Gulf on the grounds that Iran's national interests reached into the Indian Ocean.

In the mid-1970s, the shah dispatched troops to Oman to help the local sultan fight rebels. He offered Afghanistan $2 billion to break its then close ties with the Soviet Union, a move that probably prompted the Soviets to intervene militarily in that country. A U.S. congressional report summed up: "Iran in the 1970s was widely regarded as a significant regional, if not global, power. The United States relied on it, implicitly if not explicitly, to ensure the security and stability of the Persian Gulf sector and the flow of oil from the region to the industrialized Western world of Japan, Europe, and the United States, as well as to lesser powers elsewhere."[6]

These vast military expenditures, as well as the oil exports, tied Iran closely to the industrial countries of the West and to Japan. Iran was now importing millions of dollars' worth of rice, wheat, industrial tools, construction equipment, pharmaceuticals, tractors, pumps, and spare parts, the bulk of which came from the United States. Trade with neighboring and other developing countries was insignificant.

The oil revenues thus had major consequences for Iran's political economy, all of which paved the way for the Islamic Revolution. They allowed the shah to pursue ambitious programs that inadvertently widened class and regional divisions within the dual society. They drastically raised public expectations without necessarily meeting them. They made the rentier state independent of society. Economic slowdowns in the industrial countries, however, could lead to a decline in their oil demands, which could diminish Iran's ability to buy such essential goods as food, medicine, and industrial spare parts.

One of the major promises made by the Islamic Revolution was to end this economic dependency on oil and the West. The radical followers of Ayatollah Khomeini, the founder of the Islamic Republic, once denounced foreign investors as imperialist exploiters and waxed eloquent about economic self-sufficiency.

But in 2002, Iran contemplated a dramatically new law permitting foreigners to own as much as 100 percent of any firm in the country, to repatriate profits, to be free of state meddling, and to have assurances against both arbitrary confiscations and high taxation. To maintain production, Iran needs new deep-drilling technology that can be found only in the West. This goes a long way toward explaining why the regime now is eager to attract foreign investment and to rejoin the world economy.

## Summary

**resource curse**

The concept that revenue derived from abundant natural resources, such as oil, often bring unforeseen ailments to countries.

It has often been said that oil is a **resource curse** of the producing countries. It has been blamed for creating "rentier states," "dual societies," autocratic governments, unpredictable budgets, and retardation of other economic activities. Although this may be true in some parts of the world, in Iran oil has been the main engine driving state development and social modernization. It is mainly due to oil that Iran enters the twenty-first century with a strong state and a fairly modernized society in which almost all citizens have access to schools, medical clinics, modern sanitation, piped water, electricity, radios, televisions, and basic consumer goods.

# GOVERNANCE AND POLICY-MAKING

## Organization of the State

The political system of the Islamic Republic of Iran is unique. It is a theocracy with important democratic features. It is a theocracy (from the Greek, "divine rule") because the religious clerics control the most powerful political positions. But the system also contains elements of democracy with some high government officials, including the president, elected directly by the general public. All citizens, both male and female, over the age of eighteen have the right to vote.

The state rests on the Islamic constitution implemented immediately after the 1979 revolution and amended between April and June 1989 during the last months of Khomeini's life by the Council for the Revision of the Constitution, which was handpicked by Khomeini himself. The final document is a highly complex mixture of theocracy and democracy.

The preamble affirms faith in God, Divine Justice, the Qur'an, the Day of Judgment, the Prophet Muhammad, the Twelve Imams, the eventual return of the Hidden Imam (the Mahdi), and, of course, Khomeini's doctrine of jurist's guardianship that gives supreme power to senior clergy. All laws, institutions, and state organizations must conform to these "divine principles."

## The Executive

### The Leader and Major Organizations of Clerical Power

The constitution named Khomeini to be the Leader for Life on the grounds that the public overwhelmingly recognized him as the "most just, pious, informed, brave, and enterprising" of the senior clerics—the grand ayatollahs. It further described him as the Leader of the Revolution, the Founder of the Islamic Republic, and, most important, the Imam of the Muslim Community. It stipulated that if no single Leader emerged after his death, then all his authority would be passed on to a leadership council of senior clerics.

After Khomeini's death, however, his followers distrusted the other senior clerics so much that they did not set up such a council. Instead, they elected one of their own, Ali Khamenei, a middle-ranking cleric, to be the new Leader. The Islamic Republic has often been described as a regime of the ayatollahs (high-ranking clerics). It could be more aptly called a regime of the *hojjat al-Islams* (middle-ranking clerics), since few senior clerics want to be associated with it. None of the grand ayatollahs and few of the ordinary ayatollahs subscribed to Khomeini's notion of jurist's guardianship. In fact, most disliked his radical populism and political activism.

The constitution gives wide-ranging powers to the Leader, who is elected by the eighty-six member Assembly of Experts. As the vital link between the three branches of government, he can mediate between the legislature, the executive, and the judiciary. He can "determine the interests of Islam," "supervise the implementation of general policy," and "set political guidelines for the Islamic Republic." He can eliminate

**Focus Questions**

In what ways do the clergy have extraordinary powers in Iran?

How do they control the government of the Islamic Republic?

What elements of democracy are in Iran's theocratic political system?

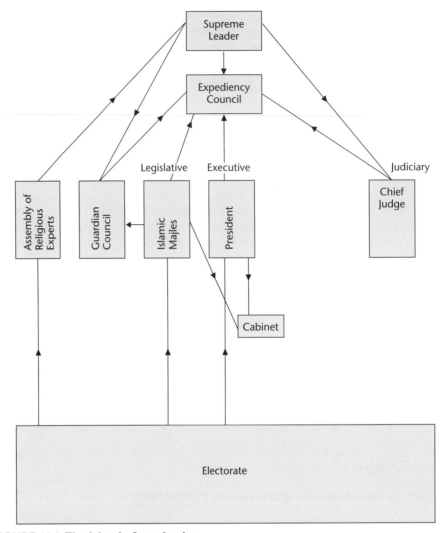

**FIGURE 13.3 The Islamic Constitution**
The general public elects the *Majles*, the president, and the Assembly of Experts. But the Leader and the Guardian Council decide who can compete in these elections.

presidential candidates and dismiss the duly elected president. He can grant amnesty. As commander-in-chief, he can mobilize the armed forces, declare war and peace, and convene the Supreme Military Council. He can appoint and dismiss the commanders of Revolutionary Guards as well as those of the regular army, navy, and air force.

The Leader has extensive power over the judicial system. He can nominate and remove the chief judge, the chief prosecutor, and the revolutionary tribunals. He can dismiss lower court judges. He also nominates six clerics to the powerful twelve-man Guardian Council, which can veto parliamentary bills. It has also obtained (through separate legislation) the right to review all candidates for elected office, including the presidency and the national legislature, the *Majles*. The other six members of the Guardian Council are jurists nominated by the chief judge and approved by the *Majles*. Furthermore, the Leader appoints the powerful **Expediency Council**, which has the authority to resolve differences between the Guardian Council and the *Majles* (the legislature) and to initiate laws on its own.

**Expediency Council**

A committee set up in Iran to resolve differences between the *Majles* (parliament) and the Guardian Council.

The Leader also fills a number of important nongovernment posts: the preachers **(Imam Jum'ehs)** at the main city mosques, the director of the national radio-television network, and the heads of the main religious endowments, especially the **Foundation of the Oppressed** (see below). By 2001, the Office of the Leader employed over six hundred in Tehran and had representatives in most sensitive institutions throughout the country. The Leader has obtained more constitutional powers than the shah ever dreamed of.

The Assembly of Experts is elected every eight years by the general public. Its members must have an advanced seminary degree, so it is packed with clerics. The Assembly has the right to oversee the work of the Leader and to dismiss him if he is found to be "mentally incapable of fulfilling his arduous duties." It has to meet at least once a year. Its deliberations are closed. In effect, the Assembly of Experts has become a second chamber to the *Majles*, the parliament of the Islamic Republic.

## The Government Executive

The constitution of the Islamic Republic reserves important executive power for the president. The president is described as the highest state official after the Leader. The office is filled every four years through a national election. If a candidate does not win a majority of the vote in the first round of the election, a run-off chooses between the two top vote-getters. The president cannot serve more than two terms.

The constitution says the president must be a pious Shi'i faithful to the principles of the Islamic Republic, of Iranian origin, and between the ages of 25 and 75. The president must also demonstrate "administrative capacity and resourcefulness" and have "a good past record." There has been some dispute about whether the language used in the constitution restricts the presidency to males.

The president has the power to

The shah turning into Khomeini from an émigré newspaper.

*Source:* Courtesy of Nashriyeh.

- Conduct the country's internal and external policies, including signing all international treaties, laws, and agreements;
- Chair the National Security Council, which is responsible for defense matters;
- Draw up the annual budget, supervise economic matters, and chair the state planning and budget organization;
- Propose legislation to the *Majles*;
- Appoint cabinet ministers, with a parliamentary stipulation that the minister of intelligence (the state security agency) must be from the ranks of the clergy;
- Appoint most other senior officials, including provincial governors, ambassadors, and the directors of some of the large public organizations, such as the National Iranian Oil Company, the National Electricity Board, and the National Bank.

Iran has no single vice president. Instead the president may select "presidential deputies" to help with "constitutional duties." There are currently ten such vice presidents.

**Imam Jum'ehs**

Prayer leaders in Iran's main urban mosques.

**Foundation of the Oppressed**

A clerically controlled foundation set up after the revolution in Iran.

## Ayatollah Ali Khamenei

Ali Khamenei succeeded Khomeini as Leader in 1989. He was born in 1939 in Mashed into a minor clerical family originally from Azerbaijan. He studied theology with Khomeini in Qom and was briefly imprisoned by the shah's regime in 1962. Active in the antishah opposition movement in 1978, he was given a series of influential positions immediately after the revolution, even though he held only the middle-level clerical rank of *hojjat al-Islam*. He became Friday prayer leader of Tehran, head of the Revolutionary Guards, and, in the last years of Khomeini's life, president of the republic. After Khomeini's death, he was elevated to the rank of Leader even though he was neither a grand ayatollah nor a recognized senior expert on Islamic law. He had not even published a theological treatise. The government-controlled media, however, began to refer to him as an ayatollah. Some ardent followers even referred to him as a grand ayatollah qualified to guide the world's whole Shi'i community. After his elevation, he built a constituency among the regime's more diehard elements: traditionalist judges, conservative war veterans, and antiliberal ideologues. Before 1989, he often sported a pipe in public, a mark of an intellectual, but gave up the habit upon becoming Leader.

One is designated as the "first vice president." The others have specific responsibilities, such as presiding over the national atomic energy organization or veterans' affairs. One is a woman. She has a Ph.D. in geology and is in charge of environmental policy.

Khomeini often promised that trained officials would run the executive branch in the Islamic Republic, but clerics—also called mullahs—have, in fact, dominated the presidency. Of the five presidents since the revolution, three have been clerics: Khamenei, Rafsanjani, and Khatami. The first president, Abol-Hassan Bani-Sadr, a lay intellectual was ousted in 1981 precisely because he denounced the regime as "a dictatorship of the mullahtariat," comparing it to a communist-led "dictatorship of the proletariat." Bani-Sadr's successor, who also was not a mullah, was assassinated shortly after taking office. The current president, Ahmadinejad, is not a cleric, but has strong support among ultra-conservative clerics.

### The Bureaucracy

As chief of the executive branch of the government, the president heads a huge bureaucracy. In fact, this bureaucracy continued to proliferate after the revolution, even though Khomeini had often criticized the shah for having a bloated government. It expanded, for the most part, to provide jobs for the many college and high school graduates. On the eve of the revolution, the state ministries had 300,000 civil servants and 1 million employees. By the early 1990s, they had over 600,000 civil servants and 1.5 million employees.

Among the most important ministries of the Islamic Republic are Culture and Islamic Guidance, which has responsibility for controlling the media and enforcing "proper conduct" in public life; Intelligence, which has replaced the shah's dreaded SAVAK as the main security organization; Heavy Industries, which manages the nationalized factories; and Reconstruction, which has the dual task of expanding social services and taking "true Islam" into the countryside. Its mission is to build bridges, roads, schools, libraries, and mosques in the villages so that the peasantry will learn the basic principles of Islam. "The peasants," declared one cleric, "are so ignorant of true Islam that they even sleep next to their unclean sheep."[7]

The clergy dominate the bureaucracy as well as the presidency. They have monopolized the most sensitive ministries—Intelligence, Interior, Justice, and Culture and Islamic Guidance—and have given posts in other ministries to relatives and protégés.

---

## PROFILE

### President Mahmoud Ahmadinejad

Ahmadinejad's inauguration as president, where he is being sworn in by Khameini.

*Source*: http://islamizationwatch. blogspot.com/2009/08/ ahmadinejad-sworn-in-as-riot-police.html.

Mahmoud Ahmadinejad was elected president in 2005 and reelected in a highly controversial election in 2009. He was born in 1956 into a working-class family in a small town in central Iran. He grew up mostly in Tehran where his father worked as a blacksmith. At the outbreak of the Islamic revolution in the late 1970s, he was studying engineering in Tehran and was active in the Islamic student movement. He volunteered to fight in the Iraqi war, and, after the cease-fire, returned to Tehran to complete a Ph.D. in urban planning.

Ahmadinejad served as governor of Ardabil province and then as mayor of Tehran (2003–2005) before running for president. As mayor of Iran's capital city, he rolled back some of the reforms implemented by Khatami's administration. For example, he ordered that men and women use separate elevators in city office buildings. This earned him a reputation as a hard-line conservative and gained him a political following among those who believed that Khatami had been too liberal. His presidential campaign was based on a combination of a pledge to restore the values of the Islamic Revolution and to attend to the needs of the poor.

After becoming president, Ahmadinejad continued to promote conservative policies. He reversed steps taken by the previous government to improve relations with the United States. He insists on Iran's right to develop nuclear power, always insisting that the country has only peaceful intentions. He has been critical of U.S. policy in the Middle East and of Israel, which he claims "was created to establish dominion of arrogant states over the region and to enable the enemy to penetrate the heart of Muslim land."[*] He has even questioned the legitimacy of the state of Israel and the historical veracity of the Holocaust.

The 2009 elections were expected to be a shoo-in for Ahmadinejad. He had spent four years campaigning in the countryside and channeling considerable amounts of the new oil bonanza into rural projects. Some four hundred foreign journalists were invited into the country to observe his expected "coronation." The election, however, produced a major surprise. A series of nationwide television debates between himself and his main reform opponent energized the whole opposition—the same opposition that had previously supported Khatami. The reform candidate was supported not only by Khatami, and many women and students, but also by the centrist politicians, the trade unions, and many reform-minded clerics. The actual results remain shrouded in mystery since the ballot boxes were quickly taken away by the Revolutionary Guards and their contents counted by the Interior Ministry packed with Ahmadinejad supporters. The Interior Ministry declared Ahmadinejad to be the clear winner—claiming he had won over 90 per cent of the vote in some constituencies. In the following days, mass protests with the slogan "What happened to my vote?" broke out in the major cities. The main protest in Tehran drew over two million—reminiscent of the 1979 mass demonstrations. These began what is now known as the Green Movement because of the color adopted by many of the protesters.

[*]Islamic Republic News Agency (IRNA), "President Ahmadinejad, Palestinian PM meet in Doha," December 2, 2006.

---

These ministers appear to be highly trained technocrats, sometimes with advanced degrees from the West. In fact, they are often fairly powerless individuals dependent on the powerful clergy—chosen by them, trusted by them, and invariably related to them.

# Other State Institutions

## The Judiciary

The constitution makes the judicial system the central pillar of the state, overshadowing the executive and the legislature. But it also gives wide-ranging judicial powers to the Leader in particular and to the clerical strata in general. Laws are supposed to conform to the religious law, and the clergy are regarded as the ultimate interpreters of the *shari'a*. Bills passed by the *Majles* are reviewed by the Guardian Council to ensure that they conform to the *shari'a*. The minister of justice is chosen by the president but needs the approval of both the *Majles* and the chief judge.

The judicial system itself has been Islamized down to the district-court level, with seminary-trained jurists replacing university-educated judges. The Pahlavis purged the clergy from the judicial system; the Islamic Republic purged the university educated.

The penal code, the Retribution Law, is based on a reading of the *shari'a* that was so narrow that it prompted many modern-educated lawyers to resign in disgust, charging that it contradicted the United Nations Charter on Human Rights. It permits injured families to demand blood money on the biblical and Qur'anic principle of "an eye for an eye, a tooth for a tooth, a life for a life." It mandates the death penalty for a long list of "moral transgressions," including adultery, homosexuality, apostasy, drug trafficking, and habitual drinking. It sanctions stoning, live burials, and finger amputations. It divides the population into male and female and Muslims and non-Muslims and treats them unequally. For example, in court, the evidence of one male Muslim is equal to that of two female Muslims. The regime also passed a "law on banking without usury" to implement the *shari'a* ban on all forms of interest taking and interest giving.

Although the law was Islamized, the modern centralized judicial system established under the shah was not dismantled. For years, Khomeini argued that in a truly Islamic society, the local *shari'a* judges would pronounce final verdicts without the intervention of the central authorities. Their verdicts would be swift and decisive. This, he insisted, was the true spirit of the *shari'a*. After the revolution, however, he discovered that the central state needed to retain ultimate control over the justice system, especially over life and death issues. Thus, the revolutionary regime retained the appeals system, the hierarchy of state courts, and the power to appoint and dismiss all judges. State interests took priority over the spirit of the *shari'a*—although religious authorities have ultimate control over the state.

Practical experience led the regime to gradually broaden the narrow interpretation of the *shari'a*. To permit the giving and taking of interest, without which modern economies would not function, the regime allowed banks to offer attractive rates as long as they avoided the taboo term *usury*. To meet public sensitivities as well as international objections, the courts rarely implemented the harsh penalties stipulated by the *shari'a*. They adopted the modern method of punishment, imprisonment, rather than the traditional one of corporal public punishment. By the early 1990s, those found guilty of breaking the law were treated much as they would be in the West: fined or imprisoned rather than flogged in the public square. Those found guilty of serious crimes, especially murder, armed violence, terrorism, and drug smuggling were often hanged. Iran, after China, has the highest number of executions per year, and the highest per capita executions in the world.

## The Military

The clergy have taken special measures to control Iran's armed forces—both the regular army of 370,000, including 220,000 conscripts, and the new forces formed of 120,000 Revolutionary Guards established immediately after 1979, and 200,000 volunteers in the Mobilization of the Oppressed (*Basej-e Mostazafin*), a volunteer militia created during the Iraqi war. The Leader, as commander-in-chief, appoints the chiefs of staff as well as the top commanders and the defense minister. He also places chaplains in military units to watch over regular officers. These chaplains act very much like the political commissars who once helped control the military in the Soviet Union.

After the revolution, the new regime purged the top ranks of the military, placed officers promoted from the ranks of the Revolutionary Guards in command positions over the regular divisions, and built up the Revolutionary Guards as a parallel force with its own uniforms, budgets, munitions factories, recruitment centers, and even small air force and navy. According to the constitution, the regular army defends the external borders, whereas the Revolutionary Guards protect the republic from internal enemies.

Political sentiments within the regular military remain unknown, if not ambivalent. In recent years, the *Basej* have been placed under the authority of the Revolutionary Guards. Although the military, especially the Revolutionary Guards, form an important pillar of the Islamic Republic, they consume only a small percentage of the annual budget. In fact, the republic spends far less on the armed forces than did the Shah—and also far less than many other states in the region, including Israel, Turkey, Pakistan, Saudi Arabia, and the Gulf sheikhdoms.

## Subnational Government

Although Iran is a highly centralized unitary state, it is divided administratively into provinces, districts, subdistricts, townships, and villages. Provinces are headed by governors-general, districts by governors, subdistricts by lieutenant governors, towns by mayors, and villages by headmen.

The constitution declares that the management of local affairs in every village, town, subdistrict, district, and province will be under the supervision of councils whose members would be elected directly by the local population. It also declares that governors-general, governors, and other regional officials appointed by the Interior Ministry have to consult local councils.

Because of conservative opposition, no steps were actually taken to hold council elections until 1999 when Khatami, the new reform-minded president, insisted on holding the country's very first nationwide local elections. Over 300,000 candidates, including 5,000 women, competed for 11,000 council seats—3,900 in towns and 34,000 in villages. Khatami's supporters won a landslide victory taking 75 percent of the seats, including twelve of the fifteen in Tehran. The top vote getter in Tehran was Khatami's former interior minister, who had been impeached by the conservative *Majles* for issuing too many publishing licenses to reform-minded journals and newspapers. Conservatives did well in the 2003 local elections, due largely to widespread voter abstention, but moderates and reformers made a comeback in 2006 when the turnout was about 60 percent of voters. With the 2009 crackdown on the Green Movement it is not clear what will happen in future local elections.

## Semipublic Institutions

The Islamic Republic has set up a number of semipublic institutions. They include the Foundation of the Oppressed, the Alavi Foundation (named after Imam Ali), the Martyrs Foundation, the Pilgrimage Foundation, the Housing Foundation, the Foundation for the Publication of Imam Khomeini's Works, and the Fifteenth of Khordad Foundation, which commemorates the date (according to the Islamic calendar) of Khomeini's 1963 denunciation of the shah's White Revolution. Although supposedly autonomous, these foundations are directed by clerics appointed personally by the Leader. According to some estimates, their annual income may be as much as half that of the government.[8] They are exempt from state taxes and are allocated foreign currencies, especially U.S. dollars, at highly favorable exchange rates subsidized by the oil revenues. Most of their assets are property confiscated from the old elite.

The largest of these institutions, the Foundation for the Oppressed, administers over 140 factories, 120 mines, 470 agribusinesses, and 100 construction companies. It also owns the country's two leading newspapers, *Ettela'at* and *Kayhan*. The Martyrs Foundation, in charge of helping war veterans, controls confiscated property that was not handed over to the Foundation for the Oppressed. It also receives an annual subsidy from the government. These foundations together control $12 billion in assets and employ over 400,000 people. They are clerical domains favored by the Leader. The recent moves to "privatize" state enterprises have tended to strengthen these foundations since these semipublic organizations are well placed and well enough financed to be able to buy shares in these new companies. Their main competitors in winning government contracts and buying privatized enterprises have been the Revolutionary Guards.

## The Policy-Making Process

Policy-making in Iran is highly complex in part because of the cumbersome constitution and in part because factionalism within the ruling clergy has resulted in more amendments, which have made the original constitution even more complicated. Laws can originate in diverse places, and they can be modified by pressures from numerous directions. They can also be blocked by a wide variety of state institutions. In short, the policy-making process is highly fluid and diffuse, often reflecting the regime's factional divisions.

The clerics who destroyed Iran's old order remained united while building the new one. They were convinced that they alone had the divine mandate to govern. They followed the same leader, admired the same texts, cited the same potent symbols, remembered the same real and imaginary indignations under the shah, and, most important, shared the same vested interest in preserving the Islamic Republic. Moreover, most had studied at the same seminaries and came from the same lower-middle-class backgrounds. Some were even related to each other through marriage and blood ties.

But once the constitution was in place, the same clerics drifted into two loose but identifiable blocs: the Society (*Majmu'eh*) of the Militant Clergy, and the Association (*Jam'eh*) of the Militant Clergy. The former can be described as statist reformers or populists, and the latter as laissez-faire (free-market) conservatives. The reformers hoped to consolidate lower-class support by using state power for redistributing wealth, eradicating unemployment, nationalizing enterprises, confiscating large estates, financing social programs, rationing and subsidizing essential goods, and placing price ceilings on essential consumer goods. In short, they espoused the creation of a comprehensive welfare state. The conservatives hoped to retain middle-class support, especially in the bazaars, by removing price controls, lowering business taxes, cutting red tape, encouraging private entrepreneurs, and balancing the budget, even at the cost of sacrificing subsidies and social programs. In recent years, the statist reformers have begun to emphasize the democratic over the theocratic features of the constitution, stressing the importance of

## THE U.S. CONNECTION

### Conservatives versus Liberals

Iran and the United States have more in common than either would admit. In both, the conservatives—calling themselves "compassionate conservatives" in the United States and "principalists" in Iran—have a core base limited to less than 30 percent of the electorate. To win national elections, they have to reach out to others while continuing to energize their supporters to vote. To reach out, they both resort to patriotic and populist language—stressing "national security," accusing "weak-kneed liberals" for not standing up to foreign enemies, claiming to represent the "ordinary folks" and appealing to cultural values. In 2005, Ahmadinejad won the presidential elections in part because he presented himself as a "man of the people." He also won partly because his liberal opposition was badly divided. But the biggest reason for the conservative victory was probably because he projected himself as a tough patriot who could better defend the nation from foreign threats—especially after President Bush named Iran as a member of the "Axis of Evil" in his 2002 State of the Union address.

individual rights, the rule of law, and government accountability to the electorate. In many ways, they have become like social democrats such as those in Britain's Labour Party.

The conservatives were originally labeled middle-of-the-roaders and traditionalists. The statists were labeled progressives, seekers of new ideas, and Followers of the Imam's Line. The former liked to denounce the latter as extremists, leftists, and pro-Soviet Muslims. The latter denounced the free-marketers as medievalists, rightists, capitalists, mafia bazaaris, and pro-American Muslims. Both could bolster their arguments with apt quotes from Khomeini.

This polarization created a major constitutional gridlock, since the early Islamic *Majles* was dominated by the reformers, whereas the Guardian Council was controlled by the conservatives appointed by Khomeini. Between 1981 and 1987, over one hundred bills passed by the reformer-dominated *Majles* were vetoed by the Guardian Council on the grounds that they violated the *shari'a*, especially the sanctity of private property. The vetoed legislation included a labor law, land reform, nationalization of foreign trade, a progressive income tax, control over urban real estate transactions, and confiscation of the property of émigrés whom the courts had not yet found guilty of counterrevolutionary activities. Introduced by individual deputies or cabinet ministers, these bills had received quick passage because reformers controlled the crucial *Majles* committees and held a comfortable majority on the *Majles* floor. Some ultraconservatives had countered by encouraging the faithful not to pay taxes and instead to contribute to the grand ayatollahs of their choice. After all, they argued, one could find no mention of income tax anywhere in the *shari'a*.

Both sides cited the Islamic constitution to support their positions. The conservative free-marketers referred to the long list of clauses protecting private property, promising balanced budgets, and placing agriculture, small industry, and retail trade in the private sector. The reformers referred to an even longer list promising education, medicine, jobs, low-income housing, unemployment benefits, disability pay, interest-free loans, and the predominance of the public sector in the economy.

To break the constitutional gridlock, Khomeini boldly introduced into Shi'ism the Sunni Islamic concept of *maslahat*—that is, "public interest" and "reasons

*maslahat*

Arabic term for "expediency," "prudence," or "advisability," now used in Iran to refer to reasons of state or what is best for the Islamic Republic.

of state." Over the centuries, Shi'i clerics had denounced this as a Sunni notion designed to bolster illegitimate rulers. Khomeini now claimed that a truly Islamic state could safeguard the public interest by suspending important religious rulings, even over prayer, fasting, and the pilgrimage to Mecca. He declared public interest to be a primary ruling and the others mere secondary rulings. In other words, the state could overrule the views of the highest-ranking clerics. In the name of public interest, it could destroy mosques, confiscate private property, and cancel religious obligations. Khomeini added that the Islamic state had absolute authority, since the Prophet Muhammad had exercised absolute (*motalaq*) power, which he had passed on to the Imams and thus eventually to the Islamic Republic. Never before had a Shi'i religious leader claimed such powers for the state, especially at the expense of fellow clerics.

As a follow-up, Khomeini set up a new institution named the Expediency Council for Determining the Public Interest of the Islamic Order—known as the Expediency Council. He entrusted it with the task of resolving conflicts between the Islamic *Majles* and the Guardian Council. He packed it with thirteen clerics, including the president, the chief judge, the Speaker of the *Majles*, and six jurists from the Guardian Council. The Expediency Council eventually passed some of the more moderate bills favored by the reformers. These included a new income tax, banking legislation, and a much-disputed labor law providing workers in large factories with a minimum wage and some semblance of job security.

Constitutional amendments introduced after Khomeini's death institutionalized the Expediency Council. The new Leader could now not only name its members but also determine its tenure and jurisdiction. Not surprisingly, Khomeini's successor as Leader, Khamenei, packed it with his supporters—none of them prominent grand ayatollahs. He also made its meetings secret and allowed it to promulgate new laws rather than restrict itself to resolving legislative differences between the Guardian Council and the *Majles*. The Expediency Council is now a secretive body that is accountable only to the Leader. It stands above the constitution. In this sense, it has become a powerful policy-making body rivaling the Islamic *Majles*, even though it did not exist in the original constitution.

There are thirty-four members of the Expediency Council. These included the president; chief judge; Speaker of the *Majles*; ministers of intelligence, oil, culture, and foreign affairs; chief of the General Staff; commander of the Revolutionary Guards; jurists from the Guardian Council; directors of radio and television as well as of the Central Bank, Atomic Energy Organization, and National Oil Company; heads of the main religious foundations; chairman of the Chamber of Commerce; and editors of the main conservative newspapers. Seventeen were clerics. These thirty-four can be considered the inner circle of Iran's policy-making elite.

## Summary

The clergy exercise authority over elected officials in three separate ways: the Leader, a cleric, supervises the three branches of government; the Guardian Council can veto legislation passed by parliament; and the same Council can vet all candidates running for high office. Despite these restrictions, the constitution—in theory—has the possibility of moving away from theocracy toward democracy. After all, the constitution enshrines the public's right to elect parliament, president, and even the Leader. The constitution even endows the public with the authority to amend the constitution. The main obstacle to democracy is the vetting process, which grants ultimate power to the Leader, not the constitution itself.

# REPRESENTATION AND PARTICIPATION

Although the Islamic Republic is a theocracy, some claim that it also has features of a democracy. According to the constitution, the voters directly choose the president and the Assembly of Experts, which in turn chooses the Leader. What is more, the elected legislature, the *Majles*, exercises considerable power. According to one of the founders of the regime, the *Majles* is the centerpiece of the Islamic constitution.[9] Another architect of the constitution has argued that the people, by carrying out the Islamic Revolution, implicitly favored a type of democracy confined within the boundaries of Islam and the guardianship of the jurist.[10] But another declared that if he had to choose between the democracy and power of the clergy as specified in the concept of jurist's guardianship, he would not hesitate to choose the latter, since it came directly from God.[11] On the eve of the initial referendum, Khomeini himself declared: "This constitution, which the people will ratify, in no way contradicts democracy. Since the people love the clergy, have faith in the clergy, want to be guided by the clergy, it is only right that the supreme religious authority oversee the work of the [government] ministers to ensure that they don't make mistakes or go against the Qur'an."[12]

**Focus Questions**

What are the powers and limitations of Iran's parliament?

What role do political parties and elections play within Iran's theocratic state?

What social groups are most likely and least likely to support the Islamic Republic?

Do discontent and protest necessarily have to take a revolutionary rather than a reform course in the Islamic Republic?

## The Legislature

According to Iran's constitution, the *Majles* "represents the nation" and possesses many powers, including making or changing ordinary laws (with the approval of the Guardian Council), investigating and supervising all affairs of state, and approving or ousting the cabinet ministers. In describing this branch of government, the constitution uses the term *qanun* (statutes) rather than *shari'a* (divine law) so as to gloss over the fundamental question of whether legislation passed by the *Majles* is derived from God or the people. It accepts the reasoning that God creates divine law (*shari'a*) but elected representatives can draw up worldly statutes (*qanuns*).

The *Majles* has 290 members and is elected by citizens over the age of eighteen. It can pass *qanuns* as long as the Guardian Council deems them compatible with the *shari'a* and the constitution. It can choose, from a list drawn up by the chief judge, six of the twelve-man Guardian Council. It can investigate at will cabinet ministers, affairs of state, and public complaints against the executive and the judiciary. It can remove cabinet members—with the exception of the president—through a parliamentary vote of no confidence. It can withhold approval for government budgets, foreign loans, international treaties, and cabinet appointments. It can hold closed debates, provide members with immunity from arrest, and regulate its own internal workings, especially the committee system.

The *Majles* plays an important role in everyday politics. It has changed government budgets, criticized cabinet policies, modified development plans, and forced the president to replace some of his ministers. In 1992, 217 deputies circulated an open letter that explicitly emphasized the powers of the *Majles* and thereby implicitly downplayed those of the Leader. Likewise, the Speaker of the House in 2002 threatened to close down the whole *Majles* if the judiciary violated parliamentary immunity and arrested one of the liberal deputies.

# Political Parties and the Party System

Iran's constitution guarantees citizens the right to organize, and a 1980 law permits the Interior Ministry to issue licenses to parties. But political parties were not encouraged until Khatami was elected president in 1997. Since then, three parties have been active: the Islamic Iran Participation Front and the Islamic Labor Party, both formed by Khatami reformist supporters, and the more centrist Servants of Reconstruction created by *Hojjat al-Islam* Ali-Akbar Hashemi Rafsanjani, the former president and now chairman of the Expediency Council.

In general, formal parties are less important in Iranian politics than reformist and conservative coalitions and groups that form along ideological and policy lines. For example, the current president, Ahmadinejad, has his power base in the Alliance of Builders of Islamic Iran, a coalition of several conservative political parties and organizations that delivered votes very effectively in recent local (2003), parliamentary (2004), and presidential (2005) elections.

According to the Interior Ministry, licenses have been granted to some seven hundred political, social, and cultural organizations, but all are led by people considered politically acceptable by the regime. Real political opposition has been forced into exile, mostly in Europe. The most important opposition groups are:

- **The Liberation Movement.** Established in 1961 by Mehdi Bazargan, the Islamic Republic's first prime minister. Bazargan had been appointed premier in February 1979 by Khomeini himself, but had resigned in disgust ten months later when the Revolutionary Guards had permitted students to take over the U.S. embassy. The Liberation Movement is a moderate Islamic party. Despite its religious orientation, it is secular and favors the strict separation of mosque from state.
- **The National Front.** Originating in the campaign to nationalize the country's oil resources in the early 1950s, the National Front remains committed to nationalism and secularism, the political ideals of Muhammad Mosaddeq, the prime minister who was overthrown in the CIA-supported coup in 1953. Because the conservative clergy feel threatened by the National Front's potential appeal, they have banned it.
- **The Mojahedin.** Formed in 1971 as a guerrilla organization to fight the shah's regime, the Mojahedin tried to synthesize Marxism and Islam. It interpreted Shi'i Islam as a radical religion favoring equality, social justice, martyrdom, and redistribution of wealth. Immediately after the revolution, the Mojahedin opposed the clerical regime and attracted a large following among students. The regime retaliated with mass executions forcing the Mojahedin to move their base of operations to Iraq. Not unexpectedly, the Mojahedin became associated with a national enemy and thereby lost much of its appeal.
- **The Fedayin.** Also formed in 1971, the Fedayin modeled itself after the Marxist guerrilla movements of the 1960s in Latin America, especially those inspired by Che Guevara and the Cuban revolution. Losing more fighters than any other organization in the struggle against the shah, the Fedayin came out of the revolution with great mystique and popular urban support. But it soon lost much of its strength because of massive government repression and a series of internal splits.
- **The Tudeh (Party of the Masses).** Established in 1941, the Tudeh is a mainstream, formerly pro-Soviet communist party. Although the Tudeh initially supported the Islamic Republic as a "popular anti-imperialist state," it was banned, and most of its organizers were executed during the 1980s.

# Elections

The constitution promises free elections. In practice, however, *Majles* elections, which are held every four years, have varied from relatively free but disorderly in the early days of the Islamic Republic to controlled and highly unfair in the middle years; back to relatively free, but orderly in the late 1990s; and back again to highly controlled—even rigged—in 2009. If the latter is asign of things to come, one can safely predict that the republic's democratic features have been sacrificed for its theocratic, authoritarian ones, in which case, the Islamic Republic has lost a major component of its legitimacy.

In the 1980s, ballot boxes were placed in mosques with Revolutionary Guards supervising the voting. Neighborhood clerics were on hand to help illiterates complete their ballots. Club-wielding gangs assaulted regime opponents. Now electoral freedom is restricted by the government-controlled radio-television network, the main source of information for the vast majority of citizens. The Interior Ministry can ban dissident organizations, especially their newspapers on the grounds they are anti-Islamic. Moreover, the electoral law, based on a winner-take-all majority system rather than on proportional representation, is designed to minimize the voice of the opposition.

But the main obstacle to fair elections has been the Guardian Council with its powers to approve all candidates. For example, the Council excluded some 3500 candidates (nearly half of the total) from running in the parliamentary elections of 2004 by questioning their loyalty to the concept of jurist's guardianship. The purge of reformers was facilitated both by President Bush's labeling of Iran as a member of the global "Axis of Evil" in 2002 and by the American military occupation of Afghanistan and Iraq. Reluctant to rock the boat at a time of apparent and imminent "national danger," most reformers restrained themselves and withdrew from active politics. Not surprisingly, the conservatives won a hollow victory in the 2004 *Majles* elections. They received a clear majority of the seats, but the voter turnout was less than 51 percent, and in Tehran only 28 percent. This was the worst showing since 1979. For a regime that liked to boast about mass participation, this was seen as a major setback—even as a crisis of legitimacy. There was a bit of an upturn, to about 60 percent, in the turnout in both rounds of the presidential election of 2005. Still this was a sharp downturn from the more than 80 percent that had voted in the 1997 presidential contest that brought the reformist Khatami to power. The 2009 elections, by reactivating the reform movement, may well have produced another record turnout, but because of government interference in tallying the vote, the facts are still unclear.

# Political Culture, Citizenship, and Identity

In theory, the Islamic Republic of Iran should be a highly viable state. After all, Shi'ism is the religion of both the state and the vast majority of the population. Shi'ism is the central component of Iranian popular culture. Also, the constitution guarantees basic rights to religious minorities as well as to individual citizens. All citizens, regardless of race, language, or religion, are promised the rights of free expression, worship, and organization. They are guaranteed freedom from arbitrary arrest, torture, and police surveillance.

The constitution extends additional rights to the recognized religious minorities: Christians, Jews, and Zoroastrians. Although Christians (Armenians and Assyrians), Jews, and Zoroastrians form just 1 percent of the total population, they are allocated five *Majles* seats. They are permitted their own community organizations, including schools, their own places of worship, and their own family laws. The constitution, however, is ominously silent about Sunnis and Baha'is. Sunni Muslims are treated in theory as full citizens, but their actual status is not spelled out. Believers in Baha'ism, a monotheistic religion founded in nineteenth-century Persia that emphasizes the spiritual unity of all humankind, are considered heretics because their founder had proclaimed his own teachings to supersede that of not only the Old and New Testaments but also of the Qur'an and the Shi'i Imams. Moreover, some ultraconservative Shi'is deem Baha'is to be part of the "international Zionist conspiracy" on the grounds their main shrine is located in modern-day Israel.

The constitution also gives guarantees to non-Persian speakers. Although 83 percent of the population understands Persian, thanks to the educational system, over 50 percent continue to speak non-Persian languages at home—languages such as Azeri, Kurdish, Turkic, Gilaki, Mazandarani, Arabic, and Baluchi. The constitution promises them rights unprecedented in Iranian history. It states that "local and native languages can be used in the press, media, and schools." It also states that local populations have the right to elect provincial, town, and village councils. These councils can watch over the governors-general and the town mayors, as well as their educational, cultural, and social programs.

These generous promises have often been honored more in theory than in practice. The local councils—the chief institution that protected minorities—were not held until twenty years after the revolution. Subsidies to non-Persian publications and radio stations remain meager. Jews have been so harassed as "pro-Israeli Zionists" that more than half—40,000 out of 80,000—have left the country since the revolution. Armenian Christians had to end coeducational classes, adopt the government curriculum, and abide by Muslim dress codes, including the veil. The Christian population has declined from over 300,000 to fewer than 200,000.

The Baha'is, however, have borne the brunt of religious persecution. Their leaders have been executed as "heretics" and "imperialist spies." Adherents have been fired from their jobs, had their property confiscated, and been imprisoned and tortured to pressure them to convert to Islam. Their schools have been closed, their community property expropriated, and their shrines and cemeteries bulldozed. It is estimated that since the revolution, one-third of the 300,000 Baha'is have left Iran. The Baha'is, like the Jews and Armenians, have migrated mostly to Canada and the United States.

The Sunni population, which forms as much as 10 percent of the total, has its own reasons for being alienated from Iran's Islamic Republic. The state religion is Shi'ism, and high officials have to be Shi'i. Citizens must abide by Khomeini's concept of jurists' guardianship, a notion derived from Shi'ism. Few institutions cater to Sunni needs. There is not a single Sunni mosque in the whole of Tehran. Iran's Kurds, Turkmans, Arabs, and Baluchis are also Sunnis, and it is no accident that immediately after the 1979 revolution, the new regime faced its most serious challenges in precisely the areas of the country where these linguistic and religious minorities lived. It crushed these revolts by sending in Revolutionary Guards from the Persian Shi'i heartland of Isfahan, Shiraz, and Qom.

Azeris, who are Shi'i but not Persian speakers, are well integrated into Iran. In the past, the Azeris, who form 24 percent of the population and dwarf the other minorities, have not posed a serious problem to the state. They are part of the Shi'i community, and have prominent figures in the Shi'i hierarchy—most notably the current

Leader, Khamenei. What is more, many Azeri merchants, professionals, and workers live and work throughout Iran.

But the 1991 creation of the Republic of Azerbaijan on Iran's northeastern border following the disintegration of the Soviet Union has raised new concerns, since some Azeris on both sides of the border have begun to talk of establishing a larger unified Azerbaijan. It is no accident that in the war between Azerbaijan and Armenia in the early 1990s, Iran favored the latter. So far, the concept of a unified Azerbaijan appears to have limited appeal among Iranian Azeris.

# Interests, Social Movements, and Protest

In the first two decades after its founding, the government of the Islamic Republic often violated its own constitution. It closed down newspapers, professional associations, labor unions, and political parties. It banned demonstrations and public meetings. It imprisoned tens of thousands without due process. It systematically tortured prisoners to extract false confessions and public recantations. And it executed some 25,000 political prisoners, most of them without due process of law. The United Nations, Amnesty International, and Human Rights Watch all took Iran to task for violating the UN Human Rights Charter as well its own Islamic constitution. Most victims were Kurds, military officers from the old regime, and leftists, especially members of the Mojahedin and Fedayin.

Although the violation of individual liberties affected the whole population, it aroused special resentment among three social groups: the modern middle class, educated women, and organized labor. The modern middle class, especially the intelligentsia, has been secular and even anticlerical ever since the 1905 revolution. Little

Executions in Kurdestan, 1979.

*Source:* Jahangir Razmi

© Bettmann/Corbis.

love is lost between it and the Islamic Republic. Not surprisingly, the vast majority of those executed in the 1980s were teachers, engineers, professionals, and college students.

Youth, especially college students, are a force to be reckoned with: Over half the current population was born after 1979 and as many as 1.15 million are enrolled in higher education. In 1999, eighteen different campuses, including Tehran University, erupted into mass demonstrations against the chief judge, who had closed down a reformist newspaper. Revolutionary Guards promptly occupied the campuses, killing or seriously injuring an unknown number of students. Again in late 2002, thousands of students protested the death sentence handed down to a reformist academic accused of insulting Islam. But in 2004, when the Guardian Council barred thousands of reformers from the parliamentary elections, the campuses remained quiet, partly out of fear, partly out of disenchantment with the reformers for failing to deliver on their promises, and partly because of the concern about the looming danger from the United States military presence in Iraq. Students, however, returned to active politics in large numbers during the 2009 presidential elections between Ahmadinejad and the reform candidates, and even more so in the mass demonstrations protesting these contested elections.

Educated women in Iran also harbor numerous grievances against the conservative clerics in the regime, especially in the judiciary. Although the Western press often dwells on the head-scarf, Iranian women consider the veil one of their less important problems. Given a choice, most would probably continue to wear it out of personal habit and national tradition. More important are work-related grievances: job security, pay scales, promotions, maternity leave, and access to prestigious professions. Despite patriarchal attitudes held by the conservative clergy, educated women have become a major factor in Iranian society. They now form 54 percent of college students, 45 percent of doctors, 25 percent of government employees, and 30 percent of the general labor force, up from 8 percent in the 1980s. They have established their own organizations and journals reinterpreting Islam to conform to modern notions of gender equality. Their main organization is known as the Women's One Million Signature Campaign. Women do serve in the *Majles* (there are ten in the current parliament, 2.8 percent of the total) and on local councils. One grand ayatollah has even argued that they should be able to hold any job, including president, court judge, and even Leader.

Factory workers in Iran are another significant social group with serious grievances. Their concerns deal mostly with high unemployment, low wages, declining incomes, lack of decent housing, and an unsatisfactory labor law, which, while giving them mandatory holidays and some semblance of job security, denies them the right to call strikes and organize independent unions. Since 1979, wage earners have had a Workers' House—a government-influenced organization—and its affiliated newspaper, *Kar va Kargar (Work and Worker)*, and since 1999 the Islamic Labor Party has represented their interests. In most years, the Workers' House flexes its political muscle by holding a May Day rally. In 1999, the rally began peacefully with a greeting from a woman reform deputy who had received the second-most votes in the 1996 Tehran municipal elections. But the rally turned into a protest when workers began to march to parliament denouncing conservatives who had spoken in favor of further watering down of the Labor Law. On May Day 2006, an estimated 10,000 workers marched to demand that the labor minister resign. Bus drivers in Tehran, who had been active in earlier protests, went on strike in January 2006 to protest the arrest and maltreatment of one of their leaders. Workers also protested the contested presidential elections of 2009 by participating in the mass demonstrations.

## Summary

The Bush administration liked to denounce Iran as a "totalitarian state" tyrannized by unelected unpopular leaders. While Iran is no liberal democracy, it hardly fits the "totalitarian" category. The clergy, despite opposition from the intelligentsia, continue to rule in part because they still enjoy some legitimacy—especially among the bazaars, rural population, and urban poor; in part because they have brought economic benefits to the wider population; and in part because they have left some room for civil society and have permitted interest groups to function so long as they do not violate red lines and directly question the clergy's legitimacy. They have also been greatly helped by the perceived notion that the nation is under siege—even under imminent threat—from the United States. The 2009 electoral rigging was a major blow to democracy, but, despite this, one should not write an obituary for democracy in Iran. Because of the long tradition of mass participation in politics, the democratic impulse remains there—however stifled at present.

# IRANIAN POLITICS IN TRANSITION

The mass demonstrations that brought down the presidents of both Tunisia and Egypt in 2011 had repercussions in Iran. The Leader praised them claiming they replicated the Islamic Revolution of 1979 in Iran. The Iranian reform movement countered that these demonstrations were inspired by the 2009 protests against the rigged elections and that they showed such protests—if continued for length of time—could bring down autocratic regimes. The Leader categorized Mubarek of Egypt and Bin Ali of Tunisia as versions of the Shah of Iran who was deposed by the Islamic Revolution of 1979. The reformers categorized Mubarek and Bin Ali as their version of current Iranian president, Ahmadinejad. Despite these polemics, there were major differences. Mubarek and Bin Ali, as well as the shah, ultimately fell from power because of the defection of their armed forces. Ahmadinejad and the Leader have survived because they have so far retained the support of critical elements of the armed forces.

### Focus Questions

What are the most important political challenges that now face Iran?

What are some of the ways in which Iran is different from other developing countries?

## Political Challenges and Changing Agendas

Contemporary Iran faces two major challenges—one internal, the other external. Internally, the Islamic Republic continues to struggle with the troubling question of how to combine theocracy with democracy, and clerical authority with mass participation. After several years when Iran's reformers seemed to be on the political rise, the conservative clerics and their supporters, who already controlled the judiciary, took over the *Majles* in 2004. In June 2005 they took over the executive as well with the election of Ahmadinejad as president. They held on to the executive in 2009 only through massive electoral rigging.

Many observers think that even though the conservatives appear to have gained the upper hand politically, they have lost touch with the grassroots of Iranian society since their political base is less than 20–25 percent of the electorate. It is estimated that over 70 percent of the public favors the reformers, and that much of this majority, if not offered real choices, will, at a minimum, protest by staying home on election days. In fact, conservatives do best when the turnout is low, reformers benefit when it is high. The ruling conservatives now face the challenge of how to maintain some semblance of legitimacy while not actually sharing power with the reformers, who most probably enjoy the support of the majority of the electorate.

This challenge is troubling to the clerical leadership since the country has in recent decades gone through a profound transformation in political values, with much of the population embracing key aspects of the democratic idea including political pluralism, mass participation, civil society, human rights, and individual liberties. Even conservatives have begun to use such terms, openly describing themselves as "neoconservatives," "constructivists," and "pragmatists."

Meanwhile, those in the general public who feel excluded from national politics remain active in influential nongovernmental organizations that make up an important part of Iranian civil society. The most visible of these is a human rights group headed by Shirin Ebadi, the winner of the Nobel Peace Prize in 2003. Ms. Ebadi has been a lawyer, judge (until the Islamic Republic barred women from holding such positions), writer, teacher, and activist, and has been most prominent in the struggle to protect the rights of women and children. Even if they are completely excluded from the political arena by the conservative religious establishment, so far concerned citizens such as Ebadi remain committed to using legal, nonviolent means to promote change. But they do not want to be associated with American projects for "regime change."

The Islamic Republic's first attempt to enter the international arena as a militant force to spread its theocratic version of Islam proved counterproductive. This effort diverted scarce resources to the military and contributed to the disastrous war with Iraq. It drove Saudi Arabia and the Gulf sheikdoms into a closer relationship with the United States. It prompted the United States to isolate Iran, discouraged foreign investment, and prevented international organizations from extending economic assistance. Iran's militancy has also alarmed nearby secular Islamic states such as Turkey, Tadzhikistan, and Azerbaijan. During the Khatami years, however, the regime managed to repair some of this damage. It won over many Arab states and established cordial relations with its neighbors. It also managed to repair some bridges to the European Community. Some of this repair work has been damaged in more recent years by the Ahmadinejad administration.

The major external challenge to the Islamic Republic comes from the United States. The Bush administration, by naming Iran as a member of the "Axis of Evil" in 2002 and openly calling for "regime change" (and promoting such change by military means in neighboring Afghanistan and Iraq) has dramatically increased pressures on Iran beyond those that already existed because of American economic sanctions, lack of diplomatic relations, and successful barring of Iran from the World Trade Organization. The United States has accused Iran of sabotaging the Arab-Israeli peace process, helping terrorist organizations, especially Hamas in Palestine and Hezbollah in Lebanon, and "grossly violating" democratic and human rights of its own citizens. More recently the United States has highlighted the danger of "weapons of mass destruction" in Iran and accused the country of intending to transform its nuclear energy program into a nuclear weapons program. Even more recently, it has accused Iran of arming and training insurgents in Iraq. Some analysts remain skeptical of such accusations.

The conservative clerics who now dominate Iranian politics have been able to transform this external threat into a political asset. They have intimidated many reformers into toning down their demands for domestic change, even silencing them, by declaring that the country was in danger, that the enemy was at the gates, and that any opposition to the government in such times would play into the hands of those who wanted to do harm to Iran. Even in the United States people have speculated about whether the Bush administration was seriously considering taking some type of military action against Iran—perhaps a preemptive air strike against its nuclear reactors. These speculations have fed the perception of threat. Few Iranians are willing to appear unpatriotic by openly criticizing their government at a time of external danger.

The Obama administration has followed a more nuanced and ambiguous policy. Before his election, Obama offered an olive branch and implicitly accepted Iran's right to enrich uranium so long as it gave verifiable guarantees it would not produce nuclear weapons. After the election, he continued to hold out an olive branch but muddied the implicit acceptance by imposing stringent economic sanctions in order to presumably bring Iran into negotiations. Unless these sanctions are at some point coupled with some form of compromise offer, they will be taken in Iran—by reformers as well as conservatives—as a continuation of Bush's threats and yet another evidence that the United States—like previous imperial powers—aspires to impose its will on Iran.

# Iranian Politics in Comparative Perspective

Unlike most developing countries, Iran was never formally colonized by the European imperial powers and has always been independent. It is, in many ways, an old state with many institutions that date back to ancient times. Furthermore, while many other Third World states have weak connections with their societies, Iran has a religion that links the elite with the masses, the cities with the villages, the government with the citizenry. Shi'ism, as well as Iranian national identity, serves as social and cultural cement, which gives the population a strong collective identity. Iran also has the advantage of abundant oil resources that can be the basis for economic growth that would be the envy of most developing countries.

Nevertheless, Iran also has much in common with other developing countries. Despite some modern aspects, its economy remains largely underdeveloped, highly dependent on one commodity, and unable to meet the rising expectations of its population. Iran's collective identity, although strong in religious terms, is strained by other internal fault lines, especially those of class, ethnicity, gender, and political differences. It wants to be an important player in the world of states, but international, domestic, and regional problems have combined to keep the country pretty much on the global sidelines.

The development of the democratic idea in Iran has been constricted by theocracy. Some argue that Islam has made this inevitable. But Islam, like the other major religions, can be interpreted in ways that either promote or hinder democracy. Some interpretations of Islam stress the importance of justice, equality, and consultation as political principles. Islam also has a tradition of tolerating other religions, and the *shari'a* explicitly protects life, property, and honor. In practice, Islam has often separated politics from religion, government legal statutes from holy laws, spiritual affairs from worldly matters, and the state from the clerical establishment.

Moreover, theocracy in Iran originates not in Islam itself but in the very specific concept of the jurist's guardianship as developed by Khomeini. On the whole, Sunni Islam considers clerics to be theological scholars, not a special political class. This helps explain why the Iranian regime has found it difficult to export its revolution to other parts of the Muslim world. The failure of democracy to take deeper root in

Iran should be attributed less to anything intrinsic in Islam than to the combination of crises between 1979 and 1981 that allowed a particular group of clerics to come to power. Whether they remain in power depends not so much on Islamic values but on how they handle socioeconomic problems, especially the demands for public participation.

Politics in the Islamic Republic of Iran is sharply divided over the question of how to govern an economy beset by rising demands, wildly fluctuating petroleum revenues, and the nightmarish prospect that in the next two generations, the oil wells will run dry. Most clerics favor a rather conventional capitalist road to development, hoping to liberalize the market, privatize industry, attract foreign capital, and encourage the propertied classes to invest. Others envisage an equally conventional statist road to development, favoring central planning, government industries, price controls, high taxes, state subsidies, national self-reliance, and ambitious programs to eliminate poverty, illiteracy, slums, and unemployment. Some are hoping to find a third way, combining elements of state intervention with free enterprise that is similar to the social democracy favored, for example, by the Labour Party in Britain.

Economic problems like those that undermined the monarchy could well undermine the Islamic Republic, particularly if there was another sharp drop in oil prices. The country's collective identity has also come under great strain in recent years. The emphasis on Shi'ism has antagonized Iran's Sunnis as well as its non-Muslim citizens. The emphasis on clerical Shi'ism has further alienated all secularists, including lay liberals and moderate nationalists, to say nothing of a large majority of Iranians who live abroad. Furthermore, the official emphasis on Khomeini's brand of Shi'ism has alienated those Shi'is who reject the whole notion of jurist's guardianship. The elevation of Khamenei as the Leader has also antagonized many early proponents of jurist's guardianship on the grounds that he lacks the scholarly qualifications to hold the position that embodies the sacred and secular power of the Islamic Republic.

Iran's ruling clerical regime has gradually eroded the broad social base that brought it to power in the Islamic Revolution nearly three decades ago. Growing discontent may be expressed through apolitical channels, such as apathy, emigration, inward-looking religion, or even drug addiction. There is also a possibility that those seeking change may turn to radical action if they cannot attain their goals through legal reformist movement. Those who want to understand the possibilities for political change in Iran would do well to remember that the country produced two popular upheavals in the twentieth century that fundamentally transformed the political system: the constitutional (1905) and the Islamic (1979) revolutions.

## Summary

To predict the future is a hazardous task. Iran could meet its internal challenge by becoming more flexible, liberalizing, giving greater scope to civil society, and allowing more public participation and competitive elections—in short, strengthening the democratic as opposed to the theocratic features of the constitution. If it did so, it would transform itself closer to democracy. If it does not, it could freeze up, alienate the public, lose legitimacy, and thereby make itself vulnerable to destruction. Iran could also meet its external challenge by following a cautious foreign policy, going slow on its nuclear program, providing verifiable guarantees that it was not building nuclear weapons, toning down its rhetoric, and assuring its neighbors as well as the United States that it was a "normal state" uninterested in exporting revolution. If it does not, it could well end up with a confrontation with the United States—a confrontation that would be disastrous for both countries.

## Key Terms

ayatollah
civil society
theocracy
*Majles*
Guardian Council
Leader/Supreme Leader
Farsi
People of the Book
Qur'an
*shari'a*
coup d'état

bazaar
fundamentalism
political Islam
jurist's guardianship
*pasdaran*
Assembly of Experts
Hezbollahis
*hojjat al-Islam*
laissez-faire
Islamism
rentier state

dual society
OPEC (Organization of
    Petroleum Exporting
    Countries)
resource curse
Expediency Council
Imam Jum'ehs
Foundation of the
    Oppressed
*maslahat*

## Suggested Readings

Abrahamian, Ervand. *Khomeinism*. Berkeley: University of California Press, 1993.

Ibid.————. *A History of Modern Iran*. New York: Cambridge University Press, 2008.

Ansari, Ali M. *Confronting Iran: The Failure of American Foreign Policy and the Next Great Crisis in the Middle East*. New York: Perseus, 2006.

Beeman, William O. *The "Great Satan" vs. the "Mad Mullahs": How the United States and Iran Demonize Each Other*. New York: Praeger, 2005.

Cook, Michael. *The Koran: A Very Short Introduction*. New York: Oxford University Press, 2000.

Cronin, Stephanie, ed. *Reformers and Revolutionaries in Modern Iran*. London: Routledge, 2004.

Ebadi, Shirin, and Azadeh Moaveni. *Iran Awakening: A Memoir of Revolution and Hope*. New York: Random House, 2006.

Garthwaite, Gene R. *The Persians*. Malden, Mass.: Blackwell, 2005.

Gheissari, Ali, ed., *Contemporary Iran: Economy, Society, Politics*. New York: Oxford University Press, 2009.

Gheissari, Ali, and Vali Nasr. *Democracy in Iran: History and the Quest for Liberty*. New York: Oxford University Press, 2006.

Keddie, Nikki. *Modern Iran: Roots and Results of Revolution*, updated ed. New Haven, Conn.: Yale University Press, 2006.

Kinzer, Stephen. *All the Shah's Men: An American Coup and the Roots of Middle East Terror*. New York: John Wiley & Sons, 2004.

Moin, Baqer. *Khomeini: Life of the Ayatollah*. New York: Thomas Dunne Books, 2000.

Nafisi, Azar. *Reading Lolita in Tehran: A Memoir in Books*. New York: Random House, 2003.

Pollack, Kenneth. *The Persian Puzzle: The Conflict between Iran and America*. New York: Random House, 2005.

Ruthven, Malise. *Islam: A Very Short Introduction*. New York: Oxford University Press, 2000.

Satrapi, Marjaneh. *Persepolis*. New York: Pantheon, 2003.

Takeyh, Ray. *Hidden Iran: Paradox and Power in the Islamic Republic*. New York: Times Books, 2006.

Wright, Robin, ed. *The Iran Primer: Power, Politics, and U.S. Policy*. Washington, D.C.: United States Institute of Peace, 2010.

## Suggested Websites

University of Texas—Iran Maps
**www.lib.utexas.edu/maps/iran.html**

Columbia University—The Gulf/2000 Project's Map
    Collection
**gulf2000.columbia.edu/maps.shtml**

The Story of the Revolution, British Broadcasting
    Corporation
**www.bbc.co.uk/persian/revolution**

Iranian Mission to the United Nations
**www.un.int/iran**

Iran Report, Radio Free Europe
**www.rferl.org/reports/iran-report**

News Related to Iran
**www.farsinews.net**

# 14 China

William A. Joseph

**Official Name:** People's Republic of China (Zhonghua Remin Gongheguo)

**Location:** East Asia

**Capital City:** Beijing

**Population (2010):** 1.3 billion

**Size:** 9,596,960 sq. km.; slightly smaller than the United States

**1912**
Sun Yat-sen founds the Nationalist Party (*Guomindang*) to oppose warlords who have seized power in the new republic

**1927**
Civil war between Nationalists (now led by Chiang Kai-shek) and Communists begins

**1937**
Japan invades China, marking the start of World War II in Asia.

| 1700 | 1900 | 1910 | 1920 | 1930 | 1940 | 1950 |

**1911**
Revolution led by Sun Yat-sen overthrows 2,000-year-old imperial system and establishes the Republic of China

**1921**
Chinese Communist Party (CCP) is founded

**1934**
Mao Zedong becomes leader of the CCP; formally elected chairman in 1943

**1949**
Chinese Communists win the civil war and establish the People's Republic of China.

SECTION

# THE MAKING OF THE MODERN CHINESE STATE

**Focus Questions**

Why did China's 2000-year old imperial system collapse in the early twentieth century?

How did the Chinese Communist Party come to power in China?

What impact did Mao Zedong and Deng Xiaoping have on China's political and economic development?

In what ways might China be compared to other countries?

## Politics in Action

In late 2010, the Nobel Peace Prize was awarded to Chinese writer and political activist Liu Xiaobo. Liu was the first citizen of the People's Republic of China (PRC) ever to win any kind of Nobel Prize,[1] which is also given in fields such as economics, medicine, and literature. The Peace Prize is one of most important global honors that can be given to anyone involved in politics. Past recipients have included Woodrow Wilson, Martin Luther King, Nelson Mandela, and Barack Obama.

According to the award citation, Liu Xiaobo received the Prize for "for his long and non-violent struggle for fundamental human rights in China." But Liu could not attend the awards ceremony in Oslo, Norway, because he was in a Chinese prison. His place at the ceremonies was symbolically filled by an empty chair. The Chinese government denounced the Nobel Peace Prize committee for insulting China by honoring a man they said was a criminal who had been tried and sentenced according to the law.

Liu was trained as a scholar of literary theory. He participated in pro-democracy demonstrations in Beijing's Tiananmen Square in 1989, which were violently crushed by the Chinese army. If not for his efforts to get many protesting students to leave the Square before the crackdown, the death toll would have been much greater. Liu was arrested for "counter-revolutionary incitement" and spent about 19 months in prison. In subsequent years, he was jailed numerous times for his political activities.

In December 2008, Liu was among the leaders of a group of prominent Chinese citizens who drafted Charter 08 calling on China's leaders to abide by the United Nations Declaration of Universal Human Rights and declaring that "democratic political reform can be delayed no longer." Even before its official public release, Liu and other activists were taken into custody. A year later he was put on trial and found guilty of "inciting subversion of state power." He was sentenced to 11 years in prison, which is why he couldn't accept the Nobel Peace Prize in person or even publically acknowledge the honor bestowed upon him.

**2002–2003**
Hu Jintao succeeds Jiang as head of the CCP and president of the People's Republic of China; re-elected to those positions in 2007–2008.

**1966–1976**
Great Proletarian Cultural Revolution

**1976**
Mao Zedong dies.

**1989**
Tiananmen massacre

1960    1970    1980    1990    2000    2010

**1958–1960**
Great Leap Forward

**1978**
Deng Xiaoping becomes China's most powerful leader and launches the nation on the path toward rapid economic growth.

**1997**
Deng Xiaoping dies; Jiang Zemin becomes China's top leader.

**2008**
Hosts the Olympic Games in Beijing

Liu Xiaobo's empty chair in Oslo spoke volumes about politics in the People's Republic of China. For all of its truly remarkable economic progress, the country remains one of the world's harshest dictatorships. The rift between China's authoritarian political system and its increasingly modern and globalized society is deep and ominous.

# Geographic Setting

China is located in the eastern part of mainland Asia, at the heart of one of the world's most strategically important regions. It is slightly smaller than the United States in land area, and is the fourth-largest country in the world, after Russia, Canada, and the United States.

**Ethnic Groups**

55 other nationalities, including Zhuang, Manchu, Hui, Miao, Uyghur, Mongal, Tibetan, and Korean, 8.5%

Han Chinese 91.5%

**Chinese Currency**
Renminbi(RMB)("People's Currency"); also called yuan
International Designation: RMB
Exchange Rate (2010): US$1 = 6.79 RMB
100 RMB Note Design: Mao Zedong (1893–1976), Chairman of Chinese Communist Party (1943–1976)

**Major Ethnic Groups**

**Languages:** Standard Chinese (Mandarin) based on the Beijing dialect; other major dialects include Cantonese and Shanghaiese. Also various minority languages, such as Tibetan and Mongolian.

**Religions:** Officially atheist; Over 16 population: Buddist, Taoists, folk religions, 21%; Christian, 4%; Muslim, 2%.

**FIGURE 14.1 The Chinese Nation at a Glance**

| Table 14.1 | Political Organization |
|---|---|
| **Political System** | Communist party-state; officially, a socialist state under the people's democratic dictatorship. |
| **Regime History** | Established in 1949 after the victory of the Chinese Communist Party (CCP) in the Chinese civil war. |
| **Administrative Structure** | Unitary system with twenty-two provinces, five autonomous regions, four centrally administrated municipalities, and two Special Administrative Regions (Hong Kong and Macao). |
| **Executive** | Premier (head of government) and president (head of state) formally elected by legislature, but only with approval of CCP leadership; the head of the CCP, the general secretary, is in effect the country's chief executive, and usually serves concurrently as president of the PRC. |
| **Legislature** | Unicameral National People's Congress; about 3,000 delegates elected indirectly from lower-level people's congresses for five-year terms. Largely a rubber-stamp body for Communist Party policies, although in recent years has become somewhat more assertive. |
| **Judiciary** | A nationwide system of people's courts, which is constitutionally independent but, in fact, largely under the control of the CCP; a Supreme People's Court supervises the country's judicial system and is formally responsible to the National People's Congress, which also elects the court's president. |
| **Party System** | A one-party system, although in addition to the ruling Chinese Communist Party, there are eight politically insignificant "democratic" parties. |

**autonomous region**

A territorial unit that is equivalent to a province and contains a large concentration of ethnic minorities. These regions, for example, Tibet, have some autonomy in the cultural sphere but in most policy matters are strictly subordinate to the central government.

The PRC consists of twenty-two provinces, five **autonomous regions**, four centrally administered cities (including the capital, Beijing), and two Special Administrative Regions (Hong Kong and Macau) that are indirectly ruled by China. The vast, sparsely populated western part of the country is mostly mountains, deserts, and high plateaus. The north is much like the U.S. plains states in its weather and topography. This wheat-growing area is also China's industrial heartland. Southern China has a much warmer climate. In places it is even semitropical, which allows year-round agriculture and intensive rice cultivation. The country is very rich in natural resources, particularly coal and petroleum (including significant, but untapped onshore and offshore reserves). It has the world's greatest potential for hydroelectric power. Still, China's astounding economic growth in recent decades has created an almost insatiable demand for energy resources. This, in turn, has led the PRC to look abroad for critical raw materials.

Although China and the United States are roughly equal in area, China's population of 1.3 billion is more than four times greater. Less than 15 percent of its land, however, can be used for agriculture. The precarious balance between people and the land needed to feed them has been a dilemma for centuries. It remains one of the government's major concerns.

China has nearly 120 cities with a population of a million or more. Beijing, the capital, has 19.6 million registered residents, while Shanghai, the economic heart of the country, has 23.0 million. Nevertheless, about 55 percent of China's people—700 million—live in rural areas. The countryside has played—and continues to play—a very important role in China's political development.

In 1997, the former British colony of Hong Kong, one of the world's great commercial centers, became a Special Administrative Region (SAR) of the PRC. Hong Kong and China's other SAR, Macau, a former Portuguese colony with a thriving casino economy that became part of the PRC in 1999, have a great deal of autonomy from the government in Beijing in most matters other than foreign relations and defense.

The great majority (about 92 percent) of China's citizens are ethnically Chinese. The remaining 8 percent is made up of more than fifty ethnic minorities. Most of these minority peoples live in the country's geopolitically sensitive border regions, including Tibet. This makes the often uneasy and sometimes hostile relationship between China's minority peoples and the central government in Beijing a crucial and volatile issue in Chinese politics today.

# Critical Junctures

Traditional Chinese culture was based on the teachings of the ancient philosopher, Confucius (551–479 BCE). Confucianism emphasizes obedience to authority, respect for superiors and elders, as well as the responsibility of rulers to govern benevolently, and the importance of education. In 221 BCE, several small kingdoms were unified by the man who would become the first emperor of China. He laid the foundation of an empire that lasted for more than twenty centuries until it was overthrown by a revolution in the early twentieth century. During those many centuries, about a dozen different family-based dynasties ruled China.

The country went through extensive geographic expansion and other significant changes during the dynastic era. But the basic political and social institutions remained remarkably consistent throughout the history of the Chinese empire. One of the most distinctive aspects of imperial China was its national bureaucracy, which developed much earlier than similar government institutions in Europe. Imperial officials were appointed by the emperor only after they had passed a series of very difficult examinations that tested their mastery of the classic teachings of Confucianism.

Imperial China experienced many internal rebellions, often quite large in scale. Some led to the downfall of the ruling dynasty. But new dynasties always kept the Confucian-based imperial political system. In the late eighteenth and nineteenth centuries, however, the Chinese empire faced an unprecedented combination of internal crises and external challenges. A population explosion (resulting from a long spell of peace and prosperity) led to economic stagnation and growing poverty. Official corruption in the bureaucracy and exploitation of the peasants by both landlords and the government increased. This caused widespread social unrest. One massive revolt, the Taiping Rebellion (1850–1864), took 20 million lives and nearly overthrew the imperial government.

By the early nineteenth century, European powers had surged far ahead of China in industrial and military development, and they were demanding that the country open its markets to foreign trade. China tried to limit the activities of Westerners. But Europe, most notably Britain, was in the midst of a great commercial and colonial expansion. Britain was exporting vast quantities of silver to China to pay for huge imports of Chinese tea. In order to balance the trade, the British used their superior military power to compel China to buy opium from the British colony of India. After a humiliating defeat by the British in the Opium War (1839–1842), China was forced to sign a series of unequal treaties. These opened its borders to foreign merchants, missionaries, and diplomats on terms dictated by Britain and other Western powers. China also lost significant pieces of its territory to foreigners (including Hong Kong). Important sectors of the Chinese economy fell under foreign control.

In the late nineteenth and early twentieth centuries, many efforts were made to revive or reform the imperial government. But political power remained in the hands of staunch conservatives who resisted fundamental change. In 1911–1912, a revolution toppled the ruling dynasty, and brought an end to the 2,000-year-old Chinese empire.

## Warlords, Nationalists, and Communists (1912–1949)

The Republic of China was established in 1912. Dr. Sun Yat-sen,[*] then China's best-known revolutionary, became president. The American-educated Sun however, could not hold on to power, and China fell into a lengthy period of conflict

---

[*] In Chinese, family names come *before* a person's given name. For example, Sun is Dr. Sun Yat-sen's family name; Yat-sen is his given name.

and disintegration. Rival military leaders, known as warlords, ruled large parts of the country.

In 1921, a few intellectuals, inspired by the Russian revolution in 1917 founded the Chinese Communist Party (CCP). They were looking for a more radical solution to China's problems than that offered by Sun Yat-sen and his Nationalist Party. The small CCP, advised by the Soviet Union, joined with the Nationalists to fight the warlords. After initial progress, this alliance came to a tragic end in 1927. Chiang Kai-shek, a military leader who had become the head of the Nationalist Party after Sun's death in 1925, turned against his communist partners. His bloody suppression nearly wiped out the CCP. By 1927, Chiang had unified the Republic of China under his personal and increasingly authoritarian rule. He did this largely by striking deals with some of the country's most powerful remaining warlords who supported him in suppressing the communists.

To survive, the Communist Party relocated its headquarters thousands of miles deep within the countryside. This retreat created the conditions for the eventual rise to power of Mao Zedong, who led the CCP to nationwide victory two decades later. Mao had been one of the junior founders of the Communist Party. Coming from a peasant background, he had strongly urged the CCP to pay more attention to China's suffering rural masses. "In a very short time," he wrote in 1927, "several hundred million peasants will rise like a mighty storm, like a hurricane, a force so swift and violent that no power, however great, will be able to hold it back."[2] While the CCP was based in the rural areas Mao began his climb to the top of the party leadership.

In late 1934, the CCP was surrounded by Chiang Kai-shek's army and forced to begin a year-long, 6000-mile journey called the Long March, which took them across some of the most remote parts of China. In October 1935, the communists established a base in an impoverished area of northwest China. There Mao consolidated his control of the CCP. He was a brilliant political and military leader, but he also sometimes used ruthless means to gain power. He was elected party chairman in 1943, a position he held until his death in 1976.

In 1937, Japan invaded China, starting World War II in Asia. The Japanese army pushed Chiang Kai-shek's government into the far southwestern part of the country. This effectively eliminated the Nationalists as an active combatant against Japanese aggression. In contrast, the CCP base in the northwest was on the front line against Japan's troops. Mao and the Communists successfully mobilized the peasants to use **guerrilla warfare** to fight the invaders. This leadership in wartime gained them a strong following among the Chinese people.

**guerrilla warfare**

A military strategy based on small, highly mobile bands of soldiers (the guerrillas, from the Spanish word for war, *guerra*) who use hit-and-run tactics like ambushes to attack a better-armed enemy.

By the end of World War II in 1945, the CCP had vastly expanded its membership. It controlled much of the countryside in north China. The Nationalists were isolated and unpopular with many Chinese because of corruption, political repression, and economic mismanagement.

After the Japanese surrender, the Chinese civil war quickly resumed. The communists won a decisive victory over the U.S.-backed Nationalists. Chiang Kai-shek and his supporters had to retreat to the island of Taiwan, 90 miles off the Chinese coast. On October 1, 1949, Mao Zedong declared the founding of the People's Republic of China (PRC).

## Mao Zedong in Power (1949–1976)

The Communist Party came to power in China on a wave of popular support because of its reputation as a party of social reformers and patriotic fighters. Chairman Mao and the CCP quickly turned their attention to some of the country's most glaring problems. A nationwide land reform campaign redistributed property from the rich

# GLOBAL CONNECTION

## The Republic of China on Taiwan

After its defeat by the Communists in 1949, Chiang Kai-shek's Nationalist Party and army retreated to the island of Taiwan, just 90 miles off the coast of central China. The Chinese communists would probably have taken over Taiwan if the United States had not intervened to prevent an invasion. More than six decades later, Taiwan remains politically separate from the People's Republic of China and still formally calls itself the Republic of China.

The Nationalists imposed a harsh dictatorship on Taiwan, which lasted until the late 1970s. This deepened the sharp divide between the Mainlanders who had arrived in large numbers with Chiang in 1949 and the native Taiwanese majority, whose ancestors had settled there centuries before and who spoke a distinctive Chinese dialect.

But with large amounts of U.S. aid and advice (and military protection), the Nationalist government promoted rural development, attracted extensive foreign investment, and presided over impressive economic growth by producing globally competitive exports. This made Taiwan a model newly industrializing country (NIC). Nationalist policies laid the foundation for health and education levels that are among the best in the world. Its standard of living is now one of the highest in Asia.

After Chiang Kai-shek died in 1975, his son, Chiang Ching-kuo, became president of the Republic of China and head of the Nationalist Party. Most people expected him to continue authoritarian rule. Instead, he permitted some opposition and dissent. He gave important government and party positions, previously dominated by mainlanders, to Taiwanese. When he died in 1988, the Taiwanese vice president, Lee Teng-hui, became president and party leader.

Under President Lee, Taiwan made great strides toward democratization. Laws used to imprison dissidents were revoked, the media was freed of all censorship, and free multiparty elections were held.

The opposition Democratic Progressive Party (DPP) won both the presidential and parliamentary elections from 2000 to 2004, a significant sign of the maturing of Taiwan's democracy. The Nationalists were returned to power in 2008.

The most divisive political issue in Taiwan is whether the island should continue to work, however slowly, towards reunification with the mainland, or should it move towards formal independence from China? The Nationalists favor eventual reunification; the DPP is regarded as a pro-independence party. Most people in Taiwan prefer the status quo in which the island is, for all intents and purposes (including its own strong military), independent of the PRC, but is not an internationally recognized country.

The PRC regards Taiwan as a part of China and has refused to renounce the use of force if the island moves toward formal separation. Nevertheless, the two have developed extensive economic relations. Large numbers of people go from Taiwan to the PRC to do business, visit relatives, or just sightsee.

The United States is committed to a "peaceful solution" of the Taiwan issue. But it continues to sell military technology to Taiwan so it can defend itself. The PRC often criticizes American policy toward Taiwan as interference in China's internal affairs. The Taiwan Straits—the ocean area between the island and the mainland—is still considered one of the world's most volatile areas in terms of the potential for military conflict.

### Taiwan

| | |
|---|---|
| **Land area** | 13,895 sq mi/35,980 sq km (slightly smaller than Maryland and Delaware combined) |
| **Population** | 23 million |
| **Ethnic composition** | Taiwanese 84%, mainland Chinese 14%, aboriginal 2% |
| **GDP at purchasing power parity (US$)** | $823.6 billion, 20th in the the world, comparable Australia (#18) and to Argentina (#24) |
| **GDP per capita at purchasing power parity (US$)** | $35,800, comparable to France and Germany |

to the poor and increased agricultural production in the countryside. Highly successful drives eliminated opium addiction and prostitution from the cities. A national law greatly improved the legal status of women in the family. The CCP often used violence to achieve its objectives and silence opponents. Nevertheless, the party gained considerable legitimacy among many parts of the population because of its successful policies during the early years of its rule.

Between 1953 and 1957, the PRC, with aid from the Soviet Union, implemented a **centrally planned economy** and took decisive steps towards **socialism**. Private property was almost completely eliminated through the takeover of industry by the government and the **collectivization** of agriculture. The Chinese economy grew significantly during this period. But Mao disliked the expansion of the government bureaucracy and the persistence of inequalities, especially those caused by a strong emphasis on industrial and urban development and the relative neglect of the countryside.

This discontent led Mao to launch the Great Leap Forward (1958–1960), which turned out to be "one of the most extreme, bizarre, and eventually catastrophic episodes in twentieth-century political history."[3] The Great Leap was a utopian effort to speed up the country's development so rapidly that China would catch up economically with Britain and the United States in just a few years. It relied on the labor power and revolutionary enthusiasm of the masses while at the same time aiming to propel China into an era of true **communism** in which there would be almost complete economic and social equality.

But irrational policies, wasted resources, poor management, and the suppression of any criticism and dissent combined with bad weather to produce a famine in the rural areas that claimed at least 40 million lives. An industrial depression followed the collapse of agriculture. China suffered a terrible setback in economic development.

In the early 1960s, Mao took a less active role in day-to-day decision-making. Two of China's other top leaders at the time, Liu Shaoqi and Deng Xiaoping, were put in charge of reviving the economy. They completely abandoned the radical strategy of the Great Leap and used a combination of government planning and market-oriented policies to stimulate production.

This approach did help the Chinese economy. Once again, however, Mao became profoundly unhappy with the consequences of China's development. By the mid-1960s, the Chairman had concluded that the policies of Liu and Deng had led to a resurgence of elitism and inequality. He thought they were threatening his communist goals by setting the country on the road to capitalism. China also broke relations with the Soviet Union, which Mao had concluded was no longer a truly revolutionary country.

The Great Proletarian Cultural Revolution (1966–1976) was Mao's ideological crusade designed to jolt China back toward his vision of communism. Like the Great Leap Forward, the Cultural Revolution was a campaign of mass mobilization and utopian idealism. But its main objective was not accelerated economic development, but the political purification of the nation through struggle against so-called class enemies. Using his unmatched political clout and charisma, Mao put together a potent coalition of radical party leaders, loyal military officers, and student rebels (called Red Guards) to support him and attack anyone thought to be guilty of betraying his version of communist ideology, known as Mao Zedong Thought.

In the Cultural Revolution's first phase (1966–1969), more than 20 million Red Guards rampaged across the country. They destroyed countless historical monuments and cultural artefacts because they were symbols of China's imperial past. They also harassed, tortured, and killed people accused of being class enemies, particularly intellectuals and discredited officials. During the next phase (1969–1971), Mao used the army to restore political order. Many Red Guards were sent to live and work in the countryside. The final phase of the Cultural Revolution (1972–1976) involved an intense power struggle over who would succeed the old and frail Mao as the leader of the Chinese Communist Party.

Mao died in September 1976 at age eighty-two. A month later, a group of relatively moderate leaders settled the power struggle. They arrested their radical rivals,

**centrally planned economy**

An economic system in which the state directs the economy through a series of bureaucratic plans for the production and distribution of goods and services. The government, rather than the market, is the major influence on the economy. Also called a command economy.

**socialism**

In a socialist regime, the state plays a leading role in organizing the economy, and most business firms are publicly owned.

**collectivization**

A process undertaken in the Soviet Union under Stalin in the late 1920s and early 1930s and in China under Mao in the 1950s, by which agricultural land was removed from private ownership and organized into large state and collective farms.

**communism**

A system of social organization based on the common ownership and coordination of production.

the so-called Gang of Four, led by Mao's wife, Jiang Qing. This marked the end of the Cultural Revolution. It had claimed at least a million lives and brought the nation close to civil war.

## Deng Xiaoping and the Transformation of Chinese Communism (1977–1997)

To repair the damage caused by the Cultural Revolution, China's new leaders restored to power many veteran officials who had been purged by Mao and the radicals. These included Deng Xiaoping. By 1978, Deng had clearly become the country's most powerful leader, although he never took for himself the formal positions of head of either the Communist Party or the Chinese government. Instead he appointed younger, loyal men to those positions.

Deng's policies were a profound break with the Maoist past. He had long believed that Mao put too much emphasis on politics and not enough on the economy. Under Deng, state control of the economy was significantly reduced. Market forces were allowed to play an increasingly important role. Private enterprise was encouraged. The government allowed unprecedented levels of foreign investment. Chinese artists and writers saw the shackles of party control that had bound them for decades greatly loosened. Deng took major steps to revitalize China's government by bringing in younger, better-educated officials. After decades of stagnation, the Chinese economy began to experience high-levels of growth in the 1980s, which became the foundation for what has been called "one of the great economic miracles of the twentieth century."[4]

Deng Xiaoping gathered global praise for his leadership of the world's most populous nation. He was named *Time* magazine's Man of the Year, first for 1978, then again for 1985. But, in spring of 1989, he and the CCP were faced with a serious challenge when large-scale demonstrations arose in Beijing and several other Chinese cities, the result of discontent over inflation and corruption, as well as a desire—especially among students and intellectuals—for more political freedom. At one point, more than a million people from all walks of life gathered in and around Tiananmen Square in the center of Beijing to voice their concerns. A very large contingent of students set up a camp in the Square, which they occupied for about two months.

For quite a while, the CCP leadership, hampered by intensive international media coverage and internal disagreements about how to handle the protests, did little more than roll out threatening rhetoric to dissuade the demonstrators. But China's leaders ran out of patience, and the army was ordered to use force to clear the square during the very early morning hours of June 4. By the time dawn broke in Beijing, Tiananmen Square had indeed been cleared, but with a death toll that still has not been revealed. The Chinese government still insists that it did the right thing in the interests of national stability.

Following the Tiananmen massacre, China went through a few years of intense political crackdown and a slowdown in the pace of economic change. Then, in early 1992, Deng Xiaoping took some bold steps to accelerate reform of the economy. He did so in large part hoping that economic progress would avoid a collapse of China's communist system such as had occurred just the year before in the Soviet Union.

## From Revolutionaries to Technocrats (1997 to the Present)

In mid-1989, Deng Xiaoping had promoted Jiang Zemin, the former mayor and Communist Party leader of Shanghai, to become the head of the CCP. Although Deng remained the power behind the throne, he gradually turned over greater authority to Jiang, who also became president of the PRC in 1993. When Deng Xiaoping died in February 1997, Jiang was secure in his position as China's top leader.

## PROFILES

# A Tale of Two Leaders

Portrait of Chinese Communist leaders Mao Tse-tung and Deng Xiaoping. 1959 photograph.
Image by © Bettmann/ CORBIS

Mao Zedong (1893–1976) and Deng Xiaoping (1904–1997) had much in common. They were both born in rural China and joined the Chinese Communist Party in their early 20s. They both participated in the CCP's "Long March" in 1934–1935 to escape annihilation by Chiang Kai-shek's Nationalist army. When Mao consolidated his power as the undisputed leader of the CCP in the 1940s, Deng became one of his most trusted comrades. Throughout the 1950s, Deng rose to the highest levels of leadership in the People's Republic of China due to his record of accomplishments in jobs assigned to him by Mao and his personal loyalty to the Chairman. And both men transformed China in ways that mark them as two of the most important figures in all of Chinese—and perhaps world—history.

But, in some ways, Mao and Deng were very different. Deng had more experience of the outside world than Mao. He had studied and traveled in Europe and the Soviet Union in the 1920s. Mao, by contrast, left China only twice in his life: in 1950 and 1957, both on official visits to Moscow. Deng was a pragmatist—someone who acts to get things done rather than dwelling on abstract ideas. Mao was an idealist who thought about the future in utopian terms and then tried to find ways to make reality fit his vision.

By the mid-1960s, Mao had decided that Deng's pragmatism was threatening his vision for China's communist future. The Chairman launched the Cultural Revolution largely to displace from power those like Deng whom he regarded as taking the "capitalist road" in promoting economic development. Deng was purged in 1966 and sent to work in a factory.

Mao restored him to office in 1973, only to purge him again in the spring of 1976 for similar reasons.

Less than a year after Mao died in September 1976, Deng was brought back to the inner circle of power by moderate leaders who had orchestrated the arrest of the top radical Maoists in the CCP (the "Gang of Four"). Deng, in turn, masterfully (and rather gently compared to Mao) pushed aside most of the colleagues who had reinstated him. By the end of the 1970s, he was clearly China's most powerful leader. He would remain so for two decades until infirmity forced him into retirement.

Deng used his power to lead the country towards spectacular economic growth by taking China in a very un-Maoist direction—some would say he took China down the capitalist road. But one other thing that Mao and Deng had in common was an unshakeable belief that communist party leadership of China should not be challenged. Mao initiated a number of ruthless campaigns to squash dissent. The brutal crackdown on the Beijing pro-democracy protests in June 1989 was Deng's response to those who questioned party rule.

Today both Mao Zedong and Deng Xiaoping are revered in China. Mao's legacy is tarnished by public memories and official acknowledgement of the tragic human cost of his utopian campaigns. But he is regarded as the founder of the People's Republic and for reestablishing China's sovereignty and dignity after more than a century of humiliation at the hands of foreign powers. Deng is, of course, seen as the architect of China's economic miracle. Few people associate him with the 1989 Beijing massacre since that remains a forbidden topic in the PRC.

The most visible monument to Mao is a large memorial hall in Tiananmen Square. Long lines form as people wait their turn to enter the hall to pay their respects to the Chairman's glass-encased embalmed corpse. When Deng died in 1997, his cremated ashes were scattered at sea according to his wishes. His most visible monument is the prosperity of the Chinese people and nation—and the continued iron-fisted rule of the Chinese Communist Party.

Under Jiang Zemin's leadership, China continued its economic reforms and remarkable growth. The PRC became an even more integral part of the global economy. It enhanced its regional and international stature. But the country also faced widening gaps between the rich and the poor, environmental degradation, and pervasive corruption. Overall, China was politically stable during the Jiang era. But the CCP still repressed any individual or group it perceived as challenging its authority.

Jiang Zemin was succeeded as head of the CCP in November 2002 and PRC president in March 2003 by Hu Jintao. The transfer of power from Jiang to Hu was remarkably predictable and orderly. Some observed that it was the first relatively peaceful top-level political succession in China in more than 200 years. Jiang had

This cartoon captures the contradiction between economic reform and political repression that characterized China under the leadership of Deng Xiaoping.

*Source:* Tribune Media Services, Inc. All Rights Reserved. Reprinted with permission

**technocrats**

Career-minded bureaucrats who administer public policy according to a technical rather than a political rationale.

retired after two terms in office, as required by new party rules and the state constitution, and Hu had, for several years, been expected to succeed Jiang.

Both Jiang and Hu also represented a new kind of leader for the PRC. Mao Zedong and Deng Xiaoping had been involved in communist politics almost their whole adult lives. They had participated in the CCP's long struggle for power dating back to the 1920s. They were among the founders of the communist regime in 1949. In contrast, Jiang and Hu were **technocrats**. They had university training (as engineers) before working their way up the ladder of success in the CCP by a combination of professional competence and political loyalty.

Hu Jintao was re-elected to second five-year terms as both CCP leader (in October 2007) and PRC president (in March 2008). He has tried to project himself as a populist leader by placing greater emphasis on dealing with the country's most serious socioeconomic problems, such as the enormous inequalities between regions and the terribly inadequate public health system. But like his predecessors, Hu has taken a hard line on political dissent and challenges to the authority of the Communist Party.

In 2008, the top leaders of the CCP began grooming Xi Jinping (b. 1953) to succeed Hu Jintao when he retires as head of the party in 2012 and president of the country in 2013. Xi is also a technocrat with a degree in chemical engineering. There is little reason to expect he will deviate significantly from the combination of economic reform and political repression that has been the CCP's formula for retaining power since the days of Deng Xiaoping.

# Themes and Implications

## Historical Junctures and Political Themes

The World of States At the time the People's Republic was established in 1949, China occupied a very weak position in the international system. For more than a century, its destiny had been shaped by interventions from abroad that it could do little to control. Mao made many tragic and terrible blunders during his years in power. But one of his great achievements was to build a strong state able to affirm and defend its sovereignty. China's international stature has increased as its economic and military strength have grown. Although still a relatively poor country by many per capita measures, the sheer size of its economy makes the PRC an economic powerhouse. Its foreign trade policies have a significant effect on many other countries and on the global economy. China is a nuclear power with the world's largest conventional military force. It is an active and influential member of the world's most important international organizations, including the United Nations, where it sits as one of the five permanent members of the Security Council. China has become a major player in the world of states.

**Governing the Economy**   Throughout its history the PRC has experimented with a series of very different approaches to economic development: a Soviet-style planning system in the early 1950s, the radical egalitarianism of the Maoist model, and the market-oriented policies implemented by Deng Xiaoping and his successors. Ideological disputes over these development strategies were the main cause of the ferocious political struggles within the CCP during the Mao era. Deng began his bold reforms in the late 1970s with the hope that improved living standards would restore the legitimacy of the CCP, which had been badly tarnished by the economic failings and political chaos of much of the previous three decades. The remarkable success of China's recent leaders in governing the economy has sustained the authority of the CCP at a time when most of the world's other communist regimes have disappeared.

**The Democratic Idea**   Any hope that the democratic idea might take root in the early years of communist rule in China quickly vanished by the mid-1950s with the building of a one-party communist state and Mao's unrelenting campaigns against alleged enemies of his revolution. The Deng Xiaoping era brought much greater economic, social, and cultural freedom, but time and again the CCP has strangled the stirrings of the democratic idea, most brutally in Tiananmen Square in 1989. Jiang Zemin and Hu Jintao have been faithful disciples of Deng. They have vigorously championed economic reform in China. They have also made sure that the CCP retains its firm grip on power.

**The Politics of Collective Identity**   Because of its long history and ancient culture, China has a very strong sense of collective national identity. Memories of past humiliations and suffering at the hands of foreigners still influence the international

Jeff Widener /AP Images.

In an act of outrage and protest, an unarmed citizen stood in front of a column of tanks leaving Tiananmen Square the day after the Chinese army had crushed the prodemocracy demonstration in 1989. This "unknown hero" disappeared into the watching crowd. Neither his identity nor his fate is known.

policies of the PRC. In addition, faith in communist ideology has weakened as the country embraces capitalist economic policies. For this reason, CCP leaders have increasingly turned to nationalism as a means to rally the Chinese people behind their government. China's cultural and ethnic homogeneity has also spared it the widespread communal violence that has plagued so many other countries. The exception has been in the border regions where there is a large concentration of minority peoples, including Tibet and the Muslim areas of China's northwest.

### Implications for Comparative Politics

**communist party-states**

A political system in which a communist party holds a monopoly on political power and controls the government (the state).

The People's Republic of China can be compared with other **communist party-states** with which it shares, or has shared, many political and ideological features. From this point of view, China raises intriguing questions: Why has China's communist party-state so far proved more durable than that of the Soviet Union and nearly all other similar regimes? By what combination of reform and repression has the CCP held on to power? What signs are there that it is likely to hold power for the foreseeable future? What signs suggest that communist rule in China may be weakening? What kind of political system might emerge if the CCP were to lose or relinquish power?

China can also be compared with other developing nations that face similar economic and political challenges. Although the PRC is part of the Third World as measured by the average standard of living of its population, its record of growth in the past several decades has far exceeded almost all other developing countries. Furthermore, the educational and health levels of the Chinese people are quite good when compared with many other countries at a similar level of development, such as India. How has China achieved such relative success in its quest for economic and social development? By contrast, much of the Third World has become more democratic in recent decades. How and why has China resisted this wave of democratization? What does the experience of other developing countries say about how economic modernization might influence the prospects for democracy in China?

Napoleon Bonaparte, emperor of France in the early nineteenth century, once remarked when looking at a map of Europe and Asia, "Let China sleep. For when China wakes, it will shake the world."[5] It has taken awhile, but China certainly has awakened. Given its geographic size, vast resources, huge population, surging economy, and formidable military, China is shaking the world.

### Summary

China has experienced more dramatic changes over the last century than almost any other country. Until 1912, it was an imperial system headed by an emperor. From then until 1949 it was known as the Republic of China, but the central government was never in full control. Warlords ruled various parts of the country. China suffered terribly from a brutal invasion by Japan during World War II. In 1949, a civil war that had been waged for two decades ended when the Chinese Communist Party under Chairman Mao Zedong defeated the Nationalist armies and established the People's Republic of China. From then until his death in 1976, Mao imposed a kind of radical communism on China. This had a mostly disastrous political and economic impact. Eventually, Deng Xiaoping became China's most powerful leader in 1978. He implemented major reforms that helped make China the fastest-growing major economy in the world. But he and his successors have suppressed all challenges to the authority of the Communist Party.

# POLITICAL ECONOMY AND DEVELOPMENT

## State and Economy

When the Chinese Communist Party came to power in 1949, China's economy was suffering from more than a hundred years of rebellion, invasion, civil war, and bad government. The country's new communist rulers seized most property from wealthy landowners, rich industrialists, and foreign companies. Nevertheless, it initially allowed some private ownership and many aspects of capitalism to continue in order to gain support for the government and revive the economy.

In the early 1950s, the CCP set up a socialist planned economy based on the Soviet model. The state owned or controlled most economic resources. Government planning and commands, not market forces, drove economic activity, including setting prices for almost all goods.

In the beginning, China's planned economy yielded impressive results. But it also created huge bureaucracies and new inequalities, especially between the heavily favored industrial cities and the investment-starved rural areas. Both the Great Leap Forward (1958–1961) and the Cultural Revolution (1966–1976) embodied the unique and radical Maoist approach to economic development that was intended to be less bureaucratic and more egalitarian than the Soviet model.

Under Mao, the PRC built a strong industrial base. The people of China became much healthier and better educated. But the Maoist economy was plagued by political interference, poor management, and ill-conceived projects. This led to wasted resources of truly staggering proportions. Overall, China's economic growth rates, especially in agriculture, barely kept pace with population increases. The average standard of living changed little between the mid-1950s and Mao's death in 1976.

### China Goes to Market

In 1962 Deng Xiaoping had remarked, "It doesn't matter whether a cat is white or black, as long as it catches mice."[6] He meant that the CCP should not be overly concerned about whether a particular policy was socialist or capitalist if it helped the economy. Such sentiments got Deng in trouble with Mao. They made Deng one of the principal targets of the Cultural Revolution.

Once he emerged as China's foremost leader in the aftermath of Mao's death in 1976, Deng let the cat loose. He spearheaded sweeping economic reforms that greatly reduced government control and increased market forces. Authority for making economic decisions passed from bureaucrats to families, factory managers, and even the owners of private businesses. Individuals were encouraged to work harder and more efficiently to make money rather than to "serve the people" as had been the slogan during the Maoist era.

In most sectors of China's economy today, the state no longer dictates what to produce and how to produce it. Almost all prices are now set according to supply and demand, as in a capitalist economy, rather than by administrative decree. Many government monopolies have given way to fierce competition between state-owned and non-state-owned firms. But there are still many thousands of **state-owned enterprises**

**state-owned enterprises (SOEs)**

Companies in which a majority of ownership control is held by the government.

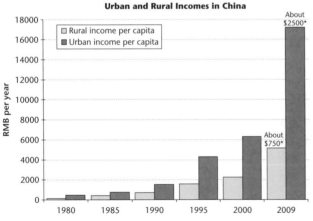

*These figures are based on official international currency exchange rates for the US dollar and the Chinese RMB. If purchasing power figures for urban and rural incomes were available, the figure in US$ would be two to four times higher.

**FIGURE 14.2 The Transformation of the Chinese Economy**

*The above charts illustrate China's phenomenal economic growth over the last three decades. The third chart also shows the growing inequality between the urban and rural areas.*

*Source:* China Statistical Yearbooks, United States–China Business Council. Chinability.com

(SOEs) with millions of employees in China. Although vastly outnumbered by private enterprises with many more workers, SOEs still dominate critical parts of the economy such as steel, petroleum, telecommunications, and transportation.

But even SOEs must now respond to market forces. Some have become very profitable, modern enterprises. But many others are overstaffed economic dinosaurs with outdated facilities and machinery. The state-owned sector remains a huge drain on the country's banks (largely government-controlled), which are still sometimes required to bail out financially failing SOEs. These large loans are rarely, if ever, paid back. Many economists think that even more drastic SOE reform is needed. But the country's leaders fear the political and social turmoil that would boil up from a massive layoff of industrial workers.

Somewhat ironically, the Chinese Communist Party now strongly encourages and supports private businesses. The private sector is the largest and fastest growing part of China's economy. The CCP even welcomes owners of private enterprises—sometimes called "red capitalists"—to join the party.[7]

The results of China's move from a planned toward a market economy have been phenomenal (see Figure 14.2). The PRC has been the fastest-growing major economy in the world for more than two decades. China's Gross Domestic Product (GDP) per capita grew at an average rate of a little over 9 percent per year from 1990 to 2009. During the same period, the per capita GDP growth of the United States was 1.5 percent per year, India's was 4.5 percent, and Brazil's 1 percent. China weathered the recession of 2009–2010 far better than any other major economy.

Nevertheless, China's GDP per capita (a rough measure of the average standard of living) is still very low when compared to that of richer countries. As of 2010, GDP per capita in the United States was $47,500. In the PRC, it was $7400, but in 1980, it was only $250, showing again how spectacular China's economic growth has been in recent decades.

Rising incomes have also led to a consumer revolution. In the late 1970s, people in the cities could only shop for most consumer goods at state-run stores. These carried a very limited range of often shoddy products. Today China's urban areas are shopping paradises. They have domestic and foreign stores of every kind, huge malls, fast-food outlets, and a great variety of entertainment. A few decades ago, hardly anyone owned a television. Now most households have a color TV. Cell phones are everywhere. In the cities, a new middle class is starting to buy houses, condominiums, and cars. China is even developing a class of "super-rich" millionaires and billionaires.

Despite these changes, economic planning has by no means disappeared. Officially, the PRC says it has a **socialist market economy**. While allowing some degree of capitalism, national and local bureaucrats continue to exercise a great deal of control over the production and distribution of goods, resources, and services. According to the country's constitution (Article 15), "The state strengthens economic legislation, improves macro-control of the economy, and, in accordance with the law, prohibits disturbance of the socioeconomic order by any organization or individual." Market reforms have gained substantial momentum that would be nearly impossible to reverse. But the CCP still determines the direction of China's economy.

> **socialist market economy**
>
> The term used by the government of China to refer to the country's current economic system.

## Remaking the Chinese Countryside

One of the first revolutionary programs launched by the Chinese Communist Party when it came to power in 1949 was land reform that confiscated the property of landlords and redistributed it as private holdings to the poorer peasants. But in the mid- to late 1950s the state reorganized peasants into collective farms and communes in which the village, not individuals, owned the land, and local officials directed all production and labor. Individuals were paid according to how much they worked on the collective land. Peasants had to sell most crops and other farm products to the state at low fixed prices. Collectivized agriculture was one of the weakest links in China's command economy because it was very inefficient in the way it used resources, including labor, and undermined incentives for farmers to work hard to benefit themselves and their families. Per capita agricultural production and rural living standards were stagnant from 1957 to 1977.

Deng Xiaoping made the revival of the rural economy one of his top priorities when he became China's most powerful leader in the late 1970s. He abolished collective farming and established a **household responsibility system**, which remains in effect today. Under this system, the village still owns the farmland. But it is contracted out by the local government to individual families, which take full charge of the production and marketing of crops. Largely because farmers are now free to earn income for themselves, agricultural productivity has sharply increased. There are still many very poor people in the Chinese countryside, but hundreds of millions have been lifted out of extreme poverty in the last two and a half decades.

> **household responsibility system**
>
> The system put into practice in China beginning in the early 1980s in which the major decisions about agricultural production are made by individual farm families based on the profit motive rather than by a people's commune or the government.

Economic life in the rural China has also been transformed by the expansion of rural industry and commerce. Rural factories and businesses range in size from a handful of employees to thousands. They employ more than 190 million people and have played a critical role in absorbing the vast pool of labor that is no longer needed in agriculture.

# Society and Economy

Economic reform has made Chinese society much more diverse and open. People are vastly freer to choose jobs, travel about the country and internationally, practice their religious beliefs, join non-political associations, and engage in a wide range of other activities that were prohibited or severely restricted during the Maoist era. But economic change has also caused serious social problems. Crime, prostitution, and drug use have sharply increased. Although such problems are still far less common in China than in many other countries, they are severe enough to worry national and local authorities.

Economic reform has created significant changes in China's basic system of social welfare. The Maoist economy provided almost all workers with what was called the **iron rice bowl**. As in other communist party-state economies, such as the Soviet Union, the government guaranteed employment, a certain standard of living, and basic cradle-to-grave benefits to most of the urban and rural labor force. The workplace was more than just a place to work and earn a living. It also provided housing, health care, day care, and other services.

China's economic reformers believed that guarantees like these led to poor work motivation and excessive costs for the government and businesses. They implemented policies designed to break the iron rice bowl. Income and employment are no longer guaranteed. They are now directly tied to individual effort.

An estimated 60 million workers have been laid off from state-owned enterprises since the early 1990s. Many are too old or too unskilled to find good jobs in the modernizing economy. They are now the core of a very large stratum of urban poor that has become a fixture in even China's most glittering cities. The PRC has very little unemployment insurance or social security for its displaced workers. Work slowdowns, strikes, and large-scale demonstrations are becoming more frequent, particularly in China's northeastern rust belt, where state-owned industries have been particularly hard hit. The official unemployment rate is about 4 percent of the urban labor force. But it is generally believed to be two to three times as high. If unemployment continues to surge, labor unrest could be a political time bomb in China's cities.

Certainly life has become much better for the vast majority of people who still live in the rural areas. But they also face serious problems. The availability of health care, educational opportunities, disability pay, and retirement funds now depends on the relative wealth of families and villages. Social services of all kinds are much poorer in the countryside than in the cities, although the Chinese government has recently said that it is committed to reducing such inequalities. Rural protests, sometimes violent, have increased significantly in recent years. The protesters have been angry about high taxes, corrupt local officials, pollution, illegal land seizures by developers, and delays in payments for agricultural products purchased by the government.

Economic changes have opened China's cities to a flood of rural migrants. After agriculture was decollectivized in the early 1980s, many peasants, no longer held back by the strict limits on internal population movement enforced in the Mao era, headed to the urban areas to look for jobs. This so-called **floating population** of about 150 million people is the biggest human migration in history. In Shanghai more than one-third of the population of 23.0 million is made up of migrants. Migrant workers are mostly employed in low-paying jobs, but fill an important niche in China's changing labor market, particularly in boom areas like construction.

Migrants also increase pressure on urban housing and social services. In some cities, many now live in "urban villages." These are areas on the fringes of cities where cheap, crowded, and substandard accommodations are available. Because the slum-like conditions sometimes breed crime and other social problems, some cities have taken to locking the gates of urban villages at night to keep residents from

---

**iron rice bowl**

A feature of China's socialist economy during the Maoist era (1949–1976) that provided guarantees of lifetime employment, income, and basic cradle-to-grave benefits to most urban and rural workers.

---

**floating population**

Migrants from the rural areas who have moved temporarily to the cities to find employment.

© Cuiphoto/Shutterstock.com

The futuristic skyline of Shanghai's Pudong district reflect the spectacular modernization of China's most prosperous areas in recent decades.

venturing out. If a stalled economy thwarts the economic aspirations of migrants or if local governments treat them too roughly or unfairly, their presence in Chinese cities could become politically destabilizing.

The benefits of economic growth have reached most of China. But the market reforms and economic boom have created sharp class differences, and inequalities between people and parts of the country have risen significantly. A huge gap separates the average incomes of urban residents from those in the countryside (see Fig. 14.2). Farmers in China's poorer areas have faced years of stagnating or even declining incomes. The gap is also widening between the prosperous coastal regions and most inland areas.

Such inequalities are an embarrassment for a political party that still claims to believe in communist ideals. The CCP has begun to promote the development of what it calls a "harmonious socialist society," which emphasizes not only achieving a higher average standard of living for the whole country, but also a more equitable distribution of income and social services. There is more investment being directed to the rural economy, and, in 2006, the government abolished taxes on agriculture, which had been in effect in some form in China for 2,600 years.

Gender inequalities have also grown in some ways since the introduction of the economic reforms. The social status, legal rights, employment opportunities, and education of women in China have improved enormously since the founding of the PRC in1949. Women have benefited from rising living standards and economic modernization. But the trend toward a market economy has not benefited men and women equally. Although China has one of the world's highest rates of female participation in the urban workforce, market reforms have "strengthened and in some cases reconstructed the sexual division of labor, keeping urban women in a transient, lower-paid, and subordinate position in the workforce."[8]

In the countryside, it is almost always the case that only male heads of households sign contracts for land and other production resources, which means that men continue to dominate the rural economy. This is true even though farm labor has become increasingly feminized as many men move to jobs in rural industry or migrate to the cities. Economic and cultural pressures have also led to an alarming suicide rate (the world's highest) among women in China's villages.

China's unique and stringent population policy has had a particularly significant impact on rural women, and certainly one that has not always been to their benefit. The government insists that without such a policy, which has been in effect since the early 1980s, China's economic development would be endangered. It has used various means to encourage or even force couples to have only a single child.

Intensive media campaigns supporting the one-child policy laud the patriotic virtues and economic benefits of small families. Positive incentives such as more farmland or preferred housing have been offered to couples with only one child. Large fines and loss of jobs have been used to punish violators. In some places, workplace medics or local doctors monitor contraceptive use and women's fertility cycles, and a couple must have official permission to have a child. Defiance has sometimes led to forced abortion or sterilization.

The combination of the one-child campaign, the modernizing economy, and a comparatively strong record in improving educational and employment opportunities for women have brought China's population growth rate to about 0.5 percent per year. This is very low for a country at its level of economic development. India, for example, has also had some success in promoting family planning. But its annual population growth rate is 1.4 percent. Nigeria's is 2.0 percent. These may not seem like big differences, but consider this: At these respective growth rates, it will take 144 years for China's population to double, whereas India's population will double in about fifty years and Nigeria's in just thirty-six years.

While the PRC government praises the success of the one-child policy, it has been met with considerable resistance in the rural areas. Because family income now depends on having more people to work, many farmers have evaded the one-child policy by not reporting births and other means. Furthermore, the still widespread belief that male children will contribute more economically to the family and that a male heir is necessary to carry on the family line causes some rural families to take drastic steps, including female infanticide and the abandonment of female babies, to make sure that their one child is a son. Ultrasound technology has led to large number of sex-selective abortions of female fetuses.

As a result, China has an unusual gender balance among its young population. Most societies have a male-female ratio of 105:100 among newborns. In the PRC, the ratio is about 120:100. Estimates suggest that there are already 30 million more males in China than females. Such a large surplus of young, unmarried males (India has a similar situation) has led to the kidnapping and selling of women—even very young girls—to provide brides for men who can pay the fee. Some scholars point out that an extreme gender imbalance is likely to cause a rise in social instability, violent crime, and gang formation. They argue that it might even make a country more authoritarian at home in order to maintain law and order and militarily adventuresome abroad as a way to channel the aggressiveness of frustrated young males.[9]

Partly in response to rural resistance and international pressure, population control policies have been somewhat relaxed. Rural couples are often allowed to have two children if their first is a girl. Ethnic minorities, such as those in Tibet, are allowed to have up to four children. But the government has announced that the one-child policy will remain basically in effect until at least 2015.

China's economic boom and mixed state-private economy have also created enormous opportunities for corruption. Officials still control numerous resources and retain power over many economic transactions from which large profits can be made. The government has repeatedly launched well-publicized campaigns against official graft, with harsh punishment, even execution, for serious offenders.

A series of recent cases involving consumer product safety revealed another problem with China's superfast economic development. Some involved faulty, even dangerous lack of quality control in Chinese exports, including toys, pet food, tires, and toothpaste. But many more—and much more severe—such cases have occurred in China, most notably one involving the addition of an industrial chemical to powdered milk in order to boost its apparent protein content. Six babies died from the contaminated products, and more than 300,000 others, mostly children, became sick. Two men who worked for the responsible dairy firm were executed, six people went to prison, including the former chairwoman of the dairy, who was given a life sentence, and several government officials were fired. The father of one sickened child, however, was jailed after setting up a website to help victims and push for compensation.

Finally, China's economic growth has seriously damaged the environment. Industrial expansion has been fuelled primarily by highly polluting coal. The air in China's cities and even many rural areas is among the dirtiest in the world. Soil erosion, the loss of arable land, water shortages, and deforestation are serious. The government does little to regulate the dumping of garbage and toxic wastes. Roughly 80 percent of China's rivers are badly polluted. Private automobile use is just starting to take off, which will greatly add to urban pollution. China has surpassed the United States as the world's largest source of carbon dioxide ($CO_2$) emissions, although per capita emissions remain much lower than in most developed countries.

The PRC is critical of rich countries that press it (and other developing countries) to slow down economic growth or invest in expensive pollution controls when those countries paid little heed to the environmental damage caused by their own industrial revolutions. Nevertheless, the Chinese government has been paying more attention to protection of the environment. Sustainable development, which balances economic growth and ecological concerns, is a key part of the CCP's current emphasis on building a "harmonious socialist society." China has also become a leader in the development of alternative clean energy, including wind and solar power.

Dealing with the negative consequences of fast growth and market reforms is one of the main challenges facing China's government. The ability of citizen associations—including labor, women's, consumer protection, and environmental organizations—to place their concerns about such problems on the nation's political agenda is strictly limited by the Communist Party's tight control of political life and by restrictions on the formation of unauthorized interest groups.

# China in the Global Economy

At the end of the Maoist era in 1976, the PRC was not deeply involved in the global economy. Total foreign trade was less 10 percent of GDP, and lingering Cold War estrangement kept trade with the United States almost to nothing. Foreign direct investment (FDI) in China was minuscule. The stagnant economy, political instability, and heavy-handed bureaucracy did not attract potential investors from abroad.

In the early 1980s, China embarked on a strategy of using trade as a central component of Deng Xiaoping's drive for economic development. In some ways it followed the model of export-led growth pioneered by Japan and newly industrializing countries (NICs) such as the Republic of Korea (South Korea) and Taiwan. This model takes advantage of low-wage domestic labor to produce goods that are in demand internationally. It then uses the earnings from those goods to modernize the economy.

Chinese exports have soared from negligible levels in the late 1970s to the world leader, ahead of Germany, the United States, and Japan. China is often referred to as the "factory to the world" because so many countries import large quantities of Chinese products.

In terms of goods and services, China is now the world's second-largest trading nation behind the United States. It is projected to surpass the United States in total trade volume sometime between 2015 and 2020. Foreign trade accounted for about 60 percent of the PRC's GDP in 2000–2009, with a relatively equal balance between imports and exports. As the following table shows, China is much more economically dependent on trade than is the United States or Japan; but, in comparison with other major economies, it is less or comparably dependent.

For the most part, China imports industrial machinery, high-level technology and scientific equipment, iron and steel, and raw materials. Despite having large domestic sources of petroleum and significant untapped reserves, China is now a net importer of oil because of the massive energy demands of its economic boom and exploding private automobile market. The PRC's hunger for oil and other raw materials has raised some concerns because of its potential to increase world prices for some commodities and put added pressure on nonrenewable resources.

Foreign investment in the PRC has also skyrocketed, topping $100 billion in 2010. More than 400 of the world's 500 top corporations have operations in the PRC. But the vast majority of investors in China are much smaller firms, producing electronics, clothing, footwear, and other consumer items for export. The low cost of labor has been a major attraction to investors from abroad, even though foreign firms generally pay their workers considerably more than the average wage of about 60 cents per hour in Chinese-owned factories. But all wages in China have been going up, and the PRC is facing increasing competition from Vietnam, Bangladesh, and other developing countries for overseas investment looking to build labor-intensive export-producing factories.

Another lure to foreign investment in China is the huge domestic market. Companies such as Coca-Cola, General Motors, Starbucks, and Wal-Mart have poured vast amounts of money into China. The American tobacco industry hopes that grabbing a share of China's 350 million smokers (one-third of the world total) can make up for sharply declining sales at home. American cigarette brands are mostly sold on the Chinese market as luxury imports, but Philip Morris recently began producing Marlboros as part of a deal with the PRC state-run tobacco monopoly.

| **Table 14.2** | Trade Dependency (2000–2009 Average) | | |
|---|---|---|---|
| | **Imports (% of GDP)** | **Exports (% of GDP)** | **Total Trade (% of GDP)** |
| Germany | 35.4 | 40.0 | 75.4 |
| Canada | 34.8 | 38.0 | 72.8 |
| **China** | **26.5** | **31.1** | **57.6** |
| Mexico | 29.4 | 27.7 | 57.1 |
| Russia | 22.5 | 34.4 | 56.9 |
| Britain | 29.6 | 27.1 | 56.7 |
| Japan | 12.5 | 13.6 | 26.1 |
| United States | 15.3 | 10.7 | 26.0 |

*Source:* World Bank World Development Indicators.

China is itself becoming a major investor in other countries as part of a government-supported "going out" strategy to diversify its economy. In a sign of how far the PRC has come as a world economic power, China's leading computer company, the Lenovo Group, bought IBM's PC division in late 2004. Lenovo is now the world's fourth-largest producer of PCs with 10.5 percent of the global market (Hewlett-Packard is number one with an 18 percent market share). At the same time, Chinese domestic brands, such a Haier refrigerators and air conditioners, are starting to find a market in the United States and elsewhere.

## THE U.S. CONNECTION

### Sino*-American Relations

China and the United States fought as allies during World War II. At that time, the Chinese government was controlled by the pro-American Nationalist Party of Chiang Kai-shek. The United States supported Chiang and the Nationalists in the civil war against the Chinese Communist Party. When the CCP took power and established the People's Republic of China in 1949, Sino-American relations plunged into a period of Cold War hostility that lasted for more than two decades.

The United States continued to support Chiang and the Nationalists after they fled to Taiwan and protected Taiwan from an attack by the PRC. China and the United States also fought to a stalemate in the Korean War (1950–1953).

Furthermore, the PRC was closely allied with its communist big brother, the Soviet Union, America's archenemy, for much of the 1950s. Relations between Moscow and Beijing soured in the early 1960s, and the two communist powers became bitter ideological rivals. But China and the United States still saw each other as enemies and, for example, backed different sides in the Vietnam War.

In the early 1970s, Sino-American relations warmed up. Each country saw the Soviet Union as its main enemy and decided to cooperate with each other in order to weaken their common foe. In 1972, Richard Nixon became the first U.S. president to visit the People's Republic (in fact, he was the first U.S. president ever to visit China). Formal diplomatic relations between Washington and Beijing were established in 1978. Since then economic, cultural, and even military ties have deepened, despite some disruptions, such as following the Tiananmen massacre in 1989, and recurring tensions over trade, human rights, and other issues. Many scholars and diplomats believe that U.S.-China relations are the most important bilateral relationship in the post–Cold War world.

Economic relations between China and the United States are particularly important and complex. China now trades with the United States more than with any other country, while China is America's second-largest trading partner (after Canada). In 2009, U.S. imports from China totalled almost $300 billion, whereas U.S. exports to the PRC were about $70 billion.

Wal-Mart alone buys over $30 billion of goods from China (about 80 percent of the company's total imports). Wal-Mart also operates about 190 stores in China and employs 50,000 people.

Many in the United States think that importing such a huge quantity of "cheap" products from China means lost jobs and lower wages for Americans. They argue that American firms can't compete with Chinese companies because labor costs in China are so much lower. They also say that the PRC engages in unfair trade practices, exploits sweatshop labor, and suppresses independent union activity. Some see the fact that China owns $900 billion of U.S. government debt (which it bought with part of the vast reserves of U.S. dollars earned from exports) as having made the United States dangerously dependent on the PRC. Critics of Sino-American economic relations want the U.S. government to put more restrictions on trade and financial dealings with China.

On the other side, many say that the benefits of U.S. trade with China far outweigh the negative impacts. First of all, consumers benefit greatly by the availability of a large variety of less-expensive products. Furthermore, in their view, the United States should focus on developing more high-tech businesses to create jobs rather than trying to compete with China and other countries in "old-fashioned" labor-intensive industries. They point out that many American firms have huge investments in China, which will grow—as will demand for American products—as that country becomes more modern and prosperous. U.S. government debt is the result of American overspending, and several other countries besides the PRC own large chunks of it, including Japan and Britain. Finally, those who oppose restrictions on Sino-American economic engagement see it as one important way to promote not only the free market in China but also a more open society and democracy.

*Sino is a term derived from Latin that is often used to refer to China. For example, scholars who specialize in the study of China are "sinologists." Sino-American relations is another way of saying United States–China relations.

China occupies an important, although somewhat contradictory, position in the global economy. On the one hand, the PRC is still a relatively poor country in terms of its level of economic and technological development compared to richer nations. On the other hand, the total output and rapid growth of its economy, expanding trade and investment, and vast resource base (including its population) has made China a rising economic superpower.

### Summary

During the Maoist era (1949–1976), the communist party-state thoroughly dominated the economy through a system of central planning in which government bureaucrats determined economic policies and by suppressing any kind of private economic activity. This approach achieved some success in promoting industrialization and raising the educational and health standards of the Chinese people. But, overall, it left China as a very poor country with little involvement in the global economy. Under Deng Xiaoping and his successors, the party-state has given up much of its control of the economy and encouraged free market forces, private ownership, international trade, and foreign investment. Living standards, modernization, and globalization have all increased dramatically. But serious problems, such as urban-rural inequality and pollution, are a challenge for China's current leaders.

# SECTION 3   GOVERNANCE AND POLICY-MAKING

**Focus Questions**

What are the most important features of a communist party-state as a type of political system?

What is the difference between the government of the People's Republic of China and the Chinese Communist Party?

How does the party control the government?

## Organization of the State

China, Cuba, Vietnam, North Korea, and Laos are the only remaining communist party-states in the world. Like the Soviet Union before its collapse in 1991, the political systems of these countries are characterized by communist party domination of all government and social institutions, the existence of an official state ideology based on Marxism-Leninism, and, to varying and changing degrees, state control of key sectors of the economy.

The Chinese Communist Party claims that only it can govern in the best interests of the entire nation and therefore has the right to exercise the "leading role" throughout Chinese society. Although China has moved sharply toward a market economy in recent decades, the CCP still asserts that it is building socialism with the ultimate objective of creating an egalitarian and classless communist society.

The underlying principles of China's party-state appear in the country's constitution.[10] The preamble of the constitution repeatedly states that the country is under "the leadership of the Communist Party of China." Article 1 defines the PRC as "a socialist state under the people's democratic dictatorship." It also declares "disruption of the socialist system by any organization or individual is prohibited." Such provisions imply that the Chinese "people" (implicitly, supporters of socialism and the leadership of the Communist Party) enjoy democratic rights and privileges under

CCP guidance. But the constitution also gives the CCP authority to exercise dictatorship over any person or organization that, it believes, opposes socialism and the party.

Marxism-Leninism, the foundation of communist ideology remains an important part of the Chinese party-state, at least officially. *Marxism* refers to the ideas of Karl Marx (1818–1883) and presents a theory of human history emphasizing economic development and the struggle between rich property-owning and poor working classes that inevitably leads to revolution. *Leninism* refers to the theories developed by Vladimir Lenin (1870–1924), the Russian revolutionary who was the leading founder of the Soviet Union. It focuses on how the workers should be organized and led by a communist party to seize political power in order to bring about socialism and communism.

The CCP says that Mao Zedong made a fundamental contribution to communist ideology. He adapted Marxism-Leninism, which evolved in Europe and Russia, to China's special circumstances. In particular, he emphasized the crucial role of peasants in the revolution that brought the Communist Party to power. Although the current CCP leadership acknowledges that Mao made serious mistakes such as the Great Leap Forward and the Cultural Revolution, the party continues to praise Mao and his ideology, which they call Mao Zedong Thought.

Communist ideology is much less important in China today than it was during the Mao era. But it still provides the framework for governance and policy-making by the Communist Party leadership and legitimizes the continuing rule of the CCP. It also sets the boundaries for what is permissible in politics.

The constitution of the PRC is more a political statement than a governing document that embodies enduring principles. Constitutional change (from minor amendments to total replacement) during the last fifty years has reflected the shifting political winds in China. The character and content of the constitution in force at any given time bear the ideological stamp of the prevailing party leadership. The constitutions of the Mao era stressed the importance of class struggle and revolutionary doctrine, while the current one (adopted in 1982) emphasizes national unity in the pursuit of economic development and modernization.

The government of the People's Republic of China (the "state) is organizationally and functionally distinct from the Chinese Communist Party. The Communist Party exercises direct or indirect control (a "leading role") over all government organizations and personnel. High-ranking government officials with any substantive authority are also members of the CCP's most powerful organizations.

The government of the PRC acts as the administrative agency for enacting, implementing, and enforcing policies made by the party. Nevertheless, to fully understand governance and policy-making in China, it is necessary to look at the structure of both the Chinese Communist Party and the government of the People's Republic of China and the relationship between the two.

## CCP Organization

According to the CCP constitution[11] (a wholly different document from the constitution of the PRC), the "highest leading bodies" of the party are the **National Party Congress** and the **Central Committee** (see Figure 14.3). But the National Party Congress meets for only one week every five years, and it has more than 2,100 delegates. This reflects the fact that the role of the Congress is more symbolic than substantive. The essential function of the National Party Congress is to approve decisions already made by the top leaders and to provide a showcase for the party's current policies. There is little debate about policy and no seriously contested voting of any

**National Party Congress**

The symbolically important meeting, held every five years for about one week, of about 2,100 delegates representatives of the Chinese Communist Party, who endorse policies and the allocation of leadership positions that have been determined beforehand by the party's much smaller ruling bodies.

**Central Committee**

The top 350 or so leaders of the Chinese Communist Party. It meets annually for about two weeks and is charged with carrying on the business of the National Party Congress when it is not in session.

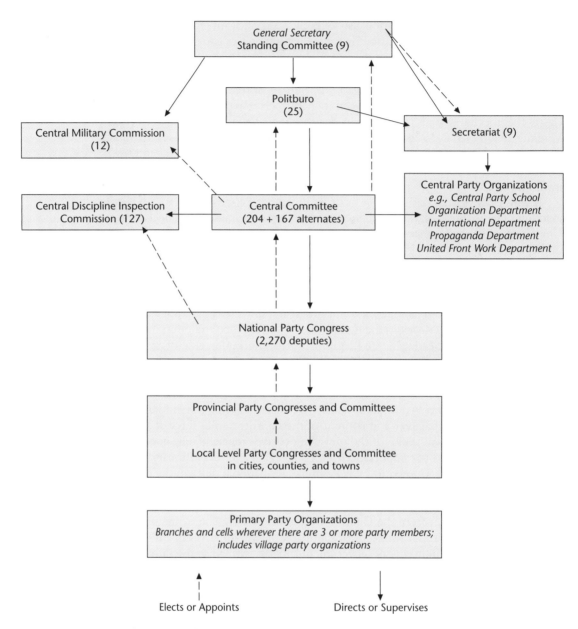

Elects or Appoints          Directs or Supervises

*Note:* Numbers in parentheses refer to the membership of the organization as of early 2008.

**FIGURE 14.3 Organization of the Chinese Communist Party (78 million members)**

consequence. The party congress does not function as a legislative check on the power of the party's executive leadership.

The Central Committee (with about 370 full and alternate members) is the next level up in the pyramid of party power. It consists of CCP leaders from around the country who meet annually for about a week. Members are elected for a five-year term by the National Party Congress by secret ballot, with a limited choice of candidates. The overall composition of the Central Committee is closely controlled by the top leaders to ensure compliance with their policies.

In principle, the Central Committee directs party affairs when the National Party Congress is not in session. But its size and short, infrequent meetings (called plenums) greatly limit its effectiveness. However, Central Committee plenums and occasional informal work conferences do represent significant gatherings of the party elite. They can be a very important arena of decision-making and political maneuvering by contending party factions.

The most powerful political organizations in China's communist party-state are two small executive bodies at the very top of the CCP's structure: the **Politburo** (or Political Bureau) and its even more exclusive **Standing Committee**. These bodies are formally elected by the Central Committee from among its own members under carefully controlled and secretive conditions. The current Politburo has twenty-five members. Nine of them also belong to the Standing Committee, the formal apex of power in the CCP.

Before 1982, the leading position in the party was the chairman of the Politburo's Standing Committee, which was occupied by Mao Zedong (hence *Chairman* Mao) for more than three decades until his death in 1976. The title of chairman was abolished in 1982 to symbolize a break with Mao's highly personal and often arbitrary style of rule. Since then, the party's leader has been the **general secretary**, who presides over the Politburo and the Standing Committee, a position most recently held by Jiang Zemin (1989–2002) and Hu Jintao (2002 to the present).

Neither Jiang nor Hu has had the personal authority or charisma of Mao or Deng Xiaoping, and therefore both have governed as part of a collective leadership that included their fellow members on the Standing Committee and Politburo. Nevertheless, both have tried to put their own stamp on the party's major policy direction, Jiang by embracing the private sector and forging sort of a partnership between the CCP and the country's entrepreneurs, and Hu by calling for attention to problems like inequality, pollution, health care, and social security as part of the development of a "harmonious socialist society."

China's leaders are, as a whole, very well educated. Seven of the nine members of the Standing Committee were trained as engineers before beginning political careers, one has a Ph.D. in economics, and another a Ph.D. in law. All but one of the remaining sixteen members of the Politburo have undergraduate or advanced degrees. This is dramatic evidence of the shift in China's ruling circles from the revolutionary leaders of the Mao and Deng generations to technocrats who place highest priority on science, technology, and higher education as the keys to the country's development.

The Politburo and Standing Committee are not accountable to the Central Committee or any other institution in any meaningful sense. Although there is now somewhat more openness about the timing and subjects covered in their meetings, the operations of the party's executive organizations are generally shrouded in secrecy. Top leaders work and often live in a huge walled compound called Zhongnanhai ("Middle and Southern Seas") on lakes in the center of Beijing. Zhongnanhai is not only heavily guarded, as any government executive headquarters would be, but it also has no identifying signs on its exterior other than some party slogans, nor is it identified on public maps.

Two other executive organizations of the party deserve brief mention. The Secretariat manages the day-to-day work of the Politburo and Standing Committee and coordinates the party's complex and far-flung structure with considerable authority in organizational and personnel matters. The Central Commission for Discipline Inspection (CCDI) is responsible for monitoring the compliance of party members with the CCP constitution and other rules. Recently, the leadership has used the commission as a vehicle against corruption within the Communist Party.

The Communist Party has an organized presence throughout Chinese society. CCP organizations in provinces, cities, and counties are headed by a party secretary and party committee. There are also about 3.6 million primary party organizations,

**Politburo**

The committee made up of the top two dozen or so leaders of the Chinese Communist Party.

**Standing Committee**

A subgroup of the Politburo, with less than a dozen members. The most powerful political organization in China.

**general secretary**

The formal title of the head of the Chinese Communist Party. From 1942 to 1982, the position was called "chairman" and was held by Mao Zedong until his death in 1976.

usually called branches. These are found throughout the country in workplaces, government offices, schools, urban neighborhoods, rural towns, villages, and army units. There is even a CCP branch organization at Wal-Mart's China headquarters. Local and primary organizations extend the CCP's reach throughout Chinese society. They are also designed to ensure coordination within the vast and complex party structure and subordination to the central party authorities in Beijing.

## PRC Organization

**National People's Congress (NPC)**

The legislature of the People's Republic of China. It is under the control of the Chinese Communist Party and is not an independent branch of government.

State authority in China is formally vested in a system of people's congresses that begins at the top with the **National People's Congress (NPC)**, which is a completely different organization from the National *Party* Congress. The NPC is China's national legislature and is discussed in more detail in Section 4.

The National People's Congress formally elects the president and vice president of China. But there is only one candidate, chosen by the Communist Party, for each office. The president's term is concurrent with that of the congress (five years). There is a two-term limit. As China's head of state, the president meets and negotiates with other world leaders. The president of the PRC has always been a high-ranking Communist Party leader. Both Jiang Zemin and Hu Jintao served concurrently as CCP general secretary and PRC president. The recent pattern is for the Communist Party to use the position of vice president to groom the country's next top leader.

The premier (prime minister) of the People's Republic has authority over the government bureaucracy and policy implementation. The premier is formally appointed by the president with the approval of the National People's Congress. But in reality, the Communist Party leadership decides which of its members will serve as premier.

**State Council**

The cabinet of the government of the People's Republic of China, headed by the premier.

The premier directs the **State Council**, which functions much like the cabinet in a parliamentary system. It includes the premier, a few vice premiers, the heads of government ministries and commissions, and several other senior officials.

The size of the State Council varies as ministries and commissions are created, merged, or disbanded to meet changing policy needs. At the height of the Maoist era planned economy, there were more than one hundred ministerial-level officials. There are now fewer than thirty, which reflects both the decreased role of central planning and the administrative streamlining undertaken to make the government more efficient. Most State Council members run functionally-specific departments, such as the Ministry of Education or the Commission on Population and Family Planning. China has also created a number of "super-ministries," such as the National Energy Commission, to coordinate policies on complex issues that cannot be managed by a single ministry.

The work of the State Council (and the CCP Politburo) is supported by flexible issue-specific task forces called "leadership small groups." These informal groups bring together top officials from various ministries, commissions, and committees in order to coordinate policy-making and implementation on matters that cross the jurisdiction of any single organization. Some groups, for example, the Central Leading Group on Foreign Affairs, are more or less permanent fixtures in the party-state structure, while others may be convened on an ad hoc basis to deal with short-term matters like a natural disaster or an epidemic. Since most of the members are high-ranking CCP officials, they are also a means to insure party supervision of policy in that particular area.

**cadre**

A person who exercises a position of authority in a communist party-state; cadres may or may not be Communist Party members.

China's bureaucracy is immense in size and in the scope of its reach throughout the country. The total number of cadres—people in positions of authority paid by the government or party—in the PRC is around 40 million. The term **cadre** applies

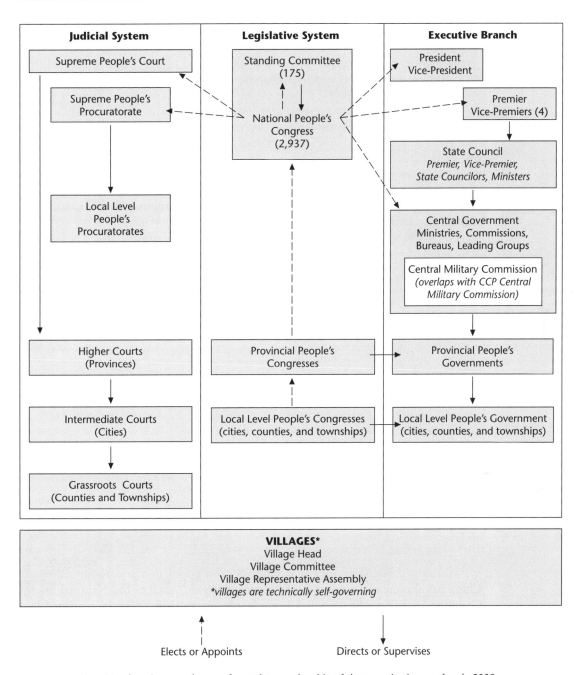

**Judicial System**

Supreme People's Court

Supreme People's Procuratorate

Local Level People's Procuratorates

Higher Courts (Provinces)

Intermediate Courts (Cities)

Grassroots Courts (Counties and Townships)

**Legislative System**

Standing Committee (175)

National People's Congress (2,937)

Provincial People's Congresses

Local Level People's Congresses (cities, counties, and townships)

**Executive Branch**

President Vice-President

Premier Vice-Premiers (4)

State Council
*Premier, Vice-Premier, State Councilors, Ministers*

Central Government Ministries, Commissions, Bureaus, Leading Groups

Central Military Commission *(overlaps with CCP Central Military Commission)*

Provincial People's Governments

Local Level People's Government (cities, counties, and townships)

**VILLAGES\***
Village Head
Village Committee
Village Representative Assembly
*\*villages are technically self-governing*

Elects or Appoints            Directs or Supervises

*Note:* Numbers in parentheses refer to the membership of the organization as of early 2008.

**FIGURE 14.4  Organization of the Government of the People's Republic of China (PRC)**

to both the most powerful leaders as well as to local-level bureaucrats. Not all cadres are party members, and not all party members are cadres. The vast majority of cadres work below the national level, and a minority work directly for the government or the CCP. The remainder occupies key posts in economic enterprises, schools, and scientific, cultural, and other institutions. There have been important moves toward professionalizing the bureaucracy. More official positions are now subject to competition through civil service exams rather than by appointment from above, and the educational level of cadres has increased significantly since the 1980s. Most cadres must now retire between the ages of sixty and seventy. A two-term limit has been set for all top cadres, including party and state leaders.

The CCP uses a weblike system of organizational controls to make sure that the government bureaucracy complies with the party's will in policy implementation. In the first place, almost all key government officials are also party members. Furthermore, the CCP exercises control over the policy process through party organizations that parallel government agencies at all levels of the system. For example, each provincial government works under the watchful eye of a provincial party committee. In addition, the Communist Party maintains an effective presence inside every government organization through a "leading party group" that is made up of key officials who are also CCP members.

The CCP also influences the policy process by means of the "cadre list," or as it was known in the Soviet Union where the practice was developed, the **nomenklatura** system. The cadre list covers millions of important positions in the government and elsewhere (including institutions such as universities, banks, trade unions, and newspapers). Any personnel decision involving an appointment, promotion, transfer, or dismissal that affects a position on this list must be approved by a party organization department, whether or not the person involved is a party member. In recent years, the growth of nonstate sectors of the economy and administrative streamlining have led to a reduction in the number of positions directly subject to party approval. Nevertheless, the *nomenklatura* system remains one of the major instruments by which the CCP tries to "ensure that leading institutions throughout the country will exercise only the autonomy granted to them by the party."[12]

**nomenklatura**

A system of personnel selection under which the Communist Party maintains control over the appointment of important officials in all spheres of social, economic, and political life. The term is also used to describe individuals chosen through this system and thus refers more broadly to the privileged circles in the Soviet Union and China.

# Other State Institutions

### The Judiciary

China has a four-tiered system of "people's courts" that reaches from a Supreme People's Court down through higher (provincial-level), intermediate (city-level), and grassroots (county- and township-level) people's courts. The Supreme People's Court supervises the work of lower courts and the application of the country's laws, but it hears few cases and does not exercise judicial review over government policies.

China's judicial system came under attack as a bastion of elitism and revisionism during the Cultural Revolution. The formal legal system pretty much ceased to operate during that period, and many of its functions were taken over by political or police organizations, which often acted arbitrarily (and brutally) in making arrests and administering punishments.

In recent decades, the legal system of the PRC has been reformed and revitalized. At the end of the Maoist era, there were only 3000 (poorly trained) lawyers in China; now there are about 200,000 (compared to more than a million lawyers in the United States), with an increasingly high level of professionalism. Advisory offices have been established throughout the country to provide citizens with legal assistance.

There has been an enormous surge in the number of lawsuits filed (and often won) by people against businesses, local officials, and government agencies. Chinese courts can provide a real avenue of redress to the public for a wide range of nonpolitical grievances, including loss of property, consumer fraud, and even unjust detention by the police.

Citizen mediation committees based in urban neighborhoods and rural villages play an important role in the judicial process by settling a majority of civil cases out of court.

China's criminal justice system is swift and harsh. Great faith is placed in the ability of an official investigation to find the facts of a case. The outcome of cases that actually do come to trial is pretty much predetermined. The conviction rate is 98–99 percent for all criminal cases. Prison terms are long and subject to only cursory appeal. A variety of offenses in addition to murder—including, in some cases, rape and especially major cases of embezzlement and other "economic crimes"—are subject to capital punishment.

All death penalty sentences must be approved by the country's Supreme People's Court. The court has recently started to be more rigorous in this review process, and quite a few death sentences have been reduced to prison terms. But appeals are handled quickly. Capital punishment cases do not linger in the courts for years, or even months. Execution is usually by a single bullet in the back of the convicted person's head, although the country is moving toward lethal injection. The number of annual executions is considered a state secret in China, but it is certainly in the thousands, and the PRC executes more people each year than the rest of the world combined.

Although the PRC constitution guarantees judicial independence, China's courts and other legal bodies remain under Communist Party control. The appointment of all judicial personnel is subject to party approval. Lawyers who displease officials are often harassed in various ways, their licenses to practice law are sometimes not renewed, and they themselves are sometimes arrested.

Legal reform in China has been undertaken because China's leaders are well aware that economic development requires professional lawyers and judicial personnel, predictable legal processes, and binding documents such as contracts. China has, by and large, become a country where there is rule *by* law, which means that the party-state uses the law to carry out its policies and enforce its rule. But it is still far from having established the rule *of* law, in which everyone and every organization, including the Communist Party, is accountable and subject to the law.

## Subnational Government

China (like France and Japan) is a unitary state in which the national government exercises a high degree of control over other levels of government. It is not a federal system (like the United States and India) that gives subnational governments considerable policy-making and financial autonomy.

There are four main layers of state structure beneath the central government in China: provinces, cities, counties, and rural towns. There are also four very large centrally administered cities (Beijing, Shanghai, Tianjin, and Chongqing) and five autonomous regions, areas of the country with large minority populations (such as Tibet).

Each level of subnational government has a people's congress that meets infrequently and plays a limited, but increasingly active, role in supervising affairs in its area. In theory, these congresses (the legislative branch) are empowered to supervise the work of the "people's governments" (the executive branch) at the various levels of the system. But in reality, subnational government executives (such as provincial governors and city mayors) are more accountable to Communist Party authority than to the people's congresses. For example, the city of Shanghai has both a mayor and a party secretary, each with distinct and important powers. But the party secretary's power is more consequential.

Government administration in China has become increasingly decentralized over the last two decades as the role of central planning has been reduced and more power has been given to provincial and local authorities, particularly in economic matters. Efforts have also been made to reduce party interference in administrative work.

Nevertheless, the central government retains considerable power to intervene in local affairs when and where it wants. This power of the central authorities derives not only from their ability to set binding national priorities, but also from their control over the military and the police, the tax system, critical energy resources, and construction of major infrastructure projects. A number of political scientists in China and abroad have suggested that the PRC, given its continental size and great regional diversity, would be better served by a federal system with a more balanced distribution of power between the national, provincial, and local levels of government. However, such a move would be inconsistent with the highly centralized structure of a communist party-state.

Under the formal layers of state administration are China's 600,000 or so rural villages, which are home to the majority of the country's population. These villages, with an average population of roughly 500–1,000 each, are technically self-governing and are not formally responsible to a higher level of state authority. In recent years, village leaders have been directly and competitively elected by local residents, and village representative assemblies have become more vocal. These trends have brought an important degree of grassroots democracy to village government. However, the most powerful organization in the village is the Communist Party committee, and the single most powerful person is the local communist party leader (the party secretary).

### The Military, Police, and Internal Security

**People's Liberation Army (PLA)**

The combined armed forces of the People's Republic of China, which includes land, sea, air, and strategic missile forces.

China's **People's Liberation Army (PLA)**, which encompasses all of the country's ground, air, and naval armed services, is, according to the PRC Ministry of Defense, "a people's army created and led by the Communist Party of China."[13]

The PLA is the world's largest military force, with about 2.3 million active personnel (down from nearly 4 million in 1989). On a per capita basis, the PRC has 1.8 active military personnel per 1,000 of its population, compared with the U.S. ratio of 5.1 per 1,000. The PLA also has a formal reserve force of another 500,000 to 800,000. A people's militia of 8 million minimally-trained civilians can be mobilized and armed by local governments in the event of war or other national emergency.

Article 55 of China's constitution states, "It is a sacred duty of every citizen...to defend the motherland and resist invasion. It is an honored obligation of the citizens to perform military service and to join the militia forces." The Military Service Law gives the government the power to conscript both men and women between the ages of eighteen and twenty-two as necessary to meet the country's security needs. But China's military has never had to rely on a draft to fill its ranks since serving in the PLA is considered a prestigious option for many young people, particularly for rural youth who might not have many other opportunities for upward mobility. All university-bound students must undergo a brief period of military training before beginning classes.

China has spent heavily over the last two decades to modernize its armed forces and raise the pay of military personnel. The PRC's official defense budget for 2010 was about $80 billion, a 7.5 percent increase over 2009 (the lowest percentage increase since 1989). Many analysts think that the PRC vastly understates its military expenditures. They estimate that it is twice the official figures. Still, China spends much less in total and vastly less per capita on its military than does the United States, which spent about $660 billion on defense in 2010.

The key organization in charge of the Chinese armed forces is the **Central Military Commission (CMC).** There are currently twelve members of the CMC, ten of whom are the highest-ranking officers of the People's Liberation Army; the other two are Hu Jintao, PRC president and CCP general secretary, who chairs the committee, and his heir-apparent, China's vice-president, Xi Jinping. The chair of the CMC is, in effect, the commander-in-chief of China's armed forces and has always been the most powerful leader of the communist party.

China's internal security apparatus consists of several different organizations. The People's Armed Police (PAP) guards public officials and buildings and carries out some border patrol and counter-terrorism functions. It has also been called in to quell public disturbances, including worker, peasant, and ethnic unrest. The Ministry of State Security, with a force of about 1.7 million, is responsible for combating espionage and gathering intelligence at home and abroad.

The Ministry of Public Security is the main policing organization in the PRC and is responsible for the prevention and investigation of crimes and for surveillance of Chinese citizens and foreigners in China suspected of being a threat to the state. Local public security bureaus, which carry out day-to-day police work, are under the command of the central ministry in Beijing. In effect, this gives China a national police force stationed throughout the country. The Ministry of Public Security has a special unit devoted to Internet surveillance with a website (http://www.cyberpolice.cn/) that allows citizens to report online activity that "endangers national security and social stability or promotes national division, cults, pornography, fraud, and other harmful information."

In addition to regular prisons, the Ministry of Public Security maintains an extensive system of labor reform (*laogai*) camps for people convicted of particularly serious crimes, including political ones, such as "endangering state and public security" or "revealing state secrets." These camps are noted for their harsh conditions and remote locations.

The Public Security Bureau also administers "reeducation through labor" (*laojiao*) centers for petty criminals, juvenile delinquents, those considered to have disrupted social order, including prostitutes and small-scale drug users, as well as political and religious dissidents. Inmates can be held in "administrative detention" for up to three years without a formal charge or trial.

# The Policy-Making Process

At the height of Mao Zedong's power in the 1950s and 1960s, many scholars described policy-making in China as a simple top-down "Mao-in-command" system. The Cultural Revolution led analysts to conclude that policy outcomes in the PRC were best understood as a result of factional and ideological struggles within the Chinese political elite. Now, a much more nuanced model, "fragmented authoritarianism," is often used to explain Chinese policy-making.[14] This model recognizes that China is still fundamentally an authoritarian state and is far from being a democracy in which public opinion, party competition, media scrutiny, and independent interest groups have an impact on policy decisions. But the model also takes into account that power in China has become much more dispersed, or fragmented, than it was during the Maoist era. It sees policy as evolving not only from commands from above, but also as a complex process of cooperation, conflict, and bargaining among political actors at various levels of the system. The decentralization of power that has accompanied economic reform has given

**Central Military Commission (CMC)**

The most important military organization in the People's Republic of China, headed by the general secretary of the Chinese Communist Party, who is the commander-in-chief of the People's Liberation Army.

provincial and local governments a lot more clout in the policy process, and the national focus on economic development has also led to the growing influence of nonparty experts, the media, and nongovernmental organizations within the policy-making loop.

The fragmented authoritarian model acknowledges that policy-making in China is still ultimately under the control of the Chinese Communist Party and that the top two dozen or so party leaders who sit on the party's Politburo wield nearly unchecked power.

The current party leadership is a balance between two major coalitions, the "elitists" who give priority to rapid economic growth and investment in China's major cities, and the "populists" who believe that more attention needs to be paid to the consequences of growth, such as urban-rural inequality and environmental degradation.[15] These coalitions appear to operate with a kind of balance-of-power understanding when it comes to allocating important leadership positions and making policy decisions.

No account of the policy process in China is complete without noting the importance of *guanxi* ("connections"), the personal relationships and mutual obligations based on family, friendship, school, military, professional, or other ties. The notion of *guanxi* has its roots in Confucian culture and has long been an important part of political, social, and economic life in China. These connections still influence the workings of the Chinese bureaucracy, where personal ties are often the key to getting things done. Depending on how they are used, *guanxi* can either help cut red tape and increase efficiency or bolster organizational rigidity and feed corruption.

The policy process in China is much more institutionalized and smoother and less personal and volatile than it was in the Maoist era. But it is still highly secretive, and leaders of the People's Republic are not accountable to the people of China. The unchallengeable power of the Communist Party is still the most basic fact of political life in the People's Republic of China. Party dominance, however, does not mean that the system "operates in a monolithic way"; in fact, it "wriggles with politics" of many kinds, formal and informal.[16] A complete picture of governance and policy-making in China must take into account how various influences, including ideology, factional maneuverings, bureaucratic interests, citizen input, and *guanxi,* shape the decisions ultimately made by Communist Party leaders and organizations.

**guanxi**

A Chinese term that means "connections" or "relationships," and describes personal ties between individuals based on such things as common birthplace or mutual acquaintances.

## Summary

China is one of the few remaining countries in the world still ruled by a communist party. Even though the CCP has moved China in the direction of a capitalist, free market economy, it proclaims it is following communist ideology and its goal is to create a socialist China. The CCP insists it is the only political party that can lead the country toward this goal, and it prohibits any serious challenge to its authority. Power is highly concentrated in the top two dozen or so leaders of the CCP, who are chosen through secretive inner-party procedures. The government of the People's Republic of China is technically separate from the CCP, and political reform in China has brought some autonomy to government institutions, such as the national legislature and the judiciary. But, in fact, the government operates only under the close supervision of the Communist Party and almost all high-ranking government officials are also members of the Communist Party.

# REPRESENTATION AND PARTICIPATION

The Chinese Communist Party claims that it represents the interests of all the people of China and describes the People's Republic as a **socialist democracy**. In the CCP's view this is superior to democracy in capitalist countries where wealthy individuals and corporations dominate politics and policy-making despite multiparty politics. China's *socialist* democracy is based on the unchallengeable role of the CCP as the country's only ruling party and should not be confused with the *social* democracy of Western European center-left political parties, which is rooted in a commitment to competitive politics.

Although power in China is highly concentrated in the hands of the top Communist Party leaders, representation and participation do play important, if limited, roles in China's political system. Legislatures, elections, and organizations like labor unions provide citizens with ways of influencing public policy-making and the selection of some leaders.

## The Legislature

The Chinese constitution grants the National People's Congress (NPC) the power to enact and amend the country's laws, approve and monitor the state budget, and declare and end war. The NPC is also empowered to elect (and recall) the president and vice president, the chair of the state Central Military Commission, the head of China's Supreme Court, and the procurator-general (something like the U.S. attorney general). The NPC has final approval over the selection of the premier and members of the State Council. On paper, China's legislature certainly looks to be the most powerful branch of government. In fact, these powers, which are not insignificant, are exercised only as allowed by the Communist Party.

The National People's Congress is a unicameral legislature with nearly 3000 members (called "deputies") who meet only for about two weeks every March. When the NPC is not in session, state power is exercised by its 175-member Standing Committee (not to be confused with the CCP Standing Committee), which convenes every other month. A council of about fifteen members conducts the day-to-day business of the NPC. The chair of the NPC is always a high-ranking Communist Party leader.

NPC deputies are elected for five-year terms. Except for those from the People's Liberation Army, they are chosen from lower-level people's congresses in China's provinces, autonomous regions, and major municipalities. There are representatives from China's two indirectly ruled Special Administrative Regions, the tiny former Portuguese colony and gambling haven of Macau and the former British colony and bustling commercial city of Hong Kong. To symbolize China's claim to Taiwan, deputies representing the island are chosen from among PRC residents with Taiwanese ancestry or other ties.

Deputies are not full-time legislators, but remain in their regular jobs and home areas except for the brief time when the congress is in session. A large majority of the deputies to the NPC are members of the CCP, but many belong to one of China's eight noncommunist (and powerless) political parties (see below) or have no party affiliation. Workers and farmers make up less than 20 percent of NPC deputies; the remainder are government and party cadres, military personnel, intellectuals, professionals, celebrities, and business people. Women make up around 20 percent of NPC deputies and ethnic minorities 15 percent. In a new category of representation, three migrant workers (out of a national total of about 150 million) were elected in 2008.

Most NPC deputies are now chosen because of their ability to contribute to China's modernization or to represent important constituencies rather than simply on the basis of political loyalty. The educational level of deputies has increased significantly in recent years, with more than 90 percent having junior college degrees or above, and more than half have advanced degrees.

Despite great fanfare in the press as examples of socialist democracy at work, legislation is passed and state leaders are elected by the National People's Congress by overwhelming majorities and with little substantive debate. The annual sessions are largely taken up by the presentation of very long reports by the premier and other state leaders. The NPC never deals with sensitive political issues. The CCP also monitors the election process to make sure that no outright dissidents are elected as deputies.

Nevertheless, some deputies have become a bit more assertive on issues like corruption and environmental problems. Government legislative initiatives have occasionally been defeated or tabled.

For example, a property rights law—which included the protection of private property—that was finally passed in March 2007 had first been put on the NPC agenda in 2002. It generated enough controversy among deputies, party-state leaders, and academics that it had to be revised several times before it was finally affirmed by 96.9 percent (2903 for, fifty-three against, and thirty-seven abstentions) of the vote. Some objected to the law because they thought providing such guarantees to private property owners was contrary to communist principles; others feared that corrupt officials would use the law to enrich themselves through the "asset-stripping" of privatized state-owned enterprises as happened on a grand scale when Russia went from a planned to a market economy. But, in a reflection of the limits on the discussion of controversial issues, the Chinese press was not allowed to cover the property law debate in the NPC or to print editorial opinions on the issue.

Legislatures in communist party-states are often called "rubber stamps," meaning they automatically and without question approve party policies. But as economics has replaced ideology as the main motivation of China's leaders, the NPC has become a more significant and lively part of the Chinese political system. It is still not, however, an independent legislative branch of government that in any way checks or balances executive power.

## Political Parties and the Party System

### The Chinese Communist Party

With about 80 million members, the Chinese Communist Party is by far the largest political party in the world. But its membership makes up a very small minority of the population (less than 10 percent of those over eighteen, the minimum age for joining the party). This is consistent with the CCP's view that it is a "vanguard" party that admits only those who are truly dedicated to the communist cause. Joining

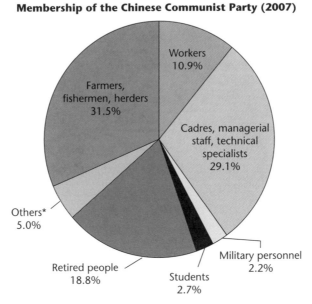

**Membership of the Chinese Communist Party (2007)**

Workers
10.9%

Farmers,
fishermen, herders
31.5%

Cadres, managerial
staff, technical
specialists
29.1%

Others*
5.0%

Military personnel
2.2%

Retired people
18.8%

Students
2.7%

*Includes private entrepreneurs, technicians, and managerial-level staff in private or foreign-funded companies and the self-employed.

**FIGURE 14.5 Membership of the Chinese Communist Party**

*Source:* http://news.xinhuanet.com/english/2007-10/09/content_6849781.htm.

the Communist Party is a time-consuming process that can last as long as two years and involves a lengthy application, interviews, references, a background check, and a probation period.

The social composition of CCP membership has changed profoundly since the party came to power in 1949. In the mid-1950s, peasants made up nearly 70 percent of party members. Figure 14.5 shows the composition of the CCP as of mid-2007.

The Chinese Communist Party now claims that rather than representing just workers and peasants, it represents the interests of the overwhelming majority of people in China and is open to all those who are committed to promoting national development and are willing to accept party leadership in achieving that goal.

The CCP welcomes members from what it calls the "new social stratum" that has emerged in the process of market reform and globalization of the Chinese economy. The new social stratum includes private business owners ("entrepreneurs") and managerial-level staff in private or foreign-funded companies. This is a dramatic change from the Maoist era when any hint of capitalism was crushed. It is also a key part of the strategy of the party to prolong its rule by adapting to a rapidly modernizing economy.

Women make up only 20 percent of the CCP membership as a whole and just 6 percent of full members of the Central Committee elected in 2007. The Politburo has one female member. No women serve on the party's most powerful organization, the Politburo Standing Committee.

Even though many Chinese believe that communist ideology is irrelevant to their lives and the nation's future, being a party member still provides unparalleled access to influence and resources. It remains a prerequisite for advancement in many careers, particularly in government. More than two million people join the CCP each year, most of them college graduates under the age of thirty-five.

### China's Non-Communist "Democratic Parties"

China is rightly called a one-party system because the country's politics are so thoroughly dominated by the Chinese Communist Party. But, in fact, China has eight political parties in addition to the CCP. These are officially referred to as China's "democratic parties," which is said to be another example of socialist democracy in the PRC. Each non-communist party represents a particular group in Chinese society. For example, the Chinese Party for the Public Interest draws on overseas Chinese who have returned to live in China. But these parties, all of which were established before the founding of the PRC in 1949 and accept the "guidance" of the CCP, have a total membership of only a little over half a million. They provide advice to the CCP on nonpolitical matters and generate support within their particular constituencies for CCP policies. Individual members of these parties may assume important government positions. But politically, these parties are relatively insignificant and function as little more than "a loyal non-opposition."[17]

New political parties are not allowed to form. When a group of activists who had been part of the 1989 Tiananmen protests tried to establish a China Democracy Party in 1998 to promote multiparty politics, they were arrested or forced into exile abroad, and the party was banned.

# Elections

Elections in the PRC are basically mechanisms to give the communist party-state greater legitimacy by allowing large numbers of citizens to participate in the political process under very controlled circumstances. But elections are becoming somewhat more democratic and more important in providing a way for citizens to express their views and hold some local officials accountable.

Most elections in China are *indirect*. In other words, the members of an already elected or established body elect those who will serve at the next-highest level in the power structure. For example, the deputies of a provincial people's congress, not all the eligible citizens of the province, elect delegates to the National People's Congress. A comparable situation would exist in the United States if members of Congress were selected by and from state legislatures rather than by popular vote.

In *direct* elections all voters in the relevant area cast ballots for candidates for a particular position. Direct elections are now quite common in China's villages, and there have been experiments with letting all voters choose officials and representatives in rural towns, counties, and urban districts. To promote "inner-party democracy," some lower-level CCP leaders are now directly elected.

The authorities have been very cautious in expanding the scope of direct elections. The Communist Party wants to prevent them from becoming a forum for dissent or a vehicle for a political movement. The most powerful positions in the government, such as city mayors and provincial governors, are appointed, not elected.

Many direct and indirect elections now have multiple candidates and open nominations, with the winner chosen by secret ballot. A significant number of independently nominated candidates have defeated official nominees, although even independent candidates also have to be approved by the CCP.

The most noteworthy steps towards democratic representation and participation have occurred in the rural villages. Laws implemented since the late 1980s have provided for direct election of the village head and other leaders. These elections are generally multicandidate with a secret ballot. Villagers have used them to remove leaders they think are incompetent or corrupt.

The village CCP committee closely monitors such grass-roots elections. In many cases, the local Communist Party leader has been chosen to serve simultaneously as the village head in a competitive election. This is often because the Communist Party leader is a well-respected person who has the confidence and support of the villagers. Only 1 percent of the village leaders (out of more than 600,000) are women.

Villager representative assemblies have members chosen from each household or group of households. The assemblies have taken a more active role in supervising the work of local officials and decision making in matters affecting community finances and welfare. Some observers believe such direct grass-roots measures are seeds of real democracy. Others see them as a façade to appease international critics and give the rural population a way to express discontent without challenging the country's fundamental political organization.

Recent electoral reform has certainly increased popular representation and participation in China's government. But elections in the PRC still do not give citizens a means by which they can exercise effective control over the party officials and organizations. Top Chinese communist leaders, from Mao to now, have repeatedly claimed that multiparty democracy is unsuited to China's traditions and socialist principles. According to an official of National People's Congress, "Western-style elections… are a game for the rich. They are affected by the resources and funding that a candidate can utilize. Those who manage to win elections are easily in the shoes of their parties or sponsors and become spokespersons for the minority…. As a socialist country, we cannot simply take the Western approach."[18]

Rural residents vote in a village election in China. In recent years, such grassroots democracy has become widespread in the countryside, although it is always closely monitored by the Chinese Communist Party.

# Political Culture, Citizenship, and Identity

## From Communism to Consumerism

Marxism-Leninism is still important in Chinese politics, since the Communist Party proclaims that it is China's official ideology. Serious challenges to that ideology or the party are not permitted. The CCP also tries to keep communist ideology viable and visible by efforts to influence public opinion and values through its control of the media, the arts, and education.

China's media is much livelier and more open than during the Maoist period when it was totally under CCP domination and did little other than convey party messages. However, freedom of the press is still quite limited. Reduced political control of the media has largely meant the freedom to publish more entertainment news, human interest stories, and nonpolitical investigative journalism in areas that are consistent with party objectives. For example, in the summer of 2007, the news media helped expose the use of slave labor (including many children) in thousands of brick kilns and coal mines in two provinces in central China. But the state does shut down media outlets that provoke its political displeasure.

In terms of political restrictions, the arts are the area of life that has seen the greatest change in China in recent years. Books, movies, plays, and other art forms are sometimes banned, but much of the artistic censorship is now self-imposed by creators who know the limits of what is acceptable to the party-state.

Educational opportunities have expanded enormously in China since 1949. Primary school enrollment is close to 100 percent of the age-eligible population (ages six to eleven), but it drops to about 75 percent in middle and high school (ages eleven to eighteen), and only 20 percent at the university level. Scoring well on a national examination is required to go to college, and Chinese schools can be pressure-cookers for those who want to move up the educational ladder, which is crucial to getting a good job in the modernizing economy.

Political study is still a required but now relatively minor part of the curriculum at all levels, and more than 80 percent of China's students between the ages of seven and fourteen belong to the Young Pioneers, an organization designed to promote good social behavior, community service, patriotism, and loyalty to the party.

At its best, China's educational system produces spectacular results. A 2010 study by the Organization for Economic Cooperation and Development (OECD) showed that students in Shanghai outperformed those in 65 countries on standardized reading, math, and science tests. But access to quality education in the PRC's most prosperous cities is light years ahead of that in the rest of the country. There are also many critics of the extreme test-centered focus of Chinese schools and the lack of attention to critical thinking and individual creativity that are essential to a hi-tech knowledge economy.

Internet access is exploding in China, with more than 400 million users by the end of 2010. Web connections are available even in some quite remote towns and villages. The government worries about the influence of e-mail and electronic information it cannot control. It has blocked access to certain foreign websites, shut down unlicensed cyber cafés, and arrested people it has accused of disseminating subversive material over the Internet.

Web access in China is tightly controlled by the licensing of just a few Internet Service Providers. They are responsible for who uses their systems and how. The government is investing huge sums to develop (with technical assistance from western companies) stronger firewalls and monitoring systems. The Chinese party-state knows that cutting-edge technology is critical to its modernization plans. The party wants citizens to become computer literate. As with so much else in China, however, the party-state wants to define the way and dictate the rules.

Alternative sources of socialization and belief are growing in importance in China. These do not often take expressly political forms, however, because of the threat of repression. In the countryside, peasants have replaced portraits of Mao and other Communist heroes with statues of folk gods and ancestor worship tablets. The influence of extended kinship groups such as clans often outweighs the formal authority of the party in the villages. In the cities, popular culture, including gigantic rock concerts, shapes youth attitudes much more profoundly than party propaganda. Consumerism ("buying things") is probably the most widely shared value in China today. Many observers have spoken of a moral vacuum. This is not uncommon for societies undergoing such rapid, multifaceted change.

Freedom of religion is guaranteed by the PRC constitution (as is the freedom not to believe in any religion). Organized religion, which was ferociously suppressed during the Mao era, is attracting an increasing number of adherents. Buddhist temples, Christian churches, and other places of worship operate more freely than they have in decades.

Religious life, however, is strictly controlled and limited to officially approved organizations and venues. Clergy of any religion who defy the authority of the party-state are still imprisoned. The Chinese Catholic Church is prohibited from recognizing the authority of the pope, although there have been recent signs of a thaw between Beijing and the Vatican.

The official number of Protestants and Catholics in China is about 14 million. But unofficial estimates put the figure at several times that and as high as 70–100 million.

Clandestine Christian communities, called house churches, have sprung up in many areas among people who reject the government's control of religious life and are unable to worship in public. Although local officials sometimes tolerate these churches, in numerous cases house church leaders and lay people have been arrested and the private homes where services are held have been bulldozed.

## Citizenship and National Identity

The views of Chinese citizens about what makes them part of the People's Republic of China—their sense of national identity—are going through a profound and uncertain transformation. Party leaders realize that most citizens are sceptical or dismissive of communist ideology and that appeals to socialist goals and revolutionary virtues no longer inspire loyalty. The CCP has turned increasingly to patriotic themes to rally the country behind its leadership. The official media put considerable emphasis on the greatness and antiquity of Chinese culture. They send the not-so-subtle message that it is time for China to reclaim its rightful place in the world order—and that only the CCP can lead the nation in achieving this goal.

In the view of some scholars and others, such officially promoted **nationalism** could lead to a more aggressive foreign and military policy—especially with the country's growing need for energy resources—toward areas such as the potentially oil-rich South China Sea, where the PRC's historical territorial claims conflict with those of other countries including Vietnam and the Philippines.

Of course, it is the cultural tie of being "Chinese" that is the most powerful collective identity that connects people to the nation. The Chinese people are intensely proud of their ancient culture and long history. Their enthusiasm for hosting the

**nationalism**

An ideology seeking to create a nation-state for a particular community; a group identity associated with membership is such a political community. Nationalists often proclaim that their state and nation are superior to others.

2008 Olympics in Beijing reflected this cultural pride. They can also be very sensitive about what they consider slights to their national dignity. Many Chinese feel that Japan has not done enough to acknowledge or apologize for the atrocities its army committed in China during World War II. This has been a strain in relations between the two countries and has sometimes led to spontaneous anti-Japanese demonstrations by Chinese students.

## China's Non-Chinese Citizens

The PRC calls itself a multinational state with fifty-six officially recognized ethnic groups, one of which is the Chinese majority, called the Han people (Han being the name of one of China's earliest dynasties). The Han make up 91.5 percent of the total population. The defining elements of a minority group involve some combination of language, culture (including religion), and race that distinguish them from the Han. The fifty-five non-Han minorities number a little more than 100 million, or about 8.5 percent of the total population. These groups range in size from 16 million (the Zhuang of southwest China) to about 2,000 (the Lhoba in the far west). Most of these minorities have come under Chinese rule over many centuries through the expansion of the Chinese state rather than through migration into China.

China's minorities are highly concentrated in the five autonomous regions of Guangxi, Inner Mongolia, Ningxia, Tibet, and Xinjiang. Only in the latter two, however, do minority people outnumber Han Chinese, who are encouraged to migrate to the autonomous regions. The five autonomous regions are sparsely populated, yet they occupy about 60 percent of the total land area of the PRC. Some of these areas are resource rich. All are located on strategically important borders of the country, including those with Vietnam, India, and Russia.

The Chinese constitution grants autonomous regions the right of self-government in certain matters. But they remain firmly under the control of the central authorities. Minority peoples enjoy some latitude to develop their local economies as they see fit. The use of minority languages in the media and literature is encouraged, as is, to a certain extent, bilingual education. Minority religions can be practiced, though only through state-approved organizations.

The most extensive ethnic conflict in China has occurred in Tibet. Tibet is located in the far west of China and has been under Chinese military occupation since the early 1950s. Tibetans practice a unique form of Buddhism, and most are fiercely loyal to the Dalai Lama, a priest they believe is the incarnation of a divine being. China has claimed authority over Tibet since long before the Communist Party came to power. Tibetans have always disputed that claim and resisted Chinese rule, sometime violently, including in 1959, when the Dalai Lama fled to exile in India following the failure of a rebellion by his followers.

During the Maoist era, traditional Tibetan culture was suppressed by the Chinese authorities. Since the late 1970s, Buddhist temples and monasteries have been allowed to reopen, and Tibetans have gained a significant degree of cultural freedom; the Chinese government has also significantly increased investment in Tibet's economic development. However, China still considers talk of Tibetan political independence to be treason, and Chinese troops have crushed several anti-China demonstrations in Lhasa, the capital of Tibet.

There are more than 20 million Muslims in China. They live in many parts of the country and belong to several different ethnic minority groups. The highest concentration of Muslims is in the far west of China in the Ningxia Hui and Xinjiang Uyghur autonomous regions.

The more secular Hui (about 10 million) are well assimilated into Han Chinese society. But there is growing unrest among Uyghurs (about 9 million) in Xinjiang, which borders several Islamic nations, including Pakistan and Afghanistan. Tensions between Uyghurs and Han Chinese exploded in Xinjiang in mid-2010, resulting in about 150 deaths and a thousand injuries. The government forcefully restored order and then arrested more than 1,500 people (almost all Uyghurs) in connection with the riots, twelve of whom were sentenced to death.

The Chinese government also has clashed with Uyghur militants who want to create a separate Islamic state of "East Turkestan" and have sometimes used violence, including bombings and assassinations, to press their cause. The PRC became an eager ally of the United States in the post–9/11 war on terrorism in part because China could then justify its crackdown on the Xinjiang-based East Turkestan Islamic Movement (ETIM). Washington has included this group on its list of organizations connected to al Qaeda.

China's minority population is relatively small and geographically isolated. Ethnic unrest has been sporadic and easily quelled. Therefore, the PRC has not had the kind of intense identity-based conflict experienced by countries with more pervasive religious and ethnic cleavages, such as India and Nigeria. But it is possible that domestic and global forces will make ethnic identity a more visible and volatile issue in Chinese politics.

# Interest Groups, Social Movements, and Protest

Truly independent interest groups and social movements are not permitted to influence the political process in the PRC in any significant way. The CCP supports official **mass organizations** as a means to provide a way for interest groups to express their views on policy matters—within strict limits.

Total membership of mass organizations in China is in the hundreds of millions. Two of the most important are the All-China Women's Federation, the only national organization representing the interests of women in general, and the All-China Federation of Trade Unions (ACFTU), to which about 90 million Chinese workers belong. Neither constitutes an autonomous political voice for the groups they are supposed to represent. But they sometimes do act as an effective lobby in promoting the non-political interests of their constituencies. For example, the Women's Federation has become a strong advocate for women on issues ranging from domestic violence to economic rights. The Trade Union Federation has pushed for legislation to reduce the standard workweek from six to five days. The ACFTU also represents individual workers with grievances against management, although its first loyalty is to the communist party-state.

Since the late 1990s, there has been a huge increase in the number of nongovernmental organizations (NGOs) less directly subordinate to the CCP than the official mass organizations. There is an enormous variety of national and local NGOs. These include ones that deal with the environment, health, charitable work, and legal issues. NGOs must register with the government, but they have considerable latitude to operate within their functional areas without direct party interference *if* they steer clear of politics and do not challenge official policies.

Although China has certainly loosened up politically since the days of Mao Zedong, the party-state is still very effective in monitoring dissent and preventing the

**mass organizations**

Organizations in a communist party-state that represent the interests of a particular social group, such as workers or women but which are controlled by the communist party.

formation of movements that might defy the CCP's authority. The extensive network of centrally-directed public security bureaus is the most formal mechanism of control. The authorities were quick to stifle responses to anonymous social networking calls for weekly peaceful gatherings in several Chinese cities to show support for the democracy movements in the Middle East and North Africa in early 2011.

In rural areas, the small-scale, closely knit nature of the village facilitates control by the local party and security organizations. Residents' committees are one of the major instruments of control in urban China. These neighborhood-based organizations, each of which covers 100 to 1,000 households depending on the size of the city, extend the unofficial reach of the party-state down to the most basic level of urban society. They used to be staffed mostly by appointed retired persons (often elderly women). But now their functions are shifting from surveillance to service. Many are led by younger and better-educated residents. In some cities, neighbors elect committee members.

The spread of private enterprises, increasing labor and residential mobility, and new forms of association (such as coffeehouses and discos) and communication (including cell phones and e-mail) are just some of the factors that are making it much harder for China's party-state to monitor citizens as closely as in the past.

## Protest and the Party-State

The Tiananmen massacre of 1989 showed the limits of protest in China. The party leadership was particularly alarmed at signs that several autonomous student and worker grass-roots organizations were emerging from the demonstrations. The brutal suppression of the democracy movement was meant to send a clear signal that neither open political protest nor the formation of independent interest groups would be tolerated.

There have been very few large-scale political demonstrations in China since 1989. Pro-democracy groups have been driven deep underground or abroad. Known dissidents are continuously watched, harassed, imprisoned, or expelled from the country.

Repression has not stopped all forms of citizen protest. The Falun Gong movement has carried out the biggest and most continuous demonstrations against the party-state. Falun Gong (FLG) is a spiritual movement with philosophical and religious elements drawn from Buddhism and Taoism along with traditional Chinese physical exercises (similar to *tai chi*) and meditation. It claims 70 million members in China and 30 million in more than seventy other countries. Its promise of inner tranquillity and good health has proven very appealing to a wide cross-section of people in China as a reaction to some of the side effects of rapid modernization.

The authorities began a crackdown on the FLG in 1999, which intensified after approximately 10,000 of its followers staged a peaceful protest in front of CCP headquarters in the center of Beijing. The authorities have destroyed FLG books and tapes, jammed websites, and arrested thousands of practitioners. Despite a few small FLG demonstrations, the crackdown seems to have been successful.

Labor unrest is growing, with reports of thousands of strikes and other actions in recent years. Workers have carried out big demonstrations at state-owned factories. They have protested the ending of the iron rice bowl system, layoffs, the nonpayment of pensions or severance packages, and the arrest of grass-roots labor leaders. Workers at some foreign-owned enterprises have gone on strike against unsafe working conditions or low wages. Most of these actions have remained limited in scope and duration, so the government has usually not cracked down on the protesters. On occasion, it has actually pressured employers to meet the workers' demands.

One of the biggest worker protests occurred in the spring of 2010 at a huge factory complex owned by a Taiwan firm in southern China where more than 300,000 workers—largely migrants from the countryside—assemble consumer electronics, including most of the world's iPhones and iPads. The protesters were targeting the 12-hour days, six-day work-weeks they say had driven several employees to commit suicide. The owners responded by putting up nets around the dormitory roofs to prevent despondent workers from jumping to their deaths, hired mental-health professionals to counsel employees, and built leisure facilities for workers. They also said that they would consult with local governments to improve conditions for its workers in China.

The countryside has also seen an upsurge of protests over corruption, exorbitant taxes and extralegal fees, and the government's failure to pay on time for agricultural products it has purchased. In areas benefiting from China's economic growth, people have protested environmental damage by factories whose owners care only for profit. Protests have also targeted illegal land seizures by greedy local officials working in cahoots with developers who want to build factories, expensive housing, or even golf courses.

Urban and rural protests in China have not spread beyond the locales where they started. They have focused on the protestors' immediate material concerns, not on grand-scale issues like democracy, and most often are aimed at corrupt local officials or unresponsive employers, not the Communist Party. By responding positively to farmer and worker concerns, the party-state can win support and turn what could be regime-threatening activities into regime-sustaining ones.

Although people are much freer than they have been in decades and most visitors find Chinese society quite open, repression can still be intense. Public political dissent is almost nonexistent. But there are many signs that the Chinese Communist Party is losing or giving up some of its ability to control the movements and associations of its citizens and can no longer easily limit access to information and ideas from abroad. Some forms of protest also appear to be increasing and may come to pose a serious challenge to the authority of the party-state.

## Summary

Representation of citizen interests and political participation in China are carried out under the watchful eye of the Chinese Communist Party. The National People's Congress, the legislature of the PRC, has become more active as the country's focus has shifted from revolutionary politics to economic development. Elections, particularly at the local level, have become more democratic. The Communist Party has also changed significantly, not just welcoming workers, peasants, and political activists into its ranks, but even recruiting members from among China's growing capitalist class of private business owners. Although they are much more open than during the Maoist era, the media, the arts, and education are still ultimately under party supervision. Communist ideology is declining as a unifying force for China's citizens, and the ability of the communist party-state to control and influence its citizens is weakening. The Internet, religion, consumerism, and popular culture are growing in influence. These all present a challenge to the CCP, which now emphasizes Chinese nationalism and pride as sources of citizen identity. Some of the greatest political tensions in China are in parts of the country with high concentrations of non-Chinese ethnic minorities, such as in Tibet and the Muslim areas of the northwest. Protests by farmers and industrial workers with economic grievances have been on the increase, but these have not become large-scale or widespread.

# CHINESE POLITICS IN TRANSITION

## Political Challenges and Changing Agendas

**Focus Questions**

What are the major economic and political challenges facing the CCP?

What factors will influence the future of the democratic idea in China?

Why has the Chinese communist party-state been more durable than other regimes of its type?

### Scenes from the Chinese Countryside[19]

China has become much more modern and urban in recent years. But a majority of its people still live in rural areas. However, depending on where you look in its vast countryside, you will see a very different China. Take, for example, the following:

**Huaxi, Jiangsu Province** This rural town, the richest in China, looks much like an American suburb: spacious roads lined with two-story townhouses, potted plants on doorsteps, green lawns, and luscious shade trees. Homes have air-conditioning, stylish furniture and modern appliances, studies with computers, and gyms. Some have swimming pools. Health care is 100 percent free. Every family has at least one car (including Mercedes, Cadillacs, and BMWs). Huaxi has grown from a small, poor agricultural village to a wealthy town of 38,000 by developing industrial and commercial enterprises that are run by residents and employ labor hired from outside.

**Changwu, Shaanxi Province** This village of 250 families is located in a mountainous region in one of the areas known as China's Third World. Persistent poverty is still the common lot. The average income is less than $100 per year. Most houses have only one or two rooms and are made of mud-brick with no running water, although electricity and telephone lines have come to the village in recent years. There are no paved roads. The poor quality land barely supports those who work it, mostly older women since the men and young women have gone to look for work in towns and cities. The children, dressed in grimy clothes and ragged cloth shoes, are not starving. But they do not seem to be flourishing either. Education, health care, and other social services are minimal or nonexistent.

**Nanhu, Shandong Province** This is a fairly typical Chinese village, nowhere near as prosperous as Huaxi or as poor as Changwu. Per capita income is about $1000 per year. Houses are now made of brick, most families have a small color TV, and there are lots of cell phones. Paved roads and public buses link the village to the nearest town where the children go to school. Most men work in small factories, while women tend the fields and farm animals. But they are worried. Local enterprises are struggling to survive fierce market competition. One village-owned factory has gone bankrupt. Recently, the village has leased out some of its land to expanding businesses from the town with the hope that this will create jobs.

**Zhaiqiao, Zhejiang Province** In late 2010, a 53-year old popular village leader, Qian Yunhui, was crushed to death by a large truck not far from his home. Evidence and eyewitness reports pointed to possibility that he was pushed beneath the truck's wheels and then deliberately run over. Qian had risen to local prominence for his role in protesting the construction of a power plant on prime village land for which the residents got no compensation. He was intensifying his efforts to expose the corrupt official and business people involved in the land grab when he was killed. Word of the incident along with graphic photos of Qian's mangled body spread rapidly via the Chinese blogosphere. The online uproar was so intense that the state-run media had to report on the incident and the provincial government launched a formal investigation, which ruled Qian's death an unfortunate accident. The truck driver was sentenced to three-and-a-half years in prison, and Qian's family was paid more than $150,000, but there is widespread skepticism about the handling of the case and many suspect a cover-up.

**Beiwang, Hebei Province**   This was one of the first villages in China to establish a representative assembly and hold democratic elections for local leaders. Among the first decisions made by the elected officials and the assembly was to give just a few families known for their farming expertise contracts to tend the village's 3000 pear trees rather giving each family in the village an equal number to look after. They believed that this would lead to better pear farming and would cause the non–pear-tending families to develop other kinds of economic activity. The local Communist Party branch objected that this would lead to too much inequality. The party leaders eventually agreed, under pressure, to go along with the new policy. In a short time, pear production zoomed. The new system proved to be beneficial not only to the families who looked after the trees, but also to the village as a whole because of economic diversification and the local government's share of the increased profits.

The above scenes reflect the enormous diversity of the Chinese countryside: prosperity and poverty, protests and peaceful politics. It is worth remembering that about 55 percent of China's population—that's more than 700 million people—live in the rural parts of the country. What happens in the rural villages and towns will obviously have a tremendous impact on China's political and economic future.

The Beiwang village case reminds us that not all politics rises to national or international significance. The question of who looks after the village pear trees may matter more to local residents than what happens in the inner sanctums of the Communist Party or U.S.-China presidential summit meetings. The victory of the Beiwang representative assembly and elected officials on the pear tree issue shows that even in a one-party state, the people sometimes prevail against those with power, and democracy can work on the local level.

The Huaxi scene shows the astonishing improvement in living standards in much of rural China. But huge pockets of severe poverty, like in Changwu, still persist, especially in inland areas far removed from the more prosperous coastal regions. Most of rural China falls between the extremes. It is in these in-between areas, such as Nanhu and Zhaiqiao, where the combination of new hopes brought about by economic progress and the tensions caused by blatant corruption, growing inequalities, and other frustrations may prove to be politically explosive.

The circumstances surrounding the death of Qian Yunhui and its aftermath also illustrate the impact of new technologies on politics in the PRC, even in the rural areas. Citizens have become empowered in ways that are difficult, if not impossible, to suppress, and the government finds itself having to be more sensitive to public opinion. The online uproar and the official response that followed, "offers a window into a new political reality in China, one that has profound implications for how the country is governed."[20]

## Economic Management, Social Tensions, and Political Legitimacy

The situation in the Chinese countryside illustrates a larger challenge facing the leaders of the PRC: how to sustain and effectively manage the economic growth that is the basis of public support for the ruling Communist Party. The CCP is gambling that continued solid economic performance will literally buy it legitimacy and that most citizens will care little about democracy or national politics if their material lives continue to get better. So far this gamble seems to have paid off.

But China's growth rate has been so high for so many years that some experts think it is unsustainable and may lead to crash landing for the economy. Soaring inflation, massive unemployment, or a burst real estate bubble could spell disaster for the country's economic miracle. How to cool growth without throttling it, will be a major test of the ability of China's technocratic leaders to govern the economy.

The government of the PRC also needs to find ways to restructure the economy so that its work force is less dependent on employment by export-oriented industries, which are very vulnerable to shifts in the global market. This will involve promoting industries that produce for the domestic economy and its huge untapped consumer market. At the same time, the Chinese government is encouraging its citizens to spend more and save less (in a way, the opposite of America's dilemma) in order to stimulate the domestic economy.

The enormous class, regional, and urban-rural inequalities that so clearly mark modernizing China have bred social instability in some parts of the country that could spread if the party-state fails to provide opportunities for advancement for the less well off. One of most formidable tasks facing the government will be to create enough jobs not only for the millions of laid-off industrial workers and the continuing flow of countryside-to-city migrants, but also for the 25 million or so new entrants to the labor force each year, including 6 million with college degrees.

China's Communist Party leaders will also have to decide how to further nurture the private sector, which is the most dynamic source of economic growth. Yet the government bureaucracy still puts daunting obstacles in the way of business owners and investors, and the state still directly controls vital sectors of the economy and the financial system.

Corruption affects the lives of most people much more directly than political repression. Despite well-publicized campaigns and often harsh punishments for offenders, corruption is still so blatant and widespread that it is probably the single most corrosive force eating away at the legitimacy of the Chinese Communist Party.

The public health system is in shambles, with AIDS and other infectious diseases spreading rapidly. The country lacks adequate pension and social security systems to meet the needs of its senior citizens of its rapidly "graying" population.

According to a detailed study by the World Bank, a range of indicators measuring governance—"the traditions and institutions by which authority in a country is exercised for the common good"—shows that the PRC fares considerably better than most developing countries at its level of economic development. But China has improved only slightly in some categories (overall government effectiveness and regulatory quality) or deteriorated somewhat in others (control of corruption and political stability) between 2000 and 2009.[21] These categories bear directly on the party-state's ability to manage China's rapidly modernizing economy and radically changing society and portray some of the most important challenges facing the country's leadership.

## China and the Democratic Idea

Two other World Bank governance indicators measure issues that are central to the democratic idea. The "rule of law" in the PRC has improved somewhat over the last decade, while "voice and accountability" has declined.

The PRC has evolved in recent decades toward a system of what has been called "Market-Leninism,"[22] a combination of increasing economic openness (a market economy) and continuing political rigidity under the leadership of a Leninist ruling party that adheres to a remodeled version of communist ideology. The major political challenges now facing the CCP and the country emerge from the sharpening contradictions and tensions of this hybrid system.

As the people of China become more secure economically, better educated, and more aware of the outside world, they will also likely become more politically active. Business owners may want political clout to match their rising economic and social status. Scholars, scientists, and technology specialists may become more outspoken about the limits on intellectual freedom. The many Chinese who travel or study abroad may find the political gap between their party-state and the world's democracies to be increasingly intolerable.

What are the prospects for democratization in China? On the one hand, China's long history of bureaucratic and authoritarian rule and the hierarchical values of still-influential Confucian culture seem to be heavy counterweights to democracy. And, although some aspects of its social control have broken down, the coercive power of China's communist party-state remains formidable. The PRC's relatively low per capita standard of living, large rural population and vast areas of extreme poverty, and state-dominated media and means of communications also impose some impediments to the spread of the democratic idea. Finally, many in China are apathetic about politics or fearful of the violence and chaos that radical political change might unleash. They are quite happy with the status quo of economic growth and overall political stability of the country under the CCP.

On the other hand, the impressive success of democratization in Taiwan in the past decade, including free and fair multiparty elections from the local level up to the presidency, strongly suggests that the values, institutions, and process of democracy are not incompatible with Confucian culture. And though it is still a developing country, China has a high literacy rate, extensive industrialization and urbanization, a fast rate of economic growth, and a burgeoning middle class—conditions widely seen by social scientists as favorable to democracy.

Despite the CCP's continuing tight hold on power, there have been a number of significant political changes in China that could be harbingers of democracy: the enhanced political and economic power of local governments; the setting of a mandatory retirement age and term limits for all officials; the rise of younger, better educated, and more worldly leaders; the increasingly important role of the National People's Congress in the policy-making process; the introduction of competitive elections in rural villages; the strengthening and partial depoliticization of the legal system; tolerance of a much wider range of artistic, cultural, and religious expression; and the important freedom (unheard of in the Mao era) for individuals to be apolitical.

Furthermore, the astounding spread of the democratic idea around the globe has created a trend that will be increasingly difficult for China's leaders to resist. The PRC has become a major player in the world of states, and its government must be more responsive to international opinion in order to continue the country's deepening integration with the international economy and growing stature as a responsible and mature global power.

**civil society**

The social space outside the state occupied by voluntary associations based on shared interests, for example, non-governmental organizations (NGOs), professional associations, labor unions, and community groups. Civil society is often seen as an important part of democracy.

One of the most important political trends in China has been the resurgence of **civil society**, a sphere of independent public life and citizen association, which, if allowed to thrive and expand, could provide fertile soil for future democratization. The development of civil society among workers in Poland and intellectuals in Czechoslovakia, for example, played an important role in the collapse of communism in East-Central Europe in the late 1980s by weakening the critical underpinnings of party-state control.

The Tiananmen demonstrations of 1989 reflected the stirrings of civil society in post–Mao China. But the brutal crushing of that movement showed the CCP's determination to thwart its growth before it could seriously contest the party's authority. But as economic modernization and social liberalization have deepened in the PRC, civil society has begun to stir again. Some stirrings, like the Falun Gong movement, have met with vicious repression by the party-state. But others, such as the proliferation and growing influence of nongovernmental organizations that deal with *non-political* matters such as the enviroment, have been encouraged by the authorities. Academic journals and conferences have recently had surprisingly open, if tentative, discussions about future political options for China, including multiparty democracy.

At some point, the leaders of the CCP will face the fundamental dilemma of whether to accommodate or, as they have done so often in the past, suppress organizations, individuals, and ideas that question the principle of party leadership. Accommodation would require the party-state to cede some of its control over society and allow more meaningful citizen representation and participation. But repression would likely derail the country's economic dynamism and could have terrible costs for China.

# Chinese Politics in Comparative Perspective

## China as a Communist Party-State

The fact that the Chinese Communists won power through an indigenous revolution with widespread popular backing and did not depend on foreign military support for their victory sets China apart from the situation of most of the now-deposed East-Central European communist parties. Despite some very serious mistakes over the six decades of its rule in China, the CCP still has a deep reservoir of historical legitimacy among large segments of the population.

The PRC has also been able to avoid the kind of economic crises that greatly weakened other communist systems, including the Soviet Union, through its successful market reforms and the rapidly rising living standard of most of the Chinese people. CCP leaders believe that one of the biggest mistakes made by the last Soviet communist party chief, Mikhail Gorbachev, was that he went too far with political reform and not far enough with economic change, and they are convinced that their reverse formula is a key reason that they have not suffered the same fate.

But China also has much in common with other communist party-states past and present, including some of the basic features of a totalitarian political system. **Totalitarianism** (a term also applied to fascist regimes such as Nazi Germany) describes a system in which the ruling party prohibits all forms of meaningful political opposition and dissent, insists on obedience to a single state-determined ideology, and enforces its rule through coercion and terror. Such regimes also seek to bring all spheres of public activity (including the economy and culture) and even many parts of

**totalitarianism**

A political system in which the state attempts to exercise total control over all aspects of public and private life, including the economy, culture, education, and social organizations, through an integrated system of ideological, economic, and political control. Totalitarian states rely on extensive coercion, including terror, as a means to exercise power.

its citizens' private lives (including reproduction) under the total control of the party-state in the effort to modernize the country and, indeed, to transform human nature.

China is much less totalitarian than it was during the Maoist era. In fact, the CCP appears to be trying to save communist rule in China by moderating or abandoning many of its totalitarian features. To promote economic development, the CCP has relaxed its grip on many areas of life. Citizens can generally pursue their interests without interference by the party-state as long as they avoid sensitive political issues.

The PRC is now a "consultative authoritarian regime" that "increasingly recognizes the need to obtain information, advice, and support from key sectors of the population, but insists on suppressing dissent … and maintaining ultimate political power in the hands of the Party."[23] This regime has shown remarkable adaptability that so far has allowed it to both carry out bold economic reform and sustain a dictatorial political system.

## China as a Third World State

The development of the PRC raises many issues about the role of the state in governing the economy. It also provides an interesting comparative perspective on the complex and much-debated relationship between economic and political change in the Third World.

When the Chinese Communist Party came to power in 1949, China was a desperately poor country, with an economy devastated by a century of civil strife and world war. It was also in a weak and subordinate position in the post–World War II international order. Measured against this starting point, the PRC has made remarkable progress in improving the wellbeing of its citizens, building a strong state, and enhancing the country's global role.

Why has China been more successful than so many other nations in meeting some of the major challenges of development? Those with political power in the Third World have often served narrow class or foreign interests more than the national interest. The result is that governments of many developing countries have become **predatory states** that prey on their people and the nation's resources to enrich the few at the expense of the many. They become defenders of a status quo built on extensive inequality and poverty rather than agents of needed change. In contrast, the PRC's recent rulers have been quite successful in creating a **developmental state**, in which government power and public policy are used effectively to promote national economic growth. In this very important way, China has become a leader among developing nations.

But, in an equally important way, China is lagging behind many other countries in Africa, Asia, and Latin America. Whereas much of the Third World has been heading towards democracy, the PRC has stood firm against that wave of democratization. According to the 2010 edition of the annual Democracy Index produced by the research staff of the highly respected magazine, *The Economist*, China ranked 136 out of 167 countries in the world according to a survey that uses a variety of measures, including the fairness of elections, political participation, and civil liberties.[24]

There is a sharp and disturbing contrast between the harsh political rule of the Chinese communist party-state and its remarkable accomplishments in improving the material lives of the Chinese people. This contrast is at the heart of what one journalist called the "riddle of China" today, where the government often fights disease "as aggressively as it attacks dissent. It inoculates infants with the same fervor with which it arrests its critics. Partly as a result, a baby born in Shanghai now has a longer life expectancy than a baby born in New York City."[25]

**predatory state**

A state in which those with political power prey on the people and the nation's resources to enrich themselves rather than using their power to promote national development. Contrast with developmental state.

**developmental state**

A **nation-state** in which the government carries out policies that effectively promote national economic growth.

This "riddle" makes it difficult to settle on a clear evaluation of the overall record of communist rule in China, particularly in the post–Mao era. It also makes it hard to predict the political future of the PRC, since the regime's economic achievements may well provide it with the support, or at least compliance of its citizens, it needs to stay in power despite its deep political shortcomings.

The CCP's tough stance on political reform is in large part based on its desire for self-preservation. But in keeping firm control on political life while allowing the country to open up in other important ways, Chinese Communist Party leaders also believe they are wisely following the model of development pioneered by the newly industrializing countries (NICs) of East Asia such as South Korea, Taiwan, and Singapore.

The lesson that the CCP draws from the NIC experience is that only a strong government can provide the political stability and social peace required for rapid economic growth. According to this view, democracy—with its open debates about national priorities, political parties contesting for power, and interest groups squabbling over how to divide the economic pie—is a recipe for chaos, particularly in a huge and still relatively poor country.

But another of the lessons from the East Asian NICs—one that most Chinese leaders have been reluctant to acknowledge—is that economic development, social modernization, and global integration also create powerful pressures for political change from below and abroad. In both Taiwan and South Korea, authoritarian governments that had presided over economic miracles in the 1960s and 1970s gave way in the 1980s and 1990s to democracy. China's leaders look approvingly on the Singapore model of development with its long-lasting combination of "soft authoritarianism" and highly developed modern economy. But that city-state has a population of just 5 million (about 300 times smaller than the PRC) and an area 1/14,000th the size of China.

China is in the early to middle stages of a period of growth and modernization that are likely to lead it to NIC status within two or three decades. But in terms of the extent of industrialization, per capita income, the strength of the private sector of the economy, and the size of the middle and professional classes, China's level of development is still far below the level at which democracy succeeded in Taiwan and South Korea. Before concluding that China's communist rulers will soon yield to the forces of modernization, it is important to remember that "authoritarian governments in East Asia pursued market-driven economic growth for decades without relaxing their hold on political power."[26]

Economic reform in China has already created social groups at home and opened up the country to ideas from abroad that are likely to grow as sources of pressure for more and faster political change. And the experiences of many developing countries suggest that such pressures will intensify as the economy and society continue to modernize. Therefore, at some point in the not-too-distant future, the Chinese Communist Party is likely to again face the challenge of the democratic idea. How China's new generation of leaders responds to this challenge is perhaps the most important and uncertain question about Chinese politics in the early decades of the twenty-first century.

## Summary

A majority of China's population still lives in the rural areas, and what happens there will greatly influence the country's political future. Rapid economic development has created other major challenges, including growing inequalities, rising unemployment, deteriorating public services, and pervasive corruption. The CCP is also very likely to face increasing demands for a political voice from different sectors of society as its citizens become more prosperous, well-educated, and worldly. In comparative perspective, China has proven more economically successful and politically adaptable than other communist party-states, including the Soviet Union, which collapsed in 1991. China has also been much more successful than most other developing countries in promoting economic growth, but so far has not been part of the wave of democratization that has spread to so many other parts of the world.

## Key Terms

autonomous region
guerrilla warfare
centrally planned economy
socialism
collectivization
communism
technocrats
communist party-states
state-owned enterprises (SOEs)
socialist market economy
household responsibility system

iron rice bowl
floating population
National Party Congress
Central Committee
Politburo
Standing Committee
general secretary
National People's Congress (NPC)
State Council
cadre
*nomenklatura*

People's Liberation Army (PLA)
Central Military Commission (CMC)
*guanxi*
socialist democracy
nationalism
mass organizations
civil society
totalitarianism
predatory state
developmental state

## Suggested Readings

Blecher, Marc J. *China against the Tides: Restructuring through Revolution, Radicalism and Reform.* 3rd edition. New York: Continuum, 2009.

Chang, Jung. *Wild Swans: Three Daughters of China.* New York: Simon and Shuster, 2003.

Cheek, Timothy. *Mao Zedong and China's Revolutions: A Brief History with Documents.* New York: Bedford/St. Martin's, 2002.

Cohen, Warren I. *America's Response to China: A History of Sino-American Relations,* 5th edition. New York: Columbia University Press, 2010.

Dikotter, Frank. *Mao's Great Famine: The History of China's Most Devastating Catastrophe, 1958–1962.* New York: Walker & Company, 2010.

Fenby, Jonathan. *Modern China: The Fall and Rise of a Great Power, 1850 to the Present.* New York: Harper Collins, 2008.

Fewsmith, Joseph. *China Today, China Tomorrow: Domestic Politics, Economy, and Society.* Lanham, MD: Rowman and Littlefield, 2010.

Gao Yuan. *Born Red: A Chronicle of the Cultural Revolution.* Stanford, CA: Stanford University Press, 1987.

Grasso, June, Jay Cornin, and Michael Kort. *Modernization and Revolution in China: From the Opium Wars to the Olympics.* 4th ed. Armonk, NY: M. E. Sharpe, 2009.

Hutchings, Graham. *Modern China: A Guide to a Century of Change.* Cambridge: Harvard University Press, 2001.

Joseph, William A., ed., *Politics in China: An Introduction.* New York: Oxford University Press, 2010.

Lampton, David M. *The Three Faces of Chinese Power: Might, Money, and Minds.* Berkeley: University of California Press, 2008.

Lawrance, Alan. *China since 1919: Revolution and Reform; A Sourcebook.* New York: Routledge, 2004.

MacFarquhar, Roderick, and Michael Schoenhals. *Mao's Last Revolution.* Cambridge: Harvard University Press, 2008.

McGregor, Richard. *The Party: The Secret World of China's Communist Rulers.* New York: Harper, 2010.

Mitter, Rana. *Modern China: A Very Short Introduction.* New York: Oxford University Press, 2008.

Naughton, Barry. *The Chinese Economy: Transitions and Growth.* Cambridge: MIT Press, 2007.

Schoppa, R. Keith. *Twentieth Century China: A History in Documents.* New York: Oxford University Press, 2004.

Wasserstrom, Jeffery. *China in the 21st Century: What Everyone Needs to Know.* New York: Oxford University Press, 2010.

Whyte, Martin K., ed. *One Country, Two Societies: Rural-Urban Inequality in Contemporary China.* Cambridge: Harvard University Press, 2010.

Womack, Brantley. *China's Rise in Historical Perspective.* Lanham, MD: Rowman and Littlefield, 2010.

Zhang, Lijia. *"Socialism Is Great!" A Worker's Memoir of the New China.* New York: Atlas & Company, 2008.

## Suggested Websites

China Politics Links
http://www.wellesley.edu/Polisci/wj/chinesepolitics/

The Central Government of the People's Republic of China
http://www.gov.cn/english/

China in the News
http://chinapoliticsnews.blogspot.com/

United States Department of State
http://www.state.gov/p/eap/ci/ch/

The Jamestown Foundation China Brief:
http://www.jamestown.org/programs/chinabrief/

Hoover Institution China Leadership Monitor
http://www.hoover.org/publications/china-leadership-monitor

University of California at Berkeley, China Digital Times
http://chinadigitaltimes.net/

# Endnotes

## Chapter 1

[1] See Philippe Schmitter, "Comparative Politics," in Joel Krieger, ed., *The Oxford Companion to Politics of the World*, 2nd ed. (New York: Oxford University Press, 2001), pp. 160–165. For a more extended discussion and different approach, see David D. Laitin, "Comparative Politics: The State of the Subdiscipline," in Ira Katznelson and Helen V. Milner, eds., *Political Science: The State of the Discipline* (New York: Norton, 2002), pp. 630–659. For a collection of articles in the field of comparative politics, see Mark Kesselman, ed., *Readings in Comparative Politics*, 2nd edition (Boston: Wadsworth, 2010).

[2] See, for example, Gerhard Loewenberg, Peverill Squire, and D. Roderick Kiewiet, eds., *Legislatures: Comparative Perspectives on Representative Assemblies*. Ann Arbor: University of Michigan Press, 2002.

[3] See, for example, Merilee S. Griddle, *Despite the Odds: The Contentious Politics of Education Reform* (Princeton: Princeton University Press, 2004), which compares education policies in several Latin American countries; and Miranda A. Schreurs, *Environmental Politics in Japan, Germany, and the United States* (Cambridge: Cambridge University Press, 2002).

[4] See, for example, Benedict Anderson, *Imagined Communities: Reflections on the Origins and Spread of Nationalism*, rev. ed. (London: Verso, 1991); and Theda Skocpol, *Social Revolutions in the Modern World* (Cambridge: Cambridge University Press, 1994).

[5] Peter A. Hall, *Governing the Economy: The Politics of State Intervention in Britain and France* (New York: Oxford University Press, 1986); and Mark Blyth, *Great Transformations: Economic Ideas and Institutional Change in the Twentieth Century* (Cambridge: Cambridge University Press, 2002).

[6] See, for example, most of the chapters in William A. Joseph, ed., *Politics in China: An Introduction* (New York: Oxford University Press, 2010).

[7] For reviews of scholarly literature on the state, see Margaret Levi, "The State of the Study of the State"; Miles Kahler, "The State of the State in World Politics"; and Atul Kohli, "State, Society, and Development," in Katznelson and Milner, eds., *Political Science: State of the Discipline*.

[8] For discussions of rational choice theory in the popular press, see "Political Scientists Debate Theory of 'Rational Choice,'" in the *New York Times*, February 26, 2000, B11; and Jonathan Cohn, "Irrational Exuberance: When Did Political Science Forget About Politics?" *New Republic*, October 25, 1999, 25–31.

[9] On democratic transitions, see for example, Samuel P. Huntington, *The Third Wave: Democratization in the Late Twentieth Century* (Norman: University of Oklahoma Press, 1993); Jan Teorell, *Determinants of Democratization: Explaining Regime Change in the World, 1972–2006* (New York: Cambridge University Press, 2010); and Larry Diamond, Marc F. Plattner, and Philip J. Costopoulos, eds., *Debates on Democratization* (Baltimore: Johns Hopkins University Press, 2010).

[10] Robert I. Rotberg, "Failed States in a World of Terror," *Foreign Affairs* 81, no. 4 (July–August 2002). The article is reprinted in Kesselman, *Readings in Comparative Politics*.

[11] The Failed States Index 2010, http://www.foreignpolicy.com/failedstates/.

[12] See Joel Krieger, ed., *Globalization and State Power: A Reader* (New York: Pearson/Longman, 2006).

[13] This term is borrowed from Peter A. Hall, *Governing the Economy*.

[14]Peter A. Hall and David Soskice, eds., *Varieties of Capitalism: The Institutional Foundations of Comparative Advantage* (New York: Oxford University Press, 2001). See also David Coates, ed., *Varieties of Capitalism, Varieties of Approaches* (Basingstoke, UK: Palgrave/Macmillan, 2005).

[15]See, for example, Chalmers Johnson, *MITI and the Japanese Miracle: The Growth of Industrial Policy* (Stanford: Stanford University Press, 1982); Stephan Haggard, *Pathways from the Periphery: The Politics of Growth in the Newly Industrializing Countries* (Ithaca, NY: Cornell University Press, 1990); Peter Evans, *Embedded Autonomy: States and Industrial Transformation* (Princeton, NJ: Princeton University Press, 1995); and Meredith Woo-Cummings, ed., *The Developmental State* (Ithaca, NY: Cornell University Press, 1999); Robert Wade, *Governing the Market: Economic Theory and the Role of Government in East Asian Industrialization* (Princeton: Princeton University Press, 2003); Atul Kohli, *State-Directed Development: Political Power and Industrialization in the Global Periphery* (Cambridge: Cambridge University Press, 2004); and Yasheng Huang, *Capitalism with Chinese Characteristics: Entrepreneurship and the State* (New York: Cambridge University Press, 2008).

[16]Adam Przeworski et al, *Democracy and Development: Political Institutions and Well-Being in the World, 1950–1990* (Cambridge: Cambridge University Press, 2000).

[17]Amartya Sen, "Democracy as a Universal Value," *Journal of Democracy* 10, no. 3 (July 1999): 3–17. This article is included in Kesselman, *Readings in Comparative Politics*. For a study that finds a positive correlation between democracy and economic growth, see Yi Feng, *Democracy, Governance, and Economic Performance: Theory and Evidence* (Cambridge, Mass.: MIT Press, 2005).

[18]Freedom House's annual Freedom in World Reports are available at www.freedomhouse.org.

[19]Sen, "Democracy as a Universal Value," 3.

[20]Andrew Roberts, "Review Article: The Quality of Democracy," *Comparative Politics* 37, no. 3 (April 2005), 357.

[21]Fareed Zakaria, *The Future of Freedom: Illiberal Democracy at Home and Abroad* (New York: W. W. Norton, 2003), 248.

[22]Arend Lijphart, *Patterns of Democracy: Government Forms and Performance in Thirty-Six Countries* (New Haven: Yale University Press, 1999).

[23]Guillermo O'Donnell and Philippe Schmitter, *Transitions from Authoritarian Rule: Tentative Conclusions about Uncertain Democracies* (Baltimore: Johns Hopkins University Press, 1986). The concept of waves of democratization is taken from Huntington, *The Third Wave*.

[24]See, for example, Guillermo O'Donnell, "Illusions About Consolidation," *Journal of Democracy* 7, no. 2 (April 1996): 34–51. See also Thomas Carothers, "The End of the Transition Paradigm," *Journal of Democracy* 13, no. 1 (January 2002): 5–21; and Steven Levitsky and Lucan A. Way, "The Rise of Competitive Authoritarianism," *Journal of Democracy* 13, no. 2 (April 2002): 51–65; both are reprinted in Kesselman, *Readings in Comparative Politics*.

[25]For contrasting views on this debate, see Samuel P. Huntington, *Political Order in Changing Societies* (New Haven: Yale University Press, 1968); and Mark Kesselman, "Order or Movement?: The Literature of Political Development as Ideology," *World Politics* 26 (1973), 139–154.

[26]Przeworski et al, *Democracy and Development*.

[27]Alfred Stepan, *Arguing Comparative Politics* (New York: Oxford University Press, 2001), 184.

[28]Larry Diamond, "Thinking about Hybrid Regimes," *Journal of Democracy*, 13.2 (2002): 21–35.

# Chapter 2

[1]The Coalition: Our Programme for Government, www.hmg.gov.uk/programmeforgovernment. © Crown copyright 2010.

[2]David Cameron's speech to the Tory Conference, http://www.guardian.co.uk/politics/2010/oct06/david-cameron-speech-tory-conference.

[3]Gail Lewis, "Black Women's Employment and the British Economy," in Winston James and Clive Harris, eds., *Inside Babylon: The Caribbean Diaspora in Britain* (London: Verso, 1993), pp. 73–96.

[4]http://www.statistics.gov.uk/cci/nugget.asp?id=167.

[5]http://www.statistics.gov.uk/cci/nugget.asp?id=1654.

[6]Philip Norton, *The British Polity*, 3rd ed. (N.Y.: Longman, 1994), p. 59.

[7]Stephen Haseler, "Britain's Ancien Régime," *Parliamentary Affairs* 40, no. 4 (October 1990): 418.

[8]See Bill Jones and Philip Norton, *Politics UK*, 7th ed., (New York: Longman, 2010), pp. 475–476.

[9]Ivor Crewe, "Great Britain," in I. Crewe and D. Denver, eds., *Electoral Change in Western Democracies* (London: Croom Helm, 1985), p.107.

[10]See Gabriel A. Almond and Sidney Verba, *The Civic Culture: Political Attitudes and Democracy in Five Nations* (Princeton, N.J.: Princeton University Press, 1963); Almond and Verba, eds., *The Civic Culture Revisited* (Boston: Little, Brown, 1980); and Samuel H. Beer, *Britain Against Itself: The Political Contradictions of Collectivism* (New York: Norton, 1982), pp. 110–114.

[11]See Chris Howell, *Trade Unions and the State* (Princeton University Press, 2005), esp. Ch. 6.

[12]Bhiku Parekh et al., *The Future of Multi-Ethnic Britain: The Parekh Report* (London: Profile Books, 2000), p. 10.

[13]Samuel H. Huntington, *The Clash of Civilizations and the Remaking of World Order* (New York: Simon and Schuster, 1993).

[14]Peter Riddell, *The Thatcher Decade* (Oxford: Basil Blackwell, 1989), p. 289.

[15]Tony Blair, "Doctrine of the International Community," speech to the Economic Club of Chicago, Hilton Hotel, Chicago, April 22, 1999.

# Chapter 3

[1]Jonathan Laurence and Justin Vaisse, *Integrating Islam: Political and Religious Challenges in Contemporary France* (Washington, DC: Brookings Institution Press, 2006), p. 80.

[2]Joan Wallach Scott, *The Politics of the Veil* (Princeton: Princeton University Press, 2007), p. 40.

[3]*Le Monde*, March 20, 2007.

[4]James B. Collins, *The State in Early Modern France*, 2nd. ed (New York: Cambridge University Press, 2009), p. xiii.

[5]*Ibid.*, pp. 211, 209.

[6]*Ibid.*, p. xiv.

[7]Sophie Meunier, "The Distinctiveness of French Anti-Americanism," in Peter J. Katzenstein and Robert O. Keohane, eds., *Anti-Americanism in World Politics* (Ithaca: Cornell University Press, 2007).

[8]Henri Mendras with Alistair Cole, *Social Change in Modern France: Towards a Cultural Anthropology of the Fifth Republic* (Cambridge: Cambridge University Press, 1991), p. 1.

[9]Jonah D. Levy, "The Return of the State? French Economic Policy under Nicholas Sarkozy," unpublished paper presented at the 106th Annual Meeting of the American Political Science Association," Washington, DC, 2–5 September 2010, p. 5.

[10]Peter A. Hall described the new economic orientation since the mid-1980s as a "neo-liberal modernization strategy." Hall, "From One Modernization Strategy to Another: The Character and Consequences of Recent Economic Policy in France" (paper presented to the Tenth International Conference of Europeanists, Chicago, March 15, 1996).

[11]Vivien A. Schmidt, *From State to Market? The Transformation of French Business and Government* (Cambridge: Cambridge University Press, 1996), p. 442.

[12]Levy, "The Return of the State?" p. 8.

[13]Peter A. Hall, "Introduction: The Politics of Social Change in France," in Pepper D. Culpepper, Peter A. Hall, and Bruno Palier, eds., *Changing France: The Politics That Markets Make* (New York: Palgrave Macmillan, 2006), p. 4.

[14]*Métro*, March 15, 2007.

[15]Katrin Bennhold, "For Women in France, Dim Outlook on Equality," *New York Times*, October 12, 2010.

[16]Richard Balme, "France, Europe and the World: Foreign Policy and the Political Regime of the Fifth Republic," in Sylvain Brouard, Andrew M. Appleton, and Amy G. Mazur, eds., *The French Fifth Republic at Fifty: Beyond Stereotypes* (New York: Palgrave Macmillan, 2009), p. 141.

[17]Alistair Cole, Patrick Le Galès, and Jonah D. Levy, "From Chirac to Sarkozy: A New France?" in Cole, Le Galès, and Levy, eds., *Developments in French Politics 4* (New York: Palgrave Macmillan, 2008), p. 2.

[18]Both comments are from the *New York Times*, December 1, 2010.

[19]*Economist*, September 9, 2010.

[20]Cole, Le Galès, and Levy, *Developments in French Politics 4*, p. 21.

[21]Ezra Suleiman, "Les élites de l'administration et de la politique dans la France de la Ve République: Homogénéité, puissance, permanence," in Ezra Suleiman and Henri Mendras, eds., *Le recrutement des élites en Europe* (Paris: La Découverte, 1995), p. 33.

[22]John T. S. Keeler and Alec Stone, "Judicial-Political Confrontation in Mitterrand's France: The Emergence of the Constitutional Council as a Major Actor in the Policy-making Process," in Stanley Hoffmann, George Ross, and Sylvia Malzacher, eds., *The Mitterrand Experiment:*

*Continuity and Change in Mitterrand's France* (New York: Oxford University Press, 1987), p. 176.

[23] *Libération*, July 5, 2010.

[24] "Une majorité d'Européens estime que la pire de la crise économique est à venir," *Le Monde*, March 15, 2011, p. 16.

[25] Patrick Weil, *La France et ses étrangers* (Paris: Gallimard, 1991), p. 28.

[26] Charles Tilly's paraphrase (in the preface) of Gérard Noiriel's position, in Gérard Noiriel, *The French Melting Pot: Immigration, Citizenship, and National Identity* (Minneapolis: University of Minnesota Press, 1996), p. xii.

[27] *Humanité*, October 2, 2010; *Le Figaro*, October 9, 2010.

[28] *Le Monde*, September 15, 2010.

[29] Pierre Birnbaum, *The Idea of France* (New York: Hill & Wang, 2001), pp. 278–279.

[30] *Le Monde*, April 30, 2002.

[31] Data from a study by the Pew Research Center cited by Martin A. Schain, *The Politics of Immigration in France, Britain, and the United States: A Comparative Study* (New York: Palgrave Macmillan, 2008), pp. 19–20.

[32] Sophie Meunier, "Free-Falling France or Free-Trading France?" *French Politics, Culture and Society* 22, no. 1 (Spring 2004): 98–107.

[33] Hall, "Introduction: The Politics of Social Change in France," p. 1.

# Chapter 4

[1] Simon Bulmer, Charlie Jeffery, and Stephen Padgett, eds., *Rethinking Germany and Europe: Democracy and Diplomacy in a Semi-Sovereign State* (London: Palgrave, 2010).

[2] Charles Tilly, ed., *The Formation of National States in Western Europe* (Princeton: Princeton University Press, 1975).

[3] Tom Kemp, *Industrialization in Nineteenth Century Europe*, 2d ed. (London: Longman, 1985).

[4] Peter Liberman, *Does Conquest Pay? The Exploitation of Occupied Industrial Societies* (Princeton: Princeton University Press, 1998).

[5] Richard Deeg, "The Comeback of Modell Deutschland? The New German Political Economy in the EU," *German Politics* 14 (2005): 332–353.

[6] Ralf Dahrendorf, *Society and Democracy in Germany* (Garden City: Anchor, 1969).

[7] Alexander Gerschenkron, *Bread and Democracy in Germany*, 2d ed. (Ithaca: Cornell University Press, 1989).

[8] Christopher Allen, "Trade Unions, Worker Participation, and Flexibility: Linking the Micro to the Macro" *Comparative Politics* 22: no. 3 (1990): 253–272.

[9] Hans-Werner Sinn, *Can Germany Be Saved? The Malaise of the World's First Welfare State* (Cambridge: MIT Press, 2009).

[10] Peter Katzenstein, *Policy and Politics in West Germany: The Growth of a Semi-Sovereign State* (Philadelphia: Temple University Press, 1987).

[11] Kathleen Thelen, *How Institutions Evolve: The Political Economy of Skills in Germany, Britain, the United States and Japan* (Cambridge: Cambridge University Press, 2004).

[12] Wade Jacoby, *Imitation and Politics: Redesigning Modern Germany* (Ithaca: Cornell University Press, 2000).

[13] Richard Deeg, *Finance Capital Unveiled: Banks and Economic Adjustment in Germany* (Ann Arbor: University of Michigan Press, 1998).

[14] Marc Morjé Howard, *The Politics of Citizenship in Europe* (Cambridge: Cambridge University Press, 2009); Simon Green, *The Politics of Exclusion: Institutions and Immigration Policy in Contemporary Germany* (Manchester: Manchester University Press, 2004).

[15] Joyce Mushaben, "Challenging the Maternalist Presumption: Gender and Welfare Reform in Germany and the United States," in Ulrike Liebert and Nancy Hirschman, eds., *Women and Welfare: Theory and Practice in the U.S. and Europe* (Rutgers: Rutgers University Press, 2001).

[16] Peter Hall and David Soskice, *Varieties of Capitalism: The Institutional Foundations of Comparative Advantage* (Oxford: Oxford University Press, 2001).

[17] Sarah Wiliarty, *The CDU and the Politics of Gender: Bringing Women to the Party* (New York: Cambridge University Press, 2010).

[18] John Koehler, *Stasi: The Untold Story of the East German Secret Police* (Boulder: Westview Press, 1999).

[19] Carolyn Moore and Wade Jacoby, eds., *German Federalism in Transition: Reforms in a Consensual State* (London: Routledge, 2009).

[20]Jonathan Rodden, *Hamilton's Paradox: The Promise and Peril of Fiscal Federalism* (New York: Cambridge University Press, 2006).

[21]Christopher Allen, ed., *Transformation of the German Political Party System: Institutional Crisis or Democratic Renewal?* (New York: Berghahn, 2001).

[22]Cas Mudde, *Populist Radical Right Parties in Europe* (New York: Cambridge University Press, 2007).

[23]Wolfgang Streeck and Kathleen Thelen, eds., *Beyond Continuity: Institutional Change in Advanced Political Economies* (New York: Oxford University Press, 2005).

[24]Katzenstein, *Policy and Politics in West Germany*.

[25]Katzenstein, *Policy and Politics in West Germany*.

[26]Christian Joppke, *Mobilizing Against Nuclear Energy: A Comparison of Germany and the United States* (Berkeley: University of California, 1993).

[27]Simon Bulmer and William Paterson, "A Life More Ordinary? Ten Theses on a Normalization of Germany's Role in the EU." Paper presented at the European Union Studies Association Meetings, Boston, March 2011.

[28]Richard Katz and Peter Mair, "Changing Models of Party Organization and Party Democracy: The Emergence of the Cartel Party," *Party Politics* 1, no. 1 (1995): 5–31.

[29]Lowell Turner, ed., *Negotiating the New Germany: Can Social Partnership Survive?* (Ithaca: Cornell University Press, 1997).

[30]Wolfgang Streeck, *Re-Forming Capitalism: Institutional Change in the German Political Economy* (Oxford: Oxford University Press, 2009).

[31]Gabriel Almond and Sidney Verba, eds., *The Civic Culture Revisited* (Newbury Park: Sage, 1989).

## Chapter 5

[1]George Sansom, *A History of Japan, 1334–1615* (Stanford, Calif.: Stanford University Press, 1961); A. L. Sadler, *A Short History of Japan* (Sydney: Angus and Robertson, 1963), chs. 4–6.

[2]Ronald P. Dore, *Education in Tokugawa Japan* (London: Athlone, 1965).

[3]Peter Duus, *Party Rivalry and Political Change in Taisho Japan* (Cambridge: Harvard University Press, 1968).

[4]Sadako N. Ogata, *Defiance in Manchuria: The Making of Japanese Foreign Policy, 1931–1932* (Berkeley: University of California Press, 1964), pt. II.

[5]Ben-Ami Shillony, *Revolt in Japan: The Young Officers and the February 26, 1936 Incident* (Princeton, N.J.: Princeton University Press, 1973).

[6]Robert E. Ward and Sakamoto Yoshikazu, eds., *Democratizing Japan: The Allied Occupation* (Honolulu: University of Hawaii Press, 1987); John Dower, *Embracing Defeat: Japan in the Aftermath of World War II* (London: Penguin Books, 1999).

[7]Bernd Martin, *Japan and Germany in the Modern World* (Providence, RI: Berghahn Books, 1995).

[8]Hugh Patrick and Henry Rosovsky, "Japan's Economic Performance: An Overview," in *Asia's New Giant: How the Japanese Economy Works,* ed. Hugh Patrick and Henry Rosovsky (Washington, D.C.: Brookings Institution, 1976), pp. 7–9; Takafusa Nakamura, "'Yakushin nihon' no uraomote" (The appearance and reality of the 'advancing Japan'), in *Showa keizaishi* (An economic history of the Showa period), ed. Hiromi Arisawa (Tokyo: Nihon keizai shimbunsha, 1976), pp. 108–11; Hugh Borton, *Japan's Modern Century: From Perry to 1970,* 2nd ed. (New York: Ronald Press Co., 1970), p. 305, Table 5.

[9]William W. Lockwood, *The Economic Development of Japan: Growth and Structural Change, 1868–1938* (Princeton, N.J.: Princeton University Press, 1954), pp. 38–39.

[10]Lockwood, *The Economic Development of Japan*, pp. 14–15.

[11]Stephen D. Cohen, *Uneasy Partnership: Competition and Conflict in U.S.-Japanese Trade Relations* (Cambridge, MA: Ballinger Publishing Company, 1985); Leonard J. Schoppa, *Bargaining with Japan: What American Pressure Can and Cannot Do* (New York: Columbia University Press, 1997).

[12]Herbert P. Bix, *Hirohito and the Making of Modern Japan* (New York: HarperCollins, 2000); Stephen S. Large, *Emperor Hirohito and Showa Japan: A Political Biography* (London: Routledge, 1992).

[13]Richard J. Samuels, *Securing Japan: Tokyo's Grand Strategy and the Future of East Asia* (Ithaca: Cornell University Press, 2007).

[14]Susan J. Pharr and Ellis S. Krauss, eds., *Media and Politics in Japan* (Honolulu: University of Hawaii Press, 1996); Laurie Anne Freeman, *Closing the Shop: Information Cartels and Japan's Mass Media* (Princeton, N.J.: Princeton University Press, 2000).

[15]Frank K. Upham, *Law and Social Change in Postwar Japan* (Cambridge: Harvard University Press, 1987), ch. 2.

[16]George De Vos and Hiroshi Wagatsuma, eds., *Japan's Invisible Race: Caste in Culture and Personality* (Berkeley: University of California Press, 1966), part 1; Upham, *Law and Social Change*, ch. 3.

[17]George Hicks, *Japan's Hidden Apartheid: Korean Minority and the Japanese* (Brookfield, Vt.: Ashgate, 1997).

[18]Samuel P. Huntington, *The Third Wave: Democratization in the Late Twentieth Century* (Norman and London: University of Oklahoma Press, 1991), pp. 266–267.

## Chapter 7

[1]Rogers Smith, *Civic Ideals: Conflicting Visions of Citizenship in U.S. History* (New Haven, CT: Yale University Press, 1997).

[2] S. Karthick Ramakrishnan, *Democracy in Immigrant America: Changing Demographics and Political Participation* (Stanford, CA: Stanford University Press, 2005), chapters 4 and 5.

[3]Louis Hartz, *The Liberal Tradition in America* (New York: Harvest/HBJ, 1955).

[4]Randall Robinson, *The Debt: What America Owes to Blacks* (New York: Plume, 2001).

[5]Gary C. Bryner, *Blue Skies, Green Politics: The Clean Air Act of 1990 and Its Implementation* (Washington, D.C.: CQ Press, 1995).

[6]Randall Monger, *U.S. Legal Permanent Residents: 2009* (Washington, D.C.: Office of Immigration Statistics, U.S. Department of Homeland Security, 2010).

[7]Jeffrey S. Passel, *The Size and Characteristics of the Unauthorized Migrant Population in the U.S.: Estimates Based on the March 2005 Current Population Survey* (Washington, D.C.: Pew Hispanic Center, 2006).

[8]See *The Federalist Papers,* ed. Clinton Rossiter (New York: Mentor, 1961), particularly *Federalist* Nos. 10 and 51.

[9]Deborah Avant, *The Market for Force: The Consequences of Privatizing Security* (New York: Cambridge University Press, 2005).

[10]Kristi Anderson, *After Suffrage: Women in Partisan and Electoral Politics Before the New Deal* (Chicago: University of Chicago Press, 1996), chapters 2 and 3.

[11]Ruy A. Teixeira, *The Disappearing American Voter* (Washington, D.C.: Brookings Institution, 1992).

[12]Raymond Wolfinger and Steven Rosenstone, *Who Votes?* (New Haven, Conn.: Yale University Press. 1980), chapters 2 and 3.

[13]Sanford Levinson, *Constitutional Faith* (Princeton, N.J.: Princeton University Press, 1988).

[14]Sidney Verba, Kay Lehman Schlozman, and Henry Brady, *Voice and Equality: Civic Voluntarism in American Politics* (Cambridge: Harvard University Press, 1995).

[15]Robert D. Putnam, *Bowling Alone: The Collapse and Revival of American Community* (New York: Simon and Schuster, 2000).

## Chapter 8

[1]I am grateful to Mikhail Zherebtsov for research assistance for this chapter.

[2]Description of the Pikalyovo events is adapted from Joan DeBardeleben and Mikhail Zherebtsov, "The Economic Crisis, the Power Vertical and Prospects for Liberalization in Russia," unpublished paper presented at Carleton University, Ottawa, August 26–27, 2010.

[3]Some protests did erupt subsequent to Pikalyovo, feeding this apprehension. See the report by Asia Skorokhodova, "Ekho Pikalyovo' pokatilos' po strane," June 19, 2009, on the newsite MR7, www.MR7.ru/news/economy/story_14348.html, accessed February 14, 2011.

[4]Federal State Statistics Service of the Russian Federation, on-line, http://www.gks.ru/free_doc/new_site/population/demo/demo11.htm, accessed February 10 2011.

[5]Richard Pipes, *Russia under the Old Regime* (London: Widenfeld & Nicolson, 1974), pp. 22–24.

[6]Mikhail Gorbachev, *Perestroika: New Thinking for Our Country and the World* (New York: Harper, 1987).

[7]As a result of the unintended misuse of the Russian word *perezagruzka* to translate "reset," Clinton actually suggested to the Russian audience an "overload" or "overcharge" for the relationship. See "Button Gaffe Embarrasses Clinton," BBC News, March 7, 2009, http://news.bbc.co.uk/2/hi/7930047.stm, accessed January 30, 2011.

[8]Sergei Peregudov, "The Oligarchic Model of Russian Corporatism," in Archie Brown, ed., *Contemporary Russian Politics: A Reader* (New York: Oxford University Press, 2001), p. 259.

[9]The Economist Intelligence Unit, *Country Profile Russia* (London, 2008), pp. 49–50.

[10]Transparency International, Corruption Perceptions Index Results 2010, http://www.transparency.org/policy_research/surveys_indices/cpi/2010/results, accessed March 30, 2011.

[11]Joel Hellman and Daniel Kaufmann, "Confronting the Challenge of State Capture in Transition Economies," *Finance and Development* 38, no. 3 (September 2001), http://www.imf.org/external/pubs/ft/fandd/2001/09/hellman.htm, accessed May 31, 2008.

[12]Victor Zaslavsky, "From Redistribution to Marketization: Social and Attitudinal Change in Post-Soviet Russia," in Gail W. Lapidus, ed., *The New Russia: Troubled Transformation* (Boulder, CO: Westview Press, 1994), 125.

[13]Website of the Federal State Statistical Service, http://www.gks.ru/bgd/free/b10_00/IssWWW.exe/Stg/d11/8-0.htm, accessed February 10, 2011.

[14]Vladimir Popov, "Mortality Crisis in Russia Revisited: Evidence from Cross-Regional Comparison," MPRA Paper No. 21311, May 2009, http://mpra.ub.uni-muenchen.de/21311/1/MPRA_paper_21311.pdf, accessed February 11, 2011.

[15]Dmitry Medvedev, "Presidential Address to the Federal Assembly of the Russian Federation," November 30, 2010, Moscow, http://eng.news.kremlin.ru/news/1384/print, accessed January 28, 2011.

[16]*Country Analysis Report: Russia* (London: Datamonitor Plc, 2010), pp. 54–55.

[17]Amie Ferris-Rotman, "Russia could shun European rights court—top judge." Reuters, November 22, 2010, http://www.reuters.com/article/idUSTRE6AL5IW20101122 (accessed Feb. 14, 2011).

[18]Federal State Statistics Service of the Russian Federation, http://www.customs.ru/ru/stats/arhiv-stats-new/trf-goods/popup.php?id286=731, accessed 10 February 2011.

[19]Speech of President of Russia Dmitry Medvedev at plenary session of Global Policy Forum, "The Modern State: Standards of Democracy and Criteria of Efficiency," September 10, 2010, http://en.gpf-yaroslavl.ru/Media/Files/Speech-of-President-of-Russia-Dmitry-Medvedev-at-plenary-session-of-Global-Policy-Forum-The-Modern-State-Standards-of-Democracy-and-Criteria-of-Efficiency, accessed February 14, 2011.

[20]For a listing of the ministries, see the website of the Government of the Russian Federation, http://government.ru/. Some material is available in English.

[21]*EBRD Transition Report*, 2006. I am grateful to Vladimir Popov for this reference.

[22]Jim Nichol, "Russian Political, Economic, and Security Issues and U.S. Interests," Congressional Research Service, November 4, 2010, http://www.fas.org/sgp/crs/row/RL33407.pdf, accessed January 30, 2011.

[23]Fred Weir, "Putin's Endgame for Chechen Beartrap," *Christian Science Monitor*, January 25, 2001.

[24]Berezovksy was a thorn in the Kremlin's side, threatening to broadcast charges on TV-6 linking the government to 1999 apartment bombings that had been attributed to terrorists. Charges of tax evasion and fraud were brought against Berezovsky before he fled to Europe.

[25]See Joan DeBardeleben and Mikhail Zherebtsov, "The Transition to Managerial Patronage in Russia's Regions," in *The Politics of Sub-national Authoritarianism in Russia*, edited by Vladimir Gel'man and Cameron Ross (Aldershot: Ashgate, 2010).

[26]Website of the State Duma of the Russian Federation, http://www.duma.gov.ru/structure/factions/, accessed 29 January 2011.

[27]David Lane, *State and Politics in the USSR* (Oxford: Blackwell, 1985), pp. 184–185, for 1985 figures; calculated from information on the website of the State Duma for later years.

[28]For a listing of registered parties, see the website of the Federal Electoral Commission of the Russian Federation, http://www.cikrf.ru/politparty/reg_politparty.html, accessed January 28, 2011.

[29]See United Russia website, http://er.ru/text.shtml?18/2152,100056, accessed Jan. 29, 2010, also reported in the *Moscow Times*, Jan. 24, 2011, http://mnweekly.ru/politics/20110124/188356584.html, both websites accessed Jan. 28, 2011.

[30]"Russian Ruling Party Suffers Another Defeat in Siberia," Radio Free Europe/Radio Liberty, May 26, 2010, http://www.rferl.org/content/Russian_Ruling_Party_Suffers_Another_Defeat_In_Siberia/2053108.html, accessed 28 January 2011.

[31]Office for Democratic Institutions and Human Rights, "Russian Federation: Election to the State Duma 7 December 2003," OSCE/ODHIR Election Observation Mission Report" (Warsaw, January 27, 2004).

[32]See the Public Chamber's website: http://www.oprf.ru/en, accessed January 28, 2011.

[33]See Svetlana Kononova, "Bump and Protest," *Russian Profile.Org*, January 11, 2011, http://www.russiaprofile.org/page.php?pageid=Politics&articleid=a1294773645, accessed January 28, 2011.

[34]Federal State Statistical Service of the Russian Federation, *Russia in Figures 2010*, Table 6.13, http://www.gks.ru/bgd/regl/b10_12/IssWWW.exe/stg/d01/06-13.htm, accessed January 28, 2011.

[35]Committee to Protect Journalists, "52 Journalists Killed in Russia since 1992," http://cpj.org/killed/europe/russia/, accessed January 15, 2011.

[36]Reporters without Borders, Press Freedom Index, 2010, http://en.rsf.org/press-freedom-index-2010,1034.html, accessed Jan. 15, 2011.

[37]Monika Scislowska and Vanessa Gera (Associated Press), "Medvedev Trip to Warsaw Helps Polish-Russian Reset," abcNEWS, on-line, December 6, 2010, http://abcnews.go.com/Business/wireStory?id=12323733, accessed February 14, 2011.

[38]Stephen Aris, "Russia's Approach to Multilateral Cooperation in the Post-Soviet Space: CSTO, EurAsEC and SCO," *Russian Analytical Digest*, no. 76, April 2010, pp. 2–6, on-line, http://e-collection.ethbib.ethz.ch/eserv/eth:1620/eth-1620-01.pdf, accessed January 30, 2011.

[39]Vladimir Putin, "Eine Wirtschaftsgemeinschaft von Lissabon bis Wladiwostok," *Süddeutsche Zeitung*, November 25, 2010, p. 22; and Judy Dempsey, "Putin Chides E.U. Over Energy Policies," *New York Times*, November 26, 2010, http://www.nytimes.com/2010/11/27/world/europe/27iht-putin.html, accessed Feb. 14, 2011.

[40]Dmitry Medvedev, "Rossiia Vpered" (*Go Russia*), gazeta.ru 10.09.2009; http://www.kremlin.ru/news/5413, accessed January 30, 2011.

# Chapter 9

[1]IBGE (Instituto Brasileiro de Geografia e Estatística), *PNAD–Pesquisa Nacional por Amostra de Domicílios 2006* Vol 27 (Rio de Janeiro: IBGE, 2006).

[2]See Bertha K. Becker and Claudio A. G. Egler, *Brazil: A New Regional Power in the World Economy: A Regional Geography* (New York: Cambridge University Press, 1992), p. 5; and Terence Turner, "Brazil: Indigenous Rights vs. Neoliberalism," *Dissent* (Summer 1996): 67.

[3]For a complete treatment of state corporatism in Brazil during this period, see Ruth Berins Collier and David Collier, *Shaping the Political Arena: Critical Junctures, the Labor Movement, and Regime Dynamics in Latin America* (Princeton, N.J.: Princeton University Press, 1991), pp. 169–195.

[4]Thomas E. Skidmore, *Politics in Brazil, 1930–1964: An Experiment in Democracy* (New York: Oxford University Press, 1967), p. 101.

[5]Maria do Carmo Campello de Souza, *Estado e Partidos Políticos no Brasil (1930 a 1964)* (São Paulo: Editora Alfa-Omega, 1975).

[6]Guillermo O'Donnell, *Modernization and Bureaucratic Authoritarianism: Studies in South American Politics* (Berkeley: Institute of International Studies, University of California, 1973).

[7]Thomas E. Skidmore, *The Politics of Military Rule in Brazil, 1964–85* (New York: Oxford University Press, 1988), p. 49.

[8]Timothy J. Power, *The Political Right in Postauthoritarian Brazil: Elites, Institutions, and Democratization* (University Park: Pennsylvania State University Press, 2000).

[9]Margaret Keck, "The New Unionism in the Brazilian Transition," in Stepan, *Democratizing Brazil*, 284.

[10]Peter B. Evans, *Dependent Development: The Alliance of Multinational, State, and Local Capital in Brazil* (Princeton, NJ: Princeton University Press, 1979).

[11]Morsch, E., N. Chavannes, M. van den Akker, H. Sa, G. J. Dinant, "The Effects of the Family Health Program on Child Health in Ceará State, Northeastern Brazil," *Arch Public Health* 59 (2001):151–65.

[12]Kurt Weyland, *Democracy without Equity: Failures of Reform in Brazil* (Pittsburgh: University of Pittsburgh Press, 1996).

[13]See Morsch et al., "The Effects of the Family Health Program."

[14]Kathy Lindert, Anja Linder, Jason Hobbs, and Benedicte de la Briere, "The Nuts and Bolts of Brazil's *Bolsa Família* Program: Implementing Conditional Cash Transfers in a Decentralized Context," Social Protection Discussion Paper No. 0709, May 2007, pp. 18–19.

[15]Jeffry A. Frieden, *Debt, Development, and Democracy: Modern Political Economy and Latin America, 1965–1985* (Princeton, NJ: Princeton University Press, 1991), pp. 54–65.

[16]David Samuels, *Ambition, Federalism, and Legislative Politics in Brazil* (New York: Cambridge University Press, 2003).

[17]Peter B. Evans, "Predatory, Developmental, and Other Apparatuses: A Comparative Political Economy Perspective

on the Third World State," *Sociological Forum* 4, no. 4 (1989), 561–587.

[18]Human Rights Watch, *Police Brutality in Urban Brazil* (New York: Human Rights Watch, 1997), 13.

[19]See Samuels, *Ambition, Federalism, and Legislative Politics in Brazil.*

[20]Alfred P. Montero, *Shifting States in Global Markets: Subnational Industrial Policy in Contemporary Brazil and Spain* (University Park: Pennsylvania State University Press, 2002).

[21]Judith Tendler, *Good Government in the Tropics* (Baltimore: Johns Hopkins University Press, 1997).

[22]Ben Ross Schneider, *Politics within the State: Elite Bureaucrats and Industrial Policy in Authoritarian Brazil* (Pittsburgh: University of Pittsburgh Press, 1991).

[23]Barry Ames, *The Deadlock of Democracy in Brazil: Interests, Identities, and Institutions in Comparative Politics* (Ann Arbor: University of Michigan Press, 2001).

[24]See Power, *The Political Right in Postauthoritarian Brazil.*

[25]Turner, "Brazil: Indigenous Rights vs. Neoliberalism," p. 67.

# Chapter 10

[1]An excellent history of this event is presented in Wayne A. Cornelius, "Nation-Building, Participation, and Distribution: The Politics of Social Reform Under Cárdenas," in Gabriel A. Almond, Scott Flanagan, and Robert J. Mundt (eds.), *Crisis, Choice and Change: Historical Studies of Political Development* (Boston: Little, Brown, 1973).

[2]Michael C. Meyer and William K. Sherman, *The Course of Mexican History*, 5th ed. (New York: Oxford UP, 1995), pp. 598–599.

[3]Merilee S. Grindle, *State and Countryside: Development Policy and Agrarian Politics in Latin America* (Baltimore: Johns Hopkins University Press, 1986), p. 63, quoting President Avila Camacho (1940–1946).

[4]Kevin J. Middlebrook (ed.), *Unions, Workers, and the State in Mexico* (San Diego: Center for U.S.-Mexican Studies, University of California Press, 1991).

[5]Grindle, *State and Countryside,* 79–111.

[6]For a description of this process, see Carlos Bazdresch and Santiago Levy, "Populism and Economic Policy in Mexico," in Rudiger Dornbusch and Sebastian Edwards (eds.), *The Macroeconomics of Populism in Latin America* (Chicago: University of Chicago Press, 1991), 72.

[7]A classic anthropological study on the urban poor left behind by the "Mexican Miracle" is Oscar Lewis, *The Children of Sánchez: Autobiography of a Mexican Family* (New York: Random House, 1961).

[8]Joe Foweraker and Ann L. Craig (eds.), *Popular Movements and Political Change in Mexico* (Boulder, CO: Lynne Rienner, 1989).

[9]For an assessment of the mounting problems of Mexico City and efforts to deal with them, see Diane E. Davis, *Urban Leviathan: Mexico City in the Twentieth Century* (Philadelphia: Temple University Press, 1994).

[10]Roger Hansen, *The Politics of Mexican Development* (Baltimore: Johns Hopkins University Press, 1971), 75.

[11]World Bank, *World Development Indicators,* http://data.worldbank.org/indicator.

[12]World Trade Organization, *Trade Profiles: Mexico,* http://stat.wto.org/CountryProfile/WSDBCountryPFView.aspx?Language=E&Country=MX.

[13]For a recent study arguing that many Mexican farmers have been hurt by NAFTA, see Timothy A. Wise, "Agricultural Dumping Under NAFTA: Estimating the Costs of U.S. Agricultural Policies to Mexican Producers," Mexican Rural Development Research Report No. 7 (Washington, DC: Woodrow Wilson International Center for Scholars, 2010).

[14]For a description of how Mexican presidents went about the process of selecting their successors during the period of PRI dominance, see Jorge G. Castañeda, *Perpetuating Power: How Mexican Presidents Were Chosen* (New York: New Press, 2000).

[15]Daniel Levy and Gabriel Székely, *Mexico: Paradoxes of Stability and Change* (Boulder, CO: Westview Press, 1983), p. 100.

[16]See Luis Carlos Ugalde, *The Mexican Congress: Old Player, New Power* (Washington, DC: Center for International and Strategic Studies, 2000).

[17]See Chapell H. Lawson, *Building the Fourth Estate: Democratization and the Rise of a Free Press in Mexico* (Berkeley: University of California Press, 2002).

[18]Susan Eckstein (ed.), *Power and Popular Protest: Latin American Social Movements* (Berkeley: University of California Press, 1989).

# Chapter 11

[1]Shula Marks and Stanley Trapido, "Lord Milner and the South African State," *History Workshop* 8 (1979): 50–80; David Yudelman, *The Making of Modern South Africa: State, Capital, and the Incorporation of Organized Labour on the South African Gold Fields* (Westport, Conn.: Greenwood Press, 1983).

[2]Stanley Trapido, "South Africa in a Comparative Study of Industrialization," Journal of Development Studies 3 (1971): 311–320; Frederick A. Johnston, *Class, Race and Gold: A Study of Class Relations and Racial Discrimination in South Africa* (London: Routledge, 1976).

[3]Hermann Giliomee, "Constructing Afrikaner Nationalism," *Journal of Asian and African Studies* 18 (1983): 83–98; Isabel Hofmeyr, "Building a Nation from Words: Afrikaans Language, Literature and Ethnic Identity, 1902–1924," in Shula Marks and Stanley Trapido, eds., *The Politics of Race, Class and Nationalism in Twentieth Century Nationalism* (London and New York: Longman, 1987).

[4]Deborah Posel, *The Making of Apartheid, 1948–1961: Conflict and Compromise* (Oxford: Clarendon Press, 1997), chap. 9.

[5]Heribert Adam and Hermann Giliomee, *The Rise and Crisis of Afrikaner Power* (Cape Town: David Philip, 1979), pp. 169–185.

[6]Andrew Nash, "Mandela's Democracy," *Monthly Review* (April 1999): 18–28.

[7]Servaas van der Berg, "Current poverty and income distribution in the context of South African history," Department of Economics, University of Stellenbosch, 2010.

[8]Jeffrey Lewis, "Assessing the Demographic and Economic Impact of HIV/AIDS," in Kyle Dean Kauffman and David L. Lindauer, eds. *AIDS and South Africa: The Social Expression of a Pandemic* (Basingstoke, UK: Palgrave Macmillian, 2004), p. 103.

[9]Shula Marks, "An Epidemic Waiting to Happen," *African Studies* 61, no. 1 (2002): 13–26.

[10]Terence Moll, "Did the Apartheid Economy Fail?" *Journal of Southern African Studies* 17, no. 2 (1991): 289–291.

[11]Neta Crawford and Audie Klotz, *How Sanctions Work: Lessons from South Africa* (New York: St. Martin's Press, 1999).

[12]*Sunday Independent* (September 2, 2001).

[13]*Mail and Guardian* (February 2, 2001).

[14]*The Star* (December 12, 2001).

[15]Robert Mattes, "Public Opinion since 1994," in Jessica Piombo and Lia Nijzink, eds., *Electoral Politics in South Africa: Assessing the First Democratic Decade* (New York: Palgrave Macmillian, 2005), p. 55.

[16]Markinor, "SABC/Markinor Opinion 2004—Racial Relations in South Africa," (November 18, 2004), http://www.biz-community.com/Article.aspx?c511&5196&ai55200.

[17]"Volunteer Statistics in South Africa," *The Star* (December 11, 2004).

[18]Lewis, "Demographic and Economic Impact of HIV/AIDS," 111.

# Chapter 12

[1]Much of this context is recounted in James S. Coleman, *Nigeria: Background to Nationalism* (Berkeley: University of California Press, 1958).

[2]Obafemi Awolowo, *Path to Nigerian Freedom* (London: Faber and Faber, 1947), pp. 47–48.

[3]Billy Dudley, *An Introduction to Nigerian Government and Politics* (Bloomington: Indiana University Press, 1982), p. 71.

[4]Robin Luckham, *The Nigerian Military: A Sociological Analysis of Authority and Revolt 1960–67* (Cambridge: Cambridge University Press, 1971).

[5]Peter Ekeh, "Colonialism and the Two Publics in Africa: A Theoretical Statement," *Comparative Studies in Society and History* 17, no. 1 (January 1975).

[6]Richard A. Joseph, *Democracy and Prebendal Politics in Nigeria: The Rise and Fall of the Second Republic* (Cambridge: Cambridge University Press), pp. 55–58.

[7]Gavin Williams and Terisa Turner, "Nigeria," in John Dunn, ed., *West African States: Failure and Promise* (Cambridge: Cambridge University Press, 1978), pp. 156–157.

[8]Michael J. Watts, *State, Oil and Agriculture in Nigeria* (Berkeley: University of California Press, 1987), p. 71.

[9]Watts, *State Oil and Agriculture in Nigeria*, p. 67.

[10]Tom Forrest, *Politics and Economic Development in Nigeria*, 2nd ed. (Boulder, CO: Westview Press, 1995), pp. 207–212.

[11]Dele Olowu, "Centralization, Self-Governance, and Development in Nigeria," in James S. Wunsch and Dele Olowu, eds., *The Failure of the Centralized State: Institutions and Self-Governance in Africa* (Boulder, CO: Westview Press, 1991), p. 211.

[12]Robert Melson and Howard Wolpe, *Nigeria: Modernization and the Politics of Communalism* (East Lansing: Michigan State University Press, 1971).

[13]Toyin Falola, Violence in Nigeria: *The Crisis of Religious Politics and Secular Ideologies* (Rochester, NY: University of Rochester Press, 1998).

[14]Pat A. Williams, "Women and the Dilemma of Politics in Nigeria," in Crawford Young and Paul Beckett, eds., *Dilemmas of Democracy in Nigeria* (Rochester, NY: University of Rochester Press, 1997), pp. 219–241.

[15]Anthony Kirk-Greene and Douglas Rimmer, *Nigeria since 1970: A Political and Economic Outline* (London: Hodder and Stoughton, 1981), p. 49.

[16]Rotimi Suberu, *Federalism and Ethnic Conflict in Nigeria* (Washington, DC: U.S. Institute of Peace, 2001).

[17]Suberu, *Federalism and Ethnic Conflict in Nigeria,* pp. 119–120.

[18]Henry Bienen, *Armies and Parties in Africa* (New York: Africana Publishing, 1978), pp. 193–211.

[19]Richard Joseph, *Democracy and Prebendal Politics in Nigeria: The Rise and Fall of the Second Republic* (Cambridge: Cambridge University Press, 1987), pp. 55–68.

[20]Samuel DeCalo, *Coups and Army Rule in Africa* (New Haven, CT: Yale University Press, 1976), p. 18.

[21]Joseph, *Democracy and Prebendal Politics in Nigeria: The Rise and Fall of the Second Republic,* pp. 52–53.

[22]Richard Sklar, *Nigerian Political Parties* (Princeton: Princeton University Press, 1963).

[23]Babafemi Badejo, "Party Formation and Party Competition," in Larry Diamond, Anthony Kirk-Greene, and Oyeleye Oyediran, eds., *Transition without End: Nigerian Politics and Civil Society under Babangida* (Boulder, CO: Lynne Rienner Publishers, 1997), p. 179.

[24]Eghosa Osaghae, *Crippled Giant: Nigeria since Independence* (Bloomington: Indiana University Press 1999), pp. 233–239.

[25]Peter M. Lewis, Barnett Rubin, and Pearl Robinson, *Stabilizing Nigeria: Pressures, Incentives and Support for Civil Society* (New York: Council on Foreign Relations, 1998), p. 87.

[26]Donald L. Horowitz, "Making Moderation Pay: The Comparative Politics of Ethnic Conflict Management," in Joseph V. Montville, ed., *Conflict and Peacemaking in Multiethnic Societies* (New York: Lexington Books, 1991), chapter 25.

[27]Rotimi Suberu, *Public Policies and National Unity in Nigeria,* Research Report No. 19 (Ibadan: Development Policy Centre, 199), pp. 9–10.

[28]Sayre Schatz, "'Pirate Capitalism' and the Inert Economy of Nigeria," *Journal of Modern African Studies* 22, no. 1 (March 1984): 45–57.

[29]Adebayo Olukoshi, "Associational Life," in Diamond, Kirk-Greene, and Oyediran, *Transition Without End,* pp. 385–86.

[30]Peter Lewis, Etannibi Alemika, and Michael Bratton, *Down to Earth: Changes in Attitudes to Democracy and Markets in Nigeria,* Afrobarometer Working Paper No. 20, Michigan State University, August 2002.

[31]See Terry Lynn Karl, *The Paradox of Plenty* (Berkeley: University of California Press, 1997); and Michael Ross, "The Political Economy of the Resource Curse," *World Politics* 51 (January 1999), 297–322.

[32]Michael Bratton and Nicolas van de Walle, *Democratic Experiments in Africa* (Cambridge: Cambridge University Press, 1997).

# Chapter 13

[1]British Financial Adviser to the Foreign Office in Tehran, *Documents on British Foreign Policy, 1919–39* (London: Her Majesty's Stationery Office, 1963), First Series, XIII, 720, 735.

[2]M. Bazargan, "Letter to the Editor," *Ettela'at*, February 7, 1980.

[3]*Iran Times*, January 12, 1979.

[4]Cited in H. Amirahmadi, *Revolution and Economic Transition* (Albany: State University of New York Press, 1960), p. 201.

[5]International Labor Organization, "Employment and Income Policies for Iran" (unpublished report, Geneva, 1972), Appendix C, 6.

[6]U.S. Congress, *Economic Consequences of the Revolution in Iran,* 5.

[7]Cited in *Iran Times*, July 9, 1993.

[8]J. Amuzegar, *Iran's Economy under the Islamic Republic* (London: Taurus Press, 1994), p. 100.

[9]A. Rafsanjani, "The Islamic Consultative Assembly," *Kayhan*, May 23, 1987.

[10]S. Saffari, "The Legitimation of the Clergy's Right to Rule in the Iranian Constitution of 1979," *British Journal of Middle Eastern Studies* 20, no. 1 (1993): 64–81.

[11]Ayatollah Montazeri, *Ettela'at*, October 8, 1979.

[12]O. Fallaci, "Interview with Khomeini," *New York Times Magazine*, October 7, 1979.

## Chapter 14

[1]Gao Xingjian won the Nobel Prize for Literature in 2000. He was born in China (1940) and lived there until the late 1980s. He has been a French citizen since 1997, and all his works are banned in the PRC because they are seen as challenging the Chinese Communist Party.

[2]Mao Zedong, "Report on an Investigation of the Peasant Movement in Hunan," March 1927. In *Selected Readings from the Works of Mao Tsetung* (Beijing: Foreign Languages Press, 1971), p. 24.

[3]David Bachman, *Bureaucracy, Economy, and Leadership in China: The Institutional Origins of the Great Leap Forward* (Cambridge: Cambridge University Press, 1991), p. 2.

[4]"When China Wakes," *The Economist*, November 28, 1992, p. 15.

[5]See Nicholas D. Kristof and Sheryl WuDunn, *China Wakes: The Struggle for the Soul of a Rising Power* (New York: Time Books, 1994); and James Kynge, *China Shakes the World: A Titan's Rise and Troubled Future—and the Challenge for America* (Boston: Houghton Mifflin, 2006).

[6]"Restore Agricultural Production," *Selected Works of Deng Xiaoping (1938–1965)* (Beijing: Foreign Languages).

[7]See Bruce J. Dickson, *Red Capitalists in China: The Party, Private Entrepreneurs, and Prospects for Political Change* (New York: Cambridge University Press, 2003).

[8]Emily Honig and Gail Herschatter, *Personal Voices: Chinese Women in the 1980s* (Stanford, CA: Stanford University Press, 1988), p. 337.

[9]See, for example, Valerie M. Hudson and Andrea M. den Boer, *Bare Branches: The Security Implications of Asia's Surplus Male Population* (Cambridge, Mass.: 2004).

[10]The constitution of the People's Republic of China can be found online at: http://english.peopledaily.com.cn/constitution/constitution.html.

[11]The constitution of the Chinese Communist Party can be found online at: http://news.xinhuanet.com/english/2007-10/25/content_6944738.htm.

[12]John P. Burns, *The Chinese Communist Party's Nomenklatura System: A Documentary Study of Party Control of Leadership Selection, 1979–1984* (Armonk, NY: M. E. Sharpe, 1989), pp. ix–x.

[13]Ministry of National Defense of the People's Republic of China, http://eng.mod.gov.cn/Database/WhitePapers/2004-09/07/content_4005646.htm.

[14]Kenneth Lieberthal and David M. Lampton, eds., *Bureaucracy, Politics, and Decision-Making in Post-Mao China* (Berkeley: University of California Press, 1992); and Andrew Mertha, " 'Fragmented Authoritarianism 2.0': Political Pluralization in the Chinese Policy Process," *China Quarterly*, no. 200 (December 2009), pp. 995–1012.

[15]Cheng Li, "China's Communist Party-State: The Structure and Dynamics of Power," in William A. Joseph, ed., *Politics in China: An Introduction* (New York: Oxford University Press, 2010), pp. 165–191.

[16]Gordon White, *Riding the Tiger: The Politics of Economic Reform in Post-Mao China* (Palo Alto, CA: Stanford University Press, 1993), p. 20.

[17]James D. Seymour, *China's Satellite Parties* (Armonk, NY: M. E. Sharpe, 1987), p. 87.

[18]"China's elections won't be Western-style," *China Daily*, March 20, 2010.

[19]The following scenes have been adapted from a variety of sources on rural China, including Louise Lim, "Chinese Village Provides Model for Prosperity," National Public Radio, May 16, 2006, http://www.npr.org/templates/story/story.php?storyId=5406900; Maureen Fan, "Two Chinese Villages, Two Views of Rural Poverty," *The Washington Post*, August 1, 2006; Bin Wu and Shujie Yao, "Empty Villages in Poor Areas of China: A Case Study of Rural Migration in North Shaanxi," Discussion Paper 56, China Policy Institute, University of Nottingham, U.K., January 2010; Susan V. Lawrence, "Democracy, Chinese-Style: Village Representative Assemblies," *Australian Journal of Chinese Affairs*, no. 32 (July 1994), pp. 61–68; and "Sentence In Villager's Death Doesn't Satisfy Skeptics," February 1, 2011, China Real Time Report, *Wall Street Journal Digital Network*.

[20]"A Villager's Death Exposes Government Credibility Crisis," China Real Time Report, *Wall Street Journal Digital Network*, December 28, 2010.

[21]Worldwide Governance Indicators, http://info.world-bank.org/governance/wgi/index.asp.

[22]Nicholas D. Kristof, "China Sees 'Market-Leninism' as Way to Future," *New York Times*, September 6, 1993. For a fuller discussion of a variation of this idea, "market Stalinism," see Marc Blecher, *China against the Tides: Restructuring through Revolution, Radicalism and Reform*, 3rd ed. (New York: Continuum, 2009).

[23]Harry Harding, *China's Second Revolution: Reform after Mao* (Washington, D.C.: Brookings Institution, 1987), p. 200.

[24]*The Economist* Intelligence Unit, Democracy Index 2010, http://eiu.com/democracy.

[25]Nicholas D. Kristof, "Riddle of China: Repression as Standard of Living Soars," *New York Times*, September 7, 1993.

[26]Nicholas Lardy, "Is China Different? The Fate of Its Economic Reform," in Daniel Chirot, ed., *The Crisis of Leninism and the Decline of the Left* (Seattle: University of Washington Press, 1991), p. 147.

# Glossary

**5 percent clause** This rule obliges a party to get at least 5 percent of the "second votes" in order to enter the Bundestag (or the state parliaments) as a party. It tends to depress votes for "splinter" parties.

## A

*abertura* Portuguese for "opening" (*apertura* in Spanish). In Brazil, refers to the period of authoritarian liberalization begun in 1974 when the military allowed civilian politicians to compete for political office in the context of a more open political society.

**absolute veto** In areas that directly affect the states, the Bundesrat can veto any bill passed by the Bundestag.

**accommodation** An informal agreement or settlement between the government and important interest groups in response to the interest groups' concerns for policy or program benefits.

**accountability** A government's responsibility to its population, usually by periodic popular elections, transparent fiscal practices, and by parliament's having the power to dismiss the government by passing a motion of no confidence. In a political system characterized by accountability, the major actions taken by government must be known and understood by the citizenry.

**acephalous societies** Literally "headless" societies. A number of traditional Nigerian societies, such as the Igbo in the precolonial period, lacked executive rulership as we have come to conceive of it. Instead, the villages and clans were governed by committee or consensus.

**administrative guidance** Informal guidance, usually not based on statute or formal regulation, that is given by a government agency, such as a ministry and its subdivisions, to a private organization, such as a firm or a lower-level government. The lack of transparency of the practice makes it subject to criticisms as a disguised form of collusion between a government agency and a firm.

**African** South African usage refers to Bantu language speakers, the demographic majority of South African citizens.

**Afrikaner** Descendants of Dutch, French, German, and Scots settlers speaking a language (Afrikaans) derived heavily from Dutch and politically mobilized as an ethnic group through the twentieth century.

*amakudari* A Japanese practice, known as "descent from heaven," in which government officials retiring from their administrative positions take jobs in public corporations or private firms with which their own ministry has or recently had close ties.

**Amerindians** Original peoples of North and South America; indigenous people.

**anarchy** The absence of any form of political authority or effective rule.

*ancien régime* The monarchical regime that ruled France until the Revolution of 1789, when it was toppled by a popular uprising.

**anticlericalism** Opposition to the power of churches or clergy in politics. In some countries, for example, France and Mexico, this opposition has focused on the role of the Catholic Church in politics.

**Articles of Confederation** The first governing document of the United States, agreed to in 1777 and ratified in 1781. The Articles concentrated most powers in the states and made the national government largely dependent on voluntary contributions of the states.

**Asian Development Bank (ADB)** A regional bank established in 1966 to promote economic development in and cooperation among nations in Asia. The bank mediates public and private investments in, and loans for, selected developmental projects. The current members include forty-eight nations and areas within the Asian and Pacific region and nineteen outside the region, including the United States.

**Asia-Pacific Economic Cooperation (APEC)** A regional organization of Asian and Pacific Rim nations established in 1989 to promote cooperation among member states, especially in foreign investment and the standardization and compilation of statistical data. Currently composed of twenty-one members (including the United States and Canada), it advocates "open regionalism," cooperation among nations within the region that neither precludes nor impedes cooperation between them and nations outside the region.

**Assembly of Experts** Group that nominates and can remove the Supreme Leader in Iran. The assembly is elected by the general electorate, but almost all its members are clerics.

**Association of Southeast Asian Nations (ASEAN)** An organization formed in 1967 to promote regional economic and political cooperation. As of 2010, ASEAN consisted of ten member states: Brunei, Cambodia, Indonesia, Laos, Malaysia, Myanmar, the Philippines, Singapore, Thailand, and Vietnam.

**asymmetrical federalism** A form of federalism in which some subnational units in the federal system have greater or lesser powers than others.

**authoritarianism** A system of rule in which power depends not on popular legitimacy but on the coercive force of the political authorities. Hence, there are few personal and group freedoms. It is also characterized by near absolute power in the executive branch and few, if any, legislative and judicial controls.

**autocracy** A government in which one or a few rulers has absolute power, thus, a dictatorship.

**autonomous region** A territorial unit that is equivalent to a province and contains a large concentration of ethnic minorities. These regions, for example, Tibet, have some autonomy in the cultural sphere but in most policy matters are strictly subordinate to the central government.

*ayatollah* Literally, "sign of God." High-ranking cleric in Iran.

# B

**balance of payments** An indicator of international flow of funds that shows the excess or deficit in total payments of all kinds between or among countries. Included in the calculation are exports and imports, grants, and international debt payments.

**Basic Law** The 1949 proto-constitution of the Federal Republic, which continues to function today.

**bazaar** An urban marketplace where shops, workshops, small businesses, and export-importers are located.

**bicameral** A legislative body with two houses, such as the U.S. Senate and the U.S. House of Representatives. Just as the U.S. Constitution divides responsibilities between the branches of the federal government and between the federal government and the states, it divides legislative responsibilities between the Senate and the House.

**Bill of Rights** The first ten amendments to the U.S. Constitution (ratified in 1791), which established limits on the actions of government. Initially, the Bill of Rights limited only the federal government. The Fourteenth Amendment and subsequent judicial rulings extended the provisions of the Bill of Rights to the states.

**Boer** Literally "farmer"; modern usage is a derogatory reference to Afrikaners.

**brahmin** The highest caste in the Hindu caste system of India.

**bureaucracy** An organization structured hierarchically, in which lower-level officials are charged with administering regulations codified in rules that specify impersonal, objective guidelines for making decisions.

**bureaucratic authoritarianism (BA)** A term developed by Argentine sociologist Guillermo O'Donnell to interpret the common characteristics of military-led authoritarian regimes in Brazil, Argentina, Chile, and Uruguay in the 1960s and 1970s. According to O'Donnell, bureaucratic authoritarian regimes led by the armed forces and key civilian allies emerged in these countries in response to severe economic crises.

**bureaucratic rings** A term developed by the Brazilian sociologist and president Fernando Henrique Cardoso that refers to the highly permeable and fragmented structure of the state bureaucracy that allows private interests to make alliances with midlevel bureaucratic officers. By shaping public policy to benefit these interests, bureaucrats gain the promise of future employment in the private sector. While in positions of responsibility, bureaucratic rings are ardent defenders of their own interests.

*bushi* (samurai) The warrior class in medieval Japan, also known as samurai. The class emerged around the tenth century CE, and a dominant band established Japan's first warrior government in the twelfth century. The last warrior government was overthrown in the Meiji Restoration of the mid-nineteenth century.

# C

**cabinet** The body of officials (e.g., ministers, secretaries) who direct executive departments presided over by the chief executive (e.g., prime minister, president).

**cabinet government** A system of government in which most executive power is held by the cabinet, headed by a prime minister.

**cadre** A person who exercises a position of authority in a communist party-state; cadres may or may not be Communist Party members.

**caste system** India's Hindu society is divided into castes. According to the Hindu religion, membership in a caste is determined at birth. Castes form a rough social and economic hierarchy.

**causal theories** An influential approach in comparative politics that involves trying to explain why "if X happens, then Y is the result."

**Central Committee** The top 350 or so leaders of the Chinese Communist Party. It meets annually for about two weeks and is charged with carrying on the business of the National Party Congress when it is not in session.

**Central Military Commission (CMC)** The most important military organization in the People's Republic of China, headed by the general secretary of the Chinese Communist Party, who is the commander-in-chief of the People's Liberation Army.

**centrally planned economy** An economic system in which the state directs the economy through a series of bureaucratic plans for the production and distribution of goods and services. The government, rather, than the market, is the major influence on the economy. Also called a command economy.

**chancellor** An old German title now used by the German head of government and essentially the same as "prime minister."

**checks and balances** A governmental system of divided authority in which coequal branches can restrain each other's actions. For example, the U.S. president must sign legislation passed by Congress for it to become law. If the president vetoes a bill, Congress can override that veto by a two-thirds vote of the Senate and the House of Representatives.

**Citizens Action Groups** Non-party and often single-issue initiatives, often focused on concrete problems such as the environment, traffic, housing, or other social and economic issues.

**civil servants** Employees of federal, state, and municipal governments.

**civil society** refers to the space occupied by voluntary associations outside the state, for example, non-governmental organizations (NGOs), professional associations (lawyers, doctors, teachers), trade unions, student and women's groups, religious bodies, and other voluntary association groups. Civil society is often seen as an important part of democracy.

**clientelism** An informal aspect of policy-making in which a powerful patron (for example, a traditional local boss, government agency, or dominant party) offers resources such as land, contracts, protection, or jobs in return for the support and services (such as labor or votes) of lower-status and less powerful clients; corruption, preferential treatment, and inequality are characteristic of clientelist politics.

**clientelistic networks** Informal systems of asymmetrical power in which a powerful patron (e.g., the president, prime minister, or governor) offers less powerful clients resources, benefits, or career advantages in return for support, loyalty, or services.

**co-determination** The legal right of representatives of employees to help determine the direction of the company in which they work. Co-determination often takes place through works councils.

**cohabitation** The term used by the French to describe the situation in the Fifth Republic when a president and prime minister belong to opposing political coalitions.

**Cold War** The hostile relations that prevailed between the United States and the Soviet Union from the late 1940s until the demise of the USSR in 1991.

**collective identities** The groups with which people identify, including gender, class, race, region, and religion, and which are the "building blocks" for social and political action.

**collectivization** A process undertaken in the Soviet Union under Stalin from 1929 into the early 1930s and in China under Mao in the l950s, by which agricultural land was removed from private ownership and organized into large state and collective farms.

**communism** A system of social organization based on the common ownership and coordination of production.

**communist party-state** A type of nation-state in which the communist party attempts to exercise a complete monopoly on political power and controls all important state institutions.

**comparative politics** The field within political science that focuses on domestic politics and analyzes patterns of similarity and difference.

**comparativist** A political scientist who studies the similarities and differences in the domestic politics of various countries.

**conservative** The belief that existing political, social, and economic arrangements should be preserved.

**consolidated democracies** Democratic political systems that have been solidly and stably established for an ample period of time and in which there is relatively consistent adherence to the core democratic principles.

**constitutional monarchy** System of government in which the head of state ascends by heredity but is limited in powers and constrained by the provisions of a constitution.

**constructive vote of no confidence** This measure requires the Bundestag to have a new chancellor in place before ousting the current one.

**corporatist state** A state in which interest groups become an institutionalized part of the state structure.

**Corruption Perceptions Index** A measure developed by Transparency International that ranks countries in terms of the degree to which corruption is perceived to exist among public officials and politicians.

**country** A territorial unit controlled by a single state.

**coup d'état** A forceful, extra-constitutional action resulting in the removal of an existing government.

**critical juncture** An important historical moment when political actors make critical choices, which shape institutions and future outcomes.

# D

*dalits* The *dalit* movement is organized by untouchables or scheduled caste against caste discrimination and oppression.

**decentralization** Policies that aim to transfer some decision-making power from higher to lower levels of government.

**Declaration of Independence** The document asserting that the British colonies in what is now the United States had declared themselves independent from Great Britain. The Declaration of Independence was signed in Philadelphia on July 4, 1776.

**democracy** From the Greek *demos* (the people) and *kratos* (rule). A political system that features the following: selection to important public offices through free and fair elections; the right of all adults to vote; political parties that are free to compete in elections; government that operates by fair and relatively open procedures; political rights and civil liberties; an independent judiciary (court system); civilian control of the military.

**democratic centralism** A system of political organization developed by V.I. Lenin and practiced, with modifications, by all communist party-states. Its principles include a hierarchical party structure.

**democratic corporatism** A bargaining system in which important policies are established and often carried out with the participation of trade unions and business associations.

**democratic transition** The process of a state moving from an authoritarian to a democratic political system.

**democratization** Transition from authoritarian rule to a democratic political order.

**dependent variable** The variable symbolized by x that is believed to influence the outcome or result.

**deregulation** The process of dismantling state regulations that govern business activities.

**developmental state** A nation-state in which the government carries out policies that effectively promote national economic growth.

# Glossary

**developmentalism** An ideology and practice in Latin America during the 1950s in which the state played a leading role in seeking to foster economic development through sponsoring vigorous industrial policy.

**dictatorships** A form of government in which power and political control are concentrated in one or a few rulers who have concentrated and nearly absolute power.

**dirigisme** A French term denoting that the state plays a leading role in supervising the economy.

**distributional politics** The use of power, particularly by the state, to allocate some kind of valued resource among competing groups.

**distributive policies** Policies that allocate state resources into an area that lawmakers perceive needs to be promoted. For example, leaders today believe that students should have access to the Internet. In order to accomplish this goal, telephone users are being taxed to provide money for schools to establish connections to the Internet (which, in large part, uses telephone lines to transfer data).

**dominant party** A political party that manages to maintain consistent control of a political system through formal and informal mechanisms of power, with or without strong support from the population.

**dual society** A society and economy that are sharply divided into a traditional, usually poorer, and a modern, usually richer, sector.

## E

**economic liberalization** The removal of government control and regulation over private enterprise.

**ejidatario** Recipient of an *ejido* land grant in Mexico.

**ejido** Land granted by Mexican government to an organized group of peasants.

**Emergency (1975–1977)** The period when Indian Prime Minister Indira Gandhi suspended many formal democratic rights and ruled in an authoritarian manner.

**Environmental Performance Index** A measure of how close countries come to meeting specific benchmarks for national pollution control and natural resource management.

**Eurozone** The 17 members of the EU (out of 27 total members) who share a common currency, the euro.

**executive** The agencies of government that implement or execute policy.

**Expediency Council** A committee set up in Iran to resolve differences between the *Majles* (parliament) and the Guardian Council.

**export-led growth** Economic growth generated by the export of a country's commodities. Export-led growth can occur at an early stage of economic development, in which case it involves primary products, such as the country's mineral resources, timber, and agricultural products; or at a later stage, when industrial goods and services are exported.

## F

**failed states** States in which the government no longer functions effectively.

**Farsi** Persian word for the Persian language. Fars is a province in Central Iran.

**favelas** A Portuguese-language term for the shantytowns that ring many of the main cities in Brazil. The shantytowns emerge where people can invade unused land and build domiciles before the authorities can remove them. Unfinished public housing projects can also become the sites of favelas. Favelas expanded after the 1970s as a response to the inadequate supply of homes in urban centers to meet the demand caused by increasing rural-urban migration.

**Federal Reserve Board** The U.S. central bank established by Congress in 1913 to regulate the banking industry and the money supply. Although the president appoints the chair of the board of governors (with Senate approval), the board operates largely independently.

**federal state** A state whose constitution divides power between a national (federal) government and lower units such as states, provinces, regions, Länder, or cantons.

**federal system** A political structure in which subnational units have significant independent powers; the powers of each level are usually specified in the federal constitution.

**federalism** A system of governance in which political authority is shared between the national government and regional or state governments. The powers of each level of government are usually specified in a federal constitution.

**floating population** Migrants from the rural areas who have moved temporarily to the cities to find employment.

**foreign direct investment** Ownership of or investment in cross-border enterprises in which the investor plays a direct managerial role.

**Foundation of the Oppressed** A clerically controlled foundation set up after the revolution in Iran.

**Four Great Pollution Trials** Includes a mercury poisoning case in Minamata City, thus known as the Minamata Disease, a very similar case in another city, thus known as the Second Minamata Disease, a cadmium poisoning case known as the itai-itai (ouch-ouch) disease, and a case of severe asthma caused by inhalation of sulfur dioxide that occurred in Yokkaichi City, hence known as the Yokkaichi Asthma.

**framework regulations** Laws that set broad parameters for economic behavior but that require subsequent elaboration, often through formal agreements between employers and employees.

**free market** A system in which government regulation of the economy is absent or limited. Relative to other advanced democracies, the United States has traditionally had a freer market economically.

**Freedom in the World rating** An annual evaluation by Freedom House of the state of freedom in countries around the world measured according to political rights and civil liberties.

**fundamentalism** A term recently popularized to describe extremist religious movements throughout the world.

**fusion of powers** A constitutional principle that merges the authority of branches of government, in contrast to the principle of separation of powers.

## G

*Gastarbeiter* (guest workers) Workers who were recruited to join the German labor force in the 1960s and early 1970s, generally from Italy, Yugoslavia, and especially Turkey.

**gender gap** Politically significant differences in social attitudes and voting behavior between men and women.

**general secretary** The formal title of the head of the Chinese Communist Party. From 1942 to 1982, the position was called "chairman" and was held by Mao Zedong.

*glasnost* Gorbachev's policy of "openness," which involved an easing of controls on the media, arts, and public discussion

**Global Gender Gap** A measure of the extent to which women in 58 countries have achieved equality with men.

**globalization** The intensification of worldwide interconnectedness associated with the increased speed and magnitude of cross-border flows of trade, investment and finance, and processes of migration, cultural diffusion, and communication.

*grandes écoles* Prestigious and highly selective schools of higher education in France that train top civil servants, engineers, and business executives.

*grands corps* Elite networks of graduates of selective training schools in France.

**grass-roots democracy** The idea that real democracy requires participation from rank-and-file members and not merely from organizational leaders.

**green revolution** A strategy for increasing agricultural (especially food) production, involving improved seeds, irrigation, and abundant use of fertilizers.

**gross domestic product (GDP)** The total of all goods and services produced within a country that is used as a broad measure of the size of its economy.

**gross national product (GNP)** GDP plus income earned by the country's residents; another broad measure of the size of an economy.

*guanxi* A Chinese term that means "connections" or "relationships," and describes personal ties between individuals based on such things as common birthplace or mutual acquaintances.

**Guardian Council** A committee created in the Iranian constitution to oversee the Majles (the parliament).

**guerrilla warfare** A military strategy based on small, highly mobile bands of soldiers (the guerrillas, from the Spanish word for war, *guerra*) who use hit-and-run tactics like ambushes to attack a better-armed enemy.

## H

**health insurance funds** Semipublic institutions that administer insurance contributions from employees and employers and thus pay for health care for covered participants.

**heavy industries** The coal, iron, and steel sectors and the machinery and armaments production associated with them.

**hegemonic power** A state that can control the pattern of alliances and terms of the international order and often shapes domestic political developments in countries throughout the world.

**hegemony** The capacity to dominate the world of states and control the terms of trade and the alliance patterns in the global order.

*Hezbollahis* Literally "partisans of God." In Iran, the term is used to describe religious vigilantes. In Lebanon, it is used to describe the Shi'i militia.

*hojjat al-Islam* Literally, "the proof of Islam." In Iran, it means a medium-ranking cleric.

**homelands** Areas reserved for exclusive African occupation, established through the provisions of the 1913 and 1936 land legislation and later developed as semi-autonomous ethnic states during the apartheid era.

**household responsibility system** The system put into practice in China beginning in the early 1980s in which the major decisions about agricultural production are made by individual farm families based on the profit motive rather than by a people's commune or the government.

**Human Development Index** A composite number used by the United Nations to measure and compare levels of achievement in health, knowledge, and standard of living. HDI is based on the following indicators: life expectancy, adult literacy rate and school enrollment statistics, and gross domestic product per capita at purchasing power parity.

**hung parliament** A situation after an election when no single party comprises a majority in the Commons.

## I

*Imam Jum'ehs* Prayer leaders in Iran's main urban mosques.

**import substitution industrialization (ISI)** Strategy for industrialization based on domestic manufacture of previously imported goods to satisfy domestic market demands.

**independent variable** The variable symbolized by y that the analyst wants to explain.

**Indian Administrative Service (IAS)** India's civil service, a highly professional and talented group of administrators who run the Indian government on a day-to-day basis.

**indicative planning** A term that describes a national plan identifying desirable priorities for economic and social development.

**indigenous groups** Population of Amerindian heritage in Mexico.

**indirect rule** A term used to describe the British style of colonialism in Nigeria and India in which local traditional rulers and political structures were used to help support the colonial governing structure.

**industrial policy** A generic term to refer to a variety of policies designed to shape leading sectors of the economy and enhance competitiveness, especially for industries that are considered strategic to national interests. Countries differ substantially regarding the degree to which their states consciously pursue industrial policies.

# Glossary

**Industrial Revolution** A period of rapid and destabilizing social, economic, and political changes caused by the introduction of large-scale factory production, originating in England in the middle of the eighteenth century.

**influx control** A system of controls that regulated African movement between cities and between towns and the countryside, enforcing residence in the homelands and restricting African choice of employment.

**informal economy** That portion of the economy largely outside government control in which employees work without contracts or benefits. Examples include casual employees in restaurants and hotels, street vendors, and day laborers in construction or agriculture.

**insider privatization** The transformation of formerly state-owned enterprises into joint-stock companies or private enterprises in which majority control is in the hands of employees and/or managers.

**institutional design** The institutional arrangements that define the relationships between executive, legislative, and judicial branches of government and between the central government and sub-central units such as states in the United States.

**interest groups** Organizations that seek to represent the interests—usually economic—of their members in dealings with the government. Important examples are associations representing people with specific occupations, business interests, racial and ethnic groups, or age groups in society.

**international financial institutions (IFIs)** This term generally refers to the International Bank for Reconstruction and Development (the World Bank) and the International Monetary Fund (IMF), but can also include other international lending institutions.

**International Monetary Fund (IMF)** The "sister organization" of the World Bank and also has more than 180 member states. It describes its mandate as "working to foster global monetary cooperation, secure financial stability, facilitate international trade, promote high employment and sustainable economic growth, and reduce poverty." It has been particularly active in helping countries that are experiencing serious financial problems. In exchange for IMF financial or technical assistance, a country must agree to a certain set of conditions that promote economic liberalization.

**interventionist** An interventionist state acts vigorously to shape the performance of major sectors of the economy.

*interventores* In Brazil, allies of Getúlio Vargas (1930–1945, 1950–1952) picked by the dictator during his first period of rulership to replace opposition governors in all the Brazilian states except Minas Gerais. The interventores represented a shift of power from subnational government to the central state.

**iron rice bowl** A feature of China's socialist economy during the Maoist era (1949–1976) that provided guarantees of lifetime employment, income, and basic cradle-to-grave benefits to most urban and rural workers.

**iron triangles** A term coined by students of American politics to refer to the relationships of mutual support formed by particular government agencies, members of congressional committees or subcommittees, and interest groups in various policy areas.

**irredentism** In this setting, irredentism is the belief that South Africa should be governed mainly or even exclusively by "indigenous' Africans."

**Islamism** A new term for the use of Islam as a political ideology. Similar to political Islam and fundamentalism.

# J

*jihad* Literally "struggle." Although often used to mean armed struggle against unbelievers, it can also mean to fight against sociopolitical corruption or a spiritual struggle for self-improvement.

**joint-stock companies** Business firms whose capital is divided into shares that can be held by individuals, groups of individuals, or governmental units.

**judicial review** The ability of a high court to nullify actions by the executive and legislative branches of government that in its judgment violate the constitution.

**judiciary** One of the primary political institutions in a country; responsible for the administration of justice and in some countries for determining the constitutionality of state decisions.

**Junkers** The land-owning nobility of Prussia, who contributed the grain component of Bismarck's "marriage of iron and rye."

**jurist's guardianship** Khomeini's concept that the Iranian clergy should rule on the grounds that they are the divinely appointed guardians of both the law and the people.

# K

*keiretsu* A group of closely allied Japanese firms that have preferential trading relationships and often interlocking directorates and stock-sharing arrangements. The relationships among keiretsu member firms have been regarded as collusive and harmful to free trade by some of Japan's principal trading partners.

**Keynesianism** Named after the British economist John Maynard Keynes, an approach to economic policy in which state economic policies are used to regulate the economy in an attempt to achieve stable economic growth. During recession, state budget deficits are used to expand demand in an effort to boost both consumption and investment, and to create employment. During periods of high growth when inflation threatens, cuts in government spending and a tightening of credit are used to reduce demand.

*koenkai* A Japanese campaign organization for a particular candidate, consisting mainly of the candidate's relatives, friends, fellow alumni, coworkers, and their acquaintances. For most conservative politicians, especially LDP and DPJ members of the Diet and local legislatures, networks of koenkai organizations are far more important and effective than political parties in assisting politicians' election campaigns. Since it costs politicians a great deal of money to maintain these networks, koenkai-centered elections encourage corruption.

*Kulturkampf* Bismarck's fight with the Catholic Church over his desire to subordinate church to state.

# L

**laissez-faire** A term taken from the French, which means, "to let do," in other words, to allow to act freely. In political economy, it refers to the pattern in which state management is limited to such matters as enforcing contracts and protecting property rights, while private market forces are free to operate with only minimal state regulation.

**Lay Judge System (***saibanin-seido***)** The quasi-jury system for major criminal cases that was introduced into Japan's judicial system in May 2009. Guilt or innocence of the accused—and, if convicted, the sentence—are determined by a judicial panel composed of three professional judges and six laypersons.

**Leader/Supreme Leader** A cleric elected to be the head of the Islamic Republic of Iran.

**legislature** One of the primary political institutions in a country, in which elected members are charged with responsibility for making laws and usually providing for the financial resources for the state to carry out its functions.

**legitimacy** A belief by powerful groups and the broad citizenry that a state exercises rightful authority. In the contemporary world, a state is said to possess legitimacy when it enjoys consent of the governed, which usually involves democratic procedures and the attempt to achieve a satisfactory level of development and equitable distribution of resources.

**liberal** Economic philosophy that stresses the important of minimizing state interference in the economy.

*Lok Sabha* The lower house of parliament in India, where all major legislation must pass before becoming law.

# M

**macroeconomic policy** Policy intended to shape the overall economic system by concentrating on policy targets such as inflation and growth.

*mafia* A term borrowed from Italy and widely used in Russia to describe networks of organized criminal activity.

*Majles* The Iranian parliament, from the Arabic term for "assembly."

**Mandal Commission** A government-appointed commission headed by J. P. Mandal to consider seat reservations and quotas to redress caste discrimination.

**manifest destiny** The public philosophy in the nineteenth century that the United States was not only entitled but also destined to occupy territory from the Atlantic to the Pacific.

*maquiladoras* Factories that produce goods for export, often located along the U.S.–Mexican border.

**Marbury v. Madison** The 1803 U.S. Supreme Court ruling that the federal courts inherently had the authority to review the constitutionality of laws passed by Congress and signed by the president. The ruling, initially used sparingly, placed the courts centrally in the system of checks and balances.

**market reform** A strategy of economic transformation that involves reducing the role of the state in managing the economy and increasing the role of market forces

*maslahat* Arabic term for "expediency," "prudence," or "advisability," now used in Iran to refer to reasons of state or what is best for the Islamic Republic.

**mass organizations** Organizations in a communist party-state that represent the interests of a particular social groups, such as workers or women but which are controlled by the communist party.

*mestizo* A person of mixed white, indigenous (Amerindian), and sometimes African descent.

**middle-level theory** seeks to explain phenomena in a limited range of cases, in particular, a specific set of countries with particular characteristics, such as parliamentary regimes, or a particular type of political institution (such as political parties) or activity (such as protest).

**migrant laborers** Laborers who move to another location to take a job, often a low-paying, temporary one.

**Mixed Member Proportional (MMP)** An electoral system that combines (mixes) the proportional features of a party list proportional representation system with the local representation features of a single-member plurality system. Under this mixed system, each voter casts one vote for a party list and another for an individual candidate in a single-member electoral district.

**Mixed Member System** An electoral system in which about half of deputies are elected from direct constituencies and the other half are drawn from closed party lists. The Bundestag uses the Mixed Member System, which is basically a form of proportional representation.

**moderating power (***poder moderador***)** A term used in Brazilian politics to refer to the situation following the 1824 constitution in which the monarchy was supposed to act as a moderating power, among the executive, legislative, and judicial branches of government, arbitrating party conflicts, and fulfilling governmental responsibilities when nonroyal agents failed.

**monetarism** An approach to economic policy that assumes a natural rate of unemployment, determined by the labor market, and rejects the instruments of government spending to run budgetary deficits for stimulating the economy and creating jobs.

# N

**National Party Congress** The symbolically important meeting, held every five years for about two weeks, of about 3000 thousand representatives of the Chinese Communist Party, who endorse policies and the allocation of leadership positions that have been determined beforehand by the party's much smaller ruling bodies.

**National People's Congress (NPC)** The legislature of the People's Republic of China. It is under the control of the Chinese Communist Party and is not an independent branch of government.

**nationalism** An ideology seeking to create a nation-state for a particular community; a group identity associated with membership is such a political community. Nationalists often proclaim that their state and nation are superior to others.

# Glossary

**nationalization** The policy by which the state assumes ownership and operation of private companies.

**nation-state** Distinct, politically defined territory in which the state and national identity coincide.

**Naxalite** The Naxalite movement emerged as a breakaway faction of the CPM in West Bengal in 1967. It is a radical, often violent, extra-parliamentary movement.

**Nazi** A German abbreviation for the National Socialist German Workers' Party, the movement led by Hitler.

**neoliberal** See neoliberalism

**neoliberalism** A term used to describe government policies aiming to promote free competition among business firms within the market, including reduced governmental regulation and social spending.

**newly industrialized countries (NICs)** A term used to describe a group of countries that achieved rapid economic development beginning in the 1960s, largely stimulated by robust international trade (particularly exports) and guided by government policies. The core NICs are usually considered to be Taiwan, South Korea, Hong Kong, and Singapore, but other countries, including Argentina, Brazil, Malaysia, Mexico, and Thailand, are often included in this category.

*nomenklatura* A system of personnel selection under which the Communist Party maintained control over the appointment of important officials in all spheres of social, economic, and political life. The term is also used to describe individuals chosen through this system and thus refers more broadly to the privileged circles in the Soviet Union and China.

**nonaligned bloc** Countries that refused to ally with either the United States or the USSR during the Cold War years.

**nontariff barriers (NTBs)** Policies—such as quotas, health and safety standards, packaging and labeling rules, and unique or unusual business practices—designed to prevent foreign imports in order to protect domestic industries. A form of protectionism that does not use formal tariffs.

**North American Free Trade Agreement (NAFTA)** A treaty between the United States, Mexico, and Canada implemented on January 1, 1994, that largely eliminates trade barriers among the three nations and establishes procedures to resolve trade disputes. NAFTA serves as a model for an eventual Free Trade Area of the Americas zone that could include most nations in the Western Hemisphere.

# O

**oligarchs** A small group of powerful and wealthy individuals who gained ownership and control of important sectors of Russia's economy in the context of privatization of state assets in the 1990s.

**oligarchy** Narrowly based, undemocratic government, often by traditional elites.

**OPEC** (Organization of Petroleum Exporting Countries). An organization dedicated to achieving stability in the price of oil, avoiding price fluctuations, and generally furthering the interests of the member states.

*Ostpolitik* The policy developed by the SPD's Willy Brandt to promote contact and commerce with the Soviet Union and its communist allies during the Cold War.

**other backward classes** The middle or intermediary castes in India that have been accorded reserved seats in public education and employment since the early 1990s.

# P

*panchayats* Elected bodies at the village, district, and state levels that have development and administrative responsibilities.

**parastatal** State-owned, or at least state-controlled, corporations, created to undertake a broad range of activities, from control and marketing of agricultural production to provision of banking services, operating airlines, and other transportation facilities and public utilities. Sometimes the government will own and manage the company outright, or only own a majority share of its stock but allow members of the private sector to run it. Parastatal institutions generally engage in or seek to promote and organize commercial activity in a particular sector. Because of their connection to the state, these enterprises can also serve as instruments of official policy, as sources of patronage opportunities, or as important generators of government revenue.

**parity law** A French law passed in 2000 that directs political parties to nominate an equal number of men and women for many elections.

**parliamentary democracy** System of government in which the chief executive is answerable to the legislature and may be dismissed by it.

**parliamentary sovereignty** The doctrine that grants the legislature the power to make or overturn any law and permits no veto or judicial review.

**party democracy** The constitutional guarantee that political parties have a privileged place in German politics, including generous subsidies for building party organizations.

*pasdaran* Persian term for guards, used to refer to the army of Revolutionary Guards formed during Iran's Islamic Revolution.

**pass laws** Laws in apartheid South Africa that required Africans to carry identity books in which were stamped the permits required for them to travel between the countryside and the cities.

**patrimonial state** A system of governance in which the ruler treats the state as personal property (patrimony).

**patronage system** A political system in which government officials appoint loyal followers to positions rather than choosing people based on their qualifications.

**People of the Book** The Muslim term for recognized religious minorities, such as Christians, Jews, and Zoroastrians.

**People's Liberation Army (PLA)** The combined armed forces of the People's Republic of China, which includes land, sea, air, and strategic missile forces.

**personalist politicians** Demagogic political leaders who use their personal charisma to mobilize their constituency.

**police powers** Powers that are traditionally held by the states to regulate public safety and welfare. Police powers are the form of interaction with government that citizens most often experience. Even with the growth in federal government powers in the twentieth century, police powers remain the primary responsibility of the states and localities.

**Politburo** The committee made up of the top two dozen or so leaders of the Chinese Communist Party.

**political action committee (PAC)** A narrow form of interest group that seeks to influence policy by making contributions to candidates and parties in U.S. politics.

**political economy** The study of the interaction between the state and the economy, that is, how the state and political processes affect the economy and how the organization of the economy and strategic choices made by the government and state actors affect political processes.

**political Islam** A term for the intermingling of religion with politics and often used as a substitute for fundamentalism.

**politics of the governors** In Brazil, refers to periods of history in which state governors acquire extraordinary powers over domains of policy that were previously claimed by the federal government. The term refers most commonly to the Old Republic and the current state of Brazilian federalism.

**populism** Gaining the support of popular sectors. When used in Latin American politics, this support is often achieved by manipulation and demagogic appeals.

**pork-barrel politics** A term originally used by students of American politics to refer to legislation that benefits particular legislators by funding public works and projects in their districts. More broadly, the term refers to preferential allocation of public benefits or resources to particular districts or regions so as to give electoral advantage to particular politicians or political parties.

**power vertical** A term introduced by Vladimir Putin when he was president to describe a unified and hierarchical structure of executive power ranging from the national to the local level.

**prebendalism** Patterns of political behavior that rest on the justification that official state offices should be utilized for the personal benefit of officeholders as well as of their support group or clients.

**predatory state** A state in which those with political power prey on the people and the nation's resources to enrich themselves rather than using their power to promote national development. Contrast with developmental state.

**predominant-party regime** A multiparty political system in which one party maintains a predominant position in parliament and control of government for a long period of time.

**prefects** French administrators appointed by the minister of the interior to coordinate state agencies and programs within the 101 French departments or localities.

**privatization** The sale of state-owned enterprises or services to private companies or investors.

**privatization voucher** A certificate worth 10,000 rubles (at various times between four and twenty U.S. dollars) issued by the government to each Russian in 1992 to be used to purchase shares in state enterprises undergoing privatization.

**procedural democracy** A system with formal procedures for popular choice of government leaders (notably free party competition) but which may lack other democratic elements.

**property taxes** Taxes levied by local governments on the assessed value of property. Property taxes are the primary way in which local jurisdictions in the United States pay for the costs of primary and secondary education. Because the value of property varies dramatically from neighborhood to neighborhood, the funding available for schools—and the quality of education—also varies from place to place.

**proportional representation (PR)** A system of political representation in which seats are allocated to parties within multimember constituencies, roughly in proportion to the votes each party receives. PR usually encourages the election to parliament of more political parties than single-member-district winner-take-all systems. In South Africa the entire country serves as a single 400-seat parliamentary constituency.

**purchasing power parity (PPP)** A method of calculating the value of a country's money based on the actual cost of buying goods and services in that country rather than how many U.S. dollars they are worth.

**pyramid debt** A situation in which a government or organization takes on debt obligations at progressively higher rates of interest in order to pay off existing debt.

# Q

**quangos** Acronym for quasi-nongovernmental organizations, the term used in Britain for nonelected bodies that are outside traditional governmental departments or local authorities.

**Qur'an** The Muslim Bible.

# R

*Rajya Sabha* India's upper house of parliament; considerably less politically powerful than the Lok Sabha.

**rational choice theory** An approach to analyzing political decision-making and behavior that assumes that individual actors rationally pursue their aims in an effort to achieve the most positive net result. The theory presupposes equilibrium and unitary actors. Rational choice is often associated with the pursuit of selfish goals, but the theory permits a wide range of motivations, including altruism.

**redistributive policies** Policies that take resources from one person or group in society and allocate them to a different, usually more disadvantaged, group. The United States has traditionally opposed redistributive policies to the disadvantaged.

**referendum** An election in which citizens are asked to approve (or reject) a policy proposal.

**regulations** The rules that explain the implementation of laws. When the legislature passes a law, it sets broad principles for implementation, but how the law is actually implemented is determined by regulations written by executive branch agencies. The regulation-writing process allows interested parties to influence the eventual shape of the law in practice.

**rentier state** a country that obtains much of its revenue from the export of oil or other natural resources.

**rents** Economic gains that do not compensate those who produced them and do not contribute to productivity, typically associated with government earnings that do not get channeled back into either investments or policies that benefit the public good. Pursuit of economic rents (or "rent-seeking") is profit seeking that takes the form of nonproductive economic activity.

**republic** In contemporary usage, a political regime in which leaders are not chosen on the basis of their inherited background (as in a monarchy).

**reservations** Jobs or admissions to colleges reserved by the government of India for specific underprivileged groups.

**resource curse** The concept that revenue derived from abundant natural resources, such as oil, often bring unforeseen ailments to countries.

**revolution** The process by which an established political regime is replaced (usually by force and with broad popular participation) and a new regime established that introduces radical changes throughout society.

# S

**sanctions** International embargos on economic and cultural contracts with a particular country; applied selectively to South Africa by various governments and the United Nations from 1948 until 1994.

*sati* Sati, or widow immolation, was outlawed by the British in the nineteenth century. Satis have occurred, although they are uncommon, in post-Independence India.

**scheduled castes** The lowest caste in India; also known as the untouchables.

**secularism** A doctrine that mandates maintaining a separation between church and state.

**Self-Defense Forces (SDF)** Inaugurated in Japan as a police reserve force with 75,000 recruits in August 1950, following the outbreak of the Korean War. Known as SDF since 1954, it today consists of approximately 250,000 troops equipped with sophisticated modern weapons and weapons systems.

**separation of powers** An organization of political institutions within the state in which the executive, legislature, and judiciary have autonomous powers and no one branch dominates the others. This is the common pattern in presidential systems, as opposed to parliamentary systems, in which there is a fusion of powers.

**Sepoy Rebellion** An armed uprising by Indian soldiers against expansion of British colonialism in India in 1857.

**settler state** Colonial or former colonial administrations controlled by the descendants of immigrants who settled in the territory.

*sexenio* The six-year term in office of Mexican presidents.

*shari'a* Islamic law derived mostly from the Qur'an and the examples set by the Prophet Muhammad in the Sunnah.

**shogun** The title, meaning general, assumed by a succession of hereditary leaders of the three military dynasties—the Minamotos, the Ashikagas, and the Tokugawas—that ruled Japan one after another from the late twelfth century to the mid-nineteenth century. Their government was called the shogunate.

**Sikhs**, a religious minority, constitute less than 2% of the Indian population and 76% of the state of Punjab. Sikhism is a monotheistic religion that was founded in the fifteenth century.

*siloviki* Derived from the Russian word *sil*, meaning "force," Russian politicians and governmental officials drawn from the security and intelligence agencies, special forces, or the military, many of whom were recruited to important political posts under Vladimir Putin.

**single-member district (SMD)** An electoral district in which only one representative is elected, most commonly by the first-past-the-post method. In a system that uses this method, the candidate who wins the most votes in each district is elected, whether or not he or she wins an absolute majority of the votes.

**single-member plurality (SMP) electoral system** An electoral system in which candidates run for a single seat from a specific geographic district. The winner is the person who receives the most votes, whether or not they amount to a majority. SMP systems, unlike systems of proportional representation, increase the likelihood that two national coalition parties will form.

**Single Non-Transferable Vote (SNTV)** A method of voting used in a multimember election district system. Each voter casts only one ballot for a particular candidate and that vote may not be transferred to another candidate even of the same party. As many candidates with the most votes are elected as the number of posts available in each district.

**social class** A group whose members share common world views and aspirations determined largely by occupation, income, and wealth.

**social market economy** A system that aims to combine the efficiency of market economies with a concern for fairness for a broad range of citizens.

**social movements** Large-scale grass-roots action that demands reforms of existing social practices and government policies.

**social security** National systems of contributory and noncontributory benefits to provide assistance for the elderly, sick, disabled, unemployed, and others similarly in need of assistance. The specific coverage of social security, a key component of the welfare state, varies by country.

**socialism** In a socialist regime, the state plays a leading role in organizing the economy, and most business firms are publicly owned.

**socialist democracy** The term used by the Chinese Communist Party to describe the political system of the People's Republic of China. The official view is that this type of system, under the leadership of the Communist Party, provides democracy for the overwhelming majority of people and suppresses (or exercises dictatorship over) only the enemies of the people.

**socialist market economy** The term used by the government of China to refer to the country's current economic system.

**socialist** The doctrine stating that the state should organize and direct the economy in order to promote equality and help low-income groups.

**soft authoritarianism** A system of political control in which a combination of formal and informal mechanisms ensure the dominance of a ruling group or dominant party, despite the existence of some forms of political competition and expressions of political opposition.

**sovereign democracy** A concept of democracy articulated by President Putin's political advisor, Vladimir Surkov, to communicate the idea that democracy in Russia should be adapted to Russian traditions and conditions rather than based on Western models.

**special relationship** Refers to relations between the United States and Britain and is meant to convey not only the largely positive, mutually beneficial nature of the relationship but also the common heritage and shared values of the two countries.

**Standing Committee** A subgroup of the Politburo, with less than a dozen members. The most powerful political organization in China.

**state** The most powerful political institutions in a country, including the executive, legislative, and judicial branches of government, the police, and armed forces.

**state capitalism** An economic system that is primarily capitalistic but in which there is some degree of government ownership of the means of production.

**state capture** The ability of firms to systematically turn state regulations to their advantage through payoffs or other benefits offered to state officials

**state corporatism** A system of interest representation in which the constituent units are organized into a limited number of singular, compulsory, noncompetitive, hierarchically ordered, and functionally differentiated categories, recognized or licensed (if not created) by the state and granted a deliberate representational monopoly within their respective categories in exchange for observing certain controls in their selection of leaders and articulation of demands and supports.

**State Council** The cabinet of the government of the People's Republic of China, headed by the premier.

**state formation** The historical development of a state, often marked by major stages, key events, or turning points (critical junctures) that influence the contemporary character of the state.

**state-led economic development** The process of promoting economic development using governmental machinery.

**state-owned enterprises** Companies in which a majority of ownership control is held by the government.

**state technocrats** Career-minded bureaucrats who administer public policy according to a technical rather than a political rationale. In Mexico and Brazil, these are known as the *técnicos*.

**statism** The doctrine that advocates firm state direction of the economy and society.

**structural adjustment program (SAP)** Programs established by the World Bank intended to alter and reform the economic structures of highly indebted Third World countries as a condition for receiving international loans. SAPs often involve the necessity for privatization, Trade liberalization, and fiscal restraint, which typically requires the dismantling of social welfare systems.

**Supreme Commander for the Allied Powers (SCAP)** The official title of General Douglas MacArthur between 1945 and 1951 when he led the Allied Occupation of Japan.

**suspensive veto** In policy areas with no direct effect on the states, the Bundesrat has the prerogative to make the Bundestag pass a bill a second time.

**sustainable development** An approach to promoting economic growth that seeks to minimize environmental degradation and depletion of natural resources.

# T

**Taisho democracy** A reference to Japanese politics in the period roughly coinciding with Emperor Taisho's reign, 1912–1926. The period was characterized by the rise of a popular movement for democratization of government by the introduction of universal manhood suffrage and the reduction of the power and influence of authoritarian institutions of the state.

**technocrats** Career-minded bureaucrats who administer public policy according to a technical rather than a political rationale.

**theocracy** A state dominated by the clergy, who rule on the grounds that they are the only interpreters of God's will and law.

**Third World** refers to countries with a low or relatively low level of economic development, particularly as measured by gross national income or gross domestic product per capita.

**Tokai Village** A seaside community lying about ninety miles northeast of Tokyo that is Japan's major nuclear research center that hosts reprocessing and enrichment plants. It is also known as the site of the two serious nuclear accidents the nation has experienced.

**totalitarianism** A political system in which the state attempts to exercise total control over all aspects of public and private life, including the economy, culture, education, and social organizations, through an integrated system of ideological, economic, and political control. Totalitarian states rely on extensive coercion, including terror, as a means to exercise power.

**township** South African usage refers to a segregated residential area reserved for Africans, during apartheid tightly controlled and constituted mainly by public housing.

**transitional democracies** Countries that have moved from an authoritarian government to a democratic one.

**two-turnover test of democratic consolidation** A test proposed by Samuel P. Huntington in *The Third Wave: Democratization in the Late Twentieth Century* (1991), which requires a new democratic regime born of a recent transition from authoritarianism to experience two peaceful changes in the party or parties in power before it is considered a consolidated, or viable, democracy.

**typology** A method of classifying by using criteria that divide a group of cases into smaller cases with common characteristics.

## U

***Umkhonto-we-Sizwe*** Zulu and Xhosa for "Spear of the Nation," the armed wing of the African National Congress, established in 1961 and integrated into the South African National Defence Force in 1994.

**unfinished state** A state characterized by instabilities and uncertainties that may render it susceptible to collapse as a coherent entity.

**unitary state** In contrast to a federal system, a system of government in which no powers are reserved for subnational units of government.

**untouchables** The lowest caste in India's caste system, whose members are among the poorest and most disadvantaged Indians.

**USA PATRIOT Act** Legislation passed by the United States Congress in the wake of the September 11, 2001 attacks on New York and Washington. The legislation dramatically expanded the federal government's ability to conduct surveillance, to enforce laws, to limit civil liberties, and to fight terrorism.

## V

**vanguard party** A political party that claims to operate in the "true" interests of the group or class that it purports to represent, even if this understanding doesn't correspond to the expressed interests of the group itself.

***voortrekkers*** Pastoralist descendants of Dutch-speaking settlers in South Africa who moved north from the British-controlled Cape in 1836 to establish independent republics; later regarded as the founders of the Afrikaner nation.

## W

**warrant chiefs** Leaders employed by the British colonial regime in Nigeria. A system in which "chiefs" were selected by the British to oversee certain legal matters and assist the colonial enterprise in governance and law enforcement in local areas.

**Weimar Republic** The constitutional system of Germany between the end of World War One in 1918 and the Nazi seizure of power in 1933. So-named because the assembly to write the constitution occurred in a German city called Weimar.

**welfare state** A set of public policies designed to provide for citizens' needs through direct or indirect provision of pensions, health care, unemployment insurance, and assistance to the poor.

**Westminster model** A form of democracy based on the supreme authority of Parliament and the accountability of its elected representatives; named after the Parliament building in London.

**works councils** Firm employees elected by their co-workers to represent the workforce in negotiations with management at that specific shop or company.

**World Bank** (officially the International Bank for Reconstruction and Development) The World Bank provides low-interest loans, no-interest credit, policy advice, and technical assistance to developing countries with the goal of reducing poverty. It is made up of more than 180 nations. All members have voting rights within the Bank, but these are weighted according to the size of each country's financial contribution to the organization.

**World Trade Organization (WTO)** A global international organization that oversees the "rules of trade" among its member states. The main functions of the WTO are to serve as a forum for its members to negotiate new agreements and resolve trade disputes. Its fundamental purpose is to lower or remove barriers to free trade.

## Z

***zaibatsu*** Giant holding companies in pre–World War II Japan, each owned by and under the control of members of a particular family. The largest were divided into a number of independent firms under the democratization program during the postwar occupation but were later revived as keiretsu, although no longer under the control of any of the original founding families.

***zamindars*** Landlords who served as tax collectors in India under the British colonial government. The *zamindari* system was abolished after independence.

***zoku*** Members of the Japanese Diet (parliament) with recognized experience and expertise in particular policy areas such as agriculture, construction, and transportation, and close personal connections with special interests in those areas.

***Zollverein*** Customs union signed in the mid-1830s between Prussia, Bavaria, Hessia, Saxony and many other German states to overcome the fragmentation of the German market.

# About the Editors and Contributors

Ervand Abrahamian is Distinguished Professor of History at Baruch College and the Graduate Center of the City University of New York. He was elected Fellow of the American Academy of the Arts and Sciences. His recent publications include *Khomeinism: Essays on the Islamic Republic* (1993), *Tortured Confessions: Prisons and Public Recantations in Modern Iran* (1999), and *A History of Modern Iran* (2008).

Amrita Basu is the Dominic Paino Professor of Political Science and Women's and Gender Studies at Amherst College. Her main areas of interest are social movements, religious nationalism, and gender politics in South Asia. She is the author of *Two Faces of Protest: Contrasting Modes of Women's Activism in India* (1992) and several edited or coedited books, including *Localizing Knowledge in a Globalizing World* (2002), *Community Conflicts and the State in India* (with Atul Kohli) (1997), *Appropriating Gender: Women's Activism and Politicized Religion in South Asia* (1998), *Beyond Exceptionalism: Violence, Religion and Democracy in India*, (2006), and *Women's Movements in a Global Era: The Power of Local Feminisms*, (2010).

Joan DeBardeleben is Chancellor's Professor of Political Science and of European, Russian, and Eurasian Studies at Carleton University in Ottawa, Canada. She has published widely on Russian politics, with a focus on Russian federalism, public opinion, and Russia's relations with the European Union. Her work includes articles in journals such as *Europe-Asia Studies, The European Political Science Review,* and *Sotsiologicheskie issledovanie (Sociological Research)*, as well as numerous chapters in edited volumes, including, most recently, in *Russian Foreign Policy in the 21ˢᵗ Century*, ed. Roger E. Kanet (2011), and *The Politics of Sub-National Authoritarianism in Russia*, eds. Vladimir Gel'man and Cameron Ross (2010). Dr. DeBardeleben is also Director of Carleton University's Centre for European Studies (EU Centre of Excellence).

Louis DeSipio is Associate Professor in the Departments of Political Science and Chicano/Latino Studies at the University of California, Irvine. He is the author of *Counting on the Latino Vote: Latinos as a New Electorate* (1996) and the coeditor (with Manuel Garcia y Griego and Sherri Kossoudji) of *Researching Migration: Stories from the Field* (2007). He is also the author and editor of an eight-volume series on Latino political values, attitudes, and behaviors. The latest volume in this series, *Beyond the Barrio: Latinos and the 2004 Elections*, was published by the University of Notre Dame Press in 2010.

Shigeko N. Fukai is Professor Emeritus of Okayama University and Visiting Professor at Chiba University (Japan). She has written a book in Japanese on a sustainable world order and a series of articles and chapters in both English and Japanese on sustainability, Japan's land problems and land policy-making, Japan's role in the emergent regional economic order in East Asia, and Japanese electoral and party politics.

Haruhiro Fukui is Professor Emeritus at the University of California, Santa Barbara, and former director of the Hiroshima Peace Institute. His most recent publications include "Why Parties Fail, Yet Survive," in Kay Lawson and Peter H. Merkl, eds., *When Parties Prosper: The Uses of Electoral Success* (2007) and "Japan: from deterrence to prevention," in Emil J. Kirchner and James Sperling, eds., *National Security Cultures: Patterns of Global Governance* (2010).

Merilee S. Grindle is the Edward S. Mason Professor of International Development at the Harvard Kennedy School of Government and the director of the David Rockefeller Center for Latin American Studies, Harvard University. She is a specialist on the comparative analysis of policy-making, implementation, and public management in developing countries and has written extensively on Mexico. Her most recent books are *Going Local: Decentralization, Democratization, and the Promise of Good Governance* (2007) and *Jobs for the Boys: The Politics of Public Sector Reform* (2012).

Wade Jacoby is professor of political science and Director of the Center for the Study of Europe at Brigham Young University. He is author of *Imitation and Politics: Redesigning Modern Germany* (2000) and *The Enlargement of the EU and NATO: Ordering from the Menu in Central Europe* (2004). His articles have appeared in *World Politics, Comparative Political Studies, Politics and Society, The Review of International Political Economy, The Review of International Organizations,* and *The British Journal of Industrial Relations*. He is co-editor of *German Politics* and received the DAAD Prize for his scholarship on Germany and the EU.

**Halbert M. Jones** is the Senior Research Fellow in North American Studies at Saint Antony's College at the University of Oxford. He is a historian whose research has focused on Mexico's political development in the twentieth century and on U.S.-Latin American relations.

**William A. Joseph** is professor of political science at Wellesley College and an associate in research of the John King Fairbank Center for Chinese Studies at Harvard University. His major areas of academic interest are contemporary Chinese politics and ideology, the political economy of development, revolutionary movements, and the Vietnam War. He is the editor of and a contributor to *Politics in China: An Introduction* (2010).

**Mark Kesselman** is editor of the *International Political Science Review* and professor emeritus of political science at Columbia University. His research and teaching focuses on the political economy of advanced capitalism, with particular attention to French politics, the Left, and organized labor in Western Europe. He has published articles in the *American Political Science Review, Comparative Politics, World Politics, Politics & Society,* and elsewhere. He is author, co-author, or editor of *The French Workers' Movement: Economic Crisis and Political Change* (1984), *European Politics in Transition* (2009), *The Politics of Globalization* (2007), *and Readings in Comparative Politics* (2010).

**Darren Kew** is Associate Professor of Conflict Resolution and Executive Director of the Center for Peace, Democracy, and Development at the University of Massachusetts, Boston. He studies the relationship between conflict resolution methods and democratic development in Africa. Much of his work focuses on the role of civil society groups in this development. He also monitored the last three Nigerian elections and the 2007 elections in Sierra Leone. Professor Kew is author of numerous works on Nigerian politics and conflict resolution, including the forthcoming book: *Democracy, Conflict Resolution, and Civil Society in Nigeria.*

**Atul Kohli** is the David K.E. Bruce Professor of International Affairs and Professor of Politics and International Affairs at Princeton University. His principal research interests are in the areas of comparative political economy with a focus on the developing countries. He is the author of *State-Directed Development: Political Power and Industrialization in the Global Periphery* (winner of the Charles Levine Award (2005) of the International Political Science Association); *Democracy and Discontent: India's Growing Crisis of Governability; The State and Poverty in India;* and the editor of six volumes: *The State and Development in the Third World; India's Democracy; State Power and Social Forces; Community Conflicts and the State in India;* and *The Success of India's Democracy; States, Markets and Just Growth.* He has also published some fifty articles. His current research focuses on the topic of "imperialism and the developing world." He is the chief editor of *World Politics.*

He has received grants and fellowships from the Social Science Research Council, Ford Foundation and Russell Sage Foundation.

**Joel Krieger** is the Norma Wilentz Hess Professor of Political Science at Wellesley College and chair of the Department of Political Science. His publications include *Globalization and State Power* (2005); *Blair's War*, coauthored with David Coates (2004), *British Politics in the Global Age: Can Social Democracy Survive?* (1999), and, *Reagan, Thatcher, and the Politics of Decline* (1986). He is editor-in-chief of *The Oxford Companion to Comparative Politics* (2012) and of *The Oxford Companion to International Relations* (2013).

**Peter M. Lewis** is Director of African Studies and Associate Professor at the Johns Hopkins University, School of Advanced International Studies (SAIS). His work focuses on economic reform and political transition in developing countries, with particular emphasis on governance and development in Sub-Saharan Africa. He has written extensively on questions of economic adjustment, democratization, and civil society in Africa; democratic reform and political economy in Nigeria; public attitudes toward reform and democracy in West Africa; and the comparative politics of economic change in Africa and Southeast Asia. His most recent book, *Growing Apart: Politics and Economic Change in Indonesia and Nigeria* (2007) is concerned with the institutional basis of economic development, drawing upon a comparative study.

**Tom Lodge** is Professor of Peace and Conflict Studies and Dean of the Faculty of Arts, Humanities and Social Sciences at the University of Limerick, Ireland. Before moving to Ireland in 2005, he was Professor of Political Studies at the University of the Witwatersrand in Johannesburg, South Africa. His publications include *Sharpeville: An Apartheid massacre and Its Consequences* (2011), *Mandela: A Critical Life* (2006) and *South African Politics from Mandela to Mbeki* (2003).

**Alfred P. Montero** is Professor of Political Science at Carleton College. His research focuses on the political economy of decentralization and comparative federalism in Latin American and European countries. He is the author of *Shifting States in Global Markets: Subnational Industrial Policy in Contemporary Brazil and Spain* (2002) and *Brazilian Politics: Reforming a Democratic State in a Changing World* (2006). He is also coeditor of *Decentralization and Democracy in Latin America* (2004). Professor Montero has also published his work in several edited volumes and journals such as *Latin American Politics and Society, Latin American Research Review, Comparative Politics, Journal of Politics in Latin America, West European Politics, Studies in Comparative International Development, Publius: The Journal of Federalism,* and the *Journal of Interamerican Studies and World Affairs.* Presently, he is working on a new book about Brazil's emergence as one of the fastest growing, large developing countries.

# Index

# Index